S0-BCW-318

INTERNET RESOURCES

Prentice Hall offers several Internet resources specifically designed for Case and Fair to help students understand and retain important economic concepts.

The Companion Website (www.prenhall.com/casefair)

The Companion Website provides free access to a wide selection of interactive learning aids including: learning objectives, current news articles, Internet exercises, practice quizzes, and solutions to the even-numbered problems in the text.

New to the Web site is eThemes of the Times for Economics, a collection of recent articles from The *New York Times*.

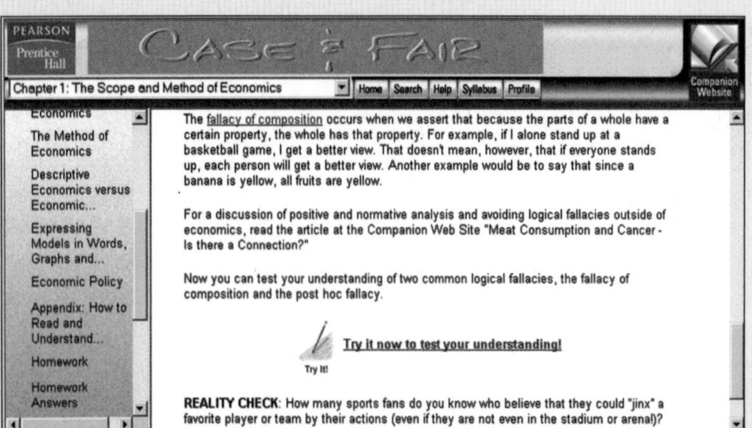

The Companion Website PLUS (www.prenhall.com/casefair)

By using the access code packaged with every new text, students get robust Web site content that includes extensive chapter notes and homework problems.

A walk-through tutorial includes detailed chapter summaries, animated figures, glossary, and additional quizzes.

The Case and Fair Web site also incorporates several types of interactive graphing exercises to help students understand the basic concepts and improve their test scores.

- **Active Graphs Level One:** JAVA-based applications invite students to change the value of variables and curves to see the effects in the movement of the graph. This is a great **tutorial** to help students understand the basic concepts being presented throughout the course and improve test scores throughout the semester.
- **Active Graphs Level Two:** require students to modify graphs based on an economic scenario. Students receive instant audio and animated feedback. This is a great **analytical tool** to further explore economics and to create strong graphing skills.

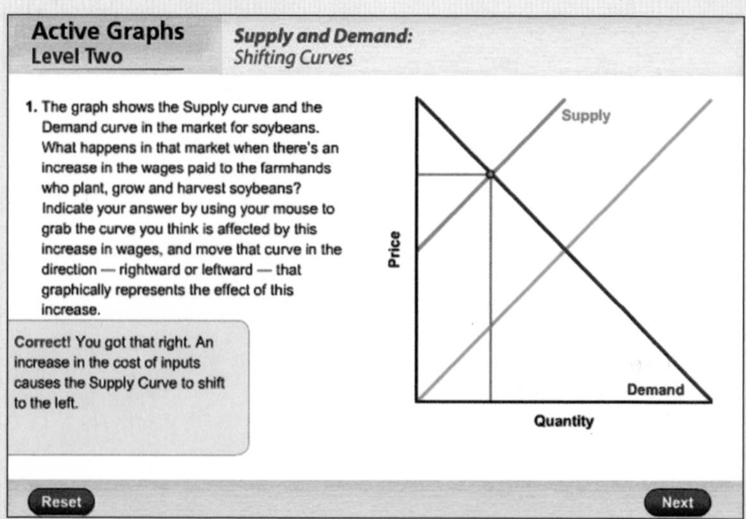

- **eGraph and Graphing Questions:** This electronic graphing tool allows students to create precise, colorful graphs using FLASH technology. The Graphing Questions require students to analyze information gathered on the Web, then create graphs using the Graphing Tool. Complete answers, with graphs, are included.

Look for this icon throughout the book to signal an interactive exercise on The Companion Website PLUS.

MACROECONOMIC STRUCTURE

The organization of the macroeconomics chapters continues to reflect the authors' view that in order for students to understand aggregate demand and aggregate supply curves, they must first understand how the goods market and the money market function. The logic behind the simple demand curve is wrong when applied to the relationship between aggregate demand and the price level. Similarly, the logic behind the simple supply curve is wrong when applied to the relationship between aggregate supply and the price level.

The authors believe the best way to teach the reasoning embodied in the aggregate demand and aggregate supply curves without creating serious confusion is to build up to them carefully. The accompanying visual gives you an overview of the macroeconomic structure.

- **Chapters 8–9** examine the market for goods and services.
- **Chapters 10–11** examine the money market.
- **Chapter 12** brings the two markets together and explains the links between aggregate output *(Y)* and the interest rate *(r)*.
- **Chapter 13** explains how the aggregate demand curve can be derived from Chapter 12, introduces the aggregate supply curve, and explains the price level *(P)*.
- **Chapter 14** shows how the labor market fits into this macroeconomic picture.

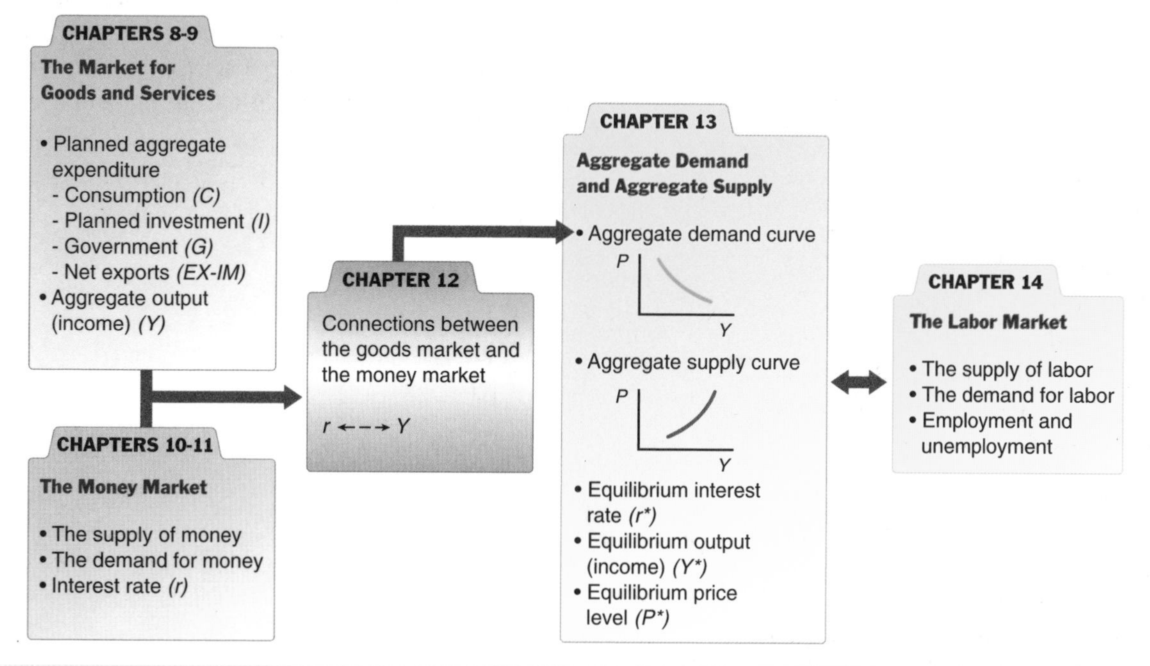

FIGURE 8.1 The Core of Macroeconomic Theory

SEVENTH EDITION

PRINCIPLES OF MACROECONOMICS

PRENTICE HALL SERIES IN ECONOMICS

Adams/Brock
The Structure of American Industry, Tenth Edition

Ayers/Collinge
Economics: Explore & Apply

Ayers/Collinge
Macroeconomics: Explore & Apply

Ayers/Collinge
Microeconomics: Explore & Apply

Blanchard
Macroeconomics, Third Edition

Blau/Ferber/Winkler
The Economics of Women, Men, and Work, Fourth Edition

Boardman/Greenberg/Vining/Weimer
Cost Benefit Analysis: Concepts and Practice, Second Edition

Bogart
The Economics of Cities and Suburbs

Case/Fair
Principles of Economics, Seventh Edition

Case/Fair
Principles of Macroeconomics, Seventh Edition

Case/Fair
Principles of Microeconomics, Seventh Edition

Caves
American Industry: Structure, Conduct, Performance, Seventh Edition

Colander/Gamber
Macroeconomics

Collinge/Ayers
Economics by Design: Principles and Issues, Third Edition

DiPasquale/Wheaton
Urban Economics and Real Estate Markets

Eaton/Eaton/Allen
Microeconomics, Fifth Edition

Folland/Goodman/Stano
Economics of Health and Health Care, Fourth Edition

Fort
Sports Economics

Froyen
Macroeconomics: Theories and Policies, Seventh Edition

Greene
Econometric Analysis, Fifth Edition

Heilbroner/Milberg
The Making of Economic Society, Eleventh Edition

Hess
Using Mathematics in Economic Analysis

Heyne/Boetke/Prychitko
The Economic Way of Thinking, Tenth Edition

Keat/Young
Managerial Economics, Fourth Edition

Lynn
Economic Development: Theory and Practice for a Divided World

Mathis/Koscianski
Microeconomic Theory: An Integrated Approach

Milgrom/Roberts
Economics, Organization, and Management

O'Sullivan/Sheffrin
Economics: Principles and Tools, Third Edition

O'Sullivan/Sheffrin
Macroeconomics: Principles and Tools, Third Edition

O'Sullivan/Sheffrin
Microeconomics: Principles and Tools, Third Edition

O'Sullivan/Sheffrin
Survey of Economics: Principles and Tools, Second Edition

Petersen/Lewis
Managerial Economics, Fifth Edition

Pindyck/Rubinfeld
Microeconomics, Fifth Edition

Reynolds/Masters/Moser
Labor Economics and Labor Relations, Eleventh Edition

Roberts
The Choice: A Fable of Free Trade and Protectionism, Revised Edition

Sawyer/Sprinkle
International Economics

Schiller
The Economics of Poverty and Discrimination, Ninth Edition

Weidenbaum
Business and Government in the Global Marketplace, Seventh Edition

SEVENTH EDITION

PRINCIPLES OF MACROECONOMICS

Karl E. Case

Wellesley College

Ray C. Fair

Yale University

Upper Saddle River, NJ 07458

Library of Congress Cataloging-in-Publication Data

Case, Karl E.
Principles of macroeconomics / Karl E. Case, Ray C. Fair.—7th ed.
p. cm.
Various multi-media instructional tools are available to supplement the text.
Includes index.
ISBN 0-13-144234-1 (pbk.)
1. Macroeconomics. I. Fair, Ray C. II. Title.

HB172.5.C375 2004
339—dc22 2003062446

AVP/Executive Editor: Rod Banister
Editor-in-Chief: P.J. Boardman
VP/Director of Development: Steve Deitmer
Managing Editor (Editorial): Gladys Soto
Project Manager: Marie McHale
Editorial Assistant: Joy Golden
Senior Developmental Editor: Lena Buonanno
Media Project Manager: Victoria Anderson
AVP/Executive Marketing Manager: Kathleen McLellan
Managing Editor (Production): Cynthia Regan
Production Editor: Carol Samet
Production Assistant: Joe DeProspero
Permissions Supervisor: Suzanne Grappi
Production Manager: Arnold Vila
Design Manager: Maria Lange
Art Director: Patricia Smythe
Interior Design: Sue Behnke
Cover Design: Joan O'Connor
Illustrator (Interior): Kenneth Batelman
Photo Researcher: Melinda Alexander
Image Permission Coordinator: Cynthia Vincenti
Manager, Print Production: Christy Mahon
Composition/Full-Service Project Management: UG / GGS Information Services, Inc.
Printer/Binder: RR Donnelley & Sons

Credits and acknowledgments borrowed from other sources and reproduced, with permission, in this textbook appear on appropriate page within text or on page P-1.

Pearson Education LTD.
Pearson Education Singapore, Pte. Ltd
Pearson Education, Canada, Ltd
Pearson Education–Japan
Pearson Education Australia PTY, Limited
Pearson Education North Asia Ltd
Pearson Educación de Mexico, S.A. de C.V.
Pearson Education Malaysia, Pte. Ltd

10 9 8 7 6 5 4 3 2
ISBN 013-144234-1

To
Professor Richard A. Musgrave
and
Professor Robert M. Solow

About the Authors

Karl E. Case is the Katharine Coman and A. Barton Hepburn Professor of Economics at Wellesley College, where he has taught for 27 years, and is a Visiting Scholar at the Federal Reserve Bank of Boston.

Before coming to Wellesley, he served as Head Tutor (director of undergraduate studies) at Harvard, where he won the Allyn Young Teaching Prize. He is Associate Editor of the *Journal of Economic Perspectives* and has been a member of the AEA's Committee on Economic Education and was Associate Editor of the *Journal of Economic Education*, responsible for the section on innovations in teaching. He teaches at least one section of the principles course every year.

Professor Case received his B.A. from Miami University in 1968, spent three years on active duty in the Army, including a year in Vietnam, and received his Ph.D. in Economics from Harvard University in 1976.

Professor Case's research has been in the areas of real estate, housing, and public finance. He is author or co-author of five books, including *Principles of Economics*, *Economics and Tax Policy*, and *Property Taxation: The Need for Reform*, and has published numerous articles in professional journals.

He is also a founding partner in the real estate research firm of Fiserv Case Shiller Weiss, Inc., and serves as a member of the Boards of Directors of the Mortgage Guaranty Insurance Corporation (MGIC), Century Bank, and The Lincoln Institute of Land Policy.

Ray C. Fair is Professor of Economics at Yale University. He is a member of the Cowles Foundation at Yale and a Fellow of the Econometric Society. He received a B.A. in economics from Fresno State College in 1964 and a Ph.D. in economics from M.I.T. in 1968. He taught at Princeton University from 1968 to 1974 and has been at Yale since 1974.

Professor Fair's research has primarily been in the areas of macroeconomics and econometrics, with particular emphasis on macroeconometric model building. His publications include *Specification, Estimation, and Analysis of Macroeconometric Models* (Harvard Press, 1984) and *Testing Macroeconometric Models* (Harvard Press, 1994).

Professor Fair has taught introductory and intermediate economics at Yale. He has also taught graduate courses in macroeconomic theory and macroeconometrics.

Professor Fair's United States and multicountry models are available for use on the Internet free of charge. The address is **http://fairmodel.econ.yale.edu**. Many teachers have found that having students work with the United States model on the Internet is a useful complement to even an introductory macroeconomics course.

Brief Contents

Contents

Global Coverage

Because the study of economics crosses national boundaries, this book includes four chapters devoted to international issues: Chapter 20 (International Trade, Comparative Advantage, and Protectionism), Chapter 21 (Open-Economy Macroeconomics: The Balance of Payments and Exchange Rates), Chapter 22 (Globalization), and Chapter 23 (Economic Growth in Developing and Transitional Economies). We also include international examples and discussions in other chapters. The following is a summary of these examples and discussions.

Chapter	Topic and Page
1	Goods and services you consume in a typical day, 1 Understanding global affairs, 4
2	Sources of growth and the dilemma of the poor countries, 32 New Analysis, *Financial Times:* Investing in Central and Eastern Europe: "Good Times Still Fail to Impress the People," 38
3	Example of the law of demand: How price changes affect number of airline flights between Mexico City and Chile, 48 Substitutes: Japanese cars and U.S. cars, 50 Changes in equilibrium: A major freeze hits Brazil and Columbia, driving up coffee prices, 63 New analysis, *New York Times:* Supply and Demand in the News in 2003: "From Steel to Copper and Zinc, Commodity Prices Surge," 66
4	New Analysis, *New York Times:* Oil Prices in 2003 Hit $40: "Oil Prices Hit Highest Levels Since the Persian Gulf War," 76 Supply and Demand Analysis: An Oil Import Fee, 78
5	Inflation, deflation, and hyperinflation around the world, 87 Labor Market: California's migrant workers from Mexico and Germany's "guest workers" from Turkey, 91 Money Market, 91 Expansion and Contraction: The Business Cycle, 94
6	Distinguishing between GDP and GNP: Japanese auto manufacturing plants in the United States, 101 Net Factor Payments to the Rest of the World, 107 The Underground Economy, 113 Table 6.7: Per Capita Gross National Income for Selected Countries, 2002, 114
7	Japanese automobile industry, 125 World Economy in Transition: Bias in the US Consumer Price Index—Why It Could Be Important, 133
8	New Analysis, *USA Today:* Inventories Rise and the Economy Slows in 2003: "Automakers' Inventories Swell," 151
10	Commodity and fiat monies, 185 News Analysis, *Economist:* A Cashless Society in Russia: "The Cashless Society," 188 New Analysis, *New York Times:* Central Banks Worry About Inflation and Deflation in 2003: "Brazil: Concern About Inflation," 196

AVAILABLE VERSIONS

Principles of Economics	Principles of Microeconomics	Principles of Macroeconomics
1 The Scope and Method of Economics	■	■
2 The Economic Problem: Scarcity and Choice	■	■
3 Demand, Supply, and Market Equilibrium	■	■
4 Demand and Supply Applications and Elasticity*	■	■
5 Household Behavior and Consumer Choice	■	
6 The Production Process: The Behavior of Profit-Maximizing Firms	■	
7 Short-Run Costs and Output Decisions	■	
8 Long-Run Costs and Output Decisions	■	
9 Input Demand: The Labor and Land Markets	■	
10 Input Demand: The Capital Market and the Investment Decision	■	
11 General Equilibrium and the Efficiency of Perfect Competition	■	
12 Monopoly and Antitrust Policy	■	
13 Monopolistic Competition and Oligopoly	■	
14 Externalities, Public Goods, Imperfect Information, and Social Choice	■	
15 Income Distribution and Poverty	■	
16 Public Finance: The Economics of Taxation	■	
17 Introduction to Macroeconomics		■
18 Measuring National Output and National Income		■
19 Long-Run and Short-Run Concerns: Growth, Productivity, Unemployment, and Inflation		■
20 Aggregate Expenditure and Equilibrium Output		■
21 The Government and Fiscal Policy		■
22 The Money Supply and the Federal Reserve System		■
23 Money Demand, the Equilibrium Interest Rate, and Monetary Policy		■
24 Money, the Interest Rate, and Output: Analysis and Policy		■
25 Aggregate Demand, Aggregate Supply, and Inflation		■
26 The Labor Market, Unemployment, and Inflation		■
27 Macroeconomic Issues and Policy		■
28 The Stock Market and the Economy		■
29 Household and Firm Behavior in the Macroeconomy: A Further Look		■
30 Long-Run Growth		■
31 Debates in Macroeconomics: Monetarism, New Classical Theory, and Supply-Side Economics		■
32 International Trade, Comparative Advantage, and Protectionism	■	■
33 Open-Economy Macroeconomics: The Balance of Payments and Exchange Rates		■
34 Globalization	■	■
35 Economic Growth in Developing and Transitional Economies	■	■

*Macro version of this chapter does not include a section on elasticity.

PREFACE

Since the publication of our sixth edition, the world economic landscape has changed significantly. In the late summer of 2003, the economic situation in the United States and the rest of the world was full of uncertainty. The U.S. economy had experienced a series of tough blows after the new millennium began in 2000. Employment in the United States fell by over three million between 2001 and 2003 after increasing by over 22 million in the previous decade. Nearly 10 million Americans were unemployed in July 2003. Between the beginning of 2000 and the beginning of 2003, the stock market declined continuously, wiping out trillions of dollars worth of wealth and retirement savings. The Standard and Poor's index of 500 stock prices declined by over 45 percent during the period. During the first three quarters of 2001, the total output of the nation fell, marking an official recession.

As the U.S. economy struggled, so too did economies around the world. Africa struggled with the massive and tragic HIV/AIDS pandemic, which continues to devastate its economy. Argentina experienced the near collapse of its economy. Russia, more than a decade after the fall of the Soviet Union, began to grow at a moderate rate. China grew rapidly but is coming under increased criticism for unfair trade practices. While Europe found itself in recession, it was also learning about the strengths and weaknesses of having a fairly new common currency, the euro.

It was also a rough time in other ways. Terrorists destroyed the World Trade Center in New York City on September 11, 2001. U.S. forces played a major role in the invasions of Afghanistan in 2002 and Iraq in 2003. These events and others pushed the federal budget from a surplus in 2001 to a deficit of over $400 billion by mid-2003.

All of this came on the heels of a major collapse of the technology sector of the economy both in the United States and abroad. Between 1991 and 2001, the United States experienced the longest economic expansion in its history. To a large extent it was based on what came to be called the "new economy." The rise of the Internet and the world of cell phones and e-commerce was thought to be a new "industrial revolution," as important as the one that transformed the world beginning in England in the eighteenth and nineteenth centuries. There can be no question that the dawn of the information age and the power of the Internet have changed the economy in ways that we do not yet fully understand. It has led to increased productivity, new products, and the transformation of many markets. But we clearly overdid it. Millions of small firms ran out of cash, new ventures failed to deliver promised profits, and the newfound riches of many successful entrepreneurs disappeared almost overnight. What we do not know is how it will play out in the long run.

How rapidly times change. In writing this seventh edition, we highlight many of these events and the debates surrounding them. It is not our role to forecast future events. It is, rather, our goal in revising the text to set the discussion in an up-to-date world context and to highlight what we do and do not understand about it.

NEW TO THE SEVENTH EDITION

More than one million students have used *Principles of Economics* or one of its split volumes. We have made every effort in this new edition to be responsive to the rapidly changing times, the recommendations we received from over 40 reviewers, and our own teaching experiences. This edition includes two new chapters and new or expanded content in several existing chapters.

TWO NEW CHAPTERS

- *Chapter 16, "The Stock Market and the Economy,"* examines the stock market boom of 1995–2000 and the stock market downturn of 2001–2002. The chapter also covers how both the boom and the bust affected GDP.

- *Chapter 22, "Globalization,"* explores the increasing economic interdependence among countries and citizens. We present the arguments for and against free trade, the link between trade and growth rates, the arguments for and against immigration, how developing countries are affected by subsidies and tariffs imposed by European countries and the United States, capital mobility, global warming, and AIDS.

NEW OR EXPANDED CONTENT

- *Chapter 2, "The Economic Problem: Scarcity and Choice,"* has a new section that uses the production possibilities frontier to illustrate the theory of comparative advantage and demonstrate gains from trade.
- *Chapter 6, "Measuring National Output and National Income,"* now covers gross national income (GNI), the World Bank's recently adopted measuring system for exchange rates.
- *Chapter 7, "Long-Run and Short-Run Concerns: Growth, Productivity, Unemployment, and Inflation,"* includes expanded coverage of the consumer price index (CPI) bias.
- *Chapter 15, "Macroeconomic Issues and Policy,"* features new coverage of how the Fed targets interest rates and how it selects the interest rate based on the state of the economy; the behavior of the Fed in 2001–2003; the increased expenditures for security and defense after September 11, 2001; deficit targeting from 1980–2003; and the 2003 tax cut.
- *Chapter 21, "Open-Economy Macroeconomics: The Balance of Payments and Exchange Rates,"* has a new section on monetary policy with fixed exchange rates.

RECENT DATA, EXAMPLES, EVENTS, AND TOPICS

Every chart, table, and graph in the book has been revised with the most recent data available. In addition, we have integrated topics that have generated a great deal of attention over the last few years—the jobless economic recovery of 2003, the 2003 tax cut, deflation, the affect of the stock market downturn on GDP, increased spending on security and defense post September 11, 2001, budget deficit, and globalization, to name just a few.

THE FOUNDATION

Despite new chapters and other revisions, the themes of *Principles of Macroeconomics, Seventh Edition,* are the same themes of the first six editions. The purpose of this book is to introduce the discipline of economics and to provide a basic understanding of how economies function. This requires a blend of economic theory, institutional material, and real-world applications. We have maintained a balance between these ingredients in every chapter in this book.

The hallmark features of our book are its

1. three-tiered explanations of key concepts (*Stories-Graphs-Equations*),
2. intuitive and accessible structure of microeconomics and macroeconomics chapters, and
3. international coverage.

THREE-TIERED EXPLANATIONS: STORIES-GRAPHS-EQUATIONS

Professors who teach principles of economics are faced with a classroom of students with different abilities, backgrounds, and learning styles. For some, analytical material is difficult no matter how it is presented; for others, graphs and equations seem to come naturally. The problem facing instructors and textbook authors is how to convey the core principles of the discipline to as many students as possible without selling the better students short. Our approach to this problem is to present most core concepts in three ways:

- First, we present each concept in the context of a simple intuitive ***story*** or example in words often followed by a table.
- Second, we use a ***graph*** in most cases to illustrate the story or example.
- And finally, in many cases where appropriate, we use an ***equation*** to present the concept with a mathematical formula.

An example of our approach using stories, graphs, and equations can be found in Chapter 8, "Aggregate Expenditure and Equilibrium Output," where we show how a household decides how much to consume and save.

A story helps capture student interest.

Macroeconomics, you will recall, is the study of behavior. To understand the functioning of the macroeconomy, we must understand the behavior of households and firms. In our simple economy in which there is no government, there are two types of spending behavior: spending by households, or *consumption*, and spending by firms, or *investment*.

Household Consumption and Saving How do households decide how much to consume? In any given period, the amount of aggregate consumption in the economy depends on a number of factors.

Some determinants of aggregate consumption include:

1. Household income
2. Household wealth
3. Interest rates
4. Households' expectations about the future

These four factors work together to determine the spending and saving behavior of households, both for individual ones and for the aggregate. This is no surprise. Households with higher income and higher wealth are likely to spend more than households with less income and less wealth. Lower interest rates reduce the cost of borrowing, so lower interest rates are likely to stimulate spending. (Higher interest rates increase the cost of borrowing and are likely to decrease spending.) Finally, positive expectations about the future are likely to increase current spending, while uncertainty about the future is likely to decrease current spending.

While all these factors are important, we will concentrate for now on the relationship between income and consumption.[1] In *The General Theory*, Keynes argued that the amount of consumption undertaken by a household is directly related to its income:

The higher your income is, the higher your consumption is likely to be. People with more income tend to consume more than people with less income.

consumption function The relationship between consumption and income.

The relationship between consumption and income is called a **consumption function**. Figure 8.3 shows a hypothetical consumption function for an individual household. The curve is labeled $c(y)$, which is read "c as a function of y," or "consumption as a function of income." There are several things you should notice about the curve. First, it has a positive

A graph illustrates the relationship between the variables in the story.

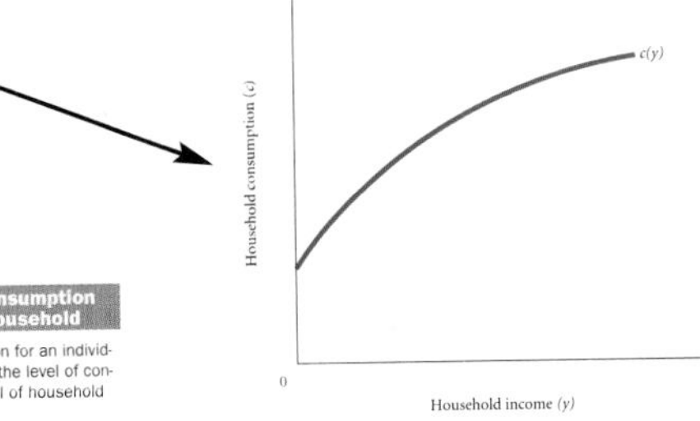

FIGURE 8.3 A Consumption Function for a Household

A consumption function for an individual household shows the level of consumption at each level of household income.

[1] The assumption that consumption is dependent solely on income is, of course, overly simplistic. Nonetheless, many important insights about how the economy works can be obtained through this simplification. In Chapter 16, we relax this assumption and consider the behavior of households and firms in the macroeconomy in more detail.

slope. In other words, as y increases, so does c. Second, the curve intersects the c-axis above zero. This means that even at an income of zero, consumption is positive. Even if a household found itself with a zero income, it still must consume to survive. It would borrow or live off its savings, but its consumption could not be zero.

Keep in mind that Figure 8.3 shows the relationship between consumption and income for an individual household, but also remember that macroeconomics is concerned with aggregate consumption. Specifically, macroeconomists want to know how *aggregate* consumption (the total consumption of all households) is likely to respond to changes in *aggregate* income. If all individual households increase their consumption as income increases, and we assume that they do, it is reasonable to assume that a positive relationship exists between aggregate consumption (C) and aggregate income (Y).

For simplicity, assume that points of aggregate consumption, when plotted against aggregate income, lie along a straight line, as in Figure 8.4. Because the aggregate consumption function is a straight line, we can write the following equation to describe it:

$$C = a + bY$$

Y is aggregate output (income), C is aggregate consumption, and a is the point at which the consumption function intersects the C-axis—a constant. The letter b is the slope of the line, in this case $\Delta C/\Delta Y$ [because consumption (C) is measured on the vertical axis, and income (Y) is measured on the horizontal axis].[2] Every time income increases (say by ΔY), consumption increases by b times ΔY. Thus, $\Delta C = b \times \Delta Y$ and $\Delta C/\Delta Y = b$. Suppose, for example, that the slope of the line in Figure 8.4 is .75 (that is, $b = .75$). An increase in income (ΔY) of \$100 would then increase consumption by $b\Delta Y = .75 \times \$100$, or \$75.

marginal propensity to consume (*MPC*) That fraction of a change in income that is consumed, or spent.

The **marginal propensity to consume (*MPC*)** is the fraction of a change in income that is consumed. In the consumption function here, b is the *MPC*. An *MPC* of .75 means consumption changes by .75 of the change in income. The slope of the consumption function is the *MPC*.

$$\text{marginal propensity to consume} \equiv \text{slope of consumption function} \equiv \frac{\Delta C}{\Delta Y}$$

marginal propensity to save (*MPS*) That fraction of a change in income that is saved.

There are only two places income can go: consumption or saving. If \$.75 of a \$1.00 increase in income goes to consumption, \$.25 must go to saving. If income decreases by \$1.00, consumption will decrease by \$.75 and saving will decrease by \$.25. The **marginal propensity to save (*MPS*)** is the fraction of a change in income that is saved: $\Delta S/\Delta Y$, where

An equation expresses the relationship mathematically.

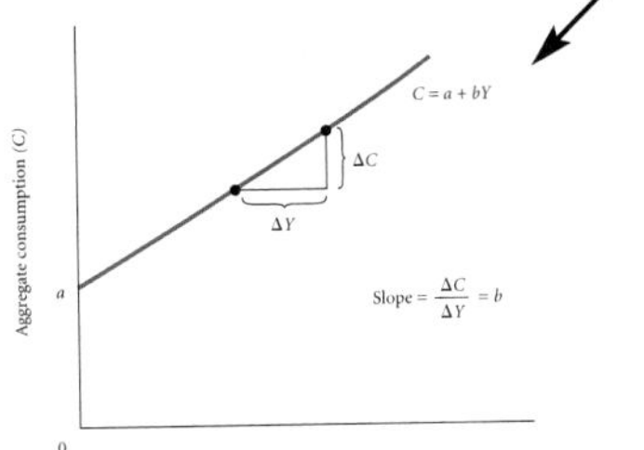

FIGURE 8.4 An Aggregate Consumption Function

The consumption function shows the level of consumption at every level of income. The upward slope indicates that higher levels of income lead to higher levels of consumption spending.

[2] The Greek letter Δ (delta) means "change in." For example, ΔY (read "delta Y") means the "change in income." If income (Y) in 2001 is \$100 and income in 2002 is \$110, then ΔY for this period is \$110 − \$100 = \$10. For a review of the concept of slope, see Appendix, Chapter 1.

MACROECONOMIC STRUCTURE

We remain committed to the view that it is a mistake simply to throw aggregate demand and aggregate supply curves at students in the first few chapters of a principles book. To understand the AS and AD curves, students need to know about the functioning of both the goods market and the money market. The logic behind the simple demand curve is wrong when applied to the relationship between aggregate demand and the price level. Similarly, the logic behind the simple supply curve is wrong when applied to the relationship between aggregate supply and the price level.

Part of teaching economics is teaching economic reasoning. Our discipline is built around deductive logic. Once we teach students a pattern of logic, we want and expect them to apply it to new circumstances. When they apply the logic of a simple demand curve or simple supply curve to the aggregate demand or aggregate supply curve, the logic does not fit. We believe the best way to teach the reasoning embodied in the aggregate demand and aggregate supply curves without creating serious confusion is to build up to them carefully.

In Chapters 8 and 9, we examine the market for goods and services. In Chapters 10 and 11 we examine the money market. We bring the two markets together in Chapter 12, which explains the links between aggregate output (Y) and the interest rate (r). In Chapter 13, we explain how the aggregate demand curve can be derived from Chapter 12, and introduce the aggregate supply curve. This allows the price level (P) to be explained. We then explain in Chapter 14 how the labor market fits into this macroeconomic picture. The accompanying visual gives you an overview of our structure.

One of the big issues in the organization of the macroeconomic material is whether long-run growth issues should be taught before short-run chapters on the determination of national income and counter-cyclical policy. In the last two editions we moved a significant discussion of growth up to Chapter 7 and highlighted it. However, while we wrote the major chapter on long-run growth (Chapter 18) so that it can be taught either before or after the short-run chapters, we remain convinced that it is easier to understand the growth issue once a student has come to grips with the logic and controversies of short-run cycles, inflation, and unemployment.

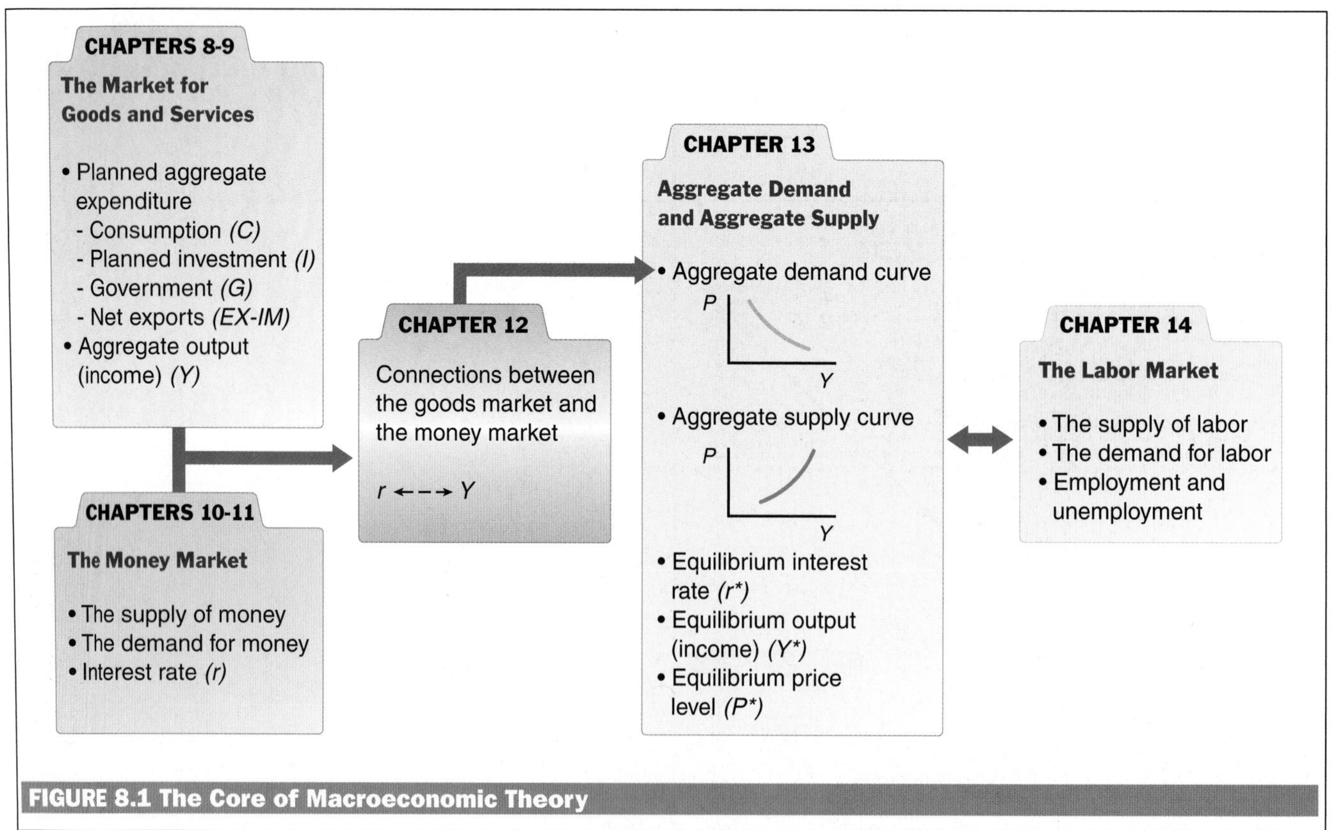

FIGURE 8.1 The Core of Macroeconomic Theory

INTERNATIONAL COVERAGE

We have expanded international coverage from previous editions by including a new chapter on globalization (Chapter 22). This chapter covers the increasing economic interdependence among countries and their citizens. We focus on the causes and consequences of increased international trade of goods and services, increased cross-border movements of labor, and expanded international financial flows.

As in previous editions, we continue to integrate international examples and applications in many chapters. All international examples are listed in a table following the book's detailed table of contents. We continue to believe that a complete treatment of open-market macroeconomics should not be taught until students have mastered the logic of a simple closed macroeconomy. For this reason, we have chosen to place the "open-economy macroeconomics" chapter in the final part of the book, entitled "The World Economy." This part also includes the trade chapter, the new globalization chapter, and the economic development chapter.

TOOLS FOR LEARNING

As authors and teachers, we understand the challenges of the principles of economics course. Our pedagogical features are designed to illustrate and reinforce key economic concepts through real-world examples and applications.

NEWS ANALYSIS

The *News Analysis* feature presents a news article that supports the key concept of the chapter and illustrates how economics is a part of students' daily lives. We have included over 20 news articles from various sources, including *The New York Times, The Economist, The Wall Street Journal,* and *The Washington Times.* Select articles include graphs or photos. Students can visit www.prenhall.com/casefair for additional and updated news articles and exercises.

News Analysis

An Economic Recovery for the United States in 2003?

DURING 2001, THE U.S. ECONOMY WAS IN RECESSION. National income declined and employment fell. Employment continued to decline well into 2003. But the end of the war in Iraq, a fall in the price of oil on world markets, and a big tax cut in the United States seemed to many economists to suggest that a recovery from the hard times was beginning. The following article from the *Economist* reflects some guarded optimism.

Poised for growth?—*Economist*

Is America's economy finally set to shake off its funk? An increasing number of economists on Wall Street and politicians in Washington seem to think so. Many number-crunchers are forecasting a sharp acceleration of economic growth in the summer. John Snow, America's treasury secretary, suggested this week that the economy could be growing by around 4% by the end of 2003, more than double its current rate. After so many false dawns, is this optimism justified?

Financial markets certainly think so. All the big stockmarket indices have risen dramatically. The Dow Jones Industrial Average is now over 9,000, up more than 20% since mid-March; the technology-laden NASDAQ is up almost 30% from three months ago. Financial conditions have loosened across the board. Not only are government bond yields at historic lows, but spreads on corporate bonds have narrowed sharply, making access to capital cheaper and easier for firms of all kinds. A weaker dollar—the greenback has dropped by 8% against the currencies of America's trading partners this year—has also added to the loose financial conditions.

And there is more to come. Judging by recent comments from its top official, America's central bank is highly likely to cut interest rates when its policy-setting Federal Open Market Committee meets on June 24 to 25.

Nor is looser monetary policy the only stimulus on the way. Mr Bush's latest tax package, signed into law on May 28, will undoubtedly give the economy a short-term boost. The huge tax package—worth $350 billion over 10 years if you believe Congress's gimmicks, and costing more than $800 billion over a decade if you take a more realistic view—may not be particularly efficient as a stimulus package. But it is big. Economists at Morgan Stanley reckon the tax cut will add about $160 billion, or 1.5% of GDP, in fiscal stimulus over the next four quarters, bigger than any tax change since the Reagan tax cut in 1981. Of that, around $64 billion will reach Americans quickly in the form of rebate cheques and less tax withheld from their pay.

Add together loose financial conditions and a fiscal boost, and it is hard to imagine that the economy will not improve at all. Lower financing costs are continuing to prop up the housing market and maintain the surge in mortgage refinancings. The weekly tally of mortgage refinancing applications reached a new high of nearly 10,000 last week.

Even in the gloomy labour market, there are glimmers of hope. True, America's jobless rate hit a cyclical peak of 6.1% in May, and weekly unemployment claims are still extremely high. But the employment report released on June 6 was in many ways less bad than expected. Although the economy lost 17,000 jobs in May, the number of private-sector jobs was flat; the drop came in government posts. The number of temporary jobs rose by a healthy 58,000, and a rise in temporary workers is often a sign that firms are thinking of hiring permanent workers again. The latest monthly survey of purchasing managers also suggests that conditions in both the manufacturing and services sector are already improving, although they are far from booming.

A trickier question is whether any rebound will last. Can America's economy expect above-trend growth next year, for instance? There, it is much harder to be optimistic. America's economy still has huge fragilities. Although firms have undergone great adjustments since the excesses of the stockmarket bubble, there is still plenty of spare capacity around, making a sustained investment boom less likely.

Source: June 12, 2003, the Economist.

Despite signs of an economic recovery, 9.4 million people remained unemployed in mid-2003.

Visit www.prenhall.com/casefair for updated articles and exercises.

FURTHER EXPLORATION

Integrated in strategic places throughout the text, the *Further Exploration* feature provides students with applications as well as practical and historical information that supports the content of the chapter. The *Further Exploration* in Chapter 1, for example, highlights the various branches of economic study including economic law, international economics, and labor economics. The *Further Exploration* in Chapter 16 shows students how to read a bond table and the stock pages.

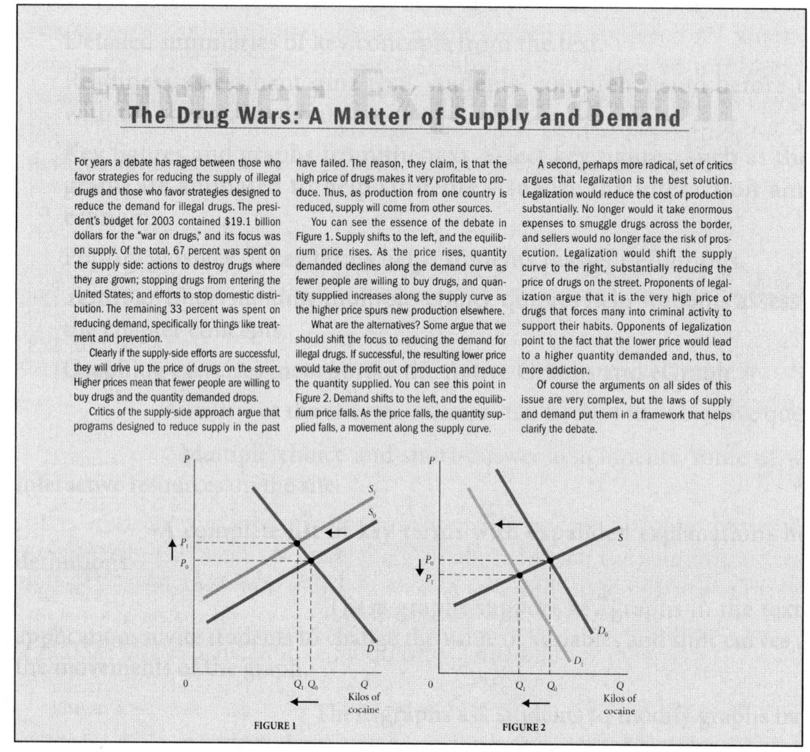

The Drug Wars: A Matter of Supply and Demand

For years a debate has raged between those who favor strategies for reducing the supply of illegal drugs and those who favor strategies designed to reduce the demand for illegal drugs. The president's budget for 2003 contained $19.1 billion dollars for the "war on drugs," and its focus was on supply. Of the total, 67 percent was spent on the supply side: actions to destroy drugs where they are grown; stopping drugs from entering the United States; and efforts to stop domestic distribution. The remaining 33 percent was spent on reducing demand, specifically for things like treatment and prevention.

Clearly if the supply-side efforts are successful, they will drive up the price of drugs on the street. Higher prices mean that fewer people are willing to buy drugs and the quantity demanded drops.

Critics of the supply-side approach argue that programs designed to reduce supply in the past have failed. The reason, they claim, is that the high price of drugs makes it very profitable to produce. Thus, as production from one country is reduced, supply will come from other sources.

You can see the essence of the debate in Figure 1. Supply shifts to the left, and the equilibrium price rises. As the price rises, quantity demanded declines along the demand curve as fewer people are willing to buy drugs, and quantity supplied increases along the supply curve as the higher price spurs new production elsewhere.

What are the alternatives? Some argue that we should shift the focus to reducing the demand for illegal drugs. If successful, the resulting lower price would take the profit out of production and reduce the quantity supplied. You can see this point in Figure 2. Demand shifts to the left, and the equilibrium price falls. As the price falls, the quantity supplied falls, a movement along the supply curve.

A second, perhaps more radical, set of critics argues that legalization is the best solution. Legalization would reduce the cost of production substantially. No longer would it take enormous expenses to smuggle drugs across the border, and sellers would no longer face the risk of prosecution. Legalization would shift the supply curve to the right, substantially reducing the price of drugs on the street. Proponents of legalization argue that it is the very high price of drugs that forces many into criminal activity to support their habits. Opponents of legalization point to the fact that the lower price would lead to a higher quantity demanded and, thus, to more addiction.

Of course the arguments on all sides of this issue are very complex, but the laws of supply and demand put them in a framework that helps clarify the debate.

GRAPHS

Reading and interpreting graphs is a key part of understanding economic concepts. The Chapter 1 appendix, "How to Read and Understand Graphs," shows readers how to interpret the graphs featured in the book. We use red curves to illustrate the behavior of firms and blue curves to show the behavior of households. We use a different shade of red and blue to signify a shift in a curve.

Forty-five graphs include an Active Graph icon. Students can visit the book's Companion Website (**www.prenhall.com/casefair**) to access interactive versions of the graphs. See the endpapers of the book for a complete list of all the Active Graphs. These graphs are categorized by level: *Active Graphs Level 1* invite students to change the value of variables and shift curves and see the effects in the movements of the graph. *Active Graphs Level 2* ask students to modify graphs based on an economic scenario or question. Students receive an instant response to their answers. If their answer is incorrect, the response will detail how they should have modified the graph.

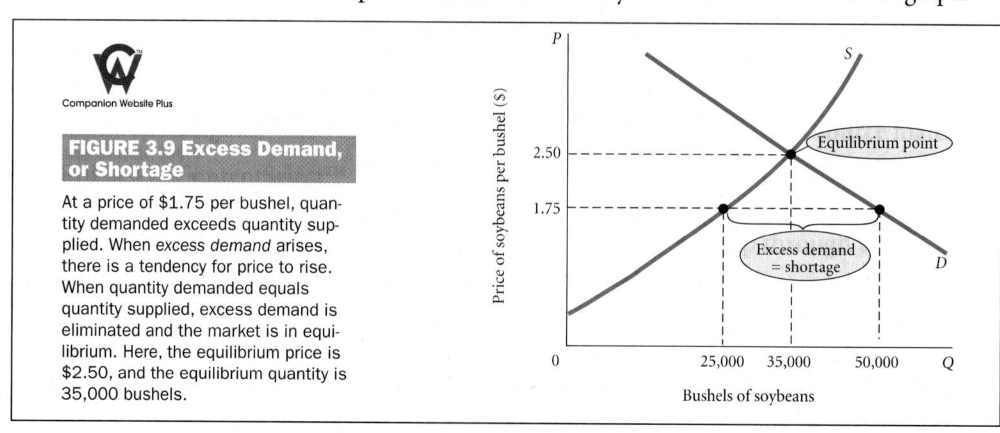

FIGURE 3.9 Excess Demand, or Shortage

At a price of $1.75 per bushel, quantity demanded exceeds quantity supplied. When *excess demand* arises, there is a tendency for price to rise. When quantity demanded equals quantity supplied, excess demand is eliminated and the market is in equilibrium. Here, the equilibrium price is $2.50, and the equilibrium quantity is 35,000 bushels.

HIGHLIGHTS OF MAJOR CONCEPTS

We have set major economic concepts off from the text in highlighted boxes. These highlights flow logically from the preceding text and into the text that follows. Students tell us that they find these very useful as a way of reviewing the key points in each chapter to prepare for exams.

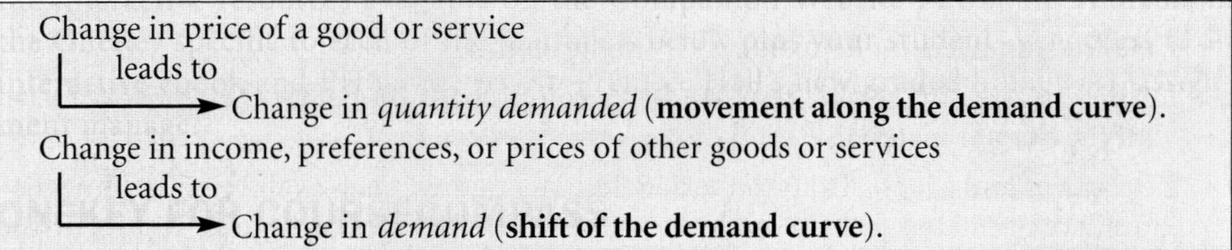
Change in price of a good or service
leads to → Change in *quantity demanded* (**movement along the demand curve**).
Change in income, preferences, or prices of other goods or services
leads to → Change in *demand* (**shift of the demand curve**).

RUNNING GLOSSARY

Definitions of key terms appear in the margin so they are easy to spot.

PROBLEM SETS AND SOLUTIONS

Each chapter and appendix ends with a problem set that asks students to think about what they've learned in the chapter. These problems are not simple memorization questions. Rather, they ask students to perform graphical analysis or to apply economics to a real-world situation or policy decision. More challenging problems are indicated by an asterisk. The worked solutions to all even-numbered problems are posted on www.prenhall.com/casefair (select "Student Resources" from the main page) so that students can check their understanding and progress. The solutions to all the problems are available in the Instructor's Manual.

INTEGRATED LEARNING PACKAGE

The integrated learning package for the seventh edition reflects changes in technology and utilizes new ways of disseminating information and resources. A customized website offers a comprehensive Internet package for the student and the instructor.

INTERNET RESOURCES

The Companion Website (www.prenhall.com/casefair) connects students to current news articles that deal with a key economic concept, Internet exercises and activities, and Practice Quizzes that include many graphs from the text. The Practice Quizzes were prepared by Fernando Quijano and Yvonn Quijano. Each chapter contains multiple-choice, true/false, and essay quizzes. These quizzes immediately grade each answer submitted, provide feedback for correct and incorrect answers, and let students e-mail results to their professors.

Also included on the Companion Website under the Student Resource link are the worked solutions to the even-numbered problems that appear at the end of each chapter of the book and current Event articles that help students see how economics affects their daily lives.

For the Instructor:

- *Syllabus Manager.* Allows instructors to create and post syllabi for their students to access. Instructors can add exams or assignments of their own, edit any of the student resources available on the Companion Website, post discussion topics, and much more.
- *Downloadable Supplements.* Instructors can access the book's PowerPoint presentations and Instructor's Manual. Please contact your Prentice Hall sales representative for password information.

COMPANION WEBSITE PLUS FOR INSTRUCTORS AND STUDENTS

Available by using the access code packaged with every new text, Companion Website PLUS uses all of the content of the Companion Website listed previously, along with many additional interactive resources. Companion Website PLUS provides the following for each chapter:

Objectives: Key questions and concepts that should be mastered by the end of the chapter.

Chapter Tutorial: A complete tutorial walk-through of the text material that includes:

- Detailed summaries of key concepts from the text.
- Readiness-assessment quiz tests student's comprehension before they move forward with the chapter material.
- Key figures and graphs from the text. Select key figures, such as the circular flow diagram, are animated to help students visualize the interaction among sectors of the economy.
- Pop-up glossary of key terms helps students master definitions.
- *Test Your Understanding* multiple-choice quizzes help students assess their progress with the chapter concepts.
- Graphing exercises incorporate the Active Graphs and eGraph.

Summary: A review of the chapter concepts ties back to the objective questions.

Homework: Multiple-choice and short-answer assignments, some of which are tied to the interactive resources on the site.

Glossary: A complete list of key terms with expanded explanations helps students retain definitions.

Active Graphs Level 1: These graphs support key graphs in the text. These JAVA-based applications invite students to change the value of variables and shift curves and see the effects in the movements of the graph.

Active Graphs Level 2: These graphs ask students to modify graphs based on an economic scenario or question. Students receive an instant response to their answers. If their answer is incorrect, the response will detail how they should have modified the graph.

eGraph and Questions: *eGraph* is an electronic tool that allows students to create precise, colorful graphs using Flash technology. Students can e-mail these graphs to their professor or print and save them. To apply this technology, we have included *Graphing Questions* that require students to analyze information gathered on the Web and then create graphs using the Graphing Tool. Complete answers, with graphs, are included.

RESEARCH NAVIGATOR™

Research Navigator™ is an online academic research service that helps students learn and master the skills needed to write effective papers and complete research assignments. Students and faculty can access Research Navigator™ through an access code found in front of *The Prentice Hall Guide to Evaluating Online Resources with Research Navigator*. This guide can be shrinkwrapped, at no additional cost, with *Economics, Seventh Edition*, by Case and Fair. Once you register, you have access to all the resources in Research Navigator™ for six months.

Research Navigator™ includes three databases of credible and reliable source material:

- EBESCO's ContentSelect™ Academic Journal database gives you instant access to thousands of academic journals and periodicals. You can search these online journals by keyword, topic, or multiple topics. It also guides students step by step through the writing of a research paper.
- *The New York Times* Search-by-Subject™ Archive allows you to search by subject and by keyword.
- Link Library is a collection of links to websites, organized by academic subject and key terms. The links are monitored and updated each week.

ONLINE COURSE OFFERINGS

ONEKEY: ALL YOU AND YOUR STUDENTS NEED TO SUCCEED

Onekey is Prentice Hall's exclusive new resource for instructors and students. OneKey gives you access to the best online teaching and learning tools–all available 24 hours a day, 7 days a week. OneKey means all your resources are in one place for maximum convenience, simplicity and success. All of the student and faculty resources, including the interactive resources available on the Companion Website PLUS, are available in the OneKey specific to each of the platforms below plus your students get access to an interactive ebook and PH Grade Assist–Prentice Hall's new graded homework assignment manager.

ONEKEY FOR COURSECOMPASS

This customizable, interactive online course-management tool, powered by Blackboard, provides the most intuitive teaching and learning environment available. Instructors can communicate with students, distribute course material, and access student progress online. For further information, please visit our website at http://www.prenhall.com/coursecompass or contact your Prentice Hall sales representative.

ONEKEY FOR WEBCT

Developed by educators, WebCT provides faculty with easy-to-use Internet tools to create online courses. Prentice Hall provides content and enhanced features to help instructors create a complete online course. Please visit our website at www.prenhall.com/webct for more information or contact your local Prentice Hall sales representative.

ONEKEY FOR BLACKBOARD

Easy to use, Blackboard's simple templates and tools make it easy to create, manage, and use online course materials. Prentice Hall provides content, and instructors can create online courses using the Blackboard tools, which include design, communications, testing, and course management tools. Please visit our website at www.prenhall.com/blackboard for more information or contact you local Prentice Hall sales representative.

TECHNOLOGY SUPPLEMENTS FOR THE INSTRUCTOR

The following technology supplements are designed to make teaching and testing flexible and easy.

INSTRUCTOR'S RESOURCE CD-ROM

The Instructor's Resource CD-ROM contains all faculty and student resources that support this text. Instructors have the ability to access and edit the Instructor's Manual, TestGen EQ, and PowerPoint presentations via this CD-ROM. Instructors can search by key term or chapter for a resource, open a file, or export a file to their own computer.

TESTGEN-EQ

Test Item File 1 and 2 appear in print and as computer files that may be used with this new TestGen-EQ test-generating software. This test-generating program permits instructors to edit, add, or delete questions from the test banks; edit or create; analyze test results; and organize a database of tests and student results. This new software allows for flexibility and ease of use. It provides many options for organizing and displaying tests, along with a search-and-sort feature. *Principles of Macroeconomics, Seventh Edition*, is supported by a comprehensive set of three test-item files. These test-item files are described in detail under the "Print Supplements" section of this preface.

POWERPOINT LECTURE PRESENTATIONS

The PowerPoint presentations, by Fernando Quijano and Yvonn Quijano, offer summaries and reinforcement of key text material. Many graphs "build" over a sequencing of slides so that students may see the step-by-step process of economic analysis. Instructors can create full-color, professional-looking presentations and customized handouts for students. The PowerPoint presentations are included in the Instructor's Resource CD-ROM and are downloadable from www.prenhall.com/casefair. Outlines of the presentations to be used for class note taking can also be found on the Companion Website PLUS.

PRINT SUPPLEMENTS

Principles of Macroeconomics, Seventh Edition, has a comprehensive print supplement package for the student and instructor.

STUDY GUIDE

The comprehensive study guide was prepared by Thomas Beveridge of North Carolina State University. This study aid reinforces the textbook and provides students with additional applications and exercises. Each chapter contains the following elements:

- *Point-by-Point Chapter Objectives.* A list of learning goals for the chapter. Each objective is followed up with a summary of the material, learning tips for each concept, and practice questions with solutions.
- *Practice Tests.* Approximately 20 multiple-choice questions and answers.
- *Application Questions.* A series of questions that require students to use graphic or numerical analysis to solve economic problems.
- *Solutions.* Worked-out solutions to all questions in the Study Guide.
- *Comprehensive Part Exams.* Exams to test the students' overall comprehension, consisting of multiple-choice and application questions. Solutions to all questions are also provided.

INSTRUCTOR'S MANUAL

The Instructor's Manual has been completely revised by Anthony Lima of California State University, Hayward. The manual is designed to provide the utmost teaching support for instructors. It includes the following:

- Detailed *chapter outlines* include key terminology, teaching notes, and lecture suggestions.
- *Topics for Class Discussion* provide topics and real-world situations that help make economic concepts resonate with students.
- *Teaching Tips* provide tips for alternative ways to cover the material or brief reminders on additional help to provide students. These tips can include suggestions for exercises or experiments to complete in class.
- *Extended Applications* include exercises, activities, and experiments to help make economics relevant to students.
- *Video Guide* provides summaries, teaching notes, and discussion questions and answers for the videos that accompany the book.
- *Solutions* to all problems in the book.

THREE TEST BANKS

The seventh edition test banks include approximately 6,500 questions. The test banks have been thoroughly revised, accuracy checked, and reviewed. To ensure the highest level of quality, a team of checkers carefully examined the content for accuracy, consistency with the text, and overall functionality for the purpose of testing student knowledge of the material. These accuracy checkers were David Boudreaux of George Mason University, Monica Cherry of St. John Fisher College, Timothy Duy of the University of Oregon, John Erkkila of Lake Superior State University, Sang Lee of Southeastern Louisiana University, Joshua Lewer of West Texas A&M University, and Robert Whaples of Wake Forest University.

To help instructors select questions more quickly and efficiently, we have used the skill descriptors of fact, definition, conceptual, and analytical. A question labeled *fact* tests a student's knowledge of factual information presented in the text. A *definition* question asks the student to define an economic term or concept. *Conceptual* questions test a student's understanding of a concept. *Analytical* questions require the student to apply an analytical procedure to answer the question.

To aid instructors in building tests, each question is also keyed by degree of difficulty as easy, moderate, or difficult. *Easy* questions involve straightforward recall of information in the text. *Moderate* questions require some analysis on the student's part. *Difficult* questions usually entail more complex analysis.

The test banks include questions with tables that students must analyze to use in solving for numerical answers. They also contain questions based on the graphs that appear in the book. The questions ask students to interpret the information presented in the graph. There are also many questions in the test banks that require students to sketch out a graph on their own and interpret curve movements.

Macroeconomics Test Bank 1 Prepared by James Swofford of University of South Alabama, this test bank includes over 3,000 questions. Types of questions include short answer, true/false, and multiple-choice. This test bank is available in a computerized format using TestGen-EQ test generating software.

Macroeconomics Test Bank 2 Prepared by Paul Kasunich of LaRoche College, this test bank includes 2,000 questions. Instructors can choose from a wide variety of short-answer, true/false, and multiple-choice questions. This test bank is also available in a computerized format using TestGen-EQ test generating software.

Macroeconomics Test Bank 3 This third test bank, prepared by Richard Gosselin of Houston Community College, includes 1,000 conceptual problems and essay questions. Application-type problems ask students to draw graphs and analyze tables. The Word files for this test bank are available on the Instructor's Resource CD-ROM.

ACETATE TRANSPARENCIES

Four-color transparencies of all figures and tables in both *Principles of Microeconomics* and *Principles of Macroeconomics* are available to adopting professors.

PEARSON HIGHER EDUCATION VIDEO PROGRAM

ABCNEWS

ABC News and Prentice Hall combine their individual expertise in academic publishing and global reporting to provide a comprehensive video ancillary for the seventh edition. The videos illustrate the vital connections between what students learn in the classroom and world events. The Instructor's Manual includes a summary of the videos, tips on how to incorporate the videos into lectures, and discussion questions and answers. Please contact your Prentice Hall representative for further details and ordering information.

SUBSCRIPTION OFFERS

Analyzing current events is an important skill for economic students to develop. To sharpen this skill, Prentice Hall offers you and your students three *news subscription* offers.

THE WALL STREET JOURNAL PRINT AND INTERACTIVE EDITIONS SUBSCRIPTION

Prentice Hall has formed a strategic alliance with *The Wall Street Journal*, the most respected and trusted daily source for information on business and economics. For a small additional charge, Prentice Hall offers your students a 10-week or 15-week subscription to *The Wall Street Journal* print edition and *The Wall Street Journal Interactive Edition*. Upon adoption of a special package containing the book and the subscription booklet, professors will receive a free one-year subscription to the print and interactive versions as well as weekly subject-specific *Wall Street Journal* educators' lesson plans. Please contact your Prentice Hall representative for further details and ordering information.

THE FINANCIAL TIMES

We are pleased to announce a special partnership with *The Financial Times*. For a small additional charge, Prentice Hall offers your students a 15-week subscription to *The Financial Times*. Upon adoption of a special package containing the book and the subscription booklet, professors will receive a free one-year subscription. Please contact your Prentice Hall representative for details and ordering information.

ECONOMIST.COM

Through a special arrangement with *Economist.com*, Prentice Hall offers your students a 12-week subscription to *Economist.com* for a small additional charge. Upon adoption of a special package containing the book and the subscription user code, professors will receive a free six-month subscription. Please contact your Prentice Hall representative for further details and ordering information.

ACKNOWLEDGMENTS

We are grateful to the many people who helped us prepare the seventh edition. We thank Rod Banister, Executive Editor for Economics at Prentice Hall, for his help and enthusiasm. We are also grateful to Lena Buonanno, Senior Developmental Editor, for overseeing the entire project. The quality of the book owes much to her guidance. The extensive print and technology supplements that accompany this book are the result of the dedication of Gladys Soto, Managing Editor, Marie McHale, Project Manager, Victoria Anderson, Media Project Manager, and Joy Golden, Editorial Assistant. Kathleen McLellan, Executive Marketing Manager, and David Theisen, National Sales Director for Key Markets, carefully crafted the marketing message.

Carol Samet, Production Editor, and Cynthia Regan, our Production Managing Editor, ensured that the production process of the book went smoothly. Melinda Alexander researched the many photographs that appear in the book.

We want to thank Maryna Marynchenko and Jenny Stack for their research assistance and proofreading of the manuscript.

We also owe a debt of gratitude to those who reviewed the seventh edition and served on our *Consultant Board* and *Accuracy Review Board*. They all provided us with valuable insight as we prepared the new edition and its supplement package.

CONSULTANT BOARD

We received continual feedback over the course of a year on content, figure treatment, and design from our *Consultant Board*:

John W. Allen, Texas A&M University
John W. Graham, Rutgers University
Arthur E. Kartman, San Diego State University
Rebecca Stein, University of Pennsylvania
Paula Worthington, Northwestern University

ACCURACY REVIEW BOARD

We have carefully evaluated the graphs, equations, and problems in each chapter. In addition, we formed an *Accuracy Review Board* of economics professors who also evaluated each chapter. The board members were:

Charles Callahan, III, State University of New York at Brockport
Sang H. Lee, Southeastern Louisiana University
Anthony K. Lima, California State University at Hayward
Karen M. Travis, Pacific Lutheran University

SUPPLEMENT AUTHORS AND ACCURACY CHECKERS

A dedicated team of economics teachers prepared a complete supplements package for the seventh edition:

Thomas Beveridge, North Carolina State University
Richard Gosselin, Houston Community College
Paul Kasunich, LaRoche College
Anthony K. Lima, California State University at Hayward
Raymond Polchow, Muskingum Tech
James Swofford, University of South Alabama
Tori Knight, Carson-Newman College

The following professors accuracy checked the test banks:

David Boudreaux, George Mason University
Monica Cherry, St. John Fisher College
Timothy Duy, University of Oregon
John Erkkila, Lake Superior State University
Sang H. Lee, Southeastern Louisiana University
Joshua Lewer, West Texas A&M University
Robert Whaples, Wake Forest University

REVIEWERS OF THE CURRENT EDITION

The guidance and recommendations of the following professors helped us develop the revision plans for our new edition and shape the content of the new chapters:

Sheri Aggarwal, University of Virginia
John W. Allen, Texas A&M University
King Banaian, St. Cloud State University
Leon Battista, Bronx Community College
Maristella Botticini, Boston University
Anne E. Bresnock, California State Polytechnic University at Pamona and the University of California at Los Angeles
Charles Callahan, III, State University of New York at Brockport
Winston W. Chang, State University of New York at Buffalo
Susan Christoffersen, Philadelphia University
Vernon J. Dixon, Haverford College
Debra Sabatini Dwyer, State University of New York at Stony Brook
David Eaton, Murray State University
Ronald D. Elkins, Central Washington University
Roger Frantz, San Diego State University
Lisa Giddings, University of Wisconsin at La Crosse
Roy Gobin, Loyola University of Chicago
John W. Graham, Rutgers University
Wayne A. Grove, Syracuse University
Russell A. Janis, University of Massachusetts at Amherst
Arthur E. Kartman, San Diego State University
Steven Kyle, Cornell University
Sang H. Lee, Southeastern Louisiana University
Robert J. Lemke, Lake Forest College
Anthony K. Lima, California State University at Hayward
Marvin S. Margolis, Millersville University of Pennsylvania
Barbara A. Moore, University of Central Florida
Niki Papadopoulou, University of Cyprus
Elizabeth Porter, University of North Florida
Michael Rolleigh, University of Minnesota
Greg Rose, Sacramento City College
Robert Rosenman, Washington State University

Jeff Rubin, Rutgers University
Jerry Schwartz, Broward Community College
David J. St. Clair, California State University at Hayward
Rebecca Stein, University of Pennsylvania
Rodney B. Swanson, University of California at Los Angeles
Karen M. Travis, Pacific Lutheran University
Lawrence Waldman, University of New Mexico
Robert Whaples, Wake Forest University
Paula Worthington, Northwestern University
Jason Zimmerman, South Dakota State University

REVIEWERS OF PREVIOUS EDITIONS

The following individuals were of immense help in reviewing all or part of this book and the teaching/learning package in various stages of development:

Lew Abernathy, University of North Texas
Jack Adams, University of Maryland
Douglas Agbetsiafa, Indiana University at South Bend
Sam Alapati, Rutgers University
Polly Allen, University of Connecticut
Stuart Allen, University of North Carolina at Greensboro
Alex Anas, SUNY at Buffalo
Jim Angresano, Hampton-Sydney College
Kenneth S. Arakelian, University of Rhode Island
Harvey Arnold, Indian River Community College
Nick Apergis, Fordham University
Richard Ashley, Virginia Technical University
Kidane Asmeron, Pennsylvania State University
James Aylesworth, Lakeland Community College
Richard J. Ballman, Jr., Augustana College
Mohammad Bajwa, Northampton Community College
Kari Battaglia, University of North Texas
Willie J. Belton, Jr., Georgia Institute of Technology
Daniel K. Benjamin, Clemson University
Charles A. Bennett, Gannon University
Daniel Berkowitz, University of Pittsburgh
Bruce Bolnick, Northeastern University
Jeffrey Bookwalter, University of Montana
G. E. Breger, University of South Carolina
Dennis Brennan, William Rainey Harper Junior College
Lindsay Caulkins, John Carroll University
Atreya Chakraborty, Boston College
Janie Chermak, University of New Mexico
Harold Christensen, Centenary College
Daniel Christiansen, Albion College
Samuel Kim-Liang Chuah, Walla Walla College
David Colander, Middlebury College
Daniel Condon, University of Illinois at Chicago; Moraine Valley Community College
David Cowen, University of Texas at Austin
Peggy Crane, Southwestern College
Minh Quang Dao, Eastern Illinois University
Michael Donihue, Colby College
Joanne M. Doyle, James Madison University
Robert Driskill, Ohio State University
James Dulgeroff, San Bernardino Valley College
Gary Dymski, University of Southern California
David Eaton, Murray State University
Jay Egger, Towson State University
Noel J. J. Farley, Bryn Mawr College
Mosin Farminesh, Temple University
Dan Feaster, Miami University of Ohio
Susan Feiner, Virginia Commonwealth University
Getachew Felleke, Albright College
Lois Fenske, South Puget Sound Community College
William Field, DePauw University
Mary Flannery, Santa Clara University
Bill Foeller, State University of New York at Fredonia
Roger Nils Folsom, San Jose State University
Richard Fowles, University of Utah
Sean Fraley, College of Mount Saint Joseph
Roger Frantz, San Diego State University
Alejandro Gallegos, Winona State University
N. Galloro, Chabot College
Martin A. Garrett, Jr., College of William and Mary
Tom Gausman, Northern Illinois University, DeKalb
Shirley J. Gedeon, University of Vermont
Gary Gigliotti, Rutgers University
Lynn Gillette, Texas A&M University
James N. Giordano, Villanova University

Sarah L. Glavin, Boston College
Bill Goffe, University of Mississippi
Devra Golbe, Hunter College
Roger Goldberg, Ohio Northern University
Richard Gosselin, Houston Community College
John W. Graham, Rutgers University
Douglas Greenley, Morrhead State University
Lisa M. Grobar, California State University at Long Beach
Benjamin Gutierrez, Indiana University at Bloomington
A. R. Gutowsky, California State University at Sacramento
David R. Hakes, University of Missouri at St. Louis
Stephen Happel, Arizona State University
Mitchell Harwitz, State University of New York at Buffalo
David Hoaas, Centenary College
Harry Holzer, Michigan State University
Bobbie Horn, University of Tulsa
John Horowitz, Ball State University
Janet Hunt, University of Georgia
E. Bruce Hutchinson, University of Tennessee at Chattanooga
Fred Inaba, Washington State University
Richard Inman, Boston College
Eric Jensen, College of William & Mary
Shirley Johnson, Vassar College
Farhoud Kafi, Babson College
R. Kallen, Roosevelt University
Arthur E. Kartman, San Diego State University
Hirshel Kasper, Oberlin College
Bruce Kaufman, Georgia State University
Dominique Khactu, University of North Dakota
Phillip King, San Francisco State University
Barbara Kneeshaw, Wayne County Community College
Inderjit Kohli, Santa Clara University
Barry Kotlove, Elmira College
David Kraybill, University of Georgia at Athens
Rosung Kwak, University of Texas at Austin
Anil K. Lal, Pittsburg State University
Melissa Lam, Wellesley College
Micheal Lawlor, Wake Forest University
Jim Lee, Fort Hays State University
Judy Lee, Leeward Community College
Don Leet, California State University at Fresno
Gary Lemon, DePauw University
Alan Leonard, Northern Illinois University
Mary Lesser, Iona College
George Lieu, Tuskegee University
Stephen E. Lile, Western Kentucky University
Jane Lillydahl, University of Colorado at Boulder
Al Link, University of North Carolina at Greensboro
Robert Litro, U.S. Air Force Academy
Burl F. Long, University of Florida
Gerald Lynch, Purdue University
Karla Lynch, University of North Texas
Marvin S. Margolis, Millserville University
Michael Magura, University of Toledo
Don Maxwell, Central State University
Nan Maxwell, California State University at Hayward
Cynthia S. McCarty, Jacksonville State University
J. Harold McClure, Jr., Villanova University
Rick McIntyre, University of Rhode Island
James J. McLain, University of New Orleans
K. Mehtaboin, College of St. Rose
Jenny Minier, University of Miami
Shahruz Mohtadi, Suffolk University
Joe L. Moore, Arkansas Technical University
Robert Moore, Occidental College
Doug Morgan, University of California at Santa Barbara
Norma C. Morgan, Curry College
John Murphy, North Shore Community College, Massachusetts
Veena Nayak, State University of New York at Buffalo
Ron Necoechea, Robert Wesleyan College
Randy Nelson, Colby College
David Nickerson, University of British Columbia
Rachel Nugent, Pacific Lutheran University
Akorlie A. Nyatepe-Coo, University of Wisconsin at LaCrosse
Norman P. Obst, Michigan State University
William C. O'Connor, Western Montana College
Martha L. Olney, University of California–Berkeley
Kent Olson, Oklahoma State University
Theresa Osborne, Hunter College
Jaime Ortiz, Florida Atlantic University
Donald J. Oswald, California State University at Bakersfield
Walter Park, American University
Carl Parker, Fort Hays State University
Spirog Patton, Neumann College
Mary Ann Pevas, Winona State University
Tony Pizelo, Spokane Community College
Kevin Quinn, St. Norbert College
Michael Rendich, Westchester Community College
Lynn Rittenoure, University of Tulsa

S. Scanlon Romer, Delta College
David C. Rose, University of Missouri at St. Louis
Richard Rosenberg, Pennsylvania State University
Paul Rothstein, Washington University
Mark Rush, University of Florida at Gainesville
Dereka Rushbrook, Ripon College
Jerard Russo, University of Hawaii
David L. Schaffer, Haverford College
Ramon Schreffler, Houston Community College System (retired)
Gary Sellers, University of Akron
Jean Shackleford, Bucknell University
Linda Shaffer, California State University at Fresno
Geoff Shepherd, University of Massachusetts at Amherst
Bih-Hay Sheu, University of Texas at Austin
Alden Shiers, California Polytechnic State University
Scott Simkins, North Carolina Agricultural and Technical State University
Sue Skeath, Wellesley College
Paula Smith, Central State University, Oklahoma
David Sobiechowski, Wayne State University
John Solow, University of Iowa at Iowa City
Susan Stojanovic, Washington University, St. Louis
Ernst W. Stromsdorfer, Washington State University
James Swofford, University of Alabama
Michael Taussig, Rutgers University
Timothy Taylor, Stanford University
Sister Beth Anne Tercek, SND, Notre Dame College of Ohio
Jack Trierweler, Northern State University
Brian M. Trinque, University of Texas at Austin
Ann Velenchik, Wellesley College
Chris Waller, Indiana University at Bloomington
Walter Wessels, North Carolina State University
Joan Whalen-Ayyappan, DeVry Institute of Technology
Robert Whaples, Wake Forest University
Leonard A. White, University of Arkansas
Ben Young, University of Missouri–Kansas City
Darrel Young, University of Texas
Michael Youngblood, Rock Valley College
Abera Zeyege, Ball State University
James Ziliak, Indiana University at Bloomington

We welcome comments about the seventh edition. Please write to us care of Economics Editor, Prentice Hall Higher Education Division, One Lake Street, Upper Saddle River, N.J. 07458.

Karl E. Case

Ray C. Fair

Save a Tree!

Many of the components of the teaching and learning package are available in electronic format. Disk-based supplements conserve paper and allow you to select and print only the material you plan to use. For more information, please ask your Prentice Hall sales representative.

The Scope and Method of Economics

1

CHAPTER OUTLINE

The study of economics should begin with a sense of wonder. Pause for a moment and consider a typical day in your life. For breakfast you might have bread made in a local bakery with flour produced in Minnesota from wheat grown in Kansas and bacon from pigs raised in Ohio packaged in plastic made in New Jersey. You spill coffee from Colombia on your shirt made in Texas from textiles shipped from South Carolina.

After class you drive with a friend in a Japanese car on an interstate highway that is part of a system that took 20 years and billions of dollars to build. You stop for gasoline refined in Louisiana from Saudi Arabian crude oil brought to the United States on a supertanker that took 3 years to build at a shipyard in Maine.

Later you log onto the Web with a laptop computer assembled in Indonesia from parts made in China and send e-mail to your brother in Mexico City, and you call a buddy on a cell phone made by a company in Finland. It is picked up by a microwave dish hiding in a church steeple rented from the church by a cellular company that was just bought by a European conglomerate.

You use or consume tens of thousands of things, both tangible and intangible, every day: buildings, rock music, compact discs (CDs), telephone services, staples, paper, toothpaste, tweezers, soap, digital watches, fire protection, antacid tablets, banks, electricity, eggs, insurance, football fields, computers, buses, rugs, subways, health services, sidewalks, and so forth. Somebody made all these things. Somebody decided to organize men and women and materials to produce them and distribute them. Thousands of decisions went into their completion. Somehow they got to you.

In the United States nearly 140 million people—almost half the total population—work at hundreds of thousands of different jobs producing over $10 trillion worth of goods and services every year. Some cannot find work; some choose not to work. Some are rich; others are poor.

The United States imports over $200 billion worth of automobiles and parts and about $100 billion worth of petroleum and petroleum products each year; it exports around $55 billion worth of agricultural products, including food. High-rise office buildings go up in central cities. Condominiums and homes are built in the suburbs. In other places homes are abandoned and boarded up.

Some countries are wealthy. Others are impoverished. Some are growing. Some are stagnating. Some businesses are doing well. Others are going bankrupt.

At any moment in time every society faces constraints imposed by nature and by previous generations. Some societies are handsomely endowed by nature with fertile land, water, sunshine, and natural resources. Others have deserts and few mineral resources. Some societies receive much from previous generations—art, music, technical knowledge, beautiful buildings, and productive factories. Others are left with overgrazed, eroded land, cities leveled by war, or polluted natural environments. *All* societies face limits.

economics The study of how individuals and societies choose to use the scarce resources that nature and previous generations have provided.

Economics is the study of how individuals and societies choose to use the scarce resources that nature and previous generations have provided. The key word in this definition is *choose*. Economics is a behavioral, or social, science. In large measure it is the study of how people make choices. The choices that people make, when added up, translate into societal choices.

The purpose of this chapter and the next is to elaborate on this definition and to introduce the subject matter of economics. What is produced? How is it produced? Who gets it? Why? Is the result good or bad? Can it be improved?

WHY STUDY ECONOMICS?

There are four main reasons to study economics: to learn a way of thinking, to understand society, to understand global affairs, and to be an informed voter.

TO LEARN A WAY OF THINKING

Probably the most important reason for studying economics is to learn a way of thinking. A good way to introduce economics is to review three of its most fundamental concepts: *opportunity cost*, *marginalism*, and *efficient markets*. If your study of economics is successful, you will use these concepts every day in making decisions.

Opportunity Cost What happens in an economy is the outcome of thousands of individual decisions. Households must decide how to divide their incomes among all the goods and services available in the marketplace. People must decide whether to work or not to work, whether to go to school, and how much to save. Businesses must decide what to produce, how much to produce, how much to charge, and where to locate. It is not surprising that economic analysis focuses on the process of decision making.

Nearly all decisions involve trade-offs. A key concept that recurs in analyzing the decision-making process is the notion of *opportunity cost*. The full "cost" of making a specific choice includes what we give up by not making the alternative choice. The best alternative that we forgo, or give up, when we make a choice or a decision is called the **opportunity cost** of that decision.

opportunity cost The best alternative that we forgo, or give up, when we make a choice or a decision.

This concept applies to individuals, businesses, and entire societies. The opportunity cost of going to a movie is the value of the other things you could have done with the same money and time. If you decide to take time off from work, the opportunity cost of your leisure is the pay that you would have earned had you worked. Part of the cost of a college education is the income you could have earned by working full time instead of going to school. If a firm purchases a new piece of equipment for $3,000, it does so because it expects that equipment to generate more profit. There is an opportunity cost, however, because that $3,000 could have been deposited in an interest-earning account. To a society, the opportunity cost of using resources to put astronauts on the moon is the value of the private/civilian or other government goods that could have been produced with the same resources.

scarce Limited.

Opportunity costs arise because resources are scarce. **Scarce** simply means "limited." Consider one of our most important resources—time. There are only 24 hours in a day, and we must live our lives under this constraint. A farmer in rural Brazil must decide whether it is better to continue to farm or to go to the city and look for a job. A hockey player at the University of Vermont must decide whether she will play on the varsity team or spend more time improving her academic work.

Marginalism and Sunk Costs A second key concept used in analyzing choices is the notion of *marginalism.* In weighing the costs and benefits of a decision, it is important to weigh only the costs and benefits that arise from the decision. Suppose, for example, that you live in New Orleans and that you are weighing the costs and benefits of visiting your mother in Iowa. If business required that you travel to Kansas City, the cost of visiting Mom would be only the additional, or *marginal,* time and money cost of getting to Iowa from Kansas City.

Consider the cost of producing this book. Assume that 10,000 copies are produced. The total cost of producing the copies includes the cost of the authors' time in writing the book, the cost of editing, the cost of making the plates for printing, and the cost of the paper and ink. If the total cost were $600,000, then the average cost of one copy would be $60, which is simply $600,000 divided by 10,000.

Although average cost is an important concept, a book publisher must know more than simply the average cost of a book. For example, suppose a second printing is being debated. That is, should another 10,000 copies be produced? In deciding whether to proceed, the costs of writing, editing, making plates, and so forth are irrelevant, because they have already been incurred—they are *sunk costs.* **Sunk costs** are costs that cannot be avoided, regardless of what is done in the future, because they have already been incurred. All that matters is the costs associated with the additional, or marginal, books to be printed. Technically, *marginal cost* is the cost of producing one more unit of output.

sunk costs Costs that cannot be avoided, regardless of what is done in the future, because they have already been incurred.

There are numerous examples in which the concept of marginal cost is useful. For an airplane that is about to take off with empty seats, the marginal cost of an extra passenger is essentially zero; the total cost of the trip is roughly unchanged by the addition of an extra passenger. Thus, setting aside a few seats to be sold at big discounts through priceline.com or other Web sites can be profitable even if the fare for those seats is far below the average cost per seat of making the trip. As long as the airline succeeds in filling seats that would otherwise have been empty, doing so is profitable.

Efficient Markets—No Free Lunch Suppose you are ready to check out of a busy grocery store on the day before a storm, and seven checkout registers are open with several people in each line. Which line should you choose? It is usually the case that the waiting time is approximately the same no matter which register you choose (assuming you have more than 12 items). If one line is much shorter than the others, people will quickly move into it until the lines are equalized again.

As you will see later, the term *profit* in economics has a very precise meaning. Economists, however, often loosely refer to "good deals" or risk-free ventures as *profit opportunities.* Using the term loosely, a profit opportunity exists at the checkout lines if one line is shorter than the others. In general, such profit opportunities are rare. At any time there are many people searching for them, and, as a consequence, few exist. Markets like this, where any profit opportunities are eliminated almost instantaneously, are said to be **efficient markets.** (We discuss *markets,* the institutions through which buyers and sellers interact and engage in exchange, in detail in Chapter 2.)

efficient market A market in which profit opportunities are eliminated almost instantaneously.

The common way of expressing the efficient markets concept is "there's no such thing as a free lunch." How should you react when a stockbroker calls up with a hot tip on the stock market? With skepticism. There are thousands of individuals each day looking for hot tips in the market. If a particular tip about a stock is valid, there will be an immediate rush to buy the stock, which will quickly drive its price up. This view that very few profit opportunities exist can, of course, be carried too far. There is a story about two people walking along, one an economist and one not. The noneconomist sees a $20 bill on the sidewalk and says, "There's a $20 bill on the sidewalk." The economist replies, "That is not possible. If there were, somebody would already have picked it up."

There are clearly times when profit opportunities exist. Someone has to be first to get the news, and some people have quicker insights than others. Nevertheless, news travels fast, and there are thousands of people with quick insights. The general view that large profit opportunities are rare is close to the mark.

The study of economics teaches us a way of thinking and helps us make decisions.

TO UNDERSTAND SOCIETY

Another reason for studying economics is to understand society better. Past and present economic decisions have an enormous influence on the character of life in a society. The current state of the physical environment, the level of material well-being, and the nature and number of jobs are all products of the economic system.

To get a sense of the ways in which economic decisions have shaped our environment, imagine looking out of a top-floor window of a high-rise office building in any large city. The workday is about to begin. All around you are other tall glass and steel buildings full of workers. In the distance you see the smoke of factories. Looking down, you see thousands of commuters pouring off trains and buses, and cars backed up on freeway exit ramps. You see trucks carrying goods from one place to another. You also see the face of urban poverty: Just beyond the freeway is a large public housing project and, beyond that, burned-out and boarded-up buildings.

What you see before you is the product of millions of economic decisions made over hundreds of years. People at some point decided to spend time and money building those buildings and factories. Somebody cleared the land, laid the tracks, built the roads, and produced the cars and buses.

Industrial Revolution The period in England during the late eighteenth and early nineteenth centuries in which new manufacturing technologies and improved transportation gave rise to the modern factory system and a massive movement of the population from the countryside to the cities.

Economic decisions not only have shaped the physical environment but also have determined the character of society. At no time has the impact of economic change on a society been more evident than in England during the late eighteenth and early nineteenth centuries, a period that we now call the **Industrial Revolution**. Increases in the productivity of agriculture, new manufacturing technologies, and development of more efficient forms of transportation led to a massive movement of the British population from the countryside to the city. At the beginning of the eighteenth century, approximately two out of three people in Great Britain worked in agriculture. By 1812, only 1 in 3 remained in agriculture; by 1900, the figure was fewer than 1 in 10. People jammed into overcrowded cities and worked long hours in factories. The world had changed completely in two centuries—a period that in the run of history was nothing more than the blink of an eye.

It is not surprising that the discipline of economics began to take shape during this period. Social critics and philosophers looked around them and knew that their philosophies must expand to accommodate the changes. Adam Smith's *Wealth of Nations* appeared in 1776. It was followed by the writings of David Ricardo, Karl Marx, Thomas Malthus, and others. Each tried to make sense out of what was happening. Who was building the factories? Why? What determined the level of wages paid to workers or the price of food? What would happen in the future, and what *should* happen? The people who asked these questions were the first economists.

Similar changes continue to affect the character of life today. In fact, many argue that the late 1990s marked the beginning of a new Industrial Revolution. As we turned the corner into the new millennium, the "e" revolution was clearly having an impact on virtually every aspect of our lives: the way we buy and sell products, the way we get news, the way we plan vacations, the way we communicate with each other, the way we teach and take classes, and on and on. These changes have had and will clearly continue to have profound impacts on societies across the globe, from Beijing to Calcutta to New York.

These changes have been driven by economics. Although the government was involved in the early years of the World Wide Web, private firms that exist to make a profit [such as Yahoo!, Microsoft, Cisco, America Online (AOL), Amazon.com, and E-Trade] created almost all the new innovations and products. How does one make sense of all this? What will the effects be on the number of jobs, the character of those jobs, the family incomes, the structure of our cities, and the political process, both in the United States and in other countries?

> The study of economics is an essential part of the study of society.

TO UNDERSTAND GLOBAL AFFAIRS

A third reason for studying economics is to understand global affairs. News headlines are filled with economic stories. International events often have enormous economic consequences. The destruction of the World Trade Center towers in New York City and the subsequent war on terror in Afghanistan and elsewhere led to a huge decline in both tourism and business travel. Several major airlines, including U.S. Airways and Swissair, went bankrupt. Hotel operators worldwide suffered huge losses. The war in Iraq and a strike in Venezuela in 2003 sent oil markets gyrating dramatically, initially increasing the cost of energy across the globe. The dramatic decline in the value of stocks traded in U.S. stock markets during the first three years of this century reduced household wealth in the United States by over $6 trillion, drove down the value of the U.S. dollar on foreign exchange markets, and had a huge effect on world trading patterns. The rapid spread of HIV and AIDS across Africa will have terrible economic consequences for the continent and ultimately for the world.

Some claim that economic considerations dominate international relations. Certainly politicians place the economic well-being of their citizens near the top of their priority lists. It would be surprising if that were not so. Thus, the economic consequences of things like environmental policy, free trade, and immigration play a huge roll in international negotiations and policies.

The events of September 11 dealt a blow to the tourism industry and left airlines in deep financial trouble.

Great Britain and the other countries of the European Union have struggled with the agreement among most members to adopt a common currency, the euro. The nations of the former Soviet Union are wrestling with a growing phenomenon that clouds their efforts to "privatize" formerly state-owned industries: organized crime.

Another important issue in today's world is the widening gap between rich and poor nations. In 2003, world population was over 6 billion. Of that number, nearly 5 billion lived in less-developed countries and 1.5 billion lived in more-developed countries. The 75 percent of the world's population that lives in the less-developed countries receives less than 20 percent of the world's income. In dozens of countries, per capita income is only a few hundred dollars a year.

An understanding of economics is essential to an understanding of global affairs.

TO BE AN INFORMED VOTER

A knowledge of economics is essential to be an informed voter. During the last 25 years, the U.S. economy has been on a roller coaster. In 1973–1974, the Organization of Petroleum Exporting Countries (OPEC) succeeded in raising the price of crude oil by 400 percent. Simultaneously, a sequence of events in the world food market drove food prices up by 25 percent. By mid-1974, prices in the United States were rising across the board at a very rapid rate. Partially as a result of government policy to fight runaway inflation, the economy went into a recession in 1975. (An *inflation* is an increase in the overall price level in the economy; a *recession* is a period of decreasing output and rising unemployment.) The recession succeeded in slowing price increases, but in the process millions found themselves unemployed.

From 1979 through 1983, it happened all over again. Prices rose rapidly, the government reacted with more policies designed to stop prices from rising, and the United States ended up with an even worse recession in 1982. By the end of that year, 10.8 percent of the workforce was unemployed. Then, in mid-1990—after almost 8 years of strong economic performance—the U.S. economy went into another recession. During the third and fourth quarters of 1990 and the first quarter of 1991, gross domestic product (GDP, a measure of the total output of the U.S. economy) fell, and unemployment again increased sharply. The election of Bill Clinton late in 1992 was no doubt in part influenced by the so-called "jobless recovery."

From the second quarter of 1991 through the early part of the new millennium, the U.S. economy experienced the longest expansion in its history. More than 24 million new jobs were created, pushing unemployment below 4 percent by the year 2000. The stock market boomed to historic levels, and the biggest worry facing the American economy was that things were too good!

The presidential election of 2000 was close, to say the least, with the outcome not known until early December. In mid December President-Elect George W. Bush and his economic advisers began to worry about the possibility of a recession occurring in 2001. The stock market was below its highs for the year; corporate profits were not coming in as well as expected; and there were some signs that demand for goods was slowing.

By the middle of 2003, focus began to shift to the 2004 presidential election. Candidates were lining up on the Democratic side of the aisle, ready to take Mr. Bush's job. But the outcome of the election may depend to a large extent on the economic conditions during the months before the election. Statistical evidence shows that good economic times prior to a presidential election give the incumbent's party a substantial edge. Similarly, a weak economy means that fewer are likely to vote for the incumbent's party.

When we participate in the political process, we are voting on issues that require a basic understanding of economics.

THE SCOPE OF ECONOMICS

Most students taking economics for the first time are surprised by the breadth of what they study. Some think that economics will teach them about the stock market or what to do with their money. Others think that economics deals exclusively with problems like inflation and unemployment. In fact, it deals with all these subjects, but they are pieces of a much larger puzzle.

Economics has deep roots in, and close ties to, social philosophy. An issue of great importance to philosophers, for example, is distributional justice. Why are some people rich and others poor, and, whatever the answer, is this fair? A number of nineteenth-century social philosophers wrestled with these questions, and out of their musings economics as a separate discipline was born.

The easiest way to get a feel for the breadth and depth of what you will be studying is to explore briefly the way economics is organized. First of all, there are two major divisions of economics: microeconomics and macroeconomics.

MICROECONOMICS AND MACROECONOMICS

microeconomics The branch of economics that examines the functioning of individual industries and the behavior of individual decision-making units—that is, business firms and households.

Microeconomics deals with the functioning of individual industries and the behavior of individual economic decision-making units: business firms and households. Firms' choices about what to produce and how much to charge, and households' choices about what and how much to buy, help to explain why the economy produces the things it does.

Another big question addressed by microeconomics is who gets the things that are produced. Wealthy households get more than poor households, and the forces that determine this distribution of output are the province of microeconomics. Why does poverty exist? Who is poor? Why do some jobs pay more than others?

Think again about all the things you consume in a day, and then think back to that view over a big city. Somebody decided to build those factories. Somebody decided to construct the roads, build the housing, produce the cars, and smoke the bacon. Why? What is going on in all those buildings? It is easy to see that understanding individual microdecisions is very important to any understanding of society.

macroeconomics The branch of economics that examines the economic behavior of aggregates—income, employment, output, and so on—on a national scale.

Macroeconomics looks at the economy as a whole. Instead of trying to understand what determines the output of a single firm or industry or the consumption patterns of a single household or group of households, macroeconomics examines the factors that determine national output, or national product. Microeconomics is concerned with *household* income; macroeconomics deals with *national* income.

Whereas microeconomics focuses on individual product prices and relative prices, macroeconomics looks at the overall price level and how quickly (or slowly) it is rising (or falling). Microeconomics questions how many people will be hired (or fired) this year in a particular industry or in a certain geographic area, and the factors that determine how much labor a firm or industry will hire. Macroeconomics deals with *aggregate* employment and unemployment: how many jobs exist in the economy as a whole, and how many people who are willing to work are not able to find work.

To summarize:

Microeconomics looks at the individual unit—the household, the firm, the industry. It sees and examines the "trees." Macroeconomics looks at the whole, the aggregate. It sees and analyzes the "forest."

TABLE 1.1 Examples of Microeconomic and Macroeconomic Concerns

DIVISION OF ECONOMICS	PRODUCTION	PRICES	INCOME	EMPLOYMENT
Microeconomics	*Production/output in individual industries and businesses* How much steel How much office space How many cars	*Prices of individual goods and services* Price of medical care Price of gasoline Food prices Apartment rents	*Distribution of income and wealth* Wages in the auto industry Minimum wage Executive salaries Poverty	*Employment by individual businesses and industries* Jobs in the steel industry Number of employees in a firm Number of accountants
Macroeconomics	*National production/output* Total industrial output Gross domestic product Growth of output	*Aggregate price level* Consumer prices Producer prices Rate of inflation	*National income* Total wages and salaries Total corporate profits	*Employment and unemployment in the economy* Total number of jobs Unemployment rate

Table 1.1 summarizes these divisions and some of the subjects with which they are concerned.

THE DIVERSE FIELDS OF ECONOMICS

Individual economists focus their research and study in many diverse areas. Many of these specialized fields are reflected in the advanced courses offered at most colleges and universities. Some are concerned with economic history or the history of economic thought. Others focus on international economics or growth in less-developed countries. Still others study the economics of cities (urban economics) or the relationship between economics and law. (See the Further Exploration box titled "The Fields of Economics" for more details.)

Economists also differ in the emphasis they place on theory. Some economists specialize in developing new theories, whereas others spend their time testing the theories of others. Some economists hope to expand the frontiers of knowledge, whereas others are more interested in applying what is already known to the formulation of public policies.

As you begin your study of economics, look through your school's course catalog and talk to the faculty about their interests. You will discover that economics encompasses a broad range of inquiry and is linked to many other disciplines.

THE METHOD OF ECONOMICS

Economics asks and attempts to answer two kinds of questions, positive and normative. **Positive economics** attempts to understand behavior and the operation of economic systems *without making judgments* about whether the outcomes are good or bad. It strives to describe what exists and how it works. What determines the wage rate for unskilled workers? What would happen if we abolished the corporate income tax? The answers to such questions are the subject of positive economics.

positive economics An approach to economics that seeks to understand behavior and the operation of systems without making judgments. It describes what exists and how it works.

In contrast, **normative economics** looks at the outcomes of economic behavior and asks whether they are good or bad and whether they can be made better. Normative economics involves judgments and prescriptions for courses of action. Should the government subsidize or regulate the cost of higher education? Should medical benefits to the elderly under Medicare be available only to those with incomes below some threshold? Should the United States allow importers to sell foreign-produced goods that compete with U.S.-produced products? Should we reduce or eliminate inheritance taxes? Normative economics is often called *policy economics.*

normative economics An approach to economics that analyzes outcomes of economic behavior, evaluates them as good or bad, and may prescribe courses of action. Also called *policy economics*.

Of course, most normative questions involve positive questions. To know whether the government *should* take a particular action, we must know first if it *can* and second what the consequences are likely to be. (For example, if we lower import fees, will there be more competition and lower prices?)

Further Exploration

The Fields of Economics

A good way to convey the diversity of economics is to describe some of its major fields of study and the issues that economists address.

- **Industrial organization** looks carefully at the structure and performance of industries and firms within an economy. How do businesses compete? Who gains and who loses?
- **Urban and regional economics** studies the spatial arrangement of economic activity. Why do we have cities? Why are manufacturing firms locating farther and farther from the center of urban areas?
- **Econometrics** applies statistical techniques and data to economic problems in an effort to test hypotheses and theories. Most schools require economics majors to take at least one course in statistics or econometrics.
- **Comparative economic systems** examine the ways alternative economic systems function. What are the advantages and disadvantages of different systems? What is the best way to convert the planned economies of the former Soviet Union to market systems?
- **Economic development** focuses on the problems of poor countries. What can be done to promote development in these nations? Important concerns of development economists include population growth and control, provision for basic needs, and strategies for international trade.
- **Labor economics** deals with the factors that determine wage rates, employment, and unemployment. How do people decide whether to work, how much to work, and at what kind of job? How have the roles of unions and management changed in recent years?
- **Finance** examines the ways in which households and firms actually pay for, or finance, their purchases. It involves the study of capital markets (including the stock and bond markets), futures and options, capital budgeting, and asset valuation.

The law has economic effects by changing the behavior of households and firms.

- **International economics** studies trade flows among countries and international financial institutions. What are the advantages and disadvantages for a country that allows its citizens to buy and sell freely in world markets? Why is the dollar strong or weak?
- **Public economics** examines the role of government in the economy. What are the economic functions of government, and what should they be? How should the government finance the services that it provides? What kinds of government programs should confront the problems of poverty, unemployment, and pollution? What problems does government involvement create?
- **Economic history** traces the development of the modern economy. What economic and political events and scientific advances caused the Industrial Revolution? What explains the tremendous growth and progress of post-World War II Japan? What caused the Great Depression of the 1930s?
- **Law and economics** analyzes the economic function of legal rules and institutions. How does the law change the behavior of individuals and businesses? Do different liability rules make accidents and injuries more or less likely? What are the economic costs of crime?
- **The history of economic thought,** which is grounded in philosophy, studies the development of economic ideas and theories over time, from Adam Smith in the eighteenth century to the works of economists such as Thomas Malthus, Karl Marx, and John Maynard Keynes. Because economic theory is constantly developing and changing, studying the history of ideas helps give meaning to modern theory and puts it in perspective.

Some claim that positive, value-free economic analysis is impossible. They argue that analysts come to problems with biases that cannot help but influence their work. Furthermore, even in choosing what questions to ask or what problems to analyze, economists are influenced by political, ideological, and moral views.

Although this argument has some merit, it is nevertheless important to distinguish between analyses that attempt to be positive and those that are intentionally and explicitly normative. Economists who ask explicitly normative questions should be forced to specify their grounds for judging one outcome superior to another.

Descriptive Economics and Economic Theory Positive economics is often divided into descriptive economics and economic theory. **Descriptive economics** is simply the compilation of data that describe phenomena and facts. Examples of such data appear in the *Statistical Abstract of the United States*, a large volume of data published by the Department of Commerce every year that describes many features of the U.S. economy. Massive volumes of data can now also be found on the World Wide Web. As an example look at www.bls.gov (Bureau of Labor Statistics).

descriptive economics The compilation of data that describe phenomena and facts.

Where do all these data come from? The Census Bureau collects an enormous amount of raw data every year, as do the Bureau of Labor Statistics, the Bureau of Economic Analysis, and nongovernment agencies such as the University of Michigan Survey Research Center. One important study now published annually is the *Survey of Consumer Expenditure*, which asks individual households to keep careful records of all their expenditures over a long period of time. Another is the *National Longitudinal Survey of Labor Force Behavior*, conducted over many years by the Center for Human Resource Development at The Ohio State University.

Economic theory attempts to generalize about data and interpret them. An **economic theory** is a statement or set of related statements about cause and effect, action and reaction. One of the first theories you will encounter in this text is the *law of demand*, which was most clearly stated by Alfred Marshall in 1890: When the price of a product rises, people tend to buy less of it; when the price of a product falls, they tend to buy more.

economic theory A statement or set of related statements about cause and effect, action and reaction.

Theories do not always arise out of formal numerical data. All of us have been collecting observations of people's behavior and their responses to economic stimuli for most of our lives. We may have observed our parents' reaction to a sudden increase—or decrease—in income or to the loss of a job or the acquisition of a new one. We all have seen people standing in line waiting for a bargain. Of course, our own actions and reactions are another important source of data.

THEORIES AND MODELS

In many disciplines, including physics, chemistry, meteorology, political science, and economics, theorists build formal models of behavior. A **model** is a formal statement of a theory. It is usually a mathematical statement of a presumed relationship between two or more variables.

model A formal statement of a theory, usually a mathematical statement of a presumed relationship between two or more variables.

A **variable** is a measure that can change from time to time or from observation to observation. Income is a variable—it has different values for different people, and different values for the same person at different times. The rental price of a movie on a videocassette is a variable; it has different values at different stores and at different times. There are countless other examples.

variable A measure that can change from time to time or from observation to observation.

Because all models simplify reality by stripping part of it away, they are abstractions. Critics of economics often point to abstraction as a weakness. Most economists, however, see abstraction as a real strength.

Maps are useful abstract representations of reality.

The easiest way to see how abstraction can be helpful is to think of a map. A map is a representation of reality that is simplified and abstract. A city or state appears on a piece of paper as a series of lines and colors. The amount of reality that the mapmaker can strip away before the map loses something essential depends on what the map will be used for. If I want to drive from St. Louis to Phoenix, I need to know only the major interstate highways and roads. I lose absolutely nothing and gain clarity by cutting out the local streets and roads. However, if I need to get around in Phoenix, I may need to see every street and alley.

Most maps are two-dimensional representations of a three-dimensional world; they show where roads and highways go but do not show hills and valleys along the way. Trail maps for hikers, however, have "contour lines" that represent changes in elevation. When you are in a car, changes in elevation matter very little; they would make a map needlessly complex and much more difficult to read. However, if you are on foot carrying a 50-pound pack, a knowledge of elevation is crucial.

Like maps, economic models are abstractions that strip away detail to expose only those aspects of behavior that are important to the question being asked. The principle that irrelevant detail should be cut away is called the principle of **Ockham's razor** after the fourteenth-century philosopher William of Ockham.

Ockham's razor The principle that irrelevant detail should be cut away.

Be careful—although abstraction is a powerful tool for exposing and analyzing specific aspects of behavior, it is possible to oversimplify. Economic models often strip away a good deal of social and political reality to get at underlying concepts. When an economic theory is used to help formulate actual government or institutional policy, political and social reality must often be reintroduced if the policy is to have a chance of working.

The key here is that the appropriate amount of simplification and abstraction depends on the use to which the model will be put. To return to the map example: You do not want to walk around San Francisco with a map made for drivers—there are too many very steep hills.

All Else Equal: *Ceteris Paribus* It is almost always true that whatever you want to explain with a model depends on more than one factor. Suppose, for example, that you want to explain the total number of miles driven by automobile owners in the United States. The number of miles driven will change from year to year or month to month; it is a variable. The issue, if we want to understand and explain changes that occur, is what factors cause those changes.

Obviously, many things might affect total miles driven. First, more or fewer people may be driving. This number, in turn, can be affected by changes in the driving age, by population growth, or by changes in state laws. Other factors might include the price of gasoline, the household's income, the number and age of children in the household, the distance from home to work, the location of shopping facilities, and the availability and quality of public transport. When any of these variables change, the members of the household may drive more or less. If changes in any of these variables affect large numbers of households across the country, the total number of miles driven will change.

Very often we need to isolate or separate these effects. For example, suppose we want to know the impact on driving of a higher tax on gasoline. This change would raise the price of gasoline at the pump, but would not (at least in the short run) affect income, workplace location, number of children, and so forth.

***ceteris paribus*, or all else equal** A device used to analyze the relationship between two variables while the values of other variables are held unchanged.

To isolate the impact of one single factor, we use the device of ***ceteris paribus***, or **all else equal**. We ask: What is the impact of a change in gasoline price on driving behavior, *ceteris paribus*, or assuming that nothing else changes? If gasoline prices rise by 10 percent, how much less driving will there be, assuming no simultaneous change in anything else—that is, assuming that income, number of children, population, laws, and so on all remain constant?

> Using the device of *ceteris paribus* is one part of the process of abstraction. In formulating economic theory, the concept helps us simplify reality to focus on the relationships that interest us.

Expressing Models in Words, Graphs, and Equations Consider the following statements: "Lower airline ticket prices cause people to fly more frequently." "Higher interest rates slow the rate of home sales." "When firms produce more output, employment increases." "Higher gasoline prices cause people to drive less and to buy more fuel-efficient cars."

Each of these statements expresses a relationship between two variables that can be quantified. In each case there is a stimulus and a response, a cause and an effect. Quantitative relationships can be expressed in a variety of ways. Sometimes words are sufficient to express the essence of a theory, but often it is necessary to be more specific about the nature of a relationship or about the size of a response. The most common method of expressing the quantitative relationship between two variables is *graphing* that relationship on a two-dimensional plane. In fact, we will use graphic analysis extensively in Chapter 2 and beyond. Because it is essential that you be familiar with the basics of graphing, the Appendix to this chapter presents a careful review of graphing techniques.

Quantitative relationships between variables can also be presented through *equations*. For example, suppose we discovered that over time, U.S. households collectively spend, or consume, 90 percent of their income and save 10 percent of their income. We could then write:

$$C = .90Y \text{ and } S = .10Y$$

where C is consumption spending, Y is income, and S is saving. Writing explicit algebraic expressions like these helps us understand the nature of the underlying process of decision making. Understanding this process is what economics is all about.

Cautions and Pitfalls In formulating theories and models, it is especially important to avoid two pitfalls: the *post hoc* fallacy and the fallacy of composition.

The* Post Hoc *Fallacy Theories often make statements, or sets of statements, about cause and effect. It can be quite tempting to look at two events that happen in sequence and assume that the first caused the second to happen. This is not always the case. This common error is called the ***post hoc, ergo propter hoc*** (or "after this, therefore because of this") fallacy.

post hoc, ergo propter hoc Literally, "after this (in time), therefore because of this." A common error made in thinking about causation: If Event A happens before Event B, it is not necessarily true that A caused B.

There are thousands of examples. The Colorado Rockies have won seven games in a row. Last night, I went to the game and they lost. I must have "jinxed" them. They lost *because* I went to the game.

Stock market analysts indulge in what is perhaps the most striking example of the *post hoc* fallacy in action. Every day the stock market goes up or down, and every day some analyst on some national news program singles out one or two of the day's events as *the* cause of some change in the market: "Today the Dow Jones industrial average rose five points on heavy trading; analysts say that the increase was due to progress in talks between Israel and Syria." Research has shown that daily changes in stock market averages are very largely random. While major news events clearly have a direct influence on certain stock prices, most daily changes cannot be directly linked to specific news stories.

Very closely related to the *post hoc* fallacy is the often erroneous link between correlation and causation. Two variables are said to be *correlated* if one variable changes when the other variable changes. However, correlation does not imply causation. Cities that have high crime rates also have lots of automobiles, so there is a very high degree of correlation between number of cars and crime rates. Can we argue, then, that cars *cause* crime? No. The reason for the correlation may have nothing to do with cause and effect. Big cities have lots of people, lots of people have lots of cars, and therefore big cities have lots of cars. Big cities also have high crime rates for many reasons—crowding, poverty, anonymity, unequal distribution of wealth, and readily available drugs, to mention only a few. However, the presence of cars is probably not one of them.

This caution must also be viewed in reverse. Sometimes events that seem entirely unconnected actually *are* connected. In 1978, Governor Michael Dukakis of Massachusetts ran for reelection. Still quite popular, Dukakis was nevertheless defeated in the Democratic primary that year by a razor-thin margin. The weekend before, the Boston Red Sox, in the thick of the division championship race, had been badly beaten by the New York Yankees in four straight games. Some very respectable political analysts believe that hundreds of thousands of Boston sports fans vented their anger on the incumbent governor the following Tuesday.

The Fallacy of Composition To conclude that what is true for a part is necessarily true for the whole is to fall into the **fallacy of composition**. Suppose that a large group of cattle ranchers graze their cattle on the same range. To an individual rancher, more cattle and more grazing mean a higher income. However, because its capacity is limited, the land can support only so many cattle. If every cattle rancher increased the number of cattle sent out to graze, the land would become overgrazed and barren, and everyone's income would fall. In short:

fallacy of composition The erroneous belief that what is true for a part is necessarily true for the whole.

> Theories that seem to work well when applied to individuals or households often break down when they are applied to the whole.

Testing Theories and Models: Empirical Economics In science, a theory is rejected when it fails to explain what is observed or when another theory better explains what is observed. Prior to the sixteenth century almost everyone believed that Earth was the center of the universe and that the Sun and stars rotated around it. The astronomer Ptolemy (A.D. 127 to 151) built a model that explained and predicted the movements of the heavenly bodies in a geocentric (Earth-centered) universe. Early in the sixteenth century, however, the Polish astronomer Nicholas Copernicus found himself dissatisfied with the Ptolemaic model and proposed an alternative theory or model, placing the Sun at the center of the known universe and relegating Earth to the status of one planet among many. The battle between the competing models was waged, at least in part, with data based on observations—actual measurements of planetary movements. The new model ultimately predicted much better than the old, and in time it came to be accepted.

In the seventeenth century, building on the works of Copernicus and others, Sir Isaac Newton constructed yet another body of theory that seemed to predict planetary motion with still more accuracy. Newtonian physics became the accepted body of theory, relied on for almost 300 years. Then Albert Einstein's theory of relativity replaced Newtonian physics for particular types of problems because it was able to explain some things that earlier theories could not.

empirical economics The collection and use of data to test economic theories.

Economic theories are also confronted with new and often conflicting data from time to time. The collection and use of data to test economic theories is called **empirical economics.**

Numerous large data sets are available to facilitate economic research. For example, economists studying the labor market can now test behavioral theories against the actual working experiences of thousands of randomly selected people who have been surveyed continuously since the 1960s by economists at The Ohio State University. Macroeconomists continuously monitoring and studying the behavior of the national economy pass thousands of items of data, collected by both government agencies and private companies, back and forth on diskettes and over the Internet.

Scientific research often seeks to isolate and measure the responsiveness of one variable to a change in another variable, *ceteris paribus.* Physical scientists, such as physicists and geologists, can often impose the condition of *ceteris paribus* by conducting controlled experiments. They can, for example, measure the effect of one chemical on another while literally holding all else constant in an environment that they control completely. Social scientists, who study people, rarely have this luxury.

Although controlled experiments are difficult in economics and other social sciences, they are not impossible. During the presidential and congressional elections in 2000, many candidates pointed to dramatic declines in crime rates in most American cities. Of course, incumbent candidates took credit, claiming that the decline was due to their policies. In fact, careful analysis shows that the decline in crime was largely due to two factors essentially beyond the control of political leaders: fewer people in the age groups that tend to commit crimes and a very strong economy with low unemployment. How do researchers know this? They look at data over time on crimes committed by people of various ages; they look at crime rates across states with different economic conditions; and they look at the pattern of crime rates nationally over time under different economic conditions. Even though economists cannot generally do controlled experiments, fluctuations in economic conditions and things like birthrate patterns in a way set up natural experiments.

ECONOMIC POLICY

Economic theory helps us understand how the world works, but the formulation of *economic policy* requires a second step. We must have objectives. What do we want to change? Why? What is good and what is bad about the way the system is operating? Can we make it better?

Such questions force us to be specific about the grounds for judging one outcome superior to another. What does it mean to be better? Four criteria are frequently applied in making these judgments:

Criteria for judging economic outcomes:
1. Efficiency
2. Equity
3. Growth
4. Stability

Efficiency In physics, "efficiency" refers to the ratio of useful energy delivered by a system to the energy supplied to it. An efficient automobile engine, for example, is one that uses up a small amount of fuel per mile for a given level of power.

efficiency In economics, allocative efficiency. An efficient economy is one that produces what people want at the least possible cost.

In economics, **efficiency** means *allocative efficiency.* An efficient economy is one that produces what people want at the least possible cost. If the system allocates resources to the production of things that nobody wants, it is inefficient. If all members of a particular society were vegetarian and somehow half of all that society's resources were used to produce meat, the result would be inefficient. It is inefficient when steel beams lie in the rain and rust because somebody fouled up a shipping schedule. If a firm could produce its product using 25 percent less labor and energy without sacrificing quality, it too is inefficient.

The clearest example of an efficient change is a voluntary exchange. If you and I each want something that the other has and we agree to exchange, we are both better off, and no one loses. When a company reorganizes its production or adopts a new technology that enables it to produce more of its product with fewer resources, without sacrificing quality, it has made an efficient change. At least potentially, the resources saved could be used to produce more of something.

Inefficiencies can arise in numerous ways. Sometimes they are caused by government regulations or tax laws that distort otherwise sound economic decisions. Suppose that land in Ohio is best suited for corn production and that land in Kansas is best suited for wheat production. A law that requires Kansas to produce only corn and Ohio to produce only wheat would be inefficient. If firms that cause environmental damage are not held accountable for their actions, the incentive to minimize those damages is lost, and the result is inefficient.

Equity While efficiency has a fairly precise definition that can be applied with some degree of rigor, **equity** (fairness) lies in the eye of the beholder. To many, fairness implies a more equal distribution of income and wealth. Fairness may imply alleviating poverty, but the extent to which the poor should receive cash benefits from the government is the subject of enormous disagreement. For thousands of years philosophers have wrestled with the principles of justice that should guide social decisions. They will probably wrestle with such questions for thousands of years to come.

equity Fairness.

Despite the impossibility of defining equity or fairness universally, public policy makers judge the fairness of economic outcomes all the time. Rent control laws were passed because some legislators thought that landlords treated low-income tenants unfairly. Certainly most social welfare programs are created in the name of equity.

Growth As the result of technological change, the building of machinery, and the acquisition of knowledge, societies learn to produce new things and to produce old things better. In the early days of the U.S. economy, it took nearly half the population to produce the required food supply. Today less than 2.5 percent of the country's population works in agriculture.

When we devise new and better ways of producing the things we use now and develop new products and services, the total amount of production in the economy increases. **Economic growth** is an increase in the total output of an economy. If output grows faster than the population, output per capita rises and standards of living increase. Presumably, when an economy grows there is more of what people want. Rural and agrarian societies become modern industrial societies as a result of economic growth and rising per capita output.

economic growth An increase in the total output of an economy.

Some policies discourage economic growth and others encourage it. Tax laws, for example, can be designed to encourage the development and application of new production techniques. Research and development in some societies are subsidized by the government. Building roads, highways, bridges, and transport systems in developing countries may speed up the process of economic growth. If businesses and wealthy people invest their wealth outside their country rather than in its own industries, growth in their home country may be slowed.

Stability Economic **stability** refers to the condition in which national output is growing steadily, with low inflation and full employment of resources. During the 1950s and 1960s, the U.S. economy experienced a long period of relatively steady growth, stable prices, and low unemployment. Between 1951 and 1969, consumer prices never rose more than 5 percent in a single year, and in only 2 years did the number of unemployed exceed 6 percent of the labor force. From the end of the Gulf War in 1991 to the beginning of 2001, the U.S. economy enjoyed price stability and strong economic growth with rising employment. It was the longest expansion in American history.

stability A condition in which national output is growing steadily, with low inflation and full employment of resources.

The decades of the 1970s and 1980s, however, were not as stable. The United States experienced two periods of rapid price inflation (over 10 percent) and two periods of severe unemployment. In 1982, for example, 12 million people (10.8 percent of the workforce) were looking for work. The beginning of the 1990s was another period of instability, with a recession occurring in 1990–1991. Around the world, economic fluctuations have

News Analysis

An Economic Recovery for the United States in 2003?

DURING 2001, THE U.S. ECONOMY WAS IN RECESSION. National income declined and employment fell. Employment continued to decline well into 2003. But the end of the war in Iraq, a fall in the price of oil on world markets, and a big tax cut in the United States seemed to many economists to suggest that a recovery from the hard times was beginning. The following article from the *Economist* reflects some guarded optimism.

Despite signs of an economic recovery, 9.4 million people remained unemployed in mid-2003.

Poised for growth?—*Economist*

Is America's economy finally set to shake off its funk? An increasing number of economists on Wall Street and politicians in Washington seem to think so. Many number-crunchers are forecasting a sharp acceleration of economic growth in the summer. John Snow, America's treasury secretary, suggested this week that the economy could be growing by around 4% by the end of 2003, more than double its current rate. After so many false dawns, is this optimism justified?

Financial markets certainly think so. All the big stockmarket indices have risen dramatically. The Dow Jones Industrial Average is now over 9,000, up more than 20% since mid-March; the technology-laden NASDAQ is up almost 30% from three months ago. Financial conditions have loosened across the board. Not only are government bond yields at historic lows, but spreads on corporate bonds have narrowed sharply, making access to capital cheaper and easier for firms of all kinds. A weaker dollar—the greenback has dropped by 8% against the currencies of America's trading partners this year—has also added to the loose financial conditions.

And there is more to come. Judging by recent comments from its top official, America's central bank is highly likely to cut interest rates when its policy-setting Federal Open Market Committee meets on June 24 to 25.

Nor is looser monetary policy the only stimulus on the way. Mr Bush's latest tax package, signed into law on May 28, will undoubtedly give the economy a short-term boost. The huge tax package—worth $350 billion over 10 years if you believe Congress's gimmicks, and costing more than $800 billion over a decade if you take a more realistic view—may not be particularly efficient as a stimulus package. But it is big. Economists at Morgan Stanley reckon the tax cut will add about $160 billion, or 1.5% of GDP, in fiscal stimulus over the next four quarters, bigger than any tax change since the Reagan tax cut in 1981. Of that, around $64 billion will reach Americans quickly in the form of rebate cheques and less tax withheld from their pay.

Add together loose financial conditions and a fiscal boost, and it is hard to imagine that the economy will not improve at all. Lower financing costs are continuing to prop up the housing market and maintain the surge in mortgage refinancings. The weekly tally of mortgage refinancing applications reached a new high of nearly 10,000 last week.

Even in the gloomy labour market, there are glimmers of hope. True, America's jobless rate hit a cyclical peak of 6.1% in May, and weekly unemployment claims are still extremely high. But the employment report released on June 6 was in many ways less bad than expected. Although the economy lost 17,000 jobs in May, the number of private-sector jobs was flat; the drop came in government posts. The number of temporary jobs rose by a healthy 58,000, and a rise in temporary workers is often a sign that firms are thinking of hiring permanent workers again. The latest monthly survey of purchasing managers also suggests that conditions in both the manufacturing and services sector are already improving, although they are far from booming.

A trickier question is whether any rebound will last. Can America's economy expect above-trend growth next year, for instance? There, it is much harder to be optimistic. America's economy still has huge fragilities. Although firms have undergone great adjustments since the excesses of the stockmarket bubble, there is still plenty of spare capacity around, making a sustained investment boom less likely.

Source: June 12, 2003, the Economist.

Visit www.prenhall.com/casefair for updated articles and exercises.

been severe in recent years. During the late 1990s, many economies in Asia fell into recessions with falling incomes and rising unemployment. The transition economies of Eastern Europe and the former Soviet Union have experienced periods of decline as well as periods of rapidly rising prices since the fall of the Berlin Wall in 1989. The U.S. economy went into recession in the first quarter of 2001, and the economy shed over 2 million jobs by 2003.

The causes of instability and the ways in which governments have attempted to stabilize the economy are the subject matter of macroeconomics.

AN INVITATION

This chapter is meant to prepare you for what is to come. The first part of the chapter invited you into an exciting discipline that deals with important issues and questions. You cannot begin to understand how a society functions without knowing something about its economic history and its economic system.

The second part of the chapter introduced the method of reasoning that economics requires and some of the tools that economics uses. We believe that learning to think in this very powerful way will help you better understand the world.

As you proceed, it is important that you keep track of what you have learned in earlier chapters. This book has a plan; it proceeds step by step, each section building on the last. It would be a good idea to read each chapter's table of contents and scan each chapter before you read it to be sure you understand where it fits in the big picture.

SUMMARY

1. *Economics* is the study of how individuals and societies choose to use the scarce resources that nature and previous generations have provided.

WHY STUDY ECONOMICS?

2. There are many reasons to study economics, including (a) to learn a way of thinking, (b) to understand society, (c) to understand global affairs, and (d) to be an informed voter.
3. The best alternative that we forgo when we make a choice or a decision is the *opportunity cost* of that decision.

THE SCOPE OF ECONOMICS

4. *Microeconomics* deals with the functioning of individual markets and industries and with the behavior of individual decision-making units: business firms and households.
5. *Macroeconomics* looks at the economy as a whole. It deals with the economic behavior of aggregates—national output, national income, the overall price level, and the general rate of inflation.
6. Economics is a broad and diverse discipline with many special fields of inquiry. These include economic history, international economics, and urban economics.

THE METHOD OF ECONOMICS

7. Economics asks and attempts to answer two kinds of questions: positive and normative. *Positive economics* attempts to understand behavior and the operation of economies without making judgments about whether the outcomes are good or bad. *Normative economics* looks at the results of economic behavior and asks whether they are good or bad and whether they can be improved.
8. Positive economics is often divided into two parts. *Descriptive economics* involves the compilation of data that accurately describe economic facts and events. *Economic theory* attempts to generalize and explain what is observed. It involves statements of cause and effect—of action and reaction.
9. An economic *model* is a formal statement of an economic theory. Models simplify and abstract from reality.
10. It is often useful to isolate the effects of one variable or another while holding "all else constant." This is the device of *ceteris paribus.*
11. Models and theories can be expressed in many ways. The most common ways are in words, in graphs, and in equations.
12. Because one event happens before another, the second event does not necessarily happen as a result of the first. To assume that "after" implies "because" is to commit the fallacy of *post hoc, ergo propter hoc.* The erroneous belief that what is true for a part is necessarily true for the whole is the *fallacy of composition.*
13. *Empirical economics* involves the collection and use of data to test economic theories. In principle, the best model is the one that yields the most accurate predictions.
14. To make policy, one must be careful to specify criteria for making judgments. Four specific criteria are used most often in economics: *efficiency, equity, growth,* and *stability.*

REVIEW TERMS AND CONCEPTS

ceteris paribus, 10
descriptive economics, 9
economic growth, 13
economic theory, 9
economics, 2
efficiency, 12
efficient market, 3
empirical economics, 12
equity, 13
fallacy of composition, 11
Industrial Revolution, 4
macroeconomics, 6
microeconomics, 6
model, 9
normative economics, 7
Ockham's razor, 9
opportunity cost, 2
positive economics, 7
post hoc, ergo propter hoc, 11
scarce, 2
stability, 13
sunk costs, 3
variable, 9

PROBLEM SET

1. One of the scarce resources that constrain our behavior is time. Each of us has only 24 hours in a day. How do you go about allocating your time in a given day among competing alternatives? How do you go about weighing the alternatives? Once you choose a most important use of time, why do you not spend all your time on it? Use the notion of opportunity cost in your answer.
2. In November 2004, the United States will elect a new president and a new Congress. What were the major economic issues debated by the candidates for national office in past elections? Look up what was written about the presidential candidate debates in back issues of the *New York Times* or a local newspaper. Do the same for a local election in your home state. What specific economic issues were discussed in the campaign?
3. Which of the following statements are examples of positive economic analysis? Which are examples of normative analysis?
   a. The inheritance tax should be repealed because it is unfair.
   b. President Clinton proposed allowing Chile to join the North American Free Trade Agreement (NAFTA) in 1998. (NAFTA is an agreement signed by the United States, Mexico, and Canada in which the countries agreed to establish all North America as a free-trade zone.) Admission of Chile should not be allowed because Chile's environmental standards are not up to those in the United States, which would give Chilean firms a cost advantage in competing with U.S. firms.
   c. Allowing Chile to join NAFTA would cause wine prices in the United States to drop.
   d. The first priorities of the new regime in the Democratic Republic of Congo (DRC, formerly Zaire) should be to rebuild schools and highways and to provide basic health care.
4. Selwyn signed up with an Internet provider for a fixed fee of $19.95 per month. For this fee he gets unlimited access to the World Wide Web. During the average month in 2003 he was logged onto the Web for 17 hours. What is the average cost of an hour of Web time to Selwyn? What is the marginal cost of an additional hour?
5. Suppose that a city is considering building a bridge across a river. The bridge will be financed by tax dollars. The city gets these revenues from a sales tax imposed on things sold in the city. The bridge would provide more direct access for commuters and shoppers. It would also alleviate the huge traffic jam that occurs every morning at the bridge down the river in another city.
   a. Who would gain if the bridge were built? Could those gains be measured? How?
   b. Who would be hurt if the bridge were built? Could those costs be measured? How?
   c. How would you determine if it is efficient to build the bridge?
6. A question facing many U.S. states is whether to allow casino gambling. States with casino gambling have seen a substantial increase in tax revenue flowing to state government. This revenue can be used to finance schools, repair roads, maintain social programs, or reduce other taxes.
   a. Recall that efficiency means producing what people want at least cost. Can you make an efficiency argument in favor of allowing casinos to operate?
   b. What nonmonetary costs might be associated with gambling? Would these costs have an impact on the efficiency argument you presented in part a?
   c. Using the concept of equity, argue for or against the legalization of casino gambling.
7. For each of the following situations, identify the full cost (opportunity costs) involved:
   a. A worker earning an hourly wage of $8.50 decides to cut back to half time to attend Houston Community College.
   b. Sue decides to drive to Los Angeles from San Francisco to visit her son, who attends UCLA.
   c. Tom decides to go to a wild fraternity party and stays out all night before his physics exam.
   d. Annie spends $200 on a new dress.
   e. The Confab Company spends $1 million to build a new branch plant that will probably be in operation for at least 10 years.
   f. Alex's father owns a small grocery store in town. Alex works 40 hours a week in the store but receives no compensation.

WWW Visit www.prenhall.com/casefair for self-test quizzes, interactive graphing exercises, and news articles.

APPENDIX

HOW TO READ AND UNDERSTAND GRAPHS

Economics is the most quantitative of the social sciences. If you flip through the pages of this or any other economics text, you will see countless tables and graphs. These serve a number of purposes. First, they illustrate important economic relationships. Second, they make difficult problems easier to understand and analyze. Finally, patterns and regularities that may not be discernible in simple lists of numbers can often be seen when those numbers are laid out in a table or on a graph.

A **graph** is a two-dimensional representation of a set of numbers, or data. There are many ways that numbers can be illustrated by a graph.

TIME SERIES GRAPHS

It is often useful to see how a single measure or variable changes over time. One way to present this information is to plot the val-

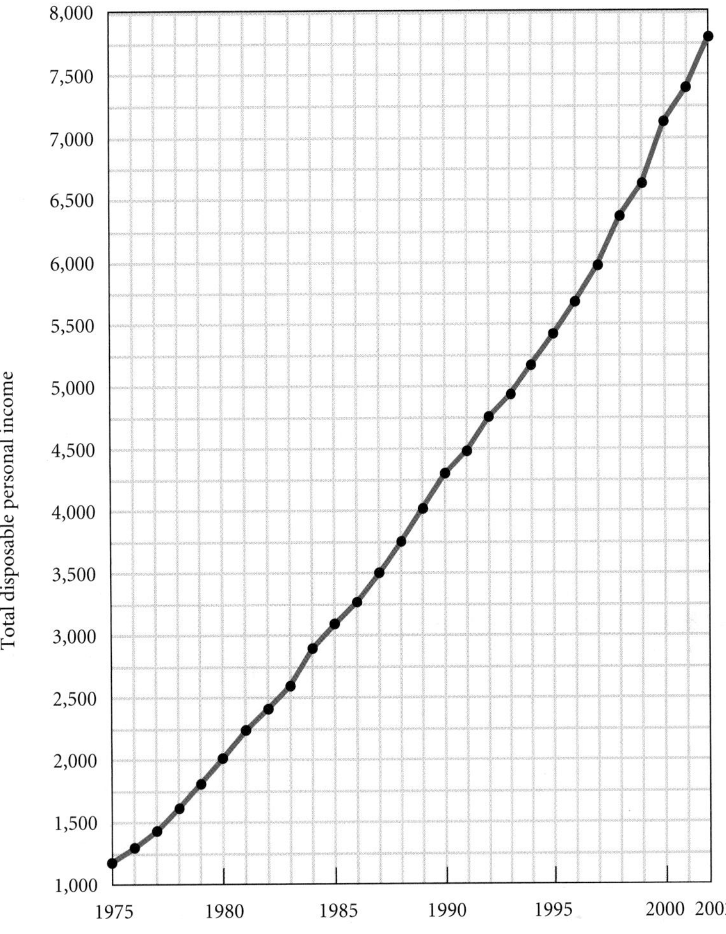

FIGURE 1A.1 Total Disposable Personal Income in the United States: 1975–2002 (in billions of dollars)

Source: See Table 1A.1.

ues of the variable on a graph, with each value corresponding to a different time period. A graph of this kind is called a **time series graph**. On a time series graph, time is measured along the horizontal scale and the variable being graphed is measured along the vertical scale. Figure 1A.1 is a time series graph that presents the total disposable personal income in the U.S. economy for each year between 1975 and 2002.[1] This graph is based on the data found in Table 1A.1. By displaying these data graphically, we can see that (1) total disposable personal income has increased steadily since 1975, and (2) during certain periods, income has increased at a faster rate than during other periods.

GRAPHING TWO VARIABLES ON A CARTESIAN COORDINATE SYSTEM

More important than simple graphs of one variable are graphs that contain information on two variables at the same time. The most common method of graphing two variables is the **Cartesian coordinate system**. This system is constructed by simply drawing two perpendicular lines: a horizontal line, or ***X*-axis**, and a vertical line, or ***Y*-axis**. The axes contain measurement scales that intersect at 0 (zero). This point is called the **origin**. On the vertical scale, positive numbers lie above the horizontal axis (that is, above the origin) and negative numbers lie below it. On the horizontal scale, positive numbers lie to the right of the vertical axis (to the right of the origin) and negative

TABLE 1A.1 Total Disposable Personal Income in the United States, 1975–2002 (in billions of dollars)

YEAR	TOTAL DISPOSABLE PERSONAL INCOME	YEAR	TOTAL DISPOSABLE PERSONAL INCOME
1975	1,181.4	1989	4,016.3
1976	1,299.9	1990	4,293.6
1977	1,436.0	1991	4,474.8
1978	1,614.8	1992	4,754.6
1979	1,808.2	1993	4,935.3
1980	2,019.8	1994	5,165.4
1981	2,247.9	1995	5,422.6
1982	2,406.8	1996	5,677.7
1983	2,586.0	1997	5,968.2
1984	2,887.6	1998	6,355.6
1985	3,086.5	1999	6,627.4
1986	3,262.5	2000	7,120.2
1987	3,459.5	2001	7,393.2
1988	3,752.4	2002	7,810.3

Source: U.S. Department of Commerce, Bureau of Economic Analysis.

[1]The measure of income presented in Table 1A.1 and in Figure 1A.1 is disposable personal income in billions of dollars. It is the total personal income received by all households in the United States minus the taxes that they pay.

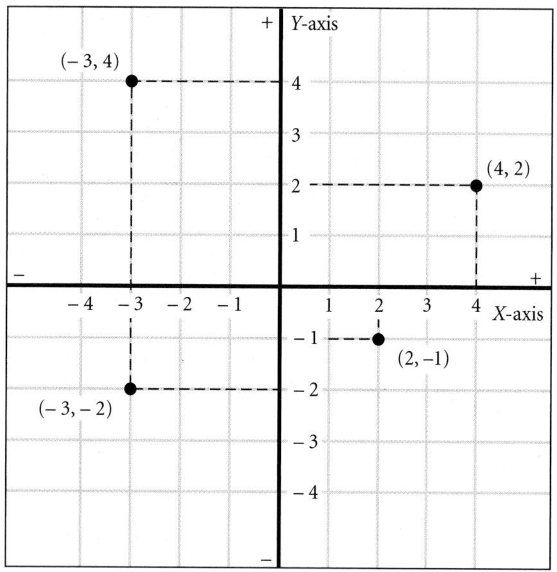

FIGURE 1A.2 A Cartesian Coordinate System

A Cartesian coordinate system is constructed by drawing two perpendicular lines: a vertical axis (the *Y*-axis) and a horizontal axis (the *X*-axis). Each axis is a measuring scale.

numbers lie to the left of it. The point at which the graph intersects the *Y*-axis is called the ***Y*-intercept**. The point at which the graph intersects the *X*-axis is called the ***X*-intercept**.

When two variables are plotted on a single graph, each point represents a *pair* of numbers. The first number is measured on the *X*-axis and the second number is measured on the *Y*-axis. For example, the following points (*X*, *Y*) are plotted on the set of axes drawn in Figure 1A.2: (4, 2), (2, –1), (–3, 4), (–3, –2). Most, but not all, of the graphs in this book are plots of two variables where both values are positive numbers [such as (4, 2) in Fig. 1A.2]. On these graphs, only the upper right quadrant of the coordinate system (i.e., the quadrant in which all *X* and *Y* values are positive) will be drawn.

PLOTTING INCOME AND CONSUMPTION DATA FOR HOUSEHOLDS

Table 1A.2 presents some data collected by the Bureau of Labor Statistics (BLS). In a recent survey, 5,000 households were asked to keep careful track of all their expenditures. Table 1A.2 shows average income and average spending for those households, ranked by income. For example, the average income for the top fifth (20 percent) of the households was $116,666. The average spending for the top 20 percent was $77,125.

Figure 1A.3 presents the numbers from Table 1A.2 graphically using the Cartesian coordinate system. Along the horizontal scale, the *X*-axis, we measure average income. Along the vertical scale, the *Y*-axis, we measure average consumption spending. Each of the five pairs of numbers from the table is represented by a point on the graph. Because all numbers are positive numbers, we need to show only the upper right quadrant of the coordinate system.

To help you read this graph, we have drawn a dotted line connecting all the points where consumption and income would be equal. *This 45° line does not represent any data.* Instead, it represents the line along which all variables on the *X*-axis correspond exactly to the variables on the *Y*-axis, for example, [10,000, 10,000], [20,000, 20,000], [37,000, 37,000] and so forth. The heavy blue line traces the data; the dotted line is only to help you read the graph.

There are several things to look for when reading a graph. The first thing you should notice is whether the line slopes upward or downward as you move from left to right. The blue line in Figure 1A.3 slopes upward, indicating that there seems to be a **positive relationship** between income and spending: The higher a household's income, the more a household tends to consume. If we had graphed the percentage of each group

TABLE 1A.2 Consumption Expenditures and Income, 2001

	AVERAGE INCOME BEFORE TAXES	AVERAGE CONSUMPTION EXPENDITURES
Bottom fifth	$ 7,946	$18,883
2nd fifth	20,319	26,492
3rd fifth	35,536	35,660
4th fifth	56,891	48,722
Top fifth	116,666	77,125

Source: U.S. BLS, *Consumer Expenditure Survey*, 2001, Table 1. "Quintiles of income before taxes: Average annual expenditures."

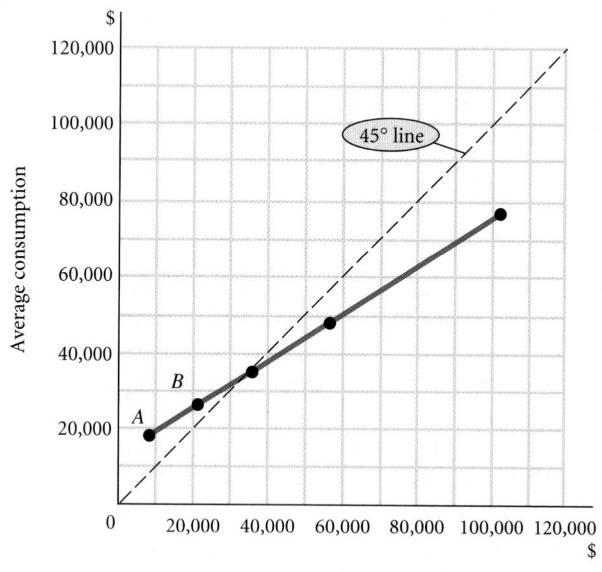

FIGURE 1A.3 Household Consumption and Income

A graph is a simple two-dimensional geometric representation of data. This graph displays the data from Table 1A.2. Along the horizontal scale (*X*-axis), we measure household income. Along the vertical scale (*Y*-axis), we measure household consumption. *Note:* At point *A*, consumption equals $18,883 and income equals $7,946. At point *B*, consumption equals $26,492 and income equals $20,319.

Source: See Table 1A.2.

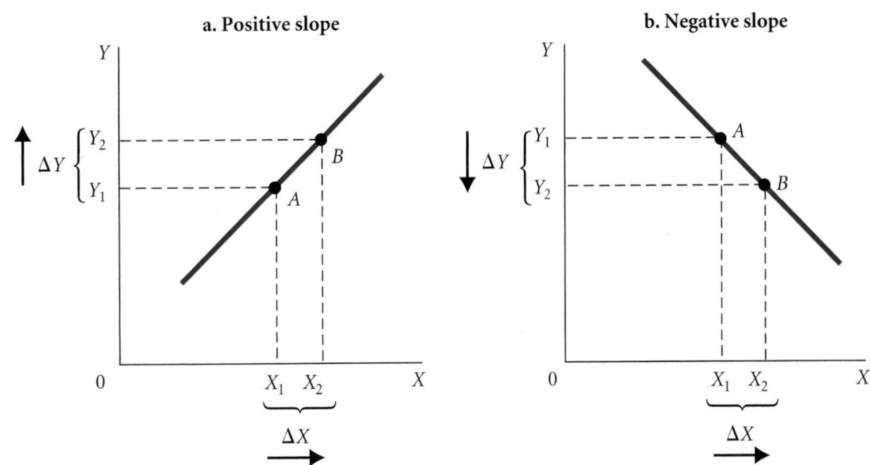

FIGURE 1A.4 A Curve with (a) Positive Slope and (b) Negative Slope

A *positive* slope indicates that increases in X are associated with increases in Y and that decreases in X are associated with decreases in Y. A *negative* slope indicates the opposite—when X increases, Y decreases and when X decreases, Y increases.

receiving welfare payments along the Y-axis, the line would presumably slope downward, indicating that welfare payments are lower at higher income levels. The income level/welfare payment relationship is thus a **negative** relationship.

SLOPE

The **slope** of a line or curve is a measure that indicates whether the relationship between the variables is positive or negative and how much of a response there is in Y (the variable on the vertical axis) when X (the variable on the horizontal axis) changes. The slope of a line between two points is the change in the quantity measured on the Y-axis divided by the change in the quantity measured on the X-axis. We will normally use Δ (the Greek letter *delta*) to refer to a change in a variable. In Figure 1A.4, the slope of the line between points A and B is ΔY divided by ΔX. Sometimes it is easy to remember slope as "the rise over the run," indicating the vertical change over the horizontal change.

To be precise, ΔX between two points on a graph is simply X_2 minus X_1, where X_2 is the X value for the second point and X_1 is the X value for the first point. Similarly, ΔY is defined as Y_2 minus Y_1, where Y_2 is the Y value for the second point and Y_1 is the Y value for the first point. Slope is equal to

$$\frac{\Delta Y}{\Delta X} = \frac{Y_2 - Y_1}{X_2 - X_1}$$

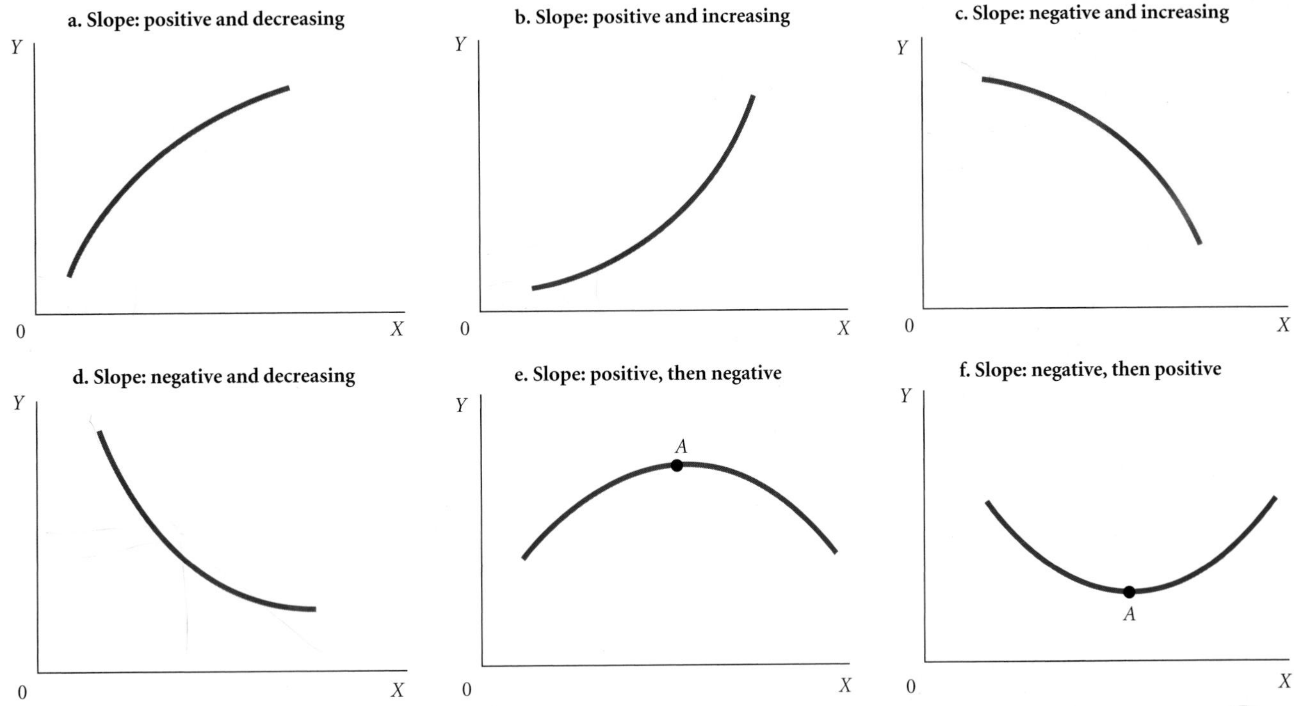

FIGURE 1A.5 Changing Slopes Along Curves

As we move from A to B in Figure 1A.4(a), both X and Y increase; the slope is thus a positive number. However, as we move from A to B in Figure 1A.4(b), X increases [$(X_2 - X_1)$ is a positive number], but Y decreases [$(Y_2 - Y_1)$ is a negative number]. The slope in Figure 1A.4(b) is thus a negative number, because a negative number divided by a positive number gives a negative quotient.

To calculate the numerical value of the slope between points A and B in Figure 1A.3, we need to calculate ΔY and ΔX. Because consumption is measured on the Y-axis, ΔY is 7,609 [$(Y_2 - Y_1) = (26{,}492 - 18{,}883)$]. Because income is measured along the X-axis, ΔX is 12,373 [$(X_2 - X_1) = (20{,}319 - 7{,}946)$]. The slope between A and B is $\Delta Y/\Delta X = 7{,}609/12{,}373 = +.615$.

Another interesting thing to note about the data graphed in Figure 1A.3 is that all the points lie roughly along a straight line. (If you look very closely, however, you can see that the slope declines as one moves from left to right; the line becomes slightly less steep.) A straight line has a constant slope. That is, if you pick any two points along it and calculate the slope, you will always get the same number. A horizontal line has a zero slope (ΔY is zero); a vertical line has an "infinite" slope, because ΔY is too big to be measured.

Unlike the slope of a straight line, the slope of a *curve* is continually changing. Consider, for example, the curves in Figure 1A.5. Figure 1A.5(a) shows a curve with a positive slope that decreases as you move from left to right. The easiest way to think about the concept of increasing or decreasing slope is to imagine what it is like walking up a hill from left to right. If the hill is steep, as it is in the first part of Figure 1A.5(a), you are moving a lot in the Y direction for each step you take in the X direction. If the hill is less steep, as it is further along in Figure 1A.5(a), you are moving less in the Y direction for every step you take in the X direction. Thus, when the hill is steep, slope ($\Delta Y/\Delta X$) is a larger number than it is when the hill is flatter. The curve in Figure 1A.5(b) has a positive slope, but its slope *increases* as you move from left to right.

The same analogy holds for curves that have a negative slope. Figure 1A.5(c) shows a curve with a negative slope that increases (in absolute value) as you move from left to right. This time think about skiing down a hill. At first, the descent in Figure 1A.5(c) is gradual (low slope), but as you proceed down the hill (to the right), you descend more quickly (high slope). Figure 1A.5(d) shows a curve with a negative slope that *decreases* in absolute value as you move from left to right.

In Figure 1A.5(e), the slope goes from positive to negative as X increases. In Figure 1A.5(f), the slope goes from negative to positive. At point A in both, the slope is zero. [Remember, slope is defined as $\Delta Y/\Delta X$. At point A, Y is not changing ($\Delta Y = 0$). Therefore, slope at point A is zero.]

SOME PRECAUTIONS

When you read a graph, it is important to think carefully about what the points in the space defined by the axes represent. Table 1A.3 and Figure 1A.6 present a graph of consumption and income that is very different from the one in Table 1A.2 and Figure 1A.3. First, each point in Figure 1A.6 represents a different year; in Figure 1A.3, each point represented a different group of households at the *same* point in time (2001). Second, the points in Figure 1A.6 represent *aggregate* consumption and income for the whole nation

TABLE 1A.3 Aggregate National Income and Consumption for the United States, 1930–2002 (in billions of dollars)

	AGGREGATE NATIONAL INCOME	AGGREGATE CONSUMPTION
1930	75.6	70.2
1940	81.1	71.2
1950	241.0	192.7
1960	427.5	332.3
1970	837.5	648.9
1980	2,243.0	1,762.9
1990	4,642.1	3,831.5
2000	7,984.4	6,683.7
2002	8,340.1	7,303.7

Source: U.S. Department of Commerce, Bureau of Economic Analysis.

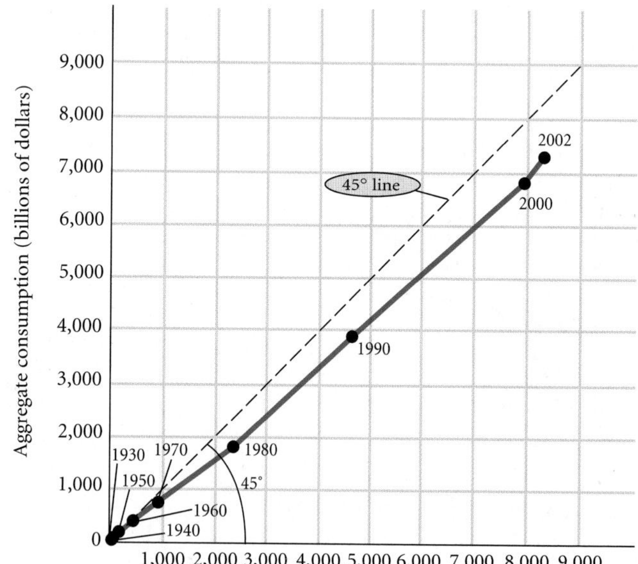

FIGURE 1A.6 National Income and Consumption

It is important to think carefully about what is represented by points in the space defined by the axes of a graph. In this graph, we have income graphed with consumption, as in Figure 1A.3, but here each observation point is national income and aggregate consumption in *different years*, measured in billions of dollars.

Source: See Table 1A.3.

measured in *billions* of dollars; in Figure 1A.3, the points represented average *household* income and consumption measured in dollars.

It is interesting to compare these two graphs. All points on the aggregate consumption curve in Figure 1A.6 lie below the 45° line, which means that aggregate consumption is always less than aggregate income. However, the graph of average household income and consumption in Figure 1A.3 crosses the 45° line, implying that for some households consumption is larger than income.

SUMMARY

1. A *graph* is a two-dimensional representation of a set of numbers, or data. A *time series graph* illustrates how a single variable changes over time.
2. The most common method of graphing two variables on one graph is the *Cartesian coordinate system*, which includes an X (horizontal)-*axis* and a Y (vertical)-*axis*. The points at which the two axes intersect is called the *origin*. The point at which a graph intersects the Y-axis is called the *Y-intercept*. The point at which a graph intersects the X-axis is called the *X-intercept*.
3. The *slope* of a line or curve indicates whether the relationship between the two variables graphed on a Cartesian coordinate system is positive or negative and how much of a response there is in Y (the variable on the vertical axis) when X (the variable on the horizontal axis) changes. The slope of a line between two points is the change in the quantity measured on the Y-axis divided by the change in the quantity measured on the X-axis.

REVIEW TERMS AND CONCEPTS

Cartesian coordinate system A common method of graphing two variables that makes use of two perpendicular lines against which the variables are plotted. 17

graph A two-dimensional representation of a set of numbers, or data. 16

negative relationship A relationship between two variables, X and Y, in which a decrease in X is associated with an increase in Y, and an increase in X is associated with a decrease in Y. 19

origin On a Cartesian coordinate system, the point at which the horizontal and vertical axes intersect. 17

positive relationship A relationship between two variables, X and Y, in which a decrease in X is associated with a decrease in Y, and an increase in X is associated with an increase in Y. 18

slope A measurement that indicates whether the relationship between variables is positive or negative and how much of a response there is in Y (the variable on the vertical axis) when X (the variable on the horizontal axis) changes. 19

times series graph A graph illustrating how a variable changes over time. 17

X-axis On a Cartesian coordinate system, the horizontal line against which a variable is plotted. 17

X-intercept The point at which a graph intersects the X-axis. 18

Y-axis On a Cartesian coordinate system, the vertical line against which a variable is plotted. 17

Y-intercept The point at which a graph intersects the Y-axis. 18

PROBLEM SET

1. Graph each of the following sets of numbers. Draw a line through the points and calculate the slope of each line.

1		2		3		4		5		6	
X	Y	X	Y	X	Y	X	Y	X	Y	X	Y
1	5	1	25	0	0	0	40	0	0	0.1	100
2	10	2	20	10	10	10	30	10	10	0.2	75
3	15	3	15	20	20	20	20	20	20	0.3	50
4	20	4	10	30	30	30	10	30	10	0.4	25
5	25	5	5	40	40	40	0	40	0	0.5	0

2. For each of the graphs in Figure 1 on the following page, say whether the curve has a positive or negative slope. Give an intuitive explanation for what is happening with the slope of each curve.
3. For each of the following equations, graph the line and calculate its slope.
   a. $P = 10 - 2q_D$ (Put q_D on the X-axis)
   b. $P = 100 - 4q_D$ (Put q_D on the X-axis)
   c. $P = 50 + 6q_S$ (Put q_S on the X-axis)
   d. $I = 10{,}000 - 500r$ (Put I on the X-axis)

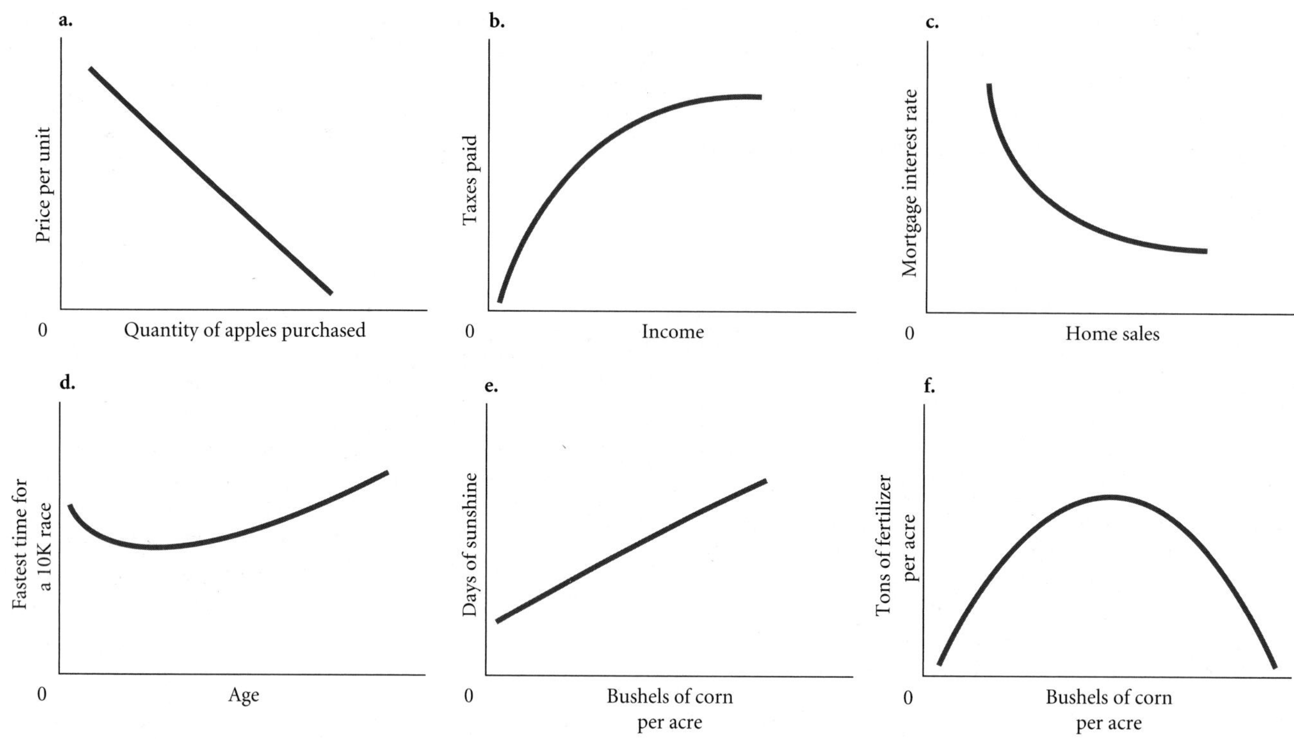
a.
Price per unit
0
Quantity of apples purchased
b.
Taxes paid
0
Income
c.
Mortgage interest rate
0
Home sales
d.
Fastest time for a 10K race
0
Age
e.
Days of sunshine
0
Bushels of corn per acre
f.
Tons of fertilizer per acre
0
Bushels of corn per acre

FIGURE 1

The Economic Problem: Scarcity and Choice

2

CHAPTER OUTLINE

Chapter 1 began with a very broad definition of economics. Every society, no matter how small or how large, no matter how simple or how complex, has a system or process that works to transform the resources that nature and previous generations provide into useful form. Economics is the study of that process and its outcomes.

Figure 2.1 illustrates three basic questions that must be answered to understand the functioning of the economic system:

- What gets produced?
- How is it produced?
- Who gets what is produced?

This chapter explores these questions in more detail. In a sense, this entire chapter *is* the definition of economics. It lays out the central problems addressed by the discipline and presents a framework that will guide you through the rest of the book. The starting point is the presumption that *human wants are unlimited, but resources are not.* Limited or scarce resources force individuals and societies to choose among competing uses of resources—alternative combinations of produced goods and services—and among alternative final distributions of what is produced among households.

These questions are *positive* or *descriptive.* That is, they ask "How does the system function?" without passing judgment about whether the result is good or bad. They must be answered first before we ask more normative questions like:

- Is the outcome good or bad?
- Can it be improved?

The term "resources" is very broad. The sketch on the left side of Figure 2.1 shows several categories of resources. Some resources are the products of nature: land, wildlife, a fertile soil, minerals, timber, energy, and even the rain and the wind. In addition, the resources available to an economy include things, like buildings and equipment, that have been produced in the past but are now being used to produce other things. And, of course, perhaps the most important resource of a society is its human workforce with people's talents, skills, and knowledge.

Things that are themselves produced and that are then used in the production of other goods and services are called capital resources, or simply **capital**. Buildings, equipment, desks, chairs, software, roads, bridges, and highways are a part of the nation's stock of capital.

capital Things that are themselves produced and that are then used in the production of other goods and services.

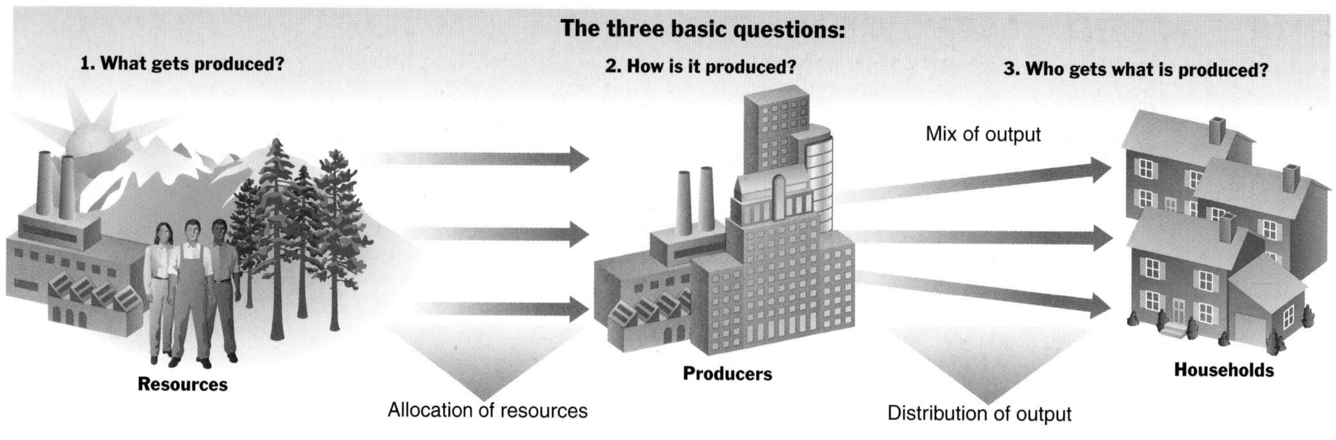

FIGURE 2.1 The Three Basic Questions

Every society has some system or process that transforms that society's scarce resources into useful goods and services. In doing so it must decide what gets produced, how it is produced, and to whom it is distributed. The primary resources that must be allocated are land, labor, and capital.

factors of production (or **factors**) The inputs into the process of production. Another word for resources.

production The process that transforms scarce resources into useful goods and services.

inputs or **resources** Anything provided by nature or previous generations that can be used directly or indirectly to satisfy human wants.

outputs Usable products.

The basic resources available to a society are often referred to as **factors of production**, or simply **factors**. The three key factors of production are land, labor, and capital. The process that transforms scarce resources into useful goods and services is called **production**. In many societies most of the production of goods and services is done by private firms. Private airlines in the United States use land (runways), labor (pilots and mechanics), as well as capital (airplanes) to produce transportation services. But in all societies some production is done by the public sector, or government. Examples of government-produced or -provided goods and services include national defense, public education, police protection, fire protection, and so forth.

Resources or factors of production are the **inputs** into the process of production; goods and services of value to households are the **outputs** of the process of production.

SCARCITY, CHOICE, AND OPPORTUNITY COST

In the second half of this chapter, we discuss the global economic landscape. Before you can understand the different types of economic systems, it is important to understand the basic economic concepts of scarcity, choice, and opportunity cost.

SCARCITY AND CHOICE IN A ONE-PERSON ECONOMY

The simplest economy is one in which a single person lives alone on an island. Consider Bill, the survivor of a plane crash, who finds himself cast ashore in such a place. Here, individual and society are one; there is no distinction between social and private. *Nonetheless, nearly all the same basic decisions that characterize complex economies must also be made in a simple economy.* That is, although Bill will get whatever he produces, he still must decide how to allocate the island's resources, what to produce, and how and when to produce it.

First, Bill must decide *what* he wants to produce. Notice that the word *needs* does not appear here. Needs are absolute requirements, but beyond just enough water, basic nutrition, and shelter to survive, they are very difficult to define. What is an "absolute necessity" for one person may not be for another. In any case, Bill must put his wants in some order of priority and make some choices.

Next he must look at the *possibilities*. What can he do to satisfy his wants, given the limits of the island? In every society, no matter how simple or complex, people are constrained in what they can do. In this society of one, Bill is constrained by time, his physical condition, his knowledge, his skills, and the resources and climate of the island.

Given that resources are limited, Bill must decide *how* to best use them to satisfy his hierarchy of wants. Food would probably come close to the top of his list. Should he spend his time simply gathering fruits and berries? Should he hunt for game? Should he clear a field and plant seeds? The answers to these questions depend on the character of the island, its climate, its flora and fauna (*are* there any fruits and berries?), the extent of his skills and knowledge (does he know anything about farming?), and his preferences (he may be a vegetarian).

Opportunity Cost The concepts of *constrained choice* and *scarcity* are central to the discipline of economics. They can be applied when discussing the behavior of individuals like Bill and when analyzing the behavior of large groups of people in complex societies.

Given the scarcity of time and resources, Bill has less time to gather fruits and berries if he chooses to hunt—he trades more meat for less fruit. There is a trade-off between food and shelter, too. If Bill likes to be comfortable, he may work on building a nice place to live, but that may require giving up the food he might have produced. As we noted in Chapter 1, the best alternative that we forgo when we make a choice is the **opportunity cost** of that choice.

opportunity cost The best alternative that we give up, or forgo, when we make a choice or decision.

Bill may occasionally decide to rest, to lie on the beach, and to enjoy the sun. In one sense, that benefit is free—he does not have to pay for the privilege. In reality, however, it does have an opportunity cost. The true cost of that leisure is the value of the other things Bill could have produced, but did not, during the time he spent on the beach.

In February 2003 the space shuttle *Columbia* broke up over Texas and seven astronauts lost their lives. That disaster set off a national debate over the "costs" of the U.S. space program. Many argued that the potential benefits of manned space exploration were not worth the costs, including human lives. More specifically they argued that the resources consumed by the program could be used for other purposes. What are the opportunity costs of continuing the manned space program? Among other things, taxes might be lower. That would mean more income for people to spend on other goods and services. Those same resources could also be used by the government to expand medical research, to improve education, to repair roads and bridges, to aid the elderly by paying for prescription drugs, or to support the arts.

In making everyday decisions, it is often helpful to think about opportunity costs. Should I go to the dorm party or not? First, it costs $4 to attend. When I pay money for anything, I give up the other things that I could have bought with that money. Second, it costs 2 or 3 hours. Time is a valuable commodity for a college student. I have exams next week and I need to study. I could go to a movie instead of the party. I could go to another party. I could sleep. Just as Bill must weigh the value of sunning on the beach against more food or better housing, so I must weight the value of the fun I may have at the party against everything else I might otherwise do with the time and money.

SCARCITY AND CHOICE IN AN ECONOMY OF TWO OR MORE

Now suppose that another survivor of the crash, Colleen, appears on the island. Now that Bill is not alone, things are more complex, and some new decisions must be made. Bill's and Colleen's preferences about what things to produce are likely to be different. They will probably not have the same knowledge or skills. Perhaps Colleen is very good at tracking animals, and Bill has a knack for building things. How should they split the work that needs to be done? Once things are produced, they must decide how to divide them. How should their products be distributed?

Education takes time. Time spent in the classroom has an opportunity cost.

The mechanism for answering these fundamental questions is clear when Bill is alone on the island. The "central plan" is his; he simply decides what he wants and what to do about it. The minute someone else appears, however, a number of decision-making arrangements immediately become possible. One or the other may take charge, in which case that person will decide for both of them. The two may agree to cooperate, with each having an equal say, and come up with a joint plan or they may agree to split the planning, as well as the production duties. Finally, they may go off to live alone at opposite ends of the island. Even if they live apart, however, they may take advantage of each other's presence by specializing and trading.

Modern industrial societies must answer exactly the same questions that Colleen and Bill must answer, but the mechanics of larger economies are naturally more complex. Instead of two people living together, the United States has over 290 million. Still decisions must be made about what to produce, how to produce it, and who gets it.

Specialization, Exchange, and Comparative Advantage The idea that members of society benefit by specializing in what they do best has a long history and is one of the most important and powerful ideas in all of economics. David Ricardo, a major nineteenth-century British economist, formalized the point precisely. According to Ricardo's **theory of comparative advantage**, specialization and free trade will benefit all trading parties, even when some are "absolutely" more efficient producers than others. Ricardo's basic point applies just as much to Colleen and Bill as it does to different nations.

theory of comparative advantage Ricardo's theory that specialization and free trade will benefit all trading parties, even those that may be absolutely more efficient producers.

To keep things simple, suppose that Colleen and Bill have only two tasks to accomplish each week: gathering food to eat and cutting logs to burn. If Colleen could cut more logs than Bill in 1 day, and Bill could gather more nuts and berries than Colleen could, specialization would clearly lead to more total production. Both would benefit if Colleen only cuts logs and Bill only gathers nuts and berries, as long as they can trade. Suppose that Bill is slow and somewhat clumsy in his nut gathering and that Colleen is better at both cutting logs *and* gathering food. Ricardo points out that it still pays for them to specialize and exchange. (Refer to Figure 2.2 in the following discussion.)

Suppose Colleen can cut 10 logs per day and Bill can cut only 4. Also suppose Colleen can gather 10 bushels of food per day and Bill can gather only 8. A producer has an **absolute advantage** over another in the production of a good or service if it can produce the good or service using fewer resources, including its time. Since Colleen can cut more logs per day than Bill, we say she has an absolute advantage in the production of logs. Similarly, Colleen has an absolute advantage over Bill in the production of food.

absolute advantage A producer has an absolute advantage over another in the production of a good or service if it can produce that product using fewer resources.

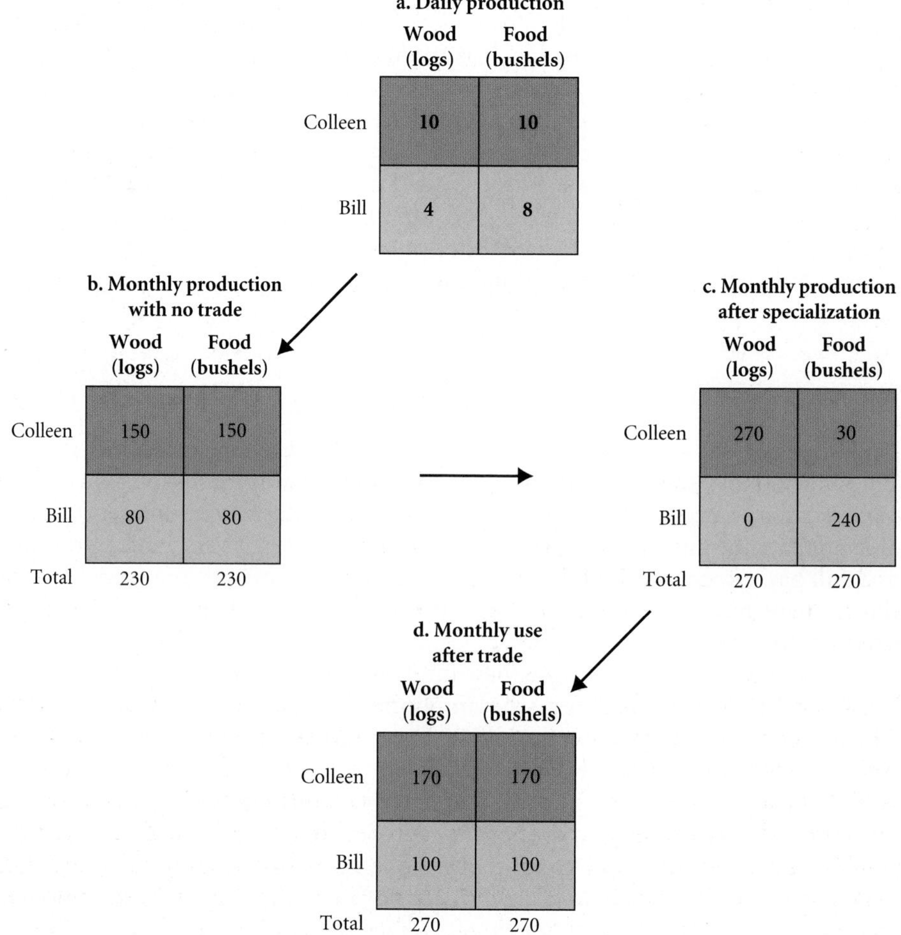

FIGURE 2.2 Comparative Advantage and the Gains from Trade

In this figure, (a) shows the number of logs and bushels of food that Colleen and Bill can produce for every day spent at the task; (b) shows how much output they could produce in a month assuming they wanted an equal number of logs and bushels. Colleen would split her time 50/50, devoting 15 days to each task and achieving total output of 150 logs and 150 bushels of food. Bill would spend 20 days on cutting wood and 10 days on gathering food. As shown in (c) and (d), by specializing and trading, both Colleen and Bill will be better off. Going from (c) to (d), Colleen trades 100 logs to Bill in exchange for 140 bushels of food.

Thinking just about productivity and the output of food and logs, it might seem that it would pay Colleen to move to the other side of the island and be by herself. Since she is more productive in cutting logs and gathering food, won't she be better off on her own? How could she benefit by hanging out with Bill and sharing what they produce?

To answer this question we must think in terms of opportunity cost. A producer has a **comparative advantage** over another in the production of a good or service if it can produce the good or service at a lower opportunity cost. First, think about Bill. He can produce 8 bushels of food per day or he can cut 4 logs. To get 8 additional bushels of food, he must give up cutting 4 logs. Thus, *for Bill the opportunity cost of 8 bushels of food is 4 logs.* Think next about Colleen. She can produce 10 bushels of food per day or she can cut 10 logs. She thus gives up 1 log for each additional bushel, and so *for Colleen the opportunity cost of 8 bushels of food is 8 logs.* Bill has a comparative advantage over Colleen in the production of food because he gives up only 4 logs for an additional 8 bushels whereas Colleen gives up 8 logs.

comparative advantage A producer has a comparative advantage over another in the production of a good or service if it can produce that product at a lower *opportunity cost.*

Think now about what Colleen must give up in terms of food to get 10 logs. To produce 10 logs she must work a whole day. If she spends a day cutting 10 logs she gives up a day of gathering 10 bushels of food. Thus *for Colleen the opportunity cost of 10 logs is 10 bushels of food.* What must Bill give up to get 10 logs? To produce 4 logs he must work a day. For each day he cuts logs he gives up 8 bushels of food. He thus gives up 2 bushels of food for each log, and so *for Bill the opportunity cost of 10 logs is 20 bushels of food.* Colleen has a comparative advantage over Bill in the production of logs since she gives up only 10 bushels of food for an additional 10 logs whereas Bill gives up 20 bushels.

Ricardo then argues that two parties can benefit from specialization and trade even if one party has an absolute advantage in the production of both goods. Suppose Colleen and Bill both want equal numbers of logs and bushels of food. If Colleen goes off on her own, in a 30-day month she can produce 150 logs and 150 bushels, devoting 15 days to each task. For Bill to produce equal numbers of logs and bushels on his own requires that he spend 10 days on food and 20 days on logs. This yields 80 bushels of food (10 days × 8 bushels per day) and 80 logs (20 days × 4 logs per day). Between the two, they produce 230 logs and 230 bushels of food.

Let's see if specialization and trade can work. If Bill spends all his time on food, he produces 240 bushels in a month (30 days × 8 bushels per day). If Colleen spends 3 days on food and 27 days on logs, she produces 30 bushels of food (3 days × 10 bushels per day) and 270 logs (27 days × 10 logs per day). Between the two, they produce 270 logs and 270 bushels of food, which is more than the 230 logs and 230 bushels they produced when not specializing. Thus, by specializing in the production of the good in which they enjoyed a comparative advantage, there is more of both goods.

Even if Colleen were to live at another place on the island, she could specialize, producing 30 bushels of food and 270 logs and then trade 100 of her logs to Bill for 140 bushels of food. This would leave her with 170 logs and 170 bushels of food, which is more than the 150 of each she could produce on her own. Bill would specialize completely in food, producing 240 bushels. Trading 140 bushels of food to Colleen for 100 logs leaves him with 100 of each, which is more than the 80 of each he could produce on his own.

The degree of specialization in modern industrial societies is breathtaking. Let your mind wander over the range of products and services available or under development today. As knowledge expands, specialization becomes a necessity. This is true not only for scientists and doctors but also in every career from tree surgeons to divorce lawyers to Web masters. Understanding specialization and trade will help you to explain much of what goes on in today's global economy.

Weighing Present and Expected Future Costs and Benefits Very often we find ourselves weighing benefits available today against benefits available tomorrow. Here too the notion of opportunity cost is helpful.

While alone on the island, Bill had to choose between cultivating a field and just gathering wild nuts and berries. Gathering nuts and berries provides food now; gathering seeds and clearing a field for planting will yield food tomorrow, if all goes well. Using today's time to farm may well be worth the effort if doing so will yield more food than Bill would otherwise have in the future. By planting, Bill is trading present value for future values.

The simplest example of trading present for future benefits is the act of saving. When I put income aside today for use in the future, I give up some things that I could have had today in exchange for something tomorrow. Because nothing is certain, some judgment about future events and expected values must be made. What will my income be in 10 years? How long am I likely to live?

We trade off present and future benefits in small ways all the time. If you decide to study instead of going to the dorm party, you are trading present fun for the expected future benefits of higher grades. If you decide to go outside on a very cold day and run 5 miles, you are trading discomfort in the present for being in better shape later.

Capital Goods and Consumer Goods A society trades present for expected future benefits when it devotes a portion of its resources to research and development or to investment in capital. As we said earlier in this chapter, *capital* in its broadest definition is anything that has already been produced that will be used to produce other valuable goods or services over time.

Building capital means trading present benefits for future ones. Bill and Colleen might trade gathering berries or lying in the sun for cutting logs to build a nicer house in the future. In a modern society, resources used to produce capital goods could have been used to produce **consumer goods**—that is, goods for present consumption. Heavy industrial machinery does not directly satisfy the wants of anyone, but producing it requires resources that could instead have gone into producing things that do satisfy wants directly—food, clothing, toys, or golf clubs.

consumer goods Goods produced for present consumption.

Capital is everywhere. A road is capital. Once it is built, we can drive on it or transport goods and services over it for many years to come. A house is also capital. Before a new manufacturing firm can start up, it must put some capital in place. The buildings, equipment, and inventories that it uses comprise its capital. As it contributes to the production process, this capital yields valuable services through time.

In Chapter 1, we talked about the enormous amount of capital—buildings, factories, housing, cars, trucks, telephone lines, and so forth—that you might see from a window high in a skyscraper. Much of it was put in place by previous generations, yet it continues to provide valuable services today; it is part of this generation's endowment of resources. To build every building, every road, every factory, every house, and every car or truck, society must forgo using resources to produce consumer goods today. To get an education, I pay tuition and put off joining the workforce for a while.

Capital does not need to be tangible. When you spend time and resources developing skills or getting an education, you are investing in human capital—your own human capital. This capital will continue to exist and yield benefits to you for years to come. A computer program produced by a software company may come on a compact disc (CD) that costs 75¢ to make, but its true intangible value comes from the ideas embodied in the program itself, which will drive computers to do valuable, time-saving tasks over time. It too is capital.

The process of using resources to produce new capital is called **investment**. (In everyday language, the term *investment* often refers to the act of buying a share of stock or a bond, as in "I invested in some Treasury bonds." In economics, however, investment *always* refers to the creation of capital: the purchase or putting in place of buildings, equipment, roads, houses, and the like.) A wise investment in capital is one that yields future benefits that are more valuable than the present cost. When you spend money for a house, for example, presumably you value its future benefits. That is, you expect to gain more from living in it than you would from the things you could buy today with the same money.

investment The process of using resources to produce new capital.

Because resources are scarce, the opportunity cost of every investment in capital is forgone present consumption.

THE PRODUCTION POSSIBILITY FRONTIER

production possibility frontier (ppf) A graph that shows all the combinations of goods and services that can be produced if all of society's resources are used efficiently.

A simple graphic device called the **production possibility frontier (ppf)** illustrates the principles of constrained choice, opportunity cost, and scarcity. The ppf is a graph that shows all the combinations of goods and services that can be produced if all society's resources are used efficiently. Figure 2.3 shows a ppf for a hypothetical economy.

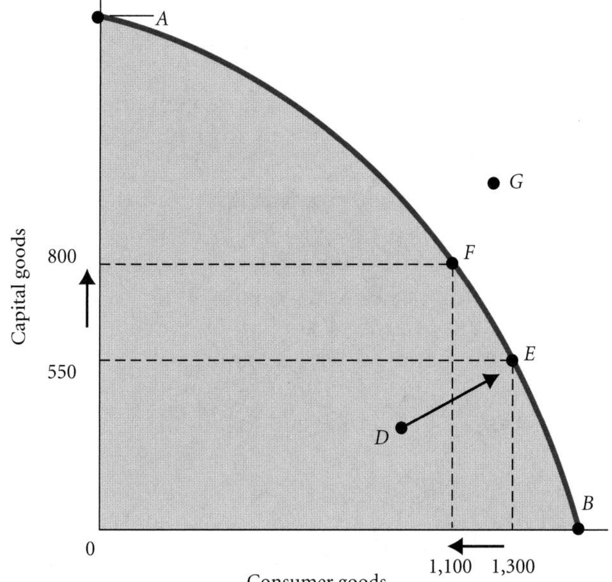

FIGURE 2.3 Production Possibility Frontier

The ppf illustrates a number of economic concepts. One of the most important is *opportunity cost.* The opportunity cost of producing more capital goods is fewer consumer goods. Moving from *E* to *F*, the number of capital goods increases from 550 to 800, but the number of consumer goods decreases from 1,300 to 1,100.

On the *Y*-axis, we measure the quantity of capital goods produced and on the *X*-axis, the quantity of consumer goods. All points below and to the left of the curve (the shaded area) represent combinations of capital and consumer goods that are possible for the society given the resources available and existing technology. Points above and to the right of the curve, such as point *G*, represent combinations that cannot be reached. If an economy were to end up at point *A* on the graph, it would be producing no consumer goods at all; all resources would be used for the production of capital. If an economy were to end up at point *B*, it would be devoting all its resources to the production of consumer goods and none of its resources to the formation of capital.

While all economies produce some of each kind of good, different economies emphasize different things. About 15.2 percent of gross output in the United States in 2002 was new capital. In Japan, capital historically accounted for a much higher percent of gross output, while in the Congo the figure was 7 percent. Japan is closer to point *A* on its ppf, the Congo is closer to *B*, and the United States is somewhere in between.

Points that are actually on the ppf are points of both full resource employment and production efficiency. (Recall from Chapter 1 that an efficient economy is one that produces the things that people want at least cost. *Production efficiency* is a state in which a given mix of outputs is produced at least cost.) Resources are not going unused, and there is no waste. Points that lie within the shaded area, but that are not on the frontier, represent either unemployment of resources or production inefficiency. An economy producing at point *D* in Figure 2.3 can produce more capital goods and more consumer goods, for example, by moving to point *E*. This is possible because resources are not fully employed at point *D* or are not being used efficiently.

Unemployment During the Great Depression of the 1930s, the U.S. economy experienced prolonged unemployment. Millions of workers found themselves without jobs. In 1933, 25 percent of the civilian labor force was unemployed. This figure stayed above 14 percent until 1940, when increased defense spending by the United States created millions of jobs. In June of 1975, the unemployment rate went over 9 percent for the first time since the 1930s. In December of 1982, when the unemployment rate hit 10.8 percent, nearly 12 million were looking for work.

In addition to the hardship that falls on the unemployed themselves, unemployment of labor means unemployment of capital. During downturns or recessions, industrial plants run at less than their total capacity. When there is unemployment of labor and capital, we are not producing all that we can.

Periods of unemployment correspond to points inside the ppf, points like *D* in Figure 2.3. Moving onto the frontier from a point like *D* means achieving full employment of resources.

Inefficiency Although an economy may be operating with full employment of its land, labor, and capital resources, it may still be operating inside its ppf (at a point like *D* in Figure 2.3). It could be using those resources *inefficiently*.

Waste and mismanagement are the results of a firm operating below its potential. If I am the owner of a bakery and I forget to order flour, my workers and ovens stand idle while I figure out what to do.

Sometimes, inefficiency results from mismanagement of the economy instead of mismanagement of individual private firms. Suppose, for example, that the land and climate in Ohio are best suited for corn production, and the land and climate in Kansas are best suited for wheat production. If Congress passes a law forcing Ohio farmers to plant 50 percent of their acreage in wheat and Kansas farmers to plant 50 percent in corn, neither corn nor wheat production will be up to potential. The economy will be at a point like *A* in Figure 2.4—inside the ppf. Allowing each state to specialize in producing the crop that it produces best increases the production of both crops and moves the economy to a point like *B* in Figure 2.4.

The Efficient Mix of Output To be efficient, an economy must produce what people want. This means that, in addition to operating *on* the ppf, the economy must be operating at the *right point* on the ppf. Suppose that an economy devotes 100 percent of its resources to beef production and that the beef industry runs efficiently, using the most modern techniques. Also suppose that everyone in the society is a vegetarian. The result is a total waste of resources (assuming that the society cannot trade its beef for vegetables produced in another country).

Both points *B* and *C* in Figure 2.4 are points of production efficiency and full employment. Whether *B* is more or less efficient than *C*, however, depends on the preferences of members of society and is not shown in the ppf graph.

Negative Slope and Opportunity Cost As we have seen, points that lie on the ppf represent points of full resource employment and production efficiency. Society can choose only one point on the curve. Because a society's choices are constrained by available resources and existing technology, when those resources are fully and efficiently employed, it can produce more capital goods only by reducing production of consumer goods. The opportunity cost of the additional capital is the forgone production of consumer goods.

The fact that scarcity exists is illustrated by the negative slope of the ppf. (If you need a review of slope, see the Appendix to Chapter 1.) In moving from point *E* to point *F* in Figure 2.3, capital production *increases* by 800 − 550 = 250 units (a positive change), but that increase in capital can be achieved only by shifting resources out of the production of consumer goods. Thus, in moving from point *E* to point *F* in Figure 2.3, consumer goods production *decreases* by 1,300 − 1,100 = 200 units of the consumer goods (a negative change).

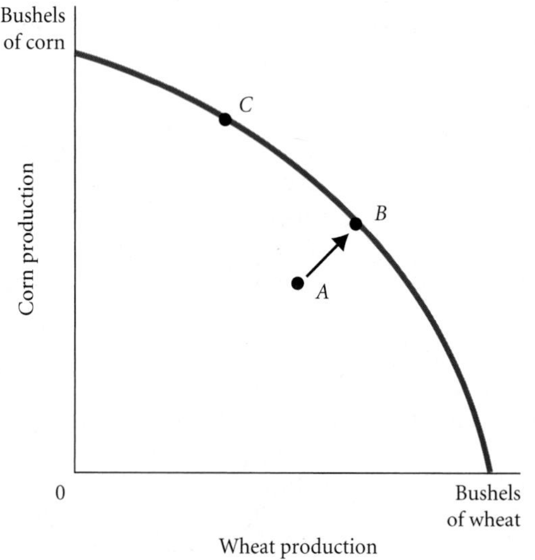

FIGURE 2.4 Inefficiency from Misallocation of Land in Farming

Society can end up inside its ppf at a point like *A* by using its resources inefficiently. If, for example, Ohio's climate and soil were best suited for corn production and those of Kansas were best suited for wheat production, a law forcing Kansas farmers to produce corn and Ohio farmers to produce wheat would result in less of both. In such a case, society might be at point *A* instead of point *B*.

TABLE 2.1 Production Possibility Schedule for Total Corn and Wheat Production in Ohio and Kansas

POINT ON PPF	TOTAL CORN PRODUCTION (MILLIONS OF BUSHELS PER YEAR)	TOTAL WHEAT PRODUCTION (MILLIONS OF BUSHELS PER YEAR)
A	700	100
B	650	200
C	510	380
D	400	500
E	300	550

The slope of the curve, the ratio of the change in capital goods to the change in consumer goods, is negative.

The value of the slope of a society's ppf is called the **marginal rate of transformation (MRT)**. In Figure 2.3, the MRT between points *E* and *F* is simply the ratio of the change in capital goods (a positive number) to the change in consumer goods (a negative number).

marginal rate of transformation (MRT) The slope of the production possibility frontier (ppf).

The Law of Increasing Opportunity Cost The negative slope of the ppf indicates the trade-off that a society faces between two goods. We can learn something further about the shape of the frontier and the terms of this trade-off. Let us look at the trade-off between corn and wheat production in Ohio and Kansas. In a recent year, Ohio and Kansas together produced 510 million bushels of corn and 380 million bushels of wheat. Table 2.1 presents these two numbers, plus some hypothetical combinations of corn and wheat production that might exist for Ohio and Kansas together. Figure 2.5 graphs the data from Table 2.1.

Suppose that society's demand for corn dramatically increases. If this happens, farmers would probably shift some of their acreage from wheat production to corn production. Such a shift is represented by a move from point *C* (where corn = 510 and wheat = 380) up and to the left along the ppf toward points *A* and *B* in Figure 2.5. As this happens, it becomes more and more difficult to produce additional corn. The best land for corn production was presumably already in corn, and the best land for wheat production already in wheat. As we try to produce more and more corn, the land is less and less well suited to that crop. As we take more and more land out of wheat production, we will be taking increasingly better wheat-producing land. All this is to say that the opportunity cost of more corn, measured in terms of wheat, increases.

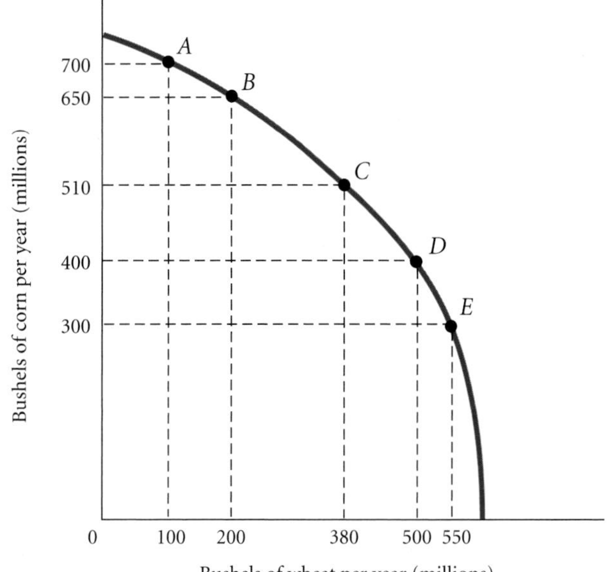

FIGURE 2.5 Corn and Wheat Production in Ohio and Kansas

The ppf illustrates that the opportunity cost of corn production increases as we shift resources from wheat production to corn production. Moving from points *E* to *D*, we get an additional 100 million bushels of corn at a cost of 50 million bushels of wheat. Moving from points *B* to *A*, we get only 50 million bushels of corn at a cost of 100 million bushels of wheat. The *cost per bushel* of corn—measured in lost wheat—has increased.

Moving from points *E* to *D*, Table 2.1 shows that we can get 100 million bushels of corn (400 – 300) by sacrificing only 50 million bushels of wheat (550 – 500)—that is, we get 2 bushels of corn for every bushel of wheat. However, when we are already stretching the ability of the land to produce corn, it becomes more difficult to produce more, and the opportunity cost increases. Moving from points *B* to *A*, we can get only 50 million bushels of corn (700 – 650) by sacrificing 100 million bushels of wheat (200 – 100). For every bushel of wheat, we now get only half a bushel of corn. However, if the demand for *wheat* were to increase substantially and we were to move down and to the right along the ppf, it would become increasingly difficult to produce wheat, and the opportunity cost of wheat, in terms of corn, would increase. This is the *law of increasing opportunity cost.*

It is important to remember that the ppf represents choices available within the constraints imposed by the current state of agricultural technology. In the long run, technology may improve, and when that happens, we have *growth.*

economic growth An increase in the total output of an economy. It occurs when a society acquires new resources or when it learns to produce more using existing resources.

Economic Growth **Economic growth** is characterized by an increase in the total output of an economy. It occurs when a society acquires new resources or when society learns to produce more with existing resources. New resources may mean a larger labor force or an increased capital stock. The production and use of new machinery and equipment (capital) increase workers' productivity. (Give a man a shovel and he can dig a bigger hole; give him a steam shovel and wow.) Improved productivity also comes from technological change and *innovation*, the discovery and application of new, more efficient production techniques.

In the past few decades, the productivity of U.S. agriculture has increased dramatically. Based on data compiled by the Department of Agriculture, Table 2.2 shows that yield per acre in corn production has increased fivefold since the late 1930s, while the labor required to produce it has dropped significantly. Productivity in wheat production has also increased, at only a slightly less remarkable rate: Output per acre has more than tripled, while labor requirements are down nearly 90 percent. These increases are the result of more efficient farming techniques, more and better capital (tractors, combines, and other equipment), and advances in scientific knowledge and technological change (hybrid seeds, fertilizers, etc.). As you can see in Figure 2.6, increases such as these shift the ppf up and to the right.

Sources of Growth and the Dilemma of the Poor Countries Economic growth arises from many sources, the two most important of which, over the years, have been the accumulation of capital and technological advances. For poor countries, capital is essential; they must build the communication networks and transportation systems necessary to develop industries that function efficiently. They also need capital goods to develop their agricultural sectors.

Recall that capital goods are produced only at a sacrifice of consumer goods. The same can be said for technological advances. Technological advances come from research and

TABLE 2.2 Increasing Productivity in Corn and Wheat Production in the United States, 1935–2001

	CORN		WHEAT	
	Yield Per Acre (Bushels)	Labor Hours Per 100 Bushels	Yield Per Acre (Bushels)	Labor Hours Per 100 Bushels
1935–1939	26.1	108	13.2	67
1945–1949	36.1	53	16.9	34
1955–1959	48.7	20	22.3	17
1965–1969	78.5	7	27.5	11
1975–1979	95.3	4	31.3	9
1981–1985	107.2	3	36.9	7
1985–1990	112.8	NA[a]	38.0	NA[a]
1990–1995	120.6	NA[a]	38.1	NA[a]
1998	134.4	NA[a]	43.2	NA[a]
2001	138.2	NA[a]	43.5	NA[a]

[a]Data not available.

Sources: U.S. Department of Agriculture, Economic Research Service, Agricultural Statistics, Crop Summary. www.ars.usda.gov/usda.html, February 2000.

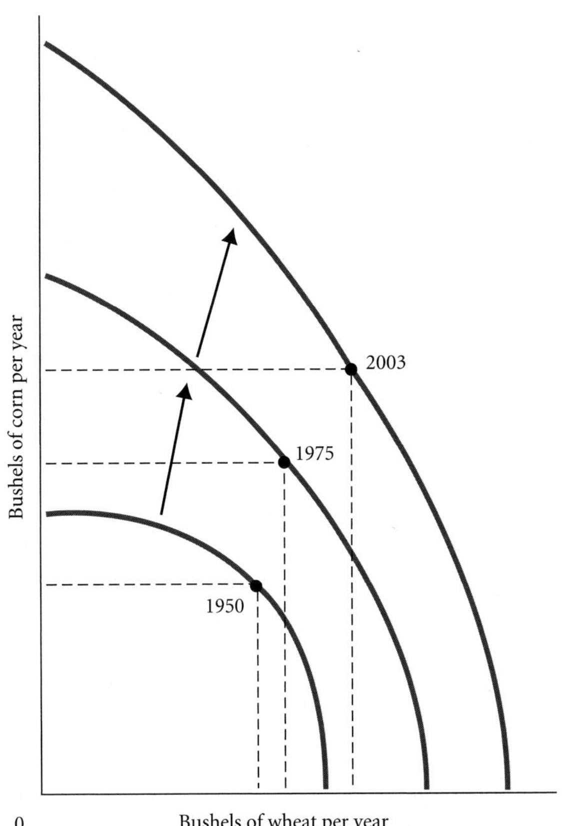

FIGURE 2.6 Economic Growth Shifts the ppf Up and to the Right

Productivity increases have enhanced the ability of the United States to produce both corn and wheat. As Table 2.2 shows, productivity increases were more dramatic for corn than for wheat. The shifts in the ppf were thus not parallel.

Note: The ppf also shifts if the amount of land or labor in corn and wheat production changes. Although we emphasize productivity increases here, the actual shifts between years were in part due to land and labor changes.

development that use resources; thus they too must be paid for. The resources used to produce capital goods—to build a road, a tractor, or a manufacturing plant—*and* to develop new technologies could have been used to produce consumer goods.

When a large part of a country's population is very poor, taking resources out of the production of consumer goods (such as food and clothing) is very difficult. In addition, in some countries those wealthy enough to invest in domestic industries choose instead to invest abroad because of political turmoil at home. As a result, it often falls to the governments of poor countries to generate revenues for capital production and research out of tax collections.

All these factors have contributed to the growing gap between some poor and rich nations. Figure 2.7 shows the result, using ppf's. On the left, the rich country devotes a larger portion of its production to capital, while the poor country produces mostly consumer goods. On the right, you see the result: The ppf of the rich country shifts up and out farther and faster.

COMPARATIVE ADVANTAGE AND THE GAINS FROM TRADE

Production possibility frontiers can also be used to show the benefits from specialization and trade. Recall the story earlier in the chapter of Colleen and Bill on a desert island. In that example we assumed that Colleen could cut 10 logs per day or she could gather 10 bushels of food per day. To construct her production possibility frontier (see Figure 2.8(a)), we start with the end points. If she were to devote an entire month (30 days) to log production, she could cut 300 logs—10 logs per day × 30 days. Similarly, if she were to devote an entire month to food gathering, she could produce 300 bushels. If she chose to split her time evenly (15 days to logs and 15 days to food), she would have 150 bushels and 150 logs. Her production possibilities are illustrated by the straight line between *A* and *B*. The ppf illustrates the trade-off that she faces between logs and food: By reducing her time spent in food gathering, she is able to devote more time to logs, and for every 10 bushels of food that she gives up she gets 10 logs.

In Figure 2.8(b), we construct Bill's ppf. Recall that Bill can produce 8 bushels of food per day, but he can only cut 4 logs. Again, starting with the end points, if Bill devoted all his

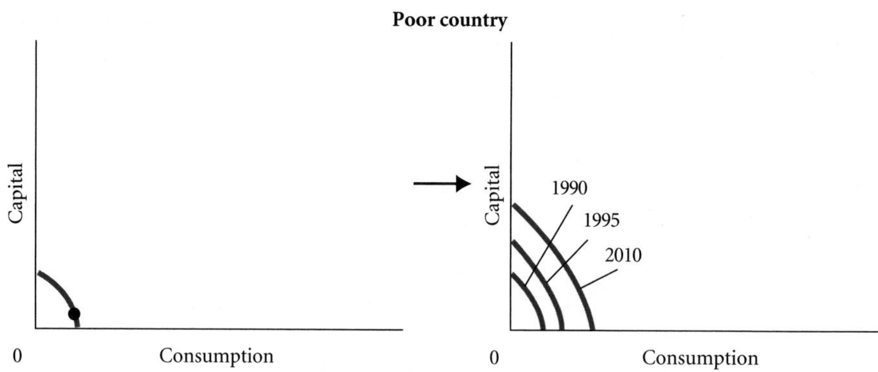

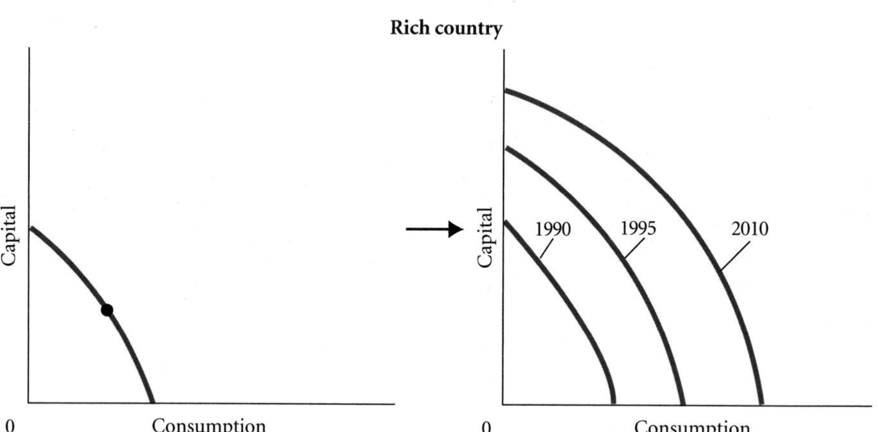

FIGURE 2.7 Capital Goods and Growth in Poor and Rich Countries

Rich countries find it easier to devote resources to the production of capital than poor countries do, but the more resources that flow into capital production, the faster the rate of economic growth. Thus the gap between poor and rich countries has grown over time.

time to food production, he could produce 240 bushels—8 bushels of food per day × 30 days. Similarly, if he were to devote the entire 30 days to log cutting, he could cut 120 logs—4 logs per day × 30 days. By splitting his time with 20 days spent on log cutting and 10 days spent gathering food, Bill could produce 80 logs and 80 bushels of food. His production possibilities are illustrated by the straight line between *D* and *E*. By shifting his resources and time from logs to food, he gets 2 bushels for every log.

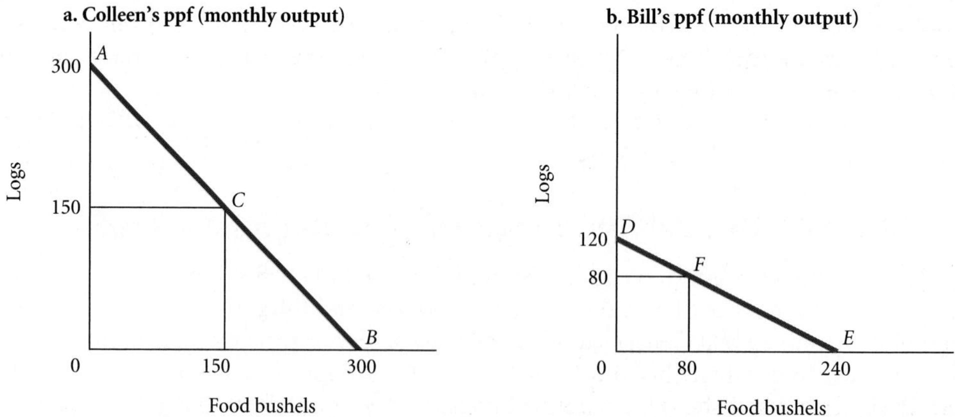

FIGURE 2.8 Production Possibility Frontiers with No Trade

The figure in (a) shows all of the combinations of logs and bushels of food that Colleen can produce by herself. If she spends all 30 days each month on logs, she produces 300 logs and no food (point *A*). If she spends all 30 days on food, she produces 300 bushels of food and no logs (point *B*). If she spends 15 days on logs and 15 days on food, she produces 150 of each (point *C*).

The figure in (b) shows all the combinations of logs and bushels of food that Bill can produce by himself. If he spends all 30 days each month on logs, he produces 120 logs and no food (point *D*). If he spends all 30 days on food, he produces 240 bushels of food and no logs (point *E*). If he spends 20 days on logs and 10 days on food, he produces 80 of each (point *F*).

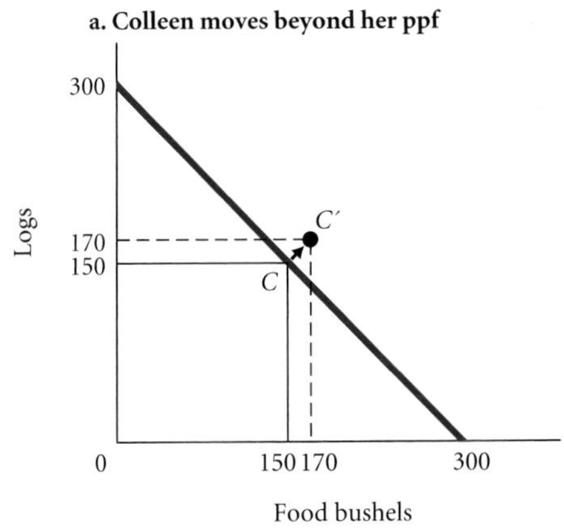

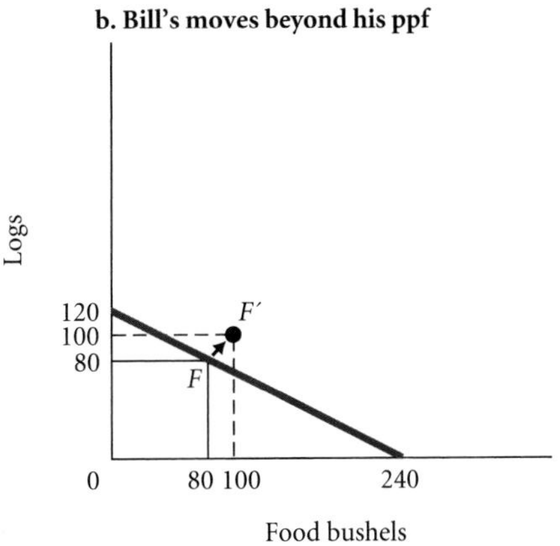

FIGURE 2.9 Colleen and Bill Gain from Trade

By specializing and engaging in trade, Colleen and Bill can move beyond their own production possibilities. If Bill spends all his time producing food, he produces 240 bushels of food and no logs. If he can trade 140 of his bushels to Colleen for 100 logs, he ends up with 100 logs and 100 bushels of food. The figure in (b) shows that he can move from point *F* on his ppf to point *F′*.

If Colleen spends 27 days cutting logs and 3 days producing food, she produces 270 logs and 30 bushels of food. If she can trade 100 of her logs to Bill for 140 bushels of food, she ends up with 170 logs and 170 bushels of food. The figure in (a) shows that she can move from point *C* on her ppf to point *C′*.

Figures 2.8(a) and 2.8(b) illustrate the maximum amounts of food and logs that Bill and Colleen can produce acting independently with no specialization or trade, which is 230 logs and 230 bushels. Let's now have each specialize in producing the good in which he or she has a comparative advantage. Back in Figure 2.2 we showed that if Bill devotes all his time to food production producing 240 bushels (30 days × 8 bushels per day) and Colleen devotes the vast majority of her time to cutting logs (27 days) and just a few days to gathering food (3 days), their combined total would be 270 logs and 270 bushels of food. Colleen would produce 270 logs and 30 bushels of food to go with Bill's 240 bushels of food.

Finally, we arrange a trade, and the result is shown in Figures 2.9(a) and 2.9(b). Bill trades 140 bushels of food to Colleen for 100 logs, and he ends up with 100 logs and 100 bushels of food, 20 more of each than he would have had before the specialization and trade. Colleen ends up with 170 logs and 170 bushels, again 20 more of each than she would have had before the specialization and trade. Both are better off. Both move out beyond their individual production possibilities.

Although it exists only as an abstraction, the ppf illustrates a number of very important concepts that we shall use throughout the rest of this book: scarcity, unemployment, inefficiency, opportunity cost, the law of increasing opportunity cost, economic growth, and the gains from trade.

THE ECONOMIC PROBLEM

Recall the three basic questions facing all economic systems: (1) What gets produced? (2) How is it produced? and (3) Who gets it?

When Bill was alone on the island, the mechanism for answering these questions was simple: He thought about his own wants and preferences, looked at the constraints imposed by the resources of the island and his own skills and time, and made his decisions. As he set about his work, he allocated available resources quite simply, more or less by dividing up his available time. Distribution of the output was irrelevant. Because Bill was the society, he got it all.

Introducing even one more person into the economy—in this case, Colleen—changed all that. With Colleen on the island, resource allocation involves deciding not only how each person spends time but also who does what; and now there are two sets of wants and preferences. If Bill and Colleen go off on their own and form two completely separate self-sufficient economies, there will be lost potential. Two people can do many more things together than one person can do alone. They may use their comparative advantages in different skills to specialize. Cooperation and coordination may give rise to gains that would otherwise not be possible.

When a society consists of millions of people, the problem of coordination and cooperation becomes enormous, but so does the potential for gain. In large, complex economies, specialization can go wild, with people working in jobs as different in their detail as an impressionist painting is from a blank page. The range of products available in a modern industrial society is beyond anything that could have been imagined a hundred years ago, and so is the range of jobs.

The amount of coordination and cooperation in a modern industrial society is almost impossible to imagine. Yet something seems to drive economic systems, if sometimes clumsily and inefficiently, toward producing the things that people want. Given scarce resources, how exactly do large, complex societies go about answering the three basic economic questions? This is the economic problem, and this is what this text is about.

ECONOMIC SYSTEMS

Now that you understand the economic problem, we can explore how different economic systems go about answering the three basic questions.

COMMAND ECONOMIES

command economy An economy in which a central government either directly or indirectly sets output targets, incomes, and prices.

In a pure **command economy**, the basic economic questions are answered by a central government. Through a combination of government ownership of state enterprises and central planning, the government, either directly or indirectly, sets output targets, incomes, and prices.

It is an understatement to say that planned economies have not in general fared well. In fact, the planned economies of Eastern Europe and the former Soviet Union—including the Russian Republic—completely collapsed. China remains committed to many of the principles of a planned economy, but reforms have moved it sharply away from pure central planning.

LAISSEZ-FAIRE ECONOMIES: THE FREE MARKET

laissez-faire economy Literally from the French: "allow [them] to do." An economy in which individual people and firms pursue their own self-interests without any central direction or regulation.

market The institution through which buyers and sellers interact and engage in exchange.

At the opposite end of the spectrum from the command economy is the **laissez-faire economy**. The term *laissez faire*, which, translated literally from French, means "allow [them] to do," implies a complete lack of government involvement in the economy. In this type of economy, individuals and firms pursue their own self-interest without any central direction or regulation; the sum total of millions of individual decisions ultimately determines all basic economic outcomes. The central institution through which a laissez-faire system answers the basic questions is the **market**, a term that is used in economics to mean an institution through which buyers and sellers interact and engage in exchange.

The interactions between buyers and sellers in any market range from simple to complex. Early explorers of the North American Midwest who wished to exchange with Native Americans did so simply by bringing their goods to a central place and trading them. Today, the World Wide Web is revolutionizing exchange. A jewelry maker in upstate Maine can exhibit wares through digital photographs on the Web. Buyers can enter orders or make bids and pay by credit card. Companies like eBay facilitate the worldwide interaction of tens of thousands of buyers and sellers sitting at their computers.

In short:

> Some markets are simple and others are complex, but they all involve buyers and sellers engaging in exchange. The behavior of buyers and sellers in a laissez-faire economy determines what gets produced, how it is produced, and who gets it.

The following chapters explore market systems in great depth. A quick preview is worthwhile here, however.

Consumer Sovereignty In a free, unregulated market, goods and services are produced and sold only if the supplier can make a profit. In simple terms, making a *profit* means selling goods or services for more than it costs to produce them. You cannot make a profit unless someone wants the product that you are selling. This logic leads to the notion of **consumer sovereignty**: The mix of output found in any free market system is dictated ultimately by the tastes and preferences of consumers, who "vote" by buying or not buying. Businesses rise and fall in response to consumer demands. No central directive or plan is necessary.

consumer sovereignty The idea that consumers ultimately dictate what will be produced (or not produced) by choosing what to purchase (and what not to purchase).

Individual Production Decisions: Free Enterprise Under a free market system, individual producers must also figure how to organize and coordinate the actual production of their products or services. The owner of a small shoe repair shop must alone buy the needed equipment and tools, hang signs, and set prices. In a big corporation, so many people are involved in planning the production process that in many ways corporate planning resembles the planning in a command economy. In a free market economy, producers may be small or large. One person who hand paints eggshells may start to sell them as a business; a person good at computers may start a business designing Web sites. On a larger scale, a group of furniture designers may put together a large portfolio of sketches, raise several million dollars, and start a bigger business. At the extreme are huge corporations like Microsoft, Mitsubishi, and Intel, each of which sells tens of billons of dollars' worth of products every year. Whether the firms are large or small, however, production decisions in a market economy are made by separate private organizations acting in what they perceive to be their own interests.

In a market economy, individuals seeking profits are free to start new businesses. Because new businesses require capital investment before they can begin operation, starting a new business involves risk. A well-run business that produces a product for which demand exists will succeed: a poorly run business or one that produces a product for which little demand exists now or in the future is likely to fail. It is through *free enterprise* that new products and new production techniques find their way into use.

Proponents of free market systems argue that free enterprise leads to more efficient production and better response to diverse and changing consumer preferences. If a producer produces inefficiently, competitors will come along, fight for the business, and eventually take it away. Thus in a free market economy, competition forces producers to use efficient techniques of production. It is competition, then, that ultimately dictates how outputs are produced.

Distribution of Output In a free market system, the distribution of output—who gets what—is also determined in a decentralized way. The amount that any one household gets depends on its income and wealth. *Income* is the amount that a household earns each year. It comes in a number of forms: wages, salaries, interest, and the like. *Wealth* is the amount that households have accumulated out of past income through savings or inheritance.

To the extent that income comes from working for a wage, it is at least in part determined by individual choice. You will work for the wages available in the market only if these wages (and the things they can buy) are sufficient to compensate you for what you give up by working. Your leisure certainly has a value also. You may discover that you can increase your income by getting more education or training. You *cannot* increase your income, however, if you acquire a skill that no one wants and can pay for.

New businesses arise each day and some go out of business in response to profit opportunities and losses.

Price Theory The basic coordinating mechanism in a free market system is price. A price is the amount that a product sells for per unit, and it reflects what society is willing to pay. Prices of inputs—labor, land, and capital—determine how much it costs to produce a product. Prices of various kinds of labor, or *wage rates*, determine the rewards for working in different jobs and professions. Many of the independent decisions made in a market economy involve the weighing of prices and costs, so it is not surprising that much of economic theory focuses on the factors that influence and determine prices. This is why microeconomic theory is often simply called *price theory*.

News Analysis

Investing in Central and Eastern Europe

DURING THE LATE 1980S, THE COMMAND ECONOMIES of Eastern Europe collapsed like a row of dominoes. The process began in November 1989, when the Berlin Wall, which had separated the communist East from the capitalist West for nearly 30 years, was torn down. Finally, in 1991, the once mighty Soviet Union disintegrated, ending 75 years of communism and nearly a half century of Cold War with the West.

More than a decade has passed, and the transition to a set of independent economies oriented to the market is nearly complete. The road to prosperity has been uneven and quite rocky. The following portion of a report in the *Financial Times* suggests real progress despite a world economic slowdown during the first years of the new century.

Good times still fail to impress the people—*Financial Times*

The countries of central and eastern Europe and the former Soviet Union have, in economic terms, never had it so good.

Neither the global economic slow down, nor terrorism in the US, nor the Argentine crisis have seriously disturbed the region's economies.

The 27 countries are this year likely to post their fourth successive year of growth, the longest sustained expansion since the fall of the Berlin Wall.

Even the countries of the Balkans, for long held back by political instability, have posted solid increases in gross national product.

Russia, fuelled by oil revenues, is generating growth, to the benefit of its own economy and its neighbours. The big exception is Poland, for long the region's economic standard-bearer, which is struggling to pull out of a sharp slowdown.

Perhaps the best example of the many problems involved in driving ahead with a second decade of economic modernisation is Poland, where, in contrast to the region as a whole, economic growth slumped last year to just 1.1 percent. Unemployment could hit 20 percent next year.

In the meantime, Russia's growth surge is helping its neighbours, by creating demand for imports and by encouraging Russian companies to seek opportunities in the former Soviet Union. Ukraine has benefited, so have parts of central Asia, including Kazakhstan which has the added advantage of its own oil boom.

Meanwhile, in much of the former Soviet Union, the concentration of wealth in the hands of a few oligarchs and their associates has left large swathes of the population untouched by progress. The gap between rich and poor is fertile ground for future social conflict.

Source: Wagstyl, Stefan, Financial Times, *May 21, 2002, p. 1. Reprinted with permission.*

Markets are playing a larger and larger role in the economies of Eastern Europe.

Visit www.prenhall.com/casefair for updated articles and exercises.

In sum:

In a free market system, the basic economic questions are answered without the help of a central government plan or directives. This is what the "free" in free market means—the system is left to operate on its own, with no outside interference. Individuals pursuing their own self-interest will go into business and produce the products and services that people want. Others will decide whether to acquire skills; whether to work; and whether to buy, sell, invest, or save the income that they earn. The basic coordinating mechanism is price.

MIXED SYSTEMS, MARKETS, AND GOVERNMENTS

The differences between command economies and laissez-faire economies in their pure forms are enormous. In fact, these pure forms do not exist in the world; all real systems are in some sense "mixed." That is, individual enterprise exists and independent choice is exercised even in economies in which the government plays the major role.

Conversely, no market economies exist without government involvement and government regulation. The United States has basically a free market economy, but government purchases accounted for about 19 percent of its total production in 2002. Governments in the United States (local, state, and federal) directly employ about 16 percent of all workers counting the military. They also redistribute income by means of taxation and social welfare expenditures, and they regulate many economic activities.

One of the major themes in this book, and indeed in economics, is the tension between the advantages of free, unregulated markets and the desire for government involvement. Advocates of free markets argue that such markets work best when left to themselves. They produce only what people want; without buyers, sellers go out of business. Competition forces firms to adopt efficient production techniques. Wage differentials lead people to acquire needed skills. Competition also leads to innovation in both production techniques and products. The result is quality and variety, but market systems have problems too.

Even staunch defenders of the free enterprise system recognize that market systems are not perfect. First, they do not always produce what people want at lowest cost—there are inefficiencies. Second, rewards (income) may be unfairly distributed, and some groups may be left out. Third, periods of unemployment and inflation recur with some regularity.

Many people point to these problems as reasons for government involvement. Indeed, for some problems government involvement may be the only solution. However, government decisions are made by people who presumably, like the rest of us, act in their own self-interest. While governments may indeed be called on to improve the functioning of the economy, there is no guarantee that they will do so. Just as markets may fail to produce an allocation of resources that is perfectly efficient and fair, governments may fail to improve matters. We return to this debate many times throughout this text.

LOOKING AHEAD

This chapter has described the economic problem in broad terms. We have outlined the questions that all economic systems must answer. We also discussed very broadly the two kinds of economic systems. In the next chapter we analyze the way market systems work.

SUMMARY

1. Every society has some system or process for transforming into useful form what nature and previous generations have provided. Economics is the study of that process and its outcomes.

2. *Producers* are those who take resources and transform them into usable products, or *outputs*. Private firms, households, and governments all produce something.

SCARCITY, CHOICE, AND OPPORTUNITY COST

3. All societies must answer *three basic questions*: What gets produced? How is it produced? Who gets what is produced? These three questions make up the *economic problem*.

4. One person alone on an island must make the same basic decisions that complex societies make. When a society consists of more than one person, questions of distribution, cooperation and specialization arise.

5. Because resources are scarce relative to human wants in all societies, using resources to produce one good or service implies *not* using them to produce something else. This concept of *opportunity cost* is central to an understanding of economics.

6. Using resources to produce *capital* that will in turn produce benefits in the future implies *not* using those resources to produce consumer goods in the present.

7. Even if one individual or nation is absolutely more efficient at producing goods than another, all parties will gain if they specialize in producing goods in which they have a *comparative advantage.*

8. A *production possibility frontier* (ppf) is a graph that shows all the combinations of goods and services that can be produced if all society's resources are used efficiently. The ppf illustrates a number of important economic concepts: scarcity, unemployment, inefficiency, increasing opportunity cost, and economic growth.

9. *Economic growth* occurs when society produces more, either by acquiring more resources or by learning to produce more with existing resources. Improved productivity may come from additional capital, or from the discovery and application of new, more efficient, techniques or production.

10. The ppf can be used to illustrate the gain from trade and the theory of comparative advantage. Trade and specialization enable people and countries to move out beyond their own productive possibilities.

ECONOMIC SYSTEMS

11. In some modern societies, government plays a big role in answering the three basic questions. In pure *command economies*, a central authority directly or indirectly sets output targets, incomes, and prices.

12. A *laissez-faire economy* is one in which individuals independently pursue their own self-interest, without any central direction or regulation and ultimately determine all basic economic outcomes.

13. A *market* is an institution through which buyers and sellers interact and engage in exchange. Some markets involve simple face-to-face exchange; others involve a complex series of transactions, often over great distance or electronically.

14. There are no purely planned economies and no pure laissez-faire economies; all economies are mixed. Individual enterprise, independent choice, and relatively free markets exist in centrally planned economies; and there is significant government involvement in market economies such as that of the United States.

15. One of the great debates in economics revolves around the tension between the advantages of free, unregulated markets and the desire for government involvement in the economy. Free markets produce what people want, and competition forces firms to adopt efficient production techniques. The need for government intervention arises because free markets are characterized by inefficiencies and an unequal distribution of income and experience regular periods of inflation and unemployment.

REVIEW TERMS AND CONCEPTS

absolute advantage, 26
capital, 23
command economy, 36
comparative advantage, 27
consumer goods, 28
consumer sovereignty, 37
economic growth, 32
factors of production (or factors), 24
inputs or resources, 24
investment, 28
laissez-faire economy, 36
marginal rate of transformation (MRT), 31
market, 36
opportunity cost, 25
outputs, 24
production, 24
production possibility frontier (ppf), 28
theory of comparative advantage, 26

PROBLEM SET

1. For each of the following, describe some of the potential opportunity costs:
   a. Studying for your economics test
   b. Spending 2 hours playing computer games
   c. Buying a new car instead of keeping the old one
   d. A local community voting to raise property taxes to increase school expenditures and to reduce class size
   e. A number of countries working together to build a space station
   f. Going to graduate school

2. "As long as all resources are fully employed, and every firm in the economy is producing its output using the best available technology, the result will be efficient." Do you agree or disagree with the statement? Explain your answer.

3. Kristen and Anna live in the beach town of Santa Monica. They own a small business in which they make wristbands and potholders and sell them to people on the beach. Kristen can make 15 wristbands per hour, but only 3 potholders. Anna is a bit slower and can make only 12 wristbands or 2 potholders in an hour.

OUTPUT PER HOUR

	Kristen	Anna
Wristbands	15	12
Potholders	3	2

   a. For Kristen and for Anna what is the opportunity cost of a potholder? Who has a comparative advantage in the production of potholders? Explain.
   b. Who has a comparative advantage in the production of wristbands? Explain.
   c. Assume that Kristen works 20 hours per week in the business. If Kristen were in business on her own, graph the possible combinations of potholders and wristbands that she could produce in a week. Do the same for Anna.
   d. If Kristen devoted half of her time (10 out of 20 hours) to wristbands and half of her time to potholders, how many of each would she produce in a week? If Anna did the same, how many of each would she produce? How many wristbands and potholders would be produced in total?
   e. Suppose that Anna spent all 20 hours of her time on wristbands and Kristen spent 17 hours on potholders and 3 hours on wristbands. How many of each would be produced?
   f. Suppose that Kristen and Anna can sell all their wristbands for $1 each and all their potholders for $5.50 each. If each of them worked 20 hours per week, how should they split their time between wristbands and potholders? What is their maximum joint revenue?

4. Briefly describe the trade-offs involved in each of the following decisions. Specifically, list some of the opportunity costs associated with the decision, paying particular attention to the trade-offs between present and future consumption.
   a. After a stressful senior year in high school, Sherice decides to take the summer off instead of working before going to college.
   b. Frank is overweight and decides to work out every day and to go on a diet.
   c. Mei is very diligent about taking her car in for routine maintenance, even though it takes 2 hours of her time and costs $100 four times each year.
   d. Jim is in a big hurry. He runs a red light on the way to work.

*5. The countries of Figistan and Blah are small island countries in the South Pacific. Both produce fruit and timber. Each island has a labor force of 1,200. The table below gives production per month for each worker in each country:

	BASKETS OF FRUIT	BOARD FEET OF TIMBER
Figistan workers	10	5
Blah workers	30	10

Productivity of one worker for one month

a. Which country has an absolute advantage in the production of fruit? Which country has an absolute advantage in the production of timber?

b. Which country has a comparative advantage in the production of fruit? Of timber?

c. Sketch the production possibility frontiers for both countries.

d. If both countries desired to have equal numbers of feet of timber and baskets of fruit, how would they allocate workers to the two sectors?

e. Show that specialization and trade can move both countries beyond their production possibility frontiers.

6. Suppose that a simple society has an economy with only one resource, labor. Labor can be used to produce only two commodities—*X*, a necessity good (food), and *Y*, a luxury good (music and merriment). Suppose that the labor force consists of 100 workers. One laborer can produce either 5 units of necessity per month (by hunting and gathering) or 10 units of luxury per month (by writing songs, playing the guitar, dancing, etc.).

a. On a graph, draw the economy's production possibility frontier (ppf). Where does the ppf intersect the *Y*-axis? Where does it intersect the *X*-axis? What meaning do those points have?

b. Suppose the economy produced at a point *inside* the ppf. Give at least two reasons why this could occur. What could be done to move the economy to a point *on* the ppf?

c. Suppose you succeeded in lifting your economy to a point on its ppf. What point would you choose? How might your small society decide the point at which it wanted to be?

d. Once you have chosen a point on the ppf, you still need to decide how your society's product will be divided. If you were a dictator, how would you decide? What would happen if you left product distribution to the free market?

7. What progress has been made during the last year in Eastern Europe? Which countries are growing? Which are in decline? What factors seem to have contributed to the differences in success across countries?

***8.** Match each diagram in Figure 1 with its description. Assume that the economy is producing or attempting to produce at point *A*, and most members of society like meat and not fish. Some descriptions apply to more than one diagram, and some diagrams have more than one description.

a. Inefficient production of meat and fish

b. Productive efficiency

c. An inefficient mix of output

d. Technological advances in the production of meat and fish

e. The law of increasing opportunity cost

f. An impossible combination of meat and fish

9. A nation with fixed quantities of resources is able to produce any of the following combinations of bread and ovens:

LOAVES OF BREAD (MILLIONS)	OVENS (THOUSANDS)
75	0
60	12
45	22
30	30
15	36
0	40

*Problems marked with an asterisk are more challenging.

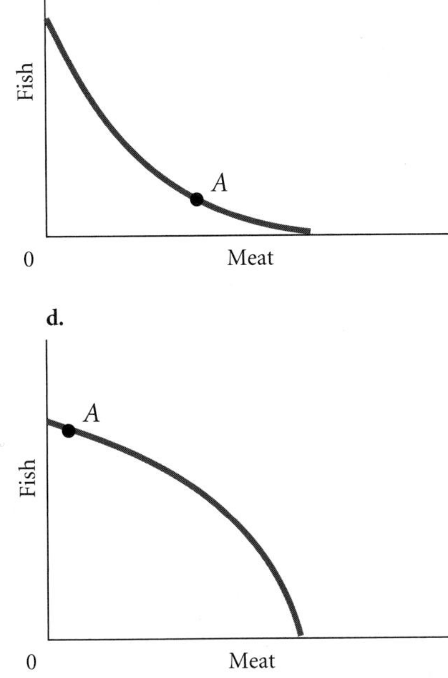

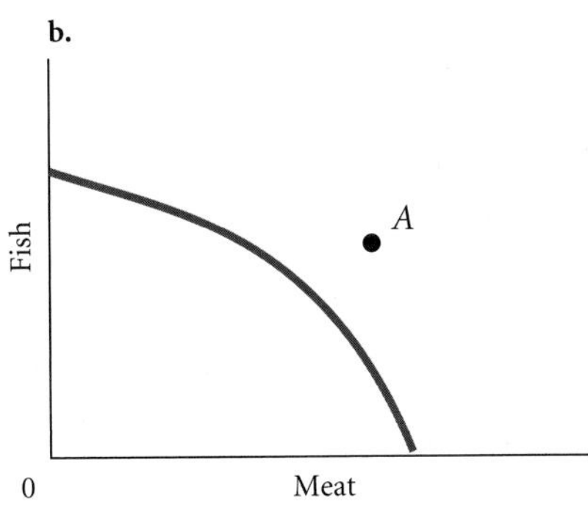

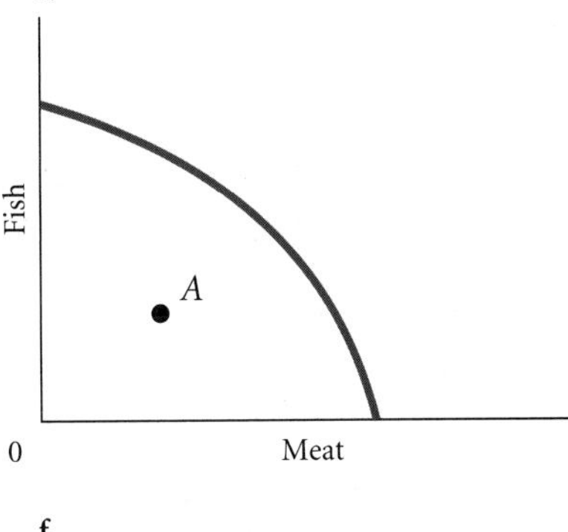

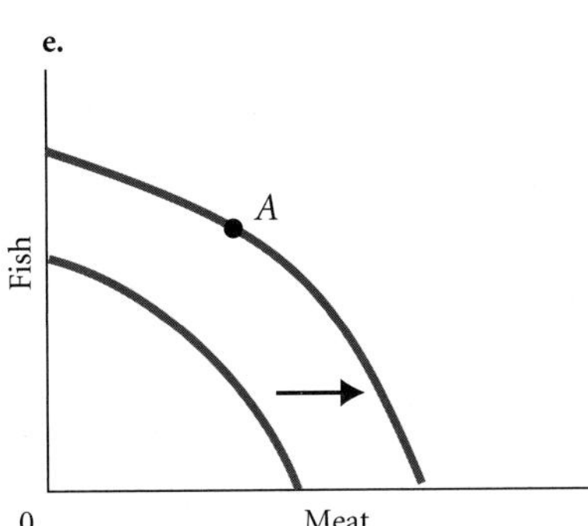

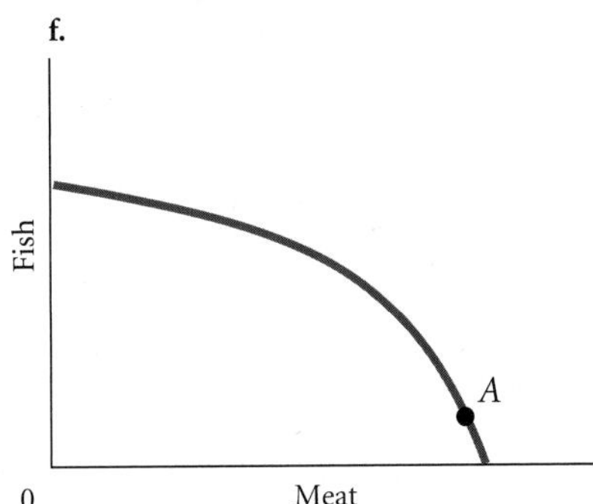

FIGURE 1

These figures assume that a certain number of previously produced ovens are available in the current period for baking bread.

a. Using the data in the table, graph the ppf (with ovens on the vertical axis).

b. Does the principle of "increasing opportunity cost" hold in this nation? Explain briefly. (*Hint:* What happens to the opportunity cost of bread—measured in number of ovens—as bread production increases?)

c. If this country chooses to produce both ovens and bread, what will happen to the ppf over time? Why?

Now suppose that a new technology is discovered that allows twice as many loaves of bread to be baked in each existing oven.

d. Illustrate (on your original graph) the effect of this new technology on the production possibilities curve.

e. Suppose that before the new technology is introduced, the nation produces 22 ovens. After the new technology is introduced, the nation produces 30 ovens. What is the effect of the new technology on the production of bread? (Give the number of loaves before and after the change.)

Demand, Supply, and Market Equilibrium

3

CHAPTER OUTLINE

Chapters 1 and 2 introduced the discipline, methodology, and subject matter of economics. We now begin the task of analyzing how a market economy actually works. This chapter and the next present an overview of the way individual markets work. They introduce some of the concepts needed to understand both microeconomics and macroeconomics.

As we proceed to define terms and make assumptions, it is important to keep in mind what we are doing. In Chapter 1 we explained what economic theory attempts to do. Theories are abstract representations of reality, like a map that represents a city. We believe that the models presented here will help you understand the workings of the economy as a map helps you find your way around a city. Just as a map presents one view of the world, so too does any given theory of the economy. Alternatives exist to the theory that we present. We believe, however, that the basic model presented here, while sometimes abstract, is useful in gaining an understanding of how the economy works.

In the simple island society discussed in Chapter 2, Bill and Colleen solved the economic problem directly. They allocated their time and used the island's resources to satisfy their wants. Bill might be a farmer, Colleen a hunter and carpenter. He might be a civil engineer, she a doctor. Exchange occurred, but complex markets were not necessary.

In societies of many people, however, production must satisfy wide-ranging tastes and preferences. Producers therefore specialize. Farmers produce more food than they can eat to sell it to buy manufactured goods. Physicians are paid for specialized services, as are attorneys, construction workers, and editors. When there is specialization, there must be exchange, and *markets* are the institutions through which exchange takes place.

This chapter begins to explore the basic forces at work in market systems. The purpose of our discussion is to explain how the individual decisions of households and firms together, without any central planning or direction, answer the three basic questions: What gets produced, how is it produced, and who gets what is produced? We begin with some definitions.

FIRMS AND HOUSEHOLDS: THE BASIC DECISION-MAKING UNITS

Throughout this book, we discuss and analyze the behavior of two fundamental decision-making units: *firms*—the primary producing units in an economy—and *households*—the consuming units in an economy. Both are made up of people performing different

firm An organization that transforms resources (inputs) into products (outputs). Firms are the primary producing units in a market economy.

entrepreneur A person who organizes, manages, and assumes the risks of a firm, taking a new idea or a new product and turning it into a successful business.

households The consuming units in an economy.

functions and playing different roles. In essence, what we are developing is a theory of human behavior.

A **firm** exists when a person or a group of people decides to produce a product or products by transforming *inputs*—that is, resources in the broadest sense—into *outputs*, the products that are sold in the market. Some firms produce goods; others produce services. Some are large, many are small, and some are in between. All firms exist to transform resources into things that people want. The Colorado Symphony Orchestra takes labor, land, a building, musically talented people, instruments, and other inputs and combines them to produce concerts. The production process can be extremely complicated. For example, the first flautist in the orchestra uses training, talent, previous performance experience, score, instrument, conductor's interpretation, and personal feelings about the music to produce just one contribution to an overall performance.

Most firms exist to make a profit for their owners, but some do not. Columbia University, for example, fits the description of a firm: It takes inputs in the form of labor, land, skills, books, and buildings and produces a service that we call education. Although it sells that service for a price, it does not exist to make a profit, but instead to provide education of the highest quality possible.

Still, most firms exist to make a profit. They engage in production because they can sell their product for more than it costs to produce it. The analysis of firm behavior that follows rests on the assumption that *firms make decisions in order to maximize profits.*

An **entrepreneur** is one who organizes, manages, and assumes the risks of a firm. When a new firm is created, someone must organize the new firm, arrange financing, hire employees, and take risks. That person is an entrepreneur. Sometimes existing companies introduce new products, and sometimes new firms develop or improve on an old idea, but at the root of it all is entrepreneurship, which some see as the core of the free enterprise system.

At the heart of the debate about the potential of free enterprise in formerly socialist Eastern Europe is the question of entrepreneurship. Does an entrepreneurial spirit exist in that part of the world? If not, can it be developed? Without it, the free enterprise system breaks down.

The consuming units in an economy are **households**. A household may consist of any number of people: a single person living alone, a married couple with four children, or 15 unrelated people sharing a house. Household decisions are presumably based on individual tastes and preferences. The household buys what it wants and can afford. In a large, heterogeneous, and open society such as the United States, wildly different tastes find expression in the marketplace. A six-block walk in any direction on any street in Manhattan or a drive from the Chicago Loop south into rural Illinois should be enough to convince someone that it is difficult to generalize about what people like and do not like.

Even though households have wide-ranging preferences, they also have some things in common. All—even the very rich—have ultimately limited incomes, and all must pay in some way for the things they consume. Although households may have some control over their incomes—they can work more hours or fewer hours—they are also constrained by the availability of jobs, current wages, their own abilities, and their accumulated and inherited wealth (or lack thereof).

INPUT MARKETS AND OUTPUT MARKETS: THE CIRCULAR FLOW

product or output markets The markets in which goods and services are exchanged.

input or factor markets The markets in which the resources used to produce products are exchanged.

Households and firms interact in two basic kinds of markets: product (or output) markets and input (or factor) markets. Goods and services that are intended for use by households are exchanged in **product** or **output markets**. In output markets, firms *supply* and households *demand.*

To produce goods and services, firms must buy resources in **input** or **factor markets**. Firms buy inputs from households, which supply these inputs. When a firm decides how much to produce (supply) in output markets, it must simultaneously decide how much of each input it needs to produce the desired level of output. To produce automobiles, Ford

Motor Company must use many inputs, including tires, steel, complicated machinery, and many different kinds of labor.

Figure 3.1 shows the *circular flow* of economic activity through a simple market economy. Note that the flow reflects the direction in which goods and services flow through input and output markets. For example, goods and services flow from firms to households through output markets. Labor services flow from households to firms through input markets. Payment (most often in money form) for goods and services flows in the opposite direction.

In input markets, households *supply* resources. Most households earn their incomes by working—they supply their labor in the **labor market** to firms that demand labor and pay workers for their time and skills. Households may also loan their accumulated or inherited savings to firms for interest, or exchange those savings for claims to future profits, as when a household buys shares of stock in a corporation. In the **capital market**, households supply the funds that firms use to buy capital goods. Households may also supply land or other real property in exchange for rent in the **land market**.

labor market The input/factor market in which households supply work for wages to firms that demand labor.

capital market The input/factor market in which households supply their savings, for interest or for claims to future profits, to firms that demand funds to buy capital goods.

land market The input/factor market in which households supply land or other real property in exchange for rent.

factors of production The inputs into the production process. Land, labor, and capital are the three key factors of production.

Inputs into the production process are also called **factors of production**. Land, labor, and capital are the three key factors of production. Throughout this text, we use the terms *input* and *factor of production* interchangeably. Thus, input markets and factor markets mean the same thing.

Early economics texts included entrepreneurship as a type of input, just like land, labor, and capital. Treating entrepreneurship as a separate factor of production has fallen out of favor, however, partially because it is unmeasurable. Most economists today implicitly assume that it is in plentiful supply. That is, if profit opportunities exist, it is likely that entrepreneurs will crop up to take advantage of them. This assumption has turned out to be a good predictor of actual economic behavior and performance.

The supply of inputs and their prices ultimately determines household income. The amount of income a household earns thus depends on the decisions it makes concerning what types of inputs it chooses to supply. Whether to stay in school, how much and what kind of training to get, whether to start a business, how many hours to work, whether to work at all, and how to invest savings are all household decisions that affect income.

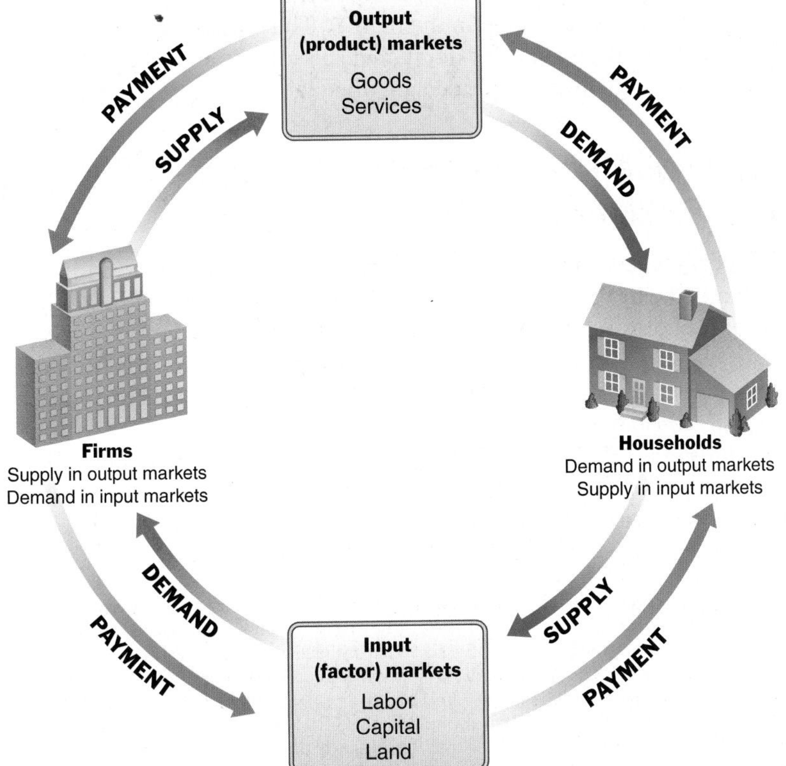

FIGURE 3.1 The Circular Flow of Economic Activity

Diagrams like this one show the circular flow of economic activity, hence the name *circular flow diagram*. Here, goods and services flow clockwise: Labor services supplied by households flow to firms, and goods and services produced by firms flow to households. Payment (usually money) flows in the opposite (counterclockwise) direction: Payment for goods and services flows from households to firms, and payment for labor services flows from firms to households.

Note: Color Guide—In Figure 3.1 households are depicted in *blue* and firms are depicted in *red*. From now on all diagrams relating to the behavior of households will be blue or shades of blue, and all diagrams relating to the behavior of firms will be in red or shades of red.

As you can see:

Input and output markets are connected through the behavior of both firms and households. Firms determine the quantities and character of outputs produced and the types of quantities of inputs demanded. Households determine the types and quantities of products demanded and the quantities and types of inputs supplied.[1]

The following analysis of demand and supply will lead up to a theory of how market prices are determined. Prices are determined by the interaction between demanders and suppliers. To understand this interaction, we first need to know how product prices influence the behavior of demanders and suppliers *separately*. We therefore discuss output markets by focusing first on demanders, then on suppliers, and finally on the interaction.

DEMAND IN PRODUCT/OUTPUT MARKETS

In real life, households make many decisions at the same time. To see how the forces of demand and supply work, however, let us focus first on the amount of a *single* product that an *individual* household decides to consume within some given period of time, such as a month or a year.

A household's decision about what quantity of a particular output, or product, to demand depends on a number of factors including:

- The *price of the product* in question
- The *income available* to the household
- The household's *amount of accumulated wealth*
- The *prices of other products* available to the household
- The household's *tastes and preferences*
- The household's *expectations* about future income, wealth, and prices

quantity demanded The amount (number of units) of a product that a household would buy in a given period if it could buy all it wanted at the current market price.

Quantity demanded is the amount (number of units) of a product that a household would buy in a given period *if it could buy all it wanted at the current market price.*

Of course, the amount of a product that households finally purchase depends on the amount of product actually available in the market. The phrase *if it could buy all it wanted* is critical to the definition of quantity demanded because it allows for the possibility that quantity supplied and quantity demanded are unequal.

CHANGES IN QUANTITY DEMANDED VERSUS CHANGES IN DEMAND

The most important relationship in individual markets is that between market price and quantity demanded. For this reason, we need to begin our discussion by analyzing the likely response of households to changes in price using the device of *ceteris paribus*, or "all else equal." That is, we will attempt to derive a relationship between the quantity demanded of a good per time period and the price of that good, holding income, wealth, other prices, tastes, and expectations constant.

It is very important to distinguish between price changes, which affect the quantity of a good demanded, and changes in other factors (such as income), which change the entire relationship between price and quantity. For example, if a family begins earning a higher

---

[1]Our description of markets begins with the behavior of firms and households. Modern orthodox economic theory essentially combines two distinct but closely related theories of behavior. The "theory of household behavior," or "consumer behavior," has its roots in the works of nineteenth-century utilitarians such as Jeremy Bentham, William Jevons, Carl Menger, Leon Walras, Vilfredo Pareto, and F. Y. Edgeworth. The "theory of the firm" developed out of the earlier classical political economy of Adam Smith, David Ricardo, and Thomas Malthus. In 1890, Alfred Marshall published the first of many editions of his *Principles of Economics*. That volume pulled together the main themes of both the classical economists and the utilitarians into what is now called "neoclassical economics." While there have been many changes over the years, the basic structure of the model that we build can be found in Marshall's work.

TABLE 3.1 Anna's Demand Schedule for Telephone Calls

PRICE (PER CALL)	QUANTITY DEMANDED (CALLS PER MONTH)
$ 0	30
.50	25
3.50	7
7.00	3
10.00	1
15.00	0

income, it might buy more of a good at every possible price. To be sure that we distinguish between changes in price and other changes that affect demand, we will throughout the rest of the text be very precise about terminology. Specifically:

> Changes in the price of a product affect the *quantity demanded* per period. Changes in any other factor, such as income or preferences, affect *demand.* Thus, we say that an increase in the price of Coca-Cola is likely to cause a decrease in the *quantity of Coca-Cola demanded.* However, we say that an increase in income is likely to cause an increase in the *demand* for most goods.

PRICE AND QUANTITY DEMANDED: THE LAW OF DEMAND

A **demand schedule** shows the quantities of a product that a household would be willing to buy at different prices. Table 3.1 presents a hypothetical demand schedule for Anna, a student who went off to college to study economics while her boyfriend went to art school. If telephone calls were free (a price of zero), Anna would call her boyfriend every day, or 30 times a month. At a price of $.50 per call, she makes 25 calls a month. When the price hits $3.50, she cuts back to seven calls a month. This same information presented graphically is called a **demand curve**. Anna's demand curve is presented in Figure 3.2.

demand schedule A table showing how much of a given product a household would be willing to buy at different prices.

demand curve A graph illustrating how much of a given product a household would be willing to buy at different prices.

You will note in Figure 3.2 that *quantity* (q) is measured along the horizontal axis, and *price* (P) is measured along the vertical axis. This is the convention we follow throughout this book.

Demand Curves Slope Downward The data in Table 3.1 show that at lower prices, Anna calls her boyfriend more frequently; at higher prices, she calls less frequently. There is thus a *negative, or inverse, relationship between quantity demanded and price.* When price

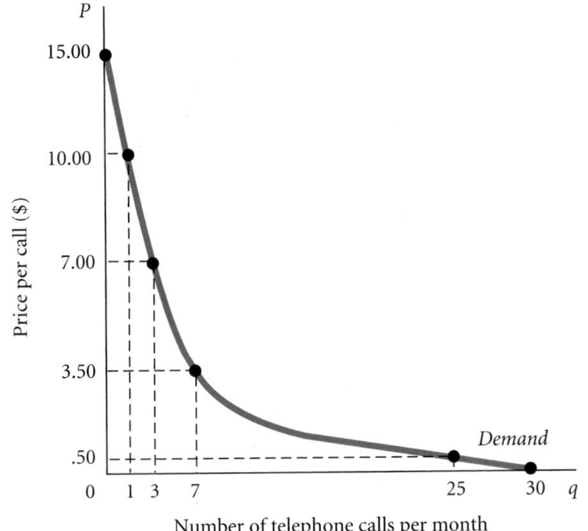

FIGURE 3.2 Anna's Demand Curve

The relationship between price (P) and quantity demanded (q) presented graphically is called a *demand curve.* Demand curves have a negative slope, indicating that lower prices cause quantity demanded to increase. Note that Anna's demand curve is blue; demand in product markets is determined by household choice.

law of demand The negative relationship between price and quantity demanded: As price rises, quantity demanded decreases. As price falls, quantity demanded increases.

rises, quantity demanded falls, and when price falls, quantity demanded rises. Thus demand curves always slope downward. This negative relationship between price and quantity demanded is often referred to as the **law of demand**, a term first used by economist Alfred Marshall in his 1890 textbook.

Some people are put off by the abstraction of demand curves. Of course, we do not actually draw our own demand curves for products. When we want to make a purchase, we usually face only a single price, and how much we would buy at other prices is irrelevant. However, demand curves help analysts understand the kind of behavior that households are *likely* to exhibit if they are actually faced with a higher or lower price. We know, for example, that if the price of a good rises enough, the quantity demanded must ultimately drop to zero. The demand curve is thus a tool that helps us explain economic behavior and predict reactions to possible price changes.

Marshall's definition of a social "law" captures the idea:

> The term "law" means nothing more than a general proposition or statement of tendencies, more or less certain, more or less definite . . . a *social law* is a statement of social tendencies; that is, that a certain course of action may be expected from the members of a social group under certain conditions.[2]

It seems reasonable to expect that consumers will demand more of a product at a lower price and less of it at a higher price. Households must divide their incomes over a wide range of goods and services. If I spend $4.50 for a pound of prime beef, I am sacrificing the other things that I might have bought with that $4.50. If the price of prime beef were to jump to $7 per pound, while chicken breasts remained at $1.99 (remember *ceteris paribus*—we are holding all else constant), I would have to give up more chicken and/or other items to buy that pound of beef. So I would probably eat more chicken and less beef. Anna calls her boyfriend three times when phone calls cost $7 each. A fourth call would mean sacrificing $7 worth of other purchases. At a price of $3.50, however, the opportunity cost of each call is lower, and she calls more frequently.

Another explanation for the fact that demand curves slope downward rests on the notion of *utility*. Economists use the concept of *utility* to mean happiness or satisfaction. Presumably we consume goods and services because they give us utility. As we consume more of a product within a given period of time, it is likely that each additional unit consumed will yield successively less satisfaction. The utility I gain from a second ice cream cone is likely to be less than the utility I gained from the first; the third is worth even less, and so forth. This *law of diminishing marginal utility* is an important concept in economics. If each successive unit of a good is worth less to me, I am not going to be willing to pay as much for it. It is thus reasonable to expect a downward slope in the demand curve for that good.

The idea of diminishing marginal utility also helps to explain Anna's behavior. The demand curve is a way of representing what she is willing to pay per phone call. At a price of $7, she calls her boyfriend three times per month. A fourth call, however, is worth less than the third—that is, the fourth call is worth less than $7 to her—so she stops at three. If the price were only $3.50, however, she would keep right on calling. Even at $3.50, she would stop at seven calls per month. This behavior reveals that the eighth call has less value to Anna than the seventh.

Thinking about the ways that people are affected by price changes also helps us see what is behind the law of demand. Consider this example: Luis lives and works in Mexico City. His elderly mother lives in Santiago, Chile. Last year, the airlines servicing South America got into a price war, and the price of flying between Mexico City and Santiago dropped from 20,000 pesos to 10,000 pesos. How might Luis's behavior change?

First, he is better off. Last year he flew home to Chile three times at a total cost of 60,000 pesos. This year he can fly to Chile the same number of times, buy exactly the same combination of other goods and services that he bought last year, and have 30,000 pesos left over. Because he is better off—his income can buy more—he may fly home more frequently. Second, the opportunity cost of flying home has changed. Before the price war, Luis had to sacrifice 20,000 pesos worth of other goods and services each time he flew to Chile. After the

---

[2]Alfred Marshall, *Principles of Economics*, 8th ed. (New York: Macmillan, 1948), p. 33. (The first edition was published in 1890.)

price war he must sacrifice only 10,000 pesos worth of other goods and services for each trip. The trade-off has changed. Both these effects are likely to lead to a higher quantity demanded in response to the lower price.

In sum:

> It is reasonable to expect quantity demanded to fall when price rises, *ceteris paribus*, and to expect quantity demanded to rise when price falls, *ceteris paribus*. Demand curves have a negative slope.

Other Properties of Demand Curves Two additional things are notable about Anna's demand curve. First, it intersects the *Y*-, or price, axis. This means that there is a price above which no calls will be made. In this case, Anna simply stops calling when the price reaches $15 per call.

> As long as households have limited incomes and wealth, all demand curves will intersect the price axis. For any commodity, there is always a price above which a household will not, or cannot, pay. Even if the good or service is very important, all households are ultimately constrained, or limited, by income and wealth.

Second, Anna's demand curve intersects the *X*-, or quantity, axis. Even at a zero price, there is a limit to the number of phone calls Anna will make. If telephone calls were free, she would call 30 times a month, but not more.

> That demand curves intersect the quantity axis is a matter of common sense. Demand in a given period of time is limited, if only by time, even at a zero price.

To summarize what we know about the shape of demand curves:

1. They have a negative slope. An increase in price is likely to lead to a decrease in quantity demanded, and a decrease in price is likely to lead to an increase in quantity demanded.
2. They intersect the quantity (*X*)-axis, a result of time limitations and diminishing marginal utility.
3. They intersect the price (*Y*)-axis, a result of limited incomes and wealth.

That is all we can say; it is not possible to generalize further. The actual shape of an individual household demand curve—whether it is steep or flat, whether it is bowed in or bowed out—depends on the unique tastes and preferences of the household and other factors. Some households may be very sensitive to price changes; other households may respond little to a change in price. In some cases, plentiful substitutes are available; in other cases they are not. Thus, to fully understand the shape and position of demand curves, we must turn to the other determinants of household demand.

OTHER DETERMINANTS OF HOUSEHOLD DEMAND

Of the many factors likely to influence a household's demand for a specific product, we have considered only the price of the product itself. Other determining factors include household income and wealth, the prices of other goods and services, tastes and preferences, and expectations.

Income and Wealth Before we proceed, we need to define two terms that are often confused, *income* and *wealth*. A household's **income** is the sum of all the wages, salaries, profits, interest payments, rents, and other forms of earnings received by the household *in a given period of time*. Income is thus a *flow* measure: We must specify a time period for it—income *per month* or *per year*. You can spend or consume more or less than your income in any given period. If you consume less than your income, you save. To consume more than your income in a period, you must either borrow or draw on savings accumulated from previous periods.

income The sum of all a household's wages, salaries, profits, interest payments, rents, and other forms of earnings in a given period of time. It is a flow measure.

wealth or **net worth** The total value of what a household owns minus what it owes. It is a stock measure.

Wealth is the total value of what a household owns less what it owes. Another word for wealth is **net worth**—the amount a household would have left if it sold off all its possessions and paid off all its debts. Wealth is a *stock* measure: It is measured at a given point in time. If, in a given period, you spend less than your income, you save; the amount that you save is added to your wealth. Saving is the flow that affects the stock of wealth. When you spend more than your income, you *dissave*—you reduce your wealth.

Households with higher incomes and higher accumulated savings or inherited wealth can afford to buy more things. In general, we would expect higher demand at higher levels of income/wealth and lower demand at lower levels of income/wealth. Goods for which demand goes up when income is higher and for which demand goes down when income is lower are called **normal goods**. Movie tickets, restaurant meals, telephone calls, and shirts are all normal goods.

normal goods Goods for which demand goes up when income is higher and for which demand goes down when income is lower.

However, generalization in economics can be hazardous. Sometimes demand for a good falls when household income rises. Consider, for example, the various qualities of meat available. When a household's income rises, it is likely to buy higher quality meats—its demand for filet mignon is likely to rise—but its demand for lower quality meats—chuck steak, for example—is likely to fall. Transportation is another example. At higher incomes, people can afford to fly. People who can afford to fly are less likely to take the bus long distances. Thus higher income may *reduce* the number of times someone takes a bus. Goods for which demand tends to fall when income rises are called **inferior goods**.

inferior goods Goods for which demand tends to fall when income rises.

Prices of Other Goods and Services No consumer decides in isolation on the amount of any one commodity to buy. Instead, each decision is part of a larger set of decisions that are made simultaneously. Households must apportion their incomes over many different goods and services. As a result, the price of any one good can and does affect the demand for other goods.

This is most obviously the case when goods are substitutes for one another. To return to our lonesome first-year student: If the price of a telephone call rises to $10, Anna will call her boyfriend only once a month (see Table 3.1). Of course, she can get in touch with him in other ways. Presumably she substitutes some other, less costly, form of communication, such as writing more letters or sending more e-mails.

When an *increase* in the price of one good causes demand for another good to *increase* (a positive relationship), we say that the goods are **substitutes**. A *fall* in the price of a good causes a *decline* in demand for its substitutes. Substitutes are goods that can serve as replacements for one another.

substitutes Goods that can serve as replacements for one another; when the price of one increases, demand for the other goes up.

perfect substitutes Identical products.

To be substitutes, two products do not need to be identical. Identical products are called **perfect substitutes**. Japanese cars are not identical to American cars. Nonetheless, all have four wheels, are capable of carrying people, and run on gasoline. Thus, significant changes in the price of one country's cars can be expected to influence demand for the other country's cars. Restaurant meals are substitutes for meals eaten at home, and flying from New York to Washington is a substitute for taking the train.

Often, two products "go together"—that is, they complement each other. Our lonesome letter writer, for example, will find her demand for stamps and stationery rising as she writes more letters, and her demand for Internet access rising as she sends more e-mails. Bacon and eggs are **complementary goods**, as are cars and gasoline, and cameras and film. When two goods are complements, a *decrease* in the price of one results in *increase* in demand for the other, and vice versa.

complements, complementary goods Goods that "go together"; a decrease in the price of one results in an increase in demand for the other, and vice versa.

Because any one good may have many potential substitutes and complements at the same time, a single price change may affect a household's demands for many goods simultaneously; the demand for some of these products may rise while the demand for others may fall. For example, consider the compact disc read-only memory (CD-ROM). Massive amounts of data can now be stored digitally on CDs that can be read by personal computers with a CD-ROM drive. When these drives first came on the market they were quite expensive, selling for several hundred dollars each. Now they are much less expensive, and most new computers have them built in. As a result, the demand for CD-ROM discs (complementary goods) is soaring. As more and more students adopt the CD technology and the price of CDs and CD hardware falls, fewer people will be buying things like encyclopedias printed on paper (substitute goods).

Tastes and Preferences Income, wealth, and prices of goods available are the three factors that determine the combinations of things that a household is *able* to buy. You know that you cannot afford to rent an apartment at $1,200 per month if your monthly income is only $400, but within these constraints, you are more or less free to choose what to buy. Your final choice depends on your individual tastes and preferences.

Changes in preferences can and do manifest themselves in market behavior. Twenty-five years ago the major big-city marathons drew only a few hundred runners. Now tens of thousands enter and run. The demand for running shoes, running suits, stopwatches, and other running items has greatly increased. For many years, people drank soda for refreshment. Today convenience stores are filled with a dizzying array of iced teas, fruit juices, natural beverages, and mineral waters.

Within the constraints of prices and incomes, preference shapes the demand curve, but it is difficult to generalize about tastes and preferences. First, they are volatile: Five years ago, more people smoked cigarettes and fewer people had computers. Second, they are idiosyncratic: Some people like to talk on the telephone, while others prefer the written word; some people prefer dogs, while others are crazy about cats; some people like chicken wings, while others prefer legs. The diversity of individual demands is almost infinite.

Perfect substitutes? On a hot day in the desert, one brand is as good as another.

Expectations What you decide to buy today certainly depends on today's prices and your current income and wealth. You also have expectations about what your position will be in the future. You may have expectations about future changes in prices, too, and these may affect your decisions today.

There are many examples of the ways expectations affect demand. When people buy a house or a car, they often must borrow part of the purchase price and repay it over a number of years. In deciding what kind of house or car to buy, they presumably must think about their income today, as well as what their income is likely to be in the future.

As another example, consider a male student in his final year of medical school living on a scholarship of $12,000. Compare him with another person earning $6 an hour at a full-time job, with no expectation of a significant change in income in the future. The two have virtually identical incomes because there are about 2,000 working hours in a year (40 hours per week × 50 work weeks per year). But even if they have the same tastes, the medical student is likely to demand different things, simply because he expects a major increase in income later on.

Increasingly, economic theory has come to recognize the importance of expectations. We will devote a good deal of time to discussing how expectations affect more than just demand. For the time being, however, it is important to understand that demand depends on more than just *current* incomes, prices, and tastes.

SHIFT OF DEMAND VERSUS MOVEMENT ALONG A DEMAND CURVE

Recall that a demand curve shows the relationship between quantity demanded and the price of a good. Such demand curves are derived while holding income, tastes, and other prices constant. If this condition of *ceteris paribus* were relaxed, we would have to derive an entirely new relationship between price and quantity.

Let us return once again to Anna (see Table 3.1 and Figure 3.2). Suppose that when we derived the demand schedule in Table 3.1, Anna had a part-time job that paid $300 per month. Now suppose that her parents inherit some money and begin sending her an additional $300 per month. Assuming that she keeps her job, Anna's income is now $ 600 per month.

With her higher income, Anna would probably call her boyfriend more frequently, regardless of the price of a call. Table 3.2 and Figure 3.3 present Anna's original-income schedule (D_0) and increased-income demand schedule (D_1). At $.50 per call, the frequency of her calls (the quantity she demands) increases from 25 to 33 calls per month; at $3.50 per call, frequency increases from 7 to 18 calls per month; at $10 per call, frequency increases from 1 to 7 calls per month. (Note in Figure 3.3 that even if calls are free, Anna's income matters; at zero price, her demand increases. With a higher income, she may visit her boyfriend more, for example, and more visits might mean more phone calls to organize and plan.)

The fact that demand *increased* when income increased implies that telephone calls are *normal goods* to Anna.

TABLE 3.2 Shift of Anna's Demand Schedule Due to Increase in Income

	SCHEDULE D_0	SCHEDULE D_1
Price (Per Call)	Quantity Demanded (Calls Per Month at an Income of \$300 Per Month)	Quantity Demanded (Calls Per Month at an Income of \$600 Per Month)
\$ 0	30	35
.50	25	33
3.50	7	18
7.00	3	12
10.00	1	7
15.00	0	2
20.00	0	0

The conditions that were in place at the time we drew the original demand curve have now changed. In other words, a factor that affects Anna's demand for telephone calls (in this case, her income) has changed, and there is now a new relationship between price and quantity demanded. Such a change is referred to as a **shift of the demand curve.**

shift of a demand curve The change that takes place in a demand curve corresponding to a new relationship between quantity demanded of a good and price of that good. The shift is brought about by a change in the original conditions.

It is very important to distinguish between a change in quantity demanded—that is, some movement *along* a demand curve—and a shift of demand. Demand schedules and demand curves show the relationship between the price of a good or service and the quantity demanded per period, *ceteris paribus.* If price changes, quantity demanded will change—this is a **movement along the demand curve**. When any of the *other* factors that influence demand change, however, a new relationship between price and quantity demanded is established—this is a *shift of the demand curve.* The result, then, is a *new* demand curve. Changes in income, preferences, or prices of other goods cause the demand curve to shift:

movement along a demand curve The change in quantity demanded brought about by a change in price.

Change in price of a good or service
leads to
→ Change in *quantity demanded* (**movement along the demand curve**).

Change in income, preferences, or prices of other goods or services
leads to
→ Change in *demand* (**shift of the demand curve**).

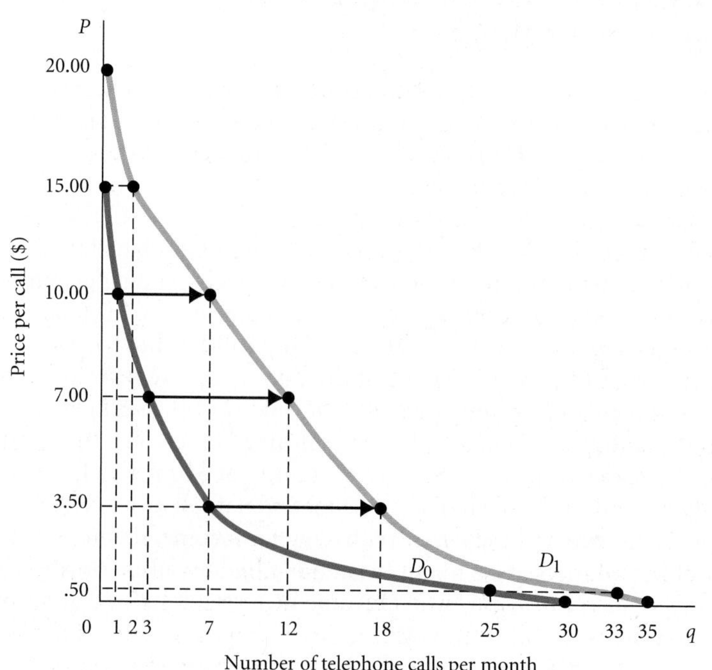

FIGURE 3.3 Shift of a Demand Curve Following a Rise in Income

When the price of a good changes, we move *along* the demand curve for that good. When any other factor that influences demand changes (income, tastes, etc.), the relationship between price and quantity is different; there is a *shift* of the demand curve, in this case from D_0 to D_1. Telephone calls are normal goods.

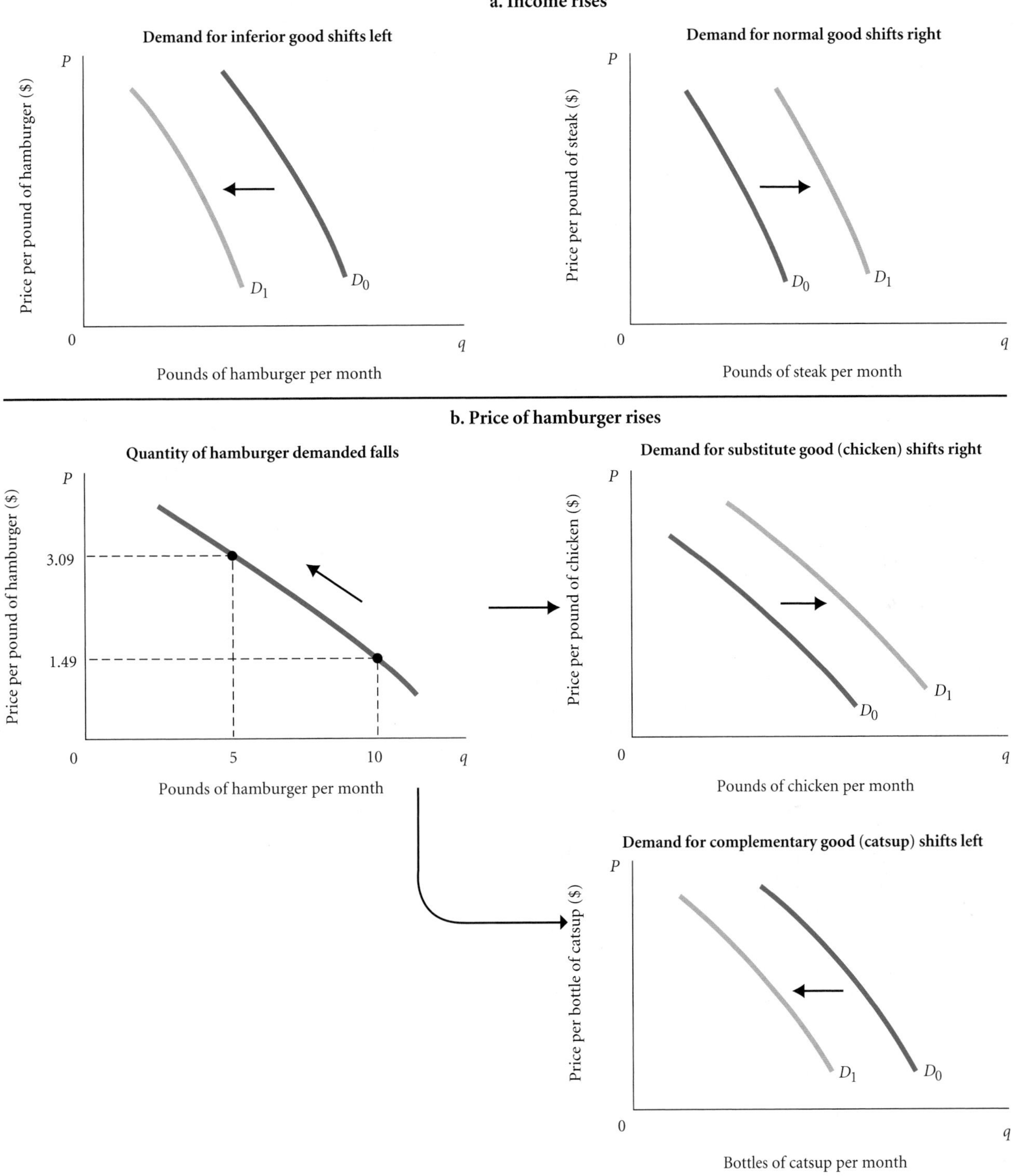

FIGURE 3.4 Shifts versus Movement along a Demand Curve

a. When income increases, the demand for inferior goods *shifts to the left* and the demand for normal goods *shifts to the right*. **b**. If the price of hamburger rises, the quantity of hamburger demanded declines—this is a movement along the demand curve. The same price rise for hamburger would shift the demand for chicken (a substitute for hamburger) to the right and the demand for catsup (a complement to hamburger) to the left.

Figure 3.4 illustrates the differences between movement along a demand curve and shifting demand curves. In Figure 3.4(a), an increase in household income causes demand for hamburger (an inferior good) to decline, or shift to the left from D_0 to D_1. (Because quantity is measured on the horizontal axis, a decrease means a *shift to the left*.) In contrast, demand for steak (a normal good) increases, or *shifts to the right*, when income rises.

In Figure 3.4(b), an increase in the price of hamburger from $1.49 to $3.09 a pound causes a household to buy fewer hamburgers each month. In other words, the higher price causes the *quantity demanded* to decline from 10 pounds to 5 pounds per month. This change represents a movement *along* the demand curve for hamburger. In place of hamburger, the household buys more chicken. The household's demand for chicken (a substitute for hamburger) rises—the demand curve shifts to the right. At the same time, the demand for catsup (a good that complements hamburger) declines—its demand curve shifts to the left.

FROM HOUSEHOLD DEMAND TO MARKET DEMAND

market demand The sum of all the quantities of a good or service demanded per period by all the households buying in the market for that good or service.

Market demand is simply the sum of all the quantities of a good or service demanded per period by all the households buying in the market for that good or service. Figure 3.5 shows the derivation of a market demand curve from three individual demand curves. (Although this market demand curve is derived from the behavior of only three people, most markets have thousands or even millions of demanders.) As the table in Figure 3.5 shows, when the price of a pound of coffee is $3.50, both A and C would purchase 4 pounds per month, while B would buy none. At that price, presumably, B drinks tea. Market demand at $3.50 would thus be a total of 4 + 4 or 8 pounds. At a price of $1.50 per pound, however, A would purchase 8 pounds per month; B, 3 pounds; and C, 9 pounds. Thus, at $1.50 per pound, market demand would be 8 + 3 + 9, or 20 pounds of coffee per month.

The total quantity demanded in the marketplace at a given price is simply the sum of all the quantities demanded by all the individual households shopping in the market *at that price.* A market demand curve shows the total amount of a product that would be sold at each price if households could buy all they wanted at that price. As Figure 3.5 shows, the

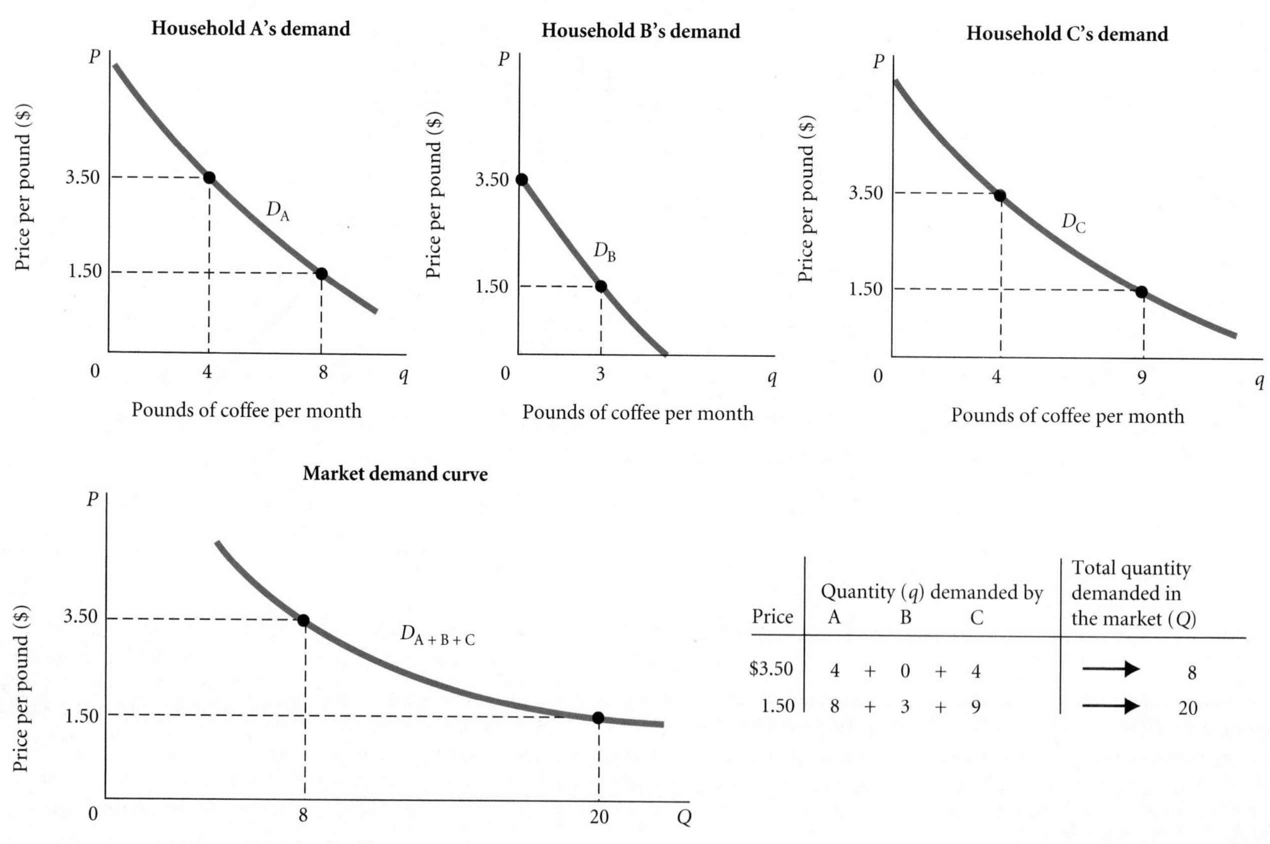

Price	Quantity (q) demanded by A	B	C		Total quantity demanded in the market (Q)
$3.50	4 +	0 +	4	→	8
1.50	8 +	3 +	9	→	20

FIGURE 3.5 Deriving Market Demand from Individual Demand Curves

Total demand in the marketplace is simply the sum of the demands of all the households shopping in a particular market. It is the sum of all the individual demand curves—that is, the sum of all the individual quantities demanded at each price.

market demand curve is the sum of all the individual demand curves—that is, the sum of all the individual quantities demanded at each price. The market demand curve thus takes its shape and position from the shapes, positions, and number of individual demand curves. If more people decide to shop in a market, more demand curves must be added, and the market demand curve will shift to the right. Market demand curves may also shift as a result of preference changes, income changes, or changes in the number of demanders.

As a general rule throughout this book, capital letters refer to the entire market and lowercase letters refer to individual households or firms. Thus, in Figure 3.5, *Q* refers to total quantity demanded in the market, while *q* refers to the quantity demanded by individual households.

SUPPLY IN PRODUCT/OUTPUT MARKETS

In addition to dealing with household demands for outputs, economic theory deals with the behavior of business firms, which supply in output markets and demand in input markets (see again Figure 3.1). Firms engage in production, and we assume that they do so for profit. Successful firms make profits because they are able to sell their products for more than it costs to produce them.

Supply decisions can thus be expected to depend on profit potential. Because **profit** is the simple difference between revenues and costs, supply is likely to react to changes in revenues and changes in production costs. The amount of revenue earned by a firm depends on the price of its product in the market and on how much it sells. Costs of production depend on many factors, the most important of which are (1) the kinds of inputs needed to produce the product, (2) the amount of each input required, and (3) the prices of inputs.

profit The difference between revenues and costs.

The supply decision is just one of several decisions that firms make to maximize profit. There are usually a number of ways to produce any given product. A golf course can be built by hundreds of workers with shovels and grass seed or by a few workers with heavy earth-moving equipment and sod blankets. Hamburgers can be individually fried by a short-order cook or grilled by the hundreds on a mechanized moving grill. Firms must choose the production technique most appropriate to their products and projected levels of production. The best method of production is the one that minimizes cost, thus maximizing profit.

Which production technique is best, in turn, depends on the prices of inputs. Where labor is cheap and machinery is expensive and difficult to transport, firms are likely to choose production techniques that use a great deal of labor. Where machines or resources to produce machines are readily available and labor is scarce or expensive, they are likely to choose more capital-intensive methods. Obviously, the technique ultimately chosen determines input requirements. Thus, by choosing an output supply target and the most appropriate technology, firms determine which inputs to demand.

With the caution that no decision exists in a vacuum, let us begin our examination of firm behavior by focusing on the output supply decision and the relationship between quantity supplied and output price, *ceteris paribus.*

PRICE AND QUANTITY SUPPLIED: THE LAW OF SUPPLY

Quantity supplied is the amount of a particular product that a firm would be willing and able to offer for sale at a particular price during a given time period. A **supply schedule** shows how much of a product a firm will sell at alternative prices. Table 3.3 itemizes the quantities of soybeans that an individual farmer such as Clarence Brown might sell at various prices. If the market paid $1.50 or less a bushel for soybeans, Brown would not supply any soybeans. For one thing, it costs more than $1.50 to produce a bushel of soybeans; for another, Brown can use his land more profitably to produce something else. At $1.75 per bushel, however, at least some soybean production takes place on Brown's farm, and a price increase from $1.75 to $2.25 per bushel causes the quantity supplied by Brown to increase from 10,000 to 20,000 bushels per year. The higher price may justify shifting land from wheat to soybean production or putting previously fallow land into soybeans, or it may lead to more intensive farming of land already in soybeans, using expensive fertilizer or equipment that was not cost-justified at the lower price.

quantity supplied The amount of a particular product that a firm would be willing and able to offer for sale at a particular price during a given time period.

supply schedule A table showing how much of a product firms will sell at different prices.

TABLE 3.3 Clarence Brown's Supply Schedule for Soybeans

PRICE (PER BUSHEL)	QUANTITY SUPPLIED (BUSHELS PER YEAR)
$1.50	0
1.75	10,000
2.25	20,000
3.00	30,000
4.00	45,000
5.00	45,000

Generalizing from Farmer Brown's experience, we can reasonably expect an increase in market price, *ceteris paribus*, to lead to an increase in quantity supplied. In other words, there is a positive relationship between the quantity of a good supplied and price. This statement sums up the **law of supply**: An increase in market price will lead to an increase in quantity supplied, and a decrease in market price will lead to a decrease in quantity supplied.

law of supply The positive relationship between price and quantity of a good supplied: An increase in market price will lead to an increase in quantity supplied, and a decrease in market price will lead to a decrease in quantity supplied.

supply curve A graph illustrating how much of a product a firm will sell at different prices.

The information in a supply schedule may be presented graphically in a **supply curve.** Supply curves slope upward. The upward, or positive, slope of Brown's curve in Figure 3.6 reflects this positive relationship between price and quantity supplied.

Note in Brown's supply schedule, however, that when price rises from $4 to $5, quantity supplied no longer increases. Often an individual firm's ability to respond to an increase in price is constrained by its existing scale of operations, or capacity, in the short run. For example, Brown's ability to produce more soybeans depends on the size of his farm, the fertility of his soil, and the types of equipment he has. The fact that output stays constant at 45,000 bushels per year suggests that he is running up against the limits imposed by the size of his farm, the quality of his soil, and his existing technology.

In the longer run, however, Brown may acquire more land, or technology may change, allowing for more soybean production. The terms *short run* and *long run* have very precise meanings in economics; we will discuss them in detail later. Here it is important only to understand that time plays a critical role in supply decisions. When prices change, firms' immediate response may be different from what they are able to do after a month or a year. Short-run and long-run supply curves are often different.

Companion Website Plus

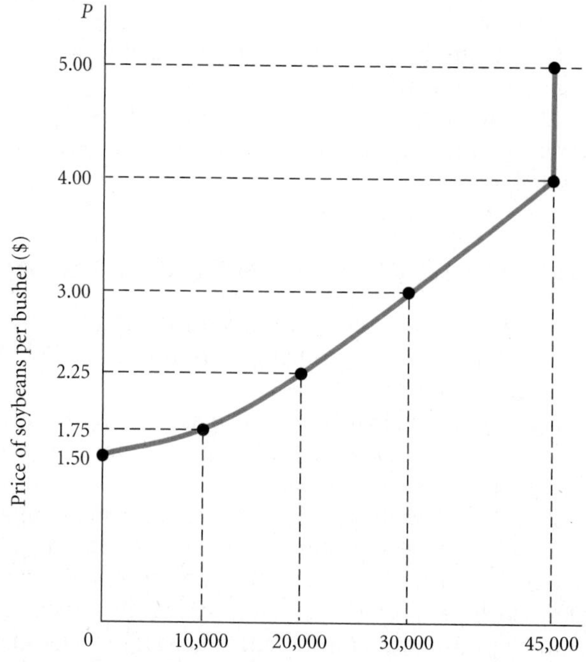

FIGURE 3.6 Clarence Brown's Individual Supply Curve

A producer will supply more when the price of output is higher. The slope of a supply curve is positive. Note that the supply curve is red: Supply is determined by choices made by firms.

OTHER DETERMINANTS OF SUPPLY

Of the factors we have listed that are likely to affect the quantity of output supplied by a given firm, we have thus far discussed only the price of output. Other factors that affect supply include the cost of producing the product and the prices of related products.

The Cost of Production Regardless of the price that a firm can command for its product, revenue must exceed the cost of producing the output for the firm to make a profit. Thus, the supply decision is likely to change in response to changes in the cost of production. Cost of production depends on a number of factors, including the available technologies and the prices and quantities of the inputs needed by the firm (labor, land, capital, energy, etc.).

Technological change can have an enormous impact on the cost of production over time. Consider agriculture. The introduction of fertilizers, the development of complex farm machinery, and the use of bioengineering to increase the yield of individual crops have all powerfully affected the cost of producing agricultural products. Farm productivity in the United States has been increasing dramatically for decades. Yield per acre of corn production has increased fivefold since the late 1930s, and the amount of labor required to produce 100 bushels of corn has fallen from 108 hours in the late 1930s, to 20 hours in the late 1950s, to less than 3 hours today.

When a technological advance lowers the cost of production, output is likely to increase. When yield per acre increases, individual farmers can and do produce more. The output of the Ford Motor Company increased substantially after the introduction of assembly line techniques. The production of electronic calculators, and later personal computers, boomed with the development of inexpensive techniques to produce microprocessors.

Cost of production is also affected directly by the price of the factors of production. In the winter of 2003, the world price of oil rose from around $24 a barrel to over $35. As a result, cab drivers faced higher gasoline prices, airlines faced higher fuel costs, and manufacturing firms faced higher heating bills. The result: Cab drivers probably spent less time driving around looking for customers, airlines cut a few low-profit routes, and some manufacturing plants stopped running extra shifts. The moral of this story: Increases in input prices raise costs of production and are likely to reduce supply.

The Prices of Related Products Firms often react to changes in the prices of related products. For example, if land can be used for either corn or soybean production, an increase in soybean prices may cause individual farmers to shift acreage out of corn production and into soybeans. Thus, an increase in soybean prices actually affects the amount of corn supplied.

Similarly, if beef prices rise, producers may respond by raising more cattle. However, leather comes from cowhide. Thus, an increase in beef prices may actually increase the supply of leather.

To summarize:

Assuming that its objective is to maximize profits, a firm's decision about what quantity of output, or product, to supply depends on

1. The price of the good or service
2. The cost of producing the product, which in turn depends on
   - The price of required inputs (labor, capital, and land)
   - The technologies that can be used to produce the product
3. The prices of related products

A soybean farm is a producer that supplies soybeans to the market.

SHIFT OF SUPPLY VERSUS MOVEMENT ALONG A SUPPLY CURVE

A supply curve shows the relationship between the quantity of a good or service supplied by a firm and the price that good or service brings in the market. Higher prices are likely to lead to an increase in quantity supplied, *ceteris paribus*. Remember: The supply curve is derived holding everything constant except price. When the price of a product changes *ceteris paribus*, a change in the quantity supplied follows—that is, a **movement along the**

TABLE 3.4 Shift of Supply Schedule for Soybeans Following Development of a New Disease-Resistant Seed Strain

	SCHEDULE S_0	SCHEDULE S_1
Price (Per Bushel)	Quantity Supplied (Bushels Per Year Using Old Seed)	Quantity Supplied (Bushels Per Year Using New Seed)
$1.50	0	5,000
1.75	10,000	23,000
2.25	20,000	33,000
3.00	30,000	40,000
4.00	45,000	54,000
5.00	45,000	54,000

movement along a supply curve The change in quantity supplied brought about by a change in price.

shift of a supply curve The change that takes place in a supply curve corresponding to a new relationship between quanity supplied of a good and the price of that good. The shift is brought about by a change in the original conditions.

supply curve takes place. As you have seen, supply decisions are also influenced by factors other than price. New relationships between price and quantity supplied come about when factors other than price change, and the result is a **shift of the supply curve**. When factors other than price cause supply curves to shift, we say that there has been a *change in supply*.

Recall that the cost of production depends on the price of inputs and the technologies of production available. Now suppose that a major breakthrough in the production of soybeans has occurred: Genetic engineering has produced a superstrain of disease- and pest-resistant seed. Such a technological change would enable individual farmers to supply more soybeans at *any* market price. Table 3.4 and Figure 3.7 describe this change. At $3 a bushel, farmers would have produced 30,000 bushels from the old seed (schedule S_0 in Table 3.4); with the lower cost of production and higher yield resulting from the new seed, they produce 40,000 bushels (schedule S_1 in Table 3.4). At $1.75 per bushel, they would have produced 10,000 bushels from the old seed; but with the lower costs and higher yields, output rises to 23,000 bushels.

Increases in input prices may also cause supply curves to shift. If Farmer Brown faces higher fuel costs, for example, his supply curve will shift to the left—that is, he will produce less at any given market price. If Brown's soybean supply curve shifted far enough to the left, it would intersect the price axis at a higher point, meaning that it would take a higher market price to induce Brown to produce any soybeans at all.

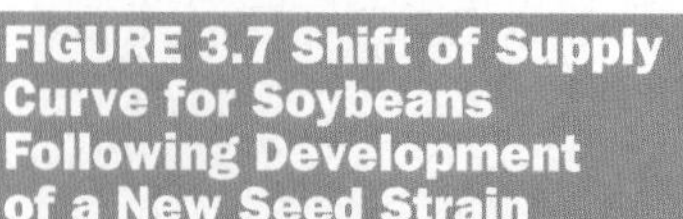

FIGURE 3.7 Shift of Supply Curve for Soybeans Following Development of a New Seed Strain

When the price of a product changes, we move *along* the supply curve for that product; the quantity supplied rises or falls. When any other factor affecting supply changes, the supply curve *shifts*.

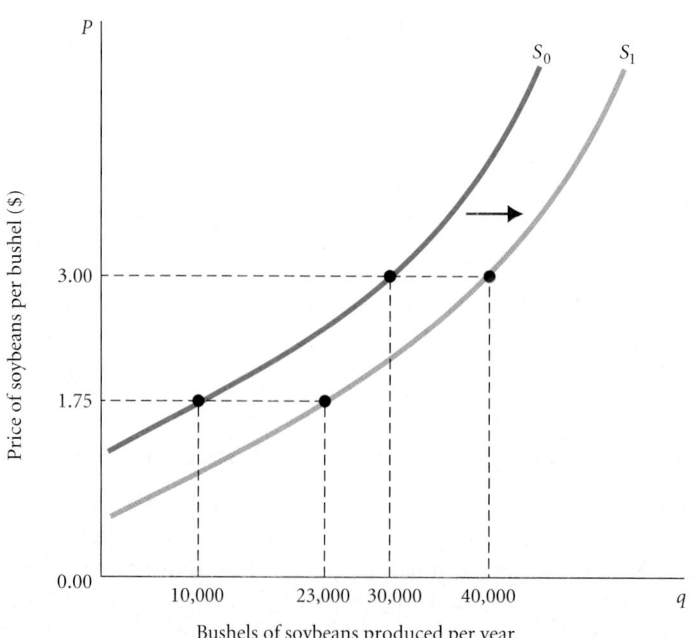

As with demand, it is very important to distinguish between *movements along* supply curves (changes in quantity supplied) and *shifts in* supply curves (changes in supply):

> Change in price of a good or service
> leads to
> → Change in *quantity supplied* (**movement along a supply curve**).
> Change in costs, input prices, technology, or prices of related goods and services
> leads to
> → Change in *supply* (**shift of a supply curve**).

FROM INDIVIDUAL SUPPLY TO MARKET SUPPLY

market supply The sum of all that is supplied each period by all producers of a single product.

Market supply is determined in the same fashion as market demand. It is simply the sum of all that is supplied each period by all producers of a single product. Figure 3.8 derives a market supply curve from the supply curves of three individual firms. (In a market with more firms, total market supply would be the sum of the amounts produced by each of the firms in that market.) As the table in Figure 3.8 shows, at a price of $3 farm A supplies 30,000 bushels of soybeans, farm B supplies 10,000 bushels, and farm C supplies 25,000 bushels. At this price, the total amount supplied in the market is 30,000 + 10,000 + 25,000, or 65,000

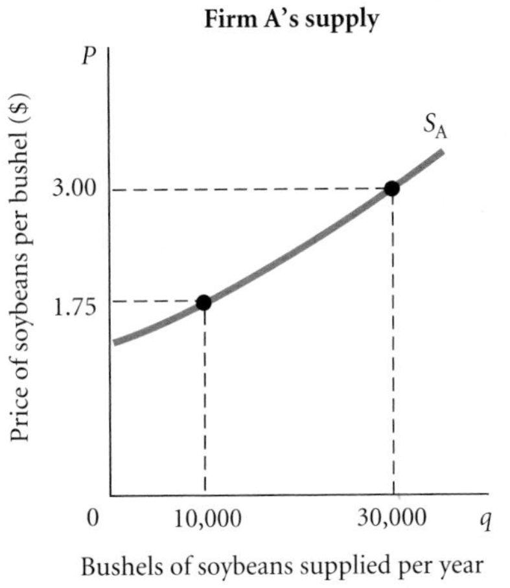

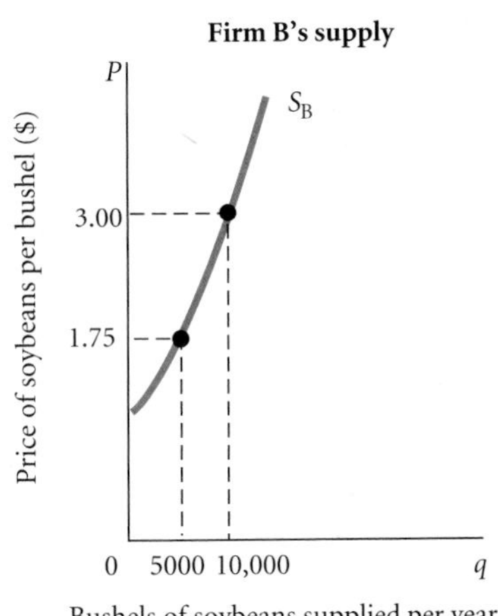

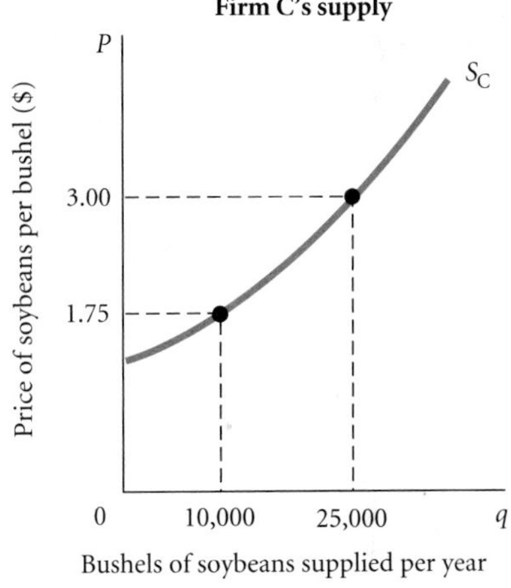

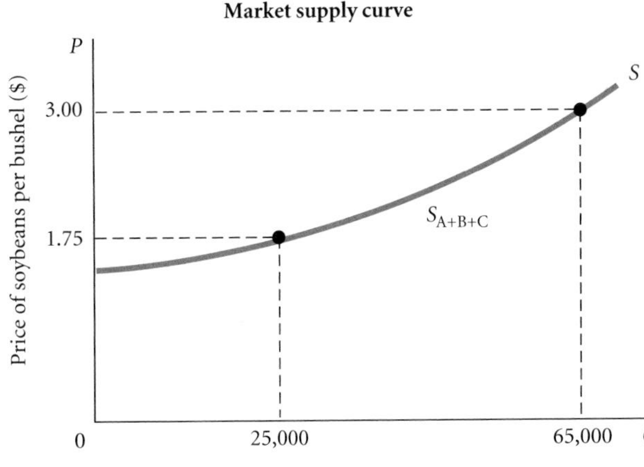

Price	Quantity (q) supplied by A	B	C		Total quantity supplied in the market (Q)
$3.00	30,000 +	10,000 +	25,000	→	65,000
1.75	10,000 +	5,000 +	10,000	→	25,000

FIGURE 3.8 Deriving Market Supply from Individual Firm Supply Curves

Total supply in the marketplace is the sum of all the amounts supplied by all the firms selling in the market. It is the sum of all the individual quantities supplied at each price.

bushels. At a price of $1.75, however, the total amount supplied is only 25,000 bushels (10,000 + 5,000 + 10,000). The market supply curve is thus the simple addition of the individual supply curves of all the firms in a particular market—that is, the sum of all the individual quantities supplied at each price.

The position and shape of the market supply curve depend on the positions and shapes of the individual firms' supply curves from which it is derived. They also depend on the number of firms that produce in that market. If firms that produce for a particular market are earning high profits, other firms may be tempted to go into that line of business. When the technology to produce computers for home use became available, literally hundreds of new firms got into the act. The popularity and profitability of professional football has three times led to the formation of new leagues. When new firms enter an industry, the supply curve shifts to the right. When firms go out of business, or "exit" the market, the supply curve shifts to the left.

MARKET EQUILIBRIUM

So far we have identified a number of factors that influence the amount that households demand and the amount that firms supply in product (output) markets. The discussion has emphasized the role of market price as a determinant both of quantity demanded and quantity supplied. We are now ready to see how supply and demand in the market interact to determine the final market price.

We have been very careful in our discussions thus far to separate household decisions about how much to demand from firm decisions about how much to supply. The operation of the market, however, clearly depends on the interaction between suppliers and demanders. At any moment, one of three conditions prevails in every market: (1) The quantity demanded exceeds the quantity supplied at the current price, a situation called *excess demand*; (2) the quantity supplied exceeds the quantity demanded at the current price, a situation called *excess supply*; or (3) the quantity supplied equals the quantity demanded at the current price, a situation called **equilibrium**. At equilibrium, no tendency for price to change exists.

equilibrium The condition that exists when quantity supplied and quantity demanded are equal. At equilibrium, there is no tendency for price to change.

EXCESS DEMAND

excess demand or shortage The condition that exists when quantity demanded exceeds quantity supplied at the current price.

Excess demand, or a **shortage**, exists when quantity demanded is greater than quantity supplied at the current price. Figure 3.9, which plots both a supply curve and a demand curve on the same graph, illustrates such a situation. As you can see, market demand at $1.75 per bushel (50,000 bushels) exceeds the amount that farmers are currently supplying (25,000 bushels).

When excess demand occurs in an unregulated market, there is a tendency for price to rise as demanders compete against each other for the limited supply. The adjustment mechanisms may differ, but the outcome is always the same. For example, consider the mechanism of an auction. In an auction, items are sold directly to the highest bidder. When the auction-

FIGURE 3.9 Excess Demand, or Shortage

At a price of $1.75 per bushel, quantity demanded exceeds quantity supplied. When excess *demand* arises, there is a tendency for price to rise. When quantity demanded equals quantity supplied, excess demand is eliminated and the market is in equilibrium. Here, the equilibrium price is $2.50, and the equilibrium quantity is 35,000 bushels.

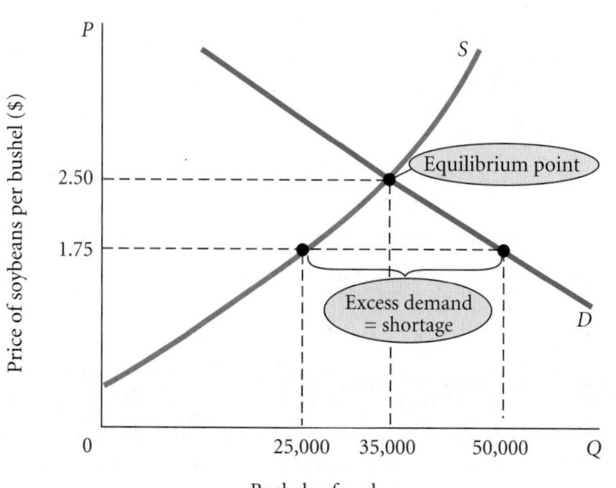

eer starts the bidding at a low price, many people bid for the item. At first there is a shortage: Quantity demanded exceeds quantity supplied. As would-be buyers offer higher and higher prices, bidders drop out, until the one who offers the most ends up with the item being auctioned. Price rises until quantity demanded and quantity supplied are equal.

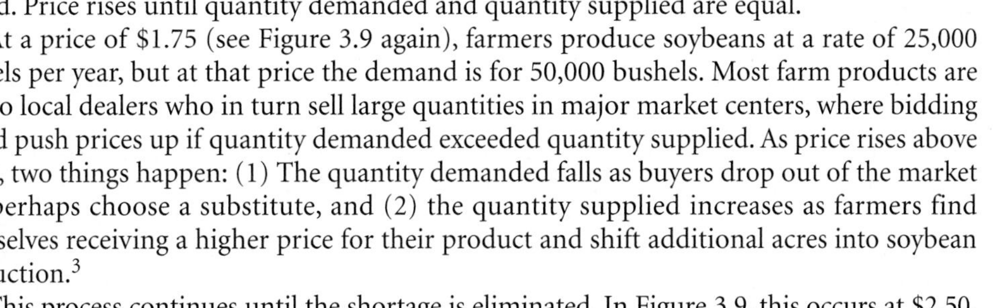

At a price of \$1.75 (see Figure 3.9 again), farmers produce soybeans at a rate of 25,000 bushels per year, but at that price the demand is for 50,000 bushels. Most farm products are sold to local dealers who in turn sell large quantities in major market centers, where bidding would push prices up if quantity demanded exceeded quantity supplied. As price rises above \$1.75, two things happen: (1) The quantity demanded falls as buyers drop out of the market and perhaps choose a substitute, and (2) the quantity supplied increases as farmers find themselves receiving a higher price for their product and shift additional acres into soybean production.[3]

Bidding at an auction starts with excess demand and ends up with quantity demanded and quantity supplied equal.

This process continues until the shortage is eliminated. In Figure 3.9, this occurs at \$2.50, where quantity demanded has fallen from 50,000 to 35,000 bushels per year and quantity supplied has increased from 25,000 to 35,000 bushels per year. When quantity demanded and quantity supplied are equal and there is no further bidding, the process has achieved an equilibrium, a situation in which *there is no natural tendency for further adjustment.* Graphically, the point of equilibrium is the point at which the supply curve and the demand curve intersect.

Increasingly, items are auctioned over the Internet. Companies like eBay connect buyers and sellers of everything from automobiles to wine and from computers to airline tickets. Auctions are occurring simultaneously with participants located across the globe. The principles through which prices are determined in these auctions are the same: When excess demand exists, prices rise.

While the principles are the same, the process through which excess demand leads to higher prices is different in different markets. Consider the market for houses in the hypothetical town of Boomville with a population of 25,000 people, most of whom live in single-family homes. Normally about 75 homes are sold in the Boomville market each year. However, last year a major business opened a plant in town, creating 1,500 new jobs that pay good wages. This attracted new residents to the area, and real estate agents now have more buyers than there are properties for sale. Quantity demanded now exceeds quantity supplied. In other words, there is a shortage.

Auctions are not unheard of in the housing market, but they are rare. This market usually works more subtly, but the outcome is the same. Properties are sold very quickly and housing prices begin to rise. Boomville sellers soon learn that there are more buyers than usual, and they begin to hold out for higher offers. As prices for Boomville houses rise, quantity demanded eventually drops off and quantity supplied increases. Quantity supplied increases in at least two ways: (1) Encouraged by the high prices, builders begin constructing new houses, and (2) some people, attracted by the higher prices their homes will fetch, put their houses on the market. Discouraged by higher prices, however, some potential buyers (demanders) may begin to look for housing in neighboring towns and settle on commuting. Eventually, equilibrium will be reestablished, with the quantity of houses demanded just equal to the quantity of houses supplied.

Although the mechanics of price adjustment in the housing market differ from the mechanics of an auction, the outcome is exactly the same:

> When quantity demanded exceeds quantity supplied, price tends to rise. When the price in a market rises, quantity demanded falls and quantity supplied rises until an equilibrium is reached at which quantity demanded and quantity supplied are equal.

This process is called *price rationing.* When a shortage exists, some people will be satisfied and some will not. When the market operates without interference, price increases will

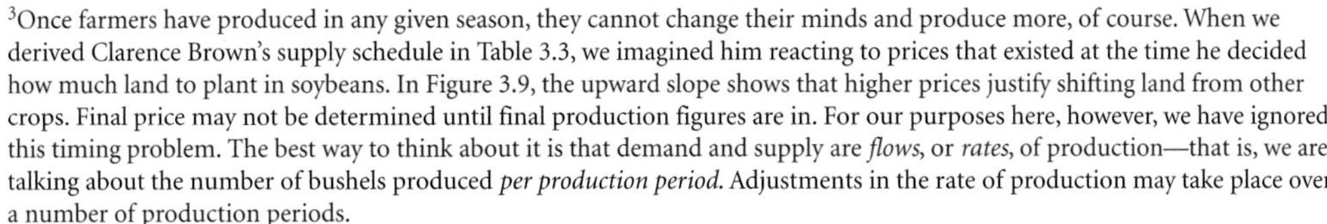

[3]Once farmers have produced in any given season, they cannot change their minds and produce more, of course. When we derived Clarence Brown's supply schedule in Table 3.3, we imagined him reacting to prices that existed at the time he decided how much land to plant in soybeans. In Figure 3.9, the upward slope shows that higher prices justify shifting land from other crops. Final price may not be determined until final production figures are in. For our purposes here, however, we have ignored this timing problem. The best way to think about it is that demand and supply are *flows,* or *rates,* of production—that is, we are talking about the number of bushels produced *per production period.* Adjustments in the rate of production may take place over a number of production periods.

distribute what is available to those who are willing and able to pay the most. As long as there is a way for buyers and sellers to interact, those who are willing to pay more will make that fact known somehow. (We discuss the nature of the price system as a rationing device in detail in Chapter 4.)

EXCESS SUPPLY

excess supply or **surplus** The condition that exists when quantity supplied exceeds quantity demanded at the current price.

Excess supply, or a **surplus**, exists when the quantity supplied exceeds the quantity demanded at the current price. As with a shortage, the mechanics of price adjustment in the face of a surplus can differ from market to market. For example, if automobile dealers find themselves with unsold cars in the fall when the new models are coming in, you can expect to see price cuts. Sometimes dealers offer discounts to encourage buyers; sometimes buyers themselves simply offer less than the price initially asked. In any event, products do no one any good sitting in dealers' lots or on warehouse shelves. The auction metaphor introduced earlier can also be applied here: If the initial asking price is too high, no one bids, and the auctioneer tries a lower price. It is almost always true, and 2002 was no exception, that certain items do not sell as well as anticipated during the Christmas holidays. After Christmas, most stores have big sales during which they lower the prices of overstocked items. Quantities supplied exceeded quantities demanded at the current prices, so stores cut prices.

Across the state from Boomville is Bustville, where last year a drug manufacturer shut down its operations and 1,500 people found themselves out of work. With no other prospects for work, many residents decided to pack up and move. They put their houses up for sale, but there were few buyers. The result was an excess supply, or surplus, of houses: The quantity of houses supplied exceeded the quantity demanded at the current prices.

As houses sit unsold on the market for months, sellers start to cut their asking prices. Potential buyers begin offering considerably less than sellers are asking. As prices fall, two things are likely to happen. First, the low housing prices may attract new buyers. People who might have bought in a neighboring town see that there are housing bargains to be had in Bustville, and quantity demanded rises in response to price decline. Second, some of those who put their houses on the market may be discouraged by the lower prices and decide to stay in Bustville. Developers are certainly not likely to be building new housing in town. Lower prices thus lead to a decline in quantity supplied as potential sellers pull their houses from the market. This was exactly the situation in New England and California in the early 1990s.

Figure 3.10 illustrates another excess supply/surplus situation. At a price of \$3 per bushel, suppose farmers are supplying soybeans at a rate of 40,000 bushels per year, but buyers are demanding only 20,000. With 20,000 (40,000 minus 20,000) bushels of soybeans going unsold, the market price falls. As price falls from \$3 to \$2.50, quantity supplied decreases from 40,000 bushels per year to 35,000. The lower price causes quantity demanded to rise from 20,000 to 35,000. At \$2.50, quantity demanded and quantity supplied are equal. For the data shown here, \$2.50 and 35,000 bushels are the equilibrium price and quantity.

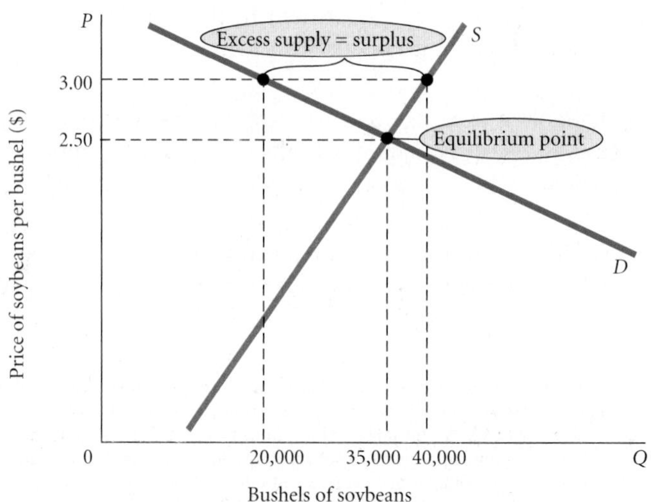

FIGURE 3.10 Excess Supply, or Surplus

At a price of \$3, quantity supplied exceeds quantity demanded by 20,000 bushels. This excess supply will cause price to fall.

Early in 1999, crude oil production worldwide exceeded the quantity demanded, and prices fell significantly as competing producer countries tried to maintain their share of world markets. Although the mechanism by which price is adjusted is different for automobiles, housing, soybeans, and crude oil, the outcome is the same:

When quantity supplied exceeds quantity demanded at the current price, the price tends to fall. When price falls, quantity supplied is likely to decrease and quantity demanded is likely to increase until an equilibrium price is reached where quantity supplied and quantity demanded are equal.

CHANGES IN EQUILIBRIUM

When supply and demand curves shift, the equilibrium price and quantity change. The following example will help to illustrate this point.

South America is a major producer of coffee beans. A cold snap there can reduce the coffee harvest enough to affect the world price of coffee beans. In the mid-1990s, a major freeze hit Brazil and Colombia and drove up the price of coffee on world markets to a record $2.40 per pound.

Figure 3.11 illustrates how the freeze pushed up coffee prices. Initially, the market was in equilibrium at a price of $1.20. At that price, the quantity demanded was equal to quantity supplied (13.2 billion pounds). At a price of $1.20 and a quantity of 13.2 billion pounds, the demand curve (labeled *D*) intersected the initial supply curve (labeled S_0). (Remember that equilibrium exists when quantity demanded equals quantity supplied—the point at which the supply and demand curves intersect.)

The freeze caused a decrease in the supply of coffee beans. That is, it caused the supply curve to shift to the left. In Figure 3.11, the new supply curve (the supply curve that shows the relationship between price and quantity supplied after the freeze) is labeled S_1.

At the initial equilibrium price, $1.20, there is now a shortage of coffee. If the price were to remain at $1.20, quantity demanded would not change; it would remain at 13.2 billion pounds. However, at that price, quantity supplied would drop to 6.6 billion pounds. At a price of $1.20, quantity demanded is greater than quantity supplied.

When excess demand exists in a market, price can be expected to rise, and rise it did. As the figure shows, price rose to a new equilibrium at $2.40. At $2.40, quantity demanded is again equal to quantity supplied, this time at 9.9 billion pounds—the point at which the new supply curve (S_1) intersects the demand curve.

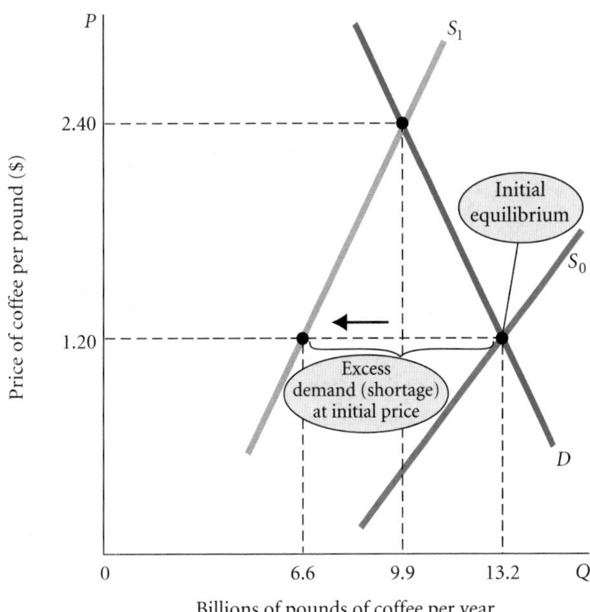

FIGURE 3.11 The Coffee Market: A Shift of Supply and Subsequent Price Adjustment

Before the freeze, the coffee market was in equilibrium at a price of $1.20. At that price, quantity demanded equaled quantity supplied. The freeze shifted the supply curve to the left (from S_0 to S_1), increasing equilibrium price to $2.40.

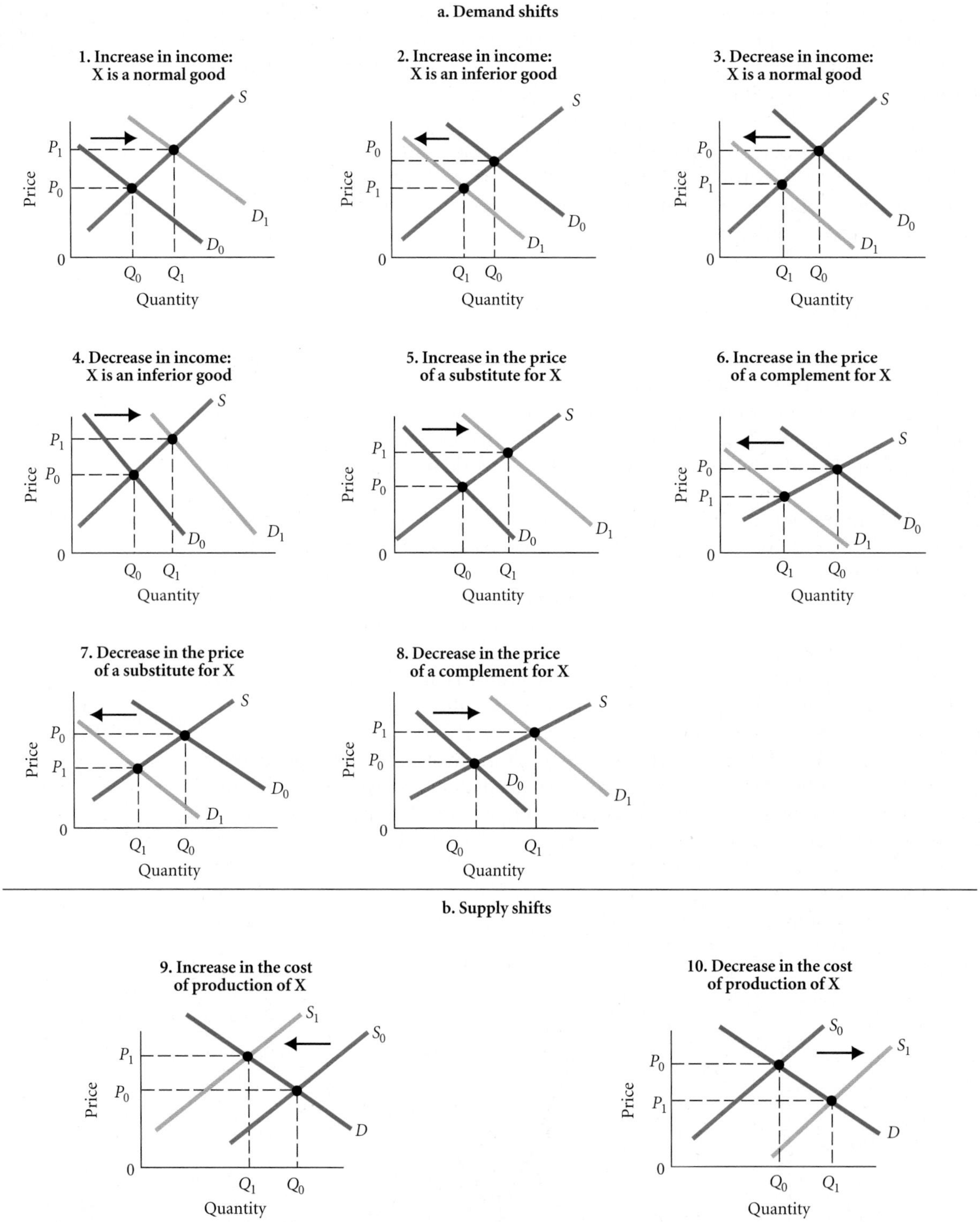

a. Demand shifts

1. Increase in income: X is a normal good

2. Increase in income: X is an inferior good

3. Decrease in income: X is a normal good

4. Decrease in income: X is an inferior good

5. Increase in the price of a substitute for X

6. Increase in the price of a complement for X

7. Decrease in the price of a substitute for X

8. Decrease in the price of a complement for X

b. Supply shifts

9. Increase in the cost of production of X

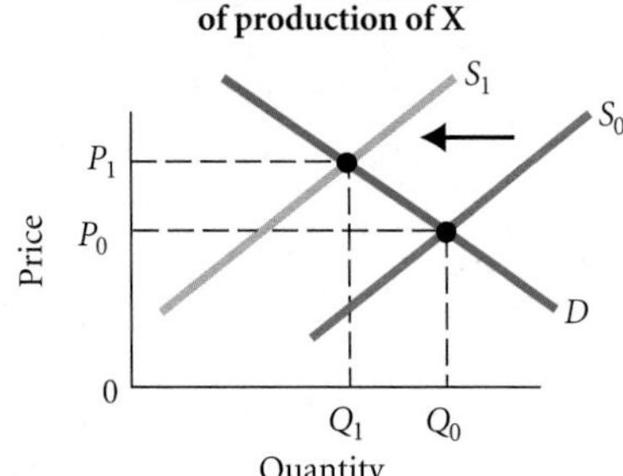

10. Decrease in the cost of production of X

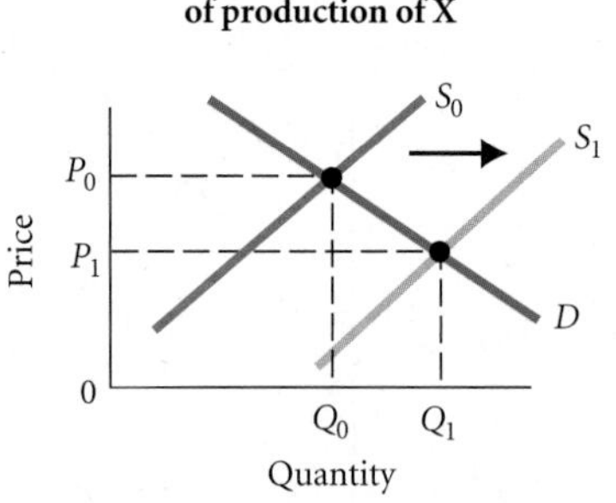

FIGURE 3.12 Examples of Supply and Demand Shifts for Product X

Notice that as the price of coffee rose from $1.20 to $2.40, two things happened. First, the quantity demanded declined (a movement along the demand curve) as people shifted to substitutes such as tea and hot cocoa. Second, the quantity supplied began to rise, but within the limits imposed by the damage from the freeze. (It might also be that some countries or areas with high costs of production, previously unprofitable, came into production and shipped to the world market at the higher price.) That is, the quantity supplied increased in response to the higher price *along* the new supply curve, which lies to the left of the old supply curve. The final result was a higher price ($2.40), a smaller quantity finally exchanged in the market (9.9 billion pounds), and coffee bought only by those willing to pay $2.40 per pound.

Since many market prices are driven by the interaction of millions of buyers and sellers, it is often hard to predict how they will change. While a series of events in the mid-1990s led to the leftward shift in supply, thus driving up the price of coffee, the opposite occurred between 1995 and 2003, when the world supply of coffee beans shifted sharply rightward. Brazil's crop was up 39 percent in 2003 alone. Brazil and the other large producing nations of Mexico, Vietnam, Indonesia, and Colombia combined to produce the largest crop ever in 2003. The result was that coffee prices fell to 40 cents per pound, the lowest price since July 1969. Very low coffee prices hurt the producing countries that rely heavily on coffee revenues.

Figure 3.12 summarizes the possible supply and demand shifts that have been discussed and the resulting changes in equilibrium price and quantity. Be sure to go through each graph carefully and ensure that you understand each.

DEMAND AND SUPPLY IN PRODUCT MARKETS: A REVIEW

As you continue your study of economics, you will discover that it is a discipline full of controversy and debate. There is, however, little disagreement about the basic way that the forces of supply and demand operate in free markets. If you hear that a freeze in Florida has destroyed a good portion of the citrus crop, you can bet that the price of oranges will rise.[4] If you read that the weather in the Midwest has been good and a record corn crop is expected, you can bet that corn prices will fall. When fishermen in Massachusetts go on strike and stop bringing in the daily catch, you can bet that the price of fish will go up. For additional examples of how the forces of supply and demand work, see the News Analysis feature titled "Supply and Demand in the News: 2003."

Here are some important points to remember about the mechanics of supply and demand in product markets:

1. A demand curve shows how much of a product a household would buy if it could buy all it wanted at the given price. A supply curve shows how much of a product a firm would supply if it could sell all it wanted at the given price.
2. Quantity demanded and quantity supplied are always per time period—that is, per day, per month, or per year.
3. The demand for a good is determined by price, household income and wealth, prices of other goods and services, tastes and preferences, and expectations.
4. The supply of a good is determined by price, costs of production, and prices of related products. Costs of production are determined by available technologies of production and input prices.
5. Be careful to distinguish between movements along supply and demand curves and shifts of these curves. When the price of a good changes, the quantity of that good demanded or supplied changes—that is, a movement occurs along the curve. When any other factor changes, the curves shift, or change position.
6. Market equilibirum exists only when quantity supplied equals quantity demanded at the current price.

LOOKING AHEAD: MARKETS AND THE ALLOCATION OF RESOURCES

You can already begin to see how markets answer the basic economic questions of what is produced, how it is produced, and who gets what is produced. A firm will produce what is profitable to produce. If it can sell a product at a price that is sufficient to leave a profit after

[4]In economics you have to think twice, however, even about a "safe" bet. If you bet that the price of frozen orange juice will rise after a freeze, you will lose your money. It turns out that much of the crop that is damaged by a freeze can be used, but for only one thing—to make frozen orange juice. Thus, a freeze actually *increases* the supply of frozen juice on the national market. Following the last two hard freezes in Florida, the price of oranges shot up, but the price of orange juice fell sharply.

News Analysis

Supply and Demand in the News: 2003

IN JANUARY 2003 THE *NEW YORK TIMES* described an increase in many commodity prices around the world including, cotton, crude oil, and steel. Price increases can almost always be traced to an increase in demand (shift of the demand curve to the right) or a decrease in supply (shift of the supply curve to the left) or some combination of the two (see diagrams below). While many hoped that the recent price increases were a sign that demand was up as the result of economic recovery and rising income, the answers seemed to be on the supply side: cotton fields were damaged by bad weather, reducing cotton production; a strike in Venezuela, the threat of war in Iraq, and OPEC production cuts reduced the supply of crude oil on world markets; and the supply of imported steel was reduced by tariffs imposed by President Bush in 2002.

From Steel to Copper and Zinc, Commodity Prices Surge—*New York Times*

The traditional interpretation for a sharp rise in commodity prices—and one occurred last year—is that the global economy is picking up speed and a rise in inflation lies ahead.

But it is not clear at all that either outcome is in store this year, despite a 15.9 percent climb in 2002 in industrial commodity prices from copper and zinc to oil and steel.

Overall commodity prices, including agricultural products and precious metals, were up 23 percent, led by a 57.3 percent surge in crude oil to $31.20 a barrel and a 24.8 percent jump in gold to $348.20 an ounce. Cotton prices, lifted by the damage to the fields in the South from a hurricane and a tropical storm in the fall and rain since, jumped 43.7 percent to 51.16 cents a pound last year.

Several economists said that prices of some industrial commodities were higher for reasons other than a rise in the producer demand that would normally be a precursor to an economic rebound, which could then be followed by a rise in inflation.

James E. Glassman, senior United States economist at J. P. Morgan, said that oil and steel prices, both of which had a big role in the jump in commodity prices, were pushed up more by changes in supply than demand. Cotton was also powered by damage to production, not demand.

Oil prices rose last year, following a sharp decline at the end of 2001, after members of the Organization of the Petroleum Exporting Countries reduced their production to stabilize the price. Since then, the threat of a war with Iraq has raised the possibility of Middle East supply disruptions. In addition, the strike that began in Venezuela late last year interrupted production there, pushing crude oil prices even higher.

A resolution of the strike in Venezuela and a quick and successful victory in a war with Iraq could end fears of oil production disruptions, pushing oil prices lower again.

Steel prices surged, in some cases as much as 60 percent, after the Bush administration imposed what it called safeguard tariffs of up to 30 percent in March on a wide range of steel products from Europe, Asia and Latin America. The intention was to protect against a flood of imports that could cripple American steel manufacturers.

The increase in the price of commodities "is not what we hoped it would be—a sign of the revival of the industrial economy," Mr. Glassman said. "This can't be an economic recovery story because the global economy is so weak, and central banks are still cutting interest rates."

Anirvan Banerji, research director for the Economic Cycle Research Institute, said that another factor that might be skewing the rise in commodity prices was the accelerating growth of China's manufacturing sector. "China, we know, is buying like crazy," he said, and is a significant cause of the surge in commodity prices. "It is a bit of a paradox," he added, "because at this point you have a global slowdown."

Source: Adapted from Fuerbringer, Jonathan, New York Times, January 2, 2003. Reprinted by permission.

a. An increase in demand

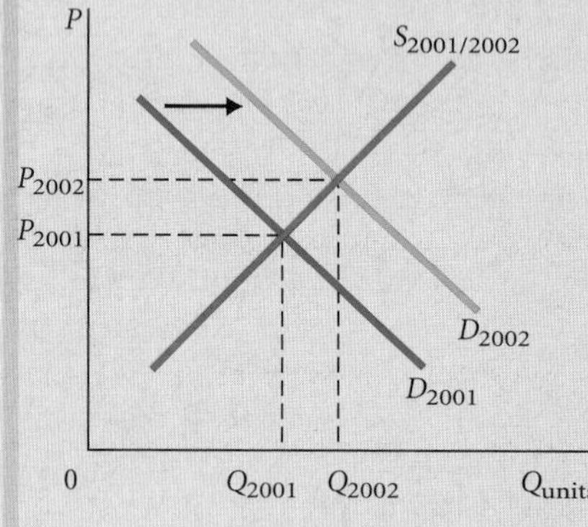

b. A decrease in supply

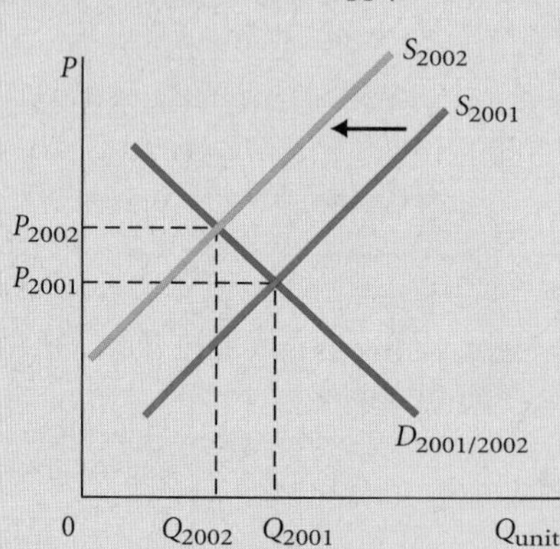

c. An increase in demand and a decrease in supply

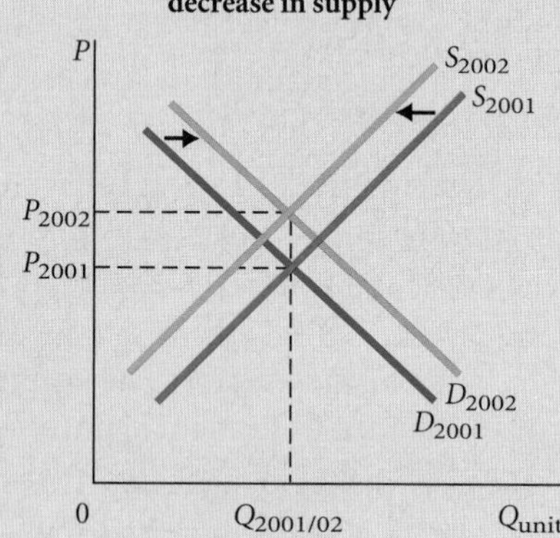

Visit www.prenhall.com/casefair for updated articles and exercises.

production costs are paid, it will in all likelihood produce that product. Resources will flow in the direction of profit opportunities.

- Demand curves reflect what people are willing and able to pay for products; they are influenced by incomes, wealth, preferences, prices of other goods, and expectations. Because product prices are determined by the interaction of supply and demand, prices reflect what people are willing to pay. If people's preferences or incomes change, resources will be allocated differently. Consider, for example, an increase in demand—a shift in the market demand curve. Beginning at an equilibrium, households simply begin buying more. At the equilibrium price, quantity demanded becomes greater than quantity supplied. When there is excess demand, prices will rise, and higher prices mean higher profits for firms in the industry. Higher profits, in turn, provide existing firms with an incentive to expand and new firms with an incentive to enter the industry. Thus, the decisions of independent private firms responding to prices and profit opportunities determine *what* will be produced. No central direction is necessary.

Adam Smith saw this self-regulating feature of markets more than 200 years ago:

> Every individual . . . by pursuing his own interest . . . promotes that of society. He is led . . . by an invisible hand to promote an end which was no part of his intention.[5]

The term Smith coined, the *invisible hand*, has passed into common parlance and is still used by economists to refer to the self-regulation of markets.

- Firms in business to make a profit have a good reason to choose the best available technology—lower costs mean higher profits. Thus, individual firms determine *how* to produce their products, again with no central direction.
- So far we have barely touched on the question of distribution—*who* gets what is produced? You can see part of the answer in the simple supply and demand diagrams. When a good is in short supply, price rises. As it does, those who are willing and able to continue buying do so; others stop buying.

The next chapter begins with a more detailed discussion of these topics. How, exactly, is the final allocation of resources (the mix of output and the distribution of output) determined in a market system?

[5]Adam Smith, *The Wealth of Nations*, Modern Library Edition (New York: Random House, 1937), p. 456 (1st ed., 1776).

SUMMARY

1. In societies with many people, production must satisfy wide-ranging tastes and preferences, and producers must therefore specialize.

FIRMS AND HOUSEHOLDS: THE BASIC DECISION-MAKING UNITS

2. A *firm* exists when a person or a group of people decides to produce a product or products by transforming resources, or *inputs*, into *outputs*—the products that are sold in the market. Firms are the primary producing units in a market economy. We assume firms make decisions to try to maximize profits.
3. *Households* are the primary consuming units in an economy. All households' incomes are subject to constraints.

INPUT MARKETS AND OUTPUT MARKETS: THE CIRCULAR FLOW

4. Households and firms interact in two basic kinds of markets: *product* or *output markets* and *input* or *factor markets*. Goods and services intended for use by households are exchanged in output markets. In output markets, competing firms supply and competing households demand. In input markets, competing firms demand and competing households supply.
5. Ultimately, firms choose the quantities and character of outputs produced, the types and quantities of inputs demanded, and the technologies used in production. Households choose the types and quantities of products demanded and the types and quantities of inputs supplied.

DEMAND IN PRODUCT/OUTPUT MARKETS

6. The quantity demanded of an individual product by an individual household depends on (1) price, (2) income, (3) wealth, (4) prices of other products, (5) tastes and preferences, and (6) expectations about the future.
7. Quantity demanded is the amount of a product that an individual household would buy in a given period if it could buy all it wanted at the current price.
8. A *demand schedule* shows the quantities of a product that a household would buy at different prices. The same information can be presented graphically in a *demand curve.*
9. The *law of demand* states that there is a negative relationship between price and quantity demanded: As price rises, quantity demanded decreases, and vice versa. Demand curves slope downward.
10. All demand curves eventually intersect the price axis because there is always a price above which a household cannot, or will not, pay. All demand curves also eventually intersect the quantity axis because demand for most goods is limited, if only by time, even at a zero price.
11. When an increase in income causes demand for a good to rise, that good is a *normal good.* When an increase in income causes demand for a good to fall, that good is an *inferior good.*
12. If a rise in the price of good X causes demand for good Y to increase, the goods are *substitutes.* If a rise in the price of X causes demand for Y to fall, the goods are *complements.*
13. Market demand is simply the sum of all the quantities of a good or service demanded per period by all the households buying in the market for that good or service. It is the sum of all the individual quantities demanded at each price.

SUPPLY IN PRODUCT/OUTPUT MARKETS

14. Quantity supplied by a firm depends on (1) the price of the good or service, (2) the cost of producing the product, which includes the prices of required inputs and the technologies that can be used to produce the product, and (3) the prices of related products.

15. Market supply is the sum of all that is supplied each period by all producers of a single product. It is the sum of all the individual quantities supplied at each price.

16. It is very important to distinguish between *movements* along demand and supply curves and *shifts* of demand and supply curves. The demand curve shows the relationship between price and quantity demanded. The supply curve shows the relationship between price and quantity supplied. A change in price is a movement along the curve. Changes in tastes, income, wealth, expectations, or prices of other goods and services cause demand curves to shift; changes in costs, input prices, technology, or prices of related goods and services cause supply curves to shift.

MARKET EQUILIBRIUM

17. When quantity demanded exceeds quantity supplied at the current price, *excess demand* (or a *shortage*) exists and the price tends to rise. When prices in a market rise, quantity demanded falls and quantity supplied rises until an equilibrium is reached at which quantity supplied and quantity demanded are equal. At *equilibrium*, there is no further tendency for price to change.

18. When quantity supplied exceeds quantity demanded at the current price, *excess supply* (or a *surplus*) exists and the price tends to fall. When price falls, quantity supplied decreases and quantity demanded increases until an equilibrium price is reached where quantity supplied and quantity demanded are equal.

REVIEW TERMS AND CONCEPTS

capital market, 45
complements, complementary goods, 50
demand curve, 47
demand schedule, 47
entrepreneur, 44
equilibrium, 60
excess demand or shortage, 60
excess supply or surplus, 62
factors of production, 45
firm, 44
households, 44
income, 49
inferior goods, 50
input or factor markets, 44
labor market, 45
land market, 45
law of demand, 48
law of supply, 56
market demand, 54
market supply, 59
movement along a demand curve, 52
movement along a supply curve, 57
normal goods, 50
perfect substitutes, 50
product or output markets, 44
profit, 55
quantity demanded, 46
quantity supplied, 55
shift of a demand curve, 52
shift of a supply curve, 58
substitutes, 50
supply curve, 56
supply schedule, 55
wealth or net worth, 50

PROBLEM SET

1. Illustrate the following with supply and demand curves:

a. Between 1999 and 2003, the demand for cell phones increased enormously. At the same time, suppliers like Nokia and Sony produced so many new cell phone units that the market price of a basic digital cell phone actually fell.

b. During the year 2002, unusually good weather conditions led to cranberry growers yielding an enormous crop; as a result the price of a 100-pound barrel of cranberries fell from $55 in 1999 to $22 in 2002.

c. During 2002 and 2003 the number of payroll jobs in the United States fell by about 1.5 million. As a result, there was a sharp drop in demand for office space in American cities. The vacancy rate in most U.S. cities increased and commercial rents fell.

d. Before economic reforms were implemented in the countries of Eastern Europe, regulation held the price of bread substantially below equilibrium. When reforms were implemented, prices were deregulated and the price of bread rose dramatically. As a result, the quantity of bread demanded fell and the quantity of bread supplied rose sharply.

e. The steel industry has been lobbying for high taxes on imported steel. Russia, Brazil, and Japan have been producing and selling steel on world markets at $22 per metric ton, well below what equilibrium would be in the United States with no imports. If no imported steel were permitted into the country, the equilibrium price would be $35 per metric ton. Show supply and demand curves for the United States assuming no imports; then show what the graph would look like if U.S. buyers could purchase all the steel that they wanted from world markets at $22; show the quantity of imported steel. In 2002 President George W. Bush imposed a 30 percent tariff on imported steel.

2. In August of 2002, the Seattle Mariners and the New York Yankees were both playoff contenders in the American League. On August 17, they played against each other at Safeco Field in Seattle. Earlier in the year on April 16, two lackluster teams, the

Detroit Tigers and the Tampa Bay Devil Rays, played in Comerica Park in Detroit. All tickets to the Seattle/Yankees game were sold out a month in advance, and many people who wanted to get tickets could not. The Detroit/Tampa Bay game attracted only 13,256 to a stadium that seats 40,000!

Safeco Field in Seattle holds 47,000. Comerica Park in Detroit holds 40,000. Assume for simplicity that tickets to all regular season games are priced at $25.

a. Draw supply and demand curves for the tickets to each of the two games. (Hint: Supply is fixed. It does not change with price.) Draw one graph for each game.

b. Is there a pricing policy that would have filled the ballpark for the Detroit Game? If the Tigers adopted such a strategy, would it bring in more or less revenue?

c. The price system was not allowed to work to ration the Seattle tickets. How do you know? How do you suppose the tickets were rationed?

3. During 2003, Orlando, Florida, was growing rapidly, with new jobs luring young people into the area. Despite increases in population and income growth that expanded demand for housing, the price of existing houses barely increased. Why? Illustrate your answer with supply and demand curves.

4. Do you agree or disagree with each of the following statements? Briefly explain your answers and illustrate with supply and demand curves.

a. The price of a good rises, causing the demand for another good to fall. The two goods are therefore substitutes.

b. A shift in supply causes the price of a good to fall. The shift must have been an increase in supply.

c. During 2003, incomes rose sharply for most Americans. This change would likely lead to an increase in the prices of both normal and inferior goods.

d. Two normal goods cannot be substitutes for each other.

e. If demand increases and supply increases at the same time, price will clearly rise.

f. The price of good A falls. This causes an increase in the price of good B. Goods A and B are therefore complements.

5. The U.S. government administers two programs that affect the market for cigarettes. Media campaigns and labeling requirements are aimed at making the public aware of the health dangers of cigarettes. At the same time, the Department of Agriculture maintains price supports for tobacco. Under this program, the supported price is above the market equilibrium price, and the government limits the amount of land that can be devoted to tobacco production. Are these two programs at odds with the goal of reducing cigarette consumption? As a part of your answer, illustrate graphically the effects of both policies on the market for cigarettes.

6. Housing prices in Boston and Los Angeles have been on a roller coaster ride. Illustrate each of the following situations with supply and demand curves:

a. In both cities an increase in income combined with expectations of a strong market shifted demand and caused prices to rise rapidly during the mid- to late 1980s.

b. By 1990, the construction industry boomed as more and more developers started new residential projects. Those new projects expanded the supply of housing just as demand was shifting as a result of falling incomes and expectations during the 1990–1991 recession.

c. In 2003, housing in higher income towns in some parts of the Midwest was experiencing price increases at the same time as housing in lower income towns was experiencing price decreases. In part this effect was due to "trade-up" buyers selling houses in lower income areas and buying houses in higher income areas.

7. The following two sets of statements contain common errors. Identify and explain each.

a. Demand increases, causing prices to rise. Higher prices cause demand to fall. Therefore, prices fall back to their original levels.

b. The supply of meat in Russia increases, causing meat prices to fall. Lower prices always mean that Russian households spend more on meat.

8. For each of the following, draw a diagram that illustrates the likely effect on the market for eggs. Indicate in each case the impact on equilibrium price and equilibrium quantity.

a. A surgeon general warns that high-cholesterol foods cause heart attacks.

b. The price of bacon, a complementary product, decreases.

c. An increase in the price of chicken feed occurs.

d. Caesar salads become trendy at dinner parties. (The dressing is made with raw eggs.)

e. A technological innovation reduces egg breakage during packing.

9. "An increase in demand causes an increase in price, but an increase in price causes a decrease in demand. Increases in demand, therefore, largely cancel themselves out." Comment.

***10.** Suppose the demand and supply curves for eggs in the United States are given by the following equations:

$$Q_d = 100 - 20P$$
$$Q_s = 10 + 40P$$

where Q_d = millions of dozens of eggs Americans would like to buy each year; Q_s = millions of dozens of eggs U.S. farms would like to sell each year; P = price per dozen eggs.

a. Fill in the following table:

PRICE (PER DOZEN)	QUANTITY DEMANDED (Q_d)	QUANTITY SUPPLIED (Q_s)
$ .50	______	______
$1.00	______	______
$1.50	______	______
$2.00	______	______
$2.50	______	______

b. Use the information in the table to find the equilibrium price and equilibrium quantity.

c. Graph the demand and supply curves, and identify the equilibrium price and quantity.

***11.** Housing policy analysts debate the best way to increase the number of housing units available to low-income households. One strategy—the demand-side strategy—is to provide people with housing "vouchers," paid for by the government, that can be used to rent housing supplied by the private market. Another—a supply-side strategy—is to have the government subsidize housing suppliers or to build public housing.

*Note: Problems marked with an asterisk are more challenging.

a. Illustrate supply- and demand-side strategies using supply and demand curves. Which results in higher rents?
b. Critics of housing vouchers (the demand-side strategy) argue that because the supply of housing to low-income households is limited and will not respond at all to higher rents, demand vouchers will serve only to drive up rents and make landlords better off. Illustrate their point with supply and demand curves.

*12. Suppose the market demand for pizza is given by $Q_d = 300 - 20P$ and the market supply for pizza is given by $Q_s = 20P - 100$, where P = price (per pizza).
a. Graph the supply and demand schedules for pizza using \$5 through \$15 as the value of P.
b. In equilibrium, how many pizzas would be sold and at what price?
c. What would happen if suppliers set the price of pizza at \$15? Explain the market adjustment process.
d. Suppose the price of hamburgers, a substitute for pizza, doubles. This leads to a doubling of the demand for pizza (at each price consumers demand twice as much pizza as before). Write the equation for the new market demand for pizza.
e. Find the new equilibrium price and quantity of pizza.

WWW

Vist www.prenhall.com/casefair for self-test quizzes, interactive graphing exercises, and new articles.

Demand and Supply Applications

4

CHAPTER OUTLINE

Every society has a system of institutions that determines what is produced, how it is produced, and who gets what is produced. In some societies, these decisions are made centrally, through planning agencies or by government directive. However, in every society many decisions are made in a *decentralized* way, through the operation of markets.

Markets exist in all societies, and Chapter 3 provided a bare-bones description of how markets operate. In this chapter, we continue our examination of demand, supply, and the price system.

THE PRICE SYSTEM: RATIONING AND ALLOCATING RESOURCES

The market system, also called the *price system*, performs two important and closely related functions. First, it provides an automatic mechanism for distributing scarce goods and services. That is, it serves as a **price rationing** device for allocating goods and services to consumers when the quantity demanded exceeds the quantity supplied. Second, the price system ultimately determines both the allocation of resources among producers and the final mix of outputs.

price rationing The process by which the market system allocates goods and services to consumers when quantity demanded exceeds quantity supplied.

PRICE RATIONING

Consider first the simple process by which the price system eliminates a shortage. Figure 4.1 shows hypothetical supply and demand curves for lobsters caught off the coast of New England.

Lobsters are considered a delicacy. Maine produces most of the lobster catch in the United States, and anyone who drives up the Maine coast cannot avoid the hundreds of restaurants selling lobster rolls, steamed lobster, and baked stuffed lobster.

As Figure 4.1 shows, the equilibrium price of live New England lobsters was $3.27 per pound in 2002. At this price, lobster boats brought in lobsters at a rate of 81 million pounds per year—an amount that was just enough to satisfy demand.

Market equilibrium existed at $3.27 per pound, because at that price quantity demanded was equal to quantity supplied. (Remember that equilibrium occurs at the point where the supply and demand curves intersect. In Figure 4.1, this occurs at point *C*.)

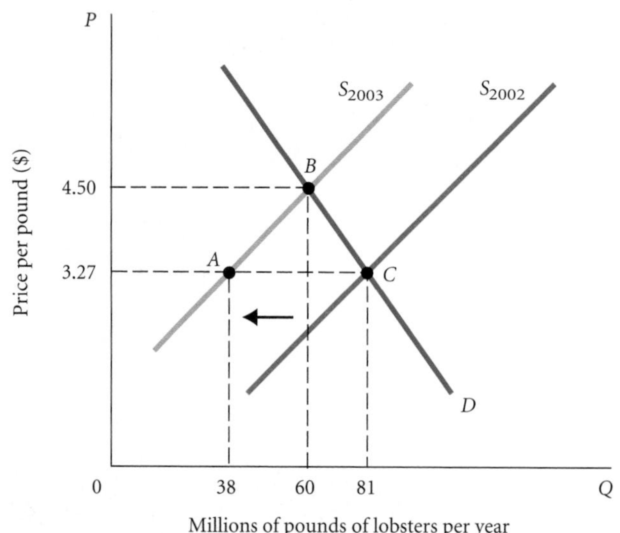

FIGURE 4.1 The Market for Lobsters

Suppose in 2003 that 15,000 square miles of lobstering waters off the coast of Maine are closed. The supply curve shifts to the left. Before the waters are closed, the lobster market is in equilibrium at the price of $3.27 and a quantity of 81 million pounds. The decreased supply of lobster leads to higher prices, and a new equilibrium is reached at $4.50 and 60 million pounds (point *B*).

Now suppose in 2003 that the waters off a section of the Maine coast become contaminated with a poisonous parasite. As a result, the Department of Agriculture is forced to close 15,000 square miles of the most productive lobstering areas. Even though many of the lobster boats shift their trapping activities to other waters, there is a sharp reduction in the quantity of lobster available for trapping. The supply curve shifts to the left, from S_{2002} to S_{2003}. This shift in the supply curve creates a situation of excess demand at $3.27. At that price, the quantity demanded is 81 million pounds and the quantity supplied is 38 million pounds. Quantity demanded exceeds quantity supplied by 43 million pounds.

The reduced supply causes the price of lobster to rise sharply. As the price rises, the available supply is "rationed." Those who are willing and able to pay the most get it.

You can see the market's price rationing function clearly in Figure 4.1. As the price rises from $3.27, the quantity demanded declines along the demand curve, moving from point *C* (81 million pounds) toward point *B* (60 million pounds). The higher prices mean that restaurants must charge much more for lobster rolls and stuffed lobsters. As a result, many people simply stop buying lobster or order it less frequently when they dine out. Some restaurants drop it from the menu entirely, and some shoppers at the fish counter turn to lobster substitutes such as swordfish and salmon.

As the price rises, lobster trappers (suppliers) also change their behavior. They stay out longer and put out more traps than they did when the price was $3.27 per pound. Quantity supplied increases from 38 million pounds to 60 million pounds. This increase in price brings about a movement along the 2003 supply curve from point *A* to point *B*.

Finally, a new equilibrium is established at a price of $4.50 per pound and a total output of 60 million pounds. The market has determined who gets the lobsters: *The lower total supply is rationed to those who are willing and able to pay the higher price.*

This idea of "willingness to pay" is central to the distribution of available supply, and willingness depends on both desire (preferences) and income/wealth. Willingness to pay does not necessarily mean that only the very rich will continue to buy lobsters when the price increases. Lower income people may continue to buy some lobster, but they will have to be willing to sacrifice more of other goods to do so.

When supply is fixed or something for sale is unique, its price is *demand determined*. Price is what the highest bidder is willing to pay. In 1990, the highest bidder was willing to pay $82.5 million for Van Gogh's (1853–1890) Dutch, *Portrait of Dr. Gachet*. Private Collection/Superstock.

In sum:

> The adjustment of price is the rationing mechanism in free markets. Price rationing means that whenever there is a need to ration a good—that is, when a shortage exists—in a free market, the price of the good will rise until quantity supplied equals quantity demanded—that is, until the market clears.

There is some price that will clear any market you can think of. Consider the market for a famous painting such as Van Gogh's *Portrait of Dr. Gachet*, illustrated in Figure 4.2. At a low

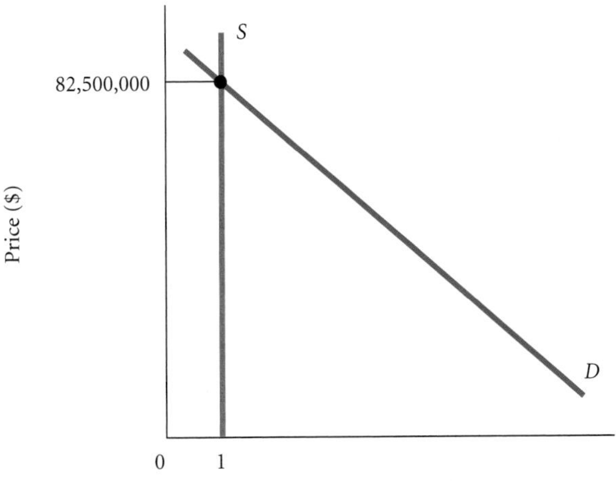

FIGURE 4.2 Market for a Rare Painting

There is some price that will clear any market, even if supply is strictly limited. In an auction for a unique painting, the price (bid) will rise to eliminate excess demand until there is only one bidder willing to purchase the single available painting.

price, there would be an enormous excess demand for such an important painting. The price would be bid up until there was only one remaining demander. Presumably, that price would be very high. In fact, Van Gogh's *Portrait of Dr. Gachet* sold for a record $82.5 million in 1990. If the product is in strictly scarce supply, as a single painting is, its price is said to be *demand determined.* That is, its price is determined solely and exclusively by the amount that the highest bidder or highest bidders are willing to pay.

One might interpret the statement that "there is some price that will clear any market" to mean "everything has its price," but that is not exactly what it means. Suppose you own a small silver bracelet that has been in your family for generations. It is quite possible that you would not sell it for *any* amount of money. Does this mean that the market is not working, or that quantity supplied and quantity demanded are not equal? Not at all. It means simply that *you* are the highest bidder. By turning down all bids, you must be willing to forgo what anybody offers for it.

CONSTRAINTS ON THE MARKET AND ALTERNATIVE RATIONING MECHANISMS

On occasion, both governments and private firms decide to use some mechanism other than the market system to ration an item for which there is excess demand at the current price. Policies designed to stop price rationing are commonly justified in a number of ways.

The rationale most often used is fairness. It is not "fair" to let landlords charge high rents, not fair for oil companies to run up the price of gasoline, not fair for insurance companies to charge enormous premiums, and so on. After all, the argument goes, we have no choice but to pay—housing and insurance are necessary, and one needs gasoline to get to work. While it is not precisely true that price rationing allocates goods and services solely on the basis of income and wealth, income and wealth do constrain our wants. Why should all the gasoline or all the tickets to the World Series go just to the rich?

Various schemes to keep price from rising to equilibrium are based on several perceptions of injustice, among them (1) that price-gouging is bad, (2) that income is unfairly distributed, and (3) that some items are necessities, and everyone should be able to buy them at a "reasonable" price. Regardless of the rationale, the following examples will make two things clear:

1. Attempts to bypass price rationing in the market and to use alternative rationing devices are much more difficult and costly than they would seem at first glance.
2. Very often, such attempts distribute costs and benefits among households in unintended ways.

Oil, Gasoline, and OPEC In 1973 and 1974, the Organization of Petroleum Exporting Countries (OPEC) imposed an embargo on shipments of crude oil to the United States.

What followed was a drastic reduction in the quantity of gasoline available at local gas pumps.

Had the market system been allowed to operate, refined gasoline prices would have increased dramatically until quantity supplied was equal to quantity demanded. However, the government decided that rationing gasoline to only those who were willing and able to pay the most was unfair, and Congress imposed a **price ceiling**, or maximum price, of 57¢ per gallon of leaded regular gasoline. That price ceiling was intended to keep gasoline "affordable," but it also perpetuated the shortage. At the restricted price, quantity demanded remained greater than quantity supplied, and the available gasoline had to be divided up somehow among all potential demanders.

price ceiling A maximum price that sellers may charge for a good, usually set by government.

You can see the effects of the price ceiling by looking carefully at Figure 4.3. If the price had been set by the interaction of supply and demand, it would have increased to approximately $1.50 per gallon. Instead, Congress made it illegal to sell gasoline for more than 57¢ per gallon. At that price, quantity demanded exceeded quantity supplied and a shortage existed. Because the price system was not allowed to function, an alternative rationing system had to be found to distribute the available supply of gasoline.

Several devices were tried. The most common of all nonprice rationing systems is **queuing**, a term that simply means waiting in line. During 1974, very long lines began to appear at gas stations, starting as early as 5 A.M. Under this system, gasoline went to those who were willing to pay the most, but the sacrifice was measured in hours and aggravation instead of dollars.[1]

queuing Waiting in line as a means of distributing goods and services; a nonprice rationing mechanism.

A second nonprice rationing device used during the gasoline crisis was that of **favored customers.** Many gas station owners decided not to sell gasoline to the general public at all but to reserve their scarce supplies for friends and favored customers. Not surprisingly, many customers tried to become "favored" by offering side payments to gas station owners.

favored customers Those who receive special treatment from dealers during situations of excess demand.

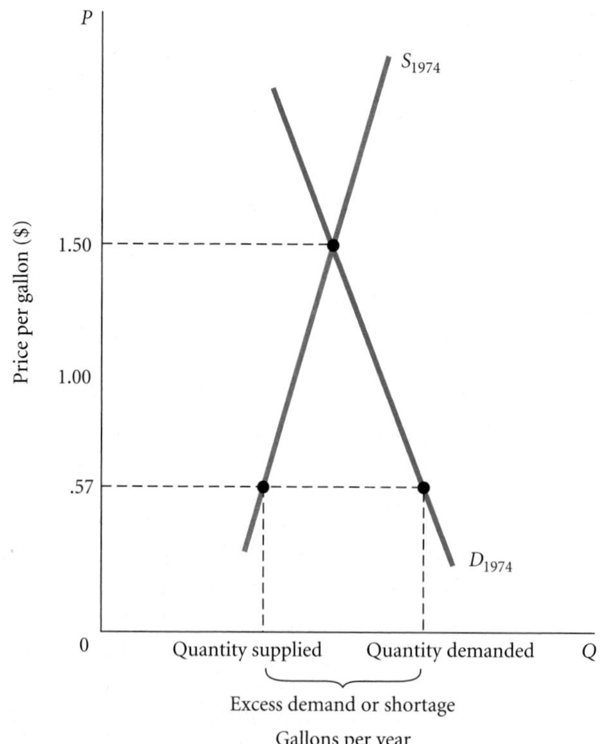

FIGURE 4.3 Excess Demand (Shortage) Created by a Price Ceiling

In 1974, a ceiling price of 57 cents per gallon of leaded regular gasoline was imposed. If the price had instead been set by the interaction of supply and demand, it would have increased to approximately $1.50 per gallon. At 57 cents per gallon, the quantity demanded exceeded the quantity supplied. Because the price system was not allowed to function, an alternative rationing system had to be found to distribute the available supply of gasoline.

[1]You can also show formally that the result is inefficient—that there is a resulting net loss of total value to society. First, there is the cost of waiting in line. Time has a value. With price rationing, no one has to wait in line and the value of that time is saved. Second, there may be additional lost value if the gasoline ends up in the hands of someone who places a lower value on it than someone else who gets no gas. Suppose, for example, that the market price of gasoline if unconstrained would rise to $2, but that the government has it fixed at $1. There will be long lines to get gas. Imagine that to motorist A, 10 gallons of gas is worth $35 but that she fails to get it because her time is too valuable to wait in line. To motorist B, 10 gallons is worth only $15, but his time is worth much less, so he gets the gas. In the end, A could pay B for the gas and both could be better off. If A pays B $30 for the gas, A is $5 better off and B is $15 better off. In addition, A does not have to wait in line. Thus, the allocation that results from nonprice rationing involves a net loss of value. Such losses are called deadweight losses.

News Analysis

Oil Prices in 2003 Hit $40

IN MARCH 2003, U.S. LIGHT CRUDE OIL hit $40 per barrel. The rise in price was driven by an extended cold blast in the U.S. Northeast, the world's largest heating oil market, which shifted the demand curve to the right, and by an 11-week-old strike in Venezuelan refineries, which shifted the supply curve to the left. The rumblings of war in Iraq and the Middle East threatened to further shift the supply curve to the left.

Clearly worried about the damage to the U.S. economy from higher oil prices, the federal government was prepared to use its own "strategic reserves" to keep supplies up and price down.

As with most commodities, oil prices are determined by world supply and demand.

Oil Prices Hit Highest Levels Since the Persian Gulf War

—New York Times

Oil prices surged yesterday to their highest levels since Iraq invaded Kuwait 12 years ago, buoyed by a combination of cold weather and a weekly government report that showed low inventories of oil and petroleum products.

In New York, crude oil for April delivery rose to $37.93 a barrel during trading yesterday before closing at $37.70, up $1.64, or 4.6 percent.

The loss of Venezuelan supplies occurred just as a cold winter settled upon much of the northern United States. Demand for heating oil grew, and profit margins increased for refiners for the first time in months. To make up for the disappearance of Venezuelan supplies, OPEC promised more oil from the Middle East to American refiners. But those shipments take about 40 days to reach the United States.

Traders also said they thought that comments made on Tuesday before the Senate by the energy secretary, Spencer Abraham, indicated a new willingness on the part of the Bush administration to release oil from the Strategic Petroleum Reserve, should a war with Iraq take place. Prices softened as a consequence. But by yesterday, Mr. Bentz and others said, traders had a chance to digest Mr. Abraham's comments and understood that the administration's approach to oil markets remained unchanged.

"Abraham said nothing new," Mr. Bentz said. "That is what he has said all along, that they would not release the oil unless it was necessary, and so far, they didn't deem it necessary."

Source: February 27, 2003, Neela Banerjee, New York Times.

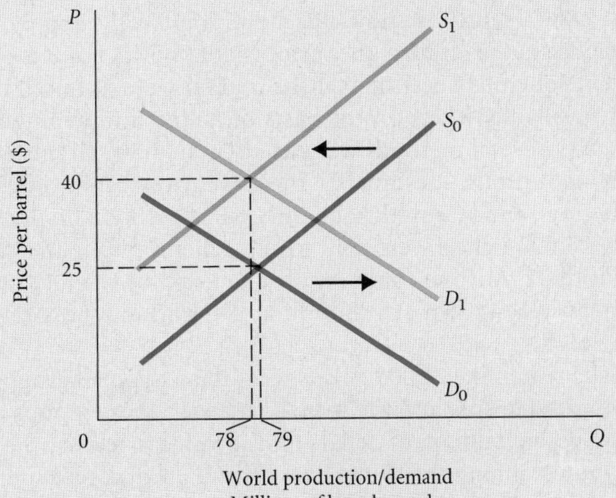

The cold winter in 2003 shifted the demand curve up (to the right); a strike in Venezuela shifted the supply curve down (to the left).

Visit www.prenhall.com/casefair for updated articles and exercises.

Owners also charged high prices for service. By doing so, they increased the real price of gasoline but hid it in service overcharges to get around the ceiling.

ration coupons Tickets or coupons that entitle individuals to purchase a certain amount of a given product per month.

Yet another method of dividing up available supply is the use of **ration coupons.** It was suggested in both 1974 and 1979 that families be given ration tickets, or coupons, that would entitle them to purchase a certain number of gallons of gasoline each month. That way, everyone would get the same amount, regardless of income. Such a system had been employed in the United States during the 1940s, when wartime price ceilings on meat, sugar, butter, tires, nylon stockings, and many other items were imposed.

When ration coupons are used with no prohibition against trading them, however, the result is almost identical to a system of price rationing. Those who are willing and able to pay the most simply buy up the coupons and use them to purchase gasoline, chocolate, fresh eggs, or anything else that is sold at a restricted price.[2] This means that the price of the restricted good will effectively rise to the market-clearing price. For instance, suppose that you decide not to sell your ration coupon. You are then forgoing what you would have received by selling the coupon. Thus the "real" price of the good you purchase will be higher (if only in opportunity cost) than the restricted price. Even when trading coupons is declared illegal, it is virtually impossible to stop black markets from developing. In a **black market**, illegal trading takes place at market-determined prices.

black market A market in which illegal trading takes place at market-determined prices.

There are many ways to deal with the excess demand to premiere sporting events such as the NCAA finals, but it is hard to keep tickets from those who are willing to pay high prices. Syracuse played Kansas in the NCAA championship game in 2003.

NCAA March Madness: College Basketball's National Championship On Sunday, March 16, 2003, The National Collegiate Athletic Association (NCAA) announced the 65 teams that would compete in the NCAA Division I Men's Basketball Championship. . . . "NCAA March Madness" had begun. The 65 teams were whittled down over the next three weeks to a final four. The semifinals were held on Saturday April 5, and the championship game took place at the Louisiana Superdome in New Orleans on Monday, April 7, between Syracuse and Kansas.

The NCAA controlled the distribution of 54,000 Final Four tickets. The face value of each ticket was between a minimum of $100 for upper-level, distant-view seats and a maximum of $160 for lower-level seats. Clearly, the potential demand for these tickets was enormous, and the NCAA made a decision to price them below equilibrium. How do we know that they were priced below equilibrium? Many ticket agencies have tickets for sale, and a check of prices being paid over the Web in mid-March of 2003 showed that upper-level tickets were being sold for over $1,750, while lower-level tickets between the baskets in the first 20 rows were going for an astonishing $10,000!

Let us say that the average price at which the original tickets were sold was $140 and that the equilibrium price that would equate the quantity supplied and the quantity demanded was $3,000. Figure 4.4 shows the story graphically. Supply is fixed at 54,000. The quantity demanded at the original sales price is not known, but it is probably a very large number.

One obvious question is if the market were not used to ration or distribute the originally available tickets on the basis of ability and willingness to pay, how were they distributed? Several methods were used. First, 4,500 tickets were saved for each of the Final Four institutions. Presumably, these went to school officials, players and their families, big donors, and season ticket holders. Each school, no doubt, had a different priority list. Next, 15,000 tickets were sold to the general public through a drawing all the way back in July 2002. Anyone could send in a check for the face amount of the tickets, the lucky winners were drawn at random, and the money was returned to those who were not drawn.

The remaining 21,000 tickets went to a variety of groups. The largest allotment went to corporate sponsors and the media. In a way, these groups "pay" for their tickets. CBS, for example, paid millions of dollars for the rights to televise the tournament. That payment was distributed among the teams by a formula. Corporate sponsors paid CBS and the NCAA millions for the rights to advertise. In return, each group received a set number of tickets to distribute as it saw fit.

[2]Of course, if you are assigned a number of tickets, and you sell them, you are better off than you would be with price rationing. Ration tickets thus serve as a way of redistributing income.

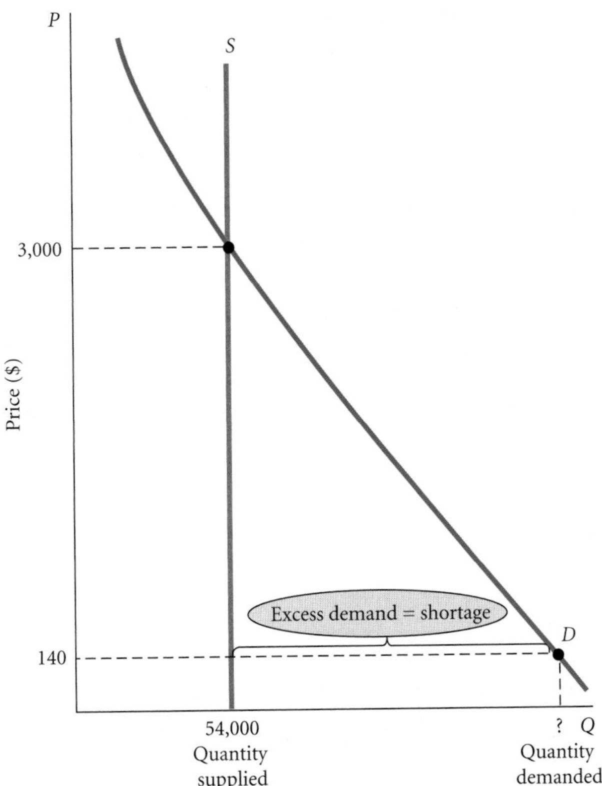

FIGURE 4.4 Supply of and Demand for a Pair of Final Four Tickets in 2003

A pair of tickets to the semi-finals and final of the NCAA men's basketball tournament in 2003 was originally priced at an average of about $140. The Superdome in New Orleans holds 54,000. Thus, the supply is vertical at 54,000. At $140, the quantity demanded far exceeded the quantity supplied. The diagram shows an equilibrium at $3,000.

What happened next was that a market arose. As long as people who are willing to pay very high prices (those who are represented by the upper left portion of the demand curve in Figure 4.4) can communicate with those who somehow were able to get tickets at face value, there will be trades! The Internet provides a convenient way for potential buyers to communicate with potential sellers. A simple search turns up dozens of organized ticket sellers.

Let us suppose that I was selected in the drawing in July and bought a pair of $100 tickets. How much must I *really* pay to go to the game? The answer is "what I can sell those tickets for." If I can sell the tickets for $4,000 a pair, I must turn down the $4,000 market price in order to go to the game. There is an opportunity cost. I must reveal that it is worth at least $4,000 because I forgo $4,000 if a friend and I go to the games.

What, then, can we conclude about alternatives to the price rationing system?

> No matter how good the intentions of private organizations and governments, it is very difficult to prevent the price system from operating and to stop willingness to pay from asserting itself. Every time an alternative is tried, the price system seems to sneak in the back door. With favored customers and black markets, the final distribution may be even more unfair than that which would result from simple price rationing.

PRICES AND THE ALLOCATION OF RESOURCES

Thinking of the market system as a mechanism for allocating scarce goods and services among competing demanders is very revealing, but the market determines much more than just the distribution of final outputs. It also determines what gets produced and how resources are allocated among competing uses.

Consider a change in consumer preferences that leads to an increase in demand for a specific good or service. During the 1980s, for example, people began going to restaurants much more frequently than before. Researchers think that this trend, which continues today, is partially the result of social changes (such as a dramatic rise in the number of two-earner families) and partially the result of rising incomes. The market responded to this change in demand by shifting resources, both capital and labor, into more and better restaurants.

With the increase in demand for restaurant meals, the price of eating out rose, and the restaurant business became more profitable. The higher profits attracted new businesses and provided old restaurants with an incentive to expand. As new capital, seeking profits, flowed into the restaurant business, so did labor. New restaurants need chefs. Chefs need training, and the higher wages that came with increased demand provided an incentive for them to get it. In response to the increase in demand for training, new cooking schools opened and existing schools began to offer courses in the culinary arts.

This story could run on and on, but the point is clear:

Price changes resulting from shifts of demand in output markets cause profits to rise or fall. Profits attract capital; losses lead to disinvestment. Higher wages attract labor and encourage workers to acquire skills. At the core of the system, supply, demand, and prices in input and output markets determine the allocation of resources and the ultimate combinations of things produced.

Companion Website Plus

PRICE FLOORS

price floor A minimum price below which exchange is not permitted.

minimum wage A price floor set under the price of labor.

As we have seen, price ceilings, often imposed because price rationing is sometimes seen as unfair, result in alternative rationing mechanisms that are inefficient and may be equally unfair. Some of the same arguments can be made for price floors. A **price floor**, is a minimum price below which exchange is not permitted. If a price floor is set above the equilibrium price, the result will be excess supply; quantity supplied will be greater than quantity demanded.

The most common example of a price floor is the **minimum wage**, which is a floor set under the price of labor. Employers (who demand labor) are not permitted under federal law to pay a wage of less than $5.15 per hour to workers (who supply labor). Critics argue that since the minimum wage is above equilibrium, the result will be wasteful unemployment. At the wage of $5.15, the quantity of labor demanded is less than the quantity of labor supplied.

Whenever a price floor is set above equilibrium, an excess supply will be on the market. A lower price would increase the quantity demanded, since buyers would pay a lower price, and quantity supplied would fall, as resources are transferred to more productive uses.

SUPPLY AND DEMAND ANALYSIS: AN OIL IMPORT FEE

The basic logic of supply and demand is a powerful tool of analysis. As an extended example of the power of this logic, we will consider a recent proposal to impose a tax on imported oil. The idea of raising the federal gasoline tax is hotly debated, with many arguing strongly for such a tax. Many economists, however, believe that a fee on imported crude oil, which is used to produce gasoline, would have better effects on the economy than would a gasoline tax.

Consider the facts. Between 1985 and 1989, the United States increased its dependence on oil imports dramatically. In 1989, total U.S. demand for crude oil was 13.6 million barrels per day. Of that amount, only 7.7 million barrels per day (57 percent) were supplied by U.S. producers, with the remaining 5.9 million barrels per day (43 percent) imported. The price of oil on world markets that year averaged about $18. This heavy dependence on foreign oil left the United States vulnerable to the price shock that followed the Iraqi invasion of Kuwait in August 1990. In the months following the invasion, the price of crude oil on world markets shot up to $40 per barrel.

Even before the invasion, many economists and some politicians had recommended a stiff oil import fee (or tax) that would, it was argued, reduce the U.S. dependence on foreign oil by (1) reducing overall consumption and (2) providing an incentive for increased domestic production. An added bonus would be improved air quality from the reduction in driving.

Supply and demand analysis makes the arguments of the import fee proponents easier to understand. Figure 4.5(a) shows the U.S. market for oil. The world price of oil is assumed to be $18, and the United States is assumed to be able to buy *all the oil that it wants* at this

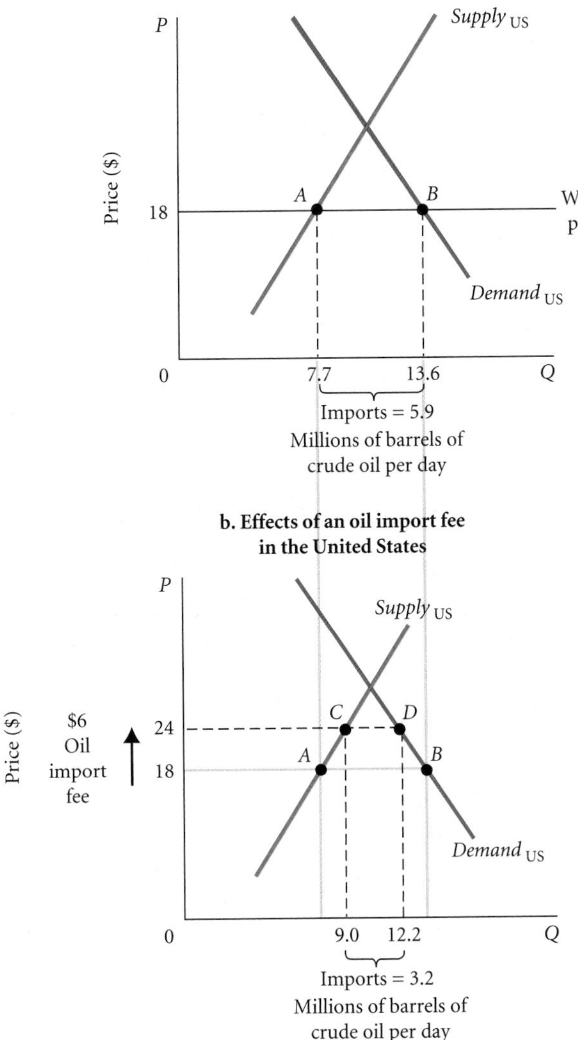

FIGURE 4.5 The U.S. Market for Crude Oil, 1989

At a world price of \$18, domestic production is 7.7 million barrels per day and the total quantity of oil demanded in the United States is 13.6 million barrels per day. The difference is total imports (5.9 million barrels per day). If the government levies a 33 percent tax on imports, the price of a barrel of oil rises to \$24. The quantity demanded falls to 12.2 million barrels per day. At the same time, the quantity supplied by domestic producers increases to 9.0 million barrels per day, and the quantity imported falls to 3.2 million barrels per day.

price. This means that domestic producers cannot get away with charging any more than \$18 per barrel. The curve labeled $Supply_{US}$ shows the amount that domestic suppliers will produce at each price level. At a price of \$18, domestic production is 7.7 million barrels. Stated somewhat differently, U.S. producers will produce at point *A* on the supply curve. The total quantity of oil demanded in the United States in 1989 was 13.6 million barrels per day. At a price of \$18, the quantity demanded in the United States is point *B* on the demand curve.

The difference between the total quantity demanded (13.6 million barrels per day) and domestic production (7.7 million barrels per day) is total imports (5.9 million barrels per day).

Now suppose that the government levies a tax of $33\frac{1}{3}$ percent on imported oil. Because the import price is \$18, a tax of \$6 (or .3333 × \$18) per barrel means that importers of oil in the United States will pay a total of \$24 per barrel (\$18 + \$6). This new higher price means that U.S. producers can also charge up to \$24 for a barrel of crude. Note, however, that the tax is paid only on imported oil. Thus the entire \$24 paid for domestic crude goes to domestic producers.

Figure 4.5(b) shows the result of the tax. First, because of higher price the quantity demanded drops to 12.2 million barrels per day. This is a movement *along* the demand curve from point *B* to point *D*. At the same time, the quantity supplied by domestic producers increases to 9.0 million barrels per day. This is a movement *along* the supply curve from

Further Exploration

The Drug Wars: A Matter of Supply and Demand

For years a debate has raged between those who favor strategies for reducing the supply of illegal drugs and those who favor strategies designed to reduce the demand for illegal drugs. The president's budget for 2003 contained $19.1 billion dollars for the "war on drugs," and its focus was on supply. Of the total, 67 percent was spent on the supply side: actions to destroy drugs where they are grown; stopping drugs from entering the United States; and efforts to stop domestic distribution. The remaining 33 percent was spent on reducing demand, specifically for things like treatment and prevention.

Clearly if the supply-side efforts are successful, they will drive up the price of drugs on the street. Higher prices mean that fewer people are willing to buy drugs and the quantity demanded drops.

Critics of the supply-side approach argue that programs designed to reduce supply in the past have failed. The reason, they claim, is that the high price of drugs makes it very profitable to produce. Thus, as production from one country is reduced, supply will come from other sources.

You can see the essence of the debate in Figure 1. Supply shifts to the left, and the equilibrium price rises. As the price rises, quantity demanded declines along the demand curve as fewer people are willing to buy drugs, and quantity supplied increases along the supply curve as the higher price spurs new production elsewhere.

What are the alternatives? Some argue that we should shift the focus to reducing the demand for illegal drugs. If successful, the resulting lower price would take the profit out of production and reduce the quantity supplied. You can see this point in Figure 2. Demand shifts to the left, and the equilibrium price falls. As the price falls, the quantity supplied falls, a movement along the supply curve.

A second, perhaps more radical, set of critics argues that legalization is the best solution. Legalization would reduce the cost of production substantially. No longer would it take enormous expenses to smuggle drugs across the border, and sellers would no longer face the risk of prosecution. Legalization would shift the supply curve to the right, substantially reducing the price of drugs on the street. Proponents of legalization argue that it is the very high price of drugs that forces many into criminal activity to support their habits. Opponents of legalization point to the fact that the lower price would lead to a higher quantity demanded and, thus, to more addiction.

Of course the arguments on all sides of this issue are very complex, but the laws of supply and demand put them in a framework that helps clarify the debate.

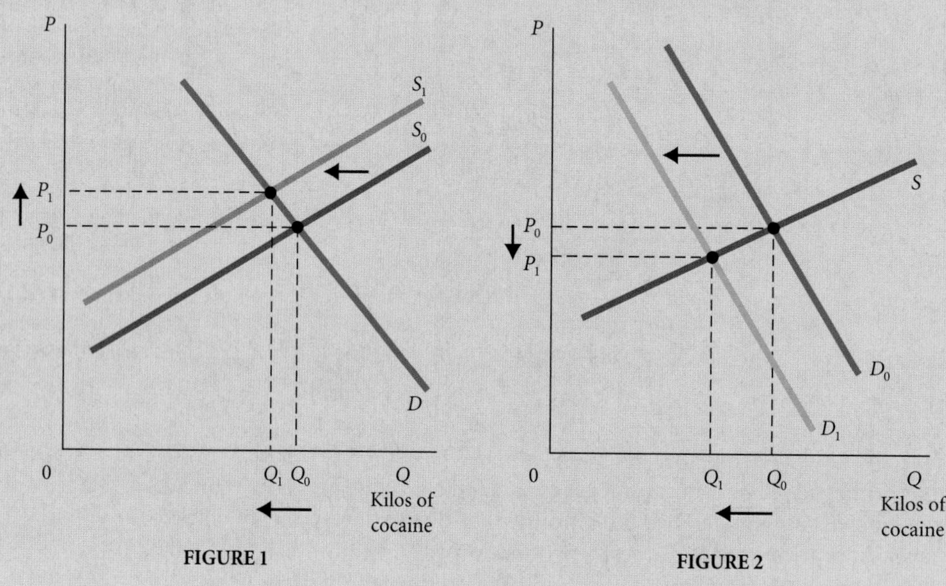

FIGURE 1

FIGURE 2

point *A* to point *C*. With an increase in domestic quantity supplied and a decrease in domestic quantity demanded, imports decrease to 3.2 million barrels per day (12.2 – 9.0).[3]

The tax also generates revenues for the federal government. The total tax revenue collected is equal to the tax per barrel ($6) times the number of imported barrels. When the quantity imported is 3.2 million barrels per day, total revenue is $6 × 3.2 million, or $19.2 million *per day* (about $7 billion per year).

What does all of this mean? In the final analysis, an oil import fee would (1) increase domestic production and (2) reduce overall consumption. This would in turn help with the problem of air pollution and simultaneously reduce U.S. dependence on foreign oil.

[3]These figures were not chosen randomly. It is interesting to note that in 1985 the world price of crude oil averaged about $24 a barrel. Domestic production was 9.0 million barrels per day, and domestic consumption was 12.2 million barrels per day, with imports of only 3.2 million. The drop in the world price between 1985 and 1989 increased imports to 5.9 million, an 84 percent increase. By 2003, domestic production had fallen to 5.9 million barrels per day, and imports were up to 8.6 million barrels per day.

LOOKING AHEAD

We have now examined the basic forces of supply and demand and discussed the market/price system. These basic concepts will serve as building blocks for what comes next. Whether you are studying microeconomics or macroeconomics, you will be studying the functions of markets and the behavior of market participants in more detail in the following chapters.

Because the concepts presented in the first four chapters are so important to your understanding of what is to come, this might be a good point for a brief review of Part I.

SUMMARY

THE PRICE SYSTEM: RATIONING AND ALLOCATING RESOURCES

1. In a market economy, the market system (or price system) serves two functions. It determines the allocation of resources among producers and the final mix of outputs. It also distributes goods and services on the basis of willingness and ability to pay. In this sense, it serves as a *price rationing* device.

2. Governments, as well as private firms, sometimes decide not to use the market system to ration an item for which there is excess demand. Examples of nonprice rationing systems include *queuing, favored customers,* and *ration coupons.* The most common rationale for such policies is "fairness."

3. Attempts to bypass the market and use alternative nonprice rationing devices are much more difficult and costly than it would seem at first glance. Schemes that open up opportunities for favored customers, black markets, and side payments often end up less "fair" than the free market.

SUPPLY AND DEMAND ANALYSIS: AN OIL IMPORT FEE

4. The basic logic of supply and demand is a powerful tool for analysis. For example, supply and demand analysis shows that an oil import tax will reduce quantity of oil demanded, increase domestic production, and generate revenues for the government.

REVIEW TERMS AND CONCEPTS

black market, 76
favored customers, 74
minimum wage, 78
price ceiling, 74
price floor, 78
price rationing, 71
queuing, 74
ration coupons, 76

PROBLEM SET

1. Illustrate the following with supply and demand curves:

a. In December 2002, a seventeenth-century portrait by Rembrandt was sold in London for $28.65 million. The price paid for *Portrait of a Lady* was a record for the Dutch master.

b. In 2003, cattle in the United States were selling for 74 cents a pound, up from 61 cents a few years ago. This was despite the fact that supply had increased during the period.

c. Early in 2004, a survey of plant stores indicated that the demand for houseplants was rising sharply. At the same time, large numbers of low-cost producers started growing plants for sale. The overall result was a drop in the average price of houseplants and an increase in the number of plants sold.

d. In 1996, several cows in Great Britain came down with "mad cow disease." As a result, the countries of the European Union banned the import of British beef. The result was a sharp increase in the price of beef in continental Europe.

2. "Every demand curve must eventually hit the quantity axis because with limited incomes there is always a price so high that there is no demand for the good." Do you agree or disagree?

3. When excess demand exists for tickets to a major sporting event or a concert, profit opportunities exist for scalpers. Explain briefly using supply and demand curves to illustrate. Some argue that scalpers work to the advantage of everyone and are "efficient." Do you agree or disagree? Explain briefly.

4. In an effort to "support" the price of some agricultural goods, the Department of Agriculture pays farmers a subsidy in cash for every acre that they leave *unplanted.* The Agriculture Department argues that the subsidy increases the "cost" of planting and that it will reduce supply and increase the price of competitively produced agricultural goods. Critics argue that because the subsidy is a payment to farmers, it will reduce costs and lead to lower prices. Which argument is correct? Explain.

5. "The rent for apartments in New York City has been rising sharply. Demand for apartments in New York City has been rising sharply as well. This is hard to explain because the law of demand says that higher prices should lead to lower demand." Do you agree or disagree? Explain your answer.

6. Illustrate the following with supply and/or demand curves:

a. The federal government "supports" the price of wheat by paying farmers not to plant wheat on some of their land.

b. The impact of an increase in the price of chicken on the price of hamburger.

c. Incomes rise, shifting the demand for gasoline. Crude oil prices rise, shifting the supply of gasoline. At the new equilibrium, the quantity of gasoline sold is less than it was before. (Crude oil is used to produce gasoline.)

7. Illustrate the following with supply and/or demand curves:
   a. A situation of excess labor supply (unemployment) caused by a "minimum wage" law.
   b. The effect of a sharp increase in heating oil prices on the demand for insulation material.

8. Suppose that the world price of oil is $30 per barrel, and suppose that the United States can buy all the oil it wants at this price. Suppose also that the demand and supply schedules for oil in the United States are as follows:

PRICE ($ PER BARREL)	U.S. QUANTITY DEMANDED	U.S.QUANTITY SUPPLIED
28	16	4
30	15	6
32	14	8
34	13	10
36	12	12

   a. On graph paper, draw the supply and demand curves for the United States.
   b. With free trade in oil, what price will Americans pay for their oil? What quantity will Americans buy? How much of this will be supplied by American producers? How much will be imported? Illustrate total imports on your graph of the U.S. oil market.
   c. Suppose the United States imposes a tax of $4 per barrel on imported oil. What quantity would Americans buy? How much of this would be supplied by American producers? How much would be imported? How much tax would the government collect?
   d. Briefly summarize the impact of an oil import tax by explaining who is helped and who is hurt among the following groups: domestic oil consumers, domestic oil producers, foreign oil producers, and the U.S. government.

9. Use the data in the preceding problem to answer the following questions. Now suppose that the United States allows no oil imports.
   a. What is the equilibrium price and quantity for oil in the United States?
   b. If the United States imposed a price ceiling of $34 per barrel on the oil market and prohibited imports would there be an excess supply or an excess demand for oil? How much?
   c. Under the price ceiling, quantity supplied and quantity demanded differ. Which of the two will determine how much oil is purchased? Briefly explain why.

10. For the following, say whether you agree or disagree and explain your answer.

If supply were to increase somewhat in the following diagram, prices would fall and firms would earn less revenue.

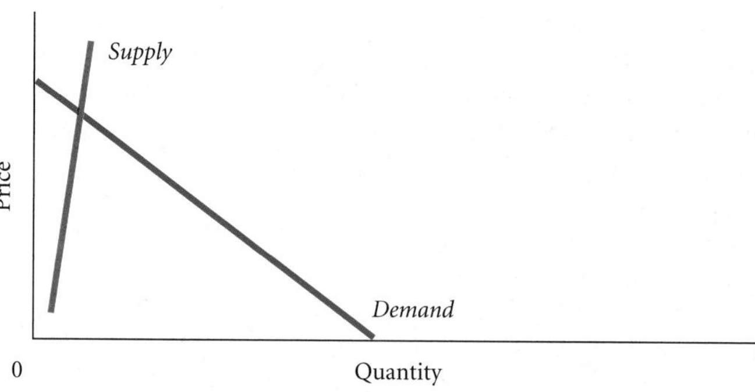

11. The box on page 80 describes the war on drugs and the potential impacts on the supply of and demand for cocaine. Suppose that the United States government simultaneously legalized drugs and launched a highly successful antidrug advertising campaign. Draw a supply and demand diagram to illustrate the effects of such changes on the price of cocaine. Proponents of legalization argue that it would reduce the crime rate. What links are likely to be between the price of drugs and the crime rate? Opponents of legalization argue that the resulting expansion of supply and decline in price would cause the quantity demanded to increase as more people become addicted. Show on a supply and demand diagram what would happen if supply shifted to the right, but the advertising campaign failed to shift demand.

Introduction to Macroeconomics

5

CHAPTER OUTLINE

Macroeconomics is part of our everyday lives. If the macroeconomy is doing well, few people do not have a job who want one, people's incomes are generally rising, and profits of corporations are generally high. In this type of an economy it is relatively easy for new entrants into the labor force, such as students who have just graduated, to find jobs. On the other hand, if the macroeconomy is in a slump, new jobs are hard to find, incomes are not growing well, and profits are low. Given the large effects that the macroeconomy can have on our lives, it is important that we understand how it works.

We begin by discussing the differences between microeconomics and macroeconomics that we glimpsed in Chapter 1. **Microeconomics** examines the functioning of individual industries and the behavior of individual decision-making units, typically business firms and households. With a few assumptions about how these units behave (firms maximize profits, households maximize utility), we can derive useful conclusions about how markets work, how resources are allocated, and so forth.

Macroeconomics, instead of focusing on the factors that influence the production of particular products and the behavior of individual industries, focuses on the determinants of total national output. Macroeconomics studies not household income but *national* income, not individual prices but the *overall* price level. It does not analyze the demand for labor in the automobile industry but instead total employment in the economy.

Both microeconomics and macroeconomics are concerned with the decisions of households and firms. Microeconomics deals with individual decisions; macroeconomics deals with the sum of these individual decisions. *Aggregate* is used in macroeconomics to refer to sums. When we speak of **aggregate behavior**, we mean the behavior of all households and firms together. We also speak of aggregate consumption and aggregate investment, which refer to total consumption and total investment in the economy.

Because microeconomists and macroeconomists look at the economy from different perspectives, you might expect they would reach somewhat different conclusions about the way the economy behaves. This is true to some extent. Microeconomists generally conclude that markets work well. They see prices as flexible, adjusting to maintain equality between quantity supplied and quantity demanded. Macroeconomists, however, observe that important prices in the economy—for example, the wage rate (or price of labor)—often seem "sticky." **Sticky prices** are prices that do not always adjust rapidly to maintain equality between quantity supplied and quantity demanded. Microeconomists do not expect to see

microeconomics Examines the functioning of individual industries and the behavior of individual decision-making units—business firms and households.

macroeconomics Deals with the economy as a whole. Macroeconomics focuses on the determinants of total national income, deals with aggregates such as aggregate consumption and investment, and looks at the overall level of prices instead of individual prices.

aggregate behavior The behavior of all households and firms together.

sticky prices Prices that do not always adjust rapidly to maintain equality between quantity supplied and quantity demanded.

microeconomic foundations of macroeconomics The microeconomic principles underlying macroeconomic analysis.

Great Depression The period of severe economic contraction and high unemployment that began in 1929 and continued throughout the 1930s.

the quantity of apples supplied exceeding the quantity of apples demanded, because the price of apples is not sticky. On the other hand, macroeconomists—who analyze aggregate behavior—examine periods of high unemployment, where the quantity of labor supplied appears to exceed the quantity of labor demanded. At such times, it appears that wage rates do not adjust fast enough to equate the quantity of labor supplied and the quantity of labor demanded.

Since about 1970, much work in macroeconomics has been concerned with making macroeconomic analysis consistent with microeconomic postulates—that is, with the idea that firms and households make their decisions along the lines suggested by microeconomic theory. If prices do not appear to equate the quantity supplied and the quantity demanded, for example, macroeconomists now look for solid microeconomic reasons why not. One of the aims of this book is to explain the **microeconomic foundations of macroeconomics.**

THE ROOTS OF MACROECONOMICS

THE GREAT DEPRESSION

Economic events of the 1930s, the decade of the **Great Depression**, spurred a great deal of thinking about macroeconomic issues, especially unemployment. The 1920s had been prosperous years for the U.S. economy. Virtually everyone who wanted a job could get one, incomes rose substantially, and prices were stable. Beginning in late 1929, things took a sudden turn for the worse. In 1929, 1.5 million people were unemployed. By 1933, that had increased to 13 million out of a labor force of 51 million. In 1933, the United States produced about 27 percent fewer goods and services than it had in 1929. In October of 1929, when stock prices collapsed on Wall Street, billions of dollars of personal wealth were lost. Unemployment remained above 14 percent of the labor force until 1940.

Classical Models Before the Great Depression, economists applied microeconomic models, sometimes referred to as "classical" or "market clearing" models, to economy-wide problems. For example, classical supply and demand analysis assumed that an excess supply of labor would drive down wages to a new equilibrium level; as a result, unemployment would not persist.

In other words, classical economists believed that *recessions* (downturns in the economy) were self-correcting. As output falls and the demand for labor shifts to the left, the argument went, the wage rate will decline, thereby raising the quantity of labor demanded by firms, who will want to hire more workers at the new lower wage rate. However, during the Great Depression unemployment levels remained very high for nearly 10 years. In large measure, the failure of simple classical models to explain the prolonged existence of high unemployment provided the impetus for the development of macroeconomics. It is not surprising that what we now call macroeconomics was born in the 1930s.

The Keynesian Revolution One of the most important works in the history of economics, *The General Theory of Employment, Interest and Money*, by John Maynard Keynes, was published in 1936. Building on what was already understood about markets and their behavior, Keynes set out to construct a theory that would explain the confusing economic events of his time.

Much of macroeconomics has roots in Keynes's work. According to Keynes, it is not prices and wages that determine the level of employment, as classical models had suggested, but instead the level of aggregate demand for goods and services. Keynes believed governments could intervene in the economy and affect the level of output and employment. The government's role during periods when private demand is low, Keynes argued, is to stimulate aggregate demand and, by so doing, to lift the economy out of recession. (See the Further Exploration box, "The Great Depression and John Maynard Keynes.")

RECENT MACROECONOMIC HISTORY

After World War II, and especially in the 1950s, Keynes's views began to gain increasing influence over both professional economists and government policy makers. Governments came to believe they could intervene in their economies to attain specific employment and

Further Exploration

The Great Depression and John Maynard Keynes

Much of the framework of modern macroeconomics comes from the works of John Maynard Keynes, whose *General Theory of Employment, Interest and Money* was published in 1936. The following excerpt by Robert L. Heilbroner provides some insights into Keynes's life and work.

The Great Depression persisted long after the stock market crash in 1929.

> By 1933 the nation was virtually prostrate. On street corners, in homes, in Hoovervilles (communities of makeshift shacks), 14 million unemployed sat, haunting the land. . . .
>
> It was the unemployment that was hardest to bear. The jobless millions were like an embolism in the nation's vital circulation; and while their indisputable existence argued more forcibly than any text that something was wrong with the system, the economists wrung their hands and racked their brains . . . but could offer neither diagnosis nor remedy. Unemployment—this kind of unemployment—was simply not listed among the possible ills of the system: it was absurd, impossible, unreasonable, and paradoxical. But it was there.
>
> It would seem logical that the man who would seek to solve this impossible paradox of not enough production existing side by side with men fruitlessly seeking work would be a Left-winger, an economist with strong sympathies for the proletariat, an angry man. Nothing could be further from the fact. The man who tackled it was almost a dilettante with nothing like a chip on his shoulder. The simple truth was that his talents inclined in every direction. He had, for example, written a most recondite book on mathematical probability, a book that Bertrand Russell had declared "impossible to praise too highly"; then he had gone on to match his skill in abstruse logic with a flair for making money—he accumulated a fortune of £500,000 by way of the most treacherous of all roads to riches: dealing in international currencies and commodities. More impressive yet, he had written his mathematics treatise on the side, as it were, while engaged in Government service, and he piled up his private wealth by applying himself for only half an hour a day while still abed.
>
> But this is only a sample of his many-sidedness. He was an economist, of course—a Cambridge don with all the dignity and erudition that go with such an appointment. . . . He managed to be simultaneously the darling of the Bloomsbury set, the cluster of Britain's most avant-garde intellectual brilliants, and also the chairman of a life insurance company, a niche in life rarely noted for its intellectual abandon. He was a pillar of stability in delicate matters of international diplomacy, but his official correctness did not prevent him from acquiring a knowledge of other European politicians that included their . . . neuroses and financial prejudices. . . . He ran a theater, and he came to be a Director of the Bank of England. He knew Roosevelt and Churchill and also Bernard Shaw and Pablo Picasso. . . .
>
> His name was John Maynard Keynes, an old British name (pronounced to rhyme with "rains") that could be traced back to one William de Cahagnes and 1066. Keynes was a traditionalist; he liked to think that greatness ran in families, and it is true that his own father was John Neville Keynes, an illustrious enough economist in his own right. But it took more than the ordinary gifts of heritage to account for the son; it was as if the talents that would have sufficed half a dozen men were by happy accident crowded into one person.
>
> By a coincidence he was born in 1883, in the very year that Karl Marx passed away. But the two economists who thus touched each other in time, although each was to exert the profoundest influence on the philosophy of the capitalist system, could hardly have differed from one another more. Marx was bitter, at bay, heavy and disappointed; as we know, he was the draftsman of Capitalism Doomed. Keynes loved life and sailed through it buoyant, at ease, and consummately successful to become the architect of Capitalism Viable.[a]

John Maynard Keynes.

Source: [a]*Reprinted with the permission of Simon & Schuster from* The Worldly Philosophers *by Robert L. Heilbroner. Copyright © 1953, 1961, 1967, 1972, 1980, 1986 by Robert L. Heilbroner. Also reprinted with permission of Penguin Books Limited, U.K.*

output goals. They began to use their powers to tax and spend, as well as their ability to affect interest rates and the money supply, for the explicit purpose of controlling the economy's ups and downs. This view of government policy became firmly established in the United States with the passage of the Employment Act of 1946. This act established the President's Council of Economic Advisors, a group of economists who advise the president on economic issues. It also committed the federal government to intervening in the economy to prevent large declines in output and employment.

Fine-Tuning in the 1960s The notion that the government could, and should, act to stabilize the macroeconomy reached the height of its popularity in the 1960s. During these years, Walter Heller, the chairman of the Council of Economic Advisors under both President Kennedy and President Johnson, alluded to **fine-tuning** as the government's role in regulating inflation and unemployment. During the 1960s, many economists believed the government could use the tools available to manipulate unemployment and inflation levels fairly precisely.

fine-tuning The phrase used by Walter Heller to refer to the government's role in regulating inflation and unemployment.

Disillusionment in the 1970s and Early 1980s In the 1970s and early 1980s, the U.S. economy had wide fluctuations in employment, output, and inflation. In 1974–1975 and again in 1980–1982, the United States experienced a severe recession. While not as catastrophic as the Great Depression of the 1930s, these two recessions left millions without jobs and resulted in billions of dollars of lost output and income. In 1974–1975 and again in 1979–1981, the United States saw very high rates of inflation.

Moreover, in the 1970s **stagflation** (stagnation + inflation) was born. Stagflation occurs when the overall price level rises rapidly (inflation) during periods of recession or high and persistent unemployment (stagnation). Until the 1970s, rapidly rising prices had been observed only in periods when the economy was prospering and unemployment was low (or at least declining). The problem of stagflation was vexing, both for macroeconomic theorists and for policy makers concerned with the health of the economy.

stagflation Occurs when the overall price level rises rapidly (inflation) during periods of recession or high and persistent unemployment (stagnation).

It was clear by 1975 that the macroeconomy was more difficult to control than either Heller's words or textbook theory had led economists to believe. The events of the 1970s and early 1980s had an important influence on macroeconomic theory. Much of the faith in the simple Keynesian model and the "conventional wisdom" of the 1960s was lost.

Good Times in the 1990s and a Pause in 2001 The economy grew well in the 1980s after the recession of 1980–1982. There was a mild recession in 1990–1991, and then the economy grew for the rest of the 1990s. Growth in 1997–1999 was particularly strong, fueled in part by the stock market boom that began in 1995. Remarkably, inflation was not a problem throughout the entire 1990s. The economy then entered into a recession in early 2001, before the terrorist attacks on September 11, 2001. In spite of the attacks, however, the economy began to pick up at the end of that year. The growth rate in 2002 and 2003 was moderate, but not large enough to prevent the unemployment rate from rising. The unemployment rate rose sharply from about 4 percent in 2000 to about 5.5 percent by the end of 2001. It then rose further to 6.2 percent by the second quarter of 2003. Inflation continued not to be a problem in the early 2000s.

The strong economy in the 1990s did *not* lead to a convergence of views of macroeconomists about how the macroeconomy works. The discipline of macroeconomics is still in flux, and many important issues have yet to be resolved. This makes it hard to teach, but exciting to study.

MACROECONOMIC CONCERNS

Three of the major concerns of macroeconomics are:

- Inflation
- Output growth
- Unemployment

Government policy makers would like to have low inflation, high output growth, and low unemployment. They may not be able to achieve these goals, but the goals themselves are clear.

INFLATION AND DEFLATION

Inflation is an increase in the overall price level. Keeping inflation low has long been a goal of government policy. Especially problematic are **hyperinflations**, or periods of very rapid increases in the overall price level.

inflation An increase in the overall price level.

hyperinflation A period of very rapid increases in the overall price level.

Most Americans are unaware of what life is like under very high inflation. In some countries at some times people were accustomed to prices rising by the day, by the hour, or even by the minute. During the hyperinflation in Bolivia in 1984 and 1985, the price of one egg rose from 3,000 pesos to 10,000 pesos in 1 week. In 1985, three bottles of aspirin sold for the same price as a luxury car had sold for in 1982. At the same time, the problem of handling money became a burden. Banks stopped counting deposits—a $500 deposit was equivalent to about 32 million pesos, and it just did not make sense to count a huge sack full of bills. Bolivia's currency, printed in West Germany and England, was the country's third biggest import in 1984, surpassed only by wheat and mining equipment.

Skyrocketing prices in Bolivia are a small part of the story. When inflation approaches rates of 2,000 percent per year, the economy and the whole organization of a country begin to break down. Workers may go on strike to demand wage increases in line with the high inflation rate, and firms may find it hard to secure credit.

Hyperinflations are rare. Nonetheless, economists have devoted much effort to identifying the costs and consequences of even moderate inflation. Does anyone gain from inflation? Who loses? What costs does inflation impose on society? How severe are they? What causes inflation? What is the best way to stop it? These are some of the main concerns of macroeconomists.

A decrease in the overall price level is called **deflation**. In some periods in U.S. history and currently in Japan, deflation has occurred over an extended period of time. The goal of policy makers is to avoid prolonged periods of deflation as well as inflation in order to pursue the macroeconomic goal of stability.

deflation A decrease in the overall price level

OUTPUT GROWTH: SHORT RUN AND LONG RUN

Instead of growing at an even rate at all times, economies tend to experience short-term ups and downs in their performance. The technical name for these ups and downs is the **business cycle**. The main measure of how an economy is doing is **aggregate output**, the total quantity of goods and services produced in the economy in a given period. When less is produced (in other words, when aggregate output decreases), there are fewer goods and services to go around, and the average standard of living declines. When firms cut back on production, they also lay off workers, increasing the rate of unemployment.

business cycle The cycle of short-term ups and downs in the economy.

aggregate output The total quantity of goods and services produced in an economy in a given period.

Recessions are periods during which aggregate output declines. It has become conventional to classify an economic downturn as a "recession" when aggregate output declines for two consecutive quarters. A prolonged and deep recession is called a **depression**, although economists do not agree on when a recession becomes a depression. Since the beginning of the twentieth century, the United States has experienced one depression (during the 1930s), three severe recessions (1946, 1974–1975, and 1980–1982), and a number of less severe, shorter recessions (1954, 1958, 1990–1991, and 2001). Other countries have also experienced recessions in the twentieth century, some roughly coinciding with U.S. recessions and some not. In 1994, while the U.S. recovery was well under way, Japan was still in a recession.

recession A period during which aggregate output declines. Conventionally, a period in which aggregate output declines for two consecutive quarters.

depression A prolonged and deep recession.

There is more to output than its up-and-down movements during business cycles. The size of the growth rate of output over a long period (longer, say, than the typical length of a business cycle) is also of concern to macroeconomists and policy makers. If the growth rate of output is greater than the growth rate of the population, there is a growing amount of goods and services produced per person. So, on average, people are becoming better off. Policy makers are thus concerned not only with smoothing fluctuations in output during a business cycle but also with policies that might increase the long-run growth rate.

UNEMPLOYMENT

unemployment rate The percentage of the labor force that is unemployed.

You cannot listen to the news or read a newspaper without noticing that data on the unemployment rate are released each month. The **unemployment rate**—the percentage of the labor force that is unemployed—is a key indicator of the economy's health. Because the unemployment rate is usually closely related to the economy's aggregate output, announcements of each month's new figure are followed with great interest by economists, politicians, and policy makers.

Although macroeconomists are interested in learning why the unemployment rate has risen or fallen in a given period, they also try to answer a more basic question: Why is there any unemployment at all? We do not expect to see zero unemployment. At any time, some firms may go bankrupt due to competition from rivals, bad management, or bad luck. Employees of such firms typically are not able to find new jobs immediately, and while they are looking for work, they will be unemployed. Also, workers entering the labor market for the first time may require a few weeks, or months, to find a job.

If we base our analysis on supply and demand, we would expect conditions to change in response to the existence of unemployed workers. Specifically, when there is unemployment beyond some minimum amount, there is an excess supply of workers—at the going wage rates, there are people who want to work who cannot find work. In microeconomic theory, the response to excess supply is a decrease in the price of the commodity in question and therefore an increase in the quantity demanded, a reduction in the quantity supplied, and the restoration of equilibrium. With the quantity supplied equal to the quantity demanded, the market clears.

The existence of unemployment seems to imply that the aggregate labor market is not in equilibrium—that something prevents the quantity supplied and the quantity demanded from equating. Why do labor markets not clear when other markets do, or is it that labor markets are clearing and the unemployment data are reflecting something different? This is another main concern of macroeconomists.

GOVERNMENT IN THE MACROECONOMY

Much of our discussion of macroeconomics concerns the potential role of government in influencing the economy. There are three kinds of policy that the government has used to influence the macroeconomy:

1. Fiscal policy
2. Monetary policy
3. Growth or supply-side policies

FISCAL POLICY

fiscal policy Government policies concerning taxes and expenditures (spending).

One way the federal government affects the economy is through its tax and expenditure (spending) decisions, or **fiscal policy**. The federal government collects taxes from households and firms and spends these funds on items ranging from missiles to parks to social security payments to interstate highways. Both the magnitude and composition of these taxes and expenditures have a major effect on the economy.

One of Keynes's main ideas in the 1930s was that fiscal policy could and should be used to stabilize the level of output and employment. Specifically, Keynes believed the government should cut taxes and/or raise spending—called *expansionary fiscal policies*—to get the economy out of a slump. Conversely, he held that the government should raise taxes and/or cut spending—called *contractionary fiscal policies*—to bring the economy out of an inflation.

MONETARY POLICY

monetary policy The tools used by the Federal Reserve to control the quantity of money in the economy.

Taxes and spending are not the only variables the government controls. The Federal Reserve, the nation's central bank, determines the quantity of money in the economy. The effects and proper role of **monetary policy** are among the most hotly debated subjects in macroeconomics. Most economists agree that the quantity of money supplied affects the overall price level, interest rates and exchange rates, unemployment rate, and level of output. The main controversies arise concerning how monetary policy manifests itself and exactly how large its effects are.

GROWTH POLICIES

Many economists are skeptical about the government's ability to regulate the business cycle with any degree of precision using monetary and fiscal policy. Their view is that the focus of government policy should be to stimulate aggregate supply—to stimulate the potential growth of aggregate output and income. A host of policies have been aimed at increasing the rate of growth. Many of these are targeted at specific markets and are largely discussed in microeconomics. One major worry of macroeconomists is that government borrowing to finance excesses of spending over tax collections (the "deficit") sops up saving that would otherwise flow to businesses to be used for investment in capital. Another focus of pro-growth government policies has been the tax system. A major goal of tax reforms in 1981 and 1986 was to increase the incentive to work, save, and invest by lowering tax rates. In addition, the Taxpayer Relief Act of 1997 included a number of progrowth measures. These types of policies are sometimes referred to as **supply-side policies**.

supply-side policies Government policies that focus on stimulating aggregate supply instead of aggregate demand.

THE COMPONENTS OF THE MACROECONOMY

Macroeconomics focuses on four groups: (1) *households* and (2) *firms*, which together comprise the private sector, (3) the *government* (the public sector), and (4) the *rest of the world* (the international sector). These four groups interact in a variety of ways, many involving either the receipt or payment of income.

THE CIRCULAR FLOW DIAGRAM

A useful way of seeing the economic interactions among the four sectors in the economy is a **circular flow** diagram, which shows the income received and payments made by each. A simple circular flow diagram is pictured in Figure 5.1.

circular flow A diagram showing the income received and payments made by each sector of the economy.

Let us walk through the circular flow step by step. Households work for firms and the government, and they receive wages for their work. Our diagram shows a flow of wages *into* the household sector as payment for those services. Households also receive interest on corporate and government bonds and dividends from firms. Many households receive other payments from the government, such as social security benefits, veterans' benefits, and welfare payments. Economists call these kinds of payments from the government (for which the recipients do not supply goods, services, or labor) **transfer payments**. Together, all these receipts make up the total income received by the households.

transfer payments Cash payments made by the government to people who do not supply goods, services, or labor in exchange for these payments. They include social security benefits, veterans' benefits, and welfare payments.

Households spend by buying goods and services from firms and by paying taxes to the government. These items make up the total amount paid out by the households. The difference between the total receipts and the total payments of the households is the amount that the households save or dissave. If households receive more than they spend, they *save* during the period. If they receive less than they spend, they *dissave*. A household can dissave by using up some of its previous savings or by borrowing. In the circular flow diagram, household spending is shown as a flow *out* of the household sector. Saving by households is sometimes termed a "leakage" from the circular flow because it withdraws income, or current purchasing power, from the system.

Firms sell goods and services to households and the government. These sales earn revenue, which shows up in the circular flow diagram as a flow *into* the firm sector. Firms pay wages, interest, and dividends to households, and they pay taxes to the government. These payments are shown flowing *out* of the firm sector.

The government collects taxes from households and firms. The government also makes payments. It buys goods and services from firms, pays wages and interest to households, and makes transfer payments to households. If the government's revenue is less than its payments, the government is dissaving.

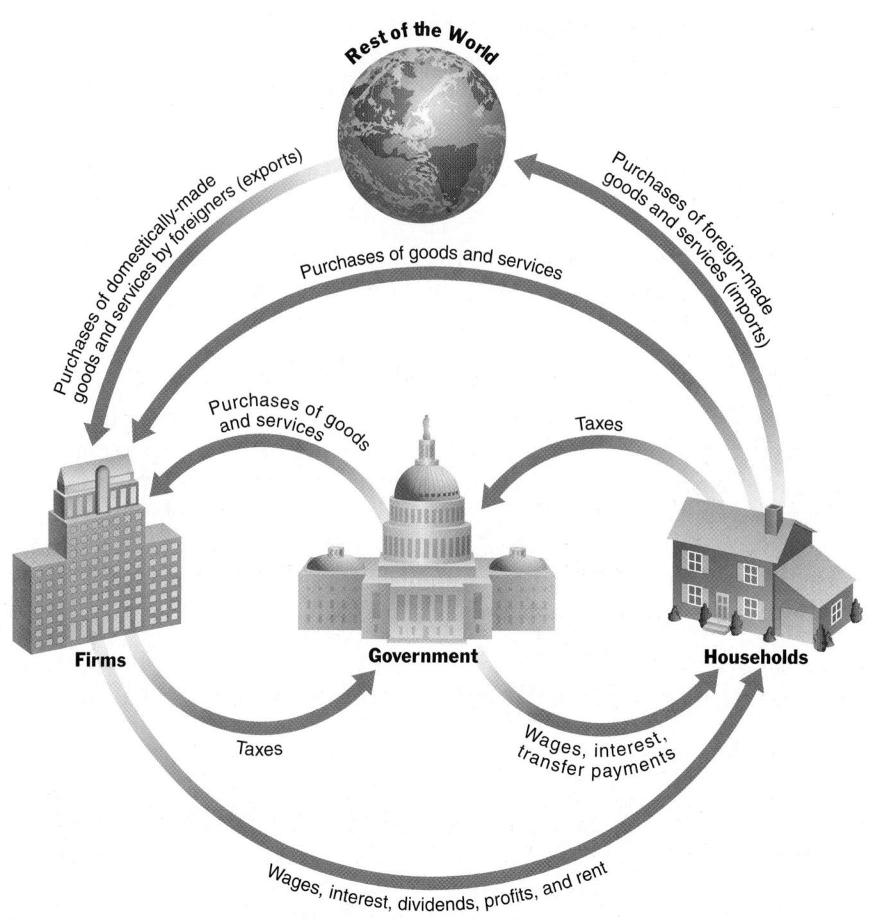

FIGURE 5.1 The Circular Flow of Payments

Households receive income from firms and the government, purchase goods and services from firms, and pay taxes to the government. They also purchase foreign-made goods and services (imports). Firms receive payments from households and the government for goods and services; they pay wages, dividends, interest, and rents to households, and taxes to the government. The government receives taxes from both firms and households, pays both firms and households for goods and services—including wages to government workers—and pays interest and transfers to households. Finally, people in other countries purchase goods and services produced domestically (exports). *Note:* Though not shown in this diagram, firms and governments also purchase imports.

Finally, households spend some of their income on *imports*—goods and services produced in the rest of the world. Similarly, people in foreign countries purchase *exports*—goods and services produced by domestic firms and sold to other countries.

One lesson of the circular flow diagram is that everyone's expenditure is someone else's receipt. If you buy a personal computer from IBM, you make a payment to IBM and IBM receives revenue. If IBM pays taxes to the government, it has made a payment and the government has received revenue.

Everyone's expenditures go somewhere. It is impossible to sell something without there being a buyer, and it is impossible to make a payment without there being a recipient. Every transaction must have two sides.

THE THREE MARKET ARENAS

Another way of looking at the ways households, firms, the government, and the rest of the world relate to each other is to consider the markets in which they interact.

The three market arenas are:

1. Goods-and-services market
2. Labor market
3. Money (financial) market

Goods-and-Services Market Households and the government purchase goods and services from firms in the *goods-and-services market.* In this market, firms also purchase goods and services from each other. For example, Levi Strauss buys denim from other firms to make its blue jeans. In addition, firms buy capital goods from other firms. If General Motors needs new robots on its assembly lines, it may buy them from another firm instead of making them.

Firms *supply* to the goods-and-services market. Households, the government, and firms *demand* from this market. Finally, the rest of the world both buys from and sells to the goods-and-services market. The United States imports hundreds of billions of dollars' worth of automobiles, DVDs, oil, and other goods. At the same time, the United States exports hundreds of billions of dollars' worth of computers, airplanes, and agricultural goods.

Labor Market Interaction in the *labor market* takes place when firms and the government purchase labor from households. In this market, households *supply* labor, and firms and the government *demand* labor. In the U.S. economy, firms are the largest demanders of labor, although the government is also a substantial employer. The total supply of labor in the economy depends on the sum of decisions made by households. Individuals must decide whether to enter the labor force (whether to look for a job at all) and how many hours to work.

Labor is also supplied to and demanded from the rest of the world. In recent years, the labor market has become an international market. For example, vegetable and fruit farmers in California would find it very difficult to bring their product to market if it were not for the labor of migrant farm workers from Mexico. For years, Turkey has provided Germany with "guest workers" who are willing to take low-paying jobs that more prosperous German workers avoid.

Money Market In the *money market*—sometimes called the *financial market*—households purchase stocks and bonds from firms. Households *supply* funds to this market in the expectation of earning income in the form of dividends on stocks and interest on bonds. Households also *demand* (borrow) funds from this market to finance various purchases. Firms borrow to build new facilities in the hope of earning more in the future. The government borrows by issuing bonds. The rest of the world both borrows from and lends to the money market; every morning there are reports on TV and radio about the Japanese and British stock markets. Much of the borrowing and lending of households, firms, the government, and the international sector are coordinated by financial institutions—commercial banks, savings and loan associations, insurance companies, and the like. These institutions take deposits from one group and lend them to others.

When a firm, a household, or the government borrows to finance a purchase, it has an obligation to pay that loan back, usually at some specified time in the future. Most loans also involve payment of interest as a fee for the use of the borrowed funds. When a loan is made, the borrower nearly always signs a "promise to repay," or *promissory note,* and gives it to the lender. When the federal government borrows, it issues "promises" called **Treasury bonds, notes,** or **bills** in exchange for money. Corporations issue **corporate bonds**. A corporate bond might state, for example, "General Electric Corporation agrees to pay $5,000 to the holder of this bond on January 1, 2001, and interest thereon at 8.3 percent annually until that time."

Instead of issuing bonds to raise funds, firms can also issue shares of stock. A **share of stock** is a financial instrument that gives the holder a share in the firm's ownership and

Treasury bonds, notes, and bills Promissory notes issued by the federal government when it borrows money.

corporate bonds Promissory notes issued by corporations when they borrow money.

shares of stock Financial instruments that give to the holder a share in the firm's ownership and therefore the right to share in the firm's profits.

therefore the right to share in the firm's profits. If the firm does well, the value of the stock increases, and the stockholder receives a *capital gain*[1] on the initial purchase. In addition, the stock may pay **dividends**—that is, the firm may return some of its profits directly to its stockholders, instead of retaining them to buy capital. If the firm does poorly, so does the stockholder. The capital value of the stock may fall, and dividends may not be paid.

dividends The portion of a corporation's profits that the firm pays out each period to its shareholders.

Stocks and bonds are simply contracts, or agreements, between parties. I agree to loan you a certain amount, and you agree to repay me this amount plus something extra at some future date, or I agree to buy part ownership in your firm, and you agree to give me a share of the firm's future profits.

A critical variable in the money market is the *interest rate.* Although we sometimes talk as if there were only one interest rate, there is never just one interest rate at any time. Instead, the interest rate on a given loan reflects the length of the loan and the perceived risk to the lender. A business that is just getting started will have to pay a higher rate than will General Motors. A 30-year mortgage has a different interest rate than a 90-day loan. Nevertheless, interest rates tend to move up and down together, and their movement reflects general conditions in the financial market.

THE METHODOLOGY OF MACROECONOMICS

Macroeconomists build models based on theories, and they test their models using data. In this sense, the methodology of macroeconomics is similar to the methodology of microeconomics.

CONNECTIONS TO MICROECONOMICS

How do macroeconomists try to explain aggregate behavior? One way assumes that the same factors that affect individual behavior also affect aggregate behavior. For example, we know from microeconomics that an individual's wage rate should affect her consumption habits and the amount of labor she is willing to supply. If we were to apply this microeconomic hypothesis to the aggregate data, we would say that the average wage rate in the economy should affect total consumption and total labor supply (which seems to be true).

The reason for looking to microeconomics for help in explaining macroeconomic events is simple:

> Macroeconomic behavior is the sum of all the microeconomic decisions made by individual households and firms. If the movements of macroeconomic aggregates, such as total output or total employment, reflect decisions made by individual firms and households, we cannot understand the former without some knowledge of the factors that influence the latter.

Consider unemployment. The unemployment rate is the number of people unemployed as a fraction of the labor force. To be classified as "in the labor force," a person must either have a job or be seeking one actively. To understand aggregate unemployment, we need to understand individual household behavior in the labor market. Why do people choose to enter the labor force? Under what circumstances will they drop out? Why does unemployment exist even when the economy seems to be doing very well? A knowledge of microeconomic behavior is the logical starting point for macroeconomic analysis.

AGGREGATE DEMAND AND AGGREGATE SUPPLY

A major concern of the next few chapters is the behavior of aggregate demand and aggregate supply. **Aggregate demand** is the total demand for goods and services. **Aggregate supply** is the total supply of goods and services.

aggregate demand The total demand for goods and services in an economy.

aggregate supply The total supply of goods and services in an economy.

Figure 5.2 shows *aggregate demand* and *aggregate supply* curves. Measured on the horizontal axis is aggregate output. Measured on the vertical axis is the *overall price level,* not the

[1] A *capital gain* occurs whenever the value of an asset increases. If you bought a stock for $1,000 and it is now worth $1,500, you have earned a capital gain of $500. A capital gain is "realized" when you sell the asset. Until you sell, the capital gain is *accrued* but not *realized.*

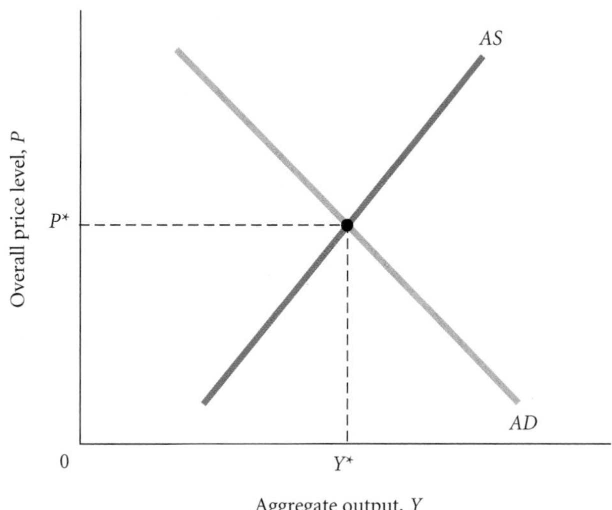

FIGURE 5.2 The Aggregate Demand and Aggregate Supply Curves

A major theme in macroeconomics is the behavior of aggregate demand and aggregate supply. The logic behind the aggregate demand and aggregate supply curves is much more complex than the logic underlying the simple demand and supply curves described in Chapters 3 and 4.

price of a particular good or service. The economy is in equilibrium at the point at which these curves intersect.

We will see that aggregate demand and supply curves are much more complicated than the simple demand and supply curves we described in Chapters 3 and 4. The simple logic of supply, demand, and equilibrium in individual markets does not explain what is depicted in Figure 5.2. It will take the entire next chapter for us to describe what is meant by "aggregate output" and the "overall price level." Furthermore, although we will look to the behavior of households and firms in individual markets for clues about how to analyze aggregate behavior, there are important differences when we move from the individual to the aggregate level.

Consider, for example, *demand*, one of the most important concepts in economics. When the price of a specific good increases, perhaps the most important determinant of consumer response is the availability of other goods that can be substituted for the good whose price has increased. Part of the reason that an increase in the price of airline tickets causes a decline in the quantity of airline tickets demanded is that a higher price relative to other goods means that the opportunity cost of buying a ticket is higher: The sacrifice required in terms of other goods and services has increased. However, when the overall price level changes, there may be no changes in the opportunity cost of goods. For example, a higher priced airline ticket when compared to higher priced other goods may involve the same trade-offs as before all prices increased.

Microeconomics teaches us that, *ceteris paribus*, the quantity demanded of a good falls when its price rises and rises when its price falls. (This is the microeconomic law of demand.) In other words, individual demand curves and market demand curves slope downward to the right. The reason the *aggregate* demand curve in Figure 5.2 slopes downward to the right is complex. As we will see later, the downward slope of the aggregate demand curve is related to what goes on in the money (financial) market.

The aggregate supply curve is very different from the supply curve of an individual firm or market. A firm's supply curve is derived under the assumption that all its input prices are fixed. In other words, the firm's input prices are assumed to remain unchanged as the price of the firm's output changes. When we derived Clarence Brown's soybean supply schedule in Chapter 3, we took his input prices as fixed. A change in an input price leads to a shift in Brown's supply curve, not a movement along it. If we are examining changes in the overall price level, however, *all* prices are changing (including input prices), so the aggregate supply curve cannot be based on the assumption of fixed input prices. We will see that the aggregate supply curve is another source of controversy in macroeconomics.

THE U.S. ECONOMY IN THE TWENTIETH CENTURY: TRENDS AND CYCLES

As we said, most macroeconomic variables go through ups and downs over time, and the economy as a whole experiences periods of prosperity and periods of recession. The trend of the U.S. economy in the twentieth century, however, has been toward prosperity. One measure of an economy's prosperity is the amount of goods and services that it produces during a year, or its gross domestic product (GDP), which is the subject of the next chapter. An economy is said to grow from one year to another if GDP is larger in the second year than in the first. Between 1900 and 2000, the U.S. economy grew at an average rate of 3.4 percent per year. This means that during those years the economy was on average 3.4 percent richer each year than it had been the year before. This is the economy's "long-run" growth rate.

Remember that we are discussing the average growth rate here. The economy did not actually grow by 3.4 percent every year. In some years, growth was less than 3 percent, and in some years growth was negative (GDP fell). In other years, the growth rate was greater than 3.4 percent. So, we need to distinguish between *long-term*, or *secular, trends* in economic performance and *short-term*, or *cyclical, variations.*

EXPANSION AND CONTRACTION: THE BUSINESS CYCLE

Macroeconomics is concerned both with long-run trends—Why has the U.S. economy done so well over the past 100 years—and with short-run fluctuations in economic performance—Why did the world experience a severe recession in the early 1980s and a mild recession in 2001? The term *business cycle* refers to the short-run fluctuations of an economy. A typical business cycle is illustrated in Figure 5.3.

Because the U.S. economy on average grows over time, the business cycle in Figure 5.3 shows a positive trend—the *peak* (the highest point) of a new business cycle is higher than the peak of the previous cycle. The period from a *trough*, or bottom of the cycle, to a peak is called an **expansion** or a **boom**. During an expansion, output and employment grow. The period from a peak to a trough is called a **contraction, recession**, or **slump**, when output and employment fall.

expansion or **boom** The period in the business cycle from a trough up to a peak, during which output and employment rise.

contraction, recession, or **slump** The period in the business cycle from a peak down to a trough, during which output and employment fall.

In judging whether an economy is expanding or contracting, note the difference between the level of economic activity and its rate of change. If the economy has just left a trough (point *A* in Figure 5.3), it will be growing (rate of change is positive), but its level of output will still be low. If the economy has just started to decline from a peak (point *B*), it will be contracting (rate of change is negative), but its level of output will still be high.

The business cycle in Figure 5.3 is symmetrical, which means the length of an expansion is the same as the length of a contraction. Most business cycles are not symmetrical, however. It is possible, for example, for the expansion phase to be longer than the contraction phase. When contraction comes, it may be fast and sharp, while expansion may be slow and gradual. Moreover, the economy is not nearly as regular as the business cycle in Figure 5.3 indicates. While there are ups and downs in the economy, they tend to be erratic.

Figure 5.4 shows the actual business cycles in the United States between 1900 and 2002. Although many business cycles have occurred in the last 100 years, each has been unique. The economy is not so simple that it has regular cycles.

The periods of the Great Depression and the two world wars show the largest fluctuations in Figure 5.4, although other large contractions and expansions have taken place. Note the expansion in the 1960s and the recessions at the beginning of the 1980s and 1990s. Some of the cycles have been long; some have been very short. Note also that GDP actually increased between 1933 and 1937, even though in 1937 it was still quite low. The economy

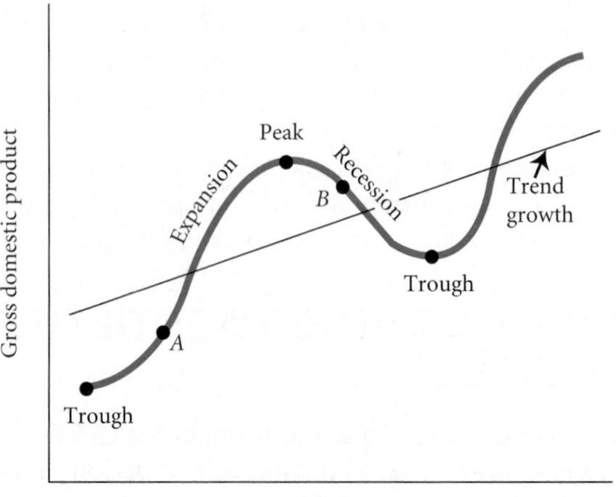

FIGURE 5.3 A Typical Business Cycle

In this business cycle, the economy is expanding as it moves through point *A* from the trough to the peak. When the economy moves from a peak down to a trough, through point *B*, the economy is in recession.

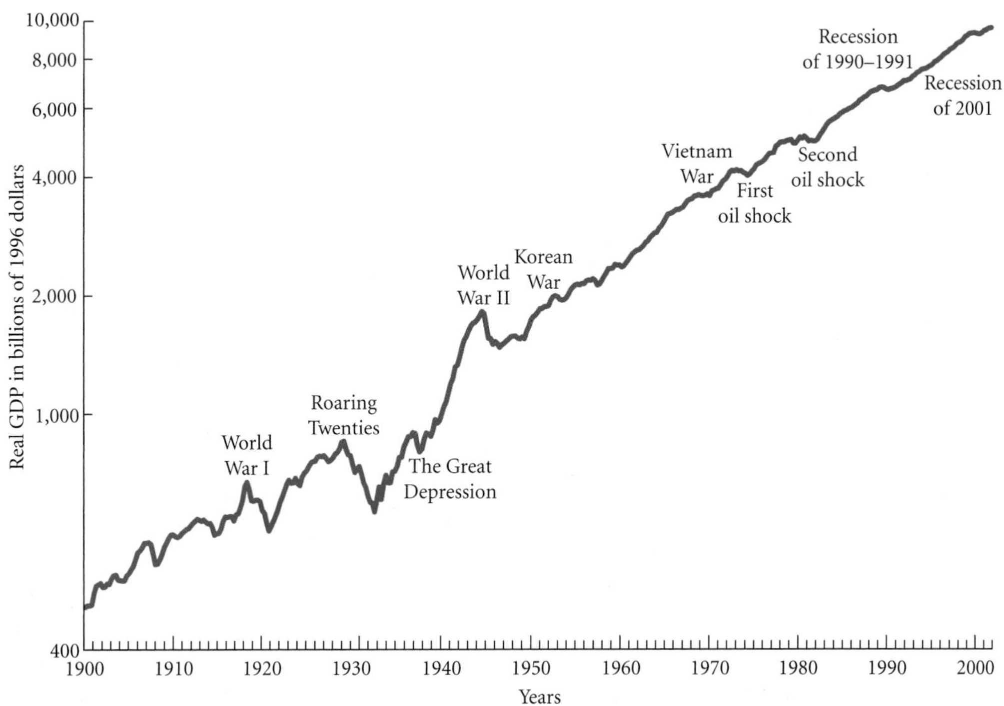

FIGURE 5.4 Real GDP, 1900–2002

The periods of the Great Depression and the two world wars show the largest fluctuations in real GDP.

did not really come out of the Depression until the defense buildup prior to the start of World War II. Note also that business cycles were more extreme before World War II than they have been since then.

THE U.S. ECONOMY SINCE 1970

Since 1970, the U.S. economy has experienced four recessions and large fluctuations in the rate of inflation. By analyzing how the various parts of the economy behaved during these hectic times, we can learn a lot about macroeconomic behavior.

Figures 5.5, 5.6, and 5.7 show the behavior of three key variables during the period since 1970: GDP, unemployment rate, and rate of inflation. These graphs are based on quarterly

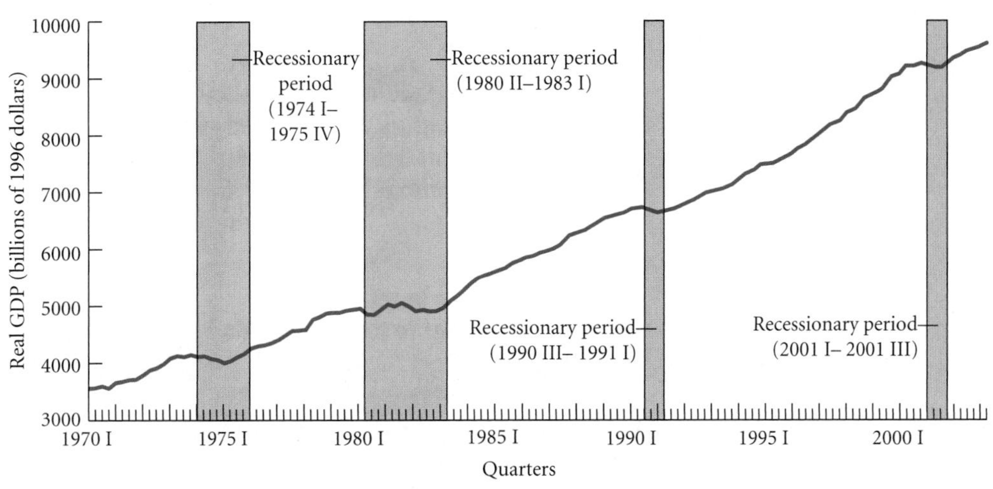

FIGURE 5.5 Real GDP, 1970 I–2003 II

Real GDP in the United States since 1970 has risen overall, but there have been four recessionary periods: 1974 I–1975 IV, 1980 II–1983 I, 1990 III–1991 I, and 2001 I–2001 III.

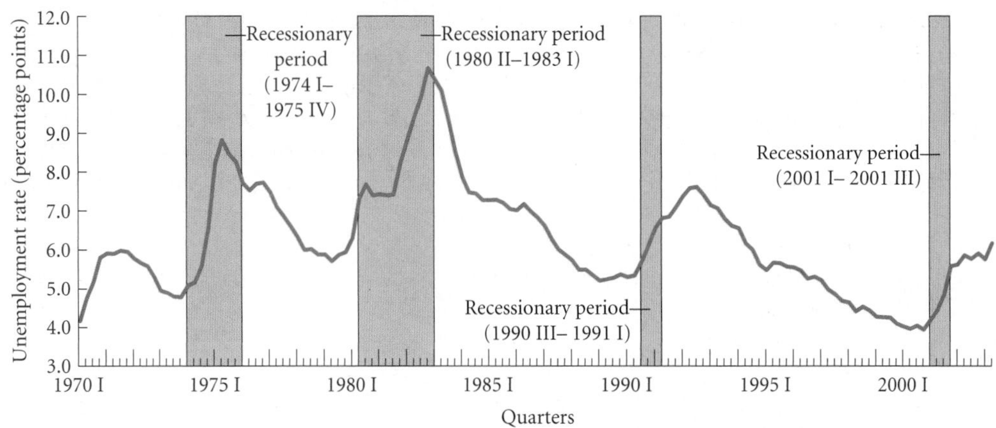

FIGURE 5.6 Unemployment Rate, 1970 I–2003 II

The U.S. unemployment rate since 1970 shows wide variations. The four recessionary reference periods show increases in the unemployment rate.

data (data compiled for each quarter of the year) instead of annual data. The first quarter of a year consists of January, February, and March; the second quarter consists of April, May, and June; and so on. The Roman numerals I, II, III, and IV denote the four quarters. For example, "1972 III" refers to the third quarter, or summer, of 1972.

Figure 5.5 plots GDP for the period 1970 I–2003 II. In the following chapters we will look at four recessionary periods within this period: 1974 I–1975 IV, 1980 II–1983 I, 1990 III–1991 I, and 2001 I–2001 III. These periods make useful reference points when we examine how other variables behaved during the four periods.[2]

One concern of macroeconomists is unemployment. Unemployment generally rises during recessions and falls during expansions. This can be seen in Figure 5.6, which plots the unemployment rate for the period 1970 I–2003 II. Note that unemployment rose in all four

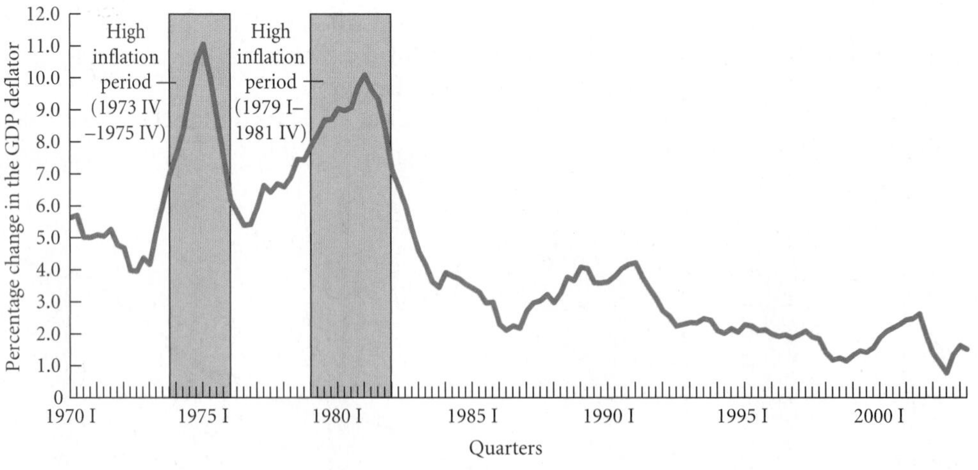

FIGURE 5.7 Percentage Change in the GDP Deflator (Four-Quarter Average), 1970 I–2003 II

The percentage change in the GDP deflator measures the overall rate of inflation. Since 1970, inflation has been high in two periods: 1973 IV–1975 IV and 1979 I–1981 IV. Inflation between 1983 and 1992 was moderate. Since 1992, it has been fairly low.

[2]As Figure 5.5 shows, GDP rose in the middle of 1981 before falling again in the last quarter of 1981. Given this fact, one possibility would be to treat the 1980 II–1983 I period as if it included two separate recessionary periods: 1980 II–1981 I and 1981 IV–1983 I. Because the expansion in 1981 was so short-lived, however, we have chosen not to separate the period into two parts.

recessions. In the 1974–1975 recession, the unemployment rate reached a maximum of 8.8 percent in the second quarter of 1975. During the 1980–1982 recession, it reached a maximum of 10.7 percent in the fourth quarter of 1982. The unemployment rate continued to rise after the 1990–1991 recession and reached a peak of 7.6 percent in 1992 III. By the end of 1994 the unemployment rate had fallen to 5.6 percent, and by the second quarter of 2000 it had fallen to 4.0 percent. The unemployment rate rose to 6.2 percent by the second quarter of 2003.

Macroeconomics is also concerned with the inflation rate. A measure of the overall price level is the GDP deflator. (The construction of the GDP deflator is discussed in the next chapter. It is an index of prices of all domestically produced goods in the economy.) The percentage change in the GDP deflator provides one measure of the overall rate of inflation. Figure 5.7 plots the percentage change in the GDP deflator for the 1970 I–2003 II period.[3] For reference purposes, we have picked two periods within this time as showing particularly high inflation: 1973 IV–1975 IV and 1979 I–1981 IV. In the first period, the inflation rate peaked at 11.0 percent in the first quarter of 1975. In the second period, it peaked at 10.1 percent in the first quarter of 1981. Since 1983, the rate of inflation has been quite low by the standards of the 1970s. Since 1994 it has been about 2.0 percent or less.

Macroeconomics tries to explain the behavior of and the connections among variables such as GDP, unemployment rate, and GDP deflator. When you can understand the forces at work in creating the movements shown in Figures 5.5 to 5.7, you will have come a long way in understanding how the economy works.

[3]The percentage change in Figure 5.7 is the percentage change over four quarters. For example, the value for 1970 I is the percentage change from 1969 I, the value for 1970 II is the percentage change from 1969 II, and so on.

SUMMARY

1. *Microeconomics* examines the functioning of individual industries and the behavior of individual decision-making units. *Macroeconomics* is concerned with the sum, or aggregate, of these individual decisions—the consumption of *all* households in the economy, the amount of labor supplied and demanded by *all* individuals and firms, and the total amount of *all* goods and services produced.

THE ROOTS OF MACROECONOMICS

2. Macroeconomics was born out of the effort to explain the *Great Depression* of the 1930s. Since that time, the discipline has evolved, concerning itself with new issues as the problems facing the economy have changed. Through the late 1960s, it was believed that the government could "fine-tune" the economy to keep it running on an even keel at all times. The poor economic performance of the 1970s, however, showed that *fine-tuning* does not always work.

MACROECONOMIC CONCERNS

3. The three topics of primary concern to macroeconomists are increases in the overall price level, or *inflation*; the growth rate of aggregate output; and the level of unemployment.

GOVERNMENT IN THE MACROECONOMY

4. Among the tools that governments have available to them for influencing the macroeconomy are *fiscal policy* (decisions on taxes and government spending); *monetary policy* (control of the money supply); and *growth or supply-side policies* (policies that focus on increasing the long-run growth rate).

THE COMPONENTS OF THE MACROECONOMY

5. The *circular flow* diagram shows the flow of income received and payments made by the three sectors of the economy—private, public, and international. Everybody's expenditure is someone else's receipt—every transaction must have two sides.
6. Another way of looking at how households, firms, the government, and the international sector relate is to consider the markets in which they interact: the goods-and-services market, labor market, and money (financial) market.

THE METHODOLOGY OF MACROECONOMICS

7. Because macroeconomic behavior is the sum of all the microeconomic decisions made by individual households and firms, we cannot possibly understand the former without some knowledge of the factors that influence the latter. The movements of macroeconomic aggregates reflect decisions made by individual firms and households.
8. A major theme in macroeconomics is understanding the behavior of *aggregate demand* and *aggregate supply*. The logic underlying the aggregate demand and supply curves is more complex than the logic underlying individual market demand and supply curves.

THE U.S. ECONOMY IN THE TWENTIETH CENTURY: TRENDS AND CYCLES

9. Macroeconomics is concerned with both long-run trends and the short-run fluctuations that are part of the *business cycle*. Since 1970, the U.S. economy has seen four *recessions* and large fluctuations in the rate of *inflation*.

REVIEW TERMS AND CONCEPTS

PROBLEM SET

1. Define inflation. Assume that you live in a simple economy in which only three goods are produced and traded: fish, fruit, and meat. Suppose that on January 1, 2003, fish sold for $2.50 per pound, meat was $3.00 per pound, and fruit was $1.50 per pound. At the end of the year, you discover that the catch was low and that fish prices had increased to $5.00 per pound, but fruit prices stayed at $1.50 and meat prices had actually fallen to $2.00. Can you say what happened to the overall "price level"? How might you construct a measure of the "change in the price level"? What additional information might you need to construct your measure?
2. Define unemployment. Should everyone who does not hold a job be considered "unemployed"? To help with your answer, draw a supply and demand diagram depicting the labor market. What is measured along the demand curve? What factors determine the quantity of labor demanded during a given period? What is measured along the labor supply curve? What factors determine the quantity of labor supplied by households during a given period? What is the opportunity cost of holding a job?
3. During 2000, the chairman of the Board of Governors of the Federal Reserve System, Alan Greenspan, voiced his concern that the unemployment rate, which was below 5 percent, was getting too low. Because employment is certainly a major concern of macroeconomic policy, and because job *creation* is considered a major goal, what is Mr. Greenspan's concern? What other goal(s) of macropolicy might be affected by very low rates of unemployment?
4. A recession occurred in the U.S. economy during the first three quarters of 2001. National output of goods and services fell during this period. But during the fourth quarter of 2001, output began to increase and it increased at a slow rate through the first quarter of 2003. At the same time, between March 2001 and April 2003, employment declined almost continuously with a loss of over 2 million jobs. How is it possible that output can rise while at the same time employment is falling?
5. Between the beginning of 2001 and late 2003, the U.S. economy continued to suffer from slow growth and a weak labor market. Over 3 million payroll jobs were lost. The decline was not uniform across sectors of the economy and across regions. The hardest-hit sector was the high-technology, new-economy made up of tens of thousands of dot-com companies. The hardest-hit regions were those with a concentration of high-tech firms, such as San Francisco and Boston.

   Describe the economy of your state. What is the most recently reported unemployment rate? How has the number of payroll jobs changed over the last 3 months, and over the last year? How does your state's performance compare to the U.S. economy's performance over the last year? What explanations have been offered in the press? How accurate are these?
6. Explain briefly how macroeconomics is different from microeconomics. How can macroeconomists use microeconomic theory to guide them in their work, and why might they wish to do so?
7. During 1993, when the economy was growing very slowly, President Clinton recommended a series of spending cuts and tax increases designed to reduce the deficit. These were passed by Congress in the Omnibus Budget Reconciliation Act of 1993. Some who opposed the bill argue that the United States was pursuing a "contractionary fiscal policy" at precisely the wrong time. Explain their logic.
8. Many of the expansionary periods during the twentieth century have occurred during wars. Why do you think this is true?
9. In the 1940s, you could buy a soda for 5 cents, eat dinner at a restaurant for less than $1, and purchase a house for $10,000. From this statement, it follows that consumers today are worse off than consumers in the 1940s. Comment.

*10. During 1994 and 1995, the Federal Reserve became increasingly concerned with inflation. As the economy grew at a more and more rapid rate, the Fed acted to raise interest rates sharply. For example, the interest rate that home buyers had to pay on 30-year fixed-rate mortgages jumped from 7 percent to over 9 percent. This policy was designed to slow the rate of spending growth in the economy. How might higher interest rates be expected to slow the rate of spending growth? Give some examples.

*Note: Problems marked with an asterisk are more challenging.

Measuring National Output and National Income

6

CHAPTER OUTLINE

Macroeconomics relies on data, much of it collected by the government. To study the economy, we need data on total output, total income, total consumption, and the like. Much of the macroeconomic data are from the **national income and product accounts**, which describe the components of national income in the economy. These accounts are produced by the Bureau of Economic Analysis (BEA) of the U.S. Department of Commerce.

The national income and product accounts do more than convey data about the performance of the economy. They also provide a conceptual framework that macroeconomists use to think about how the pieces of the economy fit together. When economists think about the macroeconomy, the categories and vocabulary they use come from the national income and product accounts.

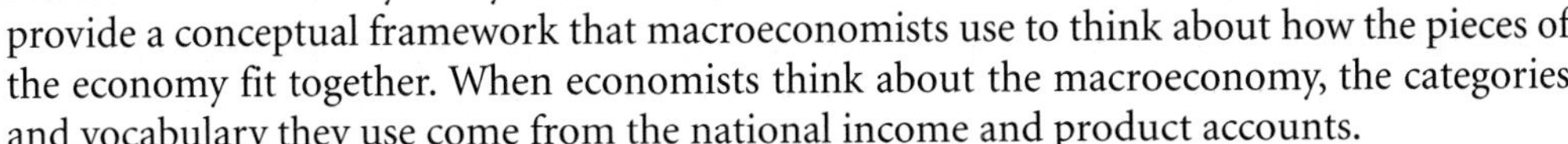

The national income and product accounts can be compared with the mechanical or wiring diagrams for an automobile engine. The diagrams do not explain how an engine works, but they identify the key parts of an engine and show how they are connected. Trying to understand the macroeconomy without understanding national income accounting is like trying to fix an engine without a mechanical diagram and with no names for the engine parts.

GROSS DOMESTIC PRODUCT

The key concept in the national income and product accounts is **gross domestic product (GDP)**.

> GDP is the total market value of a country's output. It is the market value of all final goods and services produced within a given period of time by factors of production located within a country.

national income and product accounts Data collected and published by the government describing the various components of national income and output in the economy.

U.S. GDP for 2002—the value of all the output produced by factors of production in the United States in 2002—was $10,446.2 billion.

The centrality of GDP as a working concept cannot be overestimated. Just as an individual firm needs to evaluate the success or failure of its operations each year, so the economy as a whole needs to assess itself. GDP, as a measure of the total production of an economy, provides us with a country's economic report card. Because GDP is such an important concept, we need to take some time to explain exactly what its definition means.

gross domestic product (GDP) The total market value of all final goods and services produced within a given period by factors of production located within a country.

final goods and services Goods and services produced for final use.

intermediate goods Goods that are produced by one firm for use in further processing by another firm.

value added The difference between the value of goods as they leave a stage of production and the cost of the goods as they entered that stage.

FINAL GOODS AND SERVICES

First note that the definition refers to **final goods and services.** Many goods produced in the economy are not classified as *final* goods, but instead as intermediate goods. **Intermediate goods** are produced by one firm for use in further processing by another firm. For example, tires sold to automobile manufacturers are intermediate goods. The value of intermediate goods is not counted in GDP.

Why are intermediate goods not counted in GDP? Suppose that in producing a car General Motors (GM) pays $100 to Goodyear for tires. GM uses these tires (among other components) to assemble a car, which it sells for $12,000. The value of the car (including its tires) is $12,000, not $12,000 + $100. The final price of the car already reflects the value of all its components. To count in GDP both the value of the tires sold to the automobile manufacturers and the value of the automobiles sold to the consumers would result in double counting.

Double counting can also be avoided by counting only the value added to a product by each firm in its production process. The **value added** during some stage of production is the difference between the value of goods as they leave that stage of production and the cost of the goods as they entered that stage. Value added is illustrated in Table 6.1. The four stages of the production of a gallon of gasoline are (1) oil drilling, (2) refining, (3) shipping, and (4) retail sale. In the first stage, value added is the value of sales. In the second stage, the refiner purchases the oil from the driller, refines it into gasoline, and sells it to the shipper. The refiner pays the driller $0.50 per gallon and charges the shipper $0.65. The value added by the refiner is thus $0.15 per gallon. The shipper then sells the gasoline to retailers for $0.80. The value added in the third stage of production is $0.15. Finally, the retailer sells the gasoline to consumers for $1.00. The value added at the fourth stage is $0.20, and the total value added in the production process is $1.00, the same as the value of sales at the retail level. Adding the total values of sales at each stage of production ($0.50 + $0.65 + $0.80 + $1.00 = $2.95) would significantly overestimate the value of the gallon of gasoline.

In calculating GDP, we can either sum up the value added at each stage of production or we can take the value of final sales. We do not use the value of total sales in an economy to measure how much output has been produced.

EXCLUSION OF USED GOODS AND PAPER TRANSACTIONS

GDP is concerned only with new, or current, production. Old output is not counted in current GDP because it was already counted back at the time it was produced. It would be double counting to count sales of used goods in current GDP. If someone sells a used car to you, the transaction is not counted in GDP, because no new production has taken place. Similarly, a house is counted in GDP only at the time it is built, not each time it is resold. In short:

GDP ignores all transactions in which money or goods change hands but in which no new goods and services are produced.

Sales of stocks and bonds are not counted in GDP. These exchanges are transfers of ownership of assets, either electronically or through paper exchanges, and do not correspond to current production. However, what if I sell the stock or bond for more than I originally paid

TABLE 6.1 Value Added in the Production of a Gallon of Gasoline (Hypothetical Numbers)

STAGE OF PRODUCTION	VALUE OF SALES	VALUE ADDED
(1) Oil drilling	$0.50	$0.50
(2) Refining	0.65	0.15
(3) Shipping	0.80	0.15
(4) Retail sale	1.00	0.20
Total value added		$1.00

Tires taken from that pile and mounted on the wheels of the new car before it is sold are considered intermediate goods to the auto producer. Tires from that pile to replace tires on your old car are considered final goods. If, in calculating GDP, we included the value of the tires (an intermediate good) on new cars and the value of new cars (including the tires), we would be double counting.

for it? Profits from the stock or bond market have nothing to do with current production, so they are not counted in GDP. However, if I pay a fee to a broker for selling a stock of mine to someone else, this fee is counted in GDP, because the broker is performing a service for me. This service is part of current production. Be careful to distinguish between exchanges of stocks and bonds for money (or for other stocks and bonds), which do not involve current production, and fees for performing such exchanges, which do.

EXCLUSION OF OUTPUT PRODUCED ABROAD BY DOMESTICALLY OWNED FACTORS OF PRODUCTION

GDP is the value of output produced by factors of production *located within a country.*

The three basic factors of production are land, labor, and capital. The labor of U.S. citizens counts as a domestically owned factor of production for the United States. The output produced by U.S. citizens abroad—for example, U.S. citizens working for a foreign company—is *not* counted in U.S. GDP because the output is not produced within the United States. Likewise, profits earned abroad by U.S. companies are not counted in U.S. GDP. However, the output produced by foreigners working in the United States is counted in U.S. GDP because the output is produced within the United States. Also, profits earned in the United States by foreign-owned companies are counted in U.S. GDP.

It is sometimes useful to have a measure of the output produced by factors of production owned by a country's citizens regardless of where the output is produced. This measure is called **gross national product (GNP)**. For most countries, including the United States, the difference between GDP and GNP is small. In 2002, GNP for the United States was $10,436.7 billion, which is close to the $10,446.2 billion value for U.S. GDP.

gross national product (GNP) The total market value of all final goods and services produced within a given period by factors of production owned by a country's citizens, regardless of where the output is produced.

The distinction between GDP and GNP can be tricky. Consider the Honda plant in Marysville, Ohio. The plant is owned by the Honda Corporation, a Japanese firm, but most of the workers employed at the plant are U.S. workers. Although all the output of the plant is included in U.S. GDP, only part of it is included in U.S. GNP. The wages paid to U.S. workers are part of U.S. GNP, while the profits from the plant are not. The profits from the plant are counted in Japanese GNP because this is output produced by Japanese-owned factors of production (Japanese capital in this case). The profits, however, are not counted in Japanese GDP because they were not earned in Japan.

CALCULATING GDP

expenditure approach A method of computing GDP that measures the amount spent on all final goods during a given period.

GDP can be computed in two ways. One is to add up the total amount spent on all final goods during a given period. This is the **expenditure approach** to calculating GDP. The other is to add up the income—wages, rents, interest, and profits—received by all factors of

income approach A method of computing GDP that measures the income—wages, rents, interest, and profits—received by all factors of production in producing final goods.

production in producing final goods. This is the **income approach** to calculating GDP. These two methods lead to the same value for GDP for the reason we discussed in the previous chapter: *Every payment (expenditure) by a buyer is at the same time a receipt (income) for the seller.* We can measure either income received or expenditures made, and we will end up with the same total output.

Suppose the economy is made up of just one firm and the firm's total output this year sells for $1 million. Because the total amount spent on output this year is $1 million, this year's GDP is $1 million. (Remember: The expenditure approach calculates GDP on the basis of the total amount spent on final goods and services in the economy.) However, *every one* of the million dollars of GDP is either paid to someone or remains with the owners of the firm as profit. Using the income approach, we add up the wages paid to employees of the firm, the interest paid to those who lent money to the firm, and the rents paid to those who leased land, buildings, or equipment to the firm. What is left over is profit, which is, of course, income to the owners of the firm. If we add up the incomes of all the factors of production, including profits to the owners, we get a GDP of $1 million.

THE EXPENDITURE APPROACH

Recall from the previous chapter the four main groups in the economy: households, firms, the government, and the rest of the world. There are also four main categories of expenditure:

Expenditure Categories:

- Personal consumption expenditures (*C*): household spending on consumer goods
- Gross private domestic investment (*I*): spending by firms and households on new capital, i.e., plant, equipment, inventory, and new residential structures
- Government consumption and gross investment (*G*)
- Net exports (*EX* – *IM*): net spending by the rest of the world, or exports (*EX*) minus imports (*IM*)

The expenditure approach calculates GDP by adding together these four components of spending. In equation form:

$$GDP = C + I + G + (EX - IM)$$

U.S. GDP was $10,446.2 billion in 2002. The four components of the expenditure approach are shown in Table 6.2, along with their various categories.

TABLE 6.2 Components of U.S. GDP, 2002: The Expenditure Approach

	BILLIONS OF DOLLARS		PERCENTAGE OF GDP	
Personal consumption expenditures (C)	7,303.7		69.9	
Durable goods		871.9		8.3
Nondurable goods		2,115.0		20.2
Services		4,316.8		41.3
Gross private domestic investment (I)	1,593.2		14.8	
Nonresidential		1,117.4		10.7
Residential		471.9		4.5
Change in business inventories		3.9		0
Government consumption and gross investment (G)	1,972.9		18.9	
Federal		693.7		6.6
State and local		1,279.2		12.2
Net exports(EX – IM)	–423.6		–4.1	
Exports (*EX*)		1,014.9		9.8
Imports (*IM*)		1,438.5		13.8
Total gross domestic product	10,446.2		100.0	

Note: Numbers may not add exactly because of rounding.
Source: U.S. Department of Commerce, Bureau of Economic Analysis.

Personal Consumption Expenditures (*C*) The largest part of GDP consists of **personal consumption expenditures (*C*)**. Table 6.2 shows that in 2002 the amount of personal consumption expenditures accounted for 69.9 percent of GDP. These are expenditures by consumers on goods and services.

There are three main categories of consumer expenditures: durable goods, nondurable goods, and services. **Durable goods**, such as automobiles, furniture, and household appliances, last a relatively long time. **Nondurable goods**, such as food, clothing, gasoline, and cigarettes, are used up fairly quickly. Payments for **services**—those things that we buy that do not involve the production of physical items—include expenditures for doctors, lawyers, and educational institutions. As Table 6.2 shows, in 2002 durable goods expenditures accounted for 8.3 percent of GDP, nondurables for 20.2 percent, and services for 41.3 percent.

personal consumption expenditures (*C*) A major component of GDP: expenditures by consumers on goods and services.

durable goods Goods that last a relatively long time, such as cars and household appliances.

nondurable goods Goods that are used up fairly quickly, such as food and clothing.

services The things we buy that do not involve the production of physical things, such as legal and medical services and education.

Gross Private Domestic Investment (*I*) *Investment*, as we use the term in economics, refers to the purchase of new capital—housing, plants, equipment, and inventory. The economic use of the term is in contrast to its everyday use, where *investment* often refers to purchases of stocks, bonds, or mutual funds.

Total investment in capital by the private sector is called **gross private domestic investment (*I*)**. Expenditures by firms for machines, tools, plants, and so forth make up **nonresidential investment.**[1] Because these are goods that firms buy for their own final use, they are part of "final sales" and counted in GDP. Expenditures for new houses and apartment buildings constitute **residential investment**. The third component of gross private investment, the **change in business inventories,** is the amount by which firms' inventories change during a period. Business inventories can be looked at as the goods that firms produce now but intend to sell later. In 2002, gross private investment accounted for 14.8 percent of GDP. Of this, 10.7 percent was nonresidential investment and 4.5 percent was residential investment.

gross private domestic investment (*I*) Total investment in capital—that is, the purchase of new housing, plants, equipment, and inventory by the private (or nongovernment) sector.

nonresidential investment Expenditures by firms for machines, tools, plants, and so on.

residential investment Expenditures by households and firms on new houses and apartment buildings.

change in business inventories The amount by which firms' inventories change during a period. Inventories are the goods that firms produce now but intend to sell later.

Change in Business Inventories It is sometimes confusing to students that inventories are counted as capital and that changes in inventory are counted as part of gross private domestic investment, but conceptually it makes sense. The inventory a firm owns has a value, and it serves a purpose, or provides a service, to the firm. That it has value is obvious. Think of the inventory of a new car dealer or of a clothing store, or stocks of newly produced but unsold computers awaiting shipment. All these have value.

However, what *service* does inventory provide? Firms keep stocks of inventory for a number of reasons. One is to meet unforeseen demand. Firms are never sure how much they will sell from period to period. Sales go up and down. To maintain the goodwill of their customers, firms need to be able to respond to unforeseen increases in sales. The only way to do that is with inventory.

Some firms use inventory to provide direct services to customers—the main function of a retail store. A grocery store provides a service—convenience. The store itself does not produce any food at all. It simply assembles a wide variety of items and puts them on display so consumers with varying tastes can come and shop in one place for what they want. The same is true for a clothing or hardware store. To provide their services, such stores need light fixtures, counters, cash registers, buildings, and lots of inventory.

Capital stocks are made up of plant, equipment, and inventory; inventory accumulations are part of the change in capital stocks, or investment.

Remember that GDP is not the market value of total final *sales* during a period—it is the market value of total *production*. The relationship between total production and total sales is:

GDP = final sales + change in business inventories

Total production (GDP) equals final sales of domestic goods plus the change in business inventories. In 2002, production in the United States exceeded sales by $3.9 billion. Inventories at the end of 2002 were $3.9 billion *greater* than they were at the end of 2001.

[1]The distinction between what is considered investment and what is considered consumption is sometimes fairly arbitrary. A firm's purchase of a car or a truck is counted as investment, but a household's purchase of a car or a truck is counted as consumption of durable goods. In general, expenditures by firms for items that last longer than a year are counted as investment expenditures. Expenditures for items that last less than a year are seen as purchases of intermediate goods.

Further Exploration

GDP: One of the Great Inventions of the 20th Century—Survey of Current Business

As the 20th century drew to a close, the U.S. Department of Commerce embarked on a review of its achievements. At the conclusion of this review, the Department named the development of the national income and product accounts as "its achievement of the century."

J. Steven Landefeld
Director, Bureau of Economic Analysis

While the GDP and the rest of the national income accounts may seem to be arcane concepts, they are truly among the great inventions of the twentieth century.

Paul A. Samuelson and
William D. Nordhaus

The Department of Commerce is responsible for producing and maintaining the "National Income and Product Accounts" that keep track of GDP.

HISTORY OF THE NATIONAL INCOME AND PRODUCT ACCOUNTS (NIPAs) —Prior to the development of the NIPA's, policymakers had to guide the economy using limited and fragmentary information about the state of the economy. The Great Depression underlined the problems of incomplete data and led to the development of the national accounts:

> One reads with dismay of Presidents Hoover and then Roosevelt designing policies to combat the Great Depression of the 1930's on the basis of such sketchy data as stock price indices, freight car loadings, and incomplete indices of industrial production. The fact was that comprehensive measures of national income and output did not exist at the time. The Depression, and with it the growing role of government in the economy, emphasized the need for such measures and led to the development of a comprehensive set of national income accounts.
>
> Richard T. Froyen

In response to this need in the 1930's, the Department of Commerce commissioned Nobel laureate Simon Kuznets of the National Bureau of Economic Research to develop a set of national economic accounts. . . . Professor Kuznets coordinated the work of researchers at the National Bureau of Economic Research in New York and his staff at Commerce. The original set of accounts was presented in a report to Congress in 1937 and in a research report, *National Income, 1929–35*. . . .

The national accounts have become the mainstay of modern macroeconomic analysis, allowing policymakers, economists, and the business community to analyze the impact of different tax and spending plans, the impact of oil and other price shocks, and the impact of monetary policy on the economy as a whole and on specific components of final demand, incomes, industries, and regions. . . .

> GDP! The right concept of economy-wide output, accurately measured. The U.S. and the world rely on it to tell where we are in the business cycle and to estimate long-run growth. It is the centerpiece of an elaborate and indispensable system of social accounting, the national income and product accounts. This is surely the single most innovative achievement of the Commerce Department in the 20th century. I was fortunate to become an economist in the 1930's when Kuznets, Nathan, Gilbert, and Jaszi were creating this most important set of economic time series. In economic theory, macroeconomics was just beginning at the same time. . . . These two innovations deserve much credit for the improved performance of the economy in the second half of the century.
>
> James Tobin,
> Nobel laureate
> *Yale University Professor Emeritus of Economics*

Source: U.S. Department of Commerce, Bureau of Economics, "GDP: One of the Great Inventions of the 20th Century," Survey of Current Business, *January 2000, pp. 6–9.*

depreciation The amount by which an asset's value falls in a given period.

Gross Investment versus Net Investment During the process of production, capital (especially machinery and equipment) produced in previous periods gradually wears out. GDP does not give us a true picture of the real production of an economy. GDP includes newly produced capital goods but does not take account of capital goods "consumed" in the production process.

Capital assets decline in value over time. The amount by which an asset's value falls each period is called its **depreciation**.[2] A personal computer purchased by a business today may

[2]This is the formal definition of economic depreciation. Because depreciation is difficult to measure precisely, accounting rules allow firms to use shortcut methods to approximate the amount of depreciation that they incur each period. To complicate matters even more, the U.S. tax laws allow firms to deduct depreciation for tax purposes under a different set of rules.

Investment—the purchase of new capital—includes increases in business inventories: stacks of khakis at the Gap, and lots full of cars at General Motors.

be expected to have a useful life of 4 years before becoming worn out or obsolete. Over that period, the computer steadily depreciates.

What is the relationship between gross investment (I) and depreciation? **Gross investment** is the total value of all newly produced capital goods (plant, equipment, housing, and inventory) produced in a given period. It takes no account of the fact that some capital wears out and must be replaced. **Net investment** is equal to gross investment minus depreciation. Net investment is a measure of how much the stock of capital *changes* during a period. Positive net investment means that the amount of new capital produced exceeds the amount that wears out, and negative net investment means that the amount of new capital produced is less than the amount that wears out. Therefore, if net investment is positive, the capital stock has increased, and if net investment is negative, the capital stock has decreased. Put another way, the capital stock at the end of a period is equal to the capital stock that existed at the beginning of the period plus net investment:

gross investment The total value of all newly produced capital goods (plant, equipment, housing, and inventory) produced in a given period.

net investment Gross investment minus depreciation.

$$\text{capital}_{\text{end of period}} = \text{capital}_{\text{beginning of period}} + \text{net investment}$$

Government Consumption and Gross Investment (G) **Government consumption and gross investment** (G) include expenditures by federal, state, and local governments for final goods (bombs, pencils, school buildings) and services (military salaries, congressional salaries, school teachers' salaries). Some of these expenditures are counted as government consumption and some are counted as government gross investment. Government transfer payments (Social Security benefits, veterans' disability stipends, etc.) are not included in G because these transfers are not purchases of anything currently produced. The payments are not made in exchange for any goods or services. Because interest payments on the government debt are also counted as transfers, they are also excluded from GDP on the grounds that they are not payments for current goods or services.

government consumption and gross investment (G) Expenditures by federal, state, and local governments for final goods and services.

As Table 6.2 shows, government consumption and gross investment accounted for \$1,972.9 billion, or 18.9 percent of U.S. GDP, in 2002. Federal government consumption and gross investment in 2002 accounted for 6.6 percent of GDP, and state and local government consumption and gross investment accounted for 12.2 percent.

Net Exports ($EX - IM$) The value of **net exports** ($EX - IM$) is the difference between *exports* (sales to foreigners of U.S.-produced goods and services) and *imports* (U.S. purchases of goods and services from abroad). This figure can be positive or negative. In 2002, the United States exported less than it imported, so the level of net exports was negative (–\$423.6 billion). Before 1976, the United States was generally a net exporter—exports exceeded imports, so the net export figure was positive.

net exports ($EX - IM$) The difference between exports (sales to foreigners of U.S.-produced goods and services) and imports (U.S. purchases of goods and services from abroad). The figure can be positive or negative.

The reason for including net exports in the definition of GDP is simple. Consumption, investment, and government spending (C, I, and G) include expenditures on goods produced both domestically and by foreigners. Therefore, $C + I + G$ overstates domestic production because it contains expenditures on foreign-produced goods—that is, imports (IM), which have to be subtracted out of GDP to obtain the correct figure. At the same time,

$C + I + G$ understates domestic production because some of what a nation produces is sold abroad and therefore not included in *C*, *I*, or *G*—exports (*EX*) have to be added in. If a U.S. firm produces computers and sells them in Germany, the computers are part of U.S. production and should be counted as part of U.S. GDP.

THE INCOME APPROACH

Table 6.3 presents the other approach to calculating GDP, the income approach, which looks at GDP in terms of who receives it as income, not who purchases it.

The income approach to GDP breaks down GDP into five components: national income, depreciation, indirect taxes minus subsidies, net factor payments to the rest of the world, and "other":

$$\text{GDP} = \text{national income} + \text{depreciation} + (\text{indirect taxes} - \text{subsidies}) + \text{net factor payments to the rest of the world} + \text{other}$$

As we examine each, keep in mind that total expenditures always equal total income.

national income The total income earned by the factors of production owned by a country's citizens.

compensation of employees Includes wages, salaries, and various supplements—employer contributions to social insurance and pension funds, for example—paid to households by firms and by the government.

proprietors' income The income of unincorporated businesses.

corporate profits The income of corporate businesses.

net interest The interest paid by business.

rental income The income received by property owners in the form of rent.

National Income **National income** is the total income earned by factors of production owned by a country's citizens. Table 6.3 shows that national income is the sum of five items: (1) compensation of employees, (2) proprietors' income, (3) corporate profits, (4) net interest, and (5) rental income. **Compensation of employees**, the largest of the five items by far, includes wages and salaries paid to households by firms and by the government, as well as various supplements to wages and salaries such as contributions that employers make to social insurance and private pension funds. **Proprietors' income** is the income of unincorporated businesses, and **corporate profits** are the income of corporate businesses. **Net interest** is the interest paid by business. (Interest paid by households and by the government is not counted in GDP because it is not assumed to flow from the production of goods and services.) **Rental income**, a minor item, is the income received by property owners in the form of rent.

Depreciation Recall from our discussion of net versus gross investment that when capital assets wear out or become obsolete, they decline in value. The measure of that decrease in value is called depreciation. This depreciation is a part of GDP in the income approach.

It may seem odd that we *add* depreciation to national income when we calculate GDP by the income approach. To see why depreciation is added, let us go back to the example earlier in this chapter in which the economy is made up of just one firm and total output (GDP) for the year is $1 million. Assume that after the firm pays wages, interest, and rent, it has left $100,000. Assume also that its capital stock depreciated by $40,000 during the year. National income includes corporate profits, and in calculating corporate profits the $40,000 deprecia-

TABLE 6.3 Components of GDP, 2002: The Income Approach

	BILLIONS OF DOLLARS		PERCENTAGE OF GDP	
National income	8,340.1		79.8	
Compensation of employees		5,969.5		57.1
Proprietors' income		756.5		7.2
Corporate profits		787.4		7.5
Net interest		684.2		6.5
Rental income		142.4		1.4
Depreciation	1,393.5		13.3	
Indirect taxes minus subsidies	767.9		7.4	
Net factor payments to the rest of the world	9.6		0.1	
Other	−64.9		−0.6	
Gross domestic product	10,446.2		100.0	

Source: See Table 6.2.

tion is subtracted from the $100,000, leaving profits of only $60,000. When we calculate GDP using the expenditure approach, depreciation is not subtracted. We simply add consumption, investment, government spending, and net exports. In our simple example, this is just $1 million. When we calculate GDP using the income approach, we must add depreciation because it has been subtracted from the amount that corporations actually receive (the full $100,000). This is necessary to balance the income and expenditure sides. In other words, national income as defined in Table 6.3 includes corporate profits after depreciation has been deducted, and so depreciation must be added back. In 2002, depreciation accounted for $1,393.5 billion, or 13.3 percent of U.S. GDP.

Indirect Taxes Minus Subsidies In calculating final sales on the expenditures side, **indirect taxes**—sales taxes, customs duties, and license fees, for example—are included. Because these taxes are counted on the expenditure side, they must also be counted on the income side.

indirect taxes Taxes like sales taxes, customs duties, and license fees.

To see why indirect taxes are added, let us again go back to the example of the one firm economy, where total output is $1 million. If the sales tax rate were, say, 7 percent, total sales taxes would be $70,000. These taxes would go to the government, and so the firm would receive only $930,000, to be allocated to wages, interest, rent, profits, and depreciation. Therefore, to measure total income, we must add to these items the sales taxes of $70,000.

Subsidies are payments made by the government for which it receives no goods or services in return. These subsidies are subtracted from national income to get GDP. (Remember, GDP is indirect taxes *minus* subsidies.) For example, farmers receive substantial subsidies from the government. Subsidy payments to farmers are income to farm proprietors and are thus part of national income, but they do not come from the sale of agricultural products, so are not part of GDP. To balance the expenditure side with the income side, these subsidies must be subtracted on the income side.

subsidies Payments made by the government for which it receives no goods or services in return.

Net Factor Payments to the Rest of the World **Net factor payments to the rest of the world** equal the payments of factor income (income to the factors of production) to the rest of the world *minus* the receipts of factor income from the rest of the world. This item is added for the following reason. National income is defined as the income of factors of production *owned* by the country. GDP, however, is output produced by factors of production located *within* the country. In other words, national income includes some income that should not be counted in GDP—namely, the income a country's citizens earn abroad—and this income must be subtracted. In addition, national income does not include some income that is counted in GDP—namely, the foreigners' income in the country whose GDP we are calculating—and this income must be added. Table 6.3 shows that the value of net factor payments to the rest of the world was positive in 2002 ($9.6 billion). This means that U.S. payments of factor income to the rest of the world exceeded U.S. receipts of factor income from the rest of the world in 2002.

net factor payments to the rest of the world Payments of factor income to the rest of the world minus the receipt of factor income from the rest of the world.

Other In Table 6.3, "other" includes business transfer payments and the statistical discrepancy. Business transfer payments are deducted from corporate profits and are not included as income elsewhere. Therefore, they need to be included to get total income. The statistical discrepancy adjusts for errors in the data collection.

Gross Domestic Product As you can see in Table 6.3, U.S. GDP as calculated by the income approach was $10,446.2 billion in 2002—the same amount that we calculated using the expenditure approach.

FROM GDP TO DISPOSABLE PERSONAL INCOME

Although GDP is the most important item in national income accounting, other concepts are also useful to know. Some are presented in Table 6.4. The top of the table shows how GNP is calculated from GDP. Remember that a country's GDP is total production by factors of production located within that country, while its GNP is total production by factors of production owned by that country. If we take U.S. GDP, add to it factor income earned by U.S. citizens from the rest of the world (receipts of factor income from the rest of the world),

TABLE 6.4 GDP, GNP, NNP, National Income, Personal Income, and Disposable Personal Income, 2002

	DOLLARS (BILLIONS)
GDP	**10,446.2**
Plus: receipts of factor income from the rest of the world	+278.0
Less: payments of factor income to the rest of the world	−287.6
Equals: **GNP**	**10,436.7**
Less: depreciation	−1,393.5
Equals: **net national product (NNP)**	**9,043.2**
Less: indirect taxes minus subsidies plus other	−703.1
Equals: **national income**	**8,340.1**
Less: corporate profits minus dividends	−353.6
Less: social insurance payments	−746.5
Plus: personal interest income received from the government and consumers	+394.3
Plus: transfer payments to persons	+1,288.0
Equals: **personal income**	**8,922.2**
Less: personal taxes	−1,111.9
Equals: **disposable personal income**	**7,810.3**

Source: See Table 6.2

and subtract from it factor income earned in the United States by foreigners (payments of factor income to the rest of the world), we get GNP.

net national product (NNP) Gross national product minus depreciation; a nation's total product minus what is required to maintain the value of its capital stock.

From GNP, we can calculate **net national product (NNP)**. Recall that the expenditure approach to GDP includes gross investment as one of the components of GDP (and of GNP). Gross domestic product does not account for the fact that some of the nation's capital stock is used up in the process of producing the nation's product. NNP is GNP minus depreciation. In a sense, it is a nation's total product minus (or "net of") what is required to maintain the value of its capital stock. Because GDP does not take into account any depreciation of the capital stock that may have occurred, NNP is sometimes a better measure of how the economy is doing than is GDP.

To calculate national income, we subtract indirect taxes minus subsidies from NNP (subtract indirect business taxes and add subsidies). We subtract indirect taxes because they are included in NNP but do not represent payments to factors of production and are not part of national income. We add subsidies because they are payments to factors of production but are not included in NNP.

personal income The total income of households. Equals (national income) minus (corporate profits minus dividends) minus (social insurance payments) plus (interest income received from the government and households) plus (transfer payments to households). The income received by households after paying social insurance taxes but before paying personal income taxes.

Personal income is the total income of households. To calculate personal income from national income, two items are subtracted: (1) corporate profits minus dividends, and (2) social insurance payments. Both need explanation. First, some corporate profits are paid to households in the form of dividends, and dividends are part of personal income. The profits that remain after dividends are paid—corporate profits minus dividends—are not paid to households as income. Therefore, corporate profits minus dividends must be subtracted from national income when computing personal income. Second, social insurance payments are payments made to the government, some by firms and some by employees. Because these payments are not received by households, they must be subtracted from national income when computing personal income.

Two items must be added to national income to calculate personal income: (1) personal interest income received from the government and consumers, and (2) transfer payments to persons. As we have pointed out, interest payments made by the government and consumers (households) are not counted in GDP and not reflected in national income figures.[3] However, these payments are income received by households, so they must be added to national income when computing personal income. Households can pay and receive interest. As a group, households receive more interest than they pay. Similarly, transfer payments to persons are not counted in GDP because they do not represent the production of any

[3]Interest payments on government bonds are not included in national income, while interest payments on bonds of private firms are, because government debt is assumed to be the result of activities, such as past wars, that do not add to current production. In contrast, it is presumed that firms sell bonds to finance investment that does add to current production. Interest payments by households are not included in national income because they are not considered to add to current production.

TABLE 6.5 Disposable Personal Income and Personal Saving, 2002

	DOLLARS (BILLIONS)
Disposable personal income	**7,810.3**
Less:	
Personal consumption expenditures	−7,303.7
Interest paid by consumers to business	−188.4
Personal transfer payments to foreigners	−32.3
Equals **personal saving**	**285.8**
Personal saving as a percentage of disposable personal income:	**3.7%**

Source: Table 6.2.

goods or services. Social Security checks and other cash benefits are income received by households and must also be added to national income when computing personal income.

Personal income is the income received by households before paying personal income taxes but after paying social insurance contributions. The amount of income that households have to spend or save is called **disposable personal income**, or **after-tax income**. It is equal to personal income minus personal taxes.

disposable personal income or **after-tax income** Personal income minus personal income taxes. The amount that households have to spend or save.

Because disposable personal income is the amount of income that households can spend or save, it is an important income concept. Table 6.5 shows there are three categories of spending: (1) personal consumption expenditures, (2) interest paid by consumers to business, and (3) personal transfer payments to foreigners. The amount of disposable personal income left after total personal spending is **personal saving**. If your monthly disposable income is $500 and you spend $450, you have $50 left at the end of the month. Your personal saving is $50 for the month. Your personal saving level can be negative: If you earn $500 and spend $600 during the month, you have *dissaved* $100. To spend $100 more than you earn, you will either have to borrow the $100 from someone, take the $100 from your savings account, or sell an asset you own.

personal saving The amount of disposable income that is left after total personal spending in a given period.

The **personal saving rate** is the percentage of disposable personal income saved, an important indicator of household behavior. A low saving rate means households are spending a large amount of their income. A high saving rate means households are cautious in their spending. As Table 6.5 shows, the U.S. personal saving rate in 2002 was 3.7 percent. Saving rates tend to rise during recessionary periods, when consumers become anxious about their future, and fall during boom times, as pent-up spending demand gets released.

personal saving rate The percentage of disposable personal income that is saved. If the personal saving rate is low, households are spending a large amount relative to their incomes; if it is high, households are spending cautiously.

NOMINAL VERSUS REAL GDP

So far, we have looked at GDP measured in **current dollars**, or the current prices we pay for things. When a variable is measured in current dollars, it is described in *nominal terms.* **Nominal GDP** is GDP measured in current dollars—all components of GDP valued at their current prices.

current dollars The current prices that one pays for goods and services.

nominal GDP Gross domestic product measured in current dollars.

In many applications of macroeconomics, nominal GDP is not a very desirable measure of production. Why? Assume there is only one good—say, pizza. In each year 1 and 2, 100 units (slices) of pizza were produced. Production thus remained the same for year 1 and year 2. Suppose the price of pizza increased from $1.00 per slice in year 1 to $1.10 per slice in year 2. Nominal GDP in year 1 is $100 (100 units × $1.00 per unit), and nominal GDP in year 2 is $110 (100 units × $1.10 per unit). Nominal GDP has increased by $10, even though no more slices of pizza were produced. If we use nominal GDP to measure growth, we can be misled into thinking production has grown when all that has really happened is a rise in the price level (inflation).

If there were only one good in the economy—like pizza—it would be easy to measure production and compare one year's value to another's. We would add up all the pizza slices produced each year. In the example, production is 100 in both years. If the number of slices had increased to 105 in year 2, we would say production increased by five slices between year 1 and year 2, which is a 5 percent increase. Alas, however, there is more than one good in the economy.

The following is a discussion of how the BEA adjusts nominal GDP for price changes. As you read the discussion, keep in mind that this adjustment is not easy. Even in an economy of just apples and oranges, it would not be obvious how to add up apples and oranges to get an overall measure of output. The BEA's task is to add up thousands of goods, each of whose price is changing over time.

weight The importance attached to an item within a group of items.

In the following, we will use the concept of a **weight**, either price weights or quantity weights. What is a weight? It is easiest to define the term by an example. Suppose in your economics course there is a final exam and two other tests. If the final exam counts for one-half of the grade and the other two tests for one-fourth each, the "weights" are one-half, one-fourth, and one-fourth. If instead the final exam counts for 80 percent of the grade and the other two tests for 10 percent each, the weights are .8, .1, and .1. The more important an item is in a group, the larger its weight.

CALCULATING REAL GDP

Nominal GDP adjusted for price changes is called *real GDP*. All the main issues involved in computing real GDP can be discussed using a simple three-good economy and 2 years. Table 6.6 presents all the data that we will need. The table presents price and quantity data for 2 years and three goods. The goods are labeled *A*, *B*, and *C*, and the years are labeled 1 and 2. *P* denotes price, and *Q* denotes quantity.

The first thing to note from Table 6.6 is that *nominal output*—in current dollars—in year 1 for good *A* is the price of good *A* in year 1 ($0.50) times the number of units of good *A* produced in year 1 (6), which is $3.00. Similarly, nominal output in year 1 is 7 × $0.30 = $2.10 for good *B* and 10 × $0.70 = $7.00 for good *C*. The sum of these three amounts, $12.10 in column 5, is nominal GDP in year 1 in this simple economy. Nominal GDP in year 2—calculated by using the year 2 quantities and the year 2 prices—is $19.20 (column 8). Nominal GDP has risen from $12.10 in year 1 to $19.20 in year 2, an increase of 58.7 percent.[4]

You can see that the price of each good changed between year 1 and year 2—the price of good *A* fell (from $0.50 to $0.40) and the prices of goods *B* and *C* rose (*B* from $0.30 to $1.00; *C* from $0.70 to $0.90). Some of the change in nominal GDP between years 1 and 2 is due to price changes and not production changes. How much can we attribute to price changes and how much to production changes? Here, things get tricky. The procedure that the BEA used prior to 1996 was to pick a **base year** and use the prices in that base year as weights to calculate real GDP. This is a **fixed-weight procedure** because the weights used, which are the prices, are the same for all years—namely, the prices that prevailed in the base year.

base year The year chosen for the weights in a fixed-weight procedure.

fixed-weight procedure A procedure that uses weights from a given base year.

Let us use the fixed-weight procedure and year 1 as the base year, which means using year 1 prices as the weights. Then in Table 6.6, real GDP in year 1 is $12.10 (column 5), and real GDP in year 2 is $15.10 (column 6). Note that both columns use year 1 prices, and that nominal and real GDP are the same in year 1 because year 1 is the base year. Real GDP has increased from $12.10 to $15.10, an increase of 24.8 percent.

TABLE 6.6 A Three-Good Economy

	(1) PRODUCTION YEAR 1 Q_1	(2) PRODUCTION YEAR 2 Q_2	(3) PRICE PER UNIT YEAR 1 P_1	(4) PRICE PER UNIT YEAR 2 P_2	(5) GDP IN YEAR 1 IN YEAR 1 PRICES $P_1 \times Q_1$	(6) GDP IN YEAR 2 IN YEAR 1 PRICES $P_1 \times Q_2$	(7) GDP IN YEAR 1 IN YEAR 2 PRICES $P_2 \times Q_1$	(8) GDP IN YEAR 2 IN YEAR 2 PRICES $P_2 \times Q_2$
Good *A*	6	11	$0.50	$0.40	$3.00	$5.50	$2.40	$4.40
Good *B*	7	4	0.30	1.00	2.10	1.20	7.00	4.00
Good *C*	10	12	0.70	0.90	7.00	8.40	9.00	10.80
Total					$12.10	$15.10	$18.40	$19.20
					Nominal GDP in year 1			Nominal GDP in year 2

[4]The percentage change is calculated as [(19.20 − 12.10)/12.10] × 100 = .587 × 100 = 58.7 percent.

Let us now use the fixed-weight procedure and year 2 as the base year, which means using year 2 prices as the weights. In Table 6.6, real GDP in year 1 is $18.40 (column 7), and real GDP in year 2 is $19.20 (column 8). Note that both columns use year 2 prices, and nominal and real GDP are the same in year 2 because year 2 is the base year. Real GDP has increased from $18.40 to $19.20, an increase of 4.3 percent.

This example shows that growth rates can be sensitive to the choice of the base year—24.8 percent using year 1 prices as weights and 4.3 percent using year 2 prices as weights. The old BEA procedure simply picked one year as the base year and did all the calculations using the prices in that year as weights. The new procedure makes two important changes. The first (using the current example) is to "split the difference" between 24.8 percent and 4.3 percent. What does "splitting the difference" mean? One way would be to take the average of the two numbers, which is 14.55 percent. What the BEA does is to take the *geometric* average, which for the current example is 14.09 percent.[5] These two averages (14.55 percent and 14.09 percent) are quite close, and the use of either would give similar results. The point here is not that the geometric average is used, but that the first change is to split the difference using some average. Note that this new procedure requires two "base" years, because 24.8 percent was computed using year 1 prices as weights and 4.3 percent was computed using year 2 prices as weights.

The second BEA change is to use years 1 and 2 as the base years when computing the percentage change between years 1 and 2, then use years 2 and 3 as the base years when computing the percentage change between years 2 and 3, and so on. The two base years change as the calculations move through time. The series of percentage changes computed in this way is taken to be the series of growth rates of real GDP, and so in this way nominal GDP is adjusted for price changes. To make sure you understand this, review the calculations in Table 6.6; all the data you need to see what is going on are in this table.

CALCULATING THE GDP DEFLATOR

We now switch gears from real GDP, a quantity measure, to the GDP deflator, a price measure. One of economic policy makers' goals is to keep changes in the overall price level small. For this reason policy makers need not only good measures of how real output is changing but also good measures of how the overall price level is changing. The GDP deflator is one measure of the overall price level. We can use the data in Table 6.6 to show how the GDP deflator is computed by the BEA.

In Table 6.6, the price of good *A* fell from $0.50 in year 1 to $0.40 in year 2; the price of good *B* rose from $0.30 to $1.00; and the price of good *C* rose from $0.70 to $0.90. If we were interested only in how individual prices change, this is all the information we would need. However, if we are interested in how the overall price *level* changes, we need to weight the individual prices in some way. The obvious weights to use are the quantities produced, but which quantities—those of year 1 or of year 2? The same issues arise here for the quantity weights as for the price weights in computing real GDP.

Let us first use the fixed-weight procedure and year 1 as the base year, which means using year 1 quantities as the weights. Then in Table 6.6, the "bundle" price in year 1 is $12.10 (column 5), and the bundle price in year 2 is $18.40 (column 7). Both columns use year 1 quantities. The bundle price has increased from $12.10 to $18.40, an increase of 52.1 percent.

Next use the fixed-weight procedure and year 2 as the base year, which means using year 2 quantities as the weights. Then the bundle price in year 1 is $15.10 (column 6), and the bundle price in year 2 is $19.20 (column 8). Both columns use year 2 quantities. The bundle price has increased from $15.10 to $19.20, an increase of 27.2 percent.

This example shows that overall price increases can be sensitive to the choice of the base year: 52.1 percent using year 1 quantities as weights and 27.2 percent using year 2 quantities as weights. Again, the old BEA procedure simply picked one year as the base year and did all the calculations using the quantities in the base year as weights. The new procedure first splits the difference between 52.1 percent and 27.2 percent by taking the geometric average, which is 39.1 percent. Second, it uses years 1 and 2 as the base years when computing the percentage change between years 1 and 2, years 2 and 3 as the base years when computing the

[5]The geometric average is computed as the square root of 124.8×104.3, which is 114.09.

percentage change between years 2 and 3, and so on. The series of percentage changes computed in this way is taken to be the series of percentage changes in the GDP deflator, that is, a series of inflation rates of the overall price level.

THE PROBLEMS OF FIXED WEIGHTS

To see why the BEA switched to the new procedure, let us consider a number of problems with using fixed-price weights to compute real GDP. First, 1987 price weights, the last price weights the BEA used before it changed procedures, are not likely to be very accurate for, say, the 1950s. Many structural changes have taken place in the U.S. economy in the last 30 to 40 years, and it seems unlikely that 1987 prices are good weights to use for the 1950s.

Another problem is that the use of fixed-price weights does not account for the responses in the economy to supply shifts. Say bad weather leads to a lower production of oranges in year 2. In a simple supply-and-demand diagram for oranges, this corresponds to a shift of the supply curve to the left, which leads to an increase in the price of oranges and a decrease in the quantity demanded. As consumers move up the demand curve, they are substituting away from oranges. If technical advances in year 2 result in cheaper ways of producing computers, the result is a shift of the computer supply curve to the right, which leads to a decrease in the price of computers and an increase in the quantity demanded. Consumers are substituting toward computers. (You should be able to draw supply-and-demand diagrams for both these cases.) Table 6.6 shows this tendency. The quantity of good *A* rose between years 1 and 2 and the price decreased (the computer case), whereas the quantity of good *B* fell and the price increased (the orange case). The computer supply curve has been shifting to the right over time, due primarily to technical advances. The result has been large decreases in the price of computers and large increases in the quantity demanded.

To see why these responses pose a problem for the use of fixed-price weights, consider the data in Table 6.6. Because the price of good *A* was higher in year 1, the increase in production of good *A* is weighted more if we use year 1 as the base year than if we used year 2 as the base year. Also, because the price of good *A* was lower in year 1, the decrease in production of good *B* is weighted less if we use year 1 as the base year. These effects make the overall change in real GDP larger if we use year 1 price weights than if we use year 2 price weights. Using year 1 price weights ignores the kinds of substitution responses discussed in the previous paragraph and leads to what many feel are too-large estimates of real GDP changes. In the past, the BEA tended to move the base year forward about every 5 years, resulting in the past estimates of real GDP growth being revised downward. It is undesirable to have past growth estimates change simply because of the change to a new base year. The new BEA procedure avoids many of these fixed-weight problems.

Similar problems arise when using fixed-quantity weights to compute price indexes. For example, the fixed-weight procedure ignores the substitution away from goods whose prices are increasing and toward goods whose prices are decreasing or increasing less rapidly. The procedure tends to overestimate the increase in the overall price level. As discussed in the next chapter, there are still a number of price indexes that are computed using fixed weights. The GDP deflator differs because it does not use fixed weights. It is also a price index for all the goods and services produced in the economy. Other price indexes cover fewer domestically produced goods and services but also include some imported (foreign-produced) goods and services.

It should finally be stressed that there is no "right" way of computing real GDP. The economy consists of many goods, each with its own price, and there is no exact way of adding together the production of the different goods. We can say that the BEA's new procedure for computing real GDP avoids the problems associated with the use of fixed weights, and it seems to be an improvement over the old procedure. We will see in the next chapter, however, that the consumer price index (CPI)—a widely used price index—is still computed using fixed weights.

LIMITATIONS OF THE GDP CONCEPT

We generally think of increases in GDP as good. Increasing GDP (or preventing its decrease) is usually considered one of the chief goals of the government's macroeconomic policy. Because some serious problems arise when we try to use GDP as a measure of happiness or well-being, we now point out some of the limitations of the GDP concept as a measure of welfare.

GDP AND SOCIAL WELFARE

If crime levels went down, society would be better off, but a decrease in crime is not an increase in output and is not reflected in GDP. Neither is an increase in leisure time. Yet, to the extent that households desire extra leisure time (instead of having it forced on them by a lack of jobs in the economy), an increase in leisure is also an increase in social welfare. Furthermore, some increases in social welfare are associated with a *decrease* in GDP. An increase in leisure during a time of full employment, for example, leads to a decrease in GDP because less time is spent on producing output.

Most nonmarket and domestic activities, such as housework and child care, are not counted in GDP even though they amount to real production. However, if I decide to send my children to day care or hire someone to clean my house or to drive my car for me, GDP increases. The salaries of day-care staff, cleaning people, and chauffeurs are counted in GDP, but the time I spend doing the same things is not counted. A mere change of institutional arrangements, even though no more output is being produced, can show up as a change in GDP.

Furthermore, GDP seldom reflects losses or social ills. GDP accounting rules do not adjust for production that pollutes the environment. The more production there is, the larger is GDP, regardless of how much pollution results in the process.

GDP also has nothing to say about the distribution of output among individuals in a society. It does not distinguish, for example, between the case in which most output goes to a few people and the case in which output is evenly divided among all people. We cannot use GDP to measure the effects of redistributive policies (which take income from some people and give income to others). Such policies have no direct impact on GDP. GDP is also neutral about the kinds of goods an economy produces. Symphony performances, handguns, cigarettes, professional football games, Bibles, soda pop, milk, economics textbooks, and comic books all get counted similarly without regard to their differing value to society.

In spite of these limitations, GDP is a highly useful measure of economic activity and well-being. If you doubt this, answer this simple question: Would you rather live in the United States of 200 years ago, when rivers were less polluted and crime rates were probably lower, or in the United States of today? Most people say they prefer the present. Even with all the "negatives," GDP per person and the average standard of living are much higher today than 200 years ago.

Whenever sellers looking for a profit come into contact with buyers willing to pay, markets will arise, often "underground."

THE UNDERGROUND ECONOMY

Many transactions are missed in the calculation of GDP, even though in principle they should be counted. Most illegal transactions are missed unless they are "laundered" into legitimate business. Income that is earned but not reported as income for tax purposes is usually missed, although some adjustments are made in the GDP calculations to take misreported income into account. The part of the economy that should be counted in GDP but is not is sometimes called the **underground economy**.

underground economy The part of the economy in which transactions take place and in which income is generated that is unreported and therefore not counted in GDP.

Tax evasion is usually thought to be the major incentive for people to participate in the underground economy. Studies estimate the size of the U.S. underground economy, ranging from 5 percent to 30 percent of GDP,[6] comparable to the size of the underground economy in most European countries and probably much smaller than the size of the underground economy in the Eastern European countries. Estimates of Italy's underground economy range from 10 percent to 35 percent of Italian GDP. At the lower end of the scale, estimates for Switzerland range from 3 percent to 5 percent.

[6]See, for example, Edgar L. Feige, "Defining and Estimating Underground and Informal Economies: The New Industrial Economic Approach," *World Development* 19(7) (1990); and "The Underground Economy in the United States," Occasional Paper No. 2, U.S. Department of Labor, September 1992.

TABLE 6.7 Per Capita Gross National Income for Selected Countries, 2001

COUNTRY	U.S. DOLLARS	COUNTRY	U.S. DOLLARS
Switzerland	36,970	Portugal	10,670
Japan	35,990	South Korea	9,400
Norway	35,530	Argentina	6,960
United States	34,870	Mexico	5,540
Denmark	31,090	Czech Republic	5,270
Ireland	28,880	Brazil	3,060
Sweden	25,400	South Africa	2,900
United Kingdom	24,230	Turkey	2,540
Netherlands	24,040	Colombia	1,910
Austria	23,940	Jordan	1,750
Finland	23,940	Romania	1,710
Germany	23,700	Philippines	1,050
Belgium	23,340	China	890
France	22,640	Indonesia	680
Canada	21,340	India	460
Australia	19,770	Pakistan	420
Italy	19,470	Nepal	250
Spain	14,860	Rwanda	220
Greece	11,780	Ethiopia	100

Source: The World Bank Atlas, 2002.

Why should we care about the underground economy? To the extent that GDP reflects only a part of economic activity instead of a complete measure of what the economy produces, it is misleading. Unemployment rates, for example, may be lower than officially measured if people work in the underground economy without reporting this fact to the government. Also, if the size of the underground economy varies between countries—as it does—we can be misled when we compare GDP between countries. For example, Italy's GDP would be much higher if we considered its underground sector as part of the economy, while Switzerland's GDP would change very little.

GROSS NATIONAL INCOME PER CAPITA

Making comparisons across countries is difficult because such comparisons need to be made in a single currency, generally U.S. dollars. Converting GNP numbers for Japan into dollars requires converting from yen into dollars. Since exchange rates can change quite dramatically in short periods of time, such conversions are tricky. Recently the World Bank adopted a new measuring system for international comparisons. The concept of **gross national income (GNI)** is GNP converted into dollars using an average of currency exchange rates over several years adjusted for rates of inflation. Table 6.7 lists the gross national income per capita (GNI divided by population) for various countries in 2001.

gross national income (GNI) GNP converted into dollars using an average of currency exchange rates over several years adjusted for rates of inflation.

Switzerland has the highest per capita GNI followed by Japan, Norway, and the United States. Ethiopia was estimated to have per capita GNI of only $100 in 2001.

LOOKING AHEAD

This chapter has introduced many key variables that macroeconomists are interested in, including GDP and its components. There is much more to be learned about the data that macroeconomists use. In the next chapter, we will discuss the data on employment, unemployment, and the labor force, and in Chapters 10 and 11, we will discuss the data on money and interest rates. Finally, in Chapter 20, we will discuss in more detail the data on the relationship between the United States and the rest of the world.

SUMMARY

1. One source of data on the key variables in the macroeconomy are the national income and product accounts. These accounts provide a conceptual framework that macroeconomists use to think about how the pieces of the economy fit together.

GROSS DOMESTIC PRODUCT

2. *Gross domestic product (GDP)* is the key concept in national income accounting. GDP is the total market value of all final goods and services produced within a given period by factors of production located within a country. GDP excludes intermediate goods. To include goods both when they are purchased as inputs and when they are sold as final products would be double counting and an overstatement of the value of production.
3. GDP excludes all transactions in which money or goods change hands but in which no new goods and services are produced. GDP includes the income of foreigners working in the United States and the profits that foreign companies earn in the United States. GDP excludes the income of U.S. citizens working abroad and profits earned by U.S. companies in foreign countries.
4. *Gross national product (GNP)* is the market value of all final goods and services produced during a given period by factors of production owned by a country's citizens.

CALCULATING GDP

5. The *expenditure approach* to GDP adds up the amount spent on all final goods and services during a given period. The four main categories of expenditures are *personal consumption expenditures (C)*, *gross private domestic investment (I)*, *government consumption and gross investment (G)*, and *net exports (EX – IM)*. The sum of these equals GDP.
6. The three main components of *personal consumption expenditures (C)* are *durable goods, nondurable goods,* and *services.*
7. *Gross private domestic investment (I)* is the total investment made by the private sector in a given period. There are three kinds of investment: *nonresidential investment, residential investment,* and *changes in business inventories.* Gross investment does not take *depreciation*—the decrease in the value of assets—into account. *Net investment* is equal to gross investment minus depreciation.
8. *Government consumption and gross investment (G)* include expenditures by state, federal, and local governments for final goods and services. The value of *net exports (EX – IM)* equals the differences between exports (sales to foreigners of U.S.-produced goods and services) and imports (U.S. purchases of goods and services from abroad).
9. Because every payment (expenditure) by a buyer is a receipt (income) for the seller, GDP can be computed in terms of who receives it as income—the *income approach* to calculating gross domestic product. The GDP equation using the income approach is GDP = national income + depreciation + (indirect taxes – subsidies) + net factor payments to the rest of the world + other.

FROM GDP TO DISPOSABLE PERSONAL INCOME

10. GNP minus depreciation is *net national product (NNP)*. *National income* is the total amount earned by the factors of production in the economy; it is equal to NNP less indirect taxes minus subsidies. *Personal income* is the total income of households. *Disposable personal income* is what households have to spend or save after paying their taxes. The *personal saving rate* is the percentage of disposable personal income saved instead of spent.

NOMINAL VERSUS REAL GDP

11. GDP measured in current dollars (the current prices that one pays for goods) is *nominal GDP.* If we use nominal GDP to measure growth, we can be misled into thinking that production has grown when all that has happened is a rise in the price level, or inflation. A better measure of production is *real GDP,* which is nominal GDP adjusted for price changes.
12. The GDP deflator is a measure of the overall price level.

LIMITATIONS OF THE GDP CONCEPT

13. We generally think of increases in GDP as good, but some problems arise when we try to use GDP as a measure of happiness or well-being. The peculiarities of GDP accounting mean that institutional changes can change the value of GDP even if real production has not changed. GDP ignores most social ills, such as pollution. Furthermore, GDP tells us nothing about what kinds of goods are being produced or how income is distributed across the population. GDP also ignores many transactions of the underground economy.
14. The concept of *gross national income(GNI)* is GNP converted into dollars using an average of currency exchange rates over several years adjusted for rates of inflation.

REVIEW TERMS AND CONCEPTS

base year, 110
change in business inventories, 103
compensation of employees, 106
corporate profits, 106
current dollars, 109
depreciation, 104
disposable personal income, or after-tax income, 109
durable goods, 103
expenditure approach, 101
final goods and services, 100
fixed-weight procedure, 110

government consumption and gross investment (G), 105
gross domestic product (GDP), 99
gross investment, 105
gross national income (GNI), 114
gross national product (GNP), 101
gross private domestic investment (I), 103
income approach, 102
indirect taxes, 107
intermediate goods, 100
national income, 106
national income and product accounts, 99
net exports ($EX - IM$), 105
net factor payments to the rest of the world, 107
net interest, 106
net investment, 105
net national product (NNP), 108
nominal GDP, 109
nondurable goods, 103
nonresidential investment, 103
personal consumption expenditures (C), 103
personal income, 108
personal saving, 109
personal saving rate, 109
proprietors' income, 106
rental income, 106
residential investment, 103
services, 103
subsidies, 107
underground economy, 113
value added, 100
weight, 110

Expenditure approach to GDP: GDP $= C + I + G + (EX - IM)$
GDP = final sales − change in business inventories
net investment = capital end of period − capital beginning of period
income approach to GDP:
GDP = national income + depreciation + (indirect taxes − subsidies) + net factor payments to the rest of the world + other

PROBLEM SET

1. From the following table, calculate:
   a. Gross private domestic investment
   b. Net exports
   c. Gross domestic product
   d. Gross national product
   e. Net national product
   f. National income
   g. Personal income
   h. Disposable personal income

Transfer payments	15
Subsidies	5
Social insurance payments	35
Depreciation	50
Receipts of factor income from the rest of the world	4
Government consumption and investment	75
Imports	50
Payments of factor income to the rest of the world	5
Personal interest income from government and households	35
Indirect taxes	20
Exports	60
Net private domestic investment	100
Personal taxes	60
Corporate profits	45
Personal consumption expenditures	250
Dividends	4

2. How do we know that calculating GDP by the expenditure approach yields the same answer as calculating GDP by the income approach?

3. As the following table indicates, GNP and real GNP were almost the same in 1972, but there was a \$300 billion difference by mid-1975. Explain why. Describe what the numbers here suggest about conditions in the economy at the time? How do the conditions compare with conditions today?

DATE	GNP (BILLIONS OF DOLLARS)	REAL GNP (BILLIONS OF DOLLARS)	REAL GNP (% CHANGE)	GNP DEFLATOR (% CHANGE)
72:2	1,172	1,179	7.62	2.93
72:3	1,196	1,193	5.11	3.24
72:4	1,233	1,214	7.41	5.30
73:1	1,284	1,247	10.93	5.71
73:2	1,307	1,248	.49	7.20
73:3	1,338	1,256	2.44	6.92
73:4	1,377	1,266	3.31	8.58
74:1	1,388	1,253	−4.00	7.50
74:2	1,424	1,255	.45	10.32
74:3	1,452	1,247	−2.47	10.78
74:4	1,473	1,230	−5.51	12.03
75:1	1,480	1,204	−8.27	10.86
75:2	1,517	1,219	5.00	5.07

4. What are some of the problems in using fixed weights to compute real GDP and the GDP price index? How does the BEA's approach attempt to solve these problems?

5. Explain what double counting is and discuss why GDP is not equal to total sales.

6. The following table gives some figures from a forecast of real GDP and population done in 2003. According to the forecast, approximately how much real growth will there be between 2005 and 2006? What is per capita GDP projected to be in 2005 and in 2006? Compute the forecast rate of change in real GDP and per capital real GDP between 2005 and 2006.

Real GDP 2005 (billions)	\$10,517
Real GDP 2006 (billions)	\$10,857
Population 2005 (millions)	295.3
Population 2006 (millions)	297.8

7. Look at a recent edition of *The Economist.* Go to the section on economic indicators. Go down the list of countries and make a list of the ones with the fastest and slowest GDP growth. Look also at the forecast rates of GDP growth. Go back to the table of contents at the beginning of the journal to see if there are articles about any of these countries. Write a paragraph or two describing the events or the economic conditions in one of them. Can you explain why they are growing or are not growing rapidly?
8. During 2002, real GDP in Japan rose about 1.3 percent. During the same period, retail sales in Japan fell 1.8 percent in real terms. What are some possible explanations for retail sales to consumers falling when GDP rises? (*Hint:* Think of the composition of GDP using the expenditure approach.)
9. Which of the following transactions would not be counted in GDP? Explain your answers.
   - **a.** General Motors issues new shares of stock to finance the construction of a plant.
   - **b.** General Motors builds a new plant.
   - **c.** Company A successfully launches a hostile takeover of company B, in which it purchases all the assets of company B.
   - **d.** Your grandmother wins $10 million in the lottery.
   - **e.** You buy a new copy of this textbook.
   - **f.** You buy a used copy of this textbook.
   - **g.** The government pays out social security benefits.
   - **h.** A public utility installs new antipollution equipment in its smokestacks.
   - **i.** Luigi's Pizza buys 30 pounds of mozzarella cheese, holds it in inventory for 1 month, and then uses it to make pizza (which it sells).
   - **j.** You spend the weekend cleaning your apartment.
   - **k.** A drug dealer sells $500 worth of illegal drugs.
10. If you buy a new car, the entire purchase is counted as consumption in the year in which you make the transaction. Explain briefly why this is in one sense an "error" in national income accounting. (*Hint:* How is the purchase of a car different from the purchase of a pizza?) How might you correct this error?
11. Explain why imports are subtracted in the expenditure approach to calculating GDP.
12. GDP calculations do not directly include the economic costs of environmental damage—for example, global warming, acid rain. Do you think these costs should be included in GDP? Why or why not? How could GDP be amended to include environmental damage costs?

Visit www.prenhall.com/casefair for self-test quizzes, interactive graphing exercises, and news articles.

Long-Run and Short-Run Concerns: Growth, Productivity, Unemployment, and Inflation

7

CHAPTER OUTLINE

An ideal economy is one in which there is rapid growth of output per worker, low unemployment, and low inflation. In this situation government economic policy makers can sleep well at night. Alas, however, an economy is not always in this ideal state. There can be times of low growth, high unemployment, and high inflation. A key part of macroeconomics is to consider what *determines* output, unemployment, and inflation. Why is the growth of output per worker sometimes high and sometimes low? Why are unemployment and inflation sometimes high? We begin in the next chapter the task of explaining how the macroeconomy works. Before jumping into the analysis, however, in this chapter it will be useful to spend a little more time on description.

We first discuss long-run issues, namely, the rate of growth of output and output per worker over a long period of time. We then move to the short-run issues of unemployment and inflation.

LONG-RUN OUTPUT AND PRODUCTIVITY GROWTH

Figure 5.4 in Chapter 5 shows that the average growth rate of output in the United States economy since 1900 has been about 3.4 percent per year. Some years are better than others, but on average the rate is 3.4 percent. An area of economics called "growth theory" is concerned with the question of what determines this rate. Why 3.4 percent and not 2 percent or 4 percent? We take up this question in Chapter 18, but a few points are useful to make now.

Before we begin our discussion of economic growth it is important to review what is meant by "capital." Capital is anything that is produced that is then used as an input to produce other goods and services. Capital can be tangible, such as buildings and equipment, or intangible. The knowledge and skills acquired through education and training can be thought of as intangible "human capital." Capital can be private or public. The roads and bridges that we drive and walk on are a part of the public capital stock. Capital, thus, can take many forms. To simplify the discussion, however, we will sometimes refer to capital as simply "machines."

In a simplified economy, machines (capital) and workers (labor) are needed to produce output. Suppose that an economy consists of six machines and 60 workers, with 10 workers working on each machine, and also that the length of the workweek is 40 hours, with this workweek resulting in 50 units of output per month per machine. Total output (GDP) for the month is thus 300 units (6 machines times 50 units per machine) in this simple economy.

How can output increase in this economy? There are a number of ways. One way is to add more workers. If, for example, 12 workers are added, 2 extra per machine, then more output can be produced per machine per hour worked because there are more workers helping out on each machine. Another way is to add more machines. For example, if 4 machines are added, then the 60 workers have a total of 10 machines to work with instead of 6, and more output can be produced per worker per hour worked. A third way is to increase the length of the workweek (e.g., from 40 hours to 45 hours). With workers and machines working more hours, more output can be produced. Output can thus increase if labor or capital increases or if the amount of time labor and capital are working per week increases.

Another way for output to increase in our economy is for the quality of the workers to increase. If, for example, the education of the workers increases, this may add to their skills and thus increase their ability to work on the machines. Output per machine might then rise from 50 units per month to some larger number per month. Also, if workers become more physically fit by exercising more and eating less fat and more whole grains and fresh fruits and vegetables, this may increase their output on the machines. People are sometimes said to be adding to their *human capital* when they increase their mental or physical skills.

The quality of the machines may also increase. In particular, new machines that replace old machines may allow more output to be produced per hour with the same number of workers. In our example, it may be that 55 instead of 50 units of output can be produced per month per new machine with 10 workers per machine and a 40-hour workweek. An obvious example is the replacement of an old computer with a new, faster one, which allows more to be done per minute of work on the computer.

To summarize, output can increase if there are more workers, more skills per worker, more machines, faster machines, or longer workweek.

Turning now to the actual economy, an interesting variable to look at is the ratio of total output to the total number of worker hours. Output per worker hour is called "labor productivity" or sometimes just "productivity." Output per worker hour is plotted in Figure 7.1 for the 1952 I–2003 II period. Two features are immediately clear from the figure. First, there is an upward trend, and second, there are fairly sizable short-run fluctuations around the trend. We will see in Chapter 17 why there are short-run fluctuations. This has to do with the

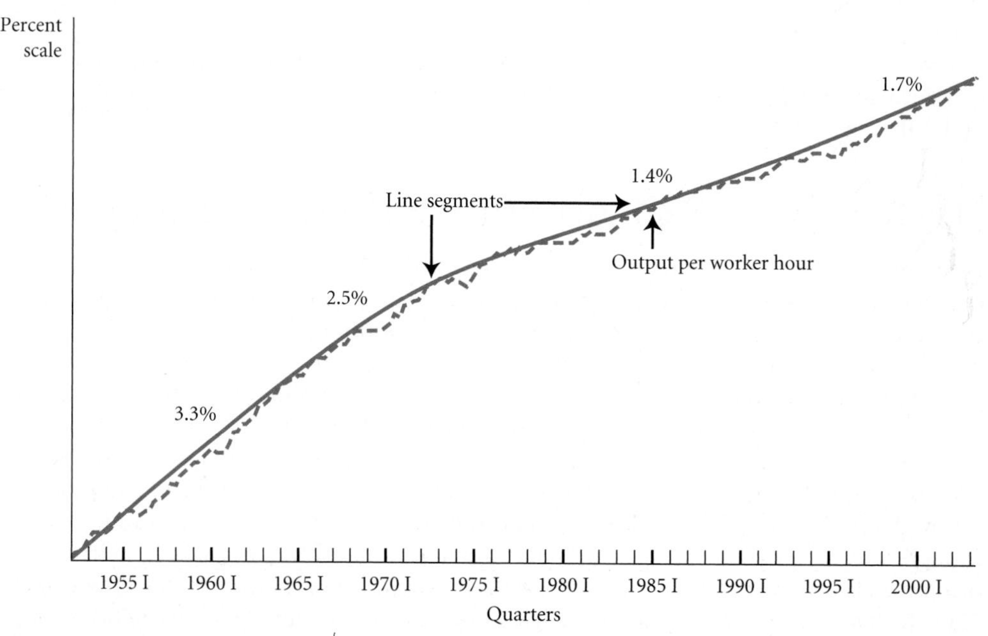

FIGURE 7.1 Output per Worker Hour (Productivity), 1952 I–2003 II

Productivity grew much faster in the 1950s and 1960s than since.

possibility that the employed workforce is not always fully utilized. For now, however, the main interest is the long-run trend.

To smooth out the short-run fluctuations in Figure 7.1, straight-line segments have been added to the figure, where the segments roughly go through the high values. The slope of each line segment is the growth rate of productivity along the segment. The growth rates are listed in the figure. The different productivity growth rates in the figure tell an interesting story. From the 1950s through the mid-1960s the growth rate was 3.3 percent. The rate then fell to 2.5 percent in the last half of the 1960s and early 1970s. Between the early 1970s and the early 1990s the growth rate was much lower at 1.4 percent. Since the early 1990s it has been 1.7 percent.

Why are the growth rates positive in Figure 7.1? In other words, why has the amount of output that a worker can produce per hour risen in the last half century? Part of the answer is that the amount of capital per worker has increased. In Figure 7.2 capital per worker is plotted for the same 1952 I–2003 II period. It is clear from the figure that the amount of capital per worker has generally been rising. Therefore, with more capital per worker, more output can be produced per worker. The other part of the answer is that quality of labor and capital has been increasing. Both the average skill of workers and the average quality of capital have been increasing. This means that more output can be produced per worker for a given quantity of capital, because both workers and capital are getting better.

A harder question to answer concerning Figure 7.1 is why the growth rate of productivity was much higher in the 1950s and 1960s than it has been since the early 1970s. Again, part of the answer is that the amount of capital per worker rose more rapidly in the 1950s and 1960s than it has since then. This can be seen in Figure 7.2. The other part of the answer is, of course, that the quality of labor and capital must have increased more in the 1950s and 1960s than later, although this to some extent begs the question. The key question is why has the quality of labor and capital grown more slowly since the early 1970s? We take up this question in Chapter 18, where we will see that there seems to be no one obvious answer. An interesting question for the future is whether the growth of the Internet will lead to a much larger productivity growth rate, perhaps as large as the growth rate in the 1950s and 1960s. In the present context you can think about the growth of the Internet as an increase in physical capital (wires, servers, switchers, etc.) and an increase in the quality of capital (an increase in what can be done per minute using the Internet). Time will tell whether the Internet will lead to a "new age" of productivity growth.

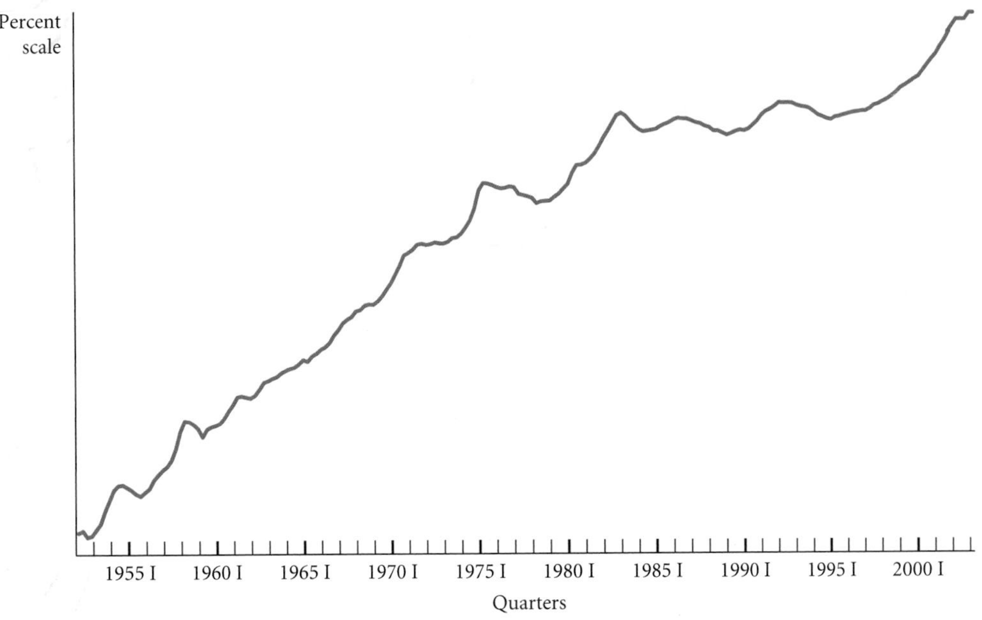

FIGURE 7.2 Capital per Worker, 1952 I–2003 II

Capital per worker grew until about 1980 and then leveled off.

RECESSIONS, DEPRESSIONS, AND UNEMPLOYMENT

We now move from considering long-run trends to considering deviations of the economy from long-run trends. In other words, we consider business cycles, the periodic ups and downs in the economy.

recession Roughly, a period in which real GDP declines for at least two consecutive quarters. Marked by falling output and rising unemployment.

Recall from Chapter 5 that a **recession** is roughly a period in which real GDP declines for at least two consecutive quarters. Also recall that real GDP is a measure of the actual output of goods and services in the economy during a given period. When real GDP falls, less is being produced. When less output is produced, fewer inputs are used, employment declines, unemployment rate rises, and a smaller percentage of the capital stock at our disposal is utilized (more plants and equipment are running at less than full capacity). When real output falls, real income declines.

depression A prolonged and deep recession. The precise definitions of prolonged and deep are debatable.

A **depression** is a prolonged and deep recession, although there is disagreement over how severe and how prolonged a recession must be to be called a depression. Nearly everyone agrees the U.S. economy experienced a depression between 1929 and the late 1930s. The most severe recession since the 1930s took place between 1980 and 1982.

In Figure 5.5, we divided the period since 1970 into four "recessionary" periods, 1974–1975, 1980–1982, 1990–1991, and 2001. Table 7.1 summarizes some of the differences between the recession of 1980–1982 and the early part of the Great Depression. Between 1929 and 1933, real GDP declined by 26.6 percent. In other words, in 1933 the United States produced 26.6 percent less than in 1929. While only 3.2 percent of the labor force was unemployed in 1929, 25.2 percent was unemployed in 1933. By contrast, between 1980 and 1982 real GDP was essentially unchanged rather than declining. The unemployment rate rose from 5.8 percent in 1979 to 9.7 percent in 1982. *Capacity utilization rates,* which show the percentage of factory capacity being used in production, are not available for the 1930s, so we have no point of comparison. However, Table 7.1 shows that capacity utilization fell from 85.2 percent in 1979 to 72.1 percent in 1982. Although the recession in the early 1980s was severe, it did not come close to the severity of the Great Depression.

DEFINING AND MEASURING UNEMPLOYMENT

The most frequently discussed symptom of a recession is unemployment. In September of 1982, the United States unemployment rate was over 10 percent for the first time since the 1930s. Although unemployment is widely discussed, most people are unaware of what unemployment statistics mean or how they are derived.

TABLE 7.1 Real GDP and Unemployment Rates, 1929–1933 and 1980–1982

THE EARLY PART OF THE GREAT DEPRESSION, 1929–1933

	Percentage Change in Real GDP	Unemployment Rate	Number of Unemployed (Millions)
1929		3.2	1.5
1930	–8.6	8.9	4.3
1931	–6.4	16.3	8.0
1932	–13.0	24.1	12.1
1933	–1.4	25.2	12.8

Note: Percentage fall in real GDP between 1929 and 1933 was 26.6 percent.

THE RECESSION OF 1980–1982

	Percentage Change in Real GDP	Unemployment Rate	Number of Unemployed (Millions)	Capacity Utilization (Percentage)
1979		5.8	6.1	85.2
1980	–0.2	7.1	7.6	80.9
1981	2.5	7.6	8.3	79.9
1982	–2.0	9.7	10.7	72.1

Note: Percentage increase in real GDP between 1979 and 1982 was 0.1 percent.
Sources: Historical Statistics of the United States and U.S. Department of Commerce, Bureau of Economic Analysis.

The unemployment statistics released to the press on the first Friday of each month are based on a survey of households conducted by the Bureau of Labor Statistics (BLS), a branch of the Department of Labor. Each month the BLS draws a sample of 65,000 households and completes interviews with all but about 2,500 of them. Each interviewed household answers questions concerning the work activity of household members 16 years of age or older during the calendar week that contains the twelfth of the month. (The survey is conducted in the week that follows the week that contains the twelfth of the month.)

If a household member 16 years of age or older worked 1 hour or more as a paid employee, either for someone else or in his own business or farm, he is classified as **employed**. A household member is also considered employed if he worked 15 hours or more without pay in a family enterprise. Finally, a household member is counted as employed if she held a job from which she was temporarily absent due to illness, bad weather, vacation, labor-management disputes, or personal reasons, whether she was paid or not.

employed Any person 16 years old or older (1) who works for pay, either for someone else or in his or her own business for 1 or more hours per week, (2) who works without pay for 15 or more hours per week in a family enterprise, or (3) who has a job but has been temporarily absent, with or without pay.

Those who are not employed fall into one of two categories: (1) unemployed or (2) not in the labor force. To be considered **unemployed**, a person must be available for work and have made specific efforts to find work during the previous 4 weeks. A person not looking for work, either because he or she does not want a job or has given up looking, is classified as **not in the labor force**. People not in the labor force include full-time students, retirees, individuals in institutions, and those staying home to take care of children or elderly parents.

unemployed A person 16 years old or older who is not working, is available for work, and has made specific efforts to find work during the previous 4 weeks.

not in the labor force A person who is not looking for work, either because he or she does not want a job or has given up looking.

The total **labor force** in the economy is the number of people employed plus the number of unemployed:

labor force The number of people employed plus the number of unemployed.

$$\text{labor force} = \text{employed} + \text{unemployed}$$

The total population 16 years of age or older is equal to the number of people in the labor force plus the number not in the labor force:

$$\text{population} = \text{labor force} + \text{not in labor force}$$

With these numbers, several ratios can be calculated. The **unemployment rate** is the ratio of the number of people unemployed to the total number of people in the labor force:

unemployment rate The ratio of the number of people unemployed to the total number of people in the labor force.

$$\text{unemployment rate} = \frac{\text{unemployed}}{\text{employed} + \text{unemployed}}$$

In July 2003, the labor force contained 146.54 million people, 137.48 million of whom were employed and 9.06 million of whom were unemployed and looking for work. The unemployment rate was 6.2 percent:

$$\frac{9.06}{137.48 + 9.06} = 6.2\%$$

The ratio of the labor force to the population 16 years old or over is called the **labor-force participation rate**:

labor-force participation rate The ratio of the labor force to the total population 16 years old or older.

$$\text{labor-force participation rate} = \frac{\text{labor force}}{\text{population}}$$

Table 7.2 shows the relationship among these numbers for selected years since 1953. The year 1982 shows the effects of the recession. Although the unemployment rate has gone up and down, the labor-force participation rate has grown steadily since 1953. Most of this increase is due to the growth in the participation rate of women between the ages of 25 and 54.

Column 3 in Table 7.2 shows how many new workers the U.S. economy has absorbed in recent years. The number of employed workers increased by about 38 million between 1953 and 1982 and by about 35 million between 1982 and 2002.

TABLE 7.2 Employed, Unemployed, and the Labor Force, 1953–2002

	(1) POPULATION 16 YEARS OLD OR OVER (MILLIONS)	(2) LABOR FORCE (MILLIONS)	(3) EMPLOYED (MILLIONS)	(4) UNEMPLOYED (MILLIONS)	(5) LABOR-FORCE PARTICIPATION RATE	(6) UNEMPLOYMENT RATE
1953	107.1	63.0	61.2	1.8	58.9	2.9
1960	117.2	69.6	65.8	3.9	59.4	5.5
1970	137.1	82.8	78.7	4.1	60.4	4.9
1980	167.7	106.9	99.3	7.6	63.8	7.1
1982	172.3	110.2	99.5	10.7	64.0	9.7
1990	189.2	125.8	118.8	7.0	66.5	5.6
2002	214.0	142.5	134.3	8.3	66.6	4.2

Note: Figures are civilian only (military excluded).
Source: Economic Report of the President, 2003, Table B-35.

COMPONENTS OF THE UNEMPLOYMENT RATE

The unemployment rate by itself conveys a limited amount of information. To understand the level of unemployment better, we must look at unemployment rates across groups of people, regions, and industries.

Unemployment Rates for Different Demographic Groups There are big differences in rates of unemployment across demographic groups. Table 7.3 shows the unemployment rate for November 1982—the worst month of the recession in 1982—and for July 2003, broken down by race, sex, and age. In November 1982, when the overall unemployment rate hit 10.8 percent, the rate for whites was 9.6 percent while the rate for African-Americans was more than twice that—20.2 percent.

During the recession in 1982, men fared worse than women. In November 1982, 9.0 percent of white men 20 years and over, but only 8.1 percent of white women 20 years and over were unemployed. For African-Americans, 19.3 percent of men 20 years and over and 16.5 percent of women 20 years and over were unemployed. Teenagers between 16 and 19 years of age fared worst. African-Americans between 16 and 19 experienced an unemployment rate of 51.1 percent in November 1982. For whites between 16 and 19 the unemployment rate was 21.8 percent.

Although the rates were lower for all groups in July 2003, the pattern was similar. The highest unemployment rates were for African-American teenagers—37.4 percent.

The main point of Table 7.3 is that an unemployment rate of, say, 6.3 percent does not mean every group in society has a 6.3 percent unemployment rate.

TABLE 7.3 Unemployment Rates by Demographic Group, 1982 and 2003

	YEARS	NOV. 1982	JULY 2003
Total		10.8	6.3
White		9.6	5.5
Men	20+	9.0	4.9
Women	20+	8.1	4.8
Both sexes	16–19	21.8	15.6
African-American		20.2	12.0
Men	20+	19.3	10.5
Women	20+	16.5	10.3
Both sexes	16–19	51.1	37.4

Source: U.S. Department of Labor, Bureau of Labor Statistics. Data are not seasonally adjusted.

There are large differences in unemployment rates across demographic groups.

Unemployment Rates in States and Regions Unemployment rates vary by geographic location. For a variety of reasons, not all states and regions have the same level of unemployment. States and regions have different combinations of industries, which do not all grow and decline at the same time and at the same rate. Also, the labor force is not completely mobile—workers often cannot or do not want to pack up and move to take advantage of job opportunities in other parts of the country.

In the last 20 years, remarkable changes have occurred in the relative prosperity of regions, particularly in the Northeast and the oil-rich Southwest. During the early 1970s, the Northeast (New England, in particular) was hit by a serious decline in its industrial base. Textile mills, leather goods plants, and furniture factories closed in the face of foreign competition or moved south to states with lower wages. During the recession of 1975, Massachusetts and Michigan had very high unemployment rates (11.2 percent and 12.5 percent, respectively). Riding the crest of rising oil prices, Texas had one of the lowest unemployment rates at that time (5.6 percent) (Table 7.4).

During the recession of 1982, Texas continued to do well, and Massachusetts took a sharp turn for the better. The unemployment rate in Massachusetts went from nearly three points above the national average during the 1975 recession to nearly two points below during the 1982 recession.

By 1987, things had changed. Although not shown in Table 7.4, Massachusetts had one of the lowest unemployment rates in the country in 1987 (an amazing 2.8 percent) and Texas (at 8.5 percent) had one of the highest. In Massachusetts, high-tech firms such as Wang Laboratories and Digital Equipment, two firms that employed a total of over 100,000 people, had grown dramatically. In contrast, the fall in crude oil prices from over $30 per barrel to under $15 per barrel in the early 1980s forced the oil-based economy of Texas into a deep and prolonged recession. Then, in 1991, Massachusetts experienced yet another reversal with an unemployment rate of 9 percent.

The economy of Michigan is heavily tied to the fortunes of the automobile industry. During the recession of 1982, Michigan had the highest unemployment rate in the country at 15.5 percent. The automobile industry not only suffered from the decline in the U.S. economy but also faced stiff foreign competition, primarily from Japan. Michigan also suffered in 1991, with an unemployment rate of 9.2 percent.

The recession of 2001 was mild by comparison and the impact was much more uniform around the country. By the first quarter of 2003, national unemployment had risen to 5.8 percent from 3.8 percent in April of 2000. The 3.8 percent figure was the lowest level of unemployment in 35 years. All the states listed in Table 7.4 had unemployment rates between 5.2 percent and 6.6 percent. Still, the largest impact on unemployment was the collapse of the dot-com bubble beginning in 2000.

TABLE 7.4 Regional Differences in Unemployment, 1975, 1982, 1991, and 2003

	1975	1982	1991	2003
U.S. avg.	8.5	9.7	6.7	5.8
Cal.	9.9	9.9	7.5	6.6
Fla.	10.7	8.2	7.3	5.2
Ill.	7.1	11.3	7.1	6.5
Mass.	11.2	7.9	9.0	5.3
Mich.	12.5	15.5	9.2	6.6
N.J.	10.2	9.0	6.6	5.7
N.Y.	9.5	8.6	7.2	6.1
N.C.	8.6	9.0	5.8	5.8
Ohio	9.1	12.5	6.4	6.0
Tex.	5.6	6.9	6.6	6.6

Sources: Statistical Abstract of the United States, various editions.

The national unemployment rate does not tell the whole story. A low national rate of unemployment does not mean that the entire nation is growing and producing at the same rate.

Discouraged-Worker Effects Remember, people who stop looking for work are classified as having dropped out of the labor force instead of being unemployed. During recessions people may become discouraged about finding a job and stop looking. This lowers the unemployment rate, because those no longer looking for work are no longer counted as unemployed.

discouraged-worker effect The decline in the measured unemployment rate that results when people who want to work but cannot find jobs grow discouraged and stop looking, thus dropping out of the ranks of the unemployed and the labor force.

To demonstrate how this **discouraged-worker effect** lowers the unemployment rate, suppose there are 10 million unemployed out of a labor force of 100 million. This means an unemployment rate of 10/100 = .10, or 10 percent. If 1 million of these 10 million unemployed people stop looking for work and drop out of the labor force, there would be 9 million unemployed out of a labor force of 99 million. The unemployment rate would then drop to 9/99 = .091, or 9.1 percent.

The BLS survey provides some evidence on the size of the discouraged-worker effect. Respondents who indicate that they have stopped searching for work are asked why they stopped. If the respondent cites inability to find employment as the sole reason for not searching, that person might be classified as a discouraged worker.

The number of discouraged workers seems to hover around 1 percent of the size of the labor force in normal times. During the 1980–1982 recession, the number of discouraged workers increased steadily to a peak of 1.5 percent. By the end of the first quarter of 1991, the recession of 1990–1991 had produced 997,000 discouraged workers. Some economists argue that adding the number of discouraged workers to the number who are now classified as unemployed gives a better picture of the unemployment situation.

The Duration of Unemployment The unemployment rate measures unemployment at a given point in time. It tells us nothing about how long the average unemployed worker is out of work.

Table 7.5 shows that during recessionary periods the average duration of unemployment rises. Between 1979 and 1983, the average duration of unemployment rose from 10.8 weeks to 20 weeks. The slow growth following the 1990–1991 recession resulted in an increase in duration of unemployment to 17.7 weeks in 1992 and to 18.8 weeks in 1994. In 2000, average duration was down to 12.6 weeks, which then rose to 16.6 weeks in 2002.

THE COSTS OF UNEMPLOYMENT

In the Employment Act of 1946, the Congress declared it was the

> continuing policy and responsibility of the federal government to use all practicable means . . . to promote maximum employment, production, and purchasing power.

TABLE 7.5 Average Duration of Unemployment, 1979–2002

	WEEKS		WEEKS
1979	10.8	1991	13.7
1980	11.9	1992	17.7
1981	13.7	1993	18.0
1982	15.6	1994	18.8
1983	20.0	1995	16.6
1984	18.2	1996	16.7
1985	15.6	1997	15.8
1986	15.0	1998	14.5
1987	14.5	1999	13.4
1988	13.5	2000	12.6
1989	11.9	2001	13.1
1990	12.0	2002	16.6

Sources: U.S. Department of Labor, Bureau of Labor Statistics.

News Analysis

Rising Unemployment in 2003

THE UNEMPLOYMENT RATE STOOD AT 3.8 PERcent in April of 2000. The nonfarm employment level stood at 132.2 million. Between April 2001 and April 2003, employment dropped by just under 2 million and the unemployment rate rose to 6.0 percent. The following article describes some of the consequences.

Unemployment Returns to Eight-Year High—*New York Times*

The nation's unemployment rate swelled to 6 percent in April, returning to an eight-year high as employers slashed payrolls even deeper. The ailing economy has lost a half million jobs in three months.

The rate was up two-tenths of a percentage point from March, with payrolls falling by 48,000, the Labor Department reported Friday.

The bottom line: Employers are handing out pink slips, not job offers, and that's not likely to change soon.

"For those who are out of work, finding a job is getting tougher," said David Rosenberg, chief economist at Merrill Lynch.

April's job losses were the third in a row, which never occurs outside of recessions, he said, adding that "we now have such a case." Job cuts were concentrated in manufacturing, airlines and retail. . . .

In April, the number of unemployed workers surged to 8.8 million, with almost 2 million without jobs for 27 weeks or more. The average duration of unemployment shot up to 19.6 weeks—a 20-year high.

"There's just no denying that these are an awful set of job figures for April," said Ken Mayland, president of ClearView Economics in Cleveland. . . .

Now that the Iraq war is over, modest hiring could resume, Mayland said. Some recent positive economic signs include lower gasoline prices, an improved stock market and elevated consumer confidence.

The report underscores the challenges facing President Bush as he turns his attention to domestic matters and a re-election campaign.

Democrats say Bush, like his father, is politically vulnerable on the economy. Some criticized his prime time speech Thursday night from the USS Abraham Lincoln, saying he should spend more energy on getting Americans back to work. . . .

April's jobless rate increase was caused in part by 680,000 people returning to the labor force. The ouster of Saddam Hussein's regime in Iraq boosted Americans' confidence, sending many unemployed people back out to look for work. But their searches yielded little results because the economy wasn't healthy enough to create new jobs.

Even before the war, businesses were wary about making big spending and hiring commitments in a struggling economy. . . .

Source: Adapted from: "Unemployment Returns to Eight-Year High," Associated Press article in the New York Times, *May 4, 2003. Reprinted by permission.*

Visit www.prenhall.com/casefair for updated articles and exercises.

In 1978, Congress passed the Full Employment and Balanced Growth Act, commonly referred to as the *Humphrey-Hawkins Act*, which formally established a specific unemployment target of 4 percent.

Why should full employment be a policy objective of the federal government? What costs does unemployment impose on society?

Some Unemployment Is Inevitable Before we discuss the costs of unemployment, we must realize that some unemployment is simply part of the natural workings of the labor market. Remember, to be classified as unemployed, a person must be looking for a job. Every year, thousands of people enter the labor force for the first time. Some have dropped out of high school, some are high school or college graduates, and still others are finishing graduate programs. At the same time, new firms are starting up and others are expanding and creating new jobs, while other firms are contracting or going out of business.

At any moment, there is a set of job seekers and a set of jobs that must be matched with one another. It is important that the right people end up in the right jobs. The right job for a person will depend on that person's skills, preferences concerning work environment (large firm or small, formal or informal), where the individual lives, and willingness to commute. At the same time, firms want workers who can meet the requirements of the job and grow with the company.

To make a good match, workers must acquire information on job availability, wage rates, location, and work environment. Firms must acquire information on worker availability and skills. Information-gathering consumes time and resources. The search may involve travel, interviewing, preparation of a résumé, telephone calls, and hours going through the newspaper. To the extent that these efforts lead to a better match of workers and jobs, they are well spent. As long as the gains to firms and workers exceed the costs of search, the result is efficient.

When considering the various costs of unemployment it is useful to categorize unemployment into three types:

- Frictional unemployment
- Structural unemployment
- Cyclical unemployment

Frictional and Structural Unemployment When the BLS does its survey about work activity for the week containing the twelfth of each month, it interviews many people who are involved in the normal search for work. Some are either entering the labor force or switching jobs. This unemployment is both natural and beneficial for the economy.

frictional unemployment The portion of unemployment that is due to the normal working of the labor market; used to denote short-run job/skill matching problems.

The portion of unemployment due to the normal working of the labor market is called **frictional unemployment**. The frictional unemployment rate can never be zero. It may, however, change over time. As jobs become more and more differentiated and the number of required skills increases, matching skills and jobs becomes more complex, and the frictional unemployment rate may rise.

The concept of frictional unemployment is somewhat abstract because it is hard to know what "the normal working of the labor market" means. The industrial structure of the U.S. economy is continually changing. Manufacturing, for instance, has yielded part of its share of total employment to services and to finance, insurance, and real estate. Within the manufacturing sector, the steel and textiles industries have contracted sharply, while high-technology sectors, such as electronic components, have expanded.

structural unemployment The portion of unemployment that is due to changes in the structure of the economy that result in a significant loss of jobs in certain industries.

Although the unemployment that arises from such structural shifts could be classified as frictional, it is usually called **structural unemployment**. The term *frictional unemployment* is used to denote short-run job/skill matching problems, problems that last a few weeks. *Structural unemployment* denotes longer run adjustment problems—those that tend to last for years.

Although structural unemployment is expected in a dynamic economy, it is painful to the workers who experience it. In some ways, those who lose their jobs because their skills are obsolete are the ones who experience the greatest pain. The fact that structural unemployment is natural and inevitable does not mean it costs society nothing.

natural rate of unemployment The unemployment that occurs as a normal part of the functioning of the economy. Sometimes taken as the sum of frictional unemployment and structural unemployment.

Economists sometimes use the phrase **natural rate of unemployment** to refer to unemployment that occurs as a normal part of the functioning of the economy. This concept is also somewhat vague, because "natural" is not a precise word. It is probably best to think of the natural rate as the sum of the frictional rate and the structural rate. Estimates of the natural rate range from 4 percent to 6 percent.

Cyclical Unemployment and Lost Output Although some unemployment is natural, there are times when the unemployment rate seems to be above the natural rate. In 1979, the unemployment rate was 5.8 percent, but it did not fall below 6 percent again until 1987, eight years later. In the meantime, the United States experienced a major recession, during which the unemployment rate rose substantially. The increase in unemployment that occurs during recessions and depressions is called **cyclical unemployment**.

cyclical unemployment The increase in unemployment that occurs during recessions and depressions.

In one sense, an increase in unemployment during a recession is simply a manifestation of a more fundamental problem. The basic problem is that firms are producing less. Remember that a recession entails a decline in real GDP, or real output. When firms cut back and produce less, they employ fewer workers and less capital. Thus, the first and most direct cost of a recession is the loss of real goods and services that otherwise would have been produced.

Never was the loss of output more dramatic than during the Great Depression. In Table 7.1 you saw that real output fell about 27 percent between 1929 and 1933. It is, of course, the real output of the economy that matters most—the food we eat, the medical care we get, the cars we drive, the movies we watch, the new houses that are built, the pots we cook in, and the education we receive. When output falls by 27 percent, life changes for a lot of people.

During the recession of 1980–1982, the growth rate of real GDP was on average roughly zero. In Table 7.1, had real GDP grown at 3 percent each year from 1979, the total growth in output in the 1980–1982 period would have been about 9 percent instead of the 0.1 percent that actually occurred. This is a substantial loss of output and, consequently, income.

Social Consequences The costs of recessions and depressions are neither evenly distributed across the population nor easily quantified. The social consequences of the Depression of the 1930s are perhaps the hardest to comprehend. Most people alive today did not live through the Great Depression and can only read about it in books or hear stories told by parents and grandparents. Few emerged from this period unscathed. At the bottom were the poor and the fully unemployed, about 25 percent of the labor force. Even those who kept their jobs found themselves working part-time. Many people lost all or part of their savings as the stock market crashed and thousands of banks failed.

Congressional committees heard story after story. In Cincinnati, where the labor force totaled about 200,000, about 48,000 were wholly unemployed, 40,000 more were on short time, and relief payments to the needy averaged $7 to $8 per week:

> Relief is given to a family one week and then they are pushed off for a week in the hope that somehow or other the breadwinner may find some kind of work. . . . We are paying no rent at all. That, of course, is a very difficult problem because we are continually having evictions, and social workers . . . are hard put to find places for people whose furniture has been put out on the street.[1]

From Birmingham, Alabama, in 1932:

> . . . we have about 108,000 wage and salary workers in my district. Of that number, it is my belief that not exceeding 8000 have their normal incomes. At least 25,000 men are altogether without work. Some of them have not had a stroke of work for more than 12 months. Perhaps 60,000 or 70,000 are working from one to five days a week, and practically all have had serious cuts in wages and many of them do not average over $1.50 per day.[2]

Economic hardship accompanied the recent recessions as well. Between 1979 and 1983, the number of people officially classified as living in poverty in the United States rose from 26.1 million (11.7 percent of the population) to 35.5 million (15.3 percent). In addition to economic hardship, prolonged unemployment may also bring with it social and personal ills: anxiety, depression, deterioration of physical and psychological health, drug abuse (including alcoholism), and suicide.

THE BENEFITS OF RECESSIONS

Do recessions have any benefits? Yes: Recessions are likely to slow the rate of inflation. We saw in Figure 5.7 two serious inflationary periods since 1970: 1974–1975 and 1979–1981. Each was followed by a recession during which the rate of inflation decreased. As Table 7.6 shows, inflation fell from a 1974 rate of 11.0 percent to 5.8 percent in 1976. In 1983, the inflation rate also fell, to 3.2 percent, from a 1980 rate of 13.5 percent.

It appears recessions do help to counteract inflation, but more analysis is needed before we can understand why (see Chapter 13). The point here is:

Recessions may help to reduce inflation.

TABLE 7.6 Inflation Rates, 1974–1976 and 1980–1983

RECESSION BEGINS	INFLATION RATE
→ 1974	11.0
1975	9.1
1976	5.8
→ 1980	13.5
1981	10.3
1982	6.2
1983	3.2

Source: See Table 7.8.

[1]U.S. Senate Hearings before a subcommittee of the Committee of Manufacturers, 72nd Congress, first session (1931), p. 239. Cited in Lester Chandler, *America's Greatest Depression, 1929–1941* (New York: Harper & Row, 1970), p. 43.

[2]Senate Hearings, in Lester Chandler, *America's Greatest Depression, 1929–1941* (New York: Harper & Row, 1970), p. 43.

Some argue recessions may increase efficiency by driving the least efficient firms in the economy out of business and forcing surviving firms to trim waste and manage their resources better. As we will discuss in Chapter 21; a recession leads to a decrease in the demand for imports, which improves a nation's balance of payments—that is, its record of trade with other countries.

INFLATION

Ups in the business cycle often, but not always, seem to encourage inflation. Table 7.7 shows the rate of inflation during the three most recent periods of expansion. The inflation rate rose from 3.2 percent to 11.0 percent from 1972 to 1974. The trend in inflation was also upward from 1976 to 1980. The sustained growth that began in 1983, however, did not seem to bring rapid inflation.

Why is inflation a problem? If you understand that wages and salaries, as well as other forms of income, increase along with prices during periods of inflation, you will see this question is more subtle than you might think. If my income doubles and the prices of the things I buy double, am I any worse off? I can buy exactly the same things that I bought yesterday, so to the extent that my well-being depends on what I am able to buy, the answer is no.

However, incomes and prices do not all increase at the same rate during inflations. For some people, income increases faster than prices; for others, prices increase faster. Some people benefit from inflations, others are hurt.

The remainder of this chapter focuses on the problem of inflation: its measurement, its costs, and the gains and losses experienced during inflationary periods.

DEFINING INFLATION

What is inflation? Not all price increases constitute inflation. Prices of individual goods and services are determined in many ways. In competitive markets, the interaction of many buyers and many sellers—the operation of supply and demand—determines prices. In imperfectly competitive markets, prices are determined by producers' decisions. (This is the core of microeconomic theory.)

In any economy, prices are continuously changing as markets adjust to changing conditions. Lack of rain may dry up corn and wheat fields, reducing supply and pushing up the price of agricultural products. At the same time, high levels of production by oil producers may be driving down the price of oil and petroleum products. Simultaneously, the United Auto Workers may be negotiating a contract with the Ford Motor Company that raises (or lowers) wage rates.

TABLE 7.7 Inflation During Three Expansions

	INFLATION RATE
1972	3.2
1973	6.2
1974	11.0
1976	5.8
1977	6.5
1978	7.6
1979	11.3
1980	13.5
1984	4.3
1985	3.6
1986	1.9
1987	3.6
1988	4.1
1989	4.8

Source: See Table 7.8.

When the price of one good rises, that price increase may or may not be part of a larger inflation. Remember, **inflation** is an increase in the overall price level. It happens when many prices increase simultaneously. We measure inflation by looking at a large number of goods and services and calculating the average increase in their prices during some period of time. **Deflation** is a decrease in the overall price level. It occurs when many prices decrease simultaneously.

inflation An increase in the overall price level.

deflation A decrease in the overall price level.

It is useful to distinguish between a *one-time* increase in the overall price level and an increase in the overall price level that continues over time. For example, the overall price level could rise 10 percent in a single month and stop rising, or it could increase steadily over some years. Economists often use *inflation* to refer only to increases in the price level that continue over some significant period. We will refer to such periods as periods of **sustained inflation.**

sustained inflation An increase in the overall price level that continues over a significant period.

PRICE INDEXES

Price indexes are used to measure overall price levels. We discussed how these indexes are constructed in the previous chapter. The price index that pertains to all goods and services in the economy is the *GDP deflator.* As we saw in Chapter 6, the Bureau of Economic Analysis (BEA) does not use fixed weights to construct the GDP deflator. Many other price indexes are constructed using fixed weights.

The most popular fixed-weight price index is the **consumer price index (CPI)**. The CPI was first constructed during World War I as a basis for adjusting shipbuilders' wages, which the government controlled during the war. Currently, the CPI is computed by the BLS each month, using a bundle of goods meant to represent the "market basket" purchased monthly by the typical urban consumer. The quantities of each good in the bundle that are used for the weights are based on extensive surveys of consumers. In fact, the BLS collects prices each month for about 71,000 goods and services from about 22,000 outlets in 44 geographic areas. For example, the cost of housing is included in the data collection by surveying about 5,000 renters and 1,000 homeowners each month. Figure 7.3 shows the CPI market basket at the end of 2002.

consumer price index (CPI) A price index computed each month by the Bureau of Labor Statistics using a bundle that is meant to represent the "market basket" purchased monthly by the typical urban consumer.

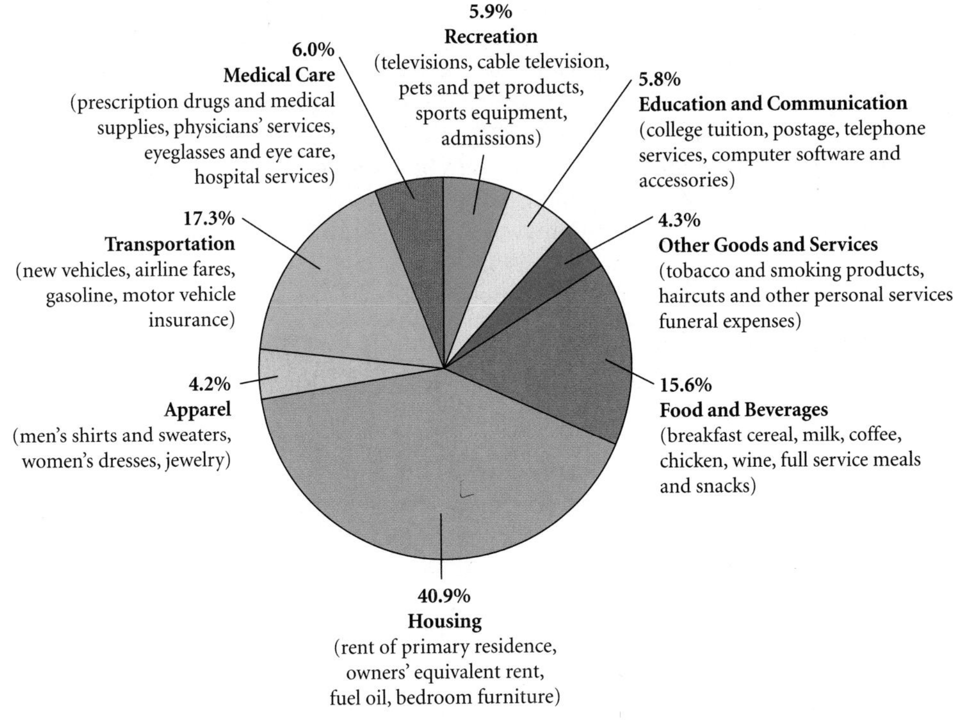

FIGURE 7.3 The CPI Market Basket

The CPI market basket shows how a typical consumer divides his or her money among various goods and services. Most of a consumer's money goes toward housing, transportation, and food and beverages.

Source: The Bureau of Labor Statistics.

TABLE 7.8 The CPI, 1950–2002

	PERCENTAGE CHANGE IN CPI	CPI		PERCENTAGE CHANGE IN CPI	CPI
1950	1.3	24.1	1977	6.5	60.6
1951	7.9	26.0	1978	7.6	65.2
1952	1.9	26.5	1979	11.3	72.6
1953	0.8	26.7	1980	13.5	82.4
1954	0.7	26.9	1981	10.3	90.9
1955	–0.4	26.8	1982	6.2	96.5
1956	1.5	27.2	1983	3.2	99.6
1957	3.3	28.1	1984	4.3	103.9
1958	2.8	28.9	1985	3.6	107.6
1959	0.7	29.1	1986	1.9	109.6
1960	1.7	29.6	1987	3.6	113.6
1961	1.0	29.9	1988	4.1	118.3
1962	1.0	30.2	1989	4.8	124.0
1963	1.3	30.6	1990	5.4	130.7
1964	1.3	31.0	1991	4.2	136.2
1965	1.6	31.5	1992	3.0	140.3
1966	2.9	32.4	1993	3.0	144.5
1967	3.1	33.4	1994	2.6	148.2
1968	4.2	34.8	1995	2.8	152.4
1969	5.5	36.7	1996	3.0	156.9
1970	5.7	38.8	1997	2.3	160.5
1971	4.4	40.5	1998	1.6	163.0
1972	3.2	41.8	1999	2.2	166.6
1973	6.2	44.4	2000	3.4	172.2
1974	11.0	49.3	2001	2.8	177.1
1975	9.1	53.8	2002	1.6	179.9
1976	5.8	56.9			

Sources: Bureau of Labor Statistics, U.S. Department of Labor.

Table 7.8 shows values of the CPI since 1950. The percentage changes in the table are calculated using the index. (The base period for this index is 3 years, 1982 to 1984, instead of the more usual 1 year.) For example, from 1970 to 1971 the CPI increased from 38.8 to 40.5. The percentage change is simply $[(40.5 - 38.8)/38.8] \times 100$, which is 4.4 percent.

Remember from the previous chapter that a fixed-weight price index like the CPI does not account for consumers' substitution away from high-priced goods. For more information, see the Further Exploration box, "World Economy in Transition: Bias in the U.S. Consumer Price Index—Why It Could Be Important."

Changes in the CPI somewhat overstate changes in the cost of living.

In response to the fixed-weight problem, in August 2002 the BLS began publishing a version of the CPI, called the "Chained Consumer Price Index," which uses changing weights. Although this version is not yet the main version, it may be that within a few years the BLS moves completely away from the fixed-weight version of the CPI. Remember, however, that even if this happens, the CPI will still differ in important ways from the GDP deflator. The CPI covers only consumer goods and services whereas the GDP deflator covers all goods and services produced in the economy. Also, the CPI includes prices of imported goods, which the GDP deflator does not. Figure 7.3 shows the market basket of goods that was used for the CPI in 2002.

producer price indexes (PPIs) Measures of prices that producers receive for products at all stages in the production process.

Other popular price indexes are **producer price indexes (PPIs)**, once called *wholesale price indexes.* These are indexes of prices that producers receive for products at all stages in the production process, not just the final stage. The indexes are calculated separately for various stages in the production process. The three main categories are *finished goods, intermediate materials,* and *crude materials,* although there are subcategories within each of these categories.

Further Exploration

World Economy in Transition: Bias in the US Consumer Price Index—Why It Could Be Important

Changes in the consumer price index (CPI) provide the most commonly used measure of inflation in all countries. . . . In a recent study, the U.S. Advisory Commission to Study the Consumer Price Index (more commonly known as the Boskin Commission, whose chairman was Michael Boskin, former chief of the U.S. Council of Economic Advisers) estimated that the US CPI overstated inflation by 1.1 percentage point in 1996 and by slightly more in each of the previous 20 years. Thus, although the official rate of inflation for 1996 was 2.9 percent, the true rate may have been in the neighborhood of 1.8 percent. This upward bias arises because the CPI methodology does not adequately capture shifts in consumer purchases when relative prices move, the effects of changes in the quality of goods and services, the introduction of new products, or the growing number of discount stores. While some experts have disputed that the upward bias is as large as has been suggested by the Commission, there is a growing consensus that there may indeed be significant bias. . . .

Not all prices rise at the same rate. When the price of beef rises, the impact on the cost of living is offset by the fact that households can substitute chicken or fish if those prices have not risen less.

Upward bias in the official inflation rate has important implications. First, real wages—which were widely thought, on the basis of official data, to have stagnated over the last two decades—may, in fact, have increased considerably. Second, in regard to fiscal policy, upward bias has considerable budgetary costs: expenditures indexed to the CPI rise by more than is needed to offset inflation, and inflation adjustments made to tax brackets are overstated, resulting in reduced tax revenues. Recent estimates indicate that if the current inflation bias continues for the next 10 years, the federal government deficit will increase on this account alone by $140 billion, and $650 billion will be added to the national debt by the end of the period. . . .

The Boskin Commission's report identified and quantified three sources of bias, all of which arise because of limitations in the methodology used to calculate the CPI . . . :

- *Quality change and new product bias*, the largest source of bias, arises because the CPI does not immediately take into account either improvements in the quality of goods and services or the introduction of new products. To the extent that the CPI fails to account for changes in quality, the index will not reflect "true" changes in prices. And new products need to be incorporated into the CPI on a timely basis, so that the early declines in price that are a normal part of the product life cycle are captured.
- *Substitution bias* occurs because the formula used for CPI calculations assumes that consumers purchase a constant mix of various goods and services despite changes in their relative prices. In actuality, if the price of one good rises relative to that of another good, consumers will tend to substitute cheaper goods for higher-priced ones. Because the weights of goods in the CPI are adjusted infrequently (about once every 10 years), substitution is not taken into account.
- *Outlet substitution bias* occurs because the CPI does not adequately take into account the extent to which new discount stores have offered lower prices and enticed consumers away from the traditional outlets that tend to be more fully represented in the CPI market basket. . . .

Source: Adapted from: Paul A. Armknecht and Paula R. De Masi, "United States: Sources and Implications of Bias in the Consumer Price Index.," World Economic Outlook, *International Monetary Fund (Washington, D.C., Spring 1997). Available at http://www.worldbank.org.*

One advantage of some of the PPIs is that they detect price increases early in the production process. Because their movements sometimes foreshadow future changes in consumer prices, they are considered to be leading indicators of future consumer prices.

THE COSTS OF INFLATION

If you asked most people why inflation is "bad," they would tell you that it lowers the overall standard of living by making goods and services more expensive. That is, it cuts into people's purchasing power. People are fond of recalling the days when a bottle of Coca-Cola cost a dime and a hamburger cost a quarter. Just think what we could buy today if prices had not changed.

What people usually do not think about is what their incomes were in the "good old days." The fact that the cost of a Coke has increased from 10 cents to 50 cents does not mean anything in real terms if people who once earned $5,000 now earn $25,000. Why? The reason is simple:

People's income from wages and salaries, profits, interest, and rent increases during inflations. The wage rate is the price of labor, rent is the price of land, and so on. During inflations, most prices—including input prices—tend to rise together, and input prices determine both the incomes of workers and the incomes of owners of capital and land.

Inflation Changes the Distribution of Income Whether you gain or lose during a period of inflation depends on whether your income rises faster or slower than the prices of the things you buy. The group most often mentioned when the impact of inflation is discussed is people living on fixed incomes. If your income is fixed and prices rise, your ability to purchase goods and services falls proportionately. Who are the fixed-income earners?

Most people think of the elderly. Many retired workers living on private pensions receive monthly checks that will never increase. Many pension plans, however, pay benefits that are *indexed* to inflation. The benefits these plans provide automatically increase when the general price level rises. If prices rise 10 percent, benefits also rise 10 percent. The biggest source of income for the elderly is social security. These benefits are fully indexed; when prices rise—that is, when the CPI rises—by 5 percent, social security benefits also increase by 5 percent.

The poor have not fared as well. Welfare benefits, which are not indexed, have not kept pace with the price level over the last two decades. Benefits to families with dependent children under the Aid to Families with Dependent Children (AFDC) program declined 33 percent in real terms between 1970 and 1988. In five states—Idaho, Illinois, Kentucky, New Jersey, and Texas—the average benefits fell by more than 50 percent in real terms.[3]

Effects on Debtors and Creditors It is also commonly believed that debtors benefit at the expense of creditors during an inflation. Certainly, if I loan you $100 to be paid back in a year, and prices increase 10 percent in the meantime, I get back 10 percent less in real terms than what I loaned you.

Suppose we had both anticipated prices would rise 10 percent. I would have taken this into consideration in the deal that I made with you. I would charge you an interest rate high enough to cover the decrease in value due to the anticipated inflation. If we agree on a 15 percent interest rate, then you must pay me $115 at the end of a year. The difference between the interest rate on a loan and the inflation rate is referred to as the **real interest rate**. In our deal, I will earn a real interest rate of 5 percent. By charging a 15 percent interest rate, I have taken into account the anticipated 10 percent inflation rate. In this sense, I am not hurt by the inflation—I keep pace with inflation and earn a profit on my money, too—despite the fact that I am a creditor.

real interest rate The difference between the interest rate on a loan and the inflation rate.

On the other hand, an unanticipated inflation—an inflation that takes people by surprise—can hurt creditors. If the actual inflation rate during the period of my loan to you turns out to be 20 percent, then I as a creditor will be hurt. I charged you 15 percent interest, expecting to get a 5 percent real rate of return, when I needed to charge you 25 percent to get the same 5 percent real rate of return. Because inflation was higher than expected, I got a negative real return of 5 percent.

Inflation that is higher than expected benefits debtors; inflation that is lower than expected benefits creditors.

Administrative Costs and Inefficiencies There are costs associated even with anticipated inflation. One is the administrative cost associated with simply keeping up. During the rapid inflation in Israel in the early 1980s, a telephone hotline was set up to give the hourly price index. Store owners have to recalculate and repost prices frequently, and this takes time that could be used more efficiently.

[3]Alicia H. Munnell, "The Current Status of Our Social Welfare System," Federal Reserve Bank of Boston, monograph (1987).

More frequent banking transactions may be required. For example, interest rates tend to rise with anticipated inflation. When interest rates are high, the opportunity costs of holding cash outside of banks is high. People therefore hold less cash and need to stop at the bank more often. (We discuss this in more detail in the next part of this book.) In addition, if people are not fully informed, or if they do not understand what is happening to prices in general, they may make mistakes in their business dealings. These mistakes can lead to a misallocation of resources.

Increased Risk and Slower Economic Growth When unanticipated inflation occurs regularly, the degree of risk associated with investments in the economy increases. Increases in uncertainty may make investors reluctant to invest in capital and to make long-term commitments. Because the level of investment falls, the prospects for long-term economic growth are lessened.

INFLATION: PUBLIC ENEMY NUMBER ONE?

Economists have debated the seriousness of the costs of inflation for decades. Some, like Alan Blinder, say, "Inflation, like every teenager, is grossly misunderstood, and this gross misunderstanding blows the political importance of inflation out of all proportion to its economic importance."[4] Others, like Phillip Cagan and Robert Lipsey, argue, "It was once thought that the economy would in time make all the necessary adjustments [to inflation], but many of them are proving to be very difficult. . . . for financial institutions and markets, the effects of inflation have been extremely unsettling."[5]

No matter what the real economic cost of inflation, people do not like it. It makes us uneasy and unhappy. In 1974, President Ford verbalized some of this discomfort when he said, "Our inflation, our public enemy number one, will unless whipped destroy our country, our homes, our liberties, our property, and finally our national pride, as surely as any well-armed wartime enemy."[6] In this belief, our elected leaders have vigorously pursued policies designed to stop inflation. This brings us to where we started. If, as we suggested earlier, the recessions of 1974 to 1975 and 1980 to 1982 were the price we had to pay to stop inflation, stopping inflation is costly.

LOOKING AHEAD

This ends our introduction to the basic concepts and problems of macroeconomics. The first chapter of this part introduced the field, the second discussed the measurement of national product and national income, and this chapter discussed some of the major concerns of macroeconomists. We are now ready to begin the analysis of how the macroeconomy works.

[4]Alan Blinder, *Hard Heads, Soft Hearts: Tough-Minded Economics for a Just Society* (Reading, MA: Addison-Wesley, 1987).
[5]Phillip Cagan and Robert Lipsey, "The Financial Effects of Inflation," National Bureau of Economic Research (Cambridge, MA: General Series No. 103, 1978), pp. 67–68.
[6]U.S. President, Weekly Compilation of Presidential Documents, vol. 10, no. 41, p. 1247. Cited in Blinder, *Hard Heads.*

SUMMARY

LONG-RUN OUTPUT AND PRODUCTIVITY GROWTH

1. Output growth depends on (1) the growth rate of the capital stock, (2) the growth rate of output per unit of the capital stock, (3) the growth rate of labor, and (4) the growth rate of output per unit of labor.
2. Output per worker hour (labor productivity) rose faster in the 1950s and 1960s than it did in the 1970s, 1980s, and 1990s. An interesting question is whether labor productivity will rise faster in the future because of the Internet.

RECESSIONS, DEPRESSIONS, AND UNEMPLOYMENT

3. A *recession* is a period in which real GDP declines for at least two consecutive quarters. When less output is produced, employment declines, unemployment rate rises, and a smaller percentage of the capital stock is used. When real output falls, real income declines.
4. A *depression* is a prolonged and deep recession, although there is disagreement over how severe and how prolonged a recession must be to be called a depression.

5. The *unemployment rate* is the ratio of the number of unemployed people to the number of people in the labor force. To be considered unemployed and in the labor force, a person must be looking for work.

6. Big differences in rates of unemployment exist across demographic groups, regions, and industries. African-Americans, for example, experience much higher unemployment rates than whites.

7. A person who decides to stop looking for work is considered to have dropped out of the labor force and is no longer classified as unemployed. People who stop looking because they are discouraged about finding a job are sometimes called *discouraged workers.*

8. Some unemployment is inevitable. Because new workers are continually entering the labor force, because industries and firms are continuously expanding and contracting, and because people switch jobs, there is a constant process of job search as workers and firms try to match the best people to the available jobs. This unemployment is both natural and beneficial for the economy.

9. The unemployment that occurs because of short-run job/skill-matching problems is called *frictional unemployment.* The unemployment that occurs because of longer run structural changes in the economy is called *structural unemployment.* The *natural rate of unemployment* is the sum of the frictional rate and the structural rate. The increase in unemployment that occurs during recessions and depressions is called *cyclical unemployment.*

10. The major costs associated with recessions and unemployment are decreased real output, the damage done to the people who are unemployed, and lost output in the future. Benefits of recessions are that they may help to reduce inflation, increase efficiency, and improve a nation's balance of payments.

INFLATION

11. An *inflation* is an increase in the overall price level. It happens when many prices increase simultaneously. Inflation is measured by calculating the average increase in the prices of a large number of goods during some period of time. A *deflation* is a decrease in the overall price level. A *sustained inflation* is an increase in the overall price level that continues over a significant period of time.

12. A number of different indexes are used to measure the overall price level. Among them are the *GDP deflator, consumer price index (CPI),* and *producer price indexes (PPIs).*

13. Whether a person gains or loses during a period of inflation depends on whether his or her income rises faster or slower than the prices of the things he or she buys. The elderly are more insulated from inflation than most people think, because social security benefits and many pensions are indexed to inflation. Welfare benefits, which are not indexed to inflation, have not kept pace with inflation since 1970.

14. Inflation that is higher than expected benefits debtors, and inflation that is lower than expected benefits creditors.

REVIEW TERMS AND CONCEPTS

consumer price index (CPI), 131
cyclical unemployment, 128
deflation, 131
depression, 122
discouraged-worker effect, 126
employed, 123
frictional unemployment, 128
inflation, 131
labor force, 123
labor-force participation rate, 123
natural rate of unemployment, 128
not in the labor force, 123
producer price indexes (PPIs), 132
real interest rate, 134
recession, 122
structural unemployment, 128
sustained inflation, 131
unemployed, 123
unemployment rate, 123

1. Labor force = employed + unemployed
2. Population = labor force + not in labor force
3. $\text{Unemployment rate} = \dfrac{\text{unemployed}}{\text{employed} + \text{unemployed}}$
4. $\text{Labor-force participation rate} = \dfrac{\text{labor force}}{\text{population}}$

PROBLEM SET

1. Suppose you are hired by the National Bureau of Economic Research to write a formal definition of a depression as distinct from a recession. What are the factors that you consider in making such a distinction formal? Prepare a formal (statistical) definition of a depression and defend it.

2. In April 2000, economists were saying that the U.S. economy was close to full employment even though the unemployment rate was 3.8 percent. How can they make this assertion?

3. In April 2003, the number of employed stood at 137.7 million while the number of unemployed stood at 8.8 million. What was the unemployment rate in April? A month earlier, in March 2003, employment stood at 137.4 and unemployment stood at 8.4 million. What was the unemployment rate in March? Did employment increase or decrease during the month? By how much? How can you reconcile the change in employment and the change in the unemployment rate?

4. "When an inefficient firm or a firm producing a product that people no longer want goes out of business, people are unemployed, but that is part of the normal process of economic growth and development; the unemployment is part of the natural rate and need not concern policy makers." Discuss this and its relevance to the economy today.

5. What is the unemployment rate in your state today? What was it in 1970, 1975, and 1982? How has your state done relative to the national average? Do you know, or can you determine, why?

6. Suppose that all wages, salaries, welfare benefits, and other sources of income were indexed to inflation. Would inflation still be considered a problem? Why or why not?

7. What do the CPI and the PPI measure? Why do we need all these price indexes? (Think about what purpose you would use each one for.)

8. The consumer price index (CPI) is a fixed-weight index. It compares the price of a fixed bundle of goods in 1 year with the price of the same bundle of goods in some base year. Calculate the price of a bundle containing 100 units of good *X*, 150 units of good *Y* and 25 units of good *Z* in years 2000, 2001, and 2002. Convert the results into an index by dividing each bundle price figure by the bundle price in year 2000. Calculate the percentage change in your index between 2000 and 2001 and again between 2001 and 2002. Was there inflation between 2001 and 2002?

GOOD	QUANTITY CONSUMED	PRICES 2000	PRICES 2001	PRICES 2002
X	100	$1.00	$1.50	$1.75
Y	150	1.50	2.00	2.00
Z	25	3.00	3.25	3.00

9. Consider the following statements:

a. "More people are employed in Tappania now than at any time in the past 50 years."

b. "The unemployment rate in Tappania is higher now than it has been in 50 years."

Can both of these statements be true at the same time? Explain.

10. Policy makers talk about the "capacity" of the economy to grow. What specifically is meant by the "capacity" of the economy? How might capacity be measured? In what ways is capacity limited by labor constraints, and by capital constraints? What are the consequences if demand in the economy exceeds capacity? What signs would you look for?

11. What was the rate of growth in real GDP during the most recent quarter? You can find the answer in publications such as the *Survey of Current Business, The Economist,* or *Businessweek.* Has growth been increasing or decreasing? What policies might you suggest for increasing the economy's potential long-run rate of growth?

12. Suppose the stock of capital and the workforce are both increasing at 3 percent annually in the country of Wholand. At the same time, real output is growing at 6 percent. How is that possible in the short run, and in the long run?

13. The table below shows that from 1969 to late 1971, real GNP grew by more than $40 billion and employment (the number of jobs) grew by 1.6 million, but the unemployment rate nearly doubled, from 3.4 percent to 5.9 percent. How can that be?

DATE	REAL GNP (BILLIONS OF DOLLARS)	REAL GNP (% CHANGE)	EMPLOYMENT (MILLIONS)	UNEMPLOYMENT (MILLIONS)	U-RATE
69:1	1,084	4.6	81.2	2.7	3.4
69:2	1,088	1.8	81.7	2.8	3.4
69:3	1,091	1.1	82.2	2.9	3.6
69:4	1,086	−2.3	82.6	2.9	3.6
70:1	1,081	−1.6	82.7	3.4	4.2
70:2	1,082	.7	82.4	4.0	4.8
70:3	1,093	3.8	82.3	4.3	5.2
70:4	1,084	−3.0	82.3	4.9	5.8
71:1	1,111	10.3	82.2	5.0	5.9
71:2	1,117	1.9	82.4	5.0	5.9
71:2	1,126	3.2	82.8	5.1	6.0

Visit www.prenhall.com/casefair for self-test quizzes, interactive graphing exercises, and news articles.

$\frac{1.5-1}{1} = 0.5$

Aggregate Expenditure and Equilibrium Output

8

CHAPTER OUTLINE

We now begin our discussion of the theory of how the macroeconomy works. We know how to calculate gross domestic product (GDP), but what factors *determine* it? We know how to define and measure inflation and unemployment, but what circumstances *cause* inflation and unemployment? What, if anything, can government do to reduce unemployment and inflation?

Analyzing the various components of the macroeconomy is a complex undertaking. The level of GDP, the overall price level, and the level of employment—three chief concerns of macroeconomists—are influenced by events in three broadly defined "markets":

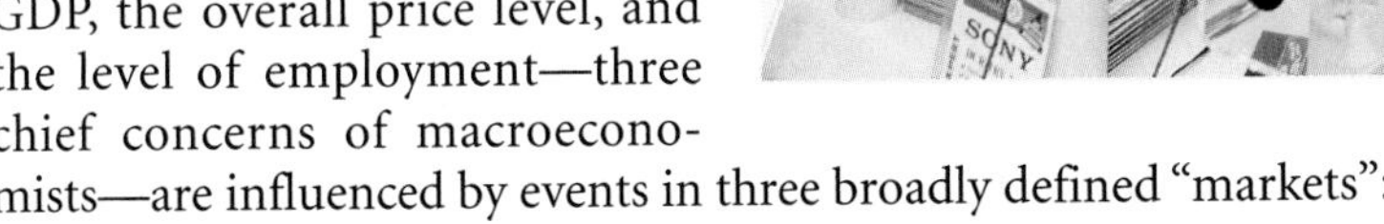

- Goods-and-services markets
- Financial (money) markets
- Labor markets

We will explore each market, as well as the links between them, in our discussion of macroeconomic theory. Figure 8.1 presents the plan of the next seven chapters, which form the core of macroeconomic theory. In Chapters 8 and 9, we describe the market for goods and services, often called the *goods market*. In Chapter 8, we explain several basic concepts and show how the equilibrium level of national income is determined in a simple economy with no government and no imports or exports. In Chapter 9, we provide a more complete picture of the economy by adding government purchases, taxes, and net exports to the analysis.

In Chapters 10 and 11, we focus on the *money market*. Chapter 10 introduces the money market and the banking system and discusses the way the U.S. central bank (the Federal Reserve) controls the money supply. Chapter 11 analyzes the demand for money and the way interest rates are determined. Chapter 12 then examines the relationship between the goods market and the money market. Chapter 13 explores the aggregate demand and supply curves first mentioned in Chapter 5. Chapter 13 also analyzes how the overall price level is determined, as well as the relationship between output and the price level. Finally, Chapter 14 discusses the supply of and demand for labor and the functioning of the *labor market* in the macroeconomy. This material is essential to an understanding of employment and unemployment.

Before we begin our discussion of aggregate output and aggregate income, we need to stress that production, consumption, and other activities that we will be discussing in the following chapters are ongoing activities. Nonetheless, it is helpful to think about these activities as if they took place in a series of *production periods*. A period might be a month long or

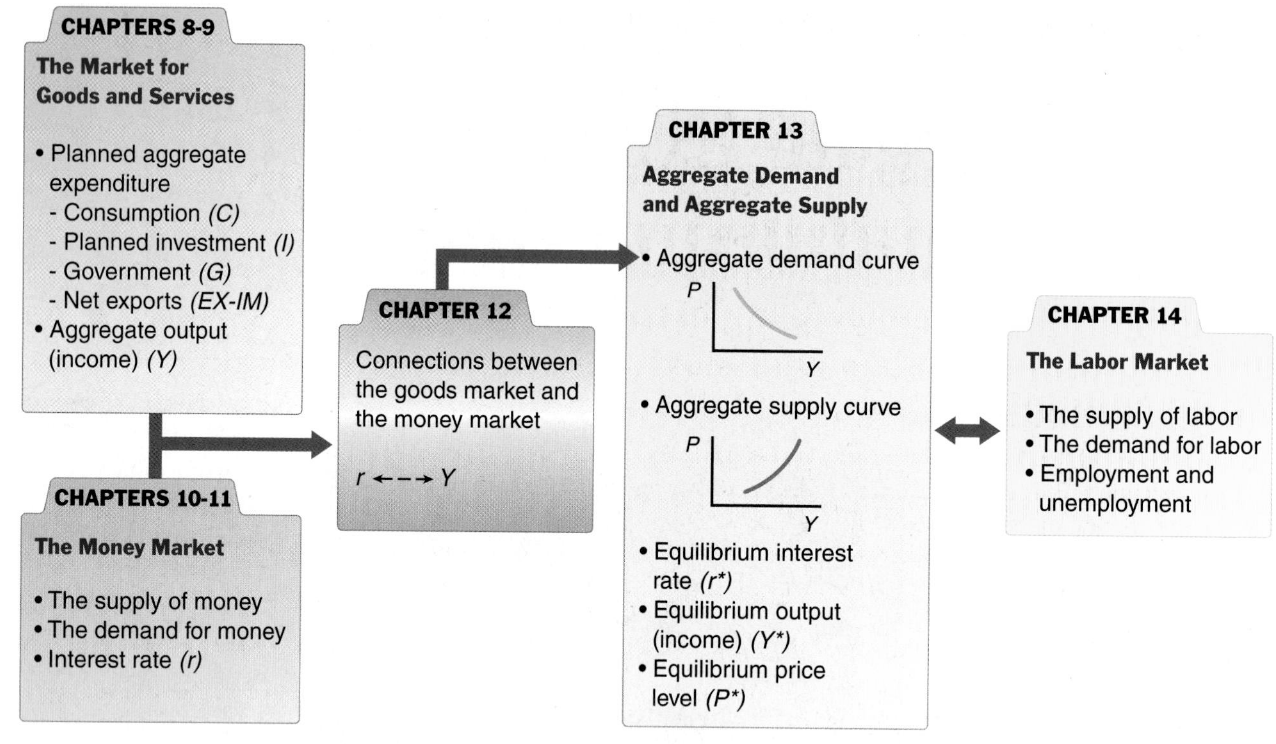

FIGURE 8.1 The Core of Macroeconomic Theory

We build up the macroeconomy slowly. In Chapters 8 and 9 we examine the market for goods and services, and in Chapters 10 and 11 we examine the money market. Then in Chapter 12 we bring the two markets together, which explains the links between aggregate output (Y) and the interest rate (r). In Chapter 13 we explain how the aggregate demand curve can be derived from Chapters 8 through 12, and we introduce the aggregate supply curve. This allows the price level (P) to be explained. We then explain in Chapter 14 how the labor market fits into the macroeconomic picture.

perhaps 3 months long. During each period, some output is produced, income is generated, and spending takes place. At the end of each period we can examine the results. Was everything that was produced in the economy sold? What percentage of income was spent? What percentage was saved? Is output (income) likely to rise or fall in the next period?

AGGREGATE OUTPUT AND AGGREGATE INCOME (*Y*)

Each period, firms produce some aggregate quantity of goods and services, which we refer to as *aggregate output* (Y). In Chapter 6, we introduced real gross domestic product as a measure of the quantity of output produced in the economy, Y. Output includes the production of services, consumer goods, and investment goods. It is important to think of these as components of "real" output.

We have already seen that GDP (Y) can be calculated in terms of either income or expenditures. Because every dollar of expenditure is received by someone as income, we can compute total GDP (Y) either by adding up the total spent on all final goods during a period *or* by adding up all the income—wages, rents, interest, and profits—received by all the factors of production.

aggregate output The total quantity of goods and services produced (or supplied) in an economy in a given period.

aggregate income The total income received by all factors of production in a given period.

aggregate output (income) (*Y*) A combined term used to remind you of the exact equality between aggregate output and aggregate income.

We will use the variable Y to refer to both **aggregate output** and **aggregate income** because they are the same seen from two different points of view. When output increases, additional income is generated. More workers may be hired and paid; workers may put in, and be paid for, more hours; and owners may earn more profits. When output is cut, income falls, workers may be laid off or work fewer hours (and be paid less), and profits may fall.

In any given period, there is an exact equality between aggregate output (production) and aggregate income. You should be reminded of this fact whenever you encounter the combined term **aggregate output (income)**.

Aggregate output can also be considered the aggregate quantity supplied, because it is the amount that firms are supplying (producing) during the period. In the discussions that follow, we use the phrase *aggregate output (income)*, instead of *aggregate quantity supplied*, but keep in mind that the two are equivalent. Also remember that "aggregate output" means "real GDP."

Think in Real Terms From the outset you must think in "real terms." For example, when we talk about output (Y), we mean real output, not nominal output. Although we discussed in Chapter 6 that the calculation of real GDP is complicated, you can ignore these complications in the following analysis. To help make things easier to read, we will frequently use dollar values for Y, but do not confuse Y with nominal output. The main point is to think of Y as being in real terms—the quantities of goods and services produced, not the dollars circulating in the economy.

INCOME, CONSUMPTION, AND SAVING (*Y*, *C*, AND *S*)

Each period (a month or 3 months) households receive some aggregate amount of income (Y). We begin our analysis in a simple world with no government and a "closed" economy, that is, no imports and no exports. In such a world, a household can do two, and only two, things with its income: It can buy goods and services—that is, it can *consume*—or it can save. This is shown in Figure 8.2. The part of its income that a household does not consume in a given period is called **saving**. Total household saving in the economy (S) is by definition equal to income minus consumption (C):

saving (S) The part of its income that a household does not consume in a given period. Distinguished from *savings*, which is the current stock of accumulated saving.

$$\text{saving} \equiv \text{income} - \text{consumption}$$
$$S \equiv Y - C$$

The triple equal sign means this is an **identity**, or something that is always true. You will encounter several identities in this chapter, which you should commit to memory.

identity Something that is always true.

Remember that saving does *not* refer to the total savings accumulated over time. Saving (without the final *s*) refers to the portion of a *single period's* income that is not spent in that period. Saving (S) is the amount added to *accumulated savings* in any given period. *Saving* is a flow variable; *savings* is a stock variable. (Review Chapter 3 if you are unsure of the difference between stock and flow variables.)

EXPLAINING SPENDING BEHAVIOR

So far, we have said nothing about behavior. We have not described the consumption and saving behavior of households, and we have not speculated about how much aggregate output firms will decide to produce in a given period. Instead, we have only a framework and a set of definitions to work with.

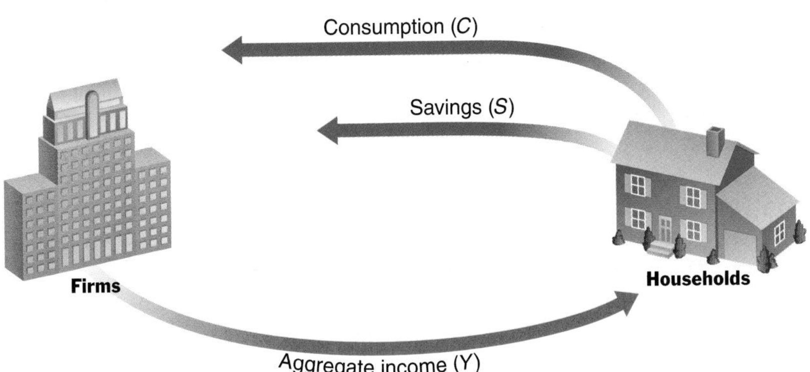

FIGURE 8.2 Saving ≡ Aggregate Income − Consumption

All income is either spent on consumption or saved in an economy in which there are no taxes. Thus, $S \equiv Y - C$.

Macroeconomics, you will recall, is the study of behavior. To understand the functioning of the macroeconomy, we must understand the behavior of households and firms. In our simple economy in which there is no government, there are two types of spending behavior: spending by households, or *consumption*, and spending by firms, or *investment.*

Household Consumption and Saving How do households decide how much to consume? In any given period, the amount of aggregate consumption in the economy depends on a number of factors.

Some determinants of aggregate consumption include:

1. Household income
2. Household wealth
3. Interest rates
4. Households' expectations about the future

These four factors work together to determine the spending and saving behavior of households, both for individual ones and for the aggregate. This is no surprise. Households with higher income and higher wealth are likely to spend more than households with less income and less wealth. Lower interest rates reduce the cost of borrowing, so lower interest rates are likely to stimulate spending. (Higher interest rates increase the cost of borrowing and are likely to decrease spending.) Finally, positive expectations about the future are likely to increase current spending, while uncertainty about the future is likely to decrease current spending.

While all these factors are important, we will concentrate for now on the relationship between income and consumption.[1] In *The General Theory*, Keynes argued that the amount of consumption undertaken by a household is directly related to its income:

The higher your income is, the higher your consumption is likely to be. People with more income tend to consume more than people with less income.

consumption function The relationship between consumption and income.

The relationship between consumption and income is called a **consumption function.** Figure 8.3 shows a hypothetical consumption function for an individual household. The curve is labeled $c(y)$, which is read "c as a function of y," or "consumption as a function of income." There are several things you should notice about the curve. First, it has a positive

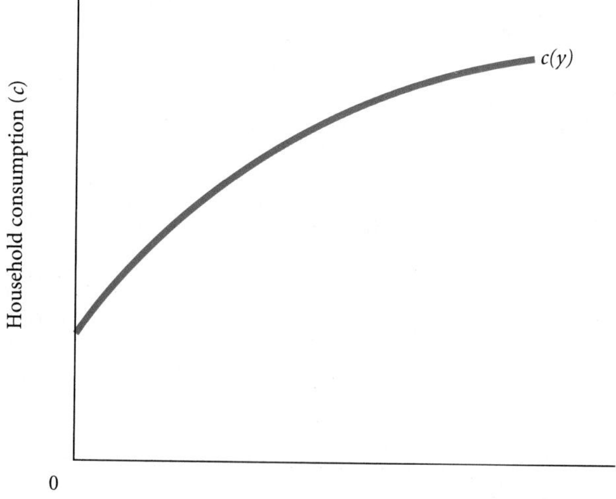

FIGURE 8.3 A Consumption Function for a Household

A consumption function for an individual household shows the level of consumption at each level of household income.

[1]The assumption that consumption is dependent solely on income is, of course, overly simplistic. Nonetheless, many important insights about how the economy works can be obtained through this simplification. In Chapter 16, we relax this assumption and consider the behavior of households and firms in the macroeconomy in more detail.

slope. In other words, as *y* increases, so does *c*. Second, the curve intersects the *c*-axis above zero. This means that even at an income of zero, consumption is positive. Even if a household found itself with a zero income, it still must consume to survive. It would borrow or live off its savings, but its consumption could not be zero.

Keep in mind that Figure 8.3 shows the relationship between consumption and income for an individual household, but also remember that macroeconomics is concerned with aggregate consumption. Specifically, macroeconomists want to know how *aggregate* consumption (the total consumption of all households) is likely to respond to changes in *aggregate* income. If all individual households increase their consumption as income increases, and we assume that they do, it is reasonable to assume that a positive relationship exists between aggregate consumption (C) and aggregate income (Y).

For simplicity, assume that points of aggregate consumption, when plotted against aggregate income, lie along a straight line, as in Figure 8.4. Because the aggregate consumption function is a straight line, we can write the following equation to describe it:

$$C = a + bY$$

Y is aggregate output (income), C is aggregate consumption, and a is the point at which the consumption function intersects the C-axis—a constant. The letter b is the slope of the line, in this case $\Delta C/\Delta Y$ [because consumption (C) is measured on the vertical axis, and income (Y) is measured on the horizontal axis].[2] Every time income increases (say by ΔY), consumption increases by b times ΔY. Thus, $\Delta C = b \times \Delta Y$ and $\Delta C/\Delta Y = b$. Suppose, for example, that the slope of the line in Figure 8.4 is .75 (that is, $b = .75$). An increase in income (ΔY) of \$100 would then increase consumption by $b\Delta Y = .75 \times \$100$, or \$75.

The **marginal propensity to consume (*MPC*)** is the fraction of a change in income that is consumed. In the consumption function here, b is the *MPC*. An *MPC* of .75 means consumption changes by .75 of the change in income. The slope of the consumption function is the *MPC*.

marginal propensity to consume (*MPC*) That fraction of a change in income that is consumed, or spent.

$$\text{marginal propensity to consume} \equiv \text{slope of consumption function} \equiv \frac{\Delta C}{\Delta Y}$$

There are only two places income can go: consumption or saving. If \$.75 of a \$1.00 increase in income goes to consumption, \$.25 must go to saving. If income decreases by \$1.00, consumption will decrease by \$.75 and saving will decrease by \$.25. The **marginal propensity to save (*MPS*)** is the fraction of a change in income that is saved: $\Delta S/\Delta Y$, where

marginal propensity to save (*MPS*) That fraction of a change in income that is saved.

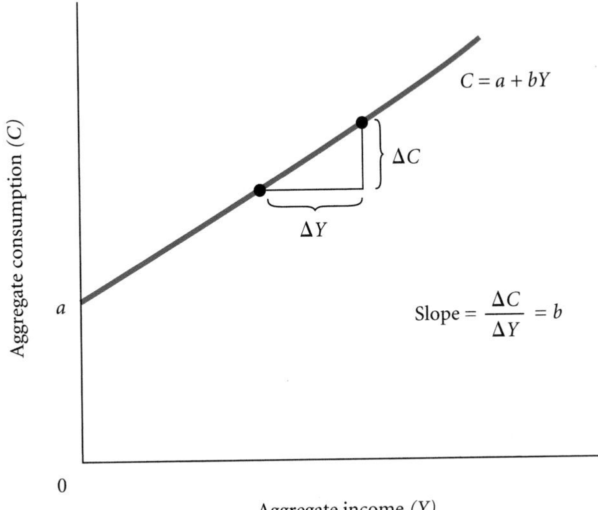

FIGURE 8.4 An Aggregate Consumption Function

The consumption function shows the level of consumption at every level of income. The upward slope indicates that higher levels of income lead to higher levels of consumption spending.

[2]The Greek letter Δ (delta) means "change in." For example, ΔY (read "delta Y") means the "change in income." If income (Y) in 2001 is \$100 and income in 2002 is \$110, then ΔY for this period is \$110 – \$100 = \$10. For a review of the concept of slope, see Appendix, Chapter 1.

ΔS is the change in saving. Because everything not consumed is saved, the *MPC* and the *MPS* must add up to one.

$$MPC + MPS \equiv 1$$

Because the *MPC* and the *MPS* are important concepts, it may help to review their definitions.

The marginal propensity to consume (*MPC*) is the fraction of an increase in income that is consumed (or the fraction of a decrease in income that comes out of consumption). The marginal propensity to save (*MPS*) is the fraction of an increase in income that is saved (or the fraction of a decrease in income that comes out of saving).

Because *C* is aggregate consumption and *Y* is aggregate income, it follows that the *MPC* is *society's* marginal propensity to consume out of national income and that the *MPS* is *society's* marginal propensity to save out of national income.

Numerical Example The numerical examples used in the rest of this chapter are based on the following consumption function:

$$C = \underbrace{100}_{a} + \underbrace{.75}_{b}Y$$

This equation is simply an extension of the generic $C = a + bY$ consumption function we have been discussing. At a national income of zero, consumption is \$100 billion (a). As income rises, so does consumption. We will assume that for every \$100 billion increase in income (ΔY), consumption rises by \$75 billion (ΔC). This means that the slope of the consumption function (b) is equal to $\Delta C/\Delta Y$, or \$75 billion/\$100 billion = .75. The marginal propensity to consume out of national income is therefore .75; the marginal propensity to save is .25. Some numbers derived from this consumption function are listed and graphed in Figure 8.5.

Now consider saving. We already know $Y \equiv C + S$, income equals consumption plus saving. Once we know how much consumption will result from a given level of income, we know how much saving there will be. Recall that saving is everything that is not consumed.

$$S \equiv Y - C$$

From the numbers in Figure 8.5, we can easily derive the saving schedule that is shown. At an income of \$200 billion, consumption is \$250 billion; saving is thus a negative \$50 billion ($S \equiv Y - C =$ \$200 billion − \$250 billion = −\$50 billion). At an aggregate income of \$400 billion, consumption is exactly \$400 billion, and saving is zero. At \$800 billion in income, saving is a positive \$100 billion.

The consumption and saving functions we have been discussing are shown in Figure 8.6. To analyze their relationship, we will use the device of the 45° line as a way of comparing *C* and *Y*. The 45° line—the solid black line in the top graph—shows all the points at which the value on the horizontal axis equals the value on the vertical axis. Thus, the 45° line in Figure 8.6 represents all the points at which aggregate income equals aggregate consumption.) Where the consumption function is *above* the 45° line, consumption exceeds income, and saving is negative. Where the consumption function *crosses* the 45° line, consumption is equal to income, and saving is zero. Where the consumption function is *below* the 45° line, consumption is less than income, and saving is positive. Note that the slope of the saving function is $\Delta S/\Delta Y$, which is equal to the marginal propensity to save (*MPS*).

The consumption function and the saving function are mirror images of one another. No information appears in one that does not also appear in the other. These functions tell us how households in the aggregate will divide income between consumption spending and saving at every possible income level. In other words, they embody aggregate household behavior.

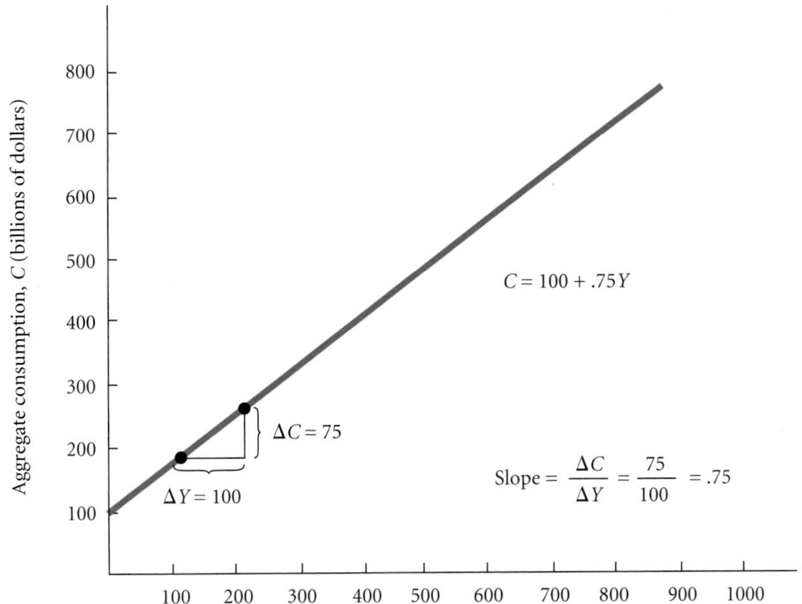

AGGREGATE INCOME, *Y* (BILLIONS OF DOLLARS)	AGGREGATE CONSUMPTION, *C* (BILLIONS OF DOLLARS)
0	100
80	160
100	175
200	250
400	400
600	550
800	700
1,000	850

FIGURE 8.5 An Aggregate Consumption Function Derived from the Equation $C = 100 + .75Y$

In this simple consumption function, consumption is $100 billion at an income of zero. As income rises, so does consumption. For every $100 billion increase in income, consumption rises by $75 billion. The slope of the line is .75.

PLANNED INVESTMENT (*I*)

Consumption, as we have seen, is the spending by households on goods and services, but what kind of spending do firms engage in? The answer is *investment.*

What Is Investment? Let us begin with a brief review of terms and concepts. In everyday language, we use *investment* to refer to what we do with our savings: "I invested in a mutual fund and some AOL stock." In the language of economics, however, *investment* always refers to the creation of capital stock. To an economist, an investment is something produced that is used to create value in the future.

You must not confuse the two uses of the term. When a firm builds a new plant or adds new machinery to its current stock, it is investing. A restaurant owner who buys tables, chairs, cooking equipment, and silverware is investing. When a college builds a new sports center, it is investing. From now on, we use **investment** only to refer to purchases by firms of new buildings and equipment and inventories, all of which add to firms' capital stocks.

investment Purchases by firms of new buildings and equipment and additions to inventories, all of which add to firms' capital stock.

Recall that inventories are part of the capital stock. When firms add to their inventories, they are investing—they are buying something that creates value in the future. Most of the capital stock of a clothing store consists of its inventories of unsold clothes in its warehouses and on its racks and display shelves. The service provided by a grocery or department store is the convenience of having a large variety of commodities in inventory available for purchase at a single location.

Manufacturing firms generally have two kinds of inventories: *inputs* and *final products.* General Motors (GM) has stocks of tires, rolled steel, engine blocks, valve covers, and thousands of other things in inventory, all waiting to be used in producing new cars. In addition, GM has an inventory of finished automobiles awaiting shipment.

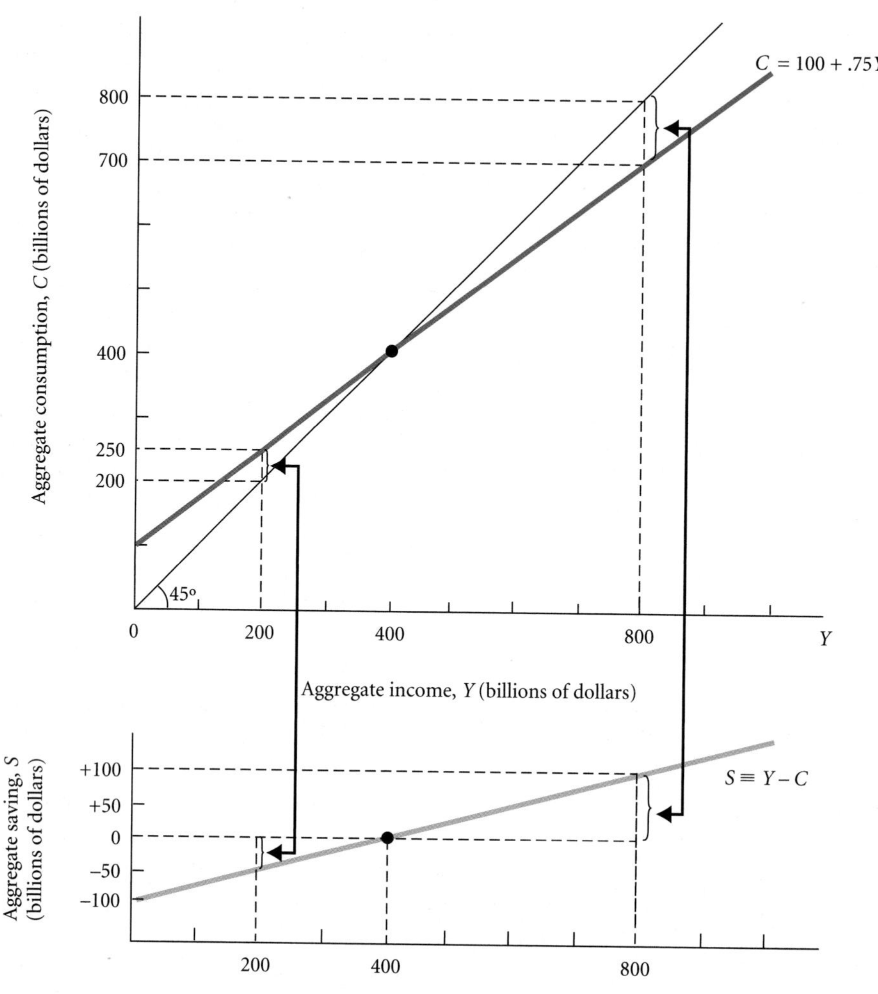

Y AGGREGATE INCOME (BILLIONS OF DOLLARS)	–	*C* AGGREGATE CONSUMPTION (BILLIONS OF DOLLARS)	=	*S* AGGREGATE SAVING (BILLIONS OF DOLLARS)
0		100		–100
80		160		–80
100		175		–75
200		250		–50
400		400		0
600		550		50
800		700		100
1,000		850		150

FIGURE 8.6 Deriving a Saving Function from a Consumption Function

Because $S \equiv Y - C$, it is easy to derive a saving function from a consumption function. A 45° line drawn from the origin can be used as a convenient tool to compare consumption and income graphically. At $Y = 200$, consumption is 250. The 45° line shows us that consumption is larger than income by 50. Thus $S \equiv Y - C = -50$. At $Y = 800$, consumption is less than income by 100. Thus, $S = 100$ when $Y = 800$.

Investment is a flow variable—it represents additions to capital stock in a specific period. A firm's decision on how much to invest each period is determined by many factors. For now, we will focus simply on the effects that given investment levels have on the rest of the economy.

Actual versus Planned Investment One of the most important insights of macroeconomics is deceptively simple: A firm may not always end up investing the exact amount that it planned to. The reason is that a firm does not have complete control over its investment decision; some parts of that decision are made by other actors in the economy. (This is not true of consumption, however. Because we assume households have complete control over their consumption, planned consumption is always equal to actual consumption.)

Generally, firms can choose how much new plant and equipment they wish to purchase in any given period. If GM wants to buy a new robot to stamp fenders or McDonald's decides to buy an extra french fry machine, it can usually do so without difficulty. There is, however, another component of investment over which firms have less control—inventory investment.

Suppose GM expects to sell 1 million cars this quarter and has inventories at a level it considers proper. If the company produces and sells 1 million cars, it will keep its inventories just where they are now (at the desired level). Now suppose GM produces 1 million cars, but due to a sudden shift of consumer interest it sells only 900,000 cars. By definition, GM's inventories of cars must go up by 100,000 cars. The firm's **change in inventory** is equal to production minus sales. The point here is:

change in inventory Production minus sales.

One component of investment—inventory change—is partly determined by how much households decide to buy, which is not under the complete control of firms. If households do not buy as much as firms expect them to, inventories will be higher than expected, and firms will have made an inventory investment that they did not plan to make.

Because involuntary inventory adjustments are neither desired nor planned, we need to distinguish between actual investment and **desired**, or **planned, investment**. We will use I to refer to desired or planned investment only. In other words, I will refer to planned purchases of plant and equipment and planned inventory changes. **Actual investment,** in contrast, is the *actual* amount of investment that takes place. If actual inventory investment turns out to be higher than firms planned, then actual investment is greater than I, planned investment.

desired, or **planned, investment** Those additions to capital stock and inventory that are planned by firms.

actual investment The actual amount of investment that takes place; it includes items such as unplanned changes in inventories.

For the purposes of this chapter, we will take the amount of investment that firms together plan to make each period (I) as fixed at some given level. We assume this level does not vary with income. In the example that follows, we will assume that I = \$25 billion, regardless of income. As Figure 8.7 shows, this means the planned investment function is a horizontal line.

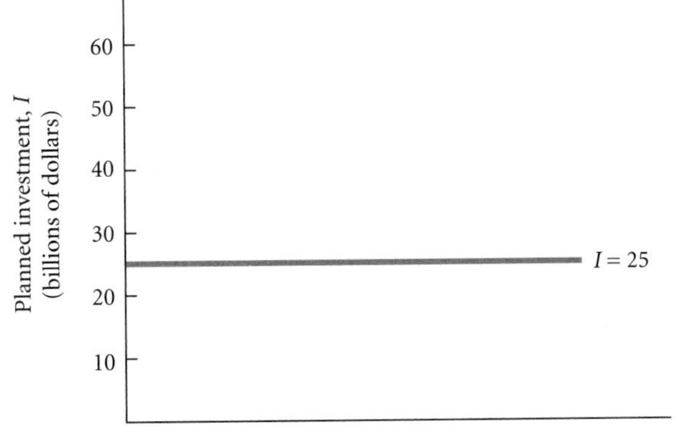

FIGURE 8.7 The Planned Investment Function

For the time being, we will assume that planned investment is fixed. It does not change when income changes, so its graph is just a horizontal line.

PLANNED AGGREGATE EXPENDITURE (*AE*)

planned aggregate expenditure (*AE*) The total amount the economy plans to spend in a given period. Equal to consumption plus planned investment: $AE \equiv C + I$.

We define total **planned aggregate expenditure (*AE*)** in the economy to be consumption (C) plus planned investment (I).[3]

$$\text{planned aggregate expenditure} \equiv \text{consumption} + \text{planned investment}$$
$$AE \equiv C + I$$

AE is the total amount that the economy plans to spend in a given period. We will now use the concept of planned aggregate expenditure to discuss the economy's equilibrium level of output.

EQUILIBRIUM AGGREGATE OUTPUT (INCOME)

Thus far, we have described the behavior of firms and households. We now discuss the nature of equilibrium and explain how the economy achieves equilibrium.

A number of definitions of *equilibrium* are used in economics. They all refer to the idea that at equilibrium, there is no tendency for change. In microeconomics, equilibrium is said to exist in a particular market (e.g., the market for bananas) at the price for which the quantity demanded is equal to the quantity supplied. At this point, both suppliers and demanders are satisfied. The equilibrium price of a good is the price at which suppliers want to furnish the amount that demanders want to buy.

equilibrium Occurs when there is no tendency for change. In the macroeconomic goods market, equilibrium occurs when planned aggregate expenditure is equal to aggregate output.

In macroeconomics, we define **equilibrium** in the goods market as that point at which planned aggregate expenditure is equal to aggregate output.

$$\text{aggregate output} \equiv Y$$
$$\text{planned aggregate expenditure} \equiv AE \equiv C + I$$
$$\text{equilibrium: } Y = AE, \text{ or } Y = C + I$$

Note that the equilibrium condition is not an identity.

This definition of equilibrium can hold if, and only if, planned investment and actual investment are equal. (Remember, we are assuming there is no unplanned consumption.) To understand why, consider Y not equal to AE. First, suppose aggregate output is greater than planned aggregate expenditure:

$$Y > C + I$$
$$\text{aggregate output} > \text{planned aggregate expenditure}$$

When output is greater than planned spending, there is unplanned inventory investment. Firms planned to sell more of their goods than they sold, and the difference shows up as an unplanned increase in inventories.

Next, suppose planned aggregate expenditure is greater than aggregate output:

$$C + I > Y$$
$$\text{planned aggregate expenditure} > \text{aggregate output}$$

When planned spending exceeds output, firms have sold more than they planned to. Inventory investment is smaller than planned. Planned and actual investment are not equal. Only when output is exactly matched by planned spending will there be no unplanned inventory investment. If there is unplanned inventory investment, this will be a state of disequilibrium. The mechanism by which the economy returns to equilibrium will be discussed later.

Equilibrium in the goods market is achieved only when aggregate output (Y) and planned aggregate expenditure ($C + I$) are equal, or when actual and planned investment are equal.

---

[3]In practice, planned aggregate expenditure also includes government spending (G) and net exports ($EX - IM$): $AE \equiv C + I + G + (EX - IM)$. In this chapter we are assuming that G and ($EX - IM$) are zero. This assumption is relaxed in the next chapter.

TABLE 8.1 Deriving the Planned Aggregate Expenditure Schedule and Finding Equilibrium (All Figures in Billions of Dollars) The Figures in Column 2 Are Based on the Equation $C = 100 + .75Y$.

(1) AGGREGATE OUTPUT (INCOME)(*Y*)	(2) AGGREGATE CONSUMPTION (*C*)	(3) PLANNED INVESTMENT (*I*)	(4) PLANNED AGGREGATE EXPENDITURE (*AE*) *C* + *I*	(5) UNPLANNED INVENTORY CHANGE *Y* − (*C* + *I*)	(6) EQUILIBRIUM? (*Y* = *AE*?)
100	175	25	200	−100	No
200	250	25	275	−75	No
400	400	25	425	−25	No
500	475	25	500	0	Yes
600	550	25	575	+25	No
800	700	25	725	+75	No
1,000	850	25	875	+125	No

Table 8.1 derives a planned aggregate expenditure schedule and shows the point of equilibrium for our numerical example. (Remember, all our calculations are based on $C = 100 + .75Y$.) To determine planned aggregate expenditure, we add consumption spending (C) to planned investment spending (I) at every level of income. Glancing down columns 1 and 4, we see one, and only one, level at which aggregate output and planned aggregate expenditure are equal: $Y = 500$.

Figure 8.8 illustrates the same equilibrium graphically. Figure 8.8(a) adds planned investment, constant at $25 billion, to consumption at every level of income. Because

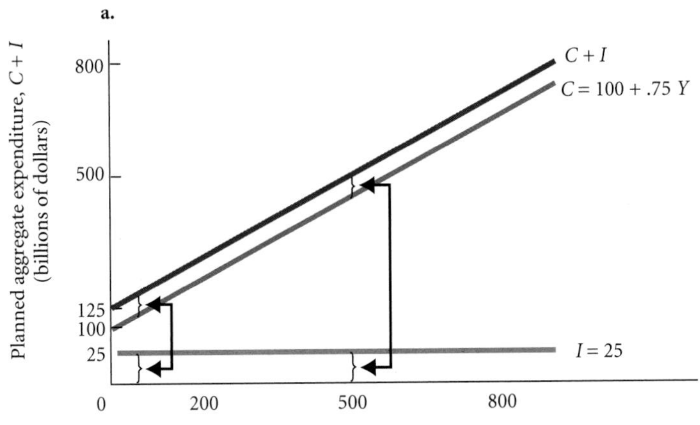

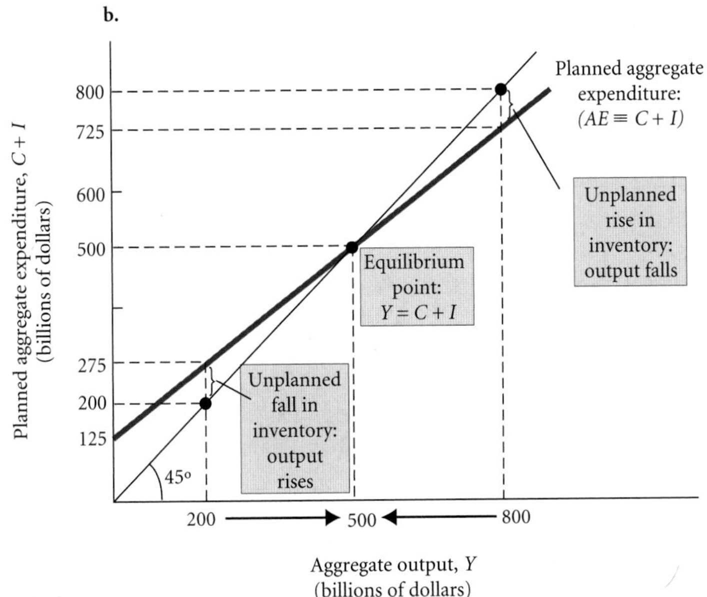

FIGURE 8.8 Equilibrium Aggregate Output

Equilibrium occurs when planned aggregate expenditure and aggregate output are equal. Planned aggregate expenditure is the sum of consumption spending and planned investment spending.

planned investment is a constant, the planned aggregate expenditure function is simply the consumption function displaced vertically by that constant amount. Figure 8.8(b) plots the planned aggregate expenditure function with the 45° line. The 45° line represents all points on the graph where the variables on the horizontal and vertical axes are equal. Any point on the 45° line is a potential equilibrium point. The planned aggregate expenditure function crosses the 45° line at a single point, where $Y = \$500$ billion. (The point at which the two lines cross is sometimes called the *Keynesian cross.*) At that point, $Y = C + I$.

Now let us look at some other levels of aggregate output (income). First, consider $Y = \$800$ billion. Is this an equilibrium output? Clearly it is not. At $Y = \$800$ billion, planned aggregate expenditure is $725 billion. (See Table 8.1.) This amount is less than aggregate output, which is $800 billion. Because output is greater than planned spending, the difference ends up in inventory as unplanned inventory investment. In this case, unplanned inventory investment is $75 billion.

Next, consider $Y = \$200$ billion. Is this an equilibrium output? No. At $Y = \$200$ billion, planned aggregate expenditure is $275 billion. Planned spending (AE) is greater than output (Y), and there is unplanned inventory disinvestment of $75 billion.

At $Y = \$200$ billion and $Y = \$800$ billion, planned investment and actual investment are unequal. There is unplanned investment, and the system is out of balance. Only at $Y = \$500$ billion, where planned aggregate expenditure and aggregate output are equal, will planned investment equal actual investment.

Finally, let us find the equilibrium level of output (income) algebraically. Recall that we know the following:

(1) $Y = C + I$	(equilibrium)
(2) $C = 100 + .75Y$	(consumption function)
(3) $I = 25$	(planned investment)

By substituting (2) and (3) into (1), we get:

$$Y = \underbrace{100 + .75Y}_{C} + \underbrace{25.}_{+\ I}$$

There is only one value of Y for which this statement is true, and we can find it by rearranging terms:

$$Y - .75Y = 100 + 25$$

$$Y - .75Y = 125$$

$$.25Y = 125$$

$$Y = \frac{125}{.25} = 500$$

The equilibrium level of output is 500, as seen in Table 8.1 and Figure 8.8.

THE SAVING/INVESTMENT APPROACH TO EQUILIBRIUM

Because aggregate income must either be saved or spent, by definition, $Y \equiv C + S$, which is an identity. The equilibrium condition is $Y = C + I$, but this is not an identity because it does not hold when we are out of equilibrium.[4] By substituting $C + S$ for Y in the equilibrium condition, we can write:

> The saving/investment approach to equilibrium is $C + S = C + I$. Because we can subtract C from both sides of this equation, we are left with $S = I$. Thus, only when planned investment equals saving will there be equilibrium.

[4]It would be an identity if I included unplanned inventory accumulations—in other words, if I were actual investment instead of planned investment.

News Analysis

Inventories Rise and the Economy Slows in 2003

WHILE THE RECESSION OF 2001 ENDED DURING the fourth quarter of 2001, the economy sputtered along, growing slowly into 2003. Employment did not recover, and many worried about a possible "double dip," a second decline in real GDP. In May of 2003, the likelihood of a drop in real GDP increased as inventories began to build.

Automakers' inventories swell

—*USA Today*

Despite unheard-of-incentives, automakers find themselves with record levels of unsold cars and trucks.

Nearly 4 million unsold vehicles are on dealer lots and storage fields, 630,000 more than a year ago. Automakers have a 74-day supply in the pipeline, 14% higher than normal for this time of year. Days supply is the number of days it would be expected to take dealers to sell current inventory if production stopped immediately. Some specifics:

- Ford has the biggest excess, 84 days of inventory, in part because it is stockpiling F-Series pickups for when it idles two plants this summer to change over to a new version of the truck. F-Series is the top-selling vehicle in the country, so supplies have to be high.
- European inventories are at a 76-day supply, 47% higher than normal. Volkswagen's inventory is an uncharacteristic 107 days. Softening sales have prompted factory shutdowns in Mexico and Germany. "Clearly, the momentum we have enjoyed in the last two years has tailed off," says Volkswagen spokesman Tony Fouladpour.

  BMW and Mercedes sales are softening too.
- Japanese and South Korean inventories are 5% and 6%, respectively, above normal levels. Asian carmakers, who have increased market share over the past two years, have upped incentives to keep inventories low.

Source: Adapted from: David Kiley, "Automakers' Inventories Swell Despite Incentives," USA Today, May 15, 2003. Reprinted by permission.

When demand for automobiles drops, the first signal is an increase in the number of cars in dealers' inventories.

Visit www.prenhall.com/casefair for updated articles and exercises.

This saving/investment approach to equilibrium stands to reason intuitively if we recall two things: (1) Output and income are equal, and (2) saving is income that is not spent. Because it is not spent, saving is like a leakage out of the spending stream. Only if that leakage is counterbalanced by some other component of planned spending can the resulting planned aggregate expenditure equal aggregate output. This other component is planned investment (I).

This counterbalancing effect can be seen in Figure 8.9. Aggregate income flows into households, and consumption and saving flow out. The diagram shows saving flowing from households into the financial market. Firms use this saving to finance investment projects. If the planned investment of firms equals the saving of households, then planned aggregate expenditure ($AE \equiv C + I$) equals aggregate output (income) (Y), and there is equilibrium: The *leakage* out of the spending stream—saving—is matched by an equal *injection* of planned investment spending into the spending stream. For this reason, the saving/investment approach to equilibrium is also called the *leakages/injections approach* to equilibrium.

Figure 8.10 reproduces the saving schedule derived in Figure 8.6 and the horizontal investment function from Figure 8.7. Notice that $S = I$ at one, and only one, level of aggregate output, $Y = 500$. At $Y = 500$, $C = 475$ and $I = 25$. In other words, $Y = C + I$, and therefore equilibrium exists.

ADJUSTMENT TO EQUILIBRIUM

We have defined equilibrium and learned how to find it, but we have said nothing about how firms might react to *disequilibrium*. Let us consider the actions firms might take when planned aggregate expenditure exceeds aggregate output (income).

We already know the only way firms can sell more than they produce is by selling some inventory. This means that when planned aggregate expenditure exceeds aggregate output, unplanned inventory reductions have occurred. It seems reasonable to assume firms will respond to unplanned inventory reductions by increasing output. If firms increase output, income must also increase (output and income are two ways of measuring the same thing).

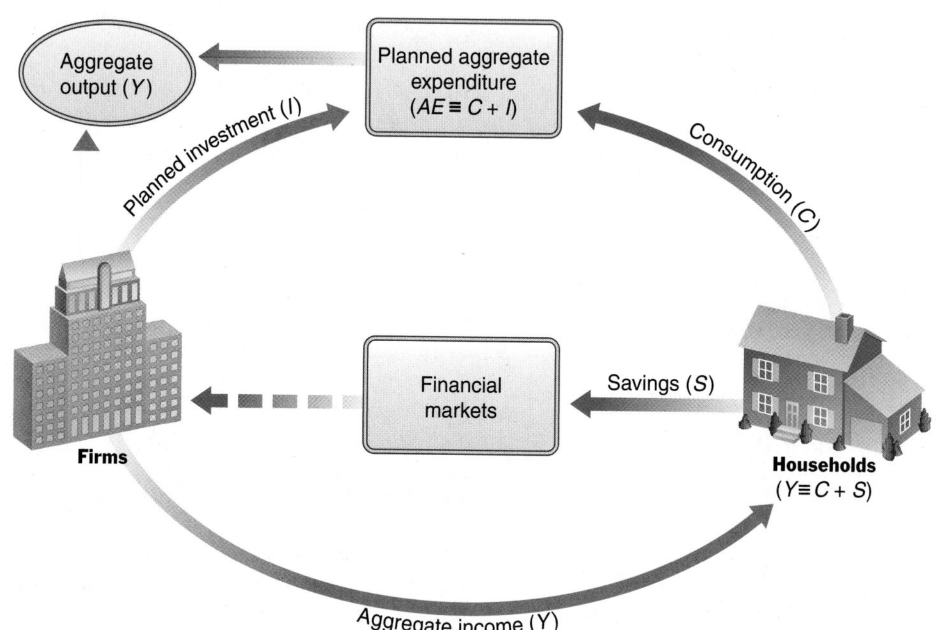

FIGURE 8.9 Planned Aggregate Expenditure and Aggregate Output (Income)

Saving is a leakage out of the spending stream. If planned investment is exactly equal to saving, then planned aggregate expenditure is exactly equal to aggregate output, and there is equilibrium.

As GM builds more cars, it hires more workers (or pays its existing workforce for working more hours), buys more steel, uses more electricity, and so on. These purchases by GM represent income for the producers of labor, steel, electricity, and so on. If GM (and all other firms) try to keep their inventories intact by increasing production, they will generate more income in the economy as a whole. This will lead to more consumption. Remember, when income rises, consumption also rises.

The adjustment process will continue as long as output (income) is below planned aggregate expenditure. If firms react to unplanned inventory reductions by increasing output, an economy with planned spending greater than output will adjust to equilibrium, with Y higher than before. If planned spending is less than output, there will be unplanned increases in inventories. In this case, firms will respond by reducing output. As output falls, income falls, consumption falls, and so forth, until equilibrium is restored, with Y lower than before.

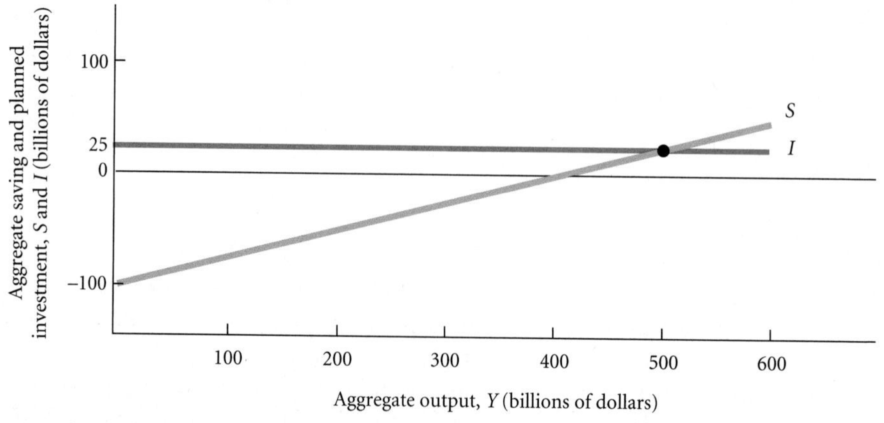

FIGURE 8.10 The $S = I$ Approach to Equilibrium

Aggregate output will be equal to planned aggregate expenditure only when saving equals planned investment ($S = I$). Saving and planned investment are equal at $Y = 500$.

As Figure 8.8 shows, at any level of output above $Y = 500$, such as $Y = 800$, output will fall until it reaches equilibrium at $Y = 500$, and at any level of output below $Y = 500$, such as $Y = 200$, output will rise until it reaches equilibrium at $Y = 500$.[5]

THE MULTIPLIER

Now that we know how the equilibrium value of income is determined, we ask: How does the equilibrium level of output change when planned investment changes? If there is a sudden change in planned investment, how will output respond, if it responds at all? As we will see, the change in equilibrium output is *greater* than the initial change in planned investment. Output changes by a multiple of the change in planned investment. So, this multiple is called the multiplier.

The **multiplier** is defined as the ratio of the change in the equilibrium level of output to a change in some autonomous variable. An **autonomous variable** is a variable that is assumed not to depend on the state of the economy—that is, a variable is autonomous if it does not change in response to changes in the economy. In this chapter, we consider planned investment to be autonomous. This simplifies our analysis and provides a foundation for later discussions.

multiplier The ratio of the change in the equilibrium level of output to a change in some autonomous variable.

autonomous variable A variable that is assumed not to depend on the state of the economy—that is, it does not change when the economy changes.

With planned investment autonomous, we can ask how much the equilibrium level of output changes when planned investment changes. Remember that we are not trying here to explain *why* planned investment changes; we are simply asking how much the equilibrium level of output changes when (for whatever reason) planned investment changes. (Beginning in Chapter 12, we will no longer take planned investment as given and will explain how planned investment is determined.)

Consider a sustained increase in planned investment of $25 billion—that is, suppose I increases from $25 billion to $50 billion and stays at $50 billion. If equilibrium existed at $I = \$25$ billion, an increase in planned investment of $25 billion will cause a disequilibrium, with planned aggregate expenditure greater than aggregate output by $25 billion. Firms immediately see unplanned reductions in their inventories, and, as a result, they begin to increase output.

Let us say the increase in planned investment comes from an anticipated increase in travel that leads airlines to purchase more airplanes, car rental companies to increase purchases of automobiles, and bus companies to purchase more buses (all capital goods). The firms experiencing unplanned inventory declines will be automobile manufacturers, bus producers, and aircraft producers—GM, Ford, McDonnell Douglas, Boeing, and so forth. In response to declining inventories of planes, buses, and cars, these firms will increase output.

Now suppose these firms raise output by the full $25 billion increase in planned investment. Does this restore equilibrium? No, it does not, because when output goes up, people earn more income and a part of that income will be spent. This increases planned aggregate expenditure even further. In other words, an increase in I also leads indirectly to an increase in C. To produce more airplanes, Boeing has to hire more workers or ask its existing employees to work more hours. It also must buy more engines from General Electric, more tires from Goodyear, and so forth. Owners of these firms will earn more profits, produce more, hire more workers, and pay out more in wages and salaries.

This added income does not vanish into thin air. It is paid to households that spend some of it and save the rest. The added production leads to added income, which leads to added consumption spending.

If planned investment (I) goes up by $25 billion initially *and is sustained at this higher level*, an increase of output of $25 billion will *not* restore equilibrium, because it generates even more consumption spending (C). People buy more consumer goods. There are

[5]In discussing simple supply and demand equilibrium in Chapters 3 and 4, we saw that when quantity supplied exceeds quantity demanded, the price falls and the quantity supplied declines. Similarly, when quantity demanded exceeds quantity supplied, the price rises and the quantity supplied increases. In the analysis here we are ignoring potential changes in prices or in the price level and focusing on changes in the level of real output (income). Later, after we have introduced money and the price level into the analysis, prices will be very important. At this stage, however, only aggregate output (income) (Y) adjusts when aggregate expenditure exceeds aggregate output (with inventory falling) or when aggregate output exceeds aggregate expenditure (with inventory rising).

unplanned reductions of inventories of basic consumption items—washing machines, food, clothing, and so forth—and this prompts other firms to increase output. The cycle starts all over again.[6]

Output and income can rise by significantly more than the initial increase in planned investment, but how much and how large is the multiplier? This is answered graphically in Figure 8.11. Assume the economy is in equilibrium at point *A*, where equilibrium output is 500. The increase in *I* of 25 shifts the $AE \equiv C + I$ curve up by 25, because *I* is higher by 25 at every level of income. The new equilibrium occurs at point *B*, where the equilibrium level of output is 600. Like point *A*, point *B* is on the 45° line and is an equilibrium value. Output (*Y*) has increased by 100 (600 – 500), or four times the initial increase in planned investment of 25, between point *A* and point *B*. The multiplier in this example is 4. At point *B*, aggregate spending is also higher by 100. If 25 of this additional 100 is investment (*I*), as we know it is,

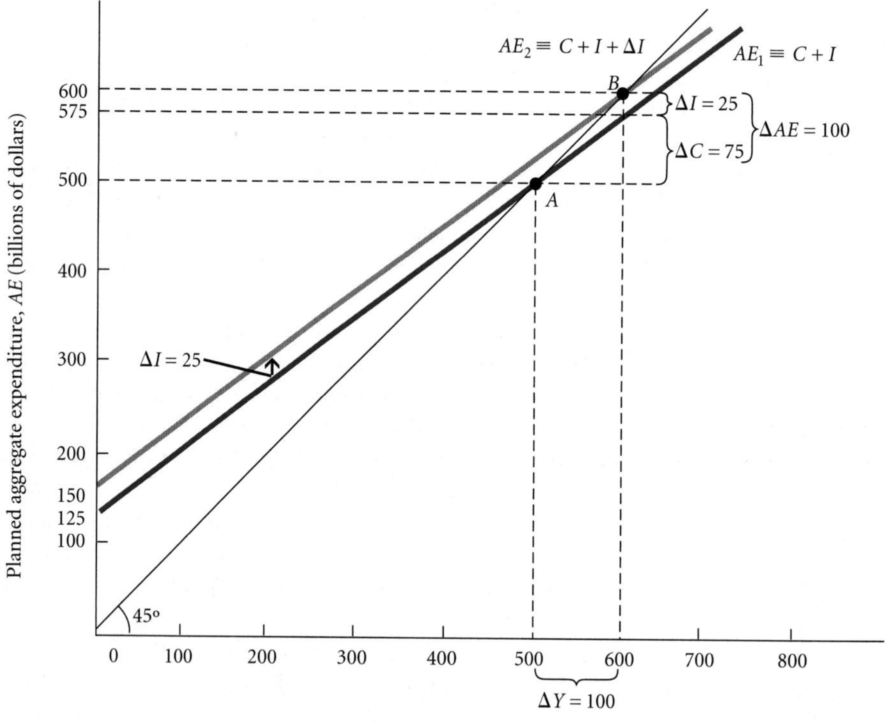

FIGURE 8.11 The Multiplier as Seen in the Planned Aggregate Expenditure Diagram

At point *A*, the economy is in equilibrium at *Y* = 500. When *I* increases by 25, planned aggregate expenditure is initially greater than aggregate output. As output rises in response, additional consumption is generated, pushing equilibrium output up by a multiple of the initial increase in *I*. The new equilibrium is found at point *B*, where *Y* = 600. Equilibrium output has increased by 100 (600 – 500), or *four times* the amount of the increase in planned investment.

---

[6]Figure 8.9 can help you understand the multiplier effect. Note in the figure how an increase in planned investment makes its way through the circular flow. Initially, aggregate output is at equilibrium with $Y = C + I$. That is, every period, aggregate output is produced by firms, and every period, planned aggregate expenditure is just sufficient to take all those goods and services off the market.

Now note what happens when planned investment spending increases and is sustained at a higher level. Firms experience unplanned declines in inventories and they increase output; more real output is produced in subsequent periods. However, the added output means more income; thus we see added income flowing to households. This means more spending. Households spend some portion of their added income (equal to the added income times the *MPC*) on consumer goods.

The higher consumption spending means that even if firms responded fully to the increase in investment spending in the first round, the economy is still out of equilibrium. Follow the added spending back over to firms in Figure 8.9 and you can see that with higher consumption, planned aggregate expenditure will be greater. Firms again see an unplanned decline in inventories and they respond by increasing the output of consumer goods. This sets off yet another round of income and expenditure increases: Output rises, and income rises as a result, thus increasing consumption. Higher consumption leads to yet another disequilibrium, inventories fall, and output (income) rises again.

the remaining 75 is added consumption (C). From point A to point B then, $\Delta Y = 100$, $\Delta I = 25$, and $\Delta C = 75$.

Why doesn't the multiplier process go on forever? The answer is because only a fraction of the increase in income is consumed in each round. Successive increases in income become smaller and smaller in each round of the multiplier process, due to leakage as saving, until equilibrium is restored.

The size of the multiplier depends on the slope of the planned aggregate expenditure line. The steeper the slope of this line is, the greater the change in output for a given change in investment. When planned investment is fixed, as in our example, the slope of the $AE \equiv C + I$ line is just the marginal propensity to consume ($\Delta C/\Delta Y$). The greater the *MPC* is, the greater the multiplier. This should not be surprising. A large *MPC* means that consumption increases a lot when income increases. The more consumption changes, the more output has to change to achieve equilibrium.

THE MULTIPLIER EQUATION

Is there a way to determine the size of the multiplier without using graphic analysis? Yes, there is.

Assume that the market is in equilibrium at an income level of $Y = 500$. Now suppose planned investment (I)—thus planned aggregate expenditure (AE)—increases and remains higher by \$25 billion. Planned aggregate expenditure is greater than output, there is an unplanned inventory reduction, and firms respond by increasing output (income) (Y). This leads to a second round of increases, and so on.

What will restore equilibrium? Look at Figure 8.10 and recall: planned aggregate expenditure ($AE \equiv C + I$) is not equal to aggregate output (Y) unless $S = I$; the leakage of saving must exactly match the injection of planned investment spending for the economy to be in equilibrium. Recall also, we assumed that planned investment jumps to a new higher level and stays there; it is a *sustained* increase of \$25 billion in planned investment spending. As income rises, consumption rises and so does saving. Our $S = I$ approach to equilibrium leads us to conclude:

> Equilibrium will be restored only when saving has increased by exactly the amount of the initial increase in I.

Otherwise, I will continue to be greater than S, and $C + I$ will continue to be greater than Y. (The $S = I$ approach to equilibrium leads to an interesting paradox in the macroeconomy. See the Further Exploration box, "The Paradox of Thrift.")

It is possible to figure how much Y must increase in response to the additional planned investment before equilibrium will be restored. Y will rise, pulling S up with it until the change in saving is exactly equal to the change in planned investment—that is, until S is again equal to I at its new higher level. Because added saving is a *fraction* of added income (the *MPS*), the increase in *income* required to restore equilibrium must be a *multiple* of the increase in planned investment.

Recall that the marginal propensity to save (*MPS*) is the fraction of a change in income that is saved. It is defined as the change in S (ΔS) over the change in income (ΔY):

$$MPS = \frac{\Delta S}{\Delta Y}$$

Because ΔS must be equal to ΔI for equilibrium to be restored, we can substitute ΔI for ΔS and solve:

$$MPS = \frac{\Delta I}{\Delta Y}$$

Therefore:

$$\Delta Y = \Delta I \times \frac{1}{MPS}$$

Further Exploration

The Paradox of Thrift

An interesting paradox can arise when households attempt to increase their saving. What happens if households become concerned about the future and want to save more today to be prepared for hard times tomorrow? If households increase their planned saving, the saving schedule in Figure 1 shifts upward from S_0 to S_1. The plan to save more is a plan to consume less, and the resulting drop in spending leads to a drop in income. Income drops by a multiple of the initial shift in the saving schedule. Before the increase in saving, equilibrium exists at point *A*, where $S_0 = I$ and Y = \$500 billion. Increased saving shifts the equilibrium to point *B*, the point at which $S_1 = I$. New equilibrium output is \$300 billion—a \$200 billion decrease (ΔY) from the initial equilibrium.

By consuming less, households have actually *caused* the hard times about which they were apprehensive. Worse, the new equilibrium finds saving at the same level as it was before consumption dropped (\$25 billion). In their attempt to save more, households have caused a contraction in output, and thus in income. They end up consuming less, but they have not saved any more.

It should be clear why saving at the new equilibrium is equal to saving at the old equilibrium. Equilibrium requires that saving equal planned investment, and because planned investment is unchanged, saving must remain unchanged for equilibrium to exist. This paradox shows that the interactions among sectors in the economy can be of crucial importance.

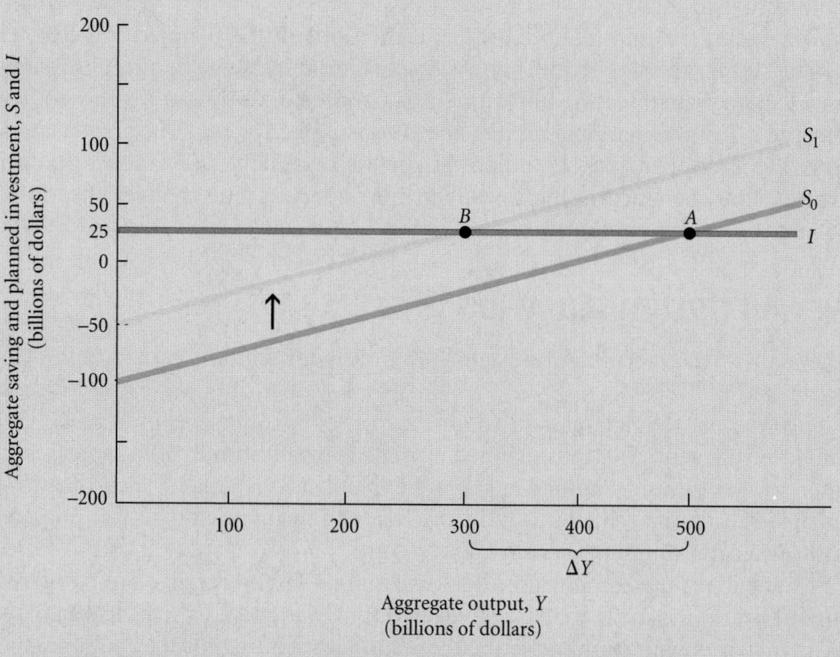

FIGURE 1 The Paradox of Thrift

An increase in planned saving from S_0 to S_1 causes equilibrium output to decrease from \$500 billion to \$300 billion. The decreased consumption that accompanies increased saving leads to a contraction of the economy and to a reduction of income, but at the new equilibrium, saving is the same as it was at the initial equilibrium. Increased efforts to save have caused a drop in income but no overall change in saving.

The **paradox of thrift** is "paradoxical" because it contradicts the widely held belief that "a penny saved is a penny earned." This may be true for an individual, but when society as a whole saves more, the result is a drop in income but no increased saving.

Does the paradox of thrift always hold? Recall our assumption that planned investment is fixed. Let us drop this assumption for a moment. If the extra saving that households want to do to ward off hard times is channeled into additional investment through financial markets, there is a shift up in the *I* schedule. The paradox could then be averted. If investment increases, a new equilibrium can be achieved at a higher level of saving and income. This result, however, depends critically on the existence of a channel through which additional household saving finances additional investment.

As you can see, the change in equilibrium income (ΔY) is equal to the initial change in planned investment (ΔI) times $1/MPS$. The multiplier is $1/MPS$:

$$\text{multiplier} \equiv \frac{1}{MPS}$$

Because $MPS + MPC \equiv 1$, $MPS \equiv 1 - MPC$. It follows that the multiplier is equal to:

$$\text{multiplier} \equiv \frac{1}{1 - MPC}$$

In our example, the *MPC* is .75, so the *MPS* must equal 1 – .75, or .25. Thus, the multiplier is 1 divided by .25, or 4. The change in the equilibrium level of *Y* is 4 × \$25 billion, or

$100 billion.[7] Also note that the same analysis holds when planned investment falls. If planned investment falls by a certain amount and is sustained at this lower level, output will fall by a multiple of the reduction in *I*. As the initial shock is felt and firms cut output, they lay people off. The result: Income, and subsequently consumption, falls.

THE SIZE OF THE MULTIPLIER IN THE REAL WORLD

In considering the size of the multiplier, it is important to realize that the multiplier we derived in this chapter is based on a *very* simplified picture of the economy. First, we have assumed that planned investment is autonomous and does not respond to changes in the economy. Second, we have thus far ignored the role of government, financial markets, and the rest of the world in the macroeconomy. For these reasons, it would be a mistake to move on from this chapter thinking that national income can be increased by $100 billion simply by increasing planned investment spending by $25 billion.

As we relax these assumptions in the following chapters, you will see that most of what we add to make our analysis more realistic has the effect of *reducing* the size of the multiplier. For example:

1. The Appendix to Chapter 9 shows that when tax payments depend on income (as they do in the real world), the size of the multiplier is reduced. As the economy expands, tax payments increase and act as a drag on the economy. The multiplier effect is smaller.
2. We will see in Chapter 12 that planned investment (*I*) is not autonomous; instead, it depends on the interest rate in the economy. This too has the effect of reducing the size of the multiplier.
3. Thus far we have not discussed how the overall price level is determined in the economy. When we do, in Chapter 13, we will see that part of an expansion of the economy is likely to take the form of an increase in the price level instead of an increase in output. When this happens, the size of the multiplier is reduced.
4. The multiplier is also reduced when imports are introduced in Chapter 21 because some domestic spending leaks into foreign markets.

These juicy tidbits give you something to look forward to as you proceed through the rest of this book. For now, however, it is enough to point out that:

> In reality, the size of the multiplier is about 1.4. That is, a sustained increase in autonomous spending of $10 billion into the U.S. economy can be expected to raise real GDP over time by about $14 billion.

This is a far cry from the value of 4.0 that we used in this chapter.

THE MULTIPLIER IN ACTION: RECOVERING FROM THE GREAT DEPRESSION

The Great Depression began in 1930 and lasted nearly a decade. Real output in 1938 was lower than real output in 1929, and the unemployment rate never fell below 14 percent of the labor force between 1930 and 1940. How did the economy get "stuck" at such a low level of income and a high level of unemployment? The model that we analyzed in this chapter can help us answer this question.

If firms do not wish to undertake much investment (*I* is low) or if consumers decide to increase their saving and cut back on consumption, then planned spending will be low. Firms do not want to produce more because, with many workers unemployed, households do not have the income to buy the extra output that firms might produce. Households, who would purchase more if they had more income, cannot find jobs that would enable them to earn additional income. The economy is caught in a vicious circle.

---

[7]The multiplier can also be derived algebraically, as the appendix to this chapter demonstrates.

How might such a cycle be broken? One way is for planned aggregate expenditure to increase, increasing aggregate output via the multiplier effect. This increase in *AE* may occur naturally, or it may be caused by a change in government policy.

In the late 1930s, for example, the economy experienced a surge of both residential and nonresidential investment. Between 1935 and 1940, total investment spending (in real terms) increased 64 percent and residential investment more than doubled. There can be no doubt that this increased investment had a multiplier effect. In just 5 years, employment in the construction industry increased by more than 400,000, employment in manufacturing industries jumped by more than 1 million, and total employment grew by more than 5 million. As more workers were employed, more income was generated, and some of this added income was spent on consumption goods. Inventories declined and firms began to expand output. Between 1935 and 1940, real output (income) increased by more than one-third and the unemployment rate dropped from 20.3 percent to 14.6 percent.

However, 14.6 percent is a very high rate of unemployment; the Depression was not yet over. Between 1940 and 1943 the Depression ended, with the unemployment rate dropping to 1.9 percent in 1943. This recovery was triggered by the mobilization for World War II and the significant increase in government purchases of goods and services, which rose from $14 billion in 1940 to $88.6 billion in 1943. In the next chapter, we will explore this *government spending multiplier*, and you will see how the government can help stimulate the economy by increasing its spending.

LOOKING AHEAD

In this chapter, we took the first step in understanding how the economy works. We described the behavior of two sectors (household and firm) and discussed how equilibrium is achieved in the market for goods and services. In the next chapter, we will relax some of the assumptions we have made and take into account the roles of government spending and net exports in the economy. This will give us a more realistic picture of how our economy works.

SUMMARY

AGGREGATE OUTPUT AND AGGREGATE INCOME (*Y*)

1. Each period, firms produce an aggregate quantity of goods and services called *aggregate output* (*Y*). Because every dollar of expenditure is received by someone as income, aggregate output and aggregate income are the same thing.
2. The total amount of aggregate consumption that takes place in any given period of time depends on factors such as household income, household wealth, interest rates, and households' expectations about the future.
3. If taxes are zero, households do only two things with their income: They can either spend on consumption or save. *C* refers to aggregate consumption by households. *S* refers to aggregate saving by households. By definition, saving equals income minus consumption: $S \equiv Y - C$.
4. The higher people's income is, the higher their consumption is likely to be. This is also true for the economy as a whole: There is a positive relationship between aggregate consumption (*C*) and aggregate income (*Y*).
5. The *marginal propensity to consume* (*MPC*) is the fraction of a change in income that is consumed, or spent. The *marginal propensity to save* (*MPS*) is the fraction of a change in income that is saved. Because all income must be either saved or spent, $MPS + MPC \equiv 1$.
6. The primary form of spending that firms engage in is investment. Strictly speaking, *investment* refers to the purchase by firms of new buildings and equipment and additions to inventories, all of which add to firms' capital stock.
7. *Actual investment* can differ from planned investment because changes in firms' inventories are part of actual investment and inventory changes are not under the complete control of firms. Inventory changes are partly determined by how much households decide to buy. *I* refers to planned investment only.

EQUILIBRIUM AGGREGATE OUTPUT (INCOME)

8. In an economy in which government spending and net exports are zero, *planned aggregate expenditure* (*AE*) equals consumption plus planned investment: $AE \equiv C + I$. *Equilibrium* in the goods market is achieved when planned aggregate expenditure equals aggregate output: $C + I = Y$. This holds if, and only if, planned investment and actual investment are equal.
9. Because aggregate income must be saved or spent, the equilibrium condition $Y = C + I$ can be rewritten as $C + S = C + I$, or $S = I$. Only when planned investment equals saving will there be equilibrium. This approach to equilibrium is the *saving/investment approach* to equilibrium or the *leakages/injections approach* to equilibrium.
10. When planned aggregate expenditure exceeds aggregate output (*income*), there is an unplanned fall in inventories. Firms will increase output. This increased output leads to increased income and even more consumption. This process will continue as long as output (income) is below planned aggregate expenditure. If firms react to unplanned inventory reduc-

tions by increasing output, an economy with planned spending greater than output will adjust to equilibrium, with Y higher than before.

THE MULTIPLIER

11. Equilibrium output changes by a multiple of the change in planned investment or any other autonomous variable. The multiplier is $1/MPS$.

12. When households increase their planned saving, income decreases and saving does not change. Saving does not increase because in equilibrium saving must equal planned investment and planned investment is fixed. If planned investment also increased, this *paradox of thrift* could be averted and a new equilibrium could be achieved at a higher level of saving and income. This result depends on the existence of a channel through which additional household saving finances additional investment.

REVIEW TERMS AND CONCEPTS

actual investment, 147
aggregate income, 140
aggregate output, 140
aggregate output (income) (Y), 140
autonomous variable, 153
change in inventory, 147
consumption function, 142
desired, or planned, investment, 147
equilibrium, 148
identity, 141
investment, 145
marginal propensity to consume (MPC), 143
marginal propensity to save (MPS), 143
multiplier, 153
paradox of thrift, 156
planned aggregate expenditure (AE), 148
saving (S), 141

1. $S \equiv Y - C$
2. $MPC \equiv$ slope of consumption function $\equiv \dfrac{\Delta C}{\Delta Y}$
3. $MPC + MPS \equiv 1$
4. $AE \equiv C + I$
5. Equilibrium condition: $Y = AE$ or $Y = C + I$
6. Saving/investment approach to equilibrium: $S = I$
7. Multiplier $\equiv \dfrac{1}{MPS} \equiv \dfrac{1}{1 - MPC}$

PROBLEM SET

1. During the first half of 2003, the following was true:

a. Inventories of unsold goods were building up on the shelves of firms (see the Further Exploration box on page 156).

b. Between 1998 and 2001, U.S. business investment (I) hit an all-time high as we replaced computer equipment and software and built record numbers of Web sites. In 2003, a good deal of that equipment needed to be replaced because it had depreciated and become obsolete. Many predicted a near-term increase in investment spending.

Discuss the likely impact of these two events on GDP.

2. Briefly define the following terms and explain the relationship between them:

MPC.............................. Multiplier
Actual investment.................... Planned investment
Aggregate expenditure................ Real GDP
Aggregate output .... Aggregate income

3. Expert econometricians in the Republic of Yuck estimate the following:

Real GNP (Y) .... 200 billion Yuck dollars
Planned investment spending .... 75 billion Yuck dollars

Yuck is a simple economy with no government, no taxes, and no imports or exports. Yuckers (citizens of Yuck) are creatures of habit. They have a rule that everyone saves exactly 25 percent of income. Assume that planned investment is fixed and remains at 75 billion Yuck dollars.

You are asked by the business editor of the *Weird Herald*, the local newspaper, to predict the economic events of the next few months. By using the data given, can you make a forecast? What is likely to happen to inventories? What is likely to happen to the level of real GDP? Is the economy at an equilibrium? When will things stop changing?

4. Log on to www.commerce.gov. Click on Economic Growth, then on Economic Analysis. Click next on National Accounts Data and then on the latest GDP release. Look through the report. Which of the components of aggregate expenditure appear to be growing or falling the fastest? What story can you tell about the current economic events from the data?

5. The following questions refer to this table:

AGGREGATE OUTPUT/INCOME	CONSUMPTION	PLANNED INVESTMENT
2,000	2,100	300
2,500	2,500	300
3,000	2,900	300
3,500	3,300	300
4,000	3,700	300
4,500	4,100	300
5,000	4,500	300
5,500	4,900	300

a. At each level of output, calculate saving. At each level of output, calculate unplanned investment (inventory change). What is likely to happen to aggregate output if the economy were producing at each of the levels indicated? What is the equilibrium level of output?

b. Over each range of income (2,000 to 2,500, 2,500 to 3,000, and so on), calculate the marginal propensity to consume. Calculate the marginal propensity to save. What is the multiplier?

c. By assuming there is no change in the level of the *MPC* and the *MPS*, and planned investment jumps by 200 and is sustained at that higher level, recompute the table. What is the new equilibrium level of *Y*? Is this consistent with what you compute using the multiplier?

6. Explain the multiplier intuitively. Why is it that an increase in planned investment of $100 raises equilibrium output by more than $100? Why is the effect on equilibrium output finite? How do we know that the multiplier is $1/MPS$?

7. You are given the following data concerning Freedonia, a legendary country:
   (1) Consumption function: $C = 200 + 0.8Y$
   (2) Investment function: $I = 100$
   (3) $AE \equiv C + I$
   (4) $AE = Y$
   a. What is the marginal propensity to consume in Freedonia, and what is the marginal propensity to save?
   b. Graph equations (3) and (4) and solve for equilibrium income.
   c. Suppose equation (2) were changed to (2′) $I = 110$.
   What is the new equilibrium level of income? By how much does the $10 increase in planned investment change equilibrium income? What is the value of the multiplier?
   d. Calculate the saving function for Freedonia. Plot this saving function on a graph with equation (2). Explain why the equilibrium income in this graph must be the same as in part b.

8. At the beginning of the section entitled "Household Consumption and Saving," it was argued that saving and spending behavior depended in part on wealth (accumulated savings and inheritance) but our simple model does not incorporate this effect. Consider the following model of a very simple economy:

$$C = 10 + .75Y + .04W$$
$$I = 100$$
$$W = 1000$$
$$Y = C + I$$
$$S = Y - C$$

If you assume that wealth (W) and investment (I) remain constant (we are ignoring the fact that saving adds to the stock of wealth), what are the equilibrium level of GDP (Y), consumption (C), and saving (S)? Now suppose that wealth increases by 50 percent to 1,500. Recalculate the equilibrium levels of Y, C, and S. What impact does wealth accumulation have on GDP? Many were concerned with the very large increase in stock values in the late 1990s. Does this present a problem for the economy?

9. You learned earlier that expenditures and income should always be equal. In this chapter, you have learned that *AE* and aggregate output (income) can be different. Is there an inconsistency here?

Visit www.prenhall.com/casefair for self-test quizzes, interactive graphing exercises, and news articles.

APPENDIX

DERIVING THE MULTIPLIER ALGEBRAICALLY

In addition to deriving the multiplier using the simple substitution we used in the chapter, we can also derive the formula for the multiplier by using simple algebra.

Recall that our consumption function is:

$$C = a + bY$$

where b is the marginal propensity to consume. In equilibrium:

$$Y = C + I$$

Now we solve these two equations for Y in terms of I. By substituting the first equation into the second, we get:

$$Y = \underbrace{a + bY}_{C} + I$$

This equation can be rearranged to yield:

$$Y - bY = a + I$$
$$Y(1 - b) = a + I$$

We can then solve for Y in terms of I by dividing through by $(1 - b)$:

$$Y = (a + I)\left(\frac{1}{1 - b}\right)$$

Now look carefully at this expression and think about increasing I by some amount, ΔI, with a held constant. If I increases by ΔI, income will increase by:

$$\Delta Y = \Delta I \times \frac{1}{1 - b}$$

Because $b \equiv MPC$, the expression becomes:

$$\Delta Y = \Delta I \times \frac{1}{1 - MPC}$$

The multiplier is:

$$\frac{1}{1 - MPC}$$

Finally, because $MPS + MPC \equiv 1$, MPS is equal to $1 - MPC$, making the alternative expression for the multiplier $1/MPS$, just as we saw in this chapter.

The Government and Fiscal Policy

9

CHAPTER OUTLINE

Nothing in macroeconomics or microeconomics arouses as much controversy as the role of government in the economy.

In microeconomics, the active presence of government in regulating competition, providing roads and education, and redistributing income is applauded by those who believe a free market simply does not work well if left to its own devices. Opponents of government intervention say it is the government, not the market, that performs badly. They say bureaucracy and inefficiency could be eliminated or reduced if the government played a smaller role in the economy.

In macroeconomics, the debate over what the government can and should do has a similar flavor, although the issues are somewhat different. At one end of the spectrum are the Keynesians and their intellectual descendants, who believe that the macroeconomy is likely to fluctuate too much if left on its own and that the government should smoothe out fluctuations in the business cycle. These ideas can be traced to Keynes's analysis in *The General Theory*, which suggests that governments can use their taxing and spending powers to increase aggregate expenditure (and thereby stimulate aggregate output) in recessions or depressions. At the other end are those who claim that government spending is incapable of stabilizing the economy, or worse, is destabilizing and harmful.

Perhaps the one thing most people can agree on is that, like it or not, governments are important actors in the economies of virtually all countries. For this alone, it is worth our while to analyze the way government influences the functioning of the macroeconomy.

While the government has a variety of powers—including regulating firms' entry into and exit from an industry, setting standards for product quality, setting minimum wage levels, and regulating the disclosure of information—in macroeconomics we study a government with general, but limited, powers. Specifically, government can affect the macroeconomy through two policy channels: fiscal policy and monetary policy. **Fiscal policy**, the focus of this chapter, refers to the government's spending and taxing behavior—in other words, its budget policy. (The word *fiscal* comes from the root *fisc*, which refers to the "treasury" of a government.) Fiscal policy is generally divided into three categories: (1) policies concerning government purchases of goods and services, (2) policies concerning taxes, and (3) policies concerning transfer payments (such as unemployment compensation, social security benefits, welfare payments, and veterans' benefits) to households. **Monetary policy**, in the next two chapters, refers to the behavior of the nation's central bank, the Federal Reserve, concerning the nation's money supply.

fiscal policy The government's spending and taxing policies.

monetary policy The behavior of the Federal Reserve concerning the nation's money supply.

GOVERNMENT IN THE ECONOMY

Given the scope and power of local, state, and federal governments, there are some matters over which they exert great control and some matters beyond their control. We need to distinguish between variables that a government controls directly and variables that are a consequence of government decisions *combined with the state of the economy.*

For example, tax rates are controlled by the government. By law, Congress has the authority to decide who and what should be taxed and at what rate. Tax *revenue*, on the other hand, is not subject to complete control by the government. Revenue from the personal income tax system depends both on personal tax rates (which Congress sets) *and* on the income of the household sector (which depends on many factors not under direct government control, such as how much households decide to work). Revenue from the corporate profits tax depends both on corporate profits tax rates and on the size of corporate profits. The government controls corporate tax rates but not the size of corporate profits.

Government expenditures also depend both on government decisions and on the state of the economy. For example, in the United States the unemployment insurance program pays benefits to unemployed people. When the economy goes into a recession, the number of unemployed workers increases and so does the level of government unemployment insurance payments.

Because taxes and expenditures often go up or down in response to changes in the economy instead of the result of deliberate decisions by policy makers, we will occasionally use **discretionary fiscal policy** to refer to changes in taxes or spending that are the result of deliberate changes in government policy.

discretionary fiscal policy Changes in taxes or spending that are the result of deliberate changes in government policy.

GOVERNMENT PURCHASES (*G*), NET TAXES (*T*), AND DISPOSABLE INCOME (Y_d)

In the previous chapter, we explored the equilibrium level of national output for a simple economy—no taxes, no government spending, and no exports—to provide a general idea of how the macroeconomy operates. To get more realistic, we need to consider an economy in which government is an active participant. We begin by adding the government sector into the simple economy in Chapter 8.

To keep things simple, we will combine two government activities—the collection of taxes and the payment of transfer payments—into a category we call **net taxes (*T*)**. Specifically, net taxes are equal to the tax payments made to the government by firms and households minus transfer payments made to households by the government. The other variable we will consider is government purchases of goods and services (*G*).

net taxes (*T*) Taxes paid by firms and households to the government minus transfer payments made to households by the government.

Our earlier discussions of household consumption did not take taxes into account. We assumed that all the income generated in the economy was spent or saved by households. When we take into account the role of government, as Figure 9.1 does, we see that as income (*Y*) flows toward households, the government takes income from households in the form of net taxes (*T*). The income that ultimately gets to households is called **disposable**, or **after-tax, income (Y_d)**:

disposable, or **after-tax, income (Y_d)** Total income minus net taxes: $Y - T$.

disposable income ≡ total income − net taxes

$$Y_d \equiv Y - T$$

Y_d excludes taxes paid by households and includes transfer payments made to households by the government. For now we are assuming that *T* does not depend on *Y*—that is, net taxes do not depend on income. This assumption is relaxed in Appendix B to this chapter. Taxes that do not depend on income are sometimes called *lump-sum taxes.*

As Figure 9.1 shows, the disposable income (Y_d) of households must end up either as consumption (*C*) or saving (*S*), Thus:

$$Y_d \equiv C + S$$

This equation is an identity—something that is always true.

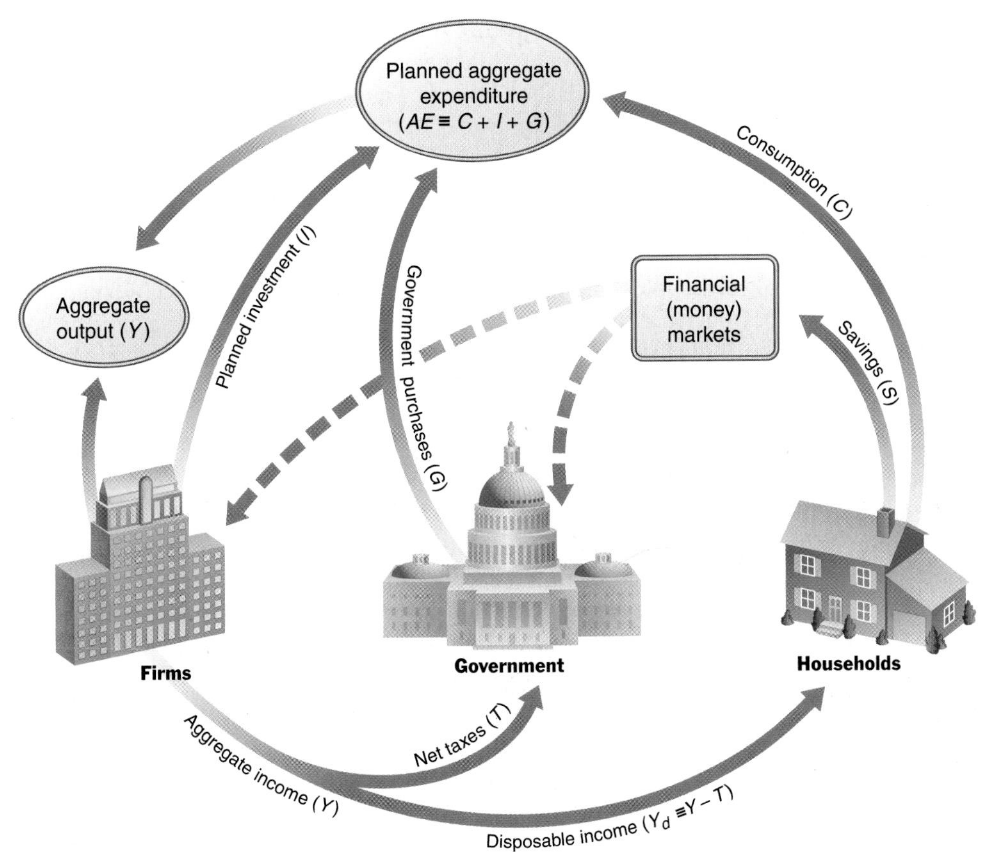

FIGURE 9.1 Adding Net Taxes (*T*) and Government Purchases (*G*) to the Circular Flow of Income

Because disposable income is aggregate income (Y) minus net taxes (T), we can write another identity:

$$Y - T \equiv C + S$$

By adding T to both sides:

$$Y \equiv C + S + T$$

This identity says aggregate income gets cut into three pieces. Government takes a slice (net taxes, T), and then households divide the rest between consumption (C) and saving (S).

Because governments spend money on goods and services, we need to expand our definition of planned aggregate expenditure. Planned aggregate expenditure (AE) is the sum of consumption spending by households (C), planned investment by business firms (I), *and* government purchases of goods and services (G).[1]

$$AE \equiv C + I + G$$

A government's **budget deficit** is the difference between what it spends (G) and what it collects in taxes (T) in a given period:

budget deficit The difference between what a government spends and what it collects in taxes in a given period: $G - T$.

$$\text{budget deficit} \equiv G - T$$

[1]We are still assuming that net exports ($EX - IM$) are zero. In practice, $AE \equiv C + I + G + (EX - IM)$. We bring net export into the analysis at the end of this chapter.

If G exceeds T, the government must borrow from the public to finance the deficit. It does so by selling Treasury bonds and bills (more on this later). In this case, a part of household saving (S) goes to the government. The dashed lines in Figure 9.1 mean that some S goes to firms to finance investment projects and some goes to the government to finance its deficit. If G is less than T, which means that the government is spending less than it is collecting in taxes, the government is running a *surplus.* A surplus is simply a negative deficit.

Adding Taxes to the Consumption Function In Chapter 8, we examined the consumption behavior of households and noted that aggregate consumption (C) depends on aggregate income (Y): In general, the higher aggregate income is, the higher aggregate consumption. For the sake of illustration, we used a specific linear consumption function:

$$C = a + bY$$

where a is the amount of consumption that would take place if national income were zero and b is the marginal propensity to consume.

We need to modify this consumption function because we have added government to the economy. With taxes a part of the picture, it makes sense to assume that disposable income (Y_d), instead of before-tax income (Y), determines consumption behavior. If you earn a million dollars, but have to pay $950,000 in taxes, you have no more disposable income than someone who earns only $50,000 but pays no taxes. What you have available for spending on current consumption is your disposable income, not your before-tax income.

To modify our aggregate consumption function to incorporate disposable income instead of before-tax income, instead of $C = a + bY$, we write

$$C = a + bY_d$$

or

$$C = a + b(Y - T)$$

Our consumption function now has consumption depending on disposable income instead of before-tax income.

Investment What about investment? The government can affect investment behavior through its tax treatment of depreciation and other tax policies. Investment may also vary with economic conditions and interest rates, as we will see later. For our present purposes, we continue to assume that planned investment (I) is autonomous.

EQUILIBRIUM OUTPUT: $Y = C + I + G$

We know from Chapter 8 that equilibrium occurs where $Y = AE$—that is, where aggregate output equals planned aggregate expenditure. Remember that planned aggregate expenditure in an economy with a government is $AE \equiv C + I + G$, so the equilibrium condition is:

$$\text{equilibrium condition: } Y = C + I + G$$

The equilibrium analysis in Chapter 8 applies here also. If output (Y) exceeds planned aggregate expenditure ($C + I + G$), there will be an unplanned increase in inventories—actual investment will exceed planned investment. Conversely, if $C + I + G$ exceeds Y, there will be an unplanned decrease in inventories.

An example will illustrate the government's effect on the macroeconomy and the equilibrium condition. First, our consumption function, $C = 100 + .75Y$ before we introduced the government sector, now becomes

$$C = 100 + .75Y_d$$

or

$$C = 100 + .75(Y - T)$$

TABLE 9.1 Finding Equilibrium for $I = 100$, $G = 100$, and $T = 100$ (All Figures in Billions of Dollars)

(1) OUTPUT (INCOME) Y	(2) NET TAXES T	(3) DISPOSABLE INCOME $Y_d \equiv Y - T$	(4) CONSUMPTION SPENDING $(C = 100 + .75\ Y_d)$	(5) SAVING S $(Y_d - C)$	(6) PLANNED INVESTMENT SPENDING I	(7) GOVERNMENT PURCHASES G	(8) PLANNED AGGREGATE EXPENDITURE $C + I + G$	(9) UNPLANNED INVENTORY CHANGE $Y - (C + I + G)$	(10) ADJUSTMENT TO DISEQUILIBRIUM
300	100	200	250	−50	100	100	450	−150	Output ↑
500	100	400	400	0	100	100	600	−100	Output ↑
700	100	600	550	50	100	100	750	−50	Output ↑
900	100	800	700	100	100	100	900	0	Equilibrium
1,100	100	1,000	850	150	100	100	1,050	+50	Output ↓
1,300	100	1,200	1,000	200	100	100	1,200	+100	Output ↓
1,500	100	1,400	1,150	250	100	100	1,350	+150	Output ↓

Second, we assume that the government is currently purchasing \$100 billion of goods and services and collecting net taxes (T) of \$100 billion.[2] In other words, the government is running a balanced budget, financing all of its spending with taxes. Third, we assume that planned investment (I) is \$100 billion.

Table 9.1 calculates planned aggregate expenditure at several levels of disposable income. For example, at $Y = 500$, disposable income is $Y - T$, or 400.[3] Therefore, $C = 100 + .75(400) = 400$. Assuming that I is fixed at 100, and assuming that G is fixed at 100, planned aggregate expenditure is 600 ($C + I + G = 400 + 100 + 100$). Because output ($Y$) is only 500, planned spending is greater than output by 100. As a result, there is an unplanned inventory decrease of 100, giving firms an incentive to raise output. Thus, output of 500 is below equilibrium.

If $Y = 1{,}300$, then $Y_d = 1{,}200$, $C = 1{,}000$, and planned aggregate expenditure is 1,200. Here, planned spending is *less* than output, there will be an unplanned inventory increase of 100, and firms have an incentive to cut back output. Thus, output of 1,300 is above equilibrium. Only when output is 900 are output and planned aggregate expenditure equal, and only at $Y = 900$ does equilibrium exist.

In Figure 9.2 we derive the same equilibrium level of output graphically. First, the consumption function is drawn, taking into account net taxes of 100. The old function was $C = 100 + .75Y$. The new function is $C = 100 + .75(Y - T)$ or $C = 100 + .75(Y - 100)$, rewritten as $C = 100 + .75Y - 75$, or $C = 25 + .75Y$. For example, consumption at an income of zero is 25 ($C = 25 + .75Y = 25 + .75(0) = 25$). The marginal propensity to consume has not changed—we assume it remains .75. Note that the consumption function in Figure 9.2 plots the points in columns 1 and 4 of Table 9.1.

Planned aggregate expenditure, recall, adds planned investment to consumption. Now, in addition to 100 in investment, we have government purchases of 100. Because I and G are constant at 100 each at all levels of income, we add $I + G = 200$ to consumption at every level of income. The result is the new AE curve. This curve is just a plot of the points in columns 1 and 8 of Table 9.1. The 45° line helps us find the equilibrium level of real output, which, we already know, is 900. If you examine any level of output above or below 900, you will find disequilibrium. Look, for example, at $Y = 500$ on the graph. At this level, planned aggregate expenditure is 600, but output is only 500. Inventories will fall below what was planned, and firms will have an incentive to increase output.

The Leakages/Injections Approach to Equilibrium As in the last chapter, we can also examine equilibrium using the leakages/injections approach. Look at the circular flow of income in Figure 9.1. The government takes out net taxes (T) from the flow of income—a leakage—and households save (S) some of their income—also a leakage from the flow of income. The planned spending injections are government purchases (G) and

[2] As we pointed out earlier, the government does not have complete control over tax revenues and transfer payments. We ignore this problem here, however, and set tax revenues minus transfers at a fixed amount. Things will become more realistic later in this chapter and in Appendix B.

[3] For the rest of this discussion, we will understand but not state that figures are in billions of dollars.

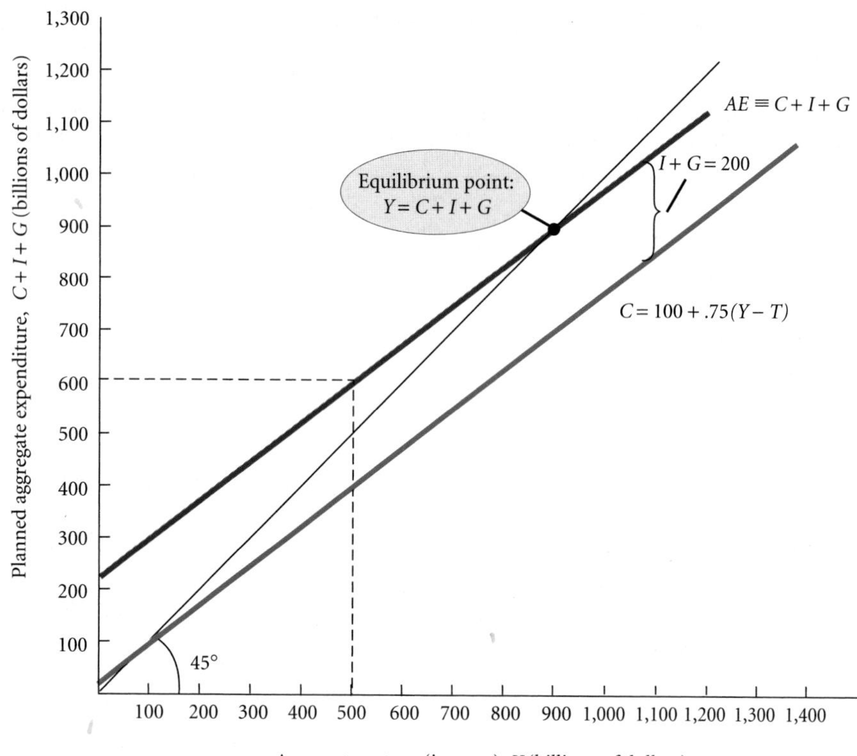

FIGURE 9.2 Finding Equilibrium Output/Income Graphically

Because G and I are both fixed at 100, the aggregate expenditure function is the new consumption function displaced upward by $I + G = 200$. Equilibrium occurs at $Y = C + I + G = 900$.

planned investment (I). If leakages ($S + T$) equal planned injections ($I + G$), there is equilibrium:

leakages/injections approach to equilibrium: $S + T = I + G$

To derive this, we know that in equilibrium, aggregate output (income) (Y) equals planned aggregate expenditure (AE). By definition, AE equals $C + I + G$, and by definition Y equals $C + S + T$. Therefore, at equilibrium:

$$C + S + T = C + I + G$$

Subtracting C from both sides leaves:

$$S + T = I + G$$

Note that equilibrium does *not* require that $G = T$ (a balanced government budget) or that $S = I$. It is only necessary that the sum of S and T equals the sum of I and G.

Column 5 of Table 9.1 calculates aggregate saving by subtracting consumption from disposal income at every level of disposable income ($S \equiv Y_d - C$). Because I and G are fixed, $I + G$ equals 200 at every level of income. Using the table to add saving and taxes ($S + T$), we see that $S + T$ equals 200 only at $Y = 900$. Thus, the equilibrium level of output (income) is 900, the same answer we arrived at through numerical and graphic analysis.

FISCAL POLICY AT WORK: MULTIPLIER EFFECTS

You can see from Figure 9.2 that if the government were able to change the levels of either G or T, it would be able to change the equilibrium level of output (income). At this point, we are assuming that the government controls G and T. In this section we will review three multipliers:

- Government spending multiplier
- Tax multiplier
- Balanced-budget multiplier

THE GOVERNMENT SPENDING MULTIPLIER

Suppose you are the chief economic adviser to the president and the economy is sitting at the equilibrium output pictured in Figure 9.2. Output and income are being produced at a rate of $900 billion per year, and the government is currently buying $100 billion worth of goods and services each year and is financing them with $100 billion in taxes. The budget is balanced. In addition, the private sector is investing (producing capital goods) at a rate of $100 billion per year.

The president calls you into the Oval Office and says, "Unemployment is too high. We need to lower unemployment by increasing output and income." After some research, you determine that an acceptable unemployment rate could be achieved only if aggregate output increases to $1,100 billion.

You now need to determine: How can the government use taxing and spending policy—fiscal policy—to increase the equilibrium level of national output? Suppose that the president has let it be known that taxes must remain at present levels—the Congress just passed a major tax reform package—so adjusting *T* is out of the question for several years. That leaves you with *G*. Your only option is to increase government spending while holding taxes constant.

To increase spending without raising taxes (which provides the government with revenue to spend), the government must borrow. When *G* is bigger than *T*, the government runs a deficit, and the difference between *G* and *T* must be borrowed. For the moment we will ignore the possible effect of the deficit and focus only on the effect of a higher *G* with *T* constant.

Meanwhile, the president is awaiting your answer. How much of an increase in spending would be required to generate a $200 billion increase in the equilibrium level of output, pushing it from $900 billion up to $1,100 billion and reducing unemployment to the president's acceptable level?

You might be tempted to say that because we need to increase income by 200 (1,100 – 900), we should increase government spending by the same amount—but what would happen? The increased government spending will throw the economy out of equilibrium. Because *G* is a component of aggregate spending, planned aggregate expenditure will increase by 200. Planned spending will be greater than output, inventories will be lower than planned, and firms will have an incentive to increase output. Suppose output rises by the desired 200. You might think, "We increased spending by 200 and output by 200, so equilibrium is restored."

There is more to the story than this. The moment output rises, the economy is generating more income. This was the desired effect: the creation of more employment. The newly employed workers are also consumers and some of their income gets spent. With higher consumption spending, planned spending will be greater than output, inventories will be lower than planned, and firms will raise output, and thus raise income, again. This time firms are responding to the new consumption spending. Already, total income is over 1,100.

This story should sound familiar. It is the multiplier in action. Although this time it is government spending (*G*) that is changed rather than planned investment (*I*), the effect is the same as the multiplier effect we described in Chapter 8. An increase in government spending has the same impact on the equilibrium level of output and income as an increase in planned investment. A dollar of extra spending from either *G* or *I* is identical with respect to its impact on equilibrium output. The equation for the government spending multiplier is the same as the equation for the multiplier for a change in planned investment.

$$\text{government spending multiplier} \equiv \frac{1}{MPS}$$

We derive the government spending multiplier algebraically in Appendix A to this chapter.

Formally, the **government spending multiplier** is defined as the ratio of the change in the equilibrium level of output to a change in government spending. This is the same definition we used in the previous chapter, but now the autonomous variable is government spending instead of planned investment.

government spending multiplier The ratio of the change in the equilibrium level of output to a change in government spending.

Remember that we were thinking of increasing government spending (*G*) by 200. We can use the multiplier analysis to see what the new equilibrium level of *Y* would be for an

TABLE 9.2 Finding Equilibrium After a $50 Billion Government Spending Increase (All Figures in Billions of Dollars; G Has Increased from 100 in Table 9.1 to 150 Here)

(1) OUTPUT (INCOME) Y	(2) NET TAXES T	(3) DISPOSABLE INCOME $Y_d \equiv Y - T$	(4) CONSUMPTION SPENDING ($C = 100 + .75\ Y_d$)	(5) SAVING S ($Y_d - C$)	(6) PLANNED INVESTMENT SPENDING I	(7) GOVERNMENT PURCHASES G	(8) PLANNED AGGREGATE EXPENDITURE $C + I + G$	(9) UNPLANNED INVENTORY CHANGE $Y - (C + I + G)$	(10) ADJUSTMENT TO DISEQUILIBRIUM
300	100	200	250	−50	100	150	500	−200	Output ↑
500	100	400	400	0	100	150	650	−150	Output ↑
700	100	600	550	50	100	150	800	−100	Output ↑
900	100	800	700	100	100	150	950	−50	Output ↑
1,100	100	1,000	850	150	100	150	1,100	0	Equilibrium
1,300	100	1,200	1,000	200	100	150	1,250	+50	Output ↓

increase in G of 200. The multiplier in our example is 4. (Because b—the *MPC*—is .75, the *MPS* must be $1 - .75 = .25$, and $1/.25 = 4$). Thus, Y will increase by 800 (4×200). Because the initial level of Y was 900, the new equilibrium level of Y is $900 + 800 = 1{,}700$ when G is increased by 200.

The level of 1,700 is much larger than the level of 1,100 that we calculated as necessary to lower unemployment to the desired level. Let us back up, then. If we want Y to increase by 200 and if the multiplier is 4, we need G to increase by only $200/4 = 50$. If G changes by 50, the equilibrium level of Y will change by 200, and the new value of Y will be 1,100 ($900 + 200$), as desired.

Looking at Table 9.2 we can check our answer to be sure that it is an equilibrium. Look first at the old equilibrium of 900. When government purchases (G) were 100, aggregate output (income) was equal to planned aggregate expenditure ($AE \equiv C + I + G$) at $Y = 900$. Now G has increased to 150. At $Y = 900$, ($C + I + G$) is greater than Y, there is an unplanned fall in inventories, and output will rise, but by how much? The multiplier told us that equilibrium income would rise by four times the 50 change in G. Y should rise by $4 \times 50 = 200$, from 900 to 1,100 before equilibrium is restored. Let us check. If $Y = 1{,}100$, then consumption is $C = 100 + .75Y_d = 100 + .75(1{,}000) = 850$. Because I equals 100 and G now equals 100 (the original level of G) + 50 (the additional G brought about by the fiscal policy change) = 150, then $C + I + G = 850 + 100 + 150 = 1{,}100$. $Y = AE$, and the economy is in equilibrium.

The graphic solution to the president's problem is presented in Figure 9.3. A 50 increase in G shifts the planned aggregate expenditure function up by 50. The new equilibrium income occurs where the new AE line (AE_2) crosses the 45° line, at $Y = 1{,}100$.

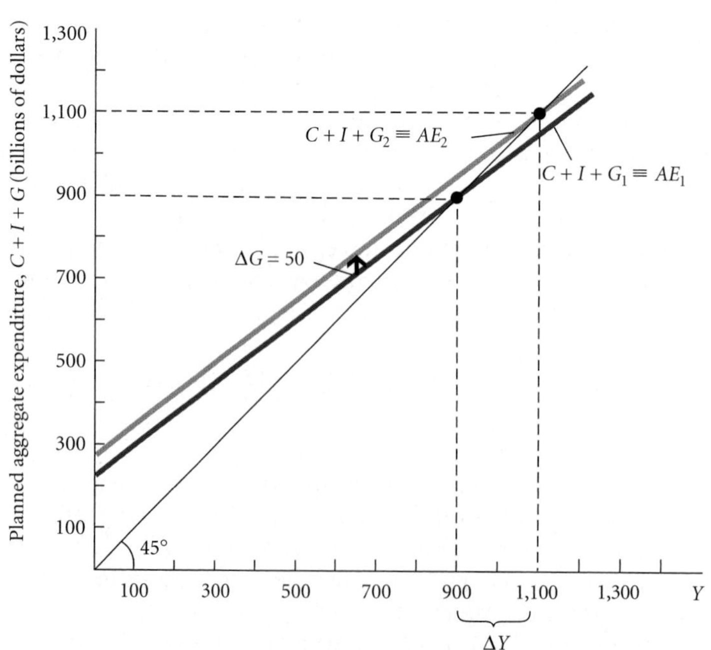

FIGURE 9.3 The Government Spending Multiplier

Increasing government spending by 50 shifts the *AE* function up by 50. As Y rises in response, additional consumption is generated. Overall, the equilibrium level of Y increases by 200, from 900 to 1,100.

THE TAX MULTIPLIER

Remember that fiscal policy comprises policies concerning government spending *and* policies concerning taxation. To see what effect a change in tax policy has on the economy, imagine the following. You are still chief economic adviser to the president, but now you are instructed to devise a plan to reduce unemployment to an acceptable level *without* increasing the level of government spending. In your plan, instead of increasing government spending (G), you decide to cut taxes and maintain the current level of spending. A tax cut increases disposable income, which is likely to lead to added consumption spending. (Remember our general rule that increased income leads to increased consumption.) Would the decrease in taxes affect aggregate output (income) the same as an increase in G?

A decrease in taxes would increase income. The government spends no less than it did before the tax cut, and households find they have a larger after-tax, or disposable, income than they had before. This leads to an increase in consumption. Planned aggregate expenditure will increase, which will lead to inventories being lower than planned, which will lead to a rise in output. When output rises, more workers will be employed and more income will be generated, causing a second-round increase in consumption, and so on. Thus, income will increase by a multiple of the decrease in taxes, but there is a "wrinkle."

> The multiplier for a change in taxes is *not the same* as the multiplier for a change in government spending.

tax multiplier The ratio of change in the equilibrium level of output to a change in taxes.

Why does the **tax multiplier**—the ratio of change in the equilibrium level of output to a change in taxes—differ from the spending multiplier? To answer this, we need to compare the ways in which a tax cut and a spending increase work their way through the economy.

Look at Figure 9.1. When the government increases spending, there is an immediate and direct impact on the economy's *total* spending. Because G is a component of planned aggregate expenditure, an increase in G leads to a dollar-for-dollar increase in planned aggregate expenditure. When taxes are cut, there is no direct impact on spending. Taxes enter the picture only because they have an effect on the household's disposable income, which influences household's consumption (which is part of total spending). As Figure 9.1 shows, the tax cut flows through households before affecting aggregate expenditure.

Let us assume the government decides to cut taxes by $1. By how much would spending increase? We already know the answer. The marginal propensity to consume (MPC) tells us how much consumption spending changes when disposable income changes. In the example running through this chapter, the marginal propensity to consume out of disposable income is .75. This means that if households' after-tax incomes rise by $1, they will increase their consumption not by the full $1, but by only $0.75.[4]

In summary, when government spending increases by $1, planned aggregate expenditure increases initially by the full amount of the rise in G, or $1. When taxes are cut, however, the initial increase in planned aggregate expenditure is only the MPC times the change in taxes. Because the initial increase in planned aggregate expenditure is smaller for a tax cut than for a government spending increase, the final effect on the equilibrium level of income will be smaller.

We figure the size of the tax multiplier in the same way we derived the multiplier for an increase in investment and an increase in government purchases. The final change in the equilibrium level of output (income) (Y) is:

$$\Delta Y = (\text{initial increase in aggregate expenditure}) \times \left(\frac{1}{MPS}\right)$$

Because the initial change in aggregate expenditure caused by a tax change of ΔT is $(-\Delta T \times MPC)$, we can solve for the tax multiplier by substitution:

$$\Delta Y = (-\Delta T \times MPC) \times \left(\frac{1}{MPS}\right) = -\Delta T \times \left(\frac{MPC}{MPS}\right)$$

[4]What happens to the other $0.25? Remember that whatever households do not consume is, by definition, saved. The other $0.25 thus gets allocated to saving.

Because a tax cut will cause an *increase* in consumption expenditures and output and a tax increase will cause a *reduction* in consumption expenditures and output, the tax multiplier is a negative multiplier:

$$\text{tax multiplier} \equiv -\left(\frac{MPC}{MPS}\right)$$

We derive the tax multiplier algebraically in Appendix A to this chapter.

If the *MPC* is .75, as in our example, the multiplier is – .75/.25 = – 3. A tax cut of 100 will increase the equilibrium level of output by – 100 × – 3 = 300. This is very different than the effect of our government spending multiplier of 4. Under these same conditions, a 100 increase in *G* will increase the equilibrium level of output by 400 or (100 × 4).

THE BALANCED-BUDGET MULTIPLIER

We have now discussed (1) changing government spending with no change in taxes, and (2) changing taxes with no change in government spending. What if government spending and taxes are increased by the same amount? That is, what if the government decides to pay for its extra spending by increasing taxes by the same amount? The government's budget deficit would not change, because the increase in expenditures would be matched by an increase in tax income.

You might think in this case that equal increases in government spending and taxes have no effect on equilibrium income. After all, the extra government spending equals the extra amount of tax revenues collected by the government. This is not so. Take, for example, a government spending increase of $40 billion. We know from the preceding analysis that an increase in *G* of 40, with taxes (*T*) held constant, should increase the equilibrium level of income by 40 × the government spending multiplier. The multiplier is 1/*MPS* or 1/.25 = 4. The equilibrium level of income should rise by 160 or (40 × 4).

Now suppose that instead of keeping tax revenues constant, we finance the 40 increase in government spending with an equal increase in taxes, so as to maintain a balanced budget. What happens to aggregate spending as a result of both the rise in *G* and the rise in *T*? There are two initial effects. First, government spending rises by 40. This effect is direct, immediate, and positive. Now the government also collects 40 more in taxes. The tax increase has a *negative* impact on overall spending in the economy, but it does not fully offset the increase in government spending.

The final impact of a tax increase on aggregate expenditure depends on how households respond to it. The only thing we know about household behavior so far is that households spend 75 percent of their added income and save 25 percent. We know that when disposable income falls, both consumption and saving are reduced. A tax *increase* of 40 reduces disposable income by 40, and that means consumption falls by 40 × *MPC*. Because *MPC* = .75, consumption falls by 30 or (40 × .75). The net result in the beginning is that government spending rises by 40 and consumption spending falls by 30. Aggregate expenditure increases by 10 right after the simultaneous balanced-budget increases in *G* and *T*.

So, a balanced-budget increase in *G* and *T* will raise output, but by how much? How large is this **balanced-budget multiplier?** The answer may surprise you:

balanced-budget multiplier The ratio of change in the equilibrium level of output to a change in government spending where the change in government spending is balanced by a change in taxes so as not to create any deficit. The balanced-budget multiplier is equal to one: The change in *Y* resulting from the change in *G* and the equal change in *T* is exactly the same size as the initial change in *G* or *T* itself.

$$\text{balanced-budget multiplier} \equiv 1$$

Let us combine what we know about the tax multiplier and the government spending multiplier to explain this. To find the final effect of a simultaneous increase in government spending and increase in net taxes, we need to add the multiplier effects of the two. The government spending multiplier is 1/*MPS*. The tax multiplier is –*MPC*/*MPS*. Their sum is (1/*MPS*) + (–*MPC*/*MPS*) ≡ (1 – *MPC*)/*MPS*. Because *MPC* + *MPS* ≡ 1, then 1 – *MPC* ≡ *MPS*. This means (1 – *MPC*)/*MPS* ≡ *MPS*/*MPS* ≡ 1. (We also derive the balanced-budget multiplier in Appendix A to this chapter.)

TABLE 9.3 Finding Equilibrium After a $200-Billion Balanced-Budget Increase in *G* and *T* (All Figures in Billions of Dollars; Both *G* and *T* Have Increased from 100 in Table 9.1 to 300 Here)

(1) OUTPUT (INCOME) Y	(2) NET TAXES T	(3) DISPOSABLE INCOME $Y_d \equiv Y - T$	(4) CONSUMPTION SPENDING ($C = 100 + .75\ Y_d$)	(5) PLANNED INVESTMENT SPENDING I	(6) GOVERNMENT PURCHASES G	(7) PLANNED AGGREGATE EXPENDITURE $C + I + G$	(8) UNPLANNED INVENTORY CHANGE $Y - (C + I + G)$	(9) ADJUSTMENT TO DISEQUILIBRIUM
500	300	200	250	100	300	650	−150	Output ↑
700	300	400	400	100	300	800	−100	Output ↑
900	300	600	550	100	300	950	−50	Output ↑
1,100	300	800	700	100	300	1,100	0	Equilibrium
1,300	300	1,000	850	100	300	1,250	+50	Output ↓
1,500	300	1,200	1,000	100	300	1,400	+100	Output ↓

Back to our example, recall that by using the government spending multiplier, a 40 increase in G would *raise* output at equilibrium by 160 (40 × the government spending multiplier of 4). By using the tax multiplier, we know that a 40 tax hike will *reduce* the equilibrium level of output by 120 (40 × the tax multiplier, −3). The net effect is 160 minus 120, or 40. It should be clear, then, that the effect on equilibrium Y is equal to the balanced increase in G and T. In other words, the net increase in the equilibrium level of Y resulting from the change in G and the change in T is exactly the size of the initial change in G or T itself.

If the president wanted to raise Y by 200 without increasing the deficit, a simultaneous increase in G and T of 200 would do it. To see why, look at the numbers in Table 9.3. In Table 9.1, we saw an equilibrium level of output at 900. With both G and T up by 200, the new equilibrium is 1,100—higher by 200. At no other level of Y do we find $(C + I + G) = Y$.

An increase in government spending has a direct initial effect on planned aggregate expenditure; a tax increase does not. The initial effect of the tax increase is that households cut consumption by the *MPC* times the change in taxes. This change in consumption is less than the change in taxes, because the *MPC* is less than 1. The positive stimulus from the government spending increase is thus greater than the negative stimulus from the tax increase. The net effect is that the balanced-budget multiplier is 1.

Table 9.4 summarizes everything we have said about fiscal policy multipliers. If anything is still unclear, review the relevant discussions in this chapter.

A Warning Although we have added government, the story we have told about the multiplier is still incomplete and oversimplified. For example, we have been treating net taxes (T) as a lump-sum, fixed amount, whereas in practice, taxes depend on income. Appendix B to this chapter shows that the size of the multiplier is reduced when we make the more realistic assumption that taxes depend on income. We continue to add more realism and difficulty to our analysis in the chapters that follow.

TABLE 9.4 Summary of Fiscal Policy Multipliers

	POLICY STIMULUS	MULTIPLIER	FINAL IMPACT ON EQUILIBRIUM Y
Government spending multiplier	Increase or decrease in the level of government purchases: ΔG	$\frac{1}{MPS}$	$\Delta G \cdot \frac{1}{MPS}$
Tax multiplier	Increase or decrease in the level of net taxes: ΔT	$\frac{-MPC}{MPS}$	$\Delta T \cdot \frac{-MPC}{MPS}$
Balanced-budget multiplier	Simultaneous balanced-budget increase or decrease in the level of government purchases and net taxes: $\Delta G = \Delta T$	1	ΔG

THE FEDERAL BUDGET

federal budget The budget of the federal government.

Because fiscal policy is the manipulation of items in the federal budget, we need to consider those aspects of the budget relevant to our study of macroeconomics. The **federal budget** is an enormously complicated document, up to thousands of pages each year. It lists in detail all the things the government plans to spend money on and all the sources of government revenues for the coming year. It is the product of a complex interplay of social, political, and economic forces.

The "budget" is really three different budgets. First, it is a *political document* that dispenses favors to certain groups or regions (the elderly benefit from social security, farmers from agricultural price supports, students from federal loan programs, and so on) and places burdens (taxes) on others. Second, it is a *reflection of goals* the government wants to achieve. For example, in addition to assisting farmers, agricultural price supports are meant to preserve the "family farm." Tax breaks for corporations engaging in research and development of new products are meant to encourage research. Finally, the budget may be an *embodiment of some beliefs about how (if at all) the government should manage the macroeconomy.* The macroeconomic aspects of the budget are only a part of a more complicated story, a story that may be of more concern to political scientists than to economists.

THE BUDGET

A highly condensed version of the federal budget is shown in Table 9.5. In 2002, the government had total receipts of $1,873.3 billion, largely from personal income taxes ($845.8 billion) and contributions for social insurance ($737.1 billion). (Contributions for social insurance are employer and employee Social Security taxes.) Receipts from corporate taxes accounted for $179.8 billion, or only 9.6 percent of total receipts. Not everyone is aware of the fact that corporate taxes as a percentage of government receipts are quite small relative to personal taxes and Social Security taxes.

The federal government also paid $2,075.4 billion in expenditures in 2002. Of this, $931.7 billion represented transfer payments (Social Security, military retirement benefits, and unemployment compensation).[5] Consumption ($586.5 billion) was the next largest

TABLE 9.5 Federal Government Receipts and Expenditures, 2002 (Billions of Dollars)

	AMOUNT	PERCENTAGE OF TOTAL
Receipts		
Personal taxes	845.8	45.2
Corporate taxes	179.8	9.6
Indirect business taxes	110.6	5.9
Contributions for social insurance	737.1	39.3
Total	1,873.3	100.0
Current expenditures		
Consumption	586.5	28.3
Transfer payments	931.7	44.9
Grants-in-aid to state and local governments	305.7	14.7
Net interest payments	207.8	10.0
Net subsidies of government enterprises	43.7	2.1
Total	2,075.4	100.0
Current surplus (+) or deficit (–) (receipts – current expenditures)	– 202.1	

Source: U.S. Department of Commerce, Bureau of Economic Analysis.

[5]Remember that there is an important difference between transfer payments and government purchases of goods and services. Much of the government budget goes for things that an economist would classify as transfers (payments that are grants or gifts) instead of purchases of goods and services. It is only the latter that are included in our variable *G*. Transfers are counted as part of net taxes.

News Analysis

Debate: Tax Cuts and the Deficit in 2003

IN MID-2003, THE PRESIDENT AND THE CONgress were in a battle over a tax cut. The proponents argued that the tax cuts were needed to stimulate the slowly growing U.S. economy. The opponents argued that the tax cuts would further increase the deficit, which was already too large.

Bush's Drive for Tax Cut

—New York Times

Two weeks into the Congressional debate on taxes, and with at least two more weeks to go, it is clear that Congress will eventually approve a big tax cut, smaller than the $726 billion, 10-year reduction President Bush proposed but still the third largest in history, on top of the largest, enacted just two years ago this month.

The linchpin of the president's plan, the elimination of taxes on most stock dividends, will be whittled down considerably, but the president will still be able to claim victory. After all, his philosophy is that lowering taxes is the best policy whether the economy is strong or weak, whether the budget is showing a surplus or a deficit.

And he will have persuaded Congress to adopt that philosophy in the face of the largest budget deficits ever, uncertain costs growing out of the war in Iraq, [and] the fiscal cloud on the horizon from the retirement of the baby boom generation.

Source: Adapted from: David E. Rosenbaum, "Bush's Drive for Tax Cut," New York Times, May 11, 2003. Reprinted by permission.

A major tax reduction bill was passed by the Congress and signed by the President in 2003.

Visit www.prenhall.com/casefair for updated articles and exercises.

component, followed by grants-in-aid to state and local governments ($305.7 billion) and interest on the federal debt ($207.8 billion).

THE SURPLUS OR DEFICIT

The difference between the federal government's receipts and its expenditures is the **federal surplus** (+) or **deficit** (−). Table 9.5 shows that the federal government spent more than it took in during 2002, resulting in a deficit of $202.1 billion.

federal surplus (+) or **deficit (−)** Federal government receipts minus expenditures.

The federal deficit was large from the early 1980s until the mid-1990s. You can see this in Figure 9.4 where the federal surplus or deficit as a percentage of gross domestic product (GDP) is plotted for 1970 I–2003 II. As the figure shows, the budget was in deficit until 1998 I, when it began to be in surplus. Except for a period in the mid-1970s, the deficit was fairly small until the early 1980s, where it reached 5.3 percent of GDP in 1982 IV. The budget improved rapidly from 1992 until 2000, but it then began falling rapidly. By the second quarter of 2003 the deficit was 3.4 percent of GDP.

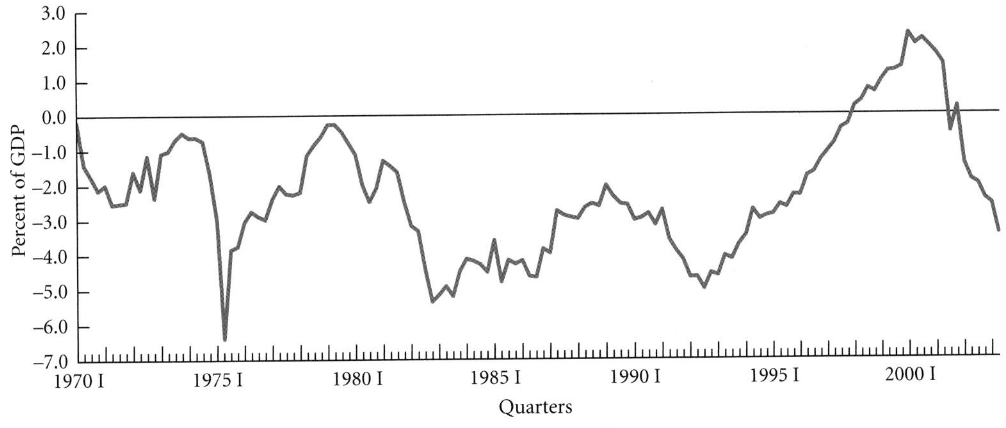

FIGURE 9.4 The Federal Government Surplus (+) or Deficit (−) as a Percentage of GDP, 1970 I–2003 II

The deficits in the 1980s were particularly large by historical standards, and they are becoming large again.

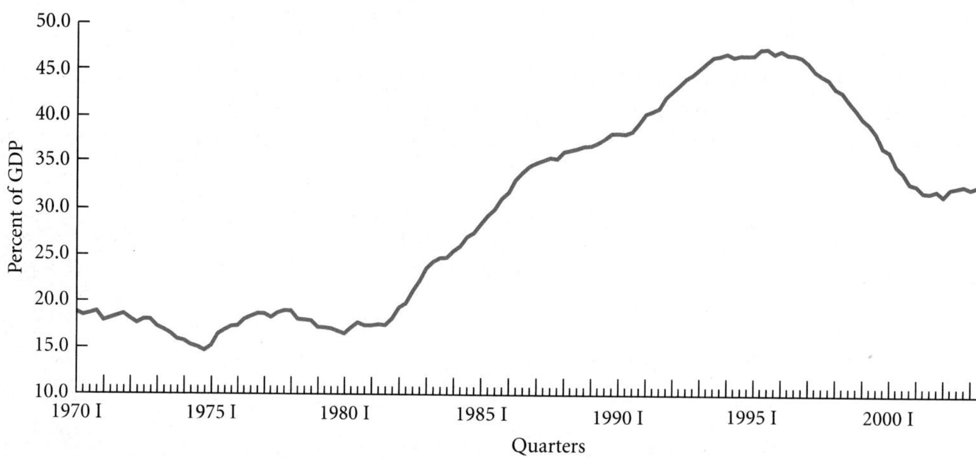

FIGURE 9.5 The Federal Government Debt as a Percentage of GDP, 1970 I–2003 II

The federal government debt increased dramatically in the 1980s as a result of the large deficits. The percentage fell sharply from the mid-1990s to 2000.

How did such large deficits in the 1980s come about? There are several reasons. First, government purchases as a percentage of GDP rose in the early 1980s and then remained high. This increase primarily reflected the defense buildup of the Reagan years. Second, interest payments as a percentage of GDP rose substantially. Third, personal income tax rates fell as a result of the Economic Recovery Tax Act of 1981. With defense spending and interest payments rising rapidly and personal tax rates falling, it is not surprising that the deficit rose substantially during the 1980s. The government simply spent a lot more than it collected in taxes.

During the two Clinton administrations (1993–2000) the deficit turned to surplus, and at its peak in the first quarter of 2000 the surplus was 2.3 percent of GDP. Some of this change was due to tax rate increases that were passed at the beginning of the first Clinton administration. The rapid movement from surplus to deficit beginning in 2001 was due in part to a number of large tax rate decreases that were passed during the G. W. Bush administration and increased government spending on Iraq.

THE DEBT

federal debt The total amount owed by the federal government.

privately held federal debt The privately held (non-government-owned) debt of the U.S. government.

When the government runs a deficit, it must borrow to finance it. To borrow, the federal government sells government securities to the public. It issues pieces of paper promising to pay a certain amount, with interest, in the future. In return, it receives funds from the buyers of the paper and uses these funds to pay its bills. This borrowing increases the **federal debt,** the total amount owed by the federal government. The federal debt is the total of all accumulated deficits minus surpluses over time.

Some of the securities that the government issues end up being held by the federal government itself at the Federal Reserve or in government trust funds. The term **privately held federal debt** refers only to the *privately held* debt of the U.S. government. At the end of March 2003, the federal debt was $6.5 trillion, of which $3.7 trillion was privately held.

Given the large deficits that the federal government had in the 1980s, it should not be surprising that the federal debt rose sharply in the 1980s. You can see this in Figure 9.5, where the privately held federal debt as a percentage of GDP is plotted for the 1970 I–2003 II period. The debt rose rapidly between 1982 and 1993—from 18.2 percent of GDP in 1981 IV to 46.7 percent in 1993 IV. From the mid-1990s until 2000 the debt as a percentage of GDP fell sharply. Since 2000 the percent has not changed much.

THE ECONOMY'S INFLUENCE ON THE GOVERNMENT BUDGET

Some parts of the government's budget depend on the state of the economy, over which the government has no direct control. The following are some of the ways in which the economy affects the budget.

TAX REVENUES DEPEND ON THE STATE OF THE ECONOMY

Consider the revenue side of the budget. The government passes laws that set tax rates and tax brackets, variables the government does control. Tax revenue, on the other hand, depends on taxable income, and income depends on the state of the economy, which the government does *not* control. The government can set a personal income tax rate of 20 percent, but the revenue that the tax brings in will depend on the average income earned by households. The government will collect more revenue when average income is $40,000 than when average income is $20,000.

SOME GOVERNMENT EXPENDITURES DEPEND ON THE STATE OF THE ECONOMY

Some items on the expenditure side of the government budget also depend on the state of the economy. As the economy expands, unemployment falls, and the result is a decrease in unemployment benefits. Welfare payments and food stamp allotments also decrease somewhat. Some of the people who receive these benefits during bad times are able to find jobs when the state of the economy improves, and they begin earning enough income that they no longer qualify. Transfer payments tend to go down automatically during an expansion. (During a slump, transfer payments tend to increase because there are more people without jobs and more poor people generally.)

Another reason government spending is not completely controllable is that inflation often picks up when the economy is expanding. This can lead the government to spend more than it had planned to spend. Suppose the government has ordered 20 planes at $2 million each and inflation causes the actual price to be higher than expected. If the government decides to go ahead and buy the planes anyway, it will be forced to increase its spending. Finally, any change in the interest rate changes government interest payments. An increase in interest rates means that the government spends more in interest payments.

AUTOMATIC STABILIZERS

As the economy expands, the government's tax receipts increase. Also, transfer payments fall as the economy expands, which leads to a decrease in government expenditures. The revenue and expenditure items that change in response to changes in economic activity in such a way as to moderate changes in GDP are known as **automatic stabilizers**. As the economy expands or contracts, "automatic" changes in government revenues and expenditures take place that tend to reduce the change in, or stabilize, GDP.

automatic stabilizers Revenue and expenditure items in the federal budget that automatically change with the state of the economy in such a way as to stabilize GDP.

The fact that some revenues *automatically* tend to rise and some expenditures *automatically* tend to fall in an expansion means that the government surplus is larger, or the deficit is smaller, in an expansion than it otherwise would be. Suppose we wanted to assess whether a government is practicing a policy designed to increase spending and income. If we looked only at the size of the government budget deficit, we might be fooled into thinking that the government is trying to stimulate the economy when, in fact, the real source of the deficit is a slump in the economy that caused revenues to fall and transfer payments to increase.

FISCAL DRAG

If the economy is doing well, income will be high and so will tax revenue. Tax revenue rises with increases in income for two reasons. First, there is more income to be taxed when people are earning more. Second, as people earn more income, they move into higher tax brackets and the average tax rate that they pay increases. This type of increase in tax rates is a **fiscal drag**, because the increase in average tax rates that results when people move into higher brackets acts as a "drag" on the economy. As the economy expands and income increases, the automatic tax increase mechanism built into the system goes to work. Tax rates go up, reducing the after-tax wage, and this slows down the expansion.

fiscal drag The negative effect on the economy that occurs when average tax rates increase because taxpayers have moved into higher income brackets during an expansion.

Before 1982, people found themselves pushed into higher tax brackets by inflation alone. Suppose my income rose 10 percent in 1981, but the price level also rose by 10 percent in that year. My income did not increase at all in real terms, but because the tax brackets were not legislated in real terms, I ended up paying more taxes. Since 1982, however, tax brackets have been indexed—that is, adjusted for inflation—and this has substantially reduced the automatic fiscal drag built into the system.

FULL-EMPLOYMENT BUDGET

Because the condition of the economy affects the budget deficit so strongly, we cannot accurately judge either the intent or the success of fiscal policies just by looking at the surplus or deficit. Instead of looking simply at the size of the surplus or deficit, economists have developed an alternative way to measure how effective fiscal policy actually is. By examining what the budget would be like if the economy were producing at the full-employment level of output—the so-called **full-employment budget**—we can establish a benchmark for evaluating fiscal policy.

full-employment budget What the federal budget would be if the economy were producing at a full-employment level of output.

The distinction between the actual and full-employment budget is important. Suppose the economy is in a slump and the deficit is $250 billion. Also suppose that if there were full employment, the deficit would fall to $75 billion. The $75 billion deficit that would remain even with full employment would be due to the structure of tax and spending programs instead of the state of the economy. This deficit—the deficit that remains at full employment—is sometimes called the **structural deficit**. The $175 billion ($250 billion – $75 billion) part of the deficit caused by the fact the economy is in a slump is known as the **cyclical deficit**. The existence of the cyclical deficit depends on where the economy is in the business cycle, and it ceases to exist when full employment is reached. By definition, the cyclical deficit of the full-employment budget is zero.

structural deficit The deficit that remains at full employment.

cyclical deficit The deficit that occurs because of a downturn in the business cycle.

LOOKING AHEAD

We have now seen how households, firms, and the government interact in the goods market, how equilibrium output (income) is determined, and how the government uses fiscal policy to influence the economy. In the following two chapters we analyze the money market and monetary policy—the government's other major tool for influencing the economy.

SUMMARY

1. The government can affect the macroeconomy through two specific policy channels. *Fiscal policy* refers to the government's taxing and spending behavior. *Discretionary fiscal policy* refers to changes in taxes or spending that are the result of deliberate changes in government policy. *Monetary policy* refers to the behavior of the Federal Reserve concerning the nation's money supply.

GOVERNMENT IN THE ECONOMY

2. The government does not have complete control over tax revenues and certain expenditures, which are partially dictated by the state of the economy.
3. As a participant in the economy, the government makes purchases of goods and services (G), collects taxes, and makes transfer payments to households. *Net taxes* (T) is equal to the tax payments made to the government by firms and households minus transfer payments made to households by the government.
4. *Disposable*, or *after-tax, income* (Y_d) is equal to the amount of income received by households after taxes: $Y_d \equiv Y - T$. After-tax income determines households' consumption behavior.
5. The *budget deficit* is equal to the difference between what the government spends and what it collects in taxes: $G - T$. When G exceeds T, the government must borrow from the public to finance its deficit.
6. In an economy in which government is a participant, planned aggregate expenditure equals consumption spending by households (C) plus planned investment spending by firms (I) plus government spending on goods and services (G): $AE \equiv C + I + G$. Because the condition $Y = AE$ is necessary for the economy to be in equilibrium, it follows that $Y = C + I + G$ is the macroeconomic equilibrium condition. The economy is also in equilibrium when leakages out of the system equal injections into the system. This occurs when savings and net taxes (the leakages) equal planned investment and government purchases (the injections): $S + T = I + G$.

FISCAL POLICY AT WORK: MULTIPLIER EFFECTS

7. Fiscal policy has a multiplier effect on the economy. A change in government spending gives rise to a multiplier equal to $1/MPS$. A change in taxation brings about a multiplier equal to $-MPC/MPS$. A simultaneous equal increase or decrease in government spending and taxes has a multiplier effect of 1.

THE FEDERAL BUDGET

8. The federal deficit was quite large in the 1980s. Reasons for the deficit include the defense buildup of the Reagan years, the high amount of interest paid on already-existing debt, and cuts in personal tax rates. With defense spending and interest payments rising rapidly and personal income tax rates falling, the government has simply been spending more than it has been collecting in taxes.

THE ECONOMY'S INFLUENCE ON THE GOVERNMENT BUDGET

9. *Automatic stabilizers* are revenue and expenditure items in the federal budget that automatically change with the state of the economy and tend to stabilize GDP. For example, during expansions the government automatically takes in more revenue, because people are making more money that is taxed. Higher income and tax brackets also mean fewer transfer payments.

10. *Fiscal drag* is the negative effect on the economy that occurs when average tax rates increase because taxpayers have moved into higher income brackets during an expansion. These higher taxes reduce disposable income and slow down the expansion. Since 1982, tax brackets have been indexed to inflation, and this has reduced the fiscal drag built into the tax system.

11. The *full-employment budget* is an economist's construction of what the federal budget would be if the economy were producing at a full-employment level of output. The *structural deficit* is the federal deficit that remains even at full employment. *Cyclical deficits* occur when there is a downturn in the business cycle.

REVIEW TERMS AND CONCEPTS

automatic stabilizers, 175
balanced-budget multiplier, 170
budget deficit, 163
cyclical deficit, 176
discretionary fiscal policy, 162
disposable, or after-tax, income (Y_d), 162
federal budget, 172
federal debt, 174
federal surplus (+) or deficit (−), 173
fiscal drag, 175
fiscal policy, 161
full-employment budget, 176
government spending multiplier, 167
monetary policy, 161
net taxes (T), 162
privately held federal debt, 174
structural deficit, 176
tax multiplier, 169

1. Disposable income $Y_d \equiv Y - T$
2. $AE \equiv C + I + G$
3. Government budget deficit $\equiv G - T$
4. Equilibrium in an economy with government: $Y = C + I + G$
5. Leakages/injections approach to equilibrium in an economy with government: $S + T = I + G$
6. Government spending multiplier $\equiv \dfrac{1}{MPS}$
7. Tax multiplier $\equiv -\dfrac{MPC}{MPS}$
8. Balanced-budget multiplier $\equiv 1$

PROBLEM SET

1. You are appointed secretary of the treasury of a recently independent country called Rugaria. The currency of Rugaria is the lav. The new nation began fiscal operations this year and the budget situation is that the government will spend 10 million lavs and taxes will be 9 million lavs. The 1-million-lav difference will be borrowed from the public by selling 10-year government bonds paying 5 percent interest. The interest on the outstanding bonds must be added to spending each year, and we assume that additional taxes are raised to cover that interest. Assuming that the budget stays the same except for the interest on the debt for 10 years, what will be the accumulated debt? What will the size of the budget be after 10 years?

2. In May 2003, the Congress and the president were debating the merits of a cut in taxes. A final tax cut was passed by the Congress and signed by the president later in the year. Research and write a short essay on the final tax bill that was passed in 2003. What taxes were cut? What were the main arguments used in favor of the tax cut? What issues did opponents raise in opposition?

3. Suppose that the government of Lumpland is enjoying a fat budget surplus with fixed government expenditures of $G = 150$ and fixed taxes of $T = 200$. Assume that consumers of Lumpland behave as described in the following consumption function:

$$C = 150 + 0.75(Y - T)$$

Suppose further that investment spending is fixed at 100. Calculate the equilibrium level of GDP in Lumpland. Solve for equilibrium levels of Y, C, and S. Next assume that the Republican Congress in Lumpland succeeds in reducing taxes by 20 to a new fixed level of 180. Recalculate the equilibrium level of GDP using the tax multiplier. Solve for equilibrium levels of Y, C, and S after the tax cut and check to ensure that the multiplier worked. What arguments are likely to be used in support of such a tax cut? What arguments might be used to oppose such a tax cut?

4. For each of the following statements, say whether you agree or disagree and explain your answer:
   a. During periods of budget surplus (when $G < T$), the government debt grows.
   b. A tax cut will increase the equilibrium level of GDP if the budget is in deficit but will decrease the equilibrium level of GDP if the budget is in surplus.
   c. If the $MPS = .90$, the tax multiplier is actually larger than the expenditure multiplier.

5. Define *saving* and *investment.* Data for the simple economy of Newt show that in 2000 saving exceeded investment and the government is running a balanced budget. What is likely to happen? What would happen instead if the government were running a deficit and saving were equal to investment?

6. Expert economists in the economy of Yuk estimate the following:

	BILLION YUKS
Real output/income	1,000
Government purchases	200
Total net taxes	200
Investment spending (planned)	100

Assume that Yukkers consume 75 percent of their disposable incomes and save 25 percent.

a. You are asked by the business editor of the *Yuk Gazette* to predict the events of the next few months. By using the data given, can you make a forecast? (Assume that investment is constant.)

b. If no changes were made, at what level of GDP (Y) would the economy of Yuk settle?

c. Some local conservatives blame Yuk's problems on the size of the government sector. They suggest cutting government purchases by 25 billion Yuks. What effect would such cuts have on the economy? (Be specific.)

7. "A \$1 increase in government spending will raise equilibrium income by more than a \$1 tax cut, yet both have the same impact on the budget deficit. So if we care about the budget deficit, the best way to stimulate the economy is through increases in spending, not cuts in taxes." Comment.

8. Assume that in 1998, the following prevails in the Republic of Nurd:

$Y = \$200$	$G = \$0$
$C = \$160$	$T = \$0$
$S = \$40$	
I (planned) $= \$30$	

Assume that households consume 80 percent of their income, they save 20 percent of their income, $MPC = .8$, and $MPS = .2$. That is, $C = .8Y_d$ and $S = .2Y_d$.

a. Is the economy of Nurd in equilibrium? What is Nurd's equilibrium level of income? What is likely to happen in the coming months if the government takes no action?

b. If \$200 is the "full-employment" level of Y, what fiscal policy might the government follow if its goal is full employment?

c. If the full-employment level of Y is \$250, what fiscal policy might the government follow?

d. Suppose $Y = \$200$, $C = \$160$, $S = \$40$, and $I = \$40$. Is Nurd's economy in equilibrium?

e. Starting with the situation in d., suppose the government starts spending \$30 each year with no taxation and continues to spend \$30 every period. If I remains constant, what will happen to the equilibrium level of Nurd's domestic product (Y)? What will the new levels of C and S be?

f. Starting with the situation in d., suppose the government starts taxing the population \$30 each year without spending anything and continues to tax at that rate every period. If I remains constant, what will happen to the equilibrium level of Nurd's domestic product (Y)? What will be the new levels of C and S? How does your answer to f. differ from your answer to e.? Why?

9. Some economists claim World War II ended the Great Depression of the 1930s. The war effort was financed by borrowing massive sums of money from the public. Explain how a war could end a recession. Look at recent and back issues of the *Economic Report of the President* or the *Statistical Abstract of the United States.* How large was the federal government's debt as a percentage of GDP in 1946? How large is it today?

10. Suppose all tax collections are fixed (instead of dependent on income), and all spending and transfer programs are also fixed (in the sense that they do not depend on the state of the economy, as, e.g., unemployment benefits now do). If this were the case, would there be any automatic stabilizers in the government budget? Would there be any distinction between the full-employment deficit and the actual budget deficit? Explain.

11. Answer the following:

a. $MPS = .4$. What is the government spending multiplier?

b. $MPC = .9$. What is the government spending multiplier?

c. $MPS = .5$. What is the government spending multiplier?

d. $MPC = .75$. What is the tax multiplier?

e. $MPS = .1$. What is the tax multiplier?

f. If the government spending multiplier is 6, what is the tax multiplier?

g. If the tax multiplier is – 2, what is the government spending multiplier?

h. If government purchases and taxes are both increased by \$100 billion simultaneously, what will the effect be on equilibrium output (income)?

Visit www.prenhall.com/casefair for self-test quizzes, interactive graphing exercises, and news articles.

APPENDIX A

DERIVING THE FISCAL POLICY MULTIPLIERS

THE GOVERNMENT SPENDING AND TAX MULTIPLIERS

In the chapter, we noted that the government spending multiplier is $1/MPS$. (This is the same as the investment multiplier.) We can also derive the multiplier algebraically using our hypothetical consumption function:

$$C = a + b(Y - T)$$

where b is the marginal propensity to consume. As you know, the equilibrium condition is:

$$Y = C + I + G$$

By substituting for C, we get:

$$Y = a + b(Y - T) + I + G$$
$$Y = a + bY - bT + I + G$$

This equation can be rearranged to yield:

$$Y - bY = a + I + G - bT$$
$$Y(1 - b) = a + I + G - bT$$

Now solve for Y by dividing through by $(1 - b)$:

$$Y = \frac{1}{(1-b)}(a + I + G - bT)$$

We see from this last equation that if G increases by 1 with the other determinants of Y (a, I, and T) remaining constant, Y increases by $1/(1 - b)$. The multiplier is, as before, simply $1/(1 - b)$, where b is the marginal propensity to consume. Of course, $1 - b$ equals the marginal propensity to save, so the government spending multiplier is $1/MPS$.

We can also derive the tax multiplier. The last equation says that when T increases by \$1, holding a, I, and G constant, income decreases by $b/(1 - b)$ dollars. The tax multiplier is $-b/(1 - b)$, or $-MPC/(1 - MPC) = -MPC/MPS$. (Remember, the negative sign in the resulting tax multiplier shows that it is a *negative* multiplier.)

THE BALANCED-BUDGET MULTIPLIER

It is easy to show formally that the balanced-budget multiplier = 1. When taxes and government spending are simultaneously increased by the same amount, there are two effects on planned aggregate expenditure: one positive and one negative. The initial impact of a balanced-budget increase in government spending and taxes on aggregate expenditure would be the *increase* in government purchases (ΔG) minus the *decrease* in consumption (ΔC) caused by the tax increase. The decrease in consumption brought about by the tax increase is equal to $\Delta C = \Delta T(MPC)$.

increase in spending:	ΔG
−decrease in spending:	$\Delta C = \Delta T(MPC)$
= net increase in spending	$\Delta G - \Delta T(MPC)$

In a balanced-budget increase, $\Delta G = \Delta T$, so we can substitute:

net initial increase in spending:

$$\Delta G - \Delta G(MPC) = \Delta G(1 - MPC)$$

Because $MPS = (1 - MPC)$, the net initial increase in spending is:

$$\Delta G(MPS)$$

We can now apply the expenditure multiplier $\left(\frac{1}{MPS}\right)$ to this net initial increase in spending:

$$\Delta Y = \Delta G(MPS)\left(\frac{1}{MPS}\right) = \Delta G$$

Thus, the final total increase in the equilibrium level of Y is just equal to the initial balanced increase in G and T. That means the balanced-budget multiplier = 1, so the final increase in real output is of the same magnitude as the initial change in spending.

APPENDIX B

THE CASE IN WHICH TAX REVENUES DEPEND ON INCOME

In this chapter, we used the simplifying assumption that the government collects taxes in a lump sum. This made our discussion of the multiplier effects somewhat easier to follow. Now suppose that the government collects taxes not solely as a lump sum that is paid regardless of income, but also partly in the form of a proportional levy against income. This is a more realistic assumption. Typically, tax collections either are based on income (as with the personal income tax) or follow the ups and downs in the economy (as with sales taxes). Instead of setting taxes equal to some fixed amount, let us say that tax revenues depend on income. If we call the amount of net taxes collected T, we can write: $T = T_0 + tY$.

This equation contains two parts. First, we note that net taxes (T) will be equal to an amount T_0 if income (Y) is zero. Second, the tax rate (t) indicates how much net taxes change as income changes. Suppose that T_0 is equal to -200 and t is 1/3. The resulting tax function is $T = -200 + 1/3Y$, which is graphed in Figure 9B.1. Note that when income is zero, the government collects "negative net taxes," which simply means that it makes transfer payments of 200. As income rises, tax collections increase because every extra dollar of income generates \$0.33 in extra revenues for the government.

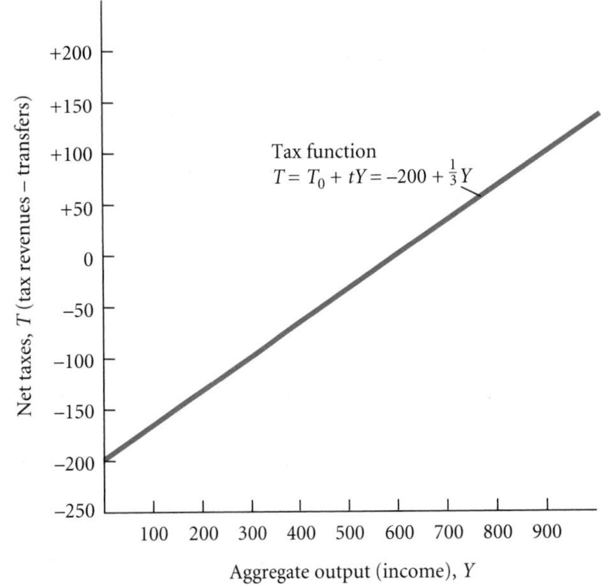

FIGURE 9B.1 The Tax Function

This graph shows net taxes (taxes minus transfer payments) as a function of aggregate income.

How do we incorporate this new tax function into our discussion? All we do is replace the old value of T (in the example in the chapter, T was set equal to 100) with the new value, $-200 + 1/3Y$. Look first at the consumption equation. Consumption (C) still depends on disposable income, as it did before. Also, disposable income is still $Y - T$, or income minus taxes. Instead of disposable income equaling $Y - 100$, however, the new equation for disposable income is:

$$Y_d \equiv Y - T$$
$$Y_d \equiv Y - (-200 + 1/3Y)$$
$$Y_d \equiv Y + 200 - 1/3Y$$

Because consumption still depends on after-tax income, exactly as it did before, we have

$$C = 100 + .75Y_d$$
$$C = 100 + .75(Y + 200 - 1/3Y)$$

Nothing else needs to be changed. We solve for equilibrium income exactly as before, by setting planned aggregate expenditure equal to aggregate output. Recall that planned aggregate expenditure is $C + I + G$, and aggregate output is Y. If we assume, as before, that $I = 100$ and $G = 100$, the equilibrium is:

$$Y = C + I + G$$
$$Y = \underbrace{100 + .75(Y + 200 - 1/3Y)}_{C} + \underbrace{100}_{I} + \underbrace{100}_{G}.$$

This equation may look difficult to solve, but it is not. It simplifies to:

$$Y = 100 + .75Y + 150 - .25Y + 100 + 100$$
$$Y = 450 + .5Y$$
$$.5Y = 450$$

This means that $Y = 450/.5 = 900$, the new equilibrium level of income.

Consider the graphic analysis of this equation as shown in Figure 9B.2 where you should note that when we make taxes a function of income (instead of a lump-sum amount), the AE function becomes *flatter* than it was before. Why? When tax collections do not depend on income, an increase in income of $1 means disposable income also increases by a dollar. Because taxes are a constant amount, adding more income does not raise the amount of taxes paid. Disposable income therefore changes dollar-for-dollar with any change in income.

When taxes depend on income, a $1 increase in income does not increase disposable income by a full dollar, because some of the additional dollar goes to pay extra taxes. Under the modified tax function of Figure 9B.2, an extra dollar of income will increase disposable income by only $0.67, because $0.33 of the extra dollar goes to the government in the form of taxes.

No matter how taxes are calculated, the marginal propensity to consume out of disposable (or after-tax) income is the same—each extra dollar of disposable income will increase consumption spending by $0.75. However, a $1 change in before-tax income does not have the same effect on disposable income in each case. Suppose we were to increase income by $1. With the lump-sum tax function, disposable income would rise by $1, and consumption would increase by the *MPC* times the change in Y_d, or $0.75. When taxes depend on income, disposable income would rise by only $0.67 from the $1 increase in income, and consumption would rise by only the *MPC* times the change in disposable income, or $0.75 × .67 = $0.50.

If a $1 increase in income raises expenditure by $0.75 in one case, and by only $0.50 in the other, the second aggregate expenditure function must be flatter than the first.

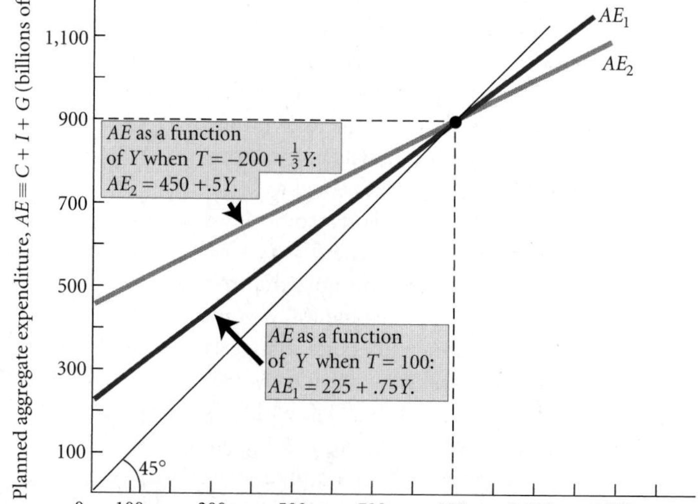

FIGURE 9B.2 Different Tax Systems

When taxes are strictly lump sum ($T = 100$) and do not depend on income, the aggregate expenditure function is steeper than when taxes depend on income.

THE GOVERNMENT SPENDING AND TAX MULTIPLIERS ALGEBRAICALLY

All this means that if taxes are a function of income, the three multipliers (investment, government spending, and tax) are less than they would be if taxes were a lump-sum amount. By using the same linear consumption function we used in Chapters 7 and 8, we can derive the multiplier:

$$C = a + b(Y - T)$$
$$C = a + b(Y - T_0 - tY)$$
$$C = a + bY - bT_0 - btY$$

We know that $Y = C + I + G$. Through substitution we get:

$$Y = \underbrace{a + bY - bT_0 - btY}_{C} + I + G$$

Solving for Y:

$$Y = \frac{1}{1 - b + bt}(a + I + G - bT_0)$$

This means that a $1 increase in G or I (holding a and T_0 constant) will increase the equilibrium level of Y by:

$$\frac{1}{1 - b + bt}$$

If $b = MPC = .75$ and $t = .20$, the spending multiplier is 2.5. (Compare this to 4, which would be the value of the spending multiplier if taxes were a lump sum, i.e., if $t = 0$.)

Holding a, I, and G constant, a fixed or lump-sum tax cut (a cut in T_0) will increase the equilibrium level of income by:

$$\frac{b}{1 - b + bt}$$

Thus, if $b = MPC = .75$ and $t = .20$, the tax multiplier is -1.875. (Compare this to -3, which would be the value of the tax multiplier if taxes were a lump sum.)

SUMMARY

1. When taxes depend on income, a $1 increase in income does not increase disposable income by a full dollar, because some of the additional dollar must go to pay extra taxes. This means that if taxes are a function of income, the three multipliers (investment, government spending, and tax) are less than they would be if taxes were a lump-sum amount.

PROBLEM SET

1. Given the following for the economy of a country:
   a. Consumption function: $C = 85 + 0.5Y_d$
   b. Investment function: $I = 85$
   c. Government spending: $G = 60$
   d. Net taxes: $T = -40 + 0.25Y$
   e. Disposable income: $Y_d \equiv Y - T$
   f. Equilibrium: $Y = C + I + G$

   Solve for equilibrium income. (*Hint*: Be very careful in doing the calculations. They are not difficult, but it is easy to make careless mistakes that produce very wrong results.) How much does the government collect in net taxes when the economy is in equilibrium? What is the government's budget deficit or surplus?

The Money Supply and the Federal Reserve System

10

CHAPTER OUTLINE

In the last two chapters, we explored how consumers, firms, and the government interact in the goods market. In this chapter and the next we show how money markets work in the macroeconomy. We begin with what money is and the role it plays in the U.S. economy. We then discuss the forces that determine the supply of money and show how banks create money. Finally, we discuss the workings of the nation's central bank, the Federal Reserve (the Fed), and the tools at its disposal to control the money supply.

Microeconomics has little to say about money. Microeconomic theories and models are concerned primarily with *real* quantities (apples, oranges, hours of labor) and *relative* prices (the price of apples relative to the price of oranges, or the price of labor relative to the prices of other goods). Most of the key ideas in microeconomics do not require that we know anything about money. As we shall see, this is not the case in macroeconomics.

AN OVERVIEW OF MONEY

You often hear people say things like, "He makes a lot of money" (in other words, "He has a high income") or "She's worth a lot of money" (meaning "She is very wealthy"). It is true that your employer uses money to pay you your income, and your wealth may be accumulated in the form of money. However, *money is not income, and money is not wealth.*

To see that money and income are not the same, think of a $20 bill. That bill may pass through a thousand hands in a year, yet never be used to pay anyone a salary. Suppose I get a $20 bill from an automatic teller machine, and I spend it on dinner. The restaurant puts that $20 bill in a bank in the next day's deposit. The bank gives it to a woman cashing a check the following day; she spends it at a baseball game that night. The bill has been through many hands but not as part of anyone's income.

WHAT IS MONEY?

We will soon get to a formal definition of money, but let us start out with the basic idea of what money is.

Money is anything that is generally accepted as a medium of exchange.

Most people take the ability to obtain and use money for granted. When the whole monetary system works well, as it generally does in the United States, the basic mechanics of the system are virtually invisible. People take for granted that they can walk into any store, restaurant, boutique, or gas station and buy whatever they want, as long as they have enough green pieces of paper.

The idea that you can buy things with money is so natural and obvious that it seems absurd to mention it, but stop and ask yourself: "How is it that a shop owner is willing to part with a steak and a loaf of bread that I can eat in exchange for some pieces of paper that are intrinsically worthless?" Why, on the other hand, are there times and places where it takes a shopping cart full of money to purchase a dozen eggs? The answers to these questions lie in what money is: a means of payment, a store of value, and a unit of account.

A Means of Payment, or Medium of Exchange Money is vital to the working of a market economy. Imagine what life would be like without it. The alternative to a monetary economy is **barter**, people exchanging goods and services for other goods and services directly instead of exchanging via the medium of money.

barter The direct exchange of goods and services for other goods and services.

How does a barter system work? Suppose you want bacon, eggs, and orange juice for breakfast. Instead of going to the store and buying these things with money, you would have to find someone who has these items and is willing to trade them. You would also have to have something the bacon seller, the orange juice purveyor, and the egg vendor want. Having pencils to trade will do you no good if the bacon, orange juice, and egg sellers do not want pencils.

A barter system requires a *double coincidence of wants* for trade to take place. That is, to effect a trade, I have to find someone who has what I want, and that person must also want what I have. Where the range of goods traded is small, as it is in relatively unsophisticated economies, it is not difficult to find someone to trade with, and barter is often used. In a complex society with many goods, barter exchanges involve an intolerable amount of effort. Imagine trying to find people who offer for sale all the things you buy in a typical trip to the grocery store, and who are willing to accept goods that you have to offer in exchange for their goods.

medium of exchange, or **means of payment** What sellers generally accept and buyers generally use to pay for goods and services.

Some agreed-to **medium of exchange** (or, **means of payment**) neatly eliminates the double-coincidence-of-wants problem. Under a monetary system, money is exchanged for goods or services when people buy things; goods or services are exchanged for money when people sell things. No one ever has to trade goods for other goods directly. Money is a lubricant in the functioning of a market economy.

A Store of Value Economists have identified other roles for money aside from its primary function as a medium of exchange. Money also serves as a **store of value**—an asset that can be used to transport purchasing power from one time period to another. If you raise chickens and at the end of the month sell them for more than you want to spend and consume immediately, you may keep some of your earnings in the form of money until the time you want to spend it.

store of value An asset that can be used to transport purchasing power from one time period to another.

There are many other stores of value besides money. You could have decided to hold your "surplus" earnings by buying such things as antique paintings, baseball cards, or diamonds, which you could sell later when you want to spend your earnings. Money has several advantages over these other stores of value. First, it comes in convenient denominations and is easily portable. You do not have to worry about making change for a Renoir painting to buy a gallon of gasoline. Second, because money is also a means of payment, it is easily exchanged for goods at all times. (A Renoir is not easily exchanged for other goods.) These two factors compose the **liquidity property of money**. Money is easily spent, flowing out of your hands like liquid. Renoirs and ancient Aztec statues are neither convenient nor portable and are not readily accepted as a means of payment.

liquidity property of money The property of money that makes it a good medium of exchange as well as a store of value: It is portable and readily accepted and thus easily exchanged for goods.

The main disadvantage of money as a store of value is that the value of money falls when the prices of goods and services rise. If the price of potato chips rises from $1 per bag to $2 per bag, the value of a dollar bill, in terms of potato chips, falls from one bag to half a bag. When this happens, it may be better to use potato chips (or antiques or real estate) as a store of value.

A Unit of Account Money also serves as a **unit of account**—a consistent way of quoting prices. All prices are quoted in monetary units. A textbook is quoted as costing $90, not 150 bananas or 5 DVDs, and a banana is quoted as costing 60 cents, not 1.4 apples or 6 pages of a textbook.

unit of account A standard unit that provides a consistent way of quoting prices.

Obviously, a standard unit of account is extremely useful when quoting prices. This function of money may have escaped your notice—what else would people quote prices in except money?

COMMODITY AND FIAT MONIES

Some of Yap's stone money wheels are so large that they are never moved.

Introductory economics textbooks are full of stories about the various items that have been used as money by various cultures—candy bars, cigarettes (in World War II prisoner-of-war camps), huge wheels of carved stone (on the island of Yap in the South Pacific), cowrie shells (in West Africa), beads (among North American Indians), cattle (in southern Africa), and small green scraps of paper (in contemporary North America). The list goes on. These various kinds of money are generally divided into two groups, commodity monies and fiat money.

Commodity monies are those items used as money that also have an intrinsic value in some other use. For example, prisoners of war made purchases with cigarettes, quoted prices in terms of cigarettes, and held their wealth in the form of accumulated cigarettes. Of course, cigarettes could also be smoked—they had an alternative use apart from serving as money. Gold represents another form of commodity money. For hundreds of years gold could be used directly to buy things, but it also had other uses, ranging from jewelry to dental fillings.

By contrast, money in the United States today is mostly fiat money. **Fiat money**, sometimes called **token money**, is money that is intrinsically worthless. The actual value of a 1-, 10-, or 50-dollar bill is basically zero; what other uses are there for a small piece of paper with some green ink on it?

Why would anyone accept worthless scraps of paper as money instead of something that has some value, such as gold, cigarettes, or cattle? If your answer is "Because the paper money is backed by gold or silver," you are wrong. There was a time when dollar bills were convertible directly into gold. The government backed each dollar bill in circulation by holding a certain amount of gold in its vaults. If the price of gold were $35 per ounce, for example, the government agreed to sell one ounce of gold for 35 dollar bills. However, dollar bills are no longer backed by any commodity—gold, silver, or anything else. They are exchangeable only for dimes, nickels, pennies, other dollars, and so on.

commodity monies Items used as money that also have intrinsic value in some other use.

fiat, or token, money Items designated as money that are intrinsically worthless.

The public accepts paper money as a means of payment and a store of value because the government has taken steps to ensure that its money is accepted. The government declares its paper money to be **legal tender**. That is, the government declares that its money must be accepted in settlement of debts. It does this by fiat (hence *fiat money*). It passes laws defining certain pieces of paper printed in certain inks on certain plates to be legal tender, and that is that. Printed on every Federal Reserve note in the United States is "This note is legal tender for all debts, public and private." Often, the government can get a start on gaining acceptance for its paper money by requiring that it be used to pay taxes. (Note that you cannot use chickens, baseball cards, or Renoir paintings to pay your taxes, only checks or currency.)

legal tender Money that a government has required to be accepted in settlement of debts.

Aside from declaring its currency legal tender, the government usually does one other thing to ensure that paper money will be accepted: It promises the public that it will not print paper money so fast that it loses its value. Expanding the supply of currency so rapidly that it loses much of its value has been a problem throughout history and is known as **currency debasement**. Debasement of the currency has been a special problem of governments that lack the strength to take the politically unpopular step of raising taxes. Printing money to be used on government expenditures of goods and services can serve as a substitute for tax increases, and weak governments have often relied on the printing press to finance their expenditures. A recent example is Bulgaria, where the inflation rate hit a record of 1,268 percent in 1997. We will discuss money and inflation at great length in later chapters.

currency debasement The decrease in the value of money that occurs when its supply is increased rapidly.

MEASURING THE SUPPLY OF MONEY IN THE UNITED STATES

We now turn to the various kinds of money in the United States. Recall that money is used: to buy things (a means of payment); to hold wealth (a store of value); and to quote prices (a unit of account). Unfortunately, these characteristics apply to a broad range of assets in the

U.S. economy. As we will see, it is not at all clear where we should draw the line and say, "Up to this is money, beyond this is something else."

To solve the problem of multiple monies, economists have given different names to different measures of money. The two most common measures of money are transactions money, also called *M*1, and broad money, also called *M*2.

_M1_: Transactions Money What should be counted as money? Coins and dollar bills, as well as higher denominations of currency, must be counted as money—they fit all the requirements. What about checking accounts? Checks, too, can be used to buy things and can serve as a store of value. In fact, bankers call checking accounts *demand deposits*, because depositors have the right to go to the bank and cash in (demand) their entire checking account balances at any time. That makes your checking account balance virtually equivalent to bills in your wallet, and it should be included as part of the amount of money you hold.

If we take the value of all currency (including coins) held outside of bank vaults and add to it the value of all demand deposits, traveler's checks, and other checkable deposits, we have defined ***M*1**, or **transactions money**. As its name suggests, this is the money that can be directly used for transactions—to buy things.

***M*1, or transactions money** Money that can be directly used for transactions.

*M*1 ≡ currency held outside banks + demand deposits + traveler's checks + other checkable deposits

A *checkable deposit* is any deposit account with a bank or other financial institution on which a check can be written. Checkable deposits include demand deposits; *negotiable order of withdrawal (NOW) accounts*, which are like checking accounts that pay interest; and *automatic-transfer savings (ATS) accounts*, which automatically transfer funds from savings to checking (or vice versa) when the balance on one of those accounts reaches a predetermined level.

*M*1 on July 28, 2003, was $1,292.4 billion. *M*1 is a stock measure—it is measured at a point in time. It is the total amount of coins and currency outside of banks and the total dollar amount in checking accounts *on a specific day*. Until now, we have considered supply as a flow—a variable with a time dimension: the quantity of wheat supplied *per year*, the quantity of automobiles supplied to the market *per year*, and so forth. However, *M*1 is a stock variable.

_M2_: Broad Money Although *M*1 is the most widely used measure of the money supply, there are others. Should savings accounts be considered money? Many of these accounts cannot be used for transactions directly, but it is easy to convert them into cash or to transfer funds from a savings account into a checking account. What about money market accounts (which allow only a few checks per month but pay market-determined interest rates) and money market mutual funds (which sell shares and use the proceeds to purchase short-term securities)? These can be used to write checks and make purchases, although only over a certain amount.

If we add **near monies**, close substitutes for transactions money, to *M*1, we get ***M*2**, called **broad money** because it includes not-quite-money monies such as savings accounts, money market accounts, and other near monies.

near monies Close substitutes for transactions money, such as savings accounts and money market accounts.

***M*2, or broad money** *M*1 plus savings accounts, money market accounts, and other near monies.

*M*2 ≡ *M*1 + savings accounts + money market accounts + other near monies

On July 28, 2003, *M*2 was $6,021.3 billion, considerably larger than the total *M*1 of $1,292.4 billion. The main advantage of looking at *M*2 instead of *M*1 is that *M*2 is sometimes more stable. For instance, when banks introduced new forms of interest-bearing checking accounts in the early 1980s, *M*1 shot up as people switched their funds from savings accounts to checking accounts. However, *M*2 remained fairly constant because the fall in savings account deposits and the rise in checking account balances were both part of *M*2, canceling each other out.

Beyond _M2_ Because a wide variety of financial instruments bear some resemblance to money, some economists have advocated including almost all of them as part of the money supply. In recent years, for example, credit cards have come to be used extensively in exchange. Everyone who has a credit card has a credit limit—you can charge only a certain amount on your card before you have to pay it off. Usually we pay our credit card bills with a check. One of the very broad definitions of money includes the amount of available credit on credit cards (your charge limit minus what you have charged but not paid) as part of the money supply.

There are no rules for deciding what is money and what is not. This poses problems for economists and those in charge of economic policy. However, *for our purposes here, "money" will always refer to transactions money, or M1.* For simplicity, we will say that *M*1 is the sum of two *general* categories: currency in circulation and deposits. Keep in mind, however, that *M*1 has *four* specific components: currency held outside banks, demand deposits, travelers checks, and other checkable deposits.

THE PRIVATE BANKING SYSTEM

Most of the money in the United States today is "bank money" of one sort or another. *M*1 is made up largely of checking account balances instead of currency, and currency makes up an even smaller part of *M*2 and other broader definitions of money. Any understanding of money requires some knowledge of the structure of the private banking system.

Banks and banklike institutions borrow from individuals or firms with excess funds and lend to those who need funds. For example, commercial banks receive funds in various forms, including deposits in checking and savings accounts. They take these funds and loan them out in the form of car loans, mortgages, commercial loans, and so forth. Banks and banklike institutions are called **financial intermediaries** because they "mediate," or act as a link between people who have funds to lend and those who need to borrow.

financial intermediaries Banks and other institutions that act as a link between those who have money to lend and those who want to borrow money.

The main types of financial intermediaries are commercial banks, followed by savings and loan associations, life insurance companies, and pension funds. Since about 1970, the legal distinctions between the different types of financial intermediaries have narrowed considerably. It used to be, for example, that checking accounts could be held only in commercial banks and that commercial banks could not pay interest on checking accounts. Savings and loan associations were prohibited from offering certain kinds of deposits and were restricted primarily to making loans for mortgages.

The Depository Institutions Deregulation and Monetary Control Act, enacted by Congress in 1980, eliminated many of the previous restrictions on the behavior of financial institutions. Many types of institutions now offer checking accounts, and interest is paid on many types of checking accounts. Savings and loan associations now make loans for many things besides home mortgages. The Sears Financial Network is one of a number of financial service firms offering, under one roof, a wide variety of services that used to be offered by separate providers such as banks, brokerage houses, insurance companies, and financial planners.

HOW BANKS CREATE MONEY

So far we have described the general way that money works and the way the supply of money is measured in the United States, but how much money is there available at a given time? Who supplies it, and how does it get supplied? We are now ready to analyze these questions in detail. In particular, we want to explore a process that many find mysterious: the way banks *create money.*

A HISTORICAL PERSPECTIVE: GOLDSMITHS

To begin to see how banks create money, consider the origins of the modern banking system. In the fifteenth and sixteenth centuries, citizens of many lands used gold as money, particularly for large transactions. Because gold is both inconvenient to carry around and susceptible to theft, people began to place their gold with goldsmiths for safekeeping. On receiving the gold, a goldsmith would issue a receipt to the depositor, charging him a small fee for looking after his gold. After a time, these receipts themselves, rather than the gold that they represented, began to be traded for goods. The receipts became a form of paper money, making it unnecessary to go to the goldsmith to withdraw gold for a transaction.

News Analysis

A Cashless Society in Russia, 1997

THE "CASHLESS SOCIETY" HAS MEANT DIFFERENT things at different times in history. The following article from the *Economist* highlights the situation in Russia in the 1990s.

The Cashless Society

—Economist

When Americans talk of the "cashless" society it conjures up images of credit cards, debit cards, Internet transactions, electronic bill paying, and so forth. Although about 80 percent of the 360 billion transactions in the United States each year are paid for with cash, the majority of which are under $20, the trend is toward on-line transfers via the computer and toward plastic cards.

However, when the Russians talk of the cashless society, they mean there is no money. Because the majority of people still work for the government in Russia, and the government is broke, millions of workers across the country have been going without cash wages for some time. How do they survive? The firms pay people in kind and they engage in barter.

The Russian-European Center for Economic Policy, a monitoring organization sponsored by the European Union, estimated that the proportion of industrial sales in Russia settled with barter rose from about 10 percent in 1993 to 40 percent in 1996. One car company is said to pay nine-tenths of its bills with finished automobiles.

In some parts of what was Russia, "Cashless Society" is literally what it says—no money. Without currency, workers may be paid in what they produce, such as the coffins "paid" to workers in Siberia in 1997.

Stories about individual household transactions abound. Siberian workers in 1997 were paid in coffins; workers at a factory in Volgograd were paid in bras. In Altai, Siberia, a local theater charged two eggs for admission, and when eggs ran out, tickets became denominated in empty bottles.

Source: "The Cashless Society," Economist, March 15, 1997.

Visit www.prenhall.com/casefair for updated articles and exercises.

At this point, all the receipts issued by goldsmiths were backed 100 percent by gold. If a goldsmith had 100 ounces of gold in his safe, he would issue receipts for 100 ounces of gold, and no more. Goldsmiths functioned as warehouses where people stored gold for safekeeping. The goldsmiths found, however, that people did not come often to withdraw gold. Why should they, when paper receipts that could easily be converted to gold were "as good as gold"? (In fact, receipts were better than gold—more portable, safer from theft, and so on.) As a result, goldsmiths had a large stock of gold continuously on hand.

Because they had what amounted to "extra" gold sitting around, goldsmiths gradually realized that they could lend out some of this gold without any fear of running out of gold. Why would they do this? Because instead of just keeping their gold idly in their vaults, they earned interest on loans. Something subtle, but dramatic, happened at this point. The goldsmiths changed from mere depositories for gold into banklike institutions that had the power to create money. This transformation occurred as soon as goldsmiths began making loans. Without adding any more real gold to the system, the goldsmiths increased the amount of money in circulation by creating additional claims to gold—that is, receipts, which entitled the bearer to receive a certain number of ounces of gold on demand.[1] Thus there were more claims than there were ounces of gold.

A detailed example may help to clarify this. Suppose you go to a goldsmith who is functioning only as a depository, or warehouse, and ask for a loan to buy a plot of land that costs

[1]Remember, these receipts circulated as money, and people used them to make transactions without feeling the need to cash them in—that is, to exchange them for gold itself.

20 ounces of gold. Also suppose that the goldsmith has 100 ounces of gold on deposit in his safe and receipts for exactly 100 ounces of gold out to the various people who deposited the gold. If the goldsmith decides he is tired of being a mere goldsmith and wants to become a real bank, he will loan you some gold. You don't want the gold itself, of course; rather, you want a slip of paper that represents 20 ounces of gold. The goldsmith in essence "creates" money for you by giving you a receipt for 20 ounces of gold (even though his entire supply of gold already belongs to various other people).[2] When he does, there will be receipts for 120 ounces of gold in circulation instead of the 100 ounces worth of receipts before your loan, and the supply of money will have increased.

People think the creation of money is mysterious. Far from it! The creation of money is simply an accounting procedure, among the most mundane of human endeavors. You may suspect the whole process is fundamentally unsound, or somehow dubious. After all, the banking system began when someone issued claims for gold that already belonged to someone else. Here you may be on slightly firmer ground.

Goldsmiths-turned-bankers did face certain problems. Once they started making loans, their receipts outstanding (claims on gold) were greater than the amount of gold they had in their vaults at any given moment. If the owners of the 120 ounces worth of gold receipts all presented their receipts and demanded their gold at the same time, the goldsmith would be in trouble. With only 100 ounces of gold on hand, people could not get their gold at once.

In normal times, people would be happy to hold receipts instead of real gold, and this problem would never arise. If, however, people began to worry about the goldsmith's financial safety, they might begin to have doubts about whether their receipts really were as good as gold. Knowing there were more receipts outstanding than there were ounces of gold in the goldsmith's vault, people might start to demand gold for receipts.

This situation leads to a paradox. It makes perfect sense to hold paper receipts (instead of gold) if you know you can always get gold for your paper. In normal times, goldsmiths could feel perfectly safe in loaning out more gold than they actually had in their possession. But once you (and everyone else) start to doubt the safety of the goldsmith, then you (and everyone else) would be foolish not to demand your gold back from the vault.

A **run** on a goldsmith (or in our day, a **run on a bank**) occurs when many people present their claims at the same time. These runs tend to feed on themselves. If I see you going to the goldsmith to withdraw your gold, I may become nervous and decide to withdraw my gold as well. It is the *fear* of a run that usually causes the run. Runs on a bank can be triggered by a variety of causes: rumors that an institution may have made loans to borrowers who cannot repay, wars, failures of other institutions that have borrowed money from the bank, and so on. As you will see later in this chapter, today's bankers differ from goldsmiths—today's banks are subject to a "required reserve ratio." Goldsmiths had no legal reserve requirements, although the amount that they loaned out was subject to the restriction imposed on them by their fear of running out of gold.

run on a bank Occurs when many of those who have claims on a bank (deposits) present them at the same time.

THE MODERN BANKING SYSTEM

To understand how the modern banking system works, you need to be familiar with some basic principles of accounting. Once you are comfortable with the way banks keep their books, the whole process of money creation will seem logical.

A Brief Review of Accounting Central to accounting practices is the statement that "the books always balance." In practice, this means that if we take a snapshot of a firm—any firm, including a bank—at a particular moment in time, then by definition:

$$\text{Assets} - \text{Liabilities} \equiv \text{Net Worth, or}$$
$$\text{Assets} \equiv \text{Liabilities} + \text{Net Worth}$$

Assets are things a firm owns that are worth something. For a bank, these assets include the bank building, its furniture, its holdings of government securities, cash in its vaults,

[2]In return for lending you the receipt for 20 ounces of gold, the goldsmith expects to get an IOU promising to repay the amount (in gold itself or with a receipt from another goldsmith) with interest after a certain period of time.

bonds, stocks, and so forth. Most important among a bank's assets, for our purposes at least, are its *loans.* A borrower gives the bank an *IOU,* a promise to repay a certain sum of money on or by a certain date. This promise is an asset of the bank because it is worth something. The bank could (and sometimes does) sell the IOU to another bank for cash.

Federal Reserve System (the Fed) The central bank of the United States.

Other bank assets include cash on hand (sometimes called *vault cash*) and deposits with the United States' central bank—the **Federal Reserve Bank (the Fed).** As we will see later in this chapter, federal banking regulations require that banks keep a certain portion of their deposits on hand as vault cash or on deposit with the Fed.

A firm's *liabilities* are its debts—what it owes. A bank's liabilities are the promises to pay, or IOUs, that it has issued. A bank's most important liabilities are its deposits. *Deposits* are debts owed to the depositors, because when you deposit money in your account, you are in essence making a loan to the bank.

The basic rule of accounting says that if we add up a firm's assets and then subtract the total amount it owes to all those who have lent it funds, the difference is the firm's net worth. *Net worth* represents the value of the firm to its stockholders or owners. How much would you pay for a firm that owns $200,000 of diamonds and had borrowed $150,000 from a bank to pay for them? The firm is worth $50,000—the difference between what it owns and what it owes. If the price of diamonds were to fall, bringing their value down to only $150,000, the firm would be worth nothing.

We can keep track of a bank's financial position using a simplified balance sheet called a T-account. By convention, the bank's assets are listed on the left side of the T-account and its liabilities and net worth, on the right side. By definition, the balance sheet always balances, so that the sum of the items on the left side of the T-account is exactly equal to the sum of the items on the right side.

reserves The deposits that a bank has at the Federal Reserve bank plus its cash on hand.

The T-account in Figure 10.1 shows a bank having $110 million in *assets,* of which $20 million are **reserves,** the deposits that the bank has made at the Fed, and its cash on hand (coins and currency). Reserves are an asset to the bank because it can go to the Fed and get cash for them, just the way you can go to the bank and get cash for the amount in your savings account. Our bank's other asset is its loans, worth $90 million.

required reserve ratio The percentage of its total deposits that a bank must keep as reserves at the Federal Reserve.

Why do banks hold reserves/deposits at the Fed? There are many reasons, but perhaps the most important is the legal requirement that they hold a certain percentage of their deposit liabilities as reserves. The percentage of its deposits that a bank must keep as reserves is known as the **required reserve ratio.** If the reserve ratio is 20 percent, then a bank with deposits of $100 million must hold $20 million as reserves, either as cash or as deposits at the Fed. To simplify, we will assume that banks hold all of their reserves in the form of deposits at the Fed.

On the liabilities side of the T-account, the bank has taken deposits of $100 million, so it owes this amount to its depositors. This means that the bank has a net worth of $10 million to its owners ($110 million in assets – $100 million in liabilities = $10 million net worth). The net worth of the bank is what "balances" the balance sheet. Remember:

> When some item on a bank's balance sheet changes, there must be at least one other change somewhere else to maintain balance.

If a bank's reserves increase by $1, then one of the following must also be true: (1) its other assets (e.g., loans) decrease by $1; (2) its liabilities (deposits) increase by $1; or (3) its net worth increases by $1. Various fractional combinations of these are also possible.

FIGURE 10.1 T-Account for a Typical Bank (millions of dollars)

The balance sheet of a bank must always balance, so that the sum of assets (reserves and loans) equals the sum of liabilities (deposits and net worth).

	Assets	Liabilities	
Reserves	20	100	Deposits
Loans	90	10	Net worth
Total	110	110	Total

THE CREATION OF MONEY

Like the goldsmiths, today's bankers seek to earn income by lending money out at a higher interest rate than they pay depositors for use of their money.

In modern times, the chances of a run on a bank are fairly small; and, even if there is a run, the central bank protects the private banks in various ways. Therefore:

> Banks usually make loans up to the point where they can no longer do so because of the reserve requirement restriction.

A bank's required amount of reserves is equal to the required reserve ratio times the total deposits in the bank. If a bank has deposits of $100 and the required ratio is 20 percent, the required amount of reserves is $20. The difference between a bank's actual reserves and its required reserves is its **excess reserves**:

excess reserves The difference between a bank's actual reserves and its required reserves.

> excess reserves ≡ actual reserves − required reserves

If banks make loans up to the point where they can no longer do so because of the reserve requirement restriction, this means that banks make loans up to the point where their excess reserves are zero.

To see why, note that when a bank has excess reserves, it has credit available, and it can make loans. Actually, a bank can make loans *only* if it has excess reserves. When a bank makes a loan, it creates a demand deposit for the borrower. This creation of a demand deposit causes the bank's excess reserves to fall because the extra deposits created by the loan use up some of the excess reserves the bank has on hand. An example will help demonstrate this.

Assume there is only one private bank in the country, the required reserve ratio is 20 percent, and the bank starts off with nothing, as shown in panel 1 of Figure 10.2. Now suppose dollar bills are in circulation and someone deposits 100 of them in the bank. The bank deposits the $100 with the central bank, so it now has $100 in reserves, as shown in panel 2. The bank now has assets (reserves) of $100 and liabilities (deposits) of $100. If the required reserve ratio is 20 percent, the bank has excess reserves of $80.

How much can the bank lend and still meet the reserve requirement? For the moment, let us suppose anyone who gets a loan keeps the entire proceeds in the bank or pays them to someone else who does. Nothing is withdrawn as cash. In this case, the bank can lend $400 and still meet the reserve requirement. Panel 3 shows the balance sheet of the bank after completing the maximum amount of loans it is allowed with a 20 percent reserve ratio. With $80 of excess reserves, the bank can have up to $400 of additional deposits. The $100 in reserves plus $400 in loans (which are made as deposits) equal $500 in deposits. With $500 in deposits and a required reserve ratio of 20 percent, the bank must have reserves of $100 (20 percent of $500)—and it does. The bank can lend no more than $400 because its reserve requirement must not exceed $100. When a bank has no excess reserves and thus can make no more loans, it is said to be *loaned up*.

Remember, the money supply ($M1$) equals cash in circulation plus deposits. Before the initial deposit, the money supply was $100 ($100 cash and no deposits). After the deposit and the loans, the money supply is $500 (no cash outside of bank vaults and $500 in

Panel 1		Panel 2		Panel 3	
Assets	Liabilities	Assets	Liabilities	Assets	Liabilities
Reserves 0	0 Deposits	Reserves 100	100 Deposits	Reserves 100 Loans 400	500 Deposits

FIGURE 10.2 Balance Sheets of a Bank in a Single-Bank Economy

In panel 2, there is an initial deposit of $100. In panel 3, the bank has made loans of $400.

deposits). It is clear, then, that when loans are converted into deposits, the supply of money can change.

The bank whose T-accounts are presented in Figure 10.2 is allowed to make loans of $400 based on the assumption that loans that are made *stay in the bank* in the form of deposits. Now suppose I borrow from the bank to buy a personal computer, and I write a check to the computer store. If the store also deposits its money in the bank, my check merely results in a reduction in my account balance and an increase to the store's account balance within the bank. No cash has left the bank. As long as the system is closed in this way—remember that we have so far assumed that there is only one bank—the bank knows that it will never be called on to release any of its $100 in reserves. It can expand its loans up to the point where its total deposits are $500.

Of course, there are many banks in the country, a situation that is depicted in Figure 10.3. As long as the banking system as a whole is closed, it is still possible for an initial deposit of $100 to result in an expansion of the money supply to $500, but more steps are involved when there is more than one bank.

To see why, assume Mary makes an initial deposit of $100 in bank 1, and the bank deposits the entire $100 with the Fed (panel 1 of Figure 10.3). All loans that a bank makes are withdrawn from the bank as the individual borrowers write checks to pay for merchandise. After Mary's deposit, bank 1 can make a loan of up to $80 to Bill, because it needs to keep only $20 of its $100 deposit as reserves. (We are assuming a 20 percent required reserve ratio.) In other words, bank 1 has $80 in excess reserves.

Bank 1's balance sheet at the moment of the loan to Bill appears in panel 2 of Figure 10.3. Bank 1 now has loans of $80. It has credited Bill's account with the $80, so its total deposits are $180 ($80 in loans plus $100 in reserves). Bill then writes a check for $80 for a set of shock absorbers for his car. Bill wrote his check to Sam's Car Shop, and Sam deposits Bill's check in bank 2. When the check clears, bank 1 transfers $80 in reserves to bank 2. Bank 1's balance sheet now looks like the top of panel 3. Its assets include reserves of $20 and loans of $80; its liabilities are $100 in deposits. Both sides of the T-account balance: The bank's reserves are 20 percent of its deposits, as required by law, and it is fully loaned up.

	Panel 1		Panel 2		Panel 3	
	Assets	Liabilities	Assets	Liabilities	Assets	Liabilities
Bank 1	Reserves 100	100 Deposits	Reserves 100 Loans 80	180 Deposits	Reserves 20 Loans 80	100 Deposits
Bank 2	Reserves 80	80 Deposits	Reserves 80 Loans 64	144 Deposits	Reserves 16 Loans 64	80 Deposits
Bank 3	Reserves 64	64 Deposits	Reserves 64 Loans 51.20	115.20 Deposits	Reserves 12.80 Loans 51.20	64 Deposits

Summary:	Loans	Deposits
Bank 1	80	100
Bank 2	64	80
Bank 3	51.20	64
Bank 4	40.96	51.20
⋮	⋮	⋮
Total	400.00	500.00

FIGURE 10.3 The Creation of Money When There Are Many Banks

In panel 1, there is an initial deposit of $100 in bank 1. In panel 2, bank 1 makes a loan of $80 by creating a deposit of $80. A check for $80 by the borrower is then written on bank 1 (panel 3) and deposited in bank 2 (panel 1). The process continues with bank 2 making loans, and so on. In the end, loans of $400 have been made, and the total level of deposits is $500.

Now look at bank 2. Because bank 1 has transferred $80 in reserves to bank 2, it now has $80 in deposits and $80 in reserves (panel 1, bank 2). Its reserve requirement is also 20 percent, so it has excess reserves of $64 on which it can make loans.

Now assume bank 2 loans the $64 to Kate to pay for a textbook and Kate writes a check for $64 payable to the Manhattan College Bookstore. The final position of bank 2, after it honors Kate's $64 check by transferring $64 in reserves to the bookstore's bank, is reserves of $16, loans of $64, and deposits of $80 (panel 3, bank 2).

The Manhattan College Bookstore deposits Kate's check in its account with bank 3. Bank 3 now has excess reserves, because it has added $64 to its reserves. With a reserve ratio of 20 percent, bank 3 can loan out $51.20 (80 percent of $64, leaving 20 percent in required reserves to back the $64 deposit).

As the process is repeated over and over, the total amount of deposits created is $500, the sum of the deposits in each of the banks. Because the banking system can be looked on as one big bank, the outcome here for many banks is the same as the outcome in Figure 10.2 for one bank.[3]

THE MONEY MULTIPLIER

In practice, the banking system is not completely closed—there is some leakage out of the system. Still, the point here is:

An increase in bank reserves leads to a greater than one-for-one increase in the money supply. Economists call the relationship between the final change in deposits and the change in reserves that caused this change the **money multiplier**. Stated somewhat differently, the money multiplier is the multiple by which deposits can increase for every dollar increase in reserves.

money multiplier The multiple by which deposits can increase for every dollar increase in reserves; equal to one divided by the required reserve ratio.

Do not confuse the money multiplier with the spending multipliers we discussed in the last two chapters. They are not the same thing.

In the example we just examined, reserves increased by $100 when the $100 in cash was deposited in a bank, and the amount of deposits increased by $500 ($100 from the initial deposit, $400 from the loans made by the various banks from their excess reserves). The money multiplier in this case is $500/$100 = 5. Mathematically, the money multiplier can be defined as:

$$\text{money multiplier} \equiv \frac{1}{\text{required reserve ratio}}$$

In the United States, the required reserve ratio varies, depending on the size of the bank and the type of deposit. For large banks and for checking deposits, the ratio is currently 10 percent, which makes the potential money multiplier 1/.10 = 10.0. This means that an increase in reserves of $1 could cause an increase in deposits of $10 if there were no leakage out of the system.

THE FEDERAL RESERVE SYSTEM

We have seen how the private banking system creates money by making loans. However, private banks are not free to create money at will. Their ability to create money is controlled by the volume of reserves in the system, which is controlled by the Fed. The Fed, therefore, has the ultimate control over the money supply. We will now examine the structure and function of the Fed.

Founded in 1913 by an act of Congress (to which major reforms were added in the 1930s), the Fed is the central bank of the United States. The Fed is a complicated institution

[3]If banks create money when they make loans, does repaying a loan "destroy" money? The answer is yes.

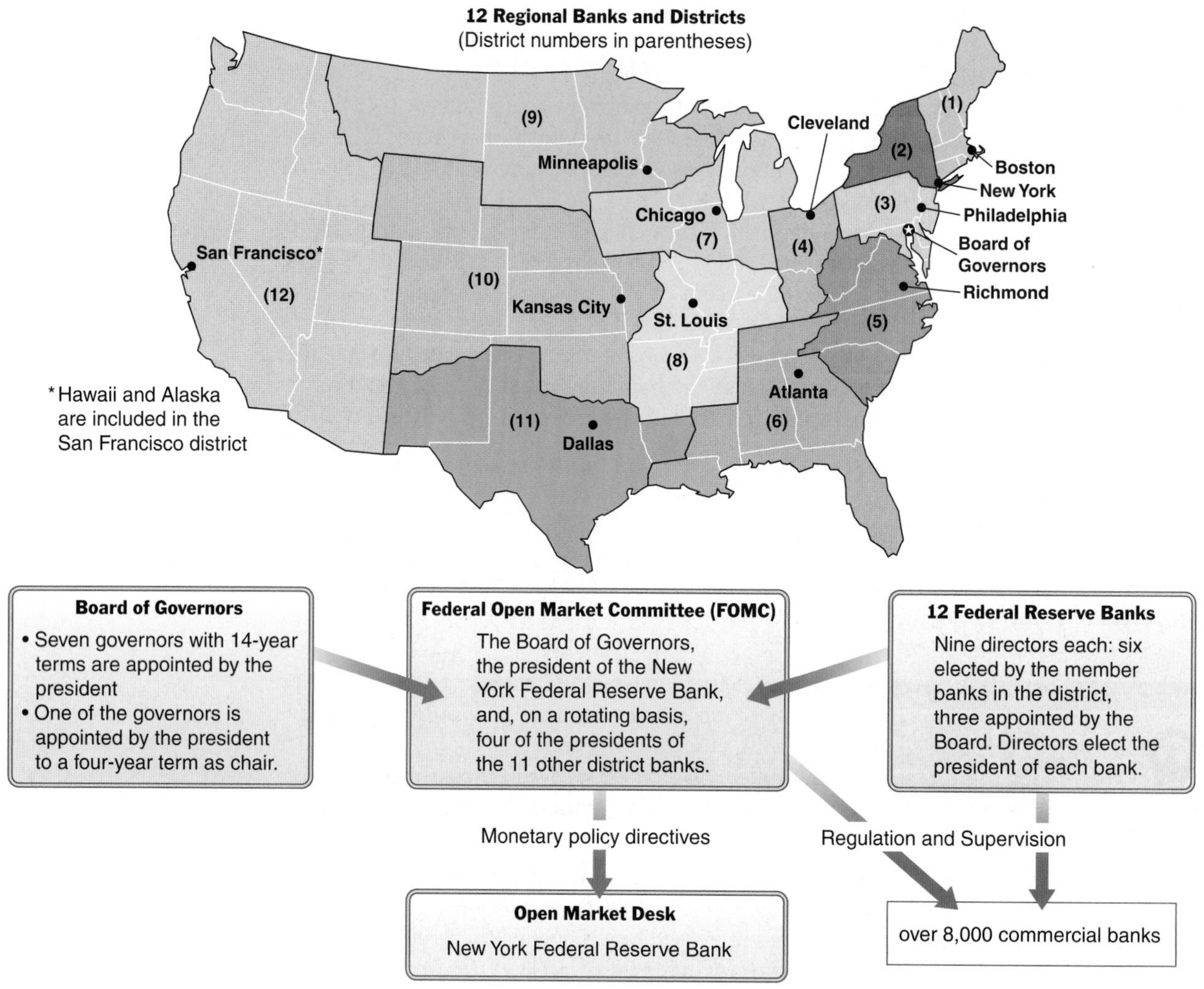

FIGURE 10.4 The Structure of the Federal Reserve System

with many responsibilities, including the regulation and supervision of over 8,000 commercial banks. The organization of the Federal Reserve System is presented in Figure 10.4.

The *Board of Governors* is the most important group within the Federal Reserve System. The board consists of seven members, each appointed for 14 years by the president of the United States. The *chair* of the Fed, who is appointed by the president and whose term runs for 4 years, usually dominates the entire Federal Reserve System and is sometimes said to be the second most powerful person in the United States. The Fed is an independent agency in that it does not take orders from the president or from Congress.

Federal Open Market Committee (FOMC) A group composed of the seven members of the Fed's Board of Governors, the president of the New York Federal Reserve Bank, and 4 of the other 11 district bank presidents on a rotating basis; it sets goals concerning the money supply and interest rates and directs the operation of the Open Market Desk in New York.

Open Market Desk The office in the New York Federal Reserve Bank from which government securities are bought and sold by the Fed.

The United States is divided into 12 Federal Reserve districts, each with its own Federal Reserve bank. These districts are indicated on the map in Figure 10.4. The district banks are like branch offices of the Fed in that they carry out the rules, regulations, and functions of the central system in their districts and report to the Board of Governors on local economic conditions.

U.S. monetary policy—the behavior of the Fed concerning the money supply—is formally set by the **Federal Open Market Committee (FOMC)**. The FOMC consists of the seven members of the Fed's Board of Governors, the president of the New York Federal Reserve Bank, and, on a rotating basis, four of the presidents of the 11 other district banks. The FOMC sets goals concerning the money supply and interest rates, and it directs the **Open Market Desk** in the New York Federal Reserve Bank to buy and/or sell government securities. (We discuss the specifics of open market operations later in this chapter.)

FUNCTIONS OF THE FEDERAL RESERVE

The Fed is the central bank of the United States. Central banks are sometimes known as "bankers's banks" because only banks (and occasionally foreign governments) can have accounts in them. As a private citizen, you cannot go to the nearest branch of the Fed and open a checking account or apply to borrow money.

Although from a macroeconomic point of view the Fed's crucial role is to control the money supply, the Fed also performs several important functions for banks. These functions include clearing interbank payments, regulating the banking system, and assisting banks in a difficult financial position. The Fed is also responsible for managing exchange rates and the nation's foreign exchange reserves.[4] In addition, it is often involved in intercountry negotiations on international economic issues.

Clearing Interbank Payments Suppose you write a $100 check, drawn on your bank, the First Bank of Fresno (FBF), to pay for tulip bulbs from Crockett Importers of Miami, Florida. Because Crockett Importers does not bank at FBF, but at Banco de Miami, how does your money get from your bank to the bank in Florida?

The answer: The Fed does it. Both FBF and Banco de Miami have accounts at the Fed. When Crockett Importers receives your check and deposits it at the Banco de Miami, the bank submits the check to the Fed, asking it to collect the funds from FBF. The Fed presents the check to FBF and is instructed to debit FBF's account for the $100 and to credit the account of Banco de Miami. Accounts at the Fed count as reserves, so FBF loses $100 in reserves and Banco de Miami gains $100 in reserves. The two banks effectively have traded ownerships of their deposits at the Fed. The *total* volume of reserves has not changed, nor has the money supply.

This function of clearing interbank payments allows banks to shift money around virtually instantaneously. All they need to do is wire the Fed and request a transfer, and the funds move at the speed of electricity from one computer account to another.

Other Duties of the Fed Besides facilitating the transfer of funds between banks, the Fed performs several other important duties. It is responsible for many of the regulations governing banking practices and standards. For example, the Fed has the authority to control mergers between banks, and it is responsible for examining banks to ensure they are financially sound and they conform to a host of government accounting regulations. As we saw earlier, the Fed also sets reserve requirements for all financial institutions.

One of the most important responsibilities of the Fed is to act as the **lender of last resort** for the banking system. As our discussion of goldsmiths suggested, banks are subject to the possibility of runs on their deposits. In the United States, most deposits of less than $100,000 are insured by the Federal Deposit Insurance Corporation (FDIC). Deposit insurance makes panics less likely. Because depositors know they can always get their money, even if the bank fails, they are less likely to withdraw their deposits. Not all deposits are insured, so the possibility of bank panics remains. However, the Fed stands ready to provide funds to a troubled bank that cannot find any other sources of funds.

lender of last resort One of the functions of the Fed: It provides funds to troubled banks that cannot find any other sources of funds.

The Fed is the ideal lender of last resort for two reasons. First, providing funds to a bank that is in dire straits is risky and not likely to be very profitable, and it is hard to find private banks or other private institutions willing to do this. The Fed is a nonprofit institution whose function is to serve the overall welfare of the public. Thus, the Fed would certainly be interested in preventing catastrophic banking panics such as those that occurred in the late 1920s and the 1930s.

Second, the Fed has an essentially unlimited supply of funds with which to bail out banks facing the possibility of runs. The reason, as we shall see, is that the Fed can create reserves at will. A promise by the Fed that it will support a bank is very convincing. Unlike any other lender, the Fed can never run out of money. Therefore, the explicit or implicit support of the Fed should be enough to assure depositors they are in no danger of losing their funds.

---

[4] *Foreign exchange reserves* are holdings of the currencies of other countries—for example, Japanese yen—by the U.S. government. We discuss exchange rates and foreign exchange markets at length in Chapter 21.

News Analysis

Central Banks Worry About Inflation and Deflation in 2003

BRAZIL HAS THE HIGHEST INFLATION IN THE world and the United States has practically none. The following two articles from the New York Times reflect the differences in interest rates and interest rate policies of two large and powerful central banks.

Brazil: Concern About Inflation—New York Times

Brazil's central bank said rising prices remained a threat and required close monitoring even though inflation had slowed recently. At its monthly Monetary Policy Committee meeting, the bank said inflation expectations had improved significantly since mid-March but the rate at which consumer prices were stabilizing merited careful monitoring. "Doubts remain regarding the speed at which inflation is falling and regarding the temporary nature of inflation's persistence," the minutes of the meeting said. Citing high inflation, the bank left its benchmark interest rate unchanged last week at 26.5 percent a year, already among the highest in the world.

Source: Adapted from: "World Business Briefing—Americas: Brazil: Concern About Inflation," New York Times, *May 13, 2003. Reprinted by permission.*

Fed Is Starting to Fret Over Falling Prices

—New York Times

In deciding this week to keep short-term interest rates at 1.25 percent, the Federal Reserve Board warned of "an unwelcome substantial fall in inflation." The topic also came up at its March meeting, according to minutes released yesterday. Economists have been talking about the dangers of falling prices for several months, but why did the Fed take note now?

First of all, some experts believe that the risk of deflation has increased of late. Commodity prices have been dropping for years, but now energy prices, after a spike leading up to the war in Iraq, have also slipped.

Most important, however, is the absence of an engine to drive the economy forward. With weak demand, prices could begin to fall in widespread fashion.

Though it took no action on Tuesday, several Wall Street banks expect it to cut short-term interest rates to 0.75 percent before July. As short-term rates edge closer to zero, expanding the money supply—the method the Fed uses for lowering rates—might have little effect on the ease of obtaining credit. Interest rates could not fall below zero, after all.

Falling prices might not sound like such a bad thing, at least from a consumer's point of view. Moreover, deflation can be a side effect of a healthy economic development, like the surges in efficiency that have steadily lowered the prices of personal computers.

But what the Fed is worried about now, the experts said, is deflation arising as a symptom of the economy's frailty. And falling prices could cause some real problems by themselves.

For example, rapid deflation can cause a huge redistribution of income and wealth from debtors to creditors, said Willem H. Buiter, a former member of the Bank of England's monetary policy committee.

Source: Adapted from: Daniel Altman, "Fed Is Starting to Fret Over Falling Prices," New York Times, *May 9, 2003. Reprinted by permission.*

Visit www.prenhall.com/casefair for updated articles and exercises.

THE FEDERAL RESERVE BALANCE SHEET

Although it is a special bank, the Fed is in some ways similar to an ordinary commercial bank. Like an ordinary bank, the Fed has a balance sheet that records its asset and liability position at any moment in time. The balance sheet for the Fed is presented in Table 10.1.

As the asset side of the balance sheet shows, the Fed owns about $11 billion of gold. *Do not think that this gold has anything to do with the supply of money.* Most of the gold was acquired during the 1930s, when it was purchased from the U.S. Treasury Department. Since 1934, the dollar has not been backed by (not convertible into) gold. You cannot take a dollar bill to the Fed to receive gold for it; all you can get for your old dollar bill is a new

TABLE 10.1 Assets and Liabilities of the Federal Reserve System, March 31, 2003 (millions of dollars)

ASSETS		LIABILITIES	
Gold	$ 11,038	$652,467	Federal Reserve notes (outstanding)
Loans to banks	31,780		Deposits:
U.S. Treasury securities	641,464	26,787	Bank reserves (from depository institutions)
		6,746	U.S. Treasury
All other assets	44,192	42,474	All other liabilities and net worth
Total	$728,474	$728,474	Total

Source: Federal Reserve Bulletin, June 2003, Table 1.18.

dollar bill.[5] Although it is unrelated to the money supply, the Fed's gold counts as an asset on its balance sheet, because it is something of value the Fed owns.

The balance sheet mentions an asset called "loans to banks." These loans are an asset of the Fed in the same way a private commercial bank's loans are among its assets. The Fed sometimes makes loans to commercial banks that are short of reserves.[6] The $31,780 billion in Table 10.1 represents these kinds of loans.

The largest of the Fed's assets by far consists of government (U.S. Treasury) securities: about $641 billion worth at the end of March 2003. Government securities are obligations of the federal government, such as Treasury bills and bonds, which the Fed has purchased over the years. The way in which these bonds are acquired has important implications for the Fed's control of the money supply. (We return to this topic after our survey of the Fed's balance sheet.)

The bulk of the Fed's liabilities are Federal Reserve notes. The dollar bill you use to buy a quart of milk is clearly an asset from your point of view—it is something you own that has value. Because every financial asset is by definition a liability of some other agent in the economy, whose liability is that dollar bill? That dollar bill, and bills of all other denominations in the economy, are a liability—an IOU—of the Fed. They are rather strange IOUs, because all they can be redeemed for are other IOUs of exactly the same type. They are, nonetheless, classified as liabilities of the Fed.

The balance sheet shows that, like an ordinary commercial bank, the Fed has accepted deposits. These deposits are liabilities. The bulk of the Fed's deposits come from commercial banks. Remember, commercial banks are required to keep a certain share of their own deposits as deposits at the Fed. A bank's deposits at the Fed (its reserves) are an asset from the bank's point of view, and those same reserves must be a liability from the Fed's point of view.

Table 10.1 shows the Fed has accepted a small volume of deposits from the U.S. Treasury. In effect, the Fed acts as the bank for the U.S. government. When the government needs to pay for something like a new aircraft carrier, it may write out a check to the supplier of the ship drawn on its "checking account" at the Fed. Similarly, when the government receives revenues from tax collections, fines, or sales of government assets, it may deposit these funds in its account at the Fed.

HOW THE FEDERAL RESERVE CONTROLS THE MONEY SUPPLY

To see how the Fed controls the supply of money in the U.S. economy we need to understand the role of reserves. As we have said, the required reserve ratio establishes a link between the reserves of the commercial banks and the deposits (money) that commercial banks are allowed to create.

The reserve requirement effectively determines how much a bank has available to lend. If the required reserve ratio is 20 percent, each $1 of reserves can support $5 in deposits. A bank that has reserves of $100,000 cannot have more than $500,000 in deposits. If it did, it would fail to meet the required reserve ratio.

If you recall that the *money supply* is equal to the sum of deposits inside banks and the currency in circulation outside of banks, you can see that reserves provide the leverage that the Fed needs to control the money supply.

> If the Fed wants to increase the supply of money, it creates more reserves, thereby freeing banks to create additional deposits by making more loans. If it wants to decrease the money supply, it reduces reserves.

[5]The fact that the Fed is not obliged to provide gold for currency means it can never go bankrupt. When the currency was backed by gold, it would have been possible for the Fed to run out of gold if too many of its depositors came to it at the same time and asked to exchange their deposits for gold. If depositors come to the Fed to withdraw their deposits today, all they can get are dollar bills. The dollar was convertible into gold internationally until August 15, 1971.

[6]Recall that commercial banks are required to keep a set percentage of their deposit liabilities on deposit at the Fed. If a bank suddenly finds itself short of reserves, one of its alternatives is to borrow the reserves it needs from the Fed.

Three tools are available to the Fed for changing the money supply: (1) changing the required reserve ratio; (2) changing the discount rate; and (3) engaging in open market operations. Although (3) is almost exclusively used to change the money supply, an understanding of how (1) and (2) work is useful in understanding how (3) works. We thus begin our discussion with the first two tools.

THE REQUIRED RESERVE RATIO

One way for the Fed to alter the supply of money is to change the required reserve ratio. This process is shown in Table 10.2. Let us assume the initial required reserve ratio is 20 percent.

In panel 1, a simplified version of the Fed's balance sheet (in billions of dollars) shows that reserves are $100 billion and currency outstanding is $100 billion. The total value of the Fed's assets is $200 billion, which we assume to be all in government securities. Assuming there are no excess reserves—banks stay fully loaned up—the $100 billion in reserves supports $500 billion in deposits at the commercial banks. [Remember, the money multiplier equals 1/required reserve ratio = 1/.20 = 5. Thus, $100 billion in reserves can support $500 billion ($100 billion × 5) in deposits when the required reserve ratio is 20 percent.] The supply of money (*M*1, or transactions money) is therefore $600 billion: $100 billion in currency and $500 billion in (checking account) deposits at the commercial banks.

Now suppose the Fed wants to increase the supply of money to $900 billion. If it lowers the required reserve ratio from 20 percent to 12.5 percent (as in panel 2 of Table 10.2), then the same $100 billion of reserves could support $800 billion in deposits instead of only $500 billion. In this case, the money multiplier is 1/.125, or 8. At a required reserve ratio of 12.5 percent, $100 billion in reserves can support $800 billion in deposits. The total money supply would be $800 billion in deposits plus the $100 billion in currency, for a total of $900 billion.[7]

Put another way, with the new lower reserve ratio, banks have excess reserves of $37.5 billion. At a required reserve ratio of 20 percent, they needed $100 billion in reserves to back their $500 billion in deposits. At the lower required reserve ratio of 12.5 percent, they need only $62.5 billion of reserves to back their $500 billion of deposits, so the remaining $37.5 billion of the existing $100 billion in reserves are "extra." With that $37.5 billion of excess reserves, banks can lend out more money. If we assume the system loans money and creates deposits to the *maximum* extent possible, the $37.5 billion of reserves will support an additional $300 billion of deposits ($37.5 billion × the money multiplier of 8 = $300 billion). The change in the required reserve ratio has injected an additional $300 billion into the banking

TABLE 10.2 A Decrease in the Required Reserve Ratio from 20 Percent to 12.5 Percent Increases the Supply of Money (All Figures in Billions of Dollars)

PANEL 1: REQUIRED RESERVE RATION = 20%

Federal Reserve Assets		Federal Reserve Liabilities		Commercial Banks Assets		Commercial Banks Liabilities	
Government securities	$200	$100	Reserves	Reserves	$100	$500	Deposits
		$100	Currency	Loans	$400		

Note: Money supply (*M*1) = Currency + Deposits = $600.

PANEL 2: REQUIRED RESERVE RATIO = 12.5%

Federal Reserve Assets		Federal Reserve Liabilities		Commercial Banks Assets		Commercial Banks Liabilities	
Government securities	$200	$100	Reserves	Reserves	$100	$800	Deposits (+$300)
		$100	Currency	Loans (+$300)	$700		

Note: Money supply (*M*1) = Currency + Deposits = $900.

[7]To find the maximum volume of deposits (D) that can be supported by an amount of reserves (R), divide R by the required reserve ratio. If the required reserve ratio is g, because $R = gD$, then $D = R/g$.

system, at which point the banks will be fully loaned up and unable to increase their deposits further.

Decreases in the required reserve ratio allow banks to have more deposits with the existing volume of reserves. As banks create more deposits by making loans, the supply of money (currency + deposits) increases. The reverse is also true: If the Fed wants to restrict the supply of money, it can raise the required reserve ratio, in which case banks will find that they have insufficient reserves and must therefore reduce their deposits by "calling in" some of their loans.[8] The result is a decrease in the money supply.

For many reasons, the Fed has tended not to use changes in the reserve requirement to control the money supply. In part, this reluctance stems from the era when only some banks were members of the Fed and, therefore, subject to reserve requirements. The Fed reasoned that if it raised the reserve requirement to contract the money supply, banks might choose to stop being members. (Because reserves pay no interest, the higher the reserve requirement, the more the penalty imposed on those banks holding reserves.) This argument no longer applies. Since the passage of the Depository Institutions Deregulation and Monetary Control Act in 1980, all depository institutions are subject to Fed requirements.

It is also true that changing the reserve requirement ratio is a crude tool. Because of lags in banks' reporting to the Fed on their reserve and deposit positions, a change in the requirement today does not affect banks for about 2 weeks. (However, the fact that changing the reserve requirement expands or reduces credit in every bank in the country makes it a very powerful tool when the Fed does use it.)

THE DISCOUNT RATE

discount rate Interest rate that banks pay to the Fed to borrow from it.

Banks may borrow from the Fed. The interest rate they pay the Fed is the **discount rate.** When banks increase their borrowing, the money supply increases. To see why this is true, assume there is only one bank in the country and the required reserve ratio is 20 percent. The initial position of the bank and the Fed appear in panel 1 of Table 10.3, where the money supply (currency + deposits) is $480. In panel 2, the bank has borrowed $20 from the Fed. By

TABLE 10.3 The Effect on the Money Supply of Commercial Bank Borrowing from the Fed (All Figures in Billions of Dollars)

PANEL 1: NO COMMERCIAL BANK BORROWING FROM THE FED

Federal Reserve				Commercial Banks			
Asset		Liabilities		Assets		Liabilities	
Securities	$160	$80	Reserves	Reserves	$80	$400	Deposits
		$80	Currency	Loans	$320		

Note: Money supply (*M1*) = Currency + Deposits = $480.

PANEL 2: COMMERCIAL BANK BORROWING $20 FROM THE FED

Federal Reserve				Commercial Banks			
Assets		Liabilities		Assets		Liabilities	
Securities	$160	$100	Reserves (+$20)	Reserves (+$20)	$100	$500	Deposits (+$300)
Loans	$20	$80	Currency	Loans (+$100)	$420	$20	Amount owed to Fed (+$20)

Note: Money supply (*M1*) = Currency + Deposits = $580.

[8]Banks never really have to "call in" loans before they are due, to reduce the money supply. First, the Fed is almost always expanding the money supply slowly because the real economy grows steadily and, as we shall see, growth brings with it the need for more circulating money. So when we speak of "contractionary monetary policy," we mean the Fed is slowing down the rate of money growth, not reducing the money supply. Second, even if the Fed were actually to cut reserves (instead of curb their expansion), banks would no doubt be able to comply by reducing the volume of new loans they make while old ones are coming due.

using this $20 as a reserve, the bank can increase its loans by $100, from $320 to $420. (Remember, a required reserve ratio of 20 percent gives a money multiplier of 5; having excess reserves of $20 allows the bank to create an additional $20 × 5, or $100, in deposits.) The money supply has thus increased from $480 to $580. Therefore:

Bank borrowing from the Fed leads to an increase in the money supply.

The Fed can influence bank borrowing, and thus the money supply, through the discount rate:

The higher the discount rate, the higher the cost of borrowing, and the less borrowing banks will want to do.

If the Fed wants to curtail the growth of the money supply, for example, it raises the discount rate and discourages banks from borrowing from it, restricting the growth of reserves (and ultimately deposits).

Historically, the Fed has not used the discount rate to control the money supply. Prior to 2003 it usually set the discount rate lower than the rate that banks had to pay to borrow money in the private market. Although this obviously provided an incentive for banks to borrow from the Fed, the Fed discouraged borrowing by putting pressure in various ways on the banks not to borrow. This pressure was sometimes called **moral suasion.**

moral suasion The pressure that in the past the Fed exerted on member banks to discourage them from borrowing heavily from the Fed.

On January 9, 2003, the Fed announced a new procedure. Henceforth the discount rate would be set above the rate that banks pay to borrow money in the private market, and moral suasion would no longer be used. Although banks can now borrow from the Fed if they wish to, they are unlikely to do so except in unusual circumstances because borrowing is cheaper in the private market. It is thus clear that the Fed is not using the discount rate as a tool to try to change the money supply on a regular basis.

OPEN MARKET OPERATIONS

open market operations The purchase and sale by the Fed of government securities in the open market; a tool used to expand or contract the amount of reserves in the system and thus the money supply.

By far the most significant of the Fed's tools for controlling the supply of money is **open market operations**. Congress has authorized the Fed to buy and sell U.S. government securities in the open market. When the Fed purchases a security, it pays for it by writing a check that, when cleared, *expands* the quantity of reserves in the system, increasing the money supply. When the Fed sells a bond, private citizens or institutions pay for it with a check that, when cleared, *reduces* the quantity of reserves in the system.

To see how open market transactions and reserve controls work, we need to review several key ideas.

Two Branches of Government Deal in Government Securities The fact that the Fed is able to buy and sell government securities—bills and bonds—may confuse students. In fact, *two* branches of government deal in financial markets for different reasons, and you must keep the two separate in your mind.

First, keep in mind that the Treasury Department is responsible for collecting taxes and paying the federal government's bills. Salary checks paid to government workers, payments to General Dynamics for a new Navy ship, social security checks to retirees, and so forth are all written on accounts maintained by the Treasury. Tax receipts collected by the Internal Revenue Service, a Treasury branch, are deposited to these accounts.

If total government spending exceeds tax receipts, the law requires the Treasury to borrow the difference. Recall that the government deficit is $(G - T)$, or government purchases minus net taxes. $(G - T)$ is the amount the Treasury must borrow each year to finance the deficit. This means:

The Treasure *cannot* print money to finance the deficit.

The Treasury borrows by issuing bills, bonds, and notes that pay interest. These government securities, or IOUs, are sold to individuals and institutions. Often foreign countries, as well as U.S. citizens, buy them. As discussed in Chapter 9, the total amount of privately held government securities is the *privately held federal debt.*

The Fed is not the Treasury. Instead, it is a quasi-independent agency authorized by Congress to buy and sell *outstanding* (preexisting) U.S. government securities on the open market. The bonds and bills initially sold by the Treasury to finance the deficit are continuously resold and traded among ordinary citizens, firms, banks, pension funds, and so forth. The Fed's participation in that trading affects the quantity of reserves in the system, as we will see.

Because the Fed owns some government securities, some of what the government owes, it owes to itself. Recall that the Federal Reserve System's largest single asset is government securities. These securities are nothing more than bills and bonds initially issued by the Treasury to finance the deficit. They were acquired by the Fed over time through direct open market purchases that the Fed made to expand the money supply as the economy expanded.

The Mechanics of Open Market Operations How do open market operations affect the money supply? Look again at Table 10.1. As you can see, most of the Fed's assets consist of the government securities we have just been talking about.

Suppose the Fed wants to decrease the supply of money. If it can reduce the volume of bank reserves on the liabilities side of its balance sheet, it will force banks in turn to reduce their own deposits (to meet the required reserve ratio). Since these deposits are part of the supply of money, the supply of money will contract.

What will happen if the Fed sells some of its holdings of government securities to the general public? The Fed's holdings of government securities must decrease, because the securities it sold will now be owned by someone else. How do the purchasers of securities pay for what they have bought? By writing checks drawn on their banks and payable to the Fed.

Let us look more carefully at how this works, with the help of Table 10.4. In panel 1, the Fed initially has $100 billion of government securities. Its liabilities consist of $20 billion of deposits (which are the reserves of commercial banks) and $80 billion of currency. With the required reserve ratio at 20 percent, the $20 billion of reserves can support $100 billion of deposits in the commercial banks. The commercial banking system is fully loaned up. Panel 1

TABLE 10.4 Open Market Operations (The Numbers in Parentheses in Panels 2 and 3 Show the Differences Between Those Panels and Panel 1. All Figures in Billions of Dollars)

PANEL 1

Federal Reserve: Assets		Federal Reserve: Liabilities		Commercial Banks: Assets		Commercial Banks: Liabilities		Jane Q. Public: Assets		Jane Q. Public: Liabilities	
Securities	$100	$20	Reserves	Reserves	$20	$100	Deposits	Deposits	$5	$0	Debts
		$80	Currency	Loans	$80					$5	Net Worth

Note: Money supply (*M*1) = Currency + Deposits = $180.

PANEL 2

Federal Reserve: Assets		Federal Reserve: Liabilities		Commercial Banks: Assets		Commercial Banks: Liabilities		Jane Q. Public: Assets		Jane Q. Public: Liabilities	
Securities (−$5)	$95	$15	Reserves (−$5)	Reserves (−$5)	$15	$95	Deposits (−$5)	Deposits (−$5)	$0	$0	Debts
		$80	Currency	Loans	$80			Securities (+$5)	$5	$5	Net Worth

Note: Money supply (*M*1) = Currency + Deposits = $175.

PANEL 3

Federal Reserve: Assets		Federal Reserve: Liabilities		Commercial Banks: Assets		Commercial Banks: Liabilities		Jane Q. Public: Assets		Jane Q. Public: Liabilities	
Securities (−$5)	$95	$15	Reserves (−$5)	Reserves (−$5)	$15	$75	Deposits (−$25)	Deposits (−$5)	$0	$0	Debts
		$80	Currency	Loans (−$20)	$60			Securities (+$5)	$5	$5	Net Worth

Note: Money supply (*M*1) = Currency + Deposits = $155.

also shows the financial position of a private citizen, Jane Q. Public. Jane has assets of $5 billion (a large checking account deposit in the bank) and no debts, so her net worth is $5 billion.

Now imagine that the Fed sells $5 billion in government securities to Jane. Jane pays for the securities by writing a check to the Fed, drawn on her bank. The Fed then reduces the reserve account of her bank by $5 billion. The balance sheets of all the participants after this transaction are shown in panel 2. Note that the supply of money (currency plus deposits) has fallen from $180 billion to $175 billion.

This is not the end of the story. As a result of the Fed's sale of securities, the amount of reserves has fallen from $20 billion to $15 billion, while deposits have fallen from $100 billion to $95 billion. With a required reserve ratio of 20 percent, banks must have .20 × $95 billion, or $19 billion in reserves. Banks are under their required reserve ratio by $4 billion [$19 billion (the amount they should have) minus $15 billion (the amount they do have)]. To comply with the federal regulations, banks must decrease their loans and their deposits.[9]

The final equilibrium position is shown in panel 3, where commercial banks have reduced their loans by $20 billion. Notice that the change in deposits from panel 1 to panel 3 is $25 billion, which is five times the size of the change in reserves that the Fed brought about through its $5 billion open market sale of securities. This corresponds exactly to our earlier analysis of the money multiplier. The change in money (–$25 billion) is equal to the money multiplier (5) times the change in reserves (–$5 billion).

Now consider what happens when the Fed *purchases* a government security. Suppose I hold $100 in Treasury bills, which the Fed buys from me. The Fed writes me a check for $100, and I turn in my Treasury bills. I then take the $100 check and deposit it in my local bank. This increases the reserves of my bank by $100 and begins a new episode in the money expansion story. With a reserve requirement of 20 percent, my bank can now lend out $80. If that $80 is spent and ends up back in a bank, that bank can lend $64, and so forth. (Review Figure 10.3.) The Fed can expand the money supply by buying government securities from people who own them, just the way it reduces the money supply by selling these securities.

Each business day, the Open Market Desk in the New York Federal Reserve Bank buys or sells millions of dollars' worth of securities, usually to large security dealers who act as intermediaries between the Fed and the private markets. We can sum up the effect of these open market operations this way:

- An open market *purchase* of securities by the Fed results in an increase in reserves and an *increase* in the supply of money by an amount equal to the money multiplier times the change in reserves.
- An open market *sale* of securities by the Fed results in a *decrease* in reserves and a *decrease* in the supply of money by an amount equal to the money multiplier times the change in reserves.

Open market operations are the Fed's preferred means of controlling the money supply for several reasons. First, open market operations can be used with some precision. If the Fed needs to change the money supply by just a small amount, it can buy or sell a small volume of government securities. If it wants a larger change in the money supply, it can buy or sell a larger amount. Second, open market operations are extremely flexible. If the Fed decides to reverse course, it can easily switch from buying securities to selling them. Finally, open market operations have a fairly predictable effect on the supply of money. Because banks are obliged to meet their reserve requirements, an open market sale of $100 in government securities will reduce reserves by $100, which will reduce the supply of money by $100 times the money multiplier.

Where does the Fed get the money to buy government securities when it wants to expand the money supply? The Fed creates it. In effect, it tells the bank from which it has bought a $100 security that its reserve account (deposit) at the Fed now contains $100 more than it did previously. This is where the power of the Fed, or any central bank, lies. The Fed has the ability to create money at will. In the United States, the Fed exercises this power when it creates money to buy government securities.

---

[9]Once again, banks never really have to call in loans. Loans and deposits would probably be reduced by slowing the rate of new lending as old loans come due and are paid off.

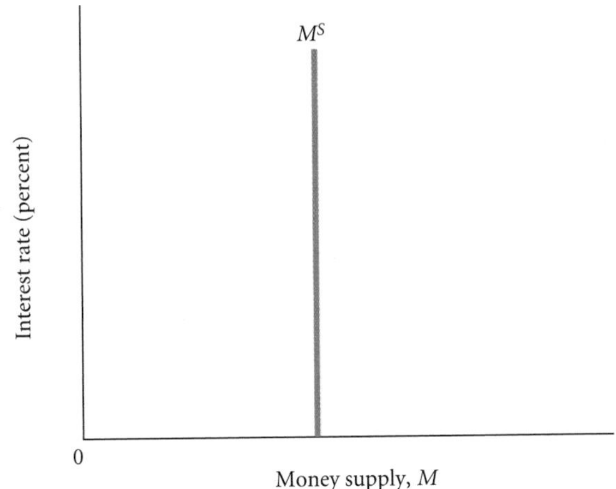

FIGURE 10.5 The Supply of Money

If the Fed's money supply behavior is not influenced by the interest rate, the money supply curve is a vertical line. Through open market operations the Fed can have the money supply be whatever value it wants.

THE SUPPLY CURVE FOR MONEY

Thus far we know how the Fed can control the money supply by controlling the amount of reserves in the economy. If the Fed wants the quantity of money to be $1,200 billion on a given date, it can aim for this target by changing the discount rate, by changing the required reserve ratio, or by engaging in open market operations. In this sense, the supply of money is completely determined by the Fed, and the money supply curve in Figure 10.5 is a vertical line.

Because the Fed, through open market operations, can choose whatever value of the money supply that it wants, it is useful to begin with the case in which the Fed picks a value independent of anything in the economy. In other words, we are assuming for now that the Fed's choice of the value of the money supply does not depend on things like inflation, unemployment, and aggregate output. This assumption is relaxed in Chapter 15. We will see in Chapter 15 that in practice the Fed chooses a value of the money supply to hit a particular value of the interest rate, where the Fed's choice for the target interest rate depends on things like inflation and unemployment. But this is jumping ahead of the story.

LOOKING AHEAD

This chapter has discussed only the supply side of the money market. We have seen what money is, how banks create money by making loans, and how the Fed controls the money supply. In the next chapter we turn to the demand side of the money market. We will examine the demand for money and how the supply of, and demand for, money determine the equilibrium interest rate.

SUMMARY

AN OVERVIEW OF MONEY

1. Money has three distinguishing characteristics: (1) a means of payment, or medium of exchange; (2) a store of value; and (3) a unit of account. The alternative to using money is *barter*, in which goods are exchanged directly for other goods. Barter is costly and inefficient in an economy with many different kinds of goods.

2. *Commodity monies* are items used as money and also have an intrinsic value in some other use—for example, gold and cigarettes. *Fiat monies* are intrinsically worthless apart from their use as money. To ensure the acceptance of fiat monies, governments use their power to declare money *legal tender* and promise the public they will not debase the currency by expanding its supply rapidly.

3. There are various definitions of money. Currency plus demand deposits plus traveler's checks plus other checkable deposits compose M1, or *transactions money*—money that can be used directly to buy things. The addition of savings accounts and money market accounts (*near monies*) to M1 gives M2, or *broad money*.

HOW BANKS CREATE MONEY

4. The *required reserve ratio* is the percentage of a bank's deposits that must be kept as reserves at the nation's central bank, the Federal Reserve.

5. Banks create money by making loans. When a bank makes a loan to a customer, it creates a deposit in that customer's account. This deposit becomes part of the money supply.

Banks can create money only when they have *excess reserves*—reserves in excess of the amount set by the required reserve ratio.

6. The *money multiplier* is the multiple by which the total supply of money can increase for every dollar increase in reserves. The money multiplier is equal to 1/required reserve ratio.

THE FEDERAL RESERVE SYSTEM

7. The Fed's most important function is controlling the nation's money supply. The Fed also performs several other functions: It clears interbank payments, is responsible for many of the regulations governing banking practices and standards, and acts as a *lender of last resort* for troubled banks that cannot find any other sources of funds. The Fed also acts as the bank for the U.S. government.

HOW THE FED CONTROLS THE MONEY SUPPLY

8. The key to understanding how the Fed controls the money supply is the role of reserves. If the Fed wants to increase the supply of money, it creates more reserves, freeing banks to create additional deposits. If it wants to decrease the money supply, it reduces reserves.

9. The Fed has three tools to control the money supply: (1) change the required reserve ratio; (2) change the *discount rate* (the interest rate member banks pay when they borrow from the Fed); or (3) engage in *open market operations* (the buying and selling of already-existing government securities). To increase the money supply, the Fed can create additional reserves by lowering the discount rate or by buying government securities, or the Fed can increase the number of deposits that can be created from a given quantity of reserves by lowering the required reserve ratio. To decrease the money supply, the Fed can reduce reserves by raising the discount rate or by selling government securities, or it can raise the required reserve ratio.

10. If the Fed's money supply behavior is not influenced by the interest rate, the supply curve for money is a vertical line.

REVIEW TERMS AND CONCEPTS

1. $M1 \equiv$ currency held outside banks + demand deposits + traveler's checks + other checkable deposits
2. $M2 \equiv M1$ + savings accounts + money market accounts + other near monies
3. Assets ≡ liabilities + capital (or net worth)
4. Excess reserves ≡ actual reserves – required reserves
5. $\text{Money multiplier} \equiv \dfrac{1}{\text{required reserve ratio}}$

PROBLEM SET

1. In the Republic of Ragu the currency is the rag. During 2004, the Treasury of Ragu sold bonds to finance the ragu budget deficit. In all, the Treasury sold 50,000 10-year bonds with a face value of 100 rags each. The total deficit was 5 million rags. Further, assume that the Ragu Central Bank reserve requirement was 20 percent, and that in the same year, the bank bought 500,000 rags' worth of outstanding bonds on the open market. Finally, assume that all of the Ragu debt is held by either the private sector (the public) or the Central Bank.
   a. What is the combined effect of the Treasury sale and the Central Bank purchase on the total Ragu debt outstanding? On the debt held by the private sector?
   b. What is the effect of the Treasury sale on the money supply in Ragu?
   c. What is the effect of the Central Bank purchase of bonds on the money supply, assuming no leakage of reserves out of the banking system?

2. In the year 2000, the federal debt was being paid down because the federal budget was in surplus. Recall this means that tax collections (T) exceed government spending (G). The surplus ($T-G$) was used to buy back government bonds from the public reducing the federal debt. As we discussed in this chapter, the main method by which the Fed increases the money supply is to buy government bonds by using open market operations. What

is the impact of using the fiscal surplus to buy back bonds on the supply of money? What is the difference between Fed open market purchases of bonds and Treasury purchases of bonds using tax revenues in term of their impacts on the money supply?

3. For each of the following, say whether it is an asset on the accounting books of a bank or a liability. Explain why in each case.

Cash in the vault
Demand deposits
Savings deposits
Reserves
Loans
Deposits at the Federal Reserve

4. If the head of the Central Bank of Japan wanted to expand the supply of money in Japan in 1999, which of the following would do it? Explain your answer.

Increase the required reserve ratio
Decrease the required reserve ratio
Increase the discount rate
Decrease the discount rate
Buy government securities in the open market
Sell government securities in the open market

5. Suppose that in the Republic of Madison, the regulation of banking rested with the Madison Congress including the determination of the reserve ratio. The Central Bank of Madison is charged with regulating the money supply by using open market operations. In April of the year 2001, the money supply was estimated to be 52 million hurls. At the same time bank reserves were 6.24 million hurls and the reserve requirement was 12 percent. The banking industry, being "loaned up," lobbied the Congress to cut the reserve ratio. The Congress yielded and cut required reserves to 10 percent. What is the potential impact on the money supply? Suppose that the Central Bank decided that the money supply should not be increased. What countermeasures could it take to prevent the Congress from expanding the money supply?

6. The U.S. money supply ($M1$) at the beginning of the year 2000 was $1,148 billion, broken down as follows: $523 billion in currency, $8 billion in traveler's checks, and $616 billion in checking deposits. Suppose the Fed has decided to reduce the money supply by increasing the reserve requirement from 10 percent to 11 percent. Assuming all banks were initially loaned up (had no excess reserves) and currency held outside of banks did not change, how large a change in the money supply would have resulted from the change in the reserve requirement?

7. "As King of Medivalia, you are constantly strapped for funds to pay your army. Your chief economic wizard suggests the following plan: "When you collect your tax payments from your subjects, insist on being paid in gold coins. Take these gold coins, melt them down, and then remint them with an extra 10 percent of brass thrown in. You will then have 10 percent more money than you started with." What do you think of the plan? Will it work?

8. "Why is $M2$ sometimes a more stable measure of money than $M1$? Explain in your own words, using the definitions of $M1$ and $M2$.

9. Do you agree or disagree with each of the following statements? Explain your answers.

a. "When the Treasury of the United States issues bonds and sells them to the public to finance the deficit, the money supply remains unchanged because every dollar of money taken in by the Treasury goes right back into circulation through government spending. This is not true when the Fed sells bonds to the public."

b. "The money multiplier depends on the marginal propensity to save."

***10.** When the Fed adds new reserves to the system, some of these new reserves find their way out of the country into foreign banks or foreign investment funds. In addition, some portion of new reserves ends up in people's pockets and mattresses instead of bank vaults. These "leakages" reduce the money multiplier and sometimes make it very difficult for the Fed to control the money supply precisely. Explain why this is true.

11. You are given this account for a bank:

ASSETS		LIABILITIES	
Reserves	$ 500	$3,500	Deposits
Loans	3,000		

The required reserve ratio is 10 percent.

a. How much is the bank required to hold as reserves, given its deposits of $3,500?

b. How much are its excess reserves?

c. By how much can the bank increase its loans?

d. Suppose a depositor comes to the bank and withdraws $200 in cash. Show the bank's new balance sheet, assuming the bank obtains the cash by drawing down its reserves. Does the bank now hold excess reserves? Is it meeting the required reserve ratio? If not, what can it do?

*Note: Problems marked with an asterisk are more challenging.

Money Demand, the Equilibrium Interest Rate, and Monetary Policy

11

CHAPTER OUTLINE

Having discussed the supply of money in the last chapter, we now turn to the *demand* for money. One goal of this and the previous chapter is to provide a theory of how the interest rate is determined in the macroeconomy. Once we have seen how the interest rate is determined, we can turn to how the Federal Reserve (Fed) affects the interest rate through **monetary policy**.

It is important that you understand exactly what the interest rate is. **Interest** is the fee borrowers pay to lenders for the use of their funds. Firms and the government borrow funds by issuing bonds, and they pay interest to the firms and households (the lenders) that purchase those bonds. Households and firms that have borrowed from a bank must pay interest on those loans to the bank.

The **interest rate** is the annual interest payment on a loan expressed as a percentage of the loan. A \$1,000 bond (representing a \$1,000 loan from a household to a firm) that pays \$100 in interest per year has an interest rate of 10 percent. The interest rate is expressed as an *annual* rate. It is the amount of interest received *per year* divided by the amount of the loan.

While there are many different interest rates, we will assume that there is only one. This simplifies our analysis yet provides a valuable tool for us to understand how the parts of the macroeconomy relate to one another. Appendix A to this chapter provides more detail on the various types of interest rates.

THE DEMAND FOR MONEY

What factors and what forces determine the demand for money are central issues in macroeconomics. As we shall see, the interest rate and the level of national income (*Y*) influence how much money households and firms wish to hold.

Before we proceed, we must stress one point students find troublesome. When we speak of the demand for money, we are not asking these questions: "How much cash do you wish you could have?" "How much income would you like to earn?" "How much wealth would you like?" (The answer to these questions is presumably "as much as possible.") Instead, we are concerned with how much of your financial assets you want to hold *in the form of money*, which does not earn interest, versus how much you want to hold in interest-bearing securities, such as bonds. We take as given the *total* amount of financial assets; our concern here is with how these assets are divided between money and interest-bearing securities.

monetary policy The behavior of the Federal Reserve concerning the money supply.

interest The fee that borrowers pay to tenders for the use of their funds.

interest rate The annual interest payment on a loan expressed as a percentage of the loan. Equal to the amount of interest received per year divided by the amount of the loan.

THE TRANSACTION MOTIVE

transaction motive The main reason that people hold money—to buy things.

How much money to hold involves a trade-off between the liquidity of money and the interest income offered by other kinds of assets. The main reason for holding money instead of interest-bearing assets is that money is useful for buying things. Economists call this the **transaction motive**. This rationale for holding money is at the heart of the discussion that follows.[1]

Assumptions To keep our analysis of the demand for money clear, we need a few simplifying assumptions. First, we assume there are only two kinds of assets available to households: bonds and money. By "bonds" we mean interest-bearing securities of all kinds. By "money" we mean currency in circulation and in deposits, neither of which is assumed to pay interest.[2]

Second, we assume that income for the typical household is "bunched up." It arrives once a month, at the beginning of the month. Spending, by contrast, is spread out over time; we assume that spending occurs at a completely uniform rate throughout the month—that is, that the same amount is spent each day (Figure 11.1). The mismatch between the timing of money inflow and the timing of money outflow is sometimes called the **nonsynchronization of income and spending**.

nonsynchronization of income and spending The mismatch between the timing of money inflow to the household and the timing of money outflow for household expenses.

Finally, we assume that spending for the month is exactly equal to income for the month. Because we are focusing on the transactions demand for money and not on its use as a store of value, this assumption is perfectly reasonable.

MONEY MANAGEMENT AND THE OPTIMAL BALANCE

Given these assumptions, how would a rational person (household) decide how much of monthly income to hold as money and how much to hold as interest-bearing bonds? Suppose Jim decides to deposit his entire paycheck in his checking account. Let us say Jim earns $1,200 per month. The pattern of Jim's bank account balance is illustrated in Figure 11.2. At the beginning of the month, Jim's balance is $1,200. As the month rolls by, Jim draws down his balance, writing checks or withdrawing cash to pay for the things he buys. At the end of the month, Jim's bank account balance is down to zero. Just in time, he receives his next month's paycheck, deposits it, and the process begins again.

One useful statistic we will need to calculate is the *average balance* in Jim's account. Jim spends his money at a constant $40 per day ($40 per day times 30 days per month = $1,200). His average balance is just his starting balance ($1,200) plus his ending balance (0) divided

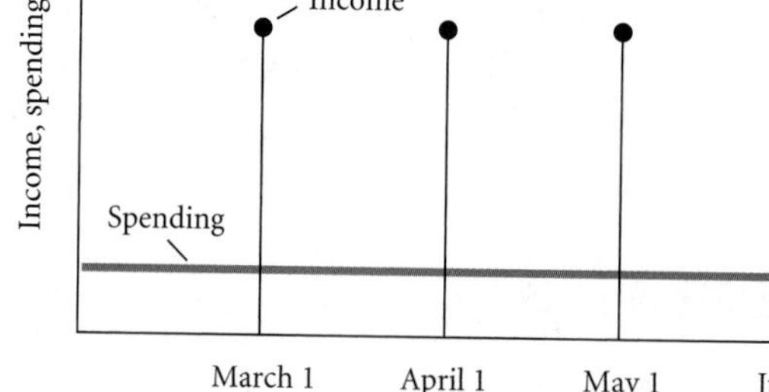

FIGURE 11.1 The Nonsynchronization of Income and Spending

Income arrives only once a month, but spending takes place continuously.

[1] The model that we discuss here is known in the economics profession as the Baumol/Tobin model, after the two economists who independently derived it, William Baumol of Princeton University and James Tobin of Yale University.

[2] Remember that the category "deposits" includes checking accounts. Many checking accounts pay interest. This will not matter for the purposes of our discussion, however. Suppose bonds pay 10 percent interest and checking accounts pay 5 percent. (Checking accounts must pay less than bonds. Otherwise, everyone would hold all their wealth in checking accounts and none in bonds, because checking accounts are more convenient.) When it comes to choosing whether to hold bonds or money, the difference in the interest rates on the two matters. People are concerned about how much extra interest they will get from holding bonds instead of money. In the preceding example we could say that bonds pay 5 percent and money pays 0 percent, which makes our discussion simpler.

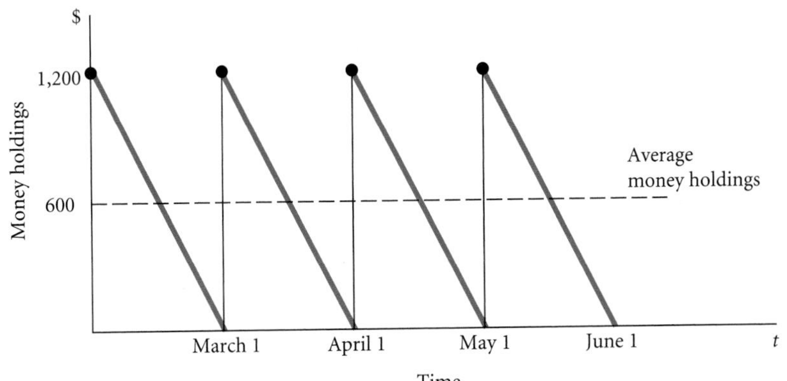

FIGURE 11.2 Jim's Monthly Checking Account Balances: Strategy 1

Jim could decide to deposit his entire paycheck ($1,200) into his checking account at the start of the month and run his balance down to zero by the end of the month. In this case, his average balance would be $600.

by 2, or ($1,200 + 0)/2 = $600. For the first half of the month Jim has more than his average of $600 on deposit, and for the second half of the month he has less than his average.

Is anything wrong with Jim's strategy? Yes. If he follows the plan described, Jim is giving up interest on his funds, interest he could be earning if he held some of his funds in interest-bearing bonds instead of in his checking account. How could he manage his funds to give himself more interest?

Instead of depositing his entire paycheck in his checking account at the beginning of the month, Jim could put half his paycheck into his checking account and buy a bond with the other half. By doing this, he would run out of money in his checking account halfway through the month. At a spending rate of $40 per day, his initial deposit of $600 would last only 15 days. Jim would have to sell his bond halfway through the month and deposit the $600 from the sale of the bond in his checking account to pay his bills during the second half of the month.

Jim's money holdings (checking account balances) if he follows this strategy are shown in Figure 11.3. When he follows the buy-a-$600-bond strategy, Jim reduces the average amount of money in his checking account. Comparing the dashed green lines (old strategy) with the solid green lines (buy-$600-bond strategy), his average bank balance is exactly half of what it was with the first strategy.[3]

The buy-a-$600-bond strategy seems sensible. The object of this strategy was to keep some funds in bonds, where they could earn interest, instead of as "idle" money. Why should he stop there? Another possibility would be for Jim to put only $400 into his checking

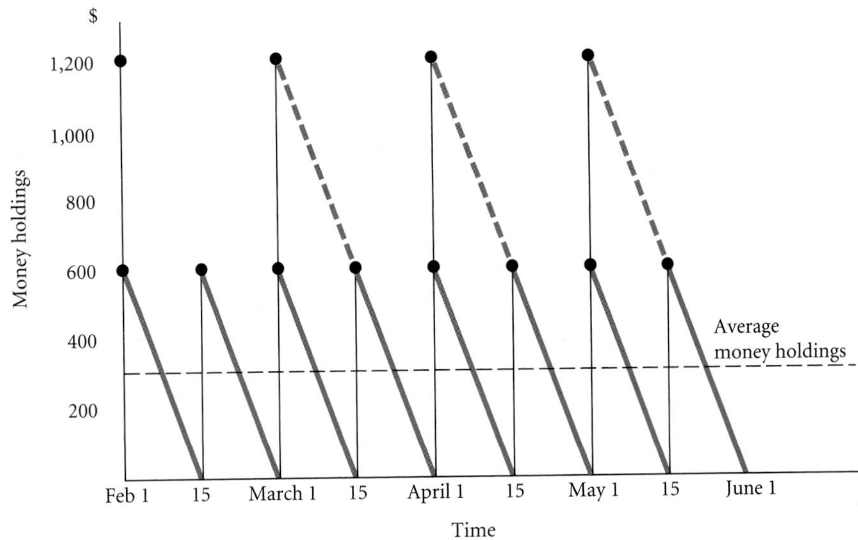

FIGURE 11.3 Jim's Monthly Checking Account Balances: Strategy 2

Jim could also choose to put one half of his paycheck into his checking account and buy a bond with the other half of his income. At mid-month, Jim would sell the bond and deposit the $600 into his checking account to pay the second half of the month's bills. Following this strategy, Jim's average money holdings would be $300.

[3]Jim's average balance for the first half of the month is (starting balance + ending balance)/2, or ($600 + 0)/2 = $300. His average for the second half of the month is also $300. His average for the month as a whole is $300.

account on the first of the month and buy two $400 bonds. The $400 in his account will last only 10 days if he spends $40 per day, so after 10 days he must sell one of the bonds and deposit the $400 from the sale in his checking account. This will last through the 20th of the month, at which point he must sell the second bond and deposit the other $400. This strategy lowers Jim's average money holding (checking account balance) even further, reducing his money holdings to an average of only $200 per month, with correspondingly higher average holdings of interest-earning bonds.

You can imagine Jim going even further. Why not hold all wealth in the form of bonds (where it earns interest) and make transfers from bonds to money every time he makes a purchase? If selling bonds, transferring funds to checking accounts, and making trips to the bank were without cost, Jim would never hold money for more than an instant. Each time he needed to pay cash for something or write a check, he would go to the bank or call the bank, transfer the exact amount of the transaction to his checking account, and either withdraw the cash or write the check to complete the transaction. If he did this constantly, he would squeeze the most interest possible out of his funds because he would never hold assets that did not earn interest.

In practice, money management of this kind is costly. There are brokerage fees and other costs to buy or sell bonds, and time must be spent waiting in line at the bank. At the same time, it is costly to hold assets in non-interest-bearing form, because they lose potential interest revenue.

We have a trade-off problem of the type that pervades economics. Switching more often from bonds to money raises the interest revenue Jim earns (because the more times he switches, the less, on average, he has to hold in his checking account and the more he can keep in bonds), but this increases his money management costs. Less switching means more interest revenue lost (because average money holdings are higher) but lower money management costs (fewer purchases and sales of bonds, less time spent waiting in bank lines, fewer trips to the bank, etc.).

The Optimal Balance There is a level of average money balances that earns Jim the most profit, taking into account both the interest earned on bonds and the costs paid for switching from bonds to money. This level is his *optimal balance.*

How does the interest rate affect the number of switches that Jim makes and thus the average money balance he chooses to hold? It is easy to see why an increase in the interest rate lowers the optimal money balance. If the interest rate were only 2 percent, it would not be worthwhile to give up much liquidity by holding bonds instead of cash or checking balances. However, if the interest rate were 30 percent, the opportunity cost of holding money instead of bonds would be quite high, and we would expect people to keep most of their funds in bonds and to spend considerable time in managing their money balances. The interest rate represents the opportunity cost of holding money (and therefore not holding bonds, which pay interest). The higher the interest rate is, the higher the opportunity cost of holding money, and the less money people will want to hold. This leads us to conclude:

When interest rates are high, people want to take advantage of the high return on bonds, so they choose to hold very little money.

Appendix B to this chapter provides a detailed example of this principle.

A demand curve for money, with the interest rate representing the "price" of money, would look like the curve labeled M^d in Figure 11.4. At higher interest rates, bonds are much more attractive than money, so people hold less money because they must make a larger sacrifice in interest for each dollar of money they hold. The curve in Figure 11.4 slopes downward, just like an ordinary demand curve for oranges or shoes. There is an inverse relationship between the interest rate and the quantity of money demanded.[4]

[4]The theory of money demand presented here assumes that people know the exact timing of their income and spending. In practice, both have some uncertainty attached to them. For example, some income payments may be unexpectedly delayed a few days or weeks, and some expenditures may arise unexpectedly (such as a plumbing problem). Because people know that this uncertainty exists, they may choose to hold more money than the strict transactions motive would suggest, as a precaution against unanticipated delays in income receipts or unanticipated expenses. This reason for holding money is sometimes called the *precautionary motive.*

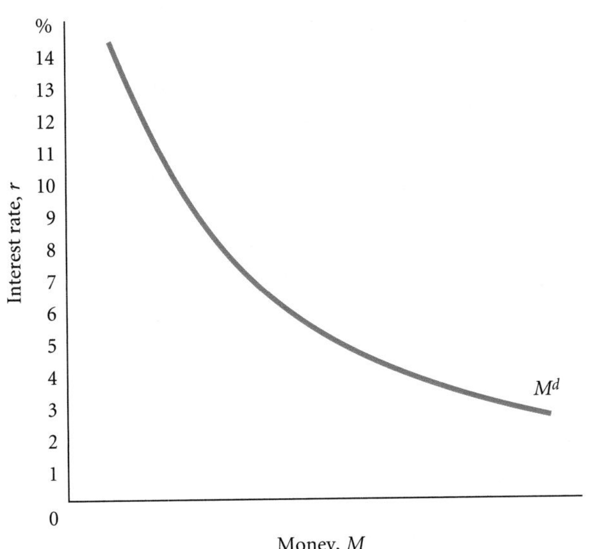

FIGURE 11.4 The Demand Curve for Money Balances

The quantity of money demanded (the amount of money households and firms wish to hold) is a function of the interest rate. Because the interest rate is the opportunity cost of holding money balances, increases in the interest rate will reduce the quantity of money that firms and households want to hold, and decreases in the interest rate will increase the quantity of money that firms and households want to hold.

THE SPECULATION MOTIVE

A number of theories have been offered to explain why the quantity of money households desire to hold may rise when interest rates fall, and fall when interest rates rise. One involves household expectations and the relationship of interest rates to bond values.

To understand this theory, you need to realize that the market value of most interest-bearing bonds is inversely related to the interest rate. Suppose I bought an 8 percent bond a year ago for $1,000. Now suppose the market interest rate rises to 10 percent. If I offered to sell my bond for $1,000, no one would buy it because anyone can buy a new bond and earn 10 percent in the market instead of 8 percent of my bond. However, at some lower selling price, my bond becomes attractive to buyers. This is because a lower price increases the actual yield to the buyer of my bond. Suppose I sell you my bond for $500. Because the bond is paying 8 percent annually on the original $1,000—that is, $80 per year—it is actually paying you an annual amount that comes to 16 percent of your investment in the bond ($500 × .16 = $80). If you bought that same bond from me for about $800, it would effectively pay you 10 percent interest ($800 × .10 = $80). The point here is simple:

When market interest rates fall, bond values rise; when market interest rates rise, bond values fall.

Now consider my desire to hold money balances instead of bonds. If market interest rates are higher than normal, I may expect them to come down in the future. If and when interest rates fall, the bonds that I bought when they were high will increase in value. When interest rates are high, the opportunity cost of holding cash balances is high and there is a **speculation motive** for holding bonds in lieu of cash. I am "speculating" that interest rates will fall in the future.

speculation motive One reason for holding bonds instead of money: Because the market value of interest-bearing bonds is inversely related to the interest rate, investors may wish to hold bonds when interest rates are high with the hope of selling them when interest rates fall.

Similarly, when market interest rates are lower than normal, I may expect them to rise in the future. Rising interest rates will bring about a decline in the value of bonds. Thus, when interest rates are low, it is a good time to be holding money and not bonds. When interest rates are low, not only is there the opportunity cost of holding cash balances low, but also there is a speculative motive for holding a larger amount of money. Why should I put money into bonds now when I expect interest rates to rise in the future? (For more on the interaction between the bond market and the money market, see the Further Exploration box "The Bond Market, the Money Market, and the Speculation Motive.")

THE TOTAL DEMAND FOR MONEY

So far we have talked only about household demand for checking account balances. However, the total quantity of money demanded in the economy is the sum of the demand for checking account balances *and cash* by both households *and firms.*

Further Exploration

The Bond Market, the Money Market, and the Speculation Motive

People are often confused when business-page headlines read "Bonds Fall, Pushing up Interest Rates" or "Bonds Rise, Driving Yields Down." Nonetheless, it is true that the current market price or value of all fixed-rate bonds, whether U.S. Treasury Bonds or German corporate bonds, fall in value when interest rates rise, and rise in value when interest rates fall.

To see why, consider Heidi, a German house painter who bought for $1,000 a 10-year German government bond with a fixed rate of 10 percent. By buying that bond, Heidi has agreed to accept a return on her money of 10 percent for 10 years. This means a check for $100 every year with a promise that her $1,000 will be returned at the end of 10 years.

Though the German government has no obligation to pay the $1,000 back before the bond matures in 10 years, Heidi may need the money before 10 years is up. To get her money back earlier, she can call a broker and sell the bond. In fact, there is a huge market for existing bonds, and existing bond prices are posted in the newspapers every day. To sell the bond, the broker has to find a buyer, and the amount that a buyer would be willing to pay depends on the current rate of interest.

Suppose Heidi wants to sell her bond 2 years after she purchased it. The bond still has 8 years left to maturity. Assume that the Bundesbank (the German central bank) has pushed rates for 8-year bonds to 12 percent. Someone who paid $1,000 for Heidi's bond today would be getting only $100 (10 percent) interest per year. The same person could be getting interest of $120 per year, or 12 percent, by buying a newly issued $1,000 bond. The result: Heidi's broker will not be able to sell her bond for $1,000. Instead, Heidi will have to take a loss because her bond's value has fallen.

Do bond values really fall in the real world? Absolutely. When the Federal Reserve raised U.S. interest rates in 1994, the value of outstanding bonds traded in the market fell substantially. Similarly, during Mexico's peso crises in 1995, Mexican interest rates shot up sharply, and Mexican government bonds lost a lot of their value. (U.S. holders of Mexican securities got hit even harder because the value of the peso fell too—but that is covered later, in the chapter on open-market macroeconomics.)

Another way to see the same connection between the bond market and the money market is to think of a case in which the demand for bonds increases. Suppose that because of excess demand for bonds in Germany, the value of Heidi's bond goes up to $1,100. Someone who is willing to pay $1,100 for Heidi's bond *must reveal a willingness to accept an annual yield of less than 10 percent*. After all, $100 is only 9.1 percent of $1,100. In addition, the buyer who pays $1,100 will get back only $1,000 when the bond matures. Higher bond prices mean the interest rate bond buyers are willing to accept is lower than before. If buyers are willing to accept 9 percent on old bonds, they will accept 9 percent on new bonds.

Bond prices and interest rates are two sides of the same coin. A rally in the bond market means bond prices have gone up and interest rates, or bond yields, have gone down. Similarly, when the bond market drops, interest rates, or yields, have gone up.

These effects have important implications for money demand. Assume households choose only between holding their assets as money (which does not earn interest) or as bonds (which do earn interest). If households and firms believe interest rates are historically high and they are likely to fall, it is a *good* time to hold bonds. This is because a drop in rates means bond values will rise, in a sense earning bondholders a bonus. When interest rates are high and expected to fall, demand for bonds is likely to be high and money demand is likely to be low. Similarly, if people see interest rates as low and expect them to rise, it is *not* a good time to be holding bonds. Why? Because if interest rates rise, bond holders suffer losses. When interest rates are low, money demand is likely to be high and the demand for bonds is likely to be low. Thus, we have another reason for the negative relationship between interest rates and money demand. As we mentioned in the text, this is the *speculation motive* for holding money.

The trade-off for firms is the same as it was for Jim. Like households, firms must manage their money. They have payrolls to meet and purchases to make; they receive cash and checks from sales; and many firms that deal with the public must make change—they need cash in the cash register. Thus, just like Jim, firms need money to engage in ordinary transactions.

However, firms as well as households can hold their assets in interest-earning form. Firms manage their assets just as households do, keeping some in cash, some in their checking accounts, and some in bonds. A higher interest rate raises the opportunity cost of money for firms as well as for households and thus reduces the demand for money.

The same trade-off holds for cash. We all walk around with some money in our pockets, but not thousands of dollars, for routine transactions. We carry, on average, about what we think we will need, not more, because there are costs—risks of being robbed and forgone interest.

At any given moment, there is a demand for money—for cash and checking account balances. Although households and firms need to hold balances for everyday transactions, their demand has a limit. For both households and firms, the quantity of money demanded at any moment depends on the opportunity cost of holding money, a cost determined by the interest rate.

TRANSACTIONS VOLUME AND THE PRICE LEVEL

The money demand curve in Figure 11.4 is a function of the interest rate. There are other factors besides the interest rate that influence total desired money holdings. One is the dollar value of transactions made during a given period of time.

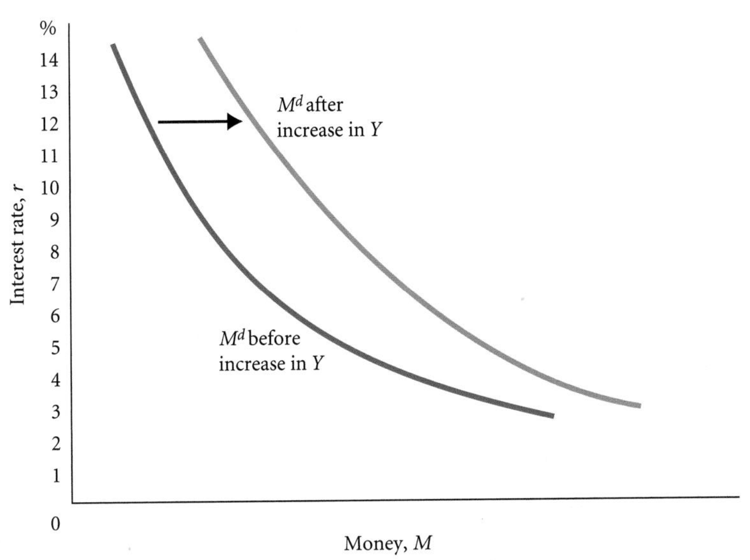

FIGURE 11.5 An increase in Aggregate Output (Income) (Y) Will Shift the Money Demand Curve to the Right

An increase in *Y* means there is more economic activity. Firms are producing and selling more, and households are earning more income and buying more. There are more transactions, for which money is needed. As a result, both firms and households are likely to increase their holdings of money balances at a given interest rate.

Suppose Jim's income were to increase. Instead of making $1,200 in purchases each month, he will now spend more. He thus needs to hold more money. The reason is simple: To buy more things, he needs more money.

What is true for Jim is true for the economy as a whole. The total demand for money in the economy depends on the total dollar volume of transactions made. The total dollar volume of transactions in the economy, in turn, depends on two things: the total *number* of transactions and the average transaction *amount.* Although there are no data on the actual number of transactions in the economy, a reasonable indicator is likely to be aggregate output (income) (*Y*). A rise in aggregate output—real gross domestic product (GDP)—means there is more economic activity. Firms are producing and selling more output, more people are on payrolls, and household incomes are higher. In short, there are more transactions, and firms and households together will hold more money when they are engaging in more transactions. Thus, an increase in aggregate output (income) will increase the demand for money.

Figure 11.5 shows a shift of the money demand curve resulting from an increase in *Y*:

> For a given interest rate, a higher level of output means an increase in the *number* of transactions and more demand for money. The money demand curve shifts to the right when *Y* rises. Similarly, a decrease in *Y* means a decrease in the number of transactions and a lower demand for money. The money demand curve shifts to the left when *Y* falls.

The amount of money needed by firms and households to facilitate their day-to-day transactions also depends on the average *dollar amount* of each transaction. In turn, the average amount of each transaction depends on prices, or instead, on the *price level.* If all prices, including the price of labor (the wage rate) were to double, firms and households would need more money balances to carry out their day-to-day transactions—each transaction would require twice as much money. If the price of your lunch increases from $3.50 to $7.00, you will begin carrying more cash. If your end-of-the-month bills are twice as high as they used to be, you will keep more money in your checking account.

> Increases in the price level shift the money demand curve to the right, and decreases in the price level shift the money demand curve to the left. Even though the number of transactions may not have changed the quantity of money needed to engage in them has.

THE DETERMINANTS OF MONEY DEMAND: REVIEW

Table 11.1 summarizes everything we have said about the demand for money. First, because the interest rate (*r*) is the opportunity cost of holding money balances for both firms and households: increases in the interest rate are likely to decrease the quantity of money demanded; decreases in the interest rate will increase the quantity of money demanded. Thus, the quantity of money demanded is a negative function of the interest rate.

TABLE 11.1 Determinants of Money Demand

1. The interest rate: r (negative effect causes downward sloping money demand)
2. The dollar volume of transactions (positive effects shift the money demand curve)
   a. Aggregate output (income): Y (positive effect: money demand shifts right when Y increases)
   b. The price level: P (positive effect: money demand shifts right when P increases)

The demand for money also depends on the dollar volume of transactions in a given period. The dollar volume of transactions depends on both aggregate output (income), Y, and the price level, P. The relationship of money demand to Y and the relationship of money demand to P are both positive. Increases in Y or in P will shift the money demand curve to the right; decreases in Y or P will shift the money demand curve to the left.

Some Common Pitfalls We need to consider several pitfalls in thinking about money demand. First, when we spoke in earlier chapters about the demand for goods and services, we were speaking of demand as a *flow variable*—something measured over a period of time. If you say your demand for coffee is three cups, you need to specify whether you are talking about three cups per hour, three cups per day, or three cups per week. In macroeconomics, consumption and saving are flow variables. We consume and save continuously, but we express consumption and saving in time-period terms, such as $600 *per month.*

Money demand is not a flow measure. Instead, it is a *stock variable,* measured at a given point in time. It answers the question: How much money do firms and households desire to hold at a specific point in time, given the current interest rate, volume of economic activity, and price level?

Second, many people think of money demand and saving as roughly the same—they are not. Suppose that in a given year a household had income of $50,000 and expenses of $47,000. It saved $3,000 during the year. At the beginning of the year the household had no debt and $100,000 in assets. Because the household saved $3,000 during the year, it has $103,000 in assets at the end of the year. Some of the $103,000 is held in stocks, some in bonds, some in other forms of securities, and some in money. How much the household chooses to hold in the form of money is its demand for money. Depending on the interest rate and the household's transactions, the amount of the $103,000 that it chooses to hold in the form of money could be anywhere from a few hundred dollars to many thousands. How much of its assets a household retains in the form of money is different from how much of its income it spends during the year.

Finally, recall the difference between a shift in a demand curve and a movement along the curve. The money demand curve in Figure 11.4 shows optimal money balances as a function of the interest rate *ceteris paribus,* all else equal. Changes in the interest rate cause movements *along* the curve—*changes in the quantity of money demanded.* Changes in real GDP (Y) or in the price level (P) cause shifts of the curve as shown in Figure 11.5—*changes in demand.*

THE EQUILIBRIUM INTEREST RATE

We are now in a position to consider one of the key questions in macroeconomics: How is the interest rate determined in the economy?

Financial markets (what we call the money market) work very well in the United States. Almost all financial markets clear—that is, almost all reach an equilibrium where quantity demanded equals quantity supplied. In the money market:

> The point at which the quantity of money demanded equals the quantity of money supplied determines the equilibrium interest rate in the economy.

This explanation sounds simple, but it requires elaboration.

SUPPLY AND DEMAND IN THE MONEY MARKET

We saw in Chapter 10 that the Fed controls the money supply through its manipulation of the amount of reserves in the economy. Because we are assuming that the Fed's money supply behavior does not depend on the interest rate, the money supply curve is a vertical line.

(Review Figure 10.5.) In other words, we are assuming that the Fed uses its three tools (the required reserve ratio, the discount rate, and open market operations) to achieve its fixed target for the money supply.

Figure 11.6 superimposes the vertical money supply curve from Figure 10.5 on the downward-sloping money demand curve. Only at interest rate r^* is the quantity of money in circulation (the money supply) equal to the quantity of money demanded. To understand why r^* is an equilibrium, we need to ask what adjustments would take place if the interest rate were not r^*.

To understand the adjustment mechanism, keep in mind that borrowing and lending is a continuous process. The Treasury sells U.S. government securities (bonds) more or less continuously to finance the deficit. When it does, it is borrowing, and must pay interest to attract bond buyers. Buyers of government bonds are, in essence, lending money to the government, just as buyers of corporate bonds are lending money to corporations that wish to finance investment projects.

Consider first r_0 in Figure 11.6. At r_0, the quantity of money demanded is M_0^d, and the quantity of money supplied exceeds the quantity of money demanded. This means there is more money in circulation than households and firms want to hold. At r_0, firms and households will attempt to reduce their money holdings by buying bonds. When there is money in circulation looking for a way to earn interest—when demand for bonds is high—those looking to borrow money by selling bonds will find that they can do so at a lower interest rate.

If the interest rate is initially high enough to create an excess supply of money, the interest rate will immediately fall, discouraging people from moving out of money and into bonds.

Now consider r_1, where the quantity of money demanded (M_1^d) exceeds the supply of money currently in circulation—households and firms do not have enough money on hand to facilitate ordinary transactions. They will try to adjust their holdings by shifting assets out of bonds and into their checking accounts. At the same time, the continuous flow of new bonds being issued must also be absorbed. The Treasury and corporations can sell bonds in an environment where people are adjusting their asset holdings to shift *out* of bonds only by offering a higher interest rate to the people who buy them.

If the interest rate is initially low enough to create an excess demand for money, the interest rate will immediately rise, discouraging people from moving out of bonds and into money.

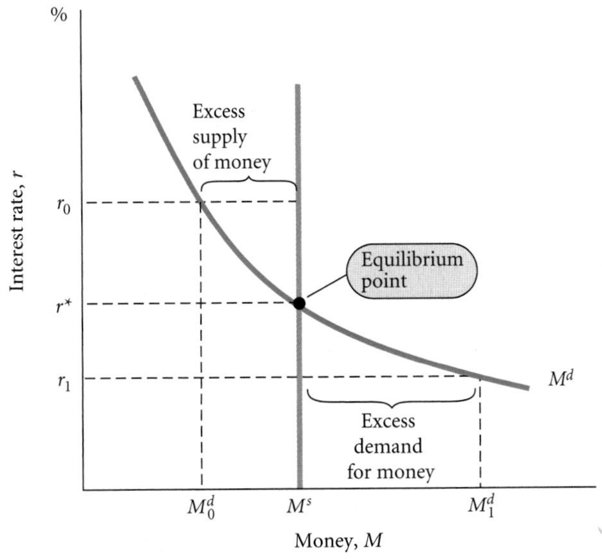

FIGURE 11.6 Adjustments in the Money Market

Equilibrium exists in the money market when the supply of money is equal to the demand for money: $M^d = M^s$. At r_0, the quantity of money supplied exceeds the quantity of money demanded, and the interest rate will fall. At r_1, the quantity demanded exceeds the quantity supplied, and the interest rate will rise. Only at r^* is equilibrium achieved.

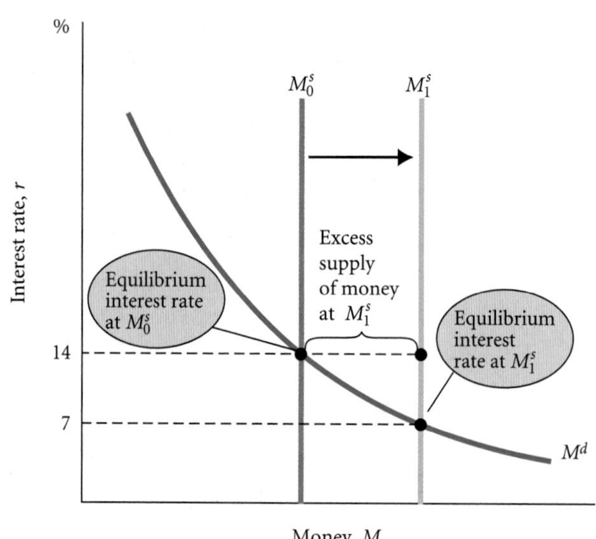

FIGURE 11.7 The Effect of an Increase in the Supply of Money on the Interest Rate

An increase in the supply of money from M_0^s to M_1^s lowers the rate of interest from 14 percent to 7 percent.

CHANGING THE MONEY SUPPLY TO AFFECT THE INTEREST RATE

With an understanding of equilibrium in the money market, we can now see how the Fed can affect the interest rate. Suppose the current interest rate is 14 percent and the Fed wants to reduce the interest rate. To do so, it would expand the money supply. Figure 11.7 shows how such an expansion would work. To expand M^s, the Fed can reduce the reserve requirement, cut the discount rate, or buy U.S. government securities on the open market. All these practices expand the quantity of reserves in the system. Banks can make more loans, and the money supply expands. (Review Chapter 10 if you are unsure why.) In Figure 11.7, the initial money supply curve, M_0^s, shifts to the right, to M_1^s.

At the 14 percent interest rate there is an excess supply of money. This immediately puts downward pressure on the interest rate as households and firms try to buy bonds with their money to earn that high interest rate. As this happens, the interest rate falls, and it will continue to fall until it reaches the new equilibrium interest rate of 7 percent. At this point, $M_1^s = M^d$, and the market is in equilibrium.

If the Fed wanted to drive the interest rate *up*, it would contract the money supply. It could do so by increasing the reserve requirement, by raising the discount rate, or by selling U.S. government securities in the open market. Whichever tool the Fed chooses, the result would be lower reserves and a lower supply of money. M_0^s in Figure 11.7 would shift to the left, and the equilibrium interest rate would rise. (As an exercise, draw a graph of this situation.)

INCREASES IN *Y* AND SHIFTS IN THE MONEY DEMAND CURVE

Changes in the supply of money are not the only factors that influence the equilibrium interest rate. Shifts in money demand can do the same thing.

Recall that the demand for money depends on both the interest rate and the volume of transactions. As a rough measure of the volume of transactions, we use *Y*, the level of aggregate output (income). Remember that the relationship between money demand and *Y* is positive—increases in *Y* mean a higher level of real economic activity. More is being produced, income is higher, and there are more transactions in the economy. Consequently, the demand for money on the part of firms and households in aggregate is higher.

> An increase in *Y* shifts the money demand curve to the right.

Figure 11.8 illustrates such a shift. *Y* increases, causing money demand to shift from M_0^d to M_1^d. The result is an increase in the equilibrium level of the interest rate from 7 percent to 14 percent. A decrease in *Y* would shift M^d to the left, and the equilibrium interest rate would fall.

The money demand curve also shifts when the price level changes. If the price level rises, the money demand curve shifts to the right, because people need more money to engage in

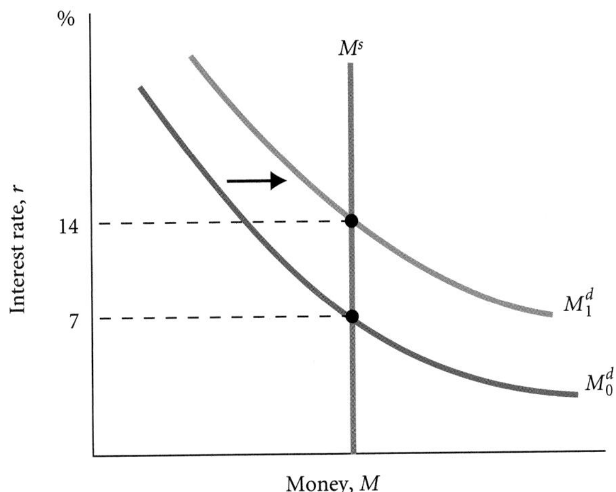

FIGURE 11.8 The Effect of an Increase in Income on the Interest Rate

An increase in aggregate output (income) shifts the money demand curve from M_0^d to M_1^d, which raises the equilibrium interest rate from 7 percent to 14 percent.

their day-to-day transactions. With the quantity of money supplied unchanged, however, the interest rate must rise to reduce the quantity of money demanded to the unchanged quantity of money supplied—a movement *along* the money demand curve.

An increase in the price level is like an increase in *Y* in that both events increase the demand for money. The result is an increase in the equilibrium interest rate.

If the price level *falls*, the money demand curve shifts to the left, because people need less money for their transactions. However, with the quantity of money supplied unchanged, the interest rate must fall to increase the quantity of money demanded to the unchanged quantity of money supplied.

A decrease in the price level leads to a decrease in the equilibrium interest rate.

We explore this relationship in more detail in Chapter 13.

LOOKING AHEAD: THE FEDERAL RESERVE AND MONETARY POLICY

We now know that the Fed can change the interest rate by changing the quantity of money supplied. If the Fed increases the quantity of money, the interest rate falls; if it decreases the quantity of money, the interest rate rises.

Nonetheless, we have not yet said *why* the Fed might want to change the interest rate or what happens to the economy when the interest rate changes. We have hinted at why: A low interest rate stimulates spending, particularly investment; a high interest rate reduces spending. By changing the interest rate the Fed can change aggregate output (income). In the next chapter, we will combine our discussions of the goods and money markets and discuss how the interest rate affects the equilibrium level of aggregate output (income) (*Y*) in the goods market.

The Fed's use of its power to influence events in the goods market, as well as in the money market, is the center of the government's monetary policy. When the Fed moves to contract the money supply in an effort to restrain the economy, economists call it a **tight monetary policy**. Conversely, when the Fed stimulates the economy by expanding the money supply, it has an **easy monetary policy**. The Fed moved aggressively to expand the money supply and lower interest rates in 1975, in 1982, and early in 1991. These easy money policies contributed to economic recovery from the recessions of those years. Tight money policies caused aggregate spending to decline in 1974 and 1981, contributing to the recessions of those years. During the summer of 1981, tight money helped to push some key interest rates above 20 percent.

tight monetary policy Fed policies that contract the money supply in an effort to restrain the economy.

easy monetary policy Fed policies that expand the money supply in an effort to stimulate the economy.

We will discuss the way in which the economy affects the Fed's behavior in Chapter 15. In that chapter, we will also discuss the Fed's recent policies and examine the effects of these policies on the economy.

SUMMARY

1. *Interest* is the fee borrowers pay to lenders for the use of their funds. The *interest rate* is the annual interest payment on a loan expressed as a percentage of the loan; it is equal to the amount of interest received per year divided by the amount of the loan. Although there are many different interest rates in the United States, we assume there is only one interest rate in the economy. This simplifies our analysis but still provides a tool for understanding how the various parts of the macroeconomy relate to each other.

THE DEMAND FOR MONEY

2. The demand for money depends negatively on the interest rate. The higher the interest rate, the higher the opportunity cost (more interest forgone) from holding money, and the less money people will want to hold. An increase in the interest rate reduces the demand for money, and the money demand curve slopes downward.
3. The volume of transactions in the economy affects money demand. The total dollar volume of transactions depends on both the total number of transactions and the average transaction amount.
4. A reasonable measure of the number of transactions in the economy is aggregate output (income) (Y). When Y rises, there is more economic activity, more is being produced and sold, and more people are on payrolls—there are more transactions in the economy. An increase in Y causes the money demand curve to shift to the right. This follows because households and firms need more money when they are engaging in more transactions. A decrease in Y causes the money demand curve to shift left.
5. Changes in the price level affect the average dollar amount of each transaction. *Increases* in the price level will increase the demand for money (shift the money demand curve to the right) because households and firms will need more money for their expenditures. *Decreases* in the price level will decrease the demand for money (shift the money demand curve to the left).

THE EQUILIBRIUM INTEREST RATE

6. The point at which the quantity of money supplied equals the quantity of money demanded determines the equilibrium interest rate in the economy. An excess supply of money will cause households and firms to buy more bonds, driving the interest rate down. An excess demand for money will cause households and firms to move out of bonds, driving the interest rate up.
7. The Fed can affect the equilibrium interest rate by changing the supply of money using one of its three tools—the required reserve ratio, the discount rate, or open market operations.
8. An increase in the price level is like an increase in Y in that both events cause an increase in money demand. The result is an increase in the equilibrium interest rate. A decrease in the price level leads to reduced money demand and a decrease in the equilibrium interest rate.
9. *Tight monetary policy* refers to Fed policies that contract the money supply in an effort to restrain the economy. *Easy monetary policy* refers to Fed policies that expand the money supply in an effort to stimulate the economy. The Fed chooses between these two types of policies for different reasons at different times.

REVIEW TERMS AND CONCEPTS

easy monetary policy, 217
interest, 207
interest rate, 207
monetary policy 207
nonsynchronization of income and spending, 208
speculation motive, 211
tight monetary policy, 217
transaction motive, 208

PROBLEM SET

1. State whether you agree or disagree with the following statements and explain why.
   a. When the real economy expands (Y rises), the demand for money expands. As a result, households hold more cash and the supply of money expands.
   b. Inflation, a rise in the price level, causes the demand for money to decline. Because inflation causes money to be worth less, households desire to hold less of it.
   c. If the Fed buys bonds in the open market and at the same time we experience a recession, interest rates will no doubt rise.
2. During 2003, we began to stop worrying that inflation was a problem. Instead we began to worry about deflation, a decline in the price level. Assume that the Fed decided to hold the money supply constant. What impact would deflation have on interest rates?
3. At the beginning of 2003, interest rates in the U.S. were very low—actually near zero. However, many households believed interest rates were likely to rise eventually. This implies that the quantity of money demanded in the beginning of 2003 was relatively high. Using the concepts of speculative motive and transaction motive for money, explain why.

4. What if, at a low level of interest rates, the money demand curve became nearly horizontal as in the figure below? That is, with interest rates so low, the public would not find it attractive to hold bonds, thus money demand would be very high. Many argue that this was the position of the U.S. economy in 2003. If the Fed decided to expand the money supply in the diagram, what would be the impact on interest rates?

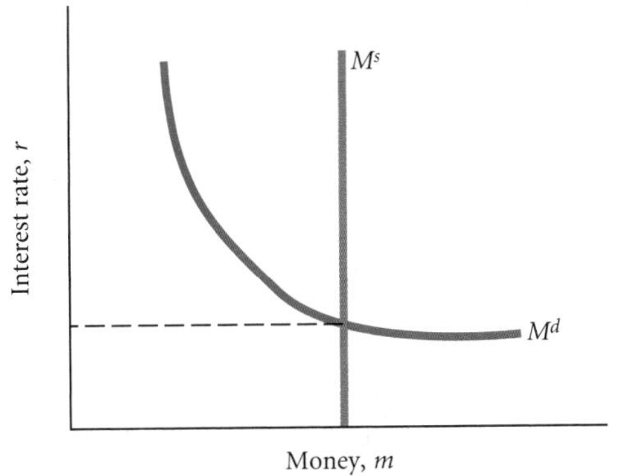

5. During the fourth quarter of 1993, real GDP in the United States grew at an annual rate of over 7 percent. During 1994, the economy continued to expand with modest inflation (Y rose at a rate of 4 percent and P increased about 3 percent). At the beginning of 1994, the prime interest rate (the interest rate that banks offer their best, least risky customers) stood at 6 percent, where it remained for over a year. By the beginning of 1995, the prime rate had increased to over 8.5 percent.
   a. By using money supply and money demand curves, show the effects of the increase in Y and P on interest rates assuming *no change* in the money supply.
   b. On a separate graph, show that the interest rate can rise even if the Federal Reserve expands the money supply as long as it does so more slowly than money demand is increasing.

6. Illustrate the following situations using supply-and-demand curves for money:
   a. The Fed buys bonds in the open market during a recession.
   b. During a period of rapid inflation, the Fed increases the reserve requirement.
   c. The Fed acts to hold interest rates constant during a period of high inflation.
   d. During a period of no growth in GDP and zero inflation, the Fed lowers the discount rate.
   e. During a period of rapid real growth of GDP, the Fed acts to increase the reserve requirement.

7. During a recession, interest rates may fall even if the Fed takes no action to expand the money supply. Why? Use a graph to explain.

8. During the summer of 1997, the Congress and the president agreed on a budget package to balance the federal budget. The "deal," signed into law by President Clinton in August as the Taxpayer Relief Act of 1997, contained substantial tax cuts and expenditure reductions. The tax reductions were scheduled to take effect immediately, however, while the expenditure cuts mostly come in the years 1999 to 2002. Thus, in 1998, the package was seen by economists to be mildly expansionary. If the result is an increase in the growth of real output/income, what would you expect to happen to interest rates if the Fed holds the money supply (or the rate of growth of the money supply) constant? What would the Fed do if it wanted to raise interest rates? What if it wanted to lower interest rates? Illustrate with graphs.

9. The demand for money in a country is given by

$$M^d = 10{,}000 - 10{,}000r + Y$$

where M^d is money demand in dollars, r is the interest rate (a 10 percent interest rate means $r = 0.1$), and Y is national income. Assume Y is initially 5,000.
   a. Graph the amount of money demanded (on the horizontal axis) against the interest rate (on the vertical axis).
   b. Suppose the money supply (M^s) is set by the Central Bank at $10,000. On the same graph you drew for part a., add the money supply curve. What is the equilibrium rate of interest? Explain how you arrived at your answer.
   c. Suppose income rises from $Y = 5{,}000$ to $Y = 7{,}500$. What happens to the money demand curve you drew in part a.? Draw the new curve, if there is one. What happens to the equilibrium interest rate if the Central Bank does not change the supply of money?
   d. If the Central Bank wants to keep the equilibrium interest rate at the same value as it was in part b., by how much should it increase or decrease the supply of money, given the new level of national income?
   e. Suppose the shift in part c has occurred, and the money supply remains at $10,000, but there is no observed change in the interest rate. What might have happened that could explain this?

Visit www.prenhall.com/casefair for self-test quizzes, interactive graphing exercises, and news articles.

APPENDIX A

THE VARIOUS INTEREST RATES IN THE U.S. ECONOMY

Although there are many different interest rates in the economy, they tend to move up or down with one another. Here, we discuss some of their differences. We will first discuss the relationship between interest rates on securities with different *maturities*, or terms. We then discuss briefly some of the main interest rates in the U.S. economy.

THE TERM STRUCTURE OF INTEREST RATES

The *term structure of interest rates* is the relationship between the interest rates offered on securities of different maturities. The key here is understanding things like: How are these different rates related? Does a 2-year security (an IOU that promises to repay principal, plus interest, after 2 years) pay a lower annual rate than a 1-year security (an IOU to be repaid, with interest, after 1 year)? What happens to the rate of interest offered on 1-year securities if the rate of interest on 2-year securities increases?

Assume you want to invest some money for 2 years and at the end of the 2 years you want it back. Assume you want to buy government securities. For this analysis, we restrict your choices to two: (1) You can buy a 2-year security today and hold it for 2 years, at which time you cash it in (we will assume that the interest rate on the 2-year security is 9 percent per year), or (2) you can buy a 1-year security today. At the end of 1 year, you must cash this security in; you can then buy another 1-year security. At the end of the second year, you will cash in the second security. Assume the interest rate on the first 1-year security is 8 percent.

Which would you prefer? Currently, you do not have enough data to answer this question. To consider choice (2) sensibly, you need to know the interest rate on the 1-year security that you intend to buy in the second year. This rate will not be known until the second year. All you know now is the rate on the 2-year security and the rate on the current 1-year security. To decide what to do, you must form an *expectation* of the rate on the 1-year security a year from now. If you expect the 1-year rate (8 percent) to remain the same in the second year, you should buy the 2-year security. You would earn 9 percent per year on the 2-year security but only 8 percent per year on the two 1-year securities. If you expect the 1-year rate to rise to 12 percent a year from now, you should make the second choice. You would earn 8 percent in the first year, and you expect to earn 12 percent in the second year. The expected rate of return over the 2 years is about 10 percent, which is better than the 9 percent you can get on the 2-year security. If you expected the 1-year rate a year from now to be 10 percent, it would not matter very much which of the two choices you made. The rate of return over the 2-year period would be roughly 9 percent for both choices.

We now alter the focus of our discussion to get to the topic we are really interested in—how the 2-year rate is determined. Assume the 1-year rate has been set by the Fed and it is 8 percent. Also assume that people expect the 1-year rate a year from now to be 10 percent. What is the 2-year rate? According to a theory called the *expectations theory of the term structure of interest rates*, the 2-year rate is equal to the average of the current 1-year rate and the 1-year rate expected a year from now. In this example, the 2-year rate would be 9 percent (the average of 8 percent and 10 percent).

If the 2-year rate were lower than the average of the two 1-year rates, people would not be indifferent as to which security they held. They would want to hold only the short-term, 1-year securities. To find a buyer for a 2-year security, the seller would be forced to increase the interest rate it offers on the 2-year security until it is equal to the average of the current 1-year rate and the expected 1-year rate for next year. The interest rate on the 2-year security will continue to rise until people are once again indifferent between one 2-year security and two 1-year securities.[1]

Let us now return to Fed behavior. We know the Fed can affect the short-term interest rate by changing the money supply, but does it also affect long-term interest rates? The answer is "somewhat." Because the 2-year rate is an average of the current 1-year rate and the expected 1-year rate a year from now, the Fed influences the 2-year rate to the extent that it influences the current 1-year rate. The same holds for 3-year rates and beyond. The current short-term rate is a means by which the Fed can influence longer term rates.

In addition, Fed behavior may directly affect people's expectations of the future short-term rates, which will then affect long-term rates. If the chair of the Fed testifies before Congress that raising short-term interest rates is under consideration, people's expectations of higher future short-term interest rates are likely to increase. These expectations will then be reflected in current long-term interest rates.

TYPES OF INTEREST RATES

The following are some widely followed interest rates in the United States.

THREE-MONTH TREASURY BILL RATE

Government securities that mature in less than a year are called *Treasury bills*, or sometimes *T-bills*. The interest rate on 3-month Treasury bills is probably the most widely followed short-term interest rate.

GOVERNMENT BOND RATE

Government securities with terms of 1 year or more are called *government bonds*. There are 1-year bonds, 2-year bonds, and so on up to 30-year bonds. Bonds of different terms have different interest rates. The relationship among the interest rates on the various maturities is the term structure of interest rates that we discussed in the first part of this appendix.

FEDERAL FUNDS RATE

Banks borrow not only from the Fed but also from each other. If one bank has excess reserves, it can lend some of those reserves to other banks through the federal funds market. The interest rate in this market is called the *federal funds rate*—the rate banks are charged to borrow reserves from other banks.

The federal funds market is really a desk in New York City. From all over the country, banks with excess reserves to lend and banks in need of reserves call the desk and negotiate a rate of interest. Account balances with the Fed are changed for the period of the loan without any physical movement of money.

[1]For longer terms, additional future rates must be averaged in. For a 3-year security, for example, the expected 1-year rate a year from now and the expected 1-year rate 2 years from now are added to the current 1-year rate and averaged.

This borrowing and lending, which takes place near the close of each working day, is generally for 1 day ("overnight"), so the federal funds rate is a 1-day rate. It is the rate that the Fed has the most effect on through its open market operations.

COMMERCIAL PAPER RATE

Firms have several alternatives for raising funds. They can sell stocks, issue bonds, or borrow from a bank. Large firms can also borrow directly from the public by issuing "commercial paper," which are essentially short-term corporate IOUs that offer a designated rate of interest. The interest rate offered on commercial paper depends on the financial condition of the firm and the maturity date of the IOU.

PRIME RATE

Banks charge different interest rates to different customers depending on how risky the banks perceive the customers to be. You would expect to pay a higher interest rate for a car loan than General Motors would pay for a $1 million loan to finance investment. Also, you would pay more interest for an unsecured loan, a "personal" loan, than for one that was secured by some asset, such as a house or car, to be used as collateral.

The *prime rate* is a benchmark that banks often use in quoting interest rates to their customers. A very low risk corporation might be able to borrow at (or even below) the prime rate. A less well known firm might be quoted a rate of "prime plus three-fourths," which means that if the prime rate is say, 10 percent, the firm would have to pay interest of 10.75 percent. The prime rate depends on the cost of funds to the bank; it moves up and down with changes in the economy.

AAA CORPORATE BOND RATE

Corporations finance much of their investment by selling bonds to the public. Corporate bonds are classified by various bond dealers according to their risk. Bonds issued by General Motors are in less risk of default than bonds issued by a new, risky biotech research firm. Bonds differ from commercial paper in one important way: Bonds have a longer maturity.

Bonds are graded in much the same way students are. The highest grade is AAA, the next highest AA, and so on. The interest rate on bonds rated AAA is the *triple A corporate bond rate*, the rate that the least risky firms pay on the bonds that they issue.

PROBLEM SET

1. The following table gives three key U.S. interest rates in 1980 and again in April 1993:

	1980 (%)	1993 (%)
Three-month U.S. government bills	11.39	2.92
Long-term U.S. government bonds	10.81	6.85
Prime rate	15.26	6.00

Can you give an explanation for the extreme differences that you see? Specifically, comment on: (1) the fact that rates in 1980 were much higher than in 1993, and (2) the long-term rate was higher than the short-term rate in 1993 but lower in 1980.

APPENDIX B

THE DEMAND FOR MONEY: A NUMERICAL EXAMPLE

This appendix presents a numerical example showing how optimal money management behavior can be derived.

We have seen that the interest rate represents the opportunity cost of holding funds in non-interest-bearing checking accounts (as opposed to bonds, which yield interest). We have also seen that there are costs involved in switching from bonds to money. Given these costs, our objective is to determine the optimum amount of money for an individual to hold. The optimal average level of money holdings is the amount that maximizes the profits from money management. Interest is earned on average bond holdings, but the cost per switch multiplied by the number of switches must be subtracted from interest revenue to obtain the net profit from money management.

Suppose the interest rate is .05 (5 percent), it costs $2 each time a bond is sold[1] and the proceeds from the sale are deposited in one's checking account. Suppose also that the individual's income is $1,200 and that this income is spent evenly throughout the period. This situation is depicted in the top half of Table 11B.1. The optimum value for average money holdings is the value that achieves the largest possible profit in column 6 of the table. When the interest rate is 5 percent, the optimum average money holdings are $150 (which means the individual makes three switches from bonds to money).

In the bottom half of Table 11B.1, the same calculations are performed for an interest rate of 3 percent instead of 5 percent.

[1]In this example we will assume the $2 cost does not apply to the original purchase of bonds.

TABLE 11B.1 Optimum Money Holdings

1 NUMBER OF SWITCHES[a]	2 AVERAGE MONEY HOLDINGS[b]	3 AVERAGE BOND HOLDINGS[c]	4 INTEREST EARNED[d]	5 COST OF SWITCHING[e]	6 NET PROFIT[f]
		r = 5 percent			
0	$600.00	$ 0.00	$ 0.00	$0.00	$ 0.00
1	300.00	300.00	15.00	2.00	13.00
2	200.00	400.00	20.00	4.00	16.00
3	150.00*	450.00	22.50	6.00	16.50
4	120.00	480.00	24.00	8.00	16.00
Assumptions: Interest rate r = 0.05. Cost of switching from bonds into money equals $2 per transaction.					
		r = 3 percent			
0	$600.00	$ 0.00	$ 0.00	$0.00	$0.00
1	300.00	300.00	9.00	2.00	7.00
2	200.00*	400.00	12.00	4.00	8.00
3	150.00	450.00	13.50	6.00	7.50
4	120.00	480.00	14.40	8.00	6.40
Assumptions: Interest rate r = 0.03. Cost of switching from bonds into money equals $2 per transaction.					

*Optimum money holdings. [a]That is, the number of times you sell a bond. [b]Calculated as 600/(col. 1 + 1). [c]Calculated as 600 – col. 2. [d]Calculated as $r \times$ col. 3, where r is the interest rate. [e]Calculated as $t \times$ col. 1, where t is the cost per switch ($2). [f]Calculated as col. 4 – col. 5

In this case, the optimum average money holding is $200 (which means the person/household makes two switches from bonds to money instead of three). The lower interest rate has led to an increase in the optimum average money holdings. Under the assumption that people behave optimally, the demand for money is a negative function of the interest rate: The lower the rate, the more money on average is held, and the higher the rate, the less money on average is held.

PROBLEM SET

1. Sherman Peabody earns a monthly salary of $1,500, which he receives at the beginning of each month. He spends the entire amount each month, at the rate of $50 per day. (Assume 30 days in a month.) The interest rate paid on bonds is 10 percent per month. It costs $4 every time Peabody sells a bond.
   a. Describe briefly how Mr. Peabody should decide how much money to hold.
   b. Calculate Peabody's optimal money holdings. (*Hint:* It may help to formulate a table such as the one in this appendix. You can round to the nearest $0.50, and you need to consider only average money holdings of more than $100.)
   c. Suppose the interest rate rises to 15 percent. Find Peabody's optimal money holdings at this new interest rate. What would happen if the interest rate increases to 20 percent?
   d. Graph your answers to b. and c. with the interest rate on the vertical axis and the amount of money demanded on the horizontal axis. Explain why your graph slopes downward.

Money, the Interest Rate, and Output: Analysis and Policy 12

CHAPTER OUTLINE

In Chapters 8 and 9, we discussed the market for goods and services—the **goods market**—without mentioning money, the money market, or the interest rate. We described how the equilibrium level of aggregate output (income) (Y) is determined in the goods market. At given levels of planned investment spending (I), government spending (G), and net taxes (T), we were able to determine the equilibrium level of output in the economy.

In Chapters 10 and 11, we discussed the financial market, or **money market**, barely referring to the goods market, as we explained how the equilibrium level of the interest rate is determined in the money market.

The goods market and the money market do not operate independently, however. Events in the money market affect what goes on in the goods market, and events in the goods market affect what goes on in the money market. Only by analyzing the two markets together can we determine the values of aggregate output (income) (Y) and the interest rate (r) that are consistent with the existence of equilibrium in *both* markets.

Looking at both markets simultaneously also reveals how fiscal policy affects the money market and how monetary policy affects the goods market. This is what we will do in this chapter. By establishing how the two markets affect each other, we will show how open market purchases of government securities (which expand the money supply) affect the equilibrium level of national output and income. Similarly, we will show how fiscal policy measures (such as tax cuts) affect interest rates and investment spending.

goods market The market in which goods and services are exchanged and in which the equilibrium level of aggregate output is determined.

money market The market in which financial instruments are exchanged and in which the equilibrium level of the interest rate is determined.

THE LINKS BETWEEN THE GOODS MARKET AND THE MONEY MARKET

There are two key *links* between the goods market and the money market:

- **Link 1: Income and the Demand for Money** The first link between the goods market and the money market exists because the demand for money depends on income. As aggregate output (income) (Y) increases, the number of transactions requiring the use of money increases. (You just saw this in Chapter 11.) An increase in output, with the interest rate held constant, leads to an increase in money demand.

FIGURE 12.1 Links between the Goods Market and the Money Market

Planned investment depends on the interest rate, and money demand depends on income.

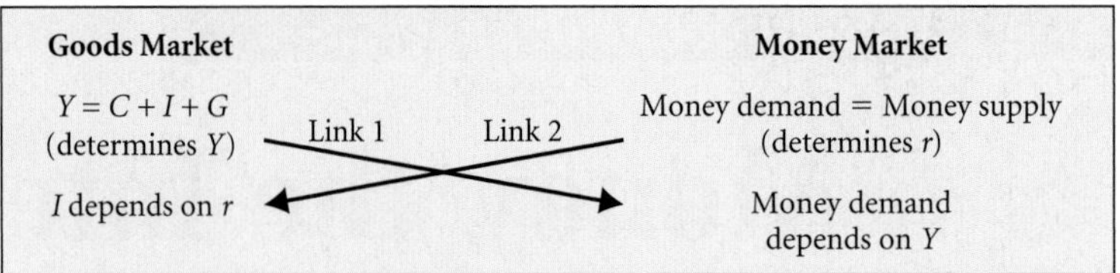

Income, which is determined in the goods market, has considerable influence on the demand for money in the money market.

- **Link 2: Planned Investment Spending and the Interest Rate** The second link between the goods market and the money market exists because planned investment spending (I) depends on the interest rate (r). In Chapters 8 and 9 we assumed that planned investment spending is fixed at a certain level, but we did so only to simplify that discussion. In practice, investment is not fixed. Instead, it depends on a number of key economic variables. One is the interest rate. The higher the interest rate is, the lower the level of planned investment spending.

The interest rate, which is determined in the money market, has significant effects on planned investment in the goods market.

These two links are summarized in Figure 12.1.

INVESTMENT, THE INTEREST RATE, AND THE GOODS MARKET

It should come as no surprise that there is an inverse relationship between the level of planned investment and the interest rate.

When the interest rate falls, planned investment rises.
When the interest rate rises, planned investment falls.

To see why this occurs, recall that *investment* refers to a firm's purchase of new capital—new machines and plants. Whether a firm decides to invest in a project depends on whether the expected profits from the project justify its costs. Usually, a big cost of an investment project is the interest cost.

Consider a firm opening a new plant, or the investment required to open a new ice cream store. When a manufacturing firm builds a new plant, the contractor must be paid at the time the plant is built. When an entrepreneur decides to open a new ice cream parlor, freezers, tables, chairs, light fixtures, and signs are needed. These too must be paid for when they are installed.

The money needed to carry out such projects is generally borrowed and paid back over an extended period. The real cost of an investment project depends in part on the interest rate—the cost of borrowing. When the interest rate rises, it becomes more expensive to borrow, and fewer projects are likely to be undertaken; increasing the interest rate, *ceteris paribus*, is likely to reduce the level of planned investment spending. When the interest rate falls, it becomes less costly to borrow, and more investment projects are likely to be undertaken; reducing the interest rate, *ceteris paribus*, is likely to increase the level of planned investment spending.

The relationship between the interest rate and planned investment is illustrated by the downward-sloping demand curve in Figure 12.2. The higher the interest rate is, the lower the level of planned investment. At an interest rate of 3 percent, planned investment is I_0. When the interest rate rises from 3 percent to 6 percent, planned investment falls from I_0 to I_1. As the interest rate falls, however, more projects become profitable, so more investment is undertaken.

We can now use the fact that planned investment depends on the interest rate to consider how this relationship affects planned aggregate expenditure (AE). Recall that planned aggregate expenditure is the sum of consumption, planned investment, and government purchases. That is:

$$AE \equiv C + I + G$$

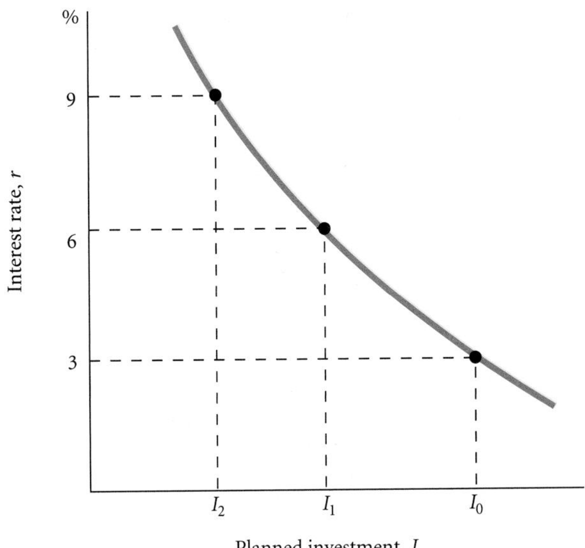

FIGURE 12.2 Planned Investment Schedule

Planned investment spending is a negative function of the interest rate. An increase in the interest rate from 3 percent to 6 percent reduces planned investment from I_0 to I_1.

We now know that there are actually many possible levels of I, each corresponding to a different interest rate. When the interest rate changes, planned investment changes. Therefore, a change in the interest rate (r) will lead to a change in total planned spending $(C + I + G)$ as well.[1]

Figure 12.3 shows what happens to planned aggregate expenditure when the interest rate rises from 3 percent to 6 percent. At the higher interest rate, planned investment is lower; planned aggregate expenditure thus shifts *downward.* Recall from Chapters 8 and 9: A fall in any component of aggregate spending has an even larger (or "multiplier") effect on equilibrium income (Y). When the interest rate rises, planned investment (and planned aggregate expenditure) falls, and equilibrium output (income) falls by even more than the fall in planned investment. In Figure 12.3, equilibrium Y falls from Y_0 to Y_1 when the interest rate rises from 3 percent to 6 percent.

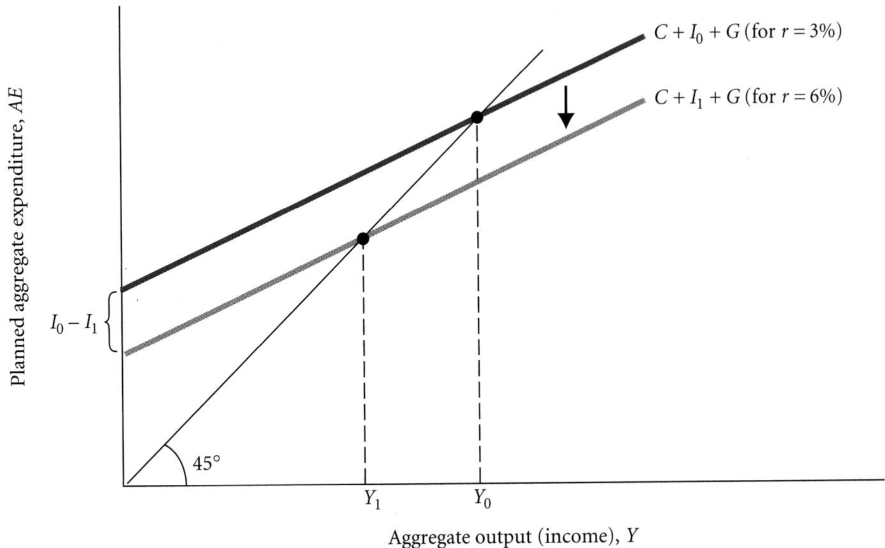

FIGURE 12.3 The Effect of an Interest Rate Increase on Planned Aggregate Expenditure

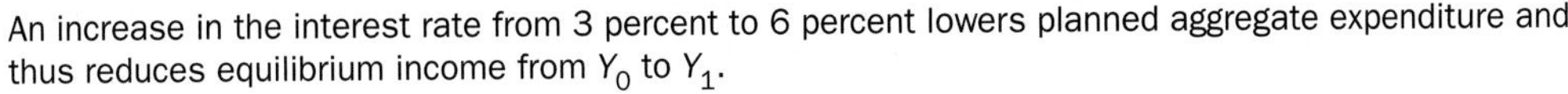
An increase in the interest rate from 3 percent to 6 percent lowers planned aggregate expenditure and thus reduces equilibrium income from Y_0 to Y_1.

[1]When we look at the behavior of households in the macroeconomy in detail in Chapter 17, you will see that consumption spending (C) is also stimulated by lower interest rates and discouraged by higher interest rates.

We can summarize the effects of a change in the interest rate on the equilibrium level of output.

The effects of a change in the interest rate include:

- A high interest rate (r) discourages planned investment (I).
- Planned investment is a part of planned aggregate expenditure (AE).
- Thus, when the interest rate rises, planned aggregate expenditure (AE) at every level of income falls.
- Finally, a decrease in planned aggregate expenditure lowers equilibrium output (income) (Y) by a multiple of the initial decrease in planned investment.

Using a convenient shorthand:

$$r\uparrow \rightarrow I\downarrow \rightarrow AE\downarrow \rightarrow Y\downarrow$$

$$r\downarrow \rightarrow I\uparrow \rightarrow AE\uparrow \rightarrow Y\uparrow$$

As you see, the equilibrium level of output (Y) is not determined solely by events in the goods market, as we assumed in our earlier simplified discussions. The reason is that the money market affects the level of the interest rate, which then affects planned investment in the goods market. There is a different equilibrium level of Y for every possible level of the interest rate (r). The final level of equilibrium Y depends on what the interest rate turns out to be, which depends on events in the money market.

MONEY DEMAND, AGGREGATE OUTPUT (INCOME), AND THE MONEY MARKET

We have just seen how the interest rate—which is determined in the money market—influences the level of planned investment spending and thus the goods market. Now let us look at the other half of the story: the ways in which the goods market affects the money market.

In Chapter 11, we explored the demand for money by households and firms and explained why the demand for money depends negatively on the interest rate. An increase in the interest rate raises the opportunity cost of holding non-interest-bearing money (as compared with interest-bearing bonds), encouraging people to keep more of their funds in bonds and less in checking account balances. The downward-sloping money demand curve (M^d) is shown in Figure 12.4.

We also saw in Chapter 11 that the demand for money depends on the level of income in the economy. More income means more transactions, and an increased volume of transactions implies a greater demand for money. With more people earning higher incomes and

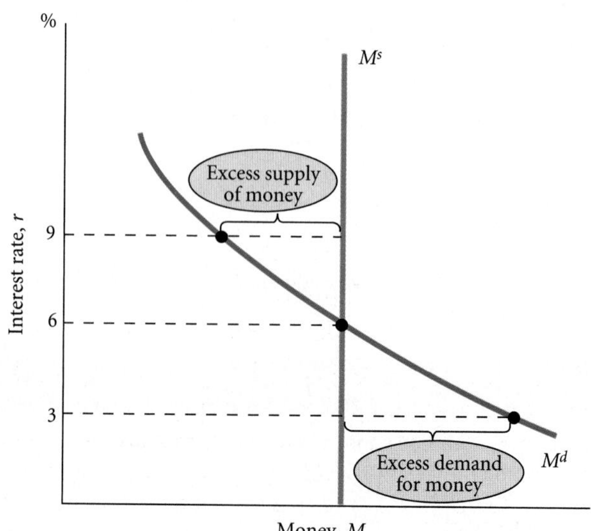

FIGURE 12.4 Equilibrium in the Money Market

If the interest rate were 9 percent, the quantity of money in circulation would exceed the amount households and firms want to hold. The excess money balances would cause the interest rate to drop as people try to shift their funds into interest-bearing bonds. At 3 percent the opposite is true. Excess demand for money balances would push interest rates up. Only at 6 percent would the actual quantity of money in circulation be equal to what the economy wants to hold in money balances.

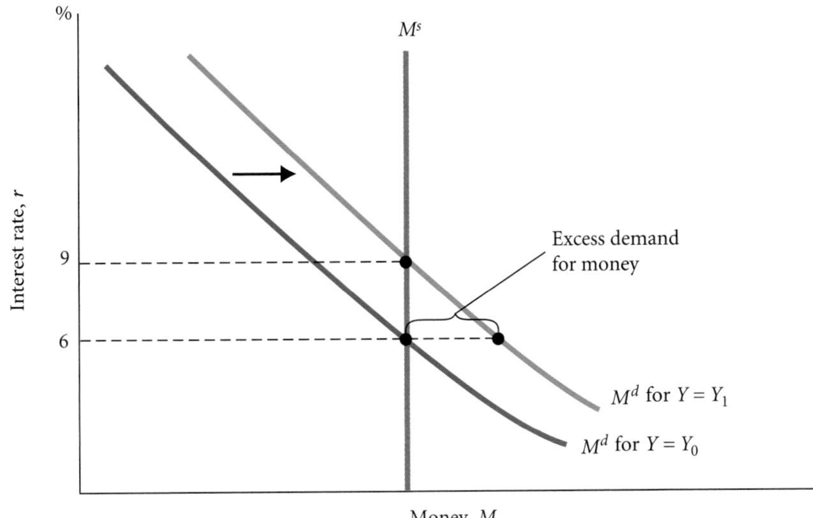

FIGURE 12.5 The Effect of an Increase in Income (Y) on the Interest Rate (r)

An increase in income from Y_0 to Y_1 shifts the M^d curve to the right. With a fixed supply of money, there is now an excess demand for money ($M^d > M^s$) at the initial interest rate of 6 percent. This causes the interest rate to rise. At an interest rate of 9 percent the money market is again in equilibrium with $M^s = M^d$, but at a higher interest rate than before the increase in income.

buying more goods and services, more money will be demanded to meet the increased volume of transactions. An increase in income therefore shifts the money demand curve to the right. (Review Figure 11.5.)

If, as we are assuming, the Federal Reserve's (Fed's) choice of the amount of money to supply does not depend on the interest rate, then the money supply curve is simply a vertical line. The equilibrium interest rate is the point at which the quantity of money demanded equals the quantity of money supplied. This equilibrium is shown at a 6 percent interest rate in Figure 12.4. If the amount of money demanded by households and firms is less than the amount in circulation as determined by the Fed, as it is at an interest rate of 9 percent in Figure 12.4, the interest rate will fall. If the amount of money demanded is greater than the amount in circulation, as it is at an interest rate of 3 percent in Figure 12.4, the interest rate will rise.

Now consider what will happen to the interest rate when there is an increase in aggregate output (income) (*Y*). This increase in *Y* will cause the money demand curve to shift to the right. This is illustrated in Figure 12.5, where an increase in income from Y_0 to Y_1 has shifted the money demand curve from M_0^d to M_1^d. At the initial interest rate of 6 percent, there is now excess demand for money, and the interest rate rises from 6 percent to 9 percent.

The equilibrium level of the interest rate is not determined exclusively in the money market. Changes in aggregate output (income) (*Y*), which take place in the goods market, shift the money demand curve and cause changes in the interest rate. With a given quantity of money supplied, higher levels of *Y* will lead to higher equilibrium levels of *r*. Lower levels of *Y* will lead to lower equilibrium levels of *r*, as represented in the following symbols:

$$Y\uparrow \rightarrow M^d\uparrow \rightarrow r\uparrow$$
$$Y\downarrow \rightarrow M^d\downarrow \rightarrow r\downarrow$$

COMBINING THE GOODS MARKET AND THE MONEY MARKET

Now that we are aware of the links between the goods market and the money market, we can examine the two markets simultaneously. To see how the two markets interact, it will be convenient to consider the effects of changes in fiscal and monetary policy on the economy. We want to examine what happens to the equilibrium levels of aggregate output (income) (*Y*) and the interest rate (*r*) when certain key variables—notably government spending (*G*), net taxes (*T*), and money supply (M^s)—increase or decrease.

EXPANSIONARY POLICY EFFECTS

expansionary fiscal policy An increase in government spending or a reduction in net taxes aimed at increasing aggregate output (income) (*Y*).

expansionary monetary policy An increase in the money supply aimed at increasing aggregate output (income) (*Y*).

Any government policy aimed at stimulating aggregate output (income) (*Y*) is said to be expansionary. An **expansionary fiscal policy** is an increase in government spending (*G*) or a reduction in net taxes (*T*) aimed at increasing aggregate output (income) (*Y*). An **expansionary monetary policy** is an increase in the money supply aimed at increasing aggregate output (income) (*Y*).

Expansionary Fiscal Policy: An Increase in Government Purchases (*G*) or Decrease in Net Taxes (*T*) As you know from Chapter 9, government purchases (*G*) and net taxes (*T*) are the two tools of government fiscal policy. The government can stimulate the economy—that is, it can increase aggregate output (income) (*Y*)—either by *increasing* government purchases or by *reducing* net taxes. Though the impact of a tax cut is somewhat smaller than the impact of an increase in *G*, both have a multiplier effect on the equilibrium level of *Y*.

Consider an increase in government purchases (*G*) of $10 billion. This increase in expenditure causes firms' inventories to be smaller than planned. Unplanned inventory reductions stimulate production, and firms increase output (*Y*). However, because added output means added income, some of which is subsequently spent, consumption spending (*C*) also increases. Again, inventories will be smaller than planned and output will rise even further. The final equilibrium level of output is higher by a multiple of the initial increase in government purchases.

This multiplier story is incomplete, however. Until this chapter, we have assumed that planned investment (*I*) is fixed at a certain level, but we now know that planned investment depends on the interest rate. We can now discuss what happens to the multiplier when investment varies because we now have an understanding of the money market, in which the interest rate is determined.

Return to our multiplier story at the point that firms first begin to raise output in response to an increase in government purchases. As aggregate output (income) (*Y*) increases, an impact is felt in the money market—the increase in income (*Y*) increases the demand for money (M^d). (For the moment, assume the Fed holds the quantity of money supplied [M^s] constant.) The resulting disequilibrium, with the quantity of money demanded greater than the quantity of money supplied, causes the interest rate to rise. The increase in *G* increases both *Y* and *r*.

The increase in *r* has a side effect—a higher interest rate causes planned investment spending (*I*) to decline. Because planned investment spending is a component of planned aggregate expenditure ($C + I + G$), the decrease in *I* works against the increase in *G*. An increase in government spending (*G*) increases planned aggregate expenditure and increases aggregate output, but a decrease in planned investment reduces planned aggregate expenditure and *decreases* aggregate output.

crowding-out effect The tendency for increases in government spending to cause reductions in private investment spending.

This tendency for increases in government spending to cause reductions in private investment spending is called the **crowding-out effect.** Without any expansion in the money supply to accommodate the rise in income and increased money demand, planned investment spending is partially crowded out by the higher interest rate. The extra spending created by the rise in government purchases is somewhat offset by the fall in planned investment spending. Income still rises, but the multiplier effect of the rise in *G* is lessened because of the higher interest rate's negative effect on planned investment.

This crowding-out effect is illustrated graphically in Figure 12.6. An increase in government purchases from G_0 to G_1 shifts the planned aggregate expenditure curve ($C + I_0 + G_0$) upward. The increase in (*Y*) from Y_0 to Y_1 causes the demand for money to rise, which results in a disequilibrium in the money market. The excess demand for money raises the interest rate, causing *I* to decrease from I_0 to I_1. The fall in *I* pulls the planned aggregate expenditure curve back down, which lowers the equilibrium level of income to Y^*. (Remember that equilibrium is achieved when $Y = AE$.)

Note that the size of the crowding-out effect and the ultimate size of the government spending multiplier depend on several things. First, we assumed the Fed did not change the quantity of money supplied. If we were to assume instead that the Fed expanded the quantity of money to accommodate the increase in *G*, the multiplier would be larger. In this case,

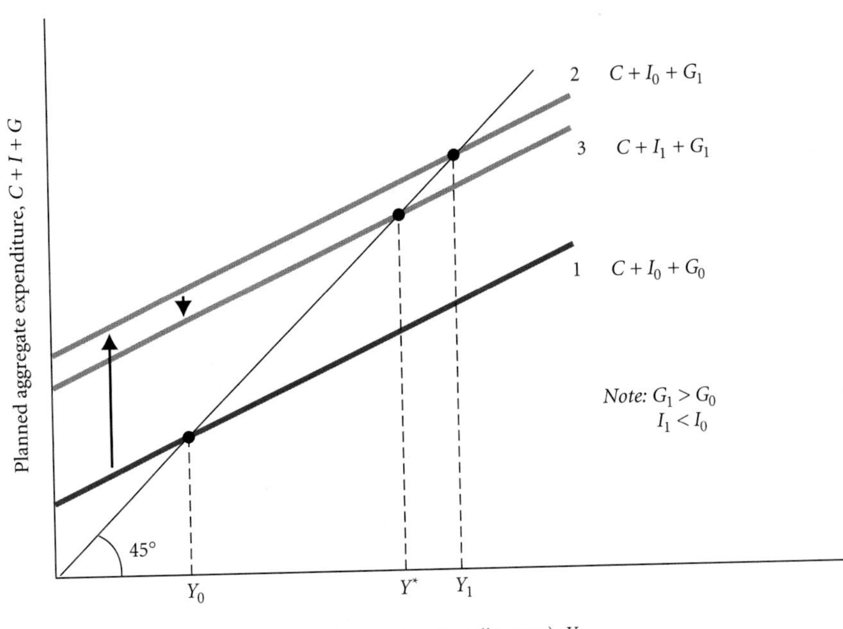

FIGURE 12.6 The Crowding-Out Effect

An increase in government spending G from G_0 to G_1 shifts the planned aggregate expenditure schedule from 1 to 2. The crowding-out effect of the decrease in planned investment (brought about by the increased interest rate) then shifts the planned aggregate expenditure schedule from 2 to 3.

the higher demand for money would be satisfied with a higher quantity of money supplied, and the interest rate would not rise. Without a higher interest rate, there would be no crowding out.

Second, the crowding-out effect depends on the **sensitivity** or **insensitivity of planned investment** spending to changes in the interest rate. Crowding out occurs because a higher interest rate reduces planned investment spending. Investment depends on factors other than the interest rate, however, and investment may at times be quite insensitive to changes in the interest rate. If planned investment does not fall when the interest rate rises, there is no crowding-out effect.

interest sensitivity or **insensitivity of planned investment** The responsiveness of planned investment spending to changes in the interest rate. *Interest sensitivity* means that planned investment spending changes a great deal in response to changes in the interest rate; *interest insensitivity* means little or no change in planned investment as a result of changes in the interest rate.

These effects are summarized next.

Effects of an expansionary fiscal policy:

$$G\uparrow \rightarrow Y\uparrow \rightarrow M^d\uparrow \rightarrow r\uparrow \rightarrow I\downarrow$$

→ Y increases less than if r did not increase

Exactly the same reasoning holds for changes in net taxes. The ultimate effect of a tax cut on the equilibrium level of output depends on how the money market reacts. The expansion of Y that a tax cut brings about will lead to an increase in the interest rate and thus a decrease in planned investment spending. The ultimate increase in Y will therefore be less than it would be if the interest rate did not rise.

Expansionary Monetary Policy: An Increase in the Money Supply Now let us consider what will happen when the Fed decides to increase the supply of money through open market operations. At first, open market operations inject new reserves into the system and expand the quantity of money supplied (the money supply curve shifts to the right). Because the quantity of money supplied is now greater than the amount households want to hold, the equilibrium rate of interest falls. Planned investment spending (which is a component of planned aggregate expenditure) increases when the interest rate falls.

Increased planned investment spending means planned aggregate expenditure is now greater than aggregate output. Firms experience unplanned decreases in inventories, and they raise output (Y). An increase in the money supply decreases the interest rate and increases Y. However, the higher level of Y increases the demand for money (the demand for money curve shifts to the right), and this keeps the interest rate from falling as far as it otherwise would.

News Analysis

Lower Interest Rates Increase Activity in the Housing Market in 2003

ONE PART OF INVESTMENT SPENDING (*I*) THAT IS quite sensitive to interest rates is investment in housing. Home purchases are generally financed with a mortgage. A mortgage is a long-term loan. Lower mortgage rates reduce the cost of buying and owning a home.

Between May of 2000 and June of 2003, the average mortgage rate on a fixed-rate 30-year mortgage fell from 8.5 percent to 5.26 percent, largely as the result of an expansionary Federal Reserve policy.

Consider the effect of such a decrease in rates on the monthly cost of buying a home. A potential buyer thinking of purchasing a home for \$150,000 and borrowing 80 percent of the purchase price, faced a \$923 monthly house payment at 8.5 percent. With rates at 5.26 percent the same buyer would face a monthly payment of just \$663. Others who bought earlier can reduce their monthly payments by refinancing their mortgage at lower rates.

All of this led to a strong housing market in 2003, which helped keep the economy out of further recession.

Home Mortgage Rates Hit Record Low—New York Times

Mortgage rates around the country tumbled to new lows this week, good news for people looking to buy homes or refinance.

The average rate on a 30-year fixed-rate mortgages dropped to a record low of 5.26 percent for the week ending June 5, Freddie Mac, the mortgage giant, reported Thursday in its weekly nationwide survey.

It marked the fourth straight week and the ninth time this year that rates on this benchmark mortgage fell to an all-time weekly low.

The previous low rate of 5.31 percent was set last week. The new rate marks the lowest since Freddie Mac began tracking 30-year mortgages in 1971. Records that reach back earlier indicate that the rate is the lowest in more than four decades, economists said.

For 15-year fixed-rate mortgages, a popular option for refinancing, rates fell to a record low of 4.66 percent this week. That surpassed last week's rate of 4.73 percent. This week's rate was the lowest level since Freddie Mac began tracking 15-year mortgages in 1991.

The housing market has managed to shine even as the national economy has struggled under numerous clouds.

Low mortgage rates propelled home sales to record levels last year. This year is shaping up to be the second-best year on record for sales of existing homes and new ones, economists say.

Refinancing activity also is booming, powered by low mortgage rates. Savings from home-mortgage refinancing has underpinned consumer spending, a main force keeping the economy going.

The drop in mortgage rates has "led to a new flood of mortgage applications," said Jay Brinkmann, vice president for research and economics at the Mortgage Bankers Association of America. "While almost 77 percent of the applications are for refinances, applications for mortgages for purchasing homes are also hitting record levels as buyers move to lock in these low rates."

Lower interest rates lower the monthly cost of owning a home and stimulate the demand for housing.

A year ago, rates on 30-year mortgages averaged 6.71 percent, 15-year mortgages were 6.18 percent and one-year adjustable mortgages stood at 4.71 percent.

"We just keep getting stunned by the performance of long-term mortgage rates," said David Seiders, chief economist at the National Association of Home Builders. "I don't know how low they can go."

Source: "Home Mortgage Rates Hit Record Low," Associated Press article in the New York Times, *June 6, 2003. Reprinted by permission.*

Visit www.prenhall.com/casefair for updated articles and exercises.

If you review the sequence of events that follows the monetary expansion, you can see the links between the injection of reserves by the Fed into the economy and the increase in output. First, the increase in the quantity of money supplied pushes down the interest rate. Second, the lower interest rate causes planned investment spending to rise. Third, the increased planned investment spending means higher planned aggregate expenditure, which means increased output as firms react to unplanned decreases in inventories. Fourth, the increase in output (income) leads to an increase in the demand for money (the demand for money curve shifts to the right), which means the interest rate decreases less than it would have if the demand for money had not increased.

Effects of an expansionary monetary policy:

$$M^s\uparrow \rightarrow r\downarrow \rightarrow I\uparrow \rightarrow Y\uparrow \rightarrow M^d\uparrow$$

$\hookrightarrow$ r decreases less than if M^d did not increase

The power of monetary policy to affect the goods market depends on how much of a reaction occurs at each link in this chain. Perhaps the most critical link is the link between r

and *I*. Monetary policy can be effective *only* if *I* reacts to changes in *r*. If firms sharply increase the number of investment projects undertaken when the interest rate falls, expansionary monetary policy works well at stimulating the economy. If, however, firms are reluctant to invest even at a low interest rate, expansionary monetary policy will have limited success. In other words, the effectiveness of monetary policy depends on the slope of the investment function. If it is nearly vertical, indicating very little responsiveness of investment to the interest rate, the middle link in this chain is weak, rendering monetary policy ineffective.

Expansionary Policy in Action: The Recessions of 1974–1975, 1980–1982, 1990–1991, and 2001 The United States has experienced four recessions since 1970. In 1974–1975 and 1980–1982 the government engaged in tax cuts that had the effect of stimulating consumer spending (*C*). Because *C* is a component of planned aggregate expenditure, these tax cuts had the effect of increasing aggregate output (income) (*Y*).

Consider the recession of 1974–1975. The Tax Reduction Act of 1975 resulted in a 1974 tax rebate of $8 billion that was paid to consumers in the second quarter of 1975. This rebate and other tax reductions led to increased consumer spending, which contributed to the economic recovery that began soon after the new tax laws went into effect.

But what about the crowding-out effect? Did the 1975 expansionary fiscal policy drive up interest rates and crowd out private spending? In this case, no. At the same time that Congress was cutting taxes to stimulate spending, the Fed was trying to stimulate the economy by expanding the money supply. Even though the increased output during the expansion caused the *demand* for money to rise, the Fed was simultaneously expanding the *supply* of money, and interest rates did not change very much. This situation is illustrated in Figure 12.7.

A similar sequence of events took place during the recession of 1980–1982. On the recommendation of President Reagan, Congress passed a huge tax cut during the summer of 1981. Like the 1975 tax cut, the 1981 tax cut led to an increase in consumer spending, which helped lift the economy out of the recession.

Recovery from the 1980–1982 recession was also helped along by the Fed, which began to increase the supply of money sharply in the spring of 1982. So, even though output and income were expanding by late 1982, thereby increasing the demand for money, interest rates actually *declined* because the supply of money was expanding at a greater rate than money demand was increasing. There was no crowding-out effect.

The recession of 1990–1991 began soon after Iraq's invasion of Kuwait in the late summer of 1990. The recession was short-lived and shallow compared with the two previous recessions. Real GDP began to rise in the second quarter of 1991, but this recovery became known as the "jobless recovery." Because productivity increased and large firms continued to trim payrolls even as output was expanding, the unemployment rate stayed high right into the presidential election of 1992.

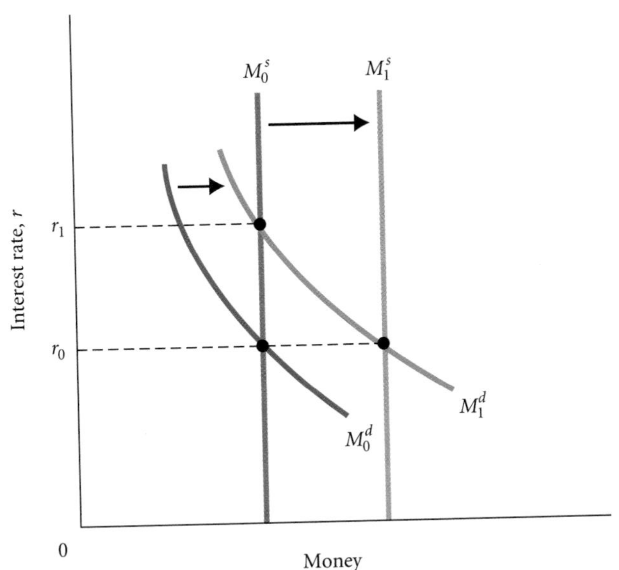

FIGURE 12.7 Fed Accommodation of an Expansionary Fiscal Policy

An expansionary fiscal policy, such as the 1975 tax cut, will increase aggregate output (income) and shift the money demand curve to the right, from M_0^d to M_1^d. If the money supply were unchanged, the interest rate would rise from r_0 to r_1 and planned investment would be negatively affected. If, however, the Fed were to "accommodate" the fiscal expansion by increasing the money supply from M_0^s to M_1^s, the interest rate would not rise.

President Bush debated calling for a tax cut to stimulate the economy, but concern with the already large government deficit and pressure from the Fed convinced him to wait. The Fed did push interest rates lower in an effort to get the economy moving. Even so, little response was evident by election time.

President Clinton called for some modest fiscal stimulus when he took office, but the Congress balked. Then, in the summer of 1993, Congress passed the Clinton deficit reduction package, which *increased* taxes and *reduced* government spending. In the meantime, monetary policy continued to be expansionary. Eventually, interest rates hit 30-year lows. For much of 1993, the 3-month T-bill rate was under 3 percent for the first time since 1962, and the 30-year bond rate fell below 6 percent for the first time since the government began selling 30-year-bonds.

In late 1994, the slow-growth recovery ended and a real expansion began, fueled in large part by the stock market boom that began in 1995. The boom ended in 2000 and the U.S. economy went into a recession in 2001. Monetary policy responded rapidly to the recession. In 2001 the Fed lowered the short-term interest rate by about 4 percentage points. This is perhaps the most expansionary monetary policy action in U.S. history. The recession was fairly mild, and by the fourth quarter of 2001 the economy was expanding again. The recovery was not, however, very strong, and the Fed kept the short-term interest rate low in 2002 and 2003.

CONTRACTIONARY POLICY EFFECTS

Any government policy that is aimed at reducing aggregate output (income) (Y) is said to be *contractionary*. Where expansionary policy is used to boost the economy, contractionary policy is used to slow the economy.

Considering that one of the four major economic goals is economic growth (Chapter 1), why would the government adopt policies designed to reduce aggregate spending? As we will see in the next two chapters, one way to fight inflation is to reduce aggregate spending. When the inflation rate is high, or the government believes it may rise soon, the government may use its powers to contract the economy. Before we discuss the contractionary policies that the government has undertaken in recent years, we need to discuss how contractionary fiscal and monetary policy work.

contractionary fiscal policy A decrease in government spending or an increase in net taxes aimed at decreasing aggregate output (income) (Y).

Contractionary Fiscal Policy: A Decrease in Government Spending (G) or an Increase in Net Taxes (T) A **contractionary fiscal policy** is a decrease in government spending (G) or an increase in net taxes (T) aimed at decreasing aggregate output (income) (Y). The effects of this policy are the opposite of the effects of an expansionary fiscal policy.

A decrease in government purchases or an increase in net taxes leads to a decrease in aggregate output (income) (Y), a decrease in the demand for money (M^d), and a decrease in the interest rate (r). The decrease in Y that accompanies a contractionary fiscal policy is less than it would be if we did not take the money market into account because the decrease in r also causes planned investment (I) to *increase*. This increase in I offsets some of the decrease in planned aggregate expenditure brought about by the decrease in G. (This also means the multiplier effect is smaller than it would be if we did not take the money market into account.) The effects of a decrease in G, or an increase in T, can be represented as shown.

Effects of a contractionary fiscal policy:

$$G\downarrow \text{ or } T\uparrow \rightarrow Y\downarrow \rightarrow M^d\downarrow \rightarrow r\downarrow \rightarrow I\uparrow$$

→ Y decreases less than if r did not decrease

contractionary monetary policy A decrease in the money supply aimed at decreasing aggregate output (income) (Y).

Contractionary Monetary Policy: A Decrease in the Money Supply A **contractionary monetary policy** is a decrease in the money supply aimed at decreasing aggregate output (income) (Y). As you recall, the level of planned investment spending is a negative function of the interest rate: The higher the interest rate, the less planned investment there will be. The less planned investment there is, the lower planned aggregate expenditure will be, and the lower the equilibrium level of output (income) (Y) will be. The lower equilibrium income results in a decrease in the demand for money, which means that the increase in the interest rate will be less than it would be if we did not take the goods market into account.

Effects of a contractionary monetary policy:

$$M^s \downarrow \rightarrow r\uparrow \rightarrow I\downarrow \rightarrow Y\downarrow \rightarrow M^d\downarrow$$

→ r increases less than if M^d did not decrease

Contractionary Policy in Action: 1973–1974 and 1979–1981 The Fed pursued strong contractionary policies twice in the 1970s and 1980s: first in 1973–1974 and again in 1979–1981. In 1974, short-term rates exceeded 12 percent, and in 1981, some short-term rates exceeded 20 percent. These high interest rates had a negative effect on planned aggregate expenditure and contributed to the recessions that followed. The Fed's purpose in following a tight monetary policy was to slow the inflation rate. (We will see in the next chapter why a contractionary policy may bring the inflation rate down.)

THE MACROECONOMIC POLICY MIX

Although we have been treating fiscal and monetary policy separately, it should be clear that fiscal and monetary policy can be used simultaneously. For example, both government purchases (G) and the money supply (M^s) can be increased at the same time. We have seen that an increase in G by itself raises both Y and r, while an increase in M^s by itself raises Y but lowers r. Therefore, if the government wanted to increase Y without changing r, it could do so by increasing both G and M^s by the appropriate amounts.

Policy mix refers to the combination of monetary and fiscal policies in use at a given time. A policy mix that consists of a decrease in government spending and an increase in the money supply would favor investment spending over government spending. This is because both the increased money supply and the fall in government purchases would cause the interest rate to fall, which would lead to an increase in planned investment. The opposite is true for a mix that consists of an expansionary fiscal policy and a contractionary monetary policy. This mix favors government spending over investment spending. Such a policy will have the effect of increasing government spending and reducing the money supply. Tight money and expanded government spending would drive the interest rate up and planned investment down.

policy mix The combination of monetary and fiscal policies in use at a given time.

There is no rule about what constitutes the "best" policy mix or the "best" composition of output. On this, as on many other issues, economists (and others) disagree. In part, someone's preference for a certain composition of output—say, one weighted heavily toward private spending with relatively little government spending—depends on how that person stands on such issues as the proper role of government in the economy.

Table 12.1 summarizes the effects of various combinations of policies on several important macroeconomic variables. If you can explain the reasoning underlying each of the

TABLE 12.1 The Effects of the Macroeconomic Policy Mix

		FISCAL POLICY	
		Expansionary ($\uparrow$ G or $\downarrow$ T)	**Contractionary ($\downarrow$ G or $\uparrow$ T)**
Monetary Policy	Expansionary ($\uparrow M^s$)	$Y\uparrow, r?, I?, C\uparrow$	$Y?, r\downarrow, I\uparrow, C?$
	Contractionary ($\downarrow M^s$)	$Y?, r\uparrow, I\downarrow, C?$	$Y\downarrow, r?, I?, C\downarrow$

Key:
$\uparrow$: Variable increases.
$\downarrow$: Variable decreases.
?: Forces push the variable in different directions. Without additional information, we cannot specify which way the variable moves.

effects shown in the table, you can be satisfied that you have a good understanding of the links between the goods market and the money market.

OTHER DETERMINANTS OF PLANNED INVESTMENT

We have assumed in this chapter that planned investment depends only on the interest rate. In reality, planned investment depends on other factors. We will discuss these factors more in Chapter 17, but provide a brief description here.

Expectations and Animal Spirits Firms' expectations about their future sales play an important role in their investment decisions. When a firm invests, it adds to its capital stock, and capital is used in the production process. If a firm expects that its sales will increase in the future, it may begin to build up its capital stock—that is, to invest—now so that it will be able to produce more in the future to meet the increased level of sales. The optimism or pessimism of entrepreneurs about the future course of the economy can have an important effect on current planned investment. Keynes used the phrase *animal spirits* to describe the feelings of entrepreneurs, and he argued that these feelings affect investment decisions.

Capital Utilization Rates The degree of utilization of a firm's capital stock is also likely to affect planned investment. If the demand for a firm's output has been decreasing and the firm has been lowering output in response to this decline, the firm may have a low rate of capital utilization. It can be costly to get rid of capital quickly once it is in place, and firms sometimes respond to a fall in output by keeping the capital in place but utilizing it less—for example, by running machines fewer hours per day or at slower speeds. Firms tend to invest less in new capital when their capital utilization rates are low than when they are high.

Relative Labor and Capital Costs The cost of capital (of which the interest rate is the main component) *relative* to the cost of labor can affect planned investment. If labor is expensive relative to capital (high wage rates), firms tend to substitute away from labor toward capital. They aim to hold more capital relative to labor when wage rates are high than when they are low.

The determinants of planned investment are:

- The interest rate
- Expectations of future sales
- Capital utilization rates
- Relative capital and labor costs

LOOKING AHEAD: THE PRICE LEVEL

Our discussion of aggregate output (income) and the interest rate in the goods market and the money market is now complete. You should now have a good understanding of how the two markets work together. However, we have not yet discussed the price level in any detail.

We cannot begin to understand the economic events of the last three decades without an understanding of the aggregate price level. The two periods of rapid increases in the price level, 1974–1975 and 1979–1981, had dramatic effects on the economy. What causes the price level to change? Are there policies that might prevent large changes in the price level or stop them once they have started? Before we can answer such questions, we must understand the factors that affect the overall price level. This is the task of the next chapter. Up to this point we have taken the price level as fixed. Now it is time to relax this assumption.

SUMMARY

1. The *goods market* and the *money market* do not operate independently. Events in the money market have considerable effects on the goods market, and events in the goods market have considerable effects on the money market.

THE LINKS BETWEEN THE GOODS MARKET AND THE MONEY MARKET

2. There are two important links between the goods market and the money market: The level of real output (income) (Y), which is determined in the goods market, determines the volume of transactions each period and thus affects the demand for money in the money market; and the interest rate (r), which is determined in the money market, affects the level of planned investment spending in the goods market.

3. There is a negative relationship between planned investment and the interest rate because the interest rate determines the cost of investment projects. When the interest rate rises, planned investment will decrease; when the interest rate falls, planned investment will increase.

4. For every value of the interest rate, there is a different level of planned investment spending and a different equilibrium level of output. The final level of equilibrium output depends on what the interest rate turns out to be, which depends on events in the money market.

5. For a given quantity of money supplied, the interest rate depends on the demand for money. Money demand depends on the level of output (income). With a given money supply, increases and decreases in Y will affect money demand, which will affect the equilibrium interest rate.

COMBINING THE GOODS MARKET AND THE MONEY MARKET

6. An *expansionary fiscal policy* is an increase in government spending (G) or a reduction in net taxes (T) aimed at increasing aggregate output (income) (Y). An expansionary fiscal policy based on increases in government spending tends to lead to a *crowding-out effect*: Because increased government expenditures mean more transactions in the economy and thus an increased demand for money, the interest rate will rise. The decrease in planned investment spending that accompanies the higher interest rate will then partially offset the increase in aggregate expenditures brought about by the increase in G.

7. The size of the crowding-out effect, affecting the size of the government spending multiplier, depends on two things: the assumption that the Fed does not change the quantity of money supplied and the *sensitivity or insensitivity of planned investment* to changes in the interest rate.

8. An *expansionary monetary policy* is an increase in the money supply aimed at increasing aggregate output (income) (Y). An increase in the money supply leads to a lower interest rate, increased planned investment, increased planned aggregate expenditure, and ultimately a higher equilibrium level of aggregate output (income) (Y). Expansionary policies have been used to lift the economy out of recessions.

9. A *contractionary fiscal policy* is a decrease in government spending or an increase in net taxes aimed at decreasing aggregate output (income) (Y). A decrease in government spending or an increase in net taxes leads to a decrease in aggregate output (income) (Y), a decrease in the demand for money, and a decrease in the interest rate. However, the decrease in Y is somewhat offset by the additional planned investment resulting from the lower interest rate.

10. A *contractionary monetary policy* is a decrease in the money supply aimed at decreasing aggregate output (income) (Y). The higher interest rate brought about by the reduced money supply causes a decrease in planned investment spending and a lower level of equilibrium output. However, the lower equilibrium level of output brings about a decrease in the demand for money, which means the increase in the interest rate will be less than it would be if we did not take the goods market into account. Contractionary policies have been used to fight inflation.

11. The *policy mix* is the combination of monetary and fiscal policies in use at a given time. There is no rule about what constitutes the best policy mix or the best composition of output. In part, one's preference for a certain composition of output depends on one's stance concerning such issues as the proper role of government in the economy.

OTHER DETERMINANTS OF PLANNED INVESTMENT

12. In addition to the interest rate, the level of planned investment in the economy also depends on expectations and animal spirits, capital utilization rates, and relative capital and labor costs.

REVIEW TERMS AND CONCEPTS

contractionary fiscal policy, 232
contractionary monetary policy, 228
crowding-out effect, 228
expansionary fiscal policy, 228
expansionary monetary policy, 232
goods market, 223
interest sensitivity or insensitivity of planned investment, 229
money market, 223
policy mix, 233

PROBLEM SET

1. On June 5, 2003, the European central bank acted to decrease the short-term interest rate in Europe by half a percentage point, to 2 percent. The bank's president, William Duisenberg, suggested that the bank could reduce rates further in the future. The rate cut was made because European countries were growing very slowly or were in recession. What effect did the bank hope the action would have on the economy? Be specific. What was the hoped-for result on *C*, *I*, and *Y*?

2. During late 1999 and early 2000, the Fed acted to slow the economy, which was growing at a blistering 7.4 percent annually at the end of 1999. At the same time Congress was debating what to do about mounting budget surpluses. The Republican members favored substantial tax cuts to "return income to the households holds that earned it." They argued that households should decide how to spend their incomes, not the government. Democrats argued that the best option was to pay down the Federal debt by buying back outstanding government bonds, not cutting taxes. Holding interest rates constant, what impacts would you expect to see on aggregate income/output from the two proposals (tax cut and debt reduction). By assuming that the Fed was determined to slow the economy regardless of Congress's choice, which of the two approaches would result in higher interest rates? Explain your answer.

3. During the third quarter of 1997, Japanese GDP was falling at an annual rate of over 11 percent. Many blame the big increase in Japan's taxes in the spring of 1997, which was designed to balance the budget. Explain how an increase in taxes with the economy growing slowly could precipitate a recession; do not skip steps in your answer. If you were head of the Japanese central bank, how would you respond? What impact would your policy have on the level of investment?

4. Some economists argue that the "animal spirits" of investors are so important in determining the level of investment in the economy that interest rates do not matter at all. Suppose that this were true—that investment in no way depends on interest rates.
   a. How would Figure 12.2 be different?
   b. What would happen to the level of planned aggregate expenditures if the interest rate changed?
   c. What would be different about the relative effectiveness of monetary and fiscal policy?

5. For each of the following, tell a story and predict the effects on the equilibrium levels of aggregate output (Y) and the interest rate (r):
   a. During 2000, the Federal Reserve was tightening monetary policy in an attempt to slow the economy. The Congress passed a substantial cut in the individual income tax at the same time.
   b. During the summer of 2003, the Congress passed and President Bush signed the third tax cut in 3 years. Many of the tax cuts took effect immediately. Assume the Fed holds M^s fixed.
   c. In 1993, the Congress and the president raised taxes. At the same time, the Fed was pursuing an expansionary monetary policy.
   d. In 2003, the Iraq War led to a sharp drop in consumer confidence and a drop in consumption. Assume the Fed holds the money supply constant.
   e. The Fed attempts to increase the money supply to stimulate the economy, but plants are operating at 65 percent of their capacities and businesses are pessimistic about the future.

6. Occasionally, the Federal Reserve Open Market Committee sets a policy designed to "track" the interest rate. This means that the OMC is pursuing policies designed to keep the interest rate constant. If, in fact, the Fed were acting to counter any increases or decreases in the interest rate to keep it constant, what specific actions would you expect to see the Fed take if the following were to occur? (In answering, indicate the effects of each set of events on Y, C, S, I, M^s, M^d, and r.)
   a. There is an unexpected increase in investor confidence, leading to a sharp increase in orders for new plants and equipment.
   b. A major New York bank fails, causing a number of worried people (not trusting even the FDIC) to withdraw a substantial amount of cash from other banks and put it in their cookie jars.

7. Paranoia, the largest country in Central Antarctica, receives word of an imminent penguin attack. The news causes expectations about the future to be shaken. As a consequence, there is a sharp decline in investment spending plans.
   a. Explain in detail the effects of such an event on the economy of Paranoia, assuming no response on the part of the Central Bank or the Treasury (M^s, T, and G all remain constant). Be sure to discuss the adjustments in the goods market and the money market.
   b. To counter the fall in investment, the king of Paranoia calls for a proposal to increase government spending. To finance the program, the Chancellor of the Exchequer has proposed three alternative options:
      (1) Finance the expenditures with an equal increase in taxes
      (2) Keep tax revenues constant and borrow the money from the public by issuing new government bonds
      (3) Keep taxes constant and finance the expenditures by printing new money

   Consider the three financing options and rank them from most expansionary to least expansionary. Explain your ranking.

8. Why might investment not respond positively to low interest rates during a recession? Why might investment not respond negatively to high interest rates during a boom?

APPENDIX

THE *IS-LM* DIAGRAM

There is a useful way of depicting graphically the determination of aggregate output (income) and the interest rate in the goods and money markets. Two curves are involved in this diagram, the *IS* curve and the *LM* curve. In this appendix, we will derive these two curves and use them to see how changes in government purchases (G) and the money supply (M^s) affect the equilibrium values of aggregate output (income) and the interest rate. The effects we describe here are the same as the effects we described in the main text; here we illustrate the effects graphically.

THE *IS* CURVE

We know that in that goods market, there is an equilibrium level of aggregate output (income) (Y) for each value of the interest rate (r). For a given value of r, we can determine the equilibrium value of Y. The equilibrium value of Y falls when r rises and rises when r falls. There is thus a *negative* relationship between the equilibrium value of Y and r. The reason for this negative relationship is the negative relationship between planned investment and the interest rate. When the interest rate rises, planned investment (I) falls, and this decrease in I leads to a decrease in the equilibrium value of Y. The negative relationship between the equilibrium value of Y and r is shown in Figure 12A.1. This curve is called the ***IS curve***.[1] Each point on the *IS* curve represents the equilibrium point in the goods market for the given interest rate.

We also know from our earlier analysis of the goods market that when government purchases (G) increase with a constant interest rate, the equilibrium value of Y increases. This means the *IS* curve shifts to the right when G increases. With the same value of r and a higher value of G, the equilibrium value of Y is larger; when G decreases, the *IS* curve shifts to the left.

THE *LM* CURVE

In the money market, there is an equilibrium value of the interest rate (r) for every value of aggregate output (income) (Y). The equilibrium value of r is determined at the point at which the quantity of money demanded equals the quantity of money supplied. For a given value of Y, we can determine the equilibrium value of r in the money market. We also know from Figure 12.5 that the equilibrium value of r rises when Y rises and falls when Y falls—a *positive* relationship between the equilibrium value of r and Y. The reason for this positive relationship is the positive relationship between the demand for money and Y. When Y increases, the demand for money increases because more money is demanded for the increased volume of transactions in the economy. An increase in the demand for money increases the equilibrium value of r—thus the positive relationship between the equilibrium value of r and Y.

The positive relationship between the equilibrium value of r and Y is shown in Figure 12A.2. This curve is called the ***LM curve***.[2] Each point on the *LM* curve represents equilibrium in the money market for the given value of aggregate output (income).

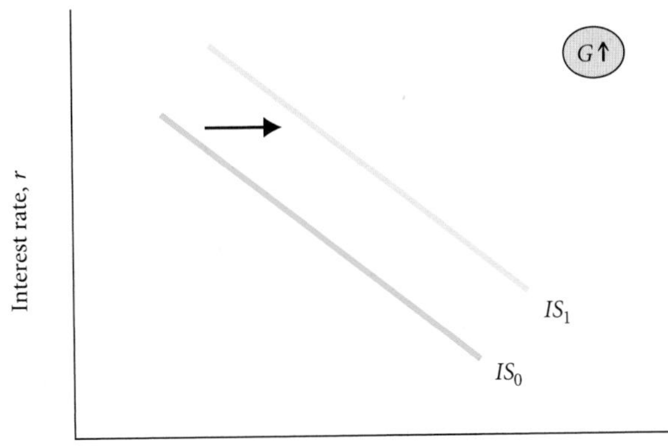

FIGURE 12A.1 The *IS* Curve

Each point on the *IS* curve corresponds to the equilibrium point in the goods market for the given interest rate. When government spending (G) increases, the *IS* curve shifts to the right, from IS_0 to IS_1.

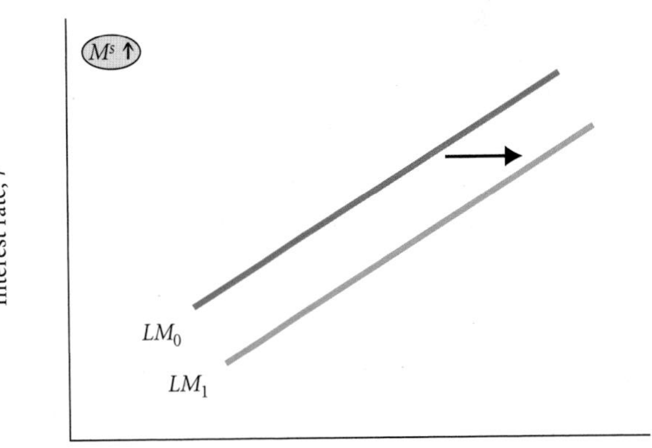

FIGURE 12A.2 The *LM* Curve

Each point on the *LM* curve corresponds to the equilibrium point in the money market for the given value of aggregate output (income). Money supply (M^S) increases shift the *LM* curve to the right, from LM_0 to LM_1.

[1] The letter I stands for investment, and the letter S stands for saving. *IS* refers to the fact that in equilibrium in the goods market, planned investment equals saving.

[2] The letter L stands for liquidity, a characteristic of money, and the letter M stands for money.

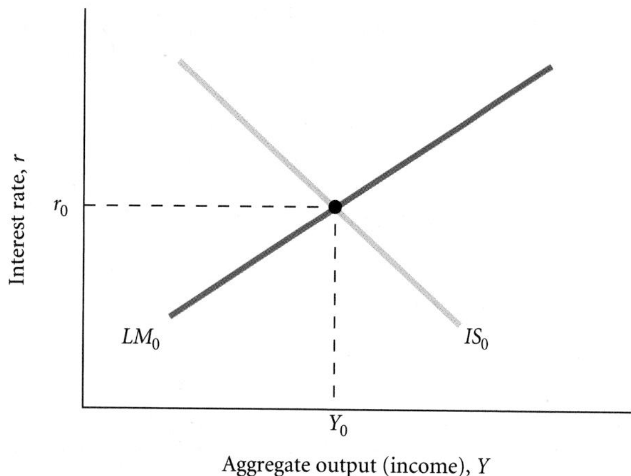

FIGURE 12A.3 The *IS-LM* Diagram

The point at which the *IS* and *LM* curves intersect corresponds to the point at which both the goods market and the money market are in equilibrium. The equilibrium values of aggregate output and the interest rate are Y_0 and r_0.

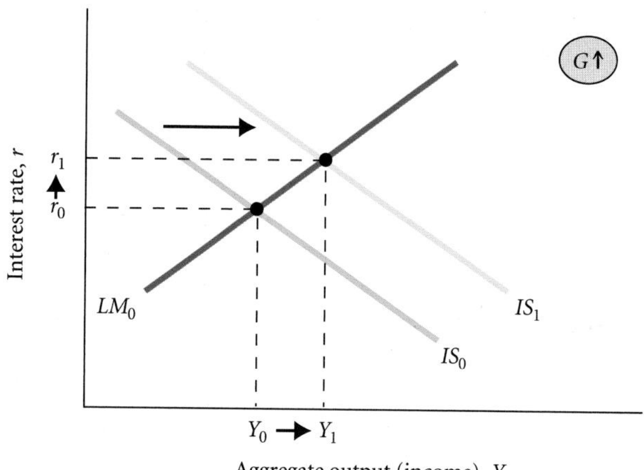

FIGURE 12A.4 An Increase in Government Purchases (*G*)

When *G* increases, the *IS* curve shifts to the right. This increases the equilibrium value of both *Y* and *r*.

We also know from our analysis of the money market that when the money supply (M^s) increases with a constant level of *Y*, the equilibrium value of *r* decreases. As Figure 12A.2 shows, this means the *LM* curve shifts to the right when M^s increases. With the same value of *Y* and a higher value of M^s, the equilibrium value of *r* is lower. When M^s decreases, the *LM* curve shifts to the left.

THE *IS-LM* DIAGRAM

Figure 12A.3 shows the *IS* and *LM* curves together on one graph. The point at which the two curves intersect is the point at which equilibrium exists in *both* the goods market and the money market. There is equilibrium in the goods market because the point is on the *IS* curve, and there is equilibrium in the money market because the point is on the *LM* curve.

We now have only two tasks left. The first is to see how the equilibrium values of *Y* and *r* are affected by changes in *G*—fiscal policy. This is easy. We have just seen that an increase in *G* shifts the *IS* curve to the right. Thus, an increase in *G* leads to higher equilibrium values of *Y* and *r*. This situation is illustrated in Figure 12A.4. Conversely, a decrease in *G* leads to lower equilibrium values of *Y* and *r* because the lower level of *G* causes the *IS* curve to shift to the left. (The direction of the effects are similar for changes in net taxes, *T*.)

Our second task is to see how the equilibrium values of *Y* and *r* are affected by changes in M^s—monetary policy. This is also easy. We have just seen that an increase in M^s shifts the *LM* curve to the right. Thus, an increase in M^s leads to a higher equilibrium value of *Y* and a lower equilibrium value of *r*. This is illustrated in Figure 12A.5. Conversely, a decrease in M^s leads to a lower equilibrium value of *Y* and a higher equilibrium value of *r* because a decreased money supply causes the *LM* curve to shift to the left.

The *IS-LM* diagram is a useful way of seeing the effects of changes in monetary and fiscal policies on equilibrium aggregate output (income) and the interest rate through shifts in the two curves. Always keep in mind the economic theory that lies *behind* the two curves. Do not memorize what curve shifts when; be able to understand and explain *why* the curves shift. This means always going back to the behavior of households and firms in the goods and money markets.

It is possible to use the *IS-LM* diagram to see how there can be a monetary and fiscal policy mix that leads to, say, an increase in aggregate output (income) but no increase in the interest rate. If both *G* and M^s increase, both curves shift to the right, and the shifts can be controlled in such a way as to bring about no change in the equilibrium value of the interest rate. Draw this case to be sure you understand this.

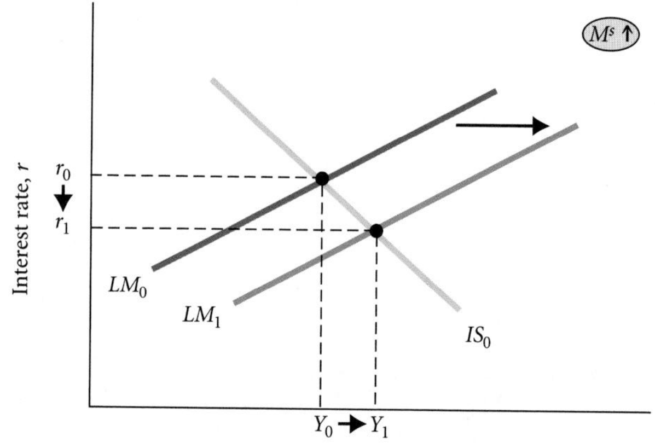

FIGURE 12A.5 An Increase in the Money Supply (M^S)

When M^s increases, the *LM* curve shifts to the right. This increases the equilibrium value of *Y* and decreases the equilibrium value of *r*.

SUMMARY

1. An *IS curve* illustrates the negative relationship between the equilibrium value of aggregate output (income) (Y) and the interest rate in the goods market. An *LM curve* illustrates the positive relationship between the equilibrium value of the interest rate and aggregate output (income) (Y) in the money market. The point at which the *IS* and *LM* curves intersect is the point at which equilibrium exists in both the goods market and the money market.

REVIEW TERMS AND CONCEPTS

***IS* curve** A curve illustrating the negative relationship between the equilibrium value of aggregate output (income) (Y) and the interest rate in the goods market. 237

***LM* curve** A curve illustrating the positive relationship between the equilibrium value of the interest rate and aggregate output (income) (Y) in the money market. 237

PROBLEM SET

1. Illustrate each of the following situations with *IS/LM* curves:
   a. An increase in G with the money supply held constant by the Fed
   b. An increase in G with the Fed changing M^S by enough to keep interest rates constant
   c. The president cuts G and increases T while the chair of the Fed expands M^S
   d. The president increasing G and holding T constant while the chair of the Fed holds M^S constant during a period of inflation

Aggregate Demand, Aggregate Supply, and Inflation

13

One of the most important issues in macroeconomics is the determination of the overall price level. Recall that inflation—an increase in the overall price level—is one of the key concerns of macroeconomists and government policy makers. Understanding the factors that affect the price level is essential to understanding macroeconomics.

In Chapter 7, we discussed how inflation is measured and the costs of inflation, but made no mention of the *causes* of inflation. For simplicity, our analysis in Chapters 8 through 12 took the price level as fixed. This allowed us to discuss the links between the goods market and the money market without the complication of a changing price level. Our having considered how the two markets work, we are ready to take up flexible prices.

We begin by discussing the *aggregate demand curve* and the *aggregate supply curve*, introduced briefly in Chapter 5. We then put the two curves together and discuss how the equilibrium price level is determined in the economy. This analysis allows us to see how the price level affects the economy and how the economy affects the price level. Finally, we consider monetary and fiscal policy effects and the causes of inflation.

THE AGGREGATE DEMAND CURVE

The place to begin our exploration of the price level is the money market. (If you have forgotten the details of how the overall price level is calculated or what it means, review Chapters 6 and 7.) As we saw in Chapter 11, people's demand for money depends on income (Y), the interest rate (r), and the price level (P).

It is not hard to understand why the price level affects the demand for money. Suppose you plan to purchase one pound of chocolate, one bag of potato chips, and a Hostess Twinkie. If these items cost \$2.00, \$1.00, and \$0.50, respectively, you would need \$3.50 in cash or in your checking account to make your purchases. Suppose that the price of these goods doubles. To make the same purchases, you will need \$7.00.

In general, the amount of money required to make a given number of transactions depends directly and proportionately on the average price of those transactions. As prices and wages rise, households will want to keep more money in their wallets and in their checking accounts, firms will need more in their cash drawers, and so forth. If prices and wages are rising at 6 percent per year, we can expect the demand for money to increase at about 6 percent per year, *ceteris paribus.*

Money demand is a function of three variables: the interest rate (r), the level of real income (Y), and the price level (P). (Remember, Y is *real* output, or income. It measures the actual volume of output, without regard to changes in the price level.) Money demand will increase if the real level of output (income) increases, the price level increases, or the interest rate declines.

DERIVING THE AGGREGATE DEMAND CURVE

aggregate demand The total demand for goods and services in the economy.

Recall that **aggregate demand** is the total demand for goods and services in the economy. To derive the aggregate demand curve, we examine what happens to aggregate output (income) (Y) when the price level (P) changes. Does it increase, decrease, or remain constant when the price level increases? Our discussions of the goods market and the money market provide the tools to answer this.

The aggregate demand curve is derived by assuming the fiscal policy variables [government purchases (G) and net taxes (T)] and the monetary policy variable (M^s) remain unchanged. In other words, the assumption is the government does not take any action to affect the economy in response to changes in the price level.

As you know, an increase in the price level increases the demand for money and shifts the money demand curve to the right, as illustrated in Figure 13.1(a). At the initial interest rate of 6 percent, an increase in the price level leads to an excess demand for money. Because of the higher price level, households and firms need to hold larger money balances than before. However, the quantity of money supplied remains the same. [Remember, we are assuming that the Federal Reserve (Fed) takes no action to change the money supply.] The money market is now out of equilibrium. Equilibrium is reestablished at a higher interest rate, 9 percent.

As indicated in Figure 13.1(b) with the interest rate now higher, fewer investment projects are desirable, and planned investment spending (I) falls from I_0 to I_1. Lower I means planned aggregate expenditure (AE) is lower, shown in Figure 13.1(c) as a downward shift of the AE curve. Lower AE means inventories are greater than planned, firms cut back on output, and Y falls from Y_0 to Y_1.

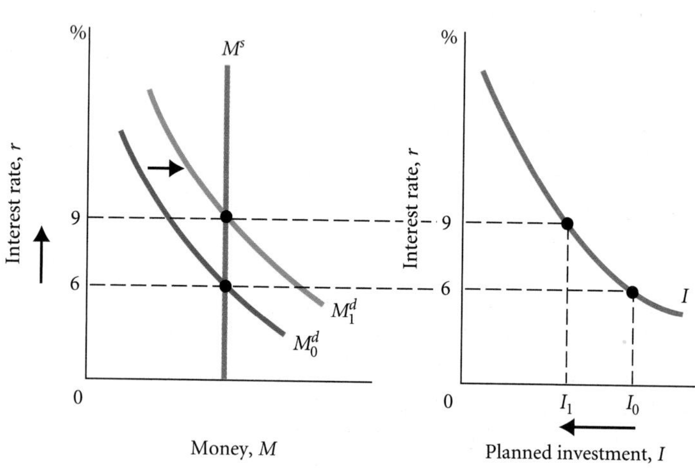

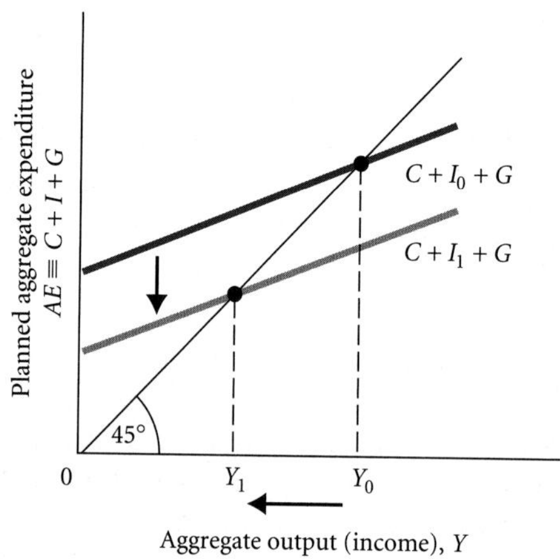

a. An increase in the price level increases the demand for money from M_0^d to M_1^d. With the supply of money unchanged, the interest rate increases from 6% to 9%.

b. The higher interest rate decreases planned investment from I_0 to I_1.

c. Decreased planned investment reduces planned aggregate expenditure and causes equilibrium output (income) to fall from Y_0 to Y_1.

FIGURE 13.1 The Impact of an Increase in the Price Level on the Economy–Assuming No Changes in *G*, *T*, and M^s

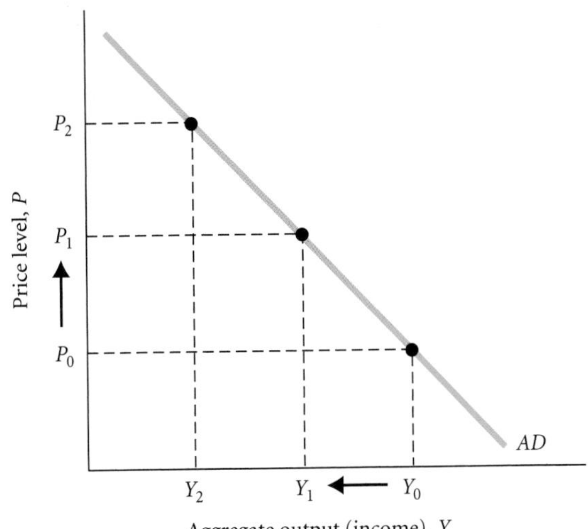

FIGURE 13.2 The Aggregate Demand (*AD*) Curve

At all points along the *AD* curve, both the goods market and the money market are in equilibrium.

An increase in the price level causes the level of aggregate output (income) to fall.

The situation is reversed when the price level declines. A lower price level causes money demand to fall, which leads to a lower interest rate. A lower interest rate stimulates planned investment spending, increasing planned aggregate expenditure, which leads to an increase in *Y*.

A decrease in the price level causes the level of aggregate output (income) to rise.

This negative relationship between aggregate output (income) and the price level is called the **aggregate demand (*AD*) curve**, shown in Figure 13.2.

aggregate demand (*AD*) curve A curve that shows the negative relationship between aggregate output (income) and the price level. Each point on the *AD* curve is a point at which both the goods market and the money market are in equilibrium.

Each point on the aggregate demand curve represents equilibrium in both the goods market *and* the money market. We have derived the *AD* curve by using the analysis we did in Chapter 12, in which the goods market and the money market were linked together. Therefore:

Each pair of values of *P* and *Y* on the aggregate demand curve corresponds to a point at which both the goods market and the money market are in equilibrium.

THE AGGREGATE DEMAND CURVE: A WARNING

It is very important that you realize what the aggregate demand curve represents. As we pointed out in Chapter 5, the aggregate demand curve is much more complex than a simple individual or market demand curve. The *AD* curve is *not* a market demand curve, and it is *not* the sum of all market demand curves in the economy.

To understand why, recall the logic behind a simple downward-sloping household demand curve. A demand curve shows the quantity of output demanded (by an individual household or in a single market) at every possible price, *ceteris paribus*. In drawing a simple demand curve, we are assuming that *other prices* and *income* are fixed. From these assumptions, it follows that one reason the quantity demanded of a particular good falls when its price rises is that other prices do *not* rise. The good in question therefore becomes more expensive relative to other goods, which leads households to substitute other goods for the good whose price increased. In addition, if income does not rise when the price of a good does, real income falls. This may also lead to a lower quantity demanded of the good whose price has risen.

Things are different when the *overall price level* rises. When the overall price level rises many prices—including many wage rates (many people's income)—rise together. For this reason, we cannot use the *ceteris paribus* assumption to draw the *AD* curve. The logic that explains why a simple demand curve slopes downward fails to explain why the *AD* curve also has a negative slope.

Aggregate demand falls when the price level increases because the higher price level causes the demand for money (M^d) to rise. With the money supply constant, the interest rate will rise to reestablish equilibrium in the money market. *It is the higher interest rate that causes aggregate output to fall.*

You do not need to understand anything about the money market to understand a simple individual or market demand curve. However, to understand what the *aggregate* demand curve represents, you must understand the interaction between the goods market and the money market. The *AD* curve in Figure 13.2 embodies everything we have learned about the goods market and the money market up to now.

The *AD* curve is *not* the sum of all the market demand curves in the economy. It is *not* a market demand curve.

OTHER REASONS FOR A DOWNWARD-SLOPING AGGREGATE DEMAND CURVE

In addition to the effects of money supply and money demand on the interest rate, two other factors lie behind the downward slope of the *AD* curve. These are the consumption link and the real wealth effect.

The Consumption Link We noted in Chapter 8 (and will discuss in detail in Chapter 17) that consumption (*C*) and planned investment (*I*) depend on the interest rate. Other things equal, consumption expenditures tend to rise when the interest rate falls and to fall when the interest rate rises—just as planned investment does. This tendency is another link between the goods market and the money market. If something happens to change the interest rate in the money market, both consumption and planned investment are affected in the goods market.

The *consumption* link provides another reason for the *AD* curve's downward slope. An increase in the price level increases the demand for money, which leads to an increase in the interest rate, which leads to a decrease in consumption (as well as planned investment), which leads to a decrease in aggregate output (income). The initial decrease in consumption (brought about by the increase in the interest rate) contributes to the overall decrease in output.

Planned investment does not bear all the burden of providing the link from a higher interest rate to a lower level of aggregate output. Decreased consumption brought about by a higher interest rate also contributes to this effect.

The Real Wealth Effect We also noted in Chapter 8 (and will discuss in detail in Chapter 17) that consumption depends on wealth. Other things equal, the more wealth households have, the more they consume. Wealth includes holdings of money, shares of stock, bonds, and housing, among other things. If household wealth decreases, the result will be less consumption now and in the future.

The price level has an effect on some kinds of wealth. Suppose you are holding $1,000 in a checking account or in a money market fund and the price level rises by 10 percent. Your holding is now worth 10 percent less because the prices of the goods that you could buy with your $1,000 have all increased by 10 percent. The purchasing power (or "real value") of your holding has decreased by 10 percent.

An increase in the price level may also lower the real value of stocks and housing, although whether it does depends on what happens to stock prices and housing prices when the overall price level rises. If stock prices and housing prices rise by the same percentage as the overall price level, the real value of stocks and housing will remain unchanged. The point is:

An increase in the price level lowers the real value of *some* types of wealth.

The fact that the price level lowers the real value of wealth provides another reason for the downward slope of the *AD* curve. An increase in the price level lowers the real value of wealth. This leads to a decrease in consumption, which leads to a decrease in aggregate output (income). So, there is a negative relationship between the price level and output through this **real wealth effect** or **real balance effect.**

real wealth, or real balance, effect The change in consumption brought about by a change in real wealth that results from a change in the price level.

AGGREGATE EXPENDITURE AND AGGREGATE DEMAND

Throughout our discussion of macroeconomics so far, we have referred to the total planned spending by households (C), firms (I), and the government (G) as planned aggregate expenditure. At equilibrium, planned aggregate expenditure ($AE \equiv C + I + G$) and aggregate output (Y) are equal:

$$\text{equilibrium condition: } C + I + G = Y$$

How does planned aggregate expenditure relate to aggregate demand?

> At every point along the aggregate demand curve, the aggregate quantity demanded is exactly equal to planned aggregate expenditure, $C + I + G$.

You can see this in Figures 13.1 and 13.2. When the price level rises, it is planned aggregate expenditure that decreases, moving us up the aggregate demand curve.

However, the aggregate demand curve represents more than just planned aggregate expenditure. Each point on the *AD* curve represents the *particular* level of planned aggregate expenditure that is consistent with equilibrium in the goods market and money market at the given price. Notice that the variable on the horizontal axis of the aggregate demand curve in Figure 13.2 is Y. At every point along the *AD* curve, $Y = C + I + G$.

SHIFTS OF THE AGGREGATE DEMAND CURVE

The aggregate demand curve in Figure 13.2 is based on the assumption that the government policy variables G, T, and M^s are fixed. If any of these variables change, the aggregate demand curve will shift.

Consider an increase in the quantity of money supplied. If the quantity of money is expanded at any given price level, the interest rate will fall, causing planned investment spending (and planned aggregate expenditure) to rise. The result is an increase in output at the given price level. As Figure 13.3 shows:

> An increase in the quantity of money supplied at a given price level shifts the aggregate demand curve to the right.

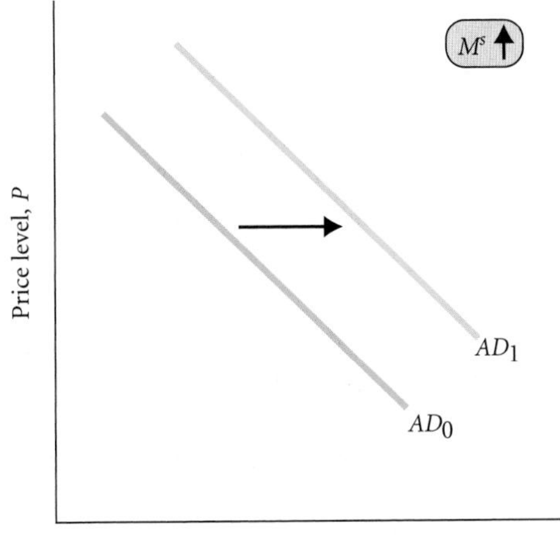

FIGURE 13.3 The Effect of an Increase in Money Supply on the *AD* Curve

An increase in the money supply (M^s) causes the aggregate demand curve to shift to the right, from AD_0 to AD_1. This shift occurs because the increase in M^s lowers the interest rate, which increases planned investment (and thus planned aggregate expenditure). The final result is an increase in output at each possible price level.

FIGURE 13.4 The Effect of an Increase in Government Purchases or a Decrease in Net Taxes on the *AD* Curve

An increase in government purchases (G) or a decrease in net taxes (*T*) causes the aggregate demand curve to shift to the right, from AD_0 to AD_1. The increase in G increases planned aggregate expenditure, which leads to an increase in output at each possible price level. A decrease in *T* causes consumption to rise. The higher consumption then increases planned aggregate expenditure, which leads to an increase in output at each possible price level.

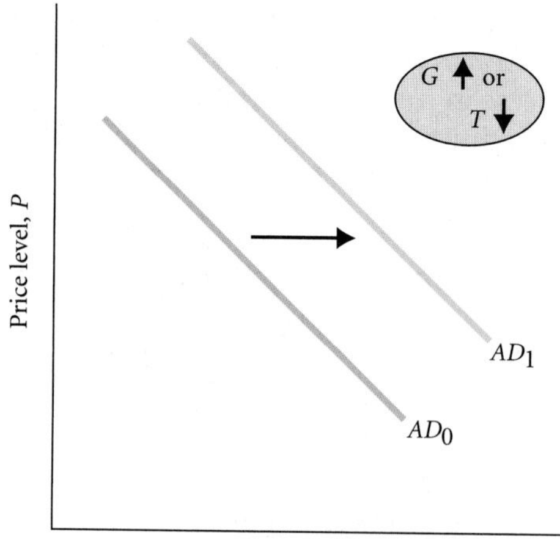

Expansionary monetary policy	**Contractionary monetary policy**
M^s ↑ → *AD* curve shifts to the right	M^s ↓ → *AD* curve shifts to the left
Expansionary fiscal policy	**Contractionary fiscal policy**
G ↑ → *AD* curve shifts to the right	*G* ↓ → *AD* curve shifts to the left
T ↓ → *AD* curve shifts to the right	*T* ↑ → *AD* curve shifts to the left

FIGURE 13.5 Factors That Shift the Aggregate Demand Curve

An increase in government purchases or a decrease in net taxes also increases aggregate output (income) at each possible price level, even though some of the increase will be crowded out if the money supply is held constant. (If you are unsure of what crowding-out is, review Chapter 11.) An increase in government purchases directly increases planned aggregate expenditure, which leads to an increase in output. A decrease in net taxes results in a rise in consumption, which increases planned aggregate expenditure, which also leads to an increase in output. As Figure 13.4 shows:

> An increase in government purchases or a decrease in net taxes shifts the aggregate demand curve to the right.

The same kind of reasoning applies to decreases in the quantity of money supplied, decreases in government purchases, and increases in net taxes. All of these shift the aggregate demand curve to the left.

Figure 13.5 summarizes the ways the aggregate demand curve shifts in response to changes in M^s, *G*, and *T*. To test your understanding of the *AD* curve, go through the figure piece by piece and explain the necessary steps for each of its components to create the shift in aggregate demand.

THE AGGREGATE SUPPLY CURVE

aggregate supply The total supply of all goods and services in an economy.

Aggregate supply is the total supply of goods and services in an economy. Although there is little disagreement among economists about the logic behind the aggregate demand curve, there is a great deal of disagreement about the logic behind the aggregate supply curve. There is also disagreement about its shape.

THE AGGREGATE SUPPLY CURVE: A WARNING

The **aggregate supply (*AS*) curve** shows the relationship between the aggregate quantity of output supplied by all the firms in an economy and the overall price level. To understand the aggregate supply curve, we need to understand something about the behavior of the individual firms that make up the economy.

aggregate supply (*AS*) curve A graph that shows the relationship between the aggregate quantity of output supplied by all firms in an economy and the overall price level.

It may seem logical to derive the aggregate supply curve by adding together the supply curves of all the individual firms in the economy. However, the logic behind the relationship between the overall price level in the economy and the level of aggregate output (income)—that is, the *AS* curve—is very different from the logic behind an individual firm's supply curve. The aggregate supply curve is *not* a market supply curve, and it is *not* the simple sum of all the individual supply curves in the economy. (Recall a similar warning for the aggregate demand curve.)

To understand why, recall the logic behind a simple supply curve, first introduced in Chapter 3. A supply curve shows the quantity of output an individual firm would supply at each possible price, *ceteris paribus.* When we draw a firm's supply curve, we assume that input prices, including wage rates, are constant. An individual firm's supply curve shows what would happen to the firm's output if the price of its output changes with *no* corresponding increase in costs. Such an assumption for an individual firm is reasonable because an individual firm is small relative to the economy as a whole. (It is unlikely that one firm raising the price of its output will lead to significant increases in input prices in the economy.) If the price of a profit-maximizing firm's output rises with *no* increase in the costs of any inputs, the firm is likely to increase output.

What would happen, however, if there were an increase in the overall price level? It is unrealistic to believe that costs are constant for individual firms if the overall price level is increasing, for two reasons. First, the outputs of some firms are the inputs of other firms. Therefore, if output prices rise, there will be an increase in at least some input prices. Second, it is unrealistic to assume that wage rates (an important input cost) do not rise at all when the overall price level rises. Because all input prices (including wage rates) are not constant as the overall price level changes, individual firms' supply curves *shift* as the overall price level changes, so we cannot sum them to get an aggregate supply curve.

Another reason the aggregate supply curve cannot be the sum of the supply curves of all the individual firms in the economy is that many firms (some would argue most firms) do not simply respond to prices determined in the market. Instead, they actually *set prices.* Only in perfectly competitive markets do firms simply react to prices determined by market forces. Firms in other kinds of industries (imperfectly competitive industries, to be exact) make both output and price decisions based on their perceptions of demand and costs. Price-setting firms do not have individual supply curves because these firms are choosing both output and price at the same time. To derive an individual supply curve, we need to imagine calling out a price to a firm and having the firm tell us how much output it will supply at that price. We cannot do this if firms are also setting prices. If supply curves do not exist for imperfectly competitive firms, we certainly cannot add them together to get an aggregate supply curve.

What can we say about the relationship between aggregate output and the overall price level? Because input prices change when the overall price level changes and because many firms in the economy set prices as well as output, it is clear that an "aggregate supply curve" in the traditional sense of the word *supply* does not exist. What does exist is what we might call a "price/output response" curve—a curve that traces out the price decisions and output decisions of all the markets and firms in the economy under a given set of circumstances.

What might such a curve look like?

AGGREGATE SUPPLY IN THE SHORT RUN

Many argue that the aggregate supply curve (or the price/output response curve) has a positive slope, at least in the short run. (We will discuss the short-run/long-run distinction in more detail later in this chapter.) In addition, many argue that at very low levels of aggregate output—for example, when the economy is in a recession—the aggregate supply curve is fairly flat, and at high levels of output—for example, when the economy is experiencing a boom—it is vertical or nearly vertical. Such a curve is shown in Figure 13.6.

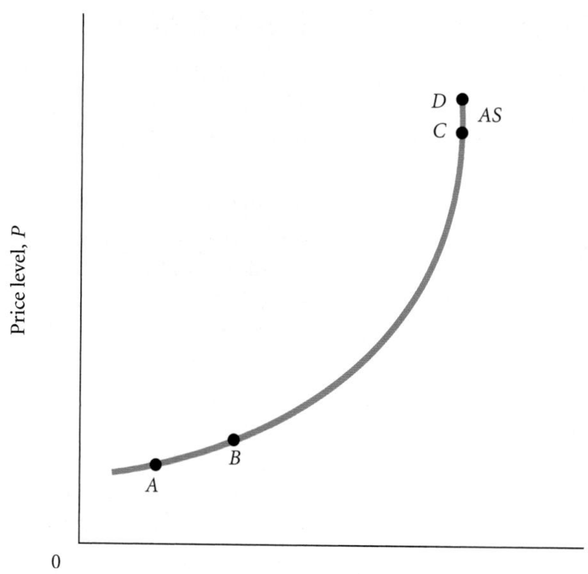

FIGURE 13.6 The Short-Run Aggregate Supply Curve

In the short run, the aggregate supply curve (the price/output response curve) has a positive slope. At low levels of aggregate output, the curve is fairly flat. As the economy approaches capacity, the curve becomes nearly vertical. At capacity, the curve is vertical.

To understand the shape of the *AS* curve in Figure 13.6, consider the output and price response of markets and firms to a steady increase in aggregate demand brought about by an increasingly expansionary fiscal or monetary policy. The reaction of firms to such an expansion is likely to depend on two factors: (1) how close the economy is to capacity at the time of the expansion, and (2) how rapidly input prices (such as wage rates) respond to increases in the overall price level.

Capacity Constraints In microeconomics, "short run" describes the time in which firms' decisions are constrained by some *fixed factor of production.* Farmers are constrained in the short run by the number of acres of land on their farm—the amount of land owned is the fixed factor of production. Manufacturing firms' short-run production decisions are constrained by the size of their physical production facilities. In the longer run, individual firms can overcome these types of constraints by investing in greater capacity—for example, by purchasing more acreage or building a new factory.

The idea of a fixed capacity in the short run also plays a role in macroeconomics. Macroeconomists tend to focus on whether or not *individual firms* are producing at or close to full capacity. A firm is producing at full capacity if it is fully utilizing the capital and labor it has on hand. As we will discuss in detail in Chapter 17, firms may at times have *excess capital* and *excess labor* on hand—amounts of capital and labor not needed to produce the current level of output. If, for example, there are costs of getting rid of capital once it is in place, a firm may choose to hold on to some of this capital, even if the economy is in a downturn and the firm has decreased its output. In this case, the firm will not be fully utilizing its capital stock. Firms may be especially likely to behave this way if they expect that the downturn will be short and that they will need the capital in the future to produce a higher level of output. Firms may have similar reasons for holding excess labor. It may be costly, both in worker morale and administrative costs, to lay off a large number of workers.

The Fed reports on the nation's "capacity utilization rate" monthly. In December of 1990, for example, during the recession of 1990–1991, the capacity utilization rate for manufacturing firms was 79.3 percent. This suggests about 20 percent of the nation's factory capacity was idle. During the recessions of 1974–1975 and 1980–1982, capacity utilization fell below 75 percent. During the 2001 recession capacity utilization also fell below 75 percent. Capacity utilization remained low throughout 2002 and 2003. In July 2003 it was only 74.6 percent.

Macroeconomists also focus on whether or not the *economy as a whole* is operating at full capacity. If there is cyclical unemployment (unemployment above the frictional and structural amounts), the economy is not fully utilizing its labor force. There are people who want to work at the current wage rates who cannot find jobs.

Even if firms are not holding excess labor and capital, the economy may be operating below its capacity if there is cyclical unemployment.

Output Levels and Price/Output Responses At low levels of output in the economy, there is likely to be excess capacity both in individual firms and in the economy as a whole. Firms are likely to be producing at levels of output below their existing capacity constraints. That is, they are likely to be holding excess capital and labor. It is also likely that there will be cyclical unemployment in the economy as a whole in periods of low output. When this is the case, it is likely that firms will respond to an increase in demand by increasing output much more than they increase prices. Firms are below capacity, so the extra cost of producing more output is likely to be small. In addition, firms can get more labor (from the ranks of the unemployed) without much, if any, increase in wage rates.

An increase in aggregate demand when the economy is operating at low levels of output is likely to result in an increase in output with little or no increase in the overall price level. That is, the aggregate supply (price/output response) curve is likely to be fairly flat at low levels of aggregate output.

Refer to Figure 13.6. Aggregate output is considerably higher at *B* than at *A*, but the price level at *B* is only slightly higher than it is at *A*.

If aggregate output continues to expand, things will change. As firms and the economy as a whole begin to move closer and closer to capacity, firms' response to an increase in demand is likely to change from mainly increasing output to mainly increasing prices. Why? As firms continue to increase their output, they will begin to bump into their short-run capacity constraints. In addition, unemployment will be falling as firms hire more workers to produce the increased output, so the economy as a whole will be approaching its capacity. As aggregate output rises, the prices of labor and capital (input costs) will begin to rise more rapidly, leading firms to increase their output prices.

At some level of output, it is virtually impossible for firms to expand any further. At this level, all sectors are fully utilizing their existing factories and equipment. Plants are running double shifts, and many workers are on overtime. In addition, there is little or no cyclical unemployment in the economy. At this point, firms will respond to any further increases in demand only by raising prices, since they are unable to expand output any further.

When the economy is producing at its maximum level of output—that is, at capacity—the aggregate supply curve becomes vertical.

Between *C* and *D* in Figure 13.6, the *AS* curve is vertical. Moving from *C* to *D* results in no increase in aggregate output but a large increase in the price level.

The Response of Input Prices to Changes in the Overall Price Level

Whether or not the economy is producing a level of output close to capacity, there must be some time lag between changes in input prices and changes in output prices for the aggregate supply (price/output response) curve to slope upward. If input prices changed at exactly the same rate as output prices, the *AS* curve would be vertical.

It is easy to see why. It is generally assumed that firms make decisions with the objective of maximizing profits. If all output and input prices increase 10 percent, no firm would find it advantageous to change its level of output. Why? Because the output level that maximized profits before the 10 percent increase will be the same as the level that maximizes profits after the 10 percent increase.[1] So, if input prices adjusted immediately to output prices, the aggregate supply (price/output response) curve would be vertical.

Wage rates may increase at exactly the same rate as the overall price level if the price level increase is *fully anticipated*. If inflation were expected to be 5 percent this year, this expected

[1] All prices going up by the same percentage is analogous to changing the monetary unit of account from, say, green dollars to red dollars, where 1.1 red dollars equals 1 green dollar. A change in the monetary unit of account has no effect on the firms' profit-maximizing decisions. If the nominal value of all output and input prices increases by 10 percent, then nothing *real* happens. When all nominal values go up by 10 percent, firms' decisions concerning *real* output will not change.

increase might be built into wage and salary contracts. Most employees, however, do not receive automatic pay raises as the overall price level increases, and sometimes increases in the price level are unanticipated. Input prices—particularly wage rates—tend to lag behind increases in output prices for a variety of reasons. (We discuss these in Chapter 14.) At least in the short run, wage rates tend to be slow to adjust to overall macroeconomic changes. It is precisely this point that has led to an important distinction between the *AS* curve in the long run and the *AS* curve in the short run.[2] We will return to this distinction shortly, but for now we will assume that the *AS* curve is shaped like the one in Figure 13.6.

SHIFTS OF THE SHORT-RUN AGGREGATE SUPPLY CURVE

Just as the aggregate demand curve can shift, so too can the aggregate supply (price/output response) curve. Recall the individual firm behavior we just considered in describing the shape of the short-run *AS* curve. Firms with the power to set prices choose the price/output combinations that maximize their profits. Firms in perfectly competitive industries choose the quantities of output to supply at given price levels. The *AS* curve traces out these price/output responses to economic conditions.

Anything that affects these individual firm decisions can shift the *AS* curve. Some of these factors include cost shocks, economic growth, stagnation, public policy, and natural disasters.

Cost Shocks Firms' decisions are heavily influenced by costs. Some costs change at the same time the overall price level changes, some costs lag behind changes in the price level, and some may not change at all. Changes in costs that occur at the same time that the price level changes are built into the shape of the short-run *AS* curve. For example, when the price level rises, wage rates might rise by half as much in the short run. (This could happen if half of all wage contracts in the economy had cost-of-living increase clauses and half did not.) The shape of the short-run *AS* curve would reflect this response.

Sometimes cost changes occur that are *not* the result of changes in the overall price level—for example, the cost of energy. During the fall of 1990, world crude oil prices doubled from about $20 to $40 a barrel. Once it became clear the Persian Gulf War would not lead to the destruction of the Saudi Arabian oil fields, the price of crude oil on world markets fell back to below $20 per barrel. In contrast, in 1973 to 1974 and again in 1979, the price of oil increased substantially and remained at a higher level. Oil is an important input in many firms and industries, and when the price of firms' inputs rises, firms respond by raising prices and lowering output. At the aggregate level, this means an increase in the price of oil (or a similar cost increase) *shifts* the *AS* curve to the left, as in Figure 13.7(a). A leftward shift of the *AS* curve means a higher price level for a given level of output.

A decrease in costs shifts the *AS* curve to the right, as in Figure 13.7(b). A rightward shift of the *AS* curve means a lower price level for a given level of output.

Shifts in the *AS* curve brought about by a change in costs are referred to as **cost shocks** or **supply shocks**.

cost shock, or **supply shock** A change in costs that shifts the aggregate supply (*AS*) curve.

Economic Growth Economic growth shifts the *AS* curve to the right. Recall that the vertical part of the short-run *AS* curve represents the economy's maximum (capacity) output. This maximum output is determined by the economy's existing resources and the current state of technology. If the supply of labor increases or the stock of capital grows, the *AS* curve will shift to the right. The labor force is expected to grow naturally with an increase in working-age population, but it can also increase for other reasons. Since the 1960s, for example, the percentage of women in the labor force has grown sharply. This increase in the supply of women workers has shifted the *AS* curve to the right.

[2]Some textbooks derive the short-run aggregate supply curve by assuming *all* input prices are fixed. "Fixed input prices" means input prices do not change as the overall price level changes. This assumption is not realistic because the outputs of some firms (such as intermediate goods and capital goods) are the inputs of other firms. It is also unrealistic to assume that wage rates do not respond at all to changes in the overall price level. It is more realistic to assume that wage rates do not *fully* respond in the short run than it is to assume no response at all.

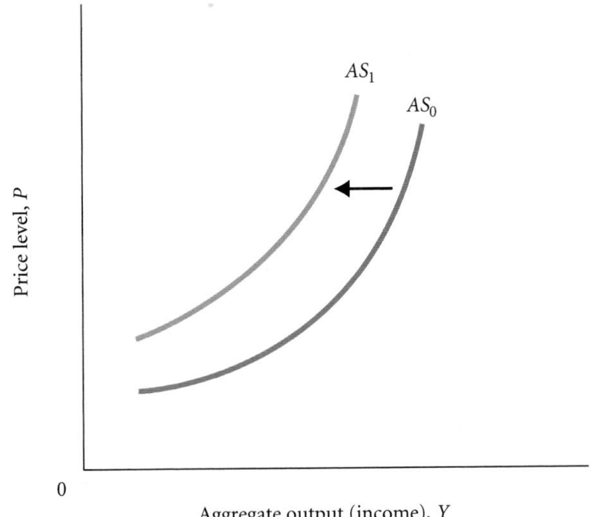

a. A decrease in aggregate supply

A leftward shift of the AS curve from AS_0 to AS_1 could be caused by an increase in costs—for example, an increase in wage rates or energy prices—natural disasters, economic stagnation, and the like.

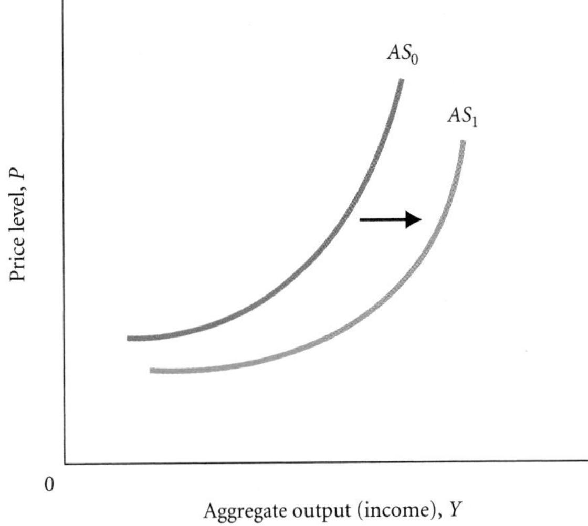

b. An increase in aggregate supply

A rightward shift of the AS curve from AS_0 to AS_1 could be caused by a decrease in costs, economic growth, public policy that stimulates supply, and the like.

FIGURE 13.7 Shifts of the Aggregate Supply Curve

Immigration can also shift the *AS* curve. During the 1970s, Germany, faced with a serious labor shortage, opened its borders to large numbers of "guest workers," largely from Turkey. The United States has recently experienced significant immigration, legal and illegal, from Mexico, from Central and South American countries, and from Asia. Increases in the stock of capital over time and technological advances can also shift the *AS* curve to the right. We will discuss economic growth in more detail in Chapter 20.

Stagnation and Lack of Investment The opposite of economic growth is stagnation and decline. Over time, capital deteriorates and eventually wears out completely if it is not properly maintained. If an economy fails to invest in both public capital (sometimes called *infrastructure*) and private capital (plant and equipment) at a sufficient rate, the stock of capital will decline. If the stock of capital declines, the *AS* curve will shift to the left.

Public Policy Public policy can shift the *AS* curve. In the 1980s, for example, the Reagan administration put into effect a form of public policy based on supply-side economics. The idea behind these supply-side policies was to deregulate the economy and reduce taxes to increase the incentives to work, engage in entrepreneurial activity, and invest. The main purpose of these policies was to shift the *AS* curve to the right. (We discuss supply-side economics in Chapter 19.)

Weather, Wars, and Natural Disasters Changes in weather can shift the *AS* curve. A severe drought will reduce the supply of agricultural goods; the perfect mix of sun and rain will produce a bountiful harvest. If an economy is damaged by war or natural disaster, the *AS* curve will shift to the left. Whenever part of the resource base of an economy is reduced or destroyed, the *AS* curve shifts to the left.

Figure 13.8 shows some factors that might cause the *AS* curve to shift.

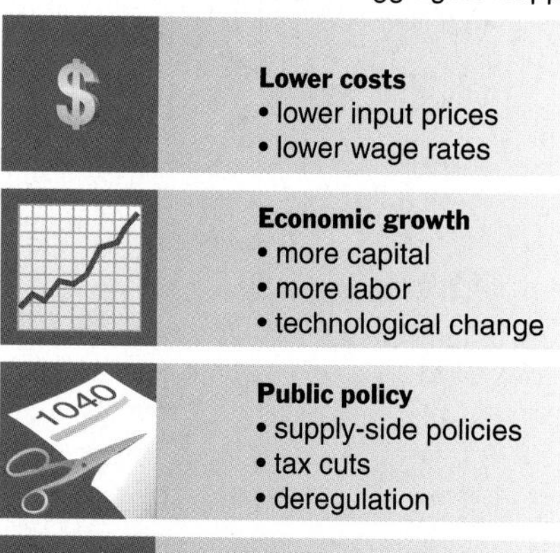
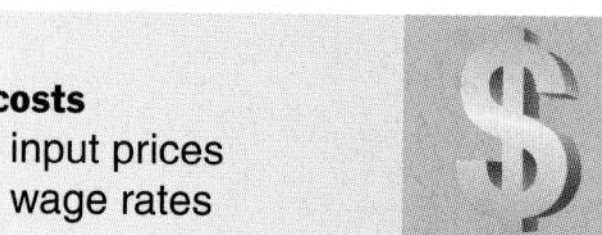

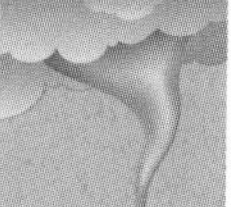

Shifts to the Right Increases in Aggregate Supply	**Shifts to the Left** Decreases in Aggregate Supply
Lower costs • lower input prices • lower wage rates	**Higher costs** • higher input prices • higher wage rates
Economic growth • more capital • more labor • technological change	**Stagnation** • capital deterioration
Public policy • supply-side policies • tax cuts • deregulation	**Public policy** • waste and inefficiency • over-regulation
Good weather	**Bad weather, natural disasters, destruction from wars**

FIGURE 13.8 Factors That Shift the Aggregate Supply Curve

THE EQUILIBRIUM PRICE LEVEL

equilibrium price level The price level at which the aggregate demand and aggregate supply curves intersect.

The **equilibrium price level** in the economy occurs at the point at which the *AD* curve and the *AS* curve intersect, shown in Figure 13.9 where the equilibrium price level is P_0 and the equilibrium level of aggregate output (income) is Y_0.

Figure 13.9 looks simple, but it is a powerful device for analyzing a number of macroeconomic questions. Consider first what is true at the intersection of the *AS* and *AD* curves. Each point on the *AD* curve corresponds to equilibrium in both the goods market and the money market. Each point on the *AS* curve represents the price/output responses of all the firms in the economy. That means:

> The point at which the *AS* and *AD* curves intersect corresponds to equilibrium in the goods and money markets and to a set of price/output decisions on the part of all the firms in the economy.

We will use this *AS*/*AD* framework to analyze the effects of monetary and fiscal policy on the economy and to analyze the causes of inflation. First we need to return to the *AS* curve and discuss its shape in the long run.

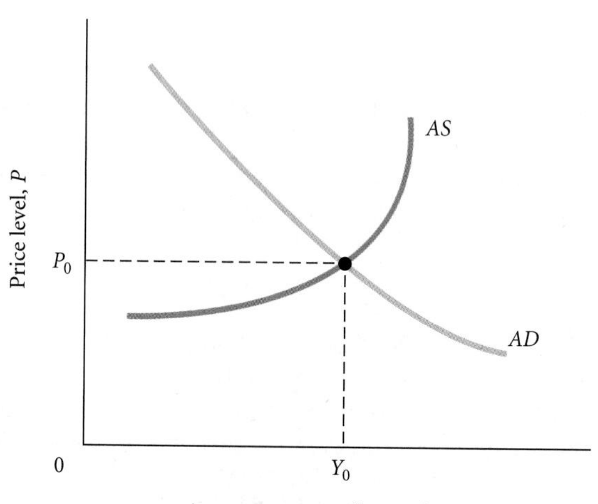

FIGURE 13.9 The Equilibrium Price Level

At each point along the *AD* curve, both the money market and the goods market are in equilibrium. Each point on the *AS* curve represents the price/output decisions of all the firms in the economy. P_0 and Y_0 correspond to equilibrium in the goods market and the money market and to a set of price/output decisions on the part of all the firms in the economy.

THE LONG-RUN AGGREGATE SUPPLY CURVE

As we noted earlier, for the *AS* curve not to be vertical, some costs must lag behind increases in the overall price level. If all prices (both input and output prices) change at the same rate, the level of aggregate output does not change. We have assumed that in the short run at least some cost changes lag behind price level changes, but what happens in the long run?

Many economists believe costs lag behind price-level changes in the short run but ultimately move with the overall price level. For example, wage rates tend to move very closely with the price level *over time*. If the price level increases at a steady rate, inflation may come to be fully anticipated and built into most labor contracts.

If costs and the price level move in tandem over a sufficient time period for these adjustments to be made, or the long run, the *AS* curve is best modeled as vertical. We can see why in Figure 13.10. Initially, the economy is in equilibrium at a price level of P_0 and aggregate output of Y_0 (the point *A* at which AD_0 and AS_0 intersect). Now imagine a shift of the *AD* curve from AD_0 to AD_1. In response to this shift, both the price level and aggregate output rise in the short run, to P_1 and Y_1, respectively (the point *B* at which AD_1 and AS_0 intersect). Recall, however, that the movement along the upward-sloping AS_0 curve as *Y* increases from Y_0 to Y_1 assumes that some costs lag behind the increase in the overall price level.

Assume now that costs fully adjust to prices in the long run, where, for example, labor unions renegotiate wage contracts to catch up with the increase in prices. These kinds of cost increases cause the *AS* curve to shift to the left, from AS_0 to AS_1. If, eventually, costs and prices have risen by exactly the same percentage, aggregate output will be back at Y_0 (the point *C* at which AD_1 and AS_1 intersect).

If wage rates and other costs fully adjust to changes in prices in the long-run, then the long-run *AS* curve is vertical.

POTENTIAL GDP

Recall that even the short-run *AS* curve becomes vertical at some particular level of output. The vertical portion of the short-run *AS* curve exists because there are physical limits to the amount that an economy can produce in any given time period. At the physical limit, all plants are operating around the clock, many workers are on overtime, and there is no cyclical unemployment.

Note that the vertical portions of the short-run *AS* curves in Figure 13.10 are to the right of Y_0. If the vertical portions of the short-run *AS* curves represent "capacity," then what is the nature of Y_0, the level of output corresponding to the long-run *AS* curve?

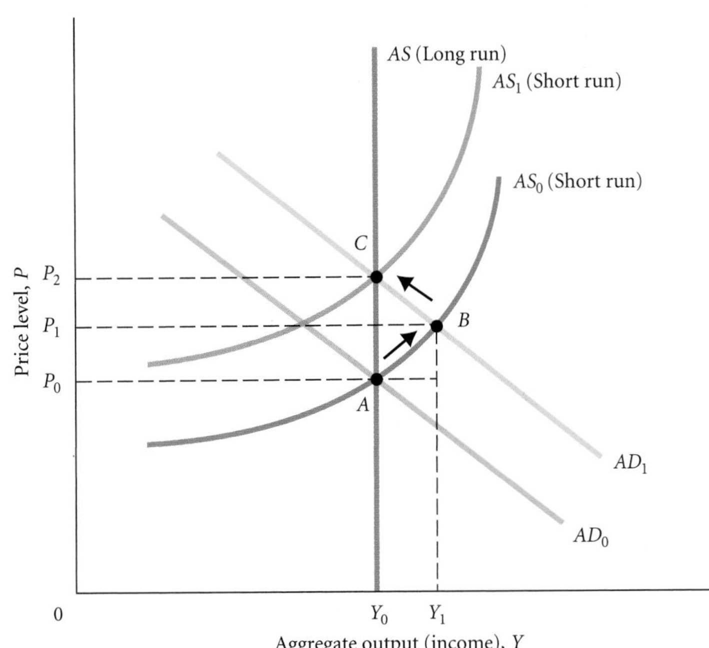

FIGURE 13.10 The Long-Run Aggregate Supply Curve

When the *AD* curve shifts from AD_0 to AD_1, the equilibrium price level initially rises from P_0 to P_1 and output rises from Y_0 to Y_1. Costs respond in the longer run, shifting the *AS* curve from AS_0 to AS_1. If costs ultimately increase by the same percentage as the price level, the quantity supplied will end up back at Y_0. Y_0 is sometimes called "potential GDP."

potential output, or **potential GDP** The level of aggregate output that can be sustained in the long run without inflation.

Y_0 represents the level of aggregate output that can be *sustained* in the long run without inflation. It is sometimes called **potential output** or **potential GDP**. Output can be pushed above Y_0 under a variety of circumstances, but when it is, there is upward pressure on costs. As the economy approaches short-run capacity, wage rates tend to rise as firms try to attract more people into the labor force and to induce more workers to work overtime. Rising costs shift the short-run *AS* curve to the left (in Figure 13.10 from AS_0 to AS_1) and drive output back to Y_0.

Short-Run Equilibrium below Potential GDP Thus far we have argued that if the short-run aggregate supply and aggregate demand curves intersect to the right of Y_0 in Figure 13.10, wages and other input prices will rise, causing the short-run *AS* curve to shift left and pushing GDP back down to Y_0. Although different economists have different opinions on how to determine whether an economy is operating at or above potential GDP, there is general agreement that there is a maximum level of output (below the vertical portion of the short-run aggregate supply curve) that can be sustained without inflation.

What about short-run equilibria that occur to the *left* of Y_0? If the short-run aggregate supply and aggregate demand curves intersect at a level of output below potential GDP, what will happen? Here again economists disagree. Those who believe the aggregate supply curve is vertical in the long run believe that when short-run equilibria exist below Y_0, GDP will tend to rise—just as GDP tends to fall when short-run equilibrium exists above Y_0. The argument is that when the economy is operating below full employment with excess capacity and high unemployment, input prices (including wages) are likely to *fall.* A decline in input prices shifts the aggregate supply curve to the *right*, causing the price level to fall and the level of real GDP to rise back to Y_0. This automatic adjustment works only if input prices fall when excess capacity and unemployment exist. We will discuss wage adjustment during periods of unemployment in detail in Chapter 14.

AGGREGATE DEMAND, AGGREGATE SUPPLY, AND MONETARY AND FISCAL POLICY

We are now ready to use the *AS/AD* framework to consider the effects of monetary and fiscal policy. We will first consider the short-run effects.

Recall that the two fiscal policy variables are government purchases (*G*) and net taxes (*T*). The monetary policy variable is the quantity of money supplied (M^s). An *expansionary* policy aims at stimulating the economy through an increase in *G* or M^s or a decrease in *T*. A *contractionary* policy aims at slowing down the economy through a decrease in *G* or M^s or an increase in *T*. We saw earlier in this chapter that an expansionary policy shifts the *AD* curve to the right and that a contractionary policy shifts the *AD* curve to the left. How do these policies affect the equilibrium values of the price level (*P*) and the level of aggregate output (income)?

When considering the effects of a policy change, we must be careful to note where along the (short-run) *AS* curve the economy is at the time of the change. If the economy is initially on the flat portion of the *AS* curve, as shown by point *A* in Figure 13.11, then an expansionary policy, which shifts the *AD* curve to the right, results in a small price increase relative to the output increase: The increase in equilibrium *Y* (from Y_0 to Y_1) is much greater than the increase in equilibrium *P* (from P_0 to P_1). This is the case in which an expansionary policy works well. There is an increase in output with little increase in the price level.

If the economy is initially on the steep portion of the *AS* curve, as shown by point *B* in Figure 13.12, then an expansionary policy results in a small increase in equilibrium output (from Y_0 to Y_1) and a large increase in the equilibrium price level (from P_0 to P_1). In this case, an expansionary policy does not work well. It results in a much higher price level with little increase in output. The multiplier is therefore close to zero: Output is initially close to capacity, and attempts to increase it further lead mostly to a higher price level.

Figures 13.11 and 13.12 show that it is important to know where the economy is *before* a policy change is put into effect. The economy is producing on the nearly flat part of the *AS* curve if most firms are producing well below capacity. When this is the case, firms will respond to an increase in demand by increasing output much more than they increase

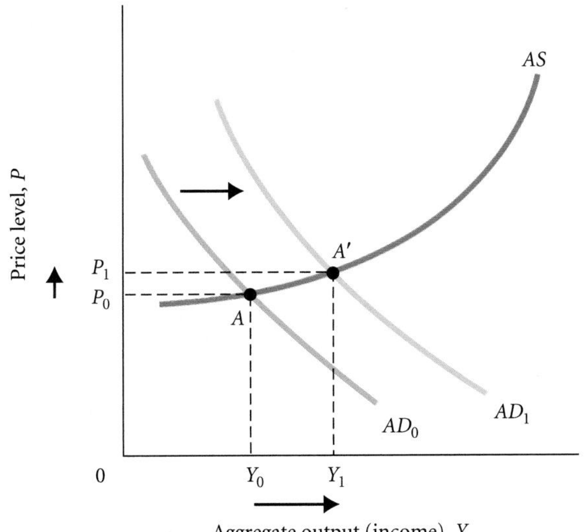

FIGURE 13.11 A Shift of the Aggregate Demand Curve When the Economy Is on the Nearly Flat Part of the *AS* Curve

Aggregate demand can shift to the right for a number of reasons, including an increase in the money supply, a tax cut, or an increase in government spending. If the shift occurs when the economy is on the nearly flat portion of the *AS* curve, the result will be an increase in output with little increase in the price level from point *A* to point *A′*.

prices. If the economy is producing on the steep part of the *AS* curve, firms are close to capacity and will respond to an increase in demand by increasing prices much more than they increase output.

To see what happens when the economy is on the steep part of the *AS* curve, consider the effects of an increase in *G* with no change in the money supply. What will happen is that when *G* is increased, there will be virtually no increase in *Y*. In other words, the expansionary fiscal policy will fail to stimulate the economy. To consider this, we need to go back to Chapter 12 and review what is behind the *AD* curve.

The first thing that happens when *G* increases is an unanticipated decline in firms' inventories. Because firms are very close to capacity output when the economy is on the steep part of the *AS* curve, they cannot increase their output very much. The result, as Figure 13.12 shows, is a substantial increase in the price level. The increase in the price level increases the demand for money, which (with a fixed money supply) leads to an increase in the interest rate, decreasing planned investment. *There is nearly complete crowding out of investment.* If firms are producing at capacity, prices and interest rates will continue to rise until the increase in *G* is completely matched by a decrease in planned investment and there is complete crowding out.

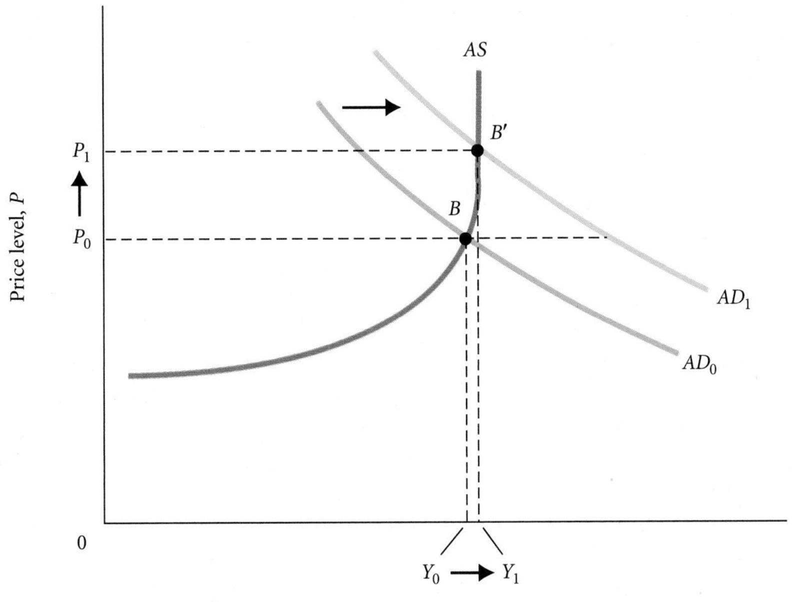

Companion Website Plus

FIGURE 13.12 A Shift of the Aggregate Demand Curve When the Economy Is Operating at or Near Maximum Capacity

If a shift of aggregate demand occurs while the economy is operating near full capacity, the result will be an increase in the price level with little increase in output from point *B* to point *B′*.

LONG-RUN AGGREGATE SUPPLY AND POLICY EFFECTS

We have so far been considering monetary and fiscal policy effects in the short-run. Concerning the long run, it is important to realize:

> If the *AS* curve is vertical in the long run, neither monetary policy nor fiscal policy has any effect on aggregate output in the long run.

Look back at Figure 13.10. Monetary and fiscal policy shift the *AD* curve. If the long-run *AS* curve is vertical, output always comes back to Y_0. In this case, policy affects *only* the price level in the long run, and the multiplier effect of a change in government spending on aggregate output in the long run is zero. Under the same circumstances, the tax multiplier is also zero.

The conclusion that policy has no effect on aggregate output in the long run is perhaps startling. Do most economists agree that the aggregate supply curve is vertical in the long run?

Most economists agree that input prices tend to lag behind output prices in the short run, giving the *AS* curve some positive slope. Most also agree the *AS* curve is likely to be steeper in the long run, but how long is the long run? The longer the lag time, the greater the potential impact of monetary and fiscal policy on aggregate output. If the long run is only 3 to 6 months, policy has little chance to affect output; if the long run is 3 or 4 years, policy can have significant effects. A good deal of research in macroeconomics focuses on the length of time lags between input and output prices. In a sense, the length of the long run is one of the most important open questions in macroeconomics.

Another source of disagreement centers on whether equilibria below potential GDP, Y_0 in Figure 13.10, are self-correcting (i.e., without government intervention). Recall that those

News Analysis

Increase in Government Spending without Fear of Inflation: 2003

On September 8, 2003, President Bush asked the Congress for $87 billion in additional funding for the military efforts in Afghanistan and Iraq. This request comes on the heals of a tax cut and a projected deficit of $475 billion in 2003. The Federal Government was running a very expansionary fiscal policy. Expansionary fiscal policy (increasing *G* and cutting *T*) shifts the aggregate demand curve to the right. Yet no one seemed to be worried about inflation. The reason was that the economy was running at a low rate of capacity utilization and the unemployment rate was relatively high. That means the economy was perceived to be on the flat part of the short run aggregate supply curve (see diagram).

US Lawmakers Back $87B Bush War Request; Questions Abound—*Wall Street Journal*

Both Republicans and Democrats predicted Monday that the U.S. Congress will approve the $87 billion President George W. Bush wants for Iraq and Afghanistan, but they said approval won't be as speedy as last spring and lawmakers will demand details.

Source: Wall Street Journal, *September 9, 2003.*

Industrial Output in U.S. Edges Up—*Wall Street Journal*

Industrial production edged up in August, but at a less vigorous pace than in July, leading some economists to question the durability of the recent manufacturing rebound.

On a day filled with conflicting economic reports, the Federal Reserve said industrial production rose 0.1%, following a revised 0.7% rise in July. That month was previously estimated as a 0.5% gain. Production of high-tech goods such as semiconductors was very strong, but other industries, including primary metals and motor vehicles, showed declines, and overall manufacturing output fell 0.1%.

Factories continue to operate with significant amounts of unused capacity, suggesting it could be a very long time before they feel the need to expand with new equipment. Capacity utilization held steady at 74.6% in August, the same as the month before.

Source: Wall Street Journal, *September 16, 2003.*

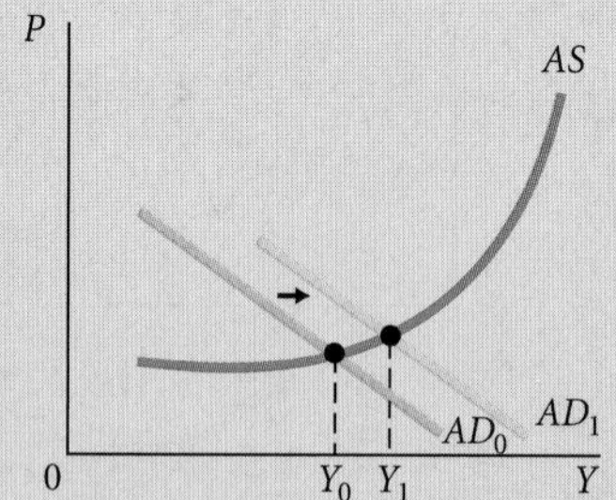

Further Exploration

The Simple "Keynesian" Aggregate Supply Curve

There is a great deal of disagreement concerning the shape of the *AS* curve. One view of the aggregate supply curve, the simple "Keynesian" view, holds that at any given moment, the economy has a clearly defined capacity, or maximum, output. This maximum output, denoted by Y_F, is defined by the existing labor force, the current capital stock, and the existing state of technology. If planned aggregate expenditure increases when the economy is producing *below* this maximum capacity, this view holds, inventories will be lower than planned and firms will increase output, but the price level will not change. Firms are operating with underutilized plants (excess capacity) and there is cyclical unemployment. Expansion does not exert any upward pressure on prices. However, if planned aggregate expenditure increases when the economy is producing near or at its maximum (Y_F), inventories will be lower than planned, but firms cannot increase their output. The result will be an increase in the price level, or inflation.

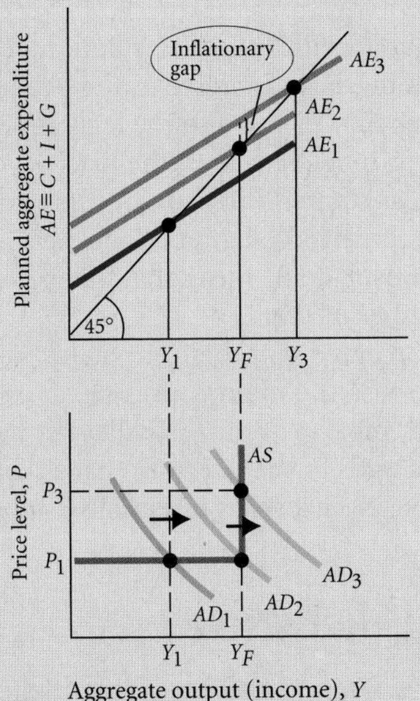

FIGURE 1

With planned aggregate expenditure of AE_1 and aggregate demand of AD_1, equilibrium output is Y_1. A shift of planned aggregate expenditure to AE_2, corresponding to a shift of the *AD* curve to AD_2, causes output to rise but the price level to remain at P_1. If planned aggregate expenditure and aggregate demand exceed Y_F, however, there is an inflationary gap and the price level rises to P_3.

This view is illustrated in Figure 1. In the top half of the diagram, aggregate output (income) (*Y*) and planned aggregate expenditure ($C + I + G \equiv AE$) are initially in equilibrium at AE_1, Y_1, and price level P_1. Now suppose a tax cut or an increase in government spending increases planned aggregate expenditure. If such an increase shifts the *AE* curve from AE_1 to AE_2 and the corresponding aggregate demand curve from AD_1 to AD_2, the equilibrium level of output will rise from Y_1 to Y_F. (Remember, an expansionary policy shifts the *AD* curve to the right.) Because we were initially producing below capacity output (Y_1 is lower than Y_F), the price level will be unaffected remaining at P_1.

Now consider what would happen if *AE* were to increase even further. Suppose planned aggregate expenditure were to shift from AE_2 to AE_3, with a corresponding shift of AD_2 to AD_3. If the economy were producing below capacity output, the equilibrium level of output would rise to Y_3. However, the output of the economy cannot exceed the maximum output of Y_F. As inventories fall below what was planned, firms encounter a fully employed labor market and fully utilized plants. Therefore, they cannot increase their output. The result is that the aggregate supply curve becomes vertical at Y_F, and the price level is driven up to P_3.

The difference between planned aggregate expenditure and aggregate output at full capacity is sometimes referred to as an **inflationary gap**. You can see the inflationary gap in the top half of Figure 1. At Y_F (capacity output), planned aggregate expenditure (shown by AE_3) is greater than Y_F. The price level rises to P_3 until the aggregate quantity supplied and the aggregate quantity demanded are equal.

Despite the fact that the kinked aggregate supply curve provides some insights, most economists find it unrealistic. It does not seem likely that the whole economy suddenly runs into a capacity "wall" at a specific level of output. As output expands, some firms and industries will hit capacity before others.

who believe in a vertical long-run *AS* curve believe that slack in the economy will put downward pressure on input prices (including wages), causing the short-run *AS* curve to shift to the right and pushing GDP back toward Y_0. However, some argue that wages and other input prices do *not* fall during slack periods and that the economy can get "stuck" at an equilibrium below potential GDP. In this case, monetary and fiscal policy would be necessary to restore full employment. We will return to this debate in Chapter 14.

The "new classical" economics, which we discuss in Chapter 19, assumes prices and wages are fully flexible and adjust very quickly to changing conditions. New classical economists believe, for example, that wage rate changes do not lag behind price changes. The new classical view is consistent with the existence of a vertical *AS* curve, even in the short run. At the other end of the spectrum is what is sometimes called the simple "Keynesian" view of aggregate supply. Those who hold this view believe there is a kink in the *AS* curve at capacity output, as we discuss in the Further Exploration box, "The Simple 'Keynesian' Aggregate Supply Curve."

CAUSES OF INFLATION

We now turn to inflation and use the *AS/AD* framework to consider the causes of inflation.

INFLATION VERSUS SUSTAINED INFLATION: A REMINDER

Inflation An increase in the overall price level.

sustained inflation Occurs when the overall price level continues to rise over some fairly long period of time.

Before we discuss the specific causes of inflation, recall the distinction we made in Chapter 7. **Inflation**, as you know, is an increase in the overall price level. Anything that shifts the *AD* curve to the right or the *AS* curve to the left causes inflation, but it is often useful to distinguish between a *one-time increase* in the price level (a one-time inflation) and an inflation that is sustained. A **sustained inflation** occurs when the overall price level continues to rise over some fairly long period of time. When we speak of a sustained inflation rate of 3 percent, for example, we generally mean that the price level has been rising at a rate of 3 percent per year over a number of years.

It is generally accepted that there are many possible causes of a one-time increase in the price level. (We discuss the main causes next.) For the price level to continue to increase period after period, most economists believe it must be "accommodated" by an expanded money supply. This leads to the assertion that a sustained inflation, whatever the initial cause of the increase in the price level, is essentially a monetary phenomenon.

DEMAND-PULL INFLATION

demand-pull inflation Inflation that is initiated by an increase in aggregate demand.

Inflation initiated by an increase in aggregate demand is called **demand-pull inflation.** You can see how demand-pull inflation works by looking at Figures 13.11 and 13.12. In both, the inflation begins with a shift of the aggregate demand schedule from AD_0 to AD_1, which causes the price level to increase from P_0 to P_1. (Output also increases, from Y_0 to Y_1.) If the economy is operating on the steep portion of the *AS* curve at the time of the increase in aggregate demand, as in Figure 13.12, most of the effect will be an increase in the price level instead of an increase in output. If the economy is operating on the flat portion of the *AS* curve, as in Figure 13.11, most of the effect will be an increase in output instead of an increase in the price level.

Remember, in the long run the initial increase in the price level will cause the *AS* curve to shift to the left as input prices (costs) respond to the increase in output prices. If the long-run *AS* curve is vertical, as depicted in Figure 13.10, the increase in costs will shift the short-run *AS* curve (AS_0) to the left to AS_1, pushing the price level even higher, to P_2. If the long-run *AS* curve is vertical, a shift in aggregate demand from AD_0 to AD_1 will result, in the long run, in *no* increase in output and a price-level increase from P_0 to P_2.

COST-PUSH, OR SUPPLY-SIDE, INFLATION

cost-push, or **supply-side, inflation** Inflation caused by an increase in costs.

stagflation Occurs when output is falling at the same time that prices are rising.

Inflation can also be caused by an increase in costs, referred to as **cost-push,** or **supply-side, inflation.** Several times in the last two decades oil prices on world markets increased sharply. Because oil is used in virtually every line of business, costs increased.

An increase in costs (a cost shock) shifts the *AS* curve to the left, as Figure 13.13 shows. If we assume the government does not react to this shift in *AS* by changing fiscal or monetary policy, the *AD* curve will not shift. The supply shift will cause the equilibrium price level to rise (from P_0 to P_1) and the level of aggregate output to decline (from Y_0 to Y_1). Recall from Chapter 5 that **stagflation** occurs when output is falling at the same time prices are rising—in other words, when the economy is experiencing both a contraction and inflation simultaneously. Figure 13.13 shows that one possible cause of stagflation is an increase in costs.

To return to monetary and fiscal policy for a moment, note from Figure 13.13 that the government could counteract the increase in costs (the cost shock) by engaging in an expansionary policy (an increase in G or M^s or a decrease in T). This would shift the *AD* curve to the right, and the new *AD* curve would intersect the new *AS* curve at a higher level of output. The problem with this policy, however, is that the intersection of the new *AS* and *AD* curves would take place at a price even higher than P_1 in Figure 13.13.

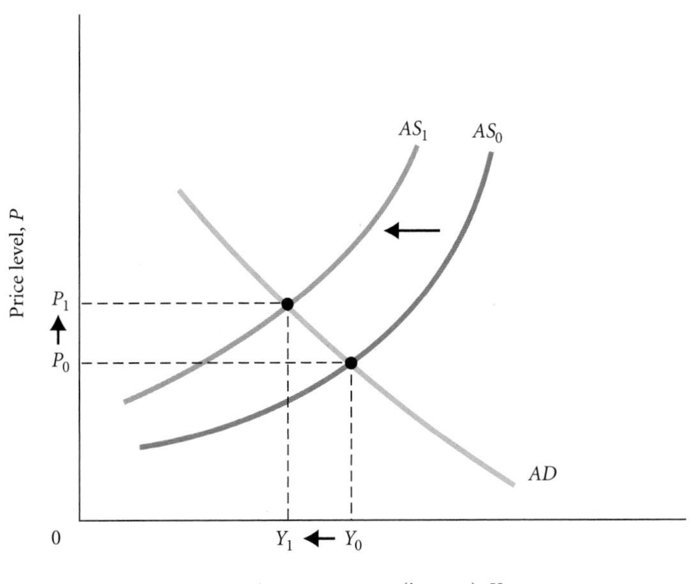

FIGURE 13.13 Cost-Push, or Supply-Side Inflation

An increase in costs shifts the *AS* curve to the left. By assuming the government does not react to this shift, the *AD* curve does not shift, the price level rises, and output falls.

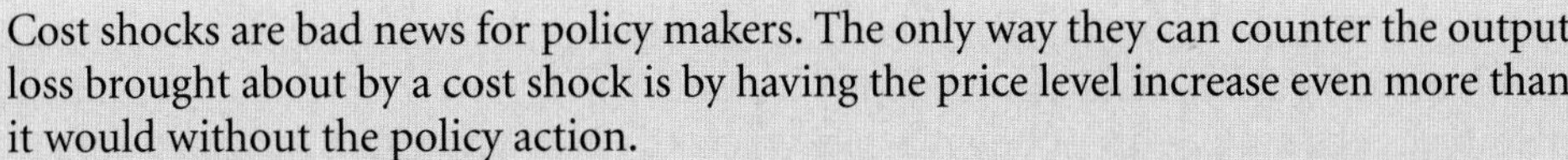
Cost shocks are bad news for policy makers. The only way they can counter the output loss brought about by a cost shock is by having the price level increase even more than it would without the policy action.

This situation is illustrated in Figure 13.14.

EXPECTATIONS AND INFLATION

When firms are making their price/output decisions, their *expectations* of future prices may affect their current decisions. If a firm expects that its competitors will raise their prices, in anticipation it may raise its own price.

Consider a firm that manufactures toasters. The toaster maker must decide what price to charge retail stores for its toaster. If it overestimates price and charges much more than other toaster manufacturers are charging, it will lose many customers. If it underestimates price and charges much less than other toaster makers are charging, it will gain customers but at a considerable loss in revenue per sale. The firm's *optimum price*—the price that maximizes the firm's profits—is presumably not too far from the average of its competitors' prices. If it

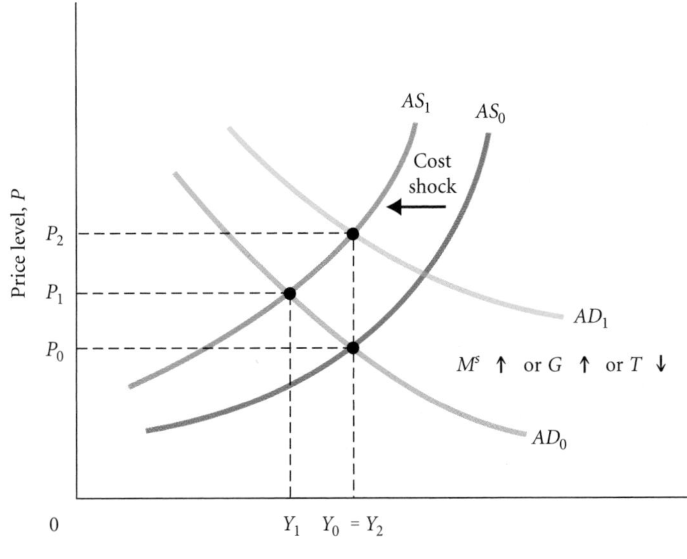

FIGURE 13.14 Cost Shocks Are Bad News for Policy Makers

A cost shock with no change in monetary or fiscal policy would shift the aggregate supply curve from AS_0 to AS_1, lower output from Y_0 to Y_1, and raise the price level from P_0 to P_1. Monetary or fiscal policy could be changed enough to have the *AD* curve shift from AD_0 to AD_1. This policy would raise aggregate output Y again, but it would raise the price level further, to P_2.

does not know its competitors' projected prices before it sets its own price, as is often the case, it must base its price on what it expects its competitors' prices to be.

Suppose inflation has been running at about 10 percent per year. Our firm probably expects its competitors will raise their prices about 10 percent this year, so it is likely to raise the price of its own toaster by about 10 percent. This is how expectations can get "built into the system." If every firm expects every other firm to raise prices by 10 percent, every firm will raise prices by about 10 percent. Every firm ends up with the price increase it expected.

The fact that expectations can affect the price level is vexing. Expectations can lead to an inertia that makes it difficult to stop an inflationary spiral. If prices have been rising, and if people's expectations are *adaptive*—that is, if they form their expectations on the basis of past pricing behavior—then firms may continue raising prices even if demand is slowing or contracting.

In terms of the *AS/AD* diagram, an increase in inflationary expectations that causes firms to increase their prices shifts the *AS* curve to the left. Remember that the *AS* curve represents the price/output responses of firms. If firms increase their prices because of a change in inflationary expectations, the result is a leftward shift of the *AS* curve.

MONEY AND INFLATION

It is easy to see that an increase in the money supply can lead to an increase in the aggregate price level. As Figures 13.11 and 13.12 show, an increase in the money supply (M^s) shifts the *AD* curve to the right and results in a higher price level. This is simply a demand-pull inflation.

However, the supply of money may also play a role in creating a sustained inflation. Consider an initial increase in government spending (G) with the money supply (M^s) unchanged. Because the money supply is unchanged, this is an increase in G that is not "accommodated" by the Fed. The increase in G shifts the *AD* curve to the right and results in a higher price level. This is shown in Figure 13.15 as a shift from AD_0 to AD_1. (In Figure 13.15, the economy is assumed to be operating on the vertical portion of the *AS* curve.)

Remember what happens when the price level increases. The higher price level causes the demand for money to increase. With an unchanged money supply and an increase in the quantity of money demanded, the interest rate will rise, and the result will be a decrease in planned investment (I) spending. The new equilibrium corresponds to higher G, lower I, a higher interest rate, and a higher price level.

Now let us take our example one step further. Suppose that the Fed is sympathetic to the expansionary fiscal policy (the increase in G we just discussed) and decides to expand the supply of money to keep the interest rate constant. As the higher price level pushes up

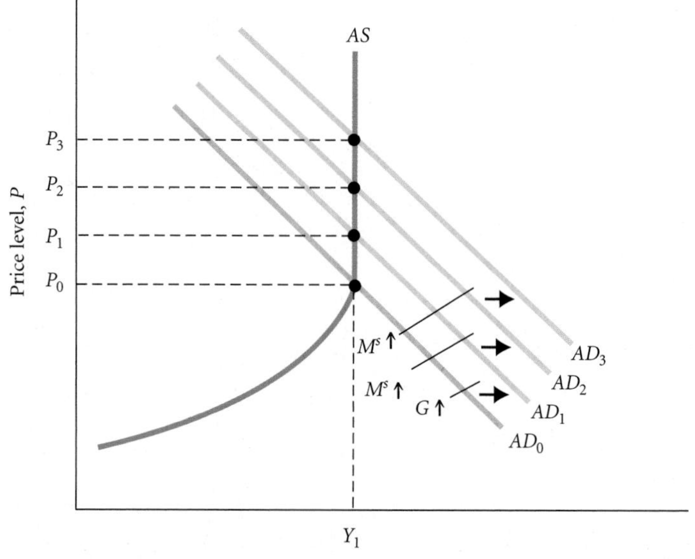

FIGURE 13.15 Sustained Inflation from an Initial Increase in G and Fed Accommodation

An increase in G with the money supply constant shifts the *AD* curve from AD_0 to AD_1. Although not shown in the figure, this leads to an increase in the interest rate and crowding out of planned investment. If the Fed tries to keep the interest rate unchanged by increasing the money supply, the *AD* curve will shift farther and farther to the right. The result is a sustained inflation, perhaps hyperinflation.

the demand for money, the Fed expands the supply of money with the goal of keeping the interest rate unchanged, eliminating the crowding-out effect of a higher interest rate.

When the supply of money is expanded, the *AD* curve shifts to the right again, from AD_1 to AD_2. This shift of the *AD* curve, brought about by the increased money supply, pushes prices up even further. Higher prices in turn increase the demand for money further, which requires a further increase in the money supply, and so on.

What would happen if the Fed tried to keep the interest rate constant when the economy is operating on the steep part of the *AS* curve? The situation could lead to a **hyperinflation**, a period of very rapid increases in the price level. If no more output can be coaxed out of the economy and if planned investment is not allowed to fall (because the interest rate is kept unchanged), then it is not possible to increase *G*. As the Fed keeps pumping more and more money into the economy to keep the interest rate unchanged, the price level will keep rising.

hyperinflation A period of very rapid increases in the price level.

SUSTAINED INFLATION AS A PURELY MONETARY PHENOMENON

Virtually all economists agree that an increase in the price level can be caused by anything that causes the *AD* curve to shift to the right or the *AS* curve to shift to the left. These include expansionary fiscal policy actions, monetary expansion, cost shocks, changes in expectations, and so forth. It is also generally agreed that for a *sustained* inflation to occur, the Fed must accommodate it. In this sense, a sustained inflation can be thought of as a purely monetary phenomenon.

This argument, first put forth by monetarists (coming in Chapter 19), has gained wide acceptance. It is easy to show, as we just did, how expanding the money supply can continuously shift the *AD* curve. It is not as easy to come up with other reasons for continued shifts of the *AD* curve if the money supply is constant. One possibility is for the government to increase spending continuously without increasing taxes, but this process cannot continue forever. To finance spending without taxes, the government must borrow. Without any expansion of the money supply, the interest rate will rise dramatically because of the increase in the supply of government bonds. Now, the public must be willing to buy the government bonds that are being issued to finance the spending increases. At some point, the public may be unwilling to buy any more bonds even though the interest rate is very high.[3] At this point, the government is no longer able to increase non-tax-financed spending without the Fed's cooperation. If this is true, then a sustained inflation cannot exist without the Fed's cooperation.

LOOKING AHEAD

In Chapters 8 and 9, we discussed the concept of an equilibrium level of aggregate output and income, the idea of the multiplier, and the basics of fiscal policy. Those two chapters centered on the workings of the goods market alone.

In Chapters 10 and 11, we analyzed the money market by discussing the supply of money, the demand for money, the equilibrium interest rate, and the basics of monetary policy. In Chapter 12 we brought our analysis of the goods market together with our analysis of the money market.

In this chapter, we used everything learned so far to discuss the aggregate supply and aggregate demand curves, first mentioned in Chapter 5. By using aggregate supply and aggregate demand curves, we can determine the equilibrium price level in the economy and understand some causes of inflation.

We have said little about employment, unemployment, and the functioning of the labor market in the macroeconomy. The next chapter will link everything we have done so far to this third major market arena—the labor market—and to the problem of unemployment.

[3]This means that the public's demand for money no longer depends on the interest rate. Even though the interest rate is very high, the public cannot be induced to have its real money balances fall any further. There is a limit concerning how much the public can be induced to have its real money balances fall.

SUMMARY

THE AGGREGATE DEMAND CURVE

1. Money demand is a function of three variables: (1) the interest rate (r); (2) the level of real income (Y); and (3) the price level (P). Money demand will increase if the real level of output (income) increases, the price level increases, or the interest rate declines.

2. At a higher price level, households and firms need to hold larger money balances. If the money supply remains the same, this increased demand for money will cause the interest rate to increase and planned investment spending to fall. As a result, planned aggregate expenditure will be lower, inventories will be greater than planned, firms will cut back on output, and Y will fall. An increase in the price level causes the level of aggregate output (income) to fall: A decrease in the price level causes the level of aggregate output (income) to rise.

3. *Aggregate demand* is the total demand for goods and services in the economy. The *aggregate demand (AD) curve* illustrates the negative relationship between aggregate output (income) and the price level. Each point on the *AD* curve is a point at which both the goods market and the money market are in equilibrium. The *AD* curve is *not* the sum of all the market demand curves in the economy.

4. At every point along the aggregate demand curve, the aggregate quantity demanded in the economy is exactly equal to planned aggregate expenditure.

5. An increase in the quantity of money supplied, an increase in government purchases, or a decrease in net taxes at a given price level shifts the aggregate demand curve to the right. A decrease in the quantity of money supplied, a decrease in government purchases, or an increase in net taxes shifts the aggregate demand curve to the left.

THE AGGREGATE SUPPLY CURVE

6. *Aggregate supply* is the total supply of goods and services in an economy. The *aggregate supply (AS) curve* shows the relationship between the aggregate quantity of output supplied by all the firms in an economy and the overall price level. The *AS* curve is *not* a market supply curve, and it is *not* the simple sum of all the individual supply curves in the economy. For this reason, it is helpful to think of the *AS* curve as a "price/output response" curve—that is, a curve that traces out the price decisions and output decisions of all the markets and firms in the economy under a given set of circumstances.

7. The shape of the short-run *AS* curve is a source of much controversy in macroeconomics. Many economists believe that at very low levels of aggregate output the *AS* curve is fairly flat, and at high levels of aggregate output the *AS* curve is vertical or nearly vertical. Thus, the *AS* curve slopes upward and becomes vertical when the economy reaches its capacity, or maximum, output.

8. Anything that affects an individual firm's decisions can shift the *AS* curve. Some of these factors include cost shocks, economic growth, stagnation, public policy, and natural disasters.

THE EQUILIBRIUM PRICE LEVEL

9. The *equilibrium price level* in the economy occurs at the point at which the *AS* and *AD* curves intersect. The intersection of the *AS* and *AD* curves corresponds to equilibrium in the goods and money markets *and* to a set of price/output decisions on the part of all the firms in the economy.

THE LONG-RUN AGGREGATE SUPPLY CURVE

10. For the *AS* curve to slope upward, some input prices must lag behind increases in the overall price level. If wage rates and other costs fully adjust to changes in prices in the long run, then the long-run *AS* curve is vertical.

11. The level of aggregate output that can be sustained in the long run without inflation is called *potential output* or *potential GDP.*

AGGREGATE DEMAND, AGGREGATE SUPPLY, AND MONETARY AND FISCAL POLICY

12. If the economy is initially producing on the flat portion of the *AS* curve, an expansionary policy—which shifts the *AD* curve to the right—will result in a small increase in the equilibrium price level relative to the increase in equilibrium output. If the economy is initially producing on the steep portion of the *AS* curve, an expansionary policy results in a small increase in equilibrium output and a large increase in the equilibrium price level.

13. If the *AS* curve is vertical in the long run, neither monetary nor fiscal policy has any effect on aggregate output in the long run. For this reason, the exact length of the long run is one of the most pressing questions in macroeconomics.

CAUSES OF INFLATION

14. *Inflation* is an increase in the overall price level. A *sustained inflation* occurs when the overall price level continues to rise over some fairly long period of time. Most economists believe that sustained inflations can occur only if the Fed continuously increases the money supply.

15. *Demand-pull inflation* is inflation initiated by an increase in aggregate demand. *Cost-push,* or *supply-side, inflation* is inflation initiated by an increase in costs. An increase in costs may also lead to *stagflation*—the situation in which the economy is experiencing both a contraction and inflation simultaneously.

16. Inflation can become "built into the system" as a result of expectations. If prices have been rising and people form their expectations on the basis of past pricing behavior, firms may continue raising prices even if demand is slowing or contracting.

17. When the price level increases, so too does the demand for money. If the economy is operating on the steep part of the *AS* curve and the Fed tries to keep the interest rate constant by increasing the supply of money, the result could be a hyperinflation—a period of very rapid increases in the price level.

REVIEW TERMS AND CONCEPTS

aggregate demand, 242
aggregate demand (*AD*) curve, 243
aggregate supply, 246
aggregate supply (*AS*) curve, 247
cost-push, or supply-side, inflation, 258
cost shock, or supply shock, 250
demand-pull inflation, 258
equilibrium price level, 252
hyperinflation, 261
inflation, 258
inflationary gap, 257
potential output, or potential GDP, 254
real wealth, or real balance, effect, 245
stagflation, 258
sustained inflation, 258

PROBLEM SET

1. In Japan during the first half of 2000, the Bank of Japan kept interest rates at a near zero level in an attempt to stimulate demand. In addition, the government passed a substantial increase in government expenditure and cut taxes. Slowly, Japanese GDP began to grow with absolutely no sign of an increase in the price level. Illustrate the position of the Japanese economy with aggregate supply-and-demand curves. Where on the short-run *AS* curve was Japan in 2000?

2. In June of 2003, with the Iraq war behind us, world oil prices declined from their highs in 2002 of $40 per barrel to $25 per barrel. What impact would you expect there to be on the aggregate price level and on real GDP? Illustrate your answer with aggregate demand-and-supply curves. What would you expect to be the effect on interest rates if the Fed held the money supply constant? Tell a complete story.

3. "The aggregate demand curve slopes downward, because when the price level is lower, people can afford to buy more, and aggregate demand rises. When prices rise, people can afford to buy less, and aggregate demand falls." Is this a good explanation of the shape of the *AD* curve? Why or why not?

4. By using aggregate supply-and-demand curves to illustrate your points, discuss the impacts of the following events on the price level and on equilibrium GDP (*Y*) in the *short run*:

a. A tax cut holding government purchases constant with the economy operating at near full capacity

b. An increase in the money supply during a period of high unemployment and excess industrial capacity

c. An increase in the price of oil caused by a war in the Middle East, assuming that the Fed attempts to keep interest rates constant by accommodating inflation

d. The Clinton plan from early 1993: an increase in taxes and a cut in government spending, supported by a cooperative Fed acting to keep output from falling

5. During 1999 and 2000, a debate raged over whether the United States was at or above potential GDP. Some economists feared the economy was operating at a level of output above potential GDP and inflationary pressures were building. They urged the Fed to tighten monetary policy and increase interest rates to slow the economy. Others argued that a worldwide glut of cheap products was causing input prices to be lower, keeping prices from rising.

By using aggregate supply-and-demand curves and other useful graphs, illustrate the following:

a. Those pushing the Fed to act were right and prices start to rise more rapidly in 2000. The Fed acts belatedly to slow money growth (contract the money supply), driving up interest rates and pushing the economy back to potential GDP.

b. The worldwide glut gets worse and the result is a *falling* price level (deflation) in the United States despite expanding aggregate demand.

6. Show the effects of the following stories on the position of the aggregate demand curve. Use graphs of the money demand curve, the investment function, and aggregate expenditure function if useful. What is likely to happen to *Y, C, I,* and *r* as a result?

a. In 2003, the Congress enacted a substantial tax cut. While the act contained some expenditure reductions, they did not kick in until 2005. Assume that the Fed expands the money supply to keep interest rates constant.

b. The Fed sharply decreases the money supply to fight inflation.

7. By using aggregate supply and aggregate demand curves to illustrate, describe the effects of the following events on the price level and on equilibrium GDP in the *long run*, assuming that input prices fully adjust to output prices after some lag:

a. An increase occurs in the money supply above potential GDP.

b. A decrease in government spending and in the money supply with GDP above potential GDP occurs.

c. Starting with the economy at potential GDP, a war in the Middle East pushes up energy prices temporarily. The Fed expands the money supply to accommodate the inflation.

8. Two separate capacity constraints are discussed in this chapter: (1) the actual physical capacity of existing plants and equipment, shown as the vertical portion of the short-run *AS* curve; and (2) potential GDP, leading to a vertical *LRAS* curve. Explain the difference between the two. Which is greater, full-capacity GDP or potential GDP? Why?

9. In country A, all wage contracts are indexed to inflation. That is, each month wages are adjusted to reflect increases in the cost of living as reflected in changes in the price level. In country B, there are no cost-of-living adjustments to wages, but the workforce is completely unionized. Unions negotiate 3-year contracts. In which country is an expansionary monetary policy likely to have a larger effect on aggregate output? Explain your answer using aggregate supply and aggregate demand curves.

The Labor Market, Unemployment, and Inflation

14

CHAPTER OUTLINE

In previous chapters we stressed the three broadly defined markets in which households, firms, the government, and the rest of the world interact: (1) the *goods market*, discussed in Chapters 8 and 9; (2) the *money market*, discussed in Chapters 10 and 11; and (3) the *labor market*. In Chapter 7 we described some features of the U.S. labor market and explained how the unemployment rate is measured. Then, in Chapter 13, we considered the labor market briefly in our discussion of the aggregate supply curve. Because labor is an input, what goes on in the labor market affects the shape of the aggregate supply (*AS*) curve. If wages and other input costs lag price increases, the *AS* curve will be upward sloping; if wages and other input costs are completely flexible and rise every time prices rise by the same percentage, the *AS* curve will be vertical.

In this chapter we look further at the labor market's role in the macroeconomy. First, we consider the classical view, which holds that wages always adjust to clear the labor market. We then consider why the labor market may not always clear and why unemployment may exist. Finally, we discuss the relationship between inflation and unemployment.

THE LABOR MARKET: BASIC CONCEPTS

Let us review briefly what the unemployment rate measures. The **unemployment rate** is the number of people unemployed as a percentage of the labor force. To be unemployed, a person must be out of a job and actively looking for work. When a person stops looking for work, he or she is considered *out of the labor force* and is no longer counted as unemployed.

unemployment rate The ratio of the number of people unemployed to the total number of people in the labor force.

It is important to realize that even if the economy is running at or near full capacity, the unemployment rate will never be zero. The economy is dynamic. Students graduate from schools and training programs; some businesses make profits and grow, while others suffer losses and go out of business; people move in and out of the labor force and change careers. It takes time for people to find the right job and for employers to match the right worker

frictional unemployment The portion of unemployment that is due to the normal working of the labor market; used to denote short-run job/skill matching problems.

structural unemployment The portion of unemployment that is due to changes in the structure of the economy that result in a significant loss of jobs in certain industries.

cyclical unemployment The increase in unemployment that occurs during recessions and depressions.

with the jobs they have. This **frictional** and **structural unemployment** is inevitable and in many ways desirable. (Review Chapter 7 if these terms are hazy to you.)

In this chapter, we are concerned with **cyclical unemployment**, the increase in unemployment that occurs during recessions and depressions. When the economy contracts, the number of people unemployed and the unemployment rate rise. The United States has experienced several periods of high unemployment. During the Great Depression, the unemployment rate remained over 17 percent for nearly a decade. In December of 1982, more than 12 million people were unemployed, putting the unemployment rate at 10.8 percent.

In one sense, the reason employment falls when the economy experiences a downturn is obvious. When firms cut back on production, they need fewer workers, so people get laid off.

> Employment tends to fall when aggregate output falls and rise when aggregate output rises.

Nevertheless, a decline in the demand for labor does not necessarily mean that unemployment will rise. If markets work as we described in Chapters 3 and 4, a decline in the demand for labor will initially create an excess supply of labor. As a result, the wage rate will fall until the quantity of labor supplied again equals the quantity of labor demanded, restoring equilibrium in the labor market. At the new lower wage rate, everyone who wants a job will have one.

If the quantity of labor demanded and the quantity of labor supplied are brought into equilibrium by rising and falling wage rates, there should be no persistent unemployment above the frictional and structural amount. This was the view held by the classical economists who preceded Keynes, and it is still the view of a number of economists today.

THE CLASSICAL VIEW OF THE LABOR MARKET

labor supply curve A graph that illustrates the amount of labor that households want to supply at each given wage rate.

The classical view of the labor market is illustrated in Figure 14.1. Classical economists assumed the wage rate adjusts to equate the quantity of labor demanded with the quantity of labor supplied, thereby implying that unemployment does not exist. To see how this adjustment takes place, assume there is a decrease in the demand for labor that shifts the demand curve in Figure 14.1 from D_0 to D_1. This decreased demand will cause the wage rate to fall from W_0 to W_1 and the amount of labor demanded to fall from L_0 to L_1. The decrease in the quantity of labor supplied is a movement along the labor supply curve.

Each point on the **labor supply curve** in Figure 14.1 represents the amount of labor households want to supply at each given wage rate. Each household's decision concerning

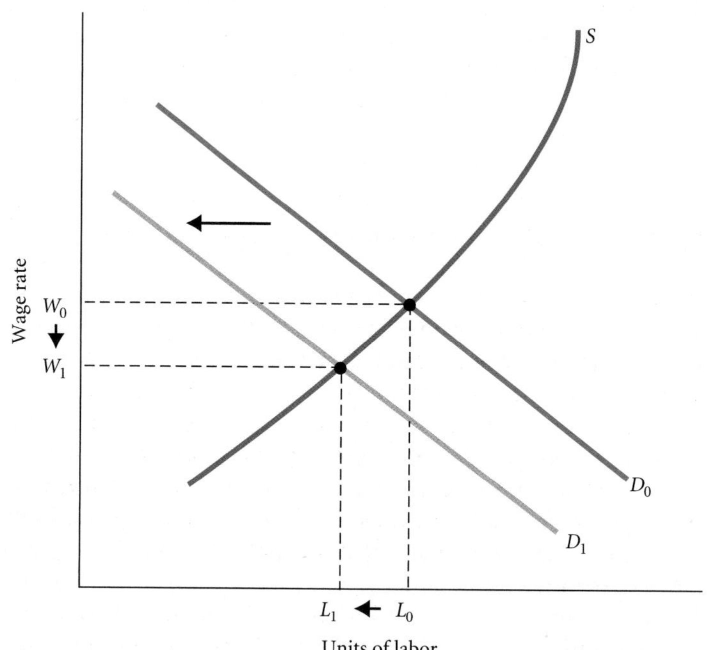

FIGURE 14.1 The Classical Labor Market

Classical economists believe that the labor market always clears. If the demand for labor shifts from D_0 to D_1, the equilibrium wage will fall from W_0 to W_1. Anyone who wants a job at W_1 will have one.

News Analysis

Employment and Unemployment in 2003

DURING 2001, GDP FELL FOR THREE CONSECUTIVE quarters, marking the end of a 10-year expansion. From 1991–2001 the U.S. economy added more than 24 million payroll jobs. But the next few years were to witness a decline in employment. The following *New York Times* article describes the situation in mid-2003.

Unemployment Rate Rises to a 9-Year High—*New York Times*

The unemployment rate rose to 6.1 percent in May, its highest level in nine years, the Labor Department reported today, as the worst jobs slump since the early 1980's continued to spread across the economy.

Still, the pace of layoffs has slowed over the last two months, suggesting that the economy might have stabilized and could begin adding jobs this summer, forecasters said.

The economy has now lost almost 2.5 million jobs since February 2001, more than the government said previously, according to annual revisions released today by the Labor Department. It is the longest sustained period without job growth since the period before World War II.

"Companies are still cutting costs," said Mark Vitner, a senior economist at the Wachovia Corporation in Charlotte, N.C. "But it looks like the worst of the layoffs are behind us."

Consumers and businesses have increased their spending somewhat in the last month, offering hope that a recovery has begun. But facing higher health care costs for employees and having become more efficient with the help of new technologies, companies have increased production without adding workers.

In perhaps the most promising sign in the jobs report, companies added a small number of jobs in both April and May after having reduced employment by more than 200,000 during the previous two months, the Labor Department said. Government cuts have caused overall employment to decline since April—including a decline of 17,000 last month—but the private sector is typically a better predictor of the economy's future, analysts say.

Some of the biggest gains came at construction companies, which are benefiting from the housing boom that is being helped by low interest rates, and financial services companies. Businesses also increased the number of temporary workers on their payrolls, by 58,000, a common sign that they are preparing for better times.

Manufacturers cut jobs in May for the 34th consecutive month. Airlines and hotels continued to reduce their work forces and have eliminated 8 percent of their jobs over the last two years. Public schools, department stores, and publishing and telecommunications companies also made cuts in May, according to the Labor Department, which adjusts its statistics to account for normal seasonal variations like the end of the school year.

To be counted in the unemployment statistics, a person must be looking for work.

In addition to the increase in the jobless rate, from 6 percent in April, to the highest since July 1994, the number of people who were not looking for work—and thus not eligible to be considered unemployed by the government—rose. The length of the current hiring slump has caused an unusually large number of workers to grow frustrated with their job search and give up temporarily, economists say.

Source: Adapted from: David Leonhardt, "Unemployment Rate Rises to a 9-Year High," New York Times, *June 7, 2003. Reprinted by permission.*

Visit www.prenhall.com/casefair for updated articles and exercises.

how much labor to supply is part of the overall consumer choice problem of a household. Each household member looks at the market wage rate, the prices of outputs, and the value of leisure time (including the value of staying at home and working in the yard or raising children) and chooses the amount of labor to supply (if any). A household member not in the labor force has decided his or her time is more valuable in nonmarket activities.

It is easy to see why. If you choose to stay out of the labor force, it is because you (a member of society) place a higher value on the use of your time than society is currently placing on the product that you would produce if you were employed. Consider households in less-developed countries. In many, the alternative to working for a wage is subsistence farming. If the wage rate in the labor market is very low, many will choose to farm for themselves. In this case, the value of what these people produce in farming must be greater than the value that society currently places on what they would produce if they worked for a wage. If this were not true, wages would rise and more people would join the labor force.

Each point on the **labor demand curve** in Figure 14.1 represents the amount of labor firms want to employ at each given wage rate. Each firm's decision about how much labor to demand is part of its overall profit-maximizing decision. A firm makes a profit by selling output to households. It will hire workers if the value of its output is sufficient to justify the wage that is being paid. Thus, the amount of labor that a firm hires depends on the value of the output that workers produce.

labor demand curve A graph that illustrates the amount of labor that firms want to employ at each given wage rate.

The classical economists saw the workings of the labor market—the behavior of labor supply and labor demand—as optimal from the standpoint of both individual households and firms and from the standpoint of society. If households want more output than is currently being produced, output demand will increase, output prices will rise, the demand for labor will increase, the wage rate will rise, and more workers will be drawn into the labor force. (Some of those who preferred not to be a part of the labor force at the lower wage rate will be lured into the labor force at the higher wage rate.) At equilibrium, prices and wages reflect a trade-off between the value households place on outputs and the value of time spent in leisure and nonmarket work. At equilibrium, the people who are not working have *chosen* not to work at that market wage. There is always *full employment* in this sense. The classical economists believed the market will achieve the optimal result if left to its own devices, and there is nothing the government can do to make things better.

THE CLASSICAL LABOR MARKET AND THE AGGREGATE SUPPLY CURVE

We can now relate the classical view of the labor market to the theory of the vertical *AS* curve in Chapter 13. The classical idea that wages adjust to clear the labor market is consistent with the view that wages respond quickly to price changes. Recall that the argument that the *AS* curve is vertical in the long run involves input-price adjustments. If the short-run *AS* and aggregate demand (*AD*) curves intersected above potential GDP (Y_0 in Figure 13.10), then input prices, *including wages*, would rise, shifting the *AS* curve to the left and pushing Y back down to Y_0. Similarly, if the short-run *AS* and *AD* curves intersected to the left of Y_0, unemployment and excess capacity would cause input prices, *including wages*, to fall, shifting the *AS* curve to the right and pushing Y back up to Y_0. Also remember, if the *AS* curve is vertical, monetary and fiscal policy cannot affect the level of output and employment in the economy. It therefore follows that those who believe the wage rate adjusts quickly to clear the labor market are likely to believe the *AS* curve is vertical (or almost vertical) and monetary and fiscal policy have little or no effect on output and employment.

THE UNEMPLOYMENT RATE AND THE CLASSICAL VIEW

If, as the classical economists assumed, the labor market works well, how can we account for the fact that the unemployment rate at times seems high? There seem to be times when millions of people who want jobs at prevailing wage rates cannot find them. How can we reconcile this situation with the classical assumption about the labor market?

Some economists answer by arguing that the unemployment rate is not a good measure of whether the labor market is working well. We know the economy is dynamic and at any given time some industries are expanding and some are contracting. In California the construction industry contracted in the mid-1990s. Consider, for example, a carpenter who is laid off because of the industry's contraction. He had probably developed specific skills related to the construction industry—skills not necessarily useful for jobs in other industries. If he were earning $40,000 per year as a carpenter, it may be that he could earn only $30,000 per year in another industry. He may eventually work his way back up to a salary of $40,000 in the new industry as he develops new skills, but this will take time. Will this carpenter take a job at $30,000? There are at least two reasons he may not. First, he may believe the slump in the construction industry is temporary and he will soon get his job back. Second, he may believe he can earn more than $30,000 in another industry and will continue to look for a better job.

If our carpenter decides to continue looking for a job paying more than $30,000 per year, he will be considered unemployed because he is actively looking for work. This does not necessarily mean the labor market is not working properly. The carpenter has *chosen* not to work for a wage of $30,000 per year, but if his value to any firm outside the construction industry is no more than $30,000 per year, we would not expect him to find a job paying more than $30,000. The unemployment rate as measured by the government is not necessarily an accurate indicator of whether the labor market is working properly.

If the degree to which industries are changing in the economy fluctuates over time, there will be more people like our carpenter at some times than at others. This will cause the measured unemployment rate to fluctuate. Some economists argue the measured unemploy-

Some economists believe unemployment is not a major problem. However, the images of the 1930s are still with us, and more than 12 million people were looking for work during the recession of 1982.

ment rate may sometimes *seem* high even though the labor market is working well. The quantity of labor supplied at the current wage is equal to the quantity demanded at the current wage. The fact that there are people willing to work at a wage higher than the current wage does not mean the labor market is not working. Whenever there is an upward-sloping supply curve in a market (as is usually the case in the labor market), the quantity supplied at a price higher than the equilibrium price is always greater than the quantity supplied at the equilibrium price.

Economists who view unemployment in this way do not see it as a major problem. Yet the images of the bread lines in the 1930s are still with us, and many find it difficult to believe everything was optimal when over 12 million people were looking for work at the end of 1982. There are other views of unemployment, as we now will see.

EXPLAINING THE EXISTENCE OF UNEMPLOYMENT

If unemployment is a major macroeconomic problem—and many economists believe it is—then we need to explore some of the reasons that have been suggested for its existence. Among these are sticky wages, efficiency wage theory, imperfect information, and minimum wage laws.

STICKY WAGES

One explanation for unemployment (above and beyond normal frictional and structural unemployment) is that wages are **"sticky"** on the downward side. That is, the equilibrium wage gets stuck at a particular level and does not fall when the demand for labor falls. This is illustrated in Figure 14.2, where the equilibrium wage gets stuck at W_0 (the original wage)

sticky wages The downward rigidity of wages as an explanation for the existence of unemployment.

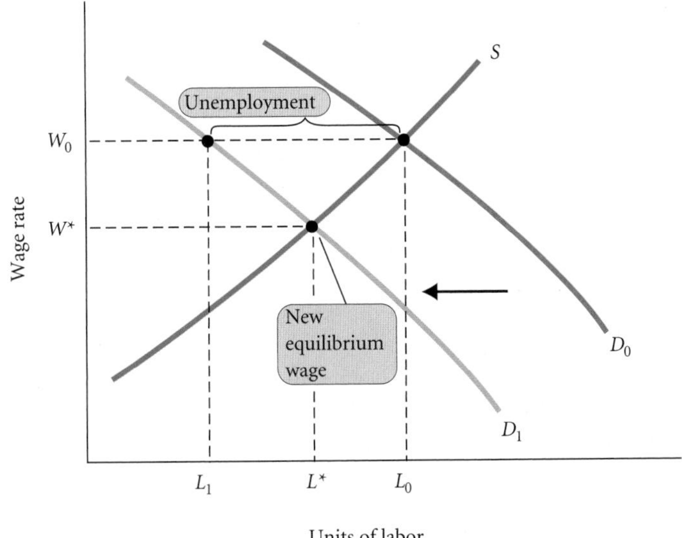

FIGURE 14.2 Sticky Wages

If wages "stick" at W_0 instead of fall to the new equilibrium wage of W^* following a shift of demand from D_0 to D_1, the result will be unemployment equal to $L_0 - L_1$.

and does not fall to W^* when demand decreases from D_0 to D_1. The result is unemployment of the amount $L_0 - L_1$, where L_0 is the quantity of labor that households want to supply at wage rate W_0 and L_1 is the amount of labor that firms want to hire at wage rate W_0. $L_0 - L_1$ is the number of workers who would like to work at W_0 but cannot find jobs.

The sticky wage explanation of unemployment begs the question. *Why* are wages sticky, if they are, and why do wages not fall to clear the labor market during periods of high unemployment? Many answers have been proposed, but as yet no one answer has been agreed on. This is one reason macroeconomics has been in a state of flux for so long. The existence of unemployment continues to be a puzzle. Although we will discuss the major theories that have been proposed to explain why wages may not clear the labor market, we can offer no conclusions. The question is still open.

social, or **implicit, contracts** Unspoken agreements between workers and firms that firms will not cut wages.

Social, or Implicit, Contracts One explanation for downwardly sticky wages is that firms enter into **social,** or **implicit, contracts** with workers not to cut wages. It seems that extreme events—deep recession, deregulation, or threat of bankruptcy—are necessary for firms to cut wages. Wage cuts did occur during the Great Depression, in the airline industry following deregulation of the industry in the 1980s, and recently when some U.S. manufacturing firms found themselves in danger of bankruptcy from stiff foreign competition. These are exceptions to the general rule. For reasons that may be more sociological than economic, cutting wages seems close to being a taboo.

relative-wage explanation of unemployment An explanation for sticky wages (and therefore unemployment): If workers are concerned about their wages relative to other workers in other firms and industries, they may be unwilling to accept a wage cut unless they know that all other workers are receiving similar cuts.

A related argument, the **relative-wage explanation of unemployment,** holds that workers are concerned about their wages *relative* to the wages of other workers in other firms and industries and may be unwilling to accept wage cuts unless they know other workers are receiving similar cuts. Because it is difficult to reassure any one group of workers that all other workers are in the same situation, workers may resist any cut in their wages. There may be an implicit understanding between firms and workers that firms will not do anything that would make their workers worse off relative to workers in other firms.

Explicit Contracts Many workers—in particular, unionized workers—sign 1- to 3-year employment contracts with firms. These contracts stipulate the workers' wages for each year of the contract. Wages set in this way do not fluctuate with economic conditions, either upward or downward. If the economy slows down and firms demand fewer workers, the wage will not fall. Instead, some workers will be laid off.

explicit contracts Employment contracts that stipulate workers' wages, usually for a period of 1 to 3 years.

Although **explicit contracts** can explain why some wages are sticky, a deeper question must also be considered. Workers and firms surely know at the time a contract is signed that unforeseen events may cause the wages set by the contract to be too high or too low. Why do firms and workers bind themselves in this way? One explanation is that negotiating wages is costly. Negotiations between unions and firms can take a considerable amount of time—time that could be spent producing output—and it would be very costly to negotiate wages weekly or monthly. Contracts are a way of bearing these costs at no more than 1-, 2-, or 3-year intervals. There is a trade-off between the costs of locking workers and firms into contracts for long periods of time and the costs of wage negotiations. The length of contracts that minimizes negotiation costs seems to be (from what we observe in practice) between 1 and 3 years.

cost-of-living adjustments (COLAs) Contract provisions that tie wages to changes in the cost of living. The greater the inflation rate, the more wages are raised.

Some multiyear contracts adjust for unforeseen events by **cost-of-living adjustments (COLAs)** written into the contract. COLAs tie wages to changes in the cost of living: The greater the rate of inflation, the more wages are raised. COLAs thus protect workers from unexpected inflation, although many COLAs adjust wages by a smaller percentage than the percentage increase in prices.

EFFICIENCY WAGE THEORY

efficiency wage theory An explanation for unemployment that holds that the productivity of workers increases with the wage rate. If this is so, firms may have an incentive to pay wages above the market-clearing rate.

Another explanation for unemployment centers on the **efficiency wage theory,** which holds that the productivity of workers increases with the wage rate. If this is true, firms may have an incentive to pay wages *above* the wage at which the quantity of labor supplied is equal to the quantity of labor demanded.

An individual firm has an incentive to hire workers as long as the value of what they produce is equal to or greater than the wage rate. With no efficiency effects, the market in Figure

14.1 would produce an equilibrium wage of $W*$. Suppose, however, the firm could increase the productivity of all its workers by raising the wage rate above $W*$. The firm's demand for labor would be no lower, but the higher wage rate would cause the quantity of labor supplied to increase. The quantity of labor supplied would exceed the quantity of labor demanded at the new higher wage—the *efficiency wage*—and the result is unemployment.

Empirical studies of labor markets have identified several potential benefits that firms receive from paying workers more than the market-clearing wage. Among them are lower turnover, improved morale, and reduced "shirking" of work. Even though the efficiency wage theory predicts some unemployment, it is unlikely that the behavior it is describing accounts for much of the observed large cyclical fluctuations in unemployment over time.

IMPERFECT INFORMATION

Thus far we have been assuming that firms know exactly what wage rates they need to set to clear the labor market. They may not choose to set their wages at this level, but at least they know what the market-clearing wage is. In practice, firms may not have enough information at their disposal to know what the market-clearing wage is. In this case, firms are said to have *imperfect information.* If firms have imperfect or incomplete information, they may simply set wages wrong—wages that do not clear the labor market.

If a firm sets its wages too high, more workers will want to work for that firm than the firm wants to employ, and some potential workers will be turned away. The result is, of course, unemployment. One objection to this explanation is that it explains the existence of unemployment only in the very short run. As soon as a firm sees that it has made a mistake, why would it not immediately correct its mistake and adjust its wage to the correct, market-clearing level? Why would unemployment *persist*?

If the economy were simple, it should take no more than a few months for firms to correct their mistakes, but the economy is complex. Although firms may be aware of their past mistakes and may try to correct them, new events are happening all the time. Because constant change—including a constantly changing equilibrium wage level—is characteristic of the economy, firms may find it hard to adjust wages to the market-clearing level. The labor market is not like the stock market or the market for wheat, where prices are determined in organized exchanges every day. Instead, thousands of firms are setting wages and millions of workers are responding to these wages. It may take considerable time for the market-clearing wages to be determined after they have been disturbed from an equilibrium position.

MINIMUM WAGE LAWS

minimum wage laws Laws that set a floor for wage rates—that is, a minimum hourly rate for any kind of labor.

Minimum wage laws explain at least a small fraction of unemployment. These laws set a floor for wage rates—a minimum hourly rate for any kind of labor. In 2003, the federal minimum wage was $5.15 per hour. If the market-clearing wage for some groups of workers is below this amount, this group will be unemployed. In Figure 14.2, if the minimum wage is W_0 and the market-clearing wage is $W*$, then the number of unemployed will be $L_0 - L_1$.

Teenagers, who have relatively little job experience, are most likely to be hurt by minimum wage laws. If some teenagers can produce only $4.50 worth of output per hour, no firm would be willing to hire them at a wage of $5.15. To do so would incur a loss of $0.65 per hour. In an unregulated market, these teenagers would be able to find work at the market-clearing wage of $4.50 per hour. If the minimum wage laws prevent the wage from falling below $5.15, these workers will not be able to find jobs, and they will be unemployed. Others who may be hurt include people with very low skills and some recent immigrants.

In response to this argument against the minimum wage, Congress established a subminimum wage for teenagers. The new law allows employers to hire teenagers at an "opportunity wage" of $4.25 for up to 90 days.

AN OPEN QUESTION

As we have seen, there are many explanations for why the labor market may not clear. The theories we have just set forth are not necessarily mutually exclusive, and there may be elements of truth in all of them. The aggregate labor market is very complicated, and there are no simple answers to why there is unemployment. Much current work in macroeconomics is concerned directly or indirectly with this question, and it is an exciting area of study. Which argument or arguments will win out in the end is an open question.

THE SHORT-RUN RELATIONSHIP BETWEEN THE UNEMPLOYMENT RATE AND INFLATION

The relationship between the unemployment rate and inflation—two of the most important variables in macroeconomics—has been the subject of much debate. We now have enough knowledge of the macroeconomy to explore this relationship.

We must begin by considering the relationship between aggregate output (income) (Y) and the unemployment rate (U). An increase in Y means firms are producing more output. To produce more output, more labor is needed in the production process. Therefore, an increase in Y leads to an increase in employment. An increase in employment means more people working (fewer people unemployed) and a lower unemployment rate. An increase in Y corresponds to a *decrease* in U. Thus U and Y are *negatively* related:

When Y rises, the unemployment rate falls, and when Y falls, the unemployment rate rises.

Next consider an upward-sloping *AS* curve, as shown in Figure 14.3. This curve represents the relationship between Y and the overall price level (P). The relationship is a positive one: When Y increases, P increases, and when Y decreases, P decreases.

As you will recall from the last chapter, the shape of the *AS* curve is determined by the behavior of firms and how they react to an increase in demand. If aggregate demand shifts to the right and the economy is operating on the nearly flat part of the *AS* curve—far from capacity—output will increase but the price level will not change much. However, if the economy is operating on the steep part of the *AS* curve—close to capacity—an increase in demand will drive up the price level, but output will be constrained by capacity and will not increase much.

Think about what will happen following an event that leads to an increase in aggregate demand. First, firms experience an unanticipated decline in inventories. They respond by increasing output (Y) and hiring workers—the unemployment rate falls. If the economy is not close to capacity, there will be little increase in the price level. If, however, aggregate demand continues to grow, the ability of the economy to increase output will eventually reach its limit. As aggregate demand shifts farther and farther to the right along the *AS* curve, the price level increases more and more, and output begins to reach its limit. At the point at which the *AS* curve becomes vertical, output cannot rise any further. If output cannot grow, the unemployment rate cannot be pushed any lower.

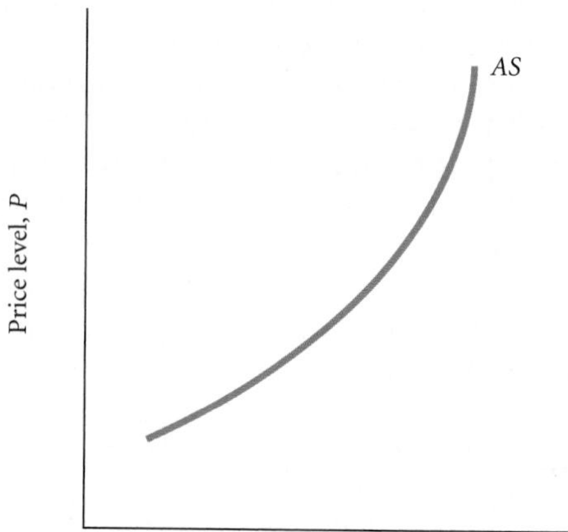

FIGURE 14.3 The Aggregate Supply Curve

The *AS* curve shows a positive relationship between the price level (P) and aggregate output (income) (Y).

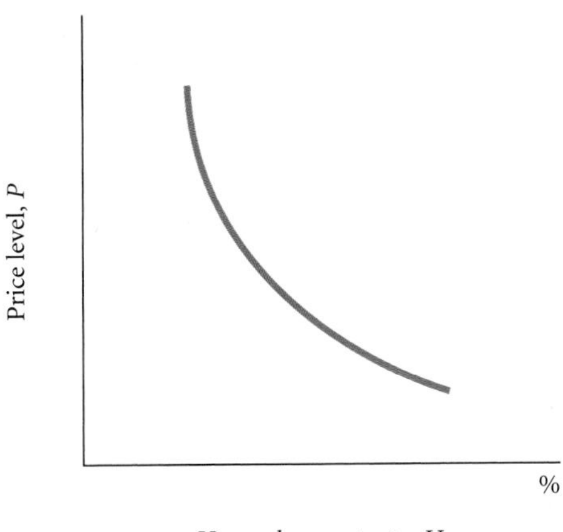

FIGURE 14.4 The Relationship Between the Price Level and the Unemployment Rate

This curve shows a negative relationship between the price level (*P*) and the unemployment rate (*U*). As the unemployment rate declines in response to the economy's moving closer and closer to capacity output, the price level rises more and more.

> There is a negative relationship between the unemployment rate and the price level. As the unemployment rate declines in response to the economy moving closer and closer to capacity output, the overall price level rises more and more, as shown in Figure 14.4.

The curve in Figure 14.4 has *not* been a major focus of attention in macroeconomics. Instead, the curve that has been extensively studied is shown in Figure 14.5, which plots the inflation rate on the vertical axis and the unemployment rate on the horizontal axis. The **inflation rate** is the percentage change in the price level, not the price level itself.

inflation rate The percentage change in the price level.

Figures 14.4 and 14.5 imply different things. Figure 14.4 shows that the *price level* remains the same if the unemployment rate remains unchanged. Figure 14.5 shows that the *inflation rate* remains the same if the unemployment rate remains unchanged. The curve in Figure 14.5 is called the **Phillips Curve**, after A. W. Phillips, who first examined it using data for the United Kingdom. In simplest terms, the Phillips Curve is a graph showing the relationship between the inflation rate and the unemployment rate.

Phillips Curve A graph showing the relationship between the inflation rate and the unemployment rate.

The rest of this chapter focuses on the Phillips Curve in Figure 14.5 because it is the macroeconomic relationship that has been studied the most. Keep in mind, however, that it is not easy to go from the *AS* curve to the Phillips Curve. We have moved from graphs in which the price level is on the vertical axis (Figures 14.3 and 14.4) to a graph in which the *percentage change* in the price level is on the vertical axis (Figure 14.5). Put another way, the theory behind the Phillips Curve is somewhat different from the theory behind the *AS* curve. Fortunately, most of the insights gained from the *AS/AD* analysis concerning the behavior of the price level also apply to the behavior of the inflation rate.

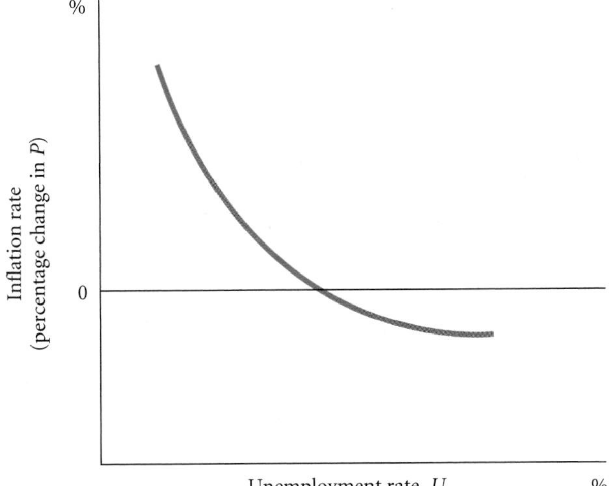

FIGURE 14.5 The Phillips Curve

The Phillips Curve shows the relationship between the inflation rate and the unemployment rate.

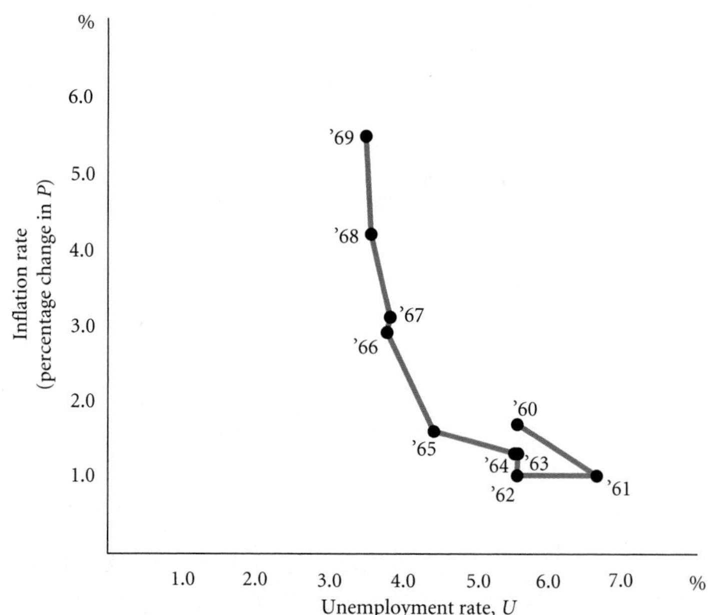

FIGURE 14.6 Unemployment and Inflation, 1960–1969

During the 1960s there seemed to be an obvious trade-off between inflation and unemployment. Policy debates during the period revolved around this apparent trade-off.

Source: See Table 7.8.

THE PHILLIPS CURVE: A HISTORICAL PERSPECTIVE

In the 1950s and 1960s, there was a remarkably smooth relationship between the unemployment rate and the rate of inflation, as Figure 14.6 shows for the 1960s. As you can see, the data points fit fairly closely around a downward-sloping curve; in general, the higher the unemployment rate is, the lower the rate of inflation. The Phillips Curve in Figure 14.6 shows a trade-off between inflation and unemployment. To lower the inflation rate, we must accept a higher unemployment rate, and to lower the unemployment rate, we must accept a higher rate of inflation.

Textbooks written in the 1960s and early 1970s relied on the Phillips Curve as the main explanation of inflation. Things seemed simple—inflation appeared to respond in a fairly predictable way to changes in the unemployment rate. For this reason, policy discussions in the 1960s revolved around the Phillips Curve. The role of the policy maker, it was thought, was to choose a point on the curve. Conservatives usually argued for choosing a point with a low rate of inflation and were willing to accept a higher unemployment rate in exchange for this. Liberals usually argued for accepting more inflation to keep unemployment at a low level.

Life did not turn out to be quite so simple. The Phillips Curve broke down in the 1970s and 1980s. This can be seen in Figure 14.7 which graphs the unemployment rate and infla-

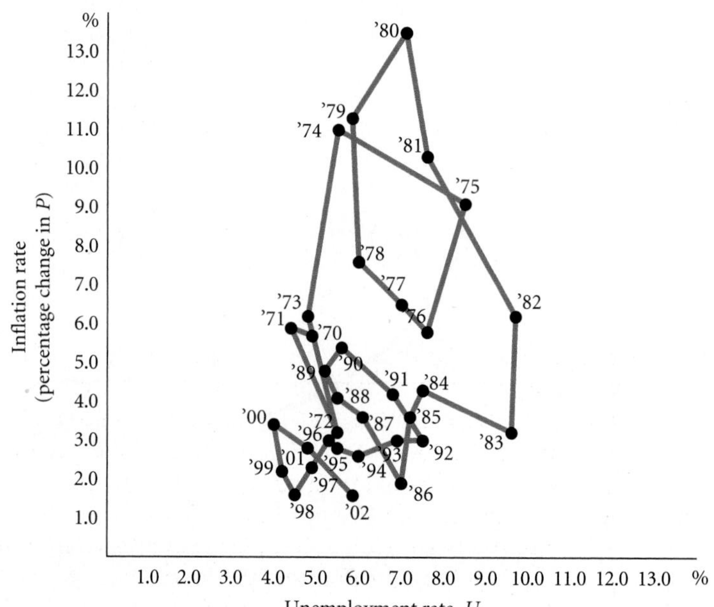

FIGURE 14.7 Unemployment and Inflation, 1970–2002

From the 1970s on, it became clear that the relationship between unemployment and inflation was anything but simple.

Source: See Table 7.8.

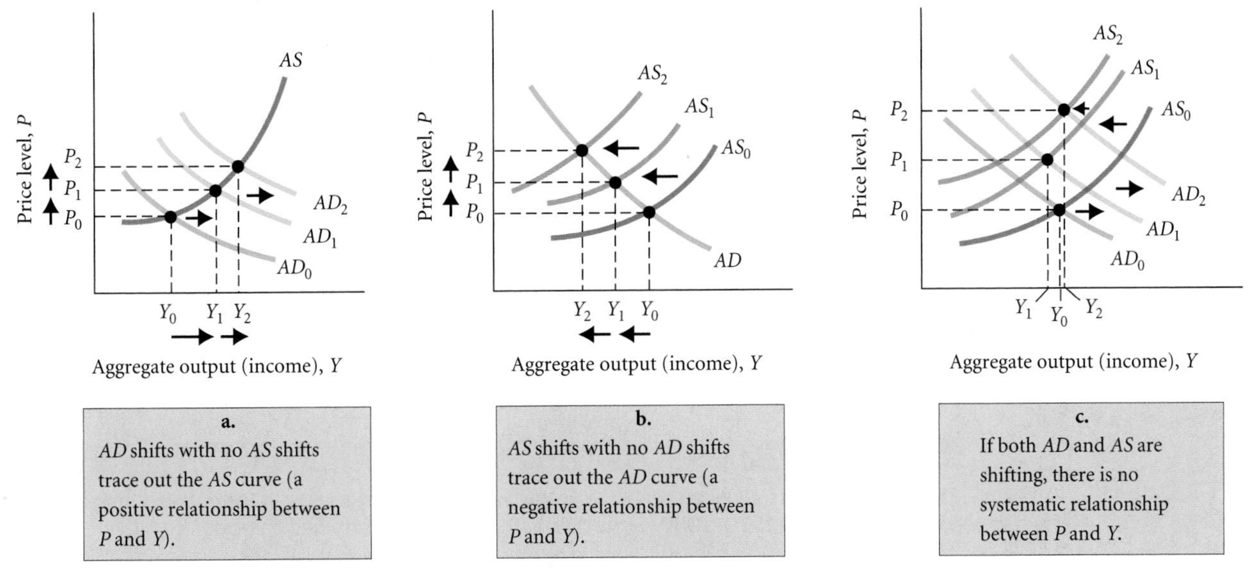

FIGURE 14.8 Changes in the Price Level and Aggregate Output Depend on Both Shifts in Aggregate Demand and Shifts in Aggregate Supply

tion rate for the period from 1970 to 2002. The points in Figure 14.7 show no particular relationship between inflation and unemployment.

AGGREGATE SUPPLY AND AGGREGATE DEMAND ANALYSIS AND THE PHILLIPS CURVE

How can we explain the stability of the Phillips Curve in the 1950s and 1960s and the lack of stability after that? To answer, we need to return to *AS*/*AD* analysis.

If the *AD* curve shifts from year to year but the *AS* curve does not, the values of *P* and *Y* each year will lie along the *AS* curve [Figure 14.8(a)]. The plot of the relationship between *P* and *Y* will be upward sloping. Correspondingly, the plot of the relationship between the unemployment rate (which decreases with increased output) and the rate of inflation will be a curve that slopes downward. In other words, we would expect to see a negative relationship between the unemployment rate and the inflation rate.

However, the relationship between the unemployment rate and the inflation rate will look different if the *AS* curve shifts from year to year but the *AD* curve does not. A leftward shift of the *AS* curve will cause an *increase* in the price level (*P*) and a *decrease* in aggregate output (*Y*) [Figure 14.8(b)]. When the *AS* curve shifts to the left, the economy experiences both inflation *and* an increase in the unemployment rate (because decreased output means increased unemployment). In other words, if the *AS* curve is shifting from year to year, we would expect to see a positive relationship between the unemployment rate and the inflation rate.

If both the *AS* and the *AD* curves are shifting simultaneously, however, there is no systematic relationship between *P* and *Y* [Figure 14.8(c)] and thus no systematic relationship between the unemployment rate and the inflation rate.

The Role of Import Prices One of the main factors that causes the *AS* curve to shift is the price of imports. (Remember, the *AS* curve shifts when input prices change, and input prices are affected by the price of imports, particularly the price of imported oil.) The price of imports is plotted in Figure 14.9 for the 1960 I–2003 II period. As you can see, the price of imports changed very little between 1960 and 1970. There were no large shifts in the *AS* curve in the 1960s due to changes in the price of imports. There were also no other large changes in input prices in the 1960s, so overall the *AS* curve shifted very little during the decade. The main variation in the 1960s was in aggregate demand, so the shifting *AD* curve traced out points along the *AS* curve.

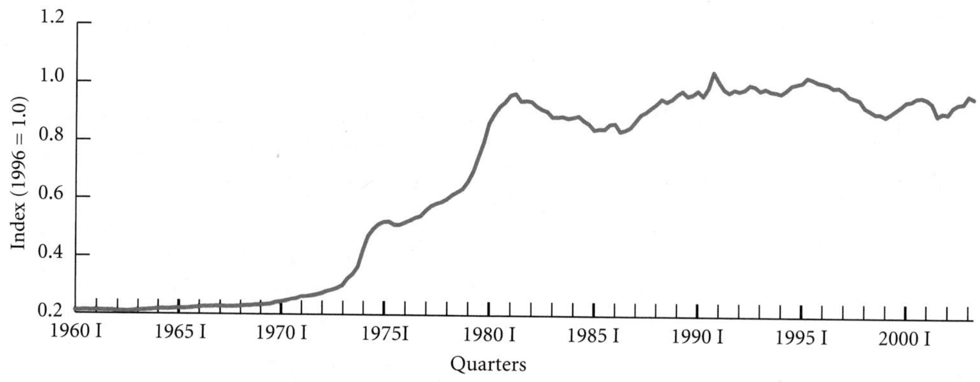

FIGURE 14.9 The Price of Imports, 1960 I–2003 II

The price of imports changed very little in the 1960s and early 1970s. It increased substantially in 1974 and again in 1979–1980. Since 1981, the price of imports has changed very little.

Figure 14.9 also shows that the price of imports increased considerably in the 1970s. This led to large shifts in the *AS* curve during the decade, but the *AD* curve was also shifting throughout the 1970s. With both curves shifting, the data points for *P* and *Y* were scattered all over the graph, and the observed relationship between *P* and *Y* was not at all systematic.

This story about import prices and the *AS* and *AD* curves in the 1960s and 1970s carries over to the Phillips Curve. The Phillips Curve was stable in the 1960s because the primary source of variation in the economy was demand, not costs. In the 1970s both demand *and* costs were varying, so no obvious relationship between the unemployment rate and the inflation rate was apparent.

To some extent, what is remarkable about the Phillips Curve is not that it was not smooth after the 1960s but that it ever was smooth.

EXPECTATIONS AND THE PHILLIPS CURVE

Another reason the Phillips Curve is not stable concerns expectations. We saw in Chapter 13 that if a firm expects other firms to raise their prices, the firm may raise the price of its own product. If all firms are behaving in this way, then prices will rise because they are expected to rise. In this sense, expectations are self-fulfilling. Similarly, if inflation is expected to be high in the future, negotiated wages are likely to be higher than if inflation is expected to be low. Wage inflation is thus affected by expectations of future price inflation. Because wages are input costs, prices rise as firms respond to the higher wage costs. Price expectations that affect wage contracts eventually affect prices themselves.

If the rate of inflation depends on expectations, then the Phillips Curve will shift as expectations change. For example, if inflationary expectations increase, the result will be an increase in the rate of inflation even though the unemployment rate may not have changed. In this case, the Phillips Curve will shift to the right. If inflationary expectations decrease, the Phillips Curve will shift to the left—there will be less inflation at any given level of the unemployment rate.

It so happened that inflationary expectations were quite stable in the 1950s and 1960s. The inflation rate was moderate during most of this period, and people expected it to remain moderate. With inflationary expectations not changing very much, there were no major shifts of the Phillips Curve, which helps explain its stability during the period.

Near the end of the 1960s, inflationary expectations began to increase, primarily in response to the actual increase in inflation that was occurring because of the tight economy caused by the Vietnam War. Inflationary expectations increased even further in the 1970s as a result of large oil price increases. These changing expectations led to shifts of the Phillips Curve, which is another reason the curve was not stable during the 1970s.

IS THERE A SHORT-RUN TRADE-OFF BETWEEN INFLATION AND UNEMPLOYMENT?

Does the fact that the Phillips Curve broke down during the 1970s mean there is no trade-off between inflation and unemployment in the short run? Not at all: It simply means other things affect inflation aside from unemployment. Just as the relationship between price and quantity demanded along a standard demand curve shifts when income or other factors change, so does the relationship between unemployment and inflation change when other factors change.

In 1975, for example, inflation and unemployment were both high. As we explained earlier, this stagflation was caused partly by an increase in oil costs that shifted the aggregate supply curve to the left and partly by expectations of continued inflation that kept prices rising despite high levels of unemployment. In response to this situation, the Federal Reserve (Fed) pursued a contractionary monetary policy, which shifted the *AD* curve to the left and led to even higher unemployment. By 1977, the rate of inflation had dropped from over 11 percent to about 6 percent. So the rise in the unemployment rate did lead to a decrease in inflation, which reflects the trade-off.

There *is* a short-run trade off between inflation and unemployment, but other factors besides unemployment affect inflation. Policy involves much more than simply choosing a point along a nice, smooth curve.

Back in Chapter 7, we mentioned that recessions may be the price that the economy pays to eliminate inflation. We can now understand this statement better. When unemployment rises, *other things being equal*, inflation falls.

THE LONG-RUN AGGREGATE SUPPLY CURVE, POTENTIAL GDP, AND THE NATURAL RATE OF UNEMPLOYMENT

Recall from Chapter 13 that many economists believe the *AS* curve is vertical in the long run. In the short run, we know that some input prices (which are costs to firms) lag behind increases in the overall price level. If the price level rises without a full adjustment of costs, firms' profits will be higher and output will increase. In the long run, however, input prices may catch up to output price increases. If input prices rise in subsequent periods, driving up costs, the short-run aggregate supply curve will shift to the left, and aggregate output will fall.

This situation is illustrated in Figure 14.10. Assume the initial equilibrium is at the intersection of AD_0 and the long-run aggregate supply curve. Now consider a shift of the aggregate demand curve from AD_0 to AD_1. If input prices lag behind changes in the overall price level, aggregate output will rise from Y_0 to Y_1. (This is a movement along the short-run *AS* curve AS_0.) In the longer run, input prices may catch up. For example, next year's labor contracts may make up for the fact that wage increases did not keep up with the cost of living this year. If input prices catch up in the longer run, the *AS* curve will shift from AS_0 to AS_1 and drive aggregate output back to Y_0. If input prices ultimately rise by exactly the same percentage as output prices, firms will produce the same level of output as they did before the increase in aggregate demand.

In Chapter 13 we said Y_0 is sometimes called *potential GDP*. Aggregate output can be pushed above Y_0 in the short run. When aggregate output exceeds Y_0, however, there is upward pressure on input prices and costs. The unemployment rate is already quite low, firms are beginning to encounter the limits of their plant capacities, and so forth. At levels of aggregate output above Y_0, costs will rise, the *AS* curve will shift to the left, and the price level will rise. Thus, potential GDP is the level of aggregate output that can be sustained in the long run without inflation.

This story is directly related to the Phillips Curve. Those who believe the *AS* curve is vertical in the long run at potential GDP also believe the Phillips Curve is vertical in the long run at some natural rate of unemployment. Recall from Chapter 7 that the **natural rate of unemployment** refers to unemployment that occurs as a normal part of the functioning of

natural rate of unemployment The unemployment that occurs as a normal part of the functioning of the economy. Sometimes taken as the sum of frictional unemployment and structural unemployment.

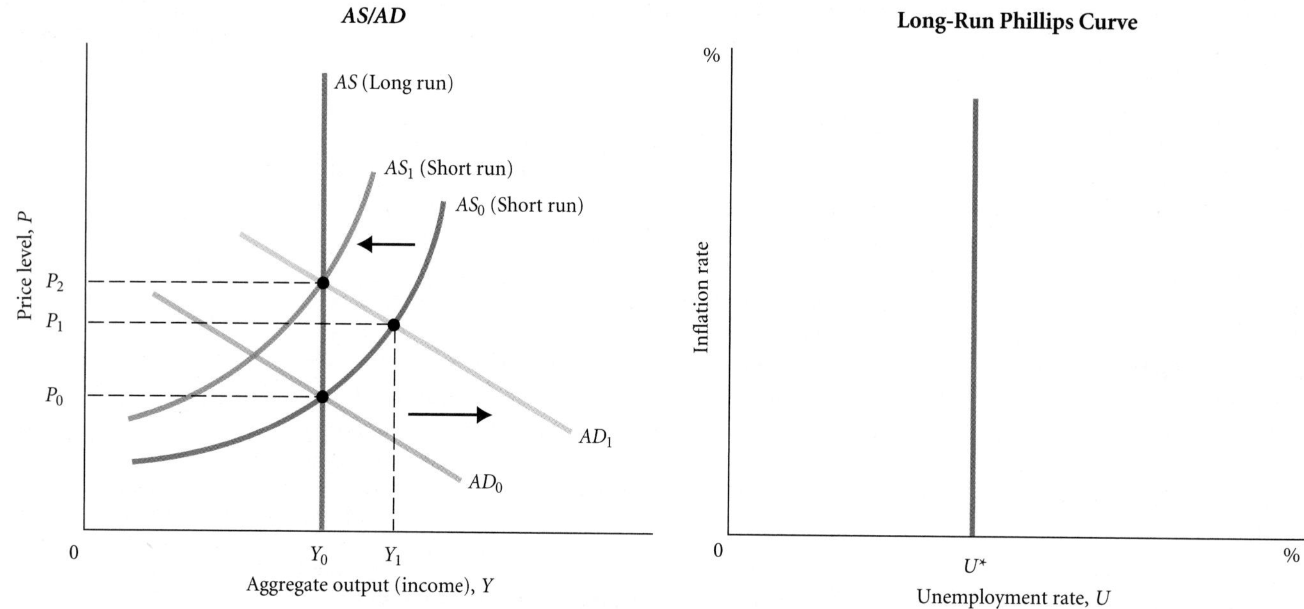

FIGURE 14.10 The Long-Run Phillips Curve: The Natural Rate of Unemployment

If the *AS* curve is vertical in the long run, so is the Phillips Curve. In the long run, the Phillips Curve corresponds to the natural rate of unemployment—that is, the unemployment rate that is consistent with the notion of a fixed long-run output at potential GDP. *U** is the natural rate of unemployment.

the economy. It is sometimes taken as the sum of frictional unemployment and structural unemployment. The logic behind the vertical Phillips Curve is that whenever the unemployment rate is pushed below the natural rate, wages begin to rise, thus pushing up costs. This leads to a *lower* level of output, which pushes the unemployment rate back up to the natural rate. At the natural rate, the economy can be considered to be at full employment.

THE NONACCELERATING INFLATION RATE OF UNEMPLOYMENT (NAIRU)

In Figure 14.10 the long-run vertical Phillips Curve is a graph with the inflation rate on the vertical axis and the unemployment rate on the horizontal axis. The natural rate of unemployment is *U**. In the long run, according to advocates of the long-run vertical Phillips Curve, the actual unemployment rate moves to *U** because of the natural workings of the economy.

NAIRU The nonaccelerating inflation rate of unemployment.

Another graph of interest is Figure 14.11 a graph with the *change in* the inflation rate on the vertical axis and the unemployment rate on the horizontal axis. Many economists believe the relationship between the change in the inflation rate and the unemployment rate is as depicted by the *PP* curve in the figure. The value of the unemployment rate where the *PP* curve crosses zero is called the "nonaccelerating inflation rate of unemployment" (**NAIRU**). If the actual unemployment rate is to the left of the NAIRU, the change in the inflation rate will be positive. As depicted in the figure, at U_1 the change in the inflation rate is 1. Conversely, if the actual unemployment rate is to the right of the NAIRU, the change in the inflation rate is negative: At U_2 the change is –1.

Consider what happens if the unemployment rate decreases from the NAIRU to U_1 and stays at U_1 for many periods. Assume also that the inflation rate at the NAIRU was 2 percent. Then in the first period the inflation rate will increase from 2 percent to 3 percent. The inflation rate does not, however, just stay at the higher 3 percent value. In the next period the inflation rate will increase from 3 percent to 4 percent, and so on. The price level will be accelerating—that is, the change in the inflation rate will be positive—when the actual unemployment rate is below the NAIRU. Conversely, the price level will be decelerating—

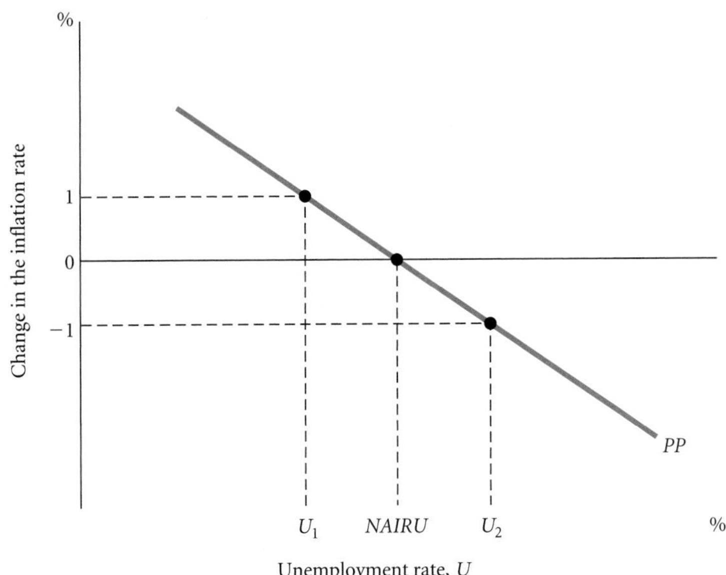

FIGURE 14.11 The NAIRU Diagram

To the left of the NAIRU the price level is accelerating (positive changes in the inflation rate), and to the right of the NAIRU the price level is decelerating (negative changes in the inflation rate). Only when the unemployment rate is equal to the NAIRU is the price level changing at a constant rate (no change in the inflation rate).

that is, the change in the inflation rate will be negative—when the actual unemployment rate is above the NAIRU.[1]

The *PP* curve in Figure 14.11 is like the *AS* curve in Figure 14.3—the same factors that shift the *AS* curve, such as cost shocks, can also shift the *PP* curve. Figure 13.8 summarizes the various factors that can cause the *AS* curve to shift, and these are also relevant for the *PP* curve. A favorable shift for the *PP* curve is to the left, because the *PP* curve crosses zero at a lower unemployment rate, which means that the NAIRU is lower. Some have argued that one possible recent source of favorable shifts is increased foreign competition, which may have kept both wage costs and other input costs down.

Before about 1995, proponents of the NAIRU theory argued that the value of the NAIRU in the United States was around 6 percent. By the end of 1995, the unemployment rate declined to 5.6 percent, and by 2000, the unemployment rate was down to 3.9 percent. If the NAIRU were 6 percent, one should have seen a continuing increase in the inflation rate beginning about 1995. In fact, the 1995 to 2003 period saw slightly declining inflation. Not only did inflation not continually increase, it did not even increase once to a new higher value and then stay there. As the unemployment rate declined during this period, proponents of the NAIRU lowered their estimates of it, more or less in line with the actual fall in the unemployment rate. This can be justified by arguing that there have been continuing favorable shifts of the *PP* curve, such as possible increased foreign competition. Critics have argued that this procedure is close to making the NAIRU theory vacuous. Can the theory really be tested if the estimate of the NAIRU is changed whenever it is not consistent with the data? How trustworthy is the appeal to favorable shifts?

Macroeconomists are currently debating whether equations estimated under the NAIRU theory are good approximations. More time is needed before any definitive answers can be given.

LOOKING AHEAD

This chapter concludes our basic analysis of how the macroeconomy works. In the preceding seven chapters, we have examined how households and firms behave in the three market arenas—the goods market, the money market, and the labor market. We have seen how aggregate output (income), the interest rate, and the price level are determined in the economy, and we have examined the relationship between two of the most important macroeconomic variables, the inflation rate and the unemployment rate. In Chapter 15, we use everything we have learned up to this point to examine a number of important policy issues.

[1]The NAIRU is actually misnamed. It is the *price level* that is accelerating or decelerating, not the inflation rate, when the actual unemployment rate differs from the NAIRU. The inflation rate is not accelerating or decelerating, but simply changing by the same amount each period. The namers of the NAIRU forgot their physics.

SUMMARY

THE LABOR MARKET: BASIC CONCEPTS

1. Because the economy is dynamic, *frictional* and *structural unemployment* are inevitable and in some ways desirable. Times of *cyclical unemployment* are of concern to macroeconomic policy makers.

2. In general, employment tends to fall when aggregate output falls and rise when aggregate output rises.

THE CLASSICAL VIEW OF THE LABOR MARKET

3. Classical economists believe the interaction of supply and demand in the labor market brings about equilibrium and that unemployment (beyond the frictional and structural amounts) does not exist.

4. The classical view of the labor market is consistent with the theory of a vertical aggregate supply curve.

EXPLAINING THE EXISTENCE OF UNEMPLOYMENT

5. Some economists argue that the unemployment rate is not an accurate indicator of whether the labor market is working properly. Unemployed people who are considered part of the labor force may be offered jobs but may be unwilling to take those jobs at the offered salaries. Some of the unemployed may have chosen not to work, but this does not mean that the labor market has malfunctioned.

6. Those who do not subscribe to the classical view of the labor market suggest several reasons why unemployment exists. Downwardly *sticky wages* may be brought about by *implicit* or *explicit contracts* not to cut wages. If the equilibrium wage rate falls but wages are prevented from falling also, the result will be unemployment.

7. *Efficiency wage theory* holds that the productivity of workers increases with the wage rate. If this is true, firms may have an incentive to pay wages above the wage at which the quantity of labor supplied is equal to the quantity of labor demanded. At all wages above the equilibrium, there will be an excess supply of labor and therefore unemployment.

8. If firms are operating with incomplete or imperfect information, they may not know what the market-clearing wage is. As a result, they may set their wages incorrectly and bring about unemployment. Because the economy is so complex, it may take considerable time for firms to correct these mistakes.

9. *Minimum wage laws*, which set a floor for wage rates, are one factor contributing to unemployment of teenagers and very low skilled workers. If the market-clearing wage for some groups of workers is below the minimum wage, some members of this group will be unemployed.

THE SHORT-RUN RELATIONSHIP BETWEEN THE UNEMPLOYMENT RATE AND INFLATION

10. There is a negative relationship between the unemployment rate (U) and aggregate output (income) (Y): When Y rises, U falls. When Y falls, U rises.

11. The relationship between the unemployment rate and the price level is negative: As the unemployment rate declines and the economy moves closer to capacity, the price level rises more and more.

12. The *Phillips Curve* represents the relationship between the *inflation rate* and the *unemployment rate*. During the 1950s and 1960s, this relationship was stable, and there seemed to be a predictable trade-off between inflation and unemployment. As a result of import price increases (which led to shifts in aggregate supply) and shifts in aggregate demand brought about partially by inflationary expectations, the relationship between the inflation rate and the unemployment rate was erratic in the 1970s. There *is* a short-run trade-off between inflation and unemployment, but other things besides unemployment affect inflation.

THE LONG-RUN AGGREGATE SUPPLY CURVE, POTENTIAL GDP, AND THE NATURAL RATE OF UNEMPLOYMENT

13. Those who believe the *AS* curve is vertical in the long run also believe the Phillips Curve is vertical in the long run at the *natural rate of unemployment*. The natural rate is generally the sum of the frictional and structural rates. If the Phillips Curve is vertical in the long run, then there is a limit to how low government policy can push the unemployment rate without setting off inflation.

14. The NAIRU theory says that the price level will accelerate when the unemployment rate is below the NAIRU and decelerate when the unemployment rate is above the NAIRU.

REVIEW TERMS AND CONCEPTS

cost-of-living adjustments (COLAs), 270
cyclical unemployment, 266
efficiency wage theory, 270
explicit contracts, 270
frictional unemployment, 266
inflation rate, 273
labor demand curve, 267
labor supply curve, 266
minimum wage laws, 271
NAIRU, 278
natural rate of unemployment, 277
Phillips Curve, 273
relative-wage explanation of unemployment, 270
social, or implicit, contracts, 270
sticky wages, 269
structural unemployment, 266
unemployment rate, 265

PROBLEM SET

1. In April of 2000, the U.S. unemployment rate dropped below 4 percent for the first time in 30 years. At the same time inflation remained at a very low level by historical standards. Can you offer an explanation for what seems to be an improved trade-off between inflation and unemployment? What factors might improve the trade-off? What factors might make it worse?
2. Do some research to find out what the current federal minimum wage is. A place to start is the Department of Labor's Web site: www.labor.gov. Explain how the minimum wage might contribute to unemployment. Draw a diagram to illustrate your argument. Recently there has been a debate raging about the actual effects of the minimum wage. Write a summary of the debate. (To find information, try google: "david card" and minimum wage).
3. Obtain monthly data on the unemployment rate and the inflation rate for the last 2 years. (These data can be found in a recent issue of the *Survey of Current Business* or in the *Monthly Labor Review* or *Employment and Earnings*, all published by the government and available in many college libraries or at www.bls.gov.)
   a. What trends do you observe? Can you explain what you see using aggregate supply and aggregate demand curves?
   b. Plot the 24 monthly rates on a graph with the unemployment rate measured on the X-axis and the inflation rate on the Y-axis. Is there evidence of a trade-off between these two variables? Can you offer an explanation?
4. In 2004, the country of Ruba was suffering a period of high unemployment. The new president Clang appointed as his chief economist Laurel Tiedye. Ms. Tiedye and her staff estimated these supply-and-demand curves for labor from data obtained from the secretary of labor, Robert Small:

$$Q_D = 100 - 5W$$
$$Q_S = 10W - 20$$

   where Q is the quantity of labor supplied/demanded in millions of workers and W is the wage rate in slugs, the currency of Ruba.
   a. Currently, the law in Ruba says no worker shall be paid less than nine slugs per hour. Estimate the quantity of labor supplied, the number of unemployed, and the unemployment rate.
   b. President Clang, over the objection of Secretary Small, has recommended to the Congress that the law be changed to allow the wage rate to be determined in the market. If such a law were passed, and the market adjusted quickly, what would happen to total employment, the size of the labor force, and the unemployment rate? Show the results graphically.
   c. Will the Rubanese labor market adjust quickly to such a change in the law? Why or why not?
5. The following policies have at times been advocated for coping with unemployment. Briefly explain how each might work, and explain which type or types of unemployment (frictional, structural, or cyclical) each policy is designed to alter.
   a. A computer list of job openings and a service that matches employees with job vacancies (sometimes called an "economic dating service")
   b. Lower minimum wage for teenagers
   c. Retraining programs for workers who need to learn new skills to find employment
   d. Public employment for people without jobs
   e. Improved information about available jobs and current wage rates
   f. The president going on nationwide TV and attempting to convince firms and workers that the inflation rate next year will be low
6. Your boss offers you a wage increase of 10 percent. Is it possible that you are worse off, even with the wage increase, than you were before?
7. How will the following affect labor force participation rates, labor supply, and unemployment?
   a. Because the retired elderly are a larger and larger fraction of the U.S. population, Congress and the president decide to raise the social security tax on individuals to continue paying benefits to the elderly.
   b. A national child care program is enacted, requiring employers to provide free child care services.
   c. The U.S. government reduces restrictions on immigration into the United States.
   d. The welfare system is eliminated.
   e. The government subsidizes the purchase of new capital by firms (an investment tax credit).
8. Draw a graph to illustrate the following:
   a. A Phillips Curve based on the assumption of a vertical long-run aggregate supply curve
   b. The effect of a change in inflationary expectations on a recently stable Phillips Curve
   c. Unemployment caused by a recently enacted minimum wage law
9. Obtain data on "average hourly earnings of production workers" and the unemployment rate for your state or area over a recent 2-year period. Has unemployment increased or decreased? What has happened to wages? Does the pattern of unemployment help explain the movement of wages? Can you offer an explanation?
10. Suppose the inflation–unemployment relationship depicted by the Phillips Curve was stable. Do you think the U.S. trade-off and the Japanese trade-off would be identical? If not, what kinds of factors might make the trade-offs dissimilar?

Macroeconomic Issues and Policy

15

CHAPTER OUTLINE

Newspapers carry articles dealing with macroeconomic problems daily, and macroeconomic issues and policies are an important part of many political campaigns. By using what we have learned about how the macroeconomy works, we can now examine in greater depth various issues and problems.

In this chapter we look more deeply at monetary and fiscal policy. We first consider a problem that both types of policy makers face, but particularly fiscal policy makers, which is the problem of time lags. We will see that it is not easy to get the timing right when trying to stabilize the economy. We then turn to more detailed looks at monetary and fiscal policy.

TIME LAGS REGARDING MONETARY AND FISCAL POLICY

One of the objectives of monetary and fiscal policy is stabilization of the economy. Consider the two possible time paths for aggregate output (income) (Y) shown in Figure 15.1. In path B (the light blue line), the fluctuations in GDP are smaller than those in path A (the dark blue line). One aim of **stabilization policy** is to smooth out fluctuations in output, to try to move the economy along a path like B instead of A. Stabilization policy is also concerned with the stability of prices. Here the goal is not to prevent the overall price level from rising at all but instead to achieve an inflation rate that is as close to zero as possible given the government's other goals of high and stable levels of output and employment.

stabilization policy Describes both monetary and fiscal policy, the goals of which are to smooth out fluctuations in output and employment and to keep prices as stable as possible.

Stabilization goals are not easy to achieve. The existence of various kinds of **time lags**, or delays in the response of the economy to stabilization policies, can make the economy difficult to control. Economists generally recognize three kinds of time lags: recognition lags, implementation lags, and response lags. We will consider each, but we will begin with an analogy.

time lags Delays in the economy's response to stabilization policies.

STABILIZATION: "THE FOOL IN THE SHOWER"

Milton Friedman, a leading critic of stabilization policy, likened the government's attempts to stabilize the economy to a "fool in the shower." The shower starts out too cold, because the pipes have not yet warmed up. So the fool turns up the hot water. Nothing happens, so he

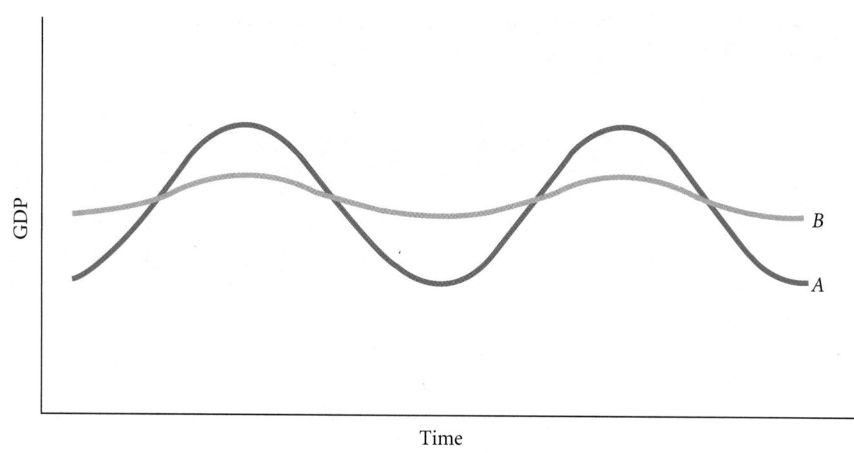

FIGURE 15.1 Two Possible Time Paths for GDP

Path *A* is less stable—it varies more over time—than path *B*. Other things being equal, society prefers path *B* to path *A*.

turns up the hot water further. The hot water comes on and scalds him. He immediately turns up the cold water. Nothing happens right away, so he turns up the cold further. When the cold water finally starts to come up, he finds the shower too cold, and so it goes.

In Friedman's view, the government is constantly behaving like the fool in the shower, stimulating or contracting the economy at the wrong time. How this might happen is shown in Figure 15.2. Suppose the economy reaches a peak and begins to slide into recession at point *A* (at time t_0). Policy makers do not observe the decline in GDP until it has sunk to point *B* (at time t_1). By the time they have begun to stimulate the economy (point *C*, time t_2), the recession is well advanced and the economy has almost bottomed out. When the policies finally begin to take effect (point *D*, time t_3), the economy is already on its road to recovery. The policies push the economy to point *F′*—a much greater fluctuation than point *F*, which is where the economy would have been without the stabilization policy. Sometime after point *D*, policy makers may begin to realize that the economy is expanding too quickly. By the time they have implemented contractionary policies and the policies have made their effects felt, the economy is starting to weaken. The contractionary policies therefore end up pushing GDP to point *G′* instead of point *G*.

Because of the various time lags, the expansionary policies that should have been instituted at time t_0 do not begin to have an effect until time t_3, when they are no longer needed. The light blue line in Figure 15.2 shows how the economy behaves as a result of the "stabilization" policies; the dark blue line shows the time path of GDP if the economy had been allowed to run its course and no stabilization policies had been attempted. In this case, stabilization policy makes income more erratic, not less—the policy results in a peak income of *F′* as opposed to *F* and a trough income of *G′* instead of *G*.

Critics of stabilization policy argue that the situation in Figure 15.2 is typical of the interaction between the government and the rest of the economy. This is not necessarily true.

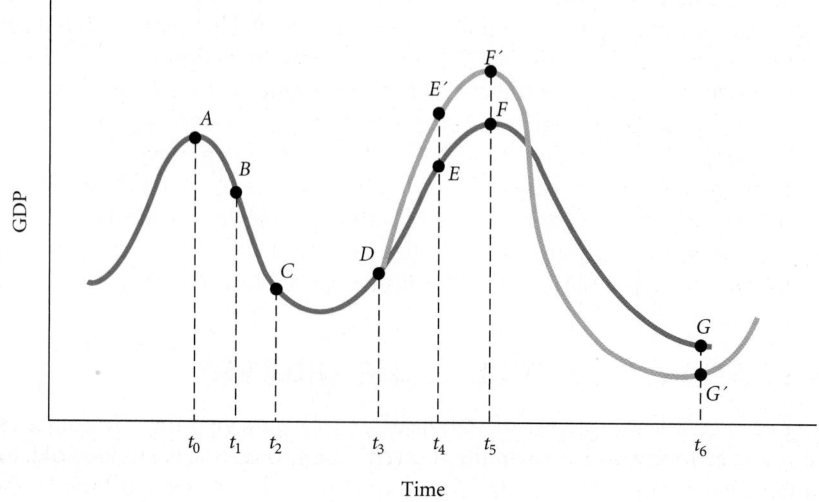

FIGURE 15.2 "The Fool in the Shower"—How Government Policy Can Make Matters Worse

Attempts to stabilize the economy can prove destabilizing because of time lags. An expansionary policy that should have begun to take effect at point *A* does not actually begin to have an impact until point *D*, when the economy is already on an upswing. Hence the policy pushes the economy to points *F′* and *G′* (instead of points *F* and G). Income varies more widely than it would have if no policy had been implemented.

We need to know more about the nature of the various kinds of lags before deciding whether stabilization policy is good or bad.

RECOGNITION LAGS

It takes time for policy makers to recognize a boom or a slump. Many important data—those from the national income and product accounts, for example—are available only quarterly. It usually takes several weeks to compile and prepare even the preliminary estimates for these figures. If the economy goes into a slump on January 1, the recession may not be detected until the data for the first quarter are available at the end of April.

Moreover, the early national income and product accounts data are only preliminary, based on an incomplete compilation of the various data sources. These estimates can, and often do, change as better data become available. This makes the interpretation of the initial estimates difficult, and **recognition lags** result.

recognition lag The time it takes for policy makers to recognize the existence of a boom or a slump.

IMPLEMENTATION LAGS

The problems that lags pose for stabilization policy do not end once economists and policy makers recognize that the economy is in a slump or a boom. Even if everyone knows that the economy needs to be stimulated or reined in, it takes time to put the desired policy into effect, especially for actions that involve fiscal policy. **Implementation lags** result.

implementation lag The time it takes to put the desired policy into effect once economists and policy makers recognize that the economy is in a boom or a slump.

Each year Congress decides on the federal government's budget for the coming year. The tax laws and spending programs embodied in this budget are not subject to change once they are in place. If it becomes clear that the economy is entering a recession and is in need of a fiscal stimulus during the middle of the year, there is little that can be done. Until Congress authorizes more spending or a cut in taxes, changes in fiscal policy are not possible.[1]

Monetary policy is less subject to the kinds of restrictions that slow down changes in fiscal policy. As we saw in Chapter 10, the Fed's chief tool to control the supply of money or the interest rate is open market operations—buying and selling government securities. Transactions in these securities take place in a highly developed market, and if the Fed wishes, it can buy or sell a large volume of securities in a very short period of time.

> The implementation lag for monetary policy is generally much shorter than for fiscal policy.

When the Fed wishes to increase the supply of money, it goes into the open market and purchases government securities. This instantly increases the stock of money (bank reserves held at the Fed), and an expansion of the money supply begins.

RESPONSE LAGS

Even after a macroeconomic problem has been recognized and the appropriate policies to correct it have been implemented, there are **response lags**—lags that occur because of the operation of the economy itself. Even after the government has formulated a policy and put it into place, the economy takes time to adjust to the new conditions. Although monetary policy can be adjusted and implemented more quickly than fiscal policy, it takes longer to make its effect felt on the economy because of response lags.

response lag The time that it takes for the economy to adjust to the new conditions after a new policy is implemented; the lag that occurs because of the operation of the economy itself.

> What is most important is the total lag between the time a problem first occurs and the time the corrective policies are felt.

---

[1]Do not forget, however, about the existence of automatic stabilizers (see Chapter 9). Many programs contain built-in countercyclical features that expand spending or cut tax collections automatically (without the need for congressional or executive action) during a recession.

Response Lags for Fiscal Policy One way to think about the response lag in fiscal policy is through the government spending multiplier. This multiplier measures the change in GDP caused by a given change in government spending or net taxes. It takes time for the multiplier to reach its full value. The result is a lag between the time a fiscal policy action is initiated and the time the full change in GDP is realized.

The reason for the response lag in fiscal policy—the delay in the multiplier process—is simple. During the first few months after an increase in government spending or a tax cut, there is not enough time for the firms or individuals who benefit directly from the extra government spending or the tax cut to increase their own spending.

Neither individuals nor firms revise their spending plans instantaneously. Until they can make those revisions, extra government spending does not stimulate extra private spending.

Changes in government purchases are a component of aggregate expenditure. When *G* rises, aggregate expenditure increases directly; when *G* falls, aggregate expenditure decreases directly. When personal taxes are changed, however, an additional step intervenes, giving rise to another lag. Suppose a tax cut has lowered personal income taxes across the board. Each household must decide what portion of its tax cut to spend and what portion to save. This decision is the extra step. Before the tax cut gets translated into extra spending, households must take the step of increasing their spending, which usually takes some time.

With a business tax cut, there is a further complication. Firms must decide what to do with their added after-tax profits. If they pay out their added profits to households as dividends, the result is the same as with a personal tax cut. Households must decide whether to spend or to save the extra funds. Firms may also retain their added profits and use them for investment, but investment is a component of aggregate expenditure that requires planning and time.

In practice, it takes about a year for a change in taxes or in government spending to have its full effect on the economy. This means that if we increase spending to counteract a recession today, the full effects will not be felt for 12 months. By that time, the state of the economy might be very different.

Response Lags for Monetary Policy Monetary policy works by changing interest rates, which then change planned investment. Interest rates can also affect consumption spending, as we discuss further in Chapter 17. For now, it is enough to know that lower interest rates usually stimulate consumption spending and higher interest rates decrease consumption spending.

The response of consumption and investment to interest rate changes takes time. Even if interest rates were to drop by 5 percent overnight, firms would not immediately increase their investment purchases. Firms generally make their investment plans several years in advance. If General Motors wants to respond to a decrease in interest rates by investing more, it will take some time—perhaps up to a year—to come up with plans for a new factory or assembly line. While such plans are being drawn, GM may spend little on new investments. The effect of the decrease in interest rates may not make itself felt for quite some time.

The response lags for monetary policy are even longer than response lags for fiscal policy. When government spending changes, there is a direct change in the sales of firms, which sell more as a result of the increased government purchases. When interest rates change, however, the sales of firms do not change until households change their consumption spending and/or firms change their investment spending. It takes time for households and firms to respond to interest rate changes. In this sense, interest rate changes are like tax-rate changes. The resulting change in firm sales must wait for households and firms to change their purchases of goods.

Summary Stabilization is not easily achieved. It takes time for policy makers to recognize the existence of a problem, more time for them to implement a solution, and yet more time for firms and households to respond to the stabilization policies taken. Monetary policy can be adjusted more quickly and easily than taxes or government spending, making it a useful instrument in stabilizing the economy. However, because the economy's response to monetary changes is probably slower than its response to changes in fiscal policy, tax and spending changes may also play a useful role in macroeconomic management.

MONETARY POLICY

We have so far in this book talked about monetary policy as consisting of changes in the money supply (M^s). We saw in Chapter 10 that the Fed can change the money supply by (1) changing the required reserve ratio, (2) changing the discount rate, and (3) engaging in open market operations (buying and selling government securities). We also pointed out that the main way in which the Fed changes the money supply is by engaging in open market operations; through these operations the Fed can achieve whatever value of the money supply that it wants.

There are two key points that we must add to the monetary policy story to make the story realistic, which we do in this section. The first point is that *in practice the Fed targets the interest rate rather than the money supply.* The second point is that *the interest rate value that the Fed chooses depends on the state of the economy.* We will first explain these two points and then turn to a discussion of actual Fed policy from 1990 on.

TARGETING THE INTEREST RATE

Figure 11.7 on page 216 in Chapter 11 shows that if the Fed increases the money supply the interest rate falls. As the money supply curve shifts to the right, there is a movement of the equilibrium interest rate down the money demand curve. The buying and selling of government securities by the Fed thus has two effects at the same time: it changes the money supply and it changes the interest rate. If the Fed buys securities, this increases the money supply and lowers the interest rate, and if the Fed sells securities, this decreases the money supply and raises the interest rate. How much the interest rate changes depends on the shape of the demand for money curve. The steeper the money demand curve, the larger is the change in the interest rate for a given size change in government securities.

What this means is that if the Fed wants to achieve a particular value of the money supply, it must accept whatever interest rate value is implied by this choice. (Again, the interest rate value depends on the shape of the demand for money curve.) Conversely, if the Fed wants to achieve a particular value of the interest rate, it must accept whatever money supply value is implied by this. If, for example, the Fed wants to lower the interest rate by one percentage point, it must keep buying government securities until the interest rate value is reached. As the Fed is buying government securities, the money supply is increasing. In short, the Fed can pick a money supply value and accept the interest rate consequences, or it can pick an interest rate value and accept the money supply consequences.

The first key point is that in practice the Fed chooses the interest rate value and accepts the money supply consequences, rather than vice versa. The Federal Open Market Committee (FOMC) meets every six weeks and sets the value of the interest rate. It then instructs the Open Market Desk at the New York Federal Reserve Bank to keep buying or selling government securities until the desired interest rate value is achieved. In other words, the Fed targets the interest rate.

The FOMC announces the interest rate value at 2:15 P.M. Eastern time on the day it meets. This is a key time for financial markets around the world. At 2:14 P.M. there are thousands of people staring at their screens waiting for the word on high. If the announcement is a surprise, this can have very large and immediate effects on bond and stock markets. We will discuss this in the next chapter.

For most of the rest of this text we will talk about monetary policy as being a change in the interest rate. Keep in mind, of course, that monetary policy also changes the money supply. We can talk about an expansionary monetary policy as either one in which the money supply is increased or one in which the interest rate is lowered. We will talk about the interest rate being lowered because the interest rate is what the Fed targets in practice. However we talk about it, an expansionary monetary policy is achieved by the Fed's buying government securities.

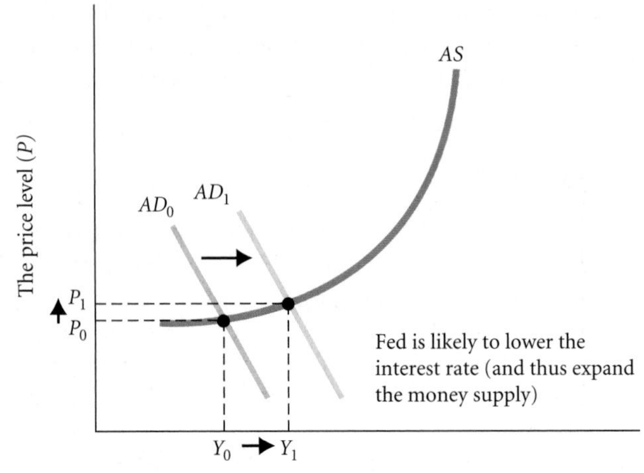

FIGURE 15.3 The Fed's Response to Low Output/Low Inflation

During periods of low output/low inflation, the economy is on the relatively flat portion of the *AS* curve. In this case, the Fed is likely to lower the interest rate (and thus expand the money supply). This will shift the *AD* curve to the right, from AD_0 to AD_1, and lead to an increase in output with very little increase in the price level.

THE FED'S RESPONSE TO THE STATE OF THE ECONOMY

When the FOMC meets every six weeks to set the value of the interest rate, it does not set the value in a vacuum. An important question in macroeconomics is what influences the interest rate decision. To answer this, we must first consider what the main goals of the Fed are. What ultimately is the Fed trying to achieve?

Two of the Fed's main goals are high levels of output and employment and a low rate of inflation. From the Fed's point of view, the best situation is a fully employed economy with an inflation rate near zero. The worst situation is *stagflation*—high unemployment and high inflation.

If the economy is in a low output/low inflation situation, it will be producing on the relatively flat portion of the aggregate supply (*AS*) curve (Figure 15.3). In this case, the Fed can increase output by lowering the interest rate (and thus increasing the money supply) with little effect on the price level. The expansionary monetary policy will shift the aggregate demand (*AD*) curve to the right, leading to an increase in output with little change in the price level.

> The Fed is likely to lower the interest rate (and thus increase the money supply) during times of low output and low inflation.

The opposite is true in times of high output and high inflation. In this situation, the economy is producing on the relatively steep portion of the *AS* curve (Figure 15.4), and the

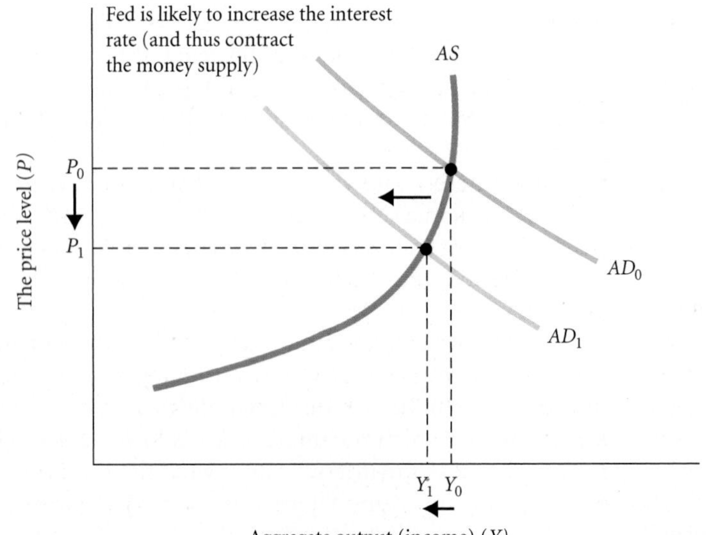

FIGURE 15.4 The Fed's Response to High Output/High Inflation

During periods of high output/high inflation, the economy is on the relatively steep portion of the *AS* curve. In this case, the Fed is likely to increase the interest rate (and thus contract the money supply). This will shift the *AD* curve to the left, from AD_0 to AD_1, and lead to a decrease in the price level with very little decrease in output.

Fed can increase the interest rate (and thus decrease the money supply) with little effect on output. The contractionary monetary policy will shift the *AD* curve to the left, which will lead to a fall in the price level and little effect on output.[2]

The Fed is likely to increase the interest rate (and thus decrease the money supply) during times of high output and high inflation.

Stagflation is a more difficult problem to solve. If the Fed lowers the interest rate, output will rise, but so will the inflation rate (which is already too high). If the Fed increases the interest rate, the inflation rate will fall, but so will output (which is already too low). (You should be able to draw *AS/AD* diagrams to see why this is true.) The Fed is faced with a trade-off. In this case, the Fed's decisions depend on how it weighs output relative to inflation. If it dislikes high inflation more than low output, it will increase the interest rate; if it dislikes low output more than high inflation, it will lower the interest rate. In practice, the Fed probably dislikes high inflation more than low output, but how the Fed behaves depends in part on the beliefs of the chair of the Fed.

The Fed sometimes "leans against the wind," meaning as the economy expands, the Fed uses open market operations to raise the interest rate gradually to try to prevent the economy from expanding too quickly. Conversely, as the economy contracts, the Fed lowers the interest rate gradually to lessen (and eventually stop) the contraction. This type of stabilization is, of course, not easily achieved, as we saw earlier in this chapter.

POLICY SINCE 1990

Table 15.1 presents data on selected variables for the 1989 I–2003 II period. This table may at first look overwhelming, but with a little study you can gain a lot of important information about the U.S. economy since 1990. We will go through it slowly. We will use the table to study the Fed's interest rate behavior. The short-term interest rate in the table is the 3-month Treasury bill rate, which we will just refer to as the "bill" rate. It is the interest rate on 3-month U.S. Treasury bills. This is not the interest rate that the FOMC directly controls each day, which is a rate called the "federal funds" rate. The federal funds interest rate is the rate on overnight loans among commercial banks. If, because of reserve requirements, a bank needs to borrow money at the end of the day, it borrows money from banks that have extra reserves, and the rate that it pays is the federal funds rate. The bill rate closely follows the federal funds rate, and we choose here to focus on the bill rate. The other interest rate in the table is the AAA bond rate, which is the interest rate on long-term (about 10 years), high grade corporate bonds.

1990–1991 Recession Table 15.1 shows that the real GDP growth rate in 1990 I was 5.1 percent, the unemployment rate was 5.3 percent, the inflation rate was 4.5 percent, and the bill rate was 7.8 percent. You can see that the Fed kept the bill rate fairly high in 1989. The economy was at or close to full employment, and the Fed wanted to keep the inflation rate in check.

In the second half of 1990, the economy went into a recession. Because inflation seemed to be under control at that time, experts expected the Fed would begin following an expansionary monetary policy to lessen the contraction of the economy. At the end of 1990, the Fed began to follow exactly this policy. Table 15.1 shows that the bill rate fell from 7.0 percent in 1990 IV to 6.1 percent in 1991 I. By 1991 IV, the bill rate was down to 4.6 percent. This lowering of interest rates was designed to stimulate private spending and bring the economy out of the recession.

The Fed's behavior during the 1990–1991 recession is an example of its tendency to lean against the wind. After the Fed became convinced a recession was at hand, it responded by engaging in open market operations to lower the interest rate. Inflation was not a problem,

[2]In practice, the price level rarely falls. What the Fed actually achieves in this case is a decrease in the *rate of inflation*—that is, in the percentage change in the price level—not a decrease in the price level itself. The discussion here is sliding over the distinction between the price level and the rate of inflation. Recall our discussion of this distinction in Chapter 14.

TABLE 15.1 Data for Selected Variables for the 1989 I–2003 II Period

DATE		REAL GDP GROWTH RATE (%)	UNEMPL. RATE (%)	INFL. RATE (%)	3-MONTH T-BILL RATE	AAA BOND RATE	FED. GOV. SURP.	SURP./GDP
1989	I	5.0	5.2	4.3	8.5	9.7	−108.8	−0.020
	II	2.2	5.2	4.0	8.4	9.5	−127.3	−0.023
	III	1.9	5.3	2.9	7.9	9.0	−140.6	−0.025
	IV	1.4	5.4	3.1	7.6	8.9	−143.4	−0.026
1990	I	5.1	5.3	4.5	7.8	9.2	−172.1	−0.030
	II	0.9	5.3	4.7	7.8	9.4	−171.2	−0.030
	III	−0.7	5.7	3.9	7.5	9.4	−164.6	−0.028
	IV	−3.2	6.1	3.5	7.0	9.3	−184.0	−0.031
1991	I	−2.0	6.6	4.7	6.1	8.9	−160.1	−0.027
	II	2.3	6.8	2.9	5.6	8.9	−213.4	−0.036
	III	1.0	6.9	2.5	5.4	8.8	−234.7	−0.039
	IV	2.2	7.1	2.3	4.6	8.4	−253.1	−0.042
1992	I	3.8	7.4	3.1	3.9	8.3	−288.3	−0.047
	II	3.8	7.6	2.2	3.7	8.3	−291.8	−0.046
	III	3.1	7.6	1.3	3.1	8.0	−316.5	−0.050
	IV	5.4	7.4	2.5	3.1	8.0	−293.5	−0.045
1993	I	−0.1	7.2	3.4	3.0	7.7	−300.9	−0.046
	II	2.5	7.1	2.2	3.0	7.4	−267.3	−0.041
	III	1.8	6.8	1.8	3.0	6.9	−275.5	−0.041
	IV	6.2	6.6	2.3	3.1	6.8	−253.0	−0.037
1994	I	3.4	6.6	2.0	3.3	7.2	−237.5	−0.034
	II	5.7	6.2	1.8	4.0	7.9	−190.6	−0.027
	III	2.2	6.0	2.4	4.5	8.2	−211.8	−0.030
	IV	5.0	5.6	1.9	5.3	8.6	−209.2	−0.029
1995	I	1.5	5.5	3.0	5.8	8.3	−208.2	−0.029
	II	0.8	5.7	1.7	5.6	7.7	−189.0	−0.026
	III	3.1	5.7	1.8	5.4	7.4	−197.5	−0.027
	IV	3.2	5.6	2.0	5.3	7.0	−173.1	−0.023
1996	I	2.9	5.6	2.5	5.0	7.0	−176.4	−0.023
	II	6.8	5.5	1.4	5.0	7.6	−137.0	−0.018
	III	2.0	5.3	1.9	5.1	7.6	−130.1	−0.017
	IV	4.6	5.3	1.6	5.0	7.2	−103.9	−0.013
1997	I	4.4	5.3	2.9	5.1	7.4	−86.5	−0.011
	II	5.9	5.0	1.9	5.1	7.6	−68.2	−0.008
	III	4.2	4.8	1.2	5.1	7.2	−33.8	−0.004
	IV	2.8	4.7	1.4	5.1	6.9	−25.0	−0.003
1998	I	6.1	4.7	1.1	5.1	6.7	19.6	0.002
	II	2.2	4.4	1.0	5.0	6.6	33.0	0.004
	III	4.1	4.5	1.4	4.8	6.5	65.7	0.007
	IV	6.7	4.4	1.1	4.3	6.3	57.1	0.006
1999	I	3.1	4.3	1.8	4.4	6.4	85.1	0.009
	II	1.7	4.3	1.3	4.5	6.9	116.5	0.013
	III	4.7	4.2	1.4	4.7	7.3	132.0	0.014
	IV	8.3	4.1	1.6	5.0	7.5	143.2	0.015
2000	I	2.3	4.1	3.8	5.5	7.7	212.8	0.022
	II	4.8	4.0	2.3	5.7	7.8	197.2	0.020
	III	0.6	4.0	1.6	6.0	7.6	213.1	0.022
	IV	1.1	3.9	2.1	6.0	7.4	193.8	0.019
2001	I	−0.6	4.2	3.6	4.8	7.1	173.8	0.017
	II	−1.6	4.4	2.5	3.7	7.2	144.6	0.014
	III	−0.3	4.8	2.2	3.2	7.1	−51.7	−0.005
	IV	2.7	5.6	−0.5	1.9	6.9	21.3	0.002
2002	I	5.0	5.6	1.4	1.8	6.6	−145.8	−0.014
	II	1.3	5.9	1.3	1.7	6.7	−195.7	−0.019
	III	4.0	5.8	1.0	1.6	6.3	−210.5	−0.020
	IV	1.4	5.9	1.8	1.3	6.3	−256.5	−0.024
2003	I	1.4	5.8	2.5	1.2	6.0	−275.4	−0.026
	II	2.4	6.2	0.8	1.0	5.3	−368.0	−0.034

Note: The inflation rate is the percentage change in the GDP price deflator.

so the Fed could expand the economy in this way without worrying much about the inflationary consequences of its actions. Some argue that the Fed should have acted sooner, but with the Persian Gulf situation uncertain until February 1991, the Fed did not want to expand too much in the face of a possibly lengthy war that could have led to inflationary pressures. Once the outcome of the Persian Gulf War was known, the Fed responded rapidly.

1993–1994 The economy was slow to recover from the 1990–1991 recession, and the growth rate did not pick up much until the beginning of 1992. Even at the end of 1992, the unemployment rate was still high at 7.4 percent (Table 15.1). The Fed kept the bill rate relatively low in 1992 and 1993 in an attempt to stimulate the economy. This was simply an extension of its expansionary policy in 1991. Again, inflation was not a problem in 1992 and 1993, so the Fed had room to stimulate. By 1993 IV the unemployment rate had fallen to 6.6 percent and the growth rate was 6.2 percent.

At the end of 1993 the Fed decided to begin slowing down the economy. The bill rate rose from 3.1 percent in 1993 IV to 5.8 percent in 1995 I. Why was the Fed pursuing a contractionary policy? You can see from the table that the inflation rate in 1993 and 1994 was quite low, and there were no signs even at the end of 1994 of any inflationary pressures building in the economy. Nevertheless, the Fed was worried about inflation picking up in the future. The real GDP growth rate in 1994 was relatively high and the unemployment rate was down to 5.6 percent by the fourth quarter, and the Fed felt these trends might spell inflation problems in the future.

The Fed's behavior in 1994 is an example of leaning against the wind quite far in advance, long before any observed sign of increasing inflation. Some people felt that the Fed was acting too hastily and should have waited for direct signs of inflationary pressures before tightening.

1995–1997 Inflation in fact did not become a problem after 1994. After slow growth in the first half of 1995, the economy picked up the pace, and by the end of 1997, the unemployment rate was down to 4.7 percent. The Fed lowered the bill rate from 5.8 percent in 1995 I to 5.0 percent in 1996 I, and then it kept the bill rate at roughly 5.0 percent throughout 1996 and 1997. You can see from Table 15.1 that the federal government deficit fell to essentially zero by the end of 1997. What better outcome could the Fed want: good growth, low unemployment, low inflation, and a balanced government budget!

1998–2000 By continuing our use of Table 15.1, you can see that the Fed kept the bill rate at about 5 percent in the first three quarters of 1998, but it then suddenly lowered the bill rate to 4.3 percent in 1998 IV. The Fed was concerned about possible negative effects on the U.S. economy from the Asian financial crisis. As it turned out, the U.S. economy was not much affected by the Asia crisis, and the growth rate in 1998–2000 was strong. By the end of 1999, the unemployment rate was down to about 4 percent. Although inflation remained very low in 1998 and 1999, the Fed got nervous in the middle of 1999 about the economy overheating. It began raising the bill rate, and at the end of 2000 the bill rate was up to 6.0 percent.

2001–2003 We will see in the next chapter that overall stock prices increased dramatically from the beginning of 1995 through the beginning of 2000. We will see that this was one of the main reasons for the strong economy in this period. The stock market boom came to an end in the beginning of 2000, and the economy began to slow down in the middle of 2000. Table 15.1 shows that the real GDP growth rate in the last half of 2000 was only about 1 percent and that real growth was negative in the first three quarters of 2001. The unemployment rate rose to 5.6 percent by 2001 IV. A recession was declared by the National Bureau of Economic Research in 2001.

The Fed responded to this slowdown by perhaps the most expansionary policy in its history. Table 15.1 shows that the bill rate fell from 6.0 percent in 2000 IV to 1.9 percent in 2001 IV, a fall of over 4 percentage points in a year! The Fed was not worried about inflation because it had not been a problem for years, and so it aggressively lowered the interest rate to try to stimulate the economy. It is interesting to note that even this aggressive policy did not avoid a recession. This shows that the ability of the Fed to stabilize the economy is limited.

Many expected after the attacks on September 11, 2001, that the economy would continue to be in a recession. You can see from Table 15.1, however, that the growth rate was positive from 2001 IV on. The growth rate in 2002 and the first half of 2003 was high enough to keep the unemployment rate roughly unchanged. Inflation continued to be low. The Fed kept the interest rate low in 2002 and 2003, as you can see from the table. In 2003 II the bill rate was only 1.0 percent. Again, the Fed was not worried about inflation and chose to keep the interest rate low to try to stimulate the economy further. Some expected that the Fed would lower the interest rate below 1 percent. The Fed did not do this, partly perhaps out of concern with the growing size of the Federal government deficit. You can see from the table that the deficit increased dramatically in 2002 and 2003.

FISCAL POLICY: DEFICIT TARGETING

Many fiscal policy discussions center around the size of the federal government surplus or deficit. You can see from Table 15.1 that there was a substantial deficit in the first half of the 1990s, which then changed to a surplus by 1998. The surplus then changed back to a deficit in 2002. By 2003 II the deficit had become fairly large again and a concern to many people.

We begin our discussion with the reaction of the federal government to the large deficits in the late 1980s and early 1990s. This material is a great macroeconomic teaching device. We then turn to a discussion of fiscal policy from 1990 on.

As just noted, the federal government deficit was large in the first half of the 1990s. In fact, the deficit began to be a problem in the early 1980s. The government was simply spending much more than it was receiving in taxes. When the deficit reached 4.7 percent of GDP in 1986, the U.S. Congress passed and President Reagan signed the **Gramm-Rudman-Hollings Bill** (named for its three congressional sponsors), referred to as GRH.

Gramm-Rudman-Hollings Bill Passed by the U.S. Congress and signed by President Reagan in 1986, this law set out to reduce the federal deficit by $36 billion per year, with a deficit of zero slated for 1991.

GRH set a target for reducing the federal deficit by a set amount each year. Figure 15.5 shows, the deficit was to decline by $36 billion per year between 1987 and 1991, with a deficit of zero slated for fiscal year 1991. What was interesting about the GRH legislation was that the targets were not merely guidelines. If Congress, through its decisions about taxes and spending programs, produced a budget with a deficit larger than the targeted amount, GRH called for automatic spending cuts. The cuts were divided proportionately among most federal spending programs, so that a program that made up 5 percent of total spending was to endure a cut equal to 5 percent of the total spending cut.[3]

In 1986, the U.S. Supreme Court declared part of the GRH bill unconstitutional. In effect, the court said the Congress would have to approve the "automatic" spending cuts before they could take place. The law was changed in 1986 to meet the Supreme Court ruling and again in 1987, when new targets were established. The new targets had the deficit reaching zero in 1993 instead of 1991. The targets were changed again in 1991, when the year to achieve a zero deficit was changed from 1993 to 1996.

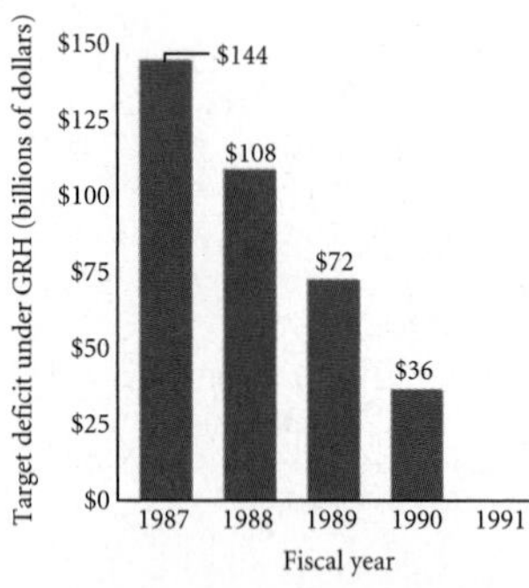

FIGURE 15.5 Deficit Reduction Targets under Gramm-Rudman-Hollings

The GRH legislation, passed in 1986, set out to lower the federal deficit by $36 billion per year. If the plan had worked, a zero deficit would have been achieved by 1991.

In practice, these targets never came close to being achieved. As time wore on, even the revised targets became completely unrealistic, and by the end of the 1980s the GRH legislation was not taken seriously.

As Table 15.1 shows, the deficit problem continued in the 1990s, and one of President Clinton's goals when he took office in 1993 was to reduce the deficit. The first step was the Omnibus Budget Reconciliation Act of 1993. The act, which barely made it through Congress, was projected to reduce the deficit in the five fiscal years 1994 to 1998 by $504.8 billion—$254.7 billion would come from cuts in federal spending, and $250.1 billion would come from tax increases. Most of the tax increases were levied on high-income taxpayers.

There was also some sentiment in the mid-1990s for the passage of a "balanced-budget amendment," intended to prevent Congress from doing what it did in the 1980s. The balanced-budget amendment passed the House in early 1995, but it failed by one vote in the Senate. It turned out that the passage of the Omnibus Budget Reconciliation Act of 1993 and a robust economy was enough to lead to a balanced budget by 1998. You can see from Table 15.1 that by 2000 there was a large budget surplus. Between 1998 and 2001 the federal

[3]Programs like Social Security were exempt from cuts or were treated differently. Interest payments on the federal debt was also immune from cuts.

News Analysis

Bush Fiscal Policy and the Deficit 2003

AT THE URGING OF PRESIDENT BUSH, THE CONGRESS passed a series of tax cuts designed to stimulate the sluggish economy between 2001 and 2003. At the same time, the events of 9/11 and wars in Afghanistan and Iraq led to increased government spending. The result was that the federal budget, which was running a surplus in the late 1990s, began to reflect huge deficits by 2003. The following *New York Times* article appeared in mid-2003.

White House Sees a $455 Billion Gap in the '03 Budget

—New York Times

The White House today projected a $455 billion budget deficit in the current fiscal year, by far the government's largest deficit ever and $150 billion higher than what the administration predicted just five months ago.

Democratic lawmakers said the new calculations showed the folly of President Bush's tax cuts and demonstrated that he was mismanaging the economy.

But Joshua B. Bolten, Mr. Bush's new budget director, said a deficit of this magnitude was "manageable if we continue pro-growth economic policies and exercise serious spending discipline."

In dollar terms, the expected deficit would be substantially higher than the previous record, $290 billion in the fiscal year 1992, the last full year of the first Bush administration.

Using what economists say is the most reliable measurement, the $455 billion represents 4.2 percent of the total economy, somewhat less than the 1983 deficit in the administration of President Ronald Reagan, which was 6 percent.

But in only six years since 1946 has the deficit been larger than 4.2 percent of the gross domestic product. Not counting the current surplus in the Social Security fund, the deficit would be 5.7 percent of the total economy, the largest since World War II except for 1983, when there was no Social Security surplus.

The projections released today by the White House's Office of Management and Budget in its midyear review showed the deficit rising to $475 billion in the 2004 fiscal year, which begins Oct. 1, then declining somewhat as a result of the stronger economy that the administration is forecasting. The deficit was also forecast to be $304 billion in 2005, $238 billion in 2006, $213 billion in 2007 and $226 billion in 2008. In all, that would be about $1.9 trillion in new debt through 2008, making for a total national debt of $8.6 trillion.

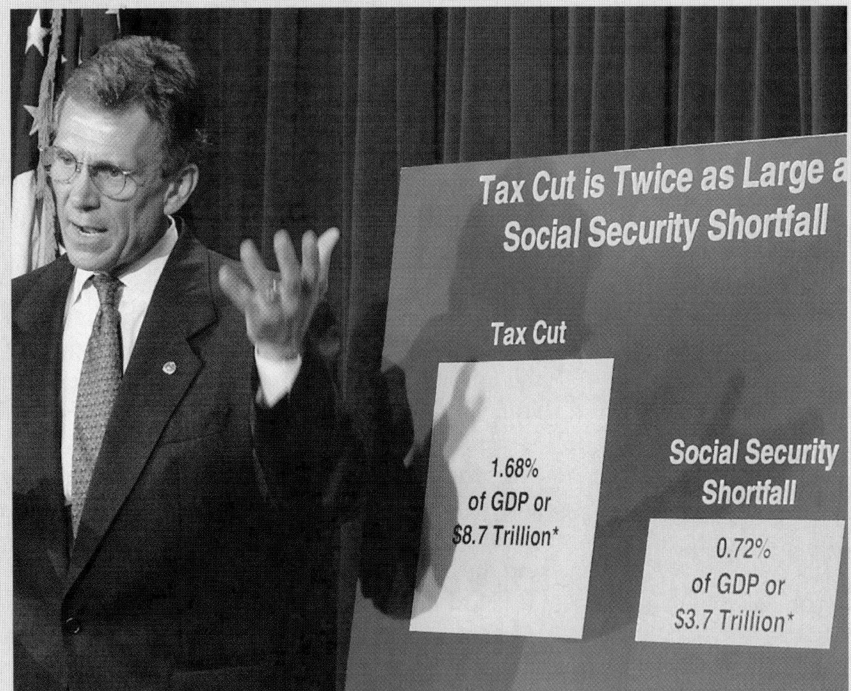

Many Democrats, including Senator Tom Daschel, opposed the President's proposed tax cut in 2003 on the grounds that it would produce big deficits.

The spending side of the budget equation for next year and afterward are almost sure to be higher than those shown in the documents, since the budget office's calculations for the fiscal years after the current one do not include the cost of maintaining troops in Iraq and Afghanistan or rebuilding those nations. Mr. Bolten said those expenses were impossible to predict. The latest Pentagon estimate is that the military costs alone in those countries are running about $5 billion a month.

"You can be sure that the president will ask Congress to spend whatever is necessary to protect our troops," Mr. Bolten said.

So far, the military campaign in Iraq has cost $48 billion, Dov Zakheim, the Pentagon comptroller, told The Associated Press today.

The deficits in future years include the president's proposal to spend $400 billion during the next decade to provide prescription drug benefits under Medicare.

The budget was in surplus by $127 billion in fiscal year 2001, the last budget prepared by the Clinton administration and the fourth consecutive year with a surplus. In April 2001, shortly after taking office, the Bush administration forecast a surplus of $334 billion in 2003.

Since then, the economy has faltered, taxes have been cut, and government spending has risen, mostly for the military and domestic security in the aftermath of Sept. 11. As a result, the deficit picture has worsened by $789 billion, from a surplus of $334 billion to a deficit of $455 billion, in just two years.

The budget office calculated that 53 percent of the deterioration was caused by the weak economy and the resulting lower tax receipts, 23 percent by tax cuts and 24 percent by higher spending for the war, domestic security and other items.

As recently as February, the White House's deficit forecast for this fiscal year was limited to $304 billion. Since then, tax revenues have been $66 billion lower than expected, Congress approved $47 billion for war costs in Iraq, taxes were cut by $13 billion and other legislation raised spending by $26 billion.

Source: David E. Rosenbaum, "White House sees a $455 Billion Gap in the '03 Budget," New York Times, *July 16, 2003. Reprinted by permission.*

Visit www.prenhall.com/casefair for updated articles and exercises.

government was in the process of paying off its debt, and there was talk of the debt being completely paid off.

Alas, surplus turned to deficit in 2002. The federal government is again beginning to worry about deficits. It is thus useful to review the approach that the government considered in the late 1980s and early 1990s to cope with the deficit problem, namely the GRH legislation and the balanced-budget amendment. In addition, this material is a great teaching device. If you understand the macroeconomic consequences of the GRH legislation and the balanced-budget amendment, you have come a long way toward being a macroeconomist.

THE EFFECTS OF SPENDING CUTS ON THE DEFICIT

Suppose the terms of the balanced-budget amendment or some other deficit-reduction measure dictate that the deficit must be cut by $20 billion. By how much must government spending be cut to achieve this goal? You might be tempted to think the spending cuts should add up to the amount the deficit is to be cut—$20 billion. (This is what GRH dictated: If the deficit needed to be cut by a certain amount, automatic spending cuts were to be equal to this amount.) This seems reasonable. If you decrease your personal spending by $100 over a year, your personal deficit will fall by the full $100 of your spending cut.

However, the government is not an individual household. A cut in government spending shifts the *AD* curve to the left and results in a decrease in aggregate output (income) (*Y*) and a contraction in the economy. When the economy contracts, both the taxable income of households and the profits of firms fall. This means revenue from the personal income tax and the corporate profits tax will fall.

How do these events affect the size of the deficit? To estimate the response of the deficit to changes in government spending, we need to go through two steps. First, we must decide how much a $1 change in government spending will change GDP. That means we need to know the size of the government spending multiplier. [Recall that the government spending multiplier measures the increase (or decrease) in GDP (*Y*) brought about by a $1 increase (or decrease) in government spending.] Based on empirical evidence, a reasonable value for the government spending multiplier seems to be around 1.4 after 1 year, and this is the value we will use. A $1 billion decrease in government spending lowers GDP by about $1.4 billion after 1 year.

Next, we must see what happens to the deficit when GDP changes. We have just noted that when GDP falls—the economy contracts—taxable income and corporate profits fall, so tax revenues fall. In addition, some categories of government expenditures tend to rise when the economy contracts. For example, unemployment insurance benefits (a transfer payment) rise as the economy contracts because more people become unemployed and eligible for benefits. Both the decrease in tax revenues and the rise in government expenditures cause the deficit to increase.

The deficit tends to rise when GDP falls, and tends to fall when GDP rises.

deficit response index (DRI) The amount by which the deficit changes with a $1 change in GDP.

Assume the **deficit response index (DRI)** is –.22. That is, for every $1 billion decrease in GDP, the deficit rises by $.22 billion. This number seems close to what is true in practice.

We can now use the multiplier and the DRI to answer the question that began this section. Suppose government spending is reduced by $20 billion, the exact amount of the necessary deficit reduction. This will lower GDP by 1.4 × $20 billion, or $28 billion, if the value of the multiplier is 1.4. A $28 billion fall in GDP will increase the deficit by .22 × $28 billion, or $6.2 billion, if the value of the DRI is –.22. Because we initially cut government spending (and therefore lowered the deficit from this source) by $20 billion, the net effect of the spending cut is to lower the deficit by $20 billion – $6.2 billion = $13.8 billion.

A $20 billion government spending cut does not lower the deficit by $20 billion. To lower the deficit by $20 billion, we need to cut government spending by about $30 billion. By using 1.4 as the value of the government spending multiplier and –.22 as the value of the DRI, we see that a spending cut of $30 billion lowers GDP by 1.4 × $30 billion, or $42 billion. This raises the deficit by .22 × $42 billion, or $9.2 billion. The net effect on the deficit is –$30 billion (from the government spending cut) + $9.2 billion, which is – $20.8 billion (slightly larger than the necessary $20 billion reduction). This means the spending cut must be nearly 50 percent larger than the deficit reduction we wish to achieve. Congress would have had trouble achieving the deficit targets under the GRH legislation even if it had allowed GRH's automatic spending cuts to take place.

Monetary Policy to the Rescue? Was Congress so poorly informed about macroeconomics that it would pass legislation that could not possibly work? In other words, are there any conditions under which it would be reasonable to assume that a spending cut needs to be only as large as the desired reduction in the deficit? If the government spending multiplier is zero, government spending cuts will not contract the economy, and the cut in the deficit will be equal to the cut in government spending.

Could the government spending multiplier ever be zero? Before the GRH bill was passed, some argued it could. The argument went as follows: If households and firms are worried about the large government deficits and hold back on consumption and investment because of these worries, the passage of GRH might make them more optimistic and induce them to consume and invest more. This increased consumption and investment would offset the effects of the decreased government spending, and the net result would be a multiplier effect of zero.

Another argument in favor of the GRH bill centered on the Fed and monetary policy. We know that an expansionary monetary policy shifts the *AD* curve to the right. Because a cut in government spending shifts the *AD* curve to the left, the Fed could respond to the spending cut enough to shift the *AD* curve back (to the right) to its original position, preventing any change in aggregate output (income). Some argued the Fed would behave in this way after the passage of the GRH bill because it would see that Congress finally "got its house in order."

How large would the interest rate cuts have to be to completely offset the decrease in *G*, thus resulting in a multiplier of zero? Studies at the time of the original GRH bill showed the decrease in the interest rate that would be necessary to have the multiplier be zero—that is, for a government spending cut to have no effect on aggregate output (income)—is quite large. The Fed would have had to engage in extreme behavior with respect to interest rate changes for the multiplier to be zero.

A zero multiplier can come about through renewed optimism on the part of households and firms or through very aggressive behavior on the part of the Fed, but because neither of these situations is very plausible, the multiplier is likely to be greater than zero. Thus, it is likely that to lower the deficit by a certain amount, the cut in government spending must be larger than that amount.

ECONOMIC STABILITY AND DEFICIT REDUCTION

So, lowering the deficit by a given amount is likely to require a government spending decrease larger than this amount. However, this is not the only point to learn from our analysis of deficit targeting. We will now show how deficit targeting can adversely affect the way the economy responds to a variety of stimuli.

In a world with no GRH, no balanced-budget amendment, no similar deficit-targeting measure, the Congress and the president make decisions each year about how much to spend and how much to tax. The federal government deficit is a result of these decisions and the state of the economy. However, with GRH or the balanced-budget amendment, the size of the deficit is set in advance. Taxes and government spending must be adjusted to produce the required deficit. In this situation, the deficit is no longer a consequence of the tax and spending decisions. Instead, taxes and spending become a consequence of the deficit decision.

What difference does it make whether Congress chooses a target deficit and adjusts government spending and taxes to achieve this target or decides how much to spend and tax and lets the deficit adjust itself? The difference may be substantial. Consider a leftward shift of the *AD* curve caused by some negative demand shock. A **negative demand shock** is something

negative demand shock Something that causes a negative shift in consumption or investment schedules or that leads to a decrease in U.S. exports.

that causes a negative shift in consumption or investment schedules or that leads to a decrease in U.S. exports.

We know that a leftward shift of the *AD* curve lowers aggregate output (income), which causes the government deficit to increase. In a world without deficit targeting, the increase in the deficit during contractions provides an **automatic stabilizer** for the economy. (Review Chapter 9 if this is hazy.) The contraction-induced decrease in tax revenues and increase in transfer payments tend to reduce the fall in after-tax income and consumer spending due to the negative demand shock. Thus, the decrease in aggregate output (income) caused by the negative demand shock is lessened somewhat by the growth of the deficit [Figure 15.6(a)].

automatic stabilizers Revenue and expenditure items in the federal budget that automatically change with the economy in such a way as to stabilize GDP.

In a world with deficit targeting, the deficit is not allowed to rise. Some combination of tax increases and government spending cuts would be needed to offset what would have otherwise been an increase in the deficit. We know that increases in taxes or cuts in spending are contractionary in themselves. The contraction in the economy will therefore be larger than it would have been without deficit targeting, because the initial effect of the negative demand shock is worsened by the rise in taxes or the cut in government spending required to keep the deficit from rising. As Figure 15.6(b) shows, deficit targeting acts as an **automatic destabilizer.** It requires taxes to be raised and government spending to be cut during a contraction. This reinforces, instead of counteracts, the shock that started the contraction.

automatic destabilizers Revenue and expenditure items in the federal budget that automatically change with the economy in such a way as to destabilize GDP.

SUMMARY

It is clear the GRH legislation, the balanced-budget amendment, and similar deficit-targeting measures have some undesirable macroeconomic consequences. Deficit targeting requires cuts in spending or increases in taxes at times when the economy is already experiencing problems. This does not mean Congress should ignore deficits when they arise. Instead, it means that locking the economy into spending cuts during periods of negative demand shocks, as deficit-targeting measures do, is not a good way to manage the economy.

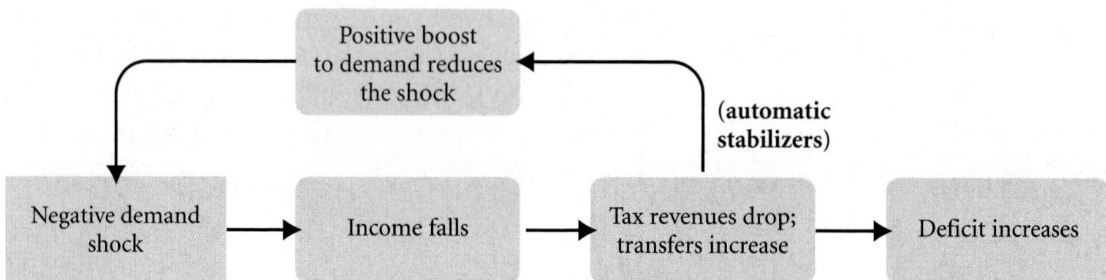

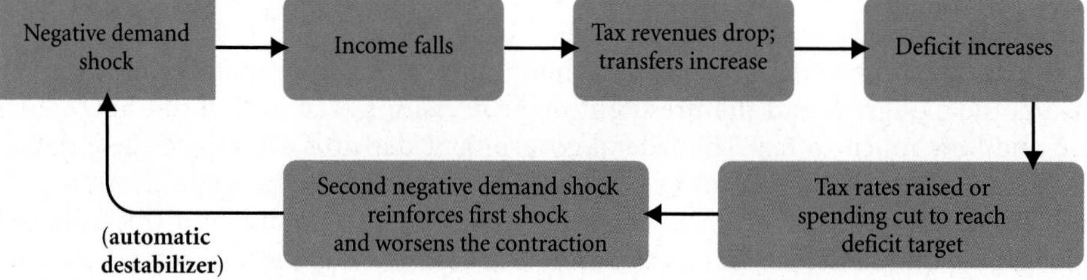

FIGURE 15.6 Deficit Targeting as an Automatic Destabilizer

Deficit targeting changes the way the economy responds to negative demand shocks because it does not allow the deficit to increase. The result is a smaller deficit, but a larger decline in income than would have otherwise occurred.

FISCAL POLICY SINCE 1990

Table 9.5 on page 172 in Chapter 9 shows the main categories of receipts and expenditures of the federal government. The primary ways the government collects money are through the personal income tax and the social security tax. Figure 15.7 plots total federal personal income taxes as a percent of total taxable income for the 1990 I–2003 II period. This is a plot of the average personal income tax rate. As the figure shows, the average tax rate increased substantially in the last half of the 1990s. Much of this increase was due to the Omnibus Budget Reconcilation Act of 1993 mentioned earlier. This act was a major change in fiscal policy.

Figure 15.7 also shows, rather dramatically, the effects of President George W. Bush's tax cuts. The large fall in the average tax rate in 2001 III was due to a tax rebate that was passed after the September 11, 2001, attacks. Although the average tax rate went back up in 2001 IV, it then fell substantially after that as the tax cuts began to be felt.

The tax policy of the federal government from 1990 on is thus rather clear from Figure 15.7. The average tax rate rose sharply under President Clinton and fell sharply under President Bush.

Fiscal policy includes spending policies as well as tax policies, and Figures 15.8 and 15.9 plot two spending variables. Figure 15.8 plots the ratio of federal government consumption expenditures to GDP. You can see from Table 9.5 that consumption expenditures make up about one-fourth of total government expenditures. Much of these expenditures are for defense. Figure 15.9 plots the ratio of federal transfer payments and grants in aid to GDP. Table 9.5 shows that these two items make up more than half of total government expenditures. Transfer payments include social security payments and medicare/medicaid payments. Grants in aid are grants to state and local government, many of which are used to fund state and local government transfer payments to households.

Figure 15.8 shows that federal consumption expenditures as a percent of GDP fell until about 1998, remained relatively constant until 2002, and then began to rise. Much of the rise since the beginning of 2002 has been increased expenditures for security and defense. Figure 15.9 shows that federal transfer payments plus grants in aid as a percent of GDP rose rapidly at the beginning of the 1990s, leveled off until about 1996, fell until about 2001, and then rose rapidly. Some of the fall between 1996 and 2000 was due to the welfare reform legislation passed under President Clinton. Some of the rise from 2001 on is due to increased medicare payments.

Given Figures 15.7, 15.8, and 15.9, it is not surprising that the federal government budget went from deficit to surplus and then back to deficit. During the last half of the 1990s, the

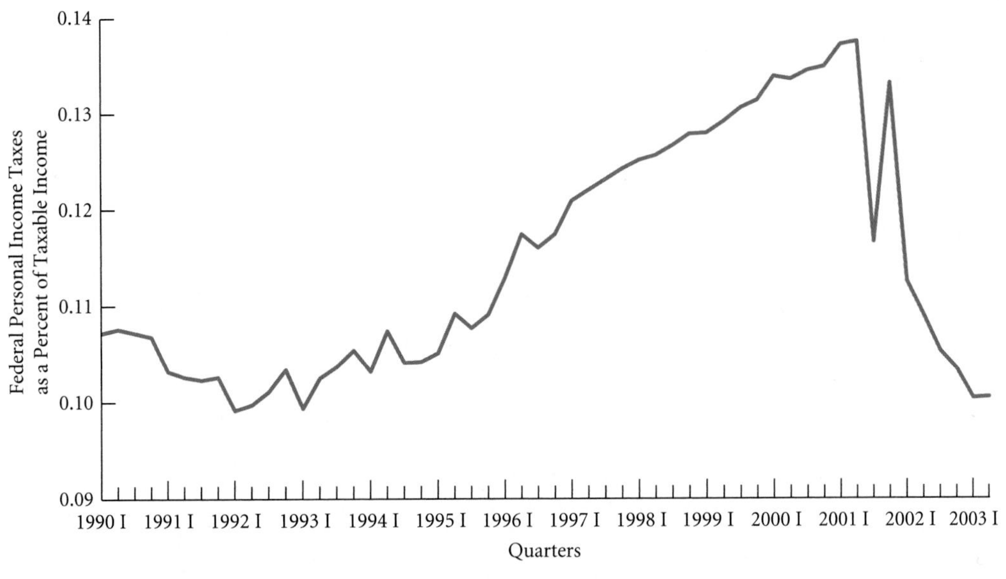

FIGURE 15.7 Federal Personal Income Taxes as a Percent of Taxable Income, 1990 I–2003 II

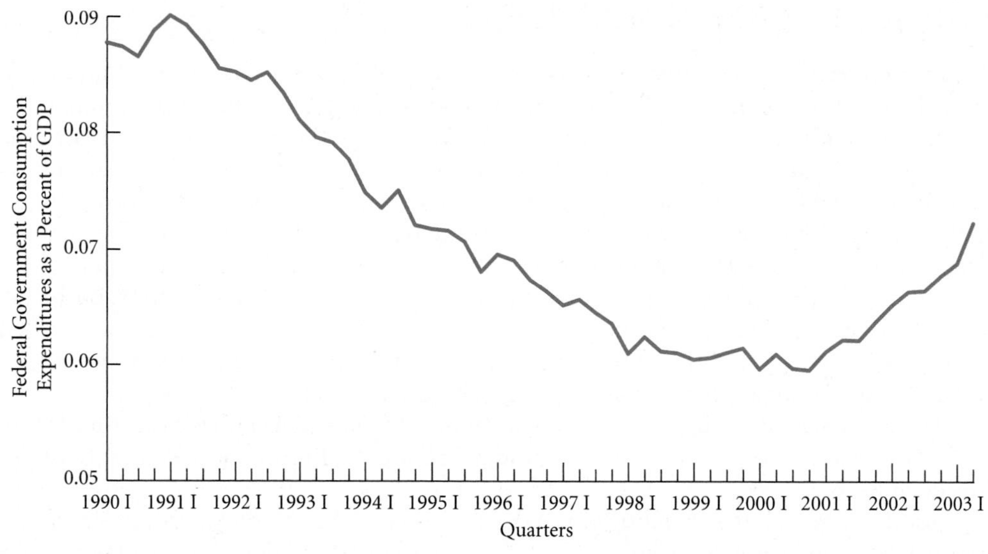

FIGURE 15.8 Federal Government Consumption Expenditures as a Percent of GDP, 1990 I–2003 II

average tax rate rose and government spending as a percent of GDP fell—both consumption expenditures and transfer payments plus grants in aid. The reverse then happened beginning in about 2001. The deficit is again a concern as tax rates are falling and spending is rising.

One final point about the federal government budget is reflected in Figure 15.10, which plots federal government interest payments as a percent of GDP. You can see that this ratio has fallen dramatically since 1995. Interest payments can fall for two reasons. One is if the size of the federal debt is decreasing, which is true if the government is running a surplus. The second is if interest rates are decreasing. Prior to the large decrease in interest rates in 2001, interest payments were falling because of the decrease in the debt. After 2001 the fall has been due to the decrease in interest rates, since the debt has in fact been increasing because of the deficits.

Regardless of why interest payments are falling, any fall is good for the federal budget. As the government spends less in interest payments, the surplus rises or the deficit falls.

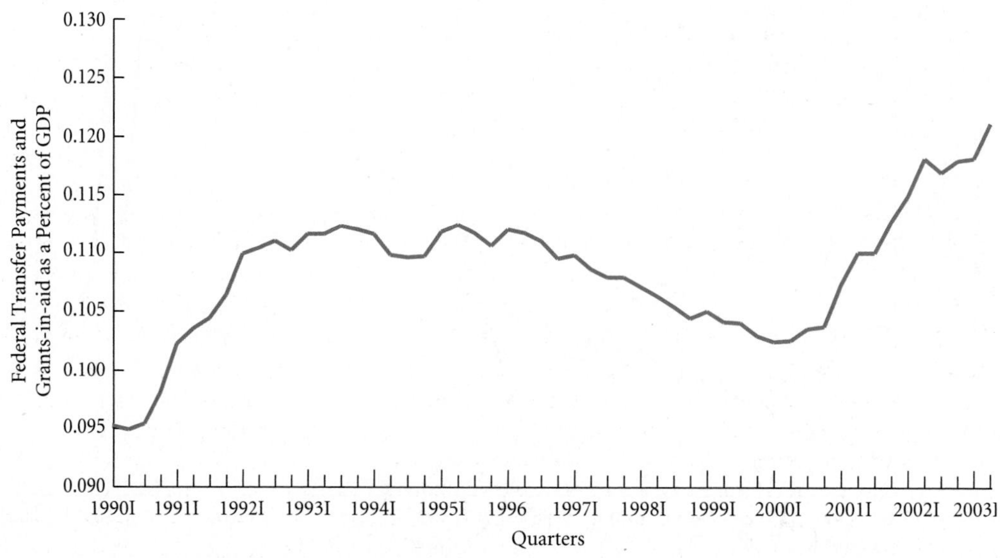

FIGURE 15.9 Federal Transfer Payments and Grants-in-aid as a Percent of GDP, 1990 I–2003 II

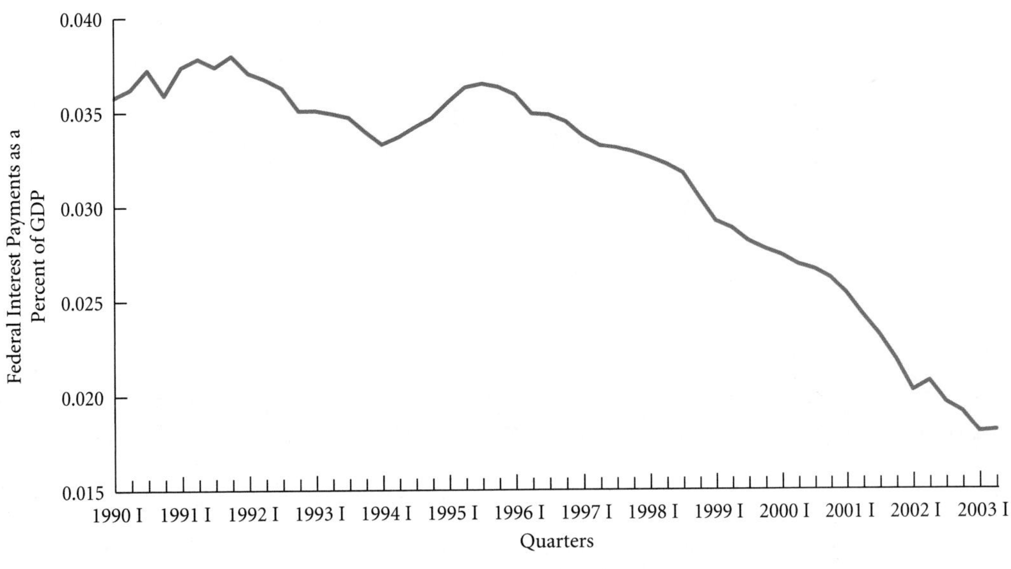

FIGURE 15.10 Federal Interest Payments as a Percent of GDP, 1990 I–2003 II

SUMMARY

TIME LAGS REGARDING MONETARY AND FISCAL POLICY

1. *Stabilization policy* describes both fiscal and monetary policy, the goals of which are to smooth out fluctuations in output and employment and to keep prices as stable as possible. Stabilization goals are not necessarily easy to achieve because of the existence of certain *time lags*, or delays in the response of the economy to macropolicies.

2. A *recognition lag* is the time it takes for policy makers to recognize the existence of a boom or a slump. An *implementation lag* is the time it takes to put the desired policy into effect once economists and policy makers recognize that the economy is in a boom or a slump. A *response lag* is the time that it takes for the economy to adjust to the new conditions after a new policy is implemented—in other words, a lag that occurs because of the operation of the economy itself. In general, monetary policy can be implemented more rapidly than fiscal policy, but fiscal policy generally has a shorter response lag than monetary policy.

MONETARY POLICY

3. In practice the Fed targets the interest rate rather than the money supply. The interest rate value that the Fed chooses depends on the state of the economy. The Fed desires high output and low inflation. The Fed is likely to decrease the interest rate during times of low output and low inflation, and it is likely to increase the interest rate during times of high output and high inflation.

4. Monetary policy since 1990 has been one of lowering interest rates to fight the 1990–1991 recession, raising rates during the boom of the last half of the 1990s, and lowering rates dramatically to fight the 2001 recession.

FISCAL POLICY: DEFICIT TARGETING

5. In fiscal year 1986, Congress passed and President Reagan signed the *Gramm-Rudman-Hollings Bill* (*GRH*), which set out to reduce the federal deficit by $36 billion per year, with a zero deficit slated for fiscal year 1991. If Congress passed a budget with a deficit larger than the targeted amount, the law called for automatic spending cuts. A Supreme Court ruling later overturned this provision, and the actual figures for each year never came close to the targets. Thanks to the Omnibus Budget Reconciliation Act of 1993, and a robust economy, the federal deficit had been eliminated by 1998.

6. The deficit tends to rise when GDP falls, and to fall when GDP rises. The *deficit response index (DRI)* is the amount by which the deficit changes with a $1 change in GDP.

7. For spending cuts of a certain amount to reduce the deficit by the same amount, the government spending multiplier must be zero. Before GRH was passed, some argued that a government spending multiplier of zero can be achieved through renewed optimism on the part of households or through very aggressive behavior by the Fed to decrease the interest rate. Empirical evidence has shown that both situations are not very plausible, so to lower the deficit by a certain amount, government spending cuts must be larger than that to lower the deficit.

8. Deficit-targeting measures that call for automatic spending cuts to eliminate or reduce the deficit may have the effect of destabilizing the economy because they prevent automatic stabilizers from working.

FISCAL POLICY SINCE 1990

9. The average personal income tax rate rose sharply under President Clinton and fell sharply under President Bush. Federal spending as a percent of GDP begin to rise rapidly in 2001. The net effect of falling tax rates and increased spending was a growing federal government deficit beginning in 2001.

REVIEW TERMS AND CONCEPTS

automatic destabilizer, 296
automatic stabilizer, 296
deficit response index (DRI), 294
Gramm-Rudman-Hollings Bill, 292
implementation lag, 285
negative demand shock, 295
recognition lag, 285
response lag, 285
stabilization policy, 283
time lags, 283

PROBLEM SET

1. During 2001, the U.S. economy slipped into a recession. For the next several years the Fed and the Congress used monetary and fiscal policy in an attempt to stimulate the economy. Obtain data on interest rates (such as the prime rate or the "fed funds rate"). Do you see evidence of the Fed's action? When did the Fed begin its expansionary policy? Obtain data on total federal expenditures, tax receipts and the deficit (try www.commerce.gov, national accounts). When did fiscal policy become "expansionary"? Which seems to have suffered more from policy lags?

2. The term *fine-tuning* was sometimes used during the 1950s and 1960s to describe federal monetary and fiscal policy. At the time the U.S. economy was on a fairly steady growth path with little inflation. The term went out of fashion during the 1970s and 1980s when the economy experienced severe inflation followed by a deep recession twice within a decade. Between 1991 and 2000, the economy once again returned to steady growth with little inflation and the term came back into use. Explain what is meant by fine-tuning. During the fall of 1999, growth accelerated. What moves would you have anticipated by the Fed in 1999? During 2000, growth slowed. What would you expect the Fed to do?

3. Explain carefully why the government deficit rises as the economy contracts.

4. You are given the following information about the economy in 2001 (all in billions of dollars):

Consumption function:	$C = 100 + (.8 \times Y_d)$
Taxes:	$T = -150 + (.25 \times Y)$
Investment function:	$I = 60$
Disposable income:	$Y_d = Y - T$
Government spending:	$G = 80$
Equilibrium:	$Y = C + I + G$

Hint: Deficit is $D = G - T = G - [-150 + (.25 \times Y)]$

   a. Find equilibrium income. Show that the government budget deficit (the difference between government spending and tax revenues) is $5 billion.

   b. Congress passes the Foghorn-Leghorn (F-L) amendment, which requires that the deficit be zero this year. If the budget adopted by Congress has a deficit that is larger than zero, the deficit target must be met by cutting spending. Suppose spending is cut by $5 billion (to $75 billion). What is the new value for equilibrium GDP? What is the new deficit? Explain carefully why the deficit is not zero.

   c. What is the deficit response index and how is it defined? Explain why the DRI must equal .25 in this example. By using this information, by how much must we cut spending to achieve a deficit of zero?

   d. Suppose the F-L amendment was not in effect and planned investment falls to $I = 55$. What is the new value of GDP? What is the new government budget deficit? What happens to GDP if the F-L amendment is in effect and spending is cut to reach the deficit target? (*Hint:* Spending must be cut by $21.666 billion to balance the budget.)

5. During the first 6 months of 2000, the U.S. economy appeared to slow. Many people point to Federal Reserve decisions made during 1999. What specific actions did the Fed take that might have caused economic slowing during 1999? Why were such actions taken? In retrospect, was the Fed right or wrong in doing what it did? Was the Fed a "fool in the shower"?

6. Some states are required to balance their budgets. Is this measure stabilizing or destabilizing? Suppose all states were committed to a balanced-budget philosophy and the economy moved into a recession. What effects would this philosophy have on the size of the federal deficit?

7. Describe the Fed's tendency to "lean against the wind." Do the Fed's policies tend to stabilize or destabilize the economy?

8. Explain why stabilization policy may be difficult to carry out. How is it possible that stabilization policies can actually be destabilizing?

9. It takes about 1 year for the multiplier to reach its full value. Explain this phenomenon. Does this have any implications for fiscal policy?

The Stock Market and the Economy

16

CHAPTER OUTLINE

Introductory macroeconomic texts written a decade ago could more or less ignore the stock market. The effects of the stock market on the macro economy were small enough to be put aside in introductory discussions. This changed in the 1990s. We will see that the stock market boom that began in 1995 had a large impact on the economy. The economy grew well in the last half of the 1990s, and many came to believe in the existence of a new economy or a "new age." How much of the growth in the last half of the 1990s was due to the stock market boom? Did the economy in fact enter a new age? We try to answer these questions in this chapter.

STOCKS AND BONDS

When a firm wishes to make a large purchase—to build a new factory or to buy an expensive piece of machinery—it often cannot pay for the purchase out of its own funds. In that case it must "finance" the investment. One possibility is simply to borrow from a bank. The bank loans the money to the firm; the firm uses the money to buy the factory or machine; and the firm pays back the loan to the bank over time with interest.

BONDS

Another possibility is for the firm to issue a **bond**. If you buy a bond from a firm, you are making a loan to the firm.

bond A document that formally promises to pay back a loan under specified terms, usually over a specific time period.

Bonds have several properties. First, they are issued with a *face value*, typically in denominations of $1,000, that represent the amount you (the buyer) agree to lend the bond issuer. They also come with a *maturity date* on which the firm promises to pay back the funds you lent it. (However, you can sell the bond to someone else before the maturity date if you want.) Finally, there is a fixed payment of a specified amount (usually made annually), paid by the bond issuer to the bondholder. This payment, known as the *coupon*, is calculated using the prevailing interest rate at the time the bond is issued. Even if interest rates change over the life of the bond, which they almost always do, the amount you receive as interest on your bond remains fixed. (This is why bonds are sometimes referred to as fixed-income securities. The bondholder receives a set amount, known in advance, no matter what happens to interest rates, stock prices, and so on.)

If you bought a $10,000, 10 percent, 15-year bond from Company XYZ on January 1, 1998, this is what would happen. You would give XYZ, or perhaps your broker, a check for $10,000. Every January for the next 14 years, XYZ would send you a check for $1,000 (10 percent of the $10,000 face value). On January 1, 2013, XYZ would send you a check for the face value of the bond—$10,000—plus the coupon for that year—$1,000—and that would square all accounts.

Does the fact that the coupon on a bond does not change with fluctuations in the interest rate mean that bonds are completely insulated from interest rate movements? Absolutely not! Instead of the coupon responding to a change in the interest rate, it is the *price of the bond* that changes. To see why, suppose you had a choice of putting $10,000 into the bond described here or into a bank account that pays 10 percent per year interest. In either case, you would earn $1,000 per year in interest payments, so you should be indifferent between the two choices.

But now suppose that the interest rate on the bank account goes up to 20 percent instead of 10 percent. The bond still promises to pay $1,000 per year. If you want to earn $1,000 in interest, you need to put only $5,000 into the bank account ($.20 \times \$5,000 = \$1,000$). You would obviously prefer to put $5,000 into the bank rather than tie up $10,000 in the bond. The only way anyone would willingly buy the bond is if it cost no more than other investments that yield the same stream of income in the future. The bond would thus be worth much less than $10,000 if the interest rate were 20 percent. It follows, then, that when interest rates rise, bond prices fall, and bondholders suffer a *loss*—that is, a reduction in the value of the securities they own.

See the Further Exploration box for a discussion of how to read bond tables in a newspaper.

STOCKS

stock A certificate that certifies ownership of a certain portion of a firm.

A third way for a firm to finance an investment is for it to issue additional shares of **stock**. When a firm issues new shares of stock, it does not add to its debt. Instead, it brings in additional owners of the firm, owners who agree to supply it with funds. Such owners are treated differently than bondholders, who are owed the amount that they have loaned.

What is a share of stock? If you buy one share of Company QRS and the firm has 1 million total shares outstanding, you have purchased a one-millionth ownership of the firm. You have a right—along with the owners of the other 999,999 shares—to select the management of the firm and to share in its profits. (This is not true of bondholders and other creditors of the firm, who have no say in its management.) Unlike bonds or direct borrowing, your stock does not promise a fixed annual payment. Rather, the returns you receive depend on how well Company QRS performs. If its profits are high, the firm may pay dividends to its shareholders, although it is not required to do so. If the firm does well, you may also find that the price of QRS stock has gone up, in which case you could have a **capital gain** by selling your stock for more than you originally paid for it. This is known as a **realized capital gain**.

capital gain An increase in the value of an asset.

realized capital gain The gain that occurs when the owner of an asset actually sells it for more than he paid for it.

Most stocks bought and sold on the stock market daily are not newly issued. Most are trades of shares issued long ago, usually when a firm "goes public." When a young firm grows enough to stimulate people to buy into it, the founders turn to the stock market and sell shares to the public.

Most bonds are promises to pay a principal amount back at a specified time in the future (here, 2032) and to pay a fixed coupon each year.

A share of stock represents part ownership of a firm and the return to shareholders depends on how profitable the firm is.

Further Exploration

Reading a Bond Table

Figure 1 shows a small section of the corporate bond price quotations in the *Wall Street Journal* for July 24, 2003. What do all these signs and symbols mean?

The first column, under "Company," gives the name of the corporation that issued the bond and certain information about the terms under which the bond was originally issued. Let's take the last bond listed in the figure as an example. This bond was issued by the Comcast Cable Communications Holding Company. The "8.375" means the bond pays a coupon of $8.375 per $100 of face value of the bond. The bond matures in 2013. The column titled "Last Yield" shows the annual rate of return on the bond if the bond were purchased at the current price. If the current price were $100, then the annual rate of return would be 8.375 percent. The bond yields only 5.485 percent, however, so the current price of the bond must be higher than its face value of $100. (Remember: A decrease in the interest rate raises the price of a bond.)

The column "Vol" tells how many thousands of dollars in bonds were traded during the day. Here we see $89.953 million (at face value) of the Comcast bond were traded on July 24, 2003.

"Last Price" is the closing price of the bond. This is how much you would have to pay for the bond per $100 of face value. The Comcast bond's closing price was $121.38, which means a $100 bond was worth $121.38 at the end of the trading day.

"Est spread" and "UST" tell us something about the risk associated with the bond. "Est spread" is the difference in yield (stated in "basis points," with 100 basis points being the same as one percentage point) between the last yield on the Comcast bond and the current yield on a 10-year U.S. Treasury bond. Since the current yield on the Comcast bond is 5.485 and the spread is 131 (or 1.31 percent), the 10-year Treasury is paying 4.175 percent. Since the U.S. Treasury is backed by the "full faith and credit of the United States Government," Treasury bonds are the benchmark for a risk-free investment. The Comcast bond pays a higher effective yield because there is a small risk that Comcast will not be able to pay when the bond comes due.

Source: Wall Street Journal, *July 25, 2003.*

When the Comcast Holdings bond was issued, it was issued at a coupon yield of 8.375 percent per year. A coupon is the annual yield expressed as a percent of the initial issue price.

The last price at which these bonds were sold was $121.384. That means that if you owned a $100 Comcast bond, you could sell it for approximately $121.384.

The bond is selling for a "spread," or premium, of 131 basis points (1.31 percent) above the current yield on the 10-year Treasury bond.

Corporate Bonds

Thursday, July 24, 2003

Forty most active fixed-coupon corporate bonds

COMPANY (TICKER)	COUPON	MATURITY	LAST PRICE	LAST YIELD	*EST SPREAD	UST†	EST $ VOL (000's)
General Motors (GM)	8.375	Jul 15, 2033	98.891	8.476	338	30	300,376
General Motors (GM)	7.125	Jul 15, 2013	99.932	7.133	297	10	215,538
Goldman Sachs Group (GS)	4.750	Jul 15, 2013	97.162	5.117	94	10	112,574
AOL Time Warner (AOL)	6.875	May 01, 2012	110.827	5.311	113	10	111,352
DaimlerChrysler North America Holding (DCX)	8.500	Jan 18, 2031	114.440	7.277	217	30	107,167
DaimlerChrysler North America Holding (DCX)	4.050	Jun 04, 2008	97.576	4.613	163	5	104,236
Morgan Stanley (MWD)	5.300	Mar 01, 2013	101.246	5.133	97	10	102,131
Comcast Cable Communications Holdings (CMCSA)	8.375	Mar 15, 2013	121.384	5.485	131	10	89,953

The bond was issued by the Comcast Cable Communications Holdings Company.

The bond will be paid off on March 15, 2013.

The last yield based on sales today was 5.485 percent.

$89,953,000 worth of the Comcast bond was sold on July 24, 2003.

FIGURE 1 New York Stock Exchange Bonds

See the Further Exploration box for a discussion of how to read the stock pages in a newspaper.

DETERMINING THE PRICE OF A STOCK

What determines the price of a stock? If a share of stock is selling for $25, why is someone willing to pay that much for it? As we have noted, when you buy a share of stock, you own part of the firm. If a firm is making profits, it may be paying dividends to its shareholders. If it is not paying dividends but is making profits, people may expect that it will pay dividends in the future. Dividends are important in thinking about stocks because dividends

Further Exploration

Reading the Stock Pages

Once you buy a stock, you are free to sell it to someone else at any time. Developments in the stock market, where such transactions take place, are constantly followed in the news.

Figure 1 reproduces part of the stock quotations from the *Wall Street Journal* for July 24, 2003. Let's take the stock of Kellogg and see what information the stock pages provide.

The first column, "YTD % Chg," gives the percent change this year to date. Kellogg stock has fallen 2.1 percent since January 1, 2003.

The next two columns, under the heading "52-Week," give the highest and lowest prices over the past year. The price of a share of Kellogg stock reached a high of $36.30 and a low of $27.85 during this period. The column "Div" gives the current annual rate of dividend payment. The current annual rate for Kellogg is $1.01 per share. What sort of return is this? The next column, "Yld %" (yield percent), takes the dividend as a percentage of the day's closing price. (The day's closing price in this case is $33.56, which is given in the column titled "Close.") For Kellogg, the yield is 3.0 percent.

The column "PE" (price-earnings ratio) calculates the ratio of the price of a share of stock to the company's *total earnings per share* (which includes not only dividends paid to shareholders but also retained earnings). The PE ratio is a measure of how highly a stock is valued. Kellogg's PE ratio is 19. The column "Vol 100s" tells how many hundreds of shares changed hands during the day's trading. On July 24, 2003, 689,300 shares of Kellogg's stock were traded.

Source: Wall Street Journal, *July 25, 2003.*

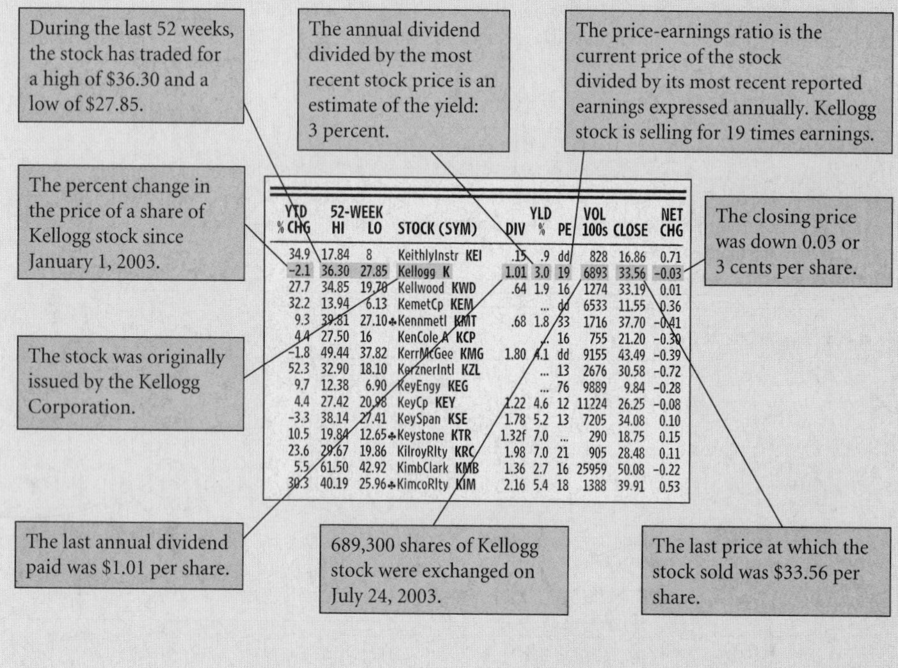

YTD % CHG	52-WEEK HI	52-WEEK LO	STOCK (SYM)	DIV	YLD %	PE	VOL 100s	CLOSE	NET CHG
34.9	17.84	8	KeithlyInstr **KEI**	.15	.9	dd	828	16.86	0.71
−2.1	36.30	27.85	Kellogg **K**	1.01	3.0	19	6893	33.56	−0.03
27.7	34.85	19.70	Kellwood **KWD**	.64	1.9	16	1274	33.19	0.01
32.2	13.94	6.13	KemetCp **KEM**		...	dd	6533	11.55	0.36
9.3	39.81	27.10	♣Kennmetl **KMT**	.68	1.8	33	1716	37.70	−0.41
4.4	27.50	16	KenCole A **KCP**		...	16	755	21.20	−0.30
−1.8	49.44	37.82	KerrMcGee **KMG**	1.80	4.1	dd	9155	43.49	−0.39
52.3	32.90	18.10	KerznerIntl **KZL**		...	13	2676	30.58	−0.72
9.7	12.38	6.90	KeyEngy **KEG**		...	76	9889	9.84	−0.28
4.4	27.42	20.98	KeyCp **KEY**	1.22	4.6	12	11224	26.25	−0.08
−3.3	38.14	27.41	KeySpan **KSE**	1.78	5.2	13	7205	34.08	0.10
10.5	19.84	12.65	♣Keystone **KTR**	1.32f	7.0	...	290	18.75	0.15
23.6	29.67	19.86	KilroyRlty **KRC**	1.98	7.0	21	905	28.48	0.11
5.5	61.50	42.92	KimbClark **KMB**	1.36	2.7	16	25959	50.08	−0.22
30.3	40.19	25.96	♣KimcoRlty **KIM**	2.16	5.4	18	1388	39.91	0.53

FIGURE 1 New York Stock Exchange Issues

are the form in which shareholders receive income from the firm. So one thing that is likely to affect the price of a stock is what people expect its future dividends will be. The larger the expected future dividends, the larger the current stock price, other things being equal.

Another important consideration in thinking about the price of a stock is when the dividends are expected to be paid. A $2 per share dividend that is expected to be paid four years from now is worth less than a $2 per share dividend that is expected to be paid next year. In other words, the further into the future the dividend is expected to be paid, the more it will be "discounted." The amount by which expected future dividends are discounted depends on the interest rate. The larger the interest rate, the more will expected future dividends be discounted. If the interest rate is 10 percent, I can invest $100.00 today and receive $110.00 a year from now. I am thus willing to pay $100.00 today to someone who will pay me $110.00

in a year. If instead, the interest rate were only 5 percent, I would be willing to pay $104.76 today to receive $110.00 a year from now because the alternative of $104.76 today at a 5 percent interest rate also yields $110.00 at the end of the year. I am thus willing to pay more for the promise of $110.00 a year from now when the interest rate is lower. In other words, I "discount" the $110.00 less when the interest rate is lower.

There is another discount factor aside from the interest rate that must be taken into account; it is the discount for risk. People prefer certain outcomes to uncertain ones for the same expected values. For example, I prefer a certain $50 over a bet in which there is a 50 percent chance I will get $100 and a 50 percent chance I will get nothing. The expected value of the bet is $50, but I prefer the certain $50 over the bet, where there is a 50 percent chance that I end up with nothing. The same reasoning holds for future dividends. If, say, I expect dividends for both firms A and B to be $2 per share next year, but firm B has a much wider range of possibilities (is riskier), I will prefer firm A. Put another way, I will "discount" firm B's expected future dividends more than firm A's because the outcome for firm B is more uncertain.

We can thus say that the price of a stock should equal the discounted value of its expected future dividends, where the discount factors depend on the interest rate and risk. If for some reason, say a positive surprise news announcement from the firm, expected future dividends increase, this should lead to an increase in the price of the stock. If the interest rate falls, this should also lead to a stock price increase. Finally, if the perceived risk of a firm falls, this should increase the firm's stock price.

Some stock analysts talk about the possibility of stock market "bubbles." Given the above discussion, what might a bubble be? Say that given your expectations about the future dividends of a firm and given the discount rate, you value the firm's stock at $20 per share. Is there any case in which you would pay more than $20 for a share? You can, of course, buy the stock and sell it later; you don't need to hold the stock forever. If the stock is currently selling for $25, which is above your value of $20, but you think that the stock will rise to $30 in the next few months, you might buy it now in anticipation of selling later for a higher price. If others have similar views, the price of the stock may be driven up.

In this case, what counts is not the discounted value of expected future dividends, but rather your view of what others will pay for the stock in the future. If everyone expects that everyone else expects that the price will be driven up, the price may be driven up. One might call this a bubble because the stock price depends on what people expect that other people expect, etc.

When a firm's stock price has risen rapidly, it is, of course, difficult to know whether this is because people have increased their expectations of the firm's future dividends or because of bubble reasons. People's expectations of future dividends are not directly observed, which makes it hard to test alternative theories.

THE STOCK MARKET SINCE 1948

If you follow the stock market at all, you know that much attention is paid to two stock price indices: the **Dow Jones Industrial Average** and the **NASDAQ Composite**. From a macroeconomic perspective, however, these two indices cover too small a sample of firms. One would like an index that includes firms whose total market value is close to the market value of all firms in the economy. For this purpose a much better measure is the **Standard and Poor's 500** stock price index, called the **S&P 500**. This index includes most of the companies in the economy by market value.

The S&P 500 index is plotted in Figure 16.1 for 1948 I–2002 III. What perhaps stands out most in this plot is the huge increase in the index between 1995 and 2000. Between December 31, 1994, and March 31, 2000, the S&P 500 index rose 226 percent, an annual rate of increase of 25 percent. This is by far the largest stock market boom in U.S. history, completely dominating the boom of the 1920s. This boom added roughly $14 trillion to household wealth, about $2.5 trillion per year.

What caused this boom? You can see from Table 15.1 in the previous chapter that interest rates did not change much in the last half of the 1990s, and so the boom cannot be explained by any large fall in interest rates. Perhaps profits rose substantially during this period, and this led to a large increase in expected future dividends? We know from the

Dow Jones Industrial Average An index based on the stock prices of 30 actively traded large companies. The oldest and most widely followed index of stock market performance.

NASDAQ Composite An index based on the stock prices of over 5,000 companies traded on the NASDAQ Stock Market. The NASDAQ market takes its name from the National Association of Securities Dealers Automated Quotation System.

Standard and Poor's 500 (S&P 500) An index based on the stock prices of the largest 500 firms traded on the New York Stock Exchange, the NASDAQ Stock Market, and the American Stock Exchange.

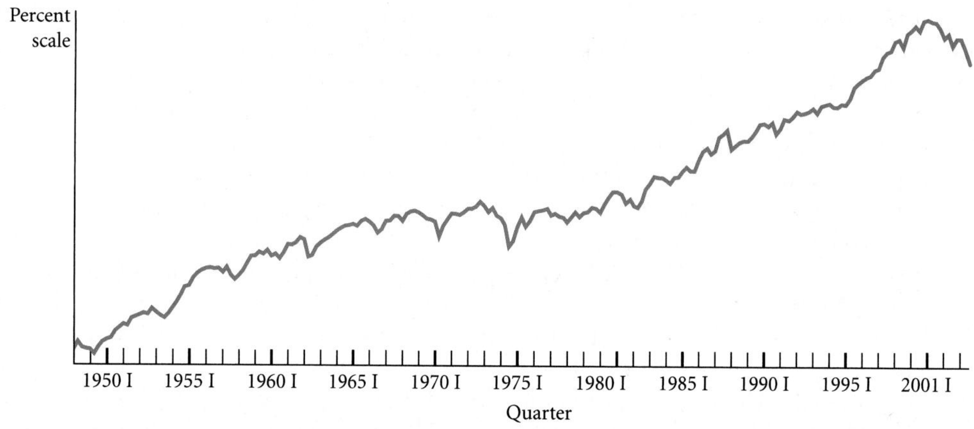

FIGURE 16.1 The S&P 500 Stock Price Index, 1948 I–2002 III

above discussion that if expected future dividends increase, stock prices should increase. Figure 16.2 plots the growth rate of S&P 500 earnings for 1948 I–2002 III, and Figure 16.3 plots the ratio of profits (as measured in the national income and product accounts) to GDP for the same period. It is clear from both figures that nothing unusual happened in the last half of the 1990s. In fact, the share of profits in GDP fell slightly. Thus there does not appear to be any surge of profits that would have led people to expect much higher future dividends.

It could be that the perceived riskiness of stocks fell in the last half of the 1990s. This would have led to smaller discount rates for stocks and thus, other things being equal, to higher stock prices. While this possibility cannot be completely ruled out, there is no strong independent evidence that perceived riskiness fell.

The stock market boom is thus a puzzle, and this has led many people to the view that it was simply a bubble. For some reason stock prices started rising rapidly in 1995, and people expected that other people expected that prices would continue to rise. This led stock prices to rise further, thus fulfilling the expectations, which led to expectations of further increases,

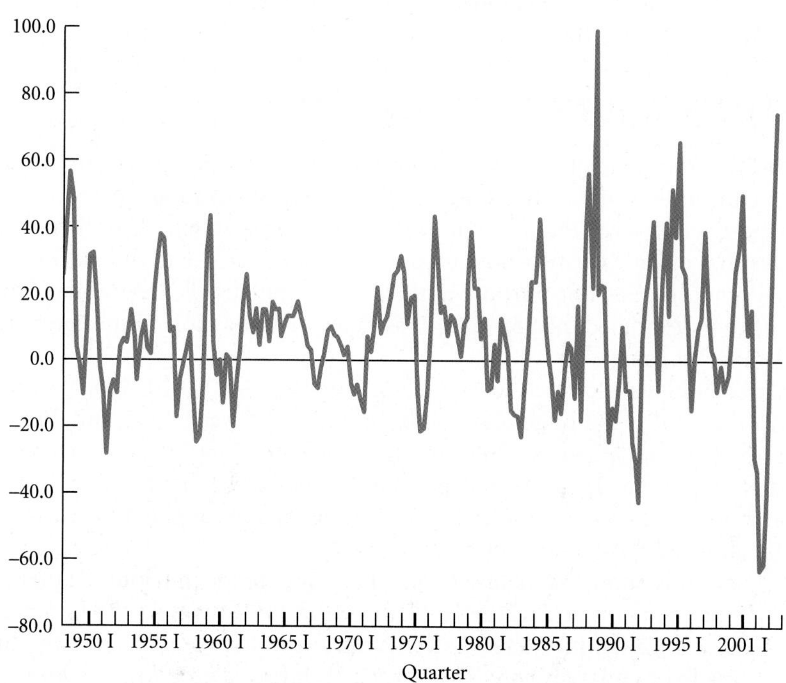

FIGURE 16.2 Growth Rate of S&P 500 Earnings, 1948 I–2002 III

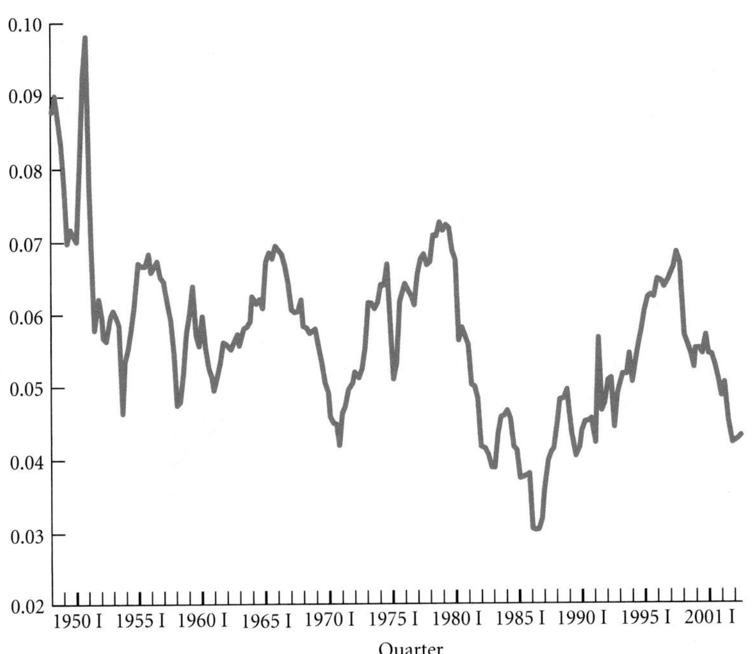

FIGURE 16.3 Ratio of Profits to GDP, 1948 I–2002 III

and so on. People of this view note that once stock prices started falling in 2000, they fell a lot. It is not the case that stock prices just leveled out in 2000; they fell rapidly. People of the bubble view argue that this is simply the bubble bursting.

Remember that we are talking about the S&P 500 index, which includes most of the firms in the U.S. economy by market value. We are not just talking about a few dot-com companies. The entire stock market went up by 25 percent per year for five years! We will see in the next section the effects that this increase in wealth had on the economy.

Before turning to the macro economy, it is of interest to reflect on the profound effect that the stock market boom had on many individuals and families. There are many stories of people putting their life savings in the stock market, many in (with hindsight) questionable dot-com companies, only to lose it all in the end. There are also stories of people who at the peak of the market were worth more than $100 million (and some more than $1 billion) and are now back to essentially nothing. Some people have had to postpone their retirement because of stock market losses. Millions of lives have been affected by the euphoria that existed during the boom and the "correction" that has occurred since.

The stock market declines between 2001 and 2003 left many people with smaller pensions and savings than they had anticipated. Some who had planned to retire had to keep working.

STOCK MARKET EFFECTS ON THE ECONOMY

We mentioned in Chapter 8 that one of the factors that affects consumption expenditures is wealth. Other things being equal, the more wealth a family has the more it spends. We discuss this in detail in the next chapter, but all we need for now is to note that an increase in wealth increases consumer spending. An increase in stock prices may also affect investment. If a firm is considering an investment project, one way in which it can finance the project is to issue additional shares of stock. The higher the price of the firm's stock, the more money it can get per additional share. A firm is thus likely to undertake more investment projects the higher its stock price. The cost of an investment project in terms of shares of stock is smaller the larger the price of the stock. This is the way in which a stock market boom may increase investment.

The effect of the stock market on the economy is thus fairly straightforward. If stock prices increase, this increases the wealth of households, which increases consumer spending. Investment also increases because firms can raise more money per share to finance investment projects. As a rough rule of thumb, a $1.00 change in the value of stocks leads to about a $0.03 to $0.04 change in consumer and investor spending per year. We will use the $0.04 number in the following discussion.

THE CRASH OF OCTOBER 1987

Before considering the boom of the late 1990s, it is useful to review a crash, namely the crash of October 1987. The value of stocks in the United States fell by about a trillion dollars between August 1987 and the end of October 1987. In one day—October 19, 1987—the value of stocks fell nearly $700 billion. If we assume that a $1 decrease in stock prices results in a $0.04 decrease in consumer and investor spending per year, we can see that the $1 trillion decrease in wealth in 1987 implies a $40 billion lower level of spending in 1988. The level of gross domestic product (GDP) was around $4 trillion in 1987, so a $40 billion decrease in spending is around 1.0 percent of GDP. A multiplier effect would also be at work here. A decrease in spending leads to a decrease in aggregate output (income), which leads to a further decrease in spending, and so on. The total decrease in GDP would be somewhat larger than the initial decrease of $40 billion. If the multiplier is 1.4, the total decrease in GDP would be about 1.4 × $40 billion = $56 billion, or about 1.4 percent of GDP.

Although 1.4 percent of GDP is a large amount, it is not large enough to imply that a recession would result from the crash. The life-cycle theory, which we will discuss in Chapter 17, helps explain why. If households are making lifetime decisions and want to have as smooth a consumption path as possible over their lifetimes, they will respond to a decrease in wealth by cutting consumption a little each year. They will *not* decrease their consumption in the current year by the full amount of the decrease in wealth.

Why were people predicting the economy would go into a recession, or worse, a depression, after the crash? The reasons all pertain to expectations. If households and firms expected the economy would contract sharply after the crash, they probably would have cut back on consumption and investment much more than otherwise. (This would be Keynes's animal spirits at work.) These expectations would have become self-fulfilling in the sense that the economy would have gone into a recession because of the cuts in consumption and investment brought about by lowered expectations.

However, the economy did not go into a recession in 1988. Expectations were not changed drastically following the crash. The Fed helped out by easing monetary policy right after the crash to counteract any large negative reaction. The 3-month Treasury bill rate fell from 6.4 percent to 5.8 percent between October and November of 1987. In addition, the value of stocks gradually increased over time to their earlier levels. Because the initial decrease in wealth turned out to be temporary, the negative wealth effect was not nearly as large as it otherwise would have been.

Stock prices are tracked by the stock exchanges on a minute-by-minute basis.

THE BOOM OF 1995–2000

We pointed out above that between 1995 and 2000 the value of stocks increased about $2.5 trillion per year. If we assume that a $1 increase in stock prices results in a $0.04 increase in consumption and investment per year and if we use a multiplier of 1.4, the added increase in

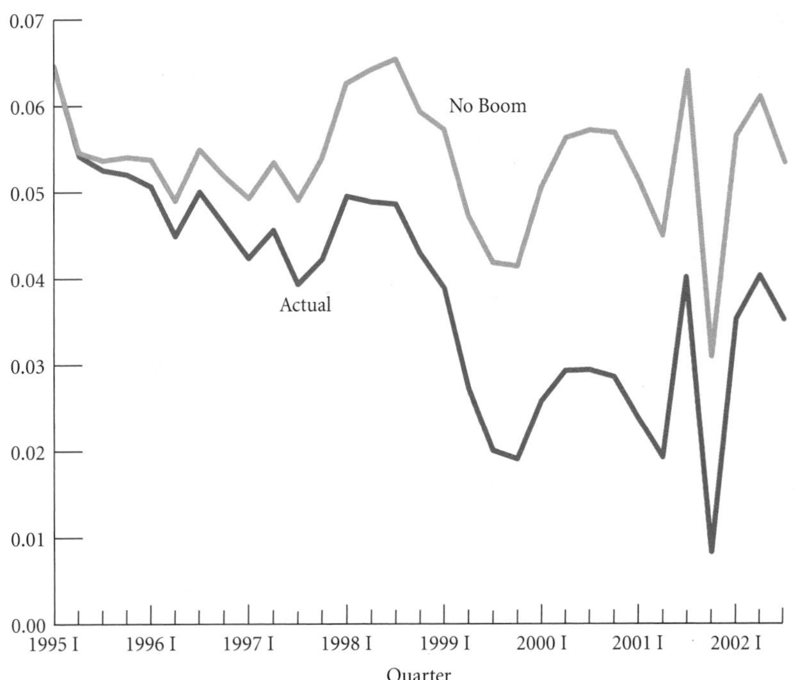

FIGURE 16.4 Personal Saving Rate, 1995 I–2002 III

spending is .04 × \$2.5 trillion × 1.4, which is \$140 billion per year. In 1998, GDP was around \$9 trillion, and so an increase of \$140 billion is 1.5 percent of GDP.

The annual growth rate of GDP from the end of 1995 to the middle of 2000 was 4.5 percent. The above numbers thus suggest that about 1.5 of the 4.5 percent was due to the stock market boom. In other words, had there been no boom, the growth rate would likely have been around 3.0 percent instead of 4.5 percent. Households simply spent much more than they would have had there been no huge increase in their wealth, and firms invested much more than they would have had stock prices not risen so much.

A more detailed analysis of the effects of the stock market boom on the economy is presented in Figures 16.4–16.10. This analysis uses a model of the economy[1] to see what the economy would have been like had there been no stock market boom. In each figure, the "actual" line represents the actual values of the variable over the 1995 I–2002 III period. These values reflect the stock market boom (since the boom actually took place!). The "no boom" line represents the values that the model estimates would have taken place had overall stock prices simply grown at a normal rate. In the no boom case, there was neither the huge increase in stock prices between 1995 and 2000 nor the large fall in prices from 2000 on.

The plots in the seven figures are interesting. They show that had there been no stock market boom, the U.S. economy would not have looked unusual in the last half of the 1990s. There would have been no talk of a "new economy" or a "new age." It would have been more or less business as usual. We will now discuss the figures one by one. Given what you have learned so far about macroeconomics, you should be able to understand the reasons for the various results.

Figure 16.4 shows that the personal saving rate is considerably higher in the no boom case. No longer are the values below the range of historical experience. This is the wealth effect on consumption at work. With no huge increase in wealth, households consume less.

Figure 16.5 shows that investment is also less in the no boom case. Firms invest less in plant and equipment because the cost to them in terms of extra shares issued is higher (the price per share is lower). Many people feel that investment was excessively high in the late 1990s, which led to the large falls in 2000 and 2001. Figure 16.5 shows that much of this would not have happened had there been no stock market boom.

---

[1]Ray C. Fair, *Estimating How the Macroeconomy Works* (Cambridge, MA: Harvard University Press, 2004).

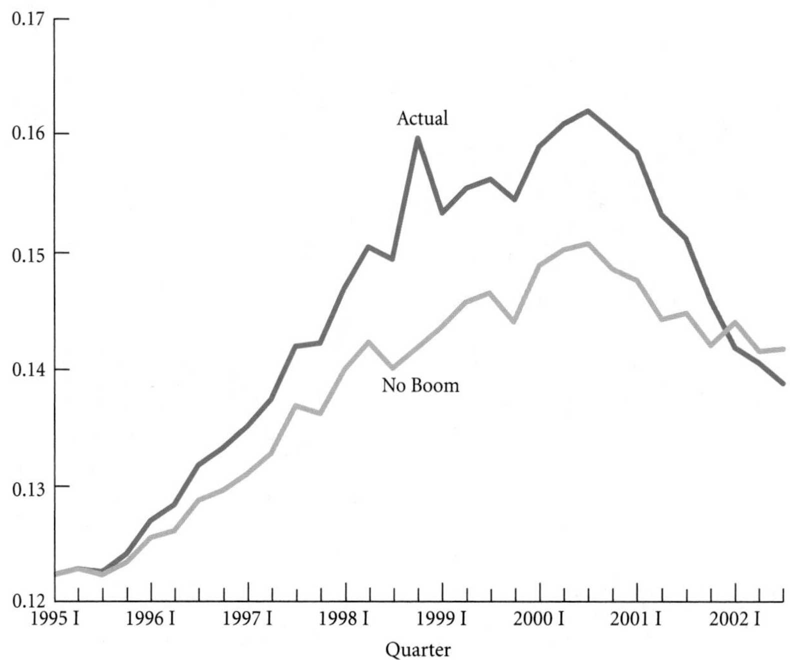

FIGURE 16.5 Investment-Output Ratio, 1995 I–2002 III

Figure 16.6 shows that the federal government surplus would not have been as high in the late 1990s and in 2000 were it not for the stock market boom. It should be clear why this is the case. In the no boom case, taxable income and profits are less, and so there is less tax revenue. Also, spending on unemployment benefits is greater because (as we will see below) unemployment is higher.

Figure 16.7 shows that real growth was higher in the last half of the 1990s than would have been the case with no boom. This figure gives a more accurate impression of the growth rate effects than the simple use of the .04 number and the 1.4 multiplier above. Note from Figure 16.7 that the growth rate is higher in the no boom case in 2001 and 2002 because in the no boom case there is no large stock market correction in these two years.

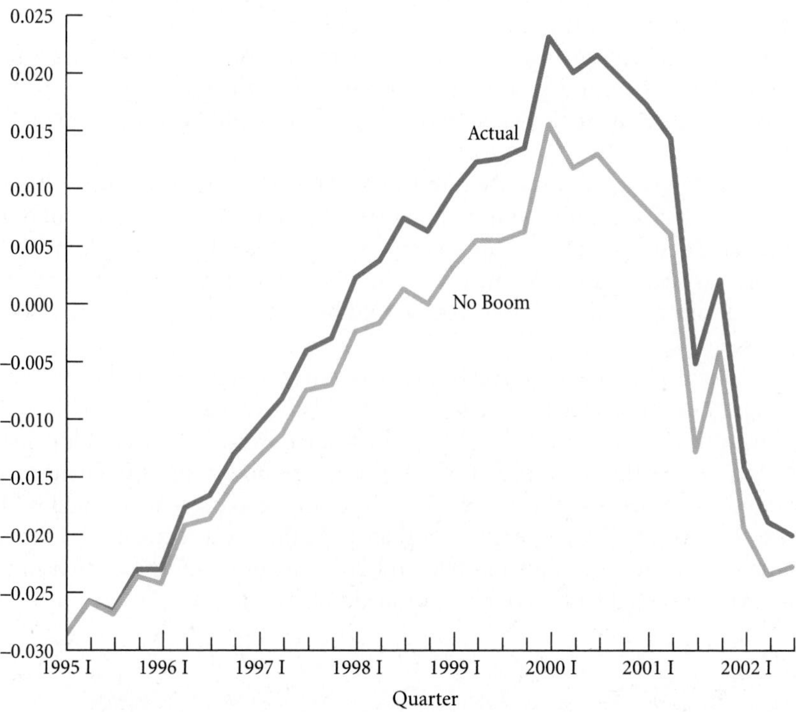

FIGURE 16.6 Ratio of Federal Government Budget Surplus to GDP, 1995 I–2002 III

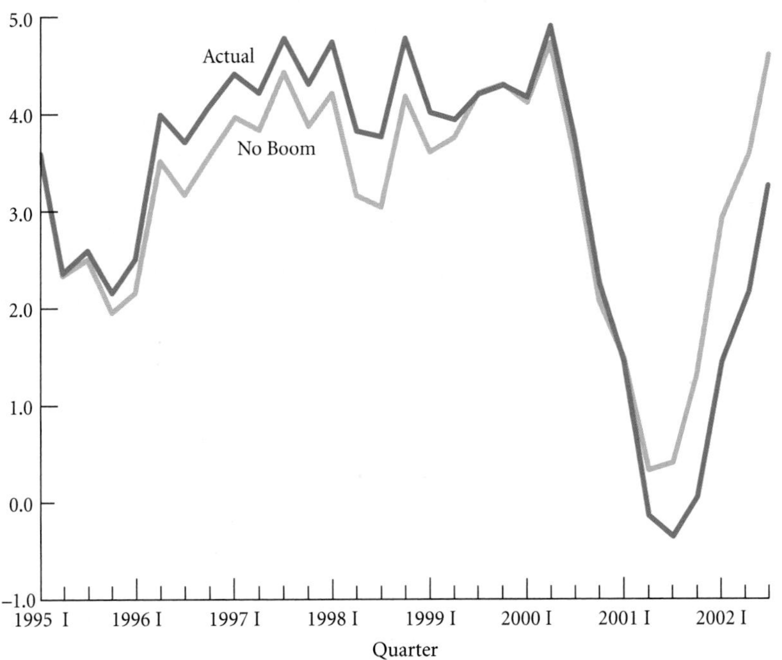

FIGURE 16.7 Growth Rate of Real GDP, 1995 I–2002 III

Figure 16.8 shows that the fall in the unemployment rate in the last half of the 1990s to 4 percent from 5.5 percent was due to the stock market boom. Had there been no boom, the unemployment rate would have remained at about 5.5 percent.

Figure 16.9 shows that inflation would have been lower in the no boom case. This is simply because output would have been lower and thus less demand pressure. In either case, however, the inflation rate is not high by historical standards.

Finally, Figure 16.10 plots the 3-month Treasury bill rate. Remember from the last chapter that this rate reflects the behavior of the Fed. The Fed essentially decides each six weeks what it wants the rate to be and uses open market operations to achieve this value. The figure shows that the interest rate would have been lower in the last half of the 1990s had there been no boom. This should make sense from the last chapter. Without the boom, real growth

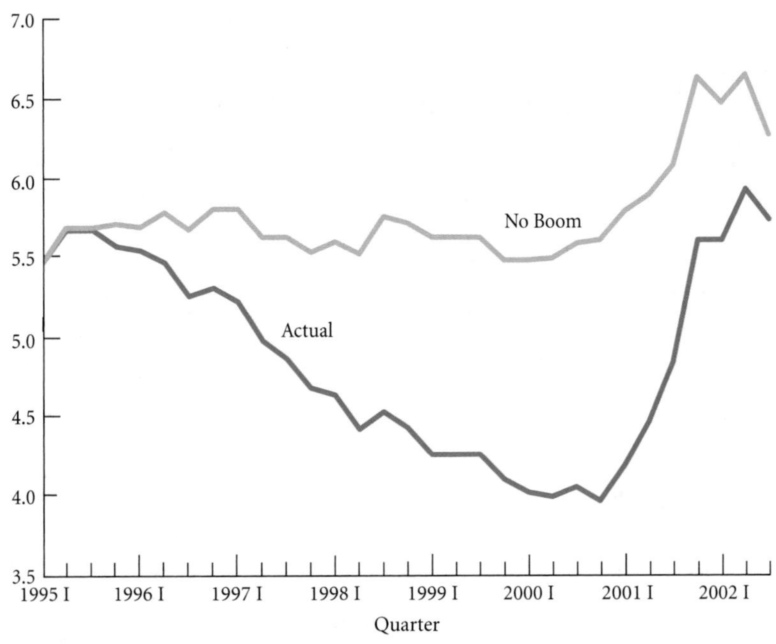

FIGURE 16.8 The Unemployment Rate, 1995 I–2002 III

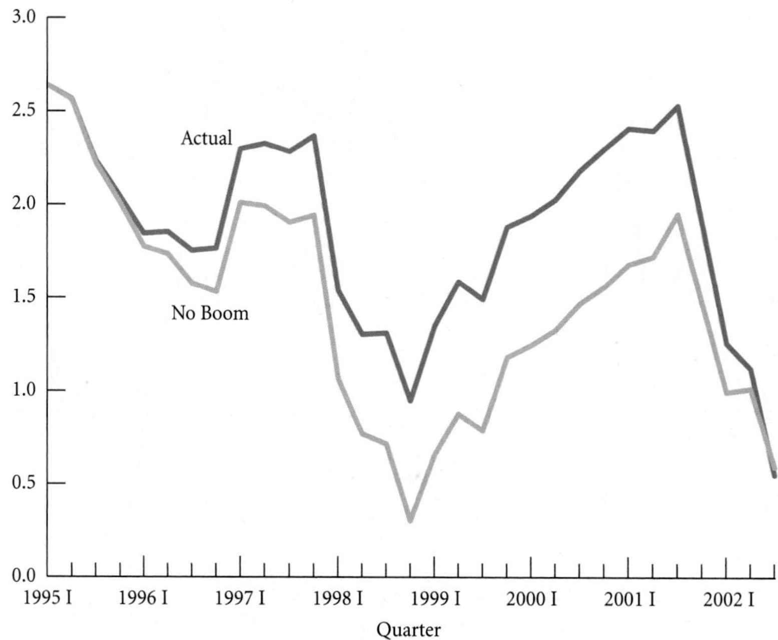

FIGURE 16.9 Inflation Rate, 1995 I–2002 III

would have been lower and the unemployment rate higher, and the Fed would have responded to this with lower interest rates.

FED POLICY AND THE STOCK MARKET

Figure 16.10 is useful for thinking about how Fed policy is related to the stock market. Policy questions arise from time to time as to whether the Fed should be influenced by the stock market. Should the Fed try to influence stock prices by changing interest rates? Figure 16.10 says that the Fed is in fact influenced by the stock market. The Fed kept the interest rate higher than it would have had there been no stock market boom. It should be clear why this is the case. If ultimately the Fed cares about output, unemployment, and inflation, and if the stock market affects these variables, the Fed will be indirectly affected by the stock market. In other words, the Fed cares about the stock market to the extent that the stock market affects the things that it ultimately cares about, namely, output, unemployment, and inflation.

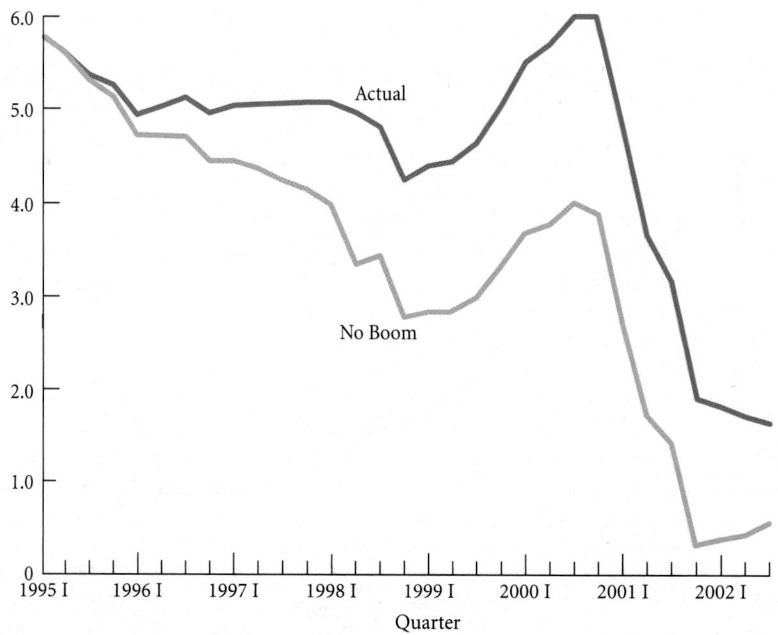

FIGURE 16.10 3-Month Treasury Bill Rate, 1995 I–2002 III

SUMMARY

STOCKS AND BONDS

1. A firm can finance an investment project by borrowing from banks, by issuing bonds, or by issuing new shares of its stock. People who own shares of stock own a fraction of the firm.
2. The price of a stock should equal the discounted value of its expected future dividends, where the discount factors depend on the interest rate and risk.
3. A bubble exists if the price of a stock exceeds the discounted value of its expected future dividends. In this case, what matters is what people expect that other people expect about how much the stock can be sold for in the future.

THE STOCK MARKET SINCE 1948

4. The largest stock market boom in U.S. history occurred between 1995 and 2000, when the S&P 500 index rose by 25 percent per year. The boom added $14 trillion to household wealth.
5. Why there was a stock market boom in 1995–2000 appears to be a puzzle. There was nothing unusual about earnings that would predict such a boom. Many people believe that the boom was merely a bubble.
6. The boom of 1995–2000 and the large fall in stock prices after that had significant effects on millions of people's lives. Many people overspent during the boom years and were seriously affected when the boom didn't last.

STOCK MARKET EFFECTS ON THE ECONOMY

7. When stock prices increase, household wealth increases, which leads to increased consumer spending. Investment also rises because firms can raise more money per share to finance investment projects. As a rough rule of thumb, a $1.00 change in the value of stocks leads to about a $0.03 to $0.04 change in consumer and investor spending per year.
8. The boom in the economy between 1995 and 2000 was fueled by the stock market boom. Estimates show that had there been no stock market boom, the economy would not have looked historically unusual in the last half of the 1990s.

REVIEW TERMS AND CONCEPTS

bond, 301
capital gain, 302
Dow Jones Industrial Average, 305
NASDAQ Composite, 305
realized capital gain, 302
Standard and Poor's 500 (S&P 500), 305
stock, 302

PROBLEM SET

1. On July 28, 2003, ~~Bank One~~ stock (stock symbol "ONE") traded for $39.50 per share. Suppose that you had bought 100 shares on that date and that you sold them today. Look up the current price of Bank One stock in the stock pages of any newspaper.
   a. How much are your shares worth today?
   b. How much did you make or lose in total dollars?
   c. Expressed as a percent of what you initially paid, how big is your gain or loss?
   d. To get a very rough annual percent increase, divide your percent change in c. by the number of years since July 2003, including fractions of a year. For example, if it is November 2004, divide by 1 and 4/12 or 1.33.
   e. What is the current dividend yield from the stock table?
   f. Now figure your total return by adding the dividend yield in e. to the annualized gain in price from d.
   g. How does your total yield compare to interest rates today? Was it a good investment?
2. In July of 2003, the S&P 500 index was at 1,000.
   a. What is the S&P 500 index?
   b. Where is the S&P today?
   c. If you had invested $10,000 in July 2003 and your investments had increased in value by the same percentage as the S&P 500 index had increased, how much would you have today?
   d. Assume that the total stock market holdings of the household sector were about $12 trillion and that the entire stock market went up/down by the same percentage as the S&P. Evidence suggests that the "wealth effect" of stock market holdings on consumer spending is about 4 percent of wealth annually. How much additional or reduced spending would you expect to see as a result of the stock market moves since July 2003? Assuming a multiplier of 2 and a GDP of $1,100 billion, how much additional/less GDP would you predict for next year if all of this were true?

3. In July 2003, the 10-year Treasury bond was paying 4.25 percent. In the corporate bond table in the box titled "Reading a Bond Table," you can see a bond sold by General Motors due in July of 2013 paying a 7.133 percent interest rate. What reasons can you give for the difference between the Treasury's borrowing rate and the rate paid by GM?

4. During 1997, stock markets in Asia collapsed. Hong Kong's was down nearly 30 percent, Thailand's down 62 percent, and Malaysia's down 60 percent. Big drops were also experienced in Japan and Korea. What impacts would these events have on the economies of the countries themselves? Explain your answer. In what ways would you have expected these events to influence the U.S. economy? How might the spending of Asians on American goods be affected? What about Americans who have invested in these countries?

Visit www.prenhall.com/casefair for self-test quizzes, interactive graphing exercises, and news articles.

Household and Firm Behavior in the Macroeconomy: A Further Look*

17

CHAPTER OUTLINE

In Chapters 8 through 14, we considered the interactions of households, firms, and the government in the goods, money, and labor markets. The macroeconomy is complicated, and there is a lot to learn about these interactions. To keep our discussions as uncomplicated as possible, we have so far assumed simple behavior of households and firms—the two basic decision-making units in the economy. We assumed household consumption (C) depends only on income, and firms' planned investment (I) depends only on the interest rate. We did not consider that households make consumption and labor supply decisions simultaneously and that firms make investment and employment decisions simultaneously.

Now that we understand the basic interactions in the economy, we must relax these assumptions. In the first part of this chapter, we present a more realistic picture of the influences on households' consumption and labor supply decisions. In the second part, we present a more detailed and realistic picture of the influences on firms' investment and employment decisions. We then use what we have learned to analyze more macroeconomic issues.

HOUSEHOLDS: CONSUMPTION AND LABOR SUPPLY DECISIONS

Before discussing household behavior, let us review what we have learned so far.

THE KEYNESIAN THEORY OF CONSUMPTION: A REVIEW

The assumption that household consumption (C) depends on income, which we have used as the basis of our analysis so far, is one that Keynes stressed in his *General Theory of Employment, Interest, and Money*. While Keynes believed many factors, including interest

*This chapter is somewhat more advanced, and it can be skipped, if desired.

rates and wealth, are likely to influence the level of consumption spending, he focused on current income:

> The amount of aggregate consumption depends mainly on the amount of aggregate income. The fundamental psychological law, upon which we are entitled to depend with great confidence both . . . from our knowledge of human nature and from the detailed facts of experience, is that men [and women, too] are disposed, as a rule and on average, to increase their consumption as their incomes increase, but not by as much as the increase in their income.[1]

Keynes is making two points here. First, he suggests that consumption is a positive function of income. The more income you have, the more consuming you are likely to do. Except for a few rich misers who save scraps of soap and bits of string despite million-dollar incomes, this proposition makes sense. Rich people typically consume more than poor people.

Second, Keynes suggests, high-income households consume a smaller proportion of their income than low-income households. (If rich households consume relatively less of their incomes, then by definition they save a higher proportion of their incomes than poor households.) The proportion of income that households spend on consumption is measured by the **average propensity to consume** (**APC**).[2] The APC is defined as consumption divided by income:

average propensity to consume (*APC*) The proportion of income households spend on consumption. Determined by dividing consumption (*C*) by income (*Y*).

$$APC = \frac{C}{Y}$$

If a household earns $30,000 per year and spends $25,000 (saving $5,000), it has an *APC* of $25,000/$30,000, or .833. Keynes argues that people who earn, for example, $30,000, are likely to spend a larger portion of their income than those who earn $100,000.

Although the idea that consumption depends on income is a useful starting point, it is far from a complete description of the consumption decision. We need to consider other theories of consumption.

THE LIFE-CYCLE THEORY OF CONSUMPTION

life-cycle theory of consumption A theory of household consumption: Households make lifetime consumption decisions based on their expectations of lifetime income.

The **life-cycle theory of consumption** is an extension of Keynes's theory. The idea of the life-cycle theory is that people make lifetime consumption plans. By realizing that they are likely to earn more in their prime working years than they earn earlier or later, they make consumption decisions based on their expectations of lifetime income. People tend to consume less than they earn during their main working years—they *save* during those years—and they tend to consume more than they earn during their early and later years—they *dissave*, or use up savings, during those years. Students in medical school generally have very low current incomes, but few live in the poverty that those incomes might predict. Instead, they borrow now and plan to pay back later when their incomes improve.

The lifetime income and consumption pattern of a representative individual is shown in Figure 17.1. As you can see, this person has a low income during the first part of her life, high income in the middle, and low income again in retirement. Her income in retirement is not zero because she has income from sources other than her own labor—Social Security payments, interest and dividends, and so forth.

The consumption path as drawn in Figure 17.1 is constant over the person's life. This is an extreme assumption, but it illustrates the point that the path of consumption over a lifetime is likely to be much more stable than the path of income. We consume an amount greater than our incomes during our early working careers. We do this by borrowing against

---

[1]John Maynard Keynes, *The General Theory of Employment, Interest, and Money (1936)*, First Harbinger Ed. (New York: Harcourt Brace Jovanovich, 1964), p. 96.

[2]Whereas the *APC* measures the proportion of total income households spend on consumption, the marginal propensity to consume (*MPC*), which we introduced in Chapter 8, measures the proportion of a *change* in income that households spend on consumption. We could interpret Keynes's theory as implying that the *MPC* falls as income rises. If the *MPC* falls as income rises, it follows that the average propensity to consume (*APC*) falls also.

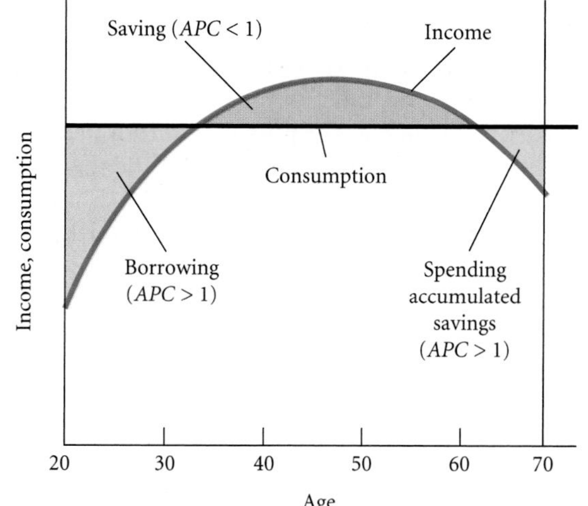

FIGURE 17.1 Life Cycle Theory of Consumption

In their early working years, people consume more than they earn. This is also true in the retirement years. In between, people save (consume less than they earn) to pay off debts from borrowing and to accumulate savings for retirement.

future income, by taking out a car loan, a mortgage to buy a house, or a loan to pay for college. This debt is repaid when our incomes have risen and we can afford to use some of our income to pay off past borrowing without substantially lowering our consumption. The reverse is true for our retirement years. Here, too, our incomes are low. Because we consume less than we earn during our prime working years, we can save up a "nest egg" that allows us to maintain an acceptable standard of living during retirement.

Fluctuations in wealth are also an important component of the life-cycle story. Many young households borrow in anticipation of higher income in the future. Some households actually have *negative wealth*—the value of their assets is less than the debts they owe. A household in its prime working years saves to pay off debts and to build up assets for its later years, when income typically goes down. Households whose assets are greater than the debts they owe have *positive wealth.* With its wage earners retired, a household consumes its accumulated wealth. Generally speaking, wealth starts out negative, turns positive, and then approaches zero near the end of life. Wealth, therefore, is intimately linked to the cumulative saving and dissaving behavior of households.

The key difference between the Keynesian theory of consumption and the life-cycle theory is that the life-cycle theory suggests consumption and saving decisions are likely to be based not just on current income but on expectations of future income as well. The consumption behavior of households immediately following World War II clearly supports the life-cycle story. Just after the war ended, income fell as wage earners moved out of war-related work. However, consumption spending did not fall commensurately, as Keynesian theory would predict. People expected to find jobs in other sectors eventually, and they did not adjust their consumption spending to the temporarily lower incomes they were earning in the meantime.

permanent income The average level of one's expected future income stream.

The phrase **permanent income** is sometimes used to refer to the average level of a person's expected future income stream. If you expect your income will be high in the future (even though it may not be high now), your permanent income is said to be high. With this concept, we can sum up the life-cycle theory by saying that current consumption decisions are likely to be based on permanent income instead of current income.[3] This means that policy changes like tax-rate changes are likely to have more of an effect on household behavior if they are expected to be permanent instead of temporary.

Although this insight enriches our understanding of the consumption behavior of households, the analysis is still missing something. What is missing is the other main decision of households: the labor supply decision.

[3]The pioneering work on this topic was done by Milton Friedman, *A Theory of the Consumption Function* (Princeton, N.J.: Princeton University Press, 1957). In the mid-1960s, Franco Modigliani did closely related work that included the formulation of the life-cycle theory.

THE LABOR SUPPLY DECISION

The size of the labor force in an economy is of obvious importance. A growing labor force is one of the ways in which national income/output can be expanded, and the larger the percentage of people who work is, the higher the potential output per capita.

So far, we have said little about the things that determine the size of the labor force. Of course, demographics are a key; the number of children born in 2003 will go a long way toward determining the potential number of 20-year-old workers in 2023. In addition, immigration, both legal and illegal, plays a role.

Also behavior plays a role. Households make decisions about whether to work and how much to work. These decisions are closely tied to consumption decisions, because for most households the bulk of their spending is financed out of wages and salaries.

> Households make consumption and labor supply decisions simultaneously. Consumption cannot be considered separately from labor supply, because it is precisely by selling your labor that you earn income to pay for your consumption.

As we discussed in Chapter 3, the alternative to supplying your labor in exchange for a wage or a salary is leisure or other nonmarket activities. Nonmarket activities include raising a child, going to school, keeping a house, or—in a developing economy—working as a subsistence farmer.

What determines the quantity of labor supplied by a household? Among the list of factors are the wage rate, prices, wealth, and nonlabor income.

The Wage Rate A changing wage rate can affect labor supply, but whether the effect is positive or negative is ambiguous. For example, an increase in the wage rate affects a household in two ways. First, work becomes more attractive relative to leisure and other nonmarket activities. Because every hour spent in leisure now requires giving up a higher wage, the opportunity cost of leisure is higher. As a result, you would expect a higher wage would lead to a larger labor supply—a larger workforce. This is called the *substitution effect of a wage rate increase.*

On the other hand, households who work are clearly better off after a wage rate increase. By working the same number of hours as they did before, they will earn more income. If we assume that leisure is a normal good, people with higher income will spend some of it on leisure by working less. This is the *income effect of a wage rate increase.*

When wage rates rise, the substitution effect suggests that people will work more, while the income effect suggests that they will work less. The ultimate effect depends on which separate effect is more powerful. The data suggest that the substitution effect seems to win in most cases. That is, higher wage rates usually lead to a larger labor supply, while lower wage rates usually lead to a lower labor supply.

Prices Prices also play a major role in the consumption/labor supply decision. In our discussions of the possible effects of an increase in the wage rate, we have been assuming that the prices of goods and services do not rise at the same time. If the wage rate and all other prices rise simultaneously, the story is different. To make things clear we need to distinguish between the nominal wage rate and the real wage rate.

nominal wage rate The wage rate in current dollars.

real wage rate The amount that the nominal wage rate can buy in terms of goods and services.

The **nominal wage rate** is the wage rate in current dollars. When we adjust the nominal wage rate for changes in the price level, we obtain the **real wage rate**. The real wage rate measures the amount that wages can buy in terms of goods and services. Workers do not care about their nominal wage—they care about the purchasing power of this wage—the real wage.

Suppose skilled workers in Indianapolis were paid a wage rate of $20 per hour in 2003. Now suppose that their wage rate rose to $22 in 2004, a 10 percent increase. If the prices of goods and services were exactly the same in 2004 as they were in 2003 the real wage rate would have increased by 10 percent. An hour of work in 2004 ($22) buys 10 percent more than an hour of work in 2003 ($20).

What if the prices of all goods and services also increased by 10 percent between 2003 and 2004? The purchasing power of an hour's wages has not changed. The real wage rate has not increased at all. In 2004, $22 bought the same quantity of goods and services that $20 bought in 2003.

To measure the real wage rate, we adjust the nominal wage rate with a price index. As we saw in Chapter 7, there are several such indexes that we might use, including the consumer price index and the GDP price index.[4]

We can now apply what we have learned from the life-cycle theory to our wage/price story. Recall the life-cycle theory says people look ahead in making their decisions. Translated to real wage rates, this idea says:

> Households look at expected future real wage rates as well as the current real wage rate in making their current consumption and labor supply decisions.

Consider medical students who expect their real wage rate will be higher in the future. This expectation obviously has an effect on current decisions about things like how much to buy and whether or not to take a part-time job.

Wealth and Nonlabor Income Life-cycle theory says wealth fluctuates over the life cycle. Households accumulate wealth during their working years to pay off debts accumulated when they were young and to support themselves in retirement. This role of wealth is clear, but the existence of wealth poses another question. Consider two households that are at the same stage in their life cycle and have pretty much the same expectations about future wage rates, prices, and so forth. They expect to live the same length of time, and both plan to leave the same amount to their children. They differ only in their wealth. Because of a past inheritance, household 1 has more wealth than household 2. Which household is likely to have a higher consumption path for the rest of its life? Household 1 is because it has more wealth to spread out over the rest of its life.

> Holding everything else constant (including the stage in the life cycle), the more wealth a household has, the more it will consume, both now and in the future.

Now consider a household that has a sudden unexpected increase in wealth, perhaps an inheritance from a distant relative. How will the household's consumption pattern be affected? The household will increase its consumption, both now and in the future, as it spends the inheritance over the course of the rest of its life.

An increase in wealth can also be looked on as an increase in nonlabor income. **Nonlabor**, or **nonwage, income** is income received from sources other than working—inheritances, interest, dividends, and transfer payments such as welfare payments and Social Security payments. As with wealth:

nonlabor, or **nonwage, income** Any income received from sources other than working—inheritances, interest, dividends, transfer payments, and so on.

> An unexpected increase in nonlabor income will have a positive effect on a household's consumption.

What about the effect of an increase in wealth or nonlabor income on labor supply? We already know an increase in income results in an increase in the consumption of normal goods, including leisure. Therefore, an unexpected increase in wealth or nonlabor income results in both an increase in consumption and an increase in leisure. With leisure increasing, labor supply must fall, so:

> An unexpected increase in wealth or nonlabor income leads to a *decrease* in labor supply.

This point should be obvious. If I suddenly win a million dollars in the state lottery or make a killing in the stock market, I will probably work less in the future than I otherwise would have.

[4]To calculate the real wage rate, we divide the nominal wage rate by the price index. Suppose the wage rate rose from $10.00 per hour in 1994 to $18.00 per hour in 2004 and the price level rose 50 percent during the same period. Using 1994 as the base year, the price index would be 1.00 in 1994 and 1.50 in 2004. The real wage rate is W/P, where W is the nominal wage rate and P is the price level. The real wage rate is $10.00 in 1994 ($10.00/1.00) and $12.00 in 2004 ($18.00/1.50), using 1994 as the base year.

INTEREST RATE EFFECTS ON CONSUMPTION

Recall from the last few chapters that the interest rate affects a firm's investment decision. A higher interest rate leads to a lower level of planned investment, and vice versa. This was a key link between the money market and the goods market, and it was the channel through which monetary policy had an impact on planned aggregate expenditure.

We can now expand on this link: The interest rate also affects household behavior. Consider the effect of a fall in the interest rate on consumption. A fall in the interest rate lowers the reward to saving. If the interest rate falls from 10 percent to 5 percent, I earn 5 cents instead of 10 cents per year on every dollar saved. This means that the opportunity cost of spending a dollar today (instead of saving it and consuming it plus the interest income a year from now) has fallen. I will substitute toward current consumption and away from future consumption when the interest rate falls: I consume more today and save less. A rise in the interest rate leads me to consume less today and save more. This effect is called the *substitution effect.*

There is also an *income effect* of an interest rate change on consumption. If a household has positive wealth and is earning interest on that wealth, a fall in the interest rate leads to a fall in interest income. This is a decrease in its nonlabor income, which, as we just saw, will have a negative effect on consumption. For households with positive wealth, the income effect works in the opposite direction from the substitution effect. On the other hand, if a household is a debtor and is paying interest on its debt, a fall in the interest rate leads to a fall in interest payments. The household is better off in this case and will consume more. In this case the income and substitution effects work in the same direction. The total household sector in the United States has positive wealth, and so in the aggregate the income and substitution effects work in the opposite direction.

On balance, the data suggest that the substitution effect dominates the income effect, so that the interest rate has a negative net effect on consumption. There is also some evidence, however, that the income effect is getting larger over time. U.S. households own most of the U.S. government debt, and the size of this debt has increased dramatically in the last 20 years. This means that the change in government interest payments, and so the change in household interest income, is now larger for a given change in interest rates than before, which leads to a larger income effect than before for a given change in interest rates.

GOVERNMENT EFFECTS ON CONSUMPTION AND LABOR SUPPLY: TAXES AND TRANSFERS

The government influences household behavior mainly through income tax rates and transfer payments.

When the government raises income tax rates, after-tax real wages decrease, lowering consumption. When the government lowers income tax rates, after-tax real wages increase, raising consumption.

A change in income tax rates also affects labor supply. If the substitution effect dominates, as we are generally assuming, then an increase in income tax rates, which lowers after-tax wages, will lower labor supply. A decrease in income tax rates will increase labor supply.

Transfer payments are payments such as Social Security benefits, veterans' benefits, and welfare benefits. An increase in transfer payments is an increase in nonlabor income, which we have seen has a positive effect on consumption and a negative effect on labor supply. Increases in transfer payments thus increase consumption and decrease labor supply, while decreases in transfer payments decrease consumption and increase labor supply. Table 17.1 summarizes these results.

A POSSIBLE EMPLOYMENT CONSTRAINT ON HOUSEHOLDS

Our discussion of the labor supply decision has so far proceeded as if households were free to choose how much to work each period. If a member of a household decides to work an additional 5 hours a week at the current wage rate, we have assumed the person *can* work 5 hours more—that work is available. If someone who has not been working decides to work at the current wage rate, we have assumed that the person *can find a job.*

News Analysis

Falling Interest Rates Designed to Stimulate Spending in 2003

ON JUNE 25, 2003, THE FED CUT THE SHORT TERM interest rates by a quarter of a point. As the following article in the *New York Times* reports, the objective of the Fed was clear.

Federal Reserve Lowers Key Rate to 1%, Lowest Level Since 1958

Trying to bring the long economic downturn to a halt at last, the Federal Reserve cut short-term interest rates by a quarter of a point today, taking them to their lowest level since 1958.

To the disappointment of the stock and bond markets, the Fed rejected a half-point cut and explained in a statement that the economy appeared to be improving but could still benefit from easier credit.

"Recent signs point to a firming in spending, markedly improved financial conditions, and labor and product markets that are stabilizing," the Fed's statement read. "The economy, nonetheless, has yet to exhibit sustainable growth." . . .

The fall in the Fed's benchmark rate, to 1 percent from 1.25 percent, will quickly reduce rates on many business, home equity and credit card loans, as well as the return on money market funds. Mortgage rates, which are set by the market, are unlikely to change significantly, economists said, because investors had expected the Fed to act.

Retirees and other people who rely on fixed investments for income will take an effective pay cut. But the overall decline in borrowing costs for households and companies is likely to help the economy, analysts said. . . .

The Fed has cut rates 13 times since the beginning of 2001, first in a failed effort to prevent a recession and more recently in hopes of halting a period of slow growth and persistent layoffs. But the hangover from the 1990's boom, combined with wars in Iraq and Afghanistan and a series of corporate scandals, has caused the worst hiring slump in 20 years and the longest one since the period before World War II. . . .

The economy has recently shown signs of improvement, like increases in manufacturing activity and retail sales, which appear to have pushed the Fed toward the smaller rate cut. A recently passed tax cut, the already low level of interest rates and this year's decline in the dollar, which helps American companies compete with foreign rivals, have also caused most economists to predict a rebound in coming months.

Alan Greenspan, Chairman of the Board of Governers of the Federal Reserve System, chairs the Federal Open Market Committee.

"There's just a lot of stimulus in the pipeline already," said James O'Sullivan, an economist at UBS Warburg. "So it's very reasonable to think that growth is going to be stronger in the second half of the year."

Source: Adapted from: David Leonhardt, "Federal Reserve Lowers Key Rate to 1%, Lowest Level Since 1958," New York Times, *June 26, 2003. Used by permission.*

Visit www.prenhall.com/casefair for updated articles and exercises.

There are times when these assumptions do not hold. The Great Depression, when unemployment rates reached 25 percent of the labor force, led to the birth of macroeconomics in the 1930s. Since the mid-1970s, the United States has experienced four recessions, with millions of unemployed workers unable to find work.

All households face a budget constraint, regardless of the state of the economy. This budget constraint, which separates those bundles of goods that are available to a household from those that are not, is determined by income, wealth, and prices. When there is unemployment, some households feel an additional constraint on their behavior. Some people may want to work 40 hours per week at the current wage rates but can find only part-time work. Others may not find any work at all.

How does a household respond when it is constrained from working as much as it would like? It consumes less. If your current wage rate is $10 per hour and you normally

TABLE 17.1 The Effects of Government on Household Consumption and Labor Supply

	Income Tax Rates		Transfer Payments	
	INCREASE	DECREASE	INCREASE	DECREASE
Effect on consumption	Negative	Positive	Positive	Negative
Effect on labor supply	Negative*	Positive*	Negative	Positive

*If the substitution effect dominates.
Note: The effects are larger if they are expected to be permanent instead of temporary.

work 40 hours a week, your normal income from wages is $400 per week. If your average tax rate is 20 percent, your after-tax wage income is $320 per week. You are likely to spend much of this income during the week. If you are prevented from working, this income will not be available to you, and you will have less to spend.

You will spend something, of course. You may receive some form of nonlabor income, and you may have assets, such as savings deposits or stocks and bonds, that can be withdrawn or sold. You may also be able to borrow during your period of unemployment. Even though you will spend something during the week, it is almost certain that you will spend less than you would have if you had your usual income of $320 in after-tax wages.

Households consume less if they are constrained from working.

A household constrained from working as much as it would like at the current wage rate faces a different decision from the decision facing a household that can work as much as it wants. The work decision of the former household is, in effect, forced on it. The household works as much as it can—a certain number of hours per week or perhaps none at all—but this amount is less than the household would choose to work at the current wage rate if it could find more work. The amount that a household would like to work at the current wage rate if it could find the work is called its **unconstrained supply of labor**. The amount that the household actually works in a given period at current wage rates is called its **constrained supply of labor**.

unconstrained supply of labor The amount a household would like to work within a given period at the current wage rate if it could find the work.

constrained supply of labor The amount a household actually works in a given period at the current wage rate.

A household's constrained supply of labor is not a variable over which it has any control. The amount of labor the household supplies is imposed on it from the outside by the workings of the economy. However, the household's consumption *is* under its control. We have just seen that the less a household works—that is, the smaller the household's constrained supply of labor is—the lower its consumption. Constraints on the supply of labor are an important determinant of consumption when there is unemployment.

Keynesian Theory Revisited Recall the Keynesian theory that current income determines current consumption. We now know the consumption decision is made jointly with the labor supply decision and the two depend on the real wage rate. It is incorrect to think consumption depends only on income, at least when there is full employment. However, if there is unemployment, Keynes is closer to being correct because income is not determined by households. When there is unemployment, the level of income (at least workers' income) depends exclusively on the employment decisions made by firms. There are unemployed workers who are willing to work at the current wage rate, and their income is in effect determined by firms' hiring decisions. This income affects current consumption, which is consistent with Keynes's theory. This is one of the reasons Keynesian theory is considered to pertain to periods of unemployment. It was, of course, precisely during such a period that the theory was developed.

A SUMMARY OF HOUSEHOLD BEHAVIOR

This completes our discussion of household behavior in the macroeconomy. Household consumption depends on more than current income. Households determine consumption and labor supply simultaneously, and they look ahead in making their decisions.

The following factors affect household consumption and labor supply decisions:

- Current and expected future real wage rates
- Initial value of wealth
- Current and expected future nonlabor income
- Interest rates
- Current and expected future tax rates and transfer payments

If households are constrained in their labor supply decisions, income is directly determined by firms' hiring decisions. In this case, we can say (in the traditional, Keynesian way) that "income" affects consumption.

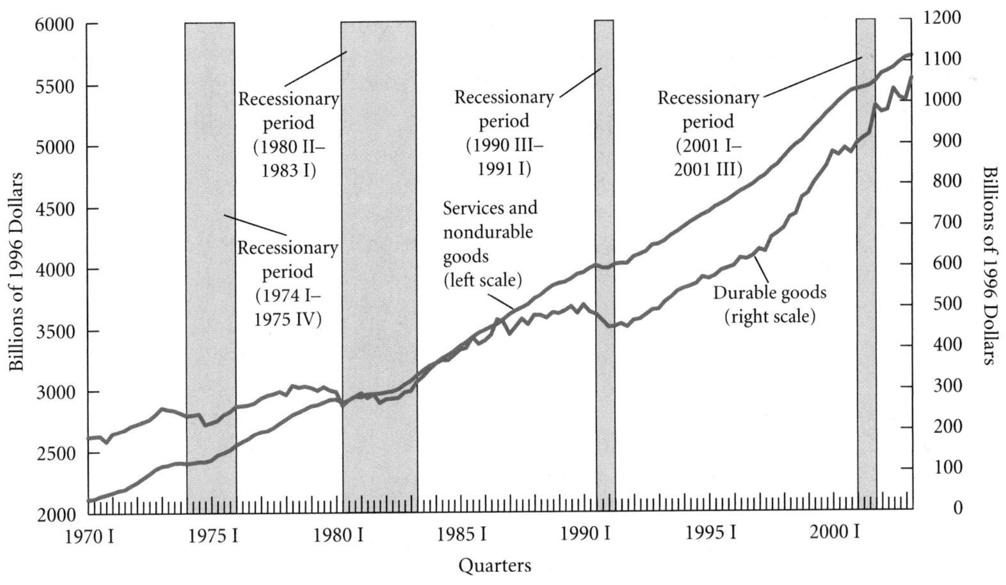

FIGURE 17.2 Consumption Expenditures, 1970 I–2003 II

Over time, expenditures on services and nondurable goods are "smoother" than expenditures on durable goods.

THE HOUSEHOLD SECTOR SINCE 1970

To better understand household behavior, let us examine how some of the aggregate household variables have changed over time. We will discuss the period 1970 I–2003 II. (Remember, Roman numerals refer to quarters, e.g., 1970 I means the first quarter of 1970.) Within this span, there have been four recessionary periods, 1974 I–1975 IV, 1980 II–1983 I, 1990 III–1991 I, and 2001 I–2001 III. How did the household variables behave during each period?

Consumption Data on the total consumption of the household sector are in the national income accounts. As we saw in Table 6.2 on page 102, personal consumption expenditures accounted for 69.9 percent of GDP in 2002. The three basic categories of consumption expenditures are services, nondurable goods, and durable goods.

Figure 17.2 plots the data for consumption expenditures on services and nondurable goods combined and for consumption expenditures on durable goods. The variables are in real terms. You can see that expenditures on services and nondurable goods are "smoother" over time than expenditures on durable goods. For example, the decrease in expenditures on services and nondurable goods was much smaller during the three recessionary periods than the decrease in expenditures on durable goods.

Why do expenditures on durables fluctuate more than expenditures on services and nondurables? When times are bad, people can postpone the purchase of durable goods, and they do. It follows that expenditures on these goods change the most. When times are tough, you do not *have* to have a new car or a new washer-dryer; you can make do with your old Chevy or Maytag until things get better. When your income falls, it is less easy to postpone the service costs of day care or health care. Nondurables fall into an intermediate category, with some items (like new clothes) easier to postpone than others (like food).

Housing Investment Another important expenditure of the household sector is housing investment (purchases of new housing), plotted in Figure 17.3. This variable fluctuates greatly, for at least two reasons. Housing investment is the most easily postponable of all household expenditures. Also, housing investment is sensitive to the general level of interest rates, and interest rates fluctuate considerably over time. When interest rates are low, housing investment is high, and vice versa.

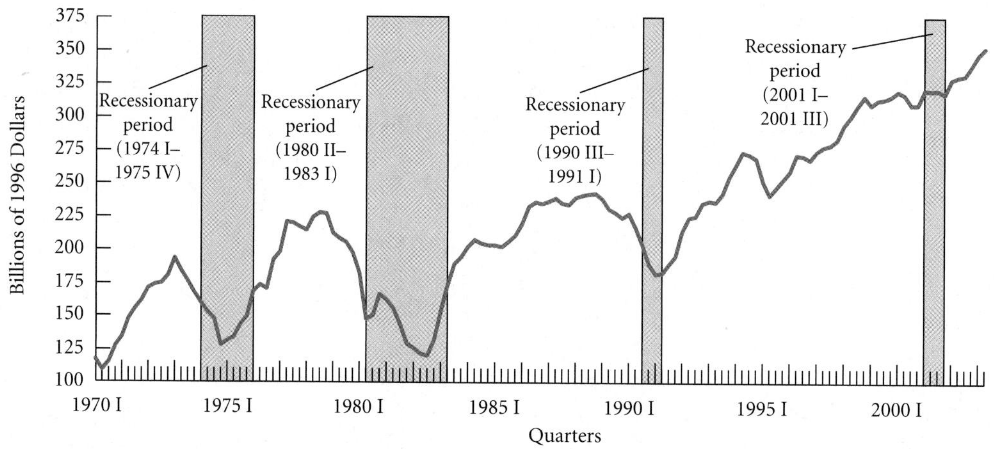

FIGURE 17.3 Housing Investment of the Household Sector, 1970 I–2003 II

Housing investment fell sharply during the four recessionary periods since 1970. Like expenditures for durable goods, expenditures for housing investment are postponable.

Labor Supply As we noted in Chapters 7 and 14, a person is considered a part of the labor force when he or she either is working or has been actively looking for work in the past few weeks. The ratio of the labor force to the total working-age population—those 16 and over—is the *labor-force participation rate.*

It is informative to divide the labor force into three categories: males 25 to 54, females 25 to 54, and all others 16 and over. Ages 25 to 54 are sometimes called "prime" ages, presuming that a person is in the prime of working life during these ages. The participation rates for these three groups are plotted in Figure 17.4.

As the figure shows, most men of prime age are in the labor force, although the participation rate has fallen slightly since 1970—from .961 in 1970 I to .908 in 2003 II. (A rate of

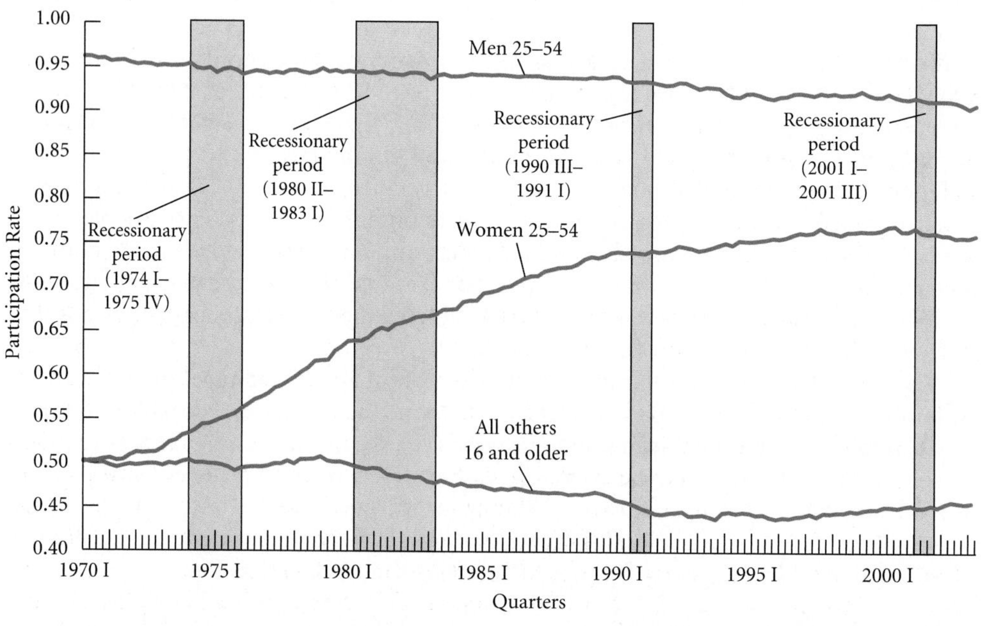

FIGURE 17.4 Labor-Force Participation Rates for Men 25 to 54, Women 25 to 54, and All Others 16 and Over, 1970 I–2003 II

Since 1970, the labor-force participation rate for prime-age men has been decreasing slightly. The rate for prime-age women has been increasing dramatically. The rate for all others 16 and over has been declining since 1979 and shows a tendency to fall during recessions (the discouraged-worker effect).

.908 means that 90.8 percent of prime-age men were in the labor force.) The participation rate for prime-age women, on the other hand, has risen dramatically since 1970—from .501 in 1970 I to .760 in 2003 II. Although economic factors account for some of this increase, a change in social attitudes and preferences probably explains much of the increase. Although the participation rate of prime-age women is still below the rate for prime-age men, this difference will narrow even further in the future if the rate for men keeps falling and the rate for women keeps rising.

Figure 17.4 also shows the participation rate for all individuals 16 and over except prime-age men and women. This rate has some cyclical features—it tends to fall in recessions and to rise or fall less during expansions. These features reveal the operation of the *discouraged-worker effect*, discussed in Chapter 7. During recessions, some people get discouraged about ever finding a job. They stop looking and are then not considered a part of the labor force. During expansions, people become encouraged again. Once they begin looking for jobs, they are again considered a part of the labor force. Because prime-age women and men are likely to be fairly attached to the labor force, the discouraged-worker effect for them is quite small.

The participation rate for non-prime-age men and women has fallen since 1970. Part of this decrease reflects an increase in early retirement. When people retire, they are no longer considered a part of the labor force.

FIRMS: INVESTMENT AND EMPLOYMENT DECISIONS

Having taken a closer look at the behavior of households in the macroeconomy, we now look more closely at the behavior of firms—the other major decision-making unit in the economy. In discussing firm behavior earlier, we assumed that planned investment depends only on the interest rate. However, there are several other determinants of planned investment. We now discuss them and the factors that affect firms' employment decisions. Once again, microeconomic theory can help us gain some insights into the working of the macroeconomy.

In a market economy, firms determine which goods and services are available to consumers today and which will be available in the future, how many workers are needed for what kinds of jobs, and how much investment will be undertaken. Stated in macroeconomic terms, the decisions of firms, taken together, determine output, labor demand, and investment.

In this section, we concentrate on the input choices made by firms. By **inputs**, we mean the goods and services that firms purchase and turn into output. Two important inputs that firms use are capital and labor. (Other inputs are energy, raw materials, and semifinished goods.) Each period, firms must decide how much capital and labor to use in producing output. Let us look first at the decision about how much capital to use.

inputs The goods and services that firms purchase and turn into output.

Investment Decisions At any point in time a firm has a certain stock of capital on hand. *Stock of capital* means the factories and buildings (sometimes called "plants") firms own, the equipment they need to do business, and their inventories of partly or wholly finished goods. There are two basic ways a firm can add to its capital stock. One is to buy more machinery or build new factories or buildings. This kind of addition to the capital stock is **plant-and-equipment investment**.

plant-and-equipment investment Purchases by firms of additional machines, factories, or buildings within a given period.

The other way a firm adds to its capital stock is to increase its inventories. When a firm produces more than it sells in a given period, the firm's stock of inventories increases.[5] This type of addition to the capital stock is **inventory investment**. Recall from Chapter 8 that unplanned inventory investment is different from planned inventory investment. When a firm sells less than it expected to, it experiences an unplanned increase in its inventories and is forced to invest more than it planned to. Unplanned increases in inventories result from factors beyond the firm's control. (We take up inventory investment in detail later in this chapter.)

inventory investment Occurs when a firm produces more output than it sells within a given period.

[5]The change in inventories is exactly equal to the difference between production and sales. If a firm sells 20 units more than it produces in the course of a month, its inventories fall by 20 units; if it produces 20 units more than it sells, its inventories rise by 20 units.

Employment Decisions In addition to investment decisions, firms make *employment* decisions. At the beginning of each period, a firm has a certain number of workers on its payroll. On the basis of its current situation and its upcoming plans, the firm must decide whether to hire additional workers, keep the same number, or reduce its workforce by laying off some employees.

Until this point, our description of firm behavior has been quite simple. In Chapter 8 we argued that firms increase production when they experience unplanned decreases in inventory and reduce production when they experience unplanned increases in inventory. We have also alluded to the fact that the demand for labor increases when output grows. In reality, the set of decisions facing firms is much more complex. A decision to produce additional output is likely to involve additional demand for both labor *and* capital.

The demand for labor is quite important in macroeconomics. If the demand for labor increases at a time of less-than-full employment, the unemployment rate will fall. If the demand for labor increases when there is full employment, wage rates will rise. The demand for capital (which is partly determined by the interest rate) is important as well. Recall, planned investment spending is a component of planned aggregate expenditure. When planned investment spending (I, the demand for new capital) increases, the result is additional output (income). We discussed the investment multiplier effect in Chapter 8.

Decision Making and Profit Maximization To understand the complex behavior of firms in input markets, we must assume that firms make decisions to maximize their profits. One of the most important profit-maximizing decisions that a firm must make is how to produce its output. In most cases, a firm must choose among alternative methods of production, or *technologies.* Different technologies generally require different combinations of capital and labor.

Consider a factory that manufactures shirts. Shirts can be made entirely by hand, with workers cutting the pieces of fabric and sewing them together. However, shirts exactly like those can be made on huge complex machines that cut and sew and produce shirts with very little human supervision. Between these two extremes are dozens of alternative technologies. Shirts can be partly hand sewn, with the stitching done on electric sewing machines.

Firms' decisions concerning the amount of capital and labor that they will use in production are closely related. If firms maximize profits, they will choose the technology that minimizes the cost of production. That is, it is logical to assume that firms will choose the technology that is most efficient.

The most efficient technology depends on the relative prices of capital and labor. A shirt factory in the Philippines that decides to increase its production faces a large supply of relatively inexpensive labor. Wage rates in the Philippines are quite low. Capital equipment must be imported and is very expensive. A shirt factory in the Philippines is likely to choose a **labor-intensive technology**—a large amount of labor relative to capital. When labor-intensive technologies are used, expansion is likely to increase the demand for labor substantially while increasing the demand for capital only modestly.

labor-intensive technology A production technique that uses a large amount of labor relative to capital.

A shirt factory in Germany that decides to expand production is likely to buy a large amount of capital equipment and to hire relatively few new workers. It will probably choose a **capital-intensive technology**—a large amount of capital relative to labor. German wage rates are quite high, higher in many occupations than in the United States. Capital, however, is plentiful.

capital-intensive technology A production technique that uses a large amount of capital relative to labor.

Firms' decisions about labor demand and investment are likely to depend on the relative costs of labor and capital. The relative impact of an expansion of output on employment and on investment demand depends on the wage rate and the cost of capital.

EXPECTATIONS AND ANIMAL SPIRITS

In addition to the cost of capital and the cost of labor, firms' expectations about the future play a big role in investment and employment decisions.

Time is a key factor in investment decisions. Capital has a life that typically extends over many years. A developer who decides to build an office tower is making an investment that will be around (barring earthquakes, floods, or tornadoes) for several decades. In deciding where to build a plant, a manufacturing firm is committing a large amount of resources to purchase capital that will presumably yield services over a long time. Furthermore, the decision to build a plant or to purchase large equipment must often be made years before the actual project is completed. While the acquisition of a small business computer may take only a few days, the planning process for downtown developments in large U.S. cities has been known to take decades.

For these reasons, investment decisions require looking into the future and forming expectations about it. In forming their expectations, firms consider numerous factors. At a minimum, they gather information about the demand for their specific products, about what their competitors are planning, and about the macroeconomy's overall health. A firm is not likely to increase its production capacity if it does not expect to sell more of its product in the future. Hilton will not put up a new hotel if it does not expect to fill the rooms at a profitable rate. Ford will not build a new plant if it expects the economy to enter a long recession.

Forecasting the future is fraught with dangers. Many events cannot be foreseen. Investments are therefore always made with imperfect knowledge. Keynes pointed this out in 1936:

> The outstanding fact is the extreme precariousness of the basis of knowledge on which our estimates of prospective yield have to be made. Our knowledge of the factors which will govern the yield of an investment some years hence is usually very slight and often negligible. If we speak frankly, we have to admit that our basis of knowledge for estimating the yield ten years hence of a railway, a copper mine, a textile factory, the goodwill of a patent medicine, an Atlantic liner, a building in the City of London amounts to little and sometimes nothing.

Keynes concludes from this that much investment activity depends on psychology and on what he calls the **animal spirits of entrepreneurs**:

animal spirits of entrepreneurs A phrase coined by Keynes to describe investors' feelings.

> Our decisions . . . can only be taken as a result of animal spirits. In estimating the prospects of investment, we must have regard, therefore, to nerves and hysteria and even the digestions and reactions to the weather of those upon whose spontaneous activity it largely depends.[6]

Because expectations about the future are, as Keynes points out, subject to great uncertainty, they may change often. Thus animal spirits help to make investment a volatile component of GDP.

The Accelerator Effect Expectations, at least in part, determine the level of planned investment spending. At any interest rate, the level of investment is likely to be higher if businesses are optimistic. If businesses are pessimistic, the level of planned investment will be lower, but what determines expectations?

One possibility borne out empirically is that expectations are optimistic when aggregate output (Y) is rising and pessimistic when aggregate output is falling.

> At any given level of the interest rate, expectations are likely to be more optimistic and planned investment is likely to be higher when output is growing rapidly than when it is growing slowly or falling.

It is easy to see why. If firms expect future output to grow, they must plan now to add productive capacity. One indicator of future prospects is the current growth rate.

If this is the case in reality, and evidence indicates it is, the ultimate result will be an **accelerator effect**. If aggregate output (income) (Y) is rising, investment will increase even though the level of Y may be low. Higher investment spending leads to an added increase in output, further "accelerating" the growth of aggregate output. If Y is falling, expectations are

accelerator effect The tendency for investment to increase when aggregate output increases and decrease when aggregate output decreases, accelerating the growth or decline of output.

---

[6]John Maynard Keynes, *The General Theory of Employment, Interest, and Money (1936)*, First Harbinger Ed. (New York: Harcourt Brace Jovanovich, 1964), pp. 149, 152.

dampened, and investment spending will be cut even though the level of Y may be high, accelerating the decline.

EXCESS LABOR AND EXCESS CAPITAL EFFECTS

excess labor, excess capital Labor and capital that are not needed to produce the firm's current level of output.

We need to make one more point about firms' investment and employment decisions: Firms may sometimes choose to hold **excess labor** and/or **excess capital**. A firm holds excess labor (or capital) if it could reduce the amount of labor it employs (or capital it holds) and still produce the same amount of output.

Why would a firm want to employ more workers or have more capital on hand than it needs? Both labor and capital are costly—a firm has to pay wages to its workers, and it forgoes interest on funds tied up in machinery or buildings. Why would a firm want to incur costs that do not yield revenue?

To see why, suppose a firm suffers a sudden and large decrease in sales, but it expects the lower sales level to last only a few months, after which it believes sales will pick up again. In this case, the firm is likely to lower production in response to the sales change to avoid too large an increase in its stock of inventories. This decrease in production means the firm could get rid of some workers and some machines, because it now needs less labor and less capital to produce the now-lower level of output.

adjustment costs The costs that a firm incurs when it changes its production level—for example, the administration costs of laying off employees or the training costs of hiring new workers.

However, things are not this simple. Decreasing its workforce and capital stock quickly can be costly for a firm. Abrupt cuts in the workforce hurt worker morale and may increase personnel administration costs, and abrupt reductions in capital stock may be disadvantageous because of the difficulty of selling used machines. These types of costs are sometimes called **adjustment costs** because they are the costs of adjusting to the new level of output. There are also adjustment costs to increasing output. For example, it is usually costly to recruit and train new workers.

Adjustment costs may be large enough that a firm chooses not to decrease its workforce and capital stock when production falls. The firm may at times choose to have more labor and capital on hand than it needs to produce its current amount of output, simply because it would be more costly to get rid of them than to keep them. In practice, excess labor takes the form of workers not working at their normal level of activity (more coffee breaks and more idle time, for instance). Some of this excess labor may receive new training so that productivity will be higher when production picks up again.

The existence of excess labor and capital at any given moment is likely to affect future employment and investment decisions. Suppose a firm already has excess labor and capital due to a fall in its sales and production. When production picks up again, the firm will not need to hire as many new workers or acquire as much new capital as it otherwise would need to.

> The more excess capital a firm already has, the less likely it is to invest in new capital in the future. The more excess labor it has, the less likely it is to hire new workers in the future.

INVENTORY INVESTMENT

We now turn to a brief discussion of the inventory investment decision. This decision is quite different from the plant-and-equipment investment decision.

The Role of Inventories Recall the distinction between a firm's sales and its output. If a firm can hold goods in inventory, which is usually the case unless the good is perishable or unless the firm produces services, then within a given period it can sell a quantity of goods that differs from the quantity of goods it produces during that period. When a firm sells more than it produces, its stock of inventories decreases; when it sells less than it produces, its stock of inventories increases.

> stock of inventories (end of period) = stock of inventories (beginning of period)
> + production − sales

If a firm starts a period with 100 umbrellas in inventory, produces 15 umbrellas during the period, and sells 10 umbrellas in this same interval, it will have 105 umbrellas (100 + 15 – 10) in inventory at the end of the period. A change in the stock of inventories is actually investment because inventories are counted as part of a firm's capital stock. In our example, inventory investment during the period is a positive number, 5 umbrellas (105 – 100). When the number of goods produced is less than the number of goods sold, such as 5 produced and 10 sold, inventory investment is negative.

The Optimal Inventory Policy We can now consider firms' inventory decisions. Firms are concerned with what they are going to sell and produce in the future, as well as what they are selling and producing currently. At each point in time, a firm has some idea of how much it is going to sell in the current period and in future periods. Given these expectations and its knowledge of how much of its good it already has in stock, a firm must decide how much to produce in the current period.

Inventories are costly to a firm because they take up space and they tie up funds that could be earning interest. However, if a firm's stock of inventories gets too low, the firm may have difficulty meeting the demand for its product, especially if demand increases unexpectedly. The firm may lose sales. The point between too low and too high a stock of inventory is called the **desired**, or **optimal, level of inventories**. This is the level at which the extra cost (in lost sales) from decreasing inventories by a small amount is just equal to the extra gain (in interest revenue and decreased storage costs).

desired, or **optimal, level of inventories** The level of inventory at which the extra cost (in lost sales) from lowering inventories by a small amount is just equal to the extra gain (in interest revenue and decreased storage costs).

A firm that had no costs other than inventory costs would always aim to produce in a period exactly the volume of goods necessary to make its stock of inventories at the end of the period equal to the desired stock. If the stock of inventory fell lower than desired, the firm would produce more than it expected to sell to bring the stock up. If the stock of inventory grew above the desired level, the firm would produce less than it expected to sell to reduce the stock.

There are other costs to running a firm besides inventory costs. In particular, large and abrupt changes in production can be very costly because it is often disruptive to change a production process geared to a certain rate of output. If production is to be increased, there may be adjustment costs for hiring more labor and increasing the capital stock. If production is to be decreased, there may be adjustment costs in laying off workers and decreasing the capital stock.

Because holding inventories and changing production levels are both costly, firms face a trade-off between them. Because of adjustment costs, a firm is likely to smooth its production path relative to its sales path. This means a firm is likely to have its production fluctuate less than its sales, with changes in inventories to absorb the difference each period. However, because there are incentives not to stray too far from the optimal level of inventories, fluctuations in production are not eliminated completely. Production is still likely to fluctuate, just not as much as sales fluctuate.

Two other points need to be made here. First, if a firm's stock of inventories is unusually or unexpectedly high, the firm is likely to produce less in the future than it would have, to decrease its high stock of inventories. In other words, although the stock of inventories fluctuates over time because production is smoothed relative to sales, at any point in time inventories may be unexpectedly high or low because sales have been unexpectedly low or high. An unexpectedly high stock will have a negative effect on production in the future, and an unexpectedly low stock will have a positive effect on production in the future.

An unexpected increase in inventories has a negative effect on future production, and an unexpected decrease in inventories has a positive effect on future production.

Second, firms do not know their future sales exactly. They have expectations of future sales, and these expectations may not turn out to be exactly right.

This has important consequences. If sales turn out to be less than expected, inventories will be higher than expected, and there will be less production in the future. Furthermore, *future* sales expectations are likely to have an important effect on *current* production. If a firm expects its sales to be high in the future, it will adjust its planned production path accordingly. Even though a firm smoothes production relative to sales, over a long time it must produce as much as it sells. If it did not, it would eventually run out of inventories.

The level of a firm's planned production path depends on the level of its expected future sales path. If a firm's expectations of the level of its future sales path decrease, the firm is likely to decrease the level of its planned production path, including its actual production in the current period. Current production depends on expected future sales.

Because production is likely to depend on expectations of the future, animal spirits may play a role. If firms become more optimistic about the future, they are likely to produce more now. Keynes's view that animal spirits affect investment is also likely to pertain to output.

A SUMMARY OF FIRM BEHAVIOR

The following factors affect firms' investment and employment decisions:

- Wage rate and cost of capital (the interest rate is an important component of the cost of capital)
- Firms' expectations of future output
- Amount of excess labor and excess capital on hand

The most important points to remember about the relationship between production, sales, and inventory investment are:

- Inventory investment—that is, the change in the stock of inventories—equals production minus sales
- An unexpected increase in the stock of inventories has a negative effect on future production
- Current production depends on expected future sales

THE FIRM SECTOR SINCE 1970

To close our discussion of firm behavior, we now examine some aggregate investment and employment variables for the period 1970 I–2003 II.

Plant-and-Equipment Investment Plant-and-equipment investment by the firm sector is plotted in Figure 17.5. Investment fared poorly in the four recessionary periods after 1970. This observation is consistent with the observation that investment depends in part on output. An examination of the plot of real GDP in Figure 17.6 and the plot of investment in Figure 17.5 shows investment generally does poorly when GDP does poorly, and investment generally does well when GDP does well.

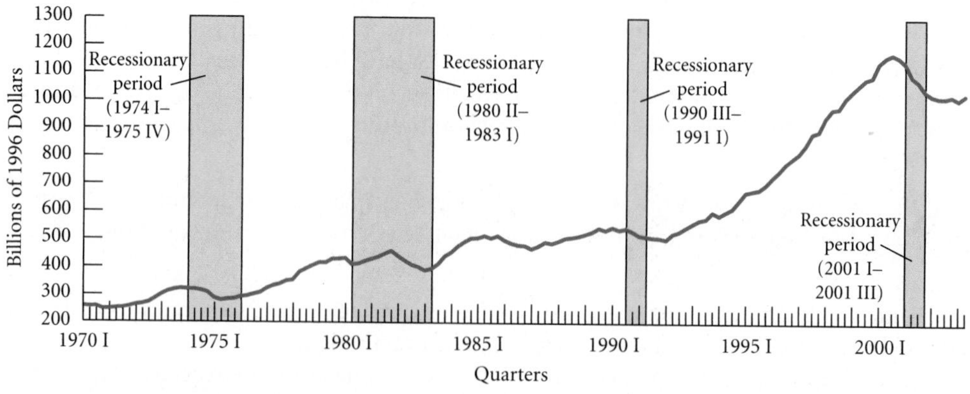

FIGURE 17.5 Plant and Equipment Investment of the Firm Sector, 1970 I–2003 II

Overall, plant and equipment investment declined in the four recessionary periods since 1970.

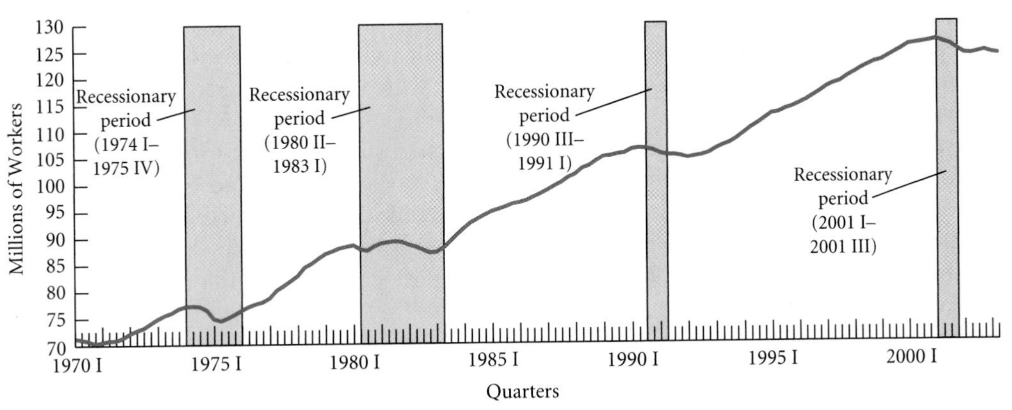

FIGURE 17.6 Employment in the Firm Sector, 1970 I–2003 II

Growth in employment was generally negative in the four recessions the U.S. economy has experienced since 1970.

Figure 17.5 also shows that investment fluctuates greatly. This is not surprising. The animal spirits of entrepreneurs are likely to be volatile, and if animal spirits affect investment, it follows that investment too will be volatile.

Despite the volatility of plant-and-equipment investment, however, it is still true that housing investment fluctuates more than plant-and-equipment investment (as you can see by comparing Figures 17.3 and 17.5). Plant-and-equipment investment is not the most volatile component of GDP.

Employment Employment in the firm sector is plotted in Figure 17.6, which shows that employment fell in all four recessionary periods. This is consistent with the theory that employment depends in part on output. Otherwise, employment has grown over time in response to the growing economy. Employment in the firm sector rose from 71.4 million in 1970 I to 124.9 million in 2003 II.

Inventory Investment Recall that *inventory investment* is the difference between the level of output and the level of sales. Recall also that some inventory investment is usually unplanned. This occurs when the actual level of sales is different from the expected level of sales.

Inventory investment of the firm sector is plotted in Figure 17.7. Also plotted in this figure is the ratio of the stock of inventories to the level of sales—the *inventory/sales ratio*. The

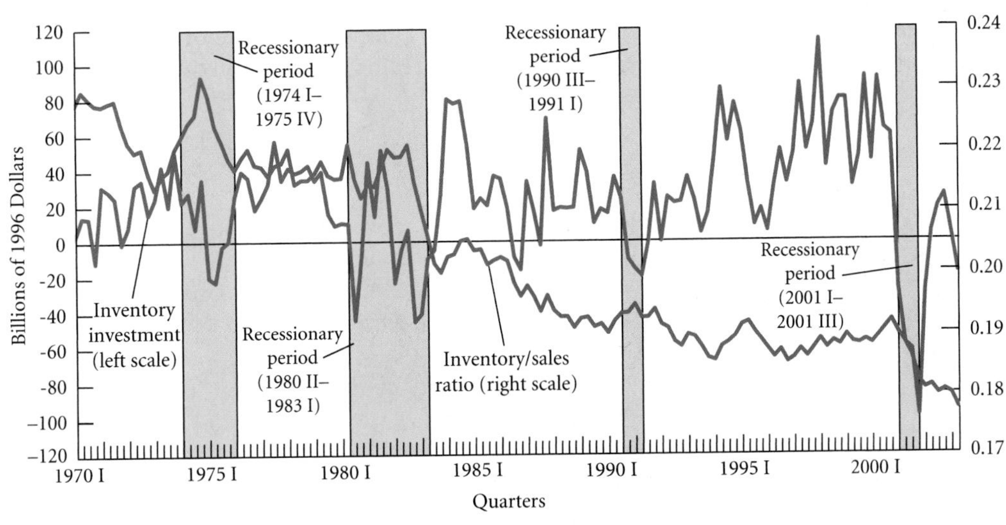

FIGURE 17.7 Inventory Investment of the Firm Sector and the Inventory/Sales Ratio, 1970 I–2003 II

The inventory/sales ratio is the ratio of the firm sector's stock of inventories to the level of sales. Inventory investment is very volatile.

figure shows that inventory investment is very volatile—more volatile than housing investment and plant-and-equipment investment. Some of this volatility is undoubtedly due to the unplanned component of inventory investment, which is likely to fluctuate greatly from one period to the next.

When the inventory/sales ratio is high, the actual stock of inventories is likely to be larger than the desired stock. In such a case, firms have overestimated demand and produced too much relative to sales, and they are likely to want to produce less in the future to draw down their stock. You can find several examples of this in Figure 17.7—the clearest occurred during the 1974–1975 period. At the end of 1974, the stock of inventories was very high relative to sales, which means that firms probably had undesired inventories at the end of 1974. In 1975, firms worked off these undesired inventories by producing less than they sold. Thus inventory investment was very low in 1975. The year 1975 is clearly a year in which output would have been higher had the stock of inventories at the beginning of the year not been so high. There was a huge fall in inventory investment in 2001.

On average the inventory/sales ratio has been declining over time, which suggests that firms are becoming more efficient in their management of inventory stocks. They are becoming more efficient in the sense of being able (other things equal) to hold smaller and smaller stocks of inventories relative to sales.

PRODUCTIVITY AND THE BUSINESS CYCLE

productivity, or **labor productivity** Output per worker hour; the amount of output produced by an average worker in 1 hour.

We can now use what we have just learned about firm behavior to analyze movements in productivity. **Productivity**, sometimes called **labor productivity**, is defined as output per worker hour. If output is Y and the number of hours worked in the economy is H, then productivity is Y/H. Simply stated, productivity measures how much output an average worker produces in 1 hour.

Productivity fluctuates over the business cycle, tending to rise during expansions and fall during contractions. The fact that firms at times hold excess labor explains why productivity fluctuates in the same direction as output.

Figure 17.8 shows the pattern of employment and output for a hypothetical economy over time. Employment does not fluctuate as much as output over the business cycle. It is precisely this pattern that leads to higher productivity during periods of high output and lower productivity during periods of low output. During expansions in the economy, output rises by a larger percentage than employment, and the ratio of output to workers rises. During downswings, output falls faster than employment and the ratio of output to workers falls.

The existence of excess labor when the economy is in a slump means productivity as measured by the ratio Y/H tends to fall at such times. Does this mean labor is in some sense "less productive" during recessions than before? Not really: It means only that firms choose

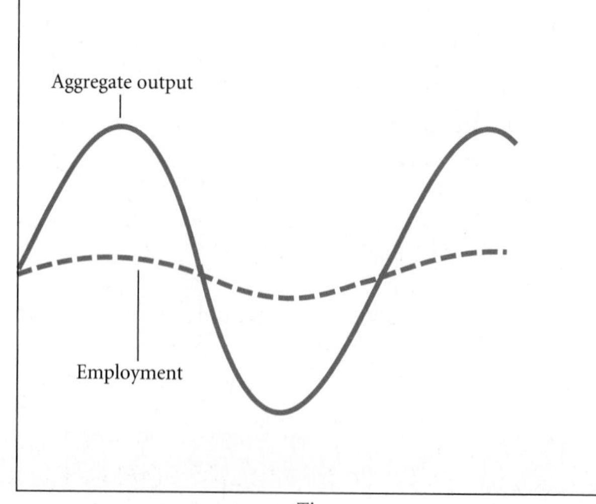

FIGURE 17.8 Employment and Output over the Business Cycle

In general, employment does not fluctuate as much as output over the business cycle. As a result, measured productivity (the output-to-labor ratio) tends to rise during expansionary periods and decline during contractionary periods.

to employ more labor than they need. For this reason, some workers are in effect idle some of the time, even though they are considered employed. They are not less productive in the sense of having less potential to produce output; they are merely not working part of the time that they are *counted* as working.

Productivity in the Long Run Theories of long-run economic behavior, which attempt to explain how and why economies grow over time, focus on productivity, usually measured in this case as *output per worker*, or its closely related measure, *GDP per capita*. Productivity defined this way is a key index of an economy's performance over the long run. For example, in comparing how the economies of the United States and Japan have performed over the past 90 years, we would probably begin by noting that although the United States had a substantially higher income per person in 1900, the two countries' incomes per person are now comparable. As we shall see in Chapter 18, the growth of output per worker depends on technological progress and on the growth of the capital stock, both of which have been more rapid in Japan than in the United States.

Productivity figures can be misleading when used to diagnose the health of the economy over the short run, because business cycles can distort the meaning of productivity measurements. Output per worker falls in recessions because firms hold excess labor during slumps. Output per worker rises in expansions because firms put the excess labor back to work. Neither of these conditions has anything to do with the economy's long-run potential to produce output.

THE RELATIONSHIP BETWEEN OUTPUT AND UNEMPLOYMENT

We can also use what we have learned about household and firm behavior to analyze the relationship between output and unemployment. When we discussed the connections between the *AS/AD* diagram and the Phillips Curve in Chapter 14, we mentioned that output (Y) and the unemployment rate (U) are inversely related. When output rises, the unemployment rate falls, and when output falls, the unemployment rate rises. At one time, it was believed that the relationship between the two variables was fairly stable. **Okun's Law** (after Arthur Okun, who first studied the relationship) stated that the unemployment rate decreased about 1 percentage point for every 3 percent increase in real GDP. As with the Phillips Curve, Okun's Law has not turned out to be a "law." The economy is far too complex for there to be such a simple and stable relationship between two macroeconomic variables.

Okun's Law The theory, put forth by Arthur Okun, that the unemployment rate decreases about 1 percentage point for every 3 percent increase in real GDP. Later research and data have shown that the relationship between output and unemployment is not as stable as Okun's "Law" predicts.

Although the relationship between output and the unemployment rate is not the simple relationship Okun believed, it is true that a 1 percent increase in output tends to correspond to a less than 1 percentage point decrease in the unemployment rate. In other words, there are a number of "slippages" between changes in output and changes in the unemployment rate.

The first slippage is between the change in output and the change in the number of jobs in the economy. When output increases by 1 percent, the number of jobs does not tend to rise by 1 percent in the short run. There are two reasons for this. First, a firm is likely to meet some of the increase in output by increasing the number of hours worked per job. Instead of having the labor force work 40 hours per week, the firm may pay overtime and have the labor force work 42 hours per week. Second, if a firm is holding excess labor at the time of the output increase, at least part of the increase in output can come from putting the excess labor back to work. For both reasons, the number of jobs is likely to rise by a smaller percentage than the increase in output.

The second slippage is between the change in the number of *jobs* and the change in the *number of people employed*. If I have two jobs, I am counted twice in the job data but only once in the persons-employed data. Because some people have two jobs, there are more jobs than there are people employed. When the number of jobs increases, some of the new jobs are filled by people who already have one job (instead of by people who are unemployed). This means the increase in the number of people employed is less than the increase in the number of jobs. This is a slippage between output and the unemployment rate because the unemployment rate is calculated from data on the number of people employed, not the number of jobs.

The third slippage concerns the response of the labor force to an increase in output. Let E denote the number of people employed, let L denote the number of people in the labor force, and let u denote the unemployment rate. In these terms, the unemployment rate is:

$$u = 1 - E/L$$

The unemployment rate is one minus the employment rate, E/L.

discouraged-worker effect The decline in the measured unemployment rate that results when people who want to work but cannot find work grow discouraged and stop looking for jobs, dropping out of the ranks of the unemployed and the labor force.

When we discussed how the unemployment rate is measured in Chapter 7, we introduced the **discouraged-worker effect**. A discouraged worker is one who would like a job but has stopped looking for one because the prospects seem so bleak. When output increases, job prospects begin to look better, and some people who had stopped looking for work begin looking again. When they do, they are once again counted as part of the labor force. The labor force increases when output increases because discouraged workers are moving back into the labor force. This is another reason the unemployment rate does not fall as much as might be expected when output increases.

These three slippages show that the link from changes in output to changes in the unemployment rate is complicated. All three combine to make the change in the unemployment rate less than the percentage change in output in the short run. They also show that the relationship between changes in output and changes in the unemployment rate is not likely to be stable. The size of the first slippage, for example, depends on how much excess labor is being held at the time of the output increase, and the size of the third slippage depends on what else is affecting the labor force (like changes in real wage rates) at the time of the output increase.

The relationship between output and unemployment depends on the state of the economy at the time of the output change.

THE SIZE OF THE MULTIPLIER

We can finally bring together the material in this chapter and in previous chapters to consider the size of the multiplier. We mentioned in Chapter 8 that much of the analysis we would do after deriving the simple multiplier would have the effect of decreasing the size of the multiplier. We can now summarize why.

- First, there are *automatic stabilizers.* We saw in the Appendix to Chapter 9 that if taxes are not a fixed amount but instead depend on income (which is surely the case in practice), the size of the multiplier is decreased. When the economy expands and income increases, the amount of taxes collected increases. This acts to offset some of the expansion (thus a smaller multiplier). When the economy contracts and income decreases, the amount of taxes collected decreases. This helps to lessen the contraction. Some transfer payments also respond to the state of the economy and act as automatic stabilizers, lowering the value of the multiplier. Unemployment benefits are the best example of transfer payments that increase during contractions and decrease during expansions.
- Second, there is the *interest rate.* We saw in Chapter 12 that if government spending increases and the money supply remains unchanged, the interest rate increases, which decreases planned investment and aggregate output (income). This *crowding out* of planned investment decreases the value of the multiplier. As we saw in Chapter 16, increases in the interest rate also have a negative effect on consumption. Consumption is also crowded out in the same way that planned investment is, and this lowers the value of the multiplier even further.
- Third, there is the response of the *price level.* We saw in Chapter 13 that some of the effect of an expansionary policy is to increase the price level. The multiplier is smaller because of this price response. The multiplier is particularly small when the economy is on the steep part of the *AS* curve, where most of the effect of an expansionary policy is to increase prices.
- Fourth, there are *excess capital* and *excess labor.* If firms are holding excess labor and capital, then part of any output increase can come from putting the excess labor and capital

back to work instead of increasing employment and investment. This lowers the value of the multiplier because (1) investment increases less than it would have if there were no excess capital, and (2) consumption increases less than it would have if employment (and thus household income) had increased more.

- Fifth, there are *inventories.* Part of any initial increase in sales can come from drawing down inventories instead of increasing output. To the extent that firms draw down their inventories in the short run, the value of the multiplier is lower because output does not respond as quickly to demand changes.
- Sixth, there are people's *expectations* about the future. People look ahead, and they respond less to temporary changes than to permanent changes. The multiplier effects for policy changes perceived to be temporary are smaller than those for policy changes perceived to be permanent.

The Size of the Multiplier in Practice In practice, the multiplier probably has a value of around 1.4. Its size also depends on how long ago the spending increase began. For example, in the first quarter of an increase in government spending, the multiplier is only about 1.1. If government spending rises by $1 billion, then GDP increases by only about $1.1 billion during the first quarter. In the second quarter, the multiplier rises to about 1.3. The multiplier then rises to its peak of about 1.4 in the third or fourth quarter.

One of the main points to remember here is that if the government is contemplating a monetary or fiscal policy change, the response of the economy to the change is not likely to be large and quick. It takes time for the full effects to be felt, and in the final analysis the effects are much smaller than the simple multiplier we discussed in Chapter 8 would lead one to believe.

A good way to review much of the material since Chapter 8 is to make sure that you clearly understand how the value of the multiplier is affected by each of the additions to the simple model in Chapter 8. We have come a long way since then, and this review may help you to put all the pieces together.

SUMMARY

HOUSEHOLDS: CONSUMPTION AND LABOR SUPPLY DECISIONS

1. The Keynesian theory of consumption holds that household consumption (*C*) is positively related to current income: The more income you have, the more you are likely to consume. Keynes also believed high-income households consume a smaller proportion of their income than low-income households. The proportion of income households spend on consumption is measured by the *average propensity to consume* (*APC*), which is equal to consumption divided by income (*C/Y*).
2. The *life-cycle theory of consumption* says households make lifetime consumption decisions based on their expectations of lifetime income. Generally, households consume an amount less than their incomes during their prime working years and an amount greater than their incomes during their early working years and after they have retired.
3. Households make consumption and labor supply decisions simultaneously. Consumption cannot be considered separately from labor supply, because it is precisely by selling your labor that you earn the income that makes consumption possible.
4. There is a trade-off between the goods and services that wage income will buy and leisure or other nonmarket activities. The wage rate is the key variable that determines how a household responds to this trade-off.
5. Changes in the wage rate have both an income effect and a substitution effect. The evidence suggests the substitution effect seems to dominate for most people, which means the aggregate labor supply responds positively to an increase in the wage rate.
6. Consumption increases when the wage rate increases.
7. The *nominal wage rate* is the wage rate in current dollars. The *real wage rate* is the amount the nominal wage can buy in terms of goods and services. Households look at expected future real wage rates as well as the current real wage rate in making their consumption and labor supply decisions.
8. Holding all else constant (including the stage in the life cycle), the more wealth a household has, the more it will consume, both now and in the future.
9. An unexpected increase in *nonlabor income* (any income received from sources other than working, such as inheritances, interest, and dividends) will have a positive effect on a household's consumption and will lead to a decrease in labor supply.
10. The interest rate also affects consumption, although the direction of the total effect depends on the relative sizes of the income and substitution effects. There is some evidence the income effect is larger now than it used to be, making monetary policy less effective than it used to be.
11. The government influences household behavior mainly through income tax rates and transfer payments. If the substitution effect dominates, an increase in tax rates lowers after-tax income, decreases consumption, and decreases the labor supply; a decrease in tax rates raises after-tax income, increases consumption, and increases labor supply. Increases in transfer payments increase consumption and decrease

labor supply; decreases in transfer payments decrease consumption and increase labor supply.

12. During times of unemployment, households' labor supply may be constrained. Households may wish to work a certain number of hours at current wage rates but may not be allowed to do so by firms. In this case, the level of income (at least workers' income) depends exclusively on the employment decisions made by firms. Households consume less if constrained from working.

FIRMS: INVESTMENT AND EMPLOYMENT DECISIONS

13. Firms purchase *inputs* and turn them into outputs. Each period, firms must decide how much capital and labor (two major inputs) to use in producing output. Firms can invest in plants and equipment or in inventory.

14. Because output can be produced using many different technologies, firms must make capital and labor decisions simultaneously. A *labor-intensive technique* uses a large amount of labor relative to capital. A *capital-intensive technique* uses a large amount of capital relative to labor. Which technology to use depends on the wage rate and the cost of capital.

15. Expectations affect investment and employment decisions. Keynes used *animal spirits of entrepreneurs* to refer to investors' feelings.

16. At any level of the interest rate, expectations are likely to be more optimistic and planned investment is likely to be higher when output is growing rapidly than when it is growing slowly or falling. The result is an *accelerator effect* that can cause the economy to expand more rapidly during an expansion and contract more quickly during a recession.

17. *Excess labor and capital* are labor and capital not needed to produce a firm's current level of output. Holding excess labor and capital may be more efficient than laying off workers or selling used equipment. The more excess capital a firm has, the less likely it is to invest in new capital in the future. The more excess labor it has, the less likely it is to hire new workers in the future.

18. Holding inventories is costly to a firm because they take up space and they tie up funds that could be earning interest. Not holding inventories can cause a firm to lose sales if demand increases. The *desired*, or *optimal, level of inventories* is the level at which the extra cost (in lost sales) from lowering inventories by a small amount is equal to the extra gain (in interest revenue and decreased storage costs).

19. An unexpected increase in inventories has a negative effect on future production, and an unexpected decrease in inventories has a positive effect on future production.

20. The level of a firm's planned production path depends on the level of its expected future sales path. If a firm's expectations of its future sales path decrease, the firm is likely to decrease the level of its planned production path, including its actual production in the current period.

PRODUCTIVITY AND THE BUSINESS CYCLE

21. *Productivity*, or *labor productivity*, is output per worker hour—the amount of output produced by an average worker in 1 hour. Productivity fluctuates over the business cycle, tending to rise during expansions and fall during contractions. That workers are less productive during contractions does not mean they have less potential to produce output; it means excess labor exists and workers are not working at their capacity.

THE RELATIONSHIP BETWEEN OUTPUT AND UNEMPLOYMENT

22. There is a negative relationship between output and unemployment: When output (Y) rises, the unemployment rate (U) falls, and when output falls, the unemployment rate rises. *Okun's Law* stated that the unemployment rate decreases about 1 percentage point for every 3 percent increase in GDP. Okun's Law is not a "law"—the economy is too complex for there to be a stable relationship between two macroeconomic variables. In general, the relationship between output and unemployment depends on the state of the economy at the time of the output change.

THE SIZE OF THE MULTIPLIER

23. There are several reasons why the actual value of the multiplier is smaller than the size that would be expected from the simple multiplier model: (1) Automatic stabilizers help to offset contractions or limit expansions. (2) When government spending increases, the increased interest rate crowds out planned investment and consumption spending. (3) Expansionary policies increase the price level. (4) Firms sometimes hold excess capital and excess labor. (5) Firms may meet increased demand by drawing down inventories instead of increasing output. (6) Households and firms change their behavior less when they expect changes to be temporary instead of permanent.

24. In practice, the size of the multiplier at its peak is about 1.4.

REVIEW TERMS AND CONCEPTS

accelerator effect, 327
adjustment costs, 328
animal spirits of entrepreneurs, 327
average propensity to consume (*APC*), 316
capital-intensive technology, 326
constrained supply of labor, 322
desired, or optimal, level of inventories, 329
discouraged-worker effect, 334
excess capital, 328
excess labor, 328
income effect of a wage rate increase, 318
inputs, 325
inventory investment, 325
labor-intensive technology, 326
life-cycle theory of consumption, 316
nominal wage rate, 318
nonlabor, or nonwage, income, 319
Okun's Law, 333
permanent income, 317
plant-and-equipment investment, 325
productivity, or labor productivity, 332
real wage rate, 318
substitution effect of a wage rate increase, 318
unconstrained supply of labor, 322

$$APC \equiv \frac{C}{Y}$$

PROBLEM SET

1. After declining for three consecutive quarters in 2001, real GDP in the United States rose 2.4 percent during 2002 and continued to rise right into 2003. Between the end of the recession in 2001 and the middle of 2003, the number of nonfarm payroll jobs as reported by the Bureau of Labor Statistics fell by more than 2 million. How is it possible for employment to be decreasing while real GDP is rising?

2. The year 2000 was an election year, and both candidates had their eyes on the economy. During that year, the Fed was attempting to slow things down with higher interest rates, and by mid-year, it was working. In July, employment fell by 430,000 and the number of unemployed went up by 67,000, but the unemployment rate stayed the same at 4 percent. How is it possible for employment to drop by that much without the unemployment rate going up? What happened to the size of the labor force in July (be specific)? What are some of the possible explanations for this?

3. During 2001–2003, the Federal Reserve Bank lowered interest rates in an effort to stimulate the U.S. economy's rate of growth.
   a. What direct effects do lower interest rates have on household and firm behavior?
   b. One of the consequences of lower interest rates was that the value of existing bonds (both corporate bonds and government bonds) rose by more than $2 trillion. Explain why lower interest rates would increase the value of existing fixed rate bonds held by the public.
   c. Some economists argue that the wealth effect of lower interest rates on consumption is as important as the direct effect of higher interest rates on investment. Explain what economists mean by "wealth effects on consumption" and illustrate with *AS/AD* curves.

4. In 1993, President Clinton proposed and Congress enacted an increase in taxes. One of the increases was in the income tax rate for higher income wage earners. Republicans claimed that reducing the rewards for working (the net after-tax wage rate), would lead to less work effort and a lower labor supply. Supporters of the tax increase replied that this criticism was baseless because it "ignored the income effect of the tax increase (net wage reduction)." Explain what these supporters meant.

5. Graph the following two consumption functions:
   $C = 300 + .5Y$
   $C = .5Y$
   a. For each function, calculate and graph the average propensity to consume (*APC*) when income is $100, $400, and $800.
   b. For each function, what happens to the *APC* as income rises?
   c. For each function, what is the relationship between the *APC* and the marginal propensity to consume?
   d. Under consumption function (1), a family with income of $50,000 consumes a smaller proportion of its income than a family with income of $20,000; yet if we take a dollar of income away from the rich family and give it to the poor family, total consumption by the two families does not change. Explain how this could be.

6. Throughout the late 1990s, the price of houses increased steadily around the country.
   a. What impact would you expect increases and decreases in home value to have on the consumption behavior of home owners? Explain.
   b. In what ways might events in the housing market have influenced the rest of the economy through their effects on consumption spending? Be specific.

*7. Adam Smith is 45 years old. He has assets (wealth) of $20,000 and has no debts or liabilities. He knows he will work for 20 more years and will live 5 years after that when he will earn nothing. His salary each year for the rest of his working career is $14,000. (There are no taxes.) He wants to distribute his consumption over the rest of his life in such a way that he consumes the same amount each year. He cannot consume in total more than his current wealth plus the sum of his income for the next 20 years. Assume the rate of interest is zero and Smith decides not to leave any inheritance to his children.
   a. How much will Adam consume this year, and next year? How did you arrive at your answer?
   b. Plot on a graph Adam's income, consumption, and wealth from the time he is 45 until he is 70 years old. What is the relationship between the annual increase in his wealth and his annual saving (income minus consumption)? In what year does Adam's wealth start to decline? Why? How much wealth does he have when he dies?
   c. Suppose Adam receives a tax rebate of $100 per year, so his income is $14,100 per year for the rest of his working career. By how much does his consumption increase this year, and next year?
   d. Now suppose Adam receives a 1-year-only tax refund of $100—his income this year is $14,100, but in all succeeding years his income is $14,000. What happens to his consumption this year? In succeeding years?

8. Explain why a household's consumption and labor supply decisions are interdependent. What impact does this interdependence have on the way in which consumption and income are related?

9. Why do expectations play such an important role in investment demand? How, if at all, does this explain why investment is so volatile?

10. How can a firm maintain a smooth production schedule even when sales are fluctuating? What are the benefits of a smooth production schedule? What are the costs?

*Note: Problems marked with an asterisk are more challenging.

Long-Run Growth

18

CHAPTER OUTLINE

The Growth Process: From Agriculture to Industry

The Sources of Economic Growth

An Increase in Labor Supply

Increases in Physical Capital

Increases in Human Capital

Increases in Productivity

Growth and Productivity in the United States

Sources of Growth in the U.S. Economy: 1929–1982

Labor Productivity: 1952 I–2003 II

Economic Growth and Public Policy

Suggested Public Policies

Growth Policy: A Long-Run Proposition

The Pros and Cons of Growth

The Progrowth Argument

The Antigrowth Argument

Summary: No Right Answer

Recall from Chapter 1 that **economic growth** occurs when an economy experiences an increase in total output. The increase in real output that began in the Western World with the Industrial Revolution and continues today has been so sustained and so rapid that economists refer to this as the period of **modern economic growth**. These three simple words describe the complex phenomenon that is the subject of this chapter.

It is through economic growth that living standards improve, but growth brings change. New things are produced, while others become obsolete. Some believe growth is the fundamental objective of a society, because it lifts people out of poverty and enhances the quality of their lives. Others say economic growth erodes traditional values and leads to exploitation, environmental destruction, and corruption.

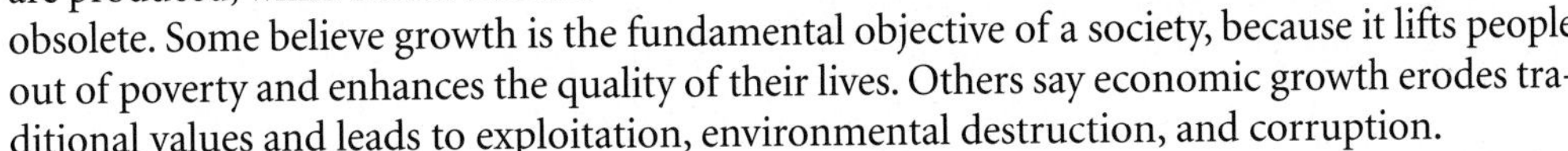

The first part of this chapter describes economic growth in some detail and identifies sources of economic growth. After a review of the U.S. economy's growth record since the nineteenth century, we examine the role of public policy in the growth process. We conclude with a review of the debate over the benefits and costs of growth.

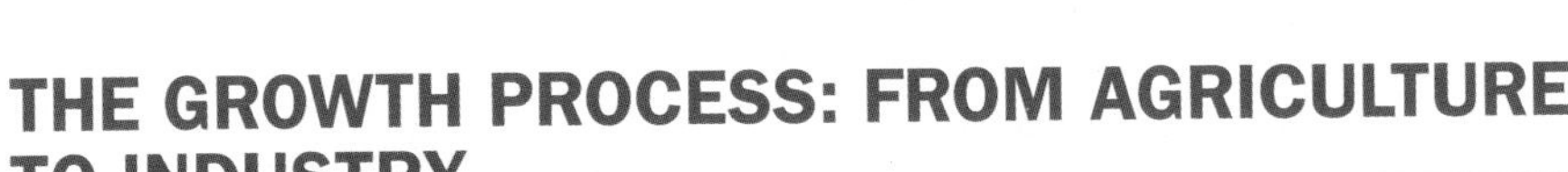

THE GROWTH PROCESS: FROM AGRICULTURE TO INDUSTRY

economic growth An increase in the total output of an economy. Defined by some economists as an increase of real GDP per capita.

modern economic growth The period of rapid and sustained increase in real output per capita that began in the Western World with the Industrial Revolution.

The easiest way to understand the growth process and to identify its causes is to think about a simple economy. Recall from Chapter 2, Colleen and Bill washed up on a deserted island. At first they had only a few simple tools and whatever human capital they brought with them to the island. They gathered nuts and berries and built a small cabin. Their "GDP" consisted of basic food and shelter.

Over time, things improved. The first year, they cleared some land and began to cultivate a few vegetables that they found growing on the island. They made some tools and dug a small reservoir to store rainwater. As their agricultural efforts became more efficient, they shifted their resources—their time—into building a larger, more comfortable home.

Colleen and Bill were accumulating capital in two forms. First, they built *physical capital*, material things used in the production of goods and services—a better house, tools, and a water system. Second, they acquired more *human capital*—knowledge, skills, and talents. Through trial and error, they learned about the island, its soil and its climate, what worked and what did not. Both kinds of capital made them more efficient and increased their productivity.

Because it took less time to produce the food they needed to survive, they could devote more energy to producing other things or to leisure.

At any given time, Colleen and Bill faced limits on what they could produce. These limits were imposed by the existing state of their technical knowledge and the resources at their disposal. Over time, they expanded their possibilities, developed new technologies, accumulated capital, and made their labor more productive. In Chapter 2 we defined a society's *production possibilities frontier* (*ppf*), which shows all possible combinations of output that can be produced given present technology and if all available resources are fully and efficiently employed. Economic growth expands those limits and shifts society's production possibilities frontier out to the right, as Figure 18.1 shows.

From Agriculture to Industry: The Industrial Revolution Before the Industrial Revolution in Great Britain, every society in the world was agrarian. Towns and cities existed here and there, but almost everyone lived in rural areas. People spent most of their time producing food and other basic subsistence goods. Then, beginning in England around 1750, technical change and capital accumulation increased productivity significantly in two important industries: agriculture and textiles. New and more efficient methods of farming were developed. New inventions and new machinery in spinning, weaving, and steel production meant that more could be produced with fewer resources. Just as new technology, capital equipment, and resulting higher productivity made it possible for Colleen and Bill to spend time working on other projects and new "products," the British turned from agricultural production to industrial production. In both cases, growth meant new products, more output, and wider choice.

There was one big difference. Colleen and Bill were fully in charge of their own lives. Peasants and workers in eighteenth-century England ended up with a very different set of choices. Those who would in the past have continued in subsistence farming could make a better living as urban workers. A rural agrarian society was very quickly transformed into an urban industrial society.

Growth in an Industrial Society The process of economic growth in an industrial society such as the United States is more complex but follows the same steps we have just described for growth in an agrarian society.

Consider the development of the electronic calculator. Prior to 1970, calculators that could add, subtract, multiply, and divide weighed 50 pounds, performed calculations slowly, and were expensive (a good calculator cost hundreds of dollars). Today, electronic calculators retail for as low as $3 or come free with a magazine subscription. Some are small enough to fit into a wristwatch.

During the past 25 years, the growth of computing technology has changed the way we live and do business. Access to the Internet is becoming cheaper and easier. Computers with

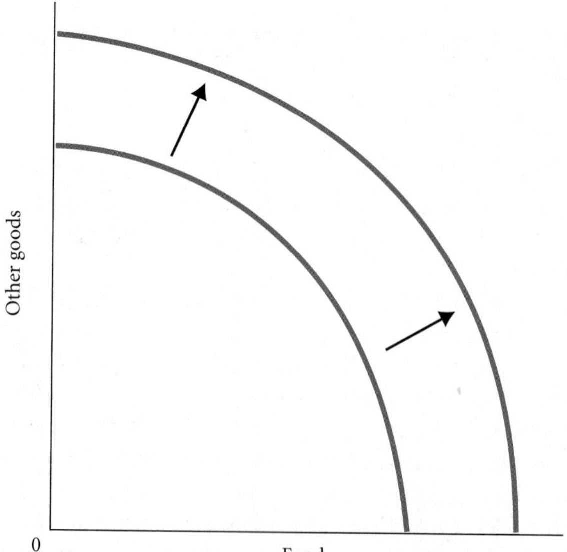

FIGURE 18.1 Economic Growth Shifts Society's Production Possibility Frontier Up and to the Right

The production possibility frontier shows all the combinations of output that can be produced if all society's scarce resources are fully and efficiently employed. Economic growth expands society's production possibilities, shifting the ppf up and to the right.

very fast processors and massive memory and storage capacity are selling for the price of small electronic calculators 35 years ago.

Technological change, innovation, and capital production (calculators, computers, and software) have increased productivity. If a diner spends less on accounting, its sandwiches will cost less. Sandwich buyers thus may go to see another movie or have another soda. The entertainment and soft drink sectors expand, and so on. That is economic growth.

THE SOURCES OF ECONOMIC GROWTH

Economic growth occurs when either (1) society acquires more resources, or (2) society discovers ways of using available resources more efficiently. For economic growth to increase living standards, the rate of growth must exceed the rate of population increase. Economic growth is generally defined as *an increase in real GDP per capita.*

As we discuss the factors that contribute to economic growth, it will be helpful to think of an **aggregate production function**. An individual firm's production function is a mathematical representation of the relationship between the firm's inputs and its output. Output for an aggregate production function is national output, or GDP. Stated simply, GDP (output) (Y), depends on the amount of labor (L) and the amount of capital (K) available in the economy (assuming the amount of land is fixed).[1]

aggregate production function The mathematical representation of the relationship between inputs and national output, or gross domestic product.

If you think of GDP as a function of both labor and capital, you can see that:

An increase in GDP can come about through:

1. An increase in the labor supply
2. An increase in physical or human capital
3. An increase in productivity (the amount of product produced by each unit of capital or labor)

AN INCREASE IN LABOR SUPPLY

Consider what would happen if another person joined Colleen and Bill on the island. That individual would join in the work and produce, and so GDP would rise. Suppose that a person who had not been a part of the labor force were to begin to work and use time and energy to produce pottery. Real output would rise in this case also. An increasing labor supply can generate more output.

Whether output *per capita* rises when the labor supply increases is another matter. If the capital stock remains fixed while labor increases, the new labor will likely be less productive than the old labor. This is called *diminishing returns,* and it worried Thomas Malthus, David Ricardo, and other early economists.

Malthus and Ricardo, who lived in England during the nineteenth century, were concerned that the fixed supply of land would lead to diminishing returns. With land in strictly limited supply, the ppf could be pushed out only so far as population increased. To increase agricultural output, people would be forced to farm less-productive land or to farm land more intensively. In either case, the returns to successive increases in population would diminish. Both Malthus and Ricardo predicted a gloomy future as population outstripped the land's capacity to produce. What both economists left out of their calculations was technological change and capital accumulation. New and better farming techniques have raised agricultural productivity so much that less than 3 percent of the U.S. population now provide enough food for the country's entire population.

Diminishing returns can also occur if a nation's capital stock grows more slowly than its workforce. Capital enhances workers' productivity. A person with a shovel digs a bigger hole than a person without one, and a person with a steam shovel outdoes them both. If a society's stock of plant and equipment does not grow and the technology of production does not change, additional workers will not be as productive, because they do not have machines to work with.

[1]All the numbers in the tables to follow were derived from the simple production function: $Y = 3 \times K^{1/3}L^{2/3}$.

TABLE 18.1 Economic Growth from an Increase in Labor—More Output but Diminishing Returns and Lower Labor Productivity

PERIOD	QUANTITY OF LABOR L (HOURS)	QUANTITY OF CAPITAL K (UNITS)	TOTAL OUTPUT Y (UNITS)	MEASURED LABOR PRODUCTIVITY Y/L
1	100	100	300	3.0
2	110	100	320	2.9
3	120	100	339	2.8
4	130	100	357	2.7

labor productivity Output per worker hour; the amount of output produced by an average worker in 1 hour.

Table 18.1 illustrates how growth in the labor force, without a corresponding increase in the capital stock or technological change, might lead to growth of output but declining productivity and a lower standard of living. As labor increases, output rises from 300 units in period 1 to 320 in period 2, to 339 in period 3, and so forth, but **labor productivity** (output per worker hour) falls. Output per worker hour, Y/L, is a measure of labor's productivity.

The fear that new workers entering the labor force will displace existing workers and generate unemployment has been with us for a long time. New workers can come from many places. They might be immigrants, young people looking for their first jobs, or older people entering the labor force for the first time. Between 1947 and 2002, the number of women in the labor force more than tripled, jumping from 17 million to 66 million. Table 18.2 shows that in the United States since World War II, the civilian noninstitutional population (those not in jails or mental institutions) over 16 years of age increased by 110.2 percent, while the labor force grew by 139.9 percent. The U.S. economy, however, has shown a remarkable ability to expand right along with the labor force. The number of persons employed jumped by 77.3 million—135.6 percent—during the same period.

As long as the economy and the capital stock are expanding rapidly enough, new entrants into the labor force do not displace other workers.

INCREASES IN PHYSICAL CAPITAL

An increase in the stock of capital can also increase output, even if it is not accompanied by an increase in the labor force. Physical capital both enhances the productivity of labor and provides valuable services directly.

It is easy to see how capital provides services directly. Consider what happened on Bill and Colleen's island. In the first few years, they built a house, putting many hours of work into it that could have gone into producing other things for immediate consumption. With the house for shelter, Colleen and Bill can spend time on other things. In the same way, cap-

TABLE 18.2 Employment, Labor Force, and Population Growth, 1947–2002

	CIVILIAN NONINSTITUTIONAL POPULATION OVER 16 YEARS OLD (MILLIONS)	CIVILIAN LABOR FORCE		EMPLOYMENT (MILLIONS)
		Number (Millions)	*Percentage of Population*	
1947	101.8	59.4	58.3	57.0
1960	117.3	69.6	59.3	65.8
1970	137.1	82.8	60.4	78.7
1980	167.7	106.9	63.7	99.3
1990	189.2	125.8	66.5	118.8
2002	214.0	142.5	66.6	134.3
Percentage change, 1947-2002	+110.2%	+139.9%		+135.6%
Annual rate	+1.4%	+1.6%		+1.6%

Source: Economic Report of the President, 2003, Table B-35.

TABLE 18.3 Economic Growth from an Increase in Capital—More Output, Diminishing Returns to Added Capital, Higher Measured Labor Productivity

PERIOD	QUANTITY OF LABOR L (HOURS)	QUANTITY OF CAPITAL K (UNITS)	TOTAL OUTPUT Y (UNITS)	MEASURED LABOR PRODUCTIVITY Y/L
1	100	100	300	3.0
2	100	110	310	3.1
3	100	120	319	3.2
4	100	130	327	3.3

Companion Website Plus

ital equipment produced in 1 year can add to the value of a product over many years. For example, we still derive use and value from bridges and tunnels built decades ago.

It is also easy to see how capital used in production enhances the productivity of labor. Computers enable us to do almost instantly tasks that once were impossible or might have taken years to complete. An airplane with a small crew can transport hundreds of people thousands of miles in a few hours. A bridge over a river at a critical location may save thousands of labor hours that would be spent transporting materials and people the long way around. It is precisely this yield in the form of future valuable services that provides both private and public investors with the incentive to devote resources to capital production.

Table 18.3 shows how an increase in capital without a corresponding increase in labor might increase output. Observe several things about these numbers. First, additional capital increases measured productivity; output per worker hour (Y/L) increases from 3.0 to 3.1, to 3.2, and finally to 3.3 as the quantity of capital (K) increases. Second, there are diminishing returns to capital. Increasing capital by 10 units first increases output by 10 units—from 300 in period 1 to 310 in period 2. However, the second increase of 10 units yields only 9 units of output, and the third increase yields only 8 units.

Table 18.4 shows the values of the private nonresidential capital stock in the United States since 1960. The increase in capital stock is the difference between gross investment and depreciation. (Remember, some capital becomes obsolete and some wears out every year.) Between 1960 and 2001, the stock of equipment has increased at a rate of 4.7 percent per year and the stock of structures has increased at a rate of 2.6 percent per year.

By comparing Tables 18.2 and 18.4, you can see that capital has been increasing faster than labor since 1960. In all economies experiencing modern economic growth, capital expands at a more rapid rate than labor. That is, the ratio of capital to labor (K/L) increases, and this too is a source of increasing productivity.

INCREASES IN HUMAN CAPITAL

Investment in human capital is another source of economic growth. People in good health are more productive than people in poor health; people with skills are more productive than people without them.

TABLE 18.4 Fixed Private Nonresidential Net Capital Stock, 1960–2001 (Billions of 1996 Dollars)

	EQUIPMENT	STRUCTURES
1960	672.7	2,015.7
1970	1,154.8	2,744.2
1980	1,989.8	3,589.1
1990	2,722.5	4,703.5
2001	4,480.0	5,682.5
Percentage change, 1960-2001	+566.0%	+181.9%
Annual rate	+4.7%	+2.6%

Source: Survey of Current Business, September 2002, Table 15, p. 37.

TABLE 18.5 Years of School Completed by People Over 25 Years Old, 1940–2001

	PERCENTAGE WITH LESS THAN 5 YEARS OF SCHOOL	PERCENTAGE WITH 4 YEARS OF HIGH SCHOOL OR MORE	PERCENTAGE WITH 4 YEARS OF COLLEGE OR MORE
1940	13.7	24.5	4.6
1950	11.1	34.3	6.2
1960	8.3	41.1	7.7
1970	5.5	52.3	10.7
1980	3.6	66.5	16.2
1990	NA	77.6	21.3
2000	NA	84.1	25.6

NA = not available.
Source: Statistical Abstract of the United States, 1990, Table 215; and 2002, Table 208.

Human capital can be produced in many ways. Individuals can invest in themselves by going to college or vocational training programs. Firms can invest in human capital through on-the-job training. The government invests in human capital with programs to improve health and to provide schooling and job training.

Table 18.5 shows that the level of educational attainment has risen significantly since 1940. The percentage of the population with at least 4 years of college rose from under 5 percent in 1940 to 25.6 percent in 2000. In 1940, less than 1 person in 4 had completed high school; in 2000, more than 8 in 10 had.

INCREASES IN PRODUCTIVITY

productivity of an input The amount of output produced per unit of an input.

Growth that cannot be explained by increases in the *quantity* of inputs can be explained only by an increase in the *productivity* of those inputs—each unit of input must be producing more output. The **productivity of an input** can be affected by factors including technological change, other advances in knowledge, and economies of scale.

Technological Change The Industrial Revolution was in part sparked by new technological developments. New techniques of spinning and weaving—the invention of the "mule" and the "spinning jenny," for example—were critical. The high-tech boom that swept the United States in the early 1980s was driven by the rapid development and dissemination of semiconductor technology.

invention An advance in knowledge.

innovation The use of new knowledge to produce a new product or to produce an existing product more efficiently.

Technological change affects productivity in two stages. First, there is an advance in knowledge, or an **invention.** However, knowledge by itself does nothing unless it is used. When new knowledge is used to produce a new product or to produce an existing product more efficiently, there is **innovation.**

Technological change cannot be measured directly. Some studies have presented data on "indicators" of the rate of technical change—the number of new patents, for example—but none are satisfactory. Still, we know technological changes that have improved productivity are all around us. Computer technology has revolutionized the office, hybrid seeds have increased the productivity of land, and more efficient and powerful aircraft have made air travel routine and inexpensive.

Other Advances in Knowledge Over and above invention and innovation, advances in other kinds of knowledge can also improve productivity. One is what we might call "managerial knowledge." For example, because of the very high cost of capital during the early 1980s, firms learned to manage their inventories much better. Many were able to keep production lines and distribution lines flowing with a much lower stock of inventories. Inventories are part of a firm's capital stock, and trimming them reduces costs and raises productivity. This is an example of a *capital-saving* innovation; many of the advances that we are used to thinking about, such as the introduction of robotics, are *labor-saving.*

In addition to managerial knowledge, improved personnel management techniques, accounting procedures, data management, and the like can also make production more efficient, reduce costs, and increase measured productivity.

Economies of Scale *External economies of scale* are cost savings that result from increases in the size of industries. The economies that accompany growth in size may arise from a variety of causes. For example, as firms in a growing industry build plants at new locations, they may lower transport costs. There may also be some economies of scale associated with research and development (R&D) spending and job-training programs.

Other Influences on Productivity In addition to technological change, other advances in knowledge, and economies of scale, other forces may affect productivity. During the 1970s and 1980s, the U.S. government required many firms to reduce the air and water pollution they were producing. These requirements diverted capital and labor from the production of measured output, therefore *reducing* measured productivity. Similarly, in recent years requirements imposed by the Occupational Safety and Health Act (OSHA) have required firms to protect workers better from accidental injuries and potential health problems. These laws also divert resources from measured output.

Negative effects such as these are more a problem of *measurement* than of truly declining productivity. The Environmental Protection Agency (EPA) regulates air and water quality because clean air and water presumably have a value to society. The resources diverted to produce that value are not wasted. A perfect measure of output produced that is of value to society would include environmental quality and good health.

The list of factors that can affect productivity is large. Weather can have a big impact on agricultural productivity. In the early 1990s, huge floods and massive crop losses occurred in the Midwest. Floods in California in 1995 had similar effects.

Having presented the major factors that influence productivity, we now turn to the growth record for the United States and how these factors have combined to produce a record of steady growth that has lasted over 100 years.

GROWTH AND PRODUCTIVITY IN THE UNITED STATES

Modern economic growth in the United States began in the middle of the nineteenth century. After the Civil War, railroads spread across the country and the economy took off. Table 18.6 shows the growth rate of real output in the United States for selected subperiods since 1871. Between 1871 and 1909, the growth rate was very strong—5.5 percent in the 1871–1889 period and 4.0 percent in the 1889–1909 period. The growth rate slowed to 2.8 percent in the 1909–1929 period and even further to 1.6 percent in the period that includes the Great Depression, 1929–1940. The growth rate was a strong 5.6 percent in the period that includes World War II, 1940–1950. It was then 3.5 percent in the 1950s, 4.2 percent in the 1960s, and 3.2 percent in the 1970s, 1980s, and 1990s.

TABLE 18.6 Growth of Real GDP in the United States, 1871–2000

PERIOD	AVERAGE GROWTH RATE PER YEAR	PERIOD	AVERAGE GROWTH RATE PER YEAR
1871–1889	5.5	1950–1960	3.5
1889–1909	4.0	1960–1970	4.2
1909–1929	2.8	1970–1980	3.2
1929–1940	1.6	1980–1990	3.2
1940–1950	5.6	1990–2000	3.2

Sources: Historical Statistics of the United States: Colonial Times to 1970, Tables F47–70, F98–124; U.S. Department of Commerce, Bureau of Economic Analysis.

TABLE 18.7 Growth of Real GDP in the United States and Other Countries, 1984–2002	
COUNTRY	**AVERAGE GROWTH RATE PER YEAR**
United States	3.2
Japan	2.3
Germany	2.2
France	2.1
Italy	2.0
United Kingdom	2.6
Canada	3.1
Africa	2.7
Asia (excluding Japan)	7.2

Source: Economic Report of the President, 2002, computed from Table B-112.

Table 18.7 compares the growth rate in the United States with the growth rates of other countries for the period 1984–2002. This period was a fairly slow time for Europe, and the U.S. growth rate exceeded the growth rates of the European countries by about 1 percentage point. The U.S. growth rate was also higher than the growth rates of Japan, Canada, and the African countries. The real winner over this period was Asia, where the average growth rate for the Asian countries (excluding Japan) was 7.2 percent.

SOURCES OF GROWTH IN THE U.S. ECONOMY: 1929–1982

For many years, Edward Denison of the Brookings Institution in Washington studied the growth process in the United States and sorted out the relative importance of the various causal factors. Table 18.8 presents some of his results.

Denison estimates that about half of U.S. growth in output over the entire period from 1929 to 1982 came from increases in factors of production and the other half from increases in productivity. Growth in the labor force accounted for about 20 percent of overall growth, while growth in capital stock (both human and physical) accounted for 33 percent. Of the capital stock growth figure, human capital (education and training) accounted for 19 percent of the total, and physical capital accounted for 14 percent. Growth of knowledge was the most important factor contributing to increases in the productivity of inputs.

The relative importance of these causes of growth varied considerably over the years. Between 1929 and 1948, for example, physical capital played a much smaller role than it did in other periods. Each period included times that were atypical for one reason or another. The period between 1929 and 1948 included the dislocations and uncertainties of the Great Depression and World War II. From 1948 to 1973, the economy enjoyed a period of unusual stability and expansion.

LABOR PRODUCTIVITY: 1952 I–2003 II

In Figure 7.1 in Chapter 7 we presented a plot of labor productivity for the 1952 I–2003 II period. It is now time to return to this figure, and it is repeated as Figure 18.2. Productivity in the figure is output per worker hour. Remember that the line segments are drawn to smooth out the short-run fluctuations in productivity. We saw in the last chapter that productivity as it is measured moves with the business cycle because firms tend to hold excess labor in recessions. We are not interested in business cycles in this chapter, and the line segments are a way of ignoring business cycle effects.

There was much talk in the late 1970s and early 1980s about the "productivity problem." Some economics textbooks published in the early 1980s had entire chapters discussing the decline in productivity that seemed to be taking place during the late 1970s. In January 1981, the Congressional Budget Office published a report, "The Productivity Problem: Alternatives for Action."

TABLE 18.8 Sources of Growth in the United States, 1929–1982

	Percent of Growth Attributable to Each Source			
	1929–1982	**1929–1948**	**1948–1973**	**1973–1979**
Increases in inputs	**53**	**49**	**45**	**94**
Labor	20	26	14	47
Capital	14	3	16	29
Education (human capital)	19	20	15	18
Increases in productivity	**47**	**51**	**55**	**6**
Advances in knowledge	31	30	39	8
Other factors[a]	16	21	16	−2
Annual growth rate in real national income	2.8	2.4	3.6	2.6

[a]Economies of scale, weather, pollution abatement, worker safety and health, crime, labor disputes, and so forth.
Source: Edward Denison, *Trends in American Economic Growth, 1929–1982* (Washington: Brookings Institution, 1985).

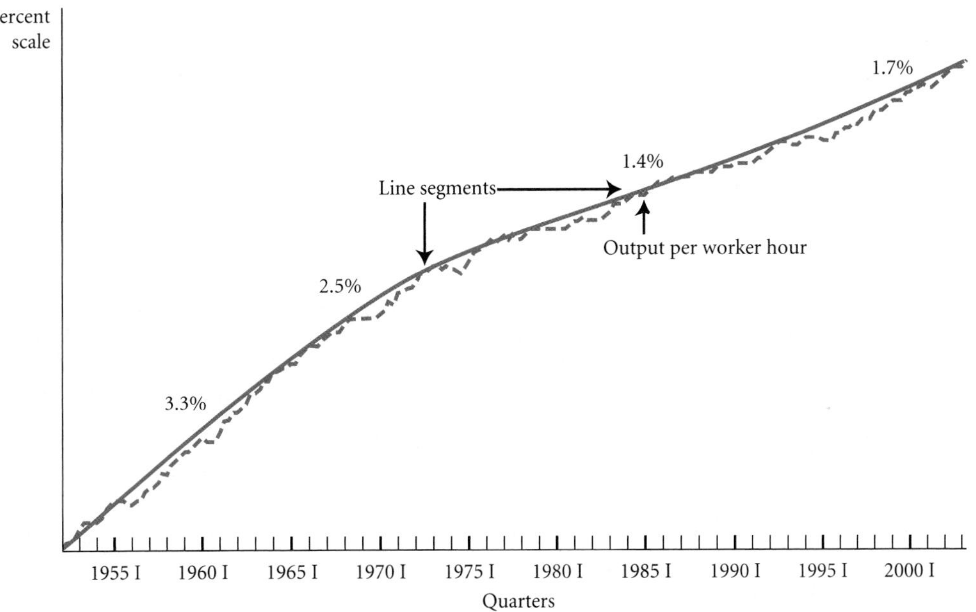

FIGURE 18.2 Output per Worker Hour (Productivity), 1952 I–2003 II

It is clear from Figure 18.2 that there was a slowdown in productivity growth in the 1970s. The growth rate went from 3.3 percent in the 1950s and first half of the 1960s to 2.5 percent in the last half of the 1960s and early 1970s and then to 1.4 percent from the early 1970s to the 1990s. Many explanations were offered at the time for the productivity slowdown of the late 1970s and early 1980s. Some economists pointed to the low rate of saving in the United States compared with other parts of the world. Others blamed increased environmental and government regulation of U.S. business. Still others argued that the country was not spending as much on R&D as it should be. Finally, some suggested that high energy costs in the 1970s led to investment designed to save energy instead of to enhance productivity. (We discuss how each of these factors influences growth later in this chapter.)

Many of these factors turned around in the 1980s and 1990s and yet, as you can see from Figure 18.2, productivity growth rose to only 1.7 percent in the 1990s. This early discussion is now quite dated. The interesting question as we move into the mid-2000s is how large an effect the Internet will have on productivity growth. Are we now in a new age, where long-run productivity growth will return to the rates of the 1950s and 1960s? Notice from Figure 18.2 that the actual growth rate of productivity between 1995 and 2000 was much larger than 1.6 percent (the growth along the 1990s line segment). The actual growth rate between the third quarter of 1995 and the second quarter of 2000 was 2.5 percent (on a per-year basis). Some have argued that this higher productivity growth is the beginning of the new age, the age of e-commerce, and so forth. However, others argue that the higher growth rate is just a cyclical phenomenon and that when actual productivity returns to the line segment (which it did in 2000), the growth rate of productivity will slow down to the rate that has existed since the early 1970s. The jury is still out on this one, so stay tuned. We need a few more years of data.

ECONOMIC GROWTH AND PUBLIC POLICY

The decline in productivity in the 1970s that caused so much concern led to a protracted national discussion about the role of government in stimulating economic growth. This debate was spurred in part by increasing concern in the United States that the United States was not doing as well as the Asian countries.

News Analysis

Productivity and Growth in the United States and Europe

THE FOLLOWING ARTICLE FROM THE *WALL STREET Journal* in June 2003 describes productivity advances in the United States, Germany, and the United Kingdom. The article discusses a number of ways that productivity can be increased, including tight or "lean management," new technology, and investment in human capital.

Manufacturers Say Productivity Rises in U.S., U.K., Germany

—Wall Street Journal

Manufacturers in the U.S., United Kingdom and Germany are reporting increases in productivity during 2002, although companies in the three nations defined productivity very differently, according to a new study.

TBM Consulting Group, a North Carolina firm, teamed with manufacturing magazines in the U.K. and Germany to conduct a joint survey of executives from a cross-section of companies in the three countries. The survey was conducted in April among a pool of more than 4,000 midsized to large manufacturing companies, with over 500 responses.

One of the major sources of labor productivity growth in all countries is additional capital per worker.

A majority of respondents—85% in the U.S., 83% in the U.K., and 68% in Germany—said their companies had seen productivity improvements in the past year.

"Companies do seem to be doing more with less in a very challenging economy," said Bill Schwartz, a senior partner at TBM and managing director of TBM's LeanSigma Institute. "They are being prudent, frugal and aggressive in understanding how to get more from the resources they need to manufacture their products."

The study found a marked difference between how German and U.S. manufacturers defined productivity. The U.S. executives primarily defined productivity as units per man-hour, while their German counterparts defined productivity as value added per employee. Using value added per employee as a measure of productivity allows companies to factor in profit margins after costs, making it a better indicator of the health of a company, said Mike Greece, a spokesman for TBM.

"We don't know if it's that the U.S. thinks if it gets down to the shop floor and focuses on the output of people, that will improve profits, or if the Germans truly do have a better understanding of how to figure productivity," Mr. Schwartz said.

The top-ranked source of productivity improvement in the U.S. was the continuous process improvement typical of so-called lean management, while German companies reported their top source of increase was technology.

Mr. Schwartz said the survey results indicate an eastward migration of the lean movement, which began in Japan more than a decade ago. Lean management is a business style that emphasizes reducing the amount of resources—materials, technology and workers—to produce a product. Companies in the U.S., and to a lesser extent in the U.K., began incorporating lean business principles years ago, but these changes have been slower to reach Germany.

"German manufacturers seem to have a technology bias and seem to rely on high-tech investments to improve productivity, whereas the U.S. has seen a tremendous return on investing in people," Mr. Schwartz said.

Source: Adapted from: Emily Anthes, "Manufacturers Say Productivity Rises in U.S., U.K., Germany," Wall Street Journal, *June 18, 2003. Reprinted by permission.*

Visit www.prenhall.com/casefair for updated articles and exercises.

SUGGESTED PUBLIC POLICIES

Several strategies for increasing the rate of growth in the United States have been suggested, and some have been enacted into law. These strategies include policies aimed toward improving the quality of education, increasing the saving rate, stimulating investment, increasing R&D, reducing regulation, and pursuing an industrial policy.

Policies to Improve the Quality of Education The Denison study shows that the contribution of education and training (human capital production) to growth in the United States has remained relatively constant at about 20 percent since 1929.

During the 1970s, public education was criticized. Teachers' salaries declined sharply in real terms, while property tax limitations and cuts in federal programs forced the curtailment of school budgets. In the last few years, battles have been waged in Congress over the

Further Exploration

Can We Really Measure Productivity Changes?

When the government publishes numbers on changes in productivity, most people take them as "true." Even though we don't really know much about how they are constructed, we assume they are the best measurements we can get.

Yet such data are often the source of controversy. Some have argued that the mix of products produced in the United States and the increased pace of technological change in recent years have made it increasingly difficult to measure productivity changes accurately. The observed productivity decline in recent decades may be measurement error.

These arguments make a certain amount of sense at an intuitive level. Even in agriculture, where it is relatively easy to measure productivity growth, the possibility of mismeasurement exists. The output of a soybean farm can be measured in bushels, and labor, capital, and land inputs present no serious measurement problems. So, over time, as farming techniques improved and farmers acquired new and better machinery, output per acre and output per worker rose and have continued to rise. But today we have biotechnology. Genetic engineering now makes it possible to make soybeans higher in protein and more disease resistant. Technology has improved and "output" has increased, but these increases do not show up in the data because of crude measures of output.

A similar problem exists with computers. If you simply counted the number of personal computers produced and measured the cost of the inputs used in their production, you would no doubt see some productivity advances. But computers being produced for under $1,000 in 1998 contained processors capable of performing tasks literally thousands of times faster than computers produced a few years earlier. If we were to measure computer outputs not in terms of units produced but in terms of the actual "services" they provide to users, we would find massive productivity advances. Most new PCs now contain CD-ROM slots and can be easily connected to the new and growing "information superhighway," a source of cheap and plentiful information. In short, the problem is that many of the products we now use are qualitatively different from the comparable products we used only a few years ago, and the standard measures of productivity miss much of these quality changes.

The problems are greater in the service sector, where output is extremely difficult to measure. It is easy to understand the problem if you think of what information technology has done for legal services. As recently as 10 years ago, a lawyer doing research to support a legal case might spend hundreds of hours looking through old cases and public documents. Today's lawyers can log on to a computer and in seconds do a key word search on a massive legal database. Such time- and labor-saving productivity advances are not counted in the official data.

One of the leading experts on technology and productivity estimates that we have reasonably good measures of output and productivity in only about 31 percent of the U.S. economy. Does this mean that productivity is not a problem? On this topic economists have agreed to disagree.[a]

[a]This argument was described most clearly by Professor Zvi Griliches of Harvard in his presidential address to the American Economic Association in January 1994. The full text, entitled "Productivity, R&D, and the Data Constraint," is published in the *American Economic Review*, March 1994. The counterargument is best advanced by Professor Dale Jorgenson in *Productivity* (Harvard University Press, 1995).

amount of federal dollars set aside for scholarships and loans to college students. Whatever the policies of the moment, however, all federal, state, and local expenditures on education acknowledge the need to build the nation's stock of human capital.

The Taxpayer Relief Act of 1997 contained provisions that focused on education. First, the HOPE Scholarship credit allows taxpayers to claim a credit up to $1,500 for postsecondary education expenses on behalf of any family member. Other provisions include a new Education Individual Retirement Account that allows savings to earn tax-free returns as long as the balance is used to pay educational expenses.

Policies to Increase the Saving Rate The amount of capital accumulation in an economy is ultimately constrained by its rate of saving. The more saving in an economy, the more funds are available for investment. Many people have argued that the tax system and the Social Security system in the United States are biased against saving. Some public finance economists favor shifting to a system of consumption taxation instead of income taxation to reduce the tax burden on saving.

Others claim the Social Security system, by providing guaranteed retirement incomes, reduces the incentive for people to save. Private pension plans make deposits to workers' accounts, the balances of which are invested in the stock market and bond market and are made available to firms for capital investment. Social Security benefits, in contrast, are paid out of current tax receipts, and no such accumulations are available for investment. Thus, the argument goes, if Social Security substitutes for private saving, the national saving rate is reduced. Evidence on the extent to which taxes and Social Security reduce the saving rate has not been clear to date.

A provision of the 1997 Taxpayer Relief Act allowed for new "backloaded" retirement accounts [the so-called Roth individual retirement accounts (IRAs)] to stimulate savings. Individuals can deposit up to $2,000 annually to specified retirement accounts that accumulate earnings without paying income tax. Withdrawals made after age $59\frac{1}{2}$ or for the purchase of a first home can be made tax free.

Policies to Stimulate Investment For the growth rate to increase, saving must be used to finance new investment. In an effort to revive a slowly growing economy in 1961, President Kennedy proposed and the Congress passed the *investment tax credit* (ITC). The ITC provided a tax reduction for firms that invest in new capital equipment. For most investments, the reduction took the form of a direct credit equal to 10 percent of the investment. A firm investing in a new computer system costing $100,000 would have its tax liability reduced by $10,000. The ITC was changed periodically over the years, and it was on the books until it was repealed in 1986. Many states have adopted ITCs against their state corporation taxes.

In 1982, the federal Economic Recovery Tax Act contained a number of provisions designed to encourage investment. Among them was the *Accelerated Cost Recovery System (ACRS)*, which gave firms the opportunity to reduce their taxes by using artificially rapid rates of depreciation for purposes of calculating taxable profits. While these rules were complicated, their effect was similar to the effect of the ITC. The government effectively reduced the cost of capital to firms that undertook investment in plant or equipment.

The Bush tax plan, which became law as the Jobs and Growth Tax Relief Reconciliation Act of 2003, was an attempt to stimulate both labor supply and investment. The centerpiece of the plan was a sharp reduction in the taxation of dividends and capital gains. While long-term capital gains have long been afforded special tax treatment, dividends have essentially always been treated as ordinary income. Under the 2003 act, both are taxed at a reduced rate of 15 percent. In addition, the act generally lowered tax rates for most taxpayers. The top rate, which was 39.6 percent just a few years ago, was reduced to 35 percent, effective in 2003.

Policies to Increase Research and Development As Table 18.8 shows, increases in knowledge accounted for 31 percent of total growth in the United States between 1929 and 1982. Although not shown in the table, during the years of high R&D expenditures, 1953 to 1973, the figure reached 40 percent. Research also shows that the rate of return on investment in R&D is quite high. Estimates place the rate of return at around 30 percent.[2]

It can be argued that new knowledge is like a public good. Although the United States has a patent system to protect the gains of R&D for inventors and innovators, many of the benefits flow to imitators and others, including the public. This logic has been used to justify public subsidization of R&D spending.

Reduced Regulations The Reagan and Bush administrations, and the Republicans' "Contract with America" in 1995, were committed to reducing government regulation, which many believe stands in the way of U.S. industry.

Critics of these policies say many regulations on the books serve legitimate economic purposes. For example, environmental regulations, if properly administered, improve efficiency. Judicious use of antitrust laws, which are designed to promote competition, can also improve the allocation of resources and stimulate investment and production.

Denison estimated that regulation of occupational health and safety, and of the environment, reduced the annual growth rate between 1973 and 1979 by 0.13 percentage points, from 2.74 percent to 2.61 percent per year. Has the value of the improved environment and increased safety been worth it?

Industrial Policy In the last few years, a number of economists have called for increased government involvement in the allocation of capital across manufacturing sectors, a practice known as **industrial policy**. Those who favor industrial policy believe that because governments of other countries are "targeting" industries for special subsidies and rapid investment, the United States should do likewise to avoid losing out in international competition. The Japanese Ministry of Trade and Industry, for example, picked the automobile industry very early on and decided to expand the automobile industry's role in world markets. The strategy succeeded very well; the Japanese auto industry has been remarkably successful.

industrial policy Government involvement in the allocation of capital across manufacturing sectors.

Critics of industrial policy argue that having the government too involved in the allocation of capital would be disastrous. Investment always involves risk, they believe, and the best

---

[2]See M. Nadiri, "Contributions and Determinants of Research and Development Expenditures in the U.S. Manufacturing Industries," in *Capital Efficiency and Growth*, George M. von Furstenberg, ed. (Cambridge, MA: Ballinger Press, 1980).

people to judge the extent and appropriateness of that risk are those making the investments and those actually involved in the industry.

GROWTH POLICY: A LONG-RUN PROPOSITION

When President Ford and Congress passed the dramatic tax cuts of 1975 to stimulate the economy and end the deep recession, the results were observable within a few months. Fiscal and monetary policies designed to counteract the cyclical up-and-down swings in the economy can produce measurable results in a short time.

However, the effects of policies designed to increase the rate of growth may not have observable effects for many years—they are by definition designed to mold the economy's long-run growth path. For example, a policy that succeeded in raising the rate of growth by 1 percentage point, for instance, from 2.5 percent to 3.5 percent, would be viewed by all as a tremendous success. Yet it would be almost a decade before such a policy would raise GDP by 10 percent.

The fact that progrowth policies can be costly in the short run and do not produce measurable results for a long time often pushes them far down on politicians' lists of priorities. Some economists who opposed the Tax Reform Act of 1986 argued that the elements of the tax code that had been favorable to capital investment and growth were cut for precisely these reasons. Defenders of the Tax Reform Act claim that it is indeed possible to oversubsidize investment and that the pre-1986 tax code had been doing just that.

Not everyone agrees that the top priority in a developed economy should be continued growth. We will see why as we close the chapter.

THE PROS AND CONS OF GROWTH

There are those who believe growth should be the primary objective of any society and those who believe the costs of growth are too great.

THE PROGROWTH ARGUMENT

Advocates of growth believe growth *is* progress. Resources in a market economy are used to produce what people want; if you produce something people do not want, you are out of business. Even in a centrally planned economy, resources are targeted to fulfill needs and wants. If a society is able to produce those things more efficiently and at less cost, how can that be bad?

By applying new technologies and better production methods, resources are freed to produce new and better products. For Colleen and Bill, accumulation of capital—a house, a water system, and so forth—and advancing knowledge were necessary to improve life on a formerly uninhabited island. In a modern industrial society, capital accumulation and new technology improve the quality of life.

One way to think about the benefits of growth is to compare two periods, for instance, 1950 and 1995. In 1995, real GDP per capita was more than twice what it was in 1950. This means incomes have grown twice as fast as prices so that we can buy that much more. (Remember, no one is telling anyone what to buy, and most people can spend much more now than they could then.)

Although things available in both periods are not exactly the same, growth has given us *more* choice, not less. Consider transportation. In the 1950s, the interstate highway system (social capital) had not been built. Driving from Chicago to New York took several days. We had automobiles, but the highway system did not compare with what we have today. Greater advances also have been made in air travel. Flying between the two cities was possible, but more costly, less comfortable, and slower in 1950 than it is today.

Do these changes improve the quality of life? Yes, they do, because they give us more freedom. We can travel more frequently. I can see my mother more often. I spend less time getting where I want to go so I can spend more time there. People are able to get to more places for less money.

What about consumer durables—dishwashers, microwave ovens, compact disc players, power lawn mowers, and so forth? Do they enhance the quality of life? If not, why do we buy them? In 1950, about 3 percent of all homes had dishwashers; today close to 50 percent have them. In 1950, fewer than 2 percent of all homes had air conditioners; today over 60 percent do.

What makes a dishwasher worthwhile? It saves the most valuable commodity—*time.* Many consumer durables have no intrinsic value—they do not provide satisfaction directly. They free us from tasks and chores that are not fun (no one likes to wash clothes or dishes). If a product allows us to perform these tasks more easily and quickly, it gives us more time for other things.

Think of the improvement in the *quality* of things that yield satisfaction directly. Record players in the 1950s reproduced sound imperfectly; high fidelity was just being developed, and stereo was in the future. Today you can get a compact disc player for your car, small "boxes" available at discount stores for under $30 reproduce sound far better than the best machines available in the early 1950s, and the range of tapes and compact discs available is extraordinary.

Growth also makes it possible to improve conditions for the less fortunate. The logic is simple: When there is more to go around, the sacrifice required to help the needy is smaller. With higher incomes, we can better afford the sacrifices needed to help the poor. Growth also produces jobs. When population growth is not accompanied by growth in output, unemployment and poverty increase.

Those in advanced societies can be complacent about growth, or critical of it, but leaders of developing countries understand its benefits. When 75 percent of a country's population is poor, redistributing existing incomes does not do much. The only hope for improvement in the long run is economic growth.

THE ANTIGROWTH ARGUMENT

Those who argue against economic growth generally make four major points:

1. Any measure of output measures only the value of things exchanged in the market. Many things that affect the quality of life are not traded in the market, and those things generally lose value when growth occurs.
2. For growth to occur, industry must cause consumers to develop new tastes and preferences. Therefore, we have no real need for many of the things we now consume. Wants are created, and consumers have become the servants, instead of the masters, of the economy.
3. The world has a finite quantity of resources, and rapid growth is consuming them at a rate that cannot continue. Because the available resources impose limits to growth, we should begin now to plan for the future, when growth will be impossible.
4. Growth requires that income be distributed unfairly.

Growth Has Negative Effects on the Quality of Life Perhaps the most significant "unmeasurable" changes that affect the quality of life occur in the early stages of growth when societies become industrialized. More is produced: Agricultural productivity is higher, more manufactured goods are available, and so forth. However, most people are crowded into cities, and their lives change drastically.

Before industrialization, most people in the Western World lived in small towns in the country. Most were poor, and they worked long hours to produce enough food to survive. After industrialization and urbanization in eighteenth-century England, men, women, and children worked long hours at routine jobs in hot, crowded factories. They were paid low wages and had very little control over their lives.

Even today, growth continues to change the quality of life in ways that are observable but not taken into account when we calculate growth rates. U.S. agriculture, for example, is becoming more productive every year. As productivity goes up, food prices drop, and fewer resources are needed in the agricultural sector. States in New England that once had thriving farms have found their climates and soils not good enough to compete anymore. In 1959, 56,000 farms covered 9.3 million acres in the six New England states; in 1998, fewer than 30,000 farms covered fewer than 5 million acres. The agricultural sector had been cut in half.

During the early 1970s, small family farmers all over the United States found that making a living was becoming nearly impossible. The villain was growth and progress. The cost was the decline of a lifestyle that many people want to maintain and that many others think of as an important part of America.

There are other consequences of growth that are not counted in the growth calculation. Perhaps the most significant is environmental damage. As the industrial engine is fed, waste is produced. Often, both the feeding and the waste cause massive environmental damage. A dramatic example is the surface, or strip, mining of coal that has ravaged many parts of the United States. Another is the uncontrolled harvesting of U.S. forests. Modern growth requires paper and wood products, and large areas of timber in many states have been cleared and never replanted.

The disposal of industrial wastes has not begun to keep pace with industrial growth. It is now clear that growing and prosperous chemical companies have for decades been dumping hazardous, often carcinogenic, waste products into the nation's soil and water. It is costing billions to clean them up. Those costs were never taken into account when the market was allocating resources to the growing chemical industry.

Growth-related problems are everywhere. Japan paid little attention to the environment during the early years of its rapid economic growth. Many of the results were disastrous. The best known of these results were the horrifying birth defects following the dumping of industrial mercury into the waters of Minamata Bay. In addition to birth defects, thousands of cases of "Minamata disease" in adults have been documented, and hundreds have died.

Growth Encourages the Creation of Artificial Needs The nature of preferences has been debated within the economics profession for many years. The orthodox view, which lies at the heart of modern welfare economics, is that preferences exist among consumers and that the economy's purpose is to serve those needs. According to the notion of **consumer sovereignty**, people are free to choose, and things that people do not want will not sell. The consumer rules.

consumer sovereignty The notion that people are free to choose, and that things that people do not want will not sell. "The customer rules."

The opposite view is that preferences are formed within the economic system. To continue growing, firms need a continuously expanding set of demands. To ensure that demand grows, firms create it by managing our minds and manipulating our behavior with elaborate advertising, fancy packaging, and other marketing techniques that persuade us to buy things for which we have no intrinsic need.

Growth Means the Rapid Depletion of a Finite Quantity of Resources In 1972, the Club of Rome, a group of "concerned citizens," contracted with a group at MIT to do a study entitled *The Limits to Growth.*[3] The book-length final report presented the results of computer simulations that assumed present growth rates of population, food, industrial output, and resource exhaustion. According to these data, sometime after the year 2000 the limits will be reached, and the entire world economy will come crashing down:

> Collapse occurs because of nonrenewable resource depletion. The industrial capital stock grows to a level that requires an enormous input of resources. In the very process of that growth, it depletes a large fraction of the resource reserves available. As resource prices rise and mines are depleted, more and more capital must be used for obtaining resources, leaving less to be invested for future growth. Finally, investment cannot keep up with depreciation and the industrial base collapses, taking with it the service and agricultural systems, which have become dependent on industrial inputs (such as fertilizers, pesticides, hospital laboratories, computers, and especially energy for mechanization. . . . Population finally decreases when the death rate is driven upward by the lack of food and health services.[4]

This argument is similar to one offered almost 200 years ago by Thomas Malthus, mentioned earlier in this chapter.

In the early 1970s, many thought that the Club of Rome's predictions had come true. It seemed the world was starting to run up against the limits of world energy supplies; the prices of energy products shot up, and there were serious shortages. In the years since, new reserves have been found, new sources of energy have been discovered and developed, and conservation measures have been tremendously successful (automobile gas mileage has

[3]Dennis L. Meadows et al., *The Limits to Growth* (Washington, DC: Potomac Associates, 1972).
[4]Dennis L. Meadows et al., *The Limits of Growth* (Washington, DC: Potomac Associates, 1972) pp. 131–132.

been pushed up to levels that were inconceivable 15 years ago). Energy prices have fallen to levels that in real terms are about the same as they were before the oil price shocks of the 1970s.

A variation of the depletion-of-resources argument stops short of predicting doomsday. It does point out that unchecked growth in the developed world may have undesirable distributional consequences. To fuel our growth, we are buying vast quantities of minerals and other resources from the developing countries, which have become dependent on the proceeds of those sales to buy food and other commodities on world markets. If this continues, by the time these countries have grown to the point that they need mineral resources, their resources may be gone.

Growth Requires an Unfair Income Distribution and Propagates it One cause of growth is capital accumulation. Capital investment requires saving, and saving comes mostly from the rich. The rich save more than the poor, and in the developing countries most people are poor and need to use whatever income they have for survival.

Critics also claim that the real beneficiaries of growth are the rich. Choices open to the "haves" in society are greatly enhanced, but the choices open to the "have-nots" remain severely limited. If the benefits of growth trickle down to the poor, why are there more homeless today than there were 20 years ago?

SUMMARY: NO RIGHT ANSWER

We have presented the arguments for and against economic growth in simple terms. In reality, even those who take extreme positions in this debate acknowledge there is no "right answer." To suggest that all economic growth is bad is wrong; to suggest that economic growth should run unchecked is equally wrong. The question is: How can we derive the benefits of growth and at the same time minimize its undesirable consequences?

Society must make some hard choices, and there are many trade-offs. For example, we can grow faster if we pay less attention to environmental concerns, but how much environmental damage should we accept to get how much economic growth? Many argue that we can achieve an acceptable level of economic growth *and* protect the environment at the same time. There is also a trade-off between growth and the distribution of income. More financial inequality would probably lead to more saving and ultimately to more capital and faster growth. Using taxes and income transfers to redistribute some of the benefits of growth to the poor probably does slow the rate of growth. However, it is not a question of all or nothing; society must decide how much inequality is desirable.

As long as these trade-offs exist, people will disagree. The debate in contemporary politics is largely about the costs and benefits of shifting more effort toward the goal of economic growth and away from environmental and social welfare goals.

SUMMARY

1. *Modern economic growth* is the period of rapid and sustained increase in real output per capita that began in the Western World with the Industrial Revolution.

THE GROWTH PROCESS: FROM AGRICULTURE TO INDUSTRY

2. All societies face limits imposed by the resources and technologies available to them. Economic growth expands these limits and shifts society's production possibilities frontier up and to the right.

THE SOURCES OF ECONOMIC GROWTH

3. If growth in output outpaces growth in population, and if the economic system is producing what people want, growth will increase the standard of living. Growth occurs when (1) society acquires more resources, or (2) society discovers ways of using available resources more efficiently.

4. An *aggregate production function* embodies the relationship between inputs—the labor force and the stock of capital—and total national output.

5. A number of factors contribute to *economic growth*: (1) an increase in the labor supply; (2) an increase in physical capital—plant and equipment—and/or human capital—education, training, and health; (3) an increase in productivity brought about by technological change; other advances in knowledge (managerial skills, etc.); and/or economies of scale.

GROWTH AND PRODUCTIVITY IN THE UNITED STATES

6. Modern economic growth in the United States dates to the middle of the nineteenth century. For the last 100 years, the nation's growth in real output has averaged about 3 percent per year. Between 1929 and 1982, about half of U.S. growth in output came from increases in factors of production and half from increases in productivity.

7. There has been much concern that the rate of growth of productivity in the United States is slowing. The growth rate of labor productivity decreased from about 3.3 percent in the 1950s and 1960s to about 1.7 percent in the 1990s.

ECONOMIC GROWTH AND PUBLIC POLICY

8. A number of public policies have been pursued with the aim of improving the growth of real output. These policies include efforts to improve the quality of education, to encourage saving, to stimulate investment, to increase research and development, and to reduce regulation. Some economists also argue for increased government involvement in the allocation of capital across manufacturing sectors, a practice known as *industrial policy*.

THE PROS AND CONS OF GROWTH

9. Advocates of growth argue that growth is progress. Growth gives us more freedom—meaning more choices. It saves time, improves the standard of living, and is the only way to improve conditions for the poor. Growth creates jobs and increases income simply because there is more to go around.

10. Those who argue against growth make four points. First, many things that affect the quality of life are not traded in the market, and these things generally lose value when there is growth. Second, to have growth, industry must cause consumers to develop new tastes and preferences for many things that they have no real need for. Third, the world has a finite quantity of resources, and rapid growth is eating them up at a rate that cannot continue. Fourth, growth requires that income be distributed inequitably.

REVIEW TERMS AND CONCEPTS

aggregate production function, 341
consumer sovereignty, 353
economic growth, 339
industrial policy, 350
innovation, 344
invention, 344
labor productivity, 342
modern economic growth, 339
productivity of an input, 344

PROBLEM SET

1. During the five years leading up to the recession of 2001, real GDP grew at a very fast pace. The expansion was led by business investment spending on the "new technology." Describe how spending on computer equipment, software, Web sites, and cell phones could have an impact on productivity and the rate of growth. After 2001, however, that sector collapsed, unemployment increased, and we went into a period of decline and very slow growth. Explain how overexpansion and overinvestment can lead to a period of economic decline.

2. Tables 1, 2, and 3 present some data on three hypothetical economies. Complete the tables by figuring the measured productivity of labor and the rate of output growth. What do the data tell you about the causes of economic growth? (*Hint*: How fast are *L* and *K* growing?)

TABLE 1

Period	L	K	Y	Y/L	Growth Rate of Output
1	1,052	3,065	4,506		
2	1,105	3,095	4,674		
3	1,160	3,126	4,842		
4	1,218	3,157	5,019		

TABLE 2

Period	L	K	Y	Y/L	Growth Rate of Output
1	1,052	3,065	4,506		
2	1,062	3,371	4,683		
3	1,073	3,709	4,866		
4	1,084	4,079	5,055		

TABLE 3

Period	L	K	Y	Y/L	Growth Rate of Output
1	1,052	3,065	4,506		
2	1,062	3,095	4,731		
3	1,073	3,126	4,967		
4	1,084	3,157	5,216		

3. Go to a recent issue of *The Economist* magazine. In the back of each issue is a section called "economic indicators." That section lists the most recent growth data for a substantial number of countries. Which countries around the world are growing the most rapidly according to the most recent data? Which countries around the world are growing more slowly? Flip through the stories in *The Economist* to see if there is any explanation for the pattern that you observe. Write a brief essay on current general economic conditions around the world.

4. One of the provisions of the Jobs and Growth Tax Act of 2003 was a reduction in the rate of income taxation on capital gains to 15 percent from 20 percent. The hope is that lower capital gains taxation will lead to a higher rate of growth. How might a lower rate of tax on capital gains affect household behavior, and firm behavior? In what ways are these changes in behavior likely or not likely to lead to more growth?

5. In earlier chapters, you learned that aggregate expenditure $(C + I + G)$ must equal aggregate output for the economy to be in equilibrium. You also saw that when consumption spending rises, $C + I + G$ increases, inventories fall, and aggregate output rises. Thus, policies that simultaneously increase consumer spending and reduce saving would lead to a higher level of GDP.

In this chapter, we have argued that a higher saving rate, even with lower consumption spending, is the key to long-run GDP growth. How can both arguments be correct?

6. Suppose you have just been elected to Congress and you find yourself on the Ways and Means Committee—the committee in the House that decides on tax matters. The committee is debating a bill that would make major changes in tax policy. First, the corporate tax would be lowered substantially in an effort to stimulate investment. The bill contains a 15 percent investment tax credit—firms would be able to reduce their taxes by 15 percent of the value of investment projects that they undertake. To keep revenues constant, the bill would impose a national sales tax that would raise the price of consumer goods and reduce consumption. What trade-offs do you see implied in this bill? What are the pros and cons? How would you vote?

7. If you wanted to measure productivity (output per worker) in the following sectors over time, how would you measure "output"? How easy is it to measure productivity in each of the sectors?
   a. Software
   b. Vegetable farming
   c. Education
   d. Airline transportation

8. Economists generally agree high budget deficits today will reduce the growth rate of the economy in the future. Why? Do the reasons for the high budget deficit matter? In other words, does it matter whether the deficit is caused by lower taxes, increased defense spending, more job-training programs, and so on?

9. Why can growth lead to a more unequal distribution of income? By assuming this is true, how is it possible for the poor to benefit from economic growth?

Visit www.prenhall.com/casefair for self-test quizzes, interactive graphing exercises, and news articles.

Debates in Macroeconomics: Monetarism, New Classical Theory, and Supply-Side Economics

19

CHAPTER OUTLINE

Throughout this book, we have noted that there are many disagreements and questions in macroeconomics. For example, economists disagree on whether the aggregate supply curve is vertical, either in the short run or in the long run. Some even doubt that the aggregate supply curve is a useful macroeconomic concept. There are different views on whether cyclical employment exists and, if it does, what causes it. Economists disagree about whether monetary and fiscal policies are effective at stabilizing the economy, and they support different views on the primary determinants of consumption and investment spending.

We discussed some of these disagreements in previous chapters, but only briefly. In this chapter, we discuss in more detail a number of alternative views of how the macroeconomy works.

KEYNESIAN ECONOMICS

John Maynard Keynes's *General Theory of Employment, Interest, and Money*, published in 1936, remains one of the most important works in economics. While a great deal of the material in the previous 10 chapters is drawn from modern research that postdates Keynes, much of it is built around a framework constructed by Keynes.

What exactly is *Keynesian economics*? In one sense, it is the foundation of all of macroeconomics. Keynes was the first to stress aggregate demand and links between the money market and the goods market. Keynes also stressed the possible problem of sticky wages. Virtually all the debates in this chapter can be understood in terms of the aggregate output/aggregate expenditure framework suggested by Keynes.

In recent years, the term *Keynesian* has been used narrowly. Keynes believed in an activist federal government. He believed the government had a role to play in fighting inflation and unemployment, and he believed monetary and fiscal policy should be used to manage the macroeconomy. This is why *Keynesian* is sometimes used to refer to economists who advocate active government intervention in the macroeconomy.

During the 1970s and 1980s, it became clear that managing the macroeconomy was more easily accomplished on paper than in practice. The inflation problems of the 1970s and early 1980s and the seriousness of the recessions of 1974 to 1975 and 1980 to 1982 led many economists to challenge the idea of active government intervention in the economy. Some were simple attacks on the bureaucracy's ability to act in a timely manner. Others were theoretical assaults that claimed to show that monetary and fiscal policy could have *no effect whatsoever* on the economy, even if it were efficiently managed.

Two major schools decidedly against government intervention have developed: monetarism and new classical economics.

MONETARISM

The debate between "monetarist" and "Keynesian" economics is complicated because they mean different things to different people. If we consider the main monetarist message to be that "money matters," then almost all economists would agree. In the aggregate supply/aggregate demand (*AS/AD*) story, for example, an increase in the money supply shifts the *AD* curve to the right, which leads to an increase in both aggregate output (*Y*) and the price level (*P*). Monetary policy thus has an effect on output and the price level. *Monetarism*, however, is usually considered to go beyond the notion that money matters.

THE VELOCITY OF MONEY

velocity of money The number of times a dollar bill changes hands, on average, during a year; the ratio of nominal *GDP* to the stock of money.

To understand monetarist reasoning, you must understand the **velocity of money**. Think of velocity as the number of times a dollar bill changes hands, on average, during a year.

Suppose on January 1 you buy a new ballpoint pen with a $5 bill. The owner of the stationery store does not spend your $5 right away. She may hold it until, say, May 1, when she uses it to buy a dozen doughnuts. The doughnut store owner does not spend the $5 he receives until July 1, when he uses it (along with other cash) to buy 100 gallons of oil. The oil distributor uses the bill to buy an engagement ring for his fiancée on September 1, but the $5 bill is not used again in the remaining 3 months of the year. Because this $5 bill has changed hands four times during the year, its velocity of circulation is four. A velocity of four means the $5 bill stays with each owner for an average of 3 months, or one quarter of a year.

In practice, we use gross domestic product (GDP), instead of the total value of all transactions in the economy, to measure velocity,[1] because GDP data are more available. The income velocity of money (*V*) is the ratio of nominal GDP to the stock of money (*M*):

$$V \equiv \frac{GDP}{M}$$

If $6 trillion worth of final goods and services are produced in a year and if the money stock is $1 trillion, then the velocity of money is $6 trillion ÷ $1 trillion, or 6.0.

We can expand this definition slightly by noting that nominal income (GDP) is equal to real output (income) (*Y*) times the overall price level (*P*):

$$GDP \equiv P \times Y$$

Through substitution:

$$V \equiv \frac{P \times Y}{M}$$

or

$$M \times V \equiv P \times Y$$

At this point, it is worth pausing to ask if our definition has provided us with any insights into the workings of the economy. The answer is no. Because we defined *V* as the

[1]Recall, GDP does not include transactions in intermediate goods (e.g., flour sold to a baker to be made into bread) or in existing assets (e.g., the sale of a used car). If these transactions are made using money, however, they do influence the number of times money changes hands during the course of a year. GDP is an imperfect measure of transactions to use in calculating the velocity of money.

ratio of GDP to the money supply, the statement $M \times V \equiv P \times Y$ is an identity—it is true by definition. It contains no more useful information than the statement "a bachelor is an unmarried man." The definition does not, for example, say anything about what will happen to $P \times Y$ when M changes. The final value of $P \times Y$ depends on what happens to V. If V falls when M increases, the product $M \times V$ could stay the same, in which case the change in M would have had no effect on nominal income. To give monetarism some economic content, we turn to a simple version of monetarism known as the **quantity theory of money**.

quantity theory of money The theory based on the identity $M \times V \equiv P \times Y$ and the assumption that the velocity of money (V) is constant (or virtually constant).

THE QUANTITY THEORY OF MONEY

The key assumption of the quantity theory of money is that the velocity of money is constant (or virtually constant) over time. If we let $\overline{V}$ denote the constant value of V, the equation for the quantity theory can be written:

$$M \times \overline{V} = P \times Y$$

Note the double equal sign has replaced the triple equal sign because the equation is no longer an identity. The equation is true if velocity is constant (and equal to $\overline{V}$), but not otherwise. If the equation is true, it provides an easy way to explain nominal GDP. Given M, which can be considered a policy variable set by the Federal Reserve (Fed), nominal GDP is just $M \times \overline{V}$. In this case, the effects of monetary policy are clear. Changes in M cause equal percentage changes in nominal GDP. For example, if the money supply doubles, nominal GDP also doubles. If the money supply remains unchanged, nominal GDP remains unchanged.

The key is whether the velocity of money is really constant. Early economists believed the velocity of money was determined largely by institutional considerations, such as how often people are paid and how the banking system clears transactions between banks. Because these factors change gradually, early economists believed velocity was essentially constant.

If there is equilibrium in the money market, then the quantity of money supplied is equal to the quantity of money demanded. That could mean M in the quantity-theory equation equals both the quantity of money supplied and the quantity of money demanded. If the quantity-theory equation is looked on as a demand-for-money equation, it says that the demand for money depends on nominal income (GDP, or $P \times Y$), but *not* on the interest rate.[2] If the interest rate changes and nominal income does not, the equation says that the quantity of money demanded will not change. This is contrary to the theory of the demand for money in Chapter 11, which had the demand for money depending on both income and the interest rate.

Testing the Quantity Theory of Money One way to test the validity of the quantity theory of money is to look at the demand for money using recent data on the U.S. economy. The key is: Does money demand depend on the interest rate? Most empirical work says yes. When demand-for-money equations are estimated (or "fit to the data"), the interest rate usually turns out to be a factor. The demand for money does not appear to depend only on nominal income.

Another way of testing the quantity theory is to plot velocity over time and see how it behaves. Figure 19.1 plots the velocity of money for the 1960 I–2003 II period. The data show that velocity is far from constant. There is a long-term trend—on average, velocity has been rising during these years—but fluctuations around this trend have also occurred, and some have been quite large. Velocity rose from 6.1 in 1980 III to 6.7 in 1981 III; fell to 6.3 in 1983 I; rose to 6.7 in 1984 III; and fell to 5.7 in 1986 IV. Changes of a few tenths of a point may seem small, but they are actually large. For example, the money supply in 1986 IV was $799 billion. If velocity changes by 0.3 with a money supply of this amount, and if the money supply is unchanged, we have a change in nominal GDP ($P \times Y$) of $240 billion (0.3 × $799 billion), which is about 5 percent of the level of GDP in 1986.

[2] In terms of the Appendix to Chapter 12, this means the *LM* curve is vertical.

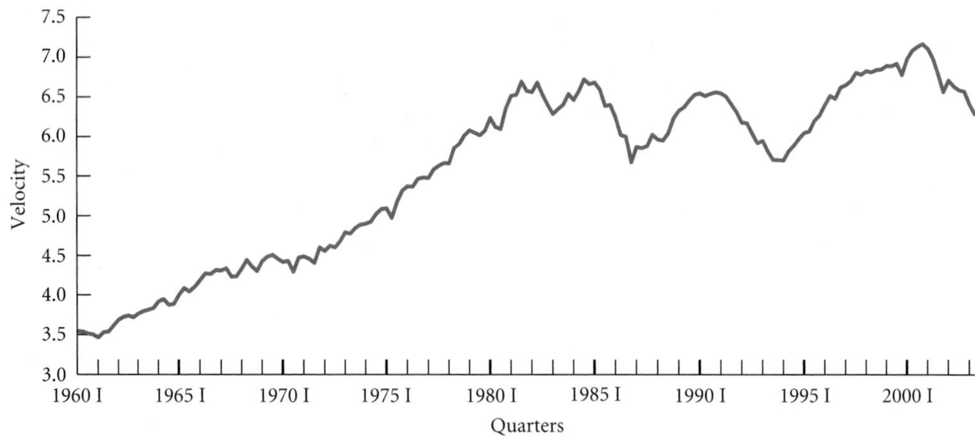

FIGURE 19.1 The Velocity of Money, 1960 I–2003 II

Velocity has not been constant over the period from 1960 to 2003. There is a long-term trend—velocity has been rising. There are also fluctuations, some of them quite large.

The debate over monetarist theories is more subtle than our discussion so far indicates. First, there are many definitions of the money supply. *M*1 is the money supply variable used for the graph in Figure 19.1, but there may be some other measure of the money supply that would lead to a smoother plot. For example, many people shifted their funds from checking account deposits to money market accounts when the latter became available in the late 1970s. Because GDP did not change as a result of this shift while *M*1 decreased, velocity—the ratio of GDP to *M*1—must have gone up. Suppose instead we measured the supply of money by *M*2 (which includes both checking accounts and money market accounts). In this case, the decrease in checking deposits would be exactly offset by the rise in money market account deposits, and *M*2 would not change. With no change in GDP and no change in *M*2, the velocity of money would not change. Whether velocity is constant or not may depend partly on how we measure the money supply.

Second, there may be a time lag between a change in the money supply and its effects on nominal GDP. Suppose we experience a 10 percent increase in the money supply today, but it takes 1 year for nominal GDP to increase by 10 percent. If we measured the ratio of today's money supply to today's GDP, it would seem that velocity had fallen by 10 percent. However, if we measured today's money supply against GDP 1 year from now, when the increase in the supply of money had its full effect on income, then velocity would have been constant.

The debate over the usefulness of monetarist theory is primarily empirical. It is a debate that can be resolved by looking at facts about the real world and seeing whether they are in accord with the predictions of theory. Is there a measure of the money supply and a choice of the time lag between a change in the money supply and its effects on nominal GDP such that *V* is in effect constant? If so, then the monetarist theory is a useful approach to understanding how the macroeconomy works. If not, then some other theory is likely to be more appropriate. (We discuss the testing of alternative theories at the end of this chapter.)

INFLATION AS A PURELY MONETARY PHENOMENON

So far we have talked only about nominal output ($P \times Y$). We have said nothing about how a monetarist would break down a change in nominal output (due to a money-supply change) into a change in *P* and a change in *Y*. Here again it is not possible to make a general statement about what all monetarists believe. Some may believe that all of the change occurs in *P*, and others may believe that at least sometimes some of the change occurs in *Y*. If all the change occurs in *P*, then there is a proportional relationship between changes in the money supply and changes in the price level. For example, a 10 percent change in *M* will lead to a 10 percent change in *P* if *Y* remains unchanged. In this case, inflation (an increase in *P*) is always a purely monetary phenomenon. The price level will not change if the money supply does not change. We will call this view, that changes in *M* affect only *P* and not *Y*, the "strict monetarist" view.

There is considerable disagreement as to whether the strict monetarist view is a good approximation of reality. For example, the strict view is not compatible with a nonvertical *AS* curve in the *AS/AD* model in Chapter 13. In the case of a nonvertical *AS* curve, an increase in *M*, which shifts the *AD* curve to the right, increases both *P* and *Y*. (You may want to review why.)

Almost all economists agree, however, that *sustained* inflation—inflation that continues over many periods—is a purely monetary phenomenon. In the context of the *AS/AD* framework, inflation cannot continue indefinitely unless the Fed "accommodates" it by increasing the money supply. Let us review this.

Consider a continuously increasing level of government spending (*G*) without any corresponding increase in taxes. The increases in *G* keep shifting the *AD* curve to the right, which leads to an increasing price level (*P*). (You may find it useful to draw a graph now.) With a fixed money supply, the increases in *P* lead to a higher and higher interest rate, but there is a limit to how far this can go. Because taxes are unchanged, the government must finance the increases in *G* by issuing bonds, and there is a limit to how many bonds the public is willing to hold regardless of how high the interest rate goes. At the point at which the public cannot be induced to hold any more bonds, the government will be unable to borrow any more to finance its expenditures. Only if the Fed is willing to increase the money supply (buy some of the government bonds) can the government spending (with its inflationary consequences) continue.

Inflation cannot continue indefinitely without increases in the money supply.

THE KEYNESIAN/MONETARIST DEBATE

The leading spokesman for monetarism over the last few decades has been Professor Milton Friedman, formerly of the University of Chicago and currently at the Hoover Institute in California. Most monetarists, including Friedman, blame most of the instability in the economy on the federal government, arguing that the inflation the United States encountered over the years could have been avoided if only the Fed had not expanded the money supply so rapidly.

Most monetarists do not advocate an activist monetary stabilization policy—expanding the money supply during bad times and slowing the growth of the money supply during good times. Monetarists tend to be skeptical of the government's ability to "manage" the macroeconomy. The most common argument against such management is the one expressed in Chapter 15: Time lags make it likely that conscious attempts to stimulate and contract the economy make the economy more, not less, unstable.

Friedman has for many years advocated a policy of steady and slow money growth—specifically, that the money supply should grow at a rate equal to the average growth of real output (income) (*Y*). That is, the Fed should pursue a constant policy that accommodates real growth but not inflation.

Keynesianism and monetarism are at odds with each other. Many Keynesians advocate the application of coordinated monetary and fiscal policy tools to reduce instability in the economy—to fight inflation and unemployment. However, not all Keynesians advocate an activist federal government. Some reject the strict monetarist position that changes in money only affect the price level in favor of the view that both monetary and fiscal policies make a difference and *at the same time* believe the best possible policy for government to pursue is basically noninterventionist.

Most Keynesians agree after the experience of the 1970s that monetary and fiscal tools are not finely calibrated. The notion that monetary and fiscal expansions and contractions can "fine-tune" the economy is gone forever. Still, many believe the experiences of the 1970s also show that stabilization policies can help prevent even bigger economic disasters. Had the government not cut taxes and expanded the money supply in 1975 and in 1982, they argue, the recessions of those years might have been significantly worse. The same people would argue that had the government not resisted the inflations of 1974 to 1975 and 1979 to 1981 with tight monetary policies, they would probably have become much worse.

News Analysis

Inflation and Money Supply Growth in Brazil: 2000

LATIN AMERICAN COUNTRIES HAVE BEEN NOTORIOUS over the years for financing public expenditure and interest payments on public debt with printed money. As recently as 1995, Brazil had inflation approaching 1,000 percent per year. Between 1995 and early 1999, inflation in Brazil fell to less than 10 percent, but an expansion early in 1999 resulted in prices rising at an accelerating rate along with real output. The central bank was very clear from the beginning that it would not accommodate inflation by expanding the money supply. With *Y* and *P* both rising, monetary restraint will lead to rising interest rates.

The following article from the *New York Times* describes the bank's strenuous efforts to resist accommodating inflation in early 2000.

International Business: Brazilians Grumble over Monetary Policy—*New York Times*

Many Brazilians are growing impatient with the austere monetary policy of the country's central bank, which left interest rates unchanged at 19 percent this week for the fifth time since September.

Under the guidance of its president, Arminio Fraga, the bank has managed to restore confidence in Brazil's currency, which was devalued a year ago. But the bank's efforts to contain inflation using interest rates that are among the highest in the world are increasingly viewed as radical medicine for an economy that has stagnated much of the last two years.

The growing irritation is perhaps made more acute because the economy is displaying its first signs of vitality since 1997. Gross domestic product rose 1.4 percent in the fourth quarter of last year, putting growth for 1999 at 0.8 percent, in sharp contrast to forecasts of a deep recession at the start of last year.

With such improving conditions, some analysts of the bank's policy are questioning whether it is prudent to remain so cautious at a time when the economy is positioned to grow.

Traditionally, the central bank has been subordinate to the finance minister and the president and has been used as a tool for political ambitions. Mr. Fraga's conservative policies are, in that sense, a break from the past. President Fernando Henrique Cardoso was re-elected to his second consecutive term only a year ago, has three years left in office and cannot run again, perhaps relieving pressure on the central bank.

The central bank does have its defenders. Albert Fishlow, an economist at the New York investment firm of Violy, Byorum & Partners, and a former thesis adviser of Pedro Malan when Mr. Malan, the finance minister, was a university student in California, said that today's high rates need to be put in perspective.

"Real interest rates, with inflation of 6 percent, are much lower than they were a year ago when the benchmark rate was above 40 percent and inflation was a lot lower," Mr. Fishlow said. "That means banks should already be channeling more capital into lending."

Still, even those who agree with the bank's recent stance say interest rates cannot remain so high if Brazil's economy is to enter into a period of sustained growth.

"Sure, there are inflationary demons that justify today's rates," said Roberto Macedo, an independent economic consultant. "But it is indecent, even disastrous, to talk of wanting stronger economic growth and improved distribution of income if rates are kept this high for much longer."[a]

Source: [a]*Simon Romero, "International Business: Brazilians Grumble over Monetary Policy,"* New York Times, *February 19, 2000. Reprinted by permission.*

Visit www.prenhall.com/casefair for updated articles and exercises.

Thirty years ago, the debate between Keynesians and monetarists was the central controversy in macroeconomics. That controversy, while still alive today, is no longer at the forefront. For the past two decades, the focus of current thinking in macroeconomics has been on the new classical macroeconomics.

NEW CLASSICAL MACROECONOMICS

The challenge to Keynesian and related theories has come from a school sometimes referred to as the *new classical macroeconomics.*[3] Like *monetarism* and *Keynesianism*, this term is vague. No two new classical macroeconomists think exactly alike, and no single model completely represents this school. The following discussion, however, conveys the flavor of the new classical views.

THE DEVELOPMENT OF NEW CLASSICAL MACROECONOMICS

New classical macroeconomics has developed from two different, though related, sources. These sources are the theoretical and the empirical critiques of existing, or traditional, macroeconomics.

On the theoretical level, there has been growing dissatisfaction with the way traditional models treat expectations. Keynes himself recognized that expectations (in the form of "ani-

[3]The term *new classical* is used because many of the assumptions and conclusions of this group of economists resemble those of the classical economists—that is, those who wrote before Keynes.

mal spirits") play a big part in economic behavior. The problem is, traditional models have assumed that expectations are formed in naive ways. A common assumption, for example, is that people form their expectations of future inflation by assuming present inflation will continue. If they turn out to be wrong, they adjust their expectations by some fraction of the difference between their original forecast and the actual inflation rate. Suppose I expect 10 percent inflation next year. When next year comes, the inflation rate turns out to be only 5 percent, so I have made an error of 5 percent. I might then predict an inflation rate for the following year of 7.5 percent, halfway between my earlier expectation (10 percent) and actual inflation last year (5 percent).

The problem with this treatment of expectations is that it is not consistent with the assumptions of microeconomics. It implies people systematically overlook information that would allow them to make better forecasts, even though there are costs to being wrong. If, as microeconomic theory assumes, people are out to maximize their satisfaction and firms are out to maximize their profits, they should form their expectations in a smarter way. Instead of naively assuming the future will be like the past, they should actively seek to forecast the future. Any other behavior is not in keeping with the microeconomic view of the forward-looking, rational people who compose households and firms.

On the empirical level, there was stagflation in the U.S. economy during the 1970s. Remember, stagflation is simultaneous high unemployment and rising prices. The Phillips Curve theory of the 1960s predicted that demand pressure pushes up prices, so that when demand is weak—in times of high unemployment, for example—prices should be stable (or perhaps even falling). The new classical theories were an attempt to explain the apparent breakdown in the 1970s of the simple inflation–unemployment trade-off predicted by the Phillips Curve. Just as the Great Depression of the 1930s motivated the development of Keynesian economics, so the stagflation of the 1970s helped motivate the formulation of new classical economics.

RATIONAL EXPECTATIONS

In previous chapters, we stressed households' and firms' expectations about the future. A firm's decision to build a new plant depends on its expectations of future sales. The amount of saving a household undertakes today depends on its expectations about future interest rates, wages, and prices.

How are expectations formed? Do people assume things will continue as they are at present (like predicting rain tomorrow because it is raining today)? What information do people use to make their guesses about the future? Questions like these have become central to current macroeconomic thinking and research. One theory, the **rational-expectations hypothesis**, offers a powerful way of thinking about expectations.

rational-expectations hypothesis The hypothesis that people know the "true model" of the economy and that they use this model to form their expectations of the future.

Suppose we want to forecast inflation. What does it mean to say that my expectations of inflation are "rational"? The rational-expectations hypothesis assumes people know the "true model" that generates inflation—they know how inflation is determined in the economy—and they use this model to forecast future inflation rates. If there were no random, unpredictable events in the economy, and if people knew the true model generating inflation, their forecasts of future inflation rates would be perfect. Because it is true, the model would not permit mistakes, and thus the people using it would not make mistakes.

However, many events that affect the inflation rate are not predictable—they are random. By "true" model, we mean a model that is *on average* correct in forecasting inflation. Sometimes the random events have a positive effect on inflation, which means the model underestimates the inflation rate, and sometimes they have a negative effect, which means the model overestimates the inflation rate. On average, the model is correct. Therefore, rational expectations are correct on average, even though their predictions are not exactly right all the time.

To see this, suppose you have to forecast how many times a fair coin will come up heads out of 100 tosses. The true model in this case is that the coin has a 50–50 chance of coming up heads on any one toss. Because the outcome of the 100 tosses is random, you cannot be sure of guessing correctly. If you know the true model—that the coin is fair—your rational expectation of the outcome of 100 tosses is 50 heads. You are not likely to be exactly right—the actual number of heads is likely to be slightly higher or slightly lower than 50—but *on average* you will be correct.

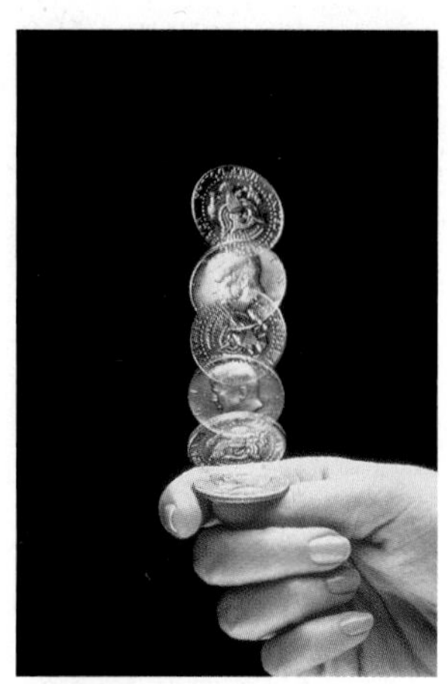

Even though uncertainty exists, if you know the "model" generating the uncertainty, it is possible to have expectations about the future that are "on average" correct. You do not know whether a random coin toss will come up heads or tails. You do know that if you toss a fair coin 1,000 times, it will come up heads about 500 times.

Sometimes people are said to have rational expectations if they use "all available information" in forming their expectations. This definition is vague, because it is not always clear what "all available information" means. The definition is precise, if by "all available information" we mean that people know and use the true model. We cannot have more or better information than the true model.

If information can be obtained at no cost, then people are not behaving rationally if they fail to use all available information. Because there are almost always costs to making a wrong forecast, it is not rational to overlook information that could help improve the accuracy of a forecast as long as the costs of acquiring that information do not outweigh the benefits of improving its accuracy.

Rational Expectations and Market Clearing If firms have rational expectations and if they set prices and wages on this basis, then, on average, prices and wages will be set at levels that ensure equilibrium in the goods and labor markets. When a firm has rational expectations, it knows the demand curve for its output and the supply curve of labor that it faces, except when random shocks disrupt those curves. Therefore, on average the firm will set the market-clearing prices and wages. The firm knows the true model, and it will not set wages different from those it expects will attract the number of workers it wants. If all firms behave this way, then wages will be set in such a way that the total amount of labor supplied will, on average, be equal to the total amount of labor that firms demand. In other words, on average there will be no unemployment.

In Chapter 14, we argued that there might be disequilibrium in the labor market (either in the form of unemployment or in excess demand for workers) because firms may make mistakes in their wage-setting behavior due to expectation errors. If, on average, firms do not make errors, then, on average, there is equilibrium. When expectations are rational, disequilibrium exists only temporarily as a result of random, unpredictable shocks—obviously an important conclusion. If true, it means disequilibrium in any market is only temporary, because firms, on average, set market-clearing wages and prices.

The assumption that expectations are rational radically changes the way we can view the economy. We go from a world in which unemployment can exist for substantial periods and the multiplier can operate to a world in which (on average) all markets clear and there is full employment. In this world there is no need for government stabilization policies. Unemployment is not a problem that governments need to worry about; if it exists at all, it is because of unpredictable shocks that, on average, amount to zero. There is no more reason for the government to try to change the outcome in the labor market than there is for it to change the outcome in the banana market. On average, prices and wages are set at market-clearing levels.

THE LUCAS SUPPLY FUNCTION

Lucas supply function The supply function embodies the idea that output (Y) depends on the difference between the actual price level and the expected price level.

The **Lucas supply function**, after Robert E. Lucas of the University of Chicago, is an important part of a number of new classical macroeconomic theories. It yields, as we shall see, a surprising policy conclusion. The function is deceptively simple. It says real output (Y) depends on (is a function of) the difference between the actual price level (P) and the expected price level (P^e):

$$Y = f(P - P^e)$$

price surprise Actual price level minus expected price level.

The actual price level minus the expected price level ($P - P^e$) is the **price surprise.** Before considering the policy implications of this function, we should look at the theory behind it.

Lucas begins by assuming people and firms are specialists in production but generalists in consumption. If someone you know is a manual laborer, the chances are she sells only one thing—labor. If she is a lawyer, she sells only legal services. In contrast, people buy a large bundle of goods—ranging from gasoline to ice cream and pretzels—on a regular basis. The same is true for firms. Most companies tend to concentrate on producing a small range of products, but they typically buy a larger range of inputs—raw materials, labor, energy, and capital. According to Lucas, this divergence between buying and selling creates an asymmetry. People know much more about the prices of the things they sell than they do about the prices of the things they buy.[4]

[4]It is not entirely obvious why this should be true, and some critics of the new classical school have argued that this is unrealistic. Some have also criticized the Lucas supply function as too simple, arguing that other things besides price surprises affect aggregate output.

At the beginning of each period, a firm has some expectation of the average price level for that period. If the actual price level turns out to be different, there is a price surprise. Suppose the average price level is higher than expected. Because the firm learns about the actual price level slowly, some time goes by before it realizes all prices have gone up. The firm *does* learn *quickly* that the price of its *output* has gone up. The firm perceives—incorrectly, it turns out—that its price has risen relative to other prices, and this leads it to produce more output.

A similar argument holds for workers. When there is a positive price surprise, workers at first believe their "price"—their wage rate—has increased relative to other prices. Workers believe their real wage rate has risen. We know from theory that an increase in the real wage is likely to encourage workers to work more hours.[5] The real wage has not actually risen, but it takes workers a while to figure this out. In the meantime, they supply more hours of work than they would have. This means the economy will produce more output when prices are unexpectedly higher than when prices are at their expected level.

This is the rationale for the Lucas supply function. Unexpected increases in the price level can fool workers and firms into thinking relative prices have changed, causing them to alter the amount of labor or goods they choose to supply.

Policy Implications of the Lucas Supply Function The Lucas supply function in combination with the assumption that expectations are rational implies that anticipated policy changes have no effect on real output. Consider a change in monetary policy. In general, the change will have some effect on the average price level. If the policy change is announced to the public, then people know what the effect on the price level will be, because they have rational expectations (and know the way changes in monetary policy affect the price level). This means the change in monetary policy affects both the actual price level and the expected price level in the same way. The new price level minus the new expected price level is zero—no price surprise. In such a case, there will be no change in real output, because the Lucas supply function states that real output can change from its fixed level only if there is a price surprise.

The general conclusion is that *any* announced policy change—in fiscal policy or any other policy—has no effect on real output, because the policy change affects both actual and expected price levels in the same way. If people have rational expectations, known policy changes can produce no price surprises—and no increases in real output. The only way any change in government policy can affect real output is if it is kept in the dark so it is not generally known. Government policy can affect real output only if it surprises people; otherwise, it cannot. Rational-expectations theory combined with the Lucas supply function proposes a very small role for government policy in the economy.

EVALUATING RATIONAL-EXPECTATIONS THEORY

What are we to make of all this? It should be clear that the key question concerning the new classical macroeconomics is how realistic is the assumption of rational expectations. If it approximates the way expectations are actually formed, then it calls into question any theory that relies at least in part on expectation errors for the existence of disequilibrium. The arguments in favor of the rational-expectations assumption sound persuasive from the perspective of microeconomic theory. If expectations are not rational, there are likely to be unexploited profit opportunities—most economists believe such opportunities are rare and short-lived.

The argument *against* rational expectations is that it requires households and firms to know too much. This argument says it is unrealistic to think these basic decision-making units know as much as they need to know to form rational expectations. People must know the true model (or at least a good approximation of the true model) to form rational expectations, and this is a lot to expect. Even if firms and households are capable of learning the true model, it may be costly to take the time and gather the relevant information to learn it. The gain from learning the true model (or a good approximation of it) may not be worth the cost. In this sense, there may not be unexploited profit opportunities around. Gathering

[5]This is true if we assume that the substitution effect dominates the income effect (see Chapter 17).

information and learning economic models may be too costly to bother with, given the expected gain from improving forecasts.

Although the assumption that expectations are rational seems consistent with the satisfaction-maximizing and profit-maximizing postulates of microeconomics, the rational-expectations assumption is more extreme and demanding because it requires more information on the part of households and firms. Consider a firm engaged in maximizing profits. In some way or other, it forms expectations of the relevant future variables, and given these expectations, it figures out the best thing to do from the point of view of maximizing profits. Given a set of expectations, the problem of maximizing profits may not be too hard. What may be hard is forming accurate expectations in the first place. This requires firms to know much more about the overall economy than they are likely to, so the assumption that their expectations are rational is not necessarily realistic. Firms, like the rest of us—so the argument goes—grope around in a world that is difficult to understand, trying to do their best but not always understanding enough to avoid mistakes.

In the final analysis, the issue is empirical. Does the assumption of rational expectations stand up well against empirical tests? This is difficult to answer. Much work is currently being done to answer it. There are no conclusive results yet, but it is one of the questions that makes macroeconomics an exciting area of research.

REAL BUSINESS CYCLE THEORY

real business cycle theory An attempt to explain business cycle fluctuations under the assumptions of complete price and wage flexibility and rational expectations. It emphasizes shocks to technology and other shocks.

Recent work in new classical macroeconomics has been concerned with whether the existence of business cycles can be explained under the assumptions of complete price and wage flexibility (market clearing) and rational expectations. This work is called **real business cycle theory**. As we discussed in Chapter 13, if prices and wages are completely flexible, then the *AS* curve is vertical, even in the short run. If the *AS* curve is vertical, then events or phenomena that shift the *AD* curve (such as changes in the money supply, changes in government spending, and shocks to consumer and investor behavior) have no effect on real output. Real output does fluctuate over time, so the puzzle is how these fluctuations can be explained if they are not due to policy changes or other shocks that shift the *AD* curve. Solving this puzzle is one of the main missions of real business cycle theory.

It is clear that if shifts of the *AD* curve cannot account for real output fluctuations (because the *AS* curve is vertical), then shifts of the *AS* curve must be responsible. However, the task is to come up with convincing explanations as to what causes these shifts and why they persist over a number of periods. The problem is particularly difficult when it comes to the labor market. If prices and wages are completely flexible, then there is never any unemployment aside from frictional unemployment. For example, because the measured U.S. unemployment rate was 9.7 percent in 1982 and 4.2 percent in 1999, the puzzle is to explain why so many more people chose not to work in 1982 than in 1999.

Early real business cycle theorists emphasized shocks to the production technology. Suppose there is a negative shock in a given year that causes the marginal product of labor to decline. This leads to a fall in the real wage, which leads to a decrease in labor supply. People have been led to work less because the negative technology shock has led to a lower return from working. The opposite happens when there is a positive shock: The marginal product of labor rises, the real wage rises, and people choose to work more. This early work was not as successful as some had hoped because it required what seemed to be unrealistically large shocks to explain the observed movements in labor supply over time.

Since this initial work, different types of shocks have been introduced, and work is actively continuing in this area. To date, fluctuations of some variables, but not all, have been explained fairly well. Some argue that this work is doomed to failure because it is based on the unrealistic assumption of complete price and wage flexibility, while others hold more hope. Real business cycle theory is another example of the current state of flux in macroeconomics.

SUPPLY-SIDE ECONOMICS

From our discussion of equilibrium in the goods market, beginning with the simple multiplier in Chapter 8 and continuing through Chapter 13, we have focused primarily on *demand*. Supply increases and decreases in response to changes in aggregate expenditure (which is closely linked to aggregate demand). Fiscal policy works by influencing aggregate expenditure through tax policy and government spending. Monetary policy works by influencing investment and consumption spending through increases and decreases in the interest rate. The theories we have been discussing are "demand oriented."

The 1970s were difficult times for the U.S. economy. The United States found itself in 1974 to 1975 with stagflation—high unemployment and inflation. In the late 1970s, inflation returned to the high levels of 1974 to 1975. It seemed as if policy makers were incapable of controlling the business cycle.

As a result of these seeming failures, orthodox economics came under fire. One assault was from a group of economists who expounded *supply-side economics.* The argument of the supply-siders was simple. Basically, they said, all the attention to demand in orthodox macroeconomic theory distracted our attention from the real problem with the U.S. economy. The real problem, said supply-siders, was that high rates of taxation and heavy regulation had reduced the incentive to work, to save, and to invest. What was needed was not a demand stimulus but better incentives to stimulate *supply.*

If we cut taxes so people take home more of their paychecks, the argument continued, they will work harder and save more. If businesses get to keep more of their profits and can get away from government regulations, they will invest more. This added labor supply and investment, or capital supply, will lead to an expansion of the supply of goods and services, which will reduce inflation and unemployment at the same time. The ultimate solution to the economy's woes, the supply-siders concluded, was on the *supply side* of the economy.

At their most extreme, supply-siders argued that the incentive effects of supply-side policies were likely to be so great that a major cut in tax rates would actually *increase* tax revenues. Even though *tax rates* would be lower, more people would be working and earning income and firms would earn more profits, so that the increases in the *tax bases* (profits, sales, and income) would outweigh the decreases in rates, resulting in increased government revenues.

The Laffer Curve Figure 19.2 presents a key diagram of supply-side economics. The tax rate is measured on the vertical axis, and tax revenue is measured on the horizontal axis. The assumption behind this curve is that there is some tax rate beyond which the supply response is large enough to lead to a decrease in tax revenue for further increases in the tax rate. There is obviously some tax rate between zero and 100 percent at which tax revenue is at a maximum. At a tax rate of zero, work effort is high, but there is no tax revenue. At a tax rate of 100, the labor supply is presumably zero, because people are not allowed to keep any of their income. Somewhere in between zero and 100 is the maximum-revenue rate.

The big debate in the 1980s was whether tax rates in the United States put the country on the upper or lower part of the curve in Figure 19.2. The supply-side school claimed the United States was around *A* and taxes should be cut. Others argued that the United States was nearer *B* and tax cuts would lead to lower tax revenue.

The diagram in Figure 19.2 is the **Laffer curve**, after Arthur Laffer, who, legend has it, first drew it on the back of a napkin at a cocktail party. The Laffer curve had some influence

Laffer curve With the tax rate measured on the vertical axis and tax revenue measured on the horizontal axis, the Laffer curve shows there is some tax rate beyond which the supply response is large enough to lead to a decrease in tax revenue for further increases in the tax rate.

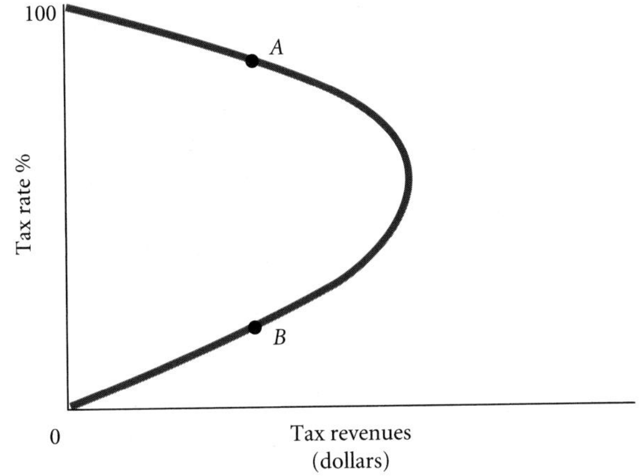

FIGURE 19.2 The Laffer Curve

The Laffer curve shows the amount of revenue the government collects is a function of the tax rate. It shows that when tax rates are very high, an increase in the tax rate could cause tax revenues to fall. Similarly, under the same circumstances, a cut in the tax rate could generate enough additional economic activity to cause revenues to rise.

on the passage of the Economic Recovery Tax Act of 1981, the tax package put forward by the Reagan administration that brought with it substantial cuts in both personal and business taxes. The individual income tax was to be cut 25 percent over 3 years. Corporate taxes were cut sharply in a way designed to stimulate capital investment. The new law allowed firms to depreciate their capital at a rapid rate for tax purposes, and the bigger deductions led to taxes that were significantly lower than before.

EVALUATING SUPPLY-SIDE ECONOMICS

Among the criticisms of supply-side economics is that it is unlikely a tax cut would substantially increase the supply of labor.

Supporters of supply-side economics claim that Reagan's tax policies were successful in stimulating the economy. They point to the fact that almost immediately after the tax cuts of 1981 were put into place, the economy expanded and the recession of 1980 to 1982 came to an end. In addition, inflation rates fell sharply from the high rates of 1980 and 1981. Except for 1 year, federal receipts continued to rise throughout the 1980s despite the cut in tax rates.

Critics of supply-side policies do not dispute these facts but offer an alternative explanation of how the economy recovered. The Reagan tax cuts were enacted just as the U.S. economy was in the middle of its deepest recession since the Great Depression. The unemployment rate stood at 10.8 percent in the fourth quarter of 1982. It was the recession, critics argue, that was responsible for the reduction in inflation—not the supply-side policies. In addition, in theory, a tax cut could even lead to a *reduction* in labor supply. Recall our discussion of income and substitution effects in Chapter 3. Although it is true a higher after-tax wage rate provides a higher reward for each hour of work and thus more incentive to work, a tax cut also means households receive a higher income for a given number of hours of work. Because they can earn the same amount of money working fewer hours, households might actually choose to work *less.* They might spend some of their added income on leisure. Research done during the 1980s suggests tax cuts seem to increase the supply of labor somewhat but the increases are very modest.

What about the recovery from the recession? Why did real output begin to grow rapidly in late 1982, precisely when the supply-side tax cuts were taking effect? Two reasons have been suggested. First, the supply-side tax cuts had large *demand*-side effects that stimulated the economy. Second, the Fed pumped up the money supply and drove interest rates down at the same time that the tax cuts were being put into effect. The money supply expanded about 20 percent between 1981 and 1983, and interest rates succumbed. In 1981, the average 3-month U.S. Treasury bill paid 14 percent interest. In 1983, the figure had dropped to 8.6 percent.

Certainly, traditional theory suggests that a huge tax cut will lead to an increase in disposable income and, in turn, an increase in consumption spending (a component of aggregate expenditure). In addition, although an increase in planned investment (brought about by a lower interest rate) leads to added productive capacity and added supply in the long run, it also increases expenditures on capital goods (new plant and equipment investment) in the short run.

Whether the recovery from the 1981–1982 recession was the result of supply-side expansion or supply-side policies that had demand-side effects, one thing is clear: The extreme promises of the supply-siders did not materialize. President Reagan argued that because of the effect depicted in the Laffer curve, the government could maintain expenditures (and even increase defense expenditures sharply), cut tax rates, *and* balance the budget. This was not the case. Government revenues fell sharply from levels that would have been realized without the tax cuts. After 1982, the federal government ran huge deficits, with nearly $2 trillion added to the national debt between 1983 and 1992.

TESTING ALTERNATIVE MACROECONOMIC MODELS

You may wonder why there is so much disagreement in macroeconomics. Why cannot macroeconomists test their models against one another and see which performs best?

One problem is that macroeconomic models differ in ways that are hard to standardize. If one model takes the price level to be given, or not explained within the model, and another one does not, the model with the given price level may do better in, for instance, predicting output—not because it is a better model but simply because the errors in predicting prices have not been allowed to affect the predictions of output. The model that takes prices as given has a head start, so to speak.

Another problem arises in the testing of the rational-expectations assumption. Remember, if people have rational expectations, they are using the true model to form their expectations. Therefore, to test this assumption we need the true model. There is no way to be sure that whatever model is taken to be the true model is in fact the true one. Any test of the rational-expectations hypothesis is therefore a *joint* test (1) that expectations are formed rationally, and (2) that the model being used is the true one. If the test rejects the hypothesis, it may be that the model is wrong instead of expectations not being rational.

Another problem for macroeconomists is the small amount of data available. Most empirical work uses data beginning about 1950, which in 2003 was about 54 years' (216 quarters) worth of data. While this may seem like a lot of data, it is not. Macroeconomic data are fairly "smooth," which means a typical variable does not vary much from quarter to quarter or year to year. For example, the number of business cycles within this 54-year period is small, about eight. Testing various macroeconomic hypotheses on the basis of seven business cycle observations is not easy, and any conclusions must be interpreted with caution.

To give an example of the problem of a small number of observations, consider trying to test the hypothesis that import prices affect domestic prices. Import prices changed very little in the 1950s and 1960s. Therefore, it would have been very difficult at the end of the 1960s to estimate the effect of import prices on domestic prices. The variation in import prices was not great enough to show any effects. We cannot demonstrate that changes in import prices help explain changes in domestic prices if import prices do not change. The situation was different by the end of the 1970s, because by then import prices had varied considerably. By the end of the 1970s, there were good estimates of the import price effect, but not before. This kind of problem is encountered again and again in empirical macroeconomics. In many cases there are not enough observations for much to be said, hence considerable room for disagreement.

We said in Chapter 1 that it is difficult in economics to perform controlled experiments. Economists are for the most part at the mercy of the historical data. If we were able to perform experiments, we could probably learn more about the economy in a shorter time. Alas, we must wait. In time, the current range of disagreements in macroeconomics should be considerably narrowed.

SUMMARY

KEYNESIAN ECONOMICS

1. In a broad sense, Keynesian economics is the foundation of modern macroeconomics. In a narrower sense, *Keynesian* refers to economists who advocate active government intervention in the economy.

MONETARISM

2. The monetarist analysis of the economy places a great deal of emphasis on the *velocity of money*, which is defined as the number of times a dollar bill changes hands, on average, during the course of a year. The velocity of money is the ratio of nominal GDP to the stock of money, or $V \equiv GDP/M \equiv (P \times Y)/M$. Alternately, $M \times V \equiv P \times Y$.
3. The *quantity theory of money* assumes that velocity is constant (or virtually constant). This implies that changes in the supply of money will lead to equal percentage changes in nominal GDP. The quantity theory of money equation is $M \times \overline{V} = P \times Y$. The equation says demand for money does not depend on the interest rate.
4. Most economists believe sustained inflation is a purely monetary phenomenon. Inflation cannot continue indefinitely unless the Fed "accommodates" it by expanding the money supply.
5. Most monetarists blame most of the instability in the economy on the federal government and are skeptical of the government's ability to manage the macroeconomy. They argue that the money supply should grow at a rate equal to the average growth of real output (income) (Y)—the Fed should expand the money supply to accommodate real growth but not inflation.

NEW CLASSICAL MACROECONOMICS

6. The *new classical macroeconomics* has developed from two different but related sources: the theoretical and the empirical critiques of traditional macroeconomics. On the theoretical level, there has been growing dissatisfaction with the way traditional models treat expectations. On the empirical level, the stagflation in the U.S. economy during the 1970s caused many people to look for alternative theories to explain the breakdown of the Phillips Curve.
7. The *rational-expectations hypothesis* assumes people know the "true model" that generates economic variables. For

example, rational expectations assumes that people know how inflation is determined in the economy and use this model to forecast future inflation rates.

8. The *Lucas supply function* assumes that real output (Y) depends on the actual price level minus the expected price level, or the *price surprise*. This function combined with the assumption that expectations are rational implies that anticipated policy changes have no effect on real output.

9. *Real business cycle theory* is an attempt to explain business-cycle fluctuations under the assumptions of complete price and wage flexibility and rational expectations. It emphasizes shocks to technology and other shocks.

SUPPLY-SIDE ECONOMICS

10. *Supply-side economics* focuses on incentives to stimulate supply. Supply-side economists believe that if we lower taxes, workers will work harder and save more and firms will invest more and produce more. At their most extreme, supply-siders argue that incentive effects are likely to be so great that a major cut in taxes will actually increase tax revenues.

11. The *Laffer curve* shows the relationship between tax rates and tax revenues. Supply-side economists use it to argue that it is possible to generate higher revenues by cutting tax rates, but evidence does not appear to support this. The lower tax rates by the Reagan administration decreased tax revenues significantly and contributed to the massive increase in the federal debt during the 1980s.

TESTING ALTERNATIVE MACRO MODELS

12. Economists disagree about which macroeconomic model is best for several reasons: (1) macroeconomic models differ in ways that are hard to standardize; (2) when testing the rational-expectations assumption, we are never sure that whatever model is taken to be the true model is the true one; (3) the amount of data available is fairly small.

REVIEW TERMS AND CONCEPTS

Laffer curve, 367
Lucas supply function, 364
price surprise, 364
quantity theory of money, 359
rational-expectations hypothesis, 363
real business cycle theory, 366
velocity of money (V), 358

$$V \equiv \frac{GDP}{M}$$

$$M \times V \equiv P \times Y$$

$$M \times \overline{V} = P \times Y$$

PROBLEM SET

1. The table gives estimates of the rate of money supply growth and the rate of real GDP growth for six countries in 2000:

	RATE OF GROWTH IN MONEY SUPPLY (*M1*)	RATE OF GROWTH OF REAL GDP
Australia	+ 9.3	+4.4
Britain	+ 7.6	+4.4
Canada	+18.7	+4.9
Japan	+ 9.0	+0.7
United States	+ 0.2	+5.1

   a. If you were a monetarist, what would you predict about the rate of inflation across the six countries?
   b. If you were a Keynesian, and assuming activist central banks, how might you interpret the same data?

2. The three diagrams in Figure 1 represent in a simplified way the predictions of the three theories presented in this chapter about the likely effects of a major tax cut.
   a. Match each of the following theories with a graph: (1) Keynesian economics, (2) supply-side economics, (3) rational expectations/monetarism. Explain the logic behind the three graphs.
   b. Which theory do you find the most convincing? Explain.

3. One of the contentious issues during the campaign for president between Al Gore and George W. Bush in 2000 was what to do with the growing budget surplus. The Republicans argued for very substantial tax reductions while the Democrats favored more modest tax reductions. The Democrats argued that the surplus should be used instead to pay down more of the national debt, reducing long-term interest rates. Write a brief essay on the pros and cons of both approaches during a period of relatively full employment.

4. In 2000, a well-known economist was heard to say, "The problem with supply-side economics is that when you cut taxes, they have both supply and demand side effects and you cannot separate them." Explain what is meant. Be specific and use either the 1997 tax cuts or the Reagan tax cuts of 1981 as an example.

5. A cornerstone of new classical economics is the notion that expectations are "rational." What do you think will happen to the prices of single-family homes in your community over the next several years? On what do you base your expectations? Is your thinking consistent with the notion of rational expectations? Explain.

6. You are a monetarist given the following information. The money supply is $1,000. The velocity of money is five. What is nominal income? Real income? What happens to nominal income if the money supply is doubled? What happens to real income?

7. When Bill Clinton took office in January 1993, he faced two major economic problems: a large federal budget deficit and

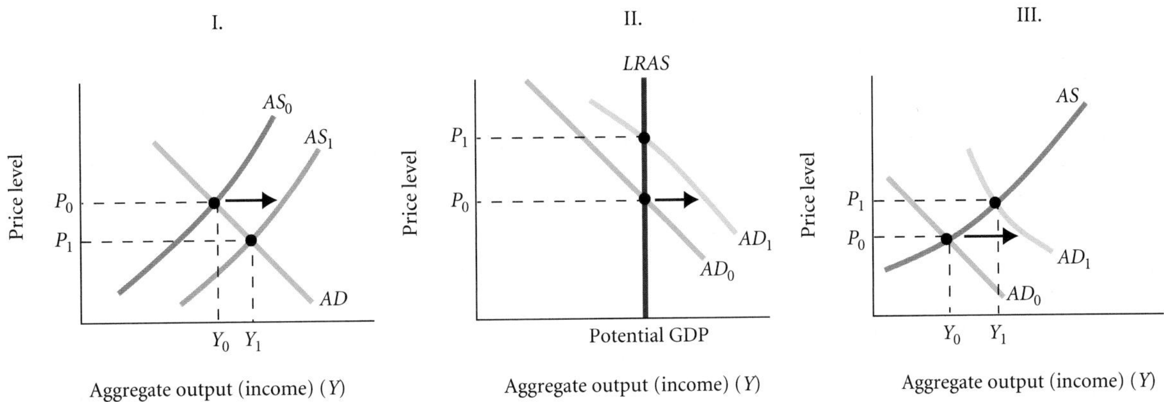

FIGURE 1

high unemployment resulting from a very slow recovery from the recession of 1990 to 1991. In his first State of the Union message, the president called for spending cuts and substantial tax increases to reduce the deficit. Most of these proposed spending cuts were in the defense budget. The following day, Alan Greenspan, chair of the Federal Reserve Board of Governors, signaled his support for the president's plan. Many elements of the president's original plan were later incorporated into the deficit reduction bill passed in 1993.

a. Some said at the time that without the Fed's support, the Clinton plan would be a disaster. Explain this argument.
b. Supply-side economists and monetarists were very worried about the plan and the support it received from the Fed. What specific problems might a monetarist, and a supply-side economist worry about?
c. Suppose you were hired by the Fed Bank of St. Louis to report on the events of 1995 and 1996. What specific evidence would you look for to see if the Clinton plan was effective or whether the critics were right to be skeptical?

8. "In an economy with reasonably flexible prices and wages, full employment is almost always maintained." Explain why this is true.

9. During the 1980 presidential campaign, Ronald Reagan promised to cut taxes, increase expenditures on national defense, and balance the budget. During the New Hampshire primary of 1980, George Bush called this policy "voodoo economics." The two men were arguing about the relative merits of supply-side economics. Explain their disagreement.

***10.** In a hypothetical economy there is a simple proportional tax on wages imposed at a rate *t*. There are plenty of jobs around so if people enter the labor force they can find work. We define total government receipts from the tax as:

$$T = t \times W \times L$$

where t = the tax rate, W = the gross wage rate, and L = the total supply of labor. The net wage rate is:

$$W_n = (1 - t)W$$

The elasticity of labor supply is defined as:

$$\frac{\text{percentage of change in } L}{\text{percentage of change in } W_n} = \frac{\Delta L / \Delta L}{\Delta W_n / W_n}$$

Suppose t were cut from .25 to .20. For such a cut to *increase* total government receipts from the tax, how elastic must the supply of labor be? (Assume a constant gross wage.) What does your answer imply about the supply-side assertion that a cut in taxes can increase tax revenues?

*Note: Problems marked with an asterisk are more challenging.

International Trade, Comparative Advantage, and Protectionism

20

CHAPTER OUTLINE

Over the last 35 years, international transactions have become increasingly important to the U.S. economy. In 1970, imports represented only about 7 percent of U.S. gross domestic product (GDP). The share is now around 14 percent. In 2002, the United States imported more than $120 billion worth of goods and services each month.

The "internationalization" or "globalization" of the U.S. economy has occurred in the private and public sectors, in input and output markets, and in business firms and households. Once uncommon, foreign products are now everywhere, from the utensils we eat with to the cars we drive. In 1970, foreign-produced cars made up only a small percentage of all the cars in the United States. At that time, it was difficult to find mechanics who knew how to repair foreign cars, and replacement parts were hard to obtain. Today the roads are full of Toyotas and Nissans from Japan, Volvos from Sweden, and BMWs from Germany, and any service station that cannot repair foreign-produced automobiles probably will not get much business. Half of all the cars and 80 percent of all the consumer electronics (televisions, CD players, and so forth) that U.S. consumers buy are produced abroad.

At the same time, the United States exports billions of dollar's worth of agricultural goods, aircraft, and industrial machinery. Financial capital flows smoothly and swiftly across international boundaries in search of high returns. In 1997, for example, a downturn in some Asian economies, including Korea and Thailand, caused an outflow of international capital and a sharp decline in stock market prices.

The inextricable connection of the U.S. economy to the economies of the rest of the world has had a profound impact on the discipline of economics and is the basis of one of its most important insights:

> All economies, regardless of their size, depend to some extent on other economies and are affected by events outside their borders.

To get you more acquainted with the international economy, this chapter discusses the economics of international trade. First, we describe the recent tendency of the United States to import more than it exports. Next, we explore the basic logic of trade. Why should the United States or any other country engage in international trade? Finally, we address the controversial issue of protectionism. Should a country provide certain industries with protection in the form of import quotas, tariffs, or subsidies?

trade surplus The situation when a country exports more than it imports.

trade deficit The situation when a country imports more than it exports.

TRADE SURPLUSES AND DEFICITS

Until the 1970s, the United States generally exported more than it imported. When a country exports more than it imports, it runs a **trade surplus**. When a country imports more than it exports, it runs a **trade deficit**. Table 20.1 shows that before 1976 the United States generally ran a trade surplus. This changed in 1976, and since 1976 the United States has run a trade deficit. The deficit reached a local peak of $142.3 billion in 1987, fell to $20.7 billion in 1991, and then rose dramatically to over $400 billion by 2002.

The large trade deficits in the middle and late 1980s touched off political controversy that continues today. Foreign competition hit U.S. markets hard. Less expensive foreign goods—among them steel, textiles, and automobiles—began driving U.S. manufacturers out of business, and thousands of jobs were lost in important industries. Cities such as Pittsburgh, Youngstown, and Detroit had major unemployment problems.

The natural reaction was to call for protection of U.S. industries. Many people wanted the president and Congress to impose taxes and import restrictions that would make foreign goods less available and more expensive, protecting U.S. jobs. This argument was not new. For hundreds of years, industries have petitioned governments for protection, and societies have debated the pros and cons of free and open trade. For the last century and a half, the

TABLE 20.1 U.S. Balance of Trade (Exports Minus Imports), 1929–2002 (Billions of Dollars)

	EXPORTS MINUS IMPORTS
1929	+0.4
1933	+0.1
1945	–0.9
1955	+0.4
1960	+2.4
1965	+3.9
1970	+1.2
1975	+13.6
1976	–2.3
1977	–23.7
1978	–26.1
1979	–24.0
1980	–14.9
1981	–15.0
1982	–20.5
1983	–51.7
1984	–102.0
1985	–114.2
1986	–131.9
1987	–142.3
1988	–106.3
1989	–80.7
1990	–71.4
1991	–20.7
1992	–27.9
1993	–60.5
1994	–87.1
1995	–84.3
1996	–89.0
1997	–89.3
1998	–151.7
1999	–249.9
2000	–365.5
2001	–348.9
2002	–423.6

Source: U.S. Department of Commerce, Bureau of Economic Analysis.

principal argument against protection has been the theory of comparative advantage, first discussed in Chapter 2.

THE ECONOMIC BASIS FOR TRADE: COMPARATIVE ADVANTAGE

Perhaps the best-known debate on the issue of free trade took place in the British Parliament during the early years of the nineteenth century. At that time, the landed gentry—the landowners—controlled Parliament. For a number of years, imports and exports of grain had been subject to a set of tariffs, subsidies, and restrictions collectively called the **Corn Laws**. Designed to discourage imports of grain and encourage exports, the Corn Laws' purpose was to keep the price of food high. The landlords' incomes, of course, depended on the prices they got for what their land produced. The Corn Laws clearly worked to the advantage of those in power.

Corn Laws The tariffs, subsidies, and restrictions enacted by the British Parliament in the early nineteenth century to discourage imports and encourage exports of grain.

With the Industrial Revolution, a class of wealthy industrial capitalists began to emerge. The industrial sector had to pay workers at least enough to live on, and a living wage depended greatly on the price of food. Tariffs on grain imports and export subsidies that kept grain and food prices high increased the wages that capitalists had to pay, cutting into their profits. The political battle raged for years. However, as time went by, the power of the landowners in the House of Lords was significantly reduced. When the conflict ended in 1848, the Corn Laws were repealed.

On the side of repeal was David Ricardo, a businessman, economist, member of Parliament, and one of the fathers of modern economics. Ricardo's principal work, *Principles of Political Economy and Taxation*, was published in 1817, 2 years before he entered Parliament. Ricardo's **theory of comparative advantage**, which he used to argue against the Corn Laws, claimed that trade enables countries to specialize in producing the products they produce best. According to the theory:

theory of comparative advantage Ricardo's theory that specialization and free trade will benefit all trading partners (real wages will rise), even those that may be absolutely less efficient producers.

> Specialization and free trade will benefit all trading partners (real wages will rise), even those that may be absolutely less efficient producers.

This basic argument remains at the heart of free-trade debates even today. It was invoked numerous times by Presidents Reagan and Bush as they wrestled with Congress over various pieces of protectionist legislation.

Specialization and Trade: The Two-Person Case The easiest way to understand the theory of comparative advantage is to examine a simple two-person society. Suppose Bill and Colleen, stranded on a deserted island in Chapter 2, have only two tasks to accomplish each week: gathering food to eat and cutting logs to construct a house. If Colleen could cut more logs than Bill in a day and Bill could gather more berries and fruits, specialization would clearly benefit both of them.

But suppose Bill is slow and clumsy and Colleen is better at both cutting logs *and* gathering food. Ricardo's point is that it still pays for them to specialize. They can produce more in total by specializing than they can by sharing the work equally. (It may be helpful to review the discussion of comparative advantage in Chapter 2 before proceeding.)

ABSOLUTE ADVANTAGE VERSUS COMPARATIVE ADVANTAGE

absolute advantage The advantage in the production of a product enjoyed by one country over another when it uses fewer resources to produce that product than the other country does.

comparative advantage The advantage in the production of a product enjoyed by one country over another when that product can be produced at lower cost in terms of other goods than it could be in the other country.

A country enjoys an **absolute advantage** over another country in the production of a product if it uses fewer resources to produce that product than the other country does. Suppose country A and country B produce wheat, but A's climate is more suited to wheat and its labor is more productive. Country A will produce more wheat per acre than country B and use less labor in growing it and bringing it to market. Country A enjoys an absolute advantage over country B in the production of wheat.

A country enjoys a **comparative advantage** in the production of a good if that good can be produced at lower cost *in terms of other goods*. Suppose countries C and D both produce wheat and corn and C enjoys an absolute advantage in the production of both—that is, C's

TABLE 20.2 Yield Per Acre of Wheat and Cotton

	NEW ZEALAND	AUSTRALIA
Wheat	6 bushels	2 bushels
Cotton	2 bales	6 bales

climate is better than D's, and fewer of C's resources are needed to produce a given quantity of both wheat and corn. Now C and D must each choose between planting land with either wheat or corn. To produce more wheat, either country must transfer land from corn production; to produce more corn, either country must transfer land from wheat production. The cost of wheat in each country can be measured in bushels of corn, and the cost of corn can be measured in bushels of wheat.

Suppose that in country C, a bushel of wheat has an opportunity cost of 2 bushels of corn. That is, to produce an additional bushel of wheat, C must give up 2 bushels of corn. At the same time, producing a bushel of wheat in country D requires the sacrifice of only 1 bushel of corn. Even though C has an *absolute* advantage in the production of both products, D enjoys a *comparative* advantage in the production of wheat because the *opportunity cost* of producing wheat is lower in D. Under these circumstances, Ricardo claims, D can benefit from trade if it specializes in the production of wheat.

Gains from Mutual Absolute Advantage To illustrate Ricardo's logic in more detail, suppose Australia and New Zealand each have a fixed amount of land and do not trade with the rest of the world. There are only two goods—wheat, to produce bread, and cotton, to produce clothing. This kind of two-country/two-good world does not exist, but its operations can be generalized to many countries and many goods.

To proceed, we have to make some assumptions about the preferences of the people living in New Zealand and the people living in Australia. If the citizens of both countries go around naked, there is no need to produce cotton; all the land can be used to produce wheat. However, assume that people in both countries have similar preferences with respect to food and clothing: The populations of both countries use both cotton and wheat, and preferences for food and clothing are such that both countries consume equal amounts of wheat and cotton.

Finally, we assume that each country has only 100 acres of land for planting and land yields are as given in Table 20.2. New Zealand can produce three times the wheat that Australia can on 1 acre of land, and Australia can produce three times the cotton that New Zealand can in the same space. New Zealand has an absolute advantage in the production of wheat, and Australia has an absolute advantage in the production of cotton. In cases like this, we say the two countries have *mutual absolute advantage.*

If there is no trade and each country divides its land to obtain equal units of cotton and wheat production, each country produces 150 bushels of wheat and 150 bales of cotton. New Zealand puts 75 acres into cotton but only 25 acres into wheat, while Australia does the reverse (Table 20.3).

We can organize the same information in graphic form as production possibility frontiers for each country. In Figure 20.1, which presents the positions of the two countries before trade, each country is constrained by its own resources and productivity. If Australia

TABLE 20.3 Total Production of Wheat and Cotton Assuming No Trade, Mutual Absolute Advantage, and 100 Available Acres

	NEW ZEALAND	AUSTRALIA
Wheat	25 acres × 6 bushels/acre 150 bushels	75 acres × 2 bushels/acre 150 bushels
Cotton	75 acres × 2 bales/acre 150 bales	25 acres × 6 bales/acre 150 bales

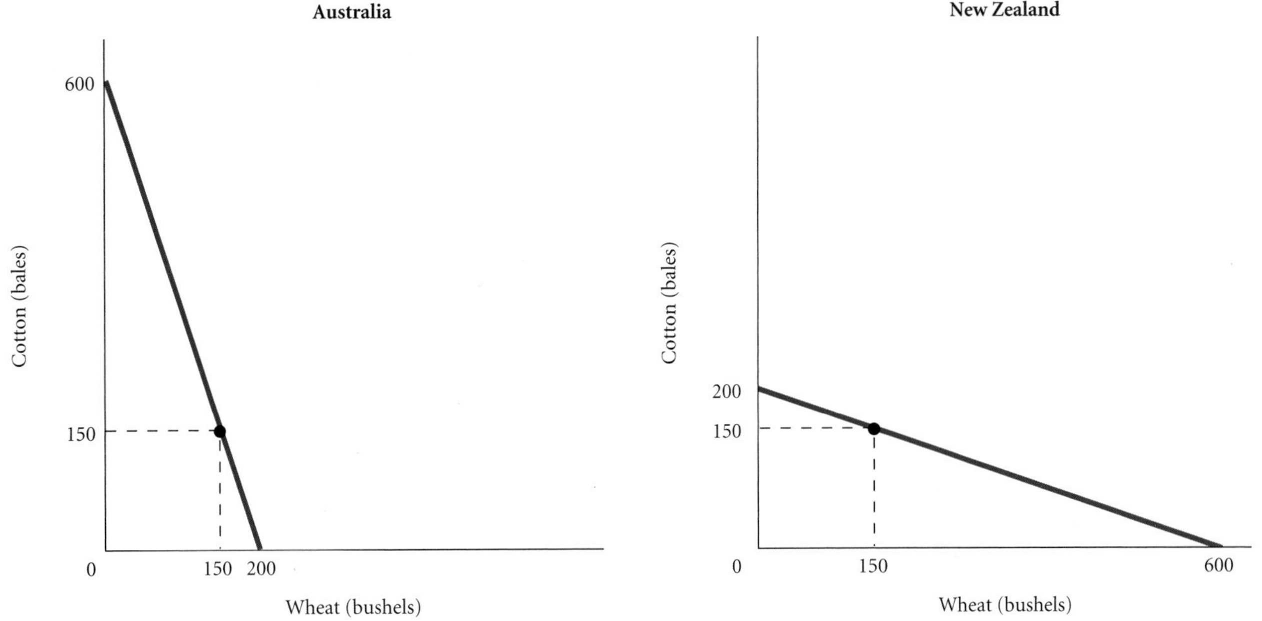

FIGURE 20.1 Production Possibility Frontiers for Australia and New Zealand before Trade

Without trade, countries are constrained by their own resources and productivity.

put all its land into cotton, it would produce 600 bales of cotton (100 acres × 6 bales/acre) and no wheat; if it put all its land into wheat, it would produce 200 bushels of wheat (100 acres × 2 bushels/acre) and no cotton. The opposite is true for New Zealand. Recall from Chapter 2, a country's production possibility frontier represents all combinations of goods that can be produced, given the country's resources and state of technology. Each country must pick a point along its own production possibility curve.

Because both countries have an absolute advantage in the production of one product, specialization and trade will benefit both. Australia should produce cotton, New Zealand should produce wheat. Transferring all land to wheat production in New Zealand yields 600 bushels; transferring all land to cotton production in Australia yields 600 bales. An agreement to trade 300 bushels of wheat for 300 bales of cotton would double both wheat and cotton consumption in both countries. (Remember, before trade both countries produced 150 bushels of wheat and 150 bales of cotton. After trade, each country will have 300 bushels of wheat and 300 bales of cotton to consume. Final production and trade figures are in Table 20.4 and Figure 20.2).

Trade enables both countries to move beyond their previous resource and productivity constraints.

The advantages of specialization and trade seem obvious when one country is technologically superior at producing one product and another country is technologically superior

TABLE 20.4 Production and Consumption of Wheat and Cotton after Specialization

	PRODUCTION			CONSUMPTION	
	New Zealand	Australia		New Zealand	Australia
Wheat	100 acres × 6 bushels/acre 600 bushels	0 acres 0	Wheat	300 bushels	300 bushels
Cotton	0 acres 0	100 acres × 6 bales/acre 600 bales	Cotton	300 bales	300 bales

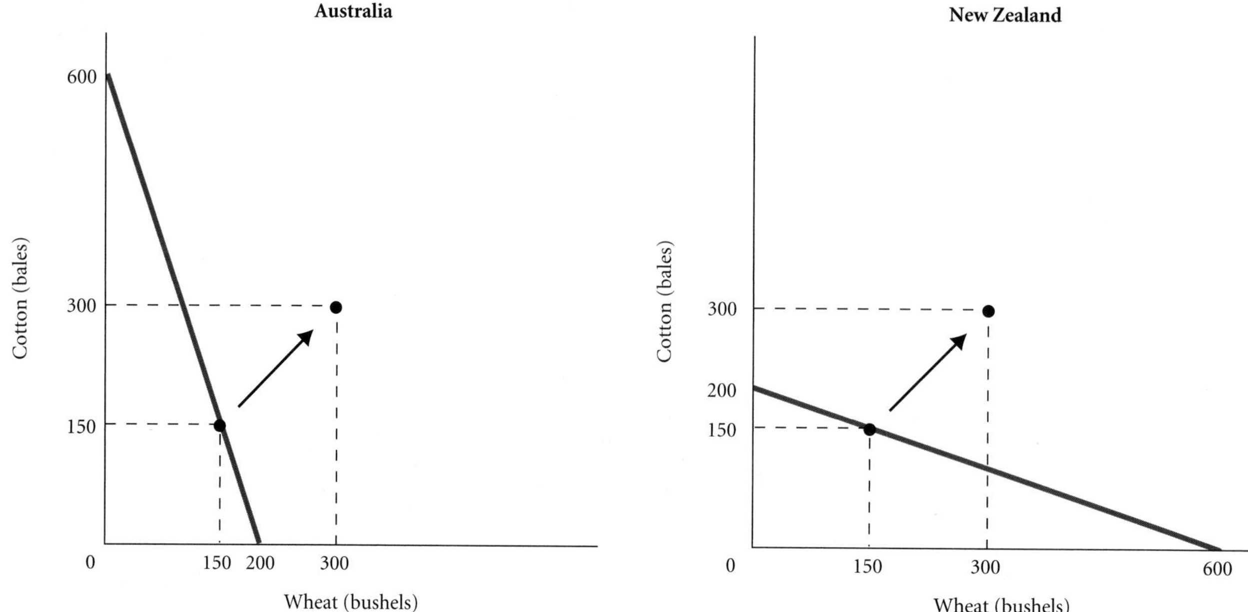

FIGURE 20.2 Expanded Possibilities after Trade

Trade enables both countries to move beyond their own resource constraints—beyond their individual production possibility frontiers.

at producing another product. However, let us turn to the case in which one country has an absolute advantage in the production of *both* goods.

Gains from Comparative Advantage Table 20.5 contains different land yield figures for New Zealand and Australia. Now New Zealand has a considerable absolute advantage in the production of both cotton and wheat, with 1 acre of land yielding six times as much wheat and twice as much cotton as 1 acre in Australia. Ricardo would argue that *specialization and trade are still mutually beneficial.*

Again, preferences imply consumption of equal units of cotton and wheat in both countries. With no trade, New Zealand would divide its 100 available acres evenly, or 50/50, between the two crops. The result would be 300 bales of cotton and 300 bushels of wheat. Australia would divide its land 75/25. Table 20.6 shows that final production in Australia would be 75 bales of cotton and 75 bushels of wheat. (Remember, we are assuming that in each country, people consume equal amounts of cotton and wheat.) Again, before any trade takes place each country is constrained by its own domestic production possibilities curve.

Imagine we are at a meeting of trade representatives of both countries. As a special adviser, David Ricardo is asked to demonstrate that trade can benefit both countries. He divides his demonstration into three stages, which you can follow in Table 20.7.

In stage 1, Australia transfers all its land into cotton production. It will have no wheat and 300 bales of cotton. New Zealand cannot completely specialize in wheat because it needs 300 bales of cotton and will not be able to get enough cotton from Australia. This is because we are assuming that each country wants to consume equal amounts of cotton and wheat.

In stage 2, New Zealand transfers 25 acres out of cotton and into wheat. Now New Zealand has 25 acres in cotton that produce 150 bales and 75 acres in wheat that produce 450 bushels.

TABLE 20.5 Yield Per Acre of Wheat and Cotton

	NEW ZEALAND	AUSTRALIA
Wheat	6 bushels	1 bushel
Cotton	6 bales	3 bales

TABLE 20.6 Total Production of Wheat and Cotton Assuming No Trade and 100 Available Acres

	NEW ZEALAND	AUSTRALIA
Wheat	50 acres × 6 bushels/acre 300 bushels	75 acres × 1 bushels/acre 75 bushels
Cotton	50 acres × 6 bales/acre 300 bales	25 acres × 3 bales/acre 75 bales

Finally, the two countries trade. We assume New Zealand ships 100 bushels of wheat to Australia in exchange for 200 bales of cotton. After the trade, New Zealand has 350 bales of cotton and 350 bushels of wheat; Australia has 100 bales of cotton and 100 bushels of wheat. Both countries are better off than they were before the trade (Table 20.6), and both have moved beyond their own production possibility frontiers.

Why Does Ricardo's Plan Work? To understand why Ricardo's scheme works, let us return to the definition of comparative advantage.

The real cost of producing cotton is the wheat that must be sacrificed to produce it. *When we think of cost this way, it is less costly to produce cotton in Australia than to produce it in New Zealand, even though an acre of land produces more cotton in New Zealand.* Consider the "cost" of 3 bales of cotton in the two countries. In terms of opportunity cost, 3 bales of cotton in New Zealand cost 3 bushels of wheat; in Australia, 3 bales of cotton cost only 1 bushel of wheat. Because 3 bales are produced by 1 acre of Australian land, to get 3 bales an Australian must transfer 1 acre of land from wheat to cotton production. Because an acre of land produces a bushel of wheat, losing 1 acre to cotton implies the loss of 1 bushel of wheat. *Australia has a comparative advantage in cotton production* because its opportunity cost, in terms of wheat, is lower than New Zealand's. This is illustrated in Figure 20.3.

Conversely, New Zealand has a comparative advantage in wheat production. A unit of wheat in New Zealand costs one unit of cotton; a unit of wheat in Australia costs three units of cotton.

> When countries specialize in producing goods in which they have a comparative advantage, they maximize their combined output and allocate their resources more efficiently.

TABLE 20.7 Realizing a Gain from Trade When One Country Has a Double Absolute Advantage

STAGE 1

	New Zealand	Australia
Wheat	50 acres × 6 bushels/acre 300 bushels	0 acres 0
Cotton	50 acres × 6 bales/acre 300 bales	100 acres × 3 bales/acre 300 bales

STAGE 2

	New Zealand	Australia
Wheat	75 acres × 6 bushels/acre 450 bushels	0 acres 0
Cotton	25 acres × 6 bales/acre 150 bales	100 acres × 3 bales/acre 300 bales

STAGE 3

	New Zealand	Australia
Wheat	100 bushels (trade) ⟶ 350 bushels (after trade)	100 bushels
Cotton	200 bales (trade) ⟵ 350 bales (after trade)	100 bales

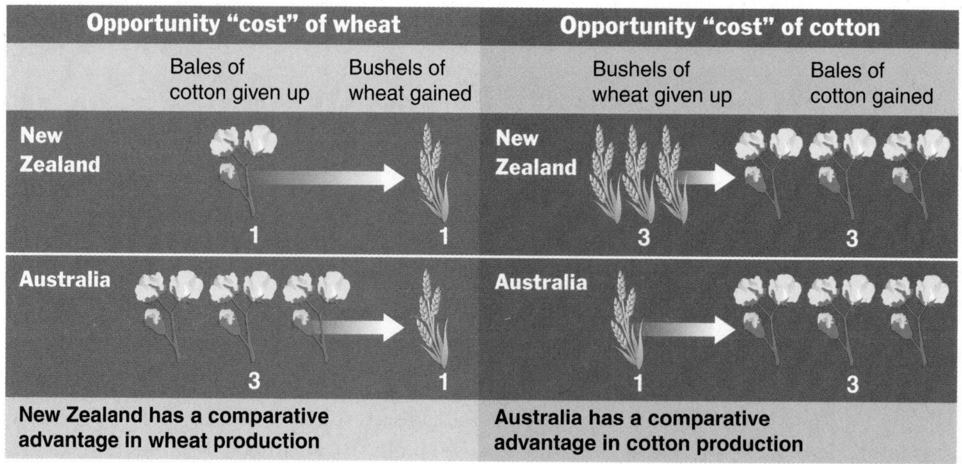

FIGURE 20.3 Comparative Advantage Means Lower Opportunity Cost

The real cost of cotton is the wheat sacrificed to obtain it. The cost of 3 bales of cotton in New Zealand is 3 bushels of wheat (a half acre of land must be transferred from wheat to cotton—refer to Table 20.5). However, the cost of 3 bales of cotton in Australia is only 1 bushel of wheat. Australia has a comparative advantage over New Zealand in cotton production, and New Zealand has a comparative advantage over Australia in wheat production.

TERMS OF TRADE

Ricardo might suggest a number of options open to the trading partners. The one we just examined benefited both partners; in percentage terms, Australia made out slightly better. Other deals might have been more advantageous to New Zealand.

terms of trade The ratio at which a country can trade domestic products for imported products.

The ratio at which a country can trade domestic products for imported products is the **terms of trade**. The terms of trade determine how the gains from trade are distributed among trading partners. In the case just considered, the agreed-to terms of trade were 1 bushel of wheat for 2 bales of cotton. Such terms of trade benefit New Zealand, which can get 2 bales of cotton for each bushel of wheat. If it were to transfer its own land from wheat to cotton, it would get only one bale of cotton. The same terms of trade benefit Australia, which can get 1 bushel of wheat for 2 bales of cotton. A direct transfer of its own land would force it to give up 3 bales of cotton for 1 bushel of wheat.

If the terms of trade changed to 3 bales of cotton for every bushel of wheat, only New Zealand would benefit. At those terms of trade *all* the gains from trade would flow to New Zealand. Such terms do not benefit Australia at all because the opportunity cost of producing wheat domestically is *exactly the same* as the trade cost: A bushel of wheat costs 3 bales of cotton. If the terms of trade went the other way—1 bale of cotton for each bushel of wheat—only Australia would benefit. New Zealand gains nothing, because it can already substitute cotton for wheat at that ratio. To get a bushel of wheat domestically, however, Australia must give up 3 bales of cotton, and one-for-one terms of trade would make wheat much less costly for Australia.

Both parties must have something to gain for trade to take place. In this case, you can see that both Australia and New Zealand will gain when the terms of trade are set between 1:1 and 3:1, cotton to wheat.

EXCHANGE RATES

The examples we have used thus far have shown that trade can result in gains to both parties. We have not yet discussed how trade actually comes about.

When trade is free—unimpeded by government-instituted barriers—patterns of trade and trade flows result from the independent decisions of thousands of importers and exporters and millions of private households and firms.

Private households decide whether to buy Toyotas or Chevrolets, and private firms decide whether to buy machine tools made in the United States or machine tools made in Taiwan, raw steel produced in Germany or raw steel produced in Pittsburgh.

Before a citizen of one country can buy a product made in, or sold by, someone in another country, a currency swap must take place. Consider Shane, who buys a Toyota from a dealer in Boston. He pays in dollars, but the Japanese workers who made the car receive their salaries in yen. Somewhere between the buyer of the car and the producer, a currency exchange must be made. The regional distributor probably takes payment in dollars and converts them into yen before remitting the proceeds to Japan.

To buy a foreign-produced good, I in effect have to buy foreign currency. The price of Shane's Toyota in dollars depends on both the price of the car stated in yen and the dollar price of yen. You probably know the ins and outs of currency exchange very well if you have ever traveled in another country.

In September 2003 the British pound was worth $1.60. Now suppose that you are in London having dinner. On the menu is a nice bottle of wine for 15 pounds. How can you figure out whether you want to buy it? You know what dollars will buy in the United States, so you have to convert the price into dollars. Each pound will cost you $1.60, so 15 pounds will cost you $1.60 × 15 = $24.00.

The attractiveness of foreign goods to U.S. buyers and of U.S. goods to foreign buyers depends in part on the **exchange rate**, the ratio at which two currencies are traded. If the price of pounds were to fall to $1.20, that same bottle of wine would cost $18.00.

exchange rate The ratio at which two currencies are traded. The price of one currency in terms of another.

To understand the patterns of trade that result from the actions of hundreds of thousands of independent buyers and sellers—households and firms—we must know something about the factors that determine exchange rates. Exchange rate determination is very complicated. Here, however, we can demonstrate two things:

> First, for any pair of countries, there is a range of exchange rates that can lead automatically to both countries realizing the gains from specialization and comparative advantage. Second, within that range, the exchange rate will determine which country gains the most from trade. In short, exchange rates determine the terms of trade.

Trade and Exchange Rates in a Two-Country/Two-Good World Consider first a simple two-country/two-good model. Suppose both the United States and Brazil produce only two goods—raw timber and rolled steel. Table 20.8 gives the current prices of both goods as domestic buyers see them. In Brazil, timber is priced at 3 reals (R) per foot, and steel is priced at 4 R per meter. In the United States, timber costs $1 per foot and steel costs $2 per meter.

Suppose U.S. and Brazilian buyers have the option of buying at home or importing to meet their needs. The options they choose will depend on the exchange rate. For the time being, we will ignore transportation costs between countries and assume that Brazilian and U.S. products are of equal quality.

Let us start with the assumption that the exchange rate is $1 = 1 R. From the standpoint of U.S. buyers, neither Brazilian steel nor Brazilian timber is competitive at this exchange rate. A dollar buys a foot of timber in the United States, but if converted into a real, it will buy only one-third of a foot. The price of Brazilian timber to an American is $3 because it will take $3 to buy the necessary 3 R. Similarly, $2 buys a meter of rolled steel in the United States, but the same $2 buys only half a meter of Brazilian steel. The price of Brazilian steel to an American is $4, twice the price of domestically produced steel.

TABLE 20.8 Domestic Prices of Timber (Per Foot) and Rolled Steel (Per Meter) in the United States and Brazil

	UNITED STATES	BRAZIL
Timber	$1	3 Reals
Rolled steel	$2	4 Reals

At this exchange rate, however, Brazilians find that U.S.-produced steel and timber are both less expensive than steel and timber produced in Brazil. Timber at home—Brazil—costs 3 R, but 3 R buys $3, which buys three times as much timber in the United States. Similarly, steel costs 4 R at home, but 4 R buys $4, which buys twice as much U.S.-made steel. At an exchange rate of $1 = 1 R, Brazil will import steel and timber and the United States will import nothing.

However, now suppose the exchange rate is 1 R = $0.25. This means that one dollar buys 4 R. At this exchange rate, the Brazilians buy timber and steel at home and the

Americans import both goods. At this exchange rate, Americans must pay a dollar for a foot of U.S. timber, but the same amount of timber can be had in Brazil for the equivalent of $0.75. (Because 1 R costs $0.25, 3 R can be purchased for $0.75.) Similarly, steel that costs $2 per meter in the United States costs an American half as much in Brazil, because $2 buys 8 R, which buys 2 meters of Brazilian steel. At the same time, Brazilians are not interested in importing, because both goods are cheaper when purchased from a Brazilian producer. In this case, the United States imports both goods and Brazil imports nothing.

So far, we can see that at exchange rates of $1 = 1 R and $1 = 4 R we get trade flowing in only one direction. Let us now try an exchange rate of $1 = 2 R, or 1 R = $0.50. First, Brazilians will buy timber in the United States. Brazilian timber costs 3 R per foot, but 3 R buys $1.50, which is enough to buy 1.5 feet of U.S. timber. Buyers in the United States will find Brazilian timber too expensive, but Brazil will import timber from the United States. At this same exchange rate, however, both Brazilian and U.S. buyers will be indifferent between Brazilian and U.S. steel. To U.S. buyers, domestically produced steel costs $2. Because $2 buys 4 R, a meter of imported Brazilian steel also costs $2. Brazilian buyers also find that steel costs 4 R, whether domestically produced or imported. Thus, there is likely to be no trade in steel.

What happens if the exchange rate changes so that $1 buys 2.1 R? While U.S. timber is still cheaper to both Brazilians and Americans, Brazilian steel begins to look good to U.S. buyers. Steel produced in the United States costs $2 per meter, but $2 buys 4.2 R, which buys more than a meter of steel in Brazil. When $1 buys more than 2 R, trade begins to flow in both directions: Brazil will import timber and the United States will import steel.

If you examine Table 20.9 carefully, you will see that trade flows in both directions as long as the exchange rate settles between $1 = 2 R and $1 = 3 R. Stated the other way around, trade will flow in both directions if the price of a real is between $0.33 and $0.50.

Exchange Rates and Comparative Advantage If the foreign exchange market drives the exchange rate to anywhere between 2 and 3 R per dollar, the countries will automatically adjust and comparative advantage will be realized. At these exchange rates, U.S. buyers begin buying all their steel in Brazil. The U.S. steel industry finds itself in trouble. Plants close, and U.S. workers begin to lobby for tariff protection against Brazilian steel. At the same time, the U.S. timber industry does well, fueled by strong export demand from Brazil. The timber-producing sector expands. Resources, including capital and labor, are attracted into timber production.

The opposite occurs in Brazil. The Brazilian timber industry suffers losses as export demand dries up and Brazilians turn to cheaper U.S. imports. In Brazil, lumber companies turn to the government and ask for protection from cheap U.S. timber. However, steel producers in Brazil are happy. Not only are they supplying 100 percent of the domestically demanded steel, but also they are selling to U.S. buyers. The steel industry expands, and the timber industry contracts. Resources, including labor, flow into steel.

With this expansion-and-contraction scenario in mind, let us look again at our original definition of comparative advantage. If we assume that prices reflect resource use and resources can be transferred from sector to sector, we can calculate the opportunity cost of

TABLE 20.9 Trade Flows Determined by Exchange Rates

EXCHANGE RATE	PRICE OF REAL	RESULT
$1 = 1 R	$ 1.00	Brazil imports timber and steel
$1 = 2 R	.50	Brazil imports timber
$1 = 2.1 R	.48	Brazil imports timber; United States imports steel
$1 = 2.9 R	.34	Brazil imports timber; United States imports steel
$1 = 3 R	.33	United States imports steel
$1 = 4 R	.25	United States imports timber and steel

steel/timber in both countries. In the United States, the production of a meter of rolled steel consumes twice the resources that the production of a foot of timber consumes. Assuming that resources can be transferred, the opportunity cost of a meter of steel is 2 feet of timber (see Table 20.8). In Brazil, a meter of steel uses resources costing 4 R, while a unit of timber costs 3 R. To produce a meter of steel means the sacrifice of only four-thirds (or one and one-third) feet of timber. Because the opportunity cost of a meter of steel (in terms of timber) is lower in Brazil, we say Brazil has a comparative advantage in steel production.

Conversely, consider the opportunity cost of timber in the two countries. Increasing timber production in the United States requires the sacrifice of half a meter of steel for every foot of timber—producing a meter of steel uses $2 worth of resources, while producing a foot of timber requires only $1 worth of resources. Nevertheless, each foot of timber production in Brazil requires the sacrifice of three-fourths of a meter of steel. Because the opportunity cost of timber is lower in the United States, the United States has a comparative advantage in the production of timber.

> If exchange rates end up in the right ranges, the free market will drive each country to shift resources into those sectors in which it enjoys a comparative advantage. Only those products in which a country has a comparative advantage will be competitive in world markets.

THE SOURCES OF COMPARATIVE ADVANTAGE

Specialization and trade can benefit all trading partners, even those that may be inefficient producers in an absolute sense. If markets are competitive, and if foreign exchange markets are linked to goods-and-services exchange, countries will specialize in producing products in which they have a comparative advantage.

So far, we have said nothing about the sources of comparative advantage. What determines whether a country has a comparative advantage in heavy manufacturing or in agriculture? What explains the actual trade flows observed around the world? Various theories and empirical work on international trade have provided some answers. Most economists look to **factor endowments**—the quantity and quality of labor, land, and natural resources—as the principal sources of comparative advantage. Factor endowments seem to explain a significant portion of actual world trade patterns.

factor endowments The quantity and quality of labor, land, and natural resources of a country.

THE HECKSCHER-OHLIN THEOREM

Eli Heckscher and Bertil Ohlin, two Swedish economists who wrote in the first half of this century, expanded and elaborated on Ricardo's theory of comparative advantage. The **Heckscher-Ohlin theorem** ties the theory of comparative advantage to factor endowments. It assumes that products can be produced using differing proportions of inputs and that inputs are mobile between sectors in each economy, but that factors are not mobile *between* economies. According to this theorem:

Heckscher-Ohlin theorem A theory that explains the existence of a country's comparative advantage by its factor endowments: A country has a comparative advantage in the production of a product if that country is relatively well endowed with inputs used intensively in the production of that product.

> A country has a comparative advantage in the production of a product if that country is relatively well endowed with inputs used intensively in the production of that product.

This idea is simple. A country with a lot of good fertile land is likely to have a comparative advantage in agriculture. A country with a large amount of accumulated capital is likely to have a comparative advantage in heavy manufacturing. A country with a lot of human capital is likely to have a comparative advantage in highly technical goods.

After an extensive study, Edward Leamer of UCLA has concluded that a short list of factors accounts for a large portion of world trade patterns. Natural resources, knowledge capital, physical capital, land, and skilled and unskilled labor, Leamer believes, explain "a large amount of the variability of net exports across countries."[1]

---

[1]Edward E. Leamer, *Sources of International Comparative Advantage: Theory and Evidence* (Cambridge, MA: MIT Press, 1984), p. 187.

OTHER EXPLANATIONS FOR OBSERVED TRADE FLOWS

Comparative advantage is not the only reason countries trade. It does not explain why many countries both import and export the same kinds of goods. The United States, for example, both exports and imports automobiles.

Just as industries within a country differentiate their products to capture a domestic market, so too do they differentiate their products to please the wide variety of tastes that exists worldwide. The Japanese automobile industry, for example, began producing small, fuel-efficient cars long before U.S. automobile makers did. In doing so, they developed expertise in creating products that attracted a devoted following and considerable brand loyalty. BMWs, made only in Germany, and Volvos, made only in Sweden, also have their champions in many countries. Just as product differentiation is a natural response to diverse preferences within an economy, it is also a natural response to diverse preferences across economies.

This idea is not inconsistent with the theory of comparative advantage. If the Japanese have developed skills and knowledge that gave them an edge in the production of fuel-efficient cars, that knowledge can be thought of as a very specific kind of capital not currently available to other producers. The Volvo company invested in a form of intangible capital that we call *goodwill.* That goodwill, which may come from establishing a reputation for safety and quality over the years, is one source of the comparative advantage that keeps Volvos selling on the international market. Some economists distinguish between gains from *acquired comparative advantages* and those from *natural comparative advantages.*

Another explanation for international trade is that some economies of scale may be available when producing for a world market that would not be available when producing for a more limited domestic market. But because the evidence suggests that economies of scale are exhausted at relatively small size in most industries, it seems unlikely that they constitute a valid explanation of world trade patterns.

Companion Website Plus

TRADE BARRIERS: TARIFFS, EXPORT SUBSIDIES, AND QUOTAS

protection The practice of shielding a sector of the economy from foreign competition.

tariff A tax on imports.

export subsidies Government payments made to domestic firms to encourage exports.

dumping A firm or industry sells products on the world market at prices below the cost of production.

Trade barriers—also called *obstacles to trade*—take many forms; the three most common are tariffs, export subsidies, and quotas. All are forms of **protection** shielding some sector of the economy from foreign competition.

A **tariff** is a tax on imports. The average tariff on imports into the United States is about 5 percent. Certain protected items have much higher tariffs. For example, the tariff rate on concentrated orange juice is a flat $0.35 per gallon. On rubber footwear, the tariff ranges from 20 percent to 48 percent, and on canned tuna it is 35 percent.

Export subsidies—government payments made to domestic firms to encourage exports—can also act as a barrier to trade. One of the provisions of the Corn Laws that stimulated Ricardo's musings was an export subsidy automatically paid to farmers by the British government when the price of grain fell below a specified level. The subsidy served to keep domestic prices high, but it flooded the world market with cheap subsidized grain. Foreign farmers who were not subsidized were driven out of the international marketplace by the artificially low prices.

Farm subsidies remain a part of the international trade landscape today. Many countries, especially in Europe, continue to appease their farmers by heavily subsidizing exports of agricultural products. The political power of the farm lobby in many countries has had an important effect on recent international trade negotiations aimed at reducing trade barriers.

Closely related to subsidies is **dumping**. Dumping takes place when a firm or an industry sells products on the world market at prices *below* the cost of production. The charge has been leveled against several specific Japanese industries, including automobiles, consumer electronics, and silicon computer chips.

Generally, a company dumps when it wants to dominate a world market. After the lower prices of the dumped goods have succeeded in driving out all the competition, the dumping company can exploit its position by raising the price of its product. A U.S. firm attempting to monopolize a domestic market violates the Sherman Antitrust Act of 1890, prohibiting predatory pricing.

The current U.S. tariff laws contain several provisions aimed at counteracting the effects of dumping. The 1974 Trade Act contains a clause that qualifies an industry for protection if it has been "injured" by foreign competition. Building on that legislation, more recent trade bills, including the Comprehensive Trade Act of 1988, contain clauses that permit the president to impose trade sanctions when investigations reveal dumping by foreign companies or countries.

A **quota** is a limit on the quantity of imports. Quotas can be mandatory or voluntary, and they may be legislated or negotiated with foreign governments. The best-known voluntary quota, or "voluntary restraint," was negotiated with the Japanese government in 1981. Japan agreed to reduce its automobile exports to the United States by 7.7 percent, from the 1980 level of 1.82 million units to 1.68 million units. In 1985, President Reagan decided not to ask Japan to continue its restraints—auto imports jumped to 2.3 million units, nearly 20 percent of the U.S. market. Quotas currently apply to such products as mushrooms, heavy motorcycles, and color TVs.

quota A limit on the quantity of imports.

U.S. Trade Policies and GATT The United States has been a high-tariff nation, with average tariffs of over 50 percent for much of its history. The highest were in effect during the Great Depression following the **Smoot-Hawley tariff**, which pushed the average tariff rate to 60 percent in 1930. The Smoot-Hawley tariff set off an international trade war when U.S. trading partners retaliated with tariffs of their own. Many economists say the decline in trade that followed was one of the causes of the worldwide depression of the 1930s.[2]

Smoot-Hawley tariff The U.S. tariff law of the 1930s, which set the highest tariffs in U.S. history (60 percent). It set off an international trade war and caused the decline in trade that is often considered a cause of the worldwide depression of the 1930s.

In 1947, the United States, with 22 other nations, agreed to reduce barriers to trade. It also established an organization to promote liberalization of foreign trade. This **General Agreement on Tariffs and Trade (GATT)**, at first considered to be an interim arrangement, continues today and has been quite effective. The most recent round of world trade talks sponsored by GATT, the "Uruguay Round," began in Uruguay in 1986. It was initialed by 116 countries on December 15, 1993, and was formally approved by the U.S. Congress after much debate following the election in 1994. The "Final Act" of the Uruguay Round of negotiations is the most comprehensive and complex multilateral trade agreement in history.

General Agreement on Tariffs and Trade (GATT) An international agreement signed by the United States and 22 other countries in 1947 to promote the liberalization of foreign trade.

Every president who has held office since the first round of this general agreement was signed has argued for free-trade policies, yet each used his powers to protect one sector or another. Eisenhower and Kennedy restricted U.S. imports of Japanese textiles; Johnson restricted meat imports; Nixon restrained imports of steel and tightened restrictions on textiles; Carter protected steel, textiles, and footwear; Reagan restricted imports of sugar and automobiles. In early 2002, President George W. Bush imposed a 30 percent tariff on steel imported into the United States. The U.S. steel industry employed 175,000 workers in 2002, but nearly 20,000 jobs had been lost during the previous 4 years due to cheaper imported steel. The Bush steel tariff was greeted with anger by the other steel producing countries, many of whom threatened a trade war.

Nevertheless, the movement in the United States has been away from tariffs and quotas and toward freer trade. The Reciprocal Trade Agreements Act of 1934 authorized the president to negotiate trade agreements on behalf of the United States. As part of trade negotiations, the president can confer *most-favored-nation status* on individual trading partners. Imports from countries with most-favored-nation status are taxed at the lowest negotiated tariff rates. In addition, in recent years several successful rounds of tariff-reduction negotiations have reduced trade barriers to their lowest levels ever.

Economic Integration **Economic integration** occurs when two or more nations join to form a free-trade zone. In 1991, the European Community (EC, or the Common Market) began forming the largest free-trade zone in the world. The economic integration process began that December, when the 12 original members (the United Kingdom, Belgium, France, Germany, Italy, the Netherlands, Luxembourg, Denmark, Greece, Ireland, Spain, and

economic integration Occurs when two or more nations join to form a free-trade zone.

[2]See especially Charles Kindleberger, *The World in Depression 1929–1939* (London: Allen Lane, 1973).

News Analysis

Trade Games

THE CONFLICT BETWEEN FREE TRADE AND OTHER national goals is most evident in agriculture. Most nations, including the United States, provide farmers with healthy subsidies. Such subsidies allow farmers who are subsidized to sell their products in world markets at low prices, often in violation of free-trade agreements like NAFTA. A big bone of contention for American farmers is the European Union's fight to keep out, or at least to label, genetically modified foods. Some feel strongly that genetic modification is dangerous and potentially harmful. Others point to the lack of evidence of harm. Is the European resistance genuine fear or a protectionist trade tactic?

U.S. Contests Europe's Ban On Some Food—*The New York Times*

The Bush administration filed suit today at the World Trade Organization to force Europe to lift its ban on genetically modified food, a move that was postponed earlier this year by the debate on Iraq.

The suit will further heighten trans-Atlantic trade tensions after several recent rulings against the United States in cases brought by Europe at the W.T.O. over United States steel tariffs and tax shelters for overseas corporations.

The administration was backed by the speaker of the House, J. Dennis Hastert of Illinois, and other senior Republican and Democratic lawmakers who have been promoting the lawsuit for months. American farmers have led the complaints, saying they have invested in the technology needed to raise genetically modified crops only to see one of the biggest markets—Europe—closed to their products.

Robert B. Zoellick, the United States trade representative, said the administration had run out of patience waiting for the European Union to lift what he called a five-year-old moratorium that blocked several hundred million dollars of American exports into Europe. Worse, he said, European attitudes were spreading unfounded fears in the developing world, where the need is greatest for the increased yield of genetically modified crops.

"In developing countries, these crops can spell the difference between life and death," he said. "The human cost of rejecting this new technology is enormous."

Mr. Hastert estimated that American farmers lost $300 million in corn exports each year because of the European policy toward genetically modified food and animal feed.

"There's no question in my mind that the European Union's protectionist, discriminatory trade policies are costing American agriculture and our nation's economy hundreds of millions of dollars each and every year," Mr. Hastert said.

But European officials said today that they were dumbfounded by the suit. They said there was no moratorium on genetically modified food.

"The U.S. claims that there is a so-called moratorium, but the fact is that the E.U. has authorized G.M. varieties in the past and is currently processing applications," said Pascal Lamy, the top European trade official. "So what is the real U.S. motive in bringing a case?"

In practice, the Europeans did have an informal moratorium on new varieties of genetically modified food from 1998 until last year, when the E.U. instituted a new regulatory system that has approved two applications, with others pending.

At the center of the debate over genetically modified crops, if not the suit filed today, is a growing disagreement between the United States and Europe over what steps are necessary to protect public health and the environment.

There is some opposition to genetically modified foods.

European consumers are far more wary of genetically modified food than are Americans, and many object to what they consider aggressive American promotion of those foods, influenced by agribusiness.

The European Union is demanding that genetically modified food be labeled as such. They also want to be able to trace the origins of the food's ingredients and are near completion of new legislation to require both.

The United States opposes such labels and tracing mechanisms, saying they are too costly and impractical.

Source: Adapted from: Elizabeth Becker, "U.S. Contests Europe's Ban On Some Food," The New York Times, *May 14, 2003. Reprinted by permission.*

Visit www.prenhall.com/casefair for updated articles and exercises.

European Union (EU) The European trading bloc composed of Austria, Belgium, Denmark, Finland, France, Germany, Greece, Ireland, Italy, Luxembourg, the Netherlands, Portugal, Spain, Sweden, and the United Kingdom.

U.S.-Canadian Free-Trade Agreement An agreement in which the United States and Canada agreed to eliminate all barriers to trade between the two countries by 1998.

North American Free-Trade Agreement (NAFTA) An agreement signed by the United States, Mexico, and Canada in which the three countries agreed to establish all North America as a free-trade zone.

Portugal) signed the Maastricht Treaty. The treaty called for the end of border controls, a common currency, an end to all tariffs, and the coordination of monetary and even political affairs. In 1995, Austria, Finland, and Sweden became members of this **European Union (EU)**, as the EC is now called, bringing the number of member countries to 15.

On January 1, 1993, all tariffs and trade barriers were dropped among the member countries. Border checkpoints were closed in early 1995. Citizens can now travel among member countries without passports.

The United States is not a part of the EU. However, in 1988 the United States (under President Reagan) and Canada (under Prime Minister Mulroney) signed the **U.S.-Canadian Free-Trade Agreement**, which removed all barriers to trade, including tariffs and quotas, between the two countries in 1998.

During the last days of the George Bush administration, the United States, Mexico, and Canada signed the **North American Free-Trade Agreement (NAFTA)**, the three countries agreeing to establish all North America as a free-trade zone. The North American free-trade area includes 360 million people and a total output of over $7 trillion—larger than the output of the EU. The agreement eliminates all tariffs over a 10- to 15-year period and removes restrictions on most investments.

During the presidential campaign of 1992, NAFTA was hotly debated. Both Bill Clinton and George Bush supported the agreement. Industrial labor unions that might be affected by increased imports from Mexico (like those in the automobile industry) opposed the agreement, while industries whose exports to Mexico might increase as a result of the agreement—for example, the machine tool industry—supported it. Another concern was that Mexican companies were not subject to the same environmental regulations as U.S. firms, so U.S. firms might move to Mexico for this reason.

NAFTA was ratified by the U.S. Congress in late 1993 and went into effect on the first day of 1994. The U.S. Department of Commerce has estimated that as a result of NAFTA, trade between the United States and Mexico increased by nearly $16 billion in 1994. In addition, exports from the United States to Mexico outpaced imports from Mexico during 1994. In 1995, however, the agreement fell under the shadow of a dramatic collapse of the value of the peso. U.S. exports to Mexico dropped sharply, and the United States shifted from a trade surplus to a large trade deficit with Mexico. Aside from a handful of tariffs, however, all of NAFTA's commitments were fully implemented by 2003, and an 8-year report signed by all three countries declared the pact a success. The report concludes, "Eight years of expanded trade, increased employment and investment, and enhanced opportunity for the citizens of all three countries have demonstrated that NAFTA works and will continue to work."

FREE TRADE OR PROTECTION?

One of the great economic debates of all time revolves around the free-trade-versus-protection controversy. We briefly summarize the arguments in favor of each.

THE CASE FOR FREE TRADE

In one sense, the theory of comparative advantage *is* the case for free trade. Trade has potential benefits for all nations. A good is not imported unless its net price to buyers is below the net price of the domestically produced alternative. When the Brazilians in our earlier example found U.S. timber less expensive than their own, they bought it, yet they continued to pay the same price for homemade steel. Americans bought less expensive Brazilian steel, but they continued to buy domestic timber at the same lower price. Under these conditions, *both Americans and Brazilians ended up paying less and consuming more.*

At the same time, resources (including labor) move out of steel production and into timber production in the United States. In Brazil, resources (including labor) move out of timber production and into steel production. The resources in both countries are more efficiently used. Tariffs, export subsidies, and quotas, which interfere with the free movement of goods and services around the world, reduce or eliminate the gains of comparative advantage.

We can use supply-and-demand curves to illustrate this. Suppose Figure 20.4 shows domestic supply and demand for textiles. In the absence of trade, the market clears at a price of $4.20. At equilibrium, 450 million yards of textiles are produced and consumed.

Assume now that textiles are available at a world price of $2. This is the price in dollars that Americans must pay for textiles from foreign sources. If we assume an unlimited amount of textiles is available at $2 and there is no difference in quality between domestic and foreign textiles, no domestic producer will be able to charge more than $2. In the absence of trade barriers, the world price sets the price in the United States. As the price in the United States falls from $4.20 to $2.00, the quantity demanded by consumers increases from 450 million yards to 700 million yards, but the quantity supplied by domestic producers drops from 450 million yards to 200 million yards. The difference, 500 million yards, is the quantity of textiles imported.

The argument for free trade is that each country should specialize in producing the goods and services in which it enjoys a comparative advantage. If foreign producers can produce textiles at a much lower price than domestic producers, they have a comparative advantage. As the world price of textiles falls to $2, domestic (U.S.) supply drops and resources are transferred to other sectors. These other sectors, which may be export industries or domestic industries, are not shown in Figure 20.4(a). It is clear that the allocation of resources is more efficient at a price of $2. Why should the United States use domestic resources to produce

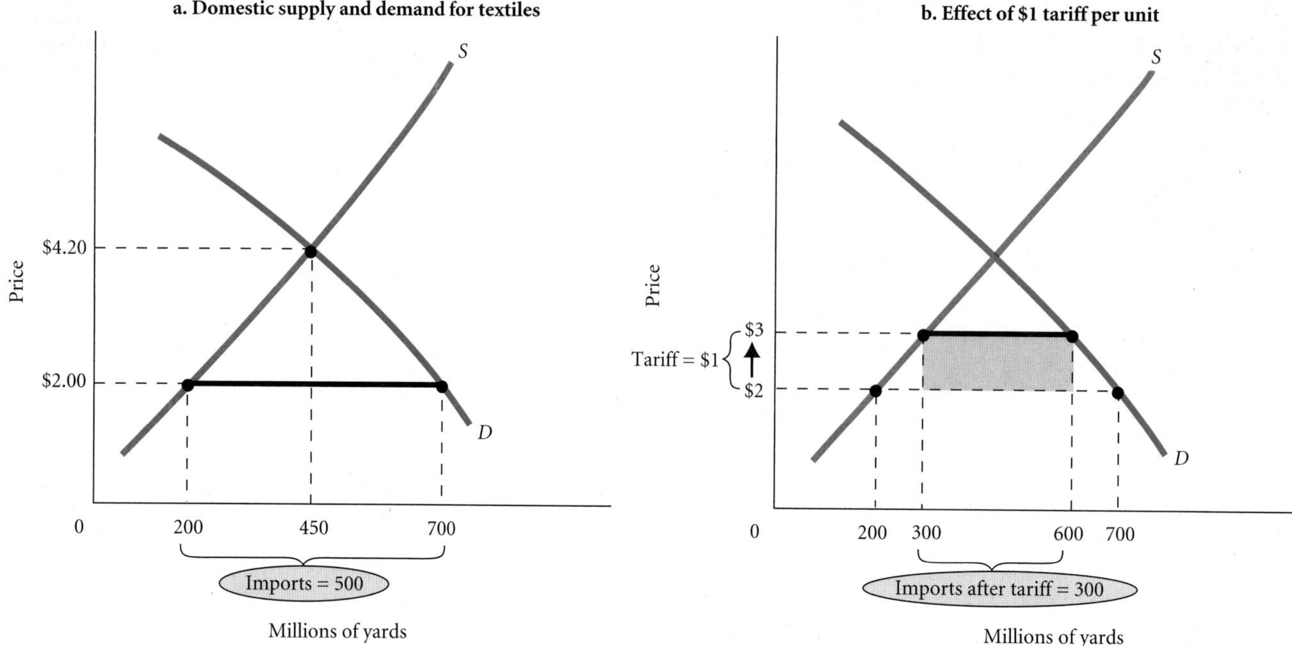

FIGURE 20.4 The Gains from Trade and Losses from the Imposition of a Tariff

A tariff of $1 increases the market price facing consumers from $2 per yard to $3 per yard. The government collects revenues equal to the gray-shaded area. The loss of efficiency has two components. First, consumers must pay a higher price for goods that could be produced at lower cost. Second, marginal producers are drawn into textiles and away from other goods, resulting in inefficient domestic production.

what foreign producers can produce at a lower cost? U.S. resources should move into the production of the things it produces best.

Now consider what happens to the domestic price of textiles when a trade barrier is imposed. Figure 20.4(b) shows the effect of a set tariff of $1 per yard imposed on imported textiles. The tariff raises the domestic price of textiles to $2 + $1 = $3. The result is that some of the gains from trade are lost. First, consumers are forced to pay a higher price for the same good; the quantity of textiles demanded drops from 700 million yards under free trade to 600 million yards because some consumers are not willing to pay the higher price.

At the same time, the higher price of textiles draws some marginal domestic producers who could not make a profit at $2 into textile production. (Recall, domestic producers do not pay a tariff.) As the price rises to $3, the quantity supplied by producers rises from 200 million yards to 300 million yards. The result is a decrease in imports from 500 million yards to 300 million yards.

Finally, the imposition of the tariff means the government collects revenue equal to the shaded blue area in Figure 20.4(b) This shaded area is equal to the tariff rate per unit ($1) times the number of units imported after the tariff is in place (300 million yards). Thus, receipts from the tariff are $300 million.

What is the final result of the tariff? Domestic producers receiving revenues of only $2 per unit before the tariff was imposed now receive a higher price and earn higher profits. However, these higher profits are achieved at a loss of efficiency.

> Trade barriers prevent a nation from reaping the benefits of specialization, push it to adopt relatively inefficient production techniques, and force consumers to pay higher prices for protected products than they would otherwise pay.

THE CASE FOR PROTECTION

Arguments can also be made in favor of tariffs and quotas. Over the course of U.S. history, these arguments have been made so many times by so many industries before so many congressional committees that it seems all pleas for protection share the same themes. We describe the most frequently heard pleas next.

Protection Saves Jobs The main argument for protection is that foreign competition costs Americans their jobs. When Americans buy Toyotas, U.S. cars go unsold. This leads to layoffs in the domestic auto industry. When Americans buy Japanese or German steel, steelworkers in Pittsburgh lose their jobs. When Americans buy shoes or textiles from Korea or Taiwan, the millworkers in Maine and Massachusetts, as well as in South Carolina and Georgia, lose their jobs.

It is true that when we buy goods from foreign producers, domestic producers suffer. However, there is no reason to believe that the workers laid off in the contracting sectors will not be ultimately reemployed in other expanding sectors. Foreign competition in textiles, for example, has meant the loss of U.S. jobs in that industry. Thousands of textile workers in New England lost their jobs as the textile mills there closed over the last 35 years. Nevertheless, with the expansion of high-tech industries, the unemployment rate in Massachusetts fell to one of the lowest in the country in the mid-1980s, and New Hampshire, Vermont, and Maine also boomed. By the 1990s, New England had suffered another severe downturn, due partly to high-technology hardware manufacturing that had moved abroad. By 1994, it became clear that small- to medium-sized companies in such newly developing areas as biotechnology and software were beginning to pick up steam just as hardware manufacturing had done a decade earlier.

The adjustment is far from costless. The knowledge that some other industry, perhaps in some other part of the country, may be expanding is of little comfort to the person whose skills become obsolete or whose pension benefits are lost when his or her company abruptly closes a plant or goes bankrupt. The social and personal problems brought about by industry-specific unemployment, obsolete skills, and bankruptcy as a result of foreign competition are significant.

These problems can be addressed in two ways. We can ban imports and give up the gains from free trade, acknowledging that we are willing to pay premium prices to save domestic jobs in industries that can produce more efficiently abroad, or we can aid the victims of free trade in a constructive way, helping to retrain them for jobs with a future. In some instances, programs to relocate people in expanding regions may be in order. Some programs deal directly with the transition without forgoing the gains from trade.

Some Countries Engage in Unfair Trade Practices Attempts by U.S. firms to monopolize an industry are illegal under the Sherman and Clayton acts. If a strong company decides to drive the competition out of the market by setting prices below cost, it would be aggressively prosecuted by the Antitrust Division of the Justice Department. However, the argument goes, if we will not allow a U.S. firm to engage in predatory pricing or monopolize an industry or market, can we stand by and let a German firm or a Japanese firm do so in the name of free trade? This is a legitimate argument and one that has gained significant favor in recent years. How should we respond when a large international company or a country behaves strategically against a domestic firm or industry? Free trade may be the best solution when everybody plays by the rules, but sometimes we have to fight back.

Cheap Foreign Labor Makes Competition Unfair Let us say that a particular country gained its "comparative advantage" in textiles by paying its workers low wages. How can U.S. textile companies compete with companies that pay wages that are less than a quarter of what U.S. companies pay?

First, remember that wages in a competitive economy reflect productivity. Workers in the United States earn higher wages because they are more productive. The United States has more capital per worker, and its workers are better trained. Second, trade flows not according to *absolute* advantage but according to *comparative* advantage: All countries benefit, even if one country is more efficient at producing everything.

Protection Safeguards National Security Beyond saving jobs, certain sectors of the economy may appeal for protection for other reasons. The steel industry has argued for years with some success that it is vital to national defense. In the event of a war, the United States would not want to depend on foreign countries for products as vital as steel. Even if we acknowledge another country's comparative advantage, we may want to protect our own resources.

Further Exploration

A Petition

From the Manufacturers of Candles, Tapers, Lanterns, Sticks, Street Lamps, Snuffers, and Extinguishers, and from Producers of Tallow, Oil, Resin, Alcohol, and Generally of Everything Connected with Lighting.

To the Honourable Members of the Chamber of Deputies.

Gentlemen:

You are on the right track. You reject abstract theories and [have] little regard for abundance and low prices. You concern yourselves mainly with the fate of the producer. You wish to free him from foreign competition, that is, to reserve the *domestic market* for *domestic industry*.

We come to offer you a wonderful opportunity for your—what shall we call it? Your theory? No, nothing is more deceptive than theory. Your doctrine? Your system? Your principle? But you dislike doctrines, you have a horror of systems, as for principles, you deny that there are any in political economy; therefore we shall call it your practice—your practice without theory and without principle.

We are suffering from the ruinous competition of a rival who apparently works under conditions so far superior to our own for the production of light that he is *flooding* the *domestic market* with it at an incredibly low price; for the moment he appears, our sales cease, all the consumers turn to him, and a branch of French industry whose ramifications are innumerable is all at once reduced to complete stagnation. This rival, which is none other than the sun, is waging war on us so mercilessly we suspect he is being stirred up against us by perfidious Albion (excellent diplomacy nowadays!), particularly because he has for that haughty island a respect that he does not show for us. [A reference to Britain's reputation as a foggy island.]

We ask you to be so good as to pass a law requiring the closing of all windows, dormers, skylights, inside and outside shutters, curtains, casements, bull's-eyes, deadlights, and blinds—in short, all openings, holes, chinks, and fissures through which the light of the sun is wont to enter houses, to the detriment of the fair industries with which, we are proud to say, we have endowed the country, a country that cannot, without betraying ingratitude, abandon us today to so unequal a combat.

Be good enough, honourable deputies, to take our request seriously, and do not reject it without at least hearing the reasons that we have to advance in its support.

First, if you shut off as much as possible all access to natural light, and thereby create a need for artificial light, what industry in France will not ultimately be encouraged? If France consumes more tallow, there will have to be more cattle and sheep, and, consequently, we shall see an increase in cleared fields, meat, wool, leather, and especially manure, the basis of all agricultural wealth.

If France consumes more oil, we shall see an expansion in the cultivation of the poppy, the olive, and rapeseed. These rich yet soil-exhausting plants will come at just the right time to enable us to put to profitable use the increased fertility that the breeding of cattle will impart to the land.

Our moors will be covered with resinous trees. Numerous swarms of bees will gather from our mountains the perfumed treasures that today waste their fragrance, like the flowers from which they emanate. Thus, there is not one branch of agriculture that would not undergo a great expansion.

The same holds true of shipping. Thousands of vessels will engage in whaling, and in a short time we shall have a fleet capable of upholding the honour of France and of gratifying the patriotic aspirations of the undersigned petitioners, chandlers, etc.

Will you tell us that, though we may gain by this protection, France will not gain at all, because the consumer will bear the expense?

We have our answer ready: You no longer have the right to invoke the interests of the consumer. You have sacrificed him whenever you have found his interests opposed to those of the producer. You have done so in order *to encourage industry and to increase employment*. For the same reason you ought to do so this time too.

Indeed, you yourselves have anticipated this objection. When told that the consumer has a stake in the free entry of iron, coal, sesame, wheat, and textiles, "Yes," you reply, "but the producer has a stake in their exclusion." Very well, surely if consumers have a stake in the admission of natural light, producers have a stake in its interdiction.

Screening out the sun would increase the demand for candles. Should candlemakers be protected from unfair competition?

"But," you may still say, "the producer and the consumer are one and the same person. If the manufacturer profits by protection, he will make the farmer prosperous. Contrariwise, if agriculture is prosperous, it will open markets for manufactured goods." Very well, if you grant us a monopoly over the production of lighting during the day, first of all we shall buy large amounts of tallow, charcoal, oil, resin, wax, alcohol, silver, iron, bronze, and crystal, to supply our industry; and, moreover, we and our numerous suppliers, having become rich, will consume a great deal and spread prosperity into all areas of domestic industry.

The question, and we pose it formally, is whether what you desire for France is the benefit of consumption free of charge or the alleged advantages of onerous production. Make your choice, but be logical; for as long as you ban, as you do, foreign coal, iron, wheat, and textiles, *in proportion* as their price approaches zero, how inconsistent it would be to admit the light of the sun, whose price is *zero* all day long!

Source: Frederic Bastiat (1801 to 1850), New Australian. *Reprinted by permission.*

No industry has ever asked for protection without invoking the national defense argument. The testimony on behalf of the scissors and shears industry argued that "in the event of a national emergency and imports cutoff, the United States would be without a source of scissors and shears, basic tools for many industries and trades essential to our national defense." The question lies not in the merit of the argument but in just how seriously it can be taken if *every* industry uses it.

Protection Discourages Dependency Closely related to the national defense argument is the claim that countries, particularly small or developing countries, may come to rely too heavily on one or more trading partners for many items. If a small country comes to rely on a major power for food or energy or some important raw material in which the large nation has a comparative advantage, it may be difficult for the smaller nation to remain politically neutral. Some critics of free trade argue that the superpowers have consciously engaged in trade with smaller countries to create these kinds of dependencies.

Therefore, should small independent countries consciously avoid trading relationships that might lead to political dependence? This may involve developing domestic industries in areas where a country has a comparative disadvantage. To do so would mean protecting that industry from international competition.

Protection Safeguards Infant Industries Young industries in a given country may have a difficult time competing with established industries in other countries. In a dynamic world, a protected **infant industry** might mature into a strong one worldwide because of an acquired, but real, comparative advantage. If such an industry is undercut and driven out of world markets at the beginning of its life, that comparative advantage might never develop.

infant industry A young industry that may need temporary protection from competition from the established industries of other countries to develop an acquired comparative advantage.

Yet efforts to protect infant industries can backfire. In July 1991, the U.S. government imposed a 62.67 percent tariff on imports of active-matrix liquid crystal display screens (also referred to as "flat-panel displays" and primarily used for laptop computers) from Japan. The Commerce Department and the International Trade Commission agreed that Japanese producers were selling their screens in the U.S. market at a price below cost and that this "dumping" threatened the survival of domestic laptop screen producers. The tariff was meant to protect the infant U.S. industry until it could compete head-on with the Japanese.

Unfortunately for U.S. producers of laptop computers and for consumers who purchase them, the tariff had an unintended (though predictable) effect on the industry. Because U.S. laptop screens were generally recognized to be of lower quality than their Japanese counter-parts, imposition of the tariff left U.S. computer manufacturers with three options: (1) They could use the screens available from U.S. producers and watch sales of their final product decline in the face of *higher quality* competition from abroad; (2) they could pay the tariff for the higher quality screens and watch sales of their final product decline in the face of *lower priced* competition from abroad; or (3) they could do what was the most profitable for them to do—move their production facilities abroad to avoid the tariff completely. The last is exactly what both Apple and IBM announced they would do. In the end, not only were the laptop industry and its consumers hurt by the imposition of the tariff (due to higher costs of production and to higher laptop computer prices), but the U.S. screen industry was hurt as well (due to its loss of buyers for its product) by a policy specifically designed to help it.

AN ECONOMIC CONSENSUS

You now know something about how international trade fits into the structure of the economy.

Critical to our study of international economics is the debate between free traders and protectionists. On one side is the theory of comparative advantage, formalized by David Ricardo in the early part of the nineteenth century. According to this view, all countries benefit from specialization and trade. The gains from trade are real, and they can be large; free international trade raises real incomes and improves the standard of living.

On the other side are the protectionists, who point to the loss of jobs and argue for the protection of workers from foreign competition. Although foreign competition can cause job loss in specific sectors, it is unlikely to cause net job loss in an economy, and workers will over time be absorbed into expanding sectors.

Foreign trade and full employment can be pursued simultaneously. Although economists disagree about many things, the vast majority of them favor free trade.

Chapter 22 picks up this debate on free trade.

SUMMARY

1. All economies, regardless of their size, depend to some extent on other economies and are affected by events outside their borders.

TRADE SURPLUSES AND DEFICITS

2. Until the 1970s, the United States generally exported more than it imported—it ran a *trade surplus.* In the mid-1970s, the United States began to import more merchandise than it exported—a *trade deficit.*

THE ECONOMIC BASIS FOR TRADE: COMPARATIVE ADVANTAGE

3. The *theory of comparative advantage*, dating to David Ricardo in the nineteenth century, holds that specialization and free trade will benefit all trading partners, even those that may be absolutely less efficient producers.
4. A country enjoys an *absolute advantage* over another country in the production of a product if it uses fewer resources to produce that product than the other country does. A country has a *comparative advantage* in the production of a product if that product can be produced at a lower cost in terms of other goods.
5. Trade enables countries to move beyond their previous resource and productivity constraints. When countries specialize in producing those goods in which they have a comparative advantage, they maximize their combined output and allocate their resources more efficiently.
6. When trade is free, patterns of trade and trade flows result from the independent decisions of thousands of importers and exporters and millions of private households and firms.
7. The relative attractiveness of foreign goods to U.S. buyers and of U.S. goods to foreign buyers depends in part on *exchange rates*, the ratios at which two currencies are traded for each other.
8. For any pair of countries, there is a range of exchange rates that will lead automatically to both countries realizing the gains from specialization and comparative advantage. Within that range, the exchange rate will determine which country gains the most from trade. This leads us to conclude that exchange rates determine the terms of trade.
9. If exchange rates end up in the right range, that is, in a range that facilitates the flow of goods between nations, the free market will drive each country to shift resources into those sectors in which it enjoys a comparative advantage. Only those products in which a country has a comparative advantage will be competitive in world markets.

THE SOURCES OF COMPARATIVE ADVANTAGE

10. The *Heckscher-Ohlin theorem* looks to relative *factor endowments* to explain comparative advantage and trade flows. According to the theorem, a country has a comparative advantage in the production of a product if that country is relatively well endowed with the inputs that are used intensively in the production of that product.
11. A relatively short list of inputs—natural resources, knowledge capital, physical capital, land, and skilled and unskilled labor—explains a surprisingly large portion of world trade patterns. However, the simple version of the theory of comparative advantage cannot explain why many countries import and export the same goods.
12. Some theories argue that comparative advantage can be acquired. Just as industries within a country differentiate their products to capture a domestic market, so too do they differentiate their products to please the wide variety of tastes that exists worldwide. This theory is consistent with the theory of comparative advantage.

TRADE BARRIERS: TARIFFS, EXPORT SUBSIDIES, AND QUOTAS

13. Trade barriers take many forms; the three most common are *tariffs, export subsidies*, and *quotas.* All are forms of *protection* through which some sector of the economy is shielded from foreign competition.
14. Although the United States has historically been a high-tariff nation, the general movement is now away from tariffs and quotas. The *General Agreement on Tariffs and Trade (GATT)*, signed by the United States and 22 other countries in 1947, continues in effect today; its purpose is to reduce barriers to world trade and keep them down. Also important are the *U.S.-Canadian Free-Trade Agreement*, signed in 1988, and the *North American Free-Trade Agreement*, signed by the United States, Mexico, and Canada in the last days of the Bush administration, taking effect in 1994.
15. The *European Union (EU)* is a free-trade bloc composed of 15 nations: Austria, Belgium, Denmark, Finland, France, Germany, Greece, Ireland, Italy, Luxembourg, the Netherlands, Portugal, Spain, Sweden, and the United Kingdom. Many economists believe that the advantages of free trade within the bloc, a reunited Germany, and the ability to work well as a bloc will make the EU the most powerful player in the international marketplace in the coming decades.

FREE TRADE OR PROTECTION?

16. In one sense, the theory of comparative advantage is the case for free trade. Trade barriers prevent a nation from reaping the benefits of specialization, push it to adopt relatively inefficient production techniques, and force consumers to pay higher prices for protected products than they would otherwise pay.

17. The case for protection rests on a number of propositions, one of which is that foreign competition results in a loss of domestic jobs, but there is no reason to believe that the workers laid off in the contracting sectors will not be ultimately reemployed in other expanding sectors. This adjustment process is far from costless, however.

18. Other arguments for protection hold that cheap foreign labor makes competition unfair; that some countries engage in unfair trade practices; and that protection safeguards the national security, discourages dependency, and shields *infant industries.* Despite these arguments, most economists favor free trade.

REVIEW TERMS AND CONCEPTS

absolute advantage, 375
comparative advantage, 375
Corn Laws, 375
dumping, 384
economic integration, 385
European Union (EU), 386
exchange rate, 381
export subsidies, 384
factor endowments, 383
General Agreement on Tariffs and Trade (GATT), 385
Heckscher-Ohlin theorem, 383
infant industry, 391
North American Free-Trade Agreement (NAFTA), 386
protection, 384
quota, 385
Smoot-Hawley tariff, 385
tariff, 384
terms of trade, 380
theory of comparative advantage, 375
trade deficit, 374
trade surplus, 374
U.S.-Canadian Free-Trade Agreement, 386

PROBLEM SET

1. Suppose Germany and France each produce only two goods, guns and butter. Both are produced using labor alone and the value of a good is equal to the number of labor units required to produce it. Assuming both countries are at full employment, you are given the following information:

Germany: 10 units of labor required to produce 1 gun
5 units of labor required to produce 1 pound of butter
Total labor force: 1,000,000 units

France: 15 units of labor required to produce 1 gun
10 units of labor required to produce 1 pound of butter
Total labor force: 750,000 units

a. Draw the production possibility frontiers for each country in the absence of trade.
b. If transportation costs are ignored and trade is allowed, will France and Germany engage in trade? Explain.
c. If a trade agreement were negotiated, at what rate (number of guns per unit of butter) would they agree to exchange?

2. In 2003, the United States began talks to create a new NAFTA-like free-trade zone in Central America including the countries of Costa Rica, El Salvador, Guatemala, Honduras, and Nicaragua. Write a short paper on the progress of those talks to date. What arguments are used by those who are in favor of this agreement? Against it? What lessons have we been taught by our experience with NAFTA?

3. The United States and Russia each produce only bearskin caps and wheat. Domestic prices are given in the following table:

	RUSSIA	UNITED STATES	
Bearskin caps	10 Ru	\$ 7	Per hat
Wheat	15 Ru	\$10	Per quart

On April 1, the Zurich exchange listed an exchange rate of \$1 = 1 Ru.

a. Which country has an absolute advantage in the production of bearskin caps? Wheat?
b. Which country has a comparative advantage in the production of bearskin caps? Wheat?
c. If the United States and Russia were the only two countries engaging in trade, what adjustments would you predict, assuming exchange rates are freely determined by the laws of supply and demand?

4. The United States imported \$27.9 billion worth of "food, feeds, and beverages" in 1996 and exported \$40.7 billion worth.

a. Name some of the imported items that you are aware of in this category. Also name some of the exported items.
b. The United States is said to have a comparative advantage in the production of agricultural goods. How would you go about testing this proposition? What data would you need?
c. Are the foregoing numbers consistent with the theory of comparative advantage? Suppose you had a more detailed breakdown of which items the United States imports and which it exports. What would you look for?
d. What else might explain why the same goods are imported and exported?

5. The following table gives 1990 figures for yield per acre in Illinois and Kansas:

	WHEAT	SOYBEANS
Illinois	48	39
Kansas	40	24

Source: U.S. Dept. of Agriculture, *Crop Production*, 1992.

a. If we assume that farmers in Illinois and Kansas use the same amount of labor, capital, and fertilizer, which state has an absolute advantage in wheat production? Soybean production?

b. If we transfer land out of wheat into soybeans, how many bushels of wheat do we give up in Illinois per additional bushel of soybeans produced? In Kansas?

c. Which state has a comparative advantage in wheat production? In soybean production?

d. The following table gives the distribution of land planted for each state in millions of acres in 1990:

	TOTAL ACRES UNDER TILL	WHEAT	SOYBEANS
Illinois	22.9	1.9 (8.3%)	9.1 (39.7%)
Kansas	20.7	11.8 (57.0%)	1.9 (9.2%)

Are these data consistent with your answer to part c? Explain.

6. You can think of the United States as a set of 50 separate economies with no trade barriers. In such an open environment, each state specializes in the products that it produces best.

a. What product or products does your state specialize in?

b. Can you identify the source of the comparative advantage that lies behind the production of one or more of these products (a natural resource, plentiful cheap labor, a skilled labor force, etc.)?

c. Do you think that the theory of comparative advantage and the Heckscher-Ohlin theorem help to explain why your state specializes in the way that it does?

7. Australia and the United States produce white and red wines. Current domestic prices for each are given in the following table:

	AUSTRALIA	UNITED STATES
White wine	5 AU$	10 US$
Red wine	10 AU$	15 US$

Suppose that the exchange rate is 1 AU$ = 1 US$.

a. If the price ratios within each country reflect resource use, which country has a comparative advantage in the production of red wine? White wine?

b. Assume there are no other trading partners and that the only motive for holding foreign currency is to buy foreign goods. Will the current exchange rate lead to trade flows in both directions between the two countries?

c. What adjustments might you expect in the exchange rate? Be specific.

d. What would you predict about trade flows between Australia and the United States after the exchange rate has adjusted?

Visit www.prenhall.com/casefair for self-test quizzes, interactive graphing exercises, and news articles.

Open-Economy Macroeconomics: The Balance of Payments and Exchange Rates

21

CHAPTER OUTLINE

The economies of the world have become increasingly interdependent over the last three decades. No economy operates in a vacuum, and economic events in one country can have significant repercussions on the economies of other countries.

International trade is a major part of today's world economy. U.S. imports now account for about 14 percent of U.S. gross domestic product (GDP), and billions of dollars flow through the international capital market each day. In Chapter 20, we explored the main reasons why there is international exchange. Countries trade with each other to obtain goods and services they cannot produce themselves or because other nations can produce goods and services at a lower cost than they can. You can see the various connections between the domestic economy and the rest of the world in the circular flow diagram in Figure 5.1. Foreign countries supply goods and services to the United States, and the United States supplies goods and services to the rest of the world.

From a macroeconomic point of view, the main difference between an international transaction and a domestic transaction concerns currency exchange:

> When people in different countries buy from and sell to each other, an exchange of currencies must also take place.

Brazilian coffee exporters cannot spend U.S. dollars in Brazil—they need Brazilian rials. A U.S. wheat exporter cannot use Brazilian rials to buy a tractor from a U.S. company or to pay the rent on warehouse facilities. Somehow, international exchange must be managed in a way that allows both partners in the transaction to wind up with their own currency.

As you know from Chapter 20, the direction of trade between two countries depends on **exchange rates**—the price of one country's currency in terms of the other country's currency. If the Japanese yen were very expensive (making the dollar cheap), both Japanese and Americans would buy from U.S. producers. If the yen were very cheap (making the U.S. dollar expensive), both Japanese and Americans would buy from Japanese producers. Within a certain range of exchange rates, trade flows in both directions, each country specializes in producing the goods in which it enjoys a comparative advantage, and trade is mutually beneficial.

exchange rate The price of one country's currency in terms of another country's currency; the ratio at which two currencies are traded for each other.

Because exchange rates are a factor in determining the flow of international trade, the way they are determined is very important. Since the turn of the century, the world monetary system has been changed several times by international agreements and events. Early in the century, nearly all currencies were backed by gold. Their values were fixed in terms of a specific number of ounces of gold, which determined their values in international trading—exchange rates.

In 1944, with the international monetary system in chaos as the end of World War II drew near, a large group of experts unofficially representing 44 countries met in Bretton Woods, New Hampshire, and drew up a number of agreements. One of these agreements established a system of essentially fixed exchange rates under which each country agreed to intervene by buying and selling currencies in the foreign exchange market when necessary to maintain the agreed-to value of its currency.

In 1971, most countries, including the United States, gave up trying to fix exchange rates formally and began allowing them to be determined essentially by supply and demand. For example, without government intervention in the marketplace, the price of British pounds in dollars is determined by the interaction of those who want to exchange dollars for pounds (those who "demand" pounds) and those who want to exchange pounds for dollars (those who "supply" pounds). If the quantity of pounds demanded exceeds the quantity of pounds supplied, the price of pounds will rise, just as the price of peanuts or paper clips would rise under similar circumstances. A more detailed discussion of the various monetary systems that have been in place since 1900 is in the Appendix to this chapter.

In this chapter, we explore what has come to be called "open-economy macroeconomics" in more detail. First, we discuss the *balance of payments*—the record of a nation's transactions with the rest of the world. We then go on to consider how the analysis changes when we allow for the international exchange of goods, services, and capital.

THE BALANCE OF PAYMENTS

foreign exchange All currencies other than the domestic currency of a given country.

We sometimes lump all foreign currencies—euros, Swiss francs, Japanese yen, Brazilian rials, and so forth—together as "foreign exchange." **Foreign exchange** is simply all currencies other than the domestic currency of a given country (in the case of the United States, the U.S. dollar). U.S. demand for foreign exchange arises because its citizens want to buy things whose prices are quoted in other currencies, such as Australian jewelry, vacations in Mexico, and bonds or stocks issued by Sony Corporation of Japan. Whenever U.S. citizens make these purchases, Australians, Mexicans, and Japanese gain U.S. dollars, which, from their point of view, are foreign exchange.

Where does the *supply* of foreign exchange come from? The answer is simple: The United States (actually, U.S. citizens or firms) earns foreign exchange when it sells products, services, or assets to another country. Just as Mexico earns foreign exchange when U.S. tourists visit Cancún, the United States earns foreign exchange (in this case, Mexican pesos) when Mexican tourists come to the United States to visit Disney World. Similarly, Saudi Arabian purchases of stock in General Motors or Colombian purchases of real estate in Miami increase the U.S. supply of foreign exchange.

Representatives of the 44 countries that met in Bretton Woods, New Hampshire, in 1944 to allay the impending chaos in the international monetary system as World War II was ending.

The record of a country's transactions in goods, services, and assets with the rest of the world is its **balance of payments.** The balance of payments is also the record of a country's sources (supply) and uses (demand) of foreign exchange.[1]

balance of payments The record of a country's transactions in goods, services, and assets with the rest of the world; also the record of a country's sources (supply) and uses (demand) of foreign exchange.

THE CURRENT ACCOUNT

The balance of payments is divided up into two major accounts, the *current account* and the *capital account.* These are shown in Table 21.1, which provides data on the U.S. balance of payments for 2002. We begin with the current account.

The first item in the current account is U.S. trade in goods. This category includes exports of computer chips, potato chips, and CDs of U.S. musicians and imports of Scotch whiskey, Japanese calculators, and Mexican oil. U.S. exports *earn* foreign exchange for the United States and are a credit (+) item on the current account. U.S. imports *use up* foreign exchange and are a debit (–) item. In 2002, the United States imported $484.3 billion more in goods than it exported.

Next in the current account is services. Like most other countries, the United States buys services from and sells services to other countries. For example, a U.S. firm shipping wheat to England might purchase insurance from a British insurance company. A Dutch flower grower may fly flowers to the United States aboard an American airliner. In the first case, the United States is importing services and therefore using up foreign exchange; in the second, it is selling services to foreigners and earning foreign exchange. In 2002, the United States exported $48.8 billion more in services than it imported.

balance of trade A country's exports of goods and services minus its imports of goods and services.

trade deficit Occurs when a country's exports of goods and services are less than its imports of goods and services in a given period.

The difference between a country's exports of goods and services and its imports of goods and services is its **balance of trade.** If exports of goods and services are less than imports of goods and services, a country has a **trade deficit.** The U.S. trade deficit in 2002 was huge: $435.5 billion (i.e., $484.3 billion less $48.8 billion).

TABLE 21.1 United States Balance of Payments, 2002

All transactions that bring foreign exchange into the United States are credited (+) to the current account; all transactions that cause the United States to lose foreign exchange are debited (–) to the current account.

CURRENT ACCOUNT	
Goods exports	682.6
Goods imports	–1,166.9
(1) Net export of goods	–484.3
Exports of services	289.3
Imports of services	–240.5
(2) Net export of services	48.8
Income received on investments	244.6
Income payments on investments	–256.5
(3) Net investment income	–11.9
(4) Net transfer payments	–56.0
(5) Balance on current account (1 + 2 + 3 + 4)	–503.4
CAPITAL ACCOUNT	
(6) Change in private U.S. assets abroad (increase is –)	–152.9
(7) Change in foreign private assets in the United States	533.7
(8) Change in U.S. government assets abroad (increase is –)	–3.3
(9) Change in foreign government assets in the United States	96.6
(10) Balance on capital account (6 + 7 + 8 + 9)	474.1
(11) Statistical discrepancy	29.3
(12) Balance of Payments (5 + 10 + 11)	0

Source: U.S. Department of Commerce, *Survey of Current Business*, April 2003.

[1]Bear in mind the distinction between the balance of payments and a balance sheet. A *balance sheet* for a firm or a country measures that entity's stock of assets and liabilities at a moment in time. The *balance of payments*, by contrast, measures *flows*, usually over a period of a month, a quarter, or a year. Despite its name, the balance of payments is *not* a balance sheet.

The third item in the current account concerns *investment income.* U.S. citizens hold foreign assets (stocks, bonds, and real assets like buildings and factories). Dividends, interest, rent, and profits paid to U.S. asset holders are a source of foreign exchange. Conversely, when foreigners earn dividends, interest, and profits on assets held in the United States, foreign exchange is used up. In 2002, investment income paid to foreigners exceeded investment income received from foreigners by $11.9 billion.

The fourth item in Table 21.1 is *net transfer payments.* Transfer payments from the United States to foreigners are another use of foreign exchange. Some of these transfer payments are from private U.S. citizens and some are from the U.S. government. You may send a check to a relief agency in Africa. Conversely, some foreigners make transfer payments to the United States. "Net" refers to the difference between payments from the United States to foreigners and payments from foreigners to the United States.

balance on current account Net exports of goods, plus net exports of services, plus net investment income, plus net transfer payments.

If we add net exports of goods, net export of services, net investment income, and net transfer payments, we get the **balance on current account**. The balance on current account shows how much a nation has spent on foreign goods, services, investment income payments, and transfers relative to how much it has earned from other countries. When the balance is negative, which it was for the United States in 2002, a nation has spent more on foreign goods and services (plus investment income and transfers paid) than it has earned through the sales of its goods and services to the rest of the world (plus investment income and transfers received). If a nation has spent more on foreign goods, services, investment income payments, and transfers than it has earned, its net wealth position vis-à-vis the rest of the world must decrease. By "net" we mean a nation's assets abroad minus its liabilities to the rest of the world. The capital account of the balance of payments records the changes in these assets and liabilities. We now turn to the capital account.

THE CAPITAL ACCOUNT

For each transaction recorded in the current account, there is an offsetting transaction recorded in the capital account. Consider the purchase of a Japanese car by a U.S. citizen. Say that the yen/dollar exchange rate is 100 yen to a dollar, and the yen price of the car is 2.0 million yen, which is $20,000. The U.S. citizen (probably an automobile dealer) takes $20,000, buys 2.0 million yen, and then buys the car. In this case, U.S. imports are increased by $20,000 in the current account and foreign assets in the United States (in this case, Japanese holdings of dollars) are increased by $20,000 in the capital account. The net wealth position of the United States vis-à-vis the rest of the world has decreased by $20,000. The key point to realize is that an increase in U.S. imports results in an increase in foreign assets in the United States. The United States must "pay" for the imports, and whatever it pays with (in this example, U.S. dollars) is an increase in foreign assets in the United States. Conversely, an increase in U.S. exports results in an increase in U.S. assets abroad, because foreigners must pay for the U.S. exports.

balance on capital account In the United States, the sum of the following (measured in a given period): the change in private U.S. assets abroad, the change in foreign private assets in the United States, the change in U.S. government assets abroad, and the change in foreign government assets in the United States.

Table 21.1 shows that U.S. assets abroad are divided into private holdings (line 6) and U.S. government holdings (line 8). Similariy, foreign assets in the United States are divided into foreign private (line 7) and foreign government (line 9). The sum of lines 6, 7, 8, and 9 is the **balance on capital account** (line 10). If there were no errors of measurement in the data collection, the balance on capital account would equal the negative of the balance on current account, because, as mentioned previously, for each transaction in the current account there is an offsetting transaction in the capital account. Another way of looking at the balance on capital account is that it is the change in the net wealth position of the country vis-à-vis the rest of the world. If the balance on capital account is positive, this means that the change in foreign assets in the country is greater than the change in the country's assets abroad, which is a decrease in the net wealth position of the country.

Table 21.1 shows that in 2002 the U.S. balance on current account was –$503.4 billion, which means that the United States spent considerably more than it made vis-à-vis the rest of the world. If the balance on current account is measured correctly, then the net wealth position of the United States vis-à-vis the rest of the world decreased by $503.4 billion in 2002. In this case, the balance on capital account should be $503.4 billion. The balance on capital account (line 10) is in fact $474.1 billion, and so the error of measurement, called the statistical discrepancy, is $29.3 billion (line 11) in 2002. The balance of payments (line 12) is the sum of the balance on current account, the balance on capital account, and the statistical discrepancy. By construction, it is always zero.

It is important to note from Table 21.1 that even though the net wealth position of the United States decreased in 2002, the change in U.S. assets abroad increased considerably ($152.9 billion private plus $3.3 billion government). How can this be? Because there was an even larger increase in foreign assets in the United States ($533.7 billion private plus $96.6 billion government). It is the *net* change (i.e., the change in foreign assets in the United States minus the change in U.S. assets abroad) that is equal to the negative of the balance on current account (aside from the statistical discrepancy), not the change in just U.S. assets abroad.

There are many transactions that get recorded in the capital account that do not pertain to the current account. Consider a purchase of a U.K. security by a U.S. resident. This is done by the U.S. resident selling dollars for pounds and using the pounds to buy the U.K. security. After this transaction, U.S. assets abroad have increased (the United States now holds more U.K. securities) and foreign assets in the United States have increased (foreigners now hold more dollars). The purchase of the U.K. security is recorded as a minus item in line 6 in Table 21.1, and the increase in foreign holdings of dollars is recorded as a plus item in line 7. These two balance out. This happens whenever there is a switch of one kind of asset for another vis-à-vis the rest of the world. When a Japanese company bought Rockefeller Center in New York City in 1990, this was an increase in foreign assets in the United States (the Japanese then owned Rockefeller Center) and an increase in U.S. assets abroad (the United States then had the yen that was used to pay for the center). If the United States then took the yen and bought Japanese securities, this was simply a switch of one kind of U.S. asset abroad (yen) for another (Japanese securities).

THE UNITED STATES AS A DEBTOR NATION

If a country has positive net wealth position vis-à-vis the rest of the world, it can be said to be a creditor nation. Conversely, if it has negative net wealth position, it can be said to be a debtor nation. Remember that a country's net wealth position increases if it has a positive current account balance and decreases if it has a negative current account balance. It is important to realize that the *only* way a country's net wealth position can change is if its current account balance is nonzero. Simply switching one form of asset for another, such as switching Rockefeller Center for Japanese securities in the preceding example, is not a change in a country's net wealth position. Another way of putting this is that a country's net wealth position is the sum of all its past current account balances.

Prior to the mid-1970s, the United States had generally run current account surpluses, and thus its net wealth position was positive. It was a creditor nation. This began to turn around in the mid-1970s, and by the mid-1980s, the United States was running large current account deficits. Some time during this period the United States changed from having a positive net wealth position vis-à-vis the rest of the world to having a negative position. In other words, the United States changed from a creditor nation to a debtor nation. The current account deficits persisted into the 1990s, and the United States is now the largest debtor nation in the world. In 2001, foreign assets in the United States totaled $9.2 trillion and U.S. assets abroad totaled $6.9 trillion.[2] The U.S. net wealth position was thus –$2.3 trillion. This large negative position reflects the fact that the United States spent much more in the 1980s and 1990s on foreign goods and services (plus investment income and transfers paid) than it earned through the sales of its goods and services to the rest of the world (plus investment income and transfers received).

EQUILIBRIUM OUTPUT (INCOME) IN AN OPEN ECONOMY

Everything we have said so far has been descriptive. Now we turn to analysis. How are all these trade and capital flows determined? What impacts do they have on the economies of

[2]U.S. Department of Commerce, *Survey of Current Business*, April 2003, Table G.1.

the countries involved? To simplify our discussion here, we will assume that exchange rates are fixed. We will relax this assumption later.

THE INTERNATIONAL SECTOR AND PLANNED AGGREGATE EXPENDITURE

Our earlier descriptions of the multiplier took into account the consumption behavior of households (C), the planned investment behavior of firms (I), and the spending of the government (G). We defined the sum of these three components as planned aggregate expenditure (AE).

To analyze the international sector, we must include the goods and services a country exports to the rest of the world, as well as what it imports. If we call our exports of goods and services EX, it should be clear that EX is a component of total output and income. A U.S. razor blade sold to a buyer in Mexico is as much a part of U.S. production as a similar blade sold in Pittsburgh. Exports simply represent demand for domestic products not by domestic households and firms and the government but by the rest of the world.

What about imports? Remember, imports are *not a part of domestic output* (Y). By definition, imports are not produced by the country that is importing them. Remember also, when we look at households' total consumption spending, firms' total investment spending, and total government spending, imports are included. Therefore, to calculate domestic output correctly, we must subtract the parts of consumption, investment, and government spending that constitute imports. The definition of planned aggregate expenditure becomes:

> Planned aggregate expenditure in an open economy:
>
> $$AE \equiv C + I + G + EX - IM$$

net exports of goods and services ($EX - IM$) The difference between a country's total exports and total imports.

The last two terms ($EX - IM$) together are the country's **net exports of goods and services.**

Determining the Level of Imports What determines the level of imports and exports in a country? For now, we assume that the level of imports is a function of income (Y). The rationale is simple: When U.S. income increases, U.S. citizens buy more of everything, including U.S. cars and peanut butter, Japanese TV sets, and Korean steel and DVD recorders. When income rises, imports tend to go up. Algebraically:

$$IM = mY$$

where Y is income and m is some positive number (m is assumed to be less than 1; otherwise, a \$1 increase in income generates an increase in imports of more than \$1, which does not make sense). Recall from Chapter 8 that the marginal propensity to consume (MPC) measures the change in consumption that results from a \$1 change in income. Similarly, the **marginal propensity to import**, abbreviated as MPM or m, is the change in imports caused by a \$1 change in income. If $m = .2$, or 20 percent, and income is \$1,000, then imports, IM, are equal to $.2 \times \$1{,}000 = \$200$. If income rises by \$100 to \$1,100, then the change in imports will equal $m \times$ (the change in income) $= .2 \times \$100 = \$20$.

marginal propensity to import (MPM) The change in imports caused by a \$1 change in income.

For now we will assume that exports (EX) are given, (i.e., that they are not affected, even indirectly, by the state of the economy.) This assumption is relaxed later in this chapter.

Solving for Equilibrium Given the assumption about how imports are determined, we can solve for equilibrium income. This procedure is illustrated in Figure 21.1. Starting from the consumption function (blue line) in Figure 21.1(a), we gradually build up the components of planned aggregate expenditure (red line). Assuming for simplicity that planned investment, government purchases, and exports are all constant and do not depend on income, we move easily from the blue line to the red line by adding the fixed amounts of I, G, and EX to consumption at every level of income. In this example, we take $I + G + EX$ to equal 80.

$C + I + G + EX$, however, includes spending on imports, which are not part of domestic production. To get spending on domestically produced goods, we must subtract the amount

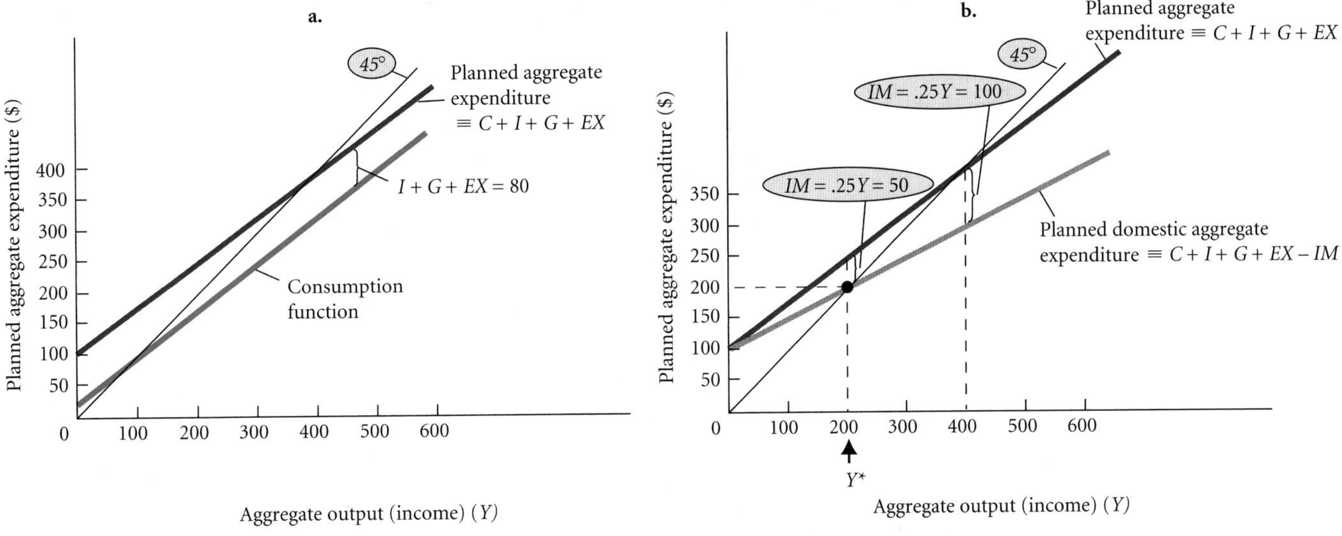

FIGURE 21.1 Determining Equilibrium Output in an Open Economy

In **a**, planned investment spending (*I*), government spending (G), and total exports (*EX*) are added to consumption (*C*) to arrive at planned aggregate expenditure. However, *C* + *I* + G + *EX* includes spending on imports. In **b**, the amount imported at every level of income is subtracted from planned aggregate expenditure. Equilibrium output occurs at $Y* = 200$, the point at which planned domestic aggregate expenditure crosses the 45-degree line.

that is imported at each level of income. In Figure 21.1(b), we assume $m = .25$, which is the assumption that 25 percent of total income is spent on goods and services produced in foreign countries. Imports under this assumption are a constant fraction of total income; therefore at higher levels of income a larger amount is spent on foreign goods and services. For example, at $Y = 200$, $IM = .25Y$, or 50. Similarly, at $Y = 400$, $IM = .25Y$, or 100. Figure 21.1(b) shows the planned *domestic* aggregate expenditure curve.

Equilibrium is reached when planned domestic aggregate expenditure equals domestic aggregate output (income). This is true at only one level of aggregate output, $Y* = 200$, in Figure 21.1(b). If *Y* were below *Y**, planned expenditure would exceed output, inventories would be lower than planned, and output would rise. At levels above *Y**, output would exceed planned expenditure, inventories would be larger than planned, and output would fall.

The Open-Economy Multiplier All of this has implications for the size of the multiplier. Recall the multiplier, introduced in Chapter 8, and consider a sustained rise in government purchases (*G*). Initially, the increase in G will cause planned aggregate expenditure to be greater than aggregate output. Domestic firms will find their inventories to be lower than planned and thus will increase their output, but added output means more income. More workers are hired and profits are higher. Some of the added income is saved, and some is spent. The added consumption spending leads to a second round of inventories being lower than planned and raising output. Equilibrium output rises by a multiple of the initial increase in government purchases. This is the multiplier.

In Chapters 8 and 9, we showed that the simple multiplier equals $1/(1 - MPC)$, or $(1/MPS)$. That is, a sustained increase in government purchases equal to ΔG will lead to an increase in aggregate output (income) of $\Delta G[1/(1 - MPC)]$. If the *MPC* were .75 and government purchases rose by \$10 billion, equilibrium income would rise by 4 × \$10 billion, or \$40 billion. The multiplier is $[1/(1 - .75)] = [1/.25] = 4.0$.

In an open economy, some of the increase in income brought about by the increase in G is spent on imports instead of domestically produced goods and services. The part of income spent on imports does not increase domestic income (*Y*) because imports are produced by foreigners. To compute the multiplier we need to know how much of the increased income is used to increase domestic consumption. (We are assuming all imports are consumption goods. In practice, some imports are investment goods and some are goods purchased by the government.) In other words, we need to know the marginal propensity to consume *domestic* goods. Domestic consumption is $C - IM$. So the marginal propensity to consume domestic goods is the marginal propensity to consume all goods (the *MPC*) minus the marginal propensity to import (the *MPM*). The marginal propensity to consume domestic goods is $(MPC - MPM)$. Consequently:

$$\text{open - economy multiplier} = \frac{1}{1-(MPC - MPM)}$$

If the *MPC* is .75 and the *MPM* is .25, then the multiplier is 1/.5, or 2.0. This multiplier is smaller than the multiplier in which imports are not taken into account, which is 1/.25, or 4.0.

The message of the open-economy multiplier model, put succinctly:

> The effect of a sustained increase in government spending (or investment) on income—that is, the multiplier—is smaller in an open economy than in a closed economy. The reason: When government spending (or investment) increases and income and consumption rises, some of the extra consumption spending that results is on foreign products and not on domestically produced goods and services.

IMPORTS AND EXPORTS AND THE TRADE FEEDBACK EFFECT

For simplicity, we have so far assumed that the level of imports depends only on income and that the level of exports is fixed. In reality the amount of spending on imports depends on factors other than income, and exports are not fixed. We will now consider the more realistic picture.

The Determinants of Imports The same factors that affect households' consumption behavior and firms' investment behavior are likely to affect the demand for imports because some imported goods are consumption goods and some are investment goods. For example, anything that increases consumption spending is likely to increase the demand for imports. We saw in Chapters 8 and 12 that such factors as the after-tax real wage, after-tax nonlabor income, and interest rates affect consumption spending; and thus these should also affect spending on imports. Similarly, anything that increases investment spending is likely to increase the demand for imports. A decrease in interest rates, for example, should encourage spending on both domestically produced goods and foreign-produced goods.

There is one additional consideration in determining spending on imports: the *relative prices* of domestically produced and foreign-produced goods. If the prices of foreign goods fall relative to the prices of domestic goods, people will consume more foreign goods relative to domestic goods. When Japanese cars are cheap relative to U.S. cars, consumption of Japanese cars should be high, and vice versa.

The Determinants of Exports We now relax our assumption that exports are fixed. The demand for U.S. exports by other countries is identical to their demand for imports from the United States. Germany imports goods, some are U.S. produced. France, Spain, and so on do the same. Total expenditure on imports in Germany is a function of the factors we have just discussed, except that the variables are German variables instead of U.S. variables. This is true for all other countries as well. The demand for U.S. exports depends on economic activity in the rest of the world—rest-of-the-world real wages, wealth, nonlabor income, interest rates, and so on—as well as on the prices of U.S. goods relative to the price of rest-of-the-world goods.

If foreign output increases, U.S. exports tend to increase. U.S. exports also tend to increase when U.S. prices fall relative to those in the rest of the world.

trade feedback effect The tendency for an increase in the economic activity of one country to lead to a worldwide increase in economic activity, which then feeds back to that country.

The Trade Feedback Effect We can now combine what we know about the demand for imports and the demand for exports to discuss the **trade feedback effect**. Suppose the United States finds its exports increasing, perhaps because the world suddenly decides it prefers U.S. computers to other computers. This will lead to an increase in U.S. output (income), which leads to an increase in U.S. imports. Here is where the trade feedback begins. Because U.S. imports are somebody else's exports, the extra import demand from the United States raises the exports of the rest of the world. When other countries' exports to the United States go up, their output and incomes also rise, which leads to an increase in the demand for imports from the rest of the world. Some of the extra imports demanded by the rest of the world come from the United States, so U.S. exports increase. The increase in U.S. exports stimulates U.S. economic activity even more, which leads to a further increase in the U.S. demand for imports, and so on.

An increase in U.S. imports increases other countries exports, which stimulates those countries' economies and increases their imports, which increases U.S. exports, which stimulates the U.S. economy and increases its imports, and so on. This is the trade feedback effect. In other words, an increase in U.S. economic activity leads to a world-wide increase in economic activity, which then "feeds back" to the United States.

IMPORT AND EXPORT PRICES AND THE PRICE FEEDBACK EFFECT

We have talked about the price of imports, but we have not yet discussed the factors that influence import prices. The consideration of import prices is complicated because more than one currency is involved. When we talk about "the price of imports," do we mean the price in dollars, in yen, in U.K. pounds, in Mexican pesos, etc? Because the exports of one country are the imports of another, the same question holds for the price of exports. When Mexico exports auto parts to the United States, Mexican manufacturers are interested in the price of auto parts in terms of pesos, because pesos are what they use for transactions in Mexico. U.S. consumers are interested in the price of auto parts in dollars, because dollars are what they use for transactions in the United States. The link between the two prices is the dollar/peso exchange rate.

Suppose Mexico is experiencing an inflation and the price of radiators in pesos rises from 1,000 pesos to 1,200 pesos per radiator. If the dollar/peso exchange rate remains unchanged at, say, $0.10 per peso, then Mexico's export price for radiators in terms of dollars will also rise, from $100 to $120 per radiator. Because Mexico's exports to the United States are by definition U.S. imports from Mexico, an increase in the dollar prices of Mexican exports to the United States means an increase in the prices of U.S. imports from Mexico. Therefore, when Mexico's export prices rise with no change in the dollar/peso exchange rate, U.S. import prices rise.

Export prices of other countries affect U.S. import prices.

A country's export prices tend to move fairly closely with the general price level in that country. If Mexico is experiencing a general increase in prices, it is likely this change will be reflected in price increases of all domestically produced goods, both exportable and nonexportable.

The general rate of inflation abroad is likely to affect U.S. import prices. If the inflation rate abroad is high, U.S. import prices are likely to rise.

The Price Feedback Effect We have just seen that when a country experiences an increase in domestic prices, the prices of its exports will increase. It is also true that when the prices of a country's *imports* increase, the prices of domestic goods may increase in response. There are at least two ways this can occur.

First, an increase in the prices of imported inputs will shift a country's aggregate supply curve to the left. In Chapter 13, we discussed the macroeconomy's response to a cost shock. Recall that a leftward shift in the aggregate supply curve due to a cost increase causes aggregate output to fall and prices to rise (stagflation).

Second, if import prices rise relative to domestic prices, households will tend to substitute domestically produced goods and services for imports. This is equivalent to a rightward shift of the aggregate demand curve. If the domestic economy is operating on the upward-sloping part of the aggregate supply curve, the overall domestic price level will rise in response to an increase in aggregate demand. Perfectly competitive firms will see market-determined prices rise, and imperfectly competitive firms will experience an increase in the demand for their products. Studies have shown, for example, that the price of automobiles produced in the United States moves closely with the price of imported cars.

Still, this is not the end of the story. Suppose a country—say, Mexico—experiences an increase in its domestic price level. This will increase the price of its exports to Canada (and to all other countries). The increase in the price of Canadian imports from Mexico will lead to an increase in domestic prices in Canada. Canada also exports to Mexico. The increase in Canadian prices causes an increase in the price of Canadian exports to Mexico, which then further increases the Mexican price level.

price feedback effect The process by which a domestic price increase in one country can "feed back" on itself through export and import prices. An increase in the price level in one country can drive up prices in other countries. This in turn further increases the price level in the first country.

This is called the **price feedback effect**, in the sense that inflation is "exportable." An increase in the price level in one country can drive up prices in other countries, which in turn further increases the price level in the first country. Through export and import prices, a domestic price increase can "feed back" on itself.

It is important to realize that the discussion so far has been based on the assumption of fixed exchange rates. Life is more complicated under flexible exchange rates, to which we now turn.

THE OPEN ECONOMY WITH FLEXIBLE EXCHANGE RATES

floating, or market-determined, exchange rates Exchange rates that are determined by the unregulated forces of supply and demand.

To a large extent, the fixed exchange rates set by the Bretton Woods agreements served as international monetary arrangements until 1971. Then, in 1971 the United States and most other countries decided to abandon the fixed exchange rate system in favor of **floating**, or **market-determined, exchange rates**. While governments still intervene to ensure that exchange rate movements are "orderly," exchange rates today are largely determined by the unregulated forces of supply and demand.

Understanding how an economy interacts with the rest of the world when exchange rates are not fixed is not as simple as when we assume fixed exchange rates. Exchange rates determine the price of imported goods relative to domestic goods and can have significant effects on the level of imports and exports. Consider a 20 percent drop in the value of the dollar against the British pound. Dollars buy fewer pounds and pounds buy more dollars. Both British residents, who now get more dollars for pounds, and U.S. residents, who get fewer pounds for dollars, find that U.S. goods and services are more attractive. Exchange rate movements have important impacts on imports, exports, and the movement of capital between countries.

THE MARKET FOR FOREIGN EXCHANGE

What determines exchange rates under a floating rate system? To explore this, we assume there are just two countries, the United States and Great Britain. It is easier to understand a world with only two countries, and most of the points we will make can be generalized to a world with many trading partners.

The Supply of, and Demand for, Pounds Governments, private citizens, banks, and corporations exchange pounds for dollars and dollars for pounds every day. In our two-country case, those who *demand* pounds are holders of dollars seeking to exchange them for pounds. Those who *supply* pounds are holders of pounds seeking to exchange them for dollars. It is important not to confuse the supply of dollars (or pounds) on the foreign exchange market with the U.S. (or British) money supply. The latter is the sum of all the money currently in circulation. The supply of dollars on the foreign exchange market is the number of dollars that holders seek to exchange for pounds in a given time period. The demand for, and supply of, dollars on foreign exchange markets determines *exchange* rates; the demand for money balances and the total domestic money supply determine the *interest* rate.

The common reason for exchanging dollars for pounds is to buy something produced in Great Britain. U.S. importers who purchase Jaguar automobiles or Scotch whiskey must pay

TABLE 21.2 Some Private Buyers and Sellers in International Exchange Markets: United States and Great Britain

THE DEMAND FOR POUNDS (SUPPLY OF DOLLARS)

1. Firms, households, or governments that import British goods into the United States or wish to buy British-made goods and services
2. U.S. citizens traveling in Great Britain
3. Holders of dollars who want to buy British stocks, bonds, or other financial instruments
4. U.S. companies that want to invest in Great Britain
5. Speculators who anticipate a decline in the value of the dollar relative to the pound

THE SUPPLY OF POUNDS (DEMAND FOR DOLLARS)

1. Firms, households, or governments that import U.S. goods into Great Britain or wish to buy U.S.-made goods and services
2. British citizens traveling in the United States
3. Holders of pounds who want to buy stocks, bonds, or other financial instruments in the United States
4. British companies that want to invest in the United States
5. Speculators who anticipate a rise in the value of the dollar relative to the pound

with pounds. U.S. citizens traveling in Great Britain who want to ride the train, stay in a hotel, or eat at a restaurant must acquire pounds for dollars to do so. If a U.S. corporation builds a plant in Great Britain, it must pay for that plant in pounds.

At the same time, some people may want to buy British stocks or bonds. Implicitly, when U.S. citizens buy a bond issued by the British government or by a British corporation, they are making a loan, but the transaction requires a currency exchange. The British bond seller must ultimately be paid in pounds.

On the supply side of the market, the situation is reversed. Here we find people—usually British citizens—holding pounds they want to use to buy dollars. Again, the common reason is to buy things produced in the United States. If a British importer decides to import golf carts made in Georgia, the producer must be paid in dollars. British tourists visiting New York may ride in cabs, eat in restaurants, and tour Ellis Island. Doing these things requires dollars. When a British firm builds an office complex in Los Angeles, it must pay the contractor in dollars.

In addition to buyers and sellers who exchange money to engage in transactions, some people and institutions hold currency balances for speculative reasons. If I think the U.S. dollar is going to decline in value relative to the pound, I may want to hold some of my wealth in the form of pounds. Table 21.2 summarizes some of the major categories of private foreign exchange demanders and suppliers in the two-country case of the United States and Great Britain.

Figure 21.2 shows the demand curve for pounds in the foreign exchange market. When the price of pounds (the exchange rate) is lower, it takes fewer dollars to buy British goods

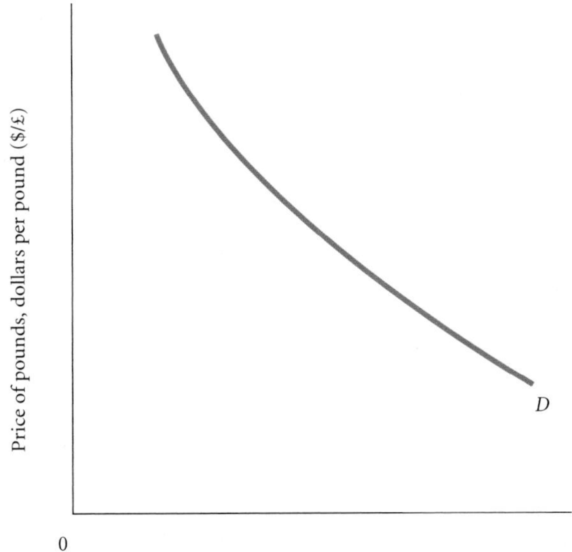

FIGURE 21.2 The Demand for Pounds in the Foreign Exchange Market

When the price of pounds falls, British-made goods and services appear less expensive to U.S. buyers. If British prices are constant, U.S. buyers will buy more British goods and services, and the quantity of pounds demanded will rise.

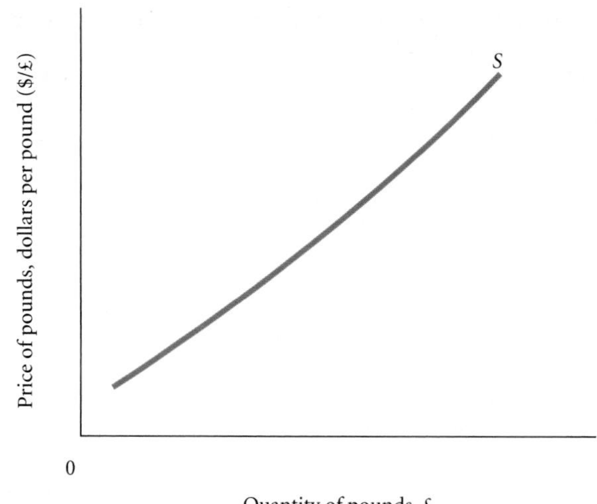

FIGURE 21.3 The Supply of Pounds in the Foreign Exchange Market

When the price of pounds rises, the British can obtain more dollars for each pound. This means that U.S.-made goods and services appear less expensive to British buyers. Thus, the quantity of pounds supplied is likely to rise with the exchange rate.

and services, to build a plant in Liverpool, to travel to London, and so forth. Lower net prices (in dollars) should increase the demand for British-made products and encourage investment and travel in Great Britain. If prices (in pounds) in Britain do not change, an increase in the quantity of British goods and services demanded by foreigners will increase the quantity of pounds demanded. The demand-for-pounds curve in the foreign exchange market has a negative slope.

Figure 21.3 shows a supply curve for pounds in the foreign exchange market. At a higher exchange rate, each pound buys more dollars, making the price of U.S.-produced goods and services lower to the British. The British are more apt to buy U.S.-made goods when the price of pounds is high (the value of the dollar is low). An increase in British demand for U.S. goods and services is likely to increase the quantity of pounds supplied. The curve representing the supply of pounds in the foreign exchange market has a positive slope.

The Equilibrium Exchange Rate When exchange rates are allowed to float, they are determined the same way other prices are determined:

> The equilibrium exchange rate occurs at the point at which the quantity demanded of a foreign currency equals the quantity of that currency supplied.

appreciation of a currency The rise in value of one currency relative to another.

This is illustrated in Figure 21.4. An excess demand for pounds (quantity demanded in excess of quantity supplied) will cause the price of pounds to rise—the pound will **appreciate** with

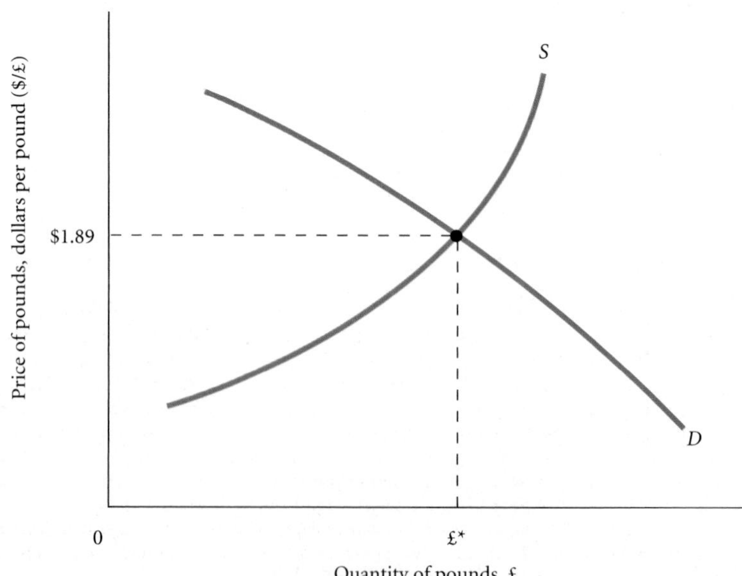

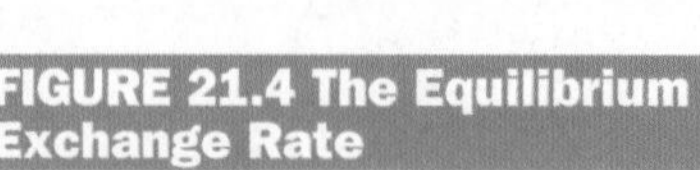
FIGURE 21.4 The Equilibrium Exchange Rate

When exchange rates are allowed to float, they are determined by the forces of supply and demand. An excess demand for pounds will cause the pound to appreciate against the dollar. An excess supply of pounds will lead to a depreciating pound.

respect to the dollar. An excess supply of pounds will cause the price of pounds to fall—the pound will **depreciate** with respect to the dollar.[3]

depreciation of a currency The fall in value of one currency relative to another.

FACTORS THAT AFFECT EXCHANGE RATES

We now know enough to discuss the factors likely to influence exchange rates. Anything that changes the behavior of the people in Table 21.2 can cause demand and supply curves to shift and the exchange rate to adjust accordingly.

Purchasing Power Parity: The Law of One Price If the costs of transporting goods between two countries are small, we would expect the price of the same good in both countries to be roughly the same. The price of basketballs should be roughly the same in Canada and the United States, for example.

It is not hard to see why. If the price of basketballs is cheaper in Canada, it will pay for someone to buy balls in Canada at a low price and sell them in the United States at a higher price. This decreases the supply and pushes up the price in Canada and increases the supply and pushes down the price in the United States. This process should continue as long as the price differential, and therefore the profit opportunity, persists. For a good with trivial transportation costs, we would expect this **law of one price** to hold. The price of a good should be the same regardless of where we buy it.

law of one price If the costs of transportation are small, the price of the same good in different countries should be roughly the same.

If the law of one price held for all goods, and if each country consumed the same market basket of goods, the exchange rate between the two currencies would be determined simply by the relative price levels in the two countries. If the price of a basketball were $10 in the United States and $12 in Canada, then the U.S.–Canada exchange rate would have to be $1 U.S. per $1.20 Canadian. If the rate were instead one to one, it would pay people to buy the balls in the United States and sell them in Canada. This would increase the demand for U.S. dollars in Canada, thereby driving up their price in terms of Canadian dollars to $1 U.S. per $1.2 Canadian, at which point no one could make a profit shipping basketballs across international lines, and the process would cease.[4]

The theory that exchange rates will adjust so that the price of similar goods in different countries is the same is known as the **purchasing-power-parity theory**. According to this theory, if it takes 10 times as many Mexican pesos to buy a pound of salt in Mexico as it takes U.S. dollars to buy a pound of salt in the United States, then the equilibrium exchange rate should be 10 pesos per dollar.

purchasing-power-parity theory A theory of international exchange holding that exchange rates are set so that the price of similar goods in different countries is the same.

In practice, transportation costs for many goods are quite large, and the law of one price does not hold for these goods. (Haircuts are often cited as a good example. The transportation costs for a U.S. resident to get a British haircut are indeed large unless that person is an airline pilot.) Also, many products that are potential substitutes for each other are not precisely identical. For instance, a Rolls Royce and a Honda are both cars, but there is no reason to expect the exchange rate between the British pound and the yen to be set so that the prices of the two are equalized. In addition, countries consume different market baskets of goods, so we would not expect the aggregate price levels to follow the law of one price. Nevertheless:

> A high rate of inflation in one country relative to another puts pressure on the exchange rate between the two countries, and there is a general tendency for the currencies of relatively high-inflation countries to depreciate.

---

[3]Although Figure 21.3 shows the supply-of-pounds curve in the foreign exchange market with a positive slope, under certain circumstances the curve may bend back. Suppose the price of a pound rises from $1.50 to $2.00. Consider a British importer who buys 10 Chevrolets each month at $15,000 each, including transportation costs. When a pound exchanges for $1.50, he will supply 100,000 pounds per month to the foreign exchange market—100,000 pounds brings $150,000, enough to buy 10 cars. Now suppose the cheaper dollar causes him to buy 12 cars. Twelve cars will cost a total of $180,000, but at $2.00 = 1 pound, he will spend only 90,000 pounds per month. The supply of pounds on the market falls when the price of pounds rises. The reason for this seeming paradox is simple. The number of pounds a British importer needs to buy U.S. goods depends on both the quantity of goods he buys and the price of those goods in pounds. If demand for imports is inelastic so that the percentage decrease in price resulting from the depreciated currency is greater than the percentage increase in the quantity of imports demanded, importers will spend fewer pounds and the quantity of pounds supplied in the foreign exchange market will fall. The supply of pounds will slope upward as long as the demand for U.S. imports is elastic.

[4]Of course, if the rate were $1 U.S. to $2 Canadian, then it would pay people to buy basketballs in Canada (at $12 Canadian, which is $6 U.S.) and sell them in the United States. This would weaken demand for the U.S. dollar, and its price would fall from $2 Canadian until it reached $1.20 Canadian.

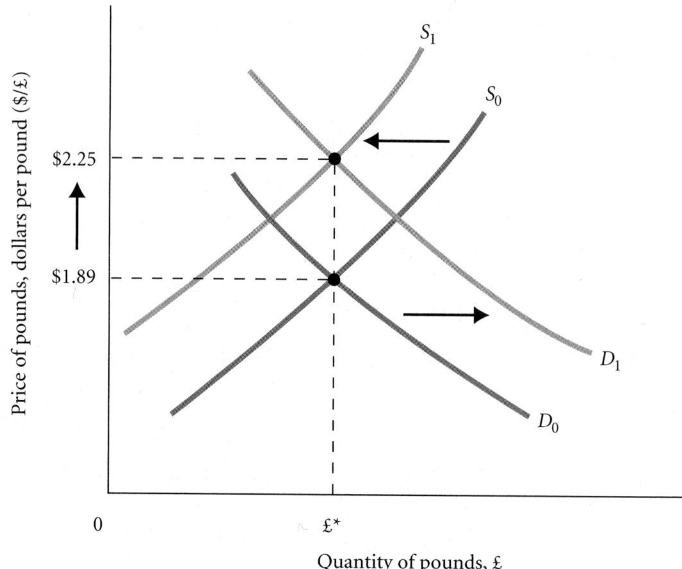

FIGURE 21.5 Exchange Rates Respond to Changes in Relative Prices

The higher price level in the United States makes imports relatively less expensive. U.S. citizens are likely to increase their spending on imports from Britain, shifting the demand for pounds to the right, from D_0 to D_1. At the same time, the British see U.S. goods getting more expensive and reduce their demand for exports from the United States. The supply of pounds shifts to the left, from S_0 to S_1. The result is an increase in the price of pounds. The pound appreciates and the dollar is worth less.

Figure 21.5 shows the adjustment likely to occur following an increase in the U.S. price level relative to the price level in Great Britain. This change in relative prices will affect citizens of both countries. Higher prices in the United States make imports relatively less expensive. U.S. citizens are likely to increase their spending on imports from Britain, shifting the demand for pounds to the right, from D_0 to D_1. At the same time, the British see U.S. goods getting more expensive and reduce their demand for exports from the United States. Consequently, the supply of pounds shifts to the left, from S_0 to S_1. The result is an increase in the price of pounds. Before the change in relative prices, 1 pound sold for $1.89; after the change, 1 pound costs $2.25. The pound appreciates and the dollar is worth less.

Relative Interest Rates Another factor that influences a country's exchange rate is the level of its interest rate relative to other countries' interest rates. If the interest rate is 6 percent in the United States and 8 percent in Great Britain, people with money to lend have an incentive to buy British securities instead of U.S. securities. Although it is sometimes difficult for individuals in one country to buy securities in another country, it is easy for international banks and investment companies to do so. If the interest rate is lower in the United States than in Britain, there will be a movement of funds out of U.S. securities into British securities as banks and firms move their funds to the higher yielding securities.

How does a U.S. bank buy British securities? It takes its dollars, buys British pounds, and uses the pounds to buy the British securities. The bank's purchase of pounds drives up the price of pounds in the foreign exchange market. The increased demand for pounds increases the price of the pound (and decreases the price of the dollar). A high interest rate in Britain relative to the interest rate in the United States tends to depreciate the dollar.

Figure 21.6 shows the effect of rising interest rates in the United States on the pound–dollar exchange rate. Higher interest rates in the United States attract British investors. To buy U.S. securities, the British need dollars. The supply of pounds (the demand for dollars) shifts to the right, from *S* to *S′*. The same relative interest rates affect the portfolio choices of U.S. banks, firms, and households. With higher interest rates at home, there is less incentive for U.S. residents to buy British securities. The demand for pounds drops at the same time as the supply increases and the demand curve shifts to the left, from *D* to *D′*. The net result is a depreciating pound and an appreciating dollar. The price of pounds falls from $1.89 to $1.25.

THE EFFECTS OF EXCHANGE RATES ON THE ECONOMY

We are now ready to discuss some of the implications of floating exchange rates. Recall, when exchange rates are fixed, households spend some of their incomes on imports and the multiplier is smaller than it would be otherwise. Imports are a "leakage" from the circular

News Analysis

The Weak U.S. Dollar and the Canadian Economy in 2003

SINCE 2001, THE FEDERAL RESERVE HAS BEEN pursuing an aggressive expansionary monetary policy designed to lower interest rates and stimulate aggregate demand. Lower interest rates stimulate investment spending by businesses and consumer spending by households. But the response of the economy was slow in coming. Another impact that low interest rates in the United States have is that fewer foreign buyers are attracted to U.S. securities, and that reduces the demand for dollars in foreign exchange markets. In fact, in 2002 and 2003, the dollar fell in value nearly 30 percent against most currencies, including the Canadian dollar. A strong (expensive) Canadian dollar, however, is bad news for Canadian producers, whose goods are less competitive on world markets. The following article from the *Wall Street Journal* tells the tale.

As Canada's Dollar Surges, Exporters Pay a Steep Price

—Wall Street Journal

The "pool noodle" isn't as profitable as it once was for Canada's Industrial Thermo Polymers Ltd.

The company, whose products include the popular floating device for children, is one of thousands of Canadian manufacturers that spent years exploiting the country's ever-weakening currency, known as the "loonie" for the diving bird on its dollar coin. Since 85% of Canada's merchandise exports go to the U.S., the weak currency meant revenues rose as costs stayed put, making the companies ever more profitable and competitive.

No more. The loonie's 16% surge this year is squeezing exporters across the country. Brampton, Ontario-based Industrial Thermal slowed its assembly line and laid off 27 of its 130 workers after the loonie's rise cut revenue by 2.3 million Canadian dollars (US$1.7 million). The loonie, which hit 75 U.S. cents this month for the first time since 1996, traded late Monday at 73.6 cents, up from 63.4 cents at the start of the year.

Of course, the euro is soaring, too. But European exporters are far less dependent on the U.S. market than Canadians. Total two-way trade in goods between the U.S. and Canada, at more than $1 billion a day, exceeds that between the U.S. and the entire European Union. Exports have grown to 41% of Canada's gross domestic product from 26% in 1990, as economic integration expanded under North American free trade. Canada, with just 30 million people, is also the biggest market for U.S. exports.

Now, the surging loonie threatens to hamper Canada's export machine and slow its economic growth. Douglas Porter, senior economist at Bank of Montreal's Nesbitt Burns securities unit, predicts the loonie's rise will shave almost 4% from Canadian export volumes and 1.2 percentage points from GDP growth by the end of 2004. "The Canadian economy has consistently outpaced its U.S. counterpart since 1999," says Mr. Porter. "Those days are now numbered."

Source: Adapted from: Christopher J. Chipello and Mark Heinzl, "As Canada's Dollar Surges, Exporters Pay a Steep Price," Wall Street Journal, *June 24, 2003. Reprinted by permission.*

Visit www.prenhall.com/casefair for updated articles and exercises.

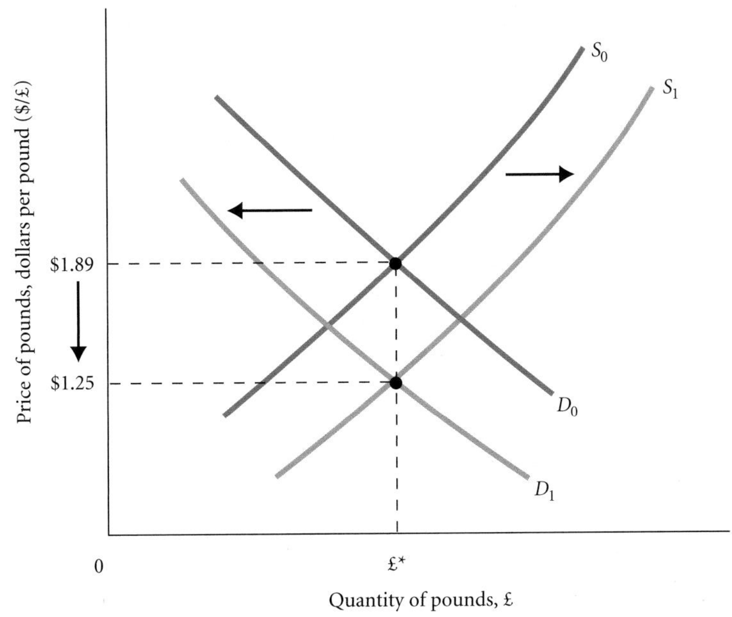

FIGURE 21.6 Exchange Rates Respond to Changes in Relative Interest Rates

If U.S. interest rates rise relative to British interest rates, British citizens holding pounds may be attracted into the U.S. securities market. To buy bonds in the United States, British buyers must exchange pounds for dollars. The supply of pounds shifts to the right, from S_0 to S_1. However, U.S. citizens are less likely to be interested in British securities, because interest rates are higher at home. The demand for pounds shifts to the left, from D_0 to D_1. The result is a depreciated pound and a stronger dollar.

flow, much like taxes and saving. Exports, in contrast, are an "injection" into the circular flow; they represent spending on U.S.-produced goods and services from abroad and can stimulate output.

The world is far more complicated when exchange rates are allowed to float. First, the level of imports and exports depends on exchange rates as well as on income and other factors. When events cause exchange rates to adjust, the levels of imports and exports will change. Changes in exports and imports can in turn affect the level of real GDP and the price level. Further, exchange rates themselves also adjust to changes in the economy. Suppose the government decides to stimulate the economy with an expansionary monetary policy. This will affect interest rates, which may affect exchange rates.

Exchange Rate Effects on Imports, Exports, and Real GDP As we already know, when a country's currency depreciates (falls in value), its import prices rise and its export prices (in foreign currencies) fall. When the U.S. dollar is cheap, U.S. products are more competitive with products produced in the rest of the world, and foreign-made goods look expensive to U.S. citizens.

A depreciation of a country's currency can serve as a stimulus to the economy. Suppose the U.S. dollar falls in value, as it did sharply between 1985 and 1988. If foreign buyers increase their spending on U.S. goods, and domestic buyers substitute U.S.-made goods for imports, aggregate expenditure on domestic output will rise, inventories will fall, and real GDP (Y) will increase.

> A depreciation of a country's currency is likely to increase its GDP.[5]

Exchange Rates and the Balance of Trade: The J Curve Because a depreciating currency tends to increase exports and decrease imports, you might think it will also reduce a country's trade deficit. In fact, the effect of a depreciation on the balance of trade is ambiguous.

J-curve effect Following a currency depreciation, a country's balance of trade may get worse before it gets better. The graph showing this effect is shaped like the letter *J*, hence the name "J-curve effect."

Many economists believe that when a currency starts to depreciate, the balance of trade is likely to worsen for the first few quarters (perhaps three to six). After that, the balance of trade may improve. This effect is graphed in Figure 21.7. The curve in this figure resembles the letter J, and the movement in the balance of trade that it describes is sometimes called the **J-curve effect**. The point of the J shape is that the balance of trade gets worse before it gets better following a currency depreciation.

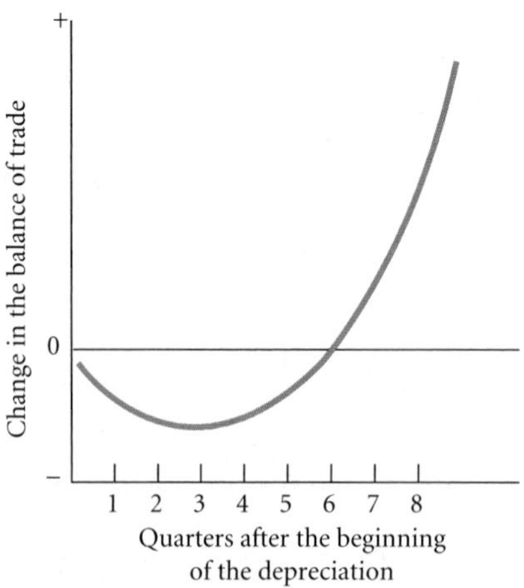

FIGURE 21.7 The Effect of a Depreciation on the Balance of Trade (the J Curve)

Initially, a depreciation of a country's currency may worsen its balance of trade. The negative effect on the price of imports may initially dominate the positive effects of an increase in exports and a decrease in imports.

[5]For this reason, some counties are tempted at times to intervene in foreign exchange markets, depreciate their currencies, and stimulate their economies. If all countries attempted to lower the value of their currencies simultaneously, there would be no gain in income for any of them. Although the exchange rate system at the time was different, such a situation actually occurred during the early years of the Great Depression. So-called *beggar-thy-neighbor* policies of competitive devaluations were practiced by many countries in a desperate attempt to maintain export sales and employment.

How does the J curve come about? Recall that the balance of trade is equal to export revenue minus import costs, including exports and imports of services:

$$\text{balance of trade} = \text{dollar price of exports} \times \text{quantity of exports} - \text{dollar price of imports} \times \text{quantity of imports}$$

A currency depreciation affects the items on the right side of this equation as follows. First, the quantity of exports increases and the quantity of imports decreases; both have a *positive* effect on the balance of trade (lowering the trade deficit or raising the trade surplus). Second, the dollar price of exports is not likely to change very much, at least not initially. The dollar price of exports changes when the U.S. price level changes, but the initial effect of a depreciation on the domestic price level is not likely to be large. Third, the dollar price of imports increases. Imports into the United States are more expensive, because $1 U.S. buys fewer yen, euros, etc. than before. An increase in the dollar price of imports has a *negative* effect on the balance of trade.

An example to clarify this last point follows: The dollar price of a Japanese car that costs 1,200,000 yen rises from $10,000 to $12,000 when the exchange rate moves from 120 yen per dollar to 100 yen per dollar. After the currency depreciation, the United States ends up spending more (in dollars) for the Japanese car than it did before. Of course, the United States will end up buying fewer Japanese cars than it did before. Does the number of cars drop enough so the quantity effect is bigger than the price effect, or vice versa? Does the value of imports increase or decrease?

The net effect of a depreciation on the balance of trade could go either way. The depreciation stimulates exports and cuts back imports, but it also increases the dollar price of imports. It seems that the negative effect dominates initially. The impact of a depreciation on the price of imports is generally felt quickly, while it takes time for export and import quantities to respond to price changes. In the short run, the value of imports increases more than the value of exports, so the balance of trade worsens. The initial effect is likely to be negative; but after exports and imports have had time to respond, the net effect turns positive. The more elastic the demand for exports and imports, the larger the eventual improvement in the balance of trade.

Exchange Rates and Prices The depreciation of a country's currency tends to increase its price level. There are two reasons for this. First, when a country's currency is less expensive, its products are more competitive on world markets, so exports rise. In addition, domestic buyers tend to substitute domestic products for the now-more-expensive imports. This means planned aggregate expenditure on domestically produced goods and services rises, and the aggregate demand curve shifts to the right. The result is a higher price level, higher output, or both. (You may want to draw an AS/AD diagram to verify this.) If the economy is close to capacity, the result is likely to be higher prices. Second, a depreciation makes imported inputs more expensive. If costs increase, the aggregate supply curve shifts to the left. If aggregate demand remains unchanged, the result is an increase in the price level.

Monetary Policy with Flexible Exchange Rates Let us now put everything in this chapter together and consider what happens when monetary policy is used first to stimulate the economy and then to contract the economy.

Suppose the economy is below full employment and the Federal Reserve (Fed) decides to expand the money supply. The volume of reserves in the system is expanded, perhaps through open market purchases of U.S. government securities by the Fed. This results in a decrease in the interest rate. The lower interest rate stimulates planned investment spending and consumption spending.

This added spending causes inventories to be lower than planned and aggregate output (income) (Y) to rise, but there are two additional effects. One, the lower interest rate has an impact in the foreign exchange market. A lower interest rate means a lower demand for U.S. securities by foreigners, so the demand for dollars drops. Two, U.S. investment managers will be more likely to buy foreign securities (which are now paying relatively higher interest rates), so the supply of dollars rises. Both events push down the value of the dollar.

A cheaper dollar is a good thing if the goal of the monetary expansion is to stimulate the domestic economy, because a cheaper dollar means more U.S. exports and fewer imports. If consumers substitute U.S.-made goods for imports, both the added exports and the decrease in imports mean more spending on domestic products, so the multiplier actually increases.

Now suppose inflation is a problem and the Fed wants to slow it down with tight money. Here again, floating exchange rates help. Tight monetary policy works through a higher interest rate. A higher interest rate lowers investment and consumption spending, reducing aggregate expenditure, reducing output, and lowering the price level. The higher interest rate also attracts foreign buyers into U.S. financial markets, driving up the value of the dollar, which reduces the price of imports. The reduction in the price of imports shifts the aggregate supply curve to the right, which helps fight inflation.

Fiscal Policy with Flexible Exchange Rates The openness of the economy and flexible exchange rates do not always work to the advantage of policy makers. Consider a policy of cutting taxes to stimulate the economy. Suppose Congress enacts a major tax cut designed to raise output. Spending by households rises, but not all this added spending is on domestic products—some leaks out of the U.S. economy, reducing the multiplier.

As income rises, so does the demand for money (M^d)—not the demand for dollars in the foreign exchange market, but the amount of money people desire to hold for transactions. Unless the Fed is fully accommodating, the interest rate will rise. A higher interest rate tends to attract foreign demand for U.S. securities. This tends to drive the price of the dollar up, which further blunts the effectiveness of the tax cut. If the value of the dollar rises, U.S. exports are less competitive in world markets, and the quantity of exports will decline. Similarly, a strong dollar makes imported goods look cheaper, and U.S. citizens spend more on foreign goods and less on U.S. goods, again reducing the multiplier.

Another caveat to the multiplier story of Chapters 8 and 9 exists. Without a fully accommodating Fed, three factors work to reduce the multiplier: (1) A higher interest rate from the increase in money demand may crowd out private investment and consumption; (2) some of the increase in income from the expansion will be spent on imports; and (3) a higher interest rate may cause the dollar to appreciate, discouraging exports and further encouraging imports.

Monetary Policy with Fixed Exchange Rates Although most major countries in the world today have a flexible exchange rate (counting for this purpose the euro zone countries as one country), it is interesting to ask what role monetary policy can play if a country has a fixed exchange rate. The answer is, no role. In order for a country to keep its exchange rate fixed to, say, the U.S. dollar, its interest rate cannot change relative to the U.S. interest rate. If the monetary authority of the country tried to lower its interest rate because it wanted to stimulate the economy, this would lead the country's currency to depreciate (assuming that the U.S. interest rate did not change). People would want to sell the country's currency and buy dollars and invest in U.S. securities, since the country's interest rate would have fallen relative to the U.S. interest rate. In other words, the monetary authority cannot change its interest rate relative to the U.S. interest rate without having its exchange rate change. The monetary authority is at the mercy of the United States, and it has no independent way of changing its interest rate if it wants to keep its exchange rate fixed to the dollar.

This restriction means that when the various European countries moved in 1999 to a common currency, the euro, each of the countries gave up its monetary policy. There is now only one monetary policy for all the euro zone countries, and it is decided by the European Central Bank (ECB).

The one case in which a country can change its interest rate and keep its exchange rate fixed is if it imposes capital controls. Imposing capital controls means that the country limits or prevents people from buying or selling its currency in the foreign exchange markets. A citizen of the country may be prevented, for example, from using the country's currency to buy dollars. The problem with capital controls is that they are hard to enforce, especially for large countries and for long periods of time.

AN INTERDEPENDENT WORLD ECONOMY

The increasing interdependence of countries in the world economy has made the problems facing policy makers more difficult. We used to be able to think of the United States as a relatively self-sufficient region. Thirty years ago, economic events outside U.S. borders had relatively little effect on its economy. This is no longer true. The events of the past three decades have taught us that the performance of the U.S. economy is heavily dependent on events outside its borders.

This chapter and the previous one have provided only the bare bones of open-market macroeconomics. If you continue your study of economics, more will be added to the basic story we have presented.

Also in the international arena, Chapter 22 deals with the problems of developing countries, and economies in transition from a noncapitalist one to a capitalist one.

SUMMARY

1. The main difference between an international transaction and a domestic transaction concerns currency exchange: When people in different countries buy from, and sell to, each other, an exchange of currencies must also take place.

2. The *exchange rate* is the price of one country's currency in terms of another country's currency.

THE BALANCE OF PAYMENTS

3. *Foreign exchange* is all currencies other than the domestic currency of a given country. The record of a nation's transactions in goods, services, and assets with the rest of the world is its *balance of payments*. The balance of payments is also the record of a country's sources (supply) and uses (demand) of foreign exchange.

EQUILIBRIUM OUTPUT (INCOME) IN AN OPEN ECONOMY

4. In an open economy, some income is spent on foreign-produced goods instead of domestically produced goods. To measure planned domestic aggregate expenditure in an open economy, we add total exports but subtract total imports: $C + I + G + EX - IM$. The open economy is in equilibrium when domestic aggregate output (income) (Y) equals planned domestic aggregate expenditure.

5. In an open economy, the multiplier equals $1/[1 - (MPC - MPM)]$, where MPC is the marginal propensity to consume and MPM is the marginal propensity to import. The *marginal propensity to import* is the change in imports caused by a $1 change in income.

6. In addition to income, other factors that affect the level of imports are the after-tax real wage rate, after-tax nonlabor income, interest rates, and relative prices of domestically produced and foreign-produced goods. The demand for exports is determined by economic activity in the rest of the world and by relative prices.

7. An increase in U.S. economic activity leads to a worldwide increase in economic activity, which then "feeds back" to the United States. An increase in U.S. imports increases other countries' exports, which stimulates economies and increases their imports, which increases U.S. exports, which stimulates the U.S. economy and increases its imports, and so on. This is the *trade feedback effect.*

8. Export prices of other countries affect U.S. import prices. The general rate of inflation abroad is likely to affect U.S. import prices. If the inflation rate abroad is high, U.S. import prices are likely to rise.

9. Because one country's exports are another country's imports, an increase in export prices increases other countries' import prices. An increase in other countries' import prices leads to an increase in their domestic prices—and their export prices. In short, export prices affect import prices, and vice versa. This *price feedback effect* shows that inflation is "exportable"; an increase in the price level in one country can drive up prices in other countries, making inflation in the first country worse.

THE OPEN ECONOMY WITH FLEXIBLE EXCHANGE RATES

10. The equilibrium exchange rate occurs when the quantity demanded of a foreign currency in the foreign exchange market equals the quantity of that currency supplied in the foreign exchange market.

11. *Depreciation of a currency occurs* when a nation's currency falls in value relative to another country's currency. *Appreciation of a currency* occurs when a nation's currency rises in value relative to another country's currency.

12. According to the *law of one price*, if the costs of transportation are small, the price of the same good in different countries should be roughly the same. The theory that exchange rates are set so that the price of similar goods in different countries is the same is known as *purchasing-power-parity* theory. In practice, transportation costs are significant for many goods, and the law of one price does not hold for these goods.

13. A high rate of inflation in one country relative to another puts pressure on the exchange rate between the two countries. There is a general tendency for the currencies of relatively high-inflation countries to depreciate.

14. A depreciation of the dollar tends to increase U.S. GDP by making U.S. exports cheaper (hence more competitive abroad) and by making U.S. imports more expensive (encouraging consumers to switch to domestically produced goods and services).

15. The effect of a depreciation of a nation's currency on its balance of trade is unclear. In the short run, a currency depreciation may increase the balance-of-trade deficit, because it raises the price of imports. Although this price increase causes a decrease in the quantity of imports demanded, the impact of a depreciation on the price of imports is generally felt quickly, but it takes time for export and import quantities to respond to price changes. The initial effect is likely to be negative; but after exports and imports have had time to respond, the net effect turns positive. The tendency for the balance-of-trade deficit to widen and then to decrease as the result of a currency depreciation is known as the *J-curve effect.*

16. The depreciation of a country's currency tends to raise its price level for two reasons. First, a currency depreciation increases planned aggregate expenditure, which shifts the aggregate demand curve to the right. If the economy is close to capacity, the result is likely to be higher prices. Second, a depreciation makes imported inputs more expensive. If costs increase, the aggregate supply curve shifts to the left. If aggregate demand remains unchanged, the result is an increase in the price level.

17. When exchange rates are flexible, a U.S. expansionary monetary policy decreases the interest rate and stimulates planned investment and consumption spending. The lower interest rate leads to a lower demand for U.S. securities by foreigners, and a higher demand for foreign securities by U.S. investment-fund managers. As a result, the dollar depreciates. A U.S. contractionary monetary policy appreciates the dollar.

18. Flexible exchange rates do not always work to the advantage of policy makers. An expansionary fiscal policy can appreciate the dollar and work to reduce the multiplier.

REVIEW TERMS AND CONCEPTS

appreciation of a currency, 406
balance of payments, 397
balance of trade, 397
balance on capital account, 398
balance on current account, 398
depreciation of a currency, 407
exchange rate, 395
floating, or market-determined, exchange rates, 404
foreign exchange, 396
J-curve effect, 410
law of one price, 407
marginal propensity to import (*MPM*), 400
net exports of goods and services (*EX – IM*), 400
price feedback effect, 404
purchasing-power-parity theory, 407
trade deficit, 397
trade feedback effect, 402

Planned domestic aggregate expenditure in an open economy:

$$C + I + G + EX - IM$$

Open-economy multiplier:

$$\frac{1}{1 - (MPC - MPM)}$$

PROBLEM SET

1. During 2003, the U.S. dollar fell sharply in value against most currencies, including the Japanese yen and the euro. Most economists point to the actions of the Federal Reserve as an explanation. For each of the following say whether you agree or disagree, and explain your answer.
   a. This is likely a result of Federal Reserve action to slow the economy with higher interest rates.
   b. This is bad news for U.S. export companies who now receive less for their dollars.
   c. This is actually good news for European exporters who will receive more dollars for their goods.
2. In July 2003, the euro was trading at $1.15. That is, the exchange rate was $1.15 = 1 euro. Check the web or any daily newspaper to see what the "price" of a euro is today. What explanations can you give for the change? Be sure to check what has happened to interest rates and economic growth.
3. Suppose the following prevailed on the foreign exchange market in 2003 with floating exchange rates:
   a. Name three phenomena that might shift the demand curve to the right.
   b. Which, if any, of these three might cause a simultaneous shift of the supply curve to the left?
   c. What effects might each of the three phenomena have on the balance of trade if the exchange rate floats?

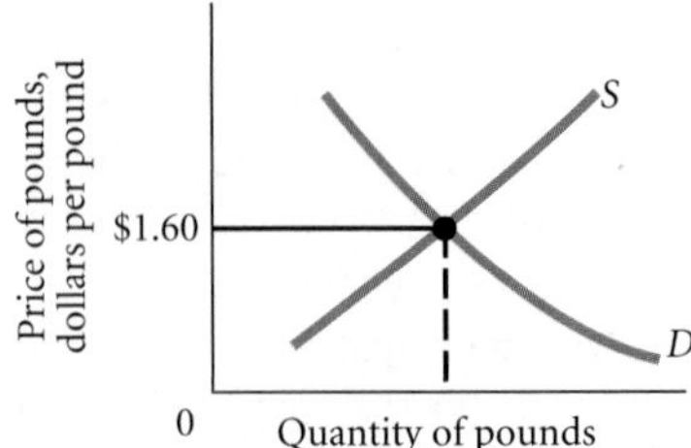

4. Obtain a recent issue of *The Economist.* Turn to the section entitled "Financial Indicators." Look at the table entitled "trade, exchange rates and budgets." Which country has the largest trade deficit over the last year and during the last month? Which country has the largest trade surplus over the last year and during the last month? How does the current account deficit/surplus compare to the overall trade balance? How can you explain the difference?

5. During 1981 and 1982, the president and the Congress were pursuing a very expansionary *fiscal* policy. In 1980 and 1981, the Federal Reserve was pursuing a very restrictive *monetary* policy in an attempt to rid the economy of inflation. Ultimately, the economy went into a deep recession, but before it did, interest rates went to record levels with the prime rate topping out at over 21 percent.
   a. Explain how this policy mix led to very high interest rates.
   b. Show graphically the effect of the high interest rates on the foreign exchange market. What do you think would happen to the value of the dollar under these circumstances?
   c. What impact was such a series of events likely to have on the trade balance in countries like Japan? Explain your answer.
6. The exchange rate between the U.S. dollar and the Japanese yen is floating freely—both governments do not intervene in the market for each currency. Suppose a large trade deficit with Japan prompts the United States to impose quotas on certain Japanese products imported into the United States and, as a result, the quantity of these imports falls.
   a. The decrease in spending on Japanese products increases spending on U.S.-made goods. Why? What effect will this have on U.S. output and employment, and on Japanese output and employment?
   b. What happens to U.S. imports from Japan when U.S. output (or income) rises? If the quotas initially reduce imports from Japan by \$25 billion, why is the final reduction in imports likely to be less than \$25 billion?
   c. Suppose the quotas do succeed in reducing imports from Japan by \$15 billion. What will happen to the demand for yen? Why?
   d. What will happen to the dollar–yen exchange rate, and why? (*Hint:* There is an excess supply of yen, or an excess demand for dollars.) What effects will the change in the value of each currency have on employment and output in the United States? What about the balance of trade? (Ignore complications such as the J curve.)
   e. Considering the macroeconomic effects of a quota on Japanese imports, could a quota actually reduce employment and output in the United States, or have no effect at all? Explain.
7. What effect will each of the following events have on the current account balance and the exchange rate if the exchange rate is fixed? If it is floating?
   a. The U.S. government cuts taxes, and income rises.
   b. The U.S. inflation rate increases, and prices in the United States rise faster than those in the countries with which the United States trades.
   c. The United States adopts an expansionary monetary policy. Interest rates fall (and are now lower than those in other countries), and income rises.
   d. The textile companies' "Buy American" campaign is successful, and U.S. consumers switch from purchasing imported products to those made in the United States.
8. You are given the following model, which describes the economy of Hypothetica.
   (1) Consumption function: $C = 100 + .8Y_d$
   (2) Planned investment: $I = 38$
   (3) Government spending: $G = 75$
   (4) Exports: $EX = 25$
   (5) Imports: $IM = .05Y_d$
   (6) Disposable income: $Y_d \equiv Y - T$
   (7) Taxes: $T = 40$
   (8) Planned aggregate expenditure:

   $$AE \equiv C + I + G + EX - IM$$

   (9) Definition of equilibrium income: $Y = AE$
   a. What is equilibrium income in Hypothetica? What is the government deficit? What is the current account balance?
   b. If government spending is increased to $G = 80$, what happens to equilibrium income? Explain, using the government spending multiplier. What happens to imports?
   c. Now suppose the amount of imports is limited to $IM = 40$ by a quota on imports. If government spending is again increased from 75 to 80, what happens to equilibrium income? Explain why the same increase in G has a bigger effect on income in the second case. What is it about the presence of imports that changes the value of the multiplier?
   d. If exports are fixed at $EX = 25$, what must income be to ensure a current account balance of zero? (*Hint:* Imports depend on income, so what must income be for imports to be equal to exports?) By how much must we cut government spending to balance the current account? (*Hint:* Use your answer to the first part of this question to determine how much of a decrease in income is needed. Then use the multiplier to calculate the decrease in G needed to reduce income by that amount.)

APPENDIX

WORLD MONETARY SYSTEMS SINCE 1900

Since the beginning of the twentieth century, the world has operated under a number of different monetary systems. This Appendix provides a brief history of each and a description of how they worked.

THE GOLD STANDARD

The gold standard was the major system of exchange rate determination before 1914. All currencies were priced in terms of gold—an ounce of gold was worth so much in each currency. When all currencies exchanged at fixed ratios to gold, exchange rates could be determined easily. For instance, one ounce of gold was worth $20 U.S.; that same ounce of gold exchange for £4 (British pounds). Because $20 and £4 were each worth one ounce of gold, the exchange rate between dollars and pounds was $20/£4, or $5 to £1.

For the gold standard to be effective it had to be backed up by the country's willingness to buy and sell gold at the determined price. As long as countries maintain their currencies at a fixed value in terms of gold *and* as long as each is willing to buy and sell gold, exchange rates are fixed. If at the given exchange rate the number of U.S. citizens who want to buy things produced in Great Britain is equal to the number of British citizens who want to buy things produced in the United States, the currencies of the two countries will simply be exchanged. What if U.S. citizens suddenly decide they want to drink imported Scotch instead of domestic bourbon? If the British do not have an increased desire for U.S. goods, they would still accept U.S. dollars because they could be redeemed in gold. This gold could then be immediately turned into pounds.

As long as a country's overall balance of payments remained in balance, no gold would enter or leave the country, and the economy would be in equilibrium. If U.S. citizens bought more from the British than the British bought from the United States, however, the U.S. balance of payments would be in deficit, and the U.S. stock of gold would begin to fall. Conversely, Britain would start to accumulate gold because it would be exporting more than it spent on imports.

Under the gold standard, gold was a big determinant of the money supply.[1] An inflow of gold into a country caused that country's money supply to expand, and an outflow of gold caused that country's money supply to contract. If gold were flowing from the United States to Great Britain, the British money supply would expand and the U.S. money supply would contract.

Now recall from earlier chapters the impacts of a change in the money supply. An expanded money supply in Britain will lower British interest rates and stimulate aggregate demand. As a result, aggregate output (income) and the price level in Britain will increase. Higher British prices will discourage U.S. citizens from buying British goods. At the same time, British citizens will have more income and will face relatively lower import prices, causing them to import more from the States.

On the other side of the Atlantic, U.S. citizens will face a contracting domestic money supply. This will cause higher interest rates, declining aggregate demand, lower prices, and falling output (income). This will lower demand in the United States for British goods. Thus, changes in relative prices and incomes that resulted from the inflow and outflow of gold would automatically bring trade back into balance.

[1]In the days when currencies were tied to gold, changes in the amount of gold influenced the supply of money in two ways. A change in the quantity of gold coins in circulation had a direct effect on the supply of money; indirectly, gold served as a backing for paper currency. A decrease in the central bank's gold holdings meant a decline in the amount of paper money that could be supported.

PROBLEMS WITH THE GOLD STANDARD

Two major problems were associated with the gold standard. First, the gold standard implied that a country had little control over its money supply. The reason, as we have just seen, is that the money stock increased when the overall balance of payments was in surplus (gold inflow) and decreased when the overall balance was in deficit (gold outflow). A country that was experiencing a balance-of-payments deficit could correct the problem only by the painful process of allowing its money supply to contract. This brought on a slump in economic activity, a slump that would eventually restore balance-of-payments equilibrium, but only after reductions in income and employment. Countries could (and often did) act to protect their gold reserves, and this prevented the adjustment mechanism from correcting the deficit.

Making the money supply depend on the amount of gold available had another disadvantage. When major new gold fields were discovered (as in California in 1849 or South Africa in 1886), the world's supply of gold (and therefore of money) increased. The price level rose and income increased. When no new gold was discovered, the supply of money remained unchanged and prices and income tended to fall.

When President Reagan took office in 1981, he established a commission to consider returning the nation to the gold standard. The final commission report recommended against such a move. An important part of the reasoning behind this was that the gold standard puts enormous economic power in the hands of gold-producing nations.

FIXED EXCHANGE RATES AND THE BRETTON WOODS SYSTEM

As World War II drew to a close, a group of economists from the United States and Europe met to formulate a new set of rules for exchange rate determination that they hoped would avoid the difficulties of the gold standard. The rules they designed became known as the **Bretton Woods system**, after the town in New Hampshire where the delegates met. The Bretton Woods system was based on two (not necessarily compatible) premises. First, countries were to maintain fixed exchange rates with each other. Instead of pegging their currencies directly to gold, however, currencies were fixed in terms of the U.S. dollar, which was fixed in value at $35 per ounce of gold. The British pound, for instance, was fixed at roughly $2.40, which meant that an ounce of gold was worth approximately £14.6. As we shall see, the pure system of fixed exchange rates would work in a manner very similar to the pre-1914 gold standard.

The second aspect of the Bretton Woods system added a new wrinkle to the operation of the international economy. Countries experiencing a "fundamental disequilibrium" in their balance of payments were allowed to change their exchange rates. (The term *fundamental disequilibrium* was necessarily vague, but it came to be interpreted as a large and persistent current account deficit.) Exchange rates were not really fixed under the Bretton Woods system; they were, as someone remarked, only "fixed until further notice."

The point of allowing countries with serious current account problems to alter the value of their currency was to avoid the harsh recessions that the operation of the gold standard would have produced under these circumstances. However, the experience of the European economies in the years between World War I and World War II suggested it might not be a good idea to give countries complete freedom to change their exchange rates whenever they wished.

During the Great Depression, many countries undertook so-called competitive devaluations to protect domestic output and employment. That is, countries would try to encourage exports—a source of output growth and employment—by attempting to set as low an exchange rate as possible, thereby making their exports competitive with foreign-produced goods. Unfortunately, such policies had a built-in flaw. A devaluation of the pound against the French franc might help encourage British exports to France, but if those additional British exports cut into French output and employment, France would likely respond by devaluing the franc against the pound, which, of course, would undo the effects of the pound's initial devaluation.

To solve this exchange rate rivalry, the Bretton Woods agreement created the International Monetary Fund (IMF). Its job was to assist countries experiencing temporary current account problems.[2] It was also supposed to certify that a "fundamental disequilibrium" existed before a country was allowed to change its exchange rate. The IMF is like an international economic traffic cop whose job is to ensure that all countries are playing the game according to the agreed-to rules and to provide emergency assistance where needed.

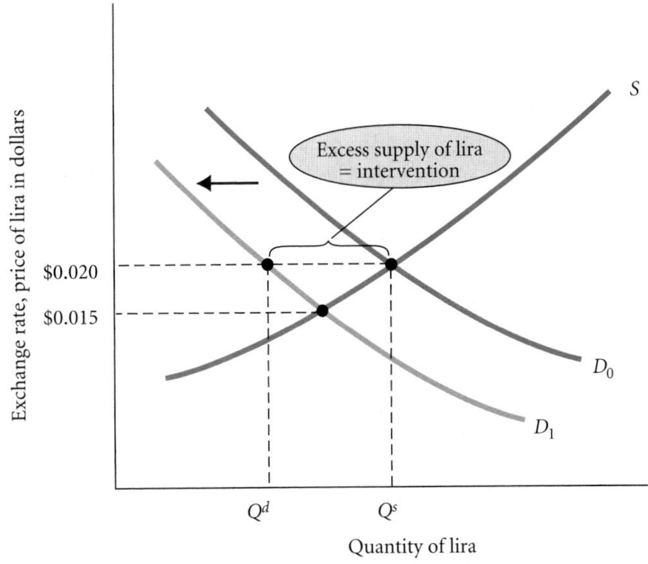

FIGURE 21A.1 Government Intervention in the Foreign Exchange Market

If the price of lira was set by a completely unfettered market, the price of a lira would be .020 when demand is D_0 and .015 when demand is D_1. If the government has committed itself to keeping the value of a lira at .020, it must buy up the excess supply of lira ($Q^s - Q^d$).

Companion Website Plus

"PURE" FIXED EXCHANGE RATES

Under a pure fixed exchange rate system, governments set a particular *fixed* rate at which their currencies will exchange for each other and then commit themselves to maintaining that rate. A true fixed exchange rate system is like the gold standard in that exchange rates are supposed to stay the same forever.[3] Because currencies are no longer backed by gold, they have no fixed, or standard, value relative to each other. There is therefore no automatic mechanism to keep exchange rates aligned with each other, as with the gold standard.

The result is that under a pure fixed exchange rate system, governments must at times intervene in the foreign exchange market to keep currencies aligned at their established values. Economists define government intervention in the foreign exchange market as the buying or selling of foreign exchange for the purpose of manipulating the exchange rate. What kind of intervention is likely to occur under a fixed exchange rate system, and how does it work?

We can see how intervention works by looking at Figure 21A.1. Initially, the market for Italian lira is in equilibrium. At the fixed exchange rate of $0.02 per lira, the supply of lira is exactly equal to the demand for lira. No government intervention is necessary to maintain the exchange rate at this level. Now suppose Italian wines are found to be contaminated with antifreeze, and U.S. citizens switch to California wines. This substitution away from the Italian product shifts the U.S. demand curve for lira to the left: The United States demands fewer lira at every exchange rate (cost of a lira) because it is purchasing less from Italy than it did before.

If the price of lira were set by a completely unfettered market, the shift in the demand curve would lead to a fall in the price of lira, just the way the price of wheat would fall if there was an excess supply of wheat. Remember, the Italian and U.S. governments have committed themselves to maintaining the rate at $0.02 per lira. To do this, either the U.S. government or Italian government (or both) must buy up the excess supply of lira to keep the price of the lira from falling. In essence, the fixed exchange rate policy commits governments to making up any difference between the supply of a currency and the demand so as to keep the price of the currency (exchange rate) at the desired level. The government promises to act as the supplier (or demander) of last resort, who will ensure that the amount of foreign exchange demanded by the private sector will equal the supply at the fixed price.

---

[2]The idea was that the IMF would make short-term loans to a country with a current account deficit. The loans would enable the country to correct the current account problem gradually, without bringing on a deep recession, running out of foreign exchange reserves, or devaluing the currency.

[3]"Forever" is a very long time. Some countries in Central America have maintained fixed exchange rates with the U.S. dollar for almost 30 years, practically forever in the world of international finance.

PROBLEMS WITH THE BRETTON WOODS SYSTEM

As it developed after the end of World War II, the system of more-or-less fixed exchange rates had some flaws that led to its abandonment in 1971.

First, there was a basic asymmetry built into the rules of international finance. Countries experiencing large and persistent current account deficits—what the Bretton Woods agreements termed "fundamental disequilibria"—were obliged to devalue their currencies and/or take measures to cut their deficits by contracting their economies. Both of these alternatives were unpleasant, because devaluation meant rising prices and contraction meant rising unemployment. However, a country with a current account deficit had no choice, since it was losing stock of foreign exchange reserves. When its stock of foreign currencies became exhausted, it had to change its exchange rate, because further intervention (selling off some of its foreign exchange reserves) became impossible.

Countries experiencing current account surpluses were in a different position, since they were gaining foreign exchange reserves. Although these countries were supposed to stimulate their economies and/or revalue their currencies to restore balance to their current account, they were not obliged to do so. They could easily maintain their fixed exchange rate by buying up any excess supply of foreign exchange with their own currency, of which they had plentiful supply.

In practice, this meant some countries—especially Germany and Japan—tended to run large and chronic current account surpluses and were under no compulsion to take steps to correct the problem. The U.S. economy, stimulated by expenditures on the Vietnam War, experienced a large and prolonged current account deficit (capital outflow) in the 1960s, which was the counterpart of these surpluses. The United States was, however, in a unique position under the Bretton Woods system. The value of gold was fixed in terms of the U.S. dollar at $35 per ounce of gold. Other countries fixed their exchange rates in terms of U.S. dollars (and therefore only indirectly in terms of gold). This meant the United States could never accomplish anything by devaluing its currency in terms of gold. If the dollar was devalued from $35 to $40 per ounce of gold, the yen, pegged at 200 yen per dollar, would move in parallel with the dollar (from 7,000 yen per ounce of gold to 8,000 yen per ounce), with the dollar–yen exchange rate unaffected. To correct its current account deficits vis-à-vis Japan and Germany, it would be necessary for those two countries to adjust their currencies' exchange rates with the dollar. These countries were reluctant to do so for a variety of reasons. As a result, the U.S. current account was chronically in deficit throughout the late 1960s.

A second flaw in the Bretton Woods system was that it permitted devaluations only if a country had a "chronic" current account deficit and was in danger of running out of foreign exchange reserves. This meant devaluations could often be predicted quite far in advance, and they usually had to be rather large if they were to correct any serious current account problem. The situation made it tempting for speculators to "attack" the currencies of countries with current account deficits.

Problems like these eventually led the United States to abandon the Bretton Woods rules in 1971. The U.S. government refused to continue pegging the value of the dollar in terms of gold. This meant the prices of all currencies were free to find their own levels.

The alternative to fixed exchange rates is a system that allows exchange rates to move freely or flexibly in response to market forces. Two types of flexible exchange rate systems are usually distinguished. In a *freely floating system*, governments do not intervene at all in the foreign exchange market.[4] They do not buy or sell currencies with the aim of manipulating the rates. In a *managed floating system*, governments intervene if markets are becoming "disorderly"—fluctuating more than a government feels is desirable. Governments may also intervene if they think a currency is increasing or decreasing too much in value, even though the day-to-day fluctuations may be small.

Since the demise of the Bretton Woods system in 1971, the world's exchange rate system can be described as "managed floating." One of the important features of this system has been times of large fluctuations in exchange rates. For example, the yen–dollar rate went from 347 in 1971 to 210 in 1978, to 125 in 1988, and to 80 in 1995. These are very large changes, changes that have important effects on the international economy, some of which we have covered in this text.

[4]However, governments may from time to time buy or sell foreign exchange for their own needs (instead of influencing the exchange rate). For example, the U.S. government might need British pounds to buy land for a U.S. embassy building in London. For our purposes, we ignore this behavior because it is not "intervention" in the strict sense of the word.

SUMMARY

1. The gold standard was the major system of exchange rate determination before 1914. All currencies were priced in terms of gold. Difficulties with the gold standard led to the *Bretton Woods* agreement following World War II. Under this system, countries maintained fixed exchange rates with each other and fixed the value of their currencies in terms of the U.S. dollar. Countries experiencing a "fundamental disequilibrium" in their current accounts were permitted to change their exchange rates.
2. The Bretton Woods system was abandoned in 1971. Since then, the world's exchange rate system has been one of managed floating rates. Under this system, governments intervene if foreign exchange markets are fluctuating more than the government thinks desirable.

REVIEW TERMS AND CONCEPTS

Bretton Woods The site in New Hampshire where a group of experts from 44 countries met in 1944 and agreed to an international monetary system of fixed exchange rates. 416

PROBLEM SET

1. The currency of Atlantis is the wimp. In 1998, Atlantis developed a balance-of-payments deficit with the United States as a result of an unanticipated decrease in exports; U.S. citizens cut back on the purchase of Atlantean goods. Assume Atlantis is operating under a system of fixed exchange rates.
   - **a.** How does the drop in exports affect the market for wimps? Identify the deficit graphically.
   - **b.** How must the government of Atlantis act (in the short run) to maintain the value of the wimp?
   - **c.** If originally Atlantis were operating at full employment (potential GDP), what impact would these events have on its economy? Explain your answer.
   - **d.** The chief economist of Atlantis suggests expansionary monetary policy to restore full employment; the secretary of commerce suggests a tax cut (expansionary fiscal policy). Given the fixed exchange rate system, describe the effects of these two policy options on Atlantis's current account.
   - **e.** How would your answers to a, b, and c change if the two countries operated under a floating rate system?

Globalization

22

CHAPTER OUTLINE

Globalization is an often-used word today. A search reveals that the term was never mentioned in the pages of the *New York Times* during the 1970s, yet it now appears in *Times* stories virtually every day. Using the search engine Google turns up 1,720,000 links using the word. Despite the fact that the word is used so frequently, it is rarely defined clearly. **Globalization** is the process of increasing interdependence among countries and their citizens.

Defined this way globalization has social, cultural, political, and economic dimensions. It includes increasing international trade, travel, the spread of American movies and music, the incredible worldwide availability of information via the Internet, the problem of disease, global climate change, terrorism, religion, war, and so forth. Any attempt to address all the issues associated with increasing interdependence in a single text chapter, or even a single book, would be hopeless.

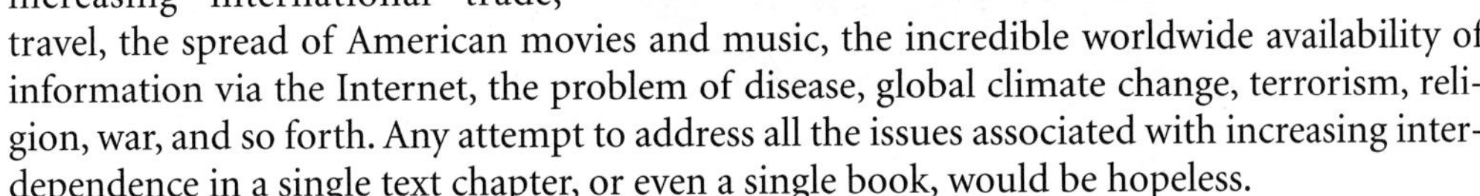

The purpose here is to explore the process of **economic globalization**. Economic globalization is the process of increasing *economic* interdependence among countries and their citizens. While the issues that we will discuss all have political and cultural dimensions, we will attempt to stick as closely as possible to economics by focusing on the causes and consequences of increased international trade of goods and services, increased cross-border movements of labor, and expanded international financial flows.

globalization The process of increasing interdependence among countries and their citizens.

economic globalization The process of increasing economic interdependence among countries and their citizens.

THE GLOBAL CIRCULAR FLOW

Figure 22-1 inserts the rest of the world on the circular flow diagram introduced in Chapter 3. It has clearly become more complex. The basic diagram of a simple closed economy includes the supply and demand for goods and services, the supply and demand for labor, and the supply and demand for capital (saving and investment). Household income comes from working and from owning assets; firms demand labor and capital and supply products; households demand goods and services and supply labor and capital.

Opening the economy adds 10 new flows to the diagram. The 10 new flows are shown in Figure 22.1: (**A.**) Domestic (in this case, U.S.) households can now buy goods and services from abroad—imports. This brings presumably greater choice and potentially lower prices. (**B.**) Domestic firms can now sell in foreign markets—exports. This opens up potential profit opportunities. (**C.**) Firms can hire workers from abroad (immigrants), in essence importing labor. (**D.**) U.S. firms can now turn to the rest of the world for capital. A U.S. firm may

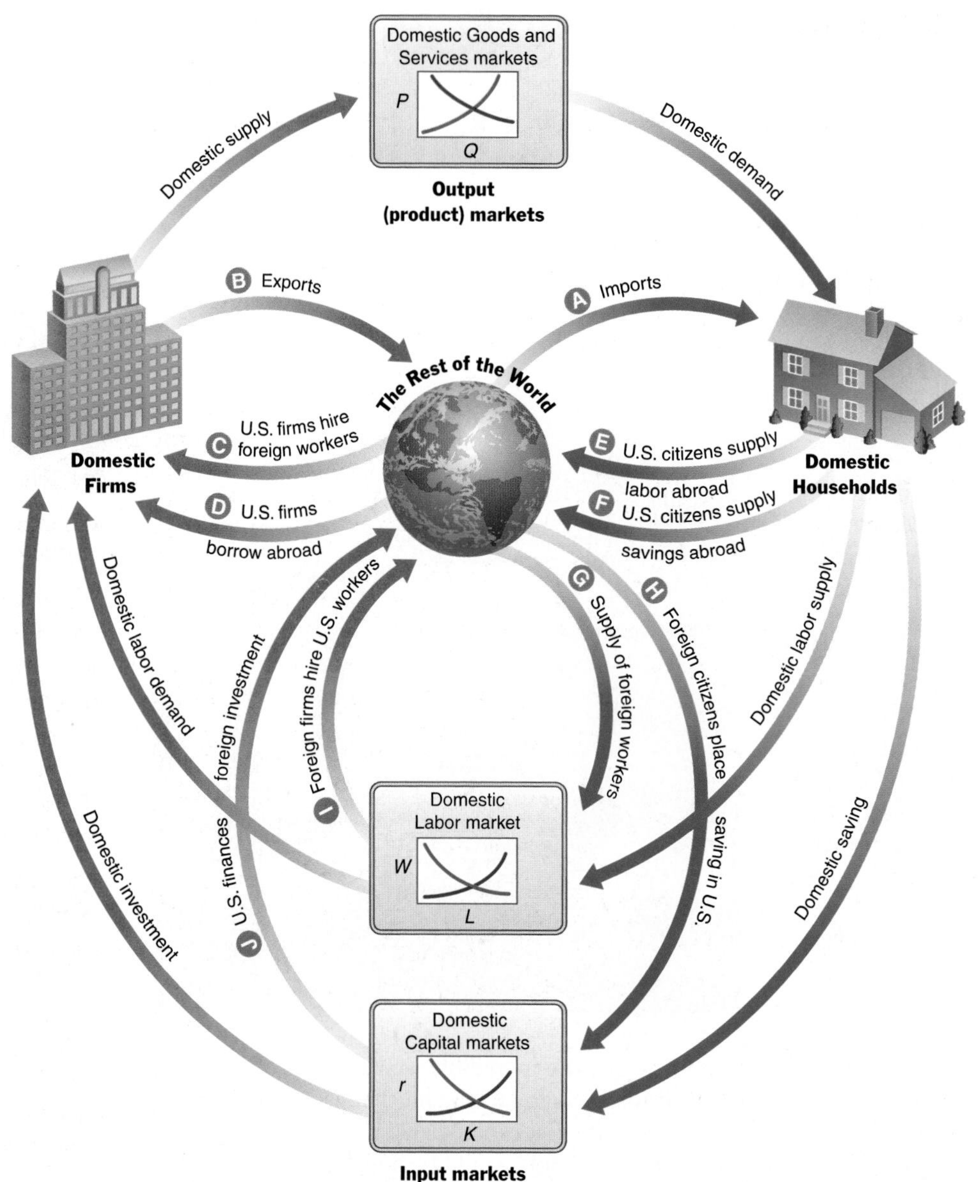

FIGURE 22.1 Economic Globalization: International Flows

A. U.S. citizens buy foreign produced goods and services (imports)
B. U.S. producers sell their goods and services abroad (exports)
C. U.S. producers hire foreign workers
D. U.S. producers finance investment with foreign savings—borrowing from a foreign bank
E. U.S. citizens supply labor to foreign companies or in foreign countries
F. U.S. citizens send savings abroad—buy foreign stocks and bonds, put money in foreign banks
G. Foreign citizens supply labor in the U.S. labor market
H. Foreign citizens place savings in the U.S.—buy U.S. stocks and bonds, put money in U.S. banks
I. Foreign producers hire workers in the U.S.
J. Foreign producers finance investment with U.S. saving

finance a new factory by borrowing from a German bank or by selling bonds in London. **(E.)** U.S. citizens can now look for a job in foreign labor markets. A laid-off high-tech worker may look for a job in Canada. **(F.)** Domestic households may put their savings into foreign stocks and bonds. During periods of low interest rates in the United States, higher rates in other countries may look attractive.

But that's not all: **(G.)** Foreign workers can work in the United States. Thousands of Mexican immigrants, many legal and many illegal, enter the United States weekly looking for work. **(H.)** Foreign citizens can buy U.S. stocks and bonds or put money into U.S. banks. One of the reasons for the big stock market boom in the late 1990s was that foreigners wanted to buy technology stocks in the United States. (**I.**) Foreign firms can demand labor, making jobs available to U.S. workers. Finally, (**J.**) Foreign firms may look to the United States for funds to use for investment in new capital. An Italian telephone company could finance the acquisition of new switching equipment with a loan from Citi Corp.

The basic argument for economic globalization can be found in the decisions behind each of these flows. A U.S. consumer buys a good or service from a foreign producer if the good being bought is cheaper than what he would have to pay for it in the United States or if it is of higher quality. Similarly, U.S. citizens put their savings into a foreign bond if it is yielding more than a similar U.S. bond. These choices are made on the basis of self interest.

Think of the United States as a set of 50 independent states that are totally integrated economically. People, financial capital, and goods and services flow freely across borders in response to people's preferences. If we didn't allow people to move freely across borders, or if we didn't let New Jersey citizens buy shares in California companies, or if we barred the export of fish from the coasts to the interior, the system would clearly be inefficient. Efficiency in any economy, even the world economy, is achieved if capital and labor can move freely to where their productivity is the highest . . . if factors of production are put to work in their "highest and best uses."

But wait a minute. If it were that simple, what is all the fuss about? Why are there such violent demonstrations over the process of globalization? Some contend that trade leads to domestic unemployment and lower wages as foreign workers compete with domestic workers. Others say that U.S. industry cannot compete with goods produced in countries with very low-wage labor. Still others contend that openness leads to unfair labor standards and sweatshop conditions in many countries or that openness leads to fierce competition and environmental degradation. Some just dislike the expansion of capitalism that they regard as inherently unjust. We will explore the objections one at a time after looking briefly at the history of globalization.

A BRIEF HISTORY OF ECONOMIC GLOBALIZATION

Economic historian Jeffrey Williamson classifies the period 1820–1914 as the first great period of globalization and the period since World War II as the second. Trade as a percent of the world's gross domestic product (GDP) rose from 5 percent in the early years of the nineteenth century to 20 percent at the beginning of World War I. The trade barriers that were imposed after 1914, the world wars, and the Great Depression all conspired to cut trade as a percent of world GDP back to around 5 percent. But the establishment of a new financial order at Bretton Woods, New Hampshire, in 1946 ushered in a new era, and trade grew back to 20 percent of world GDP by 1975.

In 1919, a young John Maynard Keynes said:

> What an extraordinary episode in the economic progress of man that age was which came to an end in August of 1914! . . . The inhabitant of London could order by telephone, sipping his morning tea in bed, the various products of the whole earth, in such quantity as he might see fit, and reasonably expect their early delivery upon his doorstep; he could at the same moment and by the same means adventure his wealth in the natural resources and new enterprices in any quarter of the world, and share, without exertion or even trouble, in their prospective fruits and advantages.[1]

While the data are difficult to get, many would argue that with respect to the international mobility of labor, we are less globalized than we were at the beginning of the twentieth century. At that time about 15 percent of the U.S. population was foreign born. The census bureau placed that number at 10.4% in 2000 up from 7.9% in 1990. Clearly, immigration has increased in recent years, but it is unclear whether we are approaching the immigration rates of the 1920s.

International capital flows were blamed for the dramatic events of 1997 in Asia. Volatile exchange rates caused by a rapid withdrawal of loans and credit to countries like Indonesia,

[1]Quoted in Stanley Fischer, "Globalization and Its Challenges," *American Economic Review*, May 2003, p. 26.

Korea, and Thailand led to dramatic swings in exchange rates and deep recessions in those countries.

Many dimensions of globalization are new today. Recent years have seen sharp reductions in trade barriers with the signing of the North American Free Trade Agreement (NAFTA) and the General Agreement on Tariffs and Trade (GATT), discussed in earlier chapters. Dramatic increases in the flows of information and commerce over the Internet and the increased speed and lower cost of travel have made the world a much smaller place—far more aware of cultural, political, and religious differences. Finally, the increase in cross-border terror has changed the nature of international relations.

THE BENEFITS AND COSTS OF GLOBALIZATION

Economic globalization has been criticized on many fronts. To keep the arguments clear, we first review the debate about free trade in goods and services. Next we turn to the debate over the mobility of labor between countries: immigration. Finally we discuss the unique problems of global financial markets.

THE FREE-TRADE DEBATE REVISITED

The potential benefits from trade have been discussed several times in this text. The simple story of comparative advantage was first discussed briefly in Chapter 2 and later in more detail in Chapter 20. The argument, first formalized by David Ricardo in the nineteenth century, is simple but powerful, and it has stood the test of time. The argument rests on two pieces of intuition. First, if you have something that I want and I have something that you want, we can exchange and both be better off. Voluntary exchange is efficient. Second, applying the concept to nations, two nations can benefit from free trade by specializing in producing those products in which they enjoy a **comparative advantage**. A country enjoys a comparative advantage in the production of a good if the production of that good has a lower opportunity cost than it would have if produced in another country.

comparative advantage A country enjoys a comparative advantage in the production of a good if the production of that good has a lower opportunity cost than it would have if produced in another country.

In both Chapter 2 and again in Chapter 20 we showed how trade between two countries allowed both to break out from behind the constraints of their production possibilities frontiers. We showed that this is true even if one country is more efficient in the production of all goods.

Perhaps even easier to understand, if consumers can buy the same good that they can buy at home at a lower cost in international markets, what is the logic for buying at home or for "protecting" domestically produced goods and services from foreign competition?

As we have seen, those who oppose trade make a number of arguments. First and foremost is that home-produced goods are produced with American workers and that buying imports simply ships jobs abroad. And besides, how can we compete with countries that pay low wages or have workers in sweatshop conditions? Not only do we lose American jobs, but we contribute to substandard working conditions in poor countries.

Proponents of free trade have a number of counterarguments:

1. We can't buy from countries unless they simultaneously buy from us. A number of years ago, presidential candidate Ross Perot opposed NAFTA on the grounds that there would be a "giant sucking sound" as all the good jobs in the United States moved to Mexico, where workers are paid a very low wage. Think about what would happen if this occurred.

   If U.S. citizens wanted to buy everything in Mexico, but the Mexicans didn't want to buy anything from us, foreign exchange markets would prevent it from happening. Mexican workers are paid in pesos. To buy a good produced in Mexico, a buyer has to obtain pesos. But if no Mexicans wanted to buy anything in the United States, there would be no one willing to exchange pesos for dollars. Simply put, there would be no supply of pesos on foreign exchange markets but there would be a big demand for them. As a result, the price of the peso . . . the exchange rate . . . would rise.

   Now think carefully about what a more expensive peso means. Since U.S. buyers have to buy pesos to buy Mexican goods, Mexican goods just became more expensive. At the same time, the increase in the price of pesos (dollars per peso) makes American goods look cheaper to Mexicans. This will have to go on until the supply and demand for pesos is equal! That means that Mexicans find some goods cheaper in the United States. In fact, exports to Mexico grew from $46 billion in 1995, just after NAFTA went into effect, to $111 billion by 2000. The exchange rate adjusts to make up for the wage differential.

There is one important exception to this story. A country can buy more goods from a second country for an extended period if those purchases are balanced by purchases of stocks and bonds. China for example sold about $9 billion per month more in goods and services to the United States during 2003 than the U.S. bought from China. To balance that while holding the value of the Chinese currency constant, China accumulated dollars and used them to buy U.S. stocks and bonds. The result is a big trade deficit for the U.S. This has been the subject of revived trade talks between the U.S. and China in recent years. Ultimately, Chinese citizens must be able to buy goods and services to enjoy the benefits of their huge exports.

2. Protecting an industry from foreign competition to save jobs will cost jobs in those sectors that would expand with free trade. Clearly, when trade opens up, some sectors are hurt by cheaper imports. In fact, that is precisely the point: to get goods at a lower price. If we spend less on vegetables from South America, we can spend more on other goods at home. In addition, demand from our trading partners will spur growth in the production of our export goods. By reducing trade with another country, we also reduce the number of jobs in its export sectors.
3. Protecting an industry can lead to inefficiency and a lack of ability to compete in world markets later on. Those industries that are subject to rigorous competition from abroad tend to adopt the newest, most efficient technology and hold costs to a minimum. The U.S. steel industry was heavily protected for many years, and it eventually lost most of the world business in steel to vigorously competitive foreign producers.
4. Keeping the unemployment rate low is a macroeconomic issue. When the economy is expanding, unemployment falls and can be low regardless of the composition of trade. The lowest rate of unemployment in decades was in the year 2000. In that year, following the expansion of trade from NAFTA and GATT, unemployment averaged just 4 percent, the lowest since 1969. The correct tools for fighting unemployment are fiscal and monetary policies, not antitrade policies.
5. If the objective is to reduce poverty, how can preventing trade help? Opening a country up to trade increases the demand for labor in the export sectors. For many countries, domestic demand is low because income is low. If export demand succeeds in increasing jobs, incomes will rise, not fall.

A second argument against free trade is that it will hurt the environment. The main thrust of this argument is that poor countries are not subject to the same environmental standards as rich countries. Lax environmental standards reduce the cost of doing business for a country's producers. Thus, countries have an incentive to ignore the environment to become more competitive in world markets.

Globalization advocates respond with two points: First, environmental regulation is a problem for all countries regardless of whether they trade. Poor countries, where people are earning subsistence wages, do not have the resources to devote to environmental protection. All you have to do is visit a major city in a poor country to be convinced that the environment is generally a problem. But the real hope for an improved environment is growth and responsible government. Clearly, environmental improvement is a luxury good. Feeding the citizenry comes first, and improving the environment comes later. Second, trade may actually be a lever to increase environmental protection. The World Trade Organization (WTO) and NAFTA have ongoing negotiations designed to pressure countries into improving environmental regulations.

A third argument is that free-trade rules and the power of organizations like the WTO can undermine national sovereignty by forcing countries to give up various things. This is, of course, true. The classic example is a farm subsidy. The farm lobbies in many countries are strong. With productivity advances, it is increasingly difficult, particularly for small farmers, to make a living farming. Many countries, including the United States, pay significant subsidies to some farmers, enabling them to produce at lower cost. Since farmers can produce at

News Analysis

Farm Subsidies and Fair Trade in 2003

ONE OF THE BIGGEST STUMBLING BLOCKS TO free and open trade is that many countries, including the United States, want to help their farmers. Farming is a very competitive business, and all countries participate. The following *New York Times* editorial appeared in July 2003. It highlights the conflict between farm subsidies and trade.

The Rigged Trade Game

—New York Times

Put simply, the Philippines got taken. A charter member of the World Trade Organization in 1995, the former American colony dutifully embraced globalization's free-market gospel over the last decade, opening its economy to foreign trade and investment. Despite widespread worries about their ability to compete, Filipinos bought the theory that their farmers' lack of good transportation and high technology would be balanced out by their cheap labor. The government predicted that access to world markets would create a net gain of a half-million farming jobs a year, and improve the country's trade balance.

It didn't happen. Small-scale farmers across the Philippine archipelago have discovered that their competitors in places like the United States or Europe do not simply have better seeds, fertilizers and equipment. Their products are also often protected by high tariffs, or underwritten by massive farm subsidies that make them artificially cheap. . . . "Farmers in the United States get help every step of the way," says Rudivico Mamac, a very typical, and very poor, Filipino sharecropper, whose 12-year-old son is embarrassed that his family cannot afford to buy him a ballpoint pen or notebooks for school.

The same sad story repeats itself around the globe, as poor countries trying to pull themselves into the world market come up against the richest nations' insistence on stacking the deck for their own farmers. President Bush deserves credit for traveling to Africa and trying to focus attention on that continent's plight. But meanwhile, struggling African cotton farmers are forced to compete with products from affluent American agribusinesses whose rock-bottom prices are made possible by as much as $3 billion in annual subsidies. Sugar producers in Africa are stymied by the European Union's insistence on subsidizing beet sugar production as part of a wasteful farming-welfare program that gobbles up half its budget. . . .

The United States, Europe and Japan funnel nearly a billion dollars a day to their farmers in taxpayer subsidies. These farmers say they will not be able to stay in business if they are left at the mercy of wildly fluctuating prices and are forced to compete against people in places like the Philippines, who are happy to work in the fields for a dollar a day. So the federal government writes out checks to Iowa corn farmers to supplement their income, and at times insures them against all sorts of risks assumed by any other business. This allows American companies to profitably dump grain on international markets for a fraction of what it cost to grow, courtesy of the taxpayer, at a price less than the break-even point for the impoverished third-world farmers. If all else fails, wealthy nations simply throw up trade barriers to lock out foreign commodities.

Farm subsidies in the United States and other countries make it difficult for farmers in the Philippines to compete in world markets.

Source: Adapted from: "The Rigged Trade Game," New York Times, *editorial, July 20, 2003. Reprinted by permission.*

Visit www.prenhall.com/casefair for updated articles and exercises.

lower cost, they enjoy a significant advantage over farmers producing in countries where there are no subsidies. This has become a huge issue between the developed and developing countries.

genetically modified (GM) foods Strains of food that have been genetically modified. Examples include insect and herbicide-resistant soybeans, corn, and cotton and rice with increased iron and vitamins.

One final issue is the debate over **genetically modified (GM) foods** or genetically modified organisms. Many companies have been experimenting with strains of food that have been genetically modified for a variety of reasons. Such crops are grown commercially in more than 40 countries. The principal crops grown include insect- and herbicide-resistant soybeans, corn, and cotton. Other GM crops include rice with increased iron and vitamins and a sweet potato resistant to a virus that could decimate much of the African harvest. Microorganisms have been genetically modified to produce enzymes that help make better wine.

The worry is that we don't know everything about the potential dangers of the newly created organisms. They may be harmful. Several European countries have in the past banned the import of GM crops despite their lower cost. As a compromise, in 2003 the European Community opted to drop the ban but to insist on mandatory labeling of any product containing even a trace of a genetically modified ingredient.

U.S. producers have taken up the case with the WTO, claiming that it is just another way to block less costly U.S. products from entering the market and again subsidizing European farmers. The proponents of free trade in GM goods say that while the benefits are clear and certain, the costs are speculative. To date there is no evidence that GM crops have caused any harmful side effects.

TRADE, GROWTH, AND POVERTY

Much of what we have said so far is theory. There is certainly a theoretical case to be made for bringing down trade barriers. But what about evidence? Do those nations that are more open to trade grow faster than countries that are less open? Has poverty declined more rapidly in countries that trade more openly? There are clearly examples of open economies that have grown rapidly and where poverty has been reduced, such as China. There are also examples of countries that trade openly that have seen little growth and increasing poverty rates, such as Haiti. But controlling for other determinants of poverty and growth, is trade a plus or a minus?

The National Bureau of Economic Research and the World Bank sponsored a number of case studies of trade liberalization in the 1970s and 1980s. Most showed that countries that were more integrated into the world economy grew faster than those that were less integrated.[2] An oft-cited study by Jeffrey Sachs and Andrew Warner concludes that open countries grew 2 percent per year more rapidly than closed economies, controlling for a number of factors.[3] While some studies challenge the strength of the relationship,[4] the bulk of the evidence supports the claim that trade liberalization was an important component of policy reforms that led to more rapid growth. Even one who challenged the strength of the relationship admits, "No country has developed successfully by turning its back on international trade and long term capital flows."[5]

But does growth necessarily reduce poverty, or do all the benefits of growth find their way into the pockets of the rich? Certainly, as Stanley Fischer states in a recent essay on globalization, "Logic dictates that there is no way of lifting the populations of poor countries out of poverty without sustained growth. Globally, the decline in poverty has been the fastest where growth has been the fastest (in developing Asia) and the slowest where growth performance has been the worst (in Africa)."[6] Empirical studies also verify that on average when countries grow, the income of the lowest fifth of the income distribution rises at about the same rate as aggregate income, including when growth is induced by more open trade.[7]

THE GLOBALIZATION OF LABOR MARKETS: THE ECONOMICS OF IMMIGRATION

Globalization also refers to the increased mobility of labor across international borders. Whenever unemployment rises, the issue of immigration takes center stage in the press. And few topics elicit as much of an emotional response. In December 1994 voters in California approved by a 3-to-2 margin Proposition 187, a highly controversial referendum that prevents illegal immigrants from receiving state education, welfare, and nonemergency medical benefits. Also in 1994, Governor Lawton Chiles of Florida declared a statewide emergency and demanded a stop to the tens of thousands of Cuban immigrants flooding into Florida. President Clinton responded by sending the Coast Guard to intercept them and take them to a detention camp at Guantanamo Naval Base in Cuba. Later, some were sent to Panama, and some were allowed to enter the United States. These events provoked memories of the 1980 Mariel boat lift, as a result of which over 125,000 refugees arrived in Florida. Many of these refugees were criminals who still reside in U.S. prisons.

What impact does immigration have on a country's economy? Is it all bad, as many would have us believe? Interestingly, one of the key elements of the agreement among the members of the European Union is the abolition of border controls to encourage the free

Many agricultural firms in Texas and California rely on immigration from Mexico, Central America, and South America to supply them with labor during the peak growing season. But does immigration reduce domestic wages and increase unemployment nationally? The evidence is mixed.

---

[2]See Jagdish Bhagwati, *Foreign Trade Regimes and Economic Development* (Cambridge, MA: Ballanger Press, 1978).

[3]Jeffrey Sachs and Andrew Warner, "Economic Reform and the Process of Global Integration," *Brookings Papers on Economic Activity*, 1995 (1).

[4]Francisco Rodriguez and Dani Rodrik, "Trade Policy and Economic Growth: A Skeptic's Guide to the Evidence," in Ben Bernanke and Kenneth Rogoff, *NBER Macroeconomics Annual*, 2000 (Cambridge, MA: MIT Press, 2001).

[5]Dani Rodrik in Rodriguez and Rodrik, p. 23.

[6]Stanley Fischer, "Globalization and Its Challenges," *American Economic Review*, May 2003, p. 13.

[7]For example, David Dollar and Aart Kraay, "Growth Is Good for the Poor," cited in Fischer, p. 13, based on data from 92 countries.

flow of labor among member countries in response to wage differentials and economic conditions. The relaxation of immigration rules in Europe was done in the name of encouraging economic growth and prosperity.

A Brief History of Immigration into the United States Immigration into the United States has come in irregular waves. The first "Great Migration" occurred between 1880 and 1924, when 25.8 million immigrants entered the country, a figure that represented more than 40 percent of the period's total population increase. During the 1920s, however, Congress established a national-origins quota system that limited the annual flow from the Eastern Hemisphere countries to 150,000. Under the new laws, visas were issued in proportion to the ethnic composition of the United States in 1920. The result was that 60 percent of the visas went to German and British immigrants.

The flow of immigrants slowed to a trickle during the 1930s but has been expanding ever since. Between 1990 and 2000 immigration averaged just under one million annually. Many of today's immigrants are illegal. Studies indicate that during the late 1980s between 2 million and 3 million people were illegally residing in the United States and 200,000 to 300,000 new illegals were arriving each year. Though the Border Patrol intercepts and returns about 1.3 million illegals per year, many illegal immigrants enter the country legally. They enter legally through customs and simply remain in the country.

Immigration Reform and Control Act (1986) Granted amnesty to about 3 million illegal aliens and imposed a strong set of employer sanctions designed to slow the flow of immigrants into the United States.

Immigration Act of 1990 Increased the number of legal immigrants allowed into the United States each year by 150,000.

In 1986 the Congress enacted the **Immigration Reform and Control Act**, which granted amnesty to about 3 million illegals and imposed a set of strong employer sanctions designed to slow the flow of immigrants into the United States. The **Immigration Act of 1990** increased the number of legal immigrants allowed in each year by 150,000.

Prior to 1960, the largest single group of immigrants into the United States came from Europe. Between 1991 and 2000 the largest group of immigrants came from the Americas, especially Mexico. Beginning in 1970, the number of immigrants from Asia began to grow rapidly. Table 22.1 shows the number of immigrants from the top 14 countries of origin between 1991 and 2000.

Economic Arguments for Free Immigration Should a country permit completely free immigration into its borders? The argument for free immigration is that it increases world output. Labor flows across borders in response to wage differentials. Consider the case of Mexico and the United States. Low-wage workers in Mexico migrate to the United States because wages are higher in the United States. If markets are basically competitive, wages reflect the workers' productivity. In other words, because the United States has more capital and uses more advanced technology than Mexico, the productivity of low-wage workers is higher in the United States than in Mexico. Thus, the same labor produces more total output after immigration, and world output rises.

TABLE 22.1 Immigrants into the United States by Country of Origin: 1991–2000

RANK	COUNTRY	THOUSANDS OF IMMIGRANTS
1	Mexico	2,251
2	Philippines	506
3	China	425
4	Vietnam	421
5	India	383
6	Dominican Republic	341
7	El Salvador	217
8	Haiti	182
9	Cuba	181
10	Jamaica	174
11	Korea	171
12	Poland	170
13	Ukraine	142
14	Canada	138

Source: *Statistical Abstract of the United States, 2002*, Table 7.

Now consider the case of France and Italy. If a labor shortage develops in France because the demand for French wine increases, French wages will rise and attract workers from other European countries. If at the same time the demand for leather goods produced in Italy drops off, Italian wages will fall, and Italian workers will move to France, where their productivity is higher.

The argument for the free movement of labor among nations is exactly the same as the argument for the free movement of labor among the sectors of the domestic economy. Suppose an economy produces only two goods, X and Y. If demand for good X picks up, the demand for labor used to produce X rises, since the gains to hiring more labor in the production of X is increasing. Labor will move out of the production of good Y if and only if its productivity is higher in X in terms of the value of output. This movement ensures efficiency. Recall the simple definition that an efficient economy is one that produces what people want at least cost.

Those who favor a looser policy toward immigrants believe that immigrants do not displace U.S. workers but rather take jobs that Americans simply do not want. Immigrants serve as domestics and low-wage farm workers producing things that the United States needs. In addition, the U.S. economy has absorbed wave after wave of immigrants while maintaining virtually full employment. Almost all U.S. citizens except Native Americans have relatively recent ancestors who came to the country as immigrants.

The Argument against Free Immigration No economist disputes the idea that the distribution of income is likely to change among countries and among groups within each country in response to immigration. Assuming that immigrants are low-wage workers, equilibrium wages in the market for low-skill labor will rise in the country of origin and fall in the country of destination. In addition, the return to capital will rise in the destination country, pushing up profits, while capital income will fall in the country of origin.

The argument in favor of free immigration assumes that all workers get jobs. However, the popular impression is certainly that immigrants (who will usually work for very low wages) take jobs away from low-income Americans and drive up unemployment rates. In addition, many believe that immigrants often end up on welfare rolls and become a burden to taxpayers. Opponents also point to crime in ethnic neighborhoods and rivalries among ethnic groups as evidence of further costs to society.

The Evidence: The Net Costs of Immigration To determine whether the net benefits of immigration outweigh its net costs, we must ask one important question: To what extent does immigration reduce domestic wages and increase unemployment? A number of recent studies have found that metropolitan areas that have greater numbers of immigrants seem to have only slightly lower wages and only slightly higher unemployment rates.

An influential study by David Card of the University of California, Berkeley, looks carefully at wages and employment opportunities in the Miami metropolitan area during and after the Mariel boat lift in 1981. Almost overnight, about 125,000 Cubans arrived in Florida and increased the labor force in Miami by over 7 percent. Card looked at trends in wages and unemployment among Miami workers between 1980 and 1985 and found virtually no effect. In addition, the data he examined mirrored the experience of workers in Los Angeles, Houston, Atlanta, and similar cities that were not hit by the same shock.[8]

However, a more recent study by Borjas, Freeman, and Katz takes issue with much of the work done to date. They argue that immigrants do not stay in the cities at which they arrive, but rather move within the United States in response to job opportunities and wage differentials. Thus, they argue that the effects of immigration on wages and unemployment must be analyzed at the national level, not at the city level. Their study points to the large decline in the wages of high school dropouts relative to workers with more education during the 1980s. Their results suggest that a third of the drop in the relative wages of high school dropouts can be attributed to lower skilled immigrants.[9]

[8]David Card, "The Impact of the Mariel Boat Lift on the Miami Labor Market," *Industrial and Labor Relations Review*, January 1990, pp. 245–257.

[9]George Borjas, Richard Freeman, and Lawrence Katz, "On the Labor Market Effects of Immigration and Trade," in *Immigration and the Work Force: Economic Consequences for the United States and Source Areas*, eds. George Borjas and Richard Freeman (Chicago: University of Chicago Press, 1992).

On the issue of immigration's effects on government costs, mixed evidence also exists. It is clear that earlier generations of immigrants have had a positive effect on both the economy as a whole and on government budgets more specifically. Studies of early immigrants' wage patterns seem to show that their wages on average exceed native workers' wages after 15 years. First-generation immigrants as a group might thus be paying more in taxes than they collect in means-tested benefits such as welfare.

But the data show that over time there has been a very dramatic drop in the level of education, experience, and skills among immigrants. At the same time, participation in welfare programs among immigrants has jumped sharply. Borjas estimates that in 1990, immigrant households in the United States contributed between $7.6 billion and $10.1 billion in tax revenues while collecting $23.8 billion in benefits from means-tested programs.

Is Immigration Bad or Good? Immigration is another of those economic issues in which no right answer clearly emerges. The evidence on the effects of immigration is mixed, and theory gives us arguments on both sides of the issue. Only time will tell whether the recent wave of immigrants will assimilate as well as past waves. In the meantime, immigration will remain a "hot button" issue politically, and the United States will be called upon to make some important decisions about the treatment of recent immigrants.

CAPITAL MOBILITY

Another important aspect of globalization is capital mobility. Look back at the circular flow diagram in Figure 22.1. Six of the 16 flows depicted in the figure refer to the supply of or demand for capital. In the global economy, domestic households can put their wealth to work in foreign or domestic financial markets; domestic firms can finance investment projects by looking to domestic or foreign financial markets. The same applies to foreign households and firms.

Banks are increasingly international institutions holding foreign saving and financing projects in many countries.

Today, virtually all well-diversified portfolios of stocks and bonds owned by households or institutions contain some foreign assets. It is as easy to buy or sell shares in an Italian textile company as it is to buy or sell shares in General Electric. In addition, most of the well-known large corporations in the United States are multinational. That is, they have extensive production, operation, or sales facilities in foreign countries. Purchases and sales of foreign stocks and bonds by U.S. citizens and purchases and sales of U.S. stocks and bonds by foreigners totaled in the trillions of dollars in 2003. One-third of all foreign holdings of U.S. securities are held by the Japanese. Foreign direct investment in the United States, that is, foreign firms' ownership of physical capital in the United States, totaled about $1.2 trillion in 2000, while U.S. firms owned about the same amount of capital in foreign countries.

The argument for free and open financial market mobility is that capital should flow to its highest and best use. Financial markets should allocate capital to those uses that have the highest returns, controlling for risks associated with those investments. If investing in a factory in Nigeria would yield a return of 20 percent annually, while a similar investment of comparable risk in the United States would yield a 14 percent return, financial markets should finance the Nigerian project first regardless of where the financing comes from.

Rapid and free flows of financial capital have, however, had adverse consequences for some nations. During the mid-1990s a tremendous volume of financial capital flowed from the United States into the countries of Thailand, Indonesia, and Korea. Mutual funds bought shares of foreign companies, banks and insurance companies financed large real estate deals, and hedge funds speculated by betting on stock markets and exchange rate movements in these countries during the years leading up to 1997.

All of this seemed good for everyone involved. The purchases of physical capital were likely to raise productivity and wages in those countries. The construction of office buildings created jobs directly and provided space for growing businesses, and new factories provided capital (machines) for workers to work with. A side effect was that the currencies of these countries became very strong. For example, the Korean won increased substantially in value. The effect was to make imports very inexpensive. The combination of cheap imports, high demand for investment goods, and prospering financial markets, including booming stock markets, fed on itself and the flows increased.

But what happens quite often in these cases is that capital markets "overshoot." Since no one coordinates the investments being made by individual investors, and since there are often long lags between the decision to invest and the actual creation of new capital, sometimes there is overinvestment. Such was the case in Thailand, Korea, and Indonesia in 1997. When things began to unwind in those countries, creditors all headed for the doors at the same time. That is, mutual funds, banks, and others who were holding assets in those countries tried to liquidate their holdings all at the same time. The result was a dramatic decline in the value of the won (Korea), the baht (Thailand), and the rupiah (Indonesia), which pushed up import prices and hurt consumption spending. Stock markets crashed, business investment dried up, aggregate spending dropped, and all three countries experienced severe recessions. Similar booms and busts in Brazil (1998), Mexico (1994), Russia (1998), Turkey (2000), and Argentina (2001) seem to have roots in similar kinds of rapid financial flows.

Partially as a reaction to these crises, some countries have "capital controls." Such controls place strict limits on the volume of financial flows into and out of a country in a given period of time. In his recent piece on globalization, Stanley Fischer makes the following argument:

> What can be done to reduce the volatility of capital flows to emerging-market countries? The first response would be for countries to shut themselves off from international capital flows. It bears emphasis that despite the crises, and the arguments of many of the critics of globalization, almost no country has taken this route; the revealed preference of the emerging-market countries is to stay involved with the international financial system.[10]

PUBLIC POLICY AND GLOBALIZATION

The increasing interdependence of nations and their citizens brings with it several specific policy debates that go beyond the issues of free trade and labor and capital mobility that we have already discussed. First, there are global public goods or externalities. How should the nations of the world respond to these large-scale problems of coordination, such as global warming? Second, a number of large and powerful institutions, often referred to as nongovernmental organizations (NGOs), play a powerful role in enforcing international monetary agreements and trade rules. The most well known are the World Bank and the International Monetary Fund (IMF). The question is, what role should institutions take in promoting world growth and eliminating poverty?

GLOBAL EXTERNALITIES AND PUBLIC GOODS

Economics by and large deals with the efficient functioning of markets both national and international. But often problems arise that are not efficiently handled by private markets. One such problem involves a class of goods called public goods.

public goods, or **social goods** Goods or services that bestow collective benefits on members of society.

Public goods, sometimes called **social goods**, are goods or services that bestow collective benefits on members of society. Generally, no one can be excluded from enjoying their benefits once they are produced. Classic examples are clean air and national defense.

Private goods, such as hamburgers, are produced by the private sector because a firm can exclude those who don't pay. If exclusion is impossible, two problems arise for markets: the "free-rider problem" and the "drop-in-the-bucket problem." Why should I pay for a good if I get the benefits whether I pay or not? Since many people benefit from production, my contribution is so small as to not matter. As a result, the private sector is powerless because it is in peoples' interests to not pay, and it falls to government to arrange for their provision. Governments can appropriate money and collect taxes for such things as national defense, a justice system, and public health, effectively forcing citizens to pay for them. Presumably, governments produce those public goods that its citizens want.

But what about public goods whose benefits are worldwide or at least cross-border? Here, even governments and nations face the "free-rider" and "drop-in-the-bucket" problems. Consider the problem of global warming. Taking action to slow global warming presumably would produce a worldwide public good. Clearly, there is no way to exclude nations

[10]Stanley Fischer, "Globalization and Its Challenges," *American Economic Review*, May 2003, p. 16.

from the benefits for not contributing, and the impact of any one nation is small. As a result, nations have an incentive to not contribute. This is particularly true for developing countries like China and India where cleanup would be costly and the sacrifice great in terms of national income.

externality A cost or a benefit resulting from some activity or transaction that is imposed or bestowed on some party outside the activity or transaction.

Another way to think of global warming is that it is the result of an externality. An **externality** is a cost or a benefit resulting from some activity or transaction that is imposed or bestowed on some party outside the activity or transaction. The classic example is pollution, but there are countless others.

For efficiency, those weighing the costs and benefits of their production or consumption decisions must weigh *all* the costs and benefits. One of the functions of government is to "internalize" externalities. In essence, the idea is to force those who generate externalities to factor those externalities into their decisions. One example of a policy designed to internalize an externality is a charge or tax imposed on a polluting firm in proportion to the damage done.

Of course this becomes very complex when one country imposes an external cost on another. If the number of countries involved is small, bargaining and negotiation may simply resolve the issue. But where large numbers of jurisdictions are involved, the public goods problems arise.

The United Nations and other international bodies exist to promote those things that have benefits for the world but that require international cooperation and contribution. One interpretation of their purpose is that they exist to ensure the production of international public goods. But their success rate has been spotty. International politics is clearly more complex and problematic than national politics. In addition, international bodies have very little in the way of taxing power.

The concept of public goods also helps to explain the HIV/AIDS pandemic. In 2003, more than 60 million people were infected with the virus. Each day approximately 14,000 infections occurred. More than 20 million have died. It is the leading cause of death in sub-Saharan Africa where the disease threatens to reverse the developmental achievements of the last 50 years.

The HIV/AIDS problem is more than just a health issue. It decimates the workforce, makes poverty and inequality much worse, creates huge numbers of orphans, and costs the poorest countries billions of dollars in health expenditures. Basic treatment for an AIDS patient can cost 3 times the per-capita gross national income.

To have an impact on the epidemic, nations must cooperate and be willing to pay. Clearly, this is a problem that will not be solved by the market. It will require a multinational effort if the pandemic is to be brought under control.

NONGOVERNMENTAL ORGANIZATIONS AND INTERNATIONAL ECONOMICS: THE WASHINGTON CONSENSUS

No single topic in international economics brings up such heated debate as the policy position taken by the IMF a few years back in setting "conditions" that had to be met for countries to qualify for development loans and grants.

Washington Consensus A set of 10 goals prescribed for countries receiving IMF grants and loans.

While there is considerable disagreement about exactly who formed it or how strongly it was designed to be enforced, a set of objectives or goals was laid down for countries that the IMF was financing. What came to be referred to as the **"Washington Consensus"** had 10 elements: (1) fiscal discipline—modest budget deficits or balanced budgets, (2) public expenditure priorities in health and education, (3) tax reform—the tax base should be broad, and marginal tax rates should be low, (4) positive but moderate market-determined interest rates, (5) a competitive—ideally floating—exchange rate as the "first essential element of an outward-oriented economic policy," (6) import liberalization—essentially a free-trade policy for reduced tariffs, (7) openness to foreign investment, (8) privatization—"based on the idea that private industry is managed more efficiently than public enterprises," (9) deregulation, and (10) protection of property rights.

Clearly, considerable room for disagreement existed about the degree to which these elements should or could be enforced. Many believed that the IMF went too far and was too rigid in its dealings with many countries. Taking a country, like one of the former communist countries of Eastern Europe, and demanding a balanced budget, openness, and privatization in rapid succession was too much too soon.

Out of the bad experiences of the 1990s has emerged a new consensus for gradualism. While the spirit of the Washington Consensus remains intact, the rigor of its application appears to be quite a bit softer.

GLOBALIZATION, CAPITALISM, AND DEMOCRACY

One final topic is important to mention before leaving the discussion of globalization. Very often the issue of openness and globalization intersects with issues concerning political and economic systems. Advocates of globalization often are staunch supporters of laissez-faire capitalism. Certainly, the 10 points of the Washington Consensus would lead one to the conclusion that its advocates are strong believers in the market system.

But does the issue of openness and the desirability of increasing interdependence among national economies depend on the kind of economic or political system that a country chooses to establish? Probably not.

First of all, it is important to separate the debate about political systems from the debate about economic systems. The terms *democracy* and *dictatorship* refer to the institutions of government and to the process of public choice. To what extent are the decisions of the government made through democratic institutions that express the will of the people?

The terms *socialism* and *capitalism* refer, on the other hand, to the economic institutions that determine the allocation of resources. A pure socialist economy is one in which the government owns the land and capital and in which resources are allocated essentially by central government plan. A laissez-faire capitalist economy is one in which the government plays virtually no role in directing the economy. Rather, resource allocation decisions are made by individual households and firms acting in their own self-interest with little or no government involvement. The essential decisions are made through the market.

In fact, most economies are mixed, and the debate is really not about government versus no government. It is instead about the role of government in the economy. Even the most conservative, free enterprise advocates believe that the government must play some role in the economy. In microeconomics we discuss the government's role in the provision of public goods, the regulation of monopoly power, internalizing external costs and benefits, and ensuring that all economic agents are well informed. We also discuss the extent to which citizens may want to get the government involved in redistribution of income. In macroeconomics we discuss the potential role of government in stabilizing the economy to hold rates of unemployment and inflation to a minimum.

Even in the strongly free enterprise economic system in the United States, fully 30 percent of total income goes to taxes to support the government, and the government plays a significant role in resource allocation choices.

There are some countries that have had very democratic political systems but that choose to have socialist-leaning economies with very substantial government direction. Examples would include Sweden and Denmark. On the other hand, there are countries that have had strong dictatorships but that choose to have very laissez-faire economic systems. Examples include Singapore and Chile under Augusto Pinochet.

While economists as a whole tend to favor globalization, there is a wide rage of opinion on the proper role of government in the economy. While many favor substantial government involvement, most economists believe that the allocation of resources should be left to the market by and large and that profit-maximizing firms and utility-maximizing households should be allowed to respond to market incentives. Those same economists tend by and large to believe that households and firms should be allowed, with as little interference as possible, to engage in trade, invest abroad, or work abroad.

A FINAL WORD

So what is the result of all of this? Is there a consensus about the desirability of globalization? There is not. Probably nothing that we have said here will convince the critics that it is a good thing. But it is important to understand that a powerful logic exists in support of economic openness—the idea that the free flow of resources and goods and services across national borders, driven by efficient economic incentives, including the desire to maximize profit, is likely to make citizens better off than if borders were closed and economies turned inward.

SUMMARY

THE GLOBAL CIRCULAR FLOW

1. *Globalization* is the process of increasing interdependence among countries and their citizens. Globalization has social, cultural, political, and economic dimensions.
2. *Economic globalization* is the process of increasing economic interdependence among countries and their citizens. It involves increased international trade of goods and services, increased cross-border movements of labor, and expanded international financial flows.
3. The global circular flow diagram shows the complexity of the interactions among economies.
4. The basic argument for economic globalization can be found in the decisions behind each of the flows in the circular flow diagram.
5. If we didn't allow people to move freely across borders, or if we didn't let New Jersey citizens invest in California companies, or if we barred the export of fish from the coasts to the interior, the system would clearly be inefficient.

A BRIEF HISTORY OF ECONOMIC GLOBALIZATION

6. Economic historian Jeffrey Williamson classifies the period 1820–1914 as the first great period of globalization and the period since World War II as the second.

THE BENEFITS AND COSTS OF GLOBALIZATION

7. The argument for free trade rests on two pieces of intuition. First, if you have something that I want and I have something that you want, we can exchange and both be better off. Voluntary exchange is efficient. Second, applying the concept to nations, two nations can benefit from free trade by specializing in producing those products in which they enjoy a *comparative advantage.*
8. Those who oppose trade make a number of arguments and proponents of free trade have a number of counterarguments.
9. There are clearly examples of open economies that have grown rapidly and where poverty has been reduced, such as China. There are also examples of countries that trade openly that have seen little growth and increasing poverty rates, such as Haiti.
10. The bulk of the evidence supports the claim that trade liberalization was an important component of policy reforms that led to more rapid growth.
11. The argument for free immigration is that it increases world output. Those who favor immigration also point out that the United States has absorbed many waves of immigrants while maintaining virtually full employment. Those who argue against immigration believe that it takes jobs away from low-income U.S. citizens.
12. Another important aspect of globalization is capital mobility. In the global economy, domestic households can put their wealth to work in foreign or domestic financial markets; domestic firms can finance investment projects by looking to domestic or foreign financial markets.
13. The argument for free and open financial market mobility is that capital should flow to its highest and best use. Rapid and free flows of financial capital have, however, had adverse consequences for some nations.

PUBLIC POLICY AND GLOBALIZATION

14. An important world policy issue concerns global public goods or externalities, such as global warming and the HIV/AIDS pandemic.

GLOBALIZATION, CAPITALISM, AND DEMOCRACY

15. Very often the issue of openness and globalization intersects with issues concerning political and economic systems. Advocates of globalization often are staunch supporters of laissez-faire capitalism.

REVIEW TERMS AND CONCEPTS

comparative advantage, 424
economic globalization, 421
externality, 432
genetically modified (GM) foods, 426
globalization, 421
Immigration Act of 1990, 428
Immigration Reform and Control Act (1986), 428
public goods, or social goods, 431
Washington Consensus, 432

PROBLEM SET

1. In a televised debate in 2004, two Senate candidates were debating the merits of a new trade agreement proposed by the president between the nations of Central America and the United States. Write a brief letter addressed to your own senator explaining the debate as it relates to jobs in your state. What industries in your state tend to export? Which goods does your state import? See if you can find out what products your state exports to the countries of Costa Rica, El Salvador, Guatemala, Honduras, and Nicaragua.
2. From which countries did the largest number of immigrants enter the United States in 2002? You may find the answer by log-

ging on to www.immigration.gov and looking for immigration statistics. Do most immigrants come from rich countries or poor countries? See if you can explain the pattern.

3. In May of 2003, the trade deficit increased modestly. Part of that increase was due to an increase in our deficit with China. The goods deficit with China increased from $9.5 billion in April to $9.9 billion in May. Exports decreased $0.1 billion (primarily iron and steel mill products; and soybeans) to $2.0 billion, while imports increased $0.3 billion (primarily camping apparel and gear and computer accessories) to $11.9 billion.

   How is it possible to import $11.9 billion worth of goods and services while exporting only $2 billion? Can it continue?

4. A huge problem for the world is the HIV/AIDS pandemic. Advocates of worldwide funding of effective but expensive drugs as well as extensive prevention argue that dealing with the crisis would be the equivalent of producing a worldwide "public good." Define "public good." In what ways would stopping HIV/AIDS be a public good? What are some of the reasons our efforts have not made significant progress in providing this public good?

Visit www.prenhall.com/casefair for self-test quizzes, interactive graphing exercises, and news articles.

Economic Growth in Developing and Transitional Economies

23

CHAPTER OUTLINE

Our primary focus in this text has been on countries with modern industrialized economies that rely heavily on markets to allocate resources, but what about the economic problems facing such countries as Somalia or Haiti? Can we apply the same economic principles that we have been studying to these less-developed nations?

Yes. All economic analysis deals with the problem of making choices under conditions of scarcity, and the problem of satisfying people's wants and needs is as real for Somalia and Haiti as it is for the United States, Germany, and Japan. The universality of scarcity is what makes economic analysis relevant to all nations, regardless of their level of material well-being or ruling political ideology.

The basic tools of supply and demand, theories about consumers and firms, and theories about the structure of markets all contribute to an understanding of the economic problems confronting the world's developing nations. However, these nations often face economic problems quite different from those faced by richer, more developed countries. In the developing nations, the economist may have to worry about chronic food shortages, explosive population growth, and hyperinflations that reach triple, and even quadruple, digits. The United States and other industrialized economies rarely encounter such difficulties.

The instruments of economic management also vary from nation to nation. The United States has well-developed financial market institutions and a strong central bank (the Federal Reserve) through which the government can control the macroeconomy to some extent. Even limited intervention is impossible in some of the developing countries. In the United States, tax laws can be changed to stimulate saving, to encourage particular kinds of investments, or to redistribute income. In most developing countries, there are neither meaningful personal income taxes nor effective tax policies.

Even though economic problems and the policy instruments available to tackle them vary across nations, economic thinking about these problems can be transferred easily from one setting to another. In this chapter we discuss several of the economic problems specific to developing nations in an attempt to capture some of the insights that economic analysis can offer.

LIFE IN THE DEVELOPING NATIONS: POPULATION AND POVERTY

In the year 2002, the population of the world reached over 6.2 billion people. Most of the world's more than 200 nations belong to the developing world, in which about three-fourths of the world's population lives.

In the early 1960s, the nations of the world could be assigned rather easily to categories: The *developed countries* included most of Europe, North America, Japan, Australia, and New Zealand; the *developing countries* included the rest of the world. The developing nations were often referred to as the "Third World" to distinguish them from the Western industrialized nations (the "First World") and the former Socialist bloc of Eastern European nations (the "Second World").

In 2002, the world did not divide easily into three neat parts. Rapid economic progress has brought some developing nations closer to developed economies. Countries such as Argentina and Korea, still considered to be "developing," are often referred to as middle-income, or newly industrialized, countries. Other countries, such as much of sub-Saharan Africa and some of South Asia, have stagnated and fallen so far behind the economic advances of the rest of the world that the "Fourth World" has been used to describe them. It is not clear yet where the republics of the former Soviet Union and other formerly Communist countries of Eastern Europe will end up. Production has fallen sharply in many of them. For example, between 1990 and 1997, real gross domestic product (GDP) fell about 40 percent in the transition economies and over 50 percent in Russia and Central Asia. One estimate puts 2002 per capita GDP in Russia below $2,500. Some of the new republics now have more in common with developing countries than with developed countries.

Although the countries of the developing world exhibit considerable diversity, both in their standards of living and in their particular experiences of growth, marked differences continue to separate them from the developed nations. The developed countries have a higher average level of material well-being (the amounts of food, clothing, shelter, and other commodities consumed by the average person). Comparisons of gross national income are often used as a crude index of the level of material well-being across nations. GNI is a new measure of a nation's income computed using a more accurate way of converting purchasing power into dollars. See Table 23.1 where GNI per capita in the industrial market economies significantly exceeds GNI of both the low- and middle-income developing economies.

Other characteristics of economic development include improvements in basic health and education. The degree of political and economic freedom enjoyed by individual citizens might also be part of what it means to be a developed nation. Some of these criteria are easier to quantify; Table 23.1 presents data for different types of economies according to some of the more easily measured indexes of development. As you see, the industrial market

TABLE 23.1 Indicators of Economic Development

COUNTRY GROUP	POPULATION (MILLIONS) 2002	GROSS NATIONAL INCOME PER CAPITA, 2002 (DOLLARS)	ANNUAL HEALTH EXPENDITURES PER CAPITA 2001 (DOLLARS)	INFANT MORTALITY, 2001 (DEATHS BEFORE AGE 5 PER 1,000 BIRTHS)	PERCENTAGE OF POPULATION IN URBAN AREAS, 2001
Low-income (e.g., China, Ethiopia, Haiti, India)	2,500	430	21.5	121.2	32
Lower middle-income (e.g., Guatemala, Poland, Philippines, Thailand)	2,400	1,390	72.3	40.6	42
Upper middle-income (e.g., Brazil, Malaysia, Mexico)	331	5,040	308.9	22.9	76
Industrial market economies (e.g., Japan, Germany, New Zealand, United States)	965	26,310	2736.0	6.6	79

Source: World Bank, www.worldbank.org.

economies enjoy higher standards of living according to whatever indicator of development is chosen.

Behind these statistics lies the reality of the very difficult life facing the people of the developing world. For most, meager incomes provide only the basic necessities. Most meals are the same, consisting of the region's food staple—rice, wheat, or corn. Shelter is primitive. Many people share a small room, usually with an earthen floor and no sanitary facilities. The great majority of the population lives in rural areas where agricultural work is hard and extremely time-consuming. Productivity (output produced per worker) is low because household plots are small and only the crudest of farm implements are available. Low productivity means farm output per person is barely sufficient to feed a farmer's own family, with nothing left to sell to others. School-age children may receive some formal education, but illiteracy remains chronic for young and old. Infant mortality runs 10 times higher than in the United States. Although parasitic infections are common and debilitating, there is only one physician per 5,000 people. In addition, many developing nations are engaged in civil and external warfare.

Life in the developing nations is a continual struggle against the circumstances of poverty, and prospects for dramatic improvements in living standards for most people are dim. As with all generalizations, there are exceptions. Some nations are better off than others, and in any given nation an elite group always lives in considerable luxury.

Poverty—not affluence—dominates the developing world. Recent studies suggest that 40 percent of the population of the developing nations have annual incomes insufficient to provide for adequate nutrition.

While the developed nations account for only about one-quarter of the world's population, they are estimated to consume three-quarters of the world's output. This leaves the developing countries with about three-fourths of the world's people, but only one-fourth of the world's income. The simple result is that most of our planet's population is poor.

In the United States, the poorest one-fifth (bottom 20 percent) of the families receives just under 5 percent of total income; the richest one-fifth receives about 46 percent. However, the inequality in the world distribution of income is much greater. When we look at the world population, the poorest one-fifth of the families earns about 0.5 percent and the richest one-fifth earn 79 percent of total world income.

ECONOMIC DEVELOPMENT: SOURCES AND STRATEGIES

Economists have been trying to understand economic growth and development since Adam Smith and David Ricardo in the eighteenth and nineteenth centuries, but the study of development economics as it applies to the developing nations has a much shorter history. The geopolitical struggles that followed World War II brought increased attention to the developing nations and their economic problems. During this period, the new field of development economics asked simply: Why are some nations poor and others rich? If economists could understand the barriers to economic growth that prevent nations from developing and the prerequisites that would help them to develop, they could prescribe strategies for achieving economic advancement.

THE SOURCES OF ECONOMIC DEVELOPMENT

Although a general theory of economic development applicable to all nations has not emerged and probably never will, some basic factors that limit a poor nation's economic growth have been suggested. These include insufficient capital formation, a shortage of human resources and entrepreneurial ability, a lack of social overhead capital, and the constraints imposed by dependency on the already developed nations.

vicious-circle-of-poverty hypothesis Suggests that poverty is self-perpetuating because poor nations are unable to save and invest enough to accumulate the capital stock that would help them grow.

capital flight The tendency for both human capital and financial capital to leave developing countries in search of higher rates of return elsewhere.

Capital Formation One explanation for low levels of output in developing nations is insufficient quantities of necessary inputs. Developing nations have diverse resource endowments—Congo, for instance, is abundant in natural resources, while Bangladesh is resource poor. Almost all developing nations have a scarcity of physical capital relative to other resources, especially labor. The small stock of physical capital (factories, machinery, farm equipment, and other productive capital) constrains labor's productivity and holds back national output.

Nevertheless, citing capital shortages as the cause of low productivity does not explain much. We need to know why capital is in such short supply in developing countries. There are many explanations. One, the **vicious-circle-of-poverty hypothesis**, suggests that a poor nation must consume most of its income just to maintain its already low standard of living. Consuming most of national income implies limited saving, and this implies low levels of investment. Without investment, the capital stock does not grow, the income remains low, and the vicious circle is complete. Poverty becomes self-perpetuating.

The difficulty with the vicious-circle argument is that if it were true, no nation could ever develop. For example, Japanese GDP per capita at the turn of the century was well below that of many of today's developing nations. The vicious-circle argument fails to recognize that every nation has some surplus above consumption needs that is available for investment. Often this surplus is most visible in the conspicuous-consumption habits of the nation's richest families.

Poverty alone cannot explain capital shortages, and poverty is not necessarily self-perpetuating.

In a developing economy, scarcity of capital may have more to do with a lack of incentives for citizens to save and invest productively than with any absolute scarcity of income available for capital accumulation. Many of the rich in developing countries invest their savings in Europe or in the United States instead of in their own country, which may have a riskier political climate. Savings transferred to the United States do not lead to physical capital growth in the developing countries. The term **capital flight** refers to the fact that both human capital and financial capital (domestic savings) leave developing countries in search of higher expected rates of return elsewhere or returns with less risk. In addition, government policies in the developing nations—including price ceilings, import controls, and even outright appropriation of private property—tend to discourage investment.

Whatever the causes of capital shortages, it is clear that the absence of productive capital prevents income from rising in any economy. The availability of capital is a necessary, but not a *sufficient*, condition for economic growth. The Third World landscape is littered with idle factories and abandoned machinery. Other ingredients are required to achieve economic progress.

Human Resources and Entrepreneurial Ability Capital is not the only factor of production required to produce output. Labor is equally important. First of all, in order to be productive the workforce must be healthy. Disease today is the leading threat to development in much of the world. The most devastating health problem in the world today is the HIV/AIDS pandemic. In 2003, more than 60 million people were infected with the virus. Each day approximately 14,000 infections occur. More than 20 million have died. It is the leading cause of death in sub-Saharan Africa, where the disease threatens to reverse the developmental achievements of the last 50 years.

Beyond AIDS, health and nutrition are essential to workforce development. Programs in nutrition and health can be seen as investments in human capital, which lead to increased productivity and higher incomes.

But health is not the only issue. To be productive the workforce must be educated and trained. The more familiar forms of human capital investment, including formal education and on-the-job training, are essential. Basic literacy, as well as specialized training in farm management, for example, can yield high returns to both the individual worker and the economy. Education has grown to become the largest category of government expenditure in many developing nations, in part because of the belief that human resources are the ultimate determinant of economic advance.

Just as financial capital seeks the highest and safest return, so does human capital. Thousands of students from developing countries, many of whom were supported by their governments, graduate every year from U.S. colleges and universities as engineers, doctors, scientists, economists, and so forth. After graduation, these people face a difficult choice: to remain in the United States and earn a high salary or to return home and accept a job at a much lower salary. Many remain in the United States. This **brain drain** siphons off many of the most talented minds from developing countries.

brain drain The tendency for talented people from developing countries to become educated in a developed country and remain there after graduation.

Innovative entrepreneurs who are willing to take risks are an essential human resource in any economy. In a developing nation, new techniques of production rarely need to be invented, because they can usually be adapted from the technology already developed by the technologically advanced nations. However, entrepreneurs who are willing and able to organize and carry out economic activity appear to be in short supply. Family and political ties often seem to be more important than ability when it comes to securing positions of authority. Whatever the explanation:

> Development cannot proceed without human resources capable of initiating and managing economic activity.

Social Overhead Capital Anyone who has spent time in a developing nation knows how difficult it can be to send a letter, make a local phone call, or travel within the country itself. Add to this problems with water supplies, frequent electrical power outages—in the few areas where electricity is available—and often ineffective mosquito and pest control, and you soon realize how deficient even the simplest, most basic government-provided goods and services can be.

In any economy, Third World or otherwise, the government has considerable opportunity and responsibility for involvement where conditions encourage natural monopoly (as in the utilities industries) and where public goods (such as roads and pest control) must be provided. In a developing economy, the government must put emphasis on creating a basic infrastructure—roads, power generation, and irrigation systems. There are often good reasons why such projects, referred to as **social overhead capital**, cannot successfully be undertaken by the private sector. First, many of these projects operate with economies of scale, which means they can be efficient only if they are very large. In that case, they may be too large for any private company or group of companies to carry out.

social overhead capital Basic infrastructure projects such as roads, power generation, and irrigation systems.

Second, many socially useful projects cannot be undertaken by the private sector because there is no way for private agents to capture enough of the returns to make such projects profitable. This so-called *free-rider problem* is common in the economics of the developed world. Consider national defense: Everyone in a country benefits from national defense, whether they have paid for it or not. Anyone who attempted to go into the private business of providing national defense would go broke. Why should I buy any national defense if your purchase of defense will also protect me? Why should you buy any if my purchase will also protect you?

> The governments of developing countries can do important and useful things to encourage development, but many of their efforts must be concentrated in areas that the private sector would never touch. If government action in these realms is not forthcoming, economic development may be curtailed by a lack of social overhead capital.

STRATEGIES FOR ECONOMIC DEVELOPMENT

Just as no single theory appears to explain lack of economic advancement, no one development strategy will likely succeed in all nations. Many alternative development strategies have been proposed over the past 40 years. Although these strategies have been very different, they all recognize that a developing economy faces basic trade-offs. An insufficient amount of both human and physical resources dictates that choices must be made, including those between agriculture and industry, exports and import substitution, and central planning and free markets.

Agriculture or Industry? Most Third World countries began to gain political independence just after World War II. The tradition of promoting industrialization as the solution to the problems of the developing world dates from this time. The early 5-year development plans of India called for promoting manufacturing; the current government in Ethiopia (an extremely poor country) has similar intentions.

Industry has several apparent attractions over agriculture. First, if it is true that capital shortages constrain economic growth, then the building of factories is an obvious step toward increasing a nation's stock of capital. Second, and perhaps most important, one of the primary characteristics of more developed economies is their structural transition away from agriculture and toward manufacturing and modern services. As Table 23.2 shows, agriculture's share in GDP declines substantially as per capita incomes increase. The share of services increases correspondingly, especially in the early phases of economic development.

Many economies have pursued industry at the expense of agriculture. In many countries, however, industrialization has been either unsuccessful or disappointing—that is, it has not brought the benefits that were expected. Experience suggests that simply trying to replicate the structure of developed economies does not in itself guarantee, or even promote, successful development.

Since the early 1970s, the agricultural sector has received considerably more attention. Agricultural development strategies have had numerous benefits. Although some agricultural projects (such as the building of major dams and irrigation networks) are very capital intensive, many others (such as services to help teach better farming techniques and small-scale fertilizer programs) have low capital and import requirements. Programs like these can affect large numbers of households, and because their benefits are directed at rural areas, they are most likely to help a country's poorest families.

Experience over the last three decades suggests that some balance between these approaches leads to the best outcome—that is, it is important and effective to pay attention to both industry and agriculture. The Chinese have referred to this dual approach to development as "walking on two legs."

Exports or Import Substitution? As developing nations expand their industrial activities, they must decide what type of trade strategy to pursue, usually one of two alternatives: import substitution or export promotion.

import substitution An industrial trade strategy that favors developing local industries that can manufacture goods to replace imports.

Import substitution is an industrial trade strategy to develop local industries that can manufacture goods to replace imports. For example, if fertilizer is imported, import substitution calls for a domestic fertilizer industry to produce replacements for fertilizer imports. This strategy gained prominence throughout South America in the 1950s. At that time, most

TABLE 23.2 The Structure of Production in Selected Developed and Developing Economies, 2001

		PERCENTAGE OF GROSS DOMESTIC PRODUCT		
COUNTRY	PER CAPITA GROSS NATIONAL INCOME (GNI)	AGRICULTURE	INDUSTRY	SERVICES
Tanzania	$ 270	45	16	39
Bangladesh	360	23	25	52
China	890	15	51	34
Thailand	1,940	10	41	49
Colombia	1,890	13	30	57
Brazil	3,070	9	34	57
Korea (Rep.)	9,460	4	42	54
United States	34,280	2	25	73
Japan	35,610	1	32	67

Source: World Bank, www.worldbank.org, 2003.

developing nations exported agricultural and mineral products, goods that faced uncertain and often unstable international markets.

Under these conditions, the call for import-substitution policies was understandable. Special government actions, including tariff and quota protection and subsidized imports of machinery, were set up to encourage new domestic industries. Multinational corporations were also invited into many countries to begin domestic operations.

Most economists believe import-substitution strategies have failed almost everywhere they have been tried. With domestic industries sheltered from international competition by high tariffs (often as high as 200 percent), major economic inefficiencies were created. For example, Peru has a population of just over 24 million, only a tiny fraction of whom could afford to buy an automobile. Yet at one time the country had five or six different automobile manufacturers, each of which produced only a few thousand cars per year. Because there are substantial economies of scale in automobile production, the cost per car was much higher than it needed to be, and valuable resources that could have been devoted to another, more productive, activity were squandered producing cars.

Furthermore, policies designed to promote import substitution often encouraged capital-intensive production methods, which limited the creation of jobs and hurt export activities. A country like Peru could not export automobiles, because it could produce them only at a cost far greater than their price on the world market. Worse still, import-substitution policies encouraged the use of expensive domestic products, such as tractors and fertilizer, instead of lower cost imports. These policies taxed the sectors that might have successfully competed in world markets. To the extent that the Peruvian sugar industry had to rely on domestically produced, high-cost fertilizer, for example, its ability to compete in international markets was reduced, because its production costs were artificially raised.

As an alternative to import substitution, some nations have pursued strategies of export promotion. **Export promotion** is simply the policy of encouraging exports. As an industrial market economy, Japan is a striking example to the developing world of the economic success that exports can provide. With an average annual per capita real GDP growth rate of roughly 6 percent per year since 1960, Japan's achievements are in part based on industrial production oriented toward foreign consumers.

export promotion A trade policy designed to encourage exports.

Several countries in the developing world have attempted to emulate Japan's success. Starting around 1970, Hong Kong, Singapore, Korea, and Taiwan (the "four little dragons" between the two big dragons, China and Japan) all began to pursue export promotion of manufactured goods. Today their growth rates have surpassed Japan's. Other nations, including Brazil, Colombia, and Turkey, have also had some success at pursuing an outward-looking trade policy.

Government support of export promotion has often taken the form of maintaining an exchange rate favorable enough to permit exports to compete with products manufactured in developed economies. For example, many people believe Japan kept the value of the yen artificially low during the 1970s. Because "cheap" yen means inexpensive Japanese goods in the United States, sales of Japanese goods (especially automobiles) increased dramatically. Governments also have provided subsidies to export industries.

A big issue for countries growing or trying to grow by selling exports on world markets is free trade. In 2003, the United States and Europe were accused of protecting their own agricultural producers with large subsidies that allowed domestic farmers a big advantage selling on world markets. The African countries in particular raised the issue during a tour of the continent by President Bush in 2003. (See the News Analysis Box titled "Trade and Development in Africa—2003.")

Central Planning or the Market? As part of its strategy for achieving economic development, a nation must decide how its economy will be directed. Its basic choices lie between a market-oriented economic system and a centrally planned one.

In the 1950s and into the 1960s, development strategies that called for national planning commanded wide support. The rapid economic growth of the Soviet Union, a centrally planned economy, provided an example of how fast a less developed agrarian nation could be transformed into a modern industrial power. (The often appalling costs of this strategy—severe discipline, gross violation of human rights, and environmental damage—were less widely known.) In addition, the underdevelopment of many commodity and asset markets

News Analysis

Trade and Development in Africa—2003

IN JULY 2003, PRESIDENT BUSH TOURED THE African continent, visiting a number of very poor countries. One topic on top of the agenda was the HIV/AIDS crisis. One of the countries on his itinerary was Botswana, where some estimates put the infection rate at 39% of adults.

One of the other issues that came up in every country on the tour was agricultural trade. Here the United States was criticized for policies that had a very negative impact on the ability of the continent to grow: agricultural subsidies. In the following piece in the *New York Times*, two African presidents state their case.

Your Farm Subsidies Are Strangling Us—*New York Times*

After too many years of Africa's being pushed to the global background, it's heartening to see the world's attention being focused on our continent. International support—both financial and otherwise—is certainly needed to help combat the severe poverty and disease gripping our nations. But first and foremost, Africa needs to be allowed to take its destiny into its own hands. Only self-reliance and economic growth and development will allow Africa to become a full member of the world community.

With the creation of the New Economic Partnership for African Development in 2001, African leaders have committed themselves to following the principles of good governance and a market economy. Nothing is more central to this goal than participating in world trade. As the presidents of two of Africa's least developed countries—Burkina Faso and Mali—we are eager to participate in the multilateral trading system and to take on its rights and obligations.

Cotton is our ticket into the world market. Its production is crucial to economic development in West and Central Africa, as well as to the livelihoods of millions of people there. Cotton accounts for up to 40 percent of export revenues and 10 percent of gross domestic product in our two countries, as well as in Benin and Chad. More than that, cotton is of paramount importance to the social infrastructure of Africa, as well as to the maintenance of its rural areas.

This vital economic sector in our countries is seriously threatened by agricultural subsidies granted by rich countries to their cotton producers. According to the International Cotton Advisory Committee, cotton subsidies amounted to about $5.8 billion in the production year of 2001 to 2002, nearly equal the amount of cotton trade for this same period. Such subsidies lead to worldwide overproduction and distort cotton prices, depriving poor African countries of their only comparative advantage in international trade.

Not only is cotton crucial to our economies, it is the sole agricultural product for our countries to trade. Although African cotton is of the highest quality, our production costs are about 50 percent lower than in developed countries even though we rely on manual labor. In wealthier countries, by contrast, lower-quality cotton is produced on large mechanized farms, generating little employment and having a questionable impact on the environment. Cotton there could be replaced by other, more valuable crops.

In the period from 2001 to 2002, America's 25,000 cotton farmers received more in subsidies—some $3 billion—than the entire economic output of Burkina Faso, where two million people depend on cotton. Further, United States subsidies are concentrated on just 10 percent of its cotton farmers. Thus, the payments to about 2,500 relatively well-off farmers has the unintended but nevertheless real effect of impoverishing some 10 million rural poor people in West and Central Africa.

Something has to be done. Along with the countries of Benin and Chad, we have submitted a proposal to the World Trade Organization—which is meeting in Cancún, Mexico, in September to discuss agricultural issues—that calls for an end to unfair subsidies granted by developed countries to their cotton producers. As an interim measure, we have also proposed that least-developed countries be granted financial compensation for lost export revenues that are due to those subsidies.

Our demand is simple: apply free trade rules not only to those products that are of interest to the rich and powerful, but also to those products where poor countries have a proven comparative advantage. We know that the world will not ignore our plea for a fair playing field. The World Trade Organization has said it is committed to addressing the problems of developing countries. The United States has convinced us that a free market economy provides the best opportunities for all members of the world community. Let us translate these principles into deeds at Cancún.

Cotton growers in Africa find that they are unable to compete with heavily subsidized U.S. growers.

Source: Amadou Toumani Touré and Blaise Compaoré, "Your Farm Subsidies Are Strangling Us," New York Times, *July 11, 2003. Reprinted by permission.*

Visit www.prenhall.com/casefair for updated articles and exercises.

in the Third World led many experts to believe that market forces could not direct an economy reliably and that major government intervention was therefore necessary. Even the United States, with its commitment to free enterprise in the marketplace, supported early central planning efforts in many developing nations.

Today, planning takes many forms in the developing nations. In some, central planning has replaced market-based outcomes with direct, administratively determined controls over such economic variables as prices, output, and employment. In others, national planning amounts to little more than the formulation of general 5- or 10-year goals as rough blueprints for a nation's economic future.

The economic appeal of planning lies theoretically in its ability to channel savings into productive investment and to coordinate economic activities that private actors in the economy might not otherwise undertake. The reality of central planning, however, is that it is a technically difficult, highly politicized, nightmare to administer. Given the scarcity of human resources and the unstable political environment in many developing nations, planning itself—let alone the execution of the plan—becomes a formidable task.

The failure of many central planning efforts has brought increasing calls for less government intervention and more market orientation in developing economies. The elimination of price controls, privatization of state-run enterprises, and reductions in import restraints are examples of market-oriented reforms recommended by such international agencies as the **International Monetary Fund** (IMF), whose primary goals are to stabilize international exchange rates and to lend money to countries that have problems financing their international transactions, and the **World Bank**, which lends money to a country for projects that promote economic development.

International Monetary Fund (IMF) An international agency whose primary goals are to stabilize international exchange rates and to lend money to countries that have problems financing their international transactions.

World Bank An international agency that lends money to individual countries for projects that promote economic development.

Members' contributions to both organizations are determined by the size of their economies. Only 20 percent of the World Bank's funding comes from contributions; 80 percent comes from retained earnings and investments in capital markets. The developing world is increasingly recognizing the value of market forces in determining the allocation of scarce resources. Nonetheless, government still has a major role to play. In the decades ahead, the governments of developing nations will need to determine those situations where planning is superior to the market and those where the market is superior to planning.

GROWTH VERSUS DEVELOPMENT: THE POLICY CYCLE

Until now, we have used *growth* and *development* as if they meant the same thing, but this may not always be the case. You can easily imagine instances in which a country has achieved higher levels of income (growth) with little or no benefit accruing to most of its citizens (development). Thus, the question is whether economic growth necessarily brings about economic development.

In the past, most development strategies were aimed at increasing the growth rate of income per capita. Many still are, based on the theory that benefits of economic growth will "trickle down" to all members of society. If this theory is correct, then growth should promote development.

By the early 1970s, the relationship between growth and development was being questioned more and more. A study by the World Bank in 1974 concluded

> It is now clear that more than a decade of rapid growth in underdeveloped countries has been of little or no benefit to perhaps a third of their population. . . . Paradoxically, while growth policies have succeeded beyond the expectations of the first development decade, the very idea of aggregate growth as a social objective has increasingly been called into question.

The World Bank study indicated that increases in GDP per capita did not guarantee significant improvements in such development indicators as nutrition, health, and education. Although GDP per capita did rise, its benefits trickled down to a small minority of the population. This prompted new development strategies that would directly address the problems of poverty. Such new strategies favored agriculture over industry, called for domestic redistribution of income and wealth (especially land), and encouraged programs to satisfy such basic needs as food and shelter.

In the late 1970s and early 1980s, the international macroeconomic crises of high oil prices, worldwide recession, and Third World debt forced attention away from programs designed to eliminate poverty directly. Then, during the 1980s and 1990s, the policy focus turned 180 degrees. The World Bank and the United States began demanding "structural adjustment" in the developing countries as a prerequisite for sending aid to them. **Structural adjustment** programs entail reducing the size of the public sector through privatization and/or expenditure reductions, substantially cutting budget deficits, reining in inflation, and encouraging private saving and investment with tax reforms. These promarket demands were an attempt to stimulate growth; distributional consequences took a back seat.

structural adjustment A series of programs in developing nations designed to (1) reduce the size of their public sectors through privatization and/or expenditure reductions, (2) decrease their budget deficits, (3) control inflation, and (4) encourage private saving and investment through tax reform.

ISSUES IN ECONOMIC DEVELOPMENT

Every developing nation has a cultural, political, and economic history all its own and therefore confronts a unique set of problems. Still, it is possible to discuss common economic issues that each nation must face in its own particular way. These issues include rapid population growth and growing debt burdens.

POPULATION GROWTH

The populations of the developing nations are estimated to be growing at about 1.7 percent per year. (Compare this with a population growth rate of only 0.5 percent per year in the industrial market economies.) If the Third World's population growth rate remains at 1.7 percent, within 41 years the population of the Third World will double from its 1990 level of 4.1 billion to over 8 billion by the year 2031. It will take the industrialized nations 139 years to double their populations. What is so immediately alarming about these numbers is that given the developing nations' current economic problems, it is hard to imagine how they can possibly absorb so many more people in such a relatively short period.

Concern over world population growth is not new. The Reverend Thomas Malthus (who became England's first professor of political economy) expressed his fears about the population increases he observed 200 years ago. Malthus believed populations grow geometrically—at a constant growth rate: Thus the absolute size of the increase each year gets larger and larger—but that food supplies grow much more slowly because of the diminishing marginal productivity of land.[1] These two phenomena led Malthus to predict the increasing impoverishment of the world's people unless population growth could be slowed.

Malthus's fears for Europe and America proved unfounded. He did not anticipate the technological changes that revolutionized agricultural productivity and the eventual decrease in population growth rates in Europe and North America. Nevertheless, Malthus's prediction may have been right, only premature. Do the circumstances in the developing world now fit his predictions? Although some contemporary observers believe the Malthusian view is correct and the earth's population will eventually grow to a level that the world's resources cannot support, others say technological change and demographic transitions (to slower population growth rates) will permit further increases in global welfare.

The Consequences of Rapid Population Growth We know far less about the economic consequences of rapid population growth than you might expect. Conventional wisdom warns of dire economic consequences from the developing nations' "population explosion," but these predictions are difficult to substantiate with the available evidence. The rapid economic growth of the United States, for example, was accompanied by relatively rapid population growth by historical standards. Any slowing of population growth has not been necessary for the economic progress achieved by many of the newly industrialized countries. Nonetheless, population expansion in many of today's poorest nations is of a magnitude unprecedented in world history, as Figure 23.1 clearly shows. From the year 1 A.D. until the mid-1600s, populations grew slowly, at rates of only about 0.04 percent per year. Since then, and especially since 1950, rates have skyrocketed. Today, populations are growing at rates of 1.5 percent to 4.0 percent per year throughout the developing world.

Because growth rates like these have never occurred before the twentieth century, no one knows what impact they will have on future economic development. However, a basic economic concern is that such rapid population growth may limit investment and restrain increases in labor productivity and income. Rapid population growth changes the age composition of a population, generating many dependent children relative to the number of productive working adults. Such a situation may diminish saving rates, and hence investment, as the immediate consumption needs of the young take priority over saving for the future.

Even if low saving rates are not a necessary consequence of rapid population growth, as some authorities contend, other economic problems remain. The ability to improve human capital through a broad range of programs, from infant nutrition to formal secondary education, may be severly limited if the population explosion continues. Such programs are

[1]The law of diminishing marginal productivity says that with a fixed amount of a resource (land), additions of more and more of a variable resource (labor) will produce smaller and smaller gains in output.

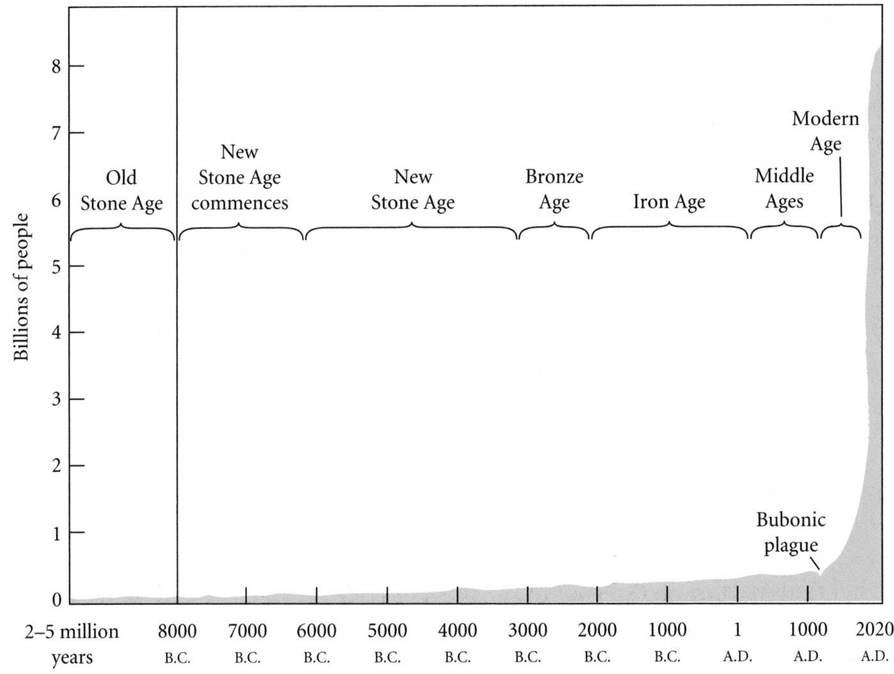

FIGURE 23.1 The Growth of World Population, Projected to 2020 A.D.

For thousands of years, population grew slowly. From 1 A.D. until the mid-1600s, population grew at about 0.04 percent per year. Since the Industrial Revolution, population growth has occurred at an unprecedented rate.

most often the responsibility of the state, and governments that are already weak cannot be expected to improve their services under the burden of population pressures that rapidly increase demands for all kinds of public goods and services.

For example, Mozambique's population growth rate—3.7 percent—is one of the highest in the world. Its 1998 population of over 17 million people grew by about 3.4 million by 2003 and will likely grow by 7 million by 2008. This is a daunting prospect, and it is hard to imagine how in so little time Mozambique, with per capita GNP under $100, will be able to provide its population with the physical and human capital needed to maintain, let alone improve, already low standards of living.

Causes of Rapid Population Growth Population growth is determined by the relationship between births and deaths—that is, between **fertility rates** and **mortality rates**. The **natural rate of population increase** is defined as the difference between the birth rate and the death rate. If the birth rate is 4 percent, for example, and the death rate is 3 percent, the population is growing at a rate of 1 percent per year.

fertility rate The birth rate. Equal to (the number of births per year divided by the population) × 100.

mortality rate The death rate. Equal to (the number of deaths per year divided by the population) × 100.

natural rate of population increase The difference between the birth rate and the death rate. It does not take migration into account.

Historically, low rates of population growth were maintained because of high mortality rates despite high levels of fertility. That is, families had many children, but average life expectancies were low, and many children (and adults) died young. In Europe and North America, improvements in nutrition, in public health programs (especially those concerned with drinking water and sanitation services), and in medical practices have led to a drop in the mortality rate and hence to more rapid population growth. Eventually fertility rates also fell, returning population growth to a low and stable rate.

Public health programs and improved nutrition over the past 30 years have brought about precipitous declines in mortality rates in the developing nations also. However, fertility rates have not declined as quickly, and the result has been high natural rates of population growth. Reduced population growth depends to some extent on decreased birth rates, but attempts to lower fertility rates must take account of how different cultures feel and behave with regard to fertility.

Family planning and modern forms of birth control are important mechanisms for decreasing fertility, but by themselves have had rather limited success in most countries where they have been tried. If family planning strategies are to be successful, they must make sense to the people who are supposed to benefit from them. The planners of such strategies must understand why families in developing nations have so many children.

To a great extent, in developing countries people want large families because they believe they need them. Economists have attempted to understand fertility patterns in the developing countries by focusing on the determinants of the demand for children. In agrarian societies, children are sources of farm labor, and they may make significant contributions to household income. In societies without public old-age support Social Security programs, children may also provide a source of income for parents who are too old to support themselves. With the high value of children enhanced by high rates of infant mortality, it is no wonder that families try to have many children to ensure that a sufficient number will survive into adulthood.

Cultural and religious values also affect the number of children families want to have, but the economic incentives to have large families are extremely powerful. Only when the relationship between the costs and benefits of having children changes will fertility rates decline. Expanding employment opportunities for women in an economy increases the opportunity costs of child rearing (by giving women a more highly valued alternative to raising children) and often leads to lower birth rates. Government incentives for smaller families, such as subsidized education for families with fewer than three children, can have a similar effect. In general, rising incomes appear to decrease fertility rates, indicating that economic development itself reduces population growth rates.

Economic theories of population growth suggest that fertility decisions made by poor families should not be viewed as uninformed and uncontrolled. An individual family may find that having many children is a rational strategy for economic survival given the conditions in which it finds itself. This does not mean, however, that having many children is a net benefit to society as a whole. When a family decides to have a large number of children, it imposes costs on the rest of society; the children must be educated, their health provided for, and so forth. In other words, what makes sense for an individual household may create negative effects for the nation as a whole.

> Any nation that wants to slow its rate of population growth will probably find it necessary to have in place economic incentives for fewer children as well as family planning programs.

DEVELOPING-COUNTRY DEBT BURDENS

In the 1970s, development experts worried about many crises facing the developing world, but not the debt crisis. Within a decade, this changed dramatically. The financial plight of nations such as Brazil, Mexico, and the Philippines has become front-page news. What alarmed those familiar with the debt situation was not only its potential impact on the developing nations, but a belief that it threatened the economic welfare of the developed nations as well.

Between 1970 and 1984, developing nations borrowed so much money from other nations that their combined debt increased by 1,000 percent, to almost $700 billion. Three nations alone—Brazil, Mexico, and Venezuela—had outstanding loans to three major U.S. banks (Citibank, Chase-Manhattan, and Manufacturer's Hanover, now part of Chemical) that were more than double the net worth of those financial institutions. As recession took hold in the economically advanced countries during the early 1980s, growth in the exports of the debtor countries slowed, and many found they could no longer pay back the money they owed.

As the situation continued to deteriorate, many feared that debtor nations might repudiate their debts outright and default on their outstanding loans. When *default* (nonpayment) occurs with domestic loans, some collateral is usually available to cover all or part of the remaining debt. For loans to another country, such collateral is virtually impossible to secure. Given their extensive involvement with developing-country borrowers, Western banks did not want to set in motion a pattern of international default and borrowers did not want to default. Leaders of the developing nations recognized that default might result in the denial of access to developed-country banking facilities and to markets in the industrial countries, posing major obstacles to further development efforts.

debt rescheduling An agreement between banks and borrowers through which a new schedule of repayments of the debt is negotiated; often some of the debt is written off and the repayment period is extended.

Various countries rescheduled their debt as an interim solution. Under a **debt rescheduling** agreement, banks and borrowers negotiate a new schedule for the repayment of existing debt, often with some of the debt written off and with repayment periods extended. In return, borrowing countries are expected to sign an agreement with the IMF to revamp their economic policies to provide incentives for higher export earnings and lower imports. This kind of agreement, referred to as a **stabilization program**, usually requires austerity measures such as currency devaluations, reduction in government expenditures, and increase in tax revenues.

stabilization program An agreement between a borrower country and the International Monetary Fund in which the country agrees to revamp its economic policies to provide incentives for higher export earnings and lower imports.

By the early 1990s, the debt crisis was not over but it had lessened, mainly as a result of macroeconomic events that led to reduced interest rates. The international economy has revived somewhat, helping some nations to increase their export earnings. Other nations have benefited from new domestic policies. Still others, including Panama, and many African nations, however, continue to face debt burdens that are unmanageable in the short run.

During 1998, a number of countries had severe economic problems that required emergency loan guarantees from the IMF. Asian economies such as Indonesia, Thailand, and Korea had sudden currency collapses as short-term loans were called by creditors and investors headed for the doors. Dramatically falling currency values made it all the more difficult to pay for the interest on dollar-denominated debt and for imports. Similar circumstances occurred in Russia and Brazil in 1998. Russia defaulted on a series of loan agreements in August of that year. In each case emergency credit guarantees were granted by the IMF in exchange for the promise of fiscal discipline and economic austerity. By 2003, these economies were recovering and growing at a fairly rapid pace but each was still saddled with a heavy debt burden.

Between 2000 and 2003, interest rates worldwide dropped considerably. In addition, the IMF and World Bank committed $41.5 billion to its Heavily Indebted Poor Country (HIPC) initiative. The result has been that Third World debt has become a manageable problem in all but a few countries, such as Guinea-Bissau and Nicaragua, where debt remains over 200% of GDP.

One economic lesson of the last two decades is that proper management of foreign capital in developing countries is essential. Much foreign borrowing was wasted on projects that had little chance of generating the returns necessary to pay back their initial costs. In other cases, domestic policies that used debt as a substitute for adjusting to new economic circumstances proved to be harmful in the long run. Overall, much optimism about the prospects of the developing economies was inappropriate. Whatever else we may have learned from these mistakes, the debt crisis underscored the growing interdependence of all economies—rich and poor, large and small.

ECONOMIES IN TRANSITION

For 40 years, between the end of World War II and the mid-1980s, a powerful rivalry existed between the Soviet Union and the United States. This "cold war" pitted the two superpowers against each other in a struggle for influence and fueled the nuclear arms race. At one time the mutual distrust between them was so strong that the concept of "mutual assured destruction" dominated international relations.

However, the world began to change in the mid-1980s as the political and economic structures of the Soviet Union and the Eastern European Communist countries started to crumble. In 1989, relatively peaceful revolutions took place in rapid succession in Poland, Hungary, and Czechoslovakia (now the Czech Republic). A bloody revolution in Romania toppled Nicolae Ceausescu, who had ruled with an iron fist for 24 years. The Berlin Wall, which had separated Berlin since 1961, was knocked down and Germany was reunited. Then, in August 1991, after a failed coup attempt by hard-line Communists, the Soviet Union itself began to come apart. By the end of 1991, the Soviet Union had dissolved into 15 independent states, the largest is the Russian Republic. Ten of these 15 republics formed the Commonwealth of Independent States (CIS) in December 1991. The Cold War was over.

We reflect on historical political rivalries in an economics text for two reasons. First, the 40-year struggle between the United States and the Soviet Union was fundamentally a struggle between two economic systems: market-based capitalism (the U.S. system) and centrally planned socialism (the Soviet system). Second, the Cold War ended so abruptly in the late 1980s because the Soviet and Eastern European economies virtually collapsed during that period. In a sense, we could say 1991 was the year that the market triumphed.

What now? The independent states of the former Soviet Union and the other former Communist economies of Eastern Europe are struggling to make the transition from centrally planned socialism to some form of market-based capitalism. In some countries, such as Serbia and Bosnia-Herzegovina, economic reforms have taken a back seat to bitter and violent ethnic and political rivalries that have been simmering for decades. In other countries, like Poland and Russia, the biggest issue continues to be economic transformation.

The success or failure of this transition from centrally planned socialism to market-based capitalism will determine the course of history. Although many countries have made the transition from a market-based system to a centrally planned system, the opposite has never occurred. The process has been and will continue to be painful and filled with ups and downs. Between 1989 and 1997, industrial production fell more than 40 percent in countries like the former East Germany, Albania, Poland, and Romania. In Russia, production decreased about 30 percent. In all these nations, fairly prosperous people suddenly found themselves with annual real incomes closer to those of people in developing countries. For many people, the issue became survival: how to get enough food and fuel to get through the winter.

By 1995, things had turned around, and though uncertainty and problems remained, output was rising in much of Eastern and Central Europe. A growing optimism seemed to be spreading. The biggest success story was in East Germany, where real output in 1994 grew by over 9 percent, the fastest growth rate of any region of Europe. A construction boom, rapid development of infrastructure, low inflation, and rising exports all contributed to the region's success. However, East Germany's situation is unique because it was absorbed by a prosperous, fully developed, and modern West Germany that has made development in the East its primary goal.

Central Europe, including Hungary, Poland, the Czech Republic, Bulgaria, and Romania, also achieved basic macroeconomic stability and began to grow in 1993 and 1994. Poland enjoyed the most rapid economic growth in the group (around 4.5 percent). Fueled by foreign investment, privatization, and entrepreneurship, the Polish private sector by 1992 accounted for well over one-third of the nation's total output, although many problems persist. Russia and the former countries of the Soviet Union have achieved less through 2000. Nonetheless, conditions have improved and prospects for success are greater than they were only a few years ago.

POLITICAL SYSTEMS AND ECONOMIC SYSTEMS: SOCIALISM, CAPITALISM, AND COMMUNISM

Every society has both a political system and an economic system. Unfortunately, the political and economic dimensions of a society are often confused.

The terms *democracy* and *dictatorship* refer to *political* systems. A *democracy* is a system of government in which ultimate power rests with the people, who make governmental decisions either directly through voting or indirectly through representatives. A *dictatorship* is a political system in which ultimate power is concentrated in either a small elite group or a single person.

Historically, two major *economic* systems have existed: socialism and capitalism. A **socialist economy** is one in which most capital—factories, equipment, buildings, railroads, and so forth—is owned by the government instead of private citizens. *Social ownership* is another term that is used to describe this kind of system. A **capitalist economy** is one in which most capital is privately owned. Beyond these systems is a purely theoretical economic system called *communism.*

socialist economy An economy in which most capital is owned by the government instead of private citizens. Also called social ownership.

capitalist economy An economy in which most capital is privately owned.

communism An economic system in which the people control the means of production (capital and land) directly, without the intervention of a government or state.

Communism is an economic system in which the people control the means of production (land and capital) directly, without the intervention of a government or state. In the world envisioned by communists, the state would wither away and society would plan the economy in the same way a collective would. Although some countries still consider themselves communist—including China, North Korea, Cuba, and Tanzania—economic planning is done by the government in all of them.

> Comparing economies today, the real distinction is between centrally planned socialism and capitalism, not between capitalism and communism.

No pure socialist economies and no pure capitalist economies exist. Even the Soviet Union, which was basically socialist, had a large private sector. Fully one-fourth of agricultural output in what was the USSR was legally produced on private plots and sold. Conversely, the strongly capitalistic United States supports many government enterprises, including the U.S. postal system. Nonetheless, public ownership is the exception in the United States and private ownership was the exception in the Soviet Union.

Whether particular kinds of political systems tend to be associated with particular kinds of economic systems is debated. The United States and Japan are countries with essentially capitalist economic systems and essentially democratic political institutions. China and North Korea have basically socialist economies with political power highly concentrated in a single political party. These observations do not imply that all capitalist countries have democratic political institutions, or that all socialist countries are subject to totalitarian party rule.

Some countries—Singapore, for example—have basically capitalist economies without democratic political systems. Other countries that are much closer to the socialist end of the economic spectrum also maintain strong democratic traditions. Sweden is an example of a democratic country that supports strong socialist institutions.

However, do certain kinds of economic systems lead to repressive governments? Austrian economist Friedrich von Hayek argues yes:

> Economic reforms and government coercion are the road to serfdom. . . . Personal and economic freedoms are inseparable. Once you start down the road to government regulation and planning of the economy, the freedom to speak minds and select political leaders will be jeopardized.[2]

The recent events in Eastern Europe and Russia seem to support Hayek's thesis. There, economic and political reforms are proceeding side by side, and the evidence is mounting that the heart of both the market system *and* democracy is individual freedom.

Nonetheless, some counter Hayek's argument by claiming that social reform and active government involvement in the economy are the only ways to prevent the rise of a totalitarian state. They argue that free and unregulated markets lead to inequality and the accumulation of economic power. Accumulated economic power, in turn, leads to political power that is inevitably used in the interests of the wealthy few, not in the interests of all.

CENTRAL PLANNING VERSUS THE MARKET

In addition to ownership of capital, economic systems also differ in the extent to which economic decisions are made through central planning instead of a market system. In some socialist economies, the allocation of resources, the mix of output, and the distribution of output are determined centrally according to a plan. The former Soviet Union, for example, generated 1-year and 5-year plans laying out specific production targets in virtually every sector of the economy. In market economies, decisions are made independently by buyers and sellers responding to market signals. Producers produce only what they expect to sell. Labor is attracted into and out of various occupations by wages that are determined by the forces of supply and demand.

Just as there are no pure capitalist and no pure socialist economies, there are no pure market economies and no pure planned economies. Even in the former Soviet Union markets existed and determined, to a large extent, the allocation of resources. Production targets in the United States are set by many agencies, including the Pentagon.

Generally, socialist economies favor central planning over market allocation, while capitalist economies rely to a much greater extent on the market. Nonetheless, some variety exists. The former Yugoslavia was a socialist country that made extensive use of the market. Ownership of capital and land rested with the government, but individual firms determined their own output levels and prices and made their own investment plans. Yugoslavian firms borrowed from banks to finance investments and paid interest on their loans. This type of system, which combines government ownership with market allocation, is referred to as a **market–socialist economy**.

market–socialist economy An economy that combines government ownership with market allocation.

[2]Friedrich Hayek, *The Road to Serfdom* (Chicago: University of Chicago Press, 1944).

THE END OF THE SOVIET UNION

No serious debate about economic matters took place in the Soviet Union until after Stalin's death in 1953. In 1965, official reforms were introduced by the government of Alexei Kosygin. Mikhail Gorbachev announced a series of reforms in 1986 and in 1987, but the structure of the economy was not changed fundamentally.

Although Gorbachev's ideas seemed promising, the situation in the Soviet Union deteriorated sharply after 1987. The attempted transition from central planning to a partly free-market system caused major problems. Growth of output slowed to a crawl in 1989 and 1990, and in 1991 the economic system collapsed. Industrial production dropped sharply, food shortages grew worse, inflation became serious, and external debt increased rapidly.

Gorbachev ran out of time in August 1991 as the struggle between the hard-liners and the radical reformers came to a head. The hard-liners took Gorbachev prisoner and assumed control of the government. The coup lasted only 3 days. People took to the streets of Moscow and resisted the tanks, the Soviet army refused to obey orders, and the hard-liners were out.

Nevertheless, the end was near for both Gorbachev and the Soviet Union. In December 1991, the Soviet Union was dissolved, 10 of the former Soviet republics formed the CIS, and Boris Yeltsin became president of the Russian Republic as Gorbachev became part of history. From the beginning, Yeltsin showed himself to be a reformer committed to converting the Russian economy rapidly into a market system while maintaining hard-won political freedoms for the people. His reform plan called for deregulating prices, privatizing public enterprises, and stabilizing the macroeconomy.

Boris Yeltsin was president of the Russian Republic and the champion of reform from 1991 to 1999. Yeltsin deregulated most prices, began the privatization process, and attempted to stabilize the macroeconomy. By 1995 progress had been slow but significant. Privatization had made steady progress, reaching a point in 1994 where the private sector was generating 60 percent of personal income. Inflation was down, and a new "economic constitution" in the form of revised laws to establish property rights and stimulate economic activity went into effect in 1995. Nevertheless, things were not going well across the board.

Most observers estimate that Russian GDP began to grow in the spring of 1997, after falling by about 50 percent from its 1989 level. However, problems remained severe into 1998. The biggest problem was attracting investment, and the biggest-barrier was crime and corruption. The Russian government was finding it very difficult to enforce the rule of law. The term *cowboy capitalism* is often used to describe the situation in Russia today.

Vladimir Putin became president in January 2000 and immediately declared his commitment to continue the reforms. The News Analysis box titled "Economic Conditions in Russia in 2003" describes recent developments in Russia.

THE TRANSITION TO A MARKET ECONOMY

The reforms under way in the Russian Republic and in the other formerly Communist countries of Eastern Europe have taken shape very slowly and amid debate about how best to proceed. Remember, there is absolutely no historical precedent to provide lessons. Despite this lack of precedent, however, there is substantial agreement among economists about what needs to be done.

SIX BASIC REQUIREMENTS FOR SUCCESSFUL TRANSITION

Economists generally agree on six basic requirements for a successful transition from socialism to a market based system: (1) macroeconomic stabilization; (2) deregulation of prices and liberalization of trade; (3) privatization of state owned enterprises and development of new private industry; (4) establishment of market-supporting institutions, such as property and contract laws, accounting systems, and so forth; (5) social safety net to deal with unemployment and poverty; and (6) external assistance.

News Analysis

Economic Conditions in Russia in 2003

THE FOLLOWING IS AN EXTRACT FROM A REVIEW of conditions in the Russian economy prepared by the Center for Strategic and International Studies in Washington.

The Russian Economy in June 2003

—Center for Strategic and International Studies

The gross domestic product (GDP) grew by 6.4, 10, 5, and 4.3 percent in 1999, 2000, 2001, and 2002. This recovery, after more than a decade of virtually uninterrupted decline, was primarily attributable to the import substitution effect after the devaluation of August 1998; the high world prices for Russia's oil, gas, and commodity exports; market-oriented restructuring; the decline in real wages leading to cost reductions; and sound fiscal and monetary policies. The Ministry of Economic Development and Trade (MEDT) foresees growth rates of 4.3-5 percent, 3.8-5.4 percent, and 4.8-5.9 percent in 2003-2005, while the stated goal of its medium-term reform program is the attainment of 7-8 percent trend rate of annual GDP growth from 2007 on. GDP growth in the first 5 months of 2003 was 7.1 percent.

Real disposable incomes rose by 9 percent in 2000, 8.5 percent in 2001, and 9 percent in 2002. During the fourth quarter of 2002, 30.9 million people or 21.6 percent of the population were living below the poverty line of 1,893 rubles ($60) a month. The average monthly calculated nominal wage due in March 2003 was 5,125 rubles ($163).

The Russian government is not expected to seek any restructuring or forgiveness of its $17.3 billion and $14.9 billion foreign debt service in 2003 and 2004. . . .

Net capital outflows declined from $16.2 billion in 2001 to $11.7 billion in 2002 and to practically zero in the first quarter of 2003.

After a decade of continuous decline, gross capital investment in 1999 rose by 5.3 percent to 670 billion rubles ($28 billion) or 15 percent of GDP, and then grew by nearly 18 percent in 2000, and by 8.7 percent in 2001 (to about 18 percent of GDP). Fixed capital investment growth in 2002 slowed to 2.6 percent, with some 60 percent going to the fuel, energy, and raw materials sectors, but surged by 10.9 percent year on year (yoy) in the first 4 months of 2003.

Cumulative foreign direct investment (FDI) since 1991 in Russia by April 1, 2003, amounted to $19.6 billion, compared with over $350 billion in China during the same period. FDI in Russia in 2000 amounted to $4.4 billion out of a global total of $1,270 billion. It declined to $2.4 billion in 2001 and to $2.6 billion (excluding banks) in 2002 (compared with $52.7 billion of FDI into China), but new foreign credits to Russian enterprises rose in 2002 to $12.4 billion.

The age of Russian manufacturing plant and equipment is, on average, more than three times higher than in the OECD. To update or replace it and the infrastructure will take trillions of dollars. This will not be available solely from domestic sources. FDI is expected to grow fast, but will remain much lower than is needed until Russia cleans up its corporate governance act and creates a welcoming environment. Much of industry is located unfavorably. Demographic trends and Russia's appalling health indicators will apply downward pressure on productivity and performance. All of which suggests that the average annual rate of Russian economic growth in the medium term will remain modest, say not more than 4 percent. This growth rate remains susceptible to the world prices of oil, gas, metals, and other Russian export commodities.

After more than a decade since the collapse of the Soviet Union, Russia is showing signs of growth.

Source: Center for Strategic and International Studies, Washington, DC, June 18, 2003.

Visit www.prenhall.com/casefair for updated articles and exercises.

We now discuss each component. Although we focus on the experience of the Russian Republic, these principles apply to all economies in transition.

Macroeconomic Stabilization Virtually every one of the countries in transition has had a problem with inflation, but nowhere has it been worse than in Russia. As economic conditions worsened, the government found itself with serious budget problems. As revenue flows slowed and expenditure commitments increased, large budget deficits resulted. At the same time, each of the new republics established its own central bank. Each central bank began issuing "ruble credits" to keep important enterprises afloat and to pay the government's bills. The issuance of these credits, which were generally accepted as a means of payment throughout the country, led to a dramatic expansion of the money supply.

Almost from the beginning, the expanded money supply meant too much money was chasing too few goods. This was made worse by government-controlled prices set substantially below market-clearing levels. The combination of monetary expansion and price control was deadly. Government-run shops that sold goods at controlled prices were empty. People waited in line for days and often became violent when their efforts to buy goods at low official prices were thwarted. At the same time, suppliers found that they could charge much higher prices for their products on the black market—which grew bigger by the day, further exacerbating the shortage of goods at government shops. Over time, the ruble became worth less and less as black market prices continued to rise more rapidly. Russia found itself with near hyperinflation in 1992.

To achieve a properly functioning market system, prices must be stabilized. To do so, the government must find a way to move toward a balanced budget and to bring the supply of money under control.

Deregulation of Prices and Liberalization of Trade To move successfully from central planning to a market system, individual prices must be deregulated. A system of freely moving prices forms the backbone of a market system. When people want more of a good than is currently being produced, its price will rise. This higher price increases producers' profits and provides an incentive for existing firms to expand production and for new firms to enter the industry. Conversely, if an industry is producing a good for which there is no market or a good that people no longer want in the same quantity, the result will be excess supply and the price of that good will fall. This reduces profits or creates losses, providing an incentive for some existing firms to cut back on production and for others to go out of business. In short, an unregulated price mechanism ensures an efficient allocation of resources across industries. Until prices are deregulated, this mechanism cannot function.

Trade barriers must also be removed. Reform-minded countries must be able to import capital, technology, and ideas. In addition, it makes no sense to continue to subsidize industries that cannot be competitive on world markets. If it is cheaper to buy steel from an efficient West German steel mill than to produce it in a subsidized antiquated Russian mill, the Russian mill should be modernized or shut down. Ultimately, as the theory of comparative advantage suggests, liberalized trade will push each country to produce the products it produces best.

Deregulating prices and eliminating subsidies can bring serious political problems. Many products in Russia and the rest of the socialist world were priced below market-clearing levels for equity reasons. Housing, food, and clothing were considered by many to be entitlements. Making them more expensive, at least relative to their prices in previous times, is not likely to be popular. In addition, forcing inefficient firms to operate without subsidies will lead many to go out of business, and jobs will be lost. So while price deregulation and trade liberalization are necessary, they are very difficult politically.

Privatization One problem with a system of central ownership is a lack of accountability. Under a system of private ownership, owners reap the rewards of their successes and suffer the consequences of their failures. Private ownership provides a strong incentive for efficient operation, innovation, and hard work that is lacking when ownership is centralized and profits are distributed to the people.

tragedy of commons The idea that collective ownership may not provide the proper private incentives for efficiency because individuals do not bear the full costs of their own decisions but do enjoy the full benefits.

The classic story to illustrate this is called the **tragedy of commons**. Suppose an agricultural community has 10,000 acres of grazing land. If the land were held in common so that all farmers had unlimited rights to graze their animals, each farmer would have an incentive to overgraze. He or she would reap the full benefits from grazing additional calves while the costs of grazing the calves would be borne collectively. The system provides no incentive to manage the land efficiently. Similarly, if the efficiency and benefits of my hard work and managerial skills accrue to others or to the state, what incentive do I have to work hard or to be efficient?

One solution to the tragedy of commons attempted in eighteenth-century Britain was to divide up the land into private holdings. Today, many economists argue, the solution to the incentive problem encountered in state-owned enterprises is to privatize them and let the owners compete.

In addition to increasing accountability, privatization means creating a climate in which new enterprises can flourish. If there is market demand for a product not currently being produced, individual entrepreneurs should be free to set up a business and make a profit. During the last months of the Soviet Union's existence, private enterprises such as taxi services, car repair services, restaurants, and even hotels began to spring up all over the country.

Like deregulation of prices, privatization is difficult politically. Privatization means many protected enterprises will go out of business because they cannot compete at world prices, resulting in a loss of jobs, at least temporarily.

Market-Supporting Institutions Between 1991 and 1997, U.S. firms raced to Eastern Europe in search of markets and investment opportunities and immediately became aware of a major obstacle. The institutions that make the market function relatively smoothly in the United States do not exist in Eastern Europe.

For example, the capital market, which channels private saving into productive capital investment in developed capitalist economies, is made up of hundreds of different institutions. The banking system, venture capital funds, stock market, bond market, commodity exchanges, brokerage houses, investment banks, and so forth, have all developed in the United States over hundreds of years, and they will not simply be replicated overnight in the formerly Communist world.

Many market-supporting institutions are so basic that Americans take them for granted. The institution of private property, for example, is a set of rights that must be protected by laws that the government must be willing to enforce. Suppose that the French hotel chain Novotel decides to build a new hotel in Moscow. Novotel must first acquire land. Then it will construct a building based on the expectation of renting rooms to customers. These investments are made with the expectation that the owner has a right to use them and a right to the profits that they produce. For such investments to be undertaken, these rights must be guaranteed by a set of property laws. This is equally true for large business firms and for Russian entrepreneurs who want to start their own enterprises.

Similarly, the law must provide for the enforcement of contracts. In the United States, a huge body of law determines what happens to you if you break a formal promise made in good faith. Businesses exist on promises to produce and promises to pay. Without recourse to the law when a contract is breached, contracts will not be entered into, goods will not be manufactured, and services will not be provided.

Another seemingly simple matter that turns out to be quite complex is the establishment of a set of accounting principles. In the United States, the rules of the accounting game are embodied in a set of generally accepted accounting principles (GAAP) that carry the force of law. Companies are required to keep track of their receipts, expenditures, and liabilities so their performance can be observed and evaluated by shareholders, taxing authorities, and others who have an interest in the company. If you have taken a course in accounting, you know how detailed these rules have become. Imagine trying to do business in a country operating under hundreds of different sets of rules. That is what has been happening in Russia.

Another institution is insurance. Whenever a venture undertakes a high-risk activity, it buys insurance to protect itself. Several years ago, Amnesty International (a nonprofit organization that works to protect civil liberties around the world) sponsored a worldwide concert tour with a number of well-known rock bands and performers. The most difficult part of organizing the tour was obtaining insurance for the artists and their equipment when they played in the then-Communist countries of Eastern Europe.

Social Safety Net In a centrally planned socialist economy, the labor market does not function freely. Everyone who wants a job is guaranteed one somewhere. The number of jobs is determined by a central plan to match the number of workers. There is essentially no unemployment. This, it has been argued, is one of the great advantages of a planned system. In addition, a central planning system provides basic housing, food, and clothing at very affordable levels for all. With no unemployment and necessities available at very low prices, there is no need for unemployment insurance, welfare, or other social programs.

Transition to a free labor market and liberalization of prices means that some workers will end up unemployed and everyone will pay higher prices for necessities. Indeed, during the early phases of the transition process, unemployment will be high. Inefficient state-owned enterprises will go out of business; some sectors will contract while others expand. As more and more people experience unemployment, popular support for reform is likely to drop unless some sort of social safety net is erected to ease the transition. This social safety net might include unemployment insurance, aid for the poor, and food and housing assistance. The experiences of the developed world have shown that such programs are expensive.

External Assistance Very few believe the transition to a market system can be achieved without outside support and some outside financing. Knowledge of, and experience with, capitalist institutions that exist in the United States, Western Europe, and Japan are of vital interest to the Eastern European nations. The basic skills of accounting, management, and enterprise development can be taught to Eastern Europe; many say it is in everyone's best interest to do so. Many also argue that the world's biggest nightmare is an economically weak or desperate Russia armed with nuclear weapons, giving up on reform or falling to a dictator.

There is little agreement about the extent of *financial* support that should be given, however. The United States has pushed for a worldwide effort to provide billions of dollars in aid. This aid, many argue, will help Russia stabilize its macroeconomy and buy desperately needed goods from abroad. However, critics in the United States and other potential donor countries say pouring money into Russia now is like pouring it into a black hole—no matter how much we donate, it will have little impact on the ultimate success or failure of the reforms.

Shock Therapy or Gradualism? Although economists generally agree on what the former socialist economies need to do, they debate the sequence and timing of specific reforms.

The popular press describes the debate as one between those who believe in "shock therapy" (sometimes called the "Big Bang" approach) and those who prefer a more gradual approach. Advocates of **shock therapy** believe that the economies in transition should proceed immediately on all fronts. They should stop printing money, deregulate prices and liberalize trade, privatize, develop market institutions, build a social safety net, and acquire external aid—all as quickly as possible. The pain will be severe, the argument goes, but in the end it will be forgotten as the transition raises living standards. Advocates of a *gradualist* approach believe the best course is to build up market institutions first, gradually decontrol prices, and privatize only the most efficient government enterprises first.

shock therapy The approach to transition from socialism to market capitalism that advocates rapid deregulation of prices, liberalization of trade, and privatization.

Those who favor moving quickly point to the apparent success of Poland, which moved rapidly through the first phases of reform. Russia's experience during the first years of its transition have demonstrated that, at least in that country, change must be to some extent gradual. In theory, stabilization and price liberalization can be achieved instantaneously. To enjoy the benefits of liberalization, a good deal of privatization must have taken place—and that will take more time. One analyst has said, privatization means "selling assets with no value to people with no money." Some estimates suggest half of Russian state-owned enterprises are incapable of making a profit at world prices. Simply cutting them loose would create chaos. In a sense, Russia had no choice but to move slowly.

SUMMARY

1. The economic problems facing the developing countries are often quite different from those confronting industrialized nations. The policy options available to governments may also differ. Nonetheless, the tools of economic analysis are as useful in understanding the economies of less developed countries as in understanding the U.S. economy.

LIFE IN THE DEVELOPING NATIONS: POPULATION AND POVERTY

2. The central reality of life in the developing countries is poverty. Although there is considerable diversity across the developing nations, most of the people in most developing countries are extremely poor by U.S. standards.

ECONOMIC DEVELOPMENT: SOURCES AND STRATEGIES

3. Almost all developing nations have a scarcity of physical capital relative to other resources, especially labor. The *vicious-circle-of-poverty hypothesis* says poor countries cannot escape from poverty because they cannot afford to postpone consumption—that is, to save—to make investments. In its crude form, the hypothesis is wrong inasmuch as some prosperous countries were at one time poorer than many developing countries are today. However, it is often difficult to mobilize savings efficiently in many developing nations.

4. Human capital—the stock of education and skills embodied in the workforce—plays a vital role in economic development.

5. Developing countries are often burdened by inadequate *social overhead capital*, ranging from poor public health and sanitation facilities to inadequate roads, telephones, and court systems. Such social overhead capital is often expensive to provide, and many governments are simply not in a position to undertake many useful projects because they are too costly.

6. Because developed economies are characterized by a large share of output and employment in the industrial sector, many developing countries seem to believe that development and industrialization are synonymous. In many cases, developing countries have pursued industry at the expense of agriculture, with mixed results. Recent evidence suggests that some balance between industry and agriculture leads to the best outcome.

7. *Import substitution* policies, a trade strategy that favors developing local industries that can manufacture goods to replace imports, were once very common in the developing nations. In general, such policies have not succeeded as well as those promoting open, export-oriented economies.
8. The failure of many central planning efforts has brought increasing calls for less government intervention and more market orientation in developing economies.

ISSUES IN ECONOMIC DEVELOPMENT

9. Rapid population growth is characteristic of many developing countries. Large families can be economically rational for parents who need support in their old age, or because children offer an important source of labor. However, having many children does not mean a net benefit to society as a whole. Rapid population growth can put a strain on already overburdened public services, such as education and health.
10. Between 1970 and 1984, the debts of the developing countries grew tenfold. As recession took hold in the advanced countries during the early 1980s, growth in the exports of the debtor countries slowed, and many found they could no longer pay back money they owed. The prospect of loan defaults by Third World nations threatened the entire international financial system and transformed the debt crisis into a global problem.

ECONOMIES IN TRANSITION

11. In a *socialist economy* most capital is owned by the government instead of private citizens. In a *capitalist economy* most capital is privately owned. *Communism* is a theoretical economic system in which the people directly control the means of production (capital and land) without the intervention of a government or state.
12. Economies differ in the extent to which decisions are made through central planning instead of a market system. Generally, socialist economies favor central planning over market allocation, and capitalist economies rely to a much greater extent on the market. Nonetheless, there are markets in all societies, and planning takes place in all economies.

THE END OF THE SOVIET UNION

13. The Soviet Union grew rapidly through the mid-1970s. During the late 1950s, the Soviet Union's economy was growing much faster than that of the United States. The key to early Soviet success was rapid planned capital accumulation. In the late 1970s, things began to deteriorate. Dramatic reforms were finally introduced by Mikhail Gorbachev after his rise to power in 1985. Nonetheless, the Soviet economy collapsed in 1991. The Soviet Union was dissolved, and the new president of the Russian Republic, Boris Yeltsin, was left to start the difficult task of transition to a market system.

THE TRANSITION TO A MARKET ECONOMY

14. Economists generally agree on six requirements for a successful transition from socialism to a market-based system: (1) macroeconomic stabilization, (2) deregulation of prices and liberalization of trade, (3) privatization, (4) establishment of market-supporting institutions, (5) social safety net, and (6) external assistance.
15. Much debate exists about the sequence and timing of specific reforms. The idea of *shock therapy* is to proceed immediately on all six fronts, including rapid deregulation of prices and privatization. The *gradualist* approach is to build up market institutions first, gradually decontrol prices, and privatize only the most efficient government enterprises first.

REVIEW TERMS AND CONCEPTS

brain drain, 441
capital flight, 440
capitalist economy, 450
communism, 450
debt rescheduling, 448
export promotion, 443
fertility rate, 447
import substitution, 442
International Monetary Fund (IMF), 445
market–socialist economy, 452
mortality rate, 447
natural rate of population increase, 447
shock therapy, 456
social overhead capital, 441
socialist economy, 450
stabilization program, 449
structural adjustment, 445
tragedy of commons, 454
vicious-circle-of-poverty hypothesis, 440
World Bank, 445

PROBLEM SET

1. The biggest problem facing developing countries across the globe in 2004 was disease. The HIV/AIDS pandemic had infected more than 60 million worldwide and up to 40 percent of the adult populations of some African countries like Botswana. Describe the effects of HIV/AIDS on the economies of these countries. Be sure to discuss the sources of economic growth and the use of scarce resources.
2. For a developing country to grow, it needs capital. The major source of capital in most countries is domestic saving, but the goal of stimulating domestic saving usually is in conflict with government policies aimed at reducing inequality in the distribution of income. Comment on this trade-off between equity and growth. How would you go about resolving the issue if you were the president of a small, poor country?

3. The GDP of any country can be divided into two kinds of goods: capital goods and consumption goods. The proportion of national output devoted to capital goods determines, to some extent, the nation's growth rate.
   a. Explain how capital accumulation leads to economic growth.
   b. Briefly describe how a market economy determines how much investment will be undertaken each period.
   c. "Consumption versus investment is a more painful conflict to resolve for developing countries." Comment on this statement.
   d. If you were the benevolent dictator of a developing country, what plans would you implement to increase per capita GDP?
4. "The main reason developing countries are poor is that they do not have enough capital. If we give them machinery, or build factories for them, we can greatly improve their situation." Comment.
5. "Poor countries are trapped in a vicious circle of poverty. For output to grow, they must accumulate capital. To accumulate capital, they must save (consume less than they produce). Because they are poor, they have little or no extra output available for savings—it must all go to feed and clothe the present generation. Thus they are doomed to stay poor forever." Comment on each step in this argument.
6. "Famines are acts of God, resulting from bad weather or other natural disasters. There is nothing we can do about them except to send food relief after they occur." Explain why this position is inaccurate. Concentrate on agricultural pricing policies and distributional issues.
7. Choose one of the transitional economies of Central Europe (Poland, Hungary, Bulgaria, the Czech Republic, Romania, Ukraine, Russia, etc.). Write a brief paper on how the transition to a market economy was proceeding in 2001 and 2002. Has the economy (prices, employment, etc.) stabilized? Has there been economic growth? How far has privatization progressed? What problems have been encountered? (A good source of information would be the chronological index to a publication like *The Economist* or the *New York Times.*)
8. "The difference between the United States and the Soviet Union is that the United States has a capitalist economic system and the Soviet Union had a totalitarian government." Explain how this comparison confuses the economic and political aspects of the two societies. What words describe the former economic system of the Soviet Union?
9. You are assigned the task of debating the strength of a socialist economy (regardless of your own viewpoint). Outline the points that you would make in the debate. Be sure to define socialism carefully in your presentation.
10. "The U.S. government should institute a policy of subsidizing those firms that are likely to be successful competitors in the international economic wars. Such an 'industrial policy' should have the authority to override the antitrust laws." Do you agree or disagree? Explain your answer.
11. The distribution of income in a capitalist economy is likely to be more unequal than it is in a socialist economy. Why is this so? Is there a tension between the goal of limiting inequality and the goal of motivating risk-taking and hard work? Explain your answer in detail.

WWW Visit www.prenhall.com/casefair for self-test quizzes, interactive graphing exercises, and news articles.

Glossary

absolute advantage The advantage in the production of a product enjoyed by one country over another when it uses fewer resources to produce that product than the other country does.

accelerator effect The tendency for investment to increase when aggregate output increases and decrease when aggregate output decreases, accelerating the growth or decline of output.

actual investment The actual amount of investment that takes place; it includes items such as unplanned changes in inventories.

adjustment costs The costs that a firm incurs when it changes its production level—for example, the administration costs of laying off employees or the training costs of hiring new workers.

aggregate behavior The behavior of all households and firms together.

aggregate demand The total demand for goods and services in an economy.

aggregate demand (AD) curve A curve that shows the negative relationship between aggregate output (income) and the price level. Each point on the AD curve is a point at which both the goods market and the money market are in equilibrium.

aggregate income The total income received by all factors of production in a given period.

aggregate output The total quantity of goods and services produced (or supplied) in an economy in a given period.

aggregate output (income) (Y) A combined term used to remind you of the exact equality between aggregate output and aggregate income.

aggregate production function The mathematical representation of the relationship between inputs and national output, or gross domestic product.

aggregate supply The total supply of all goods and services in an economy.

aggregate supply (AS) curve A graph that shows the relationship between the aggregate quantity of output supplied by all firms in an economy and the overall price level.

animal spirits of entrepreneurs A phrase coined by Keynes to describe investors' feelings.

appreciation of a currency The rise in value of one currency relative to another.

automatic destabilizers Revenue and expenditure items in the federal budget that automatically change with the economy in such a way as to destabilize GDP.

automatic stabilizers Revenue and expenditure items in the federal budget that automatically change with the state of the economy in such a way as to stabilize GDP.

autonomous variable A variable that is assumed not to depend on the state of the economy—that is, it does not change when the economy changes.

average propensity to consume (APC) The proportion of income households spend on consumption. Determined by dividing consumption (C) by income (Y).

balance of payments The record of a country's transactions in goods, services, and assets with the rest of the world; also the record of a country's sources (supply) and uses (demand) of foreign exchange.

balance of trade A country's exports of goods and services minus its imports of goods and services.

balance on capital account In the United States, the sum of the following (measured in a given period): the change in private U.S. assets abroad, the change in foreign private assets in the United States, the change in U.S. government assets abroad, and the change in foreign government assets in the United States.

balance on current account Net exports of goods, plus net exports of services, plus net investment income, plus net transfer payments.

balanced-budget multiplier The ratio of change in the equilibrium level of output to a change in government spending where the change in government spending is balanced by a change in taxes so as not to create any deficit. The balanced-budget multiplier is equal to one: The change in Y resulting from the change in G and the equal change in T is exactly the same size as the initial change in G or T itself.

barter The direct exchange of goods and services for other goods and services.

base year The year chosen for the weights in a fixed-weight procedure.

black market A market in which illegal trading takes place at market-determined prices.

bond A document that formally promises to pay back a loan under specified terms, usually over a specific time period.

brain drain The tendency for talented people from developing countries to become educated in a developed country and remain there after graduation.

budget deficit The difference between what a government spends and what it collects in taxes in a given period: $G - T$.

business cycle The cycle of short-term ups and downs in the economy.

capital flight The tendency for both human capital and financial capital to leave developing countries in search of higher rates of return elsewhere.

capital gain An increase in the value of an asset.

capital-intensive technology A production technique that uses a large amount of capital relative to labor.

capitalist economy An economy in which most capital is privately owned.

capital market The input/factor market in which households supply their savings, for interest or for claims to future profits, to firms that demand funds to buy capital goods.

***ceteris paribus*, or all else equal** A device used to analyze the relationship between two variables while the values of other variables are held unchanged.

change in business inventories The amount by which firms' inventories change during a period. Inventories are the goods that firms produce now but intend to sell later.

change in inventory Production minus sales.

circular flow A diagram showing the income received and payments made by each sector of the economy.

command economy An economy in which a central government either directly or indirectly sets output targets, incomes, and prices.

commodity monies Items used as money that also have intrinsic value in some other use.

communism An economic system in which the people control the means of production (capital and land) directly, without the intervention of a government or state.

comparative advantage The advantage in the production of a product enjoyed by one country over another when that product can be produced at lower cost in terms of other goods than it could be in the other country.

compensation of employees Includes wages, salaries, and various supplements—employer contributions to social insurance and pension funds, for example—paid to households by firms and by the government.

complements, complementary goods Goods that "go together"; a decrease in the price of one results in an increase in demand for the other, and vice versa.

constrained supply of labor The amount a household actually works in a given period at the current wage rate.

consumer goods Goods produced for present consumption.

consumer price index (CPI) A price index computed each month by the Bureau of Labor Statistics using a bundle that is meant to represent the "market basket" purchased monthly by the typical urban consumer.

consumer sovereignty The idea that consumers ultimately dictate what will be produced (or not produced) by choosing what to purchase (and what not to purchase).

consumption function The relationship between consumption and income.

contraction, recession, or slump The period in the business cycle from a peak down to a trough, during which output and employment fall.

contractionary fiscal policy A decrease in government spending or an increase in net t axes aimed at decreasing aggregate output (income) (Y).

contractionary monetary policy A decrease in the money supply aimed at decreasing aggregate output (income) (Y).

Corn Laws The tariffs, subsidies, and restrictions enacted by the British Parliament in the early nineteenth century to discourage imports and encourage exports of grain.

corporate bonds Promissory notes issued by corporations when they borrow money.

corporate profits The income of corporate businesses.

cost shock, or supply shock A change in costs that shifts the aggregate supply (AS) curve.

cost-of-living adjustments (COLAs) Contract provisions that tie wages to changes in the cost of living. The greater the inflation rate, the more wages are raised.

cost-push, or supply-side, inflation Inflation caused by an increase in costs.

crowding-out effect The tendency for increases in government spending to cause reductions in private investment spending.

currency debasement The decrease in the value of money that occurs when its supply is increased rapidly.

current dollars The current prices that one pays for goods and services.

cyclical deficit The deficit that occurs because of a downturn in the business cycle.

cyclical unemployment The increase in unemployment that occurs during recessions and depressions.

debt rescheduling An agreement between banks and borrowers through which a new schedule of repayments of the debt is negotiated; often some of the debt is written off and the repayment period is extended.

deficit response index (DRI) The amount by which the deficit changes with a $1 change in GDP.

deflation A decrease in the overall price level.

demand curve A graph illustrating how much of a given product a household would be willing to buy at different prices.

demand-pull inflation Inflation that is initiated by an increase in aggregate demand.

demand schedule A table showing how much of a given product a household would be willing to buy at different prices.

depreciation The amount by which an asset's value falls in a given period.

depreciation of a currency The fall in value of one currency relative to another.

depression A prolonged and deep recession. The precise definitions of prolonged and deep are debatable.

descriptive economics The compilation of data that describe phenomena and facts.

desired, or optimal, level of inventories The level of inventory at which the extra cost (in lost sales) from lowering inventories by a small amount is just equal to the extra gain (in interest revenue and decreased storage costs).

desired, or planned, investment Those additions to capital stock and inventory that are planned by firms.

discount rate Interest rate that banks pay to the Fed to borrow from it.

discouraged-worker effect The decline in the measured unemployment rate that results when people who want to work but cannot find jobs grow discouraged and stop looking, thus dropping out of the ranks of the unemployed and the labor force.

discretionary fiscal policy Changes in taxes or spending that are the result of deliberate changes in government policy.

disposable, or after-tax, income (Y_d) Total income minus net taxes: $Y - T$.

disposable personal income or after-tax income Personal income minus personal income taxes. The amount that households have to spend or save.

dividends The portion of a corporation's profits that the firm pays out each period to its shareholders.

Dow Jones Industrial Average An index based on the stock prices of 30 actively traded large companies. The oldest and most widely followed index of stock market performance.

dumping A firm or industry sells products on the world market at prices below the cost of production.

durable goods Goods that last a relatively long time, such as cars and household appliances.

easy monetary policy Fed policies that expand the money supply in an effort to stimulate the economy.

economic globalization The process of increasing economic interdependence among countries and their citizens.

economic growth An increase in the total output of an economy. Defined by some economists as an increase of real GDP per capita. It occurs when a society acquires new resources or when it learns to produce more using existing resources.

economic integration Occurs when two or more nations join to form a free-trade zone.

economic theory A statement or set of related statements about cause and effect, action and reaction.

economics The study of how individuals and societies choose to use the scarce resources that nature and previous generations have provided.

efficiency In economics, allocative efficiency. An efficient economy is one that produces what people want at the least possible cost.

efficiency wage theory An explanation for unemployment that holds that the productivity of workers increases with the wage rate. If this is so, firms may have an incentive to pay wages above the market-clearing rate.

efficient market A market in which profit opportunities are eliminated almost instantaneously.

empirical economics The collection and use of data to test economic theories.

employed Any person 16 years old or older (1) who works for pay, either for someone else or in his or her own business for 1 or more hours per week, (2) who works without pay for 15 or more hours per week in a family enterprise, or (3) who has a job but has been temporarily absent, with or without pay.

entrepreneur A person who organizes, manages, and assumes the risks of a firm, taking a new idea or a new product and turning it into a successful business.

equilibrium Occurs when there is no tendency for change. In the macroeconomic goods market, equilibrium occurs when planned aggregate expenditure is equal to aggregate output.

equilibrium price level The price level at which the aggregate demand and aggregate supply curves intersect.

equity Fairness.

European Union (EU) The European trading bloc composed of Austria, Belgium, Denmark, Finland, France, Germany, Greece, Ireland, Italy, Luxembourg, the Netherlands, Portugal, Spain, Sweden, and the United Kingdom.

excess demand or shortage The condition that exists when quantity demanded exceeds quantity supplied at the current price.

excess labor, excess capital Labor and capital that are not needed to produce the firm's current level of output.

excess reserves The difference between a bank's actual reserves and its required reserves.

excess supply or surplus The condition that exists when quantity supplied exceeds quantity demanded at the current price.

exchange rate The price of one country's currency in terms of another country's currency; the ratio at which two currencies are traded for each other.

expansion or boom The period in the business cycle from a trough up to a peak, during which output and employment rise.

expansionary fiscal policy An increase in government spending or a reduction in net taxes aimed at increasing aggregate output (income) (Y).

expansionary monetary policy An increase in the money supply aimed at increasing aggregate output (income) (Y).

expenditure approach A method of computing GDP that measures the amount spent on all final goods during a given period.

explicit contracts Employment contracts that stipulate workers' wages, usually for a period of 1 to 3 years.

export promotion A trade policy designed to encourage exports.

export subsidies Government payments made to domestic firms to encourage exports.

externality A cost or a benefit resulting from some activity or transaction that is imposed or bestowed on some party outside the activity or transaction.

factor endowments The quantity and quality of labor, land, and natural resources of a country.

factors of production The inputs into the production process. Land, labor, and capital are the three key factors of production.

fallacy of composition The erroneous belief that what is true for a part is necessarily true for the whole.

favored customers Those who receive special treatment from dealers during situations of excess demand.

federal budget The budget of the federal government.

federal debt The total amount owed by the federal government.

Federal Open Market Committee (FOMC) A group composed of the seven members of the Fed's Board of Governors, the president of the New York Federal Reserve Bank, and 4 of the other 11 district bank presidents on a rotating basis; it sets goals concerning the money supply and interest rates and directs the operation of the Open Market Desk in New York.

Federal Reserve System (the Fed) The central bank of the United States.

federal surplus (+) or deficit (−) Federal government receipts minus expenditures.

fertility rate The birth rate. Equal to (the number of births per year divided by the population) × 100.

fiat, or token, money Items designated as money that are intrinsically worthless.

final goods and services Goods and services produced for final use.

financial intermediaries Banks and other institutions that act as a link between those who have money to lend and those who want to borrow money.

fine-tuning The phrase used by Walter Heller to refer to the government's role in regulating inflation and unemployment.

firm An organization that transforms resources (inputs) into products (outputs). Firms are the primary producing units in a market economy.

fiscal drag The negative effect on the economy that occurs when average tax rates increase because taxpayers have moved into higher income brackets during an expansion.

fiscal policy Government policies concerning taxes and expenditures (spending).

fixed-weight procedure A procedure that uses weights from a given base year.

floating, or market-determined, exchange rates Exchange rates that are determined by the unregulated forces of supply and demand.

foreign exchange All currencies other than the domestic currency of a given country.

frictional unemployment The portion of unemployment that is due to the normal working of the labor market; used to denote short-run job/skill matching problems.

full-employment budget What the federal budget would be if the economy were producing at a full-employment level of output.

General Agreement on Tariffs and Trade (GATT) An international agreement signed by the United States and 22 other countries in 1947 to promote the liberalization of foreign trade.

genetically modified (GM) foods Strains of food that have been genetically modified. Examples include insect and herbicide-resistant soybeans, corn, and cotton and rice with increased iron and vitamins.

globalization The process of increasing interdependence among countries and their citizens.

goods market The market in which goods and services are exchanged and in which the equilibrium level of aggregate output is determined.

government consumption and gross investment (G) Expenditures by federal, state, and local governments for final goods and services.

government spending multiplier The ratio of the change in the equilibrium level of output to a change in government spending.

Gramm-Rudman-Hollings Bill Passed by the U.S. Congress and signed by President Reagan in 1986, this law set out to reduce the federal deficit by $36 billion per year, with a deficit of zero slated for 1991.

Great Depression The period of severe economic contraction and high unemployment that began in 1929 and continued throughout the 1930s.

gross investment The total value of all newly produced capital goods (plant, equipment, housing, and inventory) produced in a given period.

gross national income (GNI) GNP converted into dollars using an average of currency exchange rates over several years adjusted for rates of inflation.

gross national product (GNP) The total market value of all final goods and services produced within a given period by factors of production owned by a country's citizens, regardless of where the output is produced.

gross private domestic investment (I) Total investment in capital—that is, the purchase of new housing, plants, equipment, and inventory by the private (or nongovernment) sector.

Heckscher-Ohlin theorem A theory that explains the existence of a country's comparative advantage by its factor endowments: A country has a comparative advantage in the production of a product if that country is relatively well endowed with inputs used intensively in the production of that product.

households The consuming units in an economy.

hyperinflation A period of very rapid increases in the overall price level.

identity Something that is always true.

Immigration Act of 1990 Increased the number of legal immigrants allowed into the United States each year by 150,000.

Immigration Reform and Control Act (1986) Granted amnesty to about 3 million illegal aliens and imposed a strong set of employer sanctions designed to slow the flow of immigrants into the United States.

implementation lag The time it takes to put the desired policy into effect once economists and policy makers recognize that the economy is in a boom or a slump.

import substitution An industrial trade strategy that favors developing local industries that can manufacture goods to replace imports.

income The sum of all a household's wages, salaries, profits, interest payments, rents, and other forms of earnings in a given period of time. It is a flow measure.

income approach A method of computing GDP that measures the income—wages, rents, interest, and profits—received by all factors of production in producing final goods.

indirect taxes Taxes like sales taxes, customs duties, and license fees.

industrial policy Government involvement in the allocation of capital across manufacturing sectors.

Industrial Revolution The period in England during the late eighteenth and early nineteenth centuries in which new manufacturing technologies and improved transportation gave rise to the modern factory system and a massive movement of the population from the countryside to the cities.

infant industry A young industry that may need temporary protection from competition from the established industries of other countries to develop an acquired comparative advantage.

inferior goods Goods for which demand tends to fall when income rises.

inflation An increase in the overall price level.

inflation rate The percentage change in the price level.

innovation The use of new knowledge to produce a new product or to produce an existing product more efficiently.

input or factor markets The markets in which the resources used to produce products are exchanged.

inputs The goods and services that firms purchase and turn into output.

inputs or resources Anything provided by nature or previous generations that can be used directly or indirectly to satisfy human wants.

interest The fee that borrowers pay to tenders for the use of their funds.

interest rate The annual interest payment on a loan expressed as a percentage of the loan. Equal to the amount of interest received per year divided by the amount of the loan.

interest sensitivity or insensitivity of planned investment The responsiveness of planned investment spending to changes in the interest rate. Interest sensitivity means that planned investment spending changes a great deal in response to changes in the interest rate; interest insensitivity means little or no change in planned investment as a result of changes in the interest rate.

intermediate goods Goods that are produced by one firm for use in further processing by another firm.

International Monetary Fund (IMF) An international agency whose primary goals are to stabilize international exchange rates and to lend money to countries that have problems financing their international transactions.

invention An advance in knowledge.

inventory investment Occurs when a firm produces more output than it sells within a given period.

investment Purchases by firms of new buildings and equipment and additions to inventories, all of which add to firms' capital stock.

J-curve effect Following a currency depreciation, a country's balance of trade may get worse before it gets better. The graph showing this effect is shaped like the letter J, hence the name "J-curve effect."

labor demand curve A graph that illustrates the amount of labor that firms want to employ at each given wage rate.

labor force The number of people employed plus the number of unemployed.

labor-force participation rate The ratio of the labor force to the total population 16 years old or older.

labor-intensive technology A production technique that uses a large amount of labor relative to capital.

labor market The input/factor market in which households supply work for wages to firms that demand labor.

labor productivity Output per worker hour; the amount of output produced by an average worker in 1 hour.

labor supply curve A graph that illustrates the amount of labor that households want to supply at each given wage rate.

Laffer curve With the tax rate measured on the vertical axis and tax revenue measured on the horizontal axis, the Laffer curve shows there is some tax rate beyond which the supply response is large enough to lead to a decrease in tax revenue for further increases in the tax rate.

laissez-faire economy Literally from the French: "allow [them] to do." An economy in which individual people and firms pursue their own self-interests without any central direction or regulation.

land market The input/factor market in which households supply land or other real property in exchange for rent.

law of demand The negative relationship between price and quantity demanded: As price rises, quantity demanded decreases. As price falls, quantity demanded increases.

law of one price If the costs of transportation are small, the price of the same good in different countries should be roughly the same.

law of supply The positive relationship between price and quantity of a good supplied: An increase in market price will lead to an increase in quantity supplied, and a decrease in market price will lead to a decrease in quantity supplied.

legal tender Money that a government has required to be accepted in settlement of debts.

lender of last resort One of the functions of the Fed: It provides funds to troubled banks that cannot find any other sources of funds.

life-cycle theory of consumption A theory of household consumption: Households make lifetime consumption decisions based on their expectations of lifetime income.

liquidity property of money The property of money that makes it a good medium of exchange as well as a store of value: It is portable and readily accepted and thus easily exchanged for goods.

Lucas supply function The supply function embodies the idea that output (Y) depends on the difference between the actual price level and the expected price level.

M1, or transactions money Money that can be directly used for transactions.

M2, or broad money M1 plus savings accounts, money market accounts, and other near monies.

macroeconomics The branch of economics that examines the economic behavior of aggregates—income, employment, output, and so on—on a national scale.

marginal propensity to consume (MPC) That fraction of a change in income that is consumed, or spent.

marginal propensity to import (MPM) The change in imports caused by a $1 change in income.

marginal propensity to save (MPS) That fraction of a change in income that is saved.

marginal rate of transformation (MRT) The slope of the production possibility frontier (ppf).

market The institution through which buyers and sellers interact and engage in exchange.

market demand The sum of all the quantities of a good or service demanded per period by all the households buying in the market for that good or service.

market–socialist economy An economy that combines government ownership with market allocation.

market supply The sum of all that is supplied each period by all producers of a single product.

medium of exchange, or means of payment What sellers generally accept and buyers generally use to pay for goods and services.

microeconomic foundations of macroeconomics The microeconomic principles underlying macroeconomic analysis.

microeconomics The branch of economics that examines the functioning of individual industries and the behavior of individual decision-making units—that is, business firms and households.

minimum wage A price floor set under the price of labor.

minimum wage laws Laws that set a floor for wage rates—that is, a minimum hourly rate for any kind of labor.

model A formal statement of a theory, usually a mathematical statement of a presumed relationship between two or more variables.

modern economic growth The period of rapid and sustained increase in real output per capita that began in the Western World with the Industrial Revolution.

monetary policy The behavior of the Federal Reserve concerning the money supply.

money market The market in which financial instruments are exchanged and in which the equilibrium level of the interest rate is determined.

money multiplier The multiple by which deposits can increase for every dollar increase in reserves; equal to one divided by the required reserve ratio.

moral suasion The pressure that in the past the Fed exerted on member banks to discourage them from borrowing heavily from the Fed.

mortality rate The death rate. Equal to (the number of deaths per year divided by the population) × 100.

movement along a demand curve The change in quantity demanded brought about by a change in price.

movement along a supply curve The change in quantity supplied brought about by a change in price.

multiplier The ratio of the change in the equilibrium level of output to a change in some autonomous variable.

NAIRU The nonaccelerating inflation rate of unemployment.

NASDAQ Composite An index based on the stock prices of over 5,000 companies traded on the NASDAQ Stock Market. The NASDAQ market takes its name from the National Association of Securities Dealers Automated Quotation System.

national income The total income earned by the factors of production owned by a country's citizens.

natural rate of population increase The difference between the birth rate and the death rate. It does not take migration into account.

natural rate of unemployment The unemployment that occurs as a normal part of the functioning of the economy. Sometimes taken as the sum of frictional unemployment and structural unemployment.

near monies Close substitutes for transactions money, such as savings accounts and money market accounts.

negative demand shock Something that causes a negative shift in consumption or investment schedules or that leads to a decrease in U.S. exports.

net exports (EX − IM) The difference between exports (sales to foreigners of U.S. − produced goods and services) and imports (U.S. purchases of goods and services from abroad). The figure can be positive or negative.

net exports of goods and services (EX − IM) The difference between a country's total exports and total imports.

net factor payments to the rest of the world Payments of factor income to the rest of the world minus the receipt of factor income from the rest of the world.

net interest The interest paid by business.

net investment Gross investment minus depreciation.

net national product (NNP) Gross national product minus depreciation; a nation's total product minus what is required to maintain the value of its capital stock.

net taxes (T) Taxes paid by firms and households to the government minus transfer payments made to households by the government.

nominal GDP Gross domestic product measured in current dollars.

nominal wage rate The wage rate in current dollars.

nondurable goods Goods that are used up fairly quickly, such as food and clothing.

nonlabor, or nonwage, income Any income received from sources other than working—inheritances, interest, dividends, transfer payments, and so on.

nonresidential investment Expenditures by firms for machines, tools, plants, and so on.

nonsynchronization of income and spending The mismatch between the timing of money inflow to the household and the timing of money outflow for household expenses.

normal goods Goods for which demand goes up when income is higher and for which demand goes down when income is lower.

normative economics An approach to economics that analyzes outcomes of economic behavior, evaluates them as good or bad, and may prescribe courses of action. Also called policy economics.

North American Free-Trade Agreement (NAFTA) An agreement signed by the United States, Mexico, and Canada in which the three countries agreed to establish all North America as a free-trade zone.

not in the labor force A person who is not looking for work, either because he or she does not want a job or has given up looking.

Ockham's razor The principle that irrelevant detail should be cut away.

Okun's Law The theory, put forth by Arthur Okun, that the unemployment rate decreases about 1 percentage point for every 3 percent increase in real GDP. Later research and data have shown that the relationship between output and unemployment is not as stable as Okun's "Law" predicts.

Open Market Desk The office in the New York Federal Reserve Bank from which government securities are bought and sold by the Fed.

open market operations The purchase and sale by the Fed of government securities in the open market; a tool used to expand or contract the amount of reserves in the system and thus the money supply.

opportunity cost The best alternative that we forgo, or give up, when we make a choice or a decision.

outputs Usable products.

perfect substitutes Identical products.

permanent income The average level of one's expected future income stream.

personal consumption expenditures (C) A major component of GDP: expenditures by consumers on goods and services.

personal income The total income of households. Equals (national income) minus (corporate profits minus dividends) minus (social insurance payments) plus (interest income received from the government and households) plus (transfer payments to households). The income received by households after paying social insurance taxes but before paying personal income taxes.

personal saving The amount of disposable income that is left after total personal spending in a given period.

personal saving rate The percentage of disposable personal income that is saved. If the personal saving rate is low, households are spending a large amount relative to their incomes; if it is high, households are spending cautiously.

Phillips Curve A graph showing the relationship between the inflation rate and the unemployment rate.

planned aggregate expenditure (AE) The total amount the economy plans to spend in a given period. Equal to consumption plus planned investment: $AE \int C + I$.

plant-and-equipment investment Purchases by firms of additional machines, factories, or buildings within a given period.

policy mix The combination of monetary and fiscal policies in use at a given time.

positive economics An approach to economics that seeks to understand behavior and the operation of systems without making judgments. It describes what exists and how it works.

post hoc, ergo propter hoc Literally, "after this (in time), therefore because of this." A common error made in thinking about causation: If Event A happens before Event B, it is not necessarily true that A caused B.

potential output, or potential GDP The level of aggregate output that can be sustained in the long run without inflation.

price ceiling A maximum price that sellers may charge for a good, usually set by government.

price feedback effect The process by which a domestic price increase in one country can "feed back" on itself through export and import prices. An increase in the price level in one country can drive up prices in other countries. This in turn further increases the price level in the first country.

price floor A minimum price below which exchange is not permitted.

price rationing The process by which the market system allocates goods and services to consumers when quantity demanded exceeds quantity supplied.

price surprise Actual price level minus expected price level.

privately held federal debt The privately held (non-government-owned) debt of the U.S. government.

producer price indexes (PPIs) Measures of prices that producers receive for products at all stages in the production process.

product or output markets The markets in which goods and services are exchanged.

production The process that transforms scarce resources into useful goods and services.

production possibility frontier (ppf) A graph that shows all the combinations of goods and services that can be produced if all of society's resources are used efficiently.

productivity, or labor productivity Output per worker hour; the amount of output produced by an average worker in 1 hour.

productivity of an input The amount of output produced per unit of an input.

profit The difference between revenues and costs.

proprietors' income The income of unincorporated businesses.

protection The practice of shielding a sector of the economy from foreign competition.

public goods, or social goods Goods or services that bestow collective benefits on members of society.

purchasing-power-parity theory A theory of international exchange holding that exchange rates are set so that the price of similar goods in different countries is the same.

quantity demanded The amount (number of units) of a product that a household would buy in a given period if it could buy all it wanted at the current market price.

quantity supplied The amount of a particular product that a firm would be willing and able to offer for sale at a particular price during a given time period.

quantity theory of money The theory based on the identity $M \times V \int P \times Y$ and the assumption that the velocity of money (V) is constant (or virtually constant).

queuing Waiting in line as a means of distributing goods and services; a nonprice rationing mechanism.

quota A limit on the quantity of imports.

ration coupons Tickets or coupons that entitle individuals to purchase a certain amount of a given product per month.

rational-expectations hypothesis The hypothesis that people know the "true model" of the economy and that they use this model to form their expectations of the future.

real business cycle theory An attempt to explain business cycle fluctuations under the assumptions of complete price and wage flexibility and rational expectations. It emphasizes shocks to technology and other shocks.

real interest rate The difference between the interest rate on a loan and the inflation rate.

real wage rate The amount that the nominal wage rate can buy in terms of goods and services.

real wealth, or real balance, effect The change in consumption brought about by a change in real wealth that results from a change in the price level.

realized capital gain The gain that occurs when the owner of an asset actually sells it for more than he paid for it.

recession Roughly, a period in which real GDP declines for at least two consecutive quarters. Marked by falling output and rising unemployment.

recognition lag The time it takes for policy makers to recognize the existence of a boom or a slump.

relative-wage explanation of unemployment An explanation for sticky wages (and therefore unemployment): If workers are concerned about their wages relative to other workers in other firms and industries, they may be unwilling to accept a wage cut unless they know that all other workers are receiving similar cuts.

rental income The income received by property owners in the form of rent.

required reserve ratio The percentage of its total deposits that a bank must keep as reserves at the Federal Reserve.

reserves The deposits that a bank has at the Federal Reserve bank plus its cash on hand.

residential investment Expenditures by households and firms on new houses and apartment buildings.

response lag The time that it takes for the economy to adjust to the new conditions after a new policy is implemented; the lag that occurs because of the operation of the economy itself.

run on a bank Occurs when many of those who have claims on a bank (deposits) present them at the same time.

saving (S) The part of its income that a household does not consume in a given period. Distinguished from savings, which is the current stock of accumulated saving.

scarce Limited.

services The things we buy that do not involve the production of physical things, such as legal and medical services and education.

shares of stock Financial instruments that give to the holder a share in the firm's ownership and therefore the right to share in the firm's profits.

shift of a demand curve The change that takes place in a demand curve corresponding to a new relationship between quantity demanded of a good and price of that good. The shift is brought about by a change in the original conditions.

shift of a supply curve The change that takes place in a supply curve corresponding to a new relationship between quanity supplied of a good and the price of that good. The shift is brought about by a change in the original conditions.

shock therapy The approach to transition from socialism to market capitalism that advocates rapid deregulation of prices, liberalization of trade, and privatization.

Smoot-Hawley tariff The U.S. tariff law of the 1930s, which set the highest tariffs in U.S. history (60 percent). It set off an international trade war and caused the decline in trade that is often considered a cause of the worldwide depression of the 1930s.

social, or implicit, contracts Unspoken agreements between workers and firms that firms will not cut wages.

social overhead capital Basic infrastructure projects such as roads, power generation, and irrigation systems.

socialist economy An economy in which most capital is owned by the government instead of private citizens. Also called social ownership.

speculation motive One reason for holding bonds instead of money: Because the market value of interest-bearing bonds is inversely related to the interest rate, investors may wish to hold bonds when interest rates are high with the hope of selling them when interest rates fall.

stability A condition in which national output is growing steadily, with low inflation and full employment of resources.

stabilization policy Describes both monetary and fiscal policy, the goals of which are to smooth out fluctuations in output and employment and to keep prices as stable as possible.

stabilization program An agreement between a borrower country and the International Monetary Fund in which the country agrees to revamp its economic policies to provide incentives for higher export earnings and lower imports.

stagflation Occurs when the overall price level rises rapidly (inflation) during periods of recession or high and persistent unemployment (stagnation).

Standard and Poor's 500 (S&P 500) An index based on the stock prices of the largest 500 firms traded on the New York Stock Exchange, the NASDAQ Stock Market, and the American Stock Exchange.

sticky prices Prices that do not always adjust rapidly to maintain equality between quantity supplied and quantity demanded.

sticky wages The downward rigidity of wages as an explanation for the existence of unemployment.

stock A certificate that certifies ownership of a certain portion of a firm.

store of value An asset that can be used to transport purchasing power from one time period to another.

structural deficit The deficit that remains at full employment.

structural unemployment The portion of unemployment that is due to changes in the structure of the economy that result in a significant loss of jobs in certain industries.

subsidies Payments made by the government for which it receives no goods or services in return.

substitutes Goods that can serve as replacements for one another; when the price of one increases, demand for the other goes up.

sunk costs Costs that cannot be avoided, regardless of what is done in the future, because they have already been incurred.

supply curve A graph illustrating how much of a product a firm will sell at different prices.

supply schedule A table showing how much of a product firms will sell at different prices.

supply-side policies Government policies that focus on stimulating aggregate supply instead of aggregate demand.

sustained inflation Occurs when the overall price level continues to rise over some fairly long period of time.

tariff A tax on imports.

tax multiplier The ratio of change in the equilibrium level of output to a change in taxes.

terms of trade The ratio at which a country can trade domestic products for imported products.

theory of comparative advantage Ricardo's theory that specialization and free trade will benefit all trading partners (real wages will rise), even those that may be absolutely less efficient producers.

tight monetary policy Fed policies that contract the money supply in an effort to restrain the economy.

time lags Delays in the economy's response to stabilization policies.

trade deficit Occurs when a country's exports of goods and services are less than its imports of goods and services in a given period.

trade feedback effect The tendency for an increase in the economic activity of one country to lead to a worldwide increase in economic activity, which then feeds back to that country.

trade surplus The situation when a country exports more than it imports.

tragedy of commons The idea that collective ownership may not provide the proper private incentives for efficiency because individuals do not bear the full costs of their own decisions but do enjoy the full benefits.

transaction motive The main reason that people hold money—to buy things.

transfer payments Cash payments made by the government to people who do not supply goods, services, or labor in exchange for these payments. They include social security benefits, veterans' benefits, and welfare payments.

Treasury bonds, notes, and bills Promissory notes issued by the federal government when it borrows money.

unconstrained supply of labor The amount a household would like to work within a given period at the current wage rate if it could find the work.

underground economy The part of the economy in which transactions take place and in which income is generated that is unreported and therefore not counted in GDP.

unemployed A person 16 years old or older who is not working, is available for work, and has made specific efforts to find work during the previous 4 weeks.

unemployment rate The ratio of the number of people unemployed to the total number of people in the labor force.

unit of account A standard unit that provides a consistent way of quoting prices.

U.S.-Canadian Free-Trade Agreement An agreement in which the United States and Canada agreed to eliminate all barriers to trade between the two countries by 1998.

value added The difference between the value of goods as they leave a stage of production and the cost of the goods as they entered that stage.

variable A measure that can change from time to time or from observation to observation.

velocity of money The number of times a dollar bill changes hands, on average, during a year; the ratio of nominal GDP to the stock of money.

vicious-circle-of-poverty hypothesis Suggests that poverty is self-perpetuating because poor nations are unable to save and invest enough to accumulate the capital stock that would help them grow.

Washington Consensus A set of 10 goals prescribed for countries receiving IMF grants and loans.

wealth or net worth The total value of what a household owns minus what it owes. It is a stock measure.

weight The importance attached to an item within a group of items.

World Bank An international agency that lends money to individual countries for projects that promote economic development.

Index

D

E

F

G

S

T

U

V

W

X

Y

Z

Photo Credits

Chapter 1, page 1, Ryan McVay/Getty Images, Inc.–Photodisc.; page 5, Bob Daemmrich/The Image Works; page 8, John Neubauer/PhotoEdit; page 9; U.S. Geological Survey, Denver-page 14, AP/Wide World Photos.

Chapter 2, page 23, © ZEFA/Masterfile; page 25, © ZEFA/Masterfile; page 37, Dan Lim/Masterfile Corporation; page 38, Jeff Greenberg/PhotoEdit.

Chapter 3, page 43, AP/Wide World Photos; page 51, Churchill & Klehr Photography; page 57, Mitch Kezar/Getty Images Inc.–Stone Allstock; page 61, Steve Benbow/Stock Boston.

Chapter 4, page 71, Jeff Greenberg/PhotoEdit; page 72, Superstock, Inc.; page 75, AP/Wide World Photos; page 76, AP/Wide World Photos.

Chapter 5, page 83, Bob Daemmrich/The Image Works; page 85 (top), UPI/CORBIS BETTMANN; page 85 (bottom), National Archives and Records Administration.

Chapter 6, page 99, Bob Daemmrich/The Image Works; page 101 (left), Chris Sorensen/Corbis/Stock Market; page 101 (right), Bryan Mitchell/Getty Images, Inc.–Liaison; page 104, Cleve Bryant/PhotoEdit; page 105 (left), Rob Crandall/Stock Boston; page 105 (right), Reed Saxon/AP/Wide World Photos; page 113, Richard B. Levine/Richard B. Levine/Frances M. Roberts.

Chapter 7, page 119, AP/Wide World Photos; page 133, Syracuse Newspapers/The Image Works.

Chapter 8, page 139, Bonn Sequenz/Imapress/The Image Works; page 151, Jim Whitmer/Jim Whitner Photography.

Chapter 9, page 161, Lance Nelson/CORBIS BETTMANN; page 173, AP/Wide World Photos.

Chapter 10, page 183, John Neubauer/PhotoEdit; page 185, Jack Fields/Photo Researchers, Inc.; page 188, Reuters/Dima Korotayev/Getty Images Inc.–Hulton Archive Photos.

Chapter 11, page 207, David Young-Wolff/PhotoEdit.

Chapter 12, page 223, Jeff Greenberg/PhotoEdit; page 230, Robert W. Ginn/PhotoEdit.

Chapter 13, page 241, Layne Kennedy/CORBIS BETTMANN.

Chapter 14, page 265, Michael Newman/PhotoEdit; page 267, Richard Lord/The Image Works; page 269 (left), National Archives and Records Administration; page 269 (right), Rob Crandall/Stock Boston.

Chapter 15, page 283, AP/Wide World Photos; page 293, Dennis Cook/AP/Wide World Photos.

Chapter 16, page 301, Getty Images, Inc.–Liaison; page 302 (left), BellSouth Advertising & Publishing; page 302 (right), Amy Etra/PhotoEdit; page 307, Jack Kurtz/The Image Works; page 308, Alan Schein Photography/CORBIS-NY.

Chapter 17, page 315, Michael Newman/PhotoEdit; page 321, AP/Wide World Photos.

Chapter 18, page 339, Mark Richards/PhotoEdit; page 348, Syracuse Newspapers/David Lassman/The Image Works.

Chapter 19, page 357, AP/Wide World Photos; page 364, Al Francekevich/Corbis/Stock Market.

Chapter 20, page 373, Gary Conner/PhotoEdit; page 386, Rachel Epstein/PhotoEdit; page 390, CORBIS BETTMANN.

Chapter 21, page 395, Sang Tan/AP/Wide World Photos; page 396, PA/AP/Wide World Photos; page 409, Richard T. Nowitz/CORBIS BETTMANN.

Chapter 22, page 421, Les Stone/Corbis Sygma/Corbis/Sygma; page 426, Edwin Tuyay/Bloomberg News/Landov/Landov LLC; page 427, Peter Menzel/Stock Boston; page 430, Tom Wagner/Corbis/SABA Press Photos, Inc.

Chapter 23, page 437, Stuart Cohen/The Image Works; page 444, Albrecht G. Schaefer; page 453, Amelia Kunhardt/The Image Works.